Professional VB.NET 2nd Edition

Fred Barwell
Richard Blair
Richard Case
Jonathan Crossland
Bill Forgey
Whitney Hankison
Billy S. Hollis
Rockford Lhotka
Tim McCarthy
Jan D. Narkiewicz
Jonathan Pinnock
Rama Ramachandran
Matthew Reynolds
John Roth
Bill Sempf
Bill Sheldon

Wrox Press Ltd. ®

Professional VB.NET 2nd Edition

wrox

Published by Wrox Press Ltd,
Arden House, 1102 Warwick Road, Acocks Green,
Birmingham, B27 6BH, UK
Printed in the United States
ISBN 1861007167

Trademark Acknowledgements

Wrox has endeavored to provide trademark information about all the companies and products mentioned in this book by the appropriate use of capitals. However, Wrox cannot guarantee the accuracy of this information.

Credits

Authors
Fred Barwell
Richard Blair
Richard Case
Jonathan Crossland
Bill Forgey
Whitney Hankison
Billy S. Hollis
Rockford Lhotka
Tim McCarthy
Jan D. Narkiewicz
Jonathan Pinnock
Rama Ramachandran
Matthew Reynolds
John Roth
Bill Sempf
Bill Sheldon

Managing Editors
Viv Emery
Louay Fatoohi

Category Managers
Bruce Lawson
Sonia Mullineux

Technical Architect
Kate Hall

Commissioning Editor
Paul Jeffcoat

Technical Editors
Victoria Blackburn
Paul Jeffcoat
Allan Jones
Gareth Oakley
Daniel Richardson

Author Agents
Sarah Bowers
Avril Corbin
Laura Jones
Charlotte Smith

Project Administrator
Rob Hesketh

Project Manager
Beth Sacks

Production Coordinator
Natalie O'Donnell

Illustrations
Paul Grove

Index
Michael Brinkman
John Collin
Andrew Criddle

Proof Readers
Fiona Berryman
Keith Westmoreland

Cover
Chris Morris

Technical Reviewers
Nick Apostolopoulos
Martin Beaulieu
Maxime Bombardier
Billy Cravens
Robin Dewson
David Espinosa
Damien Foggon
Hope Hatfield
Mark Horner
Wilfried Jansoone
Kenneth Lo
Ron Miller
Matthew Milner
Paul Morris
Gerry O'Brien
Dale Onyon
Troy Proudfoot
Scott Robertson
Sean M. Schade
Larry Schoeneman
Brian Sherwin
David Schultz
Adwait Ullal
Konstantinos Vlassis
Helmut Watson
Thearon Willis
Jonathan Winer
Donald Xie

About the Authors

Fred Barwell

Fred is an MCSD and a graduate from the University of Waterloo with a Bachelor of Mathematics, Honors Computer Science and Information Systems degree. He has been developing software professionally for over 10 years, primarily with Visual Basic and SQL Server. Fred currently runs his own consulting business, working as a software architect. His experience includes small to large scale, multi-national client server applications, with more recent work involving web site development using the Microsoft DNA model. Fred was recently contracted by Microsoft to aid in the development of a .NET WinForms application to demonstrate many of the new features of the .NET Framework.

When not at his computer, he is usually tending to his aquarium or playing baseball. Fred would like to thank Alex Lisitsky, Hao Quach, Ed Musters, Craig McQueen, and Gord Schmidt for their support, and also Mark Boulter from Microsoft for his time and assistance.

You can contact Fred at fbarwell@hotmail.com.

Fred contributed Chapter 12.

Richard Blair

Richard is Web Application Architect specializing in Microsoft Web Technologies. He focuses on emerging technology and its impact on business and development. Key areas that he has helped clients evaluate include: streamlining the electronic business process, expanding access to vital information, and creating usable systems. He now works as a Senior Consultant for SEI-Information Technology. Besides his consulting work, he has also co-authored Professional ASP XML, Beginning Visual Basic .NET, and Professional VB.NET, all published by Wrox Press, Ltd.

Richard has a dual concentration bachelor's degree from the University of Michigan in English Literature and Theatre. So not only is he a Web Architect, he could play one on TV.

Richard welcomes questions and comments at richblair@hotmail.com.

I am grateful for the love and support of my family (Kathy, Graehme, Thomas) and my furry housemates (Grover, Squeakie, and Fidget). I would also like to thank all the wonderful people at Wrox Press who have allowed me to finally justify my degree in Literature.

Richard contributed material for Chapter 2.

Richard Case

Richard is a Financial Analyst Programmer with Financial Objects PLC based in Covent Garden, London, England, where he works on the company's advanced banking software. Richard is also a Microsoft Certified Developer. He has been using Visual Basic since version 3 and is looking forward to using it for many years to some. Richard can be reached at richard@vbdotnet.co.uk.

I'd like to thank Kate, my soulmate and soon to be wife, for putting up with me while I have been writing the book and for the support she has given me. I would also like to thank everyone at Wrox Press. And last, but not least, I would like to thank my parents for their encouragement throughout my life.

Richard contributed material for Chapters 2 and 25.

Jonathan Crossland

Jonathan Crossland is co-author of *Professional Windows DNA, Professional VB.NET,* and *Beginning VB.NET.* He is currently working at Yokogawa Electric Corporation in the UK, where is happily involved with the creation of software for the Batch manufacturing industry. Jonathan has been working in and out of various software technologies for eight years and now spends most of his time in C# and ASP.NET. Jonathan also works with VB, VB.NET and web technologies such as JavaScript, DHTML, XML, ASP and of course, writing Web Services.

I would like to thank all at Wrox Press for giving me the opportunity to share my knowledge with so many. I would also like to thank my wife and my son (who is currently learning his first language) who both have provided me with so much support.

Jonathan contributed Chapter 13.

Bill Forgey

I am the Technical Lead in my current position, introducing project methodology, new technologies, standards, and training to development teams. I have spent some time consulting and have been exposed to technologies such as ASP, Delphi, Pascal, COM, C/C++, SQL, Java, ADO, Visual Basic, and now .NET. I have also co-authored *Beginning Visual Basic .NET Databases.*

I currently live in Sacramento, California, and can be contacted via e-mail at bforgey@vbcentral.net.

Bill contributed some material for Chapter 21.

Whitney Hankison

Whitney is a Financial Systems Analyst with the County of Santa Barbara in California. She specializes in VB programming and System Architecture/Network Configuration. She has been working in the computer field since 1984 and holds MCP certifications in NT Server and Workstation.

Whitney can be reached at whankison@earthlink.net.

I'd like to thank Wrox Press for the opportunity to write and being wonderful people to work with. I'd also like to thank all of my friends and family who have been so patient with my work load and schedule. I also thank God for His continual help and guidance.

Whitney contributed Chapters 9 and 24, as well as Appendix A.

Billy S. Hollis

Billy Hollis first learned BASIC over 25 years ago, and is co-author of the first book ever published on Visual Basic .NET, *VB.NET Programming on the Public Beta*, as well as several other .NET books. He is a frequent speaker at conferences, including Comdex and the Visual Basic Insiders Technical Summit (VBITS), often on the topics of software design and specification, object-based development in Visual Basic, and Microsoft.NET. He was chosen by Microsoft to train all 200 instructors for their 2001 .NET Developer Tour.

Billy is MSDN Regional Director of Developer Relations in Nashville, Tennessee for Microsoft, and was named Regional Director of the Year for 2001 by Microsoft. He has hosted Developer Days in Nashville for the last four years. He has his own consulting company in Nashville that focuses on training, consultation, and software development for the Microsoft.NET platform.

> *I need to thank several folks at Microsoft who have provided me with opportunity to learn more about VB.NET, including Jennifer Ritzinger, Mike Iem, Ari Bixhorn, Susan Warren, Mark Boulter, and many others. Thanks also to Ken Spencer and Keith Pleas for getting me involved in early training projects on .NET.*
>
> *My family has been supportive, as always, as I've squeezed in the time to write for this book, often at their expense. Those of us in the software industry love this time of intense innovation, but I'm sure Cindy, Ansel, and Dyson will be happier when things get back to the normal pace of change.*

Billy contributed Chapters 1 and 21, as well as material for Chapter 2.

Rockford Lhotka

Rockford Lhotka is the Principal Technology Evangelist for Magenic Technologies, one of the nation's premiere Microsoft Gold Certified Partners dedicated to solving today's most challenging business problems using 100% Microsoft tools and technology. Rockford is an author for several Wrox Press titles, including *Professional Visual Basic Interoperability – COM and VB6 to .NET*, *VB.NET Programming on the Public Beta*, and *Visual Basic 6 Distributed Objects* and is a columnist for MSDN Online and Visual Studio Magazine. He regularly presents at major conferences around the world – including Microsoft PDC, Tech Ed, VS Live! and VS Connections. He has over 14 years experience in software development and has worked on many projects in various roles, including software architecture, design and development, network administration, and project management.

Rockford contributed Chapters 5, 6, and 7, as well as additional material to Chapter 3.

Tim McCarthy

Tim McCarthy is a Principal Engineer at InterKnowlogy, where he architects and builds highly scalable *n*-tier web applications utilizing the latest Microsoft technologies. He has been an author and technical reviewer for several books from Wrox Press, the latest of which will be *Professional ASP.NET Security*.

Tim has written numerous articles for the Developer .NET Update newsletter, and also just recently finished developing a packaged presentation for the Microsoft Field Content Team (Best Practices for .NET Development), as well as writing a whitepaper for Microsoft on using COM+ services in .NET. He also developed advanced training content for Commerce Server 2000, and delivered the content to Microsoft Certified Trainers and other companies.

Tim has been a regular speaker at Microsoft Developer Days for the past 3 years, and also spoke at the Wrox Press Web Developer's Conference 2000. He is also an instructor for UCSD in their Microsoft certification program.

Tim is currently spending his time helping companies save money by using .NET technologies. He can be reached at timm@InterKnowlogy.com.

Tim contributed Chapter 11 and material for Chapter 10.

Jan D. Narkiewicz

Jan D. Narkiewicz is Chief Technical Officer at Software Pronto, Inc (jann@softwarepronto.com). Jan began his career as a Microsoft developer thanks to basketball star, Michael Jordan. In the early 90s Jan noticed that no matter what happened during a game, Michael Jordan's team won. Similarly, no matter what happened in technology Microsoft always won (then again this strategy is ten years old and may need some revamping). Clearly there was a bandwagon to be jumped upon.

Over the years Jan managed to work on an e-mail system that resided on 17 million desktops, helped automate factories that make blue jeans you have in your closet (trust me, you own this brand) and developed defense systems. All this was achieved using technologies such as COM/DCOM, COM+, C++, VB, C#, ADO, SQL Server, Oracle, DB2, ASP.NET, ADO.NET, Java, Linux and XML.

In his spare time Jan is Academic Coordinator for the Windows curriculum at U.C. Berkeley Extension, he teaches at U.C. Santa Cruz Extension, writes for ASPToday and occasionally plays some football (a.k.a. soccer).

Jan contributed Chapter 10.

Jonathan Pinnock

Jonathan Pinnock started programming in Pal III assembler on his school's PDP 8/e, with a massive 4K of memory, back in the days before Moore's Law reached the statute books. These days he spends most of his time developing and extending the increasingly successful PlatformOne product set that his company, JPA, markets to the financial services community. He seems to spend the rest of his time writing for Wrox, although he occasionally surfaces to say "remember me?" to his wife and two children. JPA's home page is www.jpassoc.co.uk.

My heartfelt thanks go to Gail, who first suggested getting into writing, and now suffers the consequences on a fairly regular basis, and to Mark and Rachel, who just suffer the consequences.

Jonathan contributed Chapters 17 and 18.

Rama Ramachandran

Rama Ramachandran is Vice President, Technology with Imperium, *a* Microsoft Gold Certified Partner for E-Commerce. Rama is a Microsoft Certified Solution Developer and Site-Builder and has excelled in designing and developing medium to large scale web applications using .NET, ASP/+, COM, Visual Basic, SQL Server, and Windows 2000. Rama has over 15 years of experience with all facets of the Software Development lifecycle and has co-authored *Introducing .Net, Professional ASP Data Access* and *Professional Visual InterDev 6 Programming* (all from Wrox) as well as four books on Visual Basic from Que Publishing.

Rama is also the 'ASP Pro' at Devx.com where he maintains ASP related columns. He teaches Visual Basic and Web Development at Fairfield University as well as at the University of Connecticut. Rama lives in Stamford, Conn., with his wife Beena and their sons Ashish and Amit. Reach Rama at ramabeena@hotmail.com.

> *This book is dedicated to my wife Beena and our children - Ashish and Amit. They make my life whole. I'm great at writing about technology, but get tongue-tied trying to say how much I love and care about the three of you. I am grateful to our prayer-answering God for your laughing, mischievous, adoring lives. Thanks for being there, Beens. I love you.*

Rama contributed Chapter 14.

Matthew Reynolds

After working with Wrox Press on a number of projects since 1999, Matthew is now an in-house author for Wrox Press writing about and working with virtually all aspects of Microsoft.NET. He's also a regular contributor to Wrox's ASPToday, C#Today and Web Services Architect. He lives and works in North London and can be reached on matthewr@wrox.com.

> *For Fanjeev Sarin.*
>
> *Thanks very much to the following for their support and assistance in writing this book: Len, Edward, Darren, Alex, Jo, Tim, Clare, Martin, Niahm, Tom, Ollie, Amir, Gretchen, Ben, Brandon, Denise, Rob, Waggy, Mark, Elaine, James, Zoe, Faye and Sarah. And, also thanks to my new friends at Wrox, which include Rob, Charlotte, Laura, Karli, Dom S, Dom L, Ian, Kate, Joy, Pete, Helen, Vickie, John, Dave, Adam, Craig, Jake, Julian and Paul.*

Matthew contributed Chapters 16, 19, 20, and 23 as well as additional material for Chapters 10, 11, 13, and 22.

John Roth

John began his career like so many in the industry as 'that guy who knows the computer stuff', the one who could whip up a macro as fast as Julia Childs could tuck into a soufflé. Eventually, realizing that he could actually make a living having fun, John started his own company (John Roth Consulting) and he hasn't looked back in the ten years since.

He considers himself fortunate to have been able to fill the role of Senior Developer and Web Developer at Compaq, to teach both students and other instructors at institutions like the University of British Columbia and Douglas College, and to work with many other wonderful clients, big and small. Great people, cool technologies... ask John and he'll tell you, "life really doesn't suck!"

John can be reached by e-mail at john.roth@ispeakgeek.com. He's working on putting a site there he swears! Maybe after he finishes his next book... yeah, right!

> *I'd like to dedicate my part of this book to my partner, my best friend, and the love of my life. Andrea, you have no idea how much you mean to me...*

John contributed Chapter 15.

Bill Sempf

Bill Sempf is an experienced Internet strategist with a ten-year track record of using technology to help organizations accomplish specific business objectives. He is completely obsessed with the belief that Web Services are the 'next big thing', and he is usually right about stuff like that.

A Microsoft Certified Professional, Certified Internet Business Strategist, and member of the International Webmaster's Association, Bill has built nearly one hundred dynamic webs for startups and Fortune 50 companies alike. He would like to thank his wife Gabrielle for putting up with all of these projects, and ones to follow. Bill can be reached at bill@sempf.net.

Bill contributed Chapter 22.

Bill Sheldon

Bill is a software architect and engineer originally from Baltimore, Maryland, currently living with his wife in Southern California. Holding a degree in Computer Science from the Illinois Institute of Technology (IIT), he has been professionally employed since resigning his commission with the US Navy following the Gulf War. He has held his Microsoft Certified Solution Developer (MCSD) for several years, and is currently employed as a Principal Engineer with InterKnowlogy (bsheldon@InterKnowlogy.com). Bill designs software solutions and develops enterprise infrastructure components for extranets, intranets and the Internet.

> *My contributions to this book are dedicated to my loving and wonderful wife Tracie. Thanks for putting up with me, Love Always.*
>
> *And to my parents, for all the sacrifices to help us pursue our dreams and instilling for all their children with the belief that we can accomplish anything we set our minds to.*

Bill contributed Chapters 4 and 8.

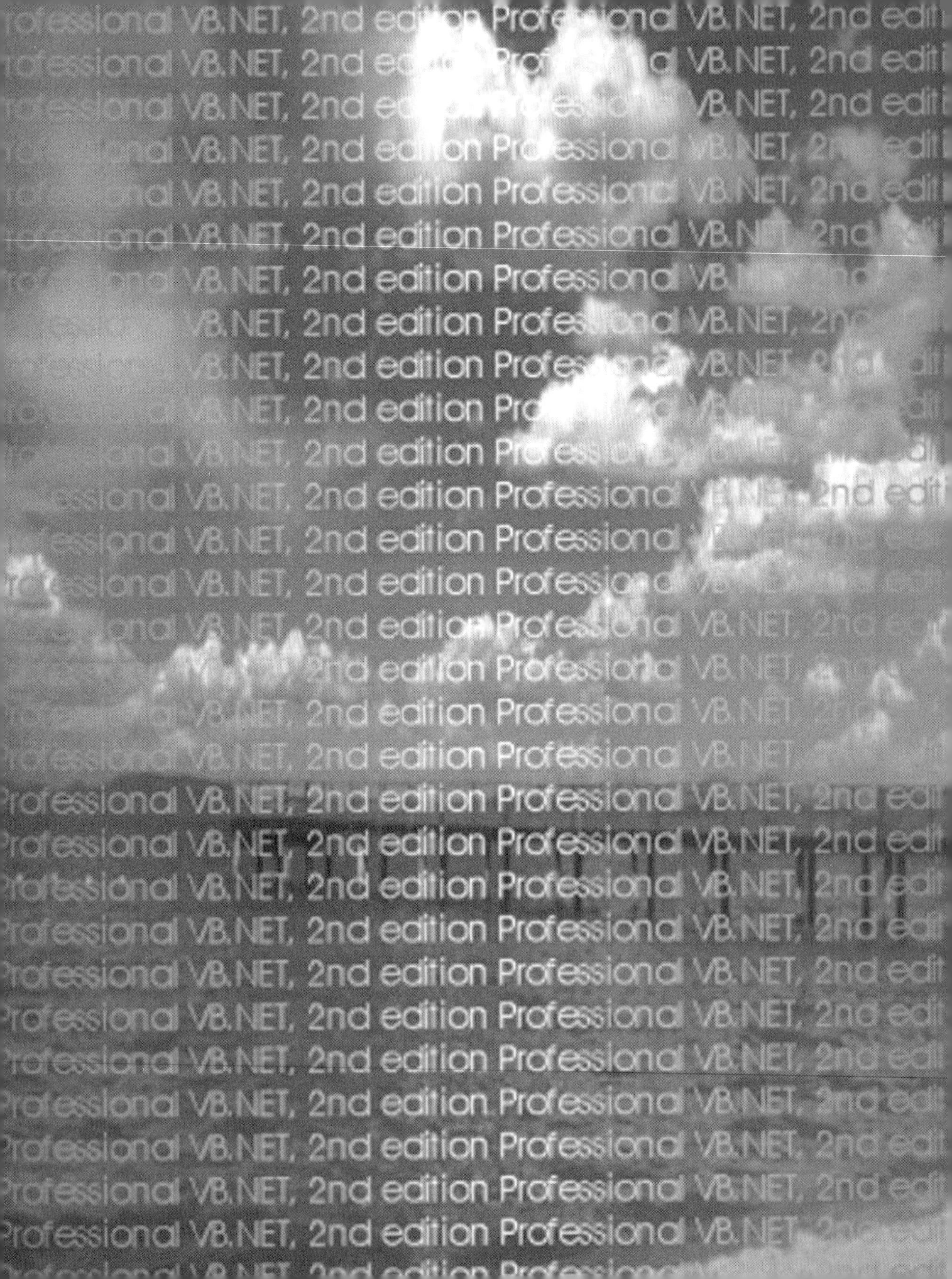
Professional VB.NET, 2nd edition

Table of Contents

Table of Contents

Table of Contents

Table of Contents

Chapter 13: Creating Windows Controls — 431

Table of Contents

Table of Contents

Table of Contents

Table of Contents

Table of Contents

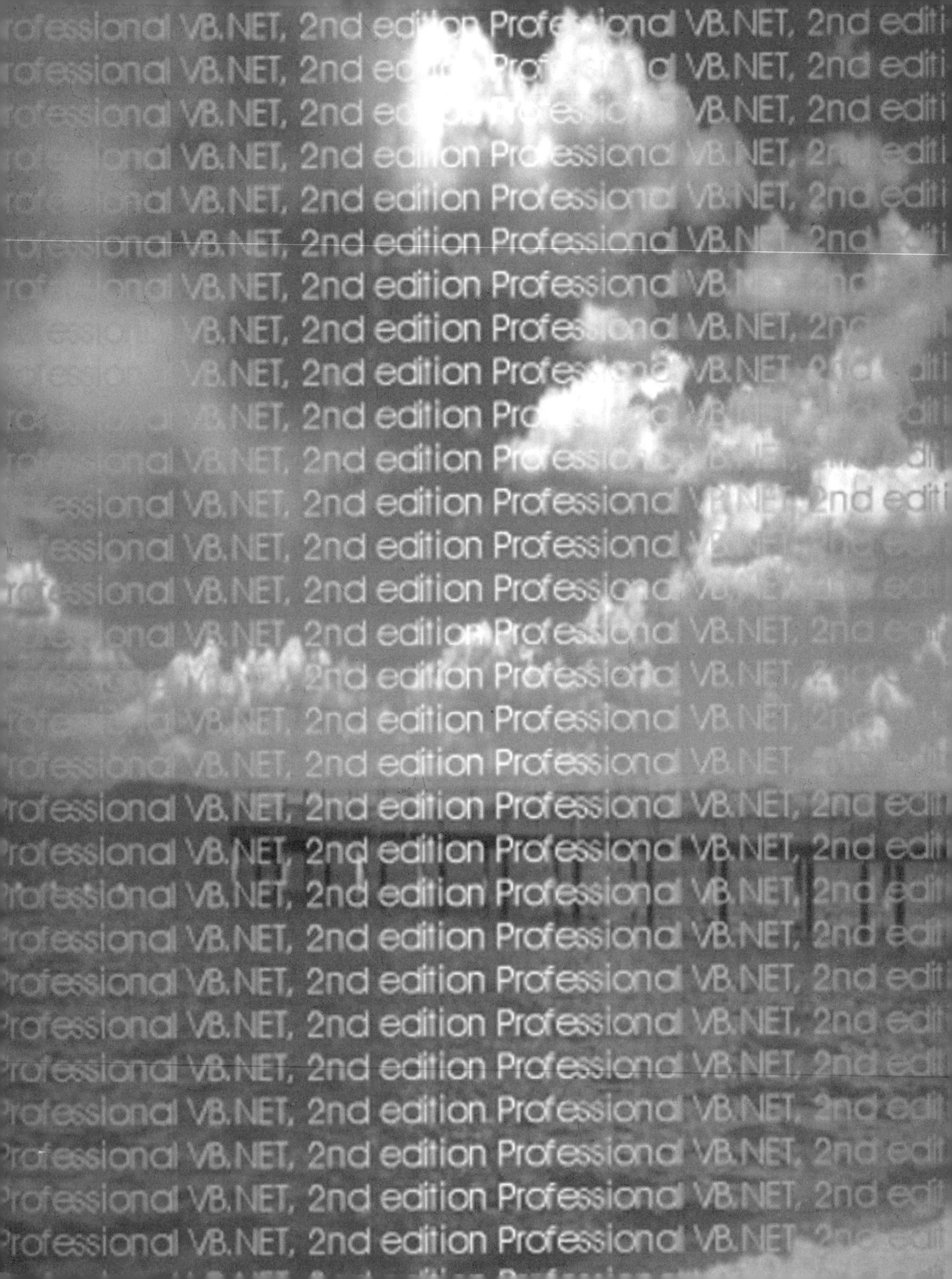
Professional VB.NET, 2nd edition

Introduction

.NET is designed to provide a new environment within which you can develop almost any application to run on Windows (and possibly in the future on other platforms). **Visual Basic .NET (VB.NET)** is likely to be a very popular development tool for use with this framework. VB.NET is a .NET compliant language and as such has (except for legacy reasons) almost identical technical functionality as the new C# language and Managed Extensions for C++. Using VB.NET, a dynamic web page, a component of a distributed application, a database access component, or a classic Windows desktop application can be developed.

In order to incorporate Visual Basic into the .NET Framework, a number of new features have been added to it. In fact, the changes are so extensive that VB.NET should be viewed as a new language rather than simply as Visual Basic 7. However, these changes were necessary to give developers the features that they have been asking for: true object orientated programming, easier deployment, better interoperability, and a cohesive environment in which to develop applications.

In this book, we cover VB.NET virtually from start to finish: we begin by looking at the .NET Framework, and end by looking at best practices for deploying .NET applications. In between, we look at everything from database access to integration with other technologies such as XML, along with investigating the new features in detail. You will see that VB.NET has emerged as a powerful yet easy to use language that will allow you to target the Internet just as easily as the desktop.

Who Is This Book For?

This book is primarily aimed at experienced Visual Basic developers who need to make the transition to VB.NET.

Although the .NET Framework provides a new and powerful way to program for the Internet, this book is not for Web developers, who should instead refer to *Professional ASP.NET 1.0 Special Edition* (Wrox Press, ISBN 1861007035).

What You Need To Use This Book

Although it is possible to create VB.NET applications using the command lines tools contained in the **.NET Framework SDK,** you will need **Visual Studio .NET** (Professional or higher), which includes the .NET Framework SDK, to use this book to the full.

In addition:

❑ Some chapters make use of **SQL Server 2000.** However, you can also run the example code using **MSDE (Microsoft Data Engine),** which ships with Visual Studio .NET.

❑ Several chapters make use of **Internet Information Services (IIS).** IIS ships with Windows 2000 Server, Windows 2000 Professional, and Windows XP, although it is not installed by default.

❑ Chapter 18 makes use of **MSMQ** to work with queued transactions. MSMQ ships with Windows 2000 Server, Windows 2000 Professional, and Windows XP, although it is not installed by default.

What Does this Book Cover?

Chapter 1, What is Microsoft .NET? – This chapter explains the importance of .NET, and just how much it changes application development. We gain an understanding of why we need .NET by looking at what's wrong with current development technologies, including COM and the DNA architectural model. Then we look at how .NET corrects the drawbacks by using the Common Language Runtime (CLR).

Chapter 2, Introducing VB.NET and VS.NET – This chapter provides our first look at a Visual Basic .NET application. As we develop this application we'll take a tour of some of the new features of Visual Studio .NET.

Chapter 3, The Common Language Runtime – This chapter examines the core of the .NET platform, the Common Language Runtime (CLR). The CLR is responsible for managing the execution of code compiled for the .NET platform. We cover versioning and deployment, memory management, cross-language integration, metadata, and the IL Disassembler.

Chapter 4, Variables and Data Types – This chapter introduces many of the types commonly used in Visual Basic .NET. The main goal of this chapter is to get you familiar with value and reference types and to help those with a background in VB 6 understand some of the key differences in how variables are defined in VB.NET.

Chapter 5, Object Syntax Introduction – This is the first of three chapters that explore object-orientated programming in VB.NET. This chapter will define objects, classes, instances, encapsulation, abstraction, polymorphism, and inheritance.

Chapter 6, Inheritance and Interfaces – This chapter examines inheritance and how it can be used within VB.NET. We create simple and abstract base classes, and understand how to create base classes from which other classes can be derived.

Chapter 7, Applying Objects and Components – This chapter puts the theory of Chapters 5 and 6 into practice. The four defining object-oriented concepts (abstraction, encapsulation, polymorphism, inheritance) are explained, and we explain how these concepts can be applied in design and development to create effective object-oriented applications.

Chapter 8, Namespaces – This chapter introduces namespaces and their hierarchical structure. An explanation of namespaces and some common ones are given. In addition, we understand how to create new namespaces, and how to import and alias existing namespaces within projects.

Chapter 9, Error Handling – This chapter covers how error handling works in VB.NET by discussing the CLR exception handler and the new `Try...Catch...Finally` structure. We also look at error handling between managed and unmanaged code, error and trace logging, and how we can use these methods to obtain feedback on how our program is working.

Chapter 10, Using XML in VB.NET – This chapter presents the features of the .NET Framework that facilitate the generation and manipulation of XML. We describe the .NET Framework's XML related namespaces and a subset of the classes exposed by these namespaces are examined in detail. This chapter also touches on a set of technologies that utilize XML, specifically ADO.NET and SQL Server.

Chapter 11, Data Access with ADO.NET – This chapter focuses on what you will need to know about the ADO.NET object model in order to be able to build flexible, fast, and scalable data access objects and applications. The evolution of ADO into ADO.NET is explored and the main objects in ADO.NET that you need to understand in order to build data access into your .NET applications are explained.

Chapter 12, Windows Forms – This chapter looks at Windows Forms, concentrating primarily on forms and built-in controls. What is new and what has been changed from previous versions of Visual Basic is discussed, along with the `System.Windows.Forms` namespace.

Chapter 13, Creating Windows Controls – This chapter looks at creating our own Windows controls. In particular, we discuss how to inherit from another control, build a composite control, and write controls from scratch based on the `Control` class.

Chapter 14, Web Forms – This chapter explores Web Forms and how you can benefit from their use. Using progressively more complex examples, this chapter explains how .NET provides the power of Rapid Application Development (normally associated with Windows applications) for the development of web applications.

Chapter 15, Creating Web Controls – This chapter looks at an entirely new form of Visual Basic control development: custom web controls. It looks at the various forms of custom web control development that are available in the .NET Framework. The basic structure of web user and sub-classed controls is examined, along with a look at composite and templated controls.

Chapter 16, Data Binding – This chapter examines how data binding in .NET makes the process of associating an underlying data store with controls easier than in previous versions of Visual Basic. We look at how .NET allows the automatic population of controls with data from an underlying data source and also provides a mechanism for updating the underlying data source in response to any changes the user may make within Windows applications.

Chapter 17, Working with Classic COM and Interfaces – This chapters discusses COM and .NET component interoperability, and what tools are provided to help link the two technologies together.

Chapter 18, Component Services – This chapter explores the .NET Component Services, in particular, transaction processing, and queued components.

Chapter 19, Threading – This chapter explores threading and explains how the various objects in the .NET Framework enable any consumer of it to develop multithreaded applications. We examine how threads can be created, how they relate to processes, and the differences between multitasking and multithreading.

Chapter 20, Remoting – This chapter takes a detailed look at how to use remoting in classic 3-tier application design. We look at the basic architecture of remoting and build a basic server and client that used a singleton object for answering client requests into the business tier. We then look at how to use serialization to return more complex objects from the server to the client and how to use the call context for passing extra data from client to server along with each call without having to change the object model.

Chapter 21, Windows Services – This chapter examines how VB.NET is used in the production of Windows Services. The creation, installation, running, and debugging of Windows Services is covered.

Chapter 22, Web Services – This chapter looks at how to create and consume Web Services using VB.NET. The abstract classes provided by the CLR to set up and work with Web Services are discussed, as well as some of the technologies that support Web Services. Finally, some of the disadvantages to using any distributed architecture and the future with Web Services are examined.

Chapter 23, VB.NET and the Internet – This chapter looks at how to download resources from the Web, how to design our own communication protocols, and how to reuse the WebBrowser control in our applications.

Chapter 24, Security in the .NET Framework – This chapter examines the additional tools and functionality with regard to security provided by .NET. `Caspol.Exe` and `Permview.exe`, which assist in establishing and maintaining security policies, are discussed. The `System.Security.Permissions` namespace is looked at and we discuss how it relates to managing permissions. Finally, we examine the `System.Security.Cryptography` namespace, and run through some code to demonstrate the capabilities of this namespace.

Chapter 25, Assemblies and Deployment in .NET – This chapter examines assemblies and their use within the CLR. The structure of an assembly, what it contains, and the information it contains is examined. In addition, the manifest of the assembly and its role in deployment will be looked at. We also look at what Visual Studio .NET and the CLR have to offer us when we come to deploy our applications.

Appendix A, Using the Visual Basic Compatibility Library – This appendix looks at the Visual Basic Compatibility Library, which is provided in order to assist in the conversion of existing code, as well as providing backward compatibility and support for developers who are transitioning to VB.NET.

Conventions

We have used a number of different styles of text and layout in the book to help differentiate between the different kinds of information. Here are examples of the styles we use and an explanation of what they mean:

Bullets appear indented, with each new bullet marked as follows:

- ❑ **Important Words** are in a bold type font
- ❑ Words that appear on the screen in menus like the File or Window are in a similar font to the one that you see on screen
- ❑ Keys that you press on the keyboard, like *Ctrl* and *Enter*, are in italics
- ❑ If you see something like, Object, you'll know that it's a filename, object name, or function name

Code in a gray box shows new, important, pertinent code:

```
Dim objMyClass as New MyClass("Hello World")

Debug.WriteLine(objMyClass.ToString)
```

Sometimes you'll see code in a mixture of styles, like this:

```
Dim objVar as Object

objVar = Me

CType(objVar, Form).Text = "New Dialog Title Text"
```

The code with a white background is code we've already looked at and that we don't wish to examine further.

Advice, hints, and background information come in an italicized, indented font like this.

> **Important pieces of information come in boxes like this.**

Customer Support

We always value hearing from our readers, and we want to know what you think about this book: what you liked, what you didn't like, and what you think we can do better next time. You can send us your comments, either by returning the reply card in the back of the book, or by e-mail to feedback@wrox.com. Please be sure to mention the book title in your message.

How to Download the Sample Code for the Book

When you visit the Wrox site, http://www.wrox.com/, simply locate the title through our Search facility or by using one of the title lists. Click on Download in the Code column, or on Download Code on the book's detail page.

The files that are available for download from our site have been archived using WinZip. When you have saved the attachments to a folder on your hard-drive, you need to extract the files using a de-compression program such as WinZip or PKUnzip. When you extract the files, the code is usually extracted into chapter folders. When you start the extraction process, ensure your software (WinZip, PKUnzip, etc.) is set to use folder names.

Errata

We've made every effort to make sure that there are no errors in the text or in the code. However, no one is perfect and mistakes do occur. If you find an error in one of our books, like a spelling mistake or a faulty piece of code, we would be very grateful for feedback. By sending in errata you may save another reader hours of frustration, and of course, you will be helping us provide even higher quality information. Simply e-mail the information to support@wrox.com, your information will be checked and if correct, posted to the errata page for that title, or used in subsequent editions of the book.

To find errata on the web site, go to http://www.wrox.com/, and simply locate the title through our Advanced Search or title list. Click on the Book Errata link, which is below the cover graphic on the book's detail page.

E-mail Support

If you wish to directly query a problem in the book with an expert who knows the book in detail then e-mail support@wrox.com, with the title of the book and the last four numbers of the ISBN in the subject field of the e-mail. A typical e-mail should include the following things:

- ❏ The **title of the book**, **last four digits of the ISBN**, and **page number** of the problem in the Subject field.

- ❏ Your **name**, **contact information**, and the **problem** in the body of the message.

We *won't* send you junk mail. We need the details to save your time and ours. When you send an e-mail message, it will go through the following chain of support:

- ❏ Customer Support – Your message is delivered to our customer support staff, who are the first people to read it. They have files on most frequently asked questions and will answer anything general about the book or the web site immediately.

- ❏ Editorial – Deeper queries are forwarded to the technical editor responsible for that book. They have experience with the programming language or particular product, and are able to answer detailed technical questions on the subject.

- ❏ The Authors – Finally, in the unlikely event that the editor cannot answer your problem, he or she will forward the request to the author. We do try to protect the author from any distractions to their writing; however, we are quite happy to forward specific requests to them. All Wrox authors help with the support on their books.

❑ They will e-mail the customer and the editor with their response, and again all readers should benefit.

The Wrox Support process can only offer support to issues that are directly pertinent to the content of our published title. Support for questions that fall outside the scope of normal book support, is provided via the community lists of our http://p2p.wrox.com/ forum.

p2p.wrox.com

For author and peer discussion join the P2P mailing lists. Our unique system provides **programmer to programmer**™ contact on mailing lists, forums, and newsgroups, all in addition to our one-to-one e-mail support system. If you post a query to P2P, you can be confident that it is being examined by the many Wrox authors and other industry experts who are present on our mailing lists. At p2p.wrox.com you will find a number of different lists that will help you, not only while you read this book, but also as you develop your own applications.

> **Particularly appropriate to this book are the vb_dotnet and pro_vb_dotnet lists.**

To subscribe to a mailing list just follow these steps:

1. Go to http://p2p.wrox.com/.

2. Choose the appropriate category from the left menu bar.

3. Click on the mailing list you wish to join.

4. Follow the instructions to subscribe and fill in your e-mail address and password.

5. Reply to the confirmation e-mail you receive.

6. Use the subscription manager to join more lists and set your e-mail preferences.

Why this System Offers the Best Support

You can choose to join the mailing lists or you can receive them as a weekly digest. If you don't have the time, or facility, to receive the mailing list, then you can search our online archives. Junk and spam mails are deleted, and your own e-mail address is protected by the unique Lyris system. Queries about joining or leaving lists, and any other general queries about lists, should be sent to listsupport@p2p.wrox.com.

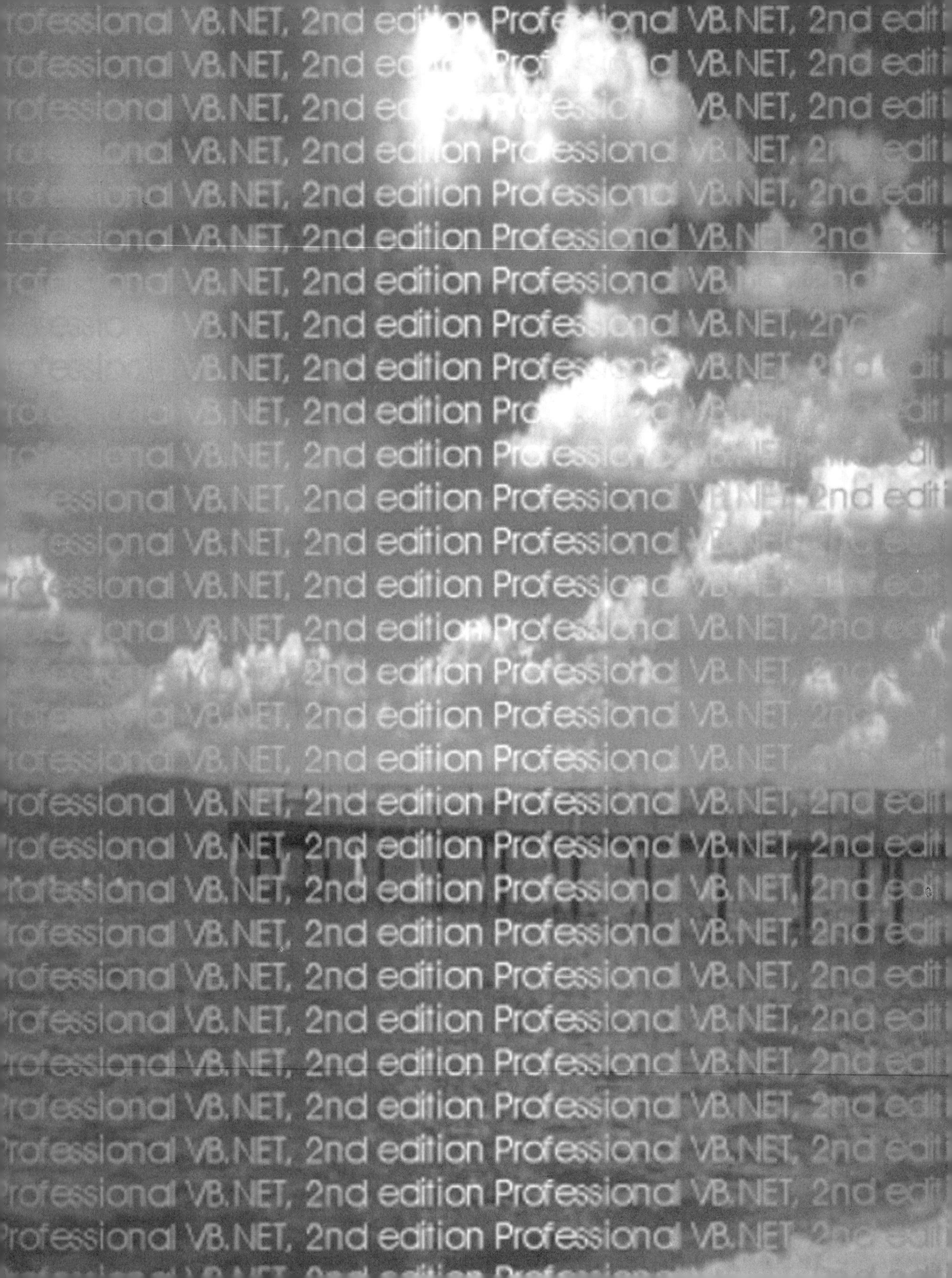
Professional VB.NET, 2nd edition

1

What is Microsoft .NET?

Microsoft began its Internet development efforts in 1995. Prior to this, Microsoft's focus had, for several years, been on moving desktop and server operating systems to 32-bit, GUI-based technologies, but once Microsoft realized the importance of the Internet, it made a dramatic shift. The company became focused on integrating its Windows platform with the Internet and it succeeded in making Windows a serious platform for the development of Internet applications.

However, it had been necessary for Microsoft to make some compromises in order to quickly produce Internet-based tools and technologies. The most glaring example was **Active Server Pages (ASP)**. While ASP was simple in concept and easily accessible to new developers, it did not encourage structured or object-oriented development. Creating user interfaces with interpreted script and limited visual elements was a real step back from the form-based user interfaces of **Visual Basic (VB)**. Many applications were written with a vast amount of interpreted script, which lead to problems of debugging and maintenance.

Visual Basic (and other languages) has continued to be used in Internet applications on Microsoft platforms, but mostly to create components that were accessed in ASP. Before Microsoft .NET, Microsoft tools were lacking in their integration and ease-of-use for web development. The few attempts that were made to place a web interface on traditional languages, such as WebClasses in VB, were compromises that never gained widespread acceptance. The result was that developing a large Internet application required the use of a large number of loosely integrated tools and technologies.

Microsoft .NET is the first software development platform to be designed from the ground up with the Internet in mind – although .NET is not exclusively for Internet development; rather it provides a consistent programming model that can be used for many types of applications. However, when an application needs Internet capabilities, access to those capabilities is almost transparent, unlike tools currently used for Internet-enabled applications.

To understand what the importance of .NET is, it's helpful to understand how current tools such as COM limit us in a development model based on the Internet. In this chapter, we'll look at what's wrong with COM and the DNA architectural model, and then examine how .NET corrects the drawbacks in these technologies.

Although we'll discuss the drawbacks of current tools in the context of the Microsoft platform, almost all apply in some form to all the platforms that are currently available for Internet development. Moreover, many of these other platforms have unique drawbacks of their own.

The DNA Programming Model

In the late 1990s, Microsoft attempted to bring some order to Internet development with the concept of **Windows DNA applications**. DNA consists of a standard three-tier development based on COM, with ASP (as well as Win32 clients) in the presentation layer, business objects in a middle layer, and a relational data store and engine in the bottom layer. The following diagram shows a generic Windows DNA application:

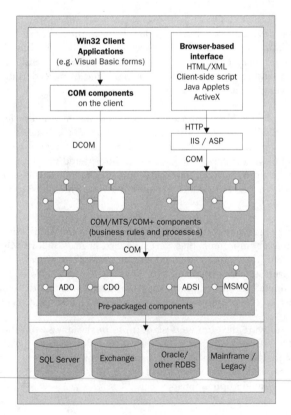

Presentation Tier

In Windows DNA, there are two types of user interfaces – **Win32 clients** and **browser-based clients**.

Win32 clients are most often produced with a visual development tool such as Visual Basic. They are simple to create, and offer a rich user interface. The drawback of such software is that it is difficult to deploy and maintain – it must be installed on every client and every installation must be altered whenever an upgrade to the software is made. In addition to these logistical difficulties, DLL conflicts frequently occur on the client because of variations in the version of the operating system and other software installed on the client. This is known as **DLL Hell**, which we'll discuss later on.

Browser-based clients are far easier to deploy than Win32 clients as the client only needs a compatible browser and a network (Internet or intranet) connection. However browser-based clients are often more difficult to create than Win32 clients, and offer a more limited user interface that has fewer controls and permits only limited control over the layout of the screen and the handling of screen events.

There are some in-between options. If clients are restricted to certain browsers, **Dynamic HTML (DHTML)** can be used to add functionality to the interface. If clients are further restricted to Internet Explorer (IE), **ActiveX controls** can be used to create an interface that is close to that available in a Win32 client. However, ActiveX controls have deployment issues of their own. VB can be used to create ActiveX controls, but then deploying the controls requires lots of supporting VB DLLs to be present on the client. Consequently, ActiveX controls are typically written in C++ to make the installation as lightweight as possible, but this adds to development time and requires a higher level of development expertise.

One important factor that is often overlooked in the DNA model is that there may be a need to implement both Win32-based and Internet-based user interfaces. Alternatively, there may be a need to have different types of user interface, perhaps one for novice or occasional users, and one for advanced users. This is practical only if the design of the system keeps the user interface layer as thin as possible. Normally, it should only contain logic that manages the user interface and performs basic validation of user data. (Such validation of data in the client layer is important as it minimizes round trips to the server.)

Middle Tier

The middle tier in a DNA application should encapsulate as much of the business logic processing as possible. Apart from those rules that are needed to validate data on the client, all the **business rules** should be in the middle layer.

The middle tier is often broken down into sub tiers. One tier may handle the interface to the client, another tier the business rules, and another tier the interface to the data repositories.

Visual Basic is the language most commonly used to write middle-tier components. This is a more sophisticated type of development than for forms-based Visual Basic programs; it requires a greater level of expertise in COM and object-oriented programming. Understanding COM is important in constructing a middle tier because the components in this layer must work together, which means that all the components must be versioned properly so that they can understand each other's interfaces. It's also important to create components that scale well, which often means developing components that are implemented using Microsoft Transaction Server (MTS) or COM+ Services. Such components typically use stateless designs, which can look very different from the stateful designs commonly used in client-based components.

Components in the middle tier may use a variety of protocols and components to communicate data to the data tier. The diagram shows examples such as HTTP, ADO (ActiveX Data Objects), ADSI (Active Directory Service Interfaces), and CDO (Collaboration Data Objects), but that list is by no means exhaustive.

Data Tier

Most business applications must store information for long-term use. The nature of the storage mechanism varies with the installation but a relational database management system (RDBMS) is often required, with the most common options being Microsoft SQL Server and Oracle. However, if the information is based around documents and messages, a messaging data store such as Exchange may be required, and many installations will depend on legacy mainframe systems.

Besides holding the data, the data tier may also contain logic that processes, retrieves, and validates data. Stored procedures, written in some variation of SQL (Structured Query Language), can be used with RDBMS databases to do this.

Issues with the DNA Model

The concept behind DNA is sound, but actually getting it to work well is overly complicated. A DNA application will often require:

- ❑ Visual Basic code in forms, as well as in components on both the client and the server
- ❑ ASP scripting code as well as client-side scripting
- ❑ HTML, DHTML, CSS (Cascading Style Sheets)
- ❑ XML, XSL
- ❑ C++ in ActiveX components
- ❑ Stored procedures (Transact-SQL in SQL Server or PL-SQL in Oracle)

With so many options, it's all too easy to make inappropriate design decisions, such as putting logic on the client that belongs on the server, or creating VBScript for formatting when CSS would work better. Designing and constructing a complex DNA-based application requires a high level of expertise in a number of different technologies.

The Limitations of COM

While COM is a viable platform for enterprise-level Internet applications, it does have some serious limitations. Let's cover some of the major ones.

DLL Hell

COM-based applications are subject to major deployment and configuration issues. Small changes in COM interfaces can render entire applications inoperable. This problem, in which small problems cascade through an entire component-based tier is often referred to as **DLL Hell** – experienced COM developers will attest to the appropriateness of the term. Getting a large set of DLLs to a compatible state of versioning requires skill and a well-controlled deployment process.

While DLL Hell is most common in the middle tier, there are also deployment issues in the client tier that are caused by COM. Any forms-based interface will depend on COM components in order to function. Some of these components arc from the tool used to create the interface (such as Visual Basic); others may be custom-written DLLs. All will need to be installed on the client.

The class IDs (which are GUID-based identifiers) of all the COM-based components must be placed in the local client's Windows Registry. Complex installation programs typically do this. Getting all the necessary components registered and properly versioned on the client is a variant of DLL Hell, and makes deploying client applications to large numbers of desktop machines an expensive process. This has driven many application designers to use browser-based interfaces whenever possible in order to avoid such deployment costs, even though the browser user interface is not as flexible.

Lack of Interoperability with Other Platforms

COM works well on pure Microsoft platforms but it doesn't provide the ability to activate or interoperate with components on other platforms such as UNIX. For enterprise-level applications, this is a significant shortcoming as large organizations often have a variety of operating platforms, and require interoperability between them.

Lack of Built-In Inheritance

One of the most important ways in which functionality can be reused is for a software component to be inherited by another component, and then extended with new functionality. (Chapter 6 covers this issue in detail.) Inheritance is crucial in developing complex application frameworks, but COM does *not* support inheritance natively.

Inheritance has been possible on Microsoft platforms at the source language level, using languages such as C++ and Delphi. However, since inheritance is not built into the basic structure of COM, many languages (such as VB6) don't support it, and there was no capability on Microsoft platforms before .NET to allow languages to inherit from components written in another language.

Limitations of VB6 for DNA Application Development

Visual Basic 6 is easily the most popular language for developing applications with the DNA model. It is used in two major roles: forms-based VB clients and COM components (either on the client or the server). There are other options, of course, including C++, J++, and various third-party languages such as Delphi and Perl, but the number of VB developers outnumbers them all put together.

However, although it's popular, VB6 isn't without its limitations, which include:

❑ **No capability for multithreading** – which implies, for example, that VB6 can't be used to write an NT-type service. There are also situations in which the apartment threading used by components created in VB6 limits performance.

❑ **A lack of implementation inheritance and other object-oriented features** – this makes VB6 unsuitable for the development of object-based frameworks.

- **Poor error-handling ability** – VB6's archaic error handling becomes especially annoying in a multi-tier environment. It's difficult in VB6 to track and pass errors through a stack of component interfaces.

- **Poor integration with other languages such as C++** – VB6's implementation of COM, although easy to use, causes problems with such integration. Class parameters (object interfaces) in VB6 are "variant compliant", forcing C++ developers who want to integrate with VB to convert parameters to less appropriate types. These varying data structures and interface conventions must be resolved before components in VB can be integrated into a multiple language project. Besides requiring extra code, these conversions may also result in a performance hit.

- **No effective user interface for Internet-based applications** – perhaps the biggest drawback to using VB6 became apparent when developing for the Internet. While VB6 forms for a Win32 client were state-of-the-art, for applications with a browser interface VB6 was mostly relegated to use in components.

Microsoft tried to address this last problem in VB6 with **WebClasses** and **DHTML Pages** but neither caught on:

- WebClasses offered an obscure programming model, and limited control over visual layout.

- DHTML Pages in VB6 had to send a (usually large) DLL to the client, and so needed a high-bandwidth connection to be practical. This limited their use mostly to intranet applications. DHTML Pages were also restricted to Internet Explorer.

Limitations of DNA Internet Development

There are a few additional areas in which previous Microsoft tools and technologies fell short of the ideal for Internet application development.

Different Programming Models

With DNA-based software development, creating software that is accessed by a user locally is done very differently from development for the Internet. The starkest example of this is the use of VB forms for client-server user interfaces versus the use of ASP for Internet user interfaces. Even though both situations involve designing and implementing GUI-based user interfaces, the tools and programming techniques used are quite different.

Having very different programming models for these similar types of development causes several problems:

- Developers have to learn multiple programming models.

- Code developed for one type of interface typically cannot be used for the other type of interface.

- It is uncommon to have both local and web-based user interfaces for an application, even though this could result in a better user experience for local users. Usually, it's simply too expensive to implement two interface tiers.

No Automatic State Management

Developers using VB6 forms and local components are accustomed to making the user interface more convenient by creating forms that remember things for the user – the interface maintains **state**. If a piece of information is placed in a text box, it stays there until it is explicitly changed or removed by the developer or user.

ASP, however, has no such capability. Every time a page is rendered, we must make sure that all the visual controls have their information loaded. It is the programmer's responsibility to manage the state in the user interface, and to transfer state information between pages.

This means that developers have to write a lot of code for Internet user interfaces that is not relevant to the business problem the application is designed to solve. In addition, if an Internet application is going to run on a group of web servers (often called a web farm), then considerable additional work is necessary to design a state management system that is independent of a particular server.

Weak User Interfaces over the Web

It is possible to produce sophisticated user interfaces for the Web by using DHTML and writing a lot of JavaScript. However, most web-based applications actually offer fairly primitive user interfaces because it takes too much time and expertise to write a sophisticated one. (Including a lot of nice graphics doesn't make a user interface sophisticated – it just makes it pretty.)

Developers who cut their teeth on producing state-of-the-art interactive user interfaces in VB during the mid-1990s were never satisfied with the compromises necessary for web interfaces. Better user interfaces on the Web would be an enormous boost for user productivity.

The Need to Abstract the Operating System

Today's applications need to use the Windows API for a variety of purposes. VB6 developers use the API to monitor Windows messages, manipulate controls, read, and write INI files, and a variety of other tasks.

This is some of the fussiest programming VB6 developers ever have to do. The Windows API is hard to program to for a variety of reasons. It isn't object-based, which means we must learn complex calls to functions with long lists of arguments. The naming scheme for the functions is inconsistent and since the whole API is written in C/C++, getting calling conventions right on data types such as strings is very messy.

There's a larger issue here as well. As hardware platforms proliferate, it's no longer enough for software just to run on desktop clients and servers. There are handheld and wireless devices of various kinds, kiosks, and other types of systems, many of which run on different processors and don't use standard Windows as an operating system. Any software written with calls to the Windows API won't be portable to any of these systems without major changes. The only way that software produced with Microsoft tools can become more portable is to abstract away the Windows API, so that application software does not write directly to it. This actually creates the possibility of an equivalent layer of abstraction on other platforms that could allow Microsoft-based software to run on them.

All of these limitations had to be addressed, but Microsoft decided to look beyond just Visual Basic and solve these problems on a global level. All of these limitations are solved in **Visual Basic .NET (VB.NET)** through the **.NET Framework**.

The Solution – Microsoft .NET

Microsoft's .NET initiative is broad-based and very ambitious. It includes the **.NET Framework**, which encompasses the languages and execution platform, plus extensive class libraries providing rich built-in functionality. Besides the core .NET Framework, the .NET initiative includes protocols (such as the **Simple Object Access Protocol**, commonly known as **SOAP**) to provide a new level of integration of software over the Internet, and a set of pre-built web-based services called **.NET My Services** (formerly codenamed Hailstorm).

Microsoft also released several products early in 2001, which were described as being part of the **.NET Enterprise Server** family: SQL Server 2000, Commerce Server 2000, BizTalk Server, Exchange 2000, Host Integration Server (the successor to SNA Server), and Internet Security and Administration (ISA) Server (the successor to Proxy Server).

Some of the marketing literature for these products emphasizes that they are part of Microsoft's .NET strategy. However, it is important to understand the difference between these products and the .NET Framework. The .NET Enterprise Servers are *not* based on the .NET Framework. Most of them are successors to previous server-based products, and they use the same COM/COM+ technologies as their predecessors.

These .NET Enterprise Servers still have a major role to play in future software development projects. When actual .NET Framework projects are developed, most will depend on the technologies in the .NET Enterprise Servers for functions like data storage and messaging.

The General Goals of .NET

Many of the goals Microsoft had in mind when designing .NET reflect the limitations we identified for their earlier tools and technologies.

Creating Highly Distributed Applications

The trend in business applications is towards a more highly distributed model. The next generation of applications may have their elements distributed among various organizations. This contrasts with today's dominant model in which all the elements of an application (except possibly a browser-based client) are located solely within a single organization.

Simplifying Software Development

Developers need to be able to concentrate on the business logic in their applications, and to stop writing logic for things like state management and scalability. Writing software for the Internet should not require expertise in a long list of Internet-specific technologies.

A related goal is to have development for the Internet look very much like development for other platforms. A component accessed over a local network or over the Internet should be manipulated with code very much like that for a component accessed on the local machine. The software platform should be able to take care of the details in transmitting information to and from the component.

Better User Interfaces over the Web

User interface development also needs to be as similar as possible for the Internet compared to local access. While using local, platform-specific interfaces will always offer more flexibility than a browser-based interface, Microsoft .NET aims to make those two types of interfaces as similar to develop as possible.

By making web-based user interfaces richer and more flexible than they are now, bringing them as close as possible to the richness of local, forms-based interfaces.

Simplifying Deployment

The problems of DLL Hell, and the need for large installs of forms-based applications, are just two examples of current deployment issues. Microsoft .NET aims to make deployment as simple as it was for DOS – just copy a compiled module over to a system and run it. No registration, no GUIDs, no special installation procedure.

Support for a Variety of Languages

While the idea of one grand, unifying language sounds good in theory, in the real world, different types of developers need different tools. Microsoft .NET is designed to support a multitude of languages, from Microsoft and third-parties. This will allow the development community to evolve languages that best fit various development needs.

An Extendable Platform for the Future

A new platform needs the capability to adapt to changing conditions through extensions and variations. .NET is designed with greater extendibility and flexibility than any previous software development platform.

Future Portability of Compiled Applications

Operating systems will make major changes and perhaps entirely new ones will be introduced in the future. Investments in software development need to be carried forward to those platforms. The goal of .NET is to allow applications to move from current platforms to future platforms, such as 64-bit operating systems with a simple copy, and no recompilation.

The Structure of Microsoft .NET

These are ambitious goals. To understand how they are accomplished, we need to understand the general structure of Microsoft .NET.

One way to look at .NET is to see how it fits into the rest of the computing world. Here is a diagram of the major layers of .NET, showing how they sit on top of an operating system, and provide various ways to interface to the outside world. Note how the entire architecture has been created to make it as easy to develop Internet applications, as it is to develop for the desktop:

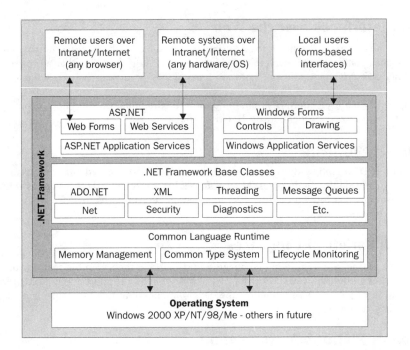

The first point of this diagram is that .NET is a framework that covers all the layers of software development above the operating system. It provides the richest level of integration among presentation technologies, component technologies, and data technologies ever seen on a Microsoft, or perhaps any, platform.

The .NET Framework wraps the operating system, insulating software developed with .NET from most operating system specifics such as file handling and memory allocation.

The .NET Framework itself starts with the execution engine, memory management, and component loading, and goes all the way up to multiple ways of rendering user and program interfaces. In between, there are layers that provide just about any system-level capability that a developer would need.

The Common Language Runtime

The **Common Language Runtime (CLR)** is at the heart of the .NET Framework. The core of the CLR is an execution engine that loads, executes, and manages code that has been compiled into an intermediate byte-code format called **Microsoft Intermediate Language** (**MSIL** and often referred to as just **IL**). This code is not interpreted – it is compiled to native binary code before execution by just-in-time compilers built into the CLR.

That means there are two levels of compilers in .NET. The language compiler takes the source code and creates MSIL. This MSIL byte code is portable to any .NET platform. At execution time, this code is then compiled by the just-in-time compilers into the native binary code of the machine the code is executed on.

> **Chapter 3 will cover the capabilities of the CLR in detail. Do not skip that chapter. Understanding the CLR is a vital step in understanding .NET as a whole.**

The .NET Framework Class Library

The next layer up in the framework provides the services and object-models for data, input/output, security, and so forth. It is called the **.NET Framework class library**, sometimes referred to as the **.NET base classes**. .NET includes functionality that is, in many cases, a duplication of existing class libraries. There are several reasons for this:

❑ The .NET Framework class library is implemented in the .NET Framework, which makes them easier to integrate with .NET-developed programs.

❑ The .NET Framework class library brings together most of the system class libraries into one location, which increases consistency and convenience.

❑ The class libraries in the .NET Framework class library are much easier to extend than older class libraries.

❑ Having the libraries as part of the .NET Framework simplifies deployment of .NET applications. Once the .NET Framework is installed on a system, individual applications don't need to install base class libraries for common functions like data access.

The .NET Framework class library contains thousands of classes and interfaces. Here is just some of the functionality it contains:

❑ Database access and manipulation

❑ Creation and management of threads

❑ Interfaces from .NET to the outside world – Windows Forms, Web Forms, Web Services, and console applications

❑ Definition, management, and enforcement of application security

❑ Application configuration

❑ Working with Directory Services, Event Logs, Processes, Message Queues and Timers

❑ Creating and working with Windows Services

❑ Encrypting and decrypting files

❑ Parsing and manipulating data in XML files

❑ Sending and receiving data with a variety of network protocols

❑ Accessing metadata information stored in assemblies, which are the execution units of .NET (think of them as DLLs and EXEs)

Much of the functionality that you might think of as being part of a language has been moved to the .NET Framework classes. For example, the `System.Math.Sqrt` method in the Framework Classes replaces the Visual Basic keyword `Sqr` for extracting a square root.

All .NET languages have these Framework classes available. That means that C#, for example, can use the same function mentioned above for getting a square root. This makes accessing base functionality highly consistent across languages. All calls to `Sqrt` look essentially the same (apart from syntactical differences between languages) and access the same underlying code. Here are examples in VB.NET and C#:

```
' Example using Sqrt in Visual Basic .NET
Dim dblNumber As Double = 200
Dim dblSquareRoot As Double
dblSquareRoot = System.Math.Sqrt(dblNumber)
```

```
// Same example in C#
Double dblNumber = 200;
Double dblSquareRoot;
dblSquareRoot = System.Math.Sqrt(dblNumber);
```

User and Program Interfaces

In a sense, the top layer of the .NET Framework is an extension of the .NET Framework Base Classes layer immediately underneath it. It comprises highly innovative user and program interfaces that allow .NET to work with the outside world. These interfacing technologies are all highly innovative:

❑ **Windows Forms** is a language-independent forms engine that brings the drag-and-drop design features of Visual Basic to all .NET-enabled languages, and also enables developers to develop forms-based interfaces with little or no access to the Win32 API. They are discussed in Chapters 12 and 13.

❑ **Web Forms** brings drag-and-drop design and an event-driven architecture to Web-based interfaces, implementing a programming model that is much like standard VB6 forms-based development. User interfaces created with Web Forms also have built-in browser independence and state management. They are discussed in Chapters 14 and 15.

❑ **Web Services** allow remote components, possibly running on completely different operating systems, to be invoked and used. This capability for communications and interoperability with remote components over the Internet serves as the mechanism by which highly-distributed applications can be built, going far beyond what is feasible with existing technologies like DCOM. Web Services are discussed in Chapter 22.

XML as the .NET Meta-Language

Much of the underlying integration of .NET is accomplished with XML:

❑ Web Services depend completely on XML for interfacing with remote objects.

❑ The information about execution modules, called **assemblies**, can be exported as XML.

❑ ADO.NET, the successor to ADO, is heavily dependent on XML for remote representation of data. Essentially, when ADO.NET creates what it calls a **DataSet** (a more complex successor to a recordset), the data is converted to XML for manipulation by ADO.NET. Then the changes to that XML are posted back to the data store by ADO.NET when remote manipulation is finished. (Chapter 11 discusses ADO.NET in more detail.)

XML, and its relationship to VB.NET, is discussed further in Chapter 10.

How Microsoft .NET Attains Its Goals

Now that we've had a short introduction to the structure of .NET, we can better understand how it meets the goals Microsoft set out for it.

Simplified Software Development

.NET simplifies the development of business application software through:

❑ **Pre-Written Functionality** – The .NET Framework Base Classes make it unnecessary to write system-level code. These classes furnish a wide array of functionality, and can be extended via inheritance if additional functionality is needed. It is no longer necessary to start over from scratch if a particular pre-built component does not do exactly what we need.

❑ **Transparent Integration of Internet Technologies** – In .NET, the protocols and mechanisms for accessing Internet resources are built into the platform in such a way that we do not need to handle the details. For example, Web Services are created by simply marking a function with a `<WebMethod>` attribute (more on this in Chapter 22). Creating simple web interfaces with Web Forms doesn't require an extensive knowledge of HTML, or how to handle information from an HTTP post operation. The controls used in Web Forms automatically produce JavaScript (if the browser in use can run it) to handle data validation on the client. If the browser does not support JavaScript, the data validation is run transparently on the server.

This integration of web technologies reduces the expertise barriers to web development. While it's still helpful to know a lot about HTML, DHTML, and so on, traditional VB developers will find that developing web software with VB.NET is much easier than with ASP.

❑ **Unified Programming Models for All Types of Development** – Web Services are just regular functions with a `<WebMethod>` attribute attached, which means they are created and consumed much like local components. Once the Web Service's location is referenced, Web Service classes are instantiated the same way as local classes, and their interface looks like a typical object interface. Web Services even have IntelliSense in the development environment, just like local components.

Likewise, developing user interfaces in Windows Forms is very similar to developing them in Web Forms. Both contain commonly used controls, such as labels and text boxes, which have similar properties and methods. Of course, not everything can be the same, because the disconnected model for Web Forms means it is impractical to have as many events as in Windows Forms. (For example, the mouse-moving events are mostly missing from Web Forms.) However, there's enough commonality between the two to make it easy to move between the two types of development, and for traditional VB developers to start using Web Forms.

Highly Distributed Systems

The vision of Microsoft .NET is of globally distributed systems that use XML as a universal glue in order to allow functions running on different computers across organizations to form a single application. In this vision, systems from servers to wireless palmtops (and everything in between) will share the same general platform, with versions of .NET available for all of them, and with each able to integrate transparently with the others.

21

Web Services are the mechanism for reaching this vision. In Web Services, software functionality is exposed as a service that doesn't care what the consumer of the service is (apart from security considerations). Web Services allow developers to build applications by combining local and remote resources to create an integrated, distributed solution.

Web Services have enormous potential. For example, a commercial software company could produce a Web Service that calculates sales tax for every jurisdiction in the nation. A subscription to that Web Service could then be sold to any company that needs to calculate sales tax. The customer has no need to deploy the sales tax calculator because is it just called over the Web. The company producing the sales tax calculator can dynamically update it to include new rates and rules for various jurisdictions and their customers that use the Web Service don't have to do anything to get these updates.

Better User Interfaces over the Web

Web Forms are a giant step towards much richer web-based user interfaces. Their built-in intelligence allows rich, browser-independent screens to be developed quickly, and to be easily integrated with compiled code.

Simplified Deployment

Executable modules in .NET are self-describing. Once the CLR knows where a module resides, it can find out everything else it needs to know to run the module, such as the module's object interface and security requirements, from the module itself. That means that a module can be copied to a new system and immediately executed.

The CLR is capable of loading multiple versions of a single DLL that can be executed side-by-side. Each executable module identifies the particular DLL it needs, and the CLR runs it against the correct one. This means that versioning difficulties are dramatically reduced with .NET.

This is a huge leap from the complex deployment of before. While advanced applications still need an installation program to accomplish tasks such as setting up database connections and other configuration information, such programs are much simpler than before. Simple applications do not need an installation program at all.

But perhaps the most radical improvement for deployment is the ability of .NET to deploy over the Internet. The components and forms for an application can be placed on a web server, and a simple launch program on the client can automatically cause elements of the application to be copied from the web server as needed, and for new versions of the application's components to be automatically updated on the client. The only requirement for the client to use this capability is to have the .NET Framework installed on it, and to have Internet connectivity. This option promises to revitalize the use of smart client interfaces, because the deployment costs associated with COM-based client applications are virtually eliminated.

Support for a Variety of Languages

The CLR executes binary code in MSIL, and that code looks the same regardless of the original source language. All .NET-enabled languages use the same data types and the same interfacing conventions. This makes it possible for all .NET languages to interoperate transparently. One language can call another easily, and languages can even inherit classes written in another language and extend them. No other platform has anywhere near this level of language interoperability.

This makes choosing a language mostly a matter of taste. .NET-enabled languages will typically have the same performance characteristics, the same overall functionality, and will interoperate with other languages the same.

One of the most important aspects of meeting this goal is that Visual Basic becomes a first-class language. It has almost exactly the same capabilities as C#. It has inheritance, structured error handling, and other advanced features. With the large number of developers who already know Visual Basic, VB.NET should set the stage for Visual Basic to continue to be the most popular programming language in the world.

Extendibility of the Platform

The completely object-based approach of .NET is designed to allow base functionality to be extended through inheritance (unlike COM), and the platform's functionality is appropriately partitioned to allow various parts (such as the just-in-time compilers discussed in Chapter 3) to be replaced as new versions are needed.

It is likely that, in the future, new ways of interfacing to the outside world will be added to the current trio of Windows Form, Web Forms, and Web Services. The architecture of .NET makes such additions quite practical.

Future Portability

By abstracting away the underlying platform as much as possible .NET makes possible a future in which software is moved to new hardware and operating system platforms. The core elements of .NET have been submitted to standards bodies, with the intent of standardizing the core of .NET on different systems. The ultimate goal is that code compiled on one implementation of .NET (such as Windows) could be moved to another implementation of .NET on a different operating system and executed without change.

The Role of COM

.NET integrates very well with COM-based software, which is fortunate because COM is not going to disappear for a while. Any COM component can be treated as a .NET component by other .NET components. The .NET Framework wraps COM components and exposes an interface that .NET components can work with. This is absolutely essential to the quick acceptance of .NET, because it makes .NET interoperable with a tremendous amount of COM-based software.

Going in the other direction, the .NET Framework can expose .NET components with a COM interface. This allows COM components to use .NET-based components as if they were developed using COM. (COM interoperability is discussed in more detail in Chapter 17).

However, native .NET components do not interface using COM. The CLR implements a new way for components to interface that is not COM-based. Use of COM is only necessary when interfacing to COM components produced by non-.NET tools.

In the long term, the fact that .NET does not use COM internally may lead to the decline of COM – but that is for the very long term. In the short to medium term, COM is definitely still important.

The Role of DNA

Earlier in the chapter, we discussed the limitations of the current DNA programming model. These limitations are mostly inherent in the technologies used to implement DNA today, not in the overall structure or philosophy. There is nothing fundamentally wrong with the multi-tiered approach to development specified by the DNA model. Many design issues, such as the need to encapsulate business rules, or to provide for multiple user interface access points to a system, apply to .NET.

In many cases, applications developed in the .NET Framework will still use a DNA model to design the appropriate tiers. However, the tiers will be a lot easier to produce in .NET:

- ❑ The presentation tier benefits from the new interface technologies, particularly Web Forms for Internet development

- ❑ The middle tier requires far less COM-related headaches to develop and implement

- ❑ Richer, more distributed middle tier designs are possible by using Web Services

The architectural skills that experienced developers have learned in the DNA world are still valuable in the .NET world.

Additional Benefits

In addition to the advantages conferred by meeting the goals we discussed previously, .NET offers a number of additional benefits. These include:

- ❑ Faster development – we have less to do as the system handles more

- ❑ More reuse because of inheritance

- ❑ Greater scalability – many capabilities to help applications scale are built into .NET

- ❑ Easier to build sophisticated development tools – debuggers and profilers can target the Common Language Runtime, and thus become accessible to all .NET-enabled languages

- ❑ Fewer bugs – whole classes of bugs should be unknown in .NET; for example, with the CLR handling memory management, memory leaks should be a thing of the past

- ❑ Potentially better performance – Microsoft's heavy investment in system level code for memory management, garbage collection, and the like have yielded an architecture that should meet or exceed performance of typical COM-based applications today

Impact on Visual Basic

Since VB.NET is built on top of the .NET framework, the shortcomings in VB6 that we discussed earlier have been eliminated. In fact, VB gets the most extensive changes of any existing language in the Visual Studio suite. These changes pull VB in line with other languages in terms of data types, calling conventions, error handling, and – most importantly – object-orientation. These changes will be covered in Chapters 5, 6, and 7.

Microsoft includes a migration tool in Visual Studio .NET, and it can assist in porting VB6 projects to .NET, but it will not do everything required. There are some areas, including unsupported, obsolete syntax such as GOSUB, where the tool merely places a note that indicates something needs to be done. You can find more information about compatibility between VB6 and VB.NET in Appendix A.

Summary

This chapter explained the importance of .NET and just how much it changes the way that applications are developed. Understanding these concepts is essential in order to use VB.NET in the most effective manner.

It is possible to use VB.NET merely to write the same kinds of software as were written in VB6, only faster and more cleanly. However, this would be failing to use much of the value of VB.NET. The real opportunities are in creating entirely new types of applications such as Web Services, and in implementing application frameworks that promote reuse of code. The rest of this book explains the concepts and technologies you'll need to do that.

In the next chapter we'll get started creating VB.NET applications, as well as take a first look at the new development environment provided by Visual Studio .NET.

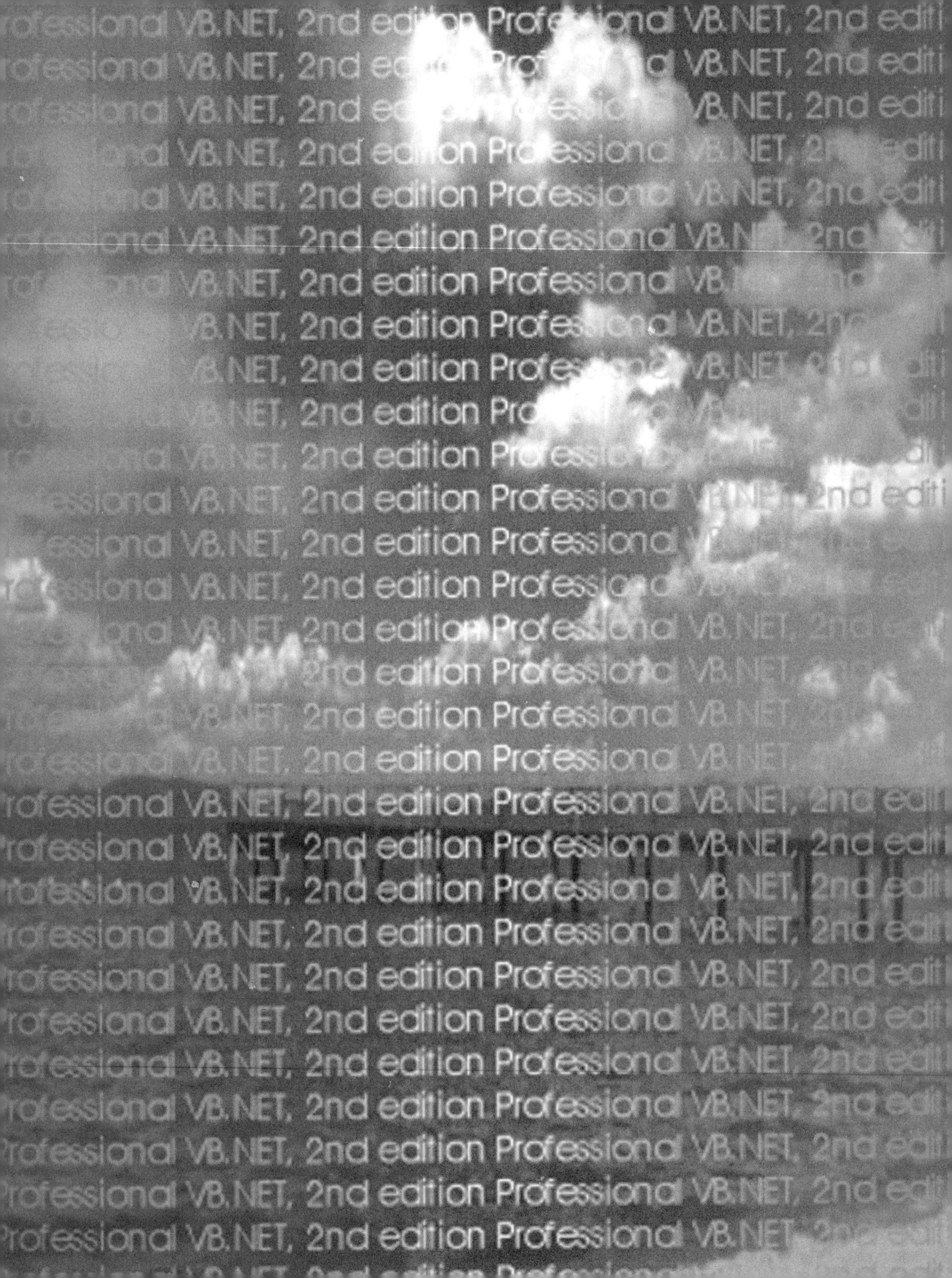
Professional VB.NET, 2nd edition

Introducing VB.NET and VS.NET

Chapter 1 introduced .NET and explained why it is an important and necessary step in the evolution of programming on the Windows platform. In this chapter, we are going to take a practical look at how these changes affect how we create applications. We'll start by walking through the creation of the standard "Hello World" Windows application with **Visual Studio .NET (VS.NET)** Then we'll make additions to this application, examining the code at each stage to understand the changes that have been made. We will cover many topics, including:

- ❏ Project types
- ❏ Generated code
- ❏ Code regions
- ❏ Forms as classes
- ❏ Class constructors
- ❏ Setting form properties

This chapter will only provide a brief introduction to VB.NET applications – we'll look at all of the subjects covered here in much more detail in later chapters.

Visual Studio .NET

When **Visual Studio .NET (VS.NET)** is first started, the following window is displayed:

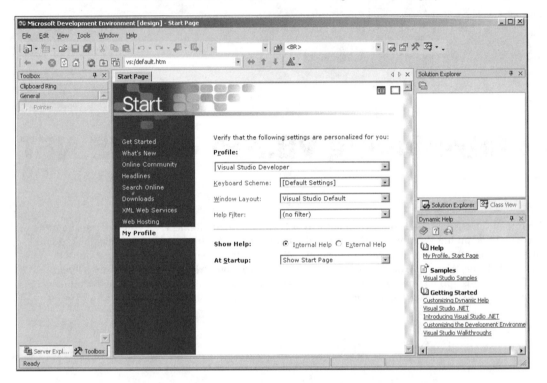

This is the VS.NET Start Page. You can use the My Profile option on the left-hand-side of this page to select an appropriate profile in order to adapt the environment to your needs.

My Profile

When a profile is chosen, several aspects of the **Integrated Development Environment (IDE)** are customized at once, such as the position of the code window and properties windows, as well as which windows take precedence in the environment. For example, if the Visual Basic Developer profile is selected, the Toolbox is, by default, always on the screen. For other profiles, such as Visual Studio Developer, the Toolbox becomes a tab on the left side of the screen that can be selected by hovering the mouse pointer over it.

Customizing Help

In answer to a long-standing gripe about Visual Studio 6, the help system can be filtered to offer help for particular languages and subjects. The My Profile page contains a Help Filter dropdown box. When VS.NET is installed, it is set to (no filter). Most of the time you'll want to set this option to Visual Basic and Related.

We also have the choice of showing help inside the IDE (as a tabbed window in the same area that code is shown), or outside the IDE as a separate window that can be positioned and manipulated independently.

New IDE Features

When you install VS.NET, one of the first things that you will notice is that there is only one entry for VS.NET in the Start menu – there are no separate entries for Visual Basic, Visual C++, or Visual C#. This is the first physical hint of the Common Language Runtime (CLR) at work. All of the Visual Studio languages share the same IDE because they can now all work together.

> **Because the .NET languages are tied to the .NET Framework, and the .NET Framework is actually installed separately for Windows, we don't need to use VS.NET to develop applications. We could simply use your favorite text editor to create the source files and use the command line compilers provided by the framework. However, this makes code management and debugging much more difficult for applications of any significant size. In this book, we'll stick to using VS.NET.**

The VB project types are different to those of VB6. VB.NET takes advantage of the .NET Framework, so there is no longer any reason to create ActiveX EXEs or DLLs, because COM is not used in the .NET Framework. However, we can still create DLLs by using a Class Library or Web Service project. These types of project will be discussed at length in later chapters.

Creating a Windows Application

Let's create our first VB.NET application. Start VS.NET and create a new project by either selecting New Project from the VS.NET start page, or by selecting New | Project from the File menu. The New Project dialog box will appear:

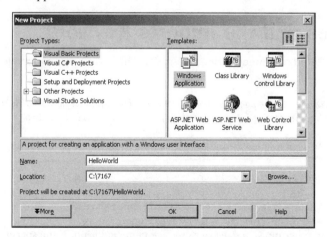

If we type HelloWorld into the Name box, and then click on the OK button, we will have created the beginnings of our Hello World example. This will launch us into the IDE itself.

The Solution Explorer

A number of files are automatically added to the project for us. The number and type of files added will depend on the type of project created. In our case, two code files (Form1.vb and AssemblyInfo.vb) have been added to the project. They can be seen in the Solution Explorer:

The Solution Explorer shows all of the projects that make up the solution. A **solution** can be thought of as a collection of projects that provide a solution to a problem.

> **A solution is similar to a VB6 project group, although solutions can contain projects from different .NET languages, as well as other files (such as images).**

In our case, a solution called HelloWorld has been created that contains one project (also called HelloWorld). The Solution Explorer also displays the references a project contains and allows us to remove a specific reference and add new ones. A reference in VS.NET allows us to access the functionality of external objects. We are able to reference type libraries (such as COM libraries and other projects created in VB6), other .NET components, and Web Services. When VS.NET created the project for the template we selected, it added a selection of references that are commonly needed for this type of project. They are listed under the References node.

Namespaces and the Imports Keyword

If you expand the References node of our project you will see that we have a reference to System.Drawing.

The `System.Drawing` component provides access to GDI+ graphics functionality, an updated version of the Graphics Device Interface functions provided by the Windows API.

Adding a reference to a component means that we can use its functionality in our applications. For example:

```
Dim CarColor As System.Drawing.Color
```

Here, the `Color` structure is in the `System.Drawing` **namespace**. A namespace is used to organize classes, structures, and other types into a single meaningful hierarchy. As well as providing a way to organize classes and other types, namespaces reduce name collision. Namespaces are covered in detail in Chapter 8.

We can omit the full namespace prefix if we import the namespace into our code by using `Imports` statements. The first two lines of the generated code in the `AssemblyInfo.vb` file are `Imports` statements:

```
Imports System.Reflection
Imports System.Runtime.InteropServices
```

`Imports` statements must be used at the beginning of a code file before any other code. In our code, the `System.Reflection` namespace is imported, so we can use the `AssemblyTitle` attribute in our code by simply using the following:

```
<Assembly: AssemblyTitle("")>
```

If the `System.Reflection` namespace had not been imported we would have had to write:

```
<Assembly: System.Reflection.AssemblyTitle("")>
```

Importing namespaces reduces the amount of code that we have to type, but we must be aware of the consequences of not using the full namespace declaration. The single biggest consequence is that if we import two namespaces that both contain types with the same name, and we try to declare a variable of this type without using the full namespace declaration, the compiler won't know which version to use. Imagine that as well as importing the `System.Drawing` namespace we import a `WroxColor` namespace that also contains a `Color` structure. If we refer to the `Color` object in our code without specifying its full namespace, we will see an error like this:

```
Protected Sub Button1_Click(ByVal sender As Object, ByVal e As System.EventArgs)
    Dim objColor As Color
End Sub
```

The name 'Color' is ambiguous, imported from the namespaces or types
'WroxColor, System.Drawing'.

The code will not compile until this ambiguity is clarified by referencing the `Color` structure's full namespace.

We can view the namespaces that are available to an application by using the **Object Browser**, which can be accessed by using the *Ctrl-Alt-J* key combination or through the **View | Other Windows** menu option:

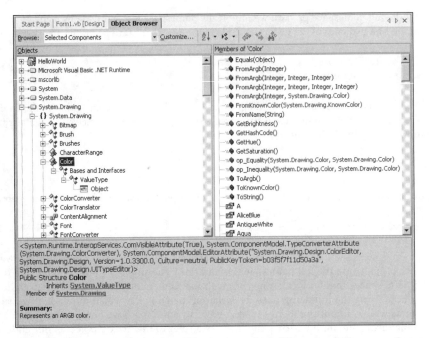

The **Object Browser** is split into two panes. The pane to the left lists the namespaces that are available to the application. We can expand the namespace nodes to reveal the classes, structures, and other types that are contained within each namespace. If we select a class or other type from the left hand pane its members will be listed in the right hand pane.

Namespaces can also be nested inside other namespaces. This nesting helps to organize classes into a more logical structure, which reduces confusion and aids the developer. For example, in the System.Drawing namespace, the Drawing namespace is a child of (is nested within) the System namespace. A parent namespace can be used across multiple components.

The Default Namespaces of a Windows Application

The references added to our project are detailed in the following table and relate directly to namespaces:

Reference	Description
System	The System namespace is often referred to as the root namespace as it provides functionality that all applications will use. All the base data types (String, Object, and so on) are contained within System namespace, along with classes that represent the garbage collector, attributes, and exceptions. It also acts as the parent namespace for a large number of child namespaces.
System.Data	The System.Data namespace consists of classes that are used to implement the functionality of ADO.NET, which is used for data access. This namespace is covered in more detail in Chapter 11.

Reference	Description
System.Drawing	The System.Drawing namespace provides access to the GDI+ graphics functionality.
System.Windows.Forms	The System.Windows.Forms namespace provides a set of classes that can be used to create traditional Windows-based applications. This namespace is covered in detail in Chapter 12.
System.XML	The System.XML namespace contains classes that can be used for processing XML. The XML processing provided is standards based and is covered in Chapter 10.

Alongside the **References** node are all of the files that make up the project. In our case, we have two: Form1.vb and AssemblyInfo.vb. Note that there is only one file extension for VB source files (.vb). We no longer have one extension for a class module and a different one for a form – any differences are held within the source files themselves.

We'll start by looking at the Form1.vb file produced for us, as it contains the code that represents the main window of our application. Later we will (briefly) discuss the AssemblyInfo.vb file that has also been created for us.

The form is visible on screen by default but if you have closed it you can easily reopen it again by right-clicking on **Form1.vb** in the **Solution Explorer** and selecting **View Designer** from the popup menu. Then bring up the code window for the form by right-clicking on it (or on the **Solution Explorer**) and selecting **View Code** from the popup menu.

Tabs versus MDI Interface

You will probably have noticed the tabs that are visible below the toolbar:

In previous versions of the VB IDE, we accessed child windows using an MDI interface. This functionality is still available in VS.NET, but the default is to use the new tabbed arrangement of child windows. We can change the arrangement that is used between the tabbed and MDI interface by using the **Options** dialog box (accessible via **Tools | Options**). We can also force the development environment to use the MDI interface as opposed to the tabbed interface by using the command line option /mdi when VS.NET is started.

The New Code Window

One of the most useful enhancements in the VS.NET IDE is the new code window. The following figure shows the code from the form (**Form1**) that was inserted automatically when the Windows Forms project was created:

```
Start Page │ Form1.vb [Design] │ Form1.vb                                    ◁ ▷ ✕

⚙Form1                              ▼    ▌▌\ (Declarations)                    ▼

  ⊟ Public Class Form1
         Inherits System.Windows.Forms.Form

  ⊞ ┌ Windows Form Designer generated code ─────────────────┐
    └──────────────────────────────────────────────────────┘

    └ End Class
```

This code editor window should look familiar from VB6, except for the gray line on the left with the plus and minus signs. This line is a visual indication that the code inside routines in VS.NET can be hidden on the screen, a feature known as **outlining**. There is a minus sign next to every routine (sub or function). This makes it easy to hide or show code on a routine-by-routine basis. If the code for a routine is hidden, the routine declaration is still shown, and has a plus sign next to it to indicate that the body code is hidden. This feature is very useful when a developer is working on a few key routines in a module, and wishes to avoid scrolling through many screens of code that are not relevant to the current task.

It is also possible to hide larger regions of code. The #Region directive is used for this within the IDE, though it has no effect on the actual application. A region of code is demarcated by the #Region directive at the top and the #End Region directive at the end. The #Region directive that begins a region should include a description, which will appear next to the plus sign shown when the code is minimized. For example, in the last screenshot, there is a code section labeled Windows Form Designer generated code. It is hidden because normally there is no need for the developer to see or manipulate this code. If the plus sign is clicked, however, it comes into view.

We can also create our own code regions by using the #Region and #End Region declarations. For example, if we wanted to create a new code region called Data Access Code, we would add the following to the source code:

```
#Region "Data Access Code"
'Include any data access code within the region tags
#End Region
```

We could, if we desired, use this method to collapse and hide the contents of a whole class.

The outlining enhancement was probably inspired by the fact that the VS.NET designers generate a lot of code when a project is first begun. Items that were hidden in Visual Basic 6 (such as the logic which sets initial form properties) are actually inside the generated code in VS.NET.

In most respects, seeing all of these functions in the code is an improvement because it is easier for the developer to understand what is happening, and possibly to manipulate the process in limited, special cases.

Outlining can also be turned off by selecting Edit | Outlining | Stop Outlining from the Visual Studio menu. That menu also contains some other useful functions. A section of code can be temporarily hidden by highlighting it and selecting Edit | Outlining | Hide Selection. The selected code will be replaced with an ellipsis with a plus sign next to it. Clicking the plus sign displays the code again. There are also options for toggling outlining on and off, and for making a block of code display only the definitions of the routines.

One additional capability of the text editor that can be useful is line numbering. Go to Tools | Options, open the Text Editor folder, and then select the All Languages folder. Checking the Line numbers checkbox will cause the editor to number all lines, which provides an easy way to unambiguously reference lines of code.

Extended IntelliSense

IntelliSense has always been a popular feature of Microsoft tools and applications and the code editor window in VS.NET includes some new IntelliSense features that take the concept even further.

For example, if you type Exit and a space, IntelliSense will display a list of keywords in a dropdown which could follow Exit. Other keywords that have dropdowns to present available options include Goto, Implements, Option, and Declare. IntelliSense also displays more tooltip information in the environment than before and helps the developer match up pairs of parentheses, braces, and brackets.

The Properties Window

The Properties window can be accessed through the View menu or by pressing the *F4* key. The Properties window is just like that of VB6. It is used to set the properties of the currently selected item – for example, a project file or a control on a form. Change the Text property of Form1 to Hello World:

> There is no **Caption** property in VB.NET. All items that had a **Caption** property in VB6 now have a **Text** property instead.

To set the caption of a Button control (the new name for Command Buttons), we would now use the Text property, rather than the Caption property, like so:

```
btnCancel.Text = "&Cancel"
```

We have now created the example project that we are going to examine and build upon for the remainder of the chapter. If you've used VB6 you may be forgiven for wondering what has changed. It is only when we look at the code that we can fully appreciate how forms in VB.NET work and how they differ from previous versions of VB.

Dynamic Help

The Properties window may not have changed much from VB6, but the Dynamic Help tab below the Properties window is new. Dynamic Help makes a guess at what you might be interested in looking at, based on what you have done recently. The options in the Dynamic Help window are categorized into three areas. The top category, entitled Help, gives a best guess on the features that the environment thinks you might be trying to use. Just below that is a section called Samples, and it points to a help page that lists a variety of sample applications. Below that is a category called Getting Started, which contains a variety of help options on introductory material.

One of the options in the Getting Started category is Visual Studio Walkthroughs. This contains step-by-step guides on how to perform the basic tasks for the different types of projects that can be created in VS.NET.

Our First Look at the Code

Let's start with the first two lines of code. These start the declaration for our form:

```
Public Class Form1
    Inherits System.Windows.Forms.Form
```

The first line declares a new class called Form1. In VB.NET, we can declare classes in any code file, not just in a class module (.cls) file as was the case in VB6. We can also declare any number of classes in a code file. The second line specifies that the class derives from the Form class contained in the System.Windows.Forms namespace.

We can deduce from these two lines of code that forms in VB.NET are classes. Specifically, forms are classes that directly or indirectly derive from the System.Windows.Forms.Form class. This class is used to create dialog boxes and windows for traditional Windows-based applications.

We can also deduce from the Inherits keyword that the VB language has been improved to provide better object-oriented features, which will be covered in Chapters 5, 6, and 7.

Because the class is declared with a name of Form1, our form will be called Form1. We can rename the file that contains the class but this does not change the actual name of the class – we must change the Public Class FormName line in order to reflect the new name.

One of the very neat outcomes of forms being implemented as classes is that we can now derive a form from another form. This technique is called **visual inheritance**. Windows Forms will be covered in much more detail in Chapter 12.

Form Properties Set in Code

VS.NET has added a routine to the code called `InitializeComponent`. As the name suggests, this handles the initialization of the components contained on the form. A comment is added before the procedure that warns us that the form designer modifies the code contained in the procedure and that we should not modify the code directly:

```
'NOTE: The following procedure is required by the Windows Form Designer
'It can be modified using the Windows Form Designer.
'Do not modify it using the code editor.
<System.Diagnostics.DebuggerStepThrough()> Private Sub _
        InitializeComponent()

    '
    'Form1
    '
    Me.AutoScaleBaseSize = New System.Drawing.Size(5, 13)
    Me.ClientSize = New System.Drawing.Size(292, 273)
    Me.Name = "Form1"
    Me.Text = "Hello World"

End Sub
```

The four lines of the `InitializeComponent` procedure assign values to properties of our `Form1` class. All the properties of the form and controls are now set directly in code. When we change the value of a property of the form or a control through the Properties window an entry will be added to `InitializeComponent` that will assign the value to the property. In our application, we set the `Text` property of the form to `Hello World`, which caused the following line of code to be added automatically:

```
Me.Text = "Hello World"
```

In previous versions of VB, the properties that were changed from the default values were stored in a region of the form file (. frm) that could not be edited directly.

The other three properties of the form class that are set in `InitializeComponent` are summarized in the following table:

Property	Description
AutoScaleBaseSize	This property is used to store the size of the font used to layout the form at design time. At runtime, the font that is actually rendered is compared to this property and the form is scaled accordingly. This helps to ensure the form looks the same at runtime as it did at design time.
ClientSize	This property is used to set the area within a form in which controls can be placed (the client area). It is the size of the form minus the size of the title bar and form borders. It is of type System.Drawing.Size.
Name	This property is used to set the textual name of the form. By default the property is set to an empty string.

The code is accessing the properties of the form using the Me keyword. The Me keyword acts as a variable that refers to the instance of the class in which it is used. This isn't entirely necessary but it can aid in the understanding of the code.

The AssemblyInfo.vb File

Let's take a brief look at the other file that was produced for us by VS.NET, AssemblyInfo.vb:

```
Imports System.Reflection
Imports System.Runtime.InteropServices

' General Information about an assembly is controlled through
' the following set of attributes. Change these attribute values
' to modify the information associated with an assembly.

' Review the values of the assembly attributes

<Assembly: AssemblyTitle("")>
<Assembly: AssemblyDescription("")>
<Assembly: AssemblyCompany("")>
<Assembly: AssemblyProduct("")>
<Assembly: AssemblyCopyright("")>
<Assembly: AssemblyTrademark("")>
<Assembly: CLSCompliant(True)>

'The following GUID is for the ID of the typelib if this project
'is exposed to COM
<Assembly: Guid("6CCAA661-F174-454C-948E-D3E25426484C")>

' Version information for an assembly consists of the following
' four values:
'
'        Major Version
'        Minor Version
'        Build Number
'        Revision
'
' You can specify all the values or you can default the Build
' and Revision Numbers by using the '*' as shown below:

<Assembly: AssemblyVersion("1.0.*")>
```

The AssemblyInfo.vb file provides a centralized place where we can set information about, and properties of, the resulting assembly. The information and properties are set using a number of **attributes**.

Assembly Attributes

The AssemblyInfo.vb file contains attribute blocks, which are used to set information about the assembly. All the attribute blocks within this file have the **assembly modifier** Assembly:

```
<Assembly: AssemblyTitle("")>
```

The assembly modifier is used to make the attribute apply to the entire assembly. The attributes set within this file all provide information that is contained within the assembly metadata. The attributes contained within the file are summarized in the following table:

Attribute	Description
AssemblyCompany	This attribute is used to set name of the company that produced the assembly. The company name set here will appear within the version resource of the compiled file. This can be seen by right-clicking the file within Windows Explorer and selecting Properties and then looking on the Version tab.
AssemblyCopyright	This attribute is used to set the copyright information of the produced assembly. The copyright information also appears within the version resource of the resulting compiled file.
AssemblyDescription	This attribute is used to provide a textual description of the assembly.
AssemblyProduct	This attribute is used to set the product name of the resulting assembly. The product name will appear within the version resource of the compiled file.
AssemblyTitle	This attribute is used to set the name of the assembly. The title will appear within the resource information of the compiled file as the Description.
AssemblyTrademark	This attribute is used to assign any trademark information to the assembly. This information also appears within the version resource of the compiled file.
AssemblyVersion	This attribute is used to set the version number of the assembly. This is a very important attribute as the version number plays a huge role in helping to avoid DLL Hell when deploying applications (and assemblies). Assembly version numbers will be covered in more detail in Chapter 25.
CLSCompliant	This attribute is used to indicate whether this assembly is compliant with the Common Language Specification (CLS). The CLS is a subset of the Common Language Runtime (see Chapter 3 for more information).
Guid	If the assembly is to be exposed as a traditional COM object then the value of this attribute will become the ID of the resulting type library.

Enhancing the Sample Application

We are going to enhance our application and examine the new code that is added for us. Before we start, make sure that the form is visible in design mode (use View I Designer).

Before we start enhancing our application, we also need to know how to access the **toolbox**. There are two ways to access the toolbox if it is not currently visible. The first is to select Toolbox from the View menu, and the second is to access the toolbox from the vertical bar that runs along the left side of VS.NET. If you look at the bar now, you will notice that there is a tab with the text Toolbox. If you move your mouse over the tab, the toolbox will slide into view from the left:

If you haven't set up the toolbox to be permanently visible, it will slide out of the way and disappear whenever focus is moved away from it. This is a new feature of the IDE that has been added to help maximize the available screen real estate. If you don't like this feature and would like the toolbox to be permanently visible, all you need to do is click the pushpin icon on the title bar of the toolbox.

Adding Controls

Now that you know how to access the toolbox, add a button control to the form and set its `Text` property to `Click Me` and its `Name` property to `btnClickMe`. Your form should look similar to this:

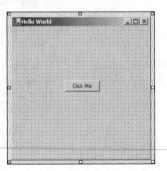

Adding an Event Handler

A button that doesn't do anything when it is clicked isn't much use. So let's add some code to respond to the button being clicked. Double-click on the button, and add the following code to the `Click` event of `btnClickMe`:

```
System.Windows.Forms.MessageBox.Show("Hello World", _
                            "A First Look at VB.NET", _
                            MessageBoxButtons.OK, _
                            MessageBoxIcon.Information)
```

This code demonstrates how we must use parentheses when calling procedures in VB.NET, even if we are not interested in the return value (and even if the procedure lacks parameters).

Changes to the Code

Let's examine the changes that have been made to the code of our application. A complete listing follows:

```
Public Class Form1
    Inherits System.Windows.Forms.Form

#Region " Windows Form Designer generated code "

    Public Sub New()
        MyBase.New()

        'This call is required by the Windows Form Designer.
        InitializeComponent()

        'Add any initialization after the InitializeComponent() call

    End Sub

    'Form overrides dispose to clean up the component list.
    Protected Overloads Overrides Sub Dispose(ByVal disposing As Boolean)
        If disposing Then
            If Not (components Is Nothing) Then
                components.Dispose()
            End If
        End If
        MyBase.Dispose(disposing)
    End Sub

    'Required by the Windows Form Designer
    Private components As System.ComponentModel.IContainer

    'NOTE: The following procedure is required by the Windows Form Designer
    'It can be modified using the Windows Form Designer.
    'Do not modify it using the code editor.
    Friend WithEvents btnClickMe As System.Windows.Forms.Button
    <System.Diagnostics.DebuggerStepThrough()> _
```

```
Private Sub InitializeComponent()
    Me.btnClickMe = New System.Windows.Forms.Button()
    Me.SuspendLayout()
    '
    'btnClickMe
    '
    Me.btnClickMe.Location = New System.Drawing.Point(112, 112)
    Me.btnClickMe.Name = "btnClickMe"
    Me.btnClickMe.TabIndex = 0
    Me.btnClickMe.Text = "Click Me"
    '
    'Form1
    '
    Me.AutoScaleBaseSize = New System.Drawing.Size(5, 13)
    Me.ClientSize = New System.Drawing.Size(292, 273)
    Me.Controls.AddRange(New System.Windows.Forms.Control() {Me.btnClickMe})
    Me.Name = "Form1"
    Me.Text = "Hello World"
    Me.ResumeLayout(False)

End Sub

#End Region

Private Sub Button1_Click(ByVal sender As System.Object, _
                        ByVal e As System.EventArgs) _
                        Handles btnClickMe.Click
    System.Windows.Forms.MessageBox.Show("Hello World", _
                            "A First Look at VB.NET", _
                            MessageBoxButtons.OK, _
                            MessageBoxIcon.Information)
End Sub

End Class
```

The first change that has been made to our code is the addition of a new variable to represent our new button:

```
Friend WithEvents btnClickMe As System.Windows.Forms.Button
```

When we add any type of control to the form, a new variable will be added to the form class. Controls are now represented by variables and, just as form properties are set in code, so form controls are added in code. The Button class in the System.Windows.Forms namespace implements the button control on the toolbox. All of the controls that can be added to a form have a class that implements the functionality of the control. These classes are usually found in the System.Windows.Forms namespace. The WithEvents keyword has been used in the declaration of the new variable so that we can respond to the events of the button.

Most of the code additions are in the InitializeComponent procedure. Eight lines of code have been added to help set up and add our button control. The first addition to the procedure is a line that creates a new instance of the Button class and assigns it to our button variable:

```
Me.btnClickMe = New System.Windows.Forms.Button()
```

Before we can add the button to the form we need to stop the layout engine of the form from working. This is accomplished by using the next line of code added for us:

```
Me.SuspendLayout()
```

The next four lines of code that have been added are setting properties of the button. The `Location` property of the `Button` class sets the location of the top left corner of the button within the form:

```
Me.btnClickMe.Location = New System.Drawing.Point(112, 112)
```

The location of a control is expressed in terms of a `Point` structure, which is a coordinate pair. The next property of the button that is set through code is the `Name` property:

```
Me.btnClickMe.Name = "btnClickMe"
```

The `Name` property acts in exactly the same way as it did for the form – it provides a way to set the textual name of the button. The `Name` property has no effect on how the button is displayed on the form. The next two lines of code assign values to the `TabIndex` and `Text` properties of the button:

```
Me.btnClickMe.TabIndex = 0
Me.btnClickMe.Text = "Click Me"
```

The `TabIndex` property of the button is used to set the order in which the control will be selected when the user cycles through the controls on the form using the *Tab* key. The higher the number, the later the control will get focus. Each control should have a unique number for its `TabIndex` property. The `Text` property of a button is used to set the text that appears on the button.

Once the properties of the button have been set it needs to be added to the form. This is accomplished with the next line of code:

```
Me.Controls.AddRange(New System.Windows.Forms.Control() {Me.btnClickMe})
```

This line of code adds the button to the collection of child controls for the form. The `System.Windows.Forms.Form` class (from which our `Form1` class is derived) has a property called `Controls` that keeps track of all of the child controls of the form. Whenever we add a control to a form, similar code to this is added automatically. The final code change to the `InitializeComponent` sub turns the layout logic of the form back on, so that our button will be correctly added to the form:

```
Me.ResumeLayout(False)
```

The final code change is the event handler we added for the button. Event handlers have a similar naming convention to that of previous versions of VB: the control name followed by an underscore and then the event name and any parameters. In our example, we added an event handler for the `Click` event of the button by double-clicking the button in the Designer. Event handlers can also be added by using the dropdown lists at the top of the code window:

The dropdown box on the left-hand-side lists the objects for which we can add event handlers. The dropdown box on the right-hand-side lists all the events for the selected object. This is exactly the same as in previous versions of VB, apart from an enhancement that allows us to handle the events of the classes that have been overridden. The overridden object is represented in the list of objects by (Overrides).

Stepping through the Hello World Example

Having written a sample "Hello World" application, the next step is to build it.

Build Configurations

In previous versions of VB, a project only had one set of properties. There was no way to have one set of properties for a debug build and one for a release build – you had to manually change all the properties as required before you built the application. This has changed with the introduction of build configurations, which allow us to have one set of project properties for a debug build and one set for a release build and we are not limited to the two default build configurations (debug and release): we can create as many different configurations as we want. The properties that can be set for a project have been split into two groups: those that are independent of build configuration and which apply to all build configurations, and those that apply to the active build configuration only. For instance, the `Project Name` and `Project Location` properties are the same irrespective of what build configuration is active, whereas the code optimization options differ depending on the active build configuration. This isn't a new concept and has been available to Visual C++ developers for some time, but it is the first time it has been available for Visual Basic developers.

This allows us to turn off optimization when we are developing our application and create symbolic debug information that will help if we encounter any errors. Once we are ready to ship the application and are happy that the application is stable, we can switch to a release build that will be optimized, smaller in size, and quicker.

We can access the project properties dialog box by right-clicking the project in the Solution Explorer and choosing Properties from the popup menu, or by selecting Properties from the Project menu:

To the left of the dialog box, there are two folders that represent the two groups of project properties. Each of the folders contains a number of sections that logically group properties together further. The first is called **Common Properties** and is where we can change those properties that are independent of build configuration.

The second folder is called **Configuration Properties** and contains a number of sections where we can change properties that are dependent on the active build configuration. When a section from the **Configuration Properties** folder is selected, the configuration dropdown box becomes enabled. This dropdown allows us to select the build configuration that we would like to set the properties of. The current configuration will be listed as **Active**, with the configuration name in brackets. There is a second dropdown box labeled **Platform**, which allows us to select the target platform for the project.

If we have more than one project in the current solution, we can choose which projects are included in a particular build configuration. Projects are assigned to build configurations through the **Configuration Manager** (available by clicking the button in the top right-hand corner of the project properties dialog).

To change the currently active build configuration, we can use the drop-box to the right of the run button on the toolbar to select the configuration that we would like to use. The dropdown contains the following options:

- Debug
- Release
- Configuration Manager...

The last option provides a way into the **Configuration Manager**, thus providing a simple two-click method for changing configurations:

The Configuration Manager contains an entry for each project in the current solution. We can include or exclude a project from the build of the selected build configuration (shown in the combo-box at the top of the window) by using the checkbox in the column of the grid labeled Build. If the checkbox is selected then the project will be built. We can also select which configuration and target platform of the project we would like to use in this particular build configuration.

Building Our Application

Next, we are now going to build our application using the Debug build configuration, so make sure this is the active build configuration. We have a whole Build menu devoted to building our project/solution:

Menu Item	Description
Build	Will use the currently active build configuration to build the project
Rebuild	Will clean all intermediate files (object files and so on) and the output directory before building the project using the active build configuration
Batch Build	Will allow us to build multiple versions of the project using one or more of the build configurations in one go
Configuration Manager	Will show the dialog box to allow edit, add, and delete build configurations

If we have more than one project in our solution, the menu will have a few more options that will allow us to either build all of the projects in the solution or to build the currently selected project only. The options presented will also vary depending on the way VS.NET is configured:

Select Build from the menu. The example project will now be built. You can keep track of what is happening by looking in the Output window:

Now you can look in the output directory (specified in the project properties) to find the executable that has been created.

If the build was unsuccessful an item is added to the Task List window (usually found along the bottom of the main VS.NET window) for each error encountered. The task will include the reason for the error and where the error occurred. By double-clicking the error task you will be taken directly to the location of the error. Now, let's run our application.

Running Our Application

To run the application, click on the Start button, select Debug | Start, or press *F5*. Once you click the Click Me button you'll see the following:

This concludes our example. For the remainder of the chapter we'll take a look at some other useful features of VS.NET.

Useful Features of VS.NET

VS.NET contains many useful tools that make the life of a developer an easier one. We'll take a look at:

- ❑   The Task List
- ❑   The Command Window
- ❑   The Server Explorer
- ❑   Macros in Visual Studio

The Task List

The Task List is a great productivity tool that tracks pending changes and additions in code. It's also a good way for the VS.NET environment to communicate information that the developer needs to know, such as errors in the current code. The Task List can show all current syntax errors in the code, so it's not necessary to do a "Run With Full Compile" and then examine them one at a time.

The Task List is displayed with the Show Tasks option on the View menu. There are several options available. The Comment option is for tasks embedded into code comments. This is done by creating a standard comment with the apostrophe, and then starting the comment with TODO:. This can be followed with any text desired. Such a comment will show up in the Task List if either the Comment option or the All option is selected.

In addition to using the TODO: token, a user can create their own comment tokens in the options for Visual Studio, via the Tools I Options I Environment I Task List menu.

Besides helping developers track these tasks, embedding the tasks in code brings another benefit. Clicking on a task in the Task List causes the code editor to jump right to the location of the task without our having to hunt through the code for it.

Another view of the Task List is Build Errors. This view summarizes all of the things that prevent a clean build of the code. As with tasks embedded in comments, clicking on a build error task takes the code editor to the location of the error. It's not necessary to explicitly choose Build for these errors to display – the environment automatically checks code continuously and inserts build errors in the list.

We can also simply type tasks into the list. These are shown when the View I Show Tasks I User option for filtering the Task List is selected, or when all tasks are displayed.

The Command Window

The Command Window is shown by selecting the menu option View I Other Windows I Command Window. When the window is displayed, a > prompt will be displayed to allow input.

The Command Window can be used to access VS.NET menu options and commands by typing them in instead of selecting them in the menu structure. For example, if you type File.AddNewProject and press *Enter* the dialog box to add a new project will appear. Note that IntelliSense is available to help enter commands in the Command Window:

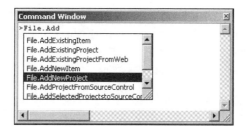

The Command Window also has an Immediate mode in which expressions can be evaluated. This mode is accessed by typing Immed at the prompt. In this mode, the window title changes to indicate that the Immediate mode is active.

> **In the Immediate mode, the window behaves very much like the Immediate window in Visual Basic 6.**

While a program is running, you can type in arithmetic expressions for evaluation, change the content of variables, and do other debugging functions. The mode can be changed back to Command mode by typing >cmd.

Other Debug-Related Windows

Once a program is running, various other windows become available for display in the same general area as the Task List and the Command Window. Most are available from the View | Other Windows menu.

Output

The compile process puts progress messages in this window, and your program can also place messages in it using the Console object. For example:

```
Console.WriteLine("This is printed in the Output Window")
```

will cause the string This is printed in the Output Window to appear in the Output Window.

Anything written to the Output window is only shown while running a program from the environment. During execution of the compiled module, no Output window is present, so nothing can be written to it.

Call Stack

The Call Stack window lists the procedures that are currently calling other procedures and waiting for their return. This was accessed in Visual Basic 6 with a menu option on the View menu.

Breakpoints

The Breakpoints window is an enhanced breakpoint handler in which breakpoints can be defined and monitored. It is improved from the breakpoint handler in VB6, for example, by having a continuous monitor on the number of times that a breakpoint has been reached. This is useful for debugging problems that only occur after a certain number of iterations of a routine. (Note that Breakpoints are saved when a solution is saved by the IDE.)

Locals

The Locals window is used to monitor the value of all variables that are currently in scope. As in VB6, even arrays can be examined, via a tree-control interface.

Autos

The Autos window displays variables used in the statement currently being executed and the statement just before it. These variables are identified and listed for you automatically, hence the window name.

Watch Windows

There are four Watch Windows, called Watch 1 to Watch 4. Each can hold a set of variables or expressions for which you want to monitor the value. Variables can also have their values changed with Watch windows. Values can be displayed in regular form or in hexadecimal. Variables can be added to Watch windows by right-clicking on the variable in the code editor, and then selecting Add Watch.

Note that the Locals, Autos, and Watch windows only automatically appear when a program is being run in the environment. Managing these windows is done via the Debug | Windows sub-menu.

The Server Explorer

As development has become more server-centric, developers have a greater need to discover and manipulate services on the network. The Server Explorer is a new feature in VS.NET that makes this easier.

Visual Interdev made a start in this direction with a Server Object section in the Interdev Toolbox. The Server Explorer is more sophisticated. It allows, for example, exploration and alteration of SQL Server database structures that would have previously been done with the SQL Enterprise Manager.

The Server Explorer looks like this:

Notice the wide variety of server resources that are available for inspection, or for use in the project. The Server Explorer means that we don't have to go to an outside resource to find, for example, what message queues are available. The Add Server option allows a new server to be selected and inspected. The Server Explorer even provides the ability to stop and restart services on the server.

The Server Explorer subsumes much of the functionality in the Data View in Visual Studio 6. However, it is far more powerful and easier to use. For example, when we right-click on the Data Connections option in the Server Explorer, and then choose the Add Connection option, the resulting screen brings together all the information needed to establish a connection to a server database in a tabbed dialog.

Recording and Using Macros in VS.NET

C++ developers have long had one feature that many Visual Basic developers craved – **macros**. In VS.NET, macros become part of the environment and are available to any language. However, as in the Microsoft Office suite, macros can only be written with Visual Basic syntax.

Macro options are accessible from the Tools | Macros menu. The concept of macros is simple: the idea is to record a series of keystrokes and/or menu actions, and then play them back by pressing a certain keystroke combination.

For example, suppose one particular function call with a complex set of arguments is constantly being called on in code, and the function call usually looks about the same except for minor variations in the arguments. The keystrokes to code the function call could be recorded and played back as necessary, which would insert code to call the function that could then be modified as necessary.

Macros can be far more complex than this, containing logic as well as keystrokes. The macro capabilities of VS.NET are so comprehensive that macros have their own Integrated Development Environment (accessed using Tools | Macros | Macros IDE…).

Macros can be developed from scratch in this environment, but more commonly they are recorded using the Record Temporary Macro option on the Macros menu, and then renamed and modified in the above development environment. Here is an example of recording and modifying a macro:

1. Start a new Windows Application project.

2. In the new project, add a button to the Form1 that was created with the project.

3. Double-click the button to get to its Click event routine.

4. Select Tools | Macros | Record Temporary Macro. A small toolbar will appear on top of the IDE with buttons to control recording of the macro (Pause, Stop, and Cancel).

5. Press the *Enter* key and then type in the following line of code:

```
Console.WriteLine("Macro test")
```

6. Press the *Enter* key again.

7. In the small toolbar, press the Stop button.

8. Select Tools | Macro | Save Temporary Macro. The Macro Explorer will appear (in the location normally occupied by the Solution Explorer), and the new macro will be in it. You can name the macro anything you like.

9. Right-click the macro and select Edit to get to the macro editor. You will see code something like this in your macro:

```
DTE.ActiveDocument.Selection.NewLine()
DTE.ActiveDocument.Selection.Text = "Console.WriteLine(""A macro test"")"
DTE.ActiveDocument.Selection.NewLine()
```

The code that appears in step 9 can vary based on how you typed in the line. If you made a mistake and backspaced, for example, those actions will have their own corresponding lines of code.

The code in a macro recorded this way is just standard VB.NET code, and it can be modified as desired. However, there are some restrictions on what you can do inside the macro IDE. For example, you cannot refer to the namespace for setting up database connections.

To run a macro, you can just double-click it in the Macro Explorer, or select Tools | Macros | Run Macro. You can also assign a keystroke to a macro in the Keyboard dialog in the Tools | Options | Environment folder.

Summary

In this chapter, we have created our first piece of VB.NET code. We've used this example to explore the new Visual Studio IDE, and to show exactly how powerful the new features of the IDE are. We've covered:

- ❑ How to create projects and the different project templates available
- ❑ Code regions and how the form designer uses them to hide code that it doesn't want the developer to change
- ❑ Namespaces and how to import them into our applications
- ❑ How forms are classes, and how the properties of forms are set in code
- ❑ New object-oriented features of VB
- ❑ Build configurations and how to build and run a project

For the first time, multiple Microsoft languages have been brought into one development environment, and it is a powerful one. While being generally familiar to users of previous versions of Visual Basic, the IDE offers many new features over VB6 that should boost programmer productivity.

The IDE is also very customizable. Various windows can be used or hidden, and can assume different positions. There are many tools in VS.NET at your disposal and its worth the effort to learn how to use them effectively.

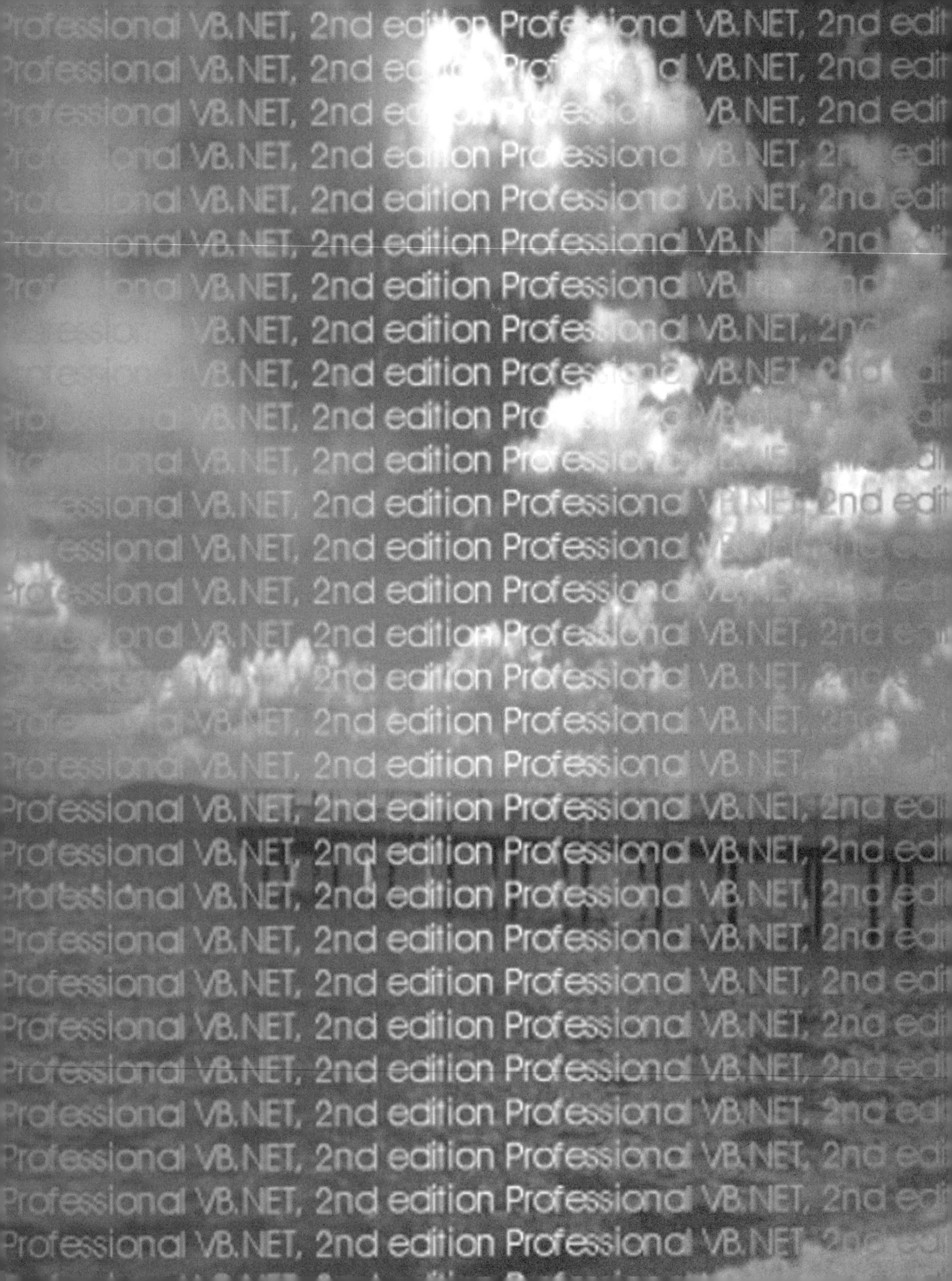
Professional VB.NET, 2nd edition

The Common Language Runtime

The architects of .NET realized that all procedural languages require certain base functionality. For example, many languages ship with their own runtime that provides features such as memory management. But instead of each language shipping with its own runtime, it would be better if all languages could use a common runtime. This is exactly what the **Common Language Runtime (CLR)** provides.

The CLR manages the execution of code on the .NET platform. In some ways the CLR can be viewed as a better VB runtime. (The VB runtime managed the execution of code that was compiled with previous versions of VB.) In this chapter we'll discuss how the features that the VB runtime provided have been enhanced by the CLR.

The functionality that the CLR exposes is available to all .NET languages. VB developers have been asking for better support for many advanced features for some time, including operator overloading, implementation inheritance, threading, and the ability to marshal objects. Building such features into a language is not trivial but as the CLR supports them, and as VB.NET is built on top of the CLR, VB.NET can use these features – eliminating many of the shortcomings of previous versions of VB.

In this chapter we'll examine the most significant features that are provided to .NET applications by the CLR. Specifically, we'll look at how:

- ❑ The CLR provides a simple and robust way to manage different versions of code, as well as how it simplifies the process of deploying an application.

- ❑ The **Garbage Collector (GC)** is responsible for freeing up memory of objects that are no longer referenced by an application.

- ❑ The CLR enables **managed code** (that is, code that is compiled to run under the control of the CLR) written in one language to integrate seamlessly with code written in another language. This includes cross-language inheritance, exception handling, marshaling of data, and debugging. (For example, create a new VB .NET class that extends a C# class.)

❏ .NET applications expose rich **metadata** that contains information about the types an application exposes, its dependencies on other .NET applications, and the memory layout for objects.

Before we explore the major features of the CLR, let's look at the major components that make up a .NET application.

An Overview of a .NET Application

A .NET application is composed of three primary entities:

❏ **Assemblies** – the primary unit of deployment of a .NET application

❏ **Modules** – the individual files that make up an assembly

❏ **Types** – the basic units that encapsulate data and behavior

Assemblies

An **assembly** is the primary unit of deployment for .NET applications – it is either a **dynamic link library (DLL)** or an **executable (EXE)**. An assembly is composed of a **manifest**, one or more modules, and other files that contain HTML, XML, images, and so on.

The manifest contains:

❏ Information about the identity of the assembly, including its textual name and version number.

❏ If the assembly is public, the manifest will contain the assembly's public key. The public key is used to help ensure that types exposed by the assembly reside within a unique namespace. It may also be used to identify the source of the assembly. (We'll learn more about namespaces in Chapter 8.)

❏ A declarative security request that describes the assembly's security requirements (the assembly is responsible for declaring the security it requires). Requests for permissions fall into three categories: required, optional, and denied. The identity information may be used as evidence by the CLR in determining whether or not to approve security requests.

❏ A list of other assemblies that the assembly depends on. The CLR uses this information to locate an appropriate version of the required assemblies at runtime. The list of dependencies also includes the exact version number of each assembly at the time that the assembly was created.

❏ A list of all types and resources exposed by the assembly. If any of the resources exposed by the assembly are localized the manifest will also contain the default culture (language, currency, date/time format, and so) that the application will target. The CLR uses this information to locate specific resources and types within the assembly.

The manifest can be stored in a separate file or in one of the modules.

Modules

A **module** contains **Microsoft Intermediate Language** (**MSIL**, often abbreviated to **IL**) code, associated metadata, and (optionally) the assembly's manifest. By default, the VB .NET compiler will create an assembly that is composed of a single module. This module contains the assembly's manifest.

> **There can only be one manifest per assembly. So, if a module contains the assembly's manifest, it must be the only one that does so in a particular assembly.**

IL is a platform independent way of representing managed code within a module. Before IL can be executed, the CLR must compile it into native machine code. The **JIT (just-in-time) compiler** will compile the IL on a method-by-method basis, as each method is called by an application for the first time.

Additional information about the types declared in the IL is provided by the associated metadata. The metadata contained within the module is used extensively by the CLR. For example, if a client and an object reside within two different processes, the CLR will use the type's metadata to marshal data between the client and the object.

Types

A **type** is a template that is used to describe the encapsulation of data and an associated set of behaviors. Unlike COM, which is scoped at the machine level, types are scoped at the assembly level. There are two kinds of type: reference and value. We'll discuss the difference between these in Chapter 4, but for the time being you can think (loosely) of reference types as classes and value types as structures (which have replaced the user-defined types of VB6).

A type has properties, methods, and fields:

❑ **Fields** are variables that are scoped to the type. For example, a Person class could declare a field called Name that holds the person's full name.

❑ **Methods** define behaviors exhibited by the type.

❑ **Properties** look like fields to clients of the type, but can have code behind them (that usually performs some sort of data validation). For example, a Dog data type could expose a property to set its gender. Code could then be placed behind the property so that it can only be set to "male" or "female".

Versioning and Deployment

Components and their clients are often installed at different times by different vendors. For example, a VB application might rely on a third-party grid control to display data. Runtime support for versioning is crucial in ensuring that an incompatible version of the grid control does not cause problems for the VB application.

As well as this issue of compatibility, the deployment of applications written in previous versions of VB was problematic. Fortunately, .NET provides a major improvement over the versioning and deployment that was offered by COM and previous versions of VB.

Better Support for Versioning

Managing the version of components was challenging in previous versions of VB. The version number of the component could be set, but this version number was not used by the runtime. COM components are often referenced by their ProgID but VB does not provide any support for appending the version number on the end of the ProgID.

> *ProgIDs are developer friendly strings that are used to identify a component, for example,* Word.Application *describes Microsoft Word. ProgIDs can be fully qualified with the targeted version of the component, for example,* Word.Application.10.

The CLR provides versioning support for all components that are loaded in the **Global Assembly Cache** (**GAC**). The GAC is used to store assemblies that are intended for use by multiple applications.

The CLR provides two features for assemblies installed within the GAC:

❑ **Side-by-side versioning** – multiple versions of the same component can be simultaneously stored in the GAC.

❑ **Automatic QFE (hotfix) support** – if a new version of a component, which is still compatible with the old version, is available in the GAC, the CLR will load the updated component. The version number, which is maintained by the developer who created the referenced assembly, drives this behavior.

The assembly's manifest contains the version numbers of referenced assemblies. The CLR uses this list at runtime to locate a compatible version of a referenced assembly. The version number of an assembly takes the following form:

```
Major.Minor.Revision.Build
```

Changes to the major and minor version numbers of the assembly indicate that the assembly is no longer compatible with previous versions. The CLR will not use versions of the assembly that have a different major or minor number unless it is explicitly told to do so. For example, if an assembly was originally compiled against a referenced assembly with a version number of 3.4.1.9, the CLR will not load an assembly stored in the GAC unless it has a major and minor number of 3 and 4.

Incrementing the revision and build numbers indicates that the new version is still compatible with the previous version. If a new assembly that has an incremented revision or build number is loaded into the GAC, the CLR can still load this assembly for clients that were compiled against a previous version.

> *Versioning is discussed in greater detail in Chapter 25, Assemblies and Deployment in .NET.*

Better Deployment

Applications that were written using previous versions of VB were often complicated to deploy. Components referenced by the application needed to be installed and registered, and the correct version of the VB runtime needed to be available. The Component Deployment tool helped in the creation of complex installation packages but applications could be easily broken if dependent components were inadvertently replaced by incompatible versions.

In .NET, components do not need to be registered. The CLR uses a set of defined search rules to locate local assemblies that are referenced by a .NET application, which allows the CLR to support the side-by-side execution of different versions of the same component. For example, an application could use a newer version of ADO.NET without adversely affecting another application that relies on a previous version.

So long as the client has the .NET runtime installed (which only has to be done once) a .NET application can be distributed using a simple command like this:

```
xcopy \\server\appDirectory "C:\Program Files\appDirectory" /E /O /I
```

This command would copy all of the files and subdirectories from \\server\appDirectory to C:\Program Files\appDirectory, and would also transfer the file's Access Control Lists (ACLs).

Deployment is discussed in greater detail in Chapter 25, Assemblies and Deployment in .NET.

Memory Management

One of the benefits of the CLR – memory management – is old news for VB developers as the VB runtime has provided memory management features for some time. However, we'll look at how the CLR **Garbage Collector (GC)** fixes the shortcomings of the VB runtime's memory management.

Better Garbage Collection

The VB6 runtime provides automatic garbage collection by automatically releasing references to objects once they are no longer referenced by the application. Once all of the references are released on an object, the runtime will automatically release the object from memory. For example, consider the following VB6 code that uses the Scripting.FileSystem object to write an entry to a log file:

```
' Requires a reference to Microsoft Scripting Runtime (scrrun.dll)
Sub WriteToLog(strLogEntry As String)
   Dim objFSO As Scripting.FileSystemObject
   Dim objTS As Scripting.TextStream

   objTS = objFSO.OpenTextFile("C:\temp\AppLog.log", ForAppending)
   Call objTS.WriteLine(Date & vbTab & strLogEntry)
End Sub
```

In WriteToLog we create two objects, a FileSystemObject and a TextStream, which are used to create an entry in the log file. Once we exit from the routine, the VB runtime will dereference the objects, which results in both being deactivated. However, there are situations in which objects that are no longer referenced by the application will not be properly cleaned up by the VB6 runtime. One of the leading causes of this is **cyclical references**.

Cyclical References

One of the most common situations in which the VB runtime is unable to ensure that objects no longer referenced by the application are deactivated is when a VB application contains a cyclical reference. An example of a cyclical reference is when object A holds a reference to object B and object B holds a reference to object A.

59

Cyclical references are problematic because the VB runtime relies on the reference counting mechanism of COM to determine whether an object can be deactivated. Each COM object is responsible for maintaining its own reference count and is responsible for destroying itself once the reference count reaches zero. Clients of the object are responsible for updating the reference count appropriately, by calling the AddRef and Release methods on the object's IUnknown interface.

Problems can occur if clients do not properly maintain the COM object's reference count. For example, an object will never get deactivated if a client forgets to call Release when the object is no longer referenced (and no other clients call Release one too many times). To avoid this, the VB6 runtime takes care of updating the reference count for us; but the object's reference count can be an invalid indicator of whether or not the object is still being used by the application. To understand why this is, we need to consider the references that objects A and B hold.

Our application can invalidate its references to A and B by setting their associated variables equal to Nothing. However, even though objects A and B are no longer referenced by the application, the VB runtime cannot ensure that the objects get deactivated because A and B still reference each other. Consider the following (VB6) code:

```
' Class:    CCyclicalRef

' Reference to another object.
Dim m_objRef As Object

Public Sub Initialize(objRef As Object)
   Set m_objRef = objRef
End Sub

Private Sub Class_Terminate()
   Call MsgBox("Terminating.")
   Set m_objRef = Nothing
End Sub
```

The CCyclicalRef class implements an Initialize method that accepts a reference to another object, and saves it as a member variable. The following code demonstrates how we can use the CCyclicalRef class to create a cyclical reference:

```
Dim objA As New CCyclicalRef
Dim objB As New CCyclicalRef

Call objA.Initialize(objB)
Call objB.Initialize(objA)

Set objA = Nothing
Set objB = Nothing
```

We create two instances (objA and objB) of CCyclicalRef, both of which have a reference count of one. Then we call the Initialize method on each object by passing it a reference to the other. Now each of the object's reference counts is equal to two: one held by the application and one held by the other object. Next we explicitly set objA and objA to Nothing, which decrements each object's reference count by one. However, since the reference count for both instances of CCyclicalRef is still greater than zero, the objects will not be released from memory until the application is terminated.

The CLR Garbage Collector solves the problem of cyclical references.

The CLR Garbage Collector

The .NET garbage collection mechanism is a very complex bit of software, and the details of its inner workings are beyond the scope of this book. We can, however, understand the principles behind its operation. The Garbage Collector (GC) is responsible for collecting objects that are no longer referenced. The GC takes a completely different approach to that of the VB runtime to accomplish this. At certain times, and based on specific rules, a task will run through all the objects, looking for those that no longer have any references. Those objects may then be terminated – the garbage is collected.

> **As long as all references to an object are either implicitly or explicitly released by the application, the GC will take care of freeing the memory allocated to it.**

Unlike COM objects, managed objects in .NET are not responsible for maintaining their reference count, and they are not responsible for destroying themselves. Instead, the GC is responsible for cleaning up objects that are no longer referenced by the application. The GC will periodically determine which objects need to be cleaned up by leveraging the information the CLR maintains about the running application. The GC obtains a list of objects that are directly referenced by the application. Then, the GC discovers all the objects that are referenced (both directly and indirectly) by each of these "root" objects. Once the GC has identified all the referenced objects, it is free to clean up any remaining objects.

> **The GC goes through a process of elimination when it locates objects that are no longer referenced by the application, so it will clean up objects that contain cyclical references.**

In some environments, such as COM, objects are destroyed in a deterministic fashion. Once the reference count reaches zero the object will destroy itself, which means that we can tell *exactly* when the object will be terminated. However, with the CLR GC, we can't tell exactly when an object will be destroyed. Just because we eliminate all references to an object doesn't mean it will be terminated immediately. It will just remain in memory until the garbage collection process gets around to locating and destroying it. This is called **nondeterministic finalization**.

This nondeterministic nature of CLR garbage collection provides a performance benefit. Rather than expending the effort to destroy objects as they are dereferenced, the destruction process can occur when the application is otherwise idle – often decreasing the impact on the user. Of course, if garbage collection must occur when the application is active, the system may start to run low on resources.

We can explicitly invoke the GC by calling the `System.GC.Collect` method. However, this process takes time, so it is not the sort of thing that should be done in a typical application. For example, we could call this method each time we set an object variable to `Nothing`, so that the object would be destroyed almost immediately. However, this would force the GC to scan all the objects in our application – a very expensive operation in terms of performance.

It's far better to design our applications so that it's acceptable for our objects to sit in memory for a time before they are terminated. That way, we can leave the garbage collector to run based on its rules – probably collecting many dereferenced objects at a time, which is far more efficient. To accomplish this goal, we need to design our objects so that they don't maintain expensive resources in instance variables. Database connections, open files on disk, or large chunks of memory (such as an image) are all examples of expensive resources. If we rely on the destruction of the object to release this type of resource, we might be keeping the resource tied up for a lot longer than we expected.

We need a way to write code so that our objects can perform any required cleanup processing before they are terminated. There are two occasions when we would probably want to perform this cleanup: when the final reference to the object is released and immediately before the GC destroys the object.

There is no automatic way to perform the cleanup when the final reference to an object is released, although implementing the IDisposable interface provides one solution. (We'll discuss this approach in Chapter 5.) However, we can run code immediately before an object is destroyed.

The Finalize Method

The GC calls the Object.Finalize method immediately before it collects an object that is no longer referenced by the application. Reference types are able to override the Finalize method to perform any necessary cleanup. For example:

```
Protected Overrides Sub Finalize()
  ' clean up code goes here
  MyBase.Finalize()
End Sub
```

This code uses both the Protected scope and Overrides keyword – concepts that we'll discuss in Chapter 6. For now, it's sufficient to know that these keywords are needed to create the Finalize method in our own classes. Notice that we not only write our own cleanup code here (as indicated by the comment), but we also call MyBase.Finalize(), which causes our base class code to do any cleanup it requires as well.

> **Class_Terminate (from earlier versions of VB) does not have a functional equivalent in .NET.**

Although we can perform cleanup in the Finalize method, we must be careful not to treat it as if it were a destructor. There are reasons for this:

❑ Since the GC has ultimate control over the lifetime of a managed object, there is likely to be a delay between when the object is no longer referenced by the application and when the GC collects it. Because of this, expensive resources that are released in the Finalize method may stay open longer than they need to be.

❑ The GC will usually be triggered when the available memory is running low. Execution of the object's Finalize method is likely to incur performance penalties because of this. Therefore the code in the Finalize method should be as short and quick as possible.

❑ There's no guarantee that a service you require is still available. For example, if the system is closing and you have a file open, .NET may have unloaded the various bits and pieces required to close the file.

All cleanup activities should be placed in the Finalize method. However, objects that require timely cleanup should implement either a Dispose method that can then be called by the client application just before setting the reference to Nothing. For example:

```
Class DemoDispose
  Private m_disposed As Boolean = False

  Public Sub Dispose()
    If (Not m_disposed) Then
      ' Call cleanup code in Finalize.
      Finalize()

      ' Record that object has been disposed.
      m_disposed = True

      ' Finalize does not need to be called.
      GC.SuppressFinalize(Me)
    End If
  End Sub

  Protected Overrides Sub Finalize()
    ' Perform cleanup here ...
  End Sub
End Class
```

The DemoDispose class overrides the Finalize method and implements code to perform any necessary cleanup. In this class, we are assuming that the cleanup code contained within the Finalize method should only be run once. We ensure that the Dispose method will only call Finalize once by checking the value of the private m_disposed field before calling Finalize, and setting it to True once Finalize has been called. Then we call GC.SuppressFinalize to ensure that the GC does not call the Finalize method on this object when the object is collected.

This example implements all of the object's cleanup code in the Finalize method to ensure that the object will be cleaned up properly before the GC collects it. The Finalize method still serves as a safety net in case the Dispose or Close methods were not called before the GC collects the object.

Faster Memory Allocation for Objects

Whenever a VB program creates an object, some memory is allocated for that object, in a region of virtual memory reserved for the program called the **heap**. The CLR introduces the concept of a **managed heap**. Objects are allocated on the managed heap and the CLR is responsible for controlling access to these objects in a type-safe manner.

One of the advantages of the managed heap is that memory allocations on it are very efficient. When unmanaged code allocates memory on the unmanaged heap, it typically scans through some sort of data structure in search of a free chunk of memory that is large enough to accommodate the allocation. The managed heap maintains a reference to the end of the most recent heap allocation. When a new object needs to be created on the heap, the CLR allocates memory on the top of memory that has previously been allocated and then increments the reference to the end of heap allocations accordingly. Let's look at an example:

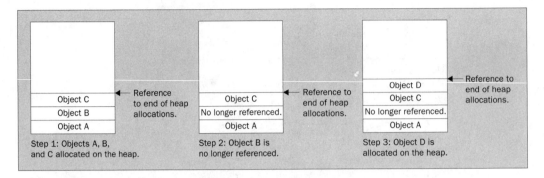

Step 1: Objects A, B, and C allocated on the heap.

Step 2: Object B is no longer referenced.

Step 3: Object D is allocated on the heap.

Step 3 shows that there is now a gap between the memory allocated for object A and object C – the memory allocation has become fragmented. After numerous allocations, there may not be sufficient memory on top of the managed heap to accommodate future requests. This is where the GC comes to the rescue. If the CLR is unable to allocate memory on the managed heap, the GC is invoked. The GC is responsible for collecting objects that are no longer referenced by the application and for compacting the heap. The GC effectively squeezes out all of the spaces between the remaining objects.

Garbage Collector Optimizations

The GC uses a concept known as **generations**, the primary purpose of which is to improve the performance of the GC. The theory behind generations is that objects that have been recently created tend to have a higher probability of being garbage collected than objects that have existed on the system for a longer time.

We can understand generations in terms of a mall parking lot – where cars represent objects created by the CLR. People have different shopping patterns when they visit the mall. Some people will spend a good portion of their day in the mall and others will only stop long enough to pick up an item or two. If we apply the theory behind generations to try to find an empty parking space to park our car, we know that we'll have a higher probability of finding a space where cars have recently parked. In other words, we're looking for a space that is occupied by someone that just needed to quickly pick up an item or two. The longer a car has been parked in the parking lot, the higher the probability is that they are an all day shopper and the lower the probability that their parking space will be freed up any time soon.

Generations provides a means for the GC to identify recently created objects versus long-lived objects. An object's generation is basically a counter that indicates how many times it has successfully avoided garbage collection. In version 1.0 of the .NET Framework, an object's generation counter starts at zero and can have a maximum value of two. The following example demonstrates this:

```
Module Module1

    Sub Main()
        Dim myObject As Object = New Object()
        Dim i As Integer

        For i = 0 To 3
            Debug.WriteLine(String.Format("Generation = {0}", _
                            GC.GetGeneration(myObject)))
            GC.Collect()
```

```
        GC.WaitForPendingFinalizers()
    Next i
  End Sub

End Module
```

This code creates an object and then iterates through a loop four times. For each loop, we display the current generation count for our object and then call the GC. The `GC.WaitForPendingFinalizers` method blocks execution until the garbage collection has been completed:

Each time the GC was run the generation counter was incremented for `myObject`, up to a maximum of 2.

Each time the GC is run, the managed heap is compacted and the reference to the end of the most recent memory allocation is updated. After compaction, objects of the same generation will be grouped together. Generation two objects will be grouped at the bottom of the managed heap and generation one objects will be grouped next. Since new generation zero objects are placed on top of the existing allocations, they will be grouped together as well.

This is significant because recently allocated objects have a higher probability of having shorter lives. Since objects on the managed heap are ordered according to generations, the GC can opt to collect newer objects. Running the GC over a portion of the heap will be quicker than running it over the entire managed heap.

We can invoke the GC with an overloaded version of the `Collect` method that accepts a generation number. The GC will then collect all objects no longer referenced by the application that belong to the specified (or younger) generation. The version of the `Collect` method that accepts no parameters collects objects that belong to all generations.

Another GC optimization is that a reference to an object may implicitly go out of scope and can therefore be collected by the GC. Consider the following code:

```
Imports System.Threading

Module Module1

  Public Class Demo
    Public Sub New()
      Debug.WriteLine("Demo.New was called on thread with hash code " _
                      & Thread.CurrentThread.GetHashCode())
    End Sub

    Protected Overrides Sub Finalize()
      Console.WriteLine("Demo.Finalize was called.")
    End Sub
```

```
    End Class


    Sub Main()
       ' Create new object.
       Dim myObject As Demo = New Demo()

       ' Force garbage collection.
       ' Since myObject is no longer referenced,
       ' it will be collected by the GC.
       GC.Collect()
       GC.WaitForPendingFinalizers()
       Debug.WriteLine("Application terminating.")
    End Sub

End Module
```

When the code is compiled and executed, the application produces the following output:

The `Finalize` method of `myObject` was called before the application terminated even though the reference to `myObject` was not explicitly released. Since `myObject` was never used by the application it implicitly went out of scope as soon as it was created.

Cross-Language Integration

In previous versions of VB, interoperating with code written in other languages was challenging. We were pretty much limited to two options if we wanted to use functionality developed in other languages: COM interfaces or DLLs with exported C functions. If we wanted to programmatically expose functionality written in VB, we were limited to creating COM interfaces.

Since VB.NET is built on top of the CLR, it's able to interoperate with code written in other .NET languages. We are even able to derive from a class written in another language. In order to support this type of functionality, the CLR relies on a common way of representing types, as well as rich metadata that can describe these types.

The Common Type System

Each programming language seems to bring its own island of data types with it. For example, VB represents strings using the `BSTR` struct (the internal representation of the `String` data type), C++ offers `char` and `wchar` data types, and MFC offers the `CString` class. And the fact that the C++ `int` data type is a 32-bit value whereas the VB6 `Integer` data type is a 16-bit value makes it difficult to pass parameters between applications written using different languages.

To help resolve this problem, C has become the lowest common denominator for interfacing between programs written in multiple languages. An exported function written in C that exposes simple C data types can be consumed by VB, Java, Delphi, and a variety of other programming languages. In fact, the Windows API is exposed as a set of C functions.

Unfortunately, in order to access a C interface, we must explicitly map C data types to a language's native data types. For example, a VB developer would use the following statement to map the `GetUserNameA` Win32 function (`GetUserNameA` is the ANSI version of the `GetUserName` function):

```
' Map GetUserName to the GetUserNameA exported function
' exported by advapi32.dll.
'    BOOL GetUserName(
'       LPTSTR lpBuffer,  // name buffer
'       LPDWORD nSize     // size of name buffer
'    );
Public Declare Function GetUserName Lib "advapi32.dll" _
Alias "GetUserNameA" (ByVal strBuffer As String, nSize As Long) As Long
```

Here, we explicitly mapped the `lpBuffer` C character array data type to the `strBuffer` VB `String` parameter. This is not only cumbersome, but also error prone. If we accidentally mapped a variable declared as `Long` to `lpBuffer` the application would not generate any compilation errors. However, calling the function at runtime would more than likely result in an access violation.

COM provides a more refined method of interoperation between languages. VB introduced a common type system for all languages that supported COM – variant compatible data types. However, variant data types are cumbersome to work with for non-VB developers as the underlying C data structures that make up the variant data types (such as `BSTR` and `SAFEARRAY`) are more complicated than they need to be.

The **Common Type System** (**CTS**) provides a set of common data types for use across all programming languages. The CTS provides every language running on top of the .NET platform with a base set of types, as well as mechanisms for extending those types.

Every type supported by the CTS is derived from `System.Object`. Therefore, every type supports the following methods:

Method	Description
`Boolean Equals(Object)`	Used to test equality with another object. Reference types should return `True` if the `Object` parameter references the same object. Value types should return `True` if the `Object` parameter has the same value. (Reference and value types will be discussed in Chapter 4.)
`Int32 GetHashCode()`	Generates a number corresponding to the value of an object. If two objects of the same type are equal, then they must return the same hash code.
`Type GetType()`	Gets a `Type` object that can be used to access metadata associated with the type. It also serves as a starting point for navigating the object hierarchy exposed by the Reflection API (which we'll discuss shortly).

Table continued on following page

Method	Description
`String ToString()`	The default implementation returns the fully qualified name of the class of the object. This method is often overridden to output data that is more meaningful to the type. For example, all base types return their value as a string.

Metadata

Metadata is information that enables components to be self-describing. Metadata is used to describe many aspects of a .NET component including classes, methods and fields, and the assembly itself. Metadata is used by the CLR to facilitate all sorts of things, such as validating an assembly before it is executed or performing garbage collection while managed code is being executed.

VB developers have used metadata for years while developing and using components within their applications:

❑ VB developers use metadata to instruct the VB runtime on how to behave. For example, we can set the Unattended Execution property to determine whether unhandled exceptions are shown on the screen in a message box or are written to the Event Log.

❑ COM components referenced within VB applications have accompanying type libraries that contain metadata about the components, their methods, and their properties. We could use the Object Browser to view this information. (The information contained within the type library is what is used to drive IntelliSense.)

❑ Additional metadata can be associated with a component by installing it within COM+. Metadata stored in COM+ is used to declare the support a component needs at runtime including transactional support, serialization support, and object pooling.

Better Support for Metadata

Metadata associated with a VB6 component was scattered in multiple locations and stored using multiple formats:

❑ Metadata instructing the VB runtime how to behave (such as the Unattended Execution property) is compiled into the VB generated executable

❑ Basic COM attributes (such as the required threading model) are stored in the registry

❑ COM+ attributes (such as the transactional support required) are stored in the COM+ catalog

.NET refines the use of metadata within applications in three significant ways:

❑ .NET consolidates the metadata associated with a component

❑ Since a .NET component does not have to be registered, installing and upgrading the component is easier and less problematic

❑ .NET makes a much clearer distinction between attributes that should only be set at compile time and those that can be modified at runtime

> **All attributes associated with VB.NET components are represented in one format and consolidated within the files that make up the assembly.**

Since much of a COM/COM+ component's metadata is stored separately from the executable, installing and upgrading components can be problematic. COM/COM+ components must be registered to update the registry/COM+ catalog before they can be used and the COM/COM+ component executable can be upgraded without upgrading its associated metadata.

The process of installing and upgrading a .NET component is greatly simplified. Since all metadata associated with a .NET component must reside within the file that contains the component, no registration is required. Once a new component is copied into an application's directory, it can be used immediately. Upgrading the component becomes much less problematic since the component and its associated metadata cannot get out of sync.

Another problem with COM+ is that attributes that should only be set at compile time may be reconfigured at runtime. For example, COM+ can provide serialization support for neutral components. A component that does not require serialization must be designed to accommodate multiple requests from multiple clients simultaneously. We should know at compile time whether or not a component requires support for serialization from the runtime. However under COM+, the attribute describing whether or not client requests should be serialized can be altered at runtime.

.NET makes a much better distinction between attributes that should be set at compile time versus those that should be set at runtime. For example, whether a .NET component is serializable is determined at compile time. This setting cannot be overridden at runtime.

Attributes

Attributes are used to decorate entities such as assemblies, classes, methods, and properties with additional information. Attributes can be used for a variety of purposes. The attribute can provide information, request a certain behavior at runtime, or even invoke a particular behavior from another application. Let's take a look at an example:

```
Module Module1

  <Serializable()> Public Class Demo

    <Obsolete("Use Method2 instead.")> Public Sub Method1()
      ' Old implementation ...
    End Sub

    Public Sub Method2()
      ' New implementation ...
    End Sub

  End Class

  Public Sub Main()
    Dim d As Demo = New Demo()
    d.Method1()
```

```
      End Sub

  End Module
```

By decorating the Demo type with the Serializable attribute, the base class library will provide serialization support for instances of the Demo type. For example, we could use the ResourceWriter type to stream an instance of the Demo type to disk.

The attribute associated with Method1 marks the method as obsolete. Visual Studio .NET will display an IntelliSense warning if Method1 is referenced within the application:

And a warning will be issued when the code is compiled:

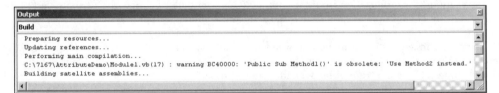

VB.NET allows us to use a shorthand notation for the name of the attribute. For example, the fully qualified name of the Obsolete attribute is System.ObsoleteAttribute but VB.NET allows us to drop the Attribute from the end of the name. A less natural, yet equivalent way of declaring an attribute would be:

```
<System.ObsoleteAttribute("Use Method2 instead.")> Public Sub Method1()
End Sub
```

There are many times when we would want to associate multiple attributes with an entity. The following is an example of how to declare multiple attributes for a class:

```
<Serializable(), Obsolete("No longer used.")> Public Class Test
   ' Implementation ...
End Class
```

The Reflection API

The .NET Framework provides the Reflection API for accessing metadata associated with managed code. We can use the Reflection API to examine the metadata associated with an assembly and its types, and even to examine the currently executing assembly.

The `Assembly` class in the `System.Reflection` namespace can be used to access the metadata in an assembly. The `LoadFrom` method can be used to load an assembly and the `GetExecutingAssembly` method can be used to access the currently executing assembly. We can then use the `GetTypes` method to obtain the collection of types defined in the assembly.

We can also access the metadata of a type directly from an instance of that type. Since every object derives from `System.Object`, every object supports the `GetType` method, which returns a `Type` object that can be used to access the metadata associated with the type.

The `Type` object exposes many methods and properties for obtaining the metadata associated with a type. For example, we can obtain a collection of properties, methods, fields, and events exposed by the type by calling the `GetMembers` method. We can also obtain the `Type` object for the object's base type by calling the `DeclaringType` property.

> **A good tool that demonstrates the power of Reflection is Lutz Roeder's Reflector for .NET. Check out http://www.aisto.com/roeder/dotnet/.**

IL Disassembler

One of the many handy tools that ships with VS.NET is the **IL Disassembler** (`ildasm.exe`). It can be used to navigate the metadata within a module including the types the module exposes as well as their properties and methods. The IL Disassembler can also be used to display the IL contained within a module.

The IL Disassembler can be found in the `FrameworkSDK\Bin` directory of your VS.NET installation. Once the IL Disassembler has been started, select **File** and then **Open**. Open `mscorlib.dll` (which will be located in `Framework` directory). Once `mscorlib.dll` has been loaded, expand the **System** folder, then the **ValueType** folder, and finally double-click on the **Equals** method. A window similar to the following one should be displayed:

This screenshot shows the IL for the Equals method. Notice how the Reflection API is used to navigate through the instance of the value type's fields in order to determine if the values of the two objects being compared are equal.

The IL Disassembler is a very useful tool for learning about how a particular module is implemented.

Summary

In this chapter, we introduced the CLR and compared and contrasted it with the VB6 runtime. We discussed the memory management features of the CLR and how they compare to the VB6 runtime including how the CLR eliminates the circular reference problem that has plagued VB6 developers. Next we examined the Finalize method and understood why it should not be treated like the Class_Terminate method. Specifically, we learned that:

❏   Whenever possible, we should not implement the Finalize method in a class as it is often called in low memory situations.

❏   If the Finalize method is used to perform necessary cleanup, we should make the code for the Finalize method as short and quick as possible.

❏   There is no way to accurately predict when the GC will collect an object that is no longer referenced by the application (unless the GC is invoked explicitly).

❏   If we implement the Finalize method, we should also implement either a Dispose or a Close method that can be called by the client when the object is no longer needed.

❏   The order in which the GC collects objects on the managed heap is non-deterministic. This means that the Finalize method should not call methods on other objects referenced by the object being collected.

We also discussed why it is important to provide a common runtime and type system that can be targeted by multiple languages.

Next, we talked about how the CLR offers better support for metadata. We discussed how metadata is used to make types "self describing". We looked at examples where metadata is used by the CLR and the .NET Class Library and we learned how to extend metadata by creating our own attributes. We briefly looked at the Reflection API and used the IL Disassembler utility (ildasm.exe) to display the IL contained within a module.

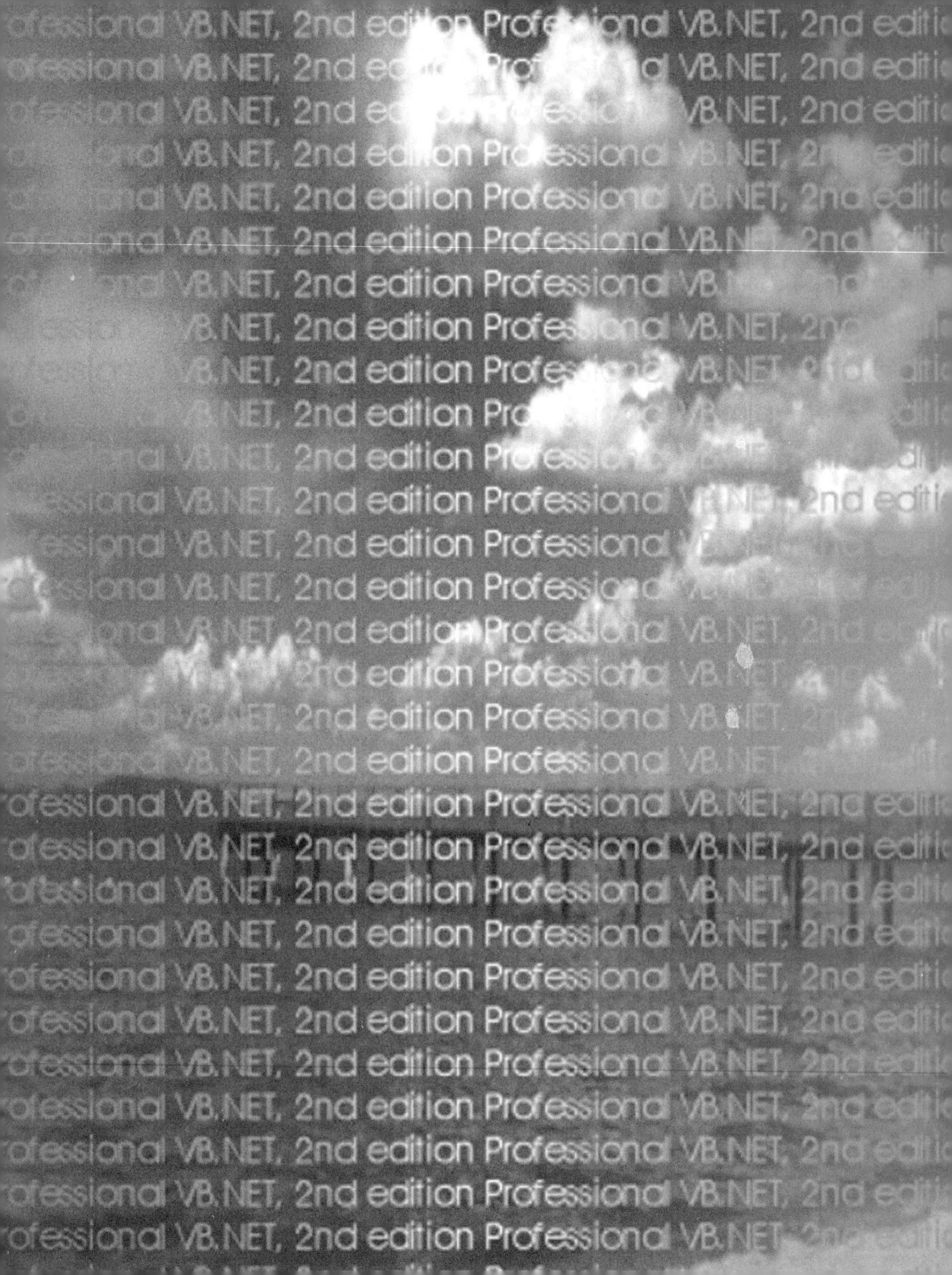
Professional VB.NET, 2nd edition

Variables and Types

In the previous chapter we introduced the Common Type System (CTS), which provides a common set of types across .NET languages. In this chapter we'll examine exactly what these types are and how we can use them.

Experienced developers generally consider integers, characters, Booleans and strings to be the basic building blocks of any language. In .NET the **structure** is the common underlying implementation of types such as Integer, Long, Character, and even Byte. However, all objects share a logical inheritance from the base Object class. The advantage of this common heritage is the ability to rely on certain common functions of every variable. However this logical inheritance does not require a common physical implementation for all variables.

.NET has only two major variable types, value and reference:

❑　**Value types** represent simple data storage located on the **stack**. They are what VB6 developers would often refer to as data types.

❑　**Reference types** are based classes and gain implementation inheritance from their parent classes.

Value and reference types are treated differently within assignment statements, and their memory management is handled differently. It is important to understand how theses differences impact the software we will write in VB.NET. Understanding the foundations of how data is manipulated in the .NET framework will enable you to build more reliable and better performing applications.

The main goal of this chapter is to get familiar with value and reference types and to understand some of the key differences in how variables are defined in VB.NET compared to VB6. We'll begin by looking at value types, followed by a clear definition of a logical grouping called primitive types. We will go on to look at classes, how they work, and how some of the basic classes are used. Specifically, we'll cover:

❑ Value types (structures)

❑ Primitive types

❑ Reference types (classes)

❑ `Option Strict` and `Option Explicit`

❑ Explicit conversions

❑ Parameter passing `ByVal` and `ByRef`

❑ Boxing

❑ Retired keywords and functions

We'll begin by discussing the difference between value and reference types.

Value and Reference Types

Value and reference types behave differently when data is assigned to them:

❑ When data is assigned to a value type the actual data is stored in the variable on the **stack**.

❑ When data is assigned to a reference type only a reference is stored in the variable. The actual data is stored on the **heap**.

We need to understand the difference between the stack and the heap. The stack is a comparatively small memory area in which processes and threads store data of fixed size. An integer or decimal value will need the same number of bytes to store their data, regardless of their actual value. This means that the location of such variables on the stack can be efficiently determined. (When a process needs to retrieve a variable it has to search the stack. If the stack contained variables that had dynamic memory sizes such a search could take a long time.)

Reference types do not have a fixed size. For example, a string could vary in size from 2 bytes to close to all the memory available on a system. The dynamic size of reference types means that the data they contain is stored on the heap rather than the stack. However, the **address** of the reference type (that is, the location of the data on the heap) does have a fixed size, and so can be stored on the stack. By only storing a reference on the stack the program as a whole runs much quicker since the process can quickly locate the data associated with a variable.

Storing the data contained in fixed- and dynamically-sized variables in different places results in differences in the way that variables behave. This can be illustrated by comparing the behavior of the `System.Drawing.Point` structure (a value type) and the `System.Text.StringBuilder` class (a reference type).

The `Point` structure is used as part of the .NET graphics library that is part of the `System.Drawing` namespace. The `StringBuilder` class is part of the `System.Text` namespace and is used to improve performance when we're editing strings. We'll learn more about namespaces in Chapter 8.

First, let's look at how we can use the `System.Drawing.Point` structure:

```
Dim ptX As New System.Drawing.Point(10, 20)
Dim ptY As New System.Drawing.Point

ptY = ptX
ptX.X = 200

Debug.WriteLine(ptY.ToString())
```

The output from this operation will be {X=10,Y=20}, which seems logical. When we copy ptX into ptY, the data contained in ptX is copied into the location on the stack that is associated with ptY. Then, when the value of ptX is changed only the memory on the stack that is associated with ptX is altered. Altering the value of ptX had no effect on ptY. This is not the case with reference types. Consider the following code, which uses the System.Test.StringBuilder class:

```
Dim objX As New System.Text.StringBuilder("Hello World")
Dim objY As System.Text.StringBuilder

objY = objX
objX.Replace("World", "Test")

Debug.WriteLine(objY.ToString())
```

The output from this operation will be "Hello Test", not "Hello World". As we saw in the previous example, when we assign one variable to another the data stored on the stack is copied. So, when objY is assigned to objX the data associated with objX on the stack is copied to the data associated with objY on the stack. However, what is copied in this case is the address to the data stored on the heap, which means that objY and objX now reference the same object. When the data on the heap is changed, the data associated with every variable that holds a reference to that memory is changed. This is the default behavior of reference types and is known as a **shallow copy**. Later in this chapter we'll see how this behavior has been overridden for strings (which perform a **deep copy**).

The differences between value types and reference types goes beyond how they behave when copied and we'll encounter some of the other features provided by objects later in this chapter. First though, we're going to take a closer look at some of the most commonly used value types, and understand how .NET works with them.

Value Types (Structures)

Value types aren't as versatile as reference types, but they can provide better performance in many circumstances. The core value types (often referred to as **primitive types**) include Boolean, Byte, Char, DateTime, Decimal, Double, Guid, Int16, Int32, Int64, SByte, Single, and TimeSpan.

Primitive Types

VB.NET, in common with other development languages, has a group of elements such as integers and strings that are termed **primitive types**. These primitive types are identified by keywords like String, Long, and Integer, which are aliases for types defined by the .NET class library. This means that writing:

```
Dim i As Long
```

is equivalent to writing:

```
Dim i As System.Int64
```

The following table lists the primitive types that VB.NET defines and the structures or classes that they map to:

Primitive Type	.NET Class or Structure
Byte	System.Byte (Structure)
Short	System.Int16 (Structure)
Integer	System.Int32 (Structure)
Long	System.Int64 (Structure)
Single	System.Single (Structure)
Double	System.Double (Structure)
Decimal	System.Decimal (Structure)
Boolean	System.Boolean (Structure)
Date	System.DateTime (Structure)
Char	System.Char (Structure)
String	System.String (Class)

> The **String** primitive type stands out from the others, as it is a class, not a structure. As such it is not a value type, but a reference type.

There are certain operations we can perform on primitive types that we cannot perform on other types. We can assign a value to a primitive type using a **literal**. For example:

```
Dim i As Integer = 32
Dim str As String = "Hello"
```

We can declare primitive types to be constant by using the Const keyword. For example:

```
Dim Const str As String = "Hello"
```

The value of the str variable cannot now be changed at runtime.

Boolean

The VB.NET Boolean type has been implemented with three values, two for `True`, and one for `False`. Two `True` values have been implemented for backward compatibility because, in contrast to most languages (in which Boolean `True` equates to 1), the Boolean `True` in VB6 equates to -1. To save developers having to examine every Boolean expression to ensure valid return values, a solution has been developed in which -1 is supported in VB.NET but the .NET standard of 1 is exposed to the rest of the world.

Of course this compromise involves making some decisions that add complexity to `True` or `False` evaluations. When we use a `True` value in a Boolean expression it equates to -1. However, if this value is converted to any other format, it equates to 1. This is best illustrated by some sample VB.NET code. Keep in mind though that this code follows poor programming practice as it references Boolean values as integers (and does so with implicit conversions):

```
Dim blnTrue As Boolean = True
Dim blnOne As Boolean = 1
Dim blnNegOne As Boolean = -1
Dim blnFalse As Boolean = False
```

The following condition, which is based on the implicit conversion of the Boolean, works even though the `blnOne` variable has been assigned a value of 1:

```
If blnOne = -1 Then
   Debug.WriteLine(blnTrue)
   Debug.WriteLine(blnOne.ToString)
   Debug.WriteLine(Convert.ToString(Convert.ToInt32(blnNegOne)))
End If
```

Now we'll explicitly convert to another integer type, and test the result. In this case the condition will fail. It is possible to use an implicit conversion and the result won't be the same. Converting `blnNegOne` to an integer results in a positive value regardless of what was originally assigned:

```
If Convert.ToInt16(blnNegOne) = 1 Then
   Debug.WriteLine(blnFalse)
   Debug.WriteLine(Convert.ToString(Convert.ToInt32(blnFalse)))
End If
```

This code will not compile if you are using `Option Strict` (more on this later) but it is a good illustration of what we should expect if we are casting implicitly rather than explicitly. The output from this code looks like this:

The first conditional expression demonstrates that if casting is performed between a Boolean and an integer value then, regardless of how a Boolean in VB.NET is initialized, True is evaluated as -1, not 1.

The second conditional expression performs an explicit cast from a Boolean to an integer value. In this case the value of 1 equates to True, even though we initialized this Boolean value with a value of -1. This is because the code used to do the explicit cast is part of .NET and, in .NET, the value of True is 1. This demonstrates the risk involved in relying on implicitly converted values. If at some point the default value associated with True were to change, this code would execute differently.

The difference between an explicit and implicit conversion is subtle, and there are two steps to take in order to avoid difficulty:

❑   Always use the True and False constants in code.

❑   If there is any doubt as to how the return value from a function will be handled, it should be assigned to a Boolean variable. That Boolean variable can then be used in conditional expressions.

To illustrate these points further let's look at a hypothetical class named MyCSharpClass (which isn't implemented here but is available in the code download) that has a single method TestTrue() that doesn't accept any parameters.

We create an instance of MyCSharpClass and make calls to the TestTrue() method:

```
Dim objMyClass as New MyCSharpClass()

If objMyClass.TestTrue() = 1 Then
  Debug.WriteLine("CSharp uses a 1 for true but does it" & _
                  " implicitly convert to a 1 in VB?")
End If

If objMyClass.TestTrue() = True Then
   Debug.WriteLine("CSharp True always converts to Visual Basic True.")
End If
```

It's unclear if the first conditional in this code will ever work. Let's look at the output this example generates:

Even when we return a Boolean using a .NET language that uses 1, not -1, to represent True, the VB.NET compiler will ensure that the value of true is converted to -1.

The behavior of the second condition is both clear and safe from future modifications of the Visual Basic language definition in which VB.NET no longer uses -1 to equate to true.

> To create reusable code it is always better to avoid implicit conversions. In the case of Booleans, if the code needs to check for an integer value, you should explicitly evaluate the Boolean and create an appropriate integer – code will be far more maintainable and prone to fewer unexpected results as a result.

The Integer Types

In VB6 there were two types of integer values: the `Integer` type was limited to a maximum value of 32767 and the `Long` type supported a maximum value of 2147483647. .NET adds a new integer type. The `Short` replaces the `Integer` value from VB6, the `Integer` has been promoted to support the range previously supported by the `Long` type, and the `Long` type is bigger then ever. In addition, each of these types also has two alternative types. In total VB.NET supports nine integer types:

Type	Allocated Memory	Min Value	Max Value
Short	2 Bytes	-32768	32767
Int16	2 Bytes	-32768	32767
UInt16	2 Bytes	0	65535
Integer	4 Bytes	-2147483648	2147483647
Int32	4 Bytes	-2147483648	2147483647
UInt32	4 Bytes	0	4294967295
Long	8 Bytes	-9223372036854775808	9223372036854775807
Int64	8 Bytes	-9223372036854775808	9223372036854775807
UInt64	8 Bytes	0	18446744073709551615

Short

A `Short` value is limited to the maximum value that can be stored in two bytes. This means there are sixteen bits and that the value can range between –32768 and 32767. This limitation may or may not be based on the amount of memory physically associated with the value, it is a definition of what must occur in .NET. This is important, because there is no guarantee that the implementation will actually use less memory than using an `Integer` value. It is possible that the operating system will, in order to optimize memory or processing, allocate the same memory used for an `Integer` type and just limit the possible value.

The `Short` (or `Int16`) value type can be used to map SQL `smallint` values.

Integer

An `Integer` is defined as a value that can be safely stored and transported in four bytes (not as a four-byte implementation). This gives the `Integer` and `Int32` value types a range from –2147483648 to 2147483647. This range is more than adequate to handle most tasks.

The main reason we would use an `Int32` in place of an `Integer` value is to ensure future portability with interfaces. For example, the `Integer` value in VB6 was limited to a two-byte value, but is now a four-byte value. In future 64 bit platforms the `Integer` value will be an eight-byte value. Problems could occur if we used this 64 bit integer with an interface that requires a 32 bit integer value. The solution is to use `Int32`, which would remain a 32 bit value on a 64 bit platform.

The new sizing of the `Integer` value type matches the size of an `int` value in SQL Server, which means that we can align the column type of a table with the variable type in our programs.

Long

The `Long` type is aligned with the `Int64` value. They have an eight-byte range, which means that their value can range from -9223372036854775808 to 9223372036854775807.

This is a big range, but if we need to add or multiply `Integer` values then we will often need a large value to contain the result. It's common when doing math operations on one type of integer to use a larger type to capture the result if there's a chance that the result could exceed the limit of the types being manipulated.

The `Long` value type now matches the `bigint` type in SQL.

Unsigned Types

Another way to gain additional space is to use one of the unsigned types. The unsigned types provide a useful buffer that will hold a result that might exceed an operation by a small amount, but that isn't the main reason they exist. The `UInt16` type happens to have the same characteristics as the `Character` type, while the `UInt32` type has the same characteristics as a system memory pointer. These types are used to interface with software that expects these values, and are the underlying implementation for other value types.

The Decimal Types

Just as we have a number of types to store integer values, we have three implementations of value types to store real number values.

The `Single` and `Double` types work the same way in VB.NET as they did in VB6. The difference is that the `Currency` type (which was a specialized version of the `Double` type) is now obsolete and a new `Decimal` value type has been added.

Type	Allocated Memory	Negative Range	Positive Range
Single	4 Bytes	-3.402823E38 to -1.401298E-45	1.401298E-45 to 3.402823E38
Double	8 Bytes	-1.79769313486231E308 to -4.94065645841247E-324	4.94065645841247E-324 to 1.79769313486232E308
Currency	Obsolete	-	-
Decimal	16 Bytes	-79228162514264337593543950335 to 0.0000000000000000000000000001	0.0000000000000000000000000001 to 79228162514264337593543950335

Single

The `Single` type contains four bytes of data and its precision can range anywhere from 1.401298E-45 to 3.402823E38 for positive values and from −3.402823E38 to −1.401298E-45 for negative values.

It can seem strange that a value that is stored using four-bytes (the same as the `Integer` type) can store a number that is larger than even the `Long` type. This is possible because of the way the numbers are stored – a real number can be stored with different levels of precision. Notice that there are six digits after the decimal point in the definition of the `Single` type. When a real number gets very large, or very small, the stored value will contain fewer significant places.

For example, while it is possible to represent a `Long` with the value of 9223372036854775805, the `Single` type rounds this value to 9.223372E18. This seems like a reasonable action to take, but it isn't a reversible action. The following code demonstrates how this loss of data can result in errors:

```
Dim l As Long
Dim s As Single

l = Long.MaxValue
Debug.WriteLine(l)

s = Convert.ToSingle(l)
s -= 1000000000000
l = Convert.ToInt64(s)

Debug.WriteLine(l)
```

This code creates a `Long` that has the maximum value possible and outputs this value. Then it stores the value in a `Short`, subtracts 1000000000000, stores the value of the `Short` in the `Long`, and outputs the result – which is probably not what we would expect:

```
Output                              ⊠
Debug                               ▼
   9223372036854775807              ▲
   9223370937343148032              ▼
◄ █                          ►
```

Double

The behavior of the previous example changes dramatically if we replace the value type of Single with Double. A Double uses eight bytes to store values and as a result has a greater precision and range. The range for a Double is from 4.94065645841247E-324 to 1.79769313486232E308 for positive values and from -1.79769313486231E308 to -4.94065645841247E-324 for negative values. The precision has increased so that a number can contain 15 digits before rounding begins. This greater level of precision makes the Double value type a much more reliable variable for use in math operations. It's possible to represent most operations with complete accuracy with this value.

Double wasn't the only eight-byte decimal value in VB6. One of the other variable types, Currency, is now obsolete. The Currency type was a specialized version of the Double type, and was designed to support numbers using nineteen available digits. While this was certainly better precision then the 15-digit precision available with the Double type, it pales in comparison to the new 28 digit Decimal type available in .NET.

Decimal

The Decimal type (new in VB.NET) is a hybrid that consists of a twelve-byte integer value combined with two additional 16-bit values that control the location of the decimal point and sign of the overall value. A Decimal value will consume sixteen bytes in total, and can store a maximum value of 79228162514264337593543950335. This value can then be manipulated by adjusting where the decimal place is located. For example, the maximum value while accounting for four decimal places is 7922816251426433759354395.0335. This is because a Decimal isn't stored as a traditional number, but is rather stored as a 12-byte integer value, and the location of the decimal in relation to the available 28 digits. This means that a Decimal does not inherently round numbers the way that a Double does.

As a result of that way values are stored, the closest precision to zero that a Decimal supports is 0.0000000000000000000000000001. And as the location of the decimal point is stored separately, it also stores a value that indicates if its value is positive or negative. This means that the positive and negative ranges are exactly the same, regardless of the number of decimal places.

If we need to store a larger number of decimal places we have to reduce the maximum size of the value. This tradeoff makes a lot of sense. After all, it's not often that we will need to store a number with fifteen digits on either side of the decimal point.

Char and Byte

The default character set under VB.NET is **Unicode**. So when we declare a variable to be of type Char we create a two-byte value, since, by default, all characters in the Unicode character set require two bytes.

We can declare a character value in two ways. Placing a c following a literal string informs the compiler that the value should be treated as a character, or we can use the Chr and ChrW functions:

```
Dim chrLtr_a As Char = "a"c
Dim chrAsc_a As Char = Chr(97)
Dim chrAsc_b as Char = ChrW(98)
```

If we needed to convert our characters into a string that was suitable for an ASCII interface the runtime library would have to check each character value in turn. Fortunately, VB.NET supports the `Byte` value type. This type contains a value between 0 and 255 that exactly matches the range of the ASCII character set. If we needed to interface with a system that uses ASCII we could use a `Byte` array. The runtime knows that there is no need to perform a Unicode to ASCII conversion for a `Byte` array, so the interface between the systems will operate significantly faster.

In VB.NET the `Byte` value type expects a numeric value. So, in order to assign the letter a to a `Byte`, we must get the appropriate character code. We can get this code using the `Asc` function, for example:

```
Dim bytLtrA as Byte = Asc("a")
```

DateTime

The Visual Basic `Date` keyword has always supported a structure of both date and time. Under VB.NET the `Date` structure continues to operate as it did in VB6 but is now implemented as part of the `DateTime` structure. We can, in fact, declare data values using both the `DateTime` and `Date` types.

The `Now()` function initializes a `Date` value with the local date and time. This function has not been changed from VB6, and `Today()` and `UtcNow()` functions have also been added. These functions can be used to initialize a `Date` object with the current local date, or the date and time based on Universal Coordinated Time (also known as Greenwich Mean Time) respectively.

Explicit Conversions

It's possible to assign the value of a smaller type into a larger type using an **implicit conversion**. For example, in the following code the value of a `Short` is assigned to a `Long`:

```
Dim shtShort As Short = 32767
Dim lnhLong As Long = shtShort
```

However, the reverse of this will result in a compilation error, since the compiler doesn't have any safe way of handling the assignment when the larger value is outside the range of the smaller value.

We can get around this restriction by performing a **cast** from a larger type to a smaller type – for example, `Long` to `Short`. However, we have to check that the value of the larger type is within the range of the smaller type, as if the value is out of range at runtime the application will throw an exception. (We'll learn more about exceptions in Chapter 9.)

To understand how explicit conversions are performed in VB.NET we need to look at an option, `Option Strict`, that we can set for our code.

Option Strict, Option Explicit, and Option Compare

When Option Strict is turned on the compiler must be able to determine the type of each variable. And if an assignment between two variables requires a type conversion – for example from Integer to Boolean – the conversion between the two types must be expressed explicitly.

We can edit the setting of this property in the Properties window of the VS solution. You can access this screen by right-clicking the project in the Solution Explorer and selecting Properties from the context menu. The left-hand-side of the resulting window contains a tree section that defaults to Common Properties. If you select the Build node you should see a window like this:

We can use this screen to set various properties for our project. In addition to Option Strict we can also set Option Explicit and Option Compare:

❑   Option Explicit – This option has not changed from VB6. When turned on it ensures that any variable name is declared. Of course, if you are using Option Strict, then this setting does not matter since the compiler would not recognize the type of an undeclared variable. There is to my knowledge no good reason to *ever* turn this option off.

❑   Option Compare – This option determines whether strings should be compared as binary strings or if the array of characters should be compared as text.

It's probably not a big surprise that the setting for comparing text can impact performance. Doing a text comparison implies that the binary values which are stored to represent a string must be converted prior to comparing them. However, the advantage of a text-based comparison is that the character "A" is equal to "a" because the comparison is case-insensitive. This allows us to perform comparisons that don't require an explicit case conversion of the compared strings. In most cases, however, this conversion will still occur, so it's better to use binary comparison and explicitly convert case as required.

It's possible to change the settings of these options in the source files of your project. However, while this ability allows you to adapt your code if you need to include a class or module that isn't up to the same standards as the rest of your project, this approach should be avoided in general.

Most experienced developers will say without fail that using Option Strict and being forced to recognize when type conversions are occurring is a good thing. Certainly, when developing software that will be deployed in a production environment anything that can be done which will help prevent runtime errors is a good thing. However, Option Strict can slow the development of a program because you are forced to explicitly define each conversion that needs to occur. If you are developing a prototype or demo component that has a limited life you might find this option limiting.

If that were the end of the argument, then many developers would simply turn the option off – as it currently defaults – and forget about it. However, Option Strict has a runtime benefit. When type conversions are explicitly identified, the system does them faster. Implicit conversions require the runtime system to first identify the types involved in a conversion and then obtain the correct handler.

Another advantage of Option Strict is that we can see where every implicit conversion might occur. Perhaps we didn't realize that some of the assignment operations we were doing involved type conversion. Setting our project for explicit conversions means that we can change certain variable types in order to avoid conversions and thus reduce the number of conversions in our project. This means that we not only get conversions that run faster but hopefully a smaller number of conversions as well.

> **My recommendation is that you should always keep Option Strict enabled and use explicit conversions.**

Performing Explicit Conversions

The following code is an example of how we can convert between different integer types when we have Option Strict enabled:

```
Dim shrShort As Short
Dim shrUInt16 As UInt16
Dim shrInt16 As Int16
Dim intInteger As Integer
Dim intUInt32 As UInt32
Dim intInt32 As Int32
Dim lngLong As Long
Dim lngInt64 As Int64

shrShort = 0
shrUInt16 = Convert.ToUInt16(shrShort)
shrInt16 = shrShort
intInteger = shrShort
intUInt32 = Convert.ToUInt32(shrShort)
intInt32 = shrShort
lngInt64 = shrShort

lngLong = lngLong.MaxValue
```

```
    If lngLong > Short.MaxValue Then
      shrShort = Convert.ToInt16(lngLong)
    End If
    intInteger = CInt(lngLong)
```

The preceding snippet provides some excellent examples of what might not be intuitive behavior. The first thing to note is that we can't implicitly cast from Short to UInt16, or any of the other unsigned types for that matter. That is because with Option Strict the compiler will not allow an implicit conversion that might result in a value out of range or loss of data. In this case, if the variable shrShort contained a –1 then the value wouldn't be in the allowable range for an unsigned type.

The second item illustrated in this code is the shared function MaxValue. All of the integer and decimal types have this method. As the name indicates it returns the maximum value for the specified type. There is a matching MinValue method for getting the minimum value. As **shared** methods, the methods can be called on either an instance of the class (LngLong.MaxValue) or by referencing the class (Short.MaxValue).

One fact that isn't apparent in the code above is that whenever possible *all* conversions should be avoided. Each of the Convert.MethodName functions has been overloaded to accept various types. However, the CInt function (which most VB6 programmers are familiar with) is defined to accept a parameter of type Object. This is important because it involves **boxing** the value type. Boxing is important because when a value type is boxed there is a performance implication.

Finally, although this code will compile, it will not execute correctly because the final statement does not check to ensure that the value being assigned to intInteger is within the maximum range for an Integer type. The assignment to intInteger will throw a runtime error when this value is out of bounds.

VB.NET has many ways to convert values. Some of them are updated versions of techniques familiar from VB6. Others, such as the ToString method, are an inherent part of every class (although we can't be sure how it will actually be implemented).

The following set of conversion methods are based on the conversions supported by VB6. They coincide with the primitive data types described earlier:

CBool()	CByte()	CChar()	CDate()
CDbl()	CDec()	CInt()	CLng()
CObj()	CShort()	CSng()	CStr()

Each of these functions has been designed to accept the input of the other primitive data types (as appropriate) and to convert that item to the type indicated by the function name. Thus, the CStr class is used to convert a primitive type to a String. The disadvantage of these functions is that they have been designed to support any object. This means that if a primitive type is used, the function automatically boxes the parameter prior to getting the new value. This results in a loss of performance. Finally, although these are available as functions within the VB language these functions are actually implemented in a class (as with everything in .NET). Because the class uses a series of type-specific overloaded functions the conversions run faster when the members of the Convert class are called explicitly.

```
Dim intMyShort As Integer = 200
Convert.ToInt32(intMyShort)
Convert.ToDateTime("9/9/2001")
```

The classes that are part of `System.Convert` implement not only the conversion methods listed above but other common conversions as well. These additional methods include standard conversions for things like unsigned integers and pointers.

All of the preceding type conversions are great for value types and the limited number of classes to which they apply. However, these implementations are oriented around a limited set of known types. It is not possible to convert a custom class to an `Integer` using these classes. More importantly, there should be no reason to have such a conversion. Instead, a particular class should provide a method that returns the appropriate type – no type conversion will be required. However, when `Option Strict` is enabled we need to cast an object to an appropriate type in order to be able to access the properties and members of that class.

Reference Types (Classes)

A lot of the power of VB.NET is harnessed in objects. An **object** is defined by its **class**, which describes what data, methods, and other attributes an instance of that class will support. There are thousands of classes provided in the .NET Framework class library.

When our code instantiates an object from a class, the object created is a **reference type**. We discussed earlier (in *Value and Reference Types*) how the data contained in value and reference types is stored in different locations, but this is not the only difference between them. Classes (which is how we will often refer to reference types) can have private and protected methods, the ability to receive events, constants, and can extend a base class via **inheritance**. Classes can also be used to define how operators such as = and + work on an instance of the class.

The intention of this chapter is to introduce you to some commonly used classes, in order to complement your knowledge of the common value types we've already covered. Chapters 5, 6, and 7 contain a detailed look a **object-orientation** in VB.NET. In this chapter, we'll take a look at the features of the `Object`, `String`, `DBNull`, and `Array` classes, as well as the Collection classes found in the `System.Collections` namespace.

The Object Class

The `Object` class is the base class for *every* type in .NET – both value and reference types. At their core, every variable is an object and can be treated as such (we'll discuss what happens when we use value types as objects in the *Boxing* section).

The VB6 runtime environment managed the interpretation of `Variant` objects for VB programmers. This is good in some ways because we could set up a situation where we knew what the contents of the variant should be and then just program as if that is what was there. So long as the content of the memory area was an object of the appropriate type then the call to a method on that object would succeed. While this was simple to do, it left VB6 programs open to some unusual runtime errors that are generally harder to track and debug. (On the other hand, when interfacing with ASP pages or other scripted code, `Variants` were a requirement due to the way that these loosely typed languages worked.)

89

You can think of the Object class (in some ways) as the replacement for the Variant type from VB6 – but take care. In VB6 a Variant type represented a variant memory location, in VB.NET an Object type represents a reference to an instance of the Object class. In VB6 a Variant was implemented to provide a reference to a memory area on the heap, but its definition didn't define any specific ways of accessing this data area.

The lines below can work equally well in VB6 and VB.NET (so long as Option Strict is not enabled in our VB.NET project):

```
Dim varObj
Dim objVar
```

Interestingly enough when we are not using Option Strict, the behavior of a VB6 Variant and a VB.NET Object is almost identical. Since the Object class is the basis of all types, you can assign any variable to an Object. Reference types will maintain their current reference and implementation but will be generically handled while value types will be packaged into a box and placed into the memory location associated with the Object. The new Object supports all of the capabilities that were available from the Variant type but it goes beyond the VB6 variant type in its support for methods. For example, there are instance methods that are available on Object, such as ToString. This method will, if implemented, return a string representation of an instance. Since the Object class defines it, it can be called on any object:

```
Dim objMyClass as New MyClass("Hello World")

Debug.WriteLine(objMyClass.ToString)
```

Which brings up the question of how does the Object class know how to convert custom classes to String objects? The answer to this question is that it doesn't. For this method to actually return the data in an instance of a String, a class must override this function. Otherwise when this code is run the default version of this function defined at the Object level will return the name of the current class as its string representation.

The Object class continues to fill the role of the Variant class even when Object Strict is enabled. The declaration is more explicit, however – anything that can be done with Object Strict disabled can be done with it enabled. The difference is that with Option Strict we must explicitly define the type of object whose property or method we wish to access if we don't want to only access those methods available from the base Object class. For example:

```
Dim objVar as Object

objVar = Me

CType(objVar, Form).Text = "New Dialog Title Text"
```

This snippet shows how to create a generic object being created under the Object Strict syntax. It is then assigned a copy of the current instance of a VB.NET form. The name Me is reserved in VB and its use will be described further in Chapter 6. Once it has been assigned, if we want to access the Text property of this class we need to cast it as something other then a base Object. The CType command (covered later) accepts the object we are interested in as its first parameter and the class to which we are casting this object as its second parameter. In this case the current form instance is of type Form, and by casting this we can reference the Text property of the current form.

This may seem difficult, but later in this chapter when we talk about explicit casting and `Option Strict` we'll show how we can modify the preceding sample to make it more generic while still maintaining the explicit declaration.

The CType Function

The `CType` function accepts two parameters. The first parameter is the object which is having its type cast. The second parameter is the name of the object to which it is being cast. There are some limits on the second parameter. The first limitation is that it can't be a variable containing the name of the casting target. Casting occurs at compile time, and any form of dynamic name selection would need to occur at runtime. If we really need runtime casting then we need to turn off `Option Strict` and pay the performance and maintenance price of allowing the runtime environment to evaluate object types.

The String Class

Another class that will play a large role in most development projects is the `String` class. Having `String`s defined as a class is more powerful then the VB6 data type of `String` with which we are familiar. The `String` class is special within .NET because it is the one primitive type that is not a value type. In order to make `String` objects compatible with some of the underlying behavior in .NET, they have some interesting characteristics.

The `String` class has the following methods and properties:

Shared Methods	Description
Empty	This is actually a property. It can be used when an empty `String` is required. It can be used for comparison or initialization of a `String`.
Compare	Compares two objects of type `String`.
CompareOrdinal	Compares two `String`s, without considering the local national language or culture.
Concat	Concatenates one or more `String`s.
Copy	Creates a new `String` with the same value as an instance provided.
Equals	Determines whether two `String`s have the same value.
Equality operator (=)	An overloaded version of the equality operator that compares two `String` objects.
Inequality operator (op_Inequality)	A method that accepts two `String` objects for comparison. The method returns true if the objects are not equal.

These methods are shared, which means that the methods are not specific to any `String`. The `String` class also contains many other methods that are called based on a specific `String` object. The methods on the `String` class replace the functions that VB6 had as part of the language for string manipulation and perform such operations as inserting strings, splitting strings and searching strings.

The String() Function

The String() function, which allows for the creation of a String with a set length and populated with a specific character, no longer exists in VB.NET. This is because String is a class and has a constructor. In fact, the String class has several different constructors:

```
Dim strConstant as String = "ABC"
Dim strRepeat as New String("A"c, 20)
```

The second example of constructing a new string imitates the VB6 String() function. Not only have creation functions been encapsulated, but other string specific functions, such as character and substring searching, and case changes are now available from String objects.

The SubString Method

Although not removed, the Left, Right, and Mid functions are deprecated in VB.NET. This is largely due to the fact that the .NET String class has a method called SubString. This single method replaces the three functions that VB6 programmers are accustomed to using to create substrings. There are two versions of this method: the first accepts a starting position and the number of characters to retrieve, while the second accepts simply the starting location. For example:

```
Dim strMyString as String = "Hello World"

Debug.WriteLine(strMystring.SubString(0,5))
Debug.WriteLine(strMyString.SubString(6))
```

The PadLeft and PadRight Methods

The LSet and RSet statements have been removed. These functions have been replaced by the PadLeft and PadRight methods. These methods allow us to justify a String so that it is left or right justified. As with SubString, the PadLeft and PadRight methods are overloaded. The first version of these methods requires only a maximum length of the String, and then uses spaces to pad the String. The other version requires two parameters, the length of the returned String, and the character that should be used to pad the original String. For example:

```
Dim strMyString as String = "Hello World"

Debug.WriteLine(strMyString.PadLeft(30))
Debug.WriteLine(strMyString.PadLeft(20,"."c))
```

The String Class is Immutable

The VB.NET String class isn't entirely different from the String type that VB programmers have used for years. The majority of String behaviors remain unchanged, and the majority of functions are now available as methods. However, in order to support the default behavior that people associate with the String primitive type, the String class isn't declared the same way many other classes are. Strings in .NET do not allow editing of their data. When a portion of a String is changed or copied, the operating system allocates a new memory location and copies the resulting String to this new location. This ensures that when a String is copied to a second variable, the new variable references its own copy.

To support this behavior in .NET, the `String` class is defined as an **immutable class**. This means that each time a change is made to the data associated with a `String`, a new instance is created, and the original referenced memory is released for garbage collection. This is an expensive operation, but the result is that the `String` class behaves as people expect a primitive type to behave. Additionally, when a copy of a `String` is made, the `String` class forces a new version of the data into the referenced memory. This ensures that each instance of a `String` will reference only its own memory. Consider the following code:

```
Dim strMyString as String
Dim intLoop as Integer

For intLoop = 1 to 1000
    strMyString = strMyString & "A very long string"
Next
Debug.WriteLine(strMyString)
```

This code does not perform well. Each time the assignment operation to `strMyString` occurs the system will allocate a new memory buffer based on the size of the new string, and copy both the current value of `strMyString` and the new text that is to be appended. The system then frees the previous memory that must be reclaimed by the Garbage Collector. As this loop continues that memory allocation requires a larger and larger chunk of memory. The result is that operations such as this can take a long time. However, .NET offers an alternative:

```
Dim objMyStrBldr as New System.Text.StringBuilder()
Dim intLoop as Integer

For intLoop = 1 to 1000
    ObjMyStrBldr.Append("A very long string")
Next
Debug.WriteLine(objMyStrBldr.ToString())
```

This code works with strings but does not use the `String` class. The .NET class library contains a class called `StringBuilder`, which performs better with strings that will be edited repeatedly. This class does not store a string in the conventional manner – editing or appending more characters does not involve allocating new memory for the entire string. Since the preceding code snippet does not need to reallocate the memory used for the entire string each time another set of characters is appended it performs significantly faster. In the end, an instance of the `String` class is never explicitly needed because the `StringBuilder` class implements the `ToString` method to roll up all of the characters into a string. While the concept of the `StringBuilder` class isn't new, the fact that it is now available as part of the VB.NET implementation means developers no longer need to create their own string memory managers.

The DBNull Class

The `IsNull` and `IsEmpty` functions from VB6 are now obsolete. VB.NET provides an alternative way of determining if a variable has not been initialized, `IsDBNull()`. The `IsDBNull` method accepts an object as its parameter and returns a Boolean that indicates if the variable has been initialized. In addition to this method, VB.NET has access to the `DBNull` class. The class is part of the `System` namespace and in order to use it you declare a local variable with the `DBNull` type. This variable is then used with an `is` comparison operator to determine if a given variable has been initialized:

```
Dim sysNull As System.DBNull
Dim strMyString As String

If strMyString Is sysNull Then
   strMyString = "Initialize my String"
End If

If Not IsDBNull(strMyString) Then
   Debug.WriteLine(strMyString)
End If
```

In this code the `strMyString` variable is declared but not yet initialized. The first conditional is evaluated to `True` and as a result the string is initialized. The second conditional then ensures that the declared variable has been initialized. Since this was accomplished in the preceding code, some output is written. In both cases, the `sysNull` value is used not to verify the type of the object, but to verify that it has not yet been instantiated with a value.

Arrays

When VB.NET was first announced, a lot of significant changes were planned to the way that arrays worked. A major reason for these changes involved getting rid of the `Variant_Array` structure. This structure, introduced with COM, was hidden from most VB programmers, but was nevertheless ever present. It was necessary because VB defined arrays in a unique way. The variant array has been removed from not only VB but from every .NET language. The reason it was removed is that under .NET, arrays are handled the same way, where they always start at an index of zero and have a defined number of elements. However, the way that an array is declared in VB.NET still varies slightly from other .NET languages like C#.

When VB.NET was announced it was said that arrays would always begin at 0 and that they would be defined based on the number of elements in the array. However, in VB6 the `Option Base` statement allowed arrays to be declared as starting at 1 or any other specified value, and this meant that they were defined based on their upper limit. The `Option Base This =` statement resulted in a problem when converting existing code. To resolve this issue the engineers at Microsoft developed a compromise. All arrays in .NET will begin at 0, but when an array is declared in VB.NET the definition is based on the upper limit of the array, not the number of elements.

The result is that while some of the more esoteric declarations that were available in VB6, such as `Dim intMyArr(15 to 30)` are no longer supported, the majority of capabilities remain unchanged. It is still possible to declare an array with multiple indices. Specifically we can declare any single type as an array. The basic `Array` class is never explicitly declared for a variable's type. The `System.Array` class that serves as the base for all arrays is defined such that it cannot be created, but must be inherited. As a result, to create an `Integer` array a set of parentheses is added to the declaration of our variable. These parentheses indicate that the system should create an array of the type specified. These parentheses may be empty or may contain the size of the array. An array can be defined as having a single dimension using a single number, or as having multiple dimensions.

Let's examine some simple examples to demonstrate five different ways of creating arrays of `Integer` objects:

```
Dim arrMyIntArray1(20) as Integer
Dim arrMyIntArray2() as Integer = {1, 2, 3, 4}
Dim arrMyIntArray3(4,2) as Integer
Dim arrMyIntArray4( , ) as Integer = _
    { {1, 2, 3, 4},{5, 6, 7, 8},{9, 10, 11, 12},{13, 14 , 15 , 16} }
Dim arrMyIntArray5() as Integer
```

In the first case we define an array of `Integers` that spans from `arrMyIntArray1(0)` to `arrMyIntArray1(20)`. This is a 21-element array, because all arrays start at 0 and end with the value defined in the declaration as the upper bound.

The UBound Function

The declaration of `arrMyIntArray2` actually defined an array that spans from `arrMyIntArray2(0)` to `arrMyIntArray1(3)`. This is because when we declare an array by specifying the set of values it still starts at 0. However, in this case we are not specifying the upper bound. If we wish to verify the upper bound, we can use the `UBound` function:

```
Debug.Writeline CStr(UBound(ArrMyIntArray2))
```

The `UBound` function has a companion called `LBound`. The `UBound` function computes the upper bound for a given array. The `LBound` function does the same thing for the lower bound, but since all arrays in VB.NET are 0-based, it doesn't have much value anymore.

Multi-Dimensional Arrays

The declaration of `arrMyIntArray3` is a multi-dimensional array. This declaration creates an array with 15 elements ranging from `arrMyIntArray3(0,0)` through `arrMyIntArray3(2,1)` to `arrMyIntArray3(4,2)`. As with all elements of an array, when it is created without specific values the values of each of these elements is created with the default value for that type. This case also demonstrates that the size of the different dimensions can vary. It is also possible to nest deeper then two levels, but this should be done with care as such code is difficult to maintain.

The fourth declaration, `arrMyIntArray4( , )` is created with values. The values are mapped based on the outer set being the first dimension and the inner values being associated with the next inner dimension. For example, the value of `arrMyIntArray4(0,1)` is 2 while the value of `arrMyIntArray4(2,3)` is 12. The following code snippet illustrates this using a set of nested loops to traverse the array. Additionally, it provides an example of calling the `UBound` function with a second parameter to specify that we are interested in the upper bound for the second dimension of the array:

```
Dim intLoop1 as Integer
Dim intLoop2 as Integer
For intLoop1 = 0 to UBound(arrMyIntArray4)
  For intLoop2 = 0 to UBound(arrMyIntArray4, 2)
    Debug.WriteLine arrMyIntArray4(intLoop1, intLoop2).ToString
  Next
Next
```

The ReDim Statement

The final declaration of `arrMyIntArray5()` is of an array which has not yet been instantiated. If an attempt were made to assign a value into this array, it would trigger an exception. The solution to this is to use the `ReDim` keyword. Although `ReDim` was part of VB6 it has changed slightly in VB.NET. The first change is that we must first `Dim` an instance of the variable; we cannot use the `ReDim` statement as the initial declaration of a variable. The second change is that we cannot change the number of dimensions in an array. For example, an array with three dimensions cannot grow an additional dimension or be reduced to only two dimensions. For example:

```
Dim arrMyIntArray5() as Integer
```

```
' The statement below would compile but would cause a runtime exception.
'arrMyIntArray5(0) = 1

ReDim arrMyIntArray5(2)
ReDim arrMyIntArray3(5,4)
ReDim Preserve arrMyIntArray4(UBound(arrMyIntArray4),2)
```

The `ReDim` of `arrMyIntArray5` instantiates values so that it can store data. Because this array was declared, but not initialized, it is not possible to use it to hold data until it has been allocated with actual data elements.

The second statement is redimensioning the `arrMyIntArray3` variable defined earlier. Note that it is changing the size of both the first and second dimension. While it is not possible to change the number of dimensions in an array it is possible to resize any of an array's dimensions. This capability is required for declarations such as `Dim arrMyIntArray6( , , ,) As Integer` to be legal.

The Preserve Keyword

The last item in the code snippet illustrates an additional keyword associated with redimensioning. The `Preserve` keyword indicates that the data that is stored in the array prior to redimensioning it should be transferred to the newly created array. If this keyword is not used then the data that was stored in an array is lost. Additionally, this statement actually reduces the second dimension of the array. While this is a perfectly legal statement it should be noted that this means that even though we have asked to preserve the data, the data values 4, 8, 12, 16 that were assigned in the original definition of this array will be discarded. These are lost because they were assigned in the highest index of the second array. Since `arrMyIntArray4(1,3)` is no longer valid, the value that resided at this location has been lost.

Arrays continue to be very powerful in VB.NET. However, the basic array class is just that, basic. While it provides a powerful framework it does not provide a lot of other features that would allow for more robust logic built into the array. To accomplish more advanced features, such as sorting and dynamic allocation, the base `Array` class has been inherited by the classes that make up the `Collections` namespace.

Collections

The `Collections` namespace is part of the `System` namespace and provides a series of classes that implement advanced array features. While being able to make an array of existing types is powerful, sometimes more power is needed in the array itself. The ability to inherently sort or dynamically add dissimilar objects in an array is provided by the classes of the `Collections` namespace:

Class	Description
ArrayList	Implements an array whose size increases automatically as elements are added.
BitArray	Manages an array of Booleans that are stored as bit values.
Hashtable	Implements a collection of values organized by key. Sorting is done based on a hash of the key.
Queue	Implements a first-in, first-out collection.
SortedList	Implements a collection of values with associated keys. The values are sorted by key, and are accessible by key or index.
Stack	Implements a last-in-first-out collection.

The preceding table contains some of the collection objects that are available as part of the System.Collections namespace. Each of these collections is based around storing a collection of objects. This means that in addition to the special capabilities each provides it also provides one capability not found in the base Array class. Since everything in .NET is based on the Object class, it is possible to have these collections contain elements that are different, and as all objects inherit from Object, these classes will be storing simply a collection of objects. However, it is possible that the actual objects being stored might be very different. Let's look at an example:

```
Dim objMyArrList As New System.Collections.ArrayList()
Dim objItem As Object
Dim intLine As Integer = 1
Dim strHello As String = "Hello"
Dim objWorld As New System.Text.StringBuilder("World")

' Add an integer value to the array list.
objMyArrList.Add(intLine)

' Add an instance of a string object
objMyArrList.Add(strHello)

' Add a single character cast as a character
objMyArrList.Add(" "c)

' Add an object that isn't a primitive type
objMyArrList.Add(objWorld)

' To balance the string, insert a break between the line
' and the string "Hello", by inserting a string constant
objMyArrList.Insert(1, ". ")

For Each objItem In objMyArrList
   ' Output the values...
   Debug.Write(objItem.ToString())
Next
```

The preceding code is an example of implementing the new `ArrayList` collection class. The collection classes, as this example shows, are more versatile than any similar structures in VB6. In this case, a new instance of an `ArrayList` is created, along with some related variables to support the demonstration. The code then shows four different types of variable being inserted into the same `ArrayList`. The code then inserts another value into the middle of the list. At no time has the size of the array been declared nor has a redefinition of the array size been required.

Part of the reason for this is that the `Add` and `Insert` methods on the `ArrayList` class are defined to accept a parameter of type `Object`. This means that the `ArrayList` object can literally accept any value in .NET. (This comes at a slight performance cost for those variables that are value types because of boxing.)

The System.Collections.Specialized Namespace

VB.NET has additional classes available as part of the `System.Collections.Specialized` namespace. These classes tend to be oriented around a specific problem. For example the `ListDictionary` class is designed to take advantage of the fact that while a hash table is very good at storing and retrieving a large number of items, it can be costly when there are only a few items. Similarly the `StringCollection` and `StringDictionary` classes are defined so that when working with strings the time spent interpreting the type of object is reduced and overall performance is improved:

Class	Description
ListDictionary	A singly linked list that allows a small number of elements to be accessed faster then other collection implementations. This collection should not be used for a large number of elements.
StringCollection	Implements a collection of strings.
StringDictionary	Implements a hash table, but the key is strongly typed as a string rather than as a base object.

Parameter Passing

When an object's methods or an assembly's procedures and functions are called, we often want to provide input for the data to be operated on by the code. VB.NET has changed the way that methods, procedures, and functions are called and how those parameters are passed. The first change actually makes writing such calls more consistent. Under VB6 the parameter list for a procedure call didn't require parentheses. On the other hand, a call to a `function` did require parentheses around the parameter list.

> In VB.NET, the parentheses are always required and the `Call` keyword is obsolete.

Another change in VB.NET is the way parameters with default values are handled. As with VB6 it is possible to define a method, procedure, or function that provides default values for the last parameter(s). This way it is possible to call a function such as `PadRight` passing either a single parameter defining the length of the string and using a default of space for the padding character, or with two parameters, the first still defining the length of the string, but the second now replacing the default of space with a dash.

```
Public Function PadRight(ByVal intSize as Integer, _
                      Optional ByVal chrPad as Char = " "c)
End Function
```

To use default parameters it is necessary to make them the last parameters in the function declaration, VB.NET also requires that every Optional parameter have a default value. It is not acceptable to just declare a parameter and assign it the Optional keyword. In VB.NET the Optional keyword must be accompanied by a value that will be assigned if the parameter is not passed in.

The most important change related to parameters in VB.NET is how the system handles them. In VB6 the default was that parameters were passed **by reference**. Passing a parameter by reference means that if changes are made to the value of a variable passed to a method, function, or procedure call, these changes were to the actual variable and therefore available to the calling routine.

Passing a parameter by reference sometimes results in unexpected changes being made to a parameter's value. It is partly due to this that parameters default to passing **by value** in VB.NET. The advantage of passing by value is that regardless of what a function might do to a variable while it is running, when the function completes, the calling code still has the original value. Making this the default results in safer code.

Under VB.NET the decision to pass something by reference not only involves the possibility of unexpected changes to the original value, but also requires significantly more system resources. The ByRef option in VB.NET will use more system resources as the parameter data is copied in for use by the function and then copied back to its original location. On the other hand, the new default of ByVal only copies the data once. When considering how to pass parameters this should be kept in mind and the ability to return data as part of a function (as opposed to using a ByRef parameter) should be considered.

Boxing

Normally when a conversion (implicit or explicit) occurs the original value is read from its current memory location and then the new value is assigned. For example to convert a Short to a Long, the system reads the two bytes of Short data, and writes them to the appropriate bytes for the Long variable. However, under VB.NET if a value type needs to be managed as an object then the system will perform an intermediate step. This intermediate step involves taking the value that is on the stack and copying it to the heap, a process referred to as **boxing**. As noted earlier, the Object class is implemented as a reference type. Therefore, the system needs to convert value types into reference types for them to be objects. This doesn't cause any problems or require any special programming, as boxing isn't something we have to declare. However, it does have an impact on performance.

In a situation where you are copying the data for a single value type this is not a significant cost. However, if you are processing an array that contains thousands of values the time spent moving between a value type and a temporary reference type can be significant.

There are ways to limit the amount of boxing that occurs. One method that has been shown to work well is to create a class based on the value type you need to work with. On first thought this seems counter intuitive because it costs more to create a class. The key though is how often we reuse the data that is contained in the class. By repeatedly using this object to interact with other objects, we will save on the creation of a temporary boxed object.

There are two important areas to examine with examples to better understand boxing. The first involves the use of arrays. When an array is created, the portion of the class which tracks the element of the array is created as a reference object, but each of the elements of the array is created directly. Thus an array of integers consists of the array object and a set of integer value types. When we update one of these values with another integer value there is no boxing involved:

```
Dim arrInt(20) as Integer
Dim intMyValue as Integer = 1

arrInt(0) = 0
arrInt(1) = intMyValue
```

Neither of the above assignments of an integer value into the integer array that was defined previously requires boxing. In each case, the array object identifies which value on the stack needs to be referenced and the value is assigned to that value type. The point here is that just because we have referenced an object doesn't mean we are going to box a value. The boxing only occurs when the values being assigned are being transitioned from a value to reference type:

```
Dim objStrBldr as New System.Text.StringBuilder()
Dim objSortedList as New System.Collections.SortedList()
Dim intCount as Integer

For intCount = 1 to 100
   objStrBldr.Append(intCount)
   objSortedList.Add(intCount, intCount)
Next
```

This code snippet illustrates two separate calls to object interfaces. One of these calls requires boxing of the value `intCount`, while the other does not. There is nothing in the code to indicate which call is which. The answer is that the `Append` method of `StringBuilder` has been overridden to include a version that accepts an `Integer`, while the `Add` method of `SortedList` collection expects two objects. While the `Integer` values can be recognized by the system as objects, doing so requires the runtime library to box up these values so that they can be added to the sorted list.

The key to boxing isn't that you are working with objects as part of an action, but that you are passing a value to a parameter that expects an object, or are taking an object and converting it to a value type. However, one time that boxing does not occur is when you call a method on a value type. There is no conversion to an object, so if we need to assign an `Integer` to a string using the `ToString` method, we will not be boxing the integer value as part of assignment of the string. On the other hand, we are explicitly creating a new object so the cost is similar. The only difference would be if the `Add` method boxes the `intCount` value twice; then, converting this value to an object before making that call would save on the creation of one of these boxes.

Retired Keywords and Functions

During the course of this chapter we have covered several changes from VB6 that are part of VB.NET. They include the removal of the `Currency` type, `String` function, `Rset`, and `Lset` functions. Other functions such as `Left`, `Right`, and `Mid` have been discussed as becoming obsolete although they may still be supported. Functions such as `IsEmpty` and `IsNull` have been replaced with new versions. We discussed the changes in the way that arrays are handled.

VB.NET has removed many keywords that won't be missed. For example the `DefType` statement has been removed. This statement was a throwback to Fortran allowing a developer to indicate for example that all variables starting with the letters I, J, K, L, M, N would be integers. Most programmers have probably never used this function and it doesn't have a logical replacement in VB.NET.

One of the real advantages of VB.NET is the way that it removed some of the more esoteric and obsolete functions from Visual Basic. The following list contains the majority of such functions. As with others that have already been discussed, some have been replaced; for example the math functions are now part of the `System.Math` library, while others such as `IsObject` really don't have much more meaning than `LBound` in the context of .NET, where everything is an object and the lower bound of all arrays is `0`.

Elements of VB6 Removed in VB.NET

`As Any`	`Now` function
`Atn` function	`Null` keyword
`Calendar` property	`On ... GoSub`
`Circle` statement	`On ... GoTo`
`Currency`	`Option Base`
`Date` function and statement	`Option Private Module`
`Date$` function	`Property Get`, `Property Let`, and `Property Set`
`Debug.Assert` method	`PSet` method
`Debug.Print` method	`Rnd` function
`DefType`	`Round` function
`DoEvents` function	`RSet`
`Empty`	`Scale` method
`Eqv` operator	`Set` statement
`GoSub` statement	`Sgn` function
`Imp` operator	`Sqr` function

Table continued on following page

Initialize event	String function
Instancing property	Terminate event
IsEmpty function	Time function and statement
IsMissing function	Time$ function
IsNull function	Timer function
IsObject function	Type statement
Let statement	Variant data type
Line statement	VarType function
LSet	Wend keyword

The User Defined Type (UDT) has also been removed from the Visual Basic vocabulary. Instead, the ability to create a user defined set of variables as a type has been replaced with the ability to create custom structures and custom classes in VB.NET.

> Remember that VB.NET isn't Visual Basic 7. It is version 1 of an entirely new language based on the .NET Framework. This new language keeps many of the syntax and coding standards of Visual Basic, but it's really a whole new language.

Summary

This chapter looked at many of the basic building blocks of VB.NET that are used throughout project development. Understanding how they work will help you to write more stable and better performing software. There are five specific points to take note of:

❑   Beware of array sizes; all arrays start at 0 and are defined not by size but by the highest index

❑   Remember to use the StringBuilder class for string manipulation

❑   Use Option Strict; it's not just about style; it's about performance

❑   Beware of parameters that are passed ByValue so changes are not returned

❑   Take advantage of the new collection classes

While this chapter covered many other items such as how the new Decimal type works and how boxing works, these five items are really the most important. Whether you are creating a new library of functions or a new user interface, these five items will consistently turn up in some form. While .NET provides a tremendous amount of power, this chapter has hopefully provided information on places where that power comes at a significant performance cost.

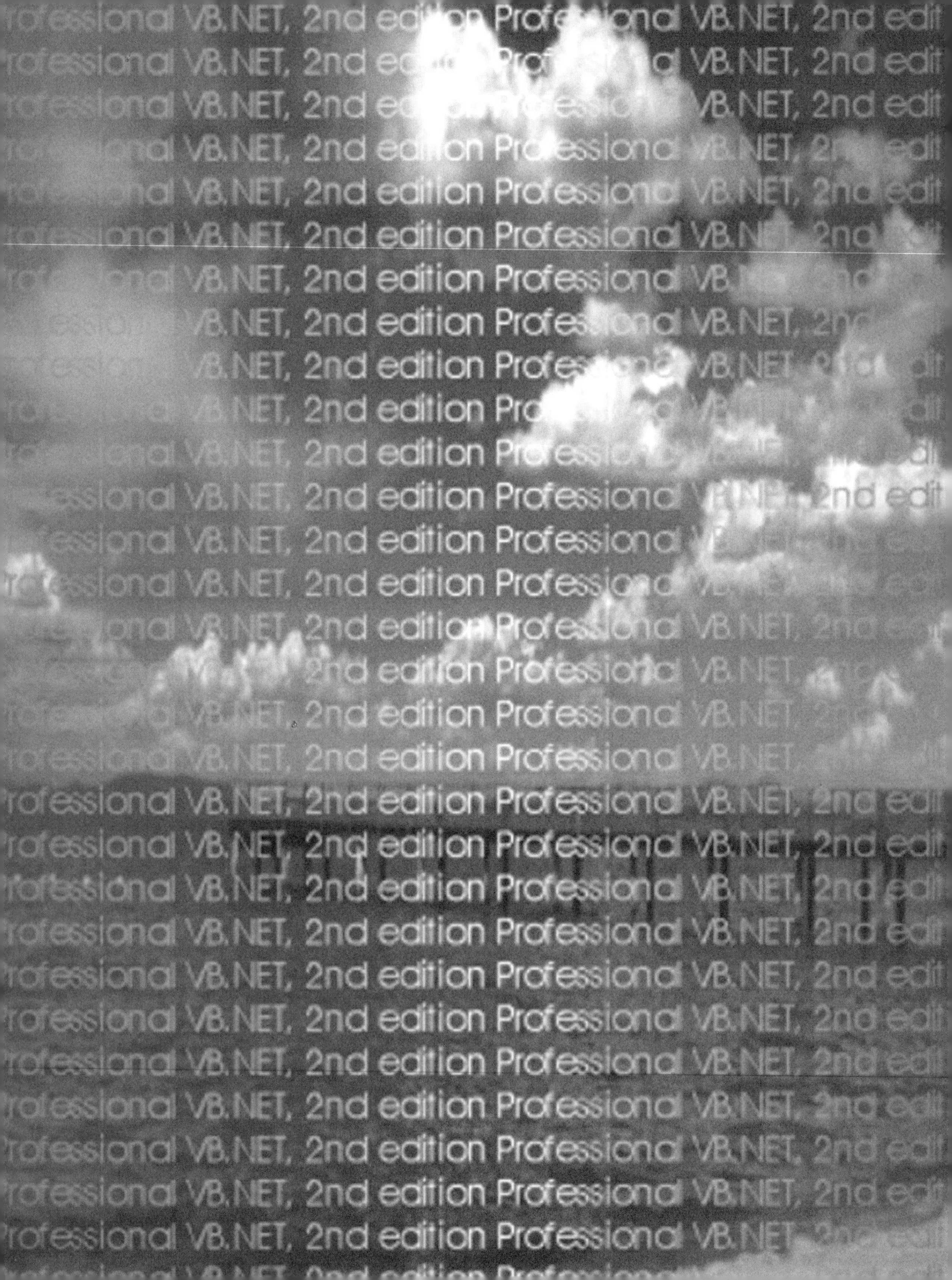
Professional VB.NET, 2nd edition

Object Syntax Introduction

Visual Basic has had powerful object-oriented capabilities since the introduction of version 4.0. VB.NET carries that tradition forward. VB.NET simplifies some of the syntax and greatly enhances these capabilities, and now supports the four major defining concepts required for a language to be fully object-oriented:

❑ **Abstraction** – VB has supported abstraction since VB4. Abstraction is merely the ability of a language to create "black box" code – to take a concept and create an abstract representation of that concept within a program. A `Customer` object, for instance, is an abstract representation of a real-world customer. A `Recordset` object is an abstract representation of a set of data.

❑ **Encapsulation** – This has also been with us since version 4.0. It's the concept of a separation between interface and implementation. The idea is that we can create an interface (`Public` methods in a class) and, as long as that interface remains consistent, the application can interact with our objects. This remains true even if we entirely rewrite the code within a given method – thus the interface is independent of the implementation.

Encapsulation allows us to hide the internal implementation details of a class. For example, the algorithm we use to compute Pi might be proprietary. We can expose a simple API to the end user, but we hide all of the logic used by our algorithm by encapsulating it within our class.

❑ **Polymorphism** – Likewise, polymorphism was introduced with VB4. Polymorphism is reflected in the ability to write one routine that can operate on objects from more than one class – treating different objects from different classes in exactly the same way. For instance, if both `Customer` and `Vendor` objects have a `Name` property, and we can write a routine that calls the `Name` property regardless of whether we're using a `Customer` or `Vendor` object, then we have polymorphism.

VB, in fact, supports polymorphism in two ways – through late binding (much like Smalltalk, a classic example of a true object-orientated language) and through the implementation of multiple interfaces. This flexibility is very powerful and is preserved within VB.NET.

❑ **Inheritance** – VB.NET is the first version of VB that supports inheritance. Inheritance is the idea that a class can gain the pre-existing interface and behaviors of an existing class. This is done by inheriting these behaviors from the existing class through a process known as subclassing. With the introduction of full inheritance, VB is now a fully **object-orientated** language by any reasonable definition.

We'll discuss these concepts in detail in Chapter 7, using this chapter and Chapter 6 to focus on the syntax that enables us to utilize these concepts.

Additionally, because VB.NET is a component-based language, we have some other capabilities that are closely related to traditional concepts of object-orientation:

❑ **Multiple interfaces** – Each class in VB.NET defines a primary interface (also called the default or native interface) through its Public methods, properties and events. Classes can also implement other, secondary interfaces in addition to this primary interface. An object based on this class then has multiple interfaces, and a client application can choose by which interface it will interact with the object.

❑ **Assembly (component) level scoping** – Not only can we define our classes and methods to be `Public` (available to anyone), `Protected` (available through inheritance) and `Private` (only available locally), but we can also define them as `Friend` – meaning they are only available within the current assembly or component. This is not a traditional object-oriented concept, but is very powerful when designing component-based applications.

In this chapter we'll explore the creation and use of classes and objects in VB.NET. In Chapter 6, we'll examine inheritance and how it can be used within VB.NET. In Chapter 7, we'll explore object-oriented programming in depth, fully defining the features listed and exploring how we can use these concepts.

Before we get too deep into code, however, it is important that we spend a little time familiarizing ourselves with basic object-oriented terms and concepts.

Object-Oriented Terminology

To start with, let's take a look at the word **object** itself, along with the related **class** and **instance** terms. Then we'll move on to discuss the four terms that define the major functionality in the object-oriented world – encapsulation, abstraction, polymorphism, and inheritance.

Objects, Classes, and Instances

An **object** is a code-based abstraction of a real-world entity or relationship. For instance, we might have a `Customer` object that represents a real-world customer – such as customer number 123 – or we might have a `File` object that represents `C:\config.sys` on our computer's hard drive.

A closely related term is **class**. A class is the code that defines our object, and all objects are created based on a class. A class is an abstraction of a real-world concept, and it provides the basis from which we create instances of specific objects. For example, in order to have a `Customer` object representing customer number 123, we must first have a `Customer` class that contains all of the code (methods, properties, events, variables, and so on) necessary to create `Customer` objects. Based on that class, we can create any number of objects – each one an **instance** of the class. Each object is identical to the others – except that it may contain different data.

We may create many instances of `Customer` objects based on the same `Customer` class. All of the `Customer` objects are identical in terms of what they can do and the code they contain, but each one contains its own unique data. This means that each object represents a different physical customer.

Composition of an Object

We use an **interface** to get access to an object's data and behavior. The object's data and behaviors are contained within the object, so a client application can treat the object like a black box accessible only through its interface. This is a key object-oriented concept called **encapsulation**. The idea is that any programs that make use of this object won't have direct access to the behaviors or data – but rather those programs must make use of our object's interface.

Let's walk through each of the three elements in detail.

Interface

The interface is defined as a set of methods (`Sub` and `Function` routines), properties (`Property` routines), events, and fields (variables or attributes) that are declared `Public` in scope.

> *The word attribute means one thing in the general object-oriented world, and something else in .NET. The OO world often refers to an object's variables as attributes, while in .NET an attribute is a coding construct that we can use to control compilation, the IDE, and so on.*

We can also have `Private` methods and properties in our code. While these methods can be called by code within our object, they are not part of the interface and cannot be called by programs written to use our object. Another option is to use the `Friend` keyword, which defines the scope to be our current project, meaning that any code within our project can call the method, but no code outside of our project (that is, from a different .NET assembly) can call the method. To complicate things a bit, we can also declare methods and properties as `Protected`, which are available to classes that inherit from our class. We'll discuss `Protected` in Chapter 6 along with inheritance.

For example, we might have the following code in a class:

```
Public Function CalculateValue() As Integer

End Function
```

Since this method is declared with the `Public` keyword, it is part of our interface and can be called by client applications that are using our object. We might also have a method such as this:

```
Private Sub DoSomething()

End Sub
```

This method is declared as being `Private` and, so, it is not part of our interface. This method can only be called by code within our class – not by any code outside of our class, such as the code in a program that is using one of our objects.

On the other hand, we can do something like this:

```
Public Function CalculateValue() As Integer
   DoSomething()
End Function
```

In this case, we're calling the `Private` method from within a `Public` method. While code using our objects can't directly call a `Private` method, we will frequently use `Private` methods to help structure the code in our class to make it more maintainable and easier to read.

Finally, we can use the `Friend` keyword:

```
Friend Sub DoSomething()

End Sub
```

In this case, the `DoSomething` method can be called by code within our class, or from other classes or modules within our current VB.NET project. Code from outside our project will not have access to the method.

The `Friend` scope is very similar to the `Public` scope, in that it makes methods available for use by code outside of our object itself. However, unlike `Public`, the `Friend` keyword restricts access to code within our current VB.NET project – preventing code in other .NET assemblies from calling the method.

> *This is very unlike the C++ `friend` keyword, which implements a form of tight coupling between objects and which is generally regarded as a bad thing to do. Instead, this is the same `Friend` keyword that VB has had for many years and which was later adopted by Java to provide component-level scoping in that language as well. It is equivalent to the `internal` keyword in C#.*

Implementation or Behavior

The code inside of a method is called the **implementation**. Sometimes it is also called **behavior** since it is this code that actually makes the object do useful work.

For instance, we may have an `Age` property as part of our object's interface. Within that method, we may have some code (perhaps written by an inexperienced developer, since it is just returning a non-calculated value):

```
Private mintAge As Integer

Public ReadOnly Property Age() As Integer
  Get
    Return mintAge
```

```
      End Get
End Sub
```

In this case, the code is returning a value directly out of a variable, rather than doing something better like calculating the value based on a birth date. However, this kind of code is often written in applications, and it seems to work fine for a while.

The key concept here is to understand that client applications can use our object even if we change the implementation – as long as we don't change the interface. As long as our method name and its parameter list and return data type remain unchanged, we can change the implementation all we want.

The code necessary to call our `Age` property would look something like this:

```
theAge = MyObject.Age
```

The result of running this code is that we get the `Age` value returned for our use. While our client application will work fine, we'll soon discover that hard coding the age into the application is a problem and so, at some point, we'll want to improve this code. Fortunately, we can change our implementation without changing the client code:

```
Private mdtBirthDate As Date

Public ReadOnly Property Age() As Integer
  Get
    Return DateDiff(DateInterval.Year, mdtBirthDate, Now())
  End Get
End Sub
```

We've changed the implementation behind the interface – effectively changing how it behaves – without changing the interface itself. Now, when our client application is run, we'll find that the `Age` value returned is accurate over time where, with the previous implementation, it was not.

It is important to keep in mind that encapsulation is a syntactic tool – it allows our code to continue to run without change. However, it is not semantic – meaning that, just because our code continues to run, doesn't mean it continues to do what we actually wanted it to do.

In this example, our client code may have been written to overcome the initial limitations of the implementation in some way, and thus might not only rely on being able to retrieve the `Age` value, but the client code might be counting on the result of that call being a fixed value over time.

While our update to the implementation won't stop the client program from running, it may very well prevent the client program from running correctly.

Member or Instance Variables

The third key part of an object is its data, or **state**. In fact, it might be argued that the only important part of an object is its data. After all, every instance of a class is absolutely identical in terms of its interface and its implementation – the only thing that can vary at all is the data contained within that particular object.

Member variables are those declared so that they are available to all code within our class. Typically member variables are `Private` in scope – available only to the code in our class itself. They are also sometimes referred to as **instance variables** or as **attributes**. The .NET Framework also refers to them as **fields**.

We shouldn't confuse instance variables with *properties*. In VB, a `Property` is a type of method that is geared around retrieving and setting values, while an instance variable is a variable within the class that may *hold* the value exposed by a `Property`.

For instance, we might have a class that has instance variables:

```
Public Class TheClass
   Private mstrName As String
   Private mdtBirthDate As Date
End Class
```

Each instance of the class – each object – will have its own set of these variables in which to store data. Because these variables are declared with the `Private` keyword, they are only available to code within each specific object.

While member variables *can* be declared as `Public` in scope, this makes them available to any code using our objects in a manner we can't control. Such a choice directly breaks the concept of encapsulation, since code outside our object can directly change data values without following any rules that might otherwise be set in our object's code.

If we want to make the value of an instance variable available to code outside of our object, we should use a **property**:

```
Public Class TheClass
   Private mstrName As String
   Private mdtBirthDate As Date

   Public ReadOnly Property Name() As String
     Get
       Return mstrName
     End Get
   End Property
End Class
```

Since the `Name` property is a method, we are not directly exposing our internal variables to client code, so we preserve encapsulation of our data. At the same time, through this mechanism we are able to safely provide access to our data as needed.

Member variables can also be declared with `Friend` scope – which means they are available to all code in our project. Like declaring them as `Public`, this breaks encapsulation and is strongly discouraged.

Now that we have a grasp on some of the basic object-oriented terminology, we're ready to explore the creation of classes and objects. First, we'll see how VB allows us to interact with objects, and then we'll dive into the actual process of authoring those objects.

Working with Objects

In the .NET environment, and within VB in particular, we use objects all the time without even thinking about it. Every control on a form – and, in fact, every form – is an object. When we open a file or interact with a database we are using objects to do that work.

Object Declaration and Instantiation

Objects are created using the New keyword – indicating that we want a new instance of a particular class. There are a number of variations on how or where we can use the New keyword in our code. Each one provides different advantages in terms of code readability or flexibility.

> *Unlike previous versions of VB, VB.NET doesn't use the CreateObject statement for object creation. CreateObject was an outgrowth of VB's relationship with COM and, since VB.NET doesn't use COM, it has no use for CreateObject. The CreateObject method still exists to support COM interoperability, but is not used to access .NET objects.*

The most obvious way to create an object is to declare an object variable and then create an instance of the object:

```
Dim obj As TheClass
obj = New TheClass()
```

The result of this code is that we have a new instance of TheClass ready for our use. To interact with this new object, we will use the obj variable that we declared. The obj variable contains a reference to the object – a concept we'll explore more later.

We can shorten this by combining the declaration of the variable with the creation of the instance:

```
Dim obj As New TheClass()
```

> *In previous versions of VB this was a very poor thing to do, as it had both negative performance and maintainability effects. However, in VB.NET, there is no difference between our first example and this one, other than that our code is shorter.*

This code both declares the variable obj as data type TheClass and also creates an instance of the class – immediately creating an object that we can use from our code.

Another variation on this theme is:

```
Dim obj As TheClass = New TheClass()
```

Again, this both declares a variable of data type TheClass and creates an instance of the class for our use.

This third syntax provides a great deal of flexibility while remaining compact. Though it is a single line of code, it separates the declaration of the variable's data type from the creation of the object.

Such flexibility is very useful when working with inheritance or with multiple interfaces. We might declare the variable to be of one type – say an interface – and instantiate the object based on a class that implements that interface. We'll cover interfaces in detail in Chapter 6 but as an example here, let's create an interface named ITheInterface:

```
Public Interface ITheInterface
   Sub DoSomething()
End Interface
```

Our class can then implement that interface, meaning that our class now has its own native interface and also has a secondary interface – ITheInterface:

```
Public Class TheClass
   Implements ITheInterface

   Public Sub DoSomething() Implements ITheInterface.DoSomething
      ' implementation goes here
   End Sub
End Class
```

We can now create an instance of TheClass, but reference it via the secondary interface by declaring the variable to be of type ITheInterface:

```
Dim obj As ITheInterface = New TheClass()
```

We can also do this using two separate lines of code:

```
Dim obj As ITheInterface
obj = New TheClass()
```

Either technique works fine and achieves the same result, which is that we have a new object of type TheClass, being accessed via its secondary interface. We'll discuss multiple interfaces in more detail in Chapter 6.

So far we've been declaring a variable for our new objects. However, sometimes we may simply need to pass an object as a parameter to a method – in which case we can create an instance of the object right in the call to that method:

```
DoSomething(New TheClass())
```

This calls the DoSomething method, passing a new instance of TheClass as a parameter.

This can be even more complex. Perhaps, instead of needing an object reference, our method needs an Integer. We can provide that Integer value from a method on our object:

```
Public Class TheClass
   Public Function GetValue() As Integer
      Return 42
   End Function
End Class
```

We can then instantiate the object and call the method all in one shot, thus passing the value returned from the method as a parameter:

```
DoSomething(New TheClass().GetValue())
```

Obviously, we need to carefully weigh the readability of such code against its compactness – at some point, having more compact code can detract from readability rather than enhancing it.

Notice that nowhere do we use the Set statement when working with objects. In VB6, any time we worked with an object reference we had to use the Set command – differentiating objects from any other data type in the language.

> In VB.NET, objects are not treated differently from any other data type, and so we can use direct assignment for objects just like we do with **Integer** or **String** data types. The **Set** command is no longer valid in VB.NET.

Object References

Typically, when we work with an object we are using a **reference** to that object. On the other hand, when we are working with simple data types such as Integer, we are working with the actual value rather than a reference. Let's explore these concepts and see how they work and interact.

When we create a new object using the New keyword, we store a reference to that object in a variable. For instance:

```
Dim obj As New TheClass()
```

This code creates a new instance of TheClass. We gain access to this new object via the obj variable. This variable holds a reference to the object. We might then do something like this:

```
Dim another As TheClass
another = obj
```

Now we have a second variable, another, which also has a reference to that same object. We can use either variable interchangeably, since they both reference the exact same object. The thing we need to remember is that the variable we have is not the object itself but, rather, is just a reference or pointer to the object itself.

Dereferencing Objects

When we are done working with an object, we can indicate that we're through with it by dereferencing the object.

To dereference an object, we need to simply set our object reference to Nothing:

```
Dim obj As TheClass

obj = New TheClass()
obj = Nothing
```

This code has no impact on our object itself. In fact, the object may remain blissfully unaware that it has been dereferenced for some time.

Once any and all variables that reference an object are set to Nothing, the .NET runtime can tell that we no longer need that object. At some point, the runtime will destroy the object and reclaim the memory and resources consumed by the object.

Between the time that we dereference the object and the time that .NET gets around to actually destroying it, the object simply sits in memory – unaware that it has been dereferenced. Right before .NET does destroy the object, the framework will call the Finalize method on the object (if it has one). We discussed the Finalize method in Chapter 3.

Early versus Late Binding

One of the strengths of Visual Basic has long been that we had access to both early and late binding when interacting with objects.

Early binding means that our code directly interacts with the object, by directly calling its methods. Since the VB compiler knows the object's data type ahead of time, it can directly compile code to invoke the methods on the object. Early binding also allows the IDE to use IntelliSense to aid our development efforts; it allows the compiler to ensure that we are referencing methods that do exist and that we are providing the proper parameter values.

> *In previous versions of VB, early binding was also known as vtable binding. The vtable was an artifact of COM, providing a list of the addresses for all the methods on an object's interface. In .NET, things are simpler and there is no real vtable. Instead, the compiler is able to generate code to directly invoke the methods on an object. From a VB coding perspective this makes no difference, but it is quite a change behind the scenes.*

Late binding means that our code interacts with an object dynamically at run-time. This provides a great deal of flexibility since our code literally doesn't care what type of object it is interacting with as long as the object supports the methods we want to call. Because the type of the object isn't known by the IDE or compiler, neither IntelliSense nor compile-time syntax checking is possible but we get unprecedented flexibility in exchange.

If we enable strict type checking by using Option Strict On at the top of our code modules, then the IDE and compiler will enforce early binding behavior. By default, Option Strict is turned off and so we have easy access to the use of late binding within our code. We discussed Option Strict in Chapter 4.

Implementing Late Binding

Late binding occurs when the compiler can't determine the type of object that we'll be calling. This level of ambiguity is achieved through the use of the Object data type. A variable of data type Object can hold virtually any value – including a reference to any type of object. Thus, code such as the following could be run against any object that implements a DoSomething method that accepts no parameters:

```
Option Strict Off

Module LateBind
  Public Sub DoWork(ByVal obj As Object)
    obj.DoSomething()
  End Sub
End Module
```

If the object passed into this routine does not have a DoSomething method that accepts no parameters, then a run-time error will result. Thus, it is recommended that any code that uses late binding always provides error trapping:

```
Option Strict Off

Module LateBind
  Public Sub DoWork(ByVal obj As Object)
    Try
      obj.DoSomething()
    Catch ex As Exception When Err.Number = 438
      ' do something appropriate given failure to call the method
    End Try
  End Sub
End Module
```

Here, we've put the call to the DoSomething method in a Try block. If it works then the code in the Catch block is ignored but, in the case of a failure, the code in the Catch block is run. We would need to write code in the Catch block to handle the case that the object did not support the DoSomething method call. This Catch block, in fact, only catches error number 438, which is the error indicating that the method doesn't exist on the object.

While late binding is flexible, it can be error prone and it is slower than early bound code. To make a late bound method call, the .NET runtime must dynamically determine if the target object actually has a method that matches the one we're calling, and then it must invoke that method on our behalf. This takes more time and effort than an early bound call where the compiler knows ahead of time that the method exists and can compile our code to make the call directly. With a late bound call, the compiler has to generate code to make the call dynamically at runtime.

Use of the CType Function

Whether we are using late binding or not, it can be useful to pass object references around using the Object data type – converting them to an appropriate type when we need to interact with them. This is particularly useful when working with objects that use inheritance or implement multiple interfaces – concepts that we'll discuss in Chapter 6.

If Option Strict is turned off, which is the default, we can write code that allows us to use a variable of type Object to make an early bound method call:

```
Module LateBind
  Public Sub DoWork(obj As Object)
    Dim local As TheClass
```

```
        local = obj
        local.DoSomething()
    End Sub
End Module
```

We are using a strongly typed variable, `local`, to reference what was a generic object value. Behind the scenes, VB.NET converts the generic type to a specific type so it can be assigned to the strongly typed variable. If the conversion can't be done we'll get a trappable runtime error.

The same thing can be done using the `CType` function. If `Option Strict` is enabled, then the previous approach will not compile and the `CType` function must be used. Here is the same code making use of `CType`:

```
Module LateBind
    Public Sub DoWork(obj As Object)
        Dim local As TheClass

        local = CType(obj, TheClass)
        local.DoSomething()
    End Sub
End Module
```

Here, we've declared a variable of type `TheClass`, which is an early bound data type that we want to use. The parameter we're accepting, though, is of the generic `Object` data type, and so we use the `CType()` method to gain an early bound reference to the object. If the object isn't of type `TheClass`, the call to `CType()` will fail with a trappable error.

Once we have a reference to the object, we can call methods by using the early bound variable, `local`.

Since all the method calls with `CType()` are early bound, this code will work even if we override the default and set `Option Strict On`.

This code can be shortened to avoid the use of the intermediate variable. Instead, we can simply call methods directly from the data type:

```
Module LateBind
    Public Sub DoWork(obj As Object)
        CType(obj, TheClass).DoSomething()
    End Sub
End Module
```

Even though the variable we're working with is of type `Object` and, thus, any calls to it will be late bound, we are using the `CType` method to temporarily convert the variable into a +specific type – in this case, the type `TheClass`.

> **If the object passed as a parameter is not of type `TheClass`, we will get a trappable error, so it is always wise to wrap this code in a `Try...Catch` block.**

The `CType` function can be very useful when working with objects that implement multiple interfaces, since we can reference a single object variable through the appropriate type as needed. For instance, as we discussed earlier, if we have an object of type `TheClass` that also implements `ITheInterface`, we can use that interface with the following code:

```
Dim obj As TheClass

obj = New TheClass
CType(obj, ITheInterface).DoSomething()
```

In this way, we can make early bound calls to other interfaces on an object without needing to declare a new variable of the interface type. We'll discuss multiple interfaces in detail in Chapter 6.

Creating Classes

Using objects is fairly straightforward and intuitive. It is the kind of thing that even the most novice programmers pick up and accept rapidly. Creating classes and objects is a bit more complex and interesting, however, and that is what we'll cover through the rest of the chapter.

Creating Basic Classes

As we discussed earlier, objects are merely instances of a specific template (a class). The class contains the code that defines the behavior of its objects, as well as defining the instance variables that will contain the object's individual data.

Classes are created using the `Class` keyword, and include definitions (declaration) and implementations (code) for the variables, methods, properties, and events that make up the class. Each object created based on this class will have the same methods, properties, and events, and will have its own set of data defined by the variables in our class.

The Class Keyword

If we wanted to create a class that represents a person – a `Person` class – we could use the `Class` keyword like so:

```
Public Class Person
  ' implementation code goes here
End Class
```

As we know, VB.NET projects are composed of a set of files with the `.vb` extension. Each file can contain multiple classes. This means that, within a single file, we could have something like this:

```
Public Class Adult
  ' implementation code goes here
End Class

Public Class Senior
  ' implementation code goes here
```

```
End Class

Public Class Child
    ' implementation code goes here
End Class
```

The most common approach is to have a single class per file. This is because the VS.NET Solution Explorer and the code-editing environment are tailored to make it easy to navigate from file to file to find our code. For instance, if we create a single class file with all these classes, the Solution Explorer simply shows a single entry:

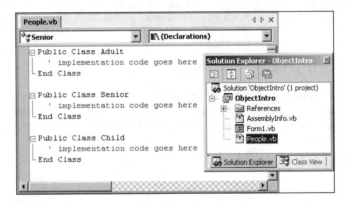

However, the VS.NET IDE does provide the **Class View** window. If we do decide to put multiple classes in each physical .vb file, we can make use of the **Class View** window to quickly and efficiently navigate through our code – jumping from class to class without having to manually locate those classes in specific code files:

> **The Class View window is incredibly useful even if we keep to one class per file, since it still provides us with a class-based view of our entire application.**

In this chapter, we'll stick with one class per file, as it is the most common approach. Open the VS.NET IDE and create a new **Windows Application** project. Name it ObjectIntro.

Choose the **Project | Add Class** menu option to add a new class module to the project. We'll be presented with the standard **Add New Item** dialog.

Change the name to `Person.vb` and click **Open**. The result will be the following code that defines our `Person` class:

```
Public Class Person

End Class
```

It is worth noting that all VB.NET source files end in a `.vb` extension, regardless of which type of VB source file we choose (form, class, module, etc.) when we are adding the file to our project. In fact, any forms, classes, components, or controls that we add to our project are actually class modules – they are just specific types of classes that provide the appropriate behaviors. Typically, these behaviors come from another class via inheritance, which we'll discuss in Chapter 6.

> *The exception is the `Module`, which is a special construct that allows us to include code within our application that is not directly contained within any class. As with previous versions of Visual Basic, methods placed in a Module can be called directly from any code within our project.*

With our `Person` class created, we're ready to start adding code to declare our interface, implement our behaviors, and to declare our instance variables.

Member Variables

Member or instance variables are variables declared in our class that will be available to each individual object when our application is run. Each object gets its own set of data – basically each object gets its own copy of the variables.

At the beginning of the chapter, we discussed how a class is simply a template from which we create specific objects. Variables that we define within our class are also simply templates – and each object gets its own copy of those variables in which to store its data.

Declaring member variables is as easy as declaring variables within the Class block structure. Add the following code to our Person class:

```
Public Class Person
    Private mstrName As String
    Private mdtBirthDate As Date

End Class
```

We can control the scope of our variables by using the following keywords:

❑ Private – available only to code within our class

❑ Friend – available only to code within our project/component

❑ Protected – available only to classes that inherit from our class – discussed in detail in Chapter 6

❑ Protected Friend – available to code within our project/component and classes that inherit from our class whether in our project or not – discussed in detail in Chapter 6

❑ Public – available to code outside our class

Typically, member variables are declared using the Private keyword – making them available only to code within each instance of our class. Choosing any other option should be done with great care, as all the other options allow code *outside* our class to directly interact with the variable – meaning that the value could be changed and our code would never know that a change took place.

One common exception to making variables Private *is the use of the* Protected *keyword, as we'll discuss in Chapter 6.*

Methods

Objects typically need to provide services (or functions) that we can call when working with the object. Using their own data, or data passed as parameters to the method, they manipulate information to yield a result or to perform a service.

Methods declared as Public, Friend, or Protected in scope define the interface of our class. Methods that are Private in scope are only available to the code within the class itself, and can be used to provide structure and organization to our code. As we discussed earlier, the actual code within each method is called *implementation*, while the declaration of the method itself is what defines our interface.

Methods are simply routines that we code within the class to implement the services that we want to provide to the users of our object. Some methods return values or provide information back to the calling code. These are called **interrogative methods**. Others, called **imperative methods**, just perform a service and return nothing to the calling code.

In VB.NET, methods are implemented using Sub (for imperative methods) or Function (for interrogative methods) routines within the class module that defines our object. Sub routines may accept parameters, but they don't return any result value when they are complete. Function routines can also accept parameters, and they always generate a result value that can be used by the calling code.

A method declared with the Sub keyword is merely one that returns no value. Add the following code to our Person class:

```
Public Sub Walk()
   ' implementation code goes here
End Sub
```

The Walk method would presumably contain some code that performed some useful work when called, but has no result value to return when it is complete.

To use this method, we might write code such as:

```
Dim myPerson As New Person()
myPerson.Walk()
```

Once we've created an instance of the Person class, we can simply invoke the Walk method.

Methods that Return Values

If we have a method that does generate some value that should be returned, we need to use the Function keyword:

```
Public Function Age() As Integer
   Return DateDiff(DateInterval.Year, mdtBirthDate, Now())
End Function
```

Notice that we need to indicate the data type of the return value when we declare a Function. In this example, we are returning the calculated age as a result of the method. We can return any value of the appropriate data type by using the Return keyword.

We can also return the value without using the Return keyword, by setting the value of the function name itself:

```
Public Function Age() As Integer
   Age = DateDiff(DateInterval.Year, mdtBirthDate, Now())
End Function
```

This is functionally equivalent to the previous code. Either way, we can use this method with code similar to the following:

```
Dim myPerson As New Person()
Dim intAge As Integer

intAge = myPerson.Age()
```

The Age method returns an Integer data value that we can use in our program as required – in this case we're just storing it into a variable.

Indicating Method Scope

Adding the appropriate keyword in front of the method declaration indicates the scope:

```
Public Sub Walk()
```

This indicates that `Walk` is a `Public` method and is thus available to code outside our class and even outside our current project. Any application that references our assembly can make use of this method. By being `Public`, this method becomes part of our object's interface.

On the other hand, we might choose to restrict the method somewhat:

```
Friend Sub Walk()
```

By declaring the method with the `Friend` keyword, we are indicating that it should be part of our object's interface only for code inside our project – any other applications or projects that make use of our assembly will not be able to call the `Walk` method.

```
Private Function Age() As Integer
```

The `Private` keyword indicates that a method is only available to the code within our particular class. `Private` methods are very useful to help us organize complex code within each class. Sometimes our methods will contain very lengthy and complex code. In order to make this code more understandable, we may choose to break it up into several smaller routines, having our main method call these routines in the proper order. Additionally, we may use these routines from several places within our class and so, by making them separate methods, we enable reuse of the code. These sub-routines should never be called by code outside our object – and so we make them `Private`.

Method Parameters

We will often want to pass information into a method as we call it. This information is provided via parameters to the method. For instance, in our `Person` class, perhaps we want our `Walk` method to track the distance the person walks over time. In such a case, the `Walk` method would need to know how far the person is to walk each time the method is called. Add the following code to our Person class:

```
Public Class Person
  Private mstrName As String
  Private mdtBirthDate As Date
  Private mintTotalDistance As Integer

  Public Sub Walk(ByVal Distance As Integer)
    mintTotalDistance += Distance
  End Sub

  Public Function Age() As Integer
    Return DateDiff(DateInterval.Year, mdtBirthDate, Now())
  End Function
End Class
```

With this implementation, a `Person` object will sum up all of the distances that are walked over time. Each time the `Walk` method is called, the calling code must pass an `Integer` value indicating the distance to be walked. Our code to call this method would be similar to the following:

```
Dim myPerson As New Person()
myPerson.Walk(12)
```

The parameter is accepted using the ByVal keyword. This indicates that the parameter value is a *copy* of the original value. This is the default way VB.NET accepts all parameters. Typically, this is desirable because it means that we can work with the parameter inside our code – including changing its value – with no risk of accidentally changing the original value back in the calling code.

If we do want to be able to change the value in the calling code, we can change the declaration to pass the parameter by reference by using the ByRef qualifier:

```
Public Sub Walk(ByRef Distance As Integer)
```

In this case, we'll get a reference (or pointer) back to the original value rather than receiving a copy. This means that any change we make to the Distance parameter will be reflected back in the calling code – very similar to the way object references work, as we discussed earlier in Chapter 4.

> **Using this technique can be dangerous, since it is not explicitly clear to the caller of our method that the value will change. Such unintended side effects can be hard to debug and should be avoided.**

Properties

The .NET environment provides for a specialized type of method called a **property**. A property is a method specifically designed for setting and retrieving data values. For instance, we declared a variable in our Person class to contain a name, so our Person class may include code to allow that name to be set and retrieved. This could be done using regular methods:

```
Public Sub SetName(ByVal Name As String)
   mstrName = Name
End Sub

Public Function GetName() As String
   Return mstrName
End Function
```

Using methods like these, we would write code to interact with our object such as:

```
Dim myPerson As New Person()

myPerson.SetName("Jones")
MsgBox(myPerson.GetName())
```

While this is perfectly acceptable, it is not as nice as it could be through the use of a property. A Property style method consolidates the setting and retrieving of a value into a single structure, and also makes the code within our class smoother overall. We can rewrite these two methods into a single property. Add the following code to the Person class:

```
Public Property Name() As String
  Get
    Return mstrName
  End Get
  Set(ByVal Value As String)
    mstrName = Value
  End Set
End Property
```

By using a property method instead, we can make our client code much more readable:

```
Dim myPerson As New Person()

myPerson.Name = "Jones"
MsgBox(myPerson.Name)
```

The `Property` method is declared with both a scope and a data type:

```
Public Property Name() As String
```

In this example, we've declared the property as `Public` in scope, but it can be declared using the same scope options as any other method – `Public`, `Friend`, `Private`, or `Protected`.

As with other methods, a `Public` property is accessible to any code outside our class, while `Friend` is available outside our class, but only to code within our VB project. `Protected` properties are available through inheritance, as we'll discuss in Chapter 6, and `Private` properties are only available to code within our class.

The return data type of this property is `String`. A property can return virtually any data type as appropriate for the nature of the value. In this regard, a property is very similar to a method declared using the `Function` keyword.

Though a `Property` method is a single structure, it is divided into two parts: a getter and a setter. The getter is contained within a `Get...End Get` block and is responsible for returning the value of the property on demand:

```
Get
  Return mstrName
End Get
```

Though the code in this example is very simple, it could be more complex – perhaps calculating the value to be returned or applying other business logic to change the value as it is returned.

Likewise, the code to change the value is contained within a `Set...End Set` block:

```
Set(ByVal Value As String)
  mstrName = Value
End Set
```

The Set statement accepts a single parameter value that stores the new value. Our code in the block can then use this value to set the property's value as appropriate. The data type of this parameter must match the data type of the property itself. By having the parameter declared in this manner, we can change the variable name used for the parameter value if needed.

By default, the parameter is named Value. However, if we dislike the name Value, we can change the parameter name to something else, for example:

```
Set(ByVal NewName As String)
   mstrName = NewName
End Set
```

In many cases, we may apply business rules or other logic within this routine to ensure that the new value is appropriate before we actually update the data within our object.

Parameterized Properties

The Name property we created is an example of a single-value property. We can also create property arrays or parameterized properties. These properties reflect a range, or array, of values. As an example, a person will often have several phone numbers. We might implement a PhoneNumber property as a parameterized property – storing not only phone numbers, but also a description of each number. To retrieve a specific phone number we'd write code such as:

```
Dim myPerson As New Person()
Dim strHomePhone As String

strHomePhone = myPerson.Phone("home")
```

Or, to add or change a specific phone number, we'd write:

```
myPerson.Phone("work") = "555-9876"
```

Not only are we retrieving and updating a phone number property, but also we're updating some specific phone number. This implies a couple of things. First off, we're no longer able to use a simple variable to hold the phone number, since we are now storing a list of numbers and their associated names. Secondly, we've effectively added a parameter to our property – we're actually passing the name of the phone number as a parameter on each property call.

To store the list of phone numbers we can use the Hashtable class. The Hashtable is very similar to the standard VB Collection object, but it is more powerful – allowing us to test for the existence of an existing element. Add the following declaration to the Person class:

```
Public Class Person
   Private mstrName As String
   Private mdtBirthDate As Date
   Private mintTotalDistance As Integer
   Private colPhones As New Hashtable()
```

We can implement the Phone property by adding the following code to our Person class:

```
Public Property Phone(ByVal Location As String) As String
  Get
    Return CStr(colPhones.Item(Location))
  End Get
  Set(ByVal Value As String)
    If colPhones.ContainsKey(Location) Then
      colPhones.Item(Location) = Value
    Else
      colPhones.Add(Location, Value)
    End If
  End Set
End Property
```

The declaration of the `Property` method itself is a bit different from what we've seen:

```
Public Property Phone(ByVal Location As String) As String
```

In particular, we've added a parameter, `Location`, to the property itself. This parameter will act as the index into our list of phone numbers and must be provided both when setting or retrieving phone number values.

Since the `Location` parameter is declared at the `Property` level, it is available to all code within the property – including both the `Get` and `Set` blocks.

Within our `Get` block, we use the `Location` parameter to select the appropriate phone number to return from the `Hashtable`:

```
Get
  Return colPhones.Item(Location)
End Get
```

With this code, if there is no value stored matching the `Location`, we'll get a trappable runtime error.

Similarly, in the `Set` block, we use the `Location` to update or add the appropriate element in the `Hashtable`. In this case, we're using the `ContainsKey` method of `Hashtable` to determine whether the phone number already exists in the list. If it does, we'll simply update the value in the list – otherwise, we'll add a new element to the list for the value:

```
Set(ByVal Value As String)
  If colPhones.ContainsKey(Location) Then
    colPhones.Item(Location) = Value
  Else
    colPhones.Add(Location, Value)
  End If
End Set
```

In this way, we're able to add or update a specific phone number entry based on the parameter passed by the calling code.

Read-Only Properties

There are times when we may want a property to be read-only – so that it can't be changed. In our `Person` class, for instance, we may have a read-write property for `BirthDate`, but just a read-only property for `Age`. In such a case, the `BirthDate` property is a normal property, as follows:

```
Public Property BirthDate() As Date
  Get
    Return mdtBirthDate
  End Get
  Set(ByVal Value As Date)
    mdtBirthDate = Value
  End Set
End Property
```

The `Age` value, on the other hand, is a derived value based on `BirthDate`. This is not a value that should ever be directly altered and, thus, is a perfect candidate for read-only status.

We already have an `Age` method – implemented as a `Function`. Remove that code from the `Person` class, as we'll be replacing it with a `Property` routine instead.

The difference between a `Function` routine and a `ReadOnly Property` is quite subtle. Both return a value to the calling code and, either way, our object is running a subroutine defined by our class module to return the value.

The difference is less a programmatic one than a design choice. We could create all our objects without any `Property` routines at all, just using methods for all interactions with the object. However, `Property` routines are obviously attributes of the object, while a `Function` might be an attribute or a method. By carefully implementing all attributes as `ReadOnly Property` routines, and any interrogative methods as `Function` routines, we will create more readable and understandable code.

To make a property read-only, we use the `ReadOnly` keyword and only implement the `Get` block:

```
Public ReadOnly Property Age() As Integer
  Get
    Return CInt(DateDiff(DateInterval.Year, mdtBirthDate, Now()))
  End Get
End Property
```

Since the property is read-only, we'll get a syntax error if we attempt to implement a `Set` block.

Write-Only Properties

As with read-only properties, there are times when a property should be write-only – where the value can be changed, but not retrieved.

Many people have allergies, so perhaps our `Person` object should have some understanding of the ambient allergens in the area. This is not a property that should be read from the `Person` object since allergens come from the environment rather than from the person, but it is data that the `Person` object needs in order to function properly. Add the following variable declaration to our class:

```
Public Class Person
  Private mstrName As String
  Private mdtBirthDate As Date
  Private mintTotalDistance As Integer
  Private colPhones As New Hashtable()
  Private mintAllergens As Integer
```

We can implement an `AmbientAllergens` property as follows:

```
Public WriteOnly Property AmbientAllergens() As Integer
  Set(ByVal Value As Integer)
    mintAllergens = Value
  End Set
End Property
```

To create a write-only property, we use the `WriteOnly` keyword and only implement a `Set` block in our code. Since the property is write-only, we'll get a syntax error if we attempt to implement a `Get` block.

The Default Property

Objects can implement a default property if desired. A default property can be used to simplify the use of our object at times, by making it appear as if our object has a native value. A good example of this behavior is the `Collection` object, which has a default property called `Item` that returns the value of a specific item, allowing us to write code similar to:

```
Dim colData As New Collection()

Return colData(Index)
```

Default properties *must be* parameterized properties. A property without a parameter cannot be marked as the default. This is a change from previous versions of VB, where any property could be marked as the default.

Our `Person` class has a parameterized property – the `Phone` property we built earlier. We can make this the default property by using the `Default` keyword:

```
Default Public Property Phone(ByVal Location As String) As String
  Get
    Return colPhones.Item(Location)
  End Get
  Set(ByVal Value As String)
    If colPhones.ContainsKey(Location) Then
      colPhones.Item(Location) = Value
    Else
      colPhones.Add(Location, Value)
    End If
  End Set
End Property
```

Prior to this change, we would need code such as the following to use the `Phone` property:

```
Dim myPerson As New Person()

MyPerson.Phone("home") = "555-1234"
```

But now, with the property marked as `Default`, we can simplify our code:

```
myPerson("home") = "555-1234"
```

By picking appropriate default properties, we can potentially make the use of our objects more intuitive.

Events

Both methods and properties allow us to write code that interacts with our objects by invoking specific functionality as needed. It is often useful for our objects to provide notification as certain activities occur during processing. We see examples of this all the time with controls, where a button indicates it was clicked via a `Click` event, or a textbox indicates its contents have changed via the `TextChanged` event.

Our objects can raise events of their own – providing a powerful and easily implemented mechanism by which objects can notify our client code of important activities or events. In VB.NET, events are provided using the standard .NET mechanism of **delegates**. We'll discuss delegates after we explore how to work with events in VB.

Handling Events

We are all used to seeing code in a form to handle the `Click` event of a button – code such as:

```
Private Sub button1_Click (ByVal sender As System.Object, _
    ByVal e As System.EventArgs) Handles button1.Click

End Sub
```

Typically we just write our code in this routine without paying a lot of attention to the code created by the VS.NET IDE. However, let's take a second look at that code, since there are a couple of important things to note here.

First off, notice the use of the `Handles` keyword. This keyword specifically indicates that this method will be handling the `Click` event from the `button1` control. Of course, a control is just an object – so what we're indicating here is that this method will be handling the `Click` event from the `button1` object.

Also notice that the method accepts two parameters. The Button control class defines these parameters. It turns out that any method that accepts two parameters with these data types can be used to handle the `Click` event. For instance, we could create a new method to handle the event:

```
Private Sub MyClickMethod(ByVal s As System.Object, _
    ByVal args As System.EventArgs) Handles button1.Click

End Sub
```

Even though we've changed the method name, and the names of the parameters, we are still accepting parameters of the same data types and we still have the `Handles` clause to indicate that this method will handle the event.

129

Handling Multiple Events

The `Handles` keyword offers even more flexibility. Not only can the method name be anything we choose, but a single method can handle multiple events if we desire. Again, the only requirement is that the method and all the events being raised must have the same parameter list.

> *This explains why all the standard events raised by the .NET system class library have exactly two parameters – the sender and an `EventArgs` object. By being so generic, it is possible to write very generic and powerful event handlers than can accept virtually any event raised by the class library.*

One common scenario where this is useful is where we have multiple instances of an object that raises events, such as two buttons on a form:

```
Private Sub MyClickMethod(ByVal sender As System.Object, _
    ByVal e As System.EventArgs) _
    Handles button1.Click, button2.Click

End Sub
```

Notice that we've modified the `Handles` clause to have a comma-separated list of events to handle. Either event will cause our method to run, giving us a central location to handle these events.

The WithEvents Keyword

The `WithEvents` keyword tells VB that we want to handle any events raised by the object within our code. For example:

```
Friend WithEvents button1 As System.Windows.Forms.Button
```

The `WithEvents` keyword makes any events from an object available for our use, while the `Handles` keyword is used to link specific events to our methods so we can receive and handle them. This is true not only for controls on forms, but also for any objects that we create.

The `WithEvents` keyword cannot be used to declare a variable of a type that doesn't raise events. In other words, if the `Button` class didn't contain code to raise events, we'd get a syntax error when we attempted to declare the variable using the `WithEvents` keyword.

The compiler can tell which classes will and won't raise events by examining their interface. Any class that will be raising an event will have that event declared as part of its interface. In VB.NET, this means that we will have used the `Event` keyword to declare at least one event as part of the interface for our class.

Raising Events

Our objects can raise events just like a control, and the code using our object can receive these events by using the `WithEvents` and `Handles` keywords. Before we can raise an event from our object, however, we need to declare the event within our class by using the `Event` keyword.

In our `Person` class, for instance, we may want to raise an event any time the `Walk` method is called. If we call this event `Walked`, we can add the following declaration to our `Person` class:

```
Public Class Person
  Private mstrName As String
  Private mdtBirthDate As Date
```

```
Private mintTotalDistance As Integer
Private colPhones As New Hashtable()
Private mintAllergens As Integer
```

```
Public Event Walked()
```

Our events can also have parameters – values that are provided to the code receiving the event. A typical button's `Click` event receives two parameters, for instance. In our `Walked` method, perhaps we want to also indicate the distance that was walked. We can do this by changing the event declaration:

```
Public Event Walked(ByVal Distance As Integer)
```

Now that our event is declared, we can raise that event within our code where appropriate. In this case, we'll raise it within the `Walk` method – so any time that a `Person` object is instructed to walk, it will fire an event indicating the distance walked. Make the following change to the `Walk` method:

```
Public Sub Walk(ByVal Distance As Integer)
  mintTotalDistance += Distance
  RaiseEvent Walked(Distance)
End Sub
```

The `RaiseEvent` keyword is used to raise the actual event. Since our event requires a parameter, that value is passed within parentheses and will be delivered to any recipient that handles the event.

In fact, the `RaiseEvent` statement will cause the event to be delivered to all code that has our object declared using the `WithEvents` keyword with a `Handles` clause for this event, or any code that has used the `AddHandler` method.

If more than one method will be receiving the event, the event will be delivered to each recipient one at a time. The order of delivery is not defined – meaning that we can't predict the order in which the recipients will receive the event – but the event will be delivered to all handlers. Note that this is a serial, synchronous process. The event is delivered to one handler at a time, and it is not delivered to the next handler until the current handler is complete. Once we call the `RaiseEvent` method, the event will be delivered to all listeners one after another until it is complete – there is no way for us to intervene and stop the process in the middle.

Receiving Events with WithEvents

Now that we've implemented an event within our `Person` class, we can write client code to declare an object using the `WithEvents` keyword. For instance, in our project's **Form1** code module, we can write the following:

```
Public Class Form1
  Inherits System.Windows.Forms.Form
```

```
Private WithEvents mobjPerson As Person
```

By declaring the variable `WithEvents`, we are indicating that we want to receive any events raised by this object.

131

We can also choose to declare the variable without the WithEvents keyword, though, in that case, we would not receive events from the object as described here. Instead we would use the AddHandler method, which we'll discuss after we cover the use of WithEvents.

We can then create an instance of the object, as the form is created, by adding the following code:

```
Private Sub Form1_Load(ByVal sender As System.Object, _
    ByVal e As System.EventArgs) Handles MyBase.Load

  mobjPerson = New Person()

End Sub
```

At this point, we've declared the object variable using WithEvents, and have created an instance of the Person class so we actually have an object with which to work. We can now proceed to write a method to handle the Walked event from the object by adding the following code to the form. We can name this method anything we like – it is the Handles clause that is important as it links the event from the object directly to this method, so it is invoked when the event is raised:

```
Private Sub OnWalk(ByVal Distance As Integer) Handles mobjPerson.Walked
  MsgBox("Person walked " & Distance)
End Sub
```

We're using the Handles keyword to indicate which event should be handled by this method. We're also receiving an Integer parameter. If the parameter list of our method doesn't match the list for the event, we'll get a compiler error indicating the mismatch.

Finally, we need to call the Walk method on our Person object. Add a button to the form and write the following code for its Click event:

```
Private Sub Button1_Click(ByVal sender As System.Object, _
    ByVal e As System.EventArgs) Handles button1.Click

  mobjPerson.Walk(42)

End Sub
```

When the button is clicked, we'll simply call the Walk method, passing an Integer value. This will cause the code in our class to be run – including the RaiseEvent statement. The result will be an event firing back into our form, since we declared the mobjPerson variable using the WithEvents keyword. Our OnWalk method will be run to handle the event, since it has the Handles clause linking it to the event.

The following diagram illustrates the flow of control:

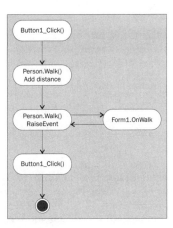

The diagram illustrates how the code in the button's click event calls the Walk method, causing it to add to the total distance walked and then to raise its event. The RaiseEvent causes the OnWalk method in the form to be invoked and, once it is done, control returns to the Walk method in the object. Since we have no code in the Walk method after we call RaiseEvent, the control returns to the Click event back in the form, and then we're all done.

> *Many people have the misconception that events use multiple threads to do their work. This is not the case. Only one thread is involved in this process. Raising an event is much like making a method call, in that our existing thread is used to run the code in the event handler. This means our application's processing is suspended until the event processing is complete.*

Receiving Events with AddHandler

Now that we've seen how to receive and handle events using the WithEvents and Handles keywords, let's take a look at an alternative approach. We can use the AddHandler method to dynamically add event handlers through our code.

WithEvents and the Handles clause require that we declare both the object variable and event handler as we build our code, effectively creating a linkage that is compiled right into our code. AddHandler, on the other hand, creates this linkage at runtime, which can provide us with more flexibility. Before we get too deep into that however, let's see how AddHandler works.

In **Form1**, we can change the way our code interacts with the Person object – first eliminating the WithEvents keyword:

```
Private mobjPerson As Person
```

and then also eliminating the Handles clause:

```
Private Sub OnWalk(ByVal Distance As Integer)
  MsgBox("Person walked " & Distance)
End Sub
```

With these changes, we've eliminated all event handling for our object and so our form will no longer receive the event, even though the `Person` object raises it.

Now we can change the code to dynamically add an event handler at runtime by using the `AddHandler` method. This method simply links an object's event to a method that should be called to handle that event. Any time after we've created our object, we can call `AddHandler` to set up the linkage:

```
Private Sub Form1_Load(ByVal sender As System.Object, _
    ByVal e As System.EventArgs) Handles MyBase.Load
  mobjPerson = New Person()
  AddHandler mobjPerson.Walked, AddressOf OnWalk
End Sub
```

This single line of code does the same thing as our earlier use of `WithEvents` and the `Handles` clause – causing the `OnWalk` method to be invoked when the `Walked` event is raised from our `Person` object.

However, this linkage is done at runtime, and so we have more control over the process than we have otherwise. For instance, we could have extra code to decide *which* event handler to link up. Suppose we have another possible method to handle the event in the case that a message box is not desirable. Add this code to **Form1**:

```
Private Sub LogOnWalk(ByVal Distance As Integer)
    System.Diagnostics.Debug.WriteLine("Person walked " & Distance)
End Sub
```

Rather than popping up a message box, this version of the handler logs the event to the **Output** window in the IDE.

Now we can enhance our `AddHandler` code to decide which handler should be used – dynamically at runtime:

```
Private Sub Form1_Load(ByVal sender As System.Object, _
    ByVal e As System.EventArgs) Handles MyBase.Load
  mobjPerson = New Person()
  If Microsoft.VisualBasic.Command = "nodisplay" Then
    AddHandler mobjPerson.Walked, AddressOf LogOnWalk
  Else
    AddHandler mobjPerson.Walked, AddressOf OnWalk
  End If
End Sub
```

If the word `nodisplay` is on the command line when our application is run, the new version of the event handler will be used – otherwise we'll continue to use the message box handler.

Constructor Methods

In VB.NET, classes can implement a special method that is always invoked *as* an object is created. This method is called the **constructor**, and it is always named `New`. We've seen this used before – most notably in a regular Windows form, where the `New` method is used to hold any initialization code for the form.

The constructor method is an ideal location for such initialization code, since it is always run before any other methods are ever invoked – and it is only ever run once for an object. Of course, we can create many objects based on a class – and the constructor method will be run for each object that is created.

The constructor method of a VB.NET class is similar to the `Class_Initialize` *event in previous versions of Visual Basic, but is far more powerful in VB.NET since we can accept parameter values as input to the method.*

We can implement a constructor in our classes as well – using it to initialize our objects as needed. This is as easy as implementing a `Public` method named `New`. Add the following to our `Person` class:

```
Public Sub New()
    Phone("home") = "555-1234"
    Phone("work") = "555-5678"
End Sub
```

In this example, we're simply using the constructor method to initialize the home and work phone numbers for any new `Person` object that is created.

Parameterized Constructors

We can also use constructors to allow parameters to be passed to our object as it is being created. This is done by simply adding parameters to the `New` method. For example, we can change the `Person` class as follows:

```
Public Sub New(ByVal Name As String, ByVal BirthDate As Date)
    mstrName = Name
    mdtBirthDate = BirthDate

    Phone("home") = "555-1234"
    Phone("work") = "555-5678"
End Sub
```

With this change, any time a `Person` object is created, we'll be provided with values for both the name and birth date. This changes how we can create a new `Person` object, however. Where we used to have code such as:

```
Dim myPerson As New Person()
```

Now we will have code such as:

```
Dim myPerson As New Person("Peter", "1/1/1960")
```

In fact, since our constructor expects these values, they are mandatory – any code wishing to create an instance of our `Person` class *must* provide these values. Fortunately, there are alternatives in the form of optional parameters and method overloading (which allows us to create multiple versions of the same method – each accepting a different parameter list – something we'll discuss later in the chapter).

Constructors with Optional Parameters

In many cases, we may want our constructor to accept parameter values for initializing new objects – but we also want to have the ability to create objects without providing those values. This is possible through method overloading, which we'll discuss later, or through the use of optional parameters.

Optional parameters on a constructor method follow the same rules as optional parameters for any other Sub routine – they must be the last parameters in the parameter list and we must provide default values for the optional parameters.

For instance, we can change our Person class as shown:

```
Public Sub New(Optional ByVal Name As String = "", _
    Optional ByVal BirthDate As Date = #1/1/1900#)
  mstrName = Name
  mdtBirthDate = BirthDate

  Phone("home") = "555-1234"
  Phone("work") = "555-5678"
End Sub
```

Here we've changed both the Name and BirthDate parameters to be optional, and we are providing default values for both of them. Now we have the option of creating a new Person object with or without the parameter values:

```
Dim myPerson As New Person("Peter", "1/1/1960")
```

or

```
Dim myPerson As New Person()
```

If we don't provide the parameter values then the default values of an empty String and 1/1/1900 will be used and our code will work just fine.

Termination and Cleanup

In the .NET environment, an object is destroyed and the memory and resources it consumes are reclaimed when there are no references remaining for the object.

As we discussed earlier in the chapter, when we are using objects, our variables actually hold a reference or pointer to the object itself. If we have code such as:

```
Dim myPerson As New Person()
```

we know that the myPerson variable is just a reference to the Person object we created. If we also have code like this:

```
Dim anotherPerson As Person
anotherPerson = myPerson
```

we know that the anotherPerson variable is also a reference to *the same object*. This means that this specific Person object is being referenced by two variables.

When there are *no* variables left referencing an object, it can be terminated by the .NET runtime environment. In particular, it is terminated and reclaimed by a mechanism called garbage collection, which we'll discuss shortly.

> Unlike COM (and thus VB6), the .NET runtime does not use reference counting to determine when an object should be terminated. Instead, it uses a scheme known as garbage collection to terminate objects. This means that, in VB.NET, we do not have deterministic finalization, so it is not possible to predict exactly when an object will be destroyed.

Before we get to garbage collection, however, let's review how we can eliminate references to an object.

We can explicitly remove a reference by setting our variable equal to `Nothing`, with code such as:

```
myPerson = Nothing
```

There are two schools of thought as to whether we should still explicitly set variables to `Nothing` even when they fall out of scope. On one hand, we can save writing extra lines of code by allowing the variable to automatically be destroyed but, on the other hand, we can explicitly show our intent to destroy the object by setting it to `Nothing` manually.

Perhaps most important is the fact that the garbage collection mechanism will sometimes reclaim our objects in the middle of our processing. This can only happen if our code doesn't use the object later in the method. Setting the variable to Nothing at the end of the method will prevent the garbage collection mechanism from proactively reclaiming our objects.

We can also remove a reference to an object by changing the variable to reference a different object. Since a variable can only point to one object at a time, it follows naturally that changing a variable to point at another object must cause it to no longer point to the first one. This means we can have code such as:

```
myPerson = New Person()
```

which causes the variable to point to a brand new object – thus releasing this reference to the prior object.

These are examples of *explicit* dereferencing. VB.NET also provides facilities for *implicit* dereferencing of objects when a variable goes out of scope. For instance, if we have a variable declared within a method, when that method completes the variable will be automatically destroyed – thus dereferencing any object to which it may have pointed. In fact, any time a variable referencing an object goes out of scope, the reference to that object is automatically eliminated.

This is illustrated by the following code:

```
Private Sub DoSomething()
  Dim myPerson As Person

  myPerson = New Person()
End Sub
```

Even though we didn't explicitly set the value of `myPerson` to `Nothing`, we know that the `myPerson` variable will be destroyed when the method is complete since it will fall out of scope. This process implicitly removes the reference to the `Person` object created within the routine.

137

Of course, another scenario where objects become dereferenced is when the application itself completes and is terminated. At that point, all variables are destroyed and so, by definition, all object references go away as well.

We discussed garbage collection and the `Finalize` method in Chapter 3. When we discussed these concepts, we mentioned that there was no automatic way to perform the cleanup when the final reference to an object is released, although implementing the `IDisposable` interface provides one solution. We'll investigate that solution now.

The IDisposable Interface

In some cases the `Finalize` behavior is not acceptable. If we have an object that is using some expensive or limited resource – such as a database connection, a file handle, or a system lock – we might need to ensure that the resource is freed as soon as the object is no longer in use.

To accomplish this, we can implement a method to be called by the client code to force our object to clean up and release its resources. This is not a perfect solution, but it is workable. The thing to remember is that this method is not called automatically by the .NET runtime environment, but instead must be called directly by the code using the object.

The .NET framework provides the `IDisposable` interface that formalizes the declaration of this cleanup method. We'll discuss creating and working with multiple interfaces in detail later so, for now, we'll just focus on the implementation of the `Dispose` method from a cleanup perspective.

Any class that derives from `System.ComponentModel.Component` automatically gains the `IDisposable` interface. This includes all of the forms and controls that are used in a Windows Forms UI, as well as various other classes within the .NET framework. For most of our custom classes, however, we'll need to implement the interface ourselves.

We can implement it in our `Person` class by adding the following code to the top of the class:

```
Public Class Person
   Implements IDisposable
```

This interface defines a single method – `Dispose` – that we need to implement in our class. It is implemented by adding the following code to the class:

```
Private Sub Dispose() Implements IDisposable.Dispose
   colPhones = Nothing
End Sub
```

In this case, we're using this method to release our reference to the `HashTable` object that the `colPhones` variable points to. While not strictly necessary, this illustrates how our code can release other objects when the `Dispose` method is called.

It is up to our client code to call this method at the appropriate time to ensure that cleanup occurs. Typically, we'll want to call the method as soon as we're done using the object.

This is not always as easy as it might sound. In particular, an object may be referenced by more than one variable and just because we're dereferencing the object from *one* variable doesn't mean it has been dereferenced by *all* the other variables. If we call the `Dispose` method while other references remain – our object may become unusable and may cause errors when invoked via those other references. There is no easy solution to this problem – so careful design is required in the case that we choose to use the `IDispose` interface.

In our application's **Form1** code, we use the `OnLoad` method of the form to create an instance of the `Person` object. In the form's `OnClosed` method, we may want to make sure to clean up by disposing of the `Person` object. To do this, add the following code to the form:

```
    Private Sub Form1_Closed(ByVal sender As Object, _
        ByVal e As System.EventArgs) Handles MyBase.Closed

      CType(mobjPerson, IDisposable).Dispose()

    End Sub
```

The `OnClosed` method runs as the form is being closed, and so it is an appropriate place to do cleanup work.

Before we can dereference the `Person` object, however, we can now call its `Dispose` method. Since this method is part of a secondary interface (something we'll discuss more later), we need to use the `CType()` method to access that specific interface in order to call the method:

```
      CType(mobjPerson(), IDisposable).Dispose()
```

`CType()` allows us to indicate the specific interface by which we want to access the object – in this case the `IDisposable` interface. Once we're using that interface, we can call the `Dispose` method to cause the object to do any cleanup before we release our reference:

```
      mobjPerson() = Nothing
```

Once we've released the reference, we know that the garbage collection mechanism will eventually find and terminate the object – thus running its `Finalize` method. In the meantime, however, we've forced the object to do any cleanup immediately, so its resources are not consumed during the time between our release of the reference and the garbage collection terminating the object.

Advanced Concepts

So far we've seen how to work with objects, how to create classes with methods, properties, and events, and how to use constructors. We've also discussed how objects are destroyed within the .NET environment and how we can hook into that process to do any cleanup required by our objects.

Now let's move on to discuss some more complex topics and variations on what we've discussed so far. First, we'll cover some advanced variations in terms of the methods we can implement in our classes, including an exploration of the underlying technology behind events.

From there we'll move on to delegates, the difference between components and classes, and .NET attributes as they pertain to classes and methods.

Advanced Methods

So far, the methods we've worked with have been quite straightforward. They've either been `Sub` or `Function` routines. We've also discussed `Property` routines, which are a specialized type of method.

Now let's take a look at some advanced concepts that provide us with a great deal more power and capability as we work with methods.

Overloading Methods

Methods often accept parameter values. Our `Person` object's `Walk` method, for instance, accepts an `Integer` parameter:

```
Public Sub Walk(ByVal Distance As Integer)
    mintTotalDistance += Distance
    RaiseEvent Walked(Distance)
End Sub
```

Sometimes we may not want to require the parameter. To solve this issue we can use the `Optional` keyword to make the parameter optional:

```
Public Sub Walk(Optional ByVal Distance As Integer = 0)
    mintTotalDistance += Distance
    RaiseEvent Walked(Distance)
End Sub
```

This doesn't provide us with a lot of flexibility, however, since the optional parameter or parameters must always be the last ones in the list. Additionally, all this allows us to do is choose to pass or not to pass the parameter – suppose we want to do something fancier such as allow different data types, or even entirely different lists of parameters?

Method **overloading** provides exactly those capabilities. By overloading methods, we can create several methods of the *same name*, with each one accepting a different set of parameters or parameters of different data types.

As a simple example, instead of using the `Optional` keyword in our `Walk` method, we could use overloading. We'll keep our original `Walk` method, but we'll also add *another* `Walk` method that accepts a different parameter list. Change the code in our `Person` class back to:

```
Public Sub Walk(ByVal Distance As Integer)
    mintTotalDistance += Distance
    RaiseEvent Walked(Distance)
End Sub
```

Then we can create another method – a method with the same name, but with a different parameter list (in this case no parameters). Add this code to the class, without removing or changing the existing `Walk` method:

```
Public Sub Walk()
    RaiseEvent Walked(0)
End Sub
```

At this point we have *two* Walk methods. The only way to tell them apart is by the list of parameters each accepts – the first requiring a single Integer parameter, the second having no parameter.

> *There is an Overloads keyword as well. This keyword is not needed for simple overloading of methods as described here, but is required when combining overloading and inheritance. We'll discuss this in Chapter 6.*

Now we have the option of calling our Walk method in a couple different ways. We can call it with a parameter:

```
objPerson.Walk(42)
```

or without a parameter:

```
objPerson.Walk()
```

We can have any number of Walk methods in our class – as long as each individual Walk method has a different **method signature**.

Method Signatures

All methods have a signature, which is defined by the method name and the data types of its parameters.

```
Public Function CalculateValue() As Integer

End Sub
```

In this example, the signature is $f()$.

The letter f is often used to indicate a method or function. It is appropriate here, because we don't care about the *name* of our function, only its parameter list is important.

If we add a parameter to the method, the signature will change. For instance, we could change the method to accept a Double:

```
Public Function CalculateValue(ByVal Value As Double) As Integer
```

Then the signature of the method is $f(Double)$.

Notice that, in VB.NET, the return value is not part of the signature. We can't overload a Function routine by just having its return value's data type vary. It is the data types in the parameter list that must vary to utilize overloading.

Also make note that the *name* of the parameter is totally immaterial – only the data type is important. This means that the following methods have identical signatures:

```
Public Sub DoWork(ByVal X As Integer, ByVal Y As Integer)

Public Sub DoWork(ByVal Value1 As Integer, ByVal Value2 As Integer)
```

141

In both cases the signature is $f(\texttt{Integer, Integer})$.

Not only do the data types of the parameters define the method signature, but whether the parameters are passed `ByVal` or `ByRef` is also important. Changing a parameter from `ByVal` to `ByRef` will change the method signature.

Combining Overloading and Optional Parameters

Overloading is more flexible than using optional parameters, but optional parameters have the advantage that they can be used to provide default values as well as making a parameter optional.

We can combine the two concepts – overloading a method and also having one or more of those methods utilize optional parameters. Obviously, this sort of thing could get very confusing if overused, since we're employing two types of method "overloading" at the same time.

The `Optional` keyword causes a single method to effectively have two signatures. This means that a method declared as:

```
Public Sub DoWork(ByVal X As Integer, Optional ByVal Y As Integer = 0)
```

has two signatures at once: $f(\texttt{Integer, Integer})$ and $f(\texttt{Integer})$.

Because of this, when we use overloading along with optional parameters, our other overloaded methods cannot match *either* of these two signatures. However, as long as our other methods don't match either signature, we can use overloading as we discussed earlier. For instance, we could implement methods with the following different signatures:

```
Public Sub DoWork(ByVal X As Integer, _
      Optional ByVal Y As Integer = 0)
```

and

```
Public Sub DoWork(ByVal Data As String)
```

since there are no conflicting method signatures. In fact, with these two methods, we've really created three signatures:

- ❑ $f(\texttt{Integer, Integer})$
- ❑ $f(\texttt{Integer})$
- ❑ $f(\texttt{String})$

The IntelliSense built into the VS.NET IDE will show that we have two overloaded methods – one of which has an optional parameter. This is different from if we'd created three different overloaded methods to match these three signatures – in which case the IntelliSense would list three variations on the method from which we can choose.

Overloading the Constructor Method

We can combine the concept of a constructor method with method overloading to allow for different ways of creating instances of our class. This can be a very powerful combination, as it allows a great deal of flexibility in object creation.

We've already explored how to use optional parameters in the constructor. Now let's change our implementation in the Person class to make use of overloading instead. Change the existing New method as follows:

```
Public Sub New(ByVal Name As String, ByVal BirthDate As Date)
    mstrName = Name
    mdtBirthDate = BirthDate

    Phone("home") = "555-1234"
    Phone("work") = "555-5678"
End Sub
```

With this change, we've returned to requiring the two parameter values be supplied.

Now add that second implementation as shown:

```
Public Sub New()
    Phone("home") = "555-1234"
    Phone("work") = "555-5678"
End Sub
```

This second implementation accepts no parameters – meaning that we can now create Person objects in two different ways – either with no parameters or by passing the name and birth date:

```
Dim myPerson As New Person()
```

or:

```
Dim myPerson As New Person("Fred", "1/11/60")
```

This type of capability is very powerful, as it allows us to define the various ways in which applications can create our objects. In fact, the VS.NET IDE takes this into account so, when we are typing the code to create an object, the IntelliSense tool tip will display the overloaded variations on the method – providing a level of automatic documentation for our class.

Shared Methods, Variables, and Events

So far, all of the methods we've built or used have been **instance methods** – methods that require us to have an actual instance of the class before they can be called. These methods have used instance variables or member variables to do their work – meaning that they have been working with a set of data that is unique to each individual object.

VB.NET allows us to create variables and methods that belong to the *class* rather than to any specific *object*. Another way to say this is that these variables and methods belong to *all* objects of a given class and are shared across all the instances of the class.

143

We can use the `Shared` keyword to indicate which variables and methods belong to the class rather than to specific objects. For instance, we may be interested in knowing the total number of `Person` objects created as our application is running – kind of a statistical counter.

Shared Variables

Since regular variables are unique to each individual `Person` object, they don't allow us to easily track the total number of `Person` objects ever created. However, if we had a variable that had a common value *across* all instances of the `Person` class, we could use that as a counter. Add the following variable declaration to our `Person` class:

```
Public Class Person
   Implements IDisposable

   Private Shared sintCounter As Integer
```

By using the `Shared` keyword, we are indicating that this variable's value should be shared across all `Person` objects within our application. This means that if one `Person` object makes the value be 42, all other `Person` objects will see the value as 42 – it is a shared piece of data.

> *We are using the letter "s" as a prefix to this variable rather than "m". The letter "m" is commonly used for member variables (or module variables), but this variable is not a member variable – it is a shared variable. Using a different prefix can help distinguish between member and shared variables within our code.*

We can now use this variable within our code. For instance, we can add code to the constructor method, `New`, to increment the variable so it acts as a counter – adding 1 each time a new `Person` object is created. Change the `New` methods as shown:

```
Public Sub New()
   Phone("home") = "555-1234"
   Phone("work") = "555-5678"
   sintCounter += 1
End Sub

Public Sub New(ByVal Name As String, ByVal BirthDate As Date)
   mstrName = Name
   mdtBirthDate = BirthDate

   Phone("home") = "555-1234"
   Phone("work") = "555-5678"
   sintCounter += 1
End Sub
```

The `sintCounter` variable will now maintain a value indicating the total number of `Person` objects created during the life of our application. We may want to add a property routine to allow access to this value by writing the following code:

```
Public ReadOnly Property PersonCount() As Integer
   Get
      Return sintCounter
```

```
      End Get
   End Property
```

Notice that we're creating a regular property that returns the value of a shared variable. This is perfectly acceptable. As we'll see shortly, we could also choose to create a shared property to return the value.

Now we could write code to use our class as follows:

```
Dim myPerson As Person

myPerson = New Person()
myPerson = New Person()
myPerson = New Person()

MsgBox(myPerson.PersonCount)
```

The resulting display would show 3 – since we've created three instances of the Person class.

Shared Methods

We cannot only share variables across all instances of our class, but we can also share methods. Where a regular method or property belongs to each specific object, a shared method or property is common across all instances of the class.

There are a couple of ramifications to this approach.

First off, since shared methods don't belong to any specific object, they can't access any instance variables from any objects. The only variables available for use within a shared method are shared variables, parameters passed into the method, or variables declared locally within the method itself. If we attempt to access an instance variable within a shared method, we'll get a compiler error.

Also, since shared methods are actually part of the *class* rather than any *object*, we can write code to call them directly from the class – without having to create an instance of the class first.

For instance, a regular instance method is invoked from an object:

```
Dim myPerson As New Person()

myPerson.Walk(42)
```

but a shared method can be invoked directly from the class itself:

```
Person.SharedMethod()
```

This saves the effort of creating an object just to invoke a method, and can be very appropriate for methods that act on shared variables, or methods that act only on values passed in via parameters. We can also invoke a shared method from an object just like a regular method. Shared methods are flexible in that they can be called with or without creating an instance of the class first.

To create a shared method we again use the `Shared` keyword. For instance, the `PersonCount` property we created earlier could easily be changed to be a shared method instead:

```
Public Shared ReadOnly Property PersonCount() As Integer
   Get
      Return sintCounter
   End Get
End Property
```

Since this property returns the value of a shared variable, it is perfectly acceptable for it to be implemented as a shared method. With this change, we can now find out how many `Person` objects have ever been created without having to actually create a `Person` object first:

```
MsgBox(Person.PersonCount)
```

As another example, in our `Person` class we could create a method that compares the ages of two people. Add a shared method with the following code:

```
Public Shared Function CompareAge(ByVal Person1 As Person, _
   ByVal Person2 As Person) As Boolean

   Return Person1.Age > Person2.Age

End Function
```

This method simply accepts two parameters – each a `Person` – and returns `True` if the first is older than the second. The use of the `Shared` keyword indicates that this method doesn't require a specific instance of the `Person` class for us to use it.

Within this code, we are invoking the `Age` property on two separate objects – the objects passed as parameters to the method. It is important to recognize that we're not *directly* using any instance variables within the method, but rather are accepting two objects as parameters and are invoking methods on those objects.

To use this method, we can call it directly from the class:

```
If Person.CompareAge(myPerson1, myPerson2) Then
```

Alternately, we can also invoke it from any `Person` object:

```
Dim myPerson As New Person()

If myPerson.CompareAge(myPerson, myPerson2) Then
```

Either way, we're invoking the same shared method and we'll get the same behavior whether we call it from the class or a specific instance of the class.

Shared Properties

As with other types of methods, we can also have shared property methods. Properties follow the same rules as regular methods – they can interact with shared variables, but not member variables, and they can invoke other shared methods or properties, but can't invoke instance methods without first creating an instance of the class.

We can add a shared property to our `Person` class with the following code:

```
Public Shared ReadOnly Property RetirementAge() As Integer
  Get
    Return 62
  End Get
End Property
```

This simply adds a property to our class that indicates the global retirement age for all people. To use this value, we can simply access it directly from the class:

```
MsgBox(Person.RetirementAge)
```

Alternately, we can also access it from any `Person` object:

```
Dim myPerson As New Person()

MsgBox(myPerson.RetirementAge)
```

Either way, we're invoking the same shared property.

Shared Events

As with other interface elements, events can also be marked as `Shared`. For instance, we could declare a shared event in the `Person` class such as:

```
Public Shared Event NewPerson()
```

Shared events can be raised from both instance methods and shared methods. Regular events can not be raised by shared methods. Since shared events can be raised by regular methods, we can raise this one from the constructors in the Person class:

```
Public Sub New()
  Phone("home") = "555-1234"
  Phone("work") = "555-5678"
  sintCounter += 1
  RaiseEvent NewPerson()
End Sub

Public Sub New(ByVal Name As String, ByVal BirthDate As Date)
  mstrName = Name
  mdtBirthDate = BirthDate

  Phone("home") = "555-1234"
```

```
    Phone("work") = "555-5678"
    sintCounter += 1
    RaiseEvent NewPerson()
End Sub
```

The interesting thing about receiving shared events is that we can get them from either an object, like a normal event, or from the *class* itself. For instance, we can use the AddHandler method in our form's code to catch this event directly from the Person class.

First let's add a method to the form to handle the event:

```
Private Sub OnNewPerson()
  MsgBox("new person " & Person.PersonCount)
End Sub
```

Then, in the form's Load event, add a statement to link the event to this method:

```
Private Sub Form1_Load(ByVal sender As System.Object, _
   ByVal e As System.EventArgs) Handles MyBase.Load

  AddHandler Person.NewPerson, AddressOf OnNewPerson

  mobjPerson = New Person()
  If Microsoft.VisualBasic.Command = "nodisplay" Then
    AddHandler mobjPerson.Walked, AddressOf LogOnWalk
  Else
    AddHandler mobjPerson.Walked, AddressOf OnWalk
  End If
End Sub
```

Notice that we are using the *class* rather than any specific object in the AddHandler statement. We could use an object as well – treating this like a normal event, but this illustrates how a class itself can raise an event.

When we run the application now, any time a Person object is created we'll see this event raised.

Delegates

There are times when it would be nice to be able to pass a procedure as a parameter to a method. The classic case is when building a generic sort routine, where we not only need to provide the data to be sorted, but we need to provide a comparison routine appropriate for the specific data.

It is easy enough to write a sort routine that sorts Person objects by name, or to write a sort routine that sorts SalesOrder objects by sales date. However, if we want to write a sort routine that can sort any type of object based on arbitrary sort criteria, that gets pretty difficult. At the same time, it would be nice to do, since some sort routines can get very complex and it would be nice to reuse that code without having to copy-and-paste it for each different sort scenario.

By using delegates, we can create such a generic routine for sorting – and in so doing we can see how delegates work and can be used to create many other types of generic routines.

The concept of a **delegate** formalizes the process of declaring a routine to be called and calling that routine.

The underlying mechanism used by the .NET environment for callback methods is the delegate. VB.NET uses delegates behind the scenes as it implements the Event, RaiseEvent, WithEvents, *and* Handles *keywords.*

Declaring a Delegate

In our code, we can declare what a delegate procedure must look like from an interface standpoint. This is done using the Delegate keyword. To see how this can work, let's create a routine to sort any kind of data.

To do this, we'll declare a delegate that defines a method signature for a method that compares the value of two objects and returns a Boolean indicating whether the first object has a larger value that the second object. We'll then create a sort algorithm that uses this generic comparison method to sort data. Finally, we'll create an actual method that *implements* the comparison and we'll pass the address of that method to the sort routine.

Add a new module to our project by choosing the Project | Add Module menu option. Name the module Sort.vb and then add the following code:

```
Module Sort

    Public Delegate Function Compare(ByVal v1 As Object, ByVal v2 As Object) _
        As Boolean

End Module
```

This line of code does something interesting. It actually defines a method signature as a *data type*. This new data type is named Compare and it can be used within our code to declare variables or parameters that will be accepted by our methods. A variable or parameter declared using this data type can actually hold the address of a method that matches the defined method signature – and we can then invoke that method by using the variable.

Any method with the signature:

f(Object, Object)

Can be viewed as being of type Compare.

Using the Delegate Data Type

We can write a routine that accepts this data type as a parameter – meaning that anyone calling our routine must pass us the address of a method that conforms to this interface. Add the following sort routine to the code module:

```
Public Sub DoSort(ByVal theData() As Object, ByVal GreaterThan As Compare)
    Dim outer As Integer
    Dim inner As Integer
    Dim temp As Object

    For outer = 0 To UBound(theData)
      For inner = outer + 1 To UBound(theData)
```

```
        If GreaterThan.Invoke(theData(outer), theData(inner)) Then
          temp = theData(outer)
          theData(outer) = theData(inner)
          theData(inner) = temp
        End If
      Next
    Next
  End Sub
```

The `GreaterThan` parameter is a variable that holds the address of a method matching the method signature defined by our `Compare` delegate. The address of any method with a matching signature can be passed as a parameter to our `Sort` routine.

Note the use of the `Invoke` method, which is the way a delegate is called from our code. Also note that the routine deals entirely with the generic `System.Object` data type rather than with any specific type of data. The specific comparison of one object to another is left to the delegate routine that is passed in as a parameter.

Implementing a Delegate Method

All that remains is to actually create the implementation of the delegate routine and call our sort method. On a very basic level, all we need to do is create a method that has a matching method signature. For instance, we could create a method such as:

```
    Public Function PersonCompare(ByVal Person1 As Object, _
      ByVal Person2 As Object) As Boolean

    End Function
```

The method signature of this method exactly matches that which we defined by our delegate earlier:

```
    Compare(Object, Object)
```

In both cases, we're defining two parameters of type `Object`.

Of course, there's more to it than simply creating the stub of a method. We know that the method needs to return a value of `True` if its first parameter is greater than the second parameter, but otherwise should be written to deal with some specific type of data.

The `Delegate` statement defines a data type based on a specific method interface. To call a routine that expects a parameter of this new data type, it must pass us the address of a method that conforms to the defined interface.

To conform to the interface, a method must have the same number of parameters with the same data types as we've defined in our `Delegate` statement. Additionally, the method must provide the same return type as defined. The actual name of the method doesn't matter – it is the number, order, and data type of the parameters and return value that count.

To find the address of a specific method, we can use the `AddressOf` operator. This operator returns the address of any procedure or method, allowing us to pass that value as a parameter to any routine that expects a delegate as a parameter.

Our `Person` class already has a shared method named `CompareAge` that generally does what we want. Unfortunately, it accepts parameters of type `Person` rather than of type `Object` as required by the `Compare` delegate. We can use method overloading to solve this problem.

Create a second implementation of `CompareAge` that accepts parameters of type `Object` as required by the delegate, rather than of type `Person` as we have in the existing implementation:

```
Public Shared Function CompareAge(ByVal Person1 As Object, _
    ByVal Person2 As Object) As Boolean

  Return CType(Person1, Person).Age > CType(Person2, Person).Age

End Function
```

This method simply returns `True` if the first `Person` object's age is greater than the second. The routine accepts two `Object` parameters rather than specific `Person` type parameters, so we have to use the `CType()` method to access those objects as type `Person`. We accept the parameters as type `Object` because that is what is defined by the `Delegate` statement. We are matching its method signature:

f(Object, Object)

Since this method's parameter data types and return value match the delegate, we can use it when calling the sort routine. Place a button on the form and write the following code behind that button:

```
Private Sub Button2_Click(ByVal sender As System.Object, _
    ByVal e As System.EventArgs) Handles button2.Click

  Dim myPeople(4) As Person

  myPeople(0) = New Person("Fred", #7/9/1960#)
  myPeople(1) = New Person("Mary", #1/21/1955#)
  myPeople(2) = New Person("Sarah", #2/1/1960#)
  myPeople(3) = New Person("George", #5/13/1970#)
  myPeople(4) = New Person("Andre", #10/1/1965#)

  DoSort(myPeople, AddressOf Person.CompareAge)
End Sub
```

This code creates an array of `Person` objects and populates them. It then calls the `DoSort` routine from our module, passing the array as the first parameter and the address of our shared `CompareAge` method as the second. To display the contents of the sorted array in the IDE's output window, we can add the following code:

```
Private Sub button2_Click(ByVal sender As System.Object, _
    ByVal e As System.EventArgs) Handles button2.Click

  Dim myPeople(4) As Person

  myPeople(0) = New Person("Fred", #7/9/1960#)
  myPeople(1) = New Person("Mary", #1/21/1955#)
  myPeople(2) = New Person("Sarah", #2/1/1960#)
```

```
myPeople(3) = New Person("George", #5/13/1970#)
myPeople(4) = New Person("Andre", #10/1/1965#)

DoSort(myPeople, AddressOf Person.CompareAge)

Dim myPerson As Person

For Each myPerson In myPeople
  System.Diagnostics.Debug.WriteLine(myPerson.Name & " " & myPerson.Age)
Next
End Sub
```

When we run the application and click the button, the output window will display a list of the people, sorted by age:

What makes this whole thing very powerful is that we can change the comparison routine without changing the sort mechanism. Simply add another comparison routine to the Person class:

```
Public Shared Function CompareName(ByVal Person1 As Object, _
    ByVal Person2 As Object) As Boolean

  Return CType(Person1, Person).Name > CType(Person2, Person).Name

End Function
```

and then change the code behind the button on the form to use that alternate comparison routine:

```
Private Sub button2_Click(ByVal sender As System.Object, _
    ByVal e As System.EventArgs) Handles button2.Click

  Dim myPeople(4) As Person

  myPeople(0) = New Person("Fred", #7/9/1960#)
  myPeople(1) = New Person("Mary", #1/21/1955#)
  myPeople(2) = New Person("Sarah", #2/1/1960#)
  myPeople(3) = New Person("George", #5/13/1970#)
  myPeople(4) = New Person("Andre", #10/1/1965#)

  DoSort(myPeople, AddressOf Person.CompareName)

  Dim myPerson As Person

  For Each myPerson In myPeople
    System.Diagnostics.Debug.WriteLine(myPerson.Name & " " & myPerson.Age)
  Next
End Sub
```

When we run this updated code, we'll find that our array contains a set of data sorted by name rather than by age:

```
Output                                          x
Debug                                           ▼
    Andre 37                                    ▲
    Fred 42
    George 32
    Mary 47
    Sarah 42                                    ▼
◄                                          ►
```

By simply creating a new compare routine and passing it as a parameter, we can entirely change the way that the data is sorted. Better still, this sort routine can operate on any type of object, as long as we provide an appropriate delegate method that knows how to compare that type of object.

Classes vs. Components

VB.NET has another concept that is very similar to a class – the component. In fact, we can pretty much use a component and a class interchangeably, though there are some differences that we'll discuss.

A component is really little more than a regular class, but it is one that supports a graphical designer within the VB.NET IDE. This means we can use drag-and-drop to provide the code in our component with access to items from the Server Explorer or from the Toolbox.

To add a component to a project, select the Project | Add Component menu option, give the component a name, and click Open in the Add New Item dialog.

When we add a class to our project we are presented with the code window. When we add a *component* on the other hand, we are presented with a graphical designer surface, much like what we'd see when adding a Web Form to the project:

```
Component1.vb [Design]                    ◄ ▷ ✕



       To add components to your class, drag them from the Server Explorer or Toolbox
         and use the Properties window to set their properties. To create methods and
                    events for your class, click here to switch to code view.


```

If we switch to the code view (by right-clicking in the designer and choosing View Code), we will see the code that is created for us automatically:

This isn't a lot more code than we'd see with a regular class, though there certainly are differences. First off, we see that this class inherits from `System.ComponentModel.Component`. While we'll discuss the concepts of inheritance in Chapters 6 and 7, it is important to note here that this `Inherits` line is what brings in all the support for the graphical designer we just saw.

There's also a collapsed region of code in a component. This region contains code generated by the graphical designer. Here's a quick look at what is included by default:

```vb
#Region " Component Designer generated code "

Public Sub New(Container As System.ComponentModel.IContainer)
    MyClass.New()

    'Required for Windows.Forms Class Composition Designer support
    Container.Add(me)
End Sub

Public Sub New()
    MyBase.New()

    'This call is required by the Component Designer.
    InitializeComponent()

    'Add any initialization after the InitializeComponent() call

End Sub

'Component overrides dispose to clean up the component list.
Protected Overloads Overrides Sub Dispose(ByVal disposing As Boolean)
    If disposing Then
        If Not (components Is Nothing) Then
            components.Dispose()
        End If
    End If
    MyBase.Dispose(disposing)
End Sub

'Required by the Component Designer
Private components As System.ComponentModel.IContainer

'NOTE: The following procedure is required by the Component Designer
'It can be modified using the Component Designer.
```

```
'Do not modify it using the code editor.
<System.Diagnostics.DebuggerStepThrough()> _
Private Sub InitializeComponent()
    components = New System.ComponentModel.Container()
End Sub
```

```
#End Region
```

As it stands, this code does very little beyond creating a single `Container` class object. However, if we switch the view back to the designer, we can drag-and-drop items onto our component. For instance, in the Toolbox there is a **Components** tab, which has entries for a variety of useful items such as a **MessageQueue**, a **DirectoryEntry**, and so forth. If we drag-and-drop a **Timer** (from the **Components** tab of the **Toolbox**) onto our component, it will be displayed in the designer:

From here, we can set its properties using the standard **Properties** window in the IDE, just like we would for a control on a form. For instance, we can set its `Name` property to `theTimer`:

If we now return to the code window and look at the automatically generated code, we'll see that the region now includes code to declare, create, and initialize the `Timer` object:

```
#Region " Component Designer generated code "

    Public Sub New(Container As System.ComponentModel.IContainer)
        MyClass.New()
```

```
            'Required for Windows.Forms Class Composition Designer support
            Container.Add(me)
    End Sub

    Public Sub New()
        MyBase.New()

        'This call is required by the Component Designer.
        InitializeComponent()

        'Add any initialization after the InitializeComponent() call

    End Sub

    'Component overrides dispose to clean up the component list.
    Protected Overloads Overrides Sub Dispose(ByVal disposing As Boolean)
        If disposing Then
            If Not (components Is Nothing) Then
                components.Dispose()
            End If
        End If
        MyBase.Dispose(disposing)
    End Sub

    'Required by the Component Designer
    Private components As System.ComponentModel.IContainer

    'NOTE: The following procedure is required by the Component Designer
    'It can be modified using the Component Designer.
    'Do not modify it using the code editor.
    Friend WithEvents theTimer As System.Windows.Forms.Timer
    <System.Diagnostics.DebuggerStepThrough()> _
    Private Sub InitializeComponent()
        Me.components = New System.ComponentModel.Container()
        Me.theTimer = New System.Windows.Forms.Timer(Me.components)

    End Sub

#End Region
```

Normally, we don't really care about the fact that this code was generated. Rather, what is important is that we now automatically, simply by dragging and dropping and setting some properties, have access to a `Timer` object named `theTimer`.

This means that we can write code within our component, just like we might in a class, to use this object:

```
    Public Sub Start()
        theTimer.Enabled = True
    End Sub

    Public Sub [Stop]()
        theTimer.Enabled = False
```

```
    End Sub

    Private Sub theTimer_Elapsed(ByVal sender As System.Object, _
      ByVal e As System.Timers.ElapsedEventArgs) Handles theTimer.Elapsed

      ' do work

    End Sub
```

Here we can see that, with a simple drag-and-drop operation, we've gained access to a variable called `theTimer` referencing a `Timer` object, and we are able to create methods that interact with and use that object much like we would with a control dropped onto a form.

For the most part, we can use a component interchangeably with a basic class, but the use of a component incurs some extra overhead that a basic class does not, since it inherits all the functionality of `System.ComponentModel.Component`.

Summary

VB.NET offers us a fully object-oriented language with all the capabilities we would expect. In this chapter, we've explored the basic concepts around classes and objects, as well as the separation of interface from implementation and data.

We've seen how to use the `Class` keyword to create classes, and how those classes can be instantiated into specific objects – each one an instance of the class. These objects have methods and properties that can be invoked by client code, and can act on data within the object stored in member or instance variables.

We also explored some more advanced concepts, including method overloading, shared or static variables and methods, and the use of delegates. Finally, we wrapped up with a brief discussion of attributes and how they can be used to affect the interaction of our class or our methods with the .NET environment.

In Chapter 6, we'll continue our discussion of object syntax as we explore the concept of inheritance and all the syntax that enables inheritance within VB.NET. We will also walk through the creation, implementation, and use of multiple interfaces – a powerful concept that allows our objects to be used in different ways depending on the interface chosen by the client application.

Then, in Chapter 7, we'll wrap up our discussion of objects and object-oriented programming by applying all of this syntax. We'll discuss the key object-oriented concepts of abstraction, encapsulation, polymorphism, and inheritance and see how they all tie together to provide a powerful way of designing and implementing applications.

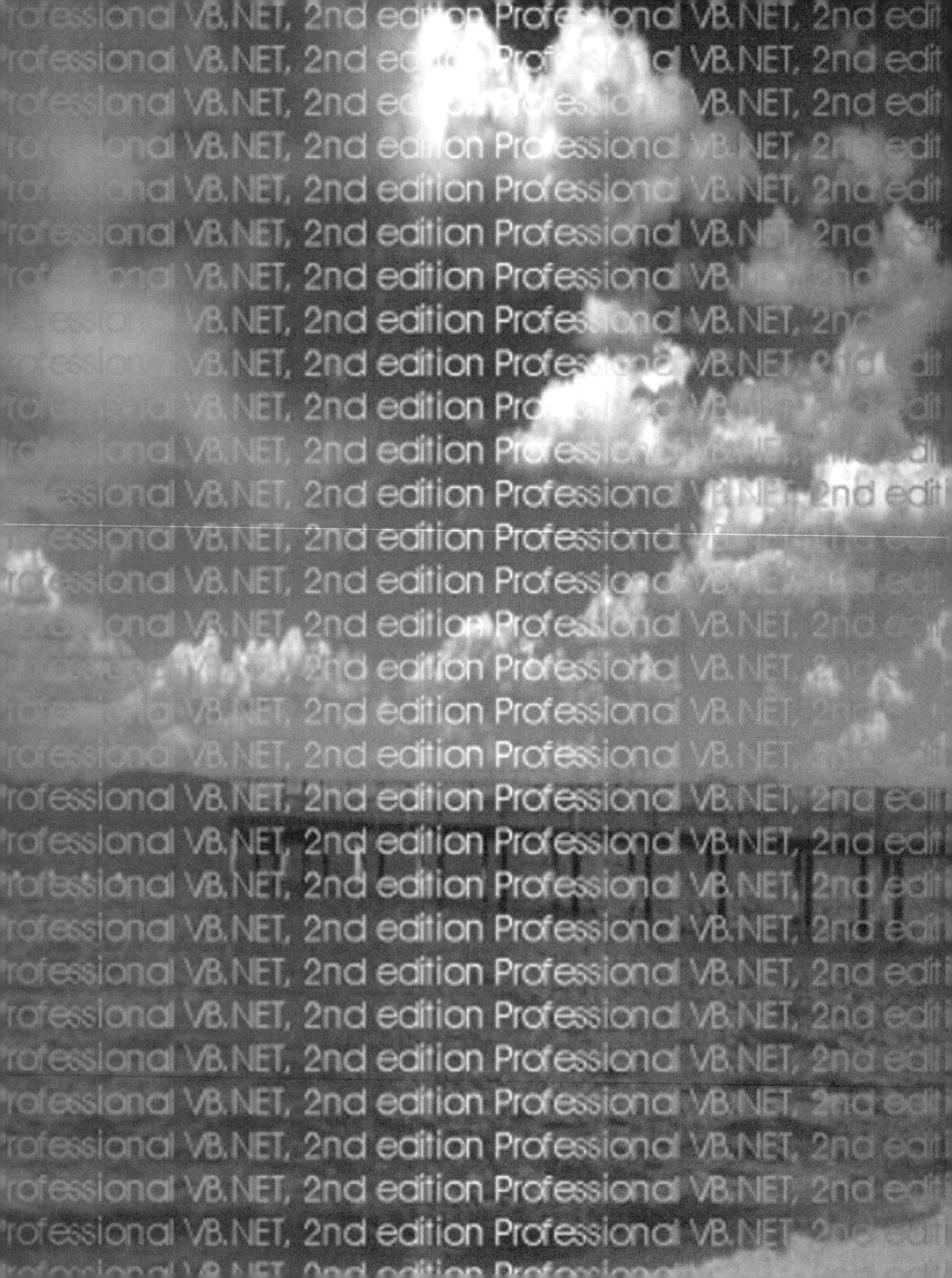
Professional VB.NET, 2nd edition

6

Inheritance and Interfaces

VB.NET is a fully object-oriented language. In Chapter 5 we covered the basics of creating classes and objects, including the creation of methods, properties, events, and instance variables. We've seen the basic building blocks for abstraction, encapsulation, and polymorphism – concepts we'll discuss in more detail in Chapter 7. The final major techniques we need to cover are inheritance and the use of multiple interfaces.

Inheritance is the idea that we can create a class that reuses methods, properties, events, and variables from another class. We can create a class with some basic functionality, then use that class as a base from which to create other, more detailed, classes. All these classes will have the same common functionality as that base class, along with new, enhanced or even completely changed functionality.

In this chapter we'll cover the syntax that supports inheritance within VB.NET. This includes creating the base classes from which other classes can be derived, as well as creating those derived classes.

VB.NET also supports a related concept – multiple interfaces. We've already seen, in Chapter 5, that all objects have a native or default interface, which is defined by the public methods, properties, and events declared in the class. In the .NET environment, an object can have other interfaces in addition to this native interface – in other words .NET objects can have multiple interfaces.

These secondary interfaces define alternate ways in which our object can be accessed by providing clearly defined sets of methods, properties, and events. Like the native interface, these secondary interfaces define how client code can interact with our object – essentially providing a "contract" that allows the client to know exactly what methods, properties and events the object will provide. When we write code to interact with an object, we can choose which of the interfaces we want to use – basically we're choosing how we want to view or interact with that object.

In this chapter, we'll be using relatively basic code examples so we can focus right in on the technical and syntactic issues surrounding inheritance and multiple interfaces. In Chapter 7, we'll revisit these concepts using a more sophisticated set of code as we continue to explore object-oriented programming and how to apply inheritance and multiple interfaces in a practical manner.

Inheritance

Inheritance is the concept that a new class can be based on an existing class, inheriting its interface and functionality from the original class. In Chapter 5 we explored the relationship between a class and an object – where the class is essentially a template from which objects can be created.

While this is very powerful, it doesn't provide all the capabilities we might like. In particular, there are many cases where a class only *partially* describes what we need for our object. We may have a class called Person, for instance, which has all the properties and methods that apply to all types of people – things like first name, last name and birth date. While useful, this class probably doesn't have everything we need to describe a *specific* type of person – such as an Employee or a Customer. An employee would have a hire date and a salary that are not included in Person, while a customer would have a credit rating – something neither the Person nor Employee classes would need.

Without inheritance, we'd probably end up replicating the code from the Person class into both the Employee and Customer classes so they'd have that same functionality as well as being able to add new functionality of their own.

Inheritance makes it very easy to create classes for Employee, Customer, and so forth. We don't have to recreate that code for an employee to be a person; it automatically gets any properties, methods, and events from the original Person class.

We can think of it this way. When we create an Employee class, which inherits from a Person class, we are effectively merging these two classes together. If we then create an object based on the Employee class, it not only has the interface (properties, methods, and events) and implementation from the Employee class, but it also has those from the Person class.

While an Employee object represents the merger between the Employee and Person classes, it is important to realize that the variables and code contained in each of those classes remain independent. There are two perspectives we need to understand.

From the outside, client code that interacts with the Employee object will see a single, unified object that represents the merger of the Employee and Person classes.

From the inside, the code in the Employee class and the code in the Person class aren't totally intermixed. Variables and methods that are `Private` are only available within the class where they were written. Variables and methods that are `Public` in one class can be called from the other class. Variables and methods that are declared as `Friend` are only available between classes if both classes are in the same VB.NET project. As we'll discuss later in the chapter there is also a `Protected` scope that is designed to work with inheritance – but again, this provides a controlled way for one class to interact with the variables and methods in the other class.

There is a standard notation called the **Universal Modeling Language (UML)** that is typically used to diagram the relationships between classes, objects and other object-oriented concepts. We can model the relationship between the Person, Employee, and Customer classes using UML:

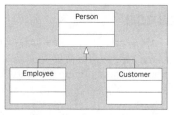

Each box in this diagram represents a class – in this case we have Person, Employee, and Customer classes. The line from Employee back up to Person, terminating in a triangle, indicates that Employee is derived from, or inherits from, Person. The same is true for the Customer class. We'll use UML through the rest of the chapter, as it is a standard diagramming notation for working with classes and objects.

> *If you'd like to learn more about UML,* Instant UML *(Wrox Press, 1861000871) is an excellent guide.*

We'll discuss when and how inheritance should be used in software design in more detail in Chapter 7. In this chapter, we'll cover the syntax and programming concepts necessary to implement inheritance. We'll create a base Person class, and then use that class to create both Employee and Customer classes that inherit behavior from Person.

Before we get into the implementation, however, we need to define some basic terms associated with inheritance. And there are a lot of terms – partly because there are often several ways to say the same thing – and the various terms are all used quite frequently and interchangeably.

> **Though we'll try to be consistent in our use of terminology in this book – it is important to note that in other books, articles and online all these various terms are used in all their various permutations.**

Inheritance, for instance, is also sometimes referred to as **generalization**. This is because the class from which we are inheriting our behavior is virtually always a more general form of our new class. A person is more general than an employee for instance.

The inheritance relationship is also referred to as an **"is-a" relationship**. When we create a Customer class that inherits from a Person class, that customer is a person. The Employee is a Person as well. Thus we have this "is-a" relationship. As we'll see later in this chapter, multiple interfaces can be used to implement something similar to the "is-a" relationship – the "act-as" relationship.

When we create a class using inheritance, we are inheriting behaviors and data from an existing class. That existing class is called the **base class**. It is also often referred to as a superclass or a parent class.

The class we create using inheritance is based on the parent class. It is called a **subclass**. Sometimes it is also called a child class or a derived class.

In fact, the process of inheriting from a base class to a subclass is often referred to as **deriving**. We are deriving a new class from the base class.

Implementing Inheritance

When we set out to implement a class using inheritance, we must first start with an existing class from which we will derive our new subclass. This existing class, or base class, may be part of the .NET system class library framework, it may be part of some other application or .NET assembly, or we may create it as part of our existing application.

Once we have a base class, we can then implement one or more subclasses based on that base class. Each of our subclasses will automatically have all of the methods, properties, and events of that base class – including the implementation behind each method, property and event. Our subclass can add new methods, properties, and events of its own – extending the original interface with new functionality. Additionally, a subclass can replace the methods and properties of the base class with its own new implementation – effectively overriding the original behavior and replacing it with new behaviors.

Essentially inheritance is a way of merging functionality from an existing class into our new subclass. Inheritance also defines rules for how these methods, properties, and events can be merged – including control over how they can be changed or replaced, and how the subclass can add new methods, properties, and events of its own. This is what we'll explore as we go forward – what these rules are and what syntax we use in VB.NET to make it all work.

Creating a Base Class

Virtually any class we create can act as a base class from which other classes can be derived. In fact, unless we specifically indicate in the code that our class *cannot* be a base class, we can derive from it (we'll come back to this later).

Create a new Windows Application project in VB.NET. Then add a class to the project using the **Project | Add Class** menu option and name it Person.vb.

We start with the following code:

```
Public Class Person

End Class
```

At this point we technically have a base class, since it is possible to inherit from this class even though it doesn't do or contain anything.

We can now add methods, properties, and events to this class as we normally would – and all of those interface elements would be inherited by any class we might create based on Person. For instance, add the following code:

```
Public Class Person
   Private mstrName As String
   Private mdtBirthDate As String

   Public Property Name() As String
      Get
         Return mstrName
      End Get
```

```
         Set(ByVal Value As String)
            mstrName = Value
         End Set
      End Property

      Public Property BirthDate() As Date
        Get
           Return mdtBirthDate
        End Get
        Set(ByVal Value As Date)
           mdtBirthDate = Value
        End Set
      End Property
   End Class
```

This gives us a simple method we can use to illustrate how basic inheritance works. This class can be represented by the following UML:

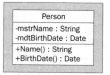

The overall box represents the `Person` class. In the top section we have the name of the class. In the middle section is a list of the instance variables, or attributes, of the class with their scope marked as `Private` due to the minus (–) symbol in front of each attribute. In the bottom section are the methods that make up the interface of the class – both marked as `Public` in scope due to the plus (+) symbol in front of each method.

Creating a Subclass

To implement inheritance we need to add a new class to our project. Use the Project | Add Class menu option and add a new class named `Employee.vb`. We'll start with the following code:

```
Public Class Employee
   Private mdtHireDate As Date
   Private mdblSalary As Double

   Public Property HireDate() As Date
     Get
        Return mdtHireDate
     End Get
     Set(ByVal Value As Date)
        mdtHireDate = Value
     End Set
   End Property

   Public Property Salary() As Double
     Get
        Return mdblSalary
     End Get
```

163

```
        Set(ByVal Value As Double)
            mdblSalary = Value
        End Set
    End Property
End Class
```

This is a regular stand-alone class with no explicit inheritance. It can be represented by the following UML:

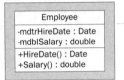

Again we can see the class name, its list of instance variables and the methods it includes as part of its interface.

It turns out that, behind the scenes, this class inherits some capabilities from System.Object. In fact every class in the entire .NET platform ultimately inherits from System.Object either implicitly or explicitly. This is why all .NET objects have a basic set of common functionality including most notably the GetType method. We'll discuss this in detail later in the chapter.

While having an Employee object with a hire date and salary is useful – it should also have Name and BirthDate properties just like we implemented for our Person class. Without inheritance we'd probably just copy and paste the code from Person directly into the new Employee class, but with inheritance we can directly reuse the code from the Person class. Let's make our new class inherit from Person.

The Inherits Keyword

To make Employee a subclass of Person we just need to add a single line of code:

```
Public Class Employee
    Inherits Person
```

The Inherits keyword is used to indicate that a class should derive from an existing class – inheriting interface and behavior from that class. We can inherit from almost any class in our project, or from the .NET system class library or from other assemblies. It is possible to *prevent* inheritance – something we'll discuss later in the chapter. When using the Inherits keyword to inherit from classes outside our current project we need to either specify the namespace that contains that class or have an Imports statement at the top of the class to import that namespace for our use.

The following UML diagram illustrates the fact that our Employee class is now a subclass of Person:

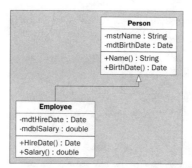

The line running from `Employee` back up to `Person` ends in an open triangle – which is the UML symbol for generalization – or inheritance. It is this line that indicates that the `Employee` class also includes all the functionality and the interface from `Person`.

This means that an object created based on the `Employee` class will not only have the methods `HireDate` and `Salary`, but will also have `Name` and `BirthDate`.

To test this, bring up the designer for `Form1` (which is automatically part of our project since we created a Windows Application project) and add the following TextBox controls along with a button to the form:

Control type	Name	Text value
TextBox	`txtName`	\<blank>
TextBox	`txtBirthDate`	\<blank>
TextBox	`txtHireDate`	\<blank>
TextBox	`txtSalary`	\<blank>
Button	`btnOK`	OK

We can also add some labels to make the form more readable. Our form designer should now look something like this:

Double-click the button to bring up the code window and enter the following code:

```
Private Sub btnOK_Click(ByVal sender As System.Object, _
                        ByVal e As System.EventArgs) Handles btnOK.Click
    Dim objEmployee As New Employee()

    With objEmployee
        .Name = "Fred"
        .BirthDate = #1/1/1960#
        .HireDate = #1/1/1980#
        .Salary = 30000

        txtName.Text = .Name
        txtBirthDate.Text = Format(.BirthDate, "Short date")
        txtHireDate.Text = Format(.HireDate, "Short date")
        txtSalary.Text = Format(.Salary, "$0.00")
    End With
End Sub
```

Even though `Employee` doesn't directly implement `Name` or `BirthDate` methods, they are available for our use through inheritance. If we run this application and click on the button our controls will be populated with the values from the `Employee` object.

When the code in `Form1` invokes the `Name` property on our `Employee` object, the code from the `Person` class is executed, since the `Employee` class has no such method built-in. However, when the `HireDate` property is invoked on the `Employee` object, the code from the `Employee` class *is* executed since it does have that method as part of its code.

From the form's perspective it doesn't matter whether a method is implemented in the `Employee` class or the `Person` class – they are all simply methods of the `Employee` object. Also, since the code in these classes is merged together to create the `Employee` object, there is no performance difference between calling a method implemented by the `Employee` class or a method implemented by the `Person` class.

Overloading Methods

Though our `Employee` class automatically gained the `Name` and `BirthDate` methods through inheritance, it also has methods of its own – `HireDate` and `Salary`. This shows how we've extended the base `Person` interface by adding methods and properties to the `Employee` subclass.

We can add new properties, methods and events to the `Employee` class – and they will be part of any object created based on `Employee`. This has no impact on the `Person` class whatsoever, only on the `Employee` class and `Employee` objects.

We can even extend the functionality of the base class by adding methods to our subclass that have the same name as methods or properties in the base class – as long as those methods or properties have different parameter lists. We are effectively overloading the existing methods from the base class – essentially the same thing as overloading regular methods as we discussed in Chapter 5.

For example, our `Person` class is currently providing our implementation for the `Name` property. Employees may have other names we also want to store – perhaps an informal name and a very formal name in addition to their normal name. One way to accommodate this requirement is to change the `Person` class itself to include an overloaded `Name` property that supports this new functionality. However, we're really only trying to enhance the `Employee` class, not the more general `Person` class, and so what we want is a way to add an overloaded method to the `Employee` class itself – even though we're overloading a method from its base class.

Overloading a method from a base class is done by using the `Overloads` keyword. The concept is the same as we discussed in Chapter 5, but in this case an extra keyword is involved. To overload the `Name` property, for instance, we can add a new property to the `Employee` class. First though, let's define an enumerated type using the `Enum` keyword. This `Enum` will list the different types of name we want to store. Add this `Enum` to the `Employee.vb` file – before the declaration of the class itself:

```
Public Enum NameTypes
   Informal = 1
   Formal = 2
End Enum
```

```
Public Class Employee
```

We can then add an overloaded `Name` property to the `Employee` class itself:

```
Public Class Employee
   Inherits Person

   Private mdtHireDate As Date
   Private mdblSalary As Double
```

```
   Private mcolNames As New Hashtable()

   Public Overloads Property Name(ByVal Type As NameTypes) As String
      Get
         Return mcolNames(Type)
      End Get
      Set(ByVal Value As String)
         If mcolNames.ContainsKey(NameTypes.Informal) Then
            mcolNames.Item(NameTypes.Informal) = Value
         Else
            mcolNames.Add(Type, Value)
         End If
      End Set
   End Property
End Property
```

This `Name` property is actually a property array – allowing us to store multiple values via the same property. In this case we're storing the values in a `Hashtable` object, which is indexed by using the `Enum` value we just defined.

> *If we omit the `Overloads` keyword here, our new implementation of the `Name` method will shadow the original implementation. Shadowing is a very different thing from overloading and is a topic we'll cover later in the chapter.*

Though this method has the same name as the method in the base class, the fact that it accepts a different parameter list allows us to use overloading to implement it here. The original `Name` property as implemented in the `Person` class remains intact and valid – but now we've added a new variation with this second `Name` property. This is illustrated by the following UML diagram:

The diagram clearly indicates that the Name method in the Person class and the Name method in the Employee class both exist, and have different method signatures.

We can now change Form1 to make use of this new version of the Name property. First off, add a couple of new text box controls and associated labels. The text box controls should be named txtFormal and txtInformal and the form should now look like this:

Now double-click on the button to bring up the code window and add code to work with the overloaded version of the Name property:

```
Private Sub btnOK_Click(ByVal sender As System.Object, _
    ByVal e As System.EventArgs) Handles btnOK.Click
  Dim objEmployee As New Employee()

  With objEmployee
    .Name = "Fred"
    .Name(NameTypes.Formal) = "Mr. Frederick R. Jones, Sr."
    .Name(NameTypes.Informal) = "Freddy"
    .BirthDate = #1/1/1960#
    .HireDate = #1/1/1980#
    .Salary = 30000

    txtName.Text = .Name
    txtFormal.Text = .Name(NameTypes.Formal)
    txtInformal.Text = .Name(NameTypes.Informal)
    txtBirthDate.Text = Format(.BirthDate, "Short date")
    txtHireDate.Text = Format(.HireDate, "Short date")
    txtSalary.Text = Format(.Salary, "$0.00")
  End With
End Sub
```

As we can see, the code still interacts with the original Name property as implemented in the Person class, but we are now also invoking the overloaded version of the property that is implemented in the Employee class.

Overriding Methods

So far we've seen how to implement a base class, and then use it to create a subclass. Finally we extended the interface by adding methods. We've also explored how to use overloading to add methods that have the same name as methods in the base class, but with different parameters.

However, there are times when we may not only want to extend the original functionality, but to actually change or entirely replace the functionality from the base class. Instead of leaving the existing functionality and just adding new methods or overloaded versions of those methods, we might want to entirely **override** the existing functionality with our own.

We can do exactly this. If the base class allows it, we can substitute our own implementation of a method in the base class – meaning that our new implementation will be used instead of the original.

The Overridable Keyword

By default we can't override the behavior of methods on a base class. The base class must be coded specifically to allow this to occur by using the Overridable keyword. This is important, since we may not always want to allow a subclass to entirely change the behavior of the methods in our base class. However, if we do wish to allow the author of a subclass to replace our implementation, we can do so by adding the Overridable keyword to our method declaration.

Returning to our Employee example, we may not like the implementation of the BirthDate method as it stands in the Person class. Say, for instance, that we can't employ anyone that is younger than 16 years of age, so any birth date value more recent than 16 years ago is invalid for an employee.

To implement this business rule, we need to change the way the BirthDate property is implemented. While we could make this change directly in the Person class, that would not be ideal. It is perfectly acceptable to have a person under age 16, just not an employee.

Open the code window for the Person class and change the BirthDate property to include the Overridable keyword:

```
Public Overridable Property BirthDate() As Date
  Get
    Return mdtBirthDate
  End Get
  Set(ByVal Value As Date)
    mdtBirthDate = Value
  End Set
End Property
```

This change allows any class that inherits from Person to entirely replace the implementation of the BirthDate property with a new implementation.

By adding the Overridable keyword to our method declaration we are indicating that we want to allow any subclass to override the behavior provided by this method. This means that we are giving permission for a subclass to totally ignore our implementation, or to extend our implementation by doing other work before or after our implementation is run.

If the subclass doesn't override this method, the method will work just like a regular method and will be automatically included as part of the subclass's interface. Putting the Overridable keyword on a method simply allows a subclass to override the method if we choose to do so.

The Overrides Keyword

In a subclass we override a method by implementing a method of the same name, and with the same parameter list as the base class and then using the Overrides keyword to indicate that we are overriding that method.

This is different from overloading, since when we *overload* a method we're adding a new method with the same name but a different parameter list. When we *override* a method we're actually replacing the original method with a new implementation.

Without the Overrides keyword we'll get a compilation error when we implement a method with the same name as one from the base class.

Open the code window for the Employee class and add a new BirthDate property:

```
Public Class Employee
   Inherits Person

   Private mdtHireDate As Date
   Private mdblSalary As Double
   Private mdtBirthDate As Date

   Private mcolNames As New Hashtable()

   Public Overrides Property BirthDate() As Date
     Get
       Return mdtBirthDate
     End Get
     Set(ByVal Value As Date)
       If DateDiff(DateInterval.Year, Value, Now()) >= 16 Then
         mdtBirthDate = Value
       Else
         Err.Raise(1001, "Employee", _
           "An employee must be at least 16 years old")
       End If
     End Set
   End Property
```

Since we're implementing our own version of the property, we have to declare a variable to store that value within the Employee class. This is not ideal, and there are a couple ways around it – including the MyBase keyword and the Protected scope.

Notice also, that we've enhanced the functionality in the Set block so it now raises an error if the new birth date value would make the employee be less than 16 years of age. With this code we've now entirely replaced the original BirthDate implementation with a new one that enforces our business rule. This is illustrated by the following UML diagram:

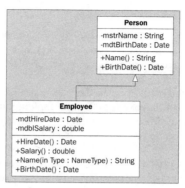

The diagram now includes a `BirthDate` method in the `Employee` class that has the same method signature as the `BirthDate` method in the `Person` class. While perhaps not entirely intuitive, this is how UML indicates that we've overridden the method.

If we now run our application and click the button on the form everything should work as it did before. This is because the birth date we're supplying conforms to our new business rule. However, we can change the code in our form to use an invalid birth date:

```
With objEmployee
    .Name = "Fred"
    .Name(NameTypes.Formal) = "Mr. Frederick R. Jones, Sr."
    .Name(NameTypes.Informal) = "Freddy"
    .BirthDate = #1/1/2000#
```

When we run the application (from within VS.NET) and click the button we'll get an error indicating that the birth date is invalid:

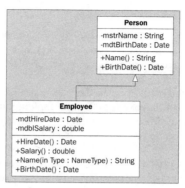

This proves that we are now using the implementation of the `BirthDate` method from the `Employee` class rather than the one from the `Person` class.

Change the date value in the form back to a valid value so our application runs properly.

The MyBase Keyword

We've just seen how we can entirely replace the functionality of a method in the base class by overriding it in our subclass. However, this can be somewhat extreme – sometimes it would be preferable to override methods such that we extend the base functionality rather than replacing the functionality.

To do this we need to override the method using the Overrides keyword like we just did, but within our new implementation we can still invoke the original implementation of the method. This allows us to add our own code before or after the original implementation is invoked – meaning we can extend the behavior, while still leveraging the code in the base class.

To invoke methods directly from the base class we can use the MyBase keyword. This keyword is available within any class, and it exposes all the methods of the base class for our use.

> *Even a base class like Person is an implicit subclass of* System.Object, *and so it can use* MyBase *to interact with its base class as well.*

This means that within the BirthDate implementation in Employee, we can invoke the BirthDate implementation in the base Person class. This is ideal, since it means we can leverage any existing functionality provided by Person, while still enforcing our Employee-specific business rules.

To take advantage of this, we can enhance the code in the Employee implementation of BirthDate. First off, remove the declaration of mdtBirthDate from the Employee class. We won't need this variable any longer, since the Person implementation will keep track of the value on our behalf. Then change the BirthDate implementation in the Employee class as follows:

```
Public Overrides Property BirthDate() As Date
  Get
    Return MyBase.BirthDate
  End Get
  Set(ByVal Value As Date)
    If DateDiff(DateInterval.Year, Value, Now()) >= 16 Then
      MyBase.BirthDate = Value
    Else
      Err.Raise(1001, "Employee", _
        "An employee must be at least 16 years old")
    End If
  End Set
End Property
```

We can now run our application and we'll see that it works just fine even though the Employee class no longer contains any code to actually keep track of the birth date value. We've effectively merged the BirthDate implementation from Person right into our enhanced implementation in Employee – creating a hybrid version of the property.

We'll discuss the MyBase keyword in some more depth later in the chapter, but here we've seen how it can be used to allow us to enhance or extend the functionality of the base class by adding our own code in the subclass, but still invoking the base class method when appropriate.

Virtual Methods

The BirthDate method is an example of a **virtual method**. Virtual methods are those that can be overridden and replaced by subclasses.

Virtual methods are more complex to understand than regular non-virtual methods. With a non-virtual method there is only one implementation that matches any given method signature, so there's no ambiguity about which specific method implementation will be invoked. With virtual methods, however, there may be several implementations of the same method, with the same method signature and so we need to understand the rules that govern which specific implementation of that method will be called.

When working with virtual methods we need to keep in mind that the data type of the *object* is used to determine the implementation of the method to call, rather than the type of the *variable* that refers to the object.

If we look at the code we've written in our form, we see that we're declaring an object variable of type Employee and we are then creating an Employee object that we can reference via that object:

```
Dim objEmployee As New Employee()
```

It is not surprising, then, that we are able to invoke any of the methods that are implemented as part of the Employee class – and through inheritance any of the methods implemented as part of the Person class:

```
With objEmployee
  .Name = "Fred"
  .Name(NameTypes.Formal) = "Mr. Frederick R. Jones, Sr."
  .Name(NameTypes.Informal) = "Freddy"
  .BirthDate = #1/1/1960#
  .HireDate = #1/1/1980#
  .Salary = 30000
```

When we call the BirthDate property we know that we're invoking the implementation contained in the Employee class – which makes sense since we know that we're using a variable of type Employee to refer to an object of type Employee.

However, because our methods are virtual methods, we can experiment with some much more interesting scenarios. For instance, suppose that we change the code in our form to interact directly with an object of type Person instead of one of type Employee:

```
Private Sub btnOK_Click(ByVal sender As System.Object, _
    ByVal e As System.EventArgs) Handles btnOK.Click

  Dim objPerson As New Person()

  With objPerson
    .Name = "Fred"
    .BirthDate = #1/1/1960#

    txtName.Text = .Name
    txtBirthDate.Text = Format(.BirthDate, "Short date")
  End With

End Sub
```

We can no longer call the methods implemented by the Employee class, because they don't exist as part of a Person object – only as part of an Employee object. However, we can see that both the Name and BirthDate properties continue to function as we'd expect. When we run the application now it will work just fine. We can even change the birth date value to something that would be invalid for Employee:

173

```
                .BirthDate = #1/1/2000#
```

The application will now accept it and work just fine, since the `BirthDate` method we're invoking is the original version from the `Person` class.

These are the two simple scenarios – where we have a variable and object of type `Employee` or a variable and object of type `Person`. However, since `Employee` is derived from `Person`, we can do something a bit more tricky. We can use a variable of type `Person` to hold a reference to an `Employee` object.

Because of this, we can change the code in `Form1` as follows:

```
Private Sub btnOK_Click(ByVal sender As System.Object, _
    ByVal e As System.EventArgs) Handles btnOK.Click
  Dim objPerson As Person
  objPerson = New Employee()

  With objPerson
    .Name = "Fred"
    .BirthDate = #1/1/2000#

    txtName.Text = .Name
    txtBirthDate.Text = Format(.BirthDate, "Short date")
  End With
End Sub
```

What we're doing now is declaring our variable to be of type `Person`, but the object itself is an instance of the `Employee` class. We've done something a bit complex here, since the data type of the variable is not the same as the data type of the object itself. The thing to remember is that a variable of a base class type can always hold a reference to an object of any subclass.

> This is the reason that a variable of type `System.Object` can hold a reference to literally anything in .NET – because all classes are ultimately derived from `System.Object`.

This technique is very useful when creating generic routines and makes use of an object-oriented concept called polymorphism that we'll discuss more thoroughly in Chapter 7. This technique allows us to create a more general routine that populates our form for any object of type `Person`. Add this code to the form:

```
Private Sub DisplayPerson(ByVal ThePerson As Person)
  With ThePerson
    txtName.Text = .Name
    txtBirthDate.Text = Format(.BirthDate, "Short date")
  End With
End Sub
```

Now we can change the code behind the button to make use of this generic routine:

```
Private Sub btnOK_Click(ByVal sender As System.Object, _
    ByVal e As System.EventArgs) Handles btnOK.Click
```

```
Dim objPerson As Person
objPerson = New Employee()

With objPerson
  .Name = "Fred"
  .BirthDate = #1/1/2000#
End With

DisplayPerson(objPerson)
End Sub
```

The benefit here is that we can pass a `Person` object, or an `Employee` object to `DisplayPerson` and the routine will work the same either way.

When we run the application now things get interesting. We'll get an error when we attempt to set the `BirthDate` property because it breaks our 16 year old business rule – which is implemented in the `Employee` class. How can this be when our `objPerson` variable is of type `Person`?

This clearly demonstrates the concept of a virtual method. It is the data type of the object, in this case `Employee`, that is important. The data type of the variable is not the deciding factor when deciding which implementation of an overridden method is invoked.

The following table illustrates which method is actually invoked based on the variable and object data types when working with virtual methods:

Variable	Object	Method invoked
Base	Base	Base
Base	Subclass	Subclass
Subclass	Subclass	Subclass

Virtual methods are very powerful and useful when we go to implement polymorphism using inheritance. A base class data type can hold a reference to any subclass object, but it is the type of that specific object that determines the implementation of the method. Because of this we can write generic routines that operate on many types of object as long as they derive from the same base class. We'll discuss this in more detail in Chapter 7.

Overriding Overloaded Methods

Earlier we wrote code in our `Employee` to overload the `Name` method in the base `Person` class. This allowed us to keep the original `Name` functionality, but also extend it by adding another `Name` method that accepted a different parameter list.

We've also overridden the `BirthDate` method. The implementation in the `Employee` class replaced the implementation in the `Person` class. Overriding is a related, but different concept from overloading. It is also possible to both overload and override a method at the same time.

In our earlier overloading example we added a new Name property to the Employee class, while retaining the functionality present in the base Person class. We may decide that we not only want to have our second overloaded implementation of the Name method, but that we also want to replace the existing one by overriding the existing method provided by the Person class.

In particular, we may want to do this so we can store the Name value in the Hashtable object along with our Formal and Informal names.

Before we can override the Name method we need to add the Overridable keyword to the base implementation in the Person class:

```
Public Overridable Property Name() As String
   Get
      Return mstrName
   End Get
   Set(ByVal Value As String)
      mstrName = Value
   End Set
End Property
```

With that done, the Name method can now be overridden by any derived classes. In the Employee class we can now override the Name method – replacing the functionality provided by the Person class. First, we'll add a Normal option to the Enum that controls the types of name value we can store:

```
Public Enum NameTypes
   Informal = 1
   Formal = 2
   Normal = 3
End Enum
```

Then we can add code to the Employee class to implement a new Name property. This is in addition to the existing Name property already implemented in the Employee class:

```
Public Overloads Overrides Property Name() As String
   Get
      Return Name(NameTypes.Normal)
   End Get
   Set(ByVal Value As String)
      Name(NameTypes.Normal) = Value
   End Set
End Property
```

Notice that we're using both the Overrides keyword to indicate that we're overriding the Name method from the base class, and also the Overloads keyword to indicate that we're overloading this method in the subclass.

This new Name property merely delegates the call to the existing version of the Name property that handles the parameter-based names. To complete the linkage between this implementation of the Name property and the parameter-based version we need to make one more change to that original overloaded version:

```
    Public Overloads Property Name(ByVal Type As NameTypes) As String
      Get
        Return mcolNames(Type)
      End Get
      Set(ByVal Value As String)
        If mcolNames.ContainsKey(NameTypes.Normal) Then
          mcolNames.Item(NameTypes.Normal) = Value
        Else
          mcolNames.Add(Type, Value)
        End If
        If Type = NameTypes.Normal Then
          MyBase.Name = Value
        End If
      End Set
    End Property
```

This way, if the client code were to set the Name property by providing the Normal index, we are still updating the name in the base class as well as in the Hashtable object maintained by the Employee class.

Shadowing

Overloading allows us to add new versions of existing methods as long as their parameter lists are different. Overriding allows our subclass to entirely replace the implementation of a base class method with a new method that has the same method signature. As we've just seen, we can even combine these concepts to not only replace the implementation of a method from the base class, but also to simultaneously overload that method with other implementations that have different method signatures.

However, any time we override a method using the Overrides keyword, we are subject to the rules governing virtual methods – meaning that the data type of the object controls which implementation of the method is invoked. Sometimes we may want to be able to create a new implementation of a method in our subclass – replacing the implementation in the base class – but we don't want to follow the rules governing virtual methods. In particular, we may want to write client code that can use our object as though it were literally of the base class data type –being able to ignore totally the implementation in the subclass. This is a primary use for the Shadows keyword.

The Shadows keyword can also be used to entirely change the nature of a method or other interface element from the base class – though that is something that should be done with great care since it can seriously reduce the maintainability of our code. Normally, when we create an Employee object, we expect that it can only act as an Employee, but also as a Person since Employee is a subclass of Person. However, with the Shadows keyword we can radically alter the behavior of an Employee class so it doesn't act like a Person. This sort of radical deviation from what is normally expected invites bugs and makes code hard to understand and maintain.

We'll explore that in more detail later. First though, let's see how Shadows can be used to override non-virtual methods.

Overriding Non-Virtual Methods

Earlier in the chapter we discussed virtual methods and how they are automatically created in VB.NET when the Overrides keyword is employed. We can also implement **non-virtual methods** in VB.NET. Non-virtual methods are methods that cannot be overridden and replaced by subclasses, and so most methods we implement are non-virtual.

> **If we don't use the `Overridable` keyword when declaring a method, it is non-virtual.**

In the typical case, non-virtual methods are easy to understand. Since they can't be overridden and replaced, we know that there's only one method by that name, with that method signature, and so when we invoke it there is no ambiguity about which specific implementation will be called. The reverse is true with virtual methods, where there may be more than one method of the same name, with the same method signature, and so we need to understand the rules governing which implementation will be invoked.

Of course nothing is simple, and it turns out that we *can* override non-virtual methods by using the `Shadows` keyword. In fact, we can use the `Shadows` keyword to override methods regardless of whether or not they have the `Overridable` keyword in the declaration.

> **The `Shadows` keyword allows us to replace methods on the base class that the base class designer didn't intend to be replaced.**

Obviously this can be *very* dangerous. The designer of a base class must use care when marking a method as `Overridable` – ensuring that the base class will continue to operate properly even when that method is replaced by a other code in a subclass. Designers of base classes typically just assume that if they *don't* mark a method as `Overridable` that it *will* be called and not overridden. Thus, overriding a non-virtual method by using the `Shadows` keyword can have unexpected and potentially dangerous side effects since we are doing something that the base class designer assumed would never happen.

If that isn't enough complexity, it turns out that shadowed methods follow different rules from virtual methods when they are invoked. In other words, they don't act like regular overridden methods, but instead they follow a different set of rules to determine which specific implementation of the method will be invoked. In particular, when we call a non-virtual method, it is the data type of the *variable* that refers to the object that indicates which implementation of the method is called – not the data type of the *object* as with virtual methods.

To override a non-virtual method we can use the `Shadows` keyword instead of the `Overrides` keyword. To see how this works, let's add a new property to our base `Person` class:

```
Public ReadOnly Property Age() As Integer
   Get
      Return DateDiff(DateInterval.Year, Now(), BirthDate())
   End Get
End Property
```

We've added a new method to our base class – and thus automatically to our subclass – called `Age`.

This code has a bug – introduced on purpose for illustration. The `DateDiff` parameters are in the wrong order, so we'll get negative age values from this routine. We introduced a bug because sometimes there are bugs in base classes that we didn't write and can't fix because we don't have the source code. In this case we'll walk through the use of the `Shadows` keyword to help address a bug in our base class – acting under the assumption that for some reason we can't actually fix the code in the `Person` class.

Notice that we're not using the `Overridable` keyword on this method, so any subclass is prevented from overriding the method by using the `Overrides` keyword. The obvious intent and expectation of this code is that all subclasses will use this implementation and will not override it with their own.

However, the base class cannot prevent a subclass from shadowing a method, and so it doesn't matter whether we use `Overridable` or not – either way works fine for shadowing.

Before we shadow the method, let's see how it works as a regular non-virtual method. First, we need to change our form to use this new value. Add a text box named `txtAge` and a related label to the form:

Next let's change the code behind the button to use the `Age` property. We'll also include the code to display the data on the form right here to keep things simple and clear:

```
Private Sub btnOK_Click(ByVal sender As System.Object, _
    ByVal e As System.EventArgs) Handles btnOK.Click

    Dim objPerson As Employee = New Employee()

    With objPerson
      .Name = "Fred"
      .BirthDate = #1/1/1960#

      txtName.Text = .Name
      txtBirthDate.Text = Format(.BirthDate, "Short date")
      txtAge.Text = .Age
    End With

End Sub
```

Also, don't forget to change the birth date value to something that will be valid for an `Employee`.

At this point we can run the application and the age field should appear in our display as expected – though with a negative value due to the bug we introduced. There's no magic or complexity here – this is basic programming with objects and basic use of inheritance as we discussed at the beginning of this chapter.

Of course we don't want a bug in our code – but if we assume we don't have access to the `Person` class, and since the `Person` class doesn't allow us to override the `Age` method – what are we to do? The answer lies in the `Shadows` keyword – which allows us to override the method anyway.

Let's shadow the `Age` method within the `Employee` class – overriding and replacing the implementation in the `Person` class even though it is not marked as `Overridable`. Add the following code to `Employee`:

```
Public Shadows ReadOnly Property Age() As Integer
  Get
      Return DateDiff(DateInterval.Year, BirthDate(), Now())
  End Get
End Property
```

In many ways this looks very similar to what we've seen with the `Overrides` keyword, in that we're implementing a method in our subclass with the same name and parameter list as a method in the base class. In this case however, we'll find some different behavior when we interact with the object in different ways.

Technically the `Shadows` keyword is not required here. Shadowing is the default behavior when a subclass implements a method that matches the name and method signature of a method in the base class. However, if we omit the `Shadows` keyword the compiler will give us a warning indicating that the method is being shadowed so it is always better to include the keyword – both to avoid the warning and to make it perfectly clear that we knew what we were doing when we chose to shadow the method.

Remember that our code in the form is currently declaring a variable of type `Employee` and is creating an instance of an `Employee` object:

```
Dim objPerson As Employee = New Employee()
```

This is the simple case, and not surprisingly when we run the application now we'll see that the value of the age field is correct – indicating that we just ran the implementation of the `Age` property from the `Employee` class. At this point we're seeing the same behavior that we got from overriding with the `Overrides` keyword.

Let's take a look at the other simple case – where we're working with a variable and object that are both of data type `Person`. Change the code in `Form1` as follows:

```
Private Sub btnOK_Click(ByVal sender As System.Object, _
    ByVal e As System.EventArgs) Handles btnOK.Click

  Dim objPerson As Person = New Person()

  With objPerson
    .Name = "Fred"
    .BirthDate = #1/1/1960#

    txtName.Text = .Name
    txtBirthDate.Text = Format(.BirthDate, "Short date")
    txtAge.Text = .Age
  End With
End Sub
```

Now we have a variable of type `Person` and an object of that same type. We would expect that the implementation in the `Person` class would be invoked in this case, and that is exactly what happens – the age field will display the original negative value, indicating that we're invoking the buggy implementation of the method directly from the `Person` class. Again this is exactly the behavior we'd expect from a method overridden via the `Overrides` keyword.

This next one is where things get truly interesting. Change the code in `Form1` as follows:

```
Private Sub btnOK_Click(ByVal sender As System.Object, _
    ByVal e As System.EventArgs) Handles btnOK.Click

    Dim objPerson As Person = New Employee()

    With objPerson
      .Name = "Fred"
      .BirthDate = #1/1/1960#

      txtName.Text = .Name
      txtBirthDate.Text = Format(.BirthDate, "Short date")
      txtAge.Text = .Age
    End With
End Sub
```

Now we are declaring the variable to be of type `Person`, but we are creating an object that is of data type `Employee`. We did this earlier in the chapter when exploring the `Overrides` keyword as well – and in that case we discovered that the version of the method that was invoked was based on the data type of the object. The `BirthDate` implementation in the `Employee` class was invoked.

If we run the application now we will find that the rules are different when the `Shadows` keyword is used. In this case, the implementation in the `Person` class is invoked – giving us the buggy negative value. The implementation in the `Employee` class is ignored – we get the exact opposite behavior to what we got with `Overrides`.

The following table summarizes which method implementation is invoked based on the variable and object data types when using shadowing:

Variable	Object	Method invoked
Base	Base	Base
Base	Subclass	Base
Subclass	Subclass	Subclass

In most cases the behavior we'll want for our methods is accomplished by the `Overrides` keyword and virtual methods. However, in those cases where the base class designer doesn't allow us to override a method and we want to do it anyway, the `Shadows` keyword provides us with the needed functionality.

Shadowing Arbitrary Elements

The Shadows keyword can be used not only to override non-virtual methods, but it can be used to totally replace and change the nature of a base class interface element. When we override a method we are providing a replacement implementation of that method with the same name and method signature. Using the Shadows keyword we can do more extreme things – like changing a method into an instance variable, or changing a Property into a Function.

However, this can be very dangerous, since any code written to use our objects will naturally assume that we implement all the same interface elements and behaviors as our base class – since that is the nature of inheritance.

> By totally changing the nature of an interface element, we can cause a great deal of confusion for programmers who will be interacting with our class in the future.

To see how we can replace an interface element from the base class, let's entirely change the nature of the Age property. In fact, let's change it from being a read-only property to being a read-write property. We could get even more extreme – changing it to a Function or Sub.

To do this, remove the Age property from the Employee class and add the following code:

```
Public Shadows Property Age() As Integer
  Get
    Return DateDiff(DateInterval.Year, BirthDate(), Now())
  End Get
  Set(ByVal Value As Integer)
    BirthDate() = DateAdd(DateInterval.Year, -Value, Now())
  End Set
End Property
```

With this change, the very nature of the Age method has changed. It is no longer a simple read only property, now it is a read-write property that includes code to calculate an approximate birth date based on the age value supplied.

As it stands, our application will continue to run just fine. This is because we're only using the read-only functionality of the property in our form. We can change the form to make use of the new read-write functionality:

```
Private Sub btnOK_Click(ByVal sender As System.Object, _
    ByVal e As System.EventArgs) Handles btnOK.Click

  Dim objPerson As Person = New Employee()

  With objPerson
    .Name = "Fred"
    .BirthDate = #1/1/1960#
    .Age = 20

    txtName.Text = .Name
    txtBirthDate.Text = Format(.BirthDate, "Short date")
```

```
        txtAge.Text = .Age
    End With
End Sub
```

This will leave us with a syntax error, however. The variable we're working with, objPerson, is of data type Person – and that data type does not provide a writable version of the Age property. This means that, in order to use our enhanced functionality, we must be using a variable and object of type Employee:

```
Dim objPerson As Employee = New Employee()
```

If we now run the application and click the button we'll see that the Age is displayed as 20, and the birth date is now a value calculated based on that age value – indicating that we are now running the shadowed version of the Age method as implemented in the Employee class.

As if that wasn't odd enough, we can do some even more strange and dangerous things. We can change Age into a *variable* and we can even change its scope. For instance, we can comment out the Age property code in the Employee class and replace it with the following:

```
Private Shadows Age As String
```

At this point we've changed everything. Age is now a String instead of an Integer. It is a variable instead of a Property or Function. It has Private scope instead of Public scope. Our Employee object is totally incompatible with the Person data type – something that shouldn't occur normally when using inheritance.

This means that the code we wrote in Form1 will no longer work. The Age property is no longer accessible and can no longer be used and so our project will no longer compile. This directly illustrates the danger in shadowing a base class element such that its very nature or scope is changed by the subclass.

Since this change prevents our application from compiling, remove the line in the Employee class that shadows Age as a String variable – and uncomment the shadowed Property routine:

```
Public Shadows Property Age() As Integer
  Get
    Return DateDiff(DateInterval.Year, BirthDate(), Now())
  End Get
  Set(ByVal Value As Integer)
    BirthDate() = DateAdd(DateInterval.Year, -Value, Now())
  End Set
End Property
```

This will restore our application to a working state and we can move on.

Levels of Inheritance

So far we've created a single base class and a single subclass – thus demonstrating that we can implement inheritance that is a single level deep. However, we can create inheritance relationships that are many levels deep. These are sometimes referred to as chains of inheritance.

In reality we've been creating a two-level inheritance hierarchy so far because we know that our base class actually derived from System.Object *– but for most purposes it is easiest to simply ignore that fact and treat only our classes as part of the inheritance hierarchy.*

Multiple Inheritance

Don't confuse multi-level inheritance with multiple inheritance, which is an entirely different concept that is not supported by either VB.NET or the .NET platform itself. The idea behind **multiple inheritance** is that we can have a single subclass that inherits from two base classes all at the same time.

For instance, we may have an application that has a class for Customer and another class for Vendor. It is quite possible that some customers are also vendors, so we might want to combine the functionality of these two classes into a CustomerVendor class. This new class would be a combination of both Customer and Vendor – so it would be nice to inherit from both of them at once – something like the following UML diagram might indicate:

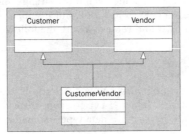

Here we see the line running from CustomerVendor back up into both Customer *and* Vendor and terminating in an open triangle in both cases. This indicates that CustomerVendor inherits from both of those classes.

While a useful concept, multiple inheritance is complex and somewhat dangerous. Within the object-oriented community there is continual debate as to whether the advantages of code reuse outweigh the complexity that comes along for the ride.

Multiple inheritance is not supported by the .NET Framework, and so it is likewise not supported by VB.NET. However, we can use multiple interfaces to achieve an effect similar to multiple inheritance – a topic we'll discuss later in the chapter when we discuss implementing multiple interfaces.

Multi-Level Inheritance

We've seen how a subclass derives from a base class with our Person and Employee classes:

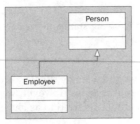

However, there's nothing to stop the Employee subclass from being the base class for yet another class – a sub-subclass so to speak. This is not at all uncommon. In our example, we may find that we have different kinds of employees – some who work in the office, and others who travel.

To accommodate this, we may want to have OfficeEmployee and TravelingEmployee classes. Of course these are both examples of an employee – and should share the functionality already present in the Employee class. The Employee class already reuses the functionality from the Person class. The following UML illustrates how these classes are interrelated:

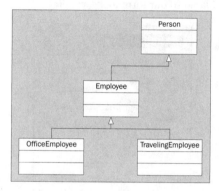

We can see that the Employee is a subclass of Person – and our two new classes are both subclasses of Employee. While both OfficeEmployee and TravelingEmployee are employees, and thus also people, they are each unique. An OfficeEmployee almost certainly has a cube or office number, while a TravelingEmployee will keep track of the number of miles traveled.

Add a new class to our project and name it OfficeEmployee. To make this class inherit from our existing Employee class, add the following code to the class:

```
Public Class OfficeEmployee
   Inherits Employee

End Class
```

With this change, the new class now has Name, BirthDate, Age, HireDate, and Salary methods. Notice that methods from both Employee and Person are inherited. A subclass always gains all the methods, properties and events of its base class.

We can now extend the interface and behavior of OfficeEmployee by adding a property to indicate which cube or office number the employee occupies:

```
Public Class OfficeEmployee
   Inherits Employee

   Private mstrOffice As String

   Public Property OfficeNumber() As String
     Get
```

```
      Return mstrOffice
    End Get
    Set(ByVal Value As String)
      mstrOffice = Value
    End Set
  End Property
End Class
```

To see how this works, let's enhance our form to display this value. Add a new text box control named txtOffice and an associated label so our form looks as follows:

Now change the code behind the button to make use of the new property:

```
Private Sub btnOK_Click(ByVal sender As System.Object, _
    ByVal e As System.EventArgs) Handles btnOK.Click

  Dim objPerson As OfficeEmployee = New OfficeEmployee()

  With objPerson
    .Name = "Fred"
    .BirthDate = #1/1/1960#
    .Age = 20
    .OfficeNumber = "A42"

    txtName.Text = .Name
    txtBirthDate.Text = Format(.BirthDate, "Short date")
    txtAge.Text = .Age
    txtOffice.Text = .OfficeNumber
  End With
End Sub
```

We've changed the routine to declare and create an object of type OfficeEmployee – thus allowing us to make use of the new property – as well as all existing properties and methods from Employee and Person since they've been "merged" into the OfficeEmployee class via inheritance.

If we now run the application we'll see that the name, birth date, age and office values are displayed in the form.

Inheritance like this can go many levels deep with each level extending and changing the behaviors of the previous levels. In fact there is no specific technical limit to the number of levels of inheritance we can implement in VB.NET. Very deep inheritance chains are typically not recommended and are often viewed as a design flaw – something we'll discuss in more detail in Chapter 7.

Interacting with the Base Class, Our Class, and Our Object

We've already seen how we can use the `MyBase` keyword to call methods on the base class from within a subclass. The `MyBase` keyword is one of three special keywords that allow us to interact with important object and class representations:

- ❑   `Me`
- ❑   `MyBase`
- ❑   `MyClass`

The Me Keyword

The `Me` keyword provides us with a reference to our current object instance. Typically, we don't need to use the `Me` keyword, since any time we want to invoke a method within our current object we can just call that method directly.

To see clearly how this works, let's add a new method to the `Person` class that returns the data of the `Person` class in the form of a `String`. This will be a bit interesting in and of itself, since the base `System.Object` class defines the `ToString` method for this exact purpose. Remember that all classes in .NET ultimately derive from `System.Object` – even if we don't explicitly indicate it with an `Inherits` statement.

This means we can simply override the `ToString` method from the `Object` class within our `Person` class by adding the following code:

```
Public Overrides Function ToString() As String
   Return Name
End Function
```

This implementation will return the person's `Name` property as a result when `ToString` is called.

> By default, `ToString` returns the class name of the class. Up to now, if we had called the `ToString` method on a `Person` object we would have gotten a result of `InheritanceAndInterfaces.Person`.

Notice that the `ToString` method is calling another method within our same class – in this case the `Name` method.

We could also write this routine using the `Me` keyword:

```
Public Overrides Function ToString() As String
   Return Me.Name
End Function
```

This is redundant, however, since Me is the default for all method calls in a class. These two implementations are identical, and so typically the Me keyword is simply left off to avoid that extra typing.

To see how the ToString method now works, we can change our code in Form1 to use this value instead of the Name property:

```
Private Sub btnOK_Click(ByVal sender As System.Object, _
    ByVal e As System.EventArgs) Handles btnOK.Click
  Dim objPerson As OfficeEmployee = New OfficeEmployee()

  With objPerson
    .Name = "Fred"
    .BirthDate = #1/1/1960#
    .Age = 20
    .OfficeNumber = "A42"

    txtName.Text = .ToString
    txtBirthDate.Text = Format(.BirthDate, "Short date")
    txtAge.Text = .Age
    txtOffice.Text = .OfficeNumber
  End With
End Sub
```

When we run the application we'll see that the person's name is displayed appropriately – which makes sense since the ToString method is simply returning the result from the Name property.

Earlier we discussed virtual methods and how they work. Since either calling a method directly or calling it using the Me keyword invokes the method on the current object this means that the method calls conform to the same rules as an external method call. In other words, our ToString method may not actually end up calling the Name method in the Person class if that method was overridden by a class further down the inheritance chain such as the Employee or OfficeEmployee classes.

For example, we could override the Name property in our OfficeEmployee class such that it always returns the informal version of the person's name rather than the regular name. We can override the Name property by adding this method to the OfficeEmployee class:

```
Public Overloads Overrides Property Name() As String
  Get
    Return MyBase.Name(NameTypes.Informal)
  End Get
  Set(ByVal Value As String)
    MyBase.Name = Value
  End Set
End Property
```

This new version of the Name method relies on the base class to actually store the value – but instead of returning the normal name on request, we are now always returning the informal name:

```
Return MyBase.Name(NameTypes.Informal)
```

Before we can test this, we need to enhance the code in our form to actually provide a value for the informal name. Make the following change to that code:

```
Private Sub btnOK_Click(ByVal sender As System.Object, _
    ByVal e As System.EventArgs) Handles btnOK.Click

  Dim objPerson As OfficeEmployee = New OfficeEmployee()

  With objPerson
    .Name = "Fred"
    .Name(NameTypes.Informal) = "Freddy"
    .BirthDate = #1/1/1960#
    .Age = 20
    .OfficeNumber = "A42"

    txtName.Text = .ToString
    txtBirthDate.Text = Format(.BirthDate, "Short date")
    txtAge.Text = .Age
    txtOffice.Text = .OfficeNumber
  End With
End Sub
```

When we run the application we'll find that the name field displays the informal name. Even though the ToString method is implemented in the Person class, it is invoking the implementation of Name from the OfficeEmployee class. This is because method calls *within* a class follow the same rules for calling virtual methods as code *outside* a class – such as our code in the form.

We'll see this behavior with or without the Me keyword, since the default behavior for method calls is to implicitly call them via the current object.

While methods called from within a class follow the same rules for virtual methods, this is not the case for shadowed methods. Here we'll find that the rules for calling a shadowed method from within our class are different from those outside our class.

To see how this works, let's make the Name property in OfficeEmployee a shadowed method instead of an overridden method:

```
Public Shadows Property Name() As String
  Get
    Return MyBase.Name(NameTypes.Informal)
  End Get
  Set(ByVal Value As String)
    MyBase.Name = Value
  End Set
End Property
```

Before we can run our application we'll have to adjust some code in the form. Because we've overridden the Name property in OfficeEmployee, we'll find that the version of Name from Employee that acts as a property array is now invalid.

> **Shadowing a method replaces *all* implementations from higher in the inheritance chain – regardless of their method signature.**

To make our application operate we'll need to change the variable declaration and object creation to declare a variable of type `Employee` so we can access the property array – while still creating an instance of `OfficeEmployee`:

```
Dim objPerson As Employee = New OfficeEmployee()
```

Since our variable is now of type `Employee`, we also need to comment out the lines that refer to the `OfficeName` property, since it is no longer available:

```
With objPerson
  .Name = "Fred"
  .Name(NameTypes.Informal) = "Freddy"
  .BirthDate = #1/1/1960#
  .Age = 20
  '.OfficeNumber = "A42"

  txtName.Text = .ToString
  txtBirthDate.Text = Format(.BirthDate, "Short date")
  txtAge.Text = .Age
  'txtOffice.Text = .OfficeNumber
End With
```

When we run the application now we'll find that it displays the name **Fred** rather than **Freddy** – meaning it is *not* calling the `Name` method from `OfficeEmployee`, but rather is calling the implementation provided by the `Employee` class. Remember that the code to make this call still resides in the `Person` class – but it now ignores the shadowed version of the `Name` method.

Shadowed implementations in subclasses are ignored when calling the method from *within* a class higher in the inheritance chain.

We'll get this same behavior with or without the `Me` keyword. So the `Me` keyword, or calling methods directly, follows the same rules for overridden methods as any other method call. For shadowed methods, however, any shadowed implementations in subclasses are ignored and the method is called from the current level in the inheritance chain.

So why does the `Me` keyword exist? Primarily for clarity and to allow us to pass a reference to the current object as a parameter to other objects or methods. As we'll see when we look at the `MyBase` and `MyClass` keywords, things can get very confusing and there is value in using the `Me` keyword when working with `MyBase` and `MyClass` to ensure that it is always clear which particular implementation of a method we intended to invoke.

The MyBase Keyword

While the `Me` keyword allows us to call methods on the current object instance, there are times we might want to explicitly call into methods in our parent class. Earlier we saw an example of this when we called back into the base class from an overridden method in the subclass.

The `MyBase` keyword references only the immediate parent class, and it works like an object reference. This means we can call methods on `MyBase`, knowing that they are being called just like we had a reference to an object of our parent class's data type.

> **There is no way to directly navigate up the inheritance chain beyond our immediate parent.**

The `MyBase` keyword can be used to invoke or use any `Public`, `Friend`, or `Protected` element from the parent class. This includes all of those elements directly on the base class, and also any elements the base class inherited from other classes higher in the inheritance chain.

We've already used `MyBase` to call back into the base `Person` class as we implemented the overridden `Name` property in the `Employee` class.

> **Any code within a subclass can call any method on the base class by using the `MyBase` keyword.**

We can also use `MyBase` to call back into the base class implementation even if we've shadowed a method. Though we didn't remark on it at the time, we've already done this in our shadowed implementation of the `Name` property in the `OfficeEmployee` class. The highlighted lines indicate where we're calling into the base class from within a shadowed method:

```
Public Shadows Property Name() As String
  Get
      Return MyBase.Name(NameTypes.Informal)
  End Get
  Set(ByVal Value As String)
      MyBase.Name = Value
  End Set
End Property
```

The `MyBase` keyword allows us to merge the functionality of the base class into our subclass code as we see fit.

The MyClass Keyword

As we've seen, when we use the `Me` keyword or call a method directly, our method call follows the rules for calling both virtual and non-virtual methods. In other words, as we discovered earlier with the `Name` property, a call to `Name` from our code in the `Person` class actually invoked the overridden version of `Name` located in the `OfficeEmployee` class.

While this behavior is useful in many cases, there are also cases where we'll want to ensure that we really are running the specific implementation from our class – where even if a subclass overrode our method we still want to ensure we're calling the version of the method that is directly in our class.

Maybe we decide that our `ToString` implementation in `Person` should always call the `Name` implementation that we write in the `Person` class – totally ignoring any overridden versions of `Name` in any subclasses.

This is where the `MyClass` keyword comes into play. This keyword is much like `MyBase`, in that it provides us with access to methods as though it were an object reference – in this case a reference to an instance of the class that contains the code we're writing when using the `MyClass` keyword. This is true even if the instantiated object is an instance of a class derived from our class.

We've seen that a call to ToString from within Person will actually invoke the implementation in Employee or OfficeEmployee if our object is an instance of either of those types. Let's restore the Name property in OfficeEmployee to be an overridden method rather than a shadowed method to see how this works:

```
Public Overloads Overrides Property Name() As String
   Get
      Return MyBase.Name(NameTypes.Informal)
   End Get
   Set(ByVal Value As String)
      MyBase.Name = Value
   End Set
End Property
```

With this change, and based on our earlier testing, we know that the ToString implementation in Person will automatically call this overridden version of the Name property, since the call to the Name method will follow the normal rules for virtual methods. In fact, if we run the application now we'll find that the name field on the form displays **Freddy** – the informal name of the person.

We can force the use of the implementation in our current class through the use of MyClass. Change the ToString method in Person as follows:

```
Public Overrides Function ToString() As String
   Return MyClass.Name
End Function
```

We are now calling the Name method, but we're doing it using the MyClass keyword. When we run the application and click on the button we'll find that the name field in the form displays **Fred** rather than **Freddy** – proving that the implementation from Person was invoked even though the data type of the object itself is OfficeEmployee.

The ToString method is invoked from Person, since neither Employee nor OfficeEmployee provide an overridden implementation. Then, because we're using the MyClass keyword, the Name method is invoked directly from Person – explicitly defeating the default behavior we'd normally expect.

Constructors

As we discussed in Chapter 5, we can provide a special constructor method, named New, on a class and it will be the first code run when an object is instantiated. We can also receive parameters via the constructor method – allowing the code that creates our object to pass data into the object during the creation process.

Constructor methods are affected by inheritance differently from regular methods. A normal Public method, such as BirthDate on our Person class, is automatically inherited by any subclass. From there we can overload, override or shadow that method as we've discussed so far in this chapter.

Simple Constructors

Constructors don't quite follow the same rules. To explore the differences, let's implement a simple constructor method in our Person class:

```
Public Sub New()
   Debug.WriteLine("Person constructor")
End Sub
```

If we now run the application we'll see the text displayed in the **Output** window in the IDE. This occurs even though the code in our form is creating an object of type `OfficeEmployee`:

```
Dim objPerson As Employee = New OfficeEmployee()
```

As we might expect, the `New` method from our base `Person` class is invoked as part of the construction process of the `OfficeEmployee` object – simple inheritance at work.

However, interesting things occur if we implement a `New` method in the `OfficeEmployee` class itself:

```
Public Sub New()
   Debug.WriteLine("OfficeEmployee constructor")
End Sub
```

Notice that we are not using the `Overrides` keyword, nor did we mark the method in `Person` as `Overridable`. These keywords have no use in this context – and in fact will cause syntax errors if we attempt to use them on constructor methods.

When we run the application now we'd probably expect that only the implementation of `New` in `OfficeEmployee` would be invoked. Certainly that is what would occur with a normal overridden method. But of course `New` isn't overridden, and so when we run the application we'll find that both implementations are run:

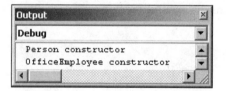

It is important to note that the implementation in the `Person` class ran first, followed by the implementation in the `OfficeEmployee` class.

This occurs because, as an object is created, all the constructors for the classes in the inheritance chain are invoked – starting with the base class and working out through all the subclasses one by one. In fact, if we implement a `New` method in the `Employee` class we can see that it too is invoked:

```
Public Sub New()
   Debug.WriteLine("Employee constructor")
End Sub
```

When the application is run and the button clicked we'll see this:

All three constructor methods were invoked – starting with the `Person` class and working down to the `OfficeEmployee` class.

Constructors in More Depth

The rules governing constructors without parameters are pretty straightforward. Things get a bit more interesting if we start requiring parameters on our constructors, however.

To understand what is going on, we need to get a slightly better understanding of how even our simple constructors are being invoked. While we see them as being invoked from the base class down through all subclasses to our final subclass, what is really happening is a bit different.

In particular, it is the subclass `New` method that is invoked first. However, VB.NET is automatically inserting a line of code into our routine at compile time. For instance, in our `OfficeEmployee` class we have a constructor:

```
Public Sub New()
   Debug.WriteLine("OfficeEmployee constructor")
End Sub
```

Behind the scenes, VB.NET inserts what is effectively a call to constructor of our parent class on our behalf. We could do this manually by using the `MyBase` keyword with the following change:

```
Public Sub New()
   MyBase.New()
   Debug.WriteLine("OfficeEmployee constructor")
End Sub
```

This call is required to be the first line in our constructor. If we put any other code before this line we'll get a syntax error indicating that our code is invalid. Since the call is always required, and since it always must be the first line in any constructor, VB.NET simply inserts it for us automatically.

It is also worth noting that if we don't explicitly provide a constructor on a class by implementing a `New` method, VB.NET creates one for us behind the scenes. The automatically created method simply has one line of code:

```
MyBase.New()
```

All classes have constructor methods, either created explicitly by us as we write a `New` method, or created implicitly by VB.NET as the class is compiled.

Constructor methods are sometimes called a ctor – short for constructor.

By always calling `Mybase.New()` as the first line in every constructor, we are guaranteed that it is the implementation of `New` in our top-level base class that will actually run first. Every subclass invokes the parent class implementation all the way up the inheritance chain until only the base class remains. Then its code runs, followed by each individual subclass as we've already seen.

Constructors with Parameters

This works great when our constructors don't require parameters. However, if our constructor does require a parameter, then it becomes impossible for VB.NET to automatically make that call on our behalf. After all, how would VB.NET know what values we want to pass as parameters?

To see how this works, let's change the `New` method in the `Person` class to require a `Name` parameter. We can use that parameter to initialize the object's `Name` property:

```
Public Sub New(ByVal Name As String)
   Me.Name = Name
   Debug.WriteLine("Person constructor")
End Sub
```

Now our constructor requires a `String` parameter and uses it to initialize the `Name` property.

We are using the `Me` keyword to make our code easier to read. Interestingly enough, the compiler will actually understand and correctly compile the following:

```
Name = Name
```

But that is not at all clear to a developer reading the code. By prefixing the property name with the `Me` keyword we've made it clear that we're invoking a property on the object and providing it with the parameter value.

At this point we'll find that our application won't compile. This is because there is an error in the `New` method of our `Employee` class. In particular, VB.NET's attempt to automatically invoke the constructor on the `Person` class is no longer workable, since it has no idea what data value to pass for this new `Name` parameter.

There are three ways we can address this error:

❑   We can make the `Name` parameter `Optional`

❑   We can overload the `New` method with another implementation that requires no parameter

❑   We can manually provide the `Name` parameter value from within the `Employee` class

If we make the `Name` parameter `Optional`, we're indicating that the `New` method can be called with or without a parameter. This means that one viable option is to call the method with no parameters – and so VB.NET's default of calling it with no parameters will work just fine.

If we overload the `New` method, we can implement a second `New` method that doesn't accept any parameters – again allowing VB.NET's default behavior to work as we've seen. Keep in mind that this solution would only invoke the overloaded version of `New` with no parameter – the version that requires a parameter would not be invoked.

The final way we can fix the error is by simply providing a parameter value ourselves from within the New method of the Employee class. To do this, change the Employee class:

```
Public Sub New()
  MyBase.New("George")
  Debug.WriteLine("Employee constructor")
End Sub
```

By explicitly calling the New method of our parent class, we are able to provide it with the required parameter value. At this point our application will compile.

Constructors, Overloading, and Variable Initialization

What isn't clear from this code is that we've now introduced a very insidious bug. The constructor in the Person class is using the Name property to set the value:

```
Public Sub New(ByVal Name As String)
  Me.Name = Name
  Debug.WriteLine("Person constructor")
End Sub
```

But the Name property is overridden by the Employee class, so it is *that* implementation which will be run. Unfortunately that implementation makes use of a Hashtable object which isn't available yet! It turns out that any member variables declared in a class with the New statement, such as our Hashtable object in Employee:

```
Private mcolNames As New Hashtable()
```

won't be initialized until after the constructor for that class has completed. Since we are still in the constructor for Person, there's no way the constructor for Employee can complete. To resolve this, we need to change the Employee class a bit so it doesn't rely on the Hashtable being created in this manner. Instead, we'll add code to create it when needed.

First change the declaration of the variable in the Employee class:

```
Private mcolNames As Hashtable
```

Then update the Name property so it creates the Hashtable object if needed:

```
Public Overloads Property Name(ByVal Type As NameTypes) As String
  Get
    If mcolNames Is Nothing Then mcolNames = New Hashtable()
    Return mcolNames(Type)
  End Get
  Set(ByVal Value As String)
    If mcolNames Is Nothing Then mcolNames = New Hashtable()
    If mcolNames.ContainsKey(NameTypes.Normal) Then
      mcolNames.Item(NameTypes.Normal) = Value
    Else
      mcolNames.Add(Type, Value)
    End If
```

```
      If Type = NameTypes.Normal Then
        MyBase.Name = Value
      End If
    End Set
  End Property
```

This will ensure that a `Hashtable` object is created in the `Employee` class code even though its constructor hasn't yet completed.

More Constructors with Parameters

Obviously we probably don't really want to hard-code a value in a constructor like we did in the `Employee` class, so we may choose instead to change this constructor to also accept a `Name` parameter. Change the `Employee` class constructor as shown:

```
    Public Sub New(ByVal Name As String)
      MyBase.New(Name)
      Debug.WriteLine("Employee constructor")
    End Sub
```

Of course this just pushed the issue deeper – and now we'll find that the `OfficeEmployee` class has a compile error in its `New` method. Again we can fix it by having that method accept a parameter so it can provide it up the chain as required. Make the following change to `OfficeEmployee`:

```
    Public Sub New(ByVal Name As String)
      MyBase.New(Name)
      Debug.WriteLine("OfficeEmployee constructor")
    End Sub
```

Now we find that the code in our form is no longer valid. We're attempting there to create an instance of `OfficeEmployee` without passing a parameter value. Let's update that code and then we can run the application:

```
    Private Sub btnOK_Click(ByVal sender As System.Object, _
        ByVal e As System.EventArgs) Handles btnOK.Click

      Dim objPerson As Employee = New OfficeEmployee("Mary")

      With objPerson
        '.Name = "Fred"
```

We're passing a name value to the constructor of `OfficeEmployee`. Also, we've commented out the line of code that sets the `Name` property directly – meaning that the value we've passed in the constructor will be displayed in our form.

The Protected Scope

We've seen how a subclass automatically gains all the `Public` methods and properties that comprise the interface of the base class. This is also true of `Friend` methods and properties – they are inherited as well, and are available only to other code in the same project as the subclass.

197

`Private` methods and properties are not exposed as part of the interface of the subclass – meaning that our code in the subclass cannot call those methods, nor can any code using our objects. These methods are only available to the code within the base class itself. This can get confusing, since the *implementation* contained in the `Private` methods are inherited and are used by any code in the base class, it is just that they aren't available to be called by any other code – including code in our subclass.

There are times when we want to create methods in our base class that *can* be called by a subclass as well as the base class, but not by code outside of those classes. Basically we want a hybrid between `Public` and `Private` – methods that are private to the classes in our inheritance chain, but are usable by any subclasses that might be created within the chain. This functionality is provided by the `Protected` scope.

`Protected` methods are very similar to `Private` methods, in that they are not available to any code that calls our objects. Instead, these methods are available to code within the base class – *and* to code within any subclass. The following table lists all the available scope options:

Scope	Description
Private	Available only to code within our class
Protected	Available only to classes that inherit from our class
Friend	Available only to code within our project/component
Protected Friend	Available to classes that inherit from our class (in any project) and to code within our project/component. This is a combination of `Protected` and `Friend`
Public	Available to code outside our class

The `Protected` scope can be applied to `Sub`, `Function`, and `Property` methods. To see how the `Protected` scope works, let's add an `Identity` field to the `Person` class:

```
Public Class Person
   Private mstrName As String
   Private mdtBirthDate As String
   Private mstrID As String

   Protected Property Identity() As String
     Get
        Return mstrID
     End Get
     Set(ByVal Value As String)
        mstrID = Value
     End Set
   End Property
```

This data field represents some arbitrary identification number or value assigned to a person. This might be a social security number, an employee number or whatever is appropriate.

The interesting thing about this value is that it is not currently accessible *outside* our inheritance chain. For instance, if we try to use it from our code in the form we'll discover that there is no `Identity` property on our `Person`, `Employee`, or `OfficeEmployee` objects.

However, there is an `Identity` property now available inside our inheritance chain. The `Identity` property is available to the code in the `Person` class just like any other method. The interesting thing is that even though `Identity` is not available to the code in our form, it is available to the code in the `Employee` and `OfficeEmployee` classes. This is because they are both subclasses of `Person`. `Employee` is directly a subclass, and `OfficeEmployee` is indirectly a subclass of `Person` because it is a subclass of `Employee`.

Thus, we can enhance our `Employee` class to implement an `EmployeeNumber` property by using the `Identity` property. To do this, add the following code to the `Employee` class:

```
Public Property EmployeeNumber() As Integer
  Get
    Return CInt(Identity)
  End Get
  Set(ByVal Value As Integer)
    Identity = CStr(Value)
  End Set
End Property
```

This new property exposes a numeric identity value for the employee – but it uses the internal `Identity` property to manage that value.

We can override and shadow `Protected` elements just as we do with elements of any other scope.

Protected Variables

Up to this point we've focused on methods and properties and how they interact through inheritance. Inheritance, and in particular the `Protected` scope, also has an impact on instance variables and how we work with them.

Though it is not recommended, we can declare variables in a class using `Public` scope. This makes the variable directly available to code both within and outside of our class – allowing any code that interacts with our objects to directly read or alter the value of that variable.

Variables can also have `Friend` scope, which likewise allows any code in our class or anywhere within our project to read or alter the value directly. This is also generally not recommended as it breaks encapsulation.

> Rather than declaring variables with **Public** or **Friend** scope it is better to expose the value using a **Property** method so we can apply any of our business rules to control how the value is altered as appropriate.

Of course we know that variables can be of `Private` scope, and this is typically the case. This makes the variables accessible only to the code within our class and is the most restrictive scope.

As with methods however, we can also use the `Protected` scope when declaring variables. This makes the variable accessible to the code in our class, and to the code in any class that derives from our class – all the way down the hierarchy chain.

There are times when this is useful, as it allows us to provide and accept data from subclasses, but act on that data from code in the base class. At the same time, exposing variables to subclasses is typically not ideal and we should use `Property` methods with `Protected` scope for this instead, since they allow our base class to enforce any business rules that are appropriate for the value, rather than just hoping that the author of the subclass only provides us with good values.

Events and Inheritance

So far we've discussed methods, properties, and variables in terms of inheritance – seeing how they can be added, overridden, extended, and shadowed. In VB.NET, events are also part of the interface of an object and they are impacted by inheritance as well.

Inheriting Events

In Chapter 5 we discussed how to declare, raise and receive events from objects. We can add such an event to our `Person` class by declaring it at the top of the class:

```
Public Class Person
   Private mstrName As String
   Private mdtBirthDate As String
   Private mstrID As String

   Public Event NameChanged(ByVal NewName As String)
```

Then we can raise this event within the class any time the person's name is changed:

```
Public Overridable Property Name() As String
  Get
    Return mstrName
  End Get
  Set(ByVal Value As String)
    mstrName = Value
    RaiseEvent NameChanged(mstrName)
  End Set
End Property
```

At this point we can receive and handle this event within our form any time we're working with a `Person` object. The nice thing about this is that our events are inherited automatically by subclasses – meaning that our `Employee` and `OfficeEmployee` objects will also raise this event. Thus, we can change the code in our form to handle the event – even though we're working with an object of type `OfficeEmployee`.

First we can add a method to handle the event to `Form1`:

```
Private Sub OnNameChanged(ByVal NewName As String)
  MsgBox("New name: " & NewName)
End Sub
```

Note that we're not using the `Handles` clause here. In this case, for simplicity, we'll use the `AddHandler` method to dynamically link the event to this method. However, we could have also chosen to use the `WithEvents` and `Handles` keywords as described in Chapter 5 – either way works.

With the handler built, we can use the `AddHandler` method to link this method to the event on our object:

```
Private Sub btnOK_Click(ByVal sender As System.Object, _
    ByVal e As System.EventArgs) Handles btnOK.Click

    Dim objPerson As Employee = New OfficeEmployee("Mary")
    AddHandler objPerson.NameChanged, AddressOf OnNameChanged

    With objPerson
        .Name = "Fred"
```

Also note that we're uncommenting the line that changes the `Name` property. With this change, we know that the event should fire when the name is changed.

When we run the application now, we'll see a message box indicating that the name has changed – and proving that the `NameChanged` event really is exposed and available even though our object is of type `OfficeEmployee` rather than of type `Person`.

Raising Events from Subclasses

One caveat we need to keep in mind is that while a subclass exposes the events of its base class, the code in the subclass cannot raise the event.

In other words, we cannot use the `RaiseEvent` method in `Employee` or `OfficeEmployee` to raise the `NameChanged` event. Only code directly in the `Person` class can raise the event.

To see this in action, let's add another event to the `Person` class – an event that can indicate the change of other arbitrary data values:

```
Public Class Person
    Private mstrName As String
    Private mdtBirthDate As String
    Private mstrID As String

    Public Event NameChanged(ByVal NewName As String)
    Public Event DataChanged(ByVal Field As String, ByVal NewValue As Object)
```

We can then raise this event when the `BirthDate` is changed:

```
Public Overridable Property BirthDate() As Date
    Get
        Return mdtBirthDate
    End Get
    Set(ByVal Value As Date)
        mdtBirthDate = Value
        RaiseEvent DataChanged("BirthDate", Value)
    End Set
End Property
```

It would also be nice to raise this event from the `Employee` class when the `Salary` value is changed. Unfortunately we can't use the `RaiseEvent` method to raise the event from a base class, so the following code won't work (don't enter this code):

```
Public Property Salary() As Double
  Get
    Return mdblSalary
  End Get
  Set(ByVal Value As Double)
    mdblSalary = Value
    RaiseEvent DataChanged("Salary", Value)
  End Set
End Property
```

Fortunately there is a relatively easy way to get around this limitation. We can simply implement a Protected method in our base class that allows any derived class to raise the method. In the Person class we can add such a method:

```
Protected Sub RaiseDataChanged(ByVal Field As String, _
    ByVal NewValue As Object)
  RaiseEvent DataChanged(Field, NewValue)
End Sub
```

Then we can use this method from within the Employee class to indicate that Salary has changed:

```
Public Property Salary() As Double
  Get
    Return mdblSalary
  End Get
  Set(ByVal Value As Double)
    mdblSalary = Value
    RaiseDataChanged("Salary", Value)
  End Set
End Property
```

Notice that the code in Employee is *not* raising the event – it is simply calling a Protected method in Person. It is the code in the Person class that actually raises the event – meaning that all will work as we desire.

We can enhance the code in Form1 to receive the event. First off, we need to create a method to handle the event:

```
Private Sub OnDataChanged(ByVal Field As String, ByVal NewValue As Object)
  MsgBox("New " & Field & ": " & NewValue)
End Sub
```

Then we can link this handler to the event using the AddHandler method:

```
Private Sub btnOK_Click(ByVal sender As System.Object, _
    ByVal e As System.EventArgs) Handles btnOK.Click
  Dim objPerson As Employee = New OfficeEmployee("Mary")
  AddHandler objPerson.NameChanged, AddressOf OnNameChanged
  AddHandler objPerson.DataChanged, AddressOf OnDataChanged
```

Finally we need to make sure we are changing and displaying the Salary property:

```
With objPerson
  .Name = "Fred"
  .Name(NameTypes.Informal) = "Freddy"
  .BirthDate = #1/1/1960#
  .Age = 20
  .Salary = 30000

  txtName.Text = .ToString
  txtBirthDate.Text = Format(.BirthDate, "Short date")
  txtAge.Text = .Age
  txtSalary.Text = Format(.Salary, "0.00")
End With
```

When we run the application and click the button now, we'll get message boxes displaying the changes to the Name property, the BirthDate property (twice – once for the BirthDate property and once for the Age property, which changes the birth date), and now the Salary.

Shared Methods

In Chapter 5 we explored shared methods and how they work – providing a set of methods that can be invoked directly from the class rather than requiring that we create an actual object.

Shared methods are inherited just like instance methods, and so are automatically available as methods on subclasses just as they are on the base class. If we implement a shared method in BaseClass, we can call that method using SubClass or any other class derived from BaseClass.

Like a regular method, shared methods can be overloaded and shadowed. They cannot, however, be overridden. If we attempt to use the Overridable keyword when declaring a Shared method we will get a syntax error.

For instance, we can implement a method in our Person class to compare two Person objects:

```
Public Shared Function Compare(ByVal Person1 As Person, _
    ByVal Person2 As Person) As Boolean

  Return (Person1.Name = Person2.Name)

End Function
```

To test this method, let's add another button to our form, name it btnCompare and set its Text value to Compare. Double-click on the button to bring up the code window and enter the following code:

```
Private Sub btnCompare_Click(ByVal sender As System.Object, _
    ByVal e As System.EventArgs) Handles btnCompare.Click
  Dim emp1 As New Employee("Fred")
  Dim emp2 As New Employee("Mary")

  MsgBox(Employee.Compare(emp1, emp2))
End Sub
```

This code simply creates two `Employee` objects and compares them. Note though, that the code uses the `Employee` class to invoke the `Compare` method – displaying the result in a message box. This establishes that the `Compare` method implemented in the `Person` class is inherited by the `Employee` class as we'd expect.

Overloading Shared Methods

Shared methods can be overloaded using the `Overloads` keyword in the same manner as we overload an instance method. This means our subclass can add new implementations of the shared method as long as the parameter list differs from the original implementation.

For example, we can add a new implementation of the `Compare` method to `Employee`:

```
Public Overloads Shared Function Compare(ByVal Employee1 As Employee, _
    ByVal Employee2 As Employee) As Boolean

  Return (Employee1.EmployeeNumber = Employee2.EmployeeNumber)

End Function
```

This new implementation compares two `Employee` objects rather than two `Person` objects – and in fact compares them based on employee number rather than by name.

We can enhance the code behind `btnCompare` in the form to set the `EmployeeNumber` properties:

```
Private Sub btnCompare_Click(ByVal sender As System.Object, _
    ByVal e As System.EventArgs) Handles btnCompare.Click
  Dim emp1 As New Employee("Fred")
  Dim emp2 As New Employee("Mary")

  emp1.EmployeeNumber = 1
  emp2.EmployeeNumber = 1

  MsgBox(Employee.Compare(emp1, emp2))
End Sub
```

While it might make little sense for these two objects to have the same `EmployeeNumber` value – it will prove a point. When we run the application now, even though the names values of the objects are different, our `Compare` routine will return `True` – proving that we're invoking the overloaded version of the method that expects two `Employee` objects as parameters.

The overloaded implementation is available on the `Employee` class or any classes derived from `Employee` such as `OfficeEmployee`. The overloaded implementation is not available if called directly from `Person`, since that class only contains the original implementation.

Shadowing Shared Methods

Shared methods can also be shadowed by a subclass. This allows us to do some very interesting things – including converting a shared method into an instance method or vice versa. We can even leave the method as shared, but change the entire way it works and is declared. In short, just as with instance methods, we can use the `Shadows` keyword to entirely replace and change a shared method in a subclass.

To see how this works, we can use the Shadows keyword to change the nature of the Compare method in OfficeEmployee:

```
Public Shared Shadows Function Compare(ByVal Person1 As Person, _
    ByVal Person2 As Person) As Boolean

  Return (Person1.Age = Person2.Age)

End Function
```

Notice that this method has the same signature as the original Compare method we implemented in the Person class, but instead of comparing by name, here we're comparing by age. With a normal method we could have done this by overriding, but since Shared methods can't be overridden the only thing we can do is shadow it.

Of course the shadowed implementation is only available via the OfficeEmployee class. Neither the Person nor Employee classes, which are higher up the inheritance chain, are aware that this shadowed version of the method exists.

To use this from our Form1 code we can change the code for btnCompare as follows:

```
Private Sub btnCompare_Click(ByVal sender As System.Object, _
    ByVal e As System.EventArgs) Handles btnCompare.Click
  Dim emp1 As New Employee("Fred")
  Dim emp2 As New Employee("Mary")

  emp1.Age = 20
  emp2.Age = 25

  MsgBox(OfficeEmployee.Compare(emp1, emp2))
End Sub
```

Instead of setting the EmployeeNumber values, we're now setting the Age values on our objects. More importantly, notice that we're now calling the Compare method via the OfficeEmployee class rather than via Employee or Person. This causes the invocation of our new version of the method – and so the ages of the objects are compared.

Shared Events

As we discussed in Chapter 5, we can create shared events – events that can be raised by shared or instance methods in a class, whereas regular events can only be raised from within instance methods.

When we inherit from a class that defines a shared event, our new subclass automatically gains that event just like it does with regular events as we discussed earlier in this chapter.

As with instance events, a shared event cannot be raised by code within our subclass – it can only be raised using the RaiseEvent keyword from code in the class where the event is declared. If we want to be able to raise the event from methods in our subclass, we need to implement a Protected method on the base class that actually makes the call to RaiseEvent.

This is no different from what we discussed earlier in the chapter other than to note that with a shared event we can use a method with protected scope that is marked as shared to raise the event rather than using an instance method.

Creating an Abstract Base Class

So far, we've seen how to inherit from a class, how to overload and override methods, and how virtual methods work. In all of our examples so far, the parent classes have been useful in their own right and could be instantiated and do some meaningful work. Sometimes, however, we want to create a class such that it can only be used as a base class for inheritance.

MustInherit Keyword

Our current Person class is not only being used as a base class, but it can also be instantiated directly to create an object of type Person. Likewise, our Employee class is also being used as a base class for the OfficeEmployee class we created that derives from it.

If we want to make a class *only* act as a base class we can use the MustInherit keyword – thereby preventing anyone from creating objects based directly on the class and requiring them instead to create a subclass and then create objects based on that subclass.

This can be very useful when we are creating object models of real-world concepts and entities and is something we'll discuss in more detail in Chapter 7.

We can change Person to use the MustInherit keyword:

```
Public MustInherit Class Person
```

This has no effect on the code within Person or any of the classes that inherit from it. However, it does mean no code can instantiate objects directly from the Person class – instead we can only create objects based on Employee or OfficeEmployee.

Keep in mind that this doesn't prevent us from declaring variables of type Person – it merely prevents us from creating an object by using New Person(). We can also continue to make use of Shared methods from the Person class without any difficulty.

MustOverride Keyword

Another option we have is to create a method (Sub, Function, or Property) that must be overridden by a subclass. We might want to do this when we are creating a base class that provides some behaviors, but relies on subclasses to also provide some behaviors in order to function properly. This is accomplished by using the MustOverride keyword on a method declaration.

If a class contains any methods marked with MustOverride, the class itself must also be declared with the MustInhert keyword or we'll get a syntax error:

```
Public MustInherit Class Person
```

This makes sense, since if we're requiring that a method be overridden in a subclass it only stands to reason that our class can't be directly instantiated but rather must be subclassed to be useful.

Let's see how this works by adding a LifeExpectancy method in Person that has no implementation and must be overridden by a subclass:

```
Public MustOverride Function LifeExpectancy() As Integer
```

Notice that there is no End Function or any other code associated with the method.

When using MustOverride, we cannot provide any implementation for the method in our class. Such a method is called an **abstract method** or **pure virtual function**, since it only defines the interface and no implementation.

Methods declared in this manner *must* be overridden in any subclass that inherits from our base class. If we don't override one of these methods, we'll generate a syntax error in the subclass and it won't compile.

This means we need to alter the Employee class to provide an implementation for this method:

```
Public Overrides Function LifeExpectancy() As Integer
  Return 90
End Function
```

Our application will compile and run at this point, since we are now overriding the LifeExpectancy method in Employee and so the required condition is met.

Abstract Base Classes

We can combine these two concepts – using both MustInherit and MustOverride – to create something called an **abstract base class**. Sometimes this is also referred to as a **virtual class**.

This is a class that provides no implementation, only the interface definitions from which a subclass can be created. An example might be as follows:

```
Public MustInherit Class AbstractBaseClass
  Public MustOverride Sub DoSomething()
  Public MustOverride Sub DoOtherStuff()
End Class
```

This technique can be very useful when creating frameworks or the high-level conceptual elements of a system. Any class that inherits AbstractBaseClass must implement both DoSomething and DoOtherStuff or a syntax error will result.

In some ways an abstract base class is very comparable to defining an interface using the Interface keyword. We'll discuss the Interface keyword in detail later in this chapter.

We could define the same interface as shown in this example with the following code:

```
Public Interface IAbstractBaseClass
  Sub DoSomething()
  Sub DoOtherStuff()
End Interface
```

Any class that implements the IAbstractBaseClass interface must implement both DoSomething and DoOtherStuff or a syntax error will result – and in that regard this technique is similar to an abstract base class.

There are differences, however. In particular, when we create a new class by subclassing the AbstractBase class, that class can in turn be subclassed. All classes derived from this base class will automatically have DoSomething and DoOtherStuff methods as part of their interface. The first non-abstract class in the inheritance chain (the first one not declared using MustInherits) will need to provide implementations for these methods. All subsequent subclasses will automatically get both the interface and implementation for the methods due to the nature of inheritance.

Contrast this with the interface approach, where each individual class must independently implement the IAbstractBase interface *and* provide its own implementation of the two methods. The implementation code in one class is never inherited by other classes that implement this interface. If we never intend to reuse the code that implements these methods as we create new classes then the interface approach is fine, but if we want code reuse within subclasses inheritance is the way to go.

Preventing Inheritance

If we want to prevent a class from being used as a base class we can use the NotInheritable keyword. For instance, we can change our OfficeEmployee as follows:

```
Public NotInheritable Class OfficeEmployee
```

At this point it is no longer possible to inherit from this class to create a new class. Our OfficeEmployee class is now **sealed** – meaning that it cannot be used as a base from which to create other classes.

If we attempt to inherit from OfficeEmployee we'll get a compile error indicating that it cannot be used as a base class. This has no effect on Person or Employee – we can continue to derive other classes from them.

Typically, we'll want to design our classes such that they can be subclassed, as that provides the greatest long-term flexibility in our overall design. There are times, however, when we will want to make sure that our class cannot be used as a base class and the NotInheritable keyword addresses that issue.

Multiple Interfaces

In VB.NET our objects can have one or more interfaces. All objects have a primary or native interface, which is composed of any methods, properties, events, or member variables declared using the Public keyword. Objects can also implement secondary interfaces in addition to their native interface by using the Implements keyword.

> *VB6 also had the concept of multiple interfaces, though the way we implemented them was not particularly intuitive or clear. The concept remains the same in VB.NET, but the syntax we use to define and implement interfaces is very clear and understandable.*

Object Interfaces

The native interface on any class is composed of all the methods, properties, events, or even variables that are declared as anything other than Private. Though this is nothing new, let's quickly review what is included in the native interface to set the stage for discussing secondary interfaces.

To include a method as part of our interface we can simply declare a `Public` routine:

```
Public Sub AMethod()

End Sub
```

Notice that there is no code in this routine. Any code would be *implementation* and is not part of the interface. Only the declaration of the method is important when we're discussing interfaces. This can seem confusing at first, but it is an important distinction since separation of the interface from its implementation is at the very core of object-oriented programming and design.

Since this method is declared as `Public` it is available to any code outside our class – including other applications that may make use of our assembly.

If our method has a property we can declare it as part of our interface by using the `Property` keyword:

```
Public Property AProperty() As String

End Property
```

We can also declare events as part of our interface by using the `Event` keyword:

```
Public Event AnEvent()
```

Finally, we can include actual variables, or attributes, as part of our interface:

```
Public AnInteger As Integer
```

This is strongly discouraged, as it directly exposes our internal variables for use by code outside our class. Since the variable is directly accessible from other code, we give up any and all control over the way the value may be changed or by which code it may be accessed.

Rather than making any variable `Public`, it is far preferable to make use of a `Property` method to expose the value. In that way we can implement code to ensure that our internal variable is only set to valid values and that only appropriate code has access to the value based on our application's logic.

Using the Native Interface

In the end, the **native** (or primary) **interface** for any class is defined by looking at all the methods, properties, events, and variables that are declared as anything other than `Private` in scope. This includes any methods, properties, events or variables that are inherited from a base class.

We're used to interacting with the default interface on most objects, and so this will seem pretty straightforward. Consider a simple class:

```
Public Class TheClass
  Public Sub DoSomething()

  End Sub
```

```
    Public Sub DoSomethingElse()

    End Sub
End Class
```

This defines a class, and by extension also defines the native interface that is exposed by any objects we instantiate based on this class. The native interface defines two methods, DoSomething and DoSomethingElse. To make use of these methods, we simply call them:

```
Dim myObject As New TheClass()

myObject.DoSomething()
myObject.DoSomethingElse()
```

This is the same thing we've been doing in Chapter 5 and so far in this chapter. However, let's take a look at creating and using secondary interfaces, as they are a bit different.

Secondary Interfaces

Sometimes it can be helpful for an object to have more than one interface – thus allowing us to interact with the object in different ways.

Inheritance allows us to create subclasses that *are* a specialized case of the base class. For example, our Employee *is-a* Person.

However, there are times when we have a group of objects that are not the same thing, but we want to be able to treat them as though they were the same. We want all these objects to *act-as* the same thing – even though they are all different.

For instance, we may have a series of different objects in an application – product, customer, invoice and so forth. Each of these would have default interfaces appropriate to each individual object – and each of them *is-a* different class – there's no natural inheritance relationship implied between these classes. At the same time, we may need to be able to generate a printed document for each type of object. So we'd like to make them all *act-as* a printable object.

> *We'll discuss the* is-a *and* act-as *relationships in more detail in Chapter 7.*

To accomplish this we can define a generic interface that would enable generating such a printed document – we can call it IPrintableObject.

> **By convention, this type of interface is typically prefixed with a capital I to indicate that it is a formal interface.**

Each of our application objects can choose to implement the IPrintableObject interface. Every object that implements this interface must provide code to provide actual *implementation* of the interface – which is unlike inheritance, where the code from a base class is automatically reused.

By implementing this common interface, however, we are able to write a routine that accepts any object that implements the `IPrintableObject` interface and print it – totally oblivious to the "real" data type of the object or the methods its native interface might expose.

Before we see how to use an interface in this manner, let's walk through the process of actually defining an interface.

Defining the Interface

We define a formal interface using the `Interface` keyword. This can be done in any code module in our project, but a good place to put this type of definition is in a standard module. An interface defines a set of methods (`Sub`, `Function`, or `Property`) and events that must be exposed by any class that chooses to implement the interface.

Add a module to the project using **Project | Add Module** and name it `Interfaces.vb`. Then add the following code to the module – outside the `Module` code block itself:

```
Public Interface IPrintableObject

End Interface

Module Interfaces

End Module
```

A code module can contain a number of interface definitions, and these definitions must exist outside any other code block. Thus, they don't go within a `Class` or `Module` block – they are at a peer level to those constructs.

Interfaces must be declared using either `Public` or `Friend` scope. Declaring a `Private` or `Protected` interface will result in a syntax error.

Within the `Interface` block of code, we can define the methods, properties and events that will make up our particular interface. Since the scope of the interface is defined by the Interface declaration itself, we can't specify scopes for individual methods and events – they are all scoped the same as the interface itself.

For instance, add the following code:

```
Public Interface IPrintableObject
    Function Label(ByVal Index As Integer) As String
    Function Value(ByVal Index As Integer) As String
    ReadOnly Property Count() As Integer
End Interface
```

This defines a new data type – somewhat like creating a class or structure – that we can use when declaring variables.

For instance, we can now declare a variable of type `IPrintableObject`:

```
Private objPrintable As IPrintableObject
```

211

We can also have our classes implement this interface – which will require each class to provide implementation code for each of the three methods defined on the interface.

Before we implement the interface in a class, let's see how we can make use of the interface to write a generic routine that can print any object that does implement IPrintableObject.

Using the Interface

Interfaces define the methods and events (including parameters and data types), which an object is required to implement if they choose to support the interface. This means that, given just the interface definition, we can easily write code that can interact with *any* object that implements the interface – even though we don't know what the native data types of those objects will be.

To see how we can write such code, let's create a simple routine in our form that can display data to the Output window in the IDE from any object that implements IPrintableObject. Bring up the code window for our form and add the following routine:

```
Public Sub PrintObject(TheObject As IPrintableObject)
   Dim intIndex As Integer

   For intIndex = 1 To TheObject.Count
     Debug.Write(TheObject.Label(intIndex) & ": ")
     Debug.WriteLine(TheObject.Value(intIndex))
   Next
End Sub
```

Notice that we're accepting a parameter of type IPrintableObject. This is how secondary interfaces are used – by treating an object of one type as though it was actually of the interface type. As long as the object passed to this routine implements the IPrintableObject interface, our code will work fine.

Within the PrintObject routine we're assuming that the object will implement three elements – Count, Label, and Value – as part of the IPrintableObject interface. Secondary interfaces can include methods, properties, and events – much like a default interface – but the interface itself is defined and implemented using some special syntax.

Now that we have a generic printing routine, we need a way to call it. Bring up the designer for Form1 and add a button and name it btnPrint. Double-click the button and put this code behind it:

```
Private Sub btnPrint_Click(ByVal sender As System.Object, _
    ByVal e As System.EventArgs) Handles btnPrint.Click
   Dim obj As New Employee("Andy")

   obj.EmployeeNumber = 123
   obj.BirthDate = #1/1/1980#
   obj.HireDate = #1/1/1996#

   PrintObject(obj)
End Sub
```

This code simply initializes an Employee object and calls the PrintObject routine.

Of course when we try to run this code we'll get a runtime error when trying to call `PrintObject`. `PrintObject` is expecting a parameter that implements `IPrintableObject` – and `Employee` implements no such interface.

If we use `Option Strict On` this will show up as a compile-time error, allowing us to catch the problem earlier in the development cycle.

Let's move on and implement that interface in `Employee` so we can see how it works.

Implementing the Interface

Any class (other than an abstract base class) can implement an interface by using the `Implements` keyword. For instance, we can implement our `IPrintableObject` interface in `Employee` by adding the following line:

```
Public Class Employee
    Inherits Person
    Implements IPrintableObject
```

This will cause the interface to be exposed by any object created as an instance of `Employee`. Of course this doesn't actually implement the interface, it just declares that we will implement it. In fact, we now have a compile error showing in the IDE, because we haven't implemented the methods and properties defined by the interface.

> **To implement an interface, we must implement *all* the methods and properties defined by that interface.**

Before we actually implement the interface, however, let's create an array to contain the labels for our data fields so we can return them via our `IPrintableObject` interface. Add the following code to the `Employee` class:

```
Public Class Employee
    Inherits Person
    Implements IPrintableObject

    Private marLabels() As String = {"ID", "Age", "HireDate"}
    Private mdtHireDate As Date
    Private mdblSalary As Double
```

To implement the interface we need to create methods and properties with the same parameter and return data types as those defined in the interface. The actual names of each method or property don't matter, because we'll be using the `Implements` keyword to link our internal method names to the external method names defined by the interface. As long as the method signatures match we are all set.

This applies to scope as well. Although the interface and its methods and properties are publicly available, we don't have to declare our actual methods and properties as `Public`. In many cases we may implement them as `Private` so they don't become part of our native interface and are only exposed via the secondary interface.

However, if we do have a `Public` method with a method signature we can use it to implement a method from the interface. This has the interesting side effect of having this method provide implementation for both a method on the object's native interface *and* on the secondary interface.

In this case we'll use a `Private` method so it is only providing implementation for the `IPrintableObject` interface. We can implement the `Label` method by adding the following code to `Employee`:

```
Private Function Label(ByVal Index As Integer) As String _
    Implements IPrintableObject.Label
  Return marLabels(Index - 1)
End Function
```

This is just a regular `Private` method that returns a `String` value. We're subtracting 1 from the `Index` value to make it appear as though our data set is 1-based rather than 0-based.

The interesting thing is that we've added the `Implements` clause to the method declaration.

```
Private Function Label(ByVal Index As Integer) As String _
    Implements IPrintableObject.Label
```

By using the `Implements` keyword in this fashion, we're indicating that this particular method is the implementation for the `Label` method on the `IPrintableObject` interface. The actual name of our private method could be anything – it is the use of the `Implements` clause that makes this work. The only requirement is that the parameter data types and the return value data type must match those defined by the `IPrintableObject` interface.

This is very similar to using the `Handles` clause to indicate which method should handle an event. In fact, like the `Handles` clause, the `Implements` clause allows us to have a comma-separated list of interface methods that should be implemented by this one function.

We can then move on to implement the other three elements defined by the `IPrintableObject` interface by adding this code to `Employee`:

```
Private Function Value(ByVal Index As Integer) As String _
    Implements IPrintableObject.Value
  Select Case Index
    Case 1
      Return EmployeeNumber()
    Case 2
      Return Age()
    Case 3
      Return Format(HireDate(), "Short date")
  End Select
End Function

Private ReadOnly Property Count() As Integer _
    Implements IPrintableObject.Count
  Get
    Return UBound(marLabels) + 1
```

```
      End Get
   End Property
```

The `Value` method returns the value based on the `Index` value, while `Count` returns the number of data elements available – again adding 1 to make it appear that our data list is 1-based like a Collection.

We can now run this application and click on the button. The Output window in the IDE will display our results – showing the ID, age, and hire date values as appropriate:

```
Output                                    ⊠
Debug                                      ▼
   ID: 123                                 ▲
   Age: 22
   HireDate: 01/01/1996                    ▼
   ◄                                    ►   //
```

Any object could create a similar implementation behind the `IPrintableObject` interface, and the `PrintObject` routine in our form would continue to work – regardless of the native data type of the object itself.

Reusing Common Implementation

Secondary interfaces provide a guarantee that all objects implementing a given interface will have exactly the same methods and events – including the same parameters. However, as we've seen, we must manually implement the behaviors to within each individual class in order to make the interface actually do anything.

Where with inheritance we automatically gain the reuse of existing code from the base class, with secondary interfaces there is virtually no inherent reuse of code within our classes.

The `Implements` clause links our actual implementation to a specific method on an interface. For instance, our `Value` method is linked to `IPrintableObject.Label` using this clause:

```
Private Function Value(ByVal Index As Integer) As String _
    Implements IPrintableObject.Value
```

Sometimes our method might be able to serve as the implementation for more than one method – either on the same interface or on different interfaces.

Add the following interface definition to `Interfaces.vb`:

```
Public Interface IValues
   Function GetValue(ByVal Idx As Integer) As String
End Interface
```

This interface defines just one method, `GetValue`. Notice that it defines a single `Integer` parameter and a return type of `String` – the same as the `Value` method from `IPrintableObject`. Even though the method name and parameter variable name don't match, what counts here is that the parameter and return value data types do match.

215

Now bring up the code window for Employee. We'll have it implement this new interface in addition to the IPrintableObject interface:

```
Public Class Employee
   Inherits Person
   Implements IPrintableObject
   Implements IValues
```

We already have a method that returns values. Rather than re-implementing that method, it would be nice to just link this new GetValues method to our existing method. We can easily do this because the Implements clause allows us to provide a comma-separated list of method names:

```
Private Function Value(ByVal Index As Integer) As String _
    Implements IPrintableObject.Value, IValues.GetValue
  Select Case Index
    Case 1
      Return EmployeeNumber()
    Case 2
      Return Age()
    Case 3
      Return Format(HireDate(), "Short date")
  End Select
End Function
```

This is very similar to the use of the Handles keyword as we discussed in Chapter 5. A single method within our class, regardless of scope or name, can be used to implement any number of methods as defined by other interfaces as long as the data types of the parameters and return values all match.

Summary

In this chapter and in Chapter 5 we've seen how VB.NET allows us to create and work with classes and objects. VB.NET provides the building blocks for abstraction, encapsulation, polymorphism and inheritance.

In this chapter we've seen how to create both simple base classes as well as abstract base classes. We've also explored how we can define formal interfaces, a concept quite similar to an abstract base class in many ways.

We've also walked through the process of subclassing – creating a new class that derives both interface and implementation from a base class. The subclass can be extended by adding new methods or altering the behavior of existing methods on the base class.

VB.NET provides us with all the capabilities we need to build robust and sophisticated object-oriented applications. In the next chapter we'll pull this all together by discussing abstraction, encapsulation, polymorphism, and inheritance as they pertain to building practical software.

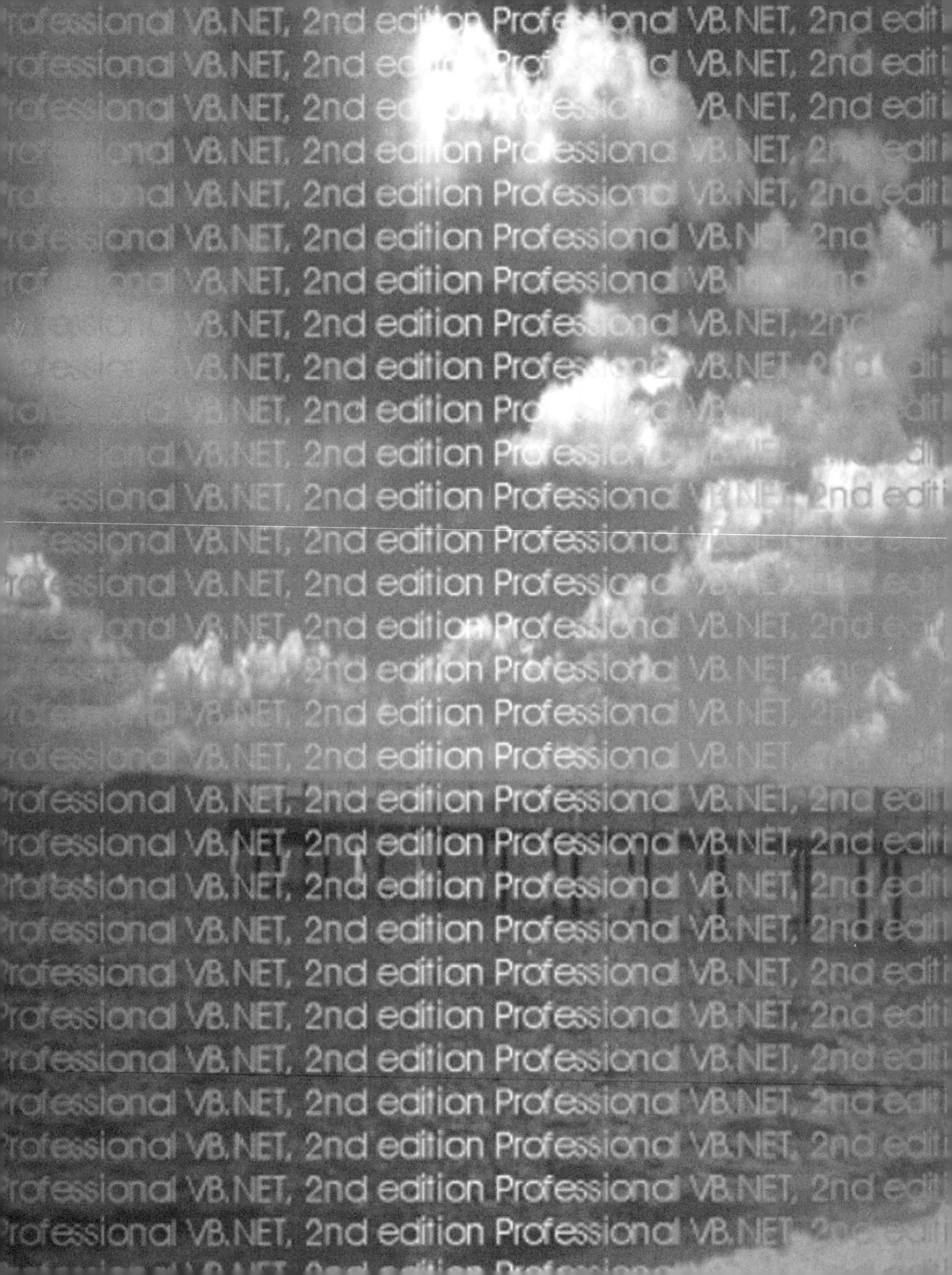
Professional VB.NET, 2nd edition

Applying Objects and Components

In Chapters 5 and 6, we explored the syntax provided by VB.NET for working with objects, creating classes, and implementing both inheritance and multiple interfaces. These are all powerful tools, providing us with the ability to create very maintainable and readable code – even for extremely complex applications.

However, just knowing the syntax and learning the tools is not enough to be successful. To successfully apply the object-oriented capabilities of VB.NET to create applications requires an understanding of object-oriented programming, which is the application of the theory we've covered in Chapters 5 and 6.

In this chapter we'll take the syntax we discussed in Chapters 5 and 6 and we'll see how it allows us to build object-oriented applications. We'll further discuss the four major object-oriented concepts – abstraction, encapsulation, polymorphism, and inheritance – that we defined in Chapter 5.

We'll understand how these concepts can be applied in our design and development to create effective object-oriented applications.

Abstraction

Abstraction, which Visual Basic has supported since version 4, is the process by which we can think about specific properties or behaviors without thinking about a particular object that has those properties or behaviors. Abstraction is merely the ability of a language to create "black box" code – to take a concept and create an abstract representation of that concept within a program.

A Customer object, for example, is an abstract representation of a real-world customer. A DataSet object is an abstract representation of a set of data.

Abstraction allows us to recognize how things are similar and to ignore differences – to think in general terms, and not the specifics. A text box control is an abstraction, because we can place it on a form, and then tailor it to our needs by setting properties. Visual Basic allows us to define abstractions using classes.

Any language that allows a developer to create a class from which objects can be instantiated meets this criterion, and Visual Basic is no exception. We can easily create a class to represent a customer, essentially providing an abstraction. We can then create instances of that class, where each object can have its own attributes such that it represents a specific customer.

In VB.NET we implement abstraction by creating a class using the Class keyword. Bring up VS.NET, and create a new VB.NET Windows Application project. Once the project is open, add a new class to the project using the **Project | Add Class** menu option. Name the new class Customer and add some code to make this class represent a real-world customer in an abstract sense:

```
Public Class Customer
    Private mgID As Guid = Guid.NewGuid
    Private mstrName As String
    Private mstrPhone As String

    Public Property ID() As Guid
      Get
        Return mgID
      End Get
      Set(ByVal Value As Guid)
        mgID = Value
      End Set
    End Property

    Public Property Name() As String
      Get
        Return mstrName
      End Get
      Set(ByVal Value As String)
        mstrName = Value
      End Set
    End Property

    Public Property Phone() As String
      Get
        Return mstrPhone
      End Get
      Set(ByVal Value As String)
        mstrPhone = Value
      End Set
    End Property
End Class
```

We know that a real customer is a lot more complex than an ID, name, and phone number. Yet at the same time, we know that in an abstract sense, our customers really do have names and phone numbers, and that we assign them unique ID numbers to keep track of them. Thus, given an ID, name, and phone number we know which customer we're dealing with and so we have a perfectly valid abstraction of a customer within our application.

We can then use this abstract representation of a customer from within our code. To do this, open the designer for Form1 and add three text box controls to the form. Then add the following code to the form. First off, we'll declare a variable and create a Customer object:

```
Public Class Form1
   Inherits System.Windows.Forms.Form

   Private mobjCustomer As New Customer()
```

Then, when the form is loaded we'll display the customer data in the text box controls:

```
   Private Sub Form1_Load(ByVal sender As System.Object, _
       ByVal e As System.EventArgs) Handles MyBase.Load

     TextBox1.DataBindings.Add("Text", mobjCustomer, "ID")
     TextBox2.DataBindings.Add("Text", mobjCustomer, "Name")
     TextBox3.DataBindings.Add("Text", mobjCustomer, "Phone")

   End Sub
```

We're using the ability of Windows Forms to data bind to a property on an object – in this case, we're binding our three text box controls' Text properties to the ID, Name, and Phone properties of our mobjCustomer object. (We'll learn more about data binding in Chapter 16.)

This code should work, but we will get a null exception error when we run the application. This appears to be because instance variables are not properly initialized prior to data binding. We can work around this by initializing the values by hand – either in the form's Load event before we data bind, or within the classes themselves. Adding the code to the class will have the least overall impact, so let's do that. In the Customer class, where we declare the mstrName instance variable, change the code to initialize it as well:

```
     Private mstrName As String = ""
```

Also, in the Customer class where we declare the mstrPhone variable we'll need to initialize it:

```
     Private mstrPhone As String = ""
```

Now we have a simple UI that both displays and updates the data in our Customer object – with that object providing the UI developer with an abstract representation of the customer. When we run the application we'll see a display similar to the following:

Here we've displayed the pre-generated ID value, and have entered values for Name and Phone directly into the form.

Encapsulation

Perhaps the most important of the object-oriented concepts is that of **encapsulation**. Encapsulation is the concept that an object should totally separate its interface from its implementation. All the data and implementation code for an object should be entirely hidden behind its interface. Another way to put this is that an object should be a **black box**.

The idea is that we can create an interface (by creating public methods in a class) and, as long as that interface remains consistent, the application can interact with our objects. This remains true even if we entirely rewrite the code within a given method. The interface is independent of the implementation.

Encapsulation allows us to hide the internal implementation details of a class. For example, the algorithm we use to find prime numbers might be proprietary. We can expose a simple API to the end user, but we hide all of the logic used in our algorithm by encapsulating it within our class.

This means that an object should completely contain any data it requires, and that it should also contain all the code required to manipulate that data. Programs should interact with an object through an interface, using the properties and methods of the object. Client code should never work directly with the data owned by the object.

> Programs interact with objects by sending messages to the object that indicate which method or property they'd like to have invoked. These messages are generated by other objects, or by external sources such as the user. The object reacts to these messages through methods or properties.

Visual Basic has provided full support for encapsulation through class modules since version 4.0. Using these modules, we can create classes that entirely hide their internal data and code, providing a well-established interface of properties and methods to the outside world.

Let's look at the following example. Add the following class to our project, the code defines its native interface:

```
Public Class Encapsulation
    Public Function DistanceTo(ByVal X As Single, Y As Single) As Single

    End Function
```

```
    Public Property CurrentX() As Single
      Get

      End Get
      Set(ByVal Value As Single)

      End Set
    End Property

    Public Property CurrentY() As Single
      Get

      End Get
      Set(ByVal Value As Single)

      End Set
    End Property
End Class
```

This creates an interface for the class. At this point we can write client code to interact with the class, since from a client perspective all we care about is the interface. Bring up the designer for `Form1` and add a button to the form, then write the following code behind the button:

```
    Private Sub Button1_Click(ByVal sender As System.Object, _
                        ByVal e As System.EventArgs) _
                        Handles button1.Click
        Dim obj As New Encapsulation()
        MsgBox(obj.DistanceTo(10, 10))
    End Sub
```

Even though we have no actual code in our `Encapsulation` class, we can still write code to *use* that class because the interface is defined.

This is a powerful idea, since it means that we can rapidly create class interfaces against which other developers can create the UI or other parts of the application – while we are still creating the implementation behind the interface.

From here, we could do virtually anything we like in terms of implementing the class. For example, we could use the values to calculate a direct distance:

```
    Imports System.Math

    Public Class Encapsulation
        Private msngX As Single
        Private msngY As Single

        Public Function DistanceTo(ByVal X As Single, Y As Single) As Single
            Return Sqrt((X - msngX) ^ 2 + (Y - msngY) ^ 2)
        End Function

        Public Property CurrentX() As Single
          Get
```

```
          Return msngX
      End Get
      Set(ByVal Value As Single)
        msngX = Value
      End Set
  End Property

  Public Property CurrentY() As Single
      Get
          Return msngY
      End Get
      Set(ByVal Value As Single)
        msngY = Value
      End Set
  End Property
End Class
```

Now when we run the application and click the button we'll get a meaningful value as a result:

Where encapsulation comes to the fore however, is that we can change the *implementation* without changing the *interface*. For example, we can change the distance calculation to find the distance between the points (assuming no diagonal travel is allowed):

```
  Public Function DistanceTo(ByVal X As Single, ByVal Y As Single) As Single
      Return Abs(X - msngX) + Abs(Y - msngY)
  End Function
```

This results in the following result being displayed if the program is run and we click the button:

We haven't changed the interface of the class, and so our client program working has no idea that we have switched from one implementation to the other. We have achieved a total change of behavior without any change to the client code. This is the essence of encapsulation.

Of course, the user might have a problem if we made such a change to our object. If applications were developed expecting the first set of behaviors, and then we changed to the second, there could be some interesting side effects. However, the key point is that the client programs would continue to function, even if the results were quite different from when we started.

Polymorphism

Polymorphism is often considered to be directly tied to inheritance (which we'll discuss next). In reality, however, it's largely independent. Polymorphism means that we can have two classes with different implementations or code, but with a common set of methods, properties or events. We can then write a program that operates upon that interface and doesn't care about which type of object it operates at runtime.

Method Signatures

To properly understand polymorphism we need to explore the concept of a **method signature**, also sometimes called a prototype. All methods have a signature, which is defined by the method's name and the data types of its parameters. We might have code such as this:

```
Public Function CalculateValue() As Integer

End Sub
```

In this example, the signature is:

f()

If we add a parameter to the method the signature will change. For example, we could change the method to accept a `Double`:

```
Public Function CalculateValue(Value As Double) As Integer
```

Then the signature of the method is:

f(Double)

Polymorphism merely says that we should be able to write some client code that calls methods on an object – and as long as the object provides our methods with the method signatures we expect, we don't care which class the object was created from. Let's look at some examples of polymorphism within VB.NET.

Implementing Polymorphism

We can use several techniques to achieve polymorphic behavior:

- ❏ Late binding
- ❏ Multiple interfaces
- ❏ .NET Reflection
- ❏ Inheritance

Late binding actually allows us to implement "pure" polymorphism – although at the cost of performance and ease of programming. Through multiple interfaces and inheritance we can also achieve polymorphism with much better performance and ease of programming. Reflection allows us to use either late binding or multiple interfaces, but against objects created in a very dynamic way – even going so far as to dynamically load a DLL into our application at runtime so we can use its classes.

We'll walk through each of these options to see how they are implemented and to explore their pros and cons.

Polymorphism through Late Binding

Typically when we interact with objects in VB.NET, we are interacting with them through strongly typed variables. For example, in Form1 we interacted with the Encapsulation object with the following code:

```
Private Sub Button1_Click(ByVal sender As System.Object, _
    ByVal e As System.EventArgs) Handles button1.Click

  Dim obj As New Encapsulation()

  MsgBox(obj.DistanceTo(10, 10))
End Sub
```

The obj variable is declared using a specific type (Encapsulation) – meaning it is strongly typed, or **early bound**.

We can also interact with objects that are **late bound**. Late binding means that our object variable has no specific data type, but rather is of type Object. VB.NET treats the Object data type in a special way – allowing us to attempt arbitrary method calls against the object even though the Object data type doesn't implement those methods.

For example, we could change the code in Form1 to be late bound as follows:

```
Private Sub Button1_Click(ByVal sender As System.Object, _
    ByVal e As System.EventArgs) Handles Button1.Click

  Dim obj As Object = New Encapsulation()

  MsgBox(obj.DistanceTo(10, 10))
End Sub
```

When this code is run, we'll get the same result as we did before – even though the Object data type has no DistanceTo method as part of its interface. The late binding mechanism, behind the scenes, dynamically determines the real type of our object and invokes the appropriate method.

> This code requires Option Strict Off in the file containing the code that is calling the objects. This is the case by default, but is required when using late binding.

When we work with objects through late binding, neither the **VB.NET IDE** nor the compiler can tell if we are or are not calling a valid method. In this case, there is no way for the compiler to know that the object referenced by our `obj` variable actually has a `DistanceTo` method. It just assumes we know what we're talking about and compiles the code.

Then at run time, when the code is actually invoked it will attempt to dynamically call the `DistanceTo` method. If that is a valid method our code will work, if it is not we'll get an error.

Obviously there is a level of danger when using late binding, since a simple typo can introduce errors that can only be discovered when the application is actually run. However, there is also a lot of flexibility, since code that makes use of late binding can talk to *any* object from *any* class as long as those objects implement the methods we require.

However, there is also a substantial performance penalty for using late binding. The existence of each method is discovered dynamically at run-time, and that discovery takes time. Additionally, the mechanism used to invoke a method through late binding is not nearly as efficient as the mechanism used to call a method that is known at compile-time.

To make this clearer, we can change the code in `Form1` by adding a generic routine that displays the distance:

```
Private Sub Button1_Click(ByVal sender As System.Object, _
    ByVal e As System.EventArgs) Handles Button1.Click

  Dim obj As New Encapsulation()
  ShowDistance(obj)
End Sub

Private Sub ShowDistance(ByVal obj As Object)
  MsgBox(obj.DistanceTo(10, 10))
End Sub
```

Notice that the new `ShowDistance` routine accepts a parameter using the generic `Object` data type – so we can pass it literally any value – `String`, `Integer`, or one of our objects. It will raise an error at run-time, however, unless the object we pass into the routine has a `DistanceTo` method that matches the required method signature.

We know our `Encapsulation` object has a method matching that signature, so our code works fine. However, let's add another simple class to demonstrate polymorphism. Add a new class to the project and name it `Poly.vb`:

```
Public Class Poly
  Public Function DistanceTo(ByVal X As Single, ByVal Y As Single) As Single
    Return X + Y
  End Function
End Class
```

This class is about as simple as we can get. It exposes a `DistanceTo` method as part of its interface and provides a very basic implementation of that interface.

227

We can use this new class in place of the `Encapsulation` class without changing the `ShowDistance` method by using polymorphism. Return to the code in `Form1` and make the following change:

```
Private Sub Button1_Click(ByVal sender As System.Object, _
    ByVal e As System.EventArgs) Handles button1.Click

  Dim obj As New Poly()

  ShowDistance(obj)
End Sub
```

Even though we changed the class of object we're passing to `ShowDistance` to one with a different overall interface and different implementation – since the method called within `ShowDistance` remains consistent so our code will run.

Polymorphism with Multiple Interfaces

Late binding is nice, because it is flexible and easy. However, it is not ideal because it defeats the IDE and compiler type checking that allows us to fix bugs due to typos during the development process, and because it has negative impact on performance.

Fortunately, VB.NET not only provides this late binding ability, but also implements a stricter form of polymorphism through its support of multiple interfaces. (We discussed multiple interfaces in Chapter 6, including the use of the `Implements` keyword and how to define interfaces.)

With late binding we've seen how to treat all objects as equals by making them all appear using the `Object` data type. With multiple interfaces, we can treat all objects as equals by making them all implement a common data type, or interface.

This approach has the benefit that it is strongly typed – meaning that the IDE and compiler can help us find errors due to typos, since the name and data types of all methods and parameters are known at design-time. It is also fast in terms of performance; since the compiler knows all about the methods, it can use optimized mechanisms for calling them – especially as compared to the dynamic mechanisms used in late binding.

Let's return to the project and implement polymorphism with multiple interfaces. First off, add a module to the project using the **Project | Add Module** menu option and name it `Interfaces.vb`. Replace the `Module` code block with an `Interface` declaration:

```
Public Interface IShared
   Function CalculateDistance(ByVal X As Single, ByVal Y As Single) As Single
End Interface
```

Now we can make both the `Encapsulation` and `Poly` classes implement this interface. First, in the `Encapsulation` class add the following code:

```
Public Class Encapsulation
   Implements IShared

   Private msngX As Single
```

```
    Private msngY As Single

    Public Function DistanceTo(ByVal X As Single, ByVal Y As Single) _
        As Single Implements IShared.CalculateDistance

      Return Sqrt((X - msngX) ^ 2 + (Y - msngY) ^ 2)
    End Function
  ...
```

We can see that we're implementing the IShared interface, and since the CalculateDistance method's signature matches that of our existing DistanceTo method, we're simply indicating that it should act as the implementation for CalculateDistance.

We can make a similar change in the Poly class:

```
  Public Class Poly
    Implements IShared

    Public Function DistanceTo(ByVal X As Single, ByVal Y As Single) As Single _
        Implements IShared.CalculateDistance

      Return X + Y
    End Function
  End Class
```

Now this class also implements the IShared interface, and we're ready to see polymorphism implemented in our code.

Bring up the code window for Form1 and change our ShowDistance method as follows:

```
    Private Sub ShowDistance(ByVal obj As IShared)
      MsgBox(obj.CalculateDistance(10, 10))
    End Sub
```

Notice that instead of accepting the parameter using the generic Object data type, we are now accepting an IShared parameter – a strong data type known by both the IDE and the compiler. Within the code itself we are now calling the CalculateDistance method as defined by that interface.

This routine can now accept any object that implements IShared – regardless of what class that object was created from, or what other interfaces that object may implement. All we care about here is that it implements IShared.

Polymorphism through .NET Reflection

We've seen how to use late binding to invoke a method on any arbitrary object – as long as that object has a method matching the method signature we're trying to call. We've also walked through the use of multiple interfaces which allows us to achieve polymorphism through a faster, early bound technique. The challenge with these techniques is that late binding can be slow and hard to debug, and multiple interfaces can be somewhat rigid and inflexible.

We can use the concept of **reflection** within .NET to overcome some of these limitations. Reflection is a technology built into .NET that allows us to write code that interrogates a .NET assembly to dynamically determine the classes and data types it contains. We can then use reflection to load the assembly into our process, create instances of those classes and invoke their methods.

When we use late binding, VB.NET is making use of the .NET System.Reflection namespace behind the scenes on our behalf. We can choose to manually use reflection as well – which allows us even more flexibility in how we interact with objects.

For example, suppose the class we want to call is located in some other assembly on disk – an assembly we didn't specifically reference from within our project when we compiled it. How can we dynamically find, load, and invoke such an assembly? Reflection allows us to do this – assuming that the assembly is polymorphic. In other words, it has either an interface we expect, or a set of methods we can invoke via late binding.

To see how reflection works with late binding, let's create a new class in a separate assembly (project) and use it from within our existing application. Choose File | Add Project | New Project to add a new Class Library project to our solution. Name it Objects. It will start with a single class module that we can use as a starting point. Change the code in that module to this:

```
Public Class External
    Public Function DistanceTo(ByVal X As Single, ByVal Y As Single) As Single
        Return X * Y
    End Function
End Class
```

Now compile the assembly by choosing the Build | Build Objects menu option.

Next, bring up the code window for Form1. Add an Imports statement at the top:

```
Imports System.Reflection
```

Then change the code behind the button to the following:

```
    Private Sub Button1_Click(ByVal sender As System.Object, _
        ByVal e As System.EventArgs) Handles button1.Click

    Dim obj As Object
    Dim myDll As [Assembly]

    myDll = [Assembly].LoadFrom("..\..\Objects\bin\Objects.dll")

    obj = myDll.CreateInstance("Objects.External")
    MsgBox(obj.DistanceTo(10, 10))
    End Sub
```

> **Assembly** is a reserved word in VB.NET, and so we surround it with square brackets so we can use the class name without conflicting with the reserved word.

There's a lot going on here, so let's walk through it a bit. First off, notice that we're reverting to late binding – our `obj` variable is declared as type `Object`. We'll take a look at using reflection and multiple interfaces in a moment – but to start with we'll use late binding.

Next, we've declared a `myDll` variable as type `Reflection.Assembly`. This variable will contain a reference to the `Objects` assembly that we'll be dynamically loading through our code. Note that we are *not* adding a reference to this assembly via **Project | Add References** – we'll get access to the assembly at runtime.

We then load the external assembly dynamically by using the `Assembly.LoadFrom` method:

```
myDll = [Assembly].LoadFrom("..\..\Objects\bin\Objects.dll")
```

This causes the reflection library to load our assembly from a file on disk at the location we specify. Once the assembly is loaded into our process, we can use the `myDll` variable to interact with it – including interrogating it to get a list of the classes it contains or to create instances of those classes.

> *We can also use the `[Assembly].Load` method, which will scan the directory where our application's EXE file is located (and the .NET global assembly cache) for any EXE or DLL containing the `Objects` assembly. When it finds the assembly, it loads it into memory – making it available for our use.*

We can then use the `CreateInstance` method on the assembly itself to create objects based on any class in that assembly. In our case, we're creating an object based on the `External` class:

```
obj = myDll.CreateInstance("Objects.External")
```

Now we have an actual object to work with – so we can use late binding to invoke its `DistanceTo` method. At this point our code is really no different from our earlier late binding example – other than that the assembly and object were created dynamically at run-time rather than being referenced directly by our project.

At this point we should be able to run the application and have it dynamically invoke the assembly at run-time.

Polymorphism through .NET Reflection and Multiple Interfaces

We can also use both reflection and multiple interfaces together. We've seen how multiple interfaces allows us to have objects from different classes implement the same interface and thus be treated identically. We've also seen how reflection allows us to load an assembly and class dynamically at run-time.

We can combine these concepts by using an interface that is common between our main application and our external assembly, and also using reflection to load that external assembly dynamically at run-time.

First off, we need to create the interface that will be shared across both application and assembly. To do this, add a new Class Library project to our solution named `Interfaces`. Once it is created, drag-and-drop the `Interfaces.vb` module from our original application into the new project. This makes the `IShared` interface part of that project and no longer part of our base application.

Of course our base application still uses IShared, so we'll want to reference the Interfaces project from our application to gain access to the interface. Do this by right-clicking on ObjectsAndComponents in the **Solution Explorer** window and selecting the **Add Reference** menu option. Then add the reference as shown in the following figure:

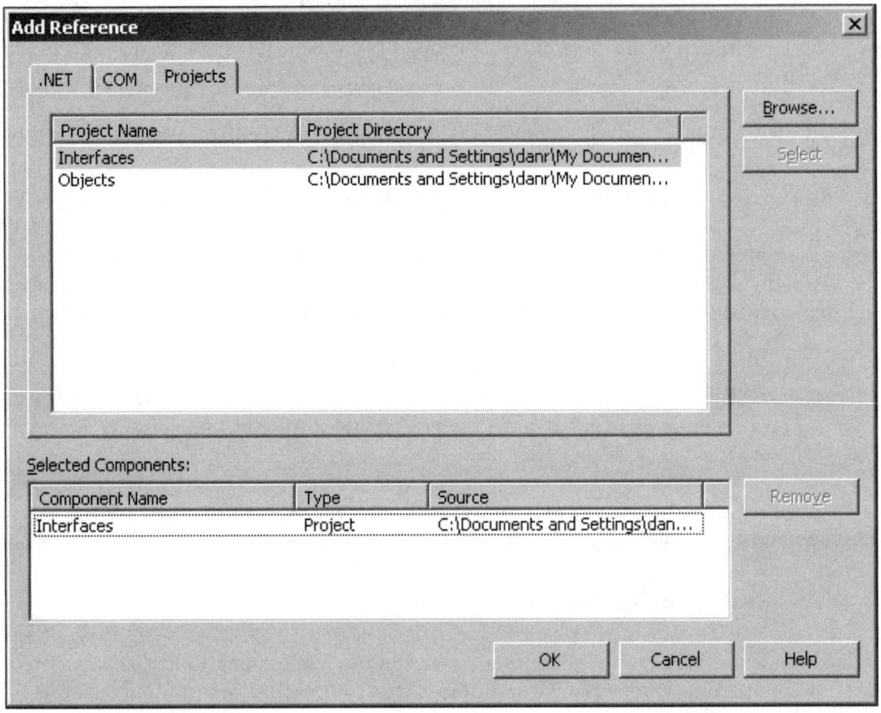

Since the IShared interface is now part of a separate assembly, we'll need to add an Imports statement to Form1, Encapsulation, and Poly so they are able to locate the IShared interface:

```
Imports Interfaces
```

Make sure to add this to the top of all three code modules.

We also need to have the Objects project reference Interfaces, so right-click on Objects in the **Solution Explorer** and choose **Add Reference** there as well. Add the reference to Interfaces and click **OK**.

At this point both our original application and our external assembly have access to the IShared interface. We can now enhance the code in Objects by changing the External class:

```
Imports Interfaces

Public Class External
    Implements IShared
```

```
      Public Function DistanceTo(ByVal X As Single, ByVal Y As Single) _
         As Single Implements IShared.CalculateDistance

      Return X * Y
   End Function
End Class
```

With both the main application and external assembly using the same data type, we are now ready to implement the polymorphic behavior using reflection.

Bring up the code window for Form1 and change the code behind the button to take advantage of the IShared interface:

```
      Private Sub Button1_Click(ByVal sender As System.Object, _
         ByVal e As System.EventArgs) Handles button1.Click

      Dim myDll As Reflection.Assembly
      Dim obj As Object

      myDll = System.Reflection.Assembly.LoadFrom( _
        "..\..\Objects\bin\Objects.dll")
      obj = myDll.CreateInstance("Objects.External")
      ShowDistance(obj)
   End Sub
```

All we've done here is to change the code so we pass our dynamically created object to the ShowDistance method – which we know requires a parameter of type IShared. Since our class implements the same IShared interface (from Interfaces) as is used by the main application this will work perfectly.

Rebuild and run the solution to see this in action.

This technique is very nice, since the code in ShowDistance is strongly typed, providing all the performance and coding benefits, but both the DLL and the object itself are loaded dynamically – providing a great deal of flexibility to our application.

Polymorphism with Inheritance

Inheritance, which we discussed in Chapter 6, can also be used to enable polymorphism. The idea here is very similar to that of multiple interfaces, since a subclass can always be treated as though it were the data type of the parent class.

> *Many people consider the concepts of inheritance and polymorphism to be tightly intertwined. As we've seen, however, it is perfectly possible to use polymorphism without inheritance – a fact that VB developers have understood since Visual Basic 4.0.*

At the moment, both our Encapsulation and Poly classes are implementing a common interface named IShared. We are able to use polymorphism to interact with objects of either class via that common interface.

The same is true if these are child classes based on the same base class through inheritance. Let's see how this works.

In the `ObjectsAndComponents` project, add a new class named `Parent`. Insert the following code into that class:

```
Public MustInherit Class Parent
  Public MustOverride Function DistanceTo(ByVal X As Single, _
     ByVal Y As Single) As Single
End Class
```

As we discussed in Chapter 6, this is an abstract base class – a class with no implementation of its own. The purpose of an abstract base class is to provide a common base from which other classes can be derived.

To implement polymorphism using inheritance we do not need to use an abstract base class. Any base class that provides overridable methods (using either `MustOverride` or `Overridable` keywords) will work fine, since all its subclasses are guaranteed to have that same set of methods as part of their interface and yet the subclasses can provide custom implementation for those methods.

In this example we're simply defining the `DistanceTo` method as being a method that must be overridden and implemented by any subclass of `Parent`.

Now we can bring up the `Encapsulation` class and change it to be a subclass of `Parent`:

```
Public Class Encapsulation
  Inherits Parent
  Implements IShared
```

We don't need to quit implementing the `IShared` interface just because we're inheriting from `Parent` – inheritance and multiple interfaces coexist nicely. We do, however, have to override the `DistanceTo` method from the `Parent` class.

The `Encapsulation` class already has a `DistanceTo` method with the proper method signature, so we can simply add the `Overrides` keyword to indicate that this method will override the declaration in the `Parent` class:

```
Public Overrides Function DistanceTo(ByVal X As Single, _
                            ByVal Y As Single) _
    As Single Implements IShared.CalculateDistance
```

At this point our `Encapsulation` class not only implements the common `IShared` interface and its own native interface, but it also can be treated as though it were of type `Parent` since it is a subclass of `Parent`.

We can do the same thing to the `Poly` class:

```
Public Class Poly
  Inherits Parent
  Implements IShared

  Public Overrides Function DistanceTo(ByVal X As Single, _
                              ByVal Y As Single) _
      As Single Implements IShared.CalculateDistance
    Return X + Y
```

```
      End Function
   End Class
```

Finally, we can see how the polymorphism works by altering the code in Form1 to take advantage of the fact that both classes can be treated as though they were of type Parent. First, we can change the ShowDistance method to accept its parameter as type Parent, and to call the DistanceTo method:

```
   Private Sub ShowDistance(ByVal obj As Parent)
     MsgBox(obj.DistanceTo(10, 10))
   End Sub
```

Then we can change the code behind our button to create an object of either type Encapsulation or Poly and pass it as a parameter to the method:

```
   Private Sub Button1_Click(ByVal sender As System.Object, _
                             ByVal e As System.EventArgs) _
                             Handles button1.Click
     ShowDistance(New Poly())
     ShowDistance(New Encapsulation())
   End Sub
```

Polymorphism Summary

Polymorphism is a very important concept in object-oriented design and programming, and VB.NET provides us with ample techniques through which it can be implemented.

The following table summarizes the different techniques, their pros and cons and provides some high level guidelines about when to use each:

Technique	Pros	Cons	Guidelines
Late binding	Flexible, "pure" polymorphism.	Slow, hard to debug, no IntelliSense.	Use to call arbitrary methods on literally any object regardless of data type or interfaces. Useful when we can't control the interfaces that will be implemented by the authors of our classes.

Table continued on following page

Technique	Pros	Cons	Guidelines
Multiple interfaces	Fast, easy to debug, full IntelliSense.	Not totally dynamic or flexible, requires class author to implement formal interface.	Use when we are creating code that interacts with clearly defined methods that can be grouped together into a formal interface. Useful when we control the interfaces that will be implemented by the classes used by our application.
Reflection and late binding	Flexible, "pure" polymorphism, dynamically load arbitrary assemblies from disk.	Slow, hard to debug, no IntelliSense.	Use to call arbitrary methods on objects, where we don't know at design time which assemblies we will be using.
Reflection and multiple interfaces	Fast, easy to debug, full IntelliSense, dynamically load arbitrary assemblies from disk.	Not totally dynamic or flexible, requires class author to implement formal interface.	Use when we are creating code that interacts with clearly defined methods that can be grouped together into a formal interface, but where we don't know at design time which assemblies we will be using.
Inheritance	Fast, easy to debug, full IntelliSense, inherits behaviors from base class.	Not totally dynamic or flexible, requires class author to inherit from common base class.	Use when we are creating objects that have an *is-a* relationship, where we have subclasses that are naturally of the same data type as a base class. Polymorphism through inheritance should occur because inheritance makes sense, *not* because we are attempting to merely achieve polymorphism.

Inheritance

Inheritance is the concept that a new class can be based on an existing class, inheriting its interface and functionality from the original class. We discussed the mechanics and syntax of inheritance in Chapter 6, so we won't rehash them here. However, in Chapter 6 we really didn't discuss inheritance from a practical perspective, and that will be the focus of this section.

When to Use Inheritance

Inheritance is one of the most powerful object-oriented features a language can support. At the same time, inheritance is one of the most dangerous and misused object-oriented features.

Properly used, inheritance allows us to increase the maintainability, readability and reusability of our application, by offering us a clear and concise way to reuse code – both via interface and implementation. Improperly used, inheritance allows us to create applications that are very fragile, where a change to a class can cause the entire application to break or require changes.

Inheritance allows us to implement an *is-a* relationship. In other words, it allows us to implement a new class that *is a* more specific type of its base class. This means that properly used, inheritance allows us to create child classes that really are the same as the base class.

Perhaps a quick example is in order. Take a duck. We know that a duck *is a* bird. However, a duck can also be food – though that is not its primary identity. Proper use of inheritance would allow us to create a `Bird` base class from which we can derive our `Duck` class. We would *not* create a `Food` class and subclass `Duck` from `Food`, since a duck isn't *really* just food – it merely acts as food sometimes.

This is the challenge. Inheritance is *not* just a mechanism for code reuse. It is a mechanism to create classes that flow naturally from some other class. If we use it anywhere we want code reuse, we'll end up with a real mess on our hands. If we use it anywhere we just want a common interface, but where the child class is not really the same as the base class then we should be using multiple interfaces – something we'll discuss shortly.

> **The question we must ask, when using inheritance, is whether the child class *is a* more specific version of the base class.**

For example, we might have different types of products in our organization. All of these products will have some common data and behaviors – they'll all have a product number and description, and they'll all have a price. However, if we have an agricultural application we might have chemical products, seed products, fertilizer products and retail products. These are all different – each having its own data and behaviors – and yet there is no doubt that each one of them really is a product. We can use inheritance to create this set of products as illustrated by the following UML diagram:

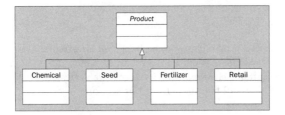

This diagram shows that we have an abstract base Product class, from which we derive the various types of product our system will actually use. This is an appropriate use of inheritance, because the child classes are obviously each a more specific form of the general Product class.

On the other hand, we might try to use inheritance just as a code sharing mechanism. For example, we may look at our application, which has Customer, Product, and SalesOrder classes, and decide that all of them need to be designed so they can be printed to a printer. The code to handle the printing will all be somewhat similar, and so to reuse that printing code we create a base PrintableObject class. This would result in the following UML:

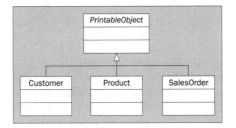

Intuitively we know that this doesn't represent an *is-a* relationship. While a Customer can be printed, and we are getting code reuse, a customer isn't really a specific case of a printable object. Implementing a system following this design will result in a fragile design and application. This is a case where multiple interfaces are a far more appropriate technology – as we'll discuss later.

To illustrate this point, we might later discover that we have other entities in our organization that are similar to a customer, but are not quite the same. Upon further analysis, we may determine that Employee, Customer, and Contact are all related because they are specific cases of a Person class. The Person class provides commonality in terms of data and behavior across all these other classes:

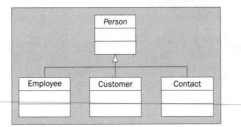

But now our `Customer` is in trouble – we've said it *is-a* `PrintableObject`, and we're now saying it *is-a* `Person`.

We *might* be able to just derive `Person` from `PrintableObject`:

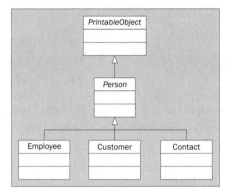

The problem with this is that now `Employee` and `Contact` are also of type `PrintableObject` – even if they shouldn't be. But we're stuck, since we unfortunately had decided early on to go against intuition and say that a `Customer` *is-a* `PrintableObject`.

This is a problem that could be solved by **multiple inheritance**, which would allow `Customer` to be a subclass of more than one base class – in this case of both `Person` and `PrintableObject`. However, the .NET platform and thus VB.NET don't support multiple inheritance in this way. Our alternative is to use inheritance for the *is-a* relationship with `Person`, and use multiple interfaces to allow the `Customer` object to *act as* a `PrintableObject` by implementing an `IPrintableObject` interface.

Application vs. Framework Inheritance

What we've just seen is how inheritance can accidentally cause reuse of code where no reuse was desired.

However, we can take a different view of this model by separating the concept of a framework from our actual application. The way we use inheritance in the design of a framework is somewhat different from how we use inheritance in the design of an actual application.

In this context, the word **framework** is being used to refer to a set of classes that provide base functionality that is not specific to our application, but rather may be used across a number of applications within our organization, or perhaps even beyond our organization. The .NET Framework class library is an example of a very broad framework we use when building our applications.

The `PrintableObject` class we discussed earlier, for example, may have little to do with our specific application, but rather may be the type of thing that is used across many applications. If so, it is a natural candidate for being part of a framework, rather than being considered part of our actual application.

Framework classes exist at a lower level than application classes. For example, the .NET system class library is a framework on which all .NET applications are built. We can layer our own framework on top of the .NET framework as well:

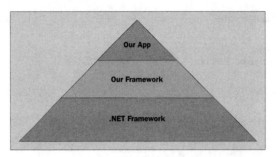

If we take this view, then the `PrintableObject` class wouldn't be part of our application at all, but rather would be part of a framework on which our application is built. In such a case, the fact that `Customer` is not a specific case of `PrintableObject` doesn't matter as much – since we're not saying it is such a thing, but rather we're saying it is leveraging that portion of the framework functionality.

To make this all work requires a lot of planning and forethought in the design of the framework itself. To see the dangers we face, consider that we might not only want to be able to print objects, but we might also want to be able to store them in a file. So we might not only have `PrintableObject`, but we might also have `SavableObject` as a base class.

The question then becomes – what do we do if `Customer` should be both printable *and* savable? If all printable objects are savable we might have:

```
SavableObject



  ↑

PrintableObject


```

Or, if all savable objects are printable we might have:

```
PrintableObject



  ↑

SavableObject


```

But really neither of these provides a decent solution, since the odds are that the concept of being printable and the concept of being savable are different and not interrelated in either of these ways.

When faced with this sort of issue, it is best to avoid using inheritance, and rather rely on multiple interfaces.

Inheritance and Multiple Interfaces

While inheritance is powerful, it is really geared around implementing the *is-a* relationship. Sometimes we will have objects that need to have a common interface, even though they aren't really a specific case of some base class that provides that interface. We've just been exploring that issue in our discussion of the `PrintableObject`, `SavableObject`, and `Customer` classes.

Sometimes multiple interfaces are a better alternative than inheritance. We discussed the syntax for creating and using secondary and multiple interfaces in Chapter 6.

Multiple interfaces can be viewed as another way of implementing the *is-a* relationship. It is often better, however, to view inheritance as an *is-a* relationship and to view multiple interfaces as a way of implementing an *act-as* relationship.

To think about this further, we can say that our `PrintableObject` concept could perhaps be better expressed as an interface – `IPrintableObject`.

When our class implements a secondary interface such as `IPrintableObject`, we're not really saying that our class *is a* printable object, we're saying that it can *act as* a printable object. A `Customer` *is-a* `Person`, but at the same time it can *act-as* a printable object. This is illustrated in UML as:

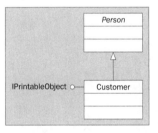

The drawback to this approach is that we get no inherited *implementation* when we implement `IPrintableObject`. In Chapter 6 we discussed how to reuse common code as we implement an interface across multiple classes. While not as automatic or easy as inheritance, it is possible to reuse implementation code with a bit of extra work.

Applying Inheritance and Multiple Interfaces

We can see how this works in code by working with our `ObjectsAndComponents` project.

Creating the Person Base Class

We already have a simple `Customer` class in the project – so now let's add a `Person` base class. Choose **Project | Add Class** and add a class named `Person`. Write the following code:

```
Public MustInherit Class Person
  Private mgID As Guid = Guid.NewGuid
  Private mstrName As String = ""

  Public Property ID() As Guid
    Get
```

```
            Return mgID
        End Get
        Set(ByVal Value As Guid)
            mgID = Value
        End Set
    End Property

    Public Property Name() As String
        Get
            Return mstrName
        End Get
        Set(ByVal Value As String)
            mstrName = Value
        End Set
    End Property
End Class
```

Subclassing Person

Now we can make the Customer class inherit from this base class, since it *is-a* Person. Also, since our base class now implements both the ID and Name properties, we can simplify the code in Customer by removing those properties and their related variables:

```
Public Class Customer
    Inherits Person

    Private mstrPhone As String = ""

    Public Property Phone() As String
        Get
            Return mstrPhone
        End Get
        Set(ByVal Value As String)
            mstrPhone = Value
        End Set
    End Property
End Class
```

This shows the benefit of subclassing Customer from Person, since we're now sharing the ID and Name code across all other types of Person as well.

Implementing IPrintableObject

However, we also know that a Customer should be able to *act-as* a printable object. To do this in a way such that the implementation is reusable requires a bit of thought. First off though, we need to define the IPrintableObject interface.

We'll use the standard printing mechanism provided by .NET from the System.Drawing namespace – and so we'll need to add a reference to System.Drawing.dll to the Interfaces project before we can define our new interface. With that done, bring up the code window for Interfaces.vb in the Interfaces project and add the following code:

```
Imports System.Drawing

Public Interface IPrintableObject
  Sub Print()
  Sub PrintPreview()
  Sub RenderPage(ByVal sender As Object, _
      ByVal ev As System.Drawing.Printing.PrintPageEventArgs)
End Interface
```

This interface ensures that any object implementing `IPrintableObject` will have `Print` and `PrintPreview` methods so we can invoke the appropriate type of printing. It also ensures the object will have a `RenderPage` method, which can be implemented by that object to render the object's data onto the printed page.

At this point we could simply implement all the code needed to handle printing directly within the `Customer` object. This isn't ideal, however, since some of the code will be common across any objects that want to implement `IPrintableObject` – and it would be nice to find a way to share that code.

To do this, let's create a new class – `ObjectPrinter`. This is a framework-style class, in that it has nothing to do with any particular application, but can be used across any application where `IPrintableObject` will be used.

Add a new class named `ObjectPrinter` to the `ObjectsAndComponents` project. This class will contain all the code common to printing any object. It makes use of the built-in printing support provided by the .NET Framework class library. To use this, we need to import a couple of namespaces, so add this code to the new class:

```
Imports System.Drawing
Imports System.Drawing.Printing
Imports Interfaces
```

We can then define a `PrintDocument` variable, which will hold the reference to our printer output. We'll also declare a variable to hold a reference to the actual object we'll be printing. Notice that we're using the `IPrintableObject` interface data type for this variable:

```
Public Class ObjectPrinter
   Private WithEvents MyDoc As PrintDocument
   Private printObject As IPrintableObject
```

Now we can create a routine to kick off the printing process for any object implementing `IPrintableObject`. This code is totally generic, so we'll write it here so it can be reused across any number of other classes:

```
   Public Sub Print(ByVal obj As IPrintableObject)
      printObject = obj

      MyDoc = New PrintDocument()
      MyDoc.Print()
   End Sub
```

Likewise, we can implement a method to show a print preview display of our object. Again, this code is totally generic, so we'll put it here for reuse:

```
Public Sub PrintPreview(ByVal obj As IPrintableObject)
  Dim PPdlg As PrintPreviewDialog = New PrintPreviewDialog()

  printObject = obj

  MyDoc = New PrintDocument()
  PPdlg.Document = MyDoc
  PPdlg.ShowDialog()
End Sub
```

Finally, we need to catch the PrintPage event that is automatically raised by the .NET printing mechanism. This event is raised by the PrintDocument object whenever the document determines that it needs data rendered onto a page. Typically it is in this routine that we'd put the code to draw our text or graphics onto the page surface. However, since this is a generic framework class, we won't do that here, but rather we'll delegate the call back into the actual application object that we want to print:

```
Private Sub PrintPage(ByVal sender As Object, _
    ByVal ev As System.Drawing.Printing.PrintPageEventArgs)
    Handles MyDoc.PrintPage

  printObject.RenderPage(sender, ev)
End Sub
End Class
```

This allows the application object itself to determine how its data should be rendered onto the output page.

Let's see how we can do that by implementing the IPrintableObject interface on our Customer class:

```
Imports Interfaces

Public Class Customer
  Inherits Person
  Implements IPrintableObject
```

By adding this code, we're requiring that our Customer class implement the Print, PrintPreview, and RenderPage methods. To avoid wasting paper as we test, let's make both the Print and PrintPreview methods the same – and have them just do a print preview display:

```
Private Sub Print() _
    Implements IPrintableObject.Print, IPrintableObject.PrintPreview

  Dim p As New ObjectPrinter()
  p.PrintPreview(Me)
End Sub
```

Notice that we're using an ObjectPrinter object to handle the common details of doing a print preview. In fact, any class we ever create that implements IPrintableObject will have this exact same code to implement a print preview function – relying on our common ObjectPrinter to take care of the details.

We also need to implement the `RenderPage` method, which is where we actually put our object's data onto the printed page:

```
Private Sub RenderPage(ByVal sender As Object, _
    ByVal ev As System.Drawing.Printing.PrintPageEventArgs) _
    Implements IPrintableObject.RenderPage

  Dim PrintFont As New Font("Arial", 10)
  Dim LineHeight As Single = PrintFont.GetHeight(ev.Graphics)
  Dim LeftMargin As Single = ev.MarginBounds.Left
  Dim yPos As Single = ev.MarginBounds.Top

  ev.Graphics.DrawString("ID: " & ID.ToString, PrintFont, Brushes.Black, _
    LeftMargin, yPos, New StringFormat())

  yPos += LineHeight
  ev.Graphics.DrawString("Name: " & Name, PrintFont, Brushes.Black, _
    LeftMargin, yPos, New StringFormat())

  ev.HasMorePages = False
End Sub
```

All of this code is unique to our object – which makes sense, since we're rendering our specific data to be printed. However, we don't need to worry about the details of whether we're doing printing to paper or print preview – that is handled by our `ObjectPrinter` class, which in turn uses the .NET framework. This allows us to just focus on generating the output to the page within our application class.

By generalizing the printing code in `ObjectPrinter`, we've achieved a level of reuse that we can tap into via the `IPrintableObject` interface. Any time we want to print a `Customer` object's data, we can have it *act-as* an `IPrintableObject` and call its `Print` or `PrintPreview` method. To see this work, let's change the code behind the button control on `Form1`:

```
Private Sub Button1_Click(ByVal sender As System.Object, _
    ByVal e As System.EventArgs) Handles Button1.Click

  Dim obj As New Customer()
  obj.Name = "Douglas Adams"
  CType(obj, IPrintableObject).PrintPreview()
End Sub
```

This code creates a new `Customer` object and sets its `Name` property. We then use the `CType()` method to access the object via its `IPrintableObject` interface to invoke the `PrintPreview` method.

When we run the application and click the button, we'll get a print preview display showing the object's data:

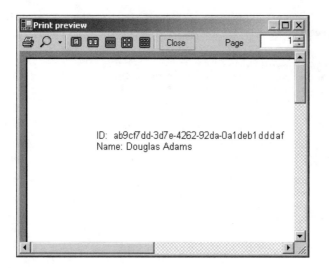

How Deep to Go?

Most of the examples we've discussed so far have illustrated how we can create a child class based on a single parent class. That is called single-level inheritance. However, inheritance can be many levels deep. For example, we might have a deep hierarchy such as:

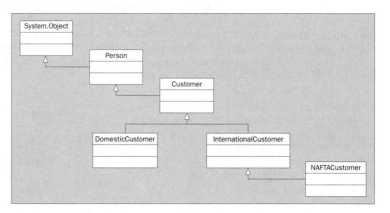

From the root of System.Object down to the NAFTACustomer we have four levels of inheritance. This can be described as a 4-level inheritance chain.

There is no hard and fast rule about how deep inheritance chains should go, but conventional wisdom and general experience with inheritance in other languages such as Smalltalk and C++ indicate that the deeper an inheritance chain becomes, the harder it is to maintain an application.

This happens for two reasons. First is the fragile base class or fragile superclass issue, which we'll discuss shortly. The second reason is that a deep inheritance hierarchy tends to seriously reduce readability of our code by scattering the code for an object across many different classes – all of which are combined together by the compiler to create our object.

One of the reasons for adopting object-oriented design and programming is to avoid so-called spaghetti code – where any bit of code we might look at does almost nothing useful, but instead calls various other procedures and routines in other parts of our application. To determine what is going on with spaghetti code, we must trace through many routines and mentally piece together what is going on.

Object-oriented programming *can* help us avoid this problem, but it is most definitely not a magic bullet. In fact, when we create deep inheritance hierarchies, we are often creating spaghetti code. This is because each level in the hierarchy not only extends the previous level's interface, but almost always also adds functionality. Thus, when we look at our final NAFTACustomer class it may have very little code. In order to figure out what it does or how it behaves, we have to trace through the code in the previous four levels of classes – and we might not even have the code for some of those classes, since they may come from other applications or class libraries we've purchased.

On one hand we have the benefit that we're reusing code, but on the other hand we have the drawback that the code for one object is actually scattered through five different classes.

It is important to keep this in mind when designing systems with inheritance – use as few levels in the hierarchy as possible to provide the required functionality.

Fragile Base Class Issue

We've explored where it is and is not appropriate to use inheritance. We've also explored how we can use inheritance and multiple interfaces in conjunction to implement both *is-a* and *act-as* relationships simultaneously within our classes.

Earlier we noted that while inheritance is an incredibly powerful and useful concept, it can also be very dangerous if used improperly. We've seen some of this danger as we discussed the misapplication of the *is-a* relationship, and how we can use multiple interfaces to avoid those issues.

However, one of the most classic and common problems with inheritance is the **fragile base class** problem. This problem is exacerbated when we have very deep inheritance hierarchies, but exists even in a single-level inheritance chain.

> **The issue we face is that a change in the base class always affects all child classes derived from that base class.**

This is a double-edged sword. On one hand we get the benefit of being able to change code in one location and have that change automatically cascade out through all derived classes. On the other hand, a change in behavior can have unintended or unexpected consequences further down the inheritance chain – and that can make our application very fragile and hard to change or maintain.

Interface Changes

There are obvious changes we might make, that require immediate attention. For example, we might change our Person class to have FirstName and LastName instead of simply Name as a property. In the Person class, replace the mstrName variable declaration with:

```
Private mstrFirstName As String = ""
Private mstrLastName As String = ""
```

Chapter 7

Now replace the Name property with the following:

```
Public Property FirstName() As String
  Get
    Return mstrFirstName
  End Get
  Set(ByVal Value As String)
    mstrFirstName = Value
  End Set
End Property

Public Property LastName() As String
  Get
    Return mstrLastName
  End Get
  Set(ByVal Value As String)
    mstrLastName = Value
  End Set
End Property
```

At this point, the Task List window in the IDE will show a list of locations where we need to change our code to compensate for the change. This is a graphic illustration of a base class change that causes cascading changes throughout our application. In this case we've changed the base class interface – thus changing the interface of all subclasses in the inheritance chain.

To avoid having to fix code throughout our application, we should always strive to keep as much consistency in our base class interface as possible. In this case, we can implement a read-only Name property that returns the full name of the Person:

```
Public ReadOnly Property Name() As String
  Get
    Return mstrFirstName & " " & mstrLastName
  End Get
End Property
```

This resolves most of the items in the Task List window. We can fix any remaining issues by using the FirstName and LastName properties. For example, in Form1 we can change the code behind our button to:

```
Private Sub Button1_Click(ByVal sender As System.Object, _
    ByVal e As System.EventArgs) Handles button1.Click

  Dim obj As New Customer()
  obj.FirstName = "Douglas"
  obj.LastName = "Adams"
  CType(obj, Interfaces.IPrintableObject).Print()
End Sub
```

Any change to a base class interface is likely to cause problems, so we must think carefully before making such a change.

Implementation Changes

Unfortunately there's another, more subtle type of change that can wreak more havoc on our application – and that is an implementation change. This is the core of the fragile base class problem.

Encapsulation provides us with separation of interface from implementation. However, keeping our interface consistent is merely a *syntactic* concept. If we change the implementation we are making a *semantic* change – a change that doesn't alter any of our syntax, but can have serious ramifications on the real behavior of the application.

In theory we can change the implementation of a class, and as long as we don't change its interface any client applications using objects based on that class will continue to operate without change. Of course reality is never as nice as theory, and more often than not a change to implementation will have some consequences in the behavior of a client application.

For example, we might use a `SortedList` to sort and display some `Customer` objects. To do this, change the code behind our button on `Form1` as follows:

```
Private Sub Button1_Click(ByVal sender As System.Object, _
    ByVal e As System.EventArgs) Handles button1.Click

    Dim col As New SortedList()
    Dim obj As Customer

    obj = New Customer()
    obj.FirstName = "Douglas"
    obj.LastName = "Adams"
    col.Add(obj.Name, obj)

    obj = New Customer()
    obj.FirstName = "Andre"
    obj.LastName = "Norton"
    col.Add(obj.Name, obj)

    Dim i As DictionaryEntry
    For Each i In col
        obj = CType(i.Value, Customer)
        System.Diagnostics.Debug.WriteLine(obj.Name)
    Next
End Sub
```

This code simply creates a couple of `Customer` objects, sets their `FirstName` and `LastName` properties and inserts them into a `SortedList` collection object from the `System.Collections` namespace.

Items in a `SortedList` are sorted based on their key value – and we are using the `Name` property to provide that key – meaning that our entries will be sorted by name. Since our `Name` property is implemented to return first name first, and last name second, our entries will be sorted by first name.

If we run the application, the Output window in the IDE will display the following:

```
Andre Norton
Douglas Adams
```

However, we can change the implementation of our `Person` class – not directly changing or impacting either the `Customer` class or our code in `Form1` – to return last name first and first name second:

```
Public ReadOnly Property Name() As String
   Get
       Return mstrLastName & ", " & mstrFirstName
   End Get
End Property
```

While no other code requires changing, and no syntax errors are flagged, the behavior of our application is changed. When we run it our output will now be:

```
Adams, Douglas
Norton, Andre
```

Maybe this change is inconsequential. Maybe it totally breaks the required behavior of our form. The developer making the change in the `Person` class might not even know that someone was using that property for sort criteria.

This illustrates how dangerous inheritance can be. Changes to implementation in a base class can cascade out to countless other classes in countless applications, having unforeseen side effects and consequences of which the base class developer is totally unaware.

Summary

Over the past three chapters we've seen how object-oriented programming flows from the four basic concepts of abstraction, encapsulation, polymorphism, and inheritance. In this chapter we've provided some basic discussion of each concept and demonstrated how to implement them using VB.NET.

We have understood how (when properly applied) object-oriented design and programming can allow us to create very large and complex applications that remain maintainable and readable over time. However, this is no magic bullet and these technologies and concepts can, if improperly applied, create the same hard to maintain code that we might create using procedural or modular design techniques.

It is not possible to fully cover all aspects of object-oriented programming in a single chapter. Before launching into a full-blown object-oriented project, I highly recommend going through other books specifically geared toward object-oriented design and programming.

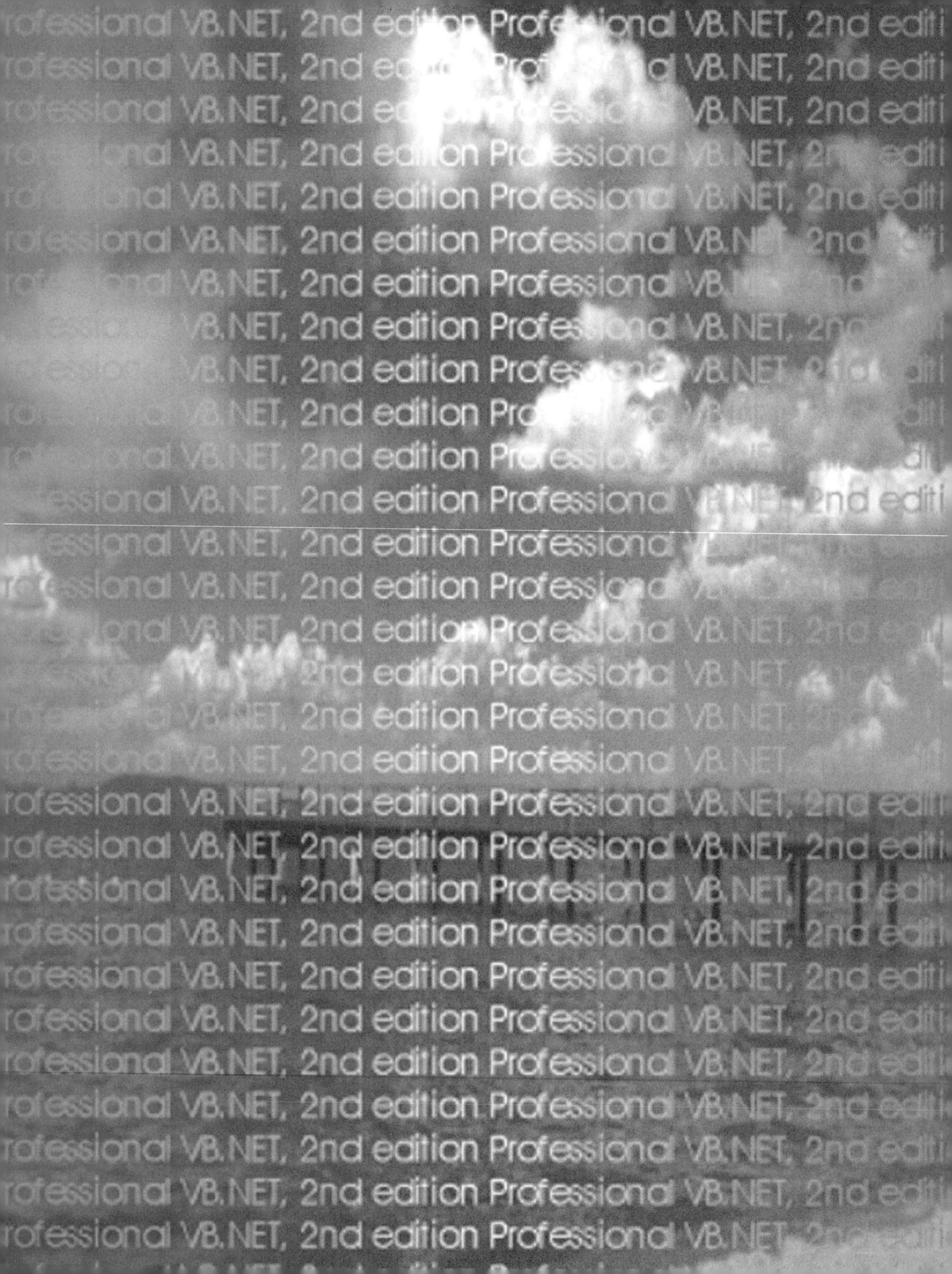
Professional VB.NET, 2nd edition

Namespaces

Even if you didn't realize it, you've been using **namespaces** since Chapter 2. For example, `System`, `System.Diagnostics`, and `System.Windows.Forms` are all namespaces. Namespaces are an easy concept to understand but in this chapter we'll put the ideas behind them on a firm footing – and clear up any misconceptions you might have about how they are used and organized.

If you're familiar with COM, you'll find that the concept of namespaces is the logical extension of programmatic identifier (ProgID) values. For example, the functionality of `Scripting.FileSystemObject` is mostly encompassed in the `System.IO` namespace, though this is not a one-to-one mapping. However, namespaces are about more than a change in name; they represent the logical extension of the COM naming structure, expanding its ease of use and extensibility.

In this chapter we'll cover:

- ❏ What namespaces are
- ❏ Which namespaces are used in VS.NET projects by default
- ❏ How we can reference namespaces and use the `Imports` statement
- ❏ How the compiler searches for class references
- ❏ How we can alias namespaces
- ❏ How we can create our own namespaces

Let's begin this chapter by defining what a namespace is (and isn't).

What is a Namespace?

Namespaces organize and simplify object references within a hierarchical structure – not only within VB.NET but across the entire Common Language Runtime (CLR). These references are typically organized by *function*. For example, the System.IO namespace contains classes, structures, and interfaces for working with input/output streams and files. These classes in this namespace *do not* necessarily inherit from the same base classes (apart from Object of course).

A namespace is a combination of a naming convention and an assembly, which organizes collections of objects and prevents ambiguity in object references. A namespace can be, and often is, implemented across several physical assemblies but, from the reference side, it is the namespace that ties these assemblies together. A namespace consists of not only classes but other (child) namespaces too – for example, the IO child namespace of the System namespace.

Namespaces provide identification beyond the component name. With a namespace, it is possible to put a more meaningful title (for example, System) followed by a grouping (for example, Text) to group together a collection of classes that contain similar functions. For example, the System.Text namespace contains a powerful class called StringBuilder. To reference this class, we can use the fully qualified namespace reference of System.Text.StringBuilder.

The structure of a namespace is not a reflection of the physical inheritance of classes that make up a namespace. For example, the System.Text namespace contains another child namespace called RegularExpressions. This namespace contains several classes, but they do not inherit or otherwise reference the classes that make up the System.Text namespace.

The following diagram shows how the System namespace contains the Text child namespace, which also has a child namespace called RegularExpressions:

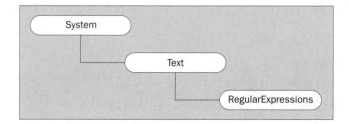

Both of these child namespaces – Text and RegularExpressions – contain a number of objects, shown here in the inheritance model for these classes:

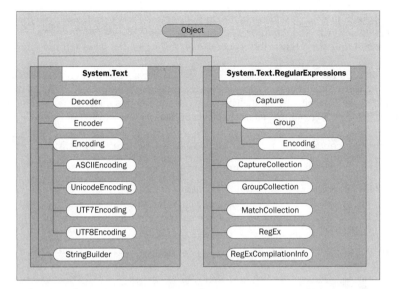

As you can see in the diagram above, while some of the classes in each namespace do inherit from each other, and while all of the classes eventually inherit from the generic `Object`, the classes in `System.Text.RegularExpressions` do not inherit from the classes in `System.Text`.

You might be wondering at this point what all the fuss is about. To emphasize the usefulness of namespaces, we can draw another good example from this diagram. The complete reference to the `Encoder` class is `System.Drawing.Imaging.Encoder`. This is not the same as the `System.Text.Encoder` class shown in the preceding diagram. Being able to clearly identify classes with the same name, but involving very different functions, is yet another advantage of namespaces.

If you are an experienced COM developer you may note that, unlike a ProgID that is a one level relationship between the project assembly and class, a single namespace can use child namespaces to extend the meaningful description of a class. The `System` namespace, imported by default as part of every project, contains not only the default `Object` class, but also many other classes that are used as the basis for every .NET language.

However, what if a class you need isn't available in your project? The problem may be with the references in your project. For example, by default the `Microsoft.VisualBasic` namespace isn't part of your assembly. Using it requires adding a **reference** to the project assembly. The concept of referencing a namespace is very similar to the ability to reference a COM object in VB6.

In fact, with all this talk about referencing, it's probably a good idea to look at an example of adding an additional namespace to a project. Before we do that, we need to know a little bit about how a namespace is implemented.

Namespaces are implemented in .NET assemblies. The `System` namespace is implemented in an assembly provided with Visual Studio called `System.dll`. By referencing this assembly, the project gains the ability to reference all of the child namespaces of `System` that happen to be implemented in this assembly. Using the preceding table, the project can import and use the `System.Text` namespace because its implementation is in the `System.dll` assembly. However, although it is listed above, the project cannot import or use the `System.Data` namespace unless it references the assembly that implements this child of the `System` namespace, `System.Data.dll`.

255

Let's create a sample project so that we can examine the role that namespaces play within it. Using VS.NET, create a new VB.NET Windows Application project called **Namespace_Sampler**. We are going to create a simple form that will retrieve some of the .NET related settings from the registry.

The `Microsoft.VisualBasic.Compatibility.VB6` library isn't part of VB projects by default. To gain access to the classes in this namespace, you need to add it to your project. You can do this by using the **Add Reference** dialog (available by right-clicking on the **References** node in the **Solution Explorer**). This dialog has three tabs, each containing elements that can be referenced from your project:

❑   The first tab contains .NET assemblies that have been provided by Microsoft

❑   The second tab contains COM components

❑   The third tab contains the custom .NET assemblies

It is also possible to browse your system for other component files if the one that you are looking for isn't listed:

The available .NET namespaces are listed by a component name. This is *not* the same as the namespace name. Selecting the **Microsoft Visual Basic.NET Compatibility Data Runtime** component will add the desired `Microsoft.VisualBasic.Compatibility.VB6` namespace. Although the lower window doesn't have enough space to fully display the path, the file name for this namespace is `Microsoft.VisualBasic.Compatibility.dll`. Also available is another compatibility library for data access, `Microsoft.VisualBasic.Compatibility.Data.dll`, which contains the second half of the compatibility library.

This implementation, while a bit surprising at first, is very powerful. Firstly, it shows the extensibility of namespaces – the single `Microsoft.VisualBasic.Compatibilty.VB6` namespace is implemented in two separate assemblies. Secondly, it allows us to include only the classes that we need – in this case, those that are related to the VB6 environment or to data base tools, or both types.

Namespaces and References

Highlighting their importance to every project, references (including namespaces) are no longer hidden from view – available only after opening a dialog box as they were in VB6. As shown in the following Solution Explorer window, every new project comes with a set of referenced namespaces:

The list of default references changes based on the type of project. For example, if the project is a VB.NET Web Application, the list of references would change appropriately – the reference to the System.Windows.Forms namespace assembly would be replaced by references to the System.Web and System.Web.Services namespaces.

In addition to making the namespaces available, references play a second important role in your project. One of the advantages of .NET is using services and components built on the CLR that allow you to avoid DLL conflicts. The various problems that can occur related to DLL versioning, commonly referred to as DLL Hell, involve two types of conflict.

The first situation occurs when you have a component that requires a minimum DLL version and an older version of the same DLL causes your product to break. The alternative situation is when you require an older version of a DLL and a new version is incompatible. In either case, the result is that a shared file, outside of your control, creates a system-wide dependency that impacts upon your software. As part of .NET, it is possible – but not required – to indicate that a DLL should be shipped as part of your project to avoid an external dependency.

In order to indicate that a referenced component should be included locally, you can select it in the Solution Explorer and then examine the properties associated with that reference. One editable property is called Copy Local. For those assemblies that are part of a VS.NET installation, this value defaults to False. However, for custom references, this property will default to True to indicate that the referenced DLL should be included as part of the assembly. Changing this property to True changes the path associated with the assembly. Instead of using the path to the referenced file's location on the system, the project creates a subdirectory based on the reference name and places the files required for the implementation of the reference in this subdirectory:

The benefit of this is that, in theory, even if another version of the DLL is later placed on the system, your project's assembly will continue to function. This protection from a conflicting version comes at a price, however. Future updates to the namespace assembly to fix flaws will be in the system version but not in the private version that is part of your project's assembly. To resolve this, Microsoft's solution is to place new versions in directories based on their version information. If you examine the path information for all of the VS.NET references, you will see that it includes a version number. As new versions of these DLLs are released, they will be installed in a separate directory. This method allows for both an escape from DLL Hell, by keeping new versions from stomping on old versions, but also allows for old versions to be easily located for maintenance updates. For this reason, in many cases, it is better to leave alone the default behavior of VS.NET to only copy locally custom components, until your organization implements a directory structure with version information similar to that of Microsoft.

The VB.NET compiler will not allow you to add a reference to your assembly if the targeted implementation includes a reference, which isn't also referenced in your assembly. The good news is that the compiler will help. If, after adding a reference, that reference doesn't appear in the IntelliSense list generated by VS.NET, go ahead and type the reference to a class from that reference. The compiler will flag it with one of its Microsoft Word-like spelling or grammar error underlines. By then clicking on the underlined text, the compiler will tell you which other assemblies need to be referenced in the project in order to use the class in question.

Common Namespaces

The generated list of references shown in the Solution Explorer for the newly created Namespace_Sampler project includes most but not all of the namespaces that are part of your Windows Application project. For example, one important namespace not displayed as a reference is `Microsoft.VisualBasic` and the accompanying `Microsoft.VisualBasic.dll`. Every VB.NET project includes the namespace `Microsoft.VisualBasic`. This namespace is part of the Visual Studio project templates for VB.NET and is, in short, what makes VB.NET different from C# or any other .NET language. The implicit inclusion of this namespace is the reason that you can call `IsDBNull` and other methods of VB.NET directly. The only difference in the default namespaces that are included with VB.NET and C# Windows Application projects is that the former use `Microsoft.VisualBasic` and the latter use `Microsoft.CSharp`.

In order to see all of the namespaces that are imported automatically, such as the `Microsoft.VisualBasic` namespace, right-click on the project name in the **Solution Explorer** and select **Properties** from the context menu. This will open the project properties dialog. Select the **Imports** node that is under the **Common Properties** node and you will see `Microsoft.VisualBasic` at the top of the list:

When looking at the project's global list of imports, you can see that, in addition to the `Microsoft.VisualBasic` namespace, the `System.Collections` and `System.Diagnostics` namespaces are also imported into the project. Unlike the other namespaces in the list, these namespaces are not listed as references. That is because the implementation of the `System.Collections` and `System.Diagnostics` namespaces is part of the referenced `System.dll`. Similar to `Microsoft.VisualBasic`, importing these namespaces allows references to the associated classes, such that a fully qualified path is not required. Since these namespaces contain commonly used classes, it is worthwhile to always include them at the project level.

The following listing brings together brief descriptions of some of the namespaces commonly used in VB.NET projects:

❑   `System.Collections` – Contains the classes that support various feature rich object collections. Included automatically, it has classes for arrays, lists, dictionaries, queues, hash tables, etc.

❑   `System.Data` – Included in all VB.NET projects; contains the classes to support the core features of ADO.NET.

❑   `System.Diagnostics` – Included in all VB.NET projects, this namespace includes the debugging classes. The `Trace` and `Debug` classes provide the primary capabilities but the namespace contains dozens of classes to support debugging.

❑   `System.Drawing` – Simple drawing classes to support Windows Application projects.

❑ `System.Windows.Forms` – The classes to create Windows Forms in Windows Application projects. This namespace contains the form elements.

❑ `System.Web.UI.HTMLControls` – Included in Web Application projects, this namespace contains classes to automatically generate standard HTML controls that support all browsers.

❑ `System.Web.UI.WebControls` – Included in Web Application projects to create server-based web controls. These controls, while not based on standard HTML, support advanced features such as validation.

❑ `System.EnterpriseServices` – Not included automatically, the `System.EnterpriseServices` implementation must be referenced to make it available. This namespace contains the classes that interface .NET assemblies with COM+.

❑ `Microsoft.VisualBasic.Compatibility.VB6` – Not included automatically. The `Microsoft.VisualBasic.Compatibility.dll` and `Microsoft.VisualBasic.Compatibility.Data.dll` implementations must be referenced to make it available.

❑ `Microsoft.Win32` – Provides classes to manage system events and the Windows registry. While not included automatically, this namespace is implemented as part of the CLR and so is available to all projects.

Of course, to really make use of the classes and other objects in the above listing, you really need more detailed information. In addition to resources such as Visual Studio's help files, the best source of information is the **Object Browser**. It is available by selecting View | Other Windows | Object Browser:

The **Object Browser** displays each of the referenced assemblies and allows you to drill down into the various namespaces. The previous screenshot illustrates how the `System.dll` implements a number of namespaces, including some that are part of the `System` namespace. By drilling down into a namespace, it is possible to see some of the classes available. By further selecting a class, the browser shows not only the methods and properties associated with the selected class but also a brief outline of what that class does.

Using the **Object Browser** is an excellent way to gain insight, not only into which classes and interfaces are available via the different assemblies included in your project, but also into how they work. As you can guess, the ability to actually see not only which classes are available but what and how to use them is important in being able to work efficiently. To work effectively in the .NET CLR environment requires finding the right class for the task.

Importing and Aliasing Namespaces

Not all namespaces should be imported at the global level. Although we have looked at namespaces that are included at this level, it is much better to import namespaces only in the module where they will be used. Importing a namespace at the module level does not change setting the reference, but does mean that you don't add it into the list of imports on the project's property page. Similar to variables used in a project, it is possible to define a namespace at the module level. The advantage of this is similar to the use of local variables in that it helps to prevent different namespaces from interfering with each other. As this section will show, it is possible for two different namespaces to contain classes or even child namespaces with the same name.

Importing Namespaces

The development environment and compiler need a way to prioritize the order that namespaces should be checked when a class is referenced. It is always possible to unequivocally specify a class by stating its complete namespace path. Using `System.Text.StringBuilder` is an example of doing this. However, if every reference to every class needed its full namespace declaration, that would make VB.NET and every other .NET language difficult to program in. After all, who would want to type `System.Collections.ArrayList` each time they wanted an instance of the `ArrayList` class. If you review the global references, you'll see the `System.Collections` namespace. Thus, you can just type `ArrayList` whenever you need an instance of this class.

In theory, another way to reference the `StringBuilder` class is to use `Text.StringBuilder` but, with all namespaces imported globally, there is a problem with this. The problem is caused by what is known as **namespace crowding**. Because there is a second namespace, `System.Drawing`, which has a child called `Text`, the compiler doesn't have a clear location for the `Text` namespace and therefore cannot resolve the `StringBuilder` class. The solution to this problem is to make it so that only a single version of the `Text` child namespace is found locally. Then the compiler will use this namespace regardless of the global availability of the `System.Drawing.Text` namespace.

`Imports` statements specify to the compiler those namespaces that the code will use. For example:

```
Imports Microsoft.Win32
Imports System
Imports SysDraw = System.Drawing
```

Each of these `Imports` statements illustrates a different facet of importing namespaces. The first, `Imports Microsoft.Win32`, is a namespace that is not imported at the global level. Looking at the reference list, you may not see the Microsoft assembly referenced directly. However, opening the **Object Browser** reveals that this namespace is actually included as part of the `System.dll`.

As noted earlier, the `StringBuilder` references become ambiguous because both `System.Text` and `System.Drawing.Text` are valid namespaces at the global level. As a result, the compiler has no way to distinguish which `Text` child-namespace is being referenced. Without any clear indication, the compiler flags `Text.StringBuilder` declarations in the command handler. However, using the `Imports System` declaration in the module tells the compiler that, before checking namespaces imported at the global level, it should attempt to match incomplete references at the module level. Since the `System` namespace is declared at this level, while `System.Drawing` (for the moment) is not, there is no ambiguity as to which child-namespace `Text.StringBuilder` belongs to.

This demonstrates how the compiler looks at each possible declaration:

- First, see if the item is a complete reference such as `System.Text.StringBuilder`

- If the declaration does not match a complete reference, then the compiler looks to see if the declaration is from a child-namespace of one of the module level imports

- Finally, if a match has not been found, the compiler looks at the global level imports to see if the declaration can be associated with a namespace imported for the entire assembly

While the preceding logical progression of moving from a full declaration through module to global level imports does resolve the majority of issues, it does not handle all possibilities. Specifically, if we imported `System.Drawing` at the module level, the **namespace collision** would return. This is where the third import statement becomes important – this import statement uses an **alias**.

Aliasing Namespaces

Aliasing has two benefits in .NET. The first is that aliasing allows a long namespace such as `System.EnterpriseServices` to be replaced with a shorthand name such as `COMPlus`. The second is that it adds a way to prevent ambiguity of child namespaces at the module level.

As noted earlier, the `System` and `System.Drawing` namespaces both contain a child-namespace of `Text`. Since we will be using a number of classes from the `System.Drawing` namespace, it follows that this namespace should be imported into the form's module. However, were this namespace imported along with the `System` namespace, the compiler would once again find references to the `Text` child-namespace to be ambiguous. However, by aliasing the `System.Drawing` namespace to `SysDraw`, the compiler knows that it should only check the `System.Drawing` namespace when a declaration begins with that alias. The result is that, although multiple namespaces with the same child-namespace are now available at the module level, the compiler knows that one (or more) of them should only be checked at this level when they are explicitly referenced.

Creating a Namespace

Every assembly created in .NET is part of some root namespace. By default, this logic actually mirrors COM in that assemblies are assigned a namespace that matches the project name. However, unlike COM, in .NET it is possible to change this default behavior. In this way, just as Microsoft has packaged the system level and common runtime language classes using well-defined names, it is possible for us to create our own namespaces. Of course, it's also possible to create projects that match existing namespaces and extend those namespaces, but that is very poor programming practice.

Creating an assembly in a custom namespace can be done at one of two levels. However, unless you want the same name for each assembly that will be used in a large namespace, you will normally reset the root namespace for the assembly. This is done through the assembly's project pages, reached by right-clicking on the assembly name in the **Solution Explorer** window:

The next step is optional but, depending on whether you want to create a class at the top level or at a child level, you can add a `Namespace` command to your code. There is a trick to being able to create top level namespaces, or multiple namespaces within the modules that make up an assembly. Instead of replacing the default namespace with another name, we can delete the default namespace and only define the namespaces in the modules using the `Namespace` command.

The `Namespace` command is accompanied by an `End Namespace` command. This `End Namespace` command must be placed after the `End Class` tag for any classes that will be part of the namespace:

```
Namespace MyMetaNamespace
    Class MyClass1
        'Code
    End Class
End Namespace
```

The Namespace command can also be nested. Using nested Namespace commands is how child namespaces are defined. The same rules apply – each Namespace must be paired with an End Namespace and must fully encompass all of the classes that are part of that namespace.

The following code demonstrates the structure used to create a MyMetaNamespace namespace, which also has a child namespace called MyMetaNamespace.MyChildNamespace:

```
Namespace MyMetaNamespace
    Class MyClass1
        'Code
    End Class
    Namespace MyChildNamespace
        Class MyClass2
            'Code
        End Class
    End Namespace
End Namespace
```

> When you create your own namespaces, Microsoft recommends that you use a convention of **CompanyName.TechnologyName** – for example, **Wrox.Books**. This helps to ensure that all libraries are organized in a consistent way.

Summary

The introduction of namespaces with .NET provides a powerful tool that helps to abstract the logical capabilities from their physical implementation. While there are differences in the syntax of referencing objects from a namespace, as opposed to referencing the same object from a COM style component implementation, overall there are several similarities. This chapter introduced namespaces and their hierarchical structure, and demonstrated:

- ❑ How namespace hierarchies are not related to class hierarchies
- ❑ How to review and add references to a project
- ❑ How to import and alias namespaces at the module level
- ❑ How to create custom namespaces

Namespaces play an important role in enterprise software development. By allowing you to separate the implementation of related functional objects, while retaining the ability to still group these objects, you improve the overall maintainability of your code. Everyone who has ever worked on a large project has been put in the situation where a fix to a component is delayed because of the potential impact on other components in the same project. Regardless of the logical separation of components in the same project, those who watched the development process worried about testing. With totally separate implementations for related components, it is not only possible to alleviate this concern, but it is easier than ever before for a team of developers to work on different parts of the same project.

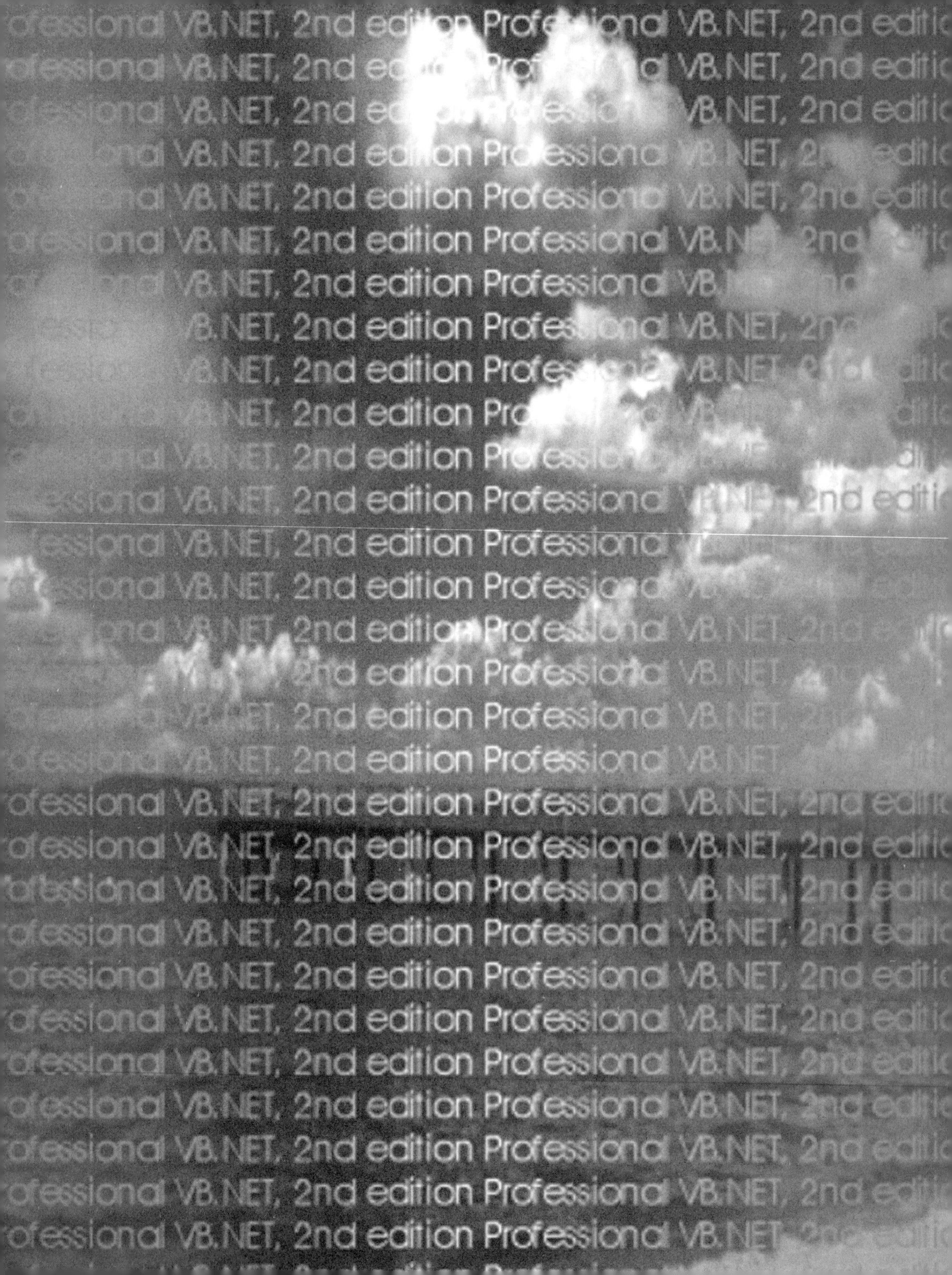
Professional VB.NET, 2nd edition

Error Handling

Error handling is an important topic in any programming language. If a program lets errors through the users will be confused and the program will not produce the results that were originally intended.

Error handling has been much improved in VB.NET compared to VB6. In this chapter, we will cover how error handling works in VB.NET by discussing the CLR exception handler in detail and the programming methods that are most efficient in catching errors. Specifically, we will discuss:

- ❑ The general principals behind error handling
- ❑ The `Try...Catch...Finally` structure, the `Exit Try` statement, and nested `Try` structures
- ❑ The exception handler's methods and properties
- ❑ Error handling between managed and unmanaged code, and how VB.NET assists us in that area
- ❑ Error and trace logging and how we can use these methods to obtain feedback on how our program is working

We'll begin by looking at how exceptions are handled by the Common Language Runtime (CLR).

The CLR Exception Handler

The error handling techniques within Visual Basic have, in the past, been very much left up to developers who came up with many very effective methods of handling exceptions and ensuring their users could report any errors to them effectively. However, there was lack of built-in VB routines to handle this.

In .NET all exceptions inherit from `System.Exception`. Extensions to the `Exception` class can be found in many namespaces. The following table lists some the most common namespaces and the classes that extend `Exception`:

Namespace	Class
System	ApplicationException SystemException VB6Exception
System.Data	InvalidConstraintException
System.IO	IOException
System.Runtime. InteropServices	COMException
System.Web.Services. Protocols	SoapException
System.XML	XmlException

The `System` namespace holds many of the classes that represent exceptions that happen on a routine basis in our applications. The following table describes some of the exception classes that exist within the `System` namespace and their descriptions:

Class	Description
ApplicationException	Occurs when a non-fatal application error occurs
ArgumentNullException	Occurs when a `Null` argument is passed and cannot be accepted as `Null`
DivideByZeroException	Occurs when a 0 is used as a divisor in an arithmetic routine
MissingFieldException	Occurs in an attempt to access a non-existent field
MissingMemberException	Indicates a DLL versioning problem
OutofMemoryException	Occurs when there is not enough memory to continue
OverflowException	Occurs in an arithmetic overflow situation
SystemException	Occurs when a recoverable exception occurs
Vb6Exception	Occurs when an exception occurs with a function within the VB6 compatibility library

Standardizing Error Handling

Standardizing error handling within our VB applications is an important consideration when writing code. If the error handling code isn't standardized, errors could happen outside our error handling structures and bring our application to an abrupt, ungraceful stop. Indeed, the whole idea behind error handling is to gracefully handle unexpected events so that the user of our application can report the error and continue without losing data.

The concept behind error handling begins with the ability to accurately trap the error. In the .NET application architecture the error will not necessarily be part of the set of modules in the current VB project, but might originate in a module on another separate machine. Our aim should be to cover any code that could raise an error and handle any errors in a uniform manner. Programmers still have to make decisions as to how to present the errors to a user in a consistent manner (say with message boxes).

VB.NET still includes the `On Error` statements familiar from VB6, which are available with the `Err` object. The `On Error` statement requires a section of code that executes the `GoTo` statement, which goes to a label that contains error handling code, which should informally handle our exception and present it to the user. Your goal should be to standardize this error handling code within your modules as well as determining how to standardize the way errors are handled in your `Try...Catch...Finally` code blocks.

The On Error Statement

When thinking about the concept of global error handling it is important to differentiate between the use of the `On Error` statement in VB and the new `Try...Catch...Finally` model available in .NET.

> Although we're going to discuss `On Error` in this section, it's very much the "old way" of doing things and where possible you should look to use `Try...Catch...Finally` blocks on your code.

In situations where there is a system error during a call to a DLL, the `On Error` statement is the only way the error will get trapped. In this case, the error can be caught by checking the `Err` object and its properties for the details of the error. The `On Error` statement is the recommended approach for error trapping from a global perspective because without it any runtime exception is fatal in our application. The traditional `On Error` statement still has a solid place in our programming environment because we want to prevent these fatal errors in situations where the `Try...Catch...Finally` block would be cumbersome to use.

> Note that the `On Error` statement cannot be used when a `Try...Catch...Finally` block is already present in a procedure.

If you've not programmed with versions of VB prior to VB.NET here's an example of an On Error statement:

```
Sub CustomErrorExample()
  On Error Goto ErrorHandler
  Dim intX As Integer
  Dim intY As Integer
  Dim intZ As Integer
  intY = 0
  intX = 5
  ' Cause a "Divide by Zero"
  intZ = CType((intX / intY), Integer)
  MessageBox.Show(Str(intZ))
  Exit Sub
ErrorHandler:
  UnhandledExceptionHandler()
End Sub
```

In this example we force a divide-by-zero error to occur by initializing our divisor variable to be zero and then using it in a division problem, but this approach would work well for any other system error that may be thrown while this procedure is running.

We start our code by setting up our On Error statement that refers to the ErrorHandler label at the bottom of our procedure:

```
On Error Goto ErrorHandler
```

Then when our divide by zero error occurs, the code after the ErrorHandler label is executed. In this case, we have referred to another subroutine within the same class. Here we have standardized the manner in which we will handle exceptions caught by our On Error statement. Any code that needs to be in the error handler to trap and handle any specific errors we would want to treat would be placed in this subroutine. The standard error handler just shows a simple message box so that the user can report the error to the programmer:

```
Sub UnhandledExceptionHandler()
  MessageBox.Show("Unhandled Error:" & Err.Description)
End Sub
```

In addition to familiar properties such as Description, the Err object now has a GetException method that returns an Exception object, which we'll be looking at shortly.

The Exception Handler

In this section, we will be going over examples that illustrate the exception handler, its structures, properties, and methods. We'll start by looking at the Try...Catch...Finally block structure and how we can include Exit Try statements and create nested Try structures. We'll then go into detail about the properties and methods within the Exception object by looking at examples that utilize them.

Try...Catch...Finally

The exception handler for VB.NET uses `Try...Catch...Finally`. Under this model a
`Try...Catch...Finally` block of code surrounds the code where an exception might occur. The simple
`Try` statement comes before the block of code, the `Catch` block of code is where we specify what types
of errors to look for, and the `Finally` block of code is always executed and contains cleanup routines
for exception situations. Since the `Catch` block is specific to the type of error we want to catch, we will
often use multiple `Catch` blocks in our `Try...Catch...Finally` structure.

Let's look at a very simple piece of code that will cause a divide-by-zero error to occur. For these
examples we need to insert an `Imports System.Windows.Forms` statement in the class declaration
section so that we can use the `Messagebox.Show` method:

```
Sub HandlerExample()
  Dim intX As Integer
  Dim intY As Integer
  Dim intZ As Integer
  intY = 0
  intX = 5
  ' First Required Error Statement.
  Try
     ' Cause a "Divide by Zero"
     intZ = CType((intX / intY), Integer)
  ' Catch the error.
  Catch objA As System.OverflowException
     Messagebox.Show("Caught the divide by zero error")
  Catch
     Messagebox.Show("Caught any other errors")
  ' Finally section always gets processed after a try
  Finally
     Messagebox.Show(Str(intZ))
  ' End of try loop
  End Try
End Sub
```

Note how we have surrounded all the code that has potential to cause an error within our
`Try...Catch...Finally` block. In our example we have two `Catch` statements. The first one is
demonstrating catching a specific error, that of an overflow caused by a divide-by-zero condition, and
allows us to use the properties of the `Exception` object by populating the variable `objA` with it:

```
Catch objA As System.OverflowException
   Messagebox.Show("Caught the divide by zero error")
```

The message box displayed when this code is run will look like the following:

The other statement that we include catches any other errors that occur in our `Try` block (this code block will be skipped over as we don't have any other errors in our code):

```
Catch
    Messagebox.Show("Caught any other errors")
```

> When we have a specific **Catch** statement, it is a good idea to also have a second statement to catch any other errors. Then, if an error passes the first **Catch**, the second will certainly catch it.

After catching the error the `Finally` block executes and displays a message box with the value of `intZ` in our code, which in this case is 0 because the integer was initialized to that and the division problem didn't complete due to our divide-by-zero error:

`Finally` blocks are optional but they are always executed if present. There is usually clean up code that needs to go at the end of our `Try` blocks that fits nicely into our `Finally` portion of the structure.

The Exit Try Statement

The `Exit Try` statement will, under a given circumstance, break out of the `Try` or `Catch` block and continue at the `Finally` block. In the following example, we are going to exit a `Catch` block if the value of `intY` value is 0 because we know that our overflow error was caused by a division by zero error:

```
Sub HandlerExample2()
    Dim intX As Integer
    Dim intY As Integer
    Dim intZ As Integer
    intY = 0
    intX = 5
    Try
        ' Cause a "Divide by Zero"
        intZ = CType((intX / intY), Integer)
    ' Catch the error.
    Catch objA As System.OverflowException
        MessageBox.Show("Caught the divide by zero error")
        If intY = 0 Then
            Exit Try
        Else
            MessageBox.Show("Error not divide by 0")
        End If
    Catch
        MessageBox.Show("Caught any other errors")
    Finally
        MessageBox.Show(Str(intZ))
```

```
          End Try
     End Sub
```

In our first `Catch` block we have inserted an `If` block, so that we can exit the block given a certain condition (in this case that the overflow exception was caused by the value of `intY` being 0). The `Exit Try` goes immediately to the `Finally` block and completes the processing there:

```
          If intY = 0 Then
            Exit Try
          Else
            MessageBox.Show("Error not divide by 0")
          End If
```

Now if the overflow exception is caused by something other than a divide-by-zero we'll get a message box displaying **Error not divide by zero**.

Nested Try Structures

Errors can occur within the `Catch` portion of the `Try` structures, and cause further exceptions to be thrown. The ability to nest `Try` structures is available so that we can use a second `Try` structure to cover exceptions that could occur in code executing within the `Catch` portion of the initial try structure.

In our example below, we will use the new `Throw` method to raise a custom error. It's often helpful to be able to throw our own more general exceptions both to make it easier for users to report an error, and also to be able to handle similar exceptions in a standard way:

```
    Sub HandlerExample3()
      Dim intX As Integer
      Dim intY As Integer
      Dim intZ As Integer
      intY = 0
      intX = 5
      ' First Required Error Statement.
      Try
        ' Cause a "Divide by Zero"
        intZ = CType((intX / intY), Integer)
      ' Catch the error.
      Catch objA As System.OverflowException
        Messagebox.Show(objA.Message)
        Try
          Throw (New Exception("0 as divisor"))
        Catch objB As Exception
          Messagebox.Show(objB.Message)
        End Try
      Catch
        Messagebox.Show("Caught any other errors")
      Finally
        Messagebox.Show(Str(intZ))
      End Try
    End Sub
```

First, note now that the `Message` property of our `objA` exception object is displaying our divide-by-zero error:

```
Messagebox.Show(objA.Message)
```

This will result in a message box that looks like this:

Next, a nested `Try` structure catches another error within our `Catch` block, which is deliberately raised by the `Throw` method. The `Throw` method requires a type of exception to be thrown. Here we have only specified a generic `Exception` object with a `Message` property of `"0 as divisor"`:

```
Try
    Throw (New Exception("0 as divisor"))
Catch objB As Exception
    Messagebox.Show(objB.Message)
End Try
```

The resulting message box would look like this; the reason for our exception is now much more obvious to the end user:

> The nested **Try** structure does not have a **Finally** statement. At a bare minimum, the **Try...Catch...Finally** structure requires a **Try** and an **End Try**, with either a **Catch** or a **Finally** block; otherwise, we'll get a syntax error.

The Exception's Properties and Methods

The `Exception` class has properties that relate to each portion of the exception. In this section, we will discuss by way of example the properties and methods of the object and how they are used. We'll start with tables of the properties and methods, and descriptions of each. We'll then continue with examples of the properties and methods, and how each can be used within our `Try...Catch...Finally` structures.

The `Exception` class has the following properties:

Property	Description
HelpLink	A string indicating the link to the help for this exception
InnerException	Returns the exception object reference to an inner (nested) exception
Message	A string that contains the error
Source	A string containing the name of an object that generated the error
StackTrace	A read-only property that holds the stack trace as a text string
TargetSite	A read-only string property that holds the method that threw the exception

The `Exception` class has the following methods:

Method	Description
Equals	Determines if one exception object is equal to another
GetBaseException	Returns the first exception in the chain
GetHashCode	Similar to a hash table, serves as a hash function
GetObjectData	Used to hold the data in the `Exception` object when serializing it
GetType	Gets the type of the object which caused the exception
ToString	Returns the error string, which might include as much information as the error message, the inner exceptions, and stack trace depending on the error

The `Message` property has been used in our previous examples of the `Try…Catch…Finally` block, so let's look at some examples of how the other properties and methods listed above can be used.

InnerException and TargetSite

The `InnerException` property is used to store an exception trail. This comes in handy when multiple exceptions occur. It's quite common for an exception to occur that sets up circumstances whereby further exceptions are raised. As exceptions occur in a sequence, we can choose to **stack** our exceptions for later reference by use of the `InnerException` property of our `Exception` object. As each exception joins the stack, the previous `Exception` object becomes the inner exception in the stack.

We'll be extending our previous code sample, but this time we'll be adding a reference to an `InnerException` object to the exception we are generating with the `Throw` method:

```
Sub HandlerExample4()
   Dim intX As Integer
   Dim intY As Integer
   Dim intZ As Integer
```

```
    intY = 0
    intX = 5
    ' First Required Error Statement.
    Try
        ' Cause a "Divide by Zero"
        intZ = CType((intX / intY), Integer)
    ' Catch the error.
    Catch objA As System.OverflowException
        Try
            Throw (New Exception("0 as divisor", objA))
        Catch objB As Exception
            Messagebox.Show(objB.Message)
            Messagebox.Show(objB.InnerException.Message)
            Messagebox.Show(objB.TargetSite.Name)
        End Try
    Catch
        Messagebox.Show("Caught any other errors")
    Finally
        Messagebox.Show(Str(intZ))
    End Try
End Sub
```

As before, we catch the divide-by-zero error in the following statement, which stores our exception in objA so that we can reference its properties later:

```
    Catch objA As System.OverflowException
```

We throw a new exception with a more general message ("0 as divisor") that is easier to interpret and we build up our stack by appending objA as the InnerException object at the end of our New Exception statement:

```
        Throw (New Exception("0 as divisor", objA))
```

We catch our newly thrown exception in another Catch statement. Note how it does not catch a specific type of error:

```
        Catch objB As Exception
```

Then we display three message boxes:

```
            Messagebox.Show(objB.Message)
            Messagebox.Show(objB.InnerException.Message)
            Messagebox.Show(objB.TargetSite.Name)
```

The message box that is produced by our custom error, which is held in the cbjB variable looks like this:

The `InnerException` property holds the exception object that was generated first. The `Message` property of the `InnerException` looks like this:

The `TargetSite` property gives us the name of the method that threw our exception. This information comes in handy when troubleshooting and could be integrated into the error message so that the end user could report the method name back to us. In our example, we have displayed the value of this property in a message box for illustration. The currently executing method is `HandlerExample4`:

Source and StackTrace

The `Source` and `StackTrace` properties provide the user with information regarding where the error occurred. This supplemental information can be invaluable for the user to pass on to the troubleshooter in order to help get errors resolved more quickly. The following example below uses these two properties and shows the feedback when the error occurs:

```
Sub HandlerExample5()
    Dim intX As Integer
    Dim intY As Integer
    Dim intZ As Integer
    intY = 0
    intX = 5
    ' First Required Error Statement.
    Try
        ' Cause a "Divide by Zero"
        intZ = CType((intX / intY), Integer)
    ' Catch the error.
    Catch objA As System.OverflowException
        objA.Source = "HandlerExample5"
        Messagebox.Show("Error Occurred at :" & _
            objA.Source & objA.StackTrace)
    Finally
        Messagebox.Show(Str(intZ))
```

```
      End Try
   End Sub
```

The output from our message box statement is very detailed and gives the entire path and line number where our error occurred:

GetBaseException, GetHashCode, and Equals

The GetBaseException method comes in very handy when we are deep in a set of thrown exceptions. This method returns the originating exception, which makes debugging easier and helps keep the troubleshooting process on track by sorting through information that can be misleading.

The GetHashCode method allows a programmer to generate a unique number for assignment to an object. An object will always return the same result to the GetHashCode method, and so can be used in comparing to see if two reference type objects are the same.

The Equals method will evaluate whether one exception is identical to another.

Here are examples of each of these methods:

```
Sub HandlerExample6()
   Dim intX As Integer
   Dim intY As Integer
   Dim intZ As Integer
   intY = 0
   intX = 5
   ' First Required Error Statement.
   Try
      ' Cause a "Divide by Zero"
      intZ = CType((intX / intY), Integer)
   ' Catch the error.
   Catch objA As System.OverflowException
      Try
         Throw (New Exception("0 as divisor", objA))
         Catch objB As Exception
            Messagebox.Show(str(objB.GetHashCode))
         If objA.Equals(objB.InnerException) Then
            Messagebox.Show("Exceptions the same")
         End If
         Try
            Throw (New Exception("New error", objB))
         Catch objC As Exception
            Messagebox.Show(objC.GetBaseException.Message)
         End Try
      End Try
   End Try
```

```
      Finally
        Messagebox.Show(Str(intZ))
      End Try
   End Sub
```

In the code where we have used `GetHashCode`, the system generates a hash code and returns it, so that we can display it in a message box that looks like this:

The hash code generated will vary on different computers and at different instances of the object. Hashcode generation is truly unique for each computer and instance of an object on each computer.

We can also evaluate whether `objA` is the same as the `InnerException` object of another exception, in this case `objB`:

```
      If objA.Equals(objB.InnerException) Then
        Messagebox.Show("Exceptions the same")
      End If
```

The two exception objects are evaluated to be the same:

The `InnerException` property provides the information that the `GetBaseException` method needs, so as our example executes the `Throw` statements it sets up the `InnerException` property. The purpose of the `GetBaseException` method is to provide the properties of the initial exception in the chain that was produced. Hence, `objC.GetBaseException.Message` returns the `Message` property of the original `OverflowException` message even though we've thrown multiple errors since the original error occurred:

```
      Messagebox.Show(objC.GetBaseException.Message)
```

To put it another way, the code traverses back to the exception caught as `objA`, and displays the same message as the `objA.Message` property would:

![Exception of type System.OverflowException was thrown.]

GetType and ToString

The GetType and ToString methods return more valuable information about the error message as well as how and when it was generated. The GetType method returns additional information about the type of error that occurred. The GetType method inherits from the Object class and has many of the Object class's properties and methods. The GetType method can return such things as the full name of the exception type, the base class of the exception type, whether the exception type is public or is an interface, and even what namespace the exception type belongs to. In the following example, we illustrate two properties of the GetType method – FullName and BaseType.FullName:

```
Sub HandlerExample7()
    Dim intX As Integer
    Dim intY As Integer
    Dim intZ As Integer
    intY = 0
    intX = 5
    ' First Required Error Statement.
    Try
        ' Cause a "Divide by Zero"
        intZ = CType((intX / intY), Integer)
    ' Catch the error.
    Catch objA As System.OverflowException
        Messagebox.Show(objA.GetType.FullName)
        Messagebox.Show(objA.GetType.BaseType.FullName)
        Messagebox.Show(objA.ToString)
    Finally
        Messagebox.Show(Str(intZ))
    End Try
End Sub
```

The first message box that we show contains the full name of our error and is displayed by the code:

```
Messagebox.Show(objA.GetType.FullName)
```

The message box itself looks like this:

Our second message box is displayed by the following code:

```
Messagebox.Show(objA.GetType.BaseType.FullName)
```

The message that shows the BaseType.FullName looks like this:

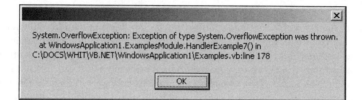

The ToString method returns a combination of the GetType.Fullname method, the Message property and the StackTrace property of the current exception. In our code, the message box that displays the ToString method is:

```
Messagebox.Show(objA.ToString)
```

The message box displayed looks like this:

System.OverflowException: Exception of type System.OverflowException was thrown.
at WindowsApplication1.ExamplesModule.HandlerExample7() in
C:\DOCS\WHIT\VB.NET\WindowsApplication1\Examples.vb:line 178

OK

HelpLink

The HelpLink property sets the help link for a specific Exception object to a string. The following example shows the syntax for the HelpLink property:

```
Sub HandlerExample8()
  Dim intX As Integer
  Dim intY As Integer
  Dim intZ As Integer
  intY = 0
  intX = 5
  ' First Required Error Statement.
  Try
    ' Cause a "Divide by Zero"
    intZ = CType((intX / intY), Integer)
  ' Catch the error.
  Catch objA As System.OverflowException
    objA.HelpLink = ("file:///C:/test/help.html")
    Messagebox.Show(objA.HelpLink)
  Finally
    Messagebox.Show(Str(intZ))
  End Try
End Sub
```

This results in the following screenshot:

Error Handling Between Managed and Unmanaged Code

The ability to trace the stack of calls in an application all the way back to the originating module and location of the module becomes a very important factor in interoperability between new VB.NET code and old VB6 code. This ability to trace the stack of calls can help us in determining our next action, based on what kind of error the application got and where it happened.

If an OLEDB error happened in a module running as a COM object on another machine while doing interactions with database data, we might want to react to the problem differently than if we got that same type of error on a local machine. In addition, as errors pass through layers of code, some errors will generate other errors, perhaps misleading us as to what the original error actually was. That is why it is so important to be able to trap the location of the error, as well as accurately being able to identify the error. We accomplish this in VB.NET by using stack-tracing properties provided in the runtime environment.

In VB.NET the error handling between managed and unmanaged code is now handled through the automatic population of an Exception object that carries through to the front-end application. We can use the properties and methods of the Exception object that we have already discussed to find out the information we need to proceed appropriately.

Our example of error handling will use an unmanaged VB6 component on the back-end that generates a divide-by-zero error. The purpose of our unmanaged component is to perform an arithmetic operation on data to derive an answer and pass the answer back to the front-end application. The VB6 DLL is called VBNet.dll and needs to be included as a reference in the VB.NET application on the front-end. The VB6 DLL has a class called Unmanaged, which has a function called CauseError. The DLL will pass the overflow error back through to the front-end application where there is code to display it accordingly.

We'll look now at the function we exposed within the VB6 DLL. The class is named Unmanaged, with the function named CauseError:

```
Function CauseError() As Integer
   Dim iResult As Integer
   Dim iDividor As Integer
   Dim iDivisor As Integer
   iDivisor = 5
   iDivisor = 0
   iResult = iDividor / iDivisor
   CauseError = iResult
End Function
```

Now as we can see in our code, it is set up to do a simple math problem, and we have forced a divide-by-zero error to occur and go un-trapped back to the calling application:

```
iDivisor = 5
iDivisor = 0
iResult = iDividor / iDivisor
```

The line of code that generates the error causes an `Exception` object to be passed back to the front-end application, where it will be handled and alert the user to do extra work to resolve our problem. The fact that an exception has been thrown takes us out of the `CauseError` function and populates an `Exception` object to return to the front-end application.

Now let's look at our front-end code; the `ComponentExample` subroutine in a VB.NET project calls our `CauseError` function and determines what to do based on whether the `Exception` object is populated:

```
Sub ComponentExample()
   Dim objX As New VBNet.Unmanaged()
   Dim intY As Integer
   Try
      intY = objX.CauseError
      MessageBox.Show("The answer is: " & intY)
   Catch a As System.Exception
      MessageBox.Show("Caught Error:" & _
         a.Message & " " & a.Source)
   End Try
   objX = Nothing
End Sub
```

If you don't have VB6, you can find VBNet.dll *in the code download from* http://www.wrox.com.

We first instantiate an instance of our unmanaged component:

```
Dim objX As New VBNet.Unmanaged()
```

We then call our component returning the numeric result to a variable so that we can deal with later:

```
intY = objX.CauseError
```

When the component returns the error, we display properties of the `Exception` object in a message box:

```
Catch a As System.Exception
   MessageBox.Show("Caught Error:" & _
      a.Message & " " & a.Source)
```

Our message box looks like this:

Error Logging

Error logging is important in many applications as an alternative way to decipher what exactly is going on when errors occur. It is common for end-users of the applications to not remember what the error said exactly and so we can trap specific errors in a log for ease of finding in such situations that we don't want to re-create the error in order to get the specific error message.

While error logging is very important, we only want to use it to trap specific levels of errors, as it carries overhead and can reduce the performance of our application. In general, the overhead it carries is writing the events to the log on a hard disk, which is an extra step in our application that isn't always necessary. The impact to our program will vary, as the hard disk speed varies on each system that the program is running on. We want to only log errors that will be critical to our application integrity, for instance an error that would cause the data that the application is working with to become invalid.

There are two main approaches to error logging:

❑ Many programmers use a trace file based approach, which would write any information in a free-form style to a simple text file located in a strategic location.

❑ We can also take advantage of the event log that is available on NT and Windows 2000 based machines. VB.NET now provides a component that can be used to write and read from the system, application, and security logs on any given machine.

The type of logging you choose depends on the categories of errors you wish to trap and the types of machines you will run your application on. If you choose to write to the event log, you need to categorize the errors and write them in the appropriate log file. Resource-, hardware-, and system-level errors would best fit into the system event log. Data access errors would fit best into the application event log. Permission errors would best fit into the security event log. Since the event log is only available on NT or Windows 2000 machines, the trace file method of logging would be a good choice if you need to support other client machines.

The Event Log

The **event log** is available on NT and Windows 2000 based machines. There are three logs on these machines: the system, application, and security logs.

The event logging operations, while available since VB6, have been greatly enhanced through an event log component that allows a programmer both read and write capabilities with all of the available logs on a machine. The `EventLog` component is part of the `System.Diagnostics` namespace and is accessed through adding the namespace as a reference to the VB.NET project. The component is what provides us with functionality such as adding and removing custom event logs, reading and writing from the standard Windows event logs and creating customized event log entries.

In contrast, Visual Basic versions 5.0 and 6.0 exposed only three methods and properties of the `App` *object by which event logging can be enabled: the* `LogMode` *property, the* `LogPath` *property, and the* `LogEvent` *method. The* `LogMode` *and* `LogPath` *properties returned information about how and where logging happened, and the* `LogEvent` *method wrote an event to the application log.*

Event logs can get full, as they have a limited amount of space, so we only want to write critical information to our event logs. We can customize each of our system event log's properties by changing the log size and determining how the system will handle events that occur when the log is full. We can configure the log to overwrite when it is full, or overwrite all events older than a given number of days. It is important to remember that the event log that is written to is based on where the code is running from, so that if there are many tiers we can locate the proper event log information to research the error further.

There are five types of event log entries we can make. These five types are separated into **event type entries** and **audit type entries**.

Event type entries are:

❏ **Information** – added when events such as a service starting or stopping occurs

❏ **Warning** – occurs when a non-critical event occurs that might cause future problems, such as disk space getting low

❏ **Error** – should be logged when something occurs that will prevent normal processing, such as a startup service not being able to start

Audit type entries will usually go into the security log and can be either:

❏ **Success audit** – for example, a success audit might be a successful login through an application to a SQL Server

❏ **Failure audit** – a failure audit might come in handy if a user doesn't have access to create an output file on a certain file system

If we don't specify the type of event log entry an information type entry is generated.

Each entry in an event log has a `Source` property. The `Source` property is required, and is a programmer-defined string that is assigned to an event that helps categorize the events in a log. A new `Source` must be defined prior to being used in an entry in an event log. The `SourceExists` method is used to determine if a particular source already exists on the given computer. We recommend that you use a string that is easily sorted based on where the error originated such as the component name, or a programmer-defined grouping for the source. For instance, packaged software often uses the software name as the Source in the application log. As shown in the following screenshot, this helps group errors that occur by any given software package:

The `EventLog` object model is based on the `System.Diagnostics` namespace. Therefore, in order to use the `EventLog` component, you need to include an `Imports System.Diagnostics` statement in the declarations section of your code.

> **Certain security rights must be obtained in order to manipulate event logs. Ordinary programs can read all of the event logs and write to the application event log. Special privileges, on the administrator level, are required to perform tasks such as clearing and deleting event logs.**

The most common events, methods, and properties are listed and described in the following tables.

Events

Event	Description
EntryWritten	Generated when an event is written to a log

Methods

Methods	Description
CreateEventSource	Creates an event source in the specified log
DeleteEventSource	Deletes an event source and associated entries
WriteEntry	Writes a string to a specified log
Exists	This can be used to determine if a specific event log exists

Methods	Description
SourceExists	Used to determine if a specific source exists in a log
GetEventLogs	Retrieves a list of all event logs on a particular computer
Delete	Deletes an entire event log – *use this method with care*

Properties

Properties	Description
Source	Specifies the source of the entry to be written.
Log	Used to specify a log to write to. The three logs are system, application, and security. The system log is the default if not specified.

Here is an example that illustrates some of these methods and properties:

```
Sub LoggingExample1()
  Dim objLog As New EventLog()
  Dim objLogEntryType As EventLogEntryType
  Try
     Throw (New EntryPointNotFoundException())
  Catch objA As System.EntryPointNotFoundException
    If Not objLog.SourceExists("Example") Then
       objLog.CreateEventSource("Example", "System")
    End If
    objLog.Source = "Example"
    objLog.Log = "System"
    objLogEntryType = EventLogEntryType.Information
    objLog.WriteEntry("Error: " & objA.Message, objLogEntryType)
  End Try
End Sub
```

We have declared two variables – one to instantiate our log and one to hold our entry's type information. Note that we need to check for the existence of a source prior to creating it. These two lines of code accomplish this:

```
If Not objLog.SourceExists("Example") Then
   objLog.CreateEventSource("Example", "System")
```

Once we have verified or created our source, we can set the Source property of the EventLog object, set the Log property to specify which log we want to write to, and EventLogEntryType to Information (other choices are Warning, Error, SuccessAudit, and FailureAudit). If we attempt to write to a source that does not exist in a specific log, we will get an error. After we have set these three properties of our EventLog object, we then can write our entry. In our example, we concatenated the word Error with the actual exception's Message property to form our string to write to our log:

```
objLog.Source = "Example"
```

287

```
objLog.Log = "System"
objLogEntryType = EventLogEntryType.Information
objLog.WriteEntry("Error: " & objA.Message, objLogEntryType)
```

The following is the copy of the event log that was generated from our example:

Event Type:	Information
Event Source:	Example
Event Category:	None
Event ID:	0
Date:	2/2/2002
Time:	9:42:54 AM
User:	N/A
Computer:	Computer01
Description:	Error: Entry point was not found

Writing to Trace Files

As an alternative for platforms that don't support event logging, or if we can't get direct access to the event log, we can write our debugging and error information to trace files. A **trace file** is a text-based file that we generate in our program to track detailed information about an error condition. Trace files are also a good way to supplement our event logging on Windows NT and Windows 2000 machines if we wish to track detailed information that would potentially fill the event log.

A more detailed explanation of the variety of trace tools and uses in debugging follows in *Measuring Performance via the Trace Class*, but we will cover some of the techniques for using the StreamWriter interface in our development of a trace file in this section.

The concepts involved in writing to text files include setting up **streamwriters** and **debug listeners**. The StreamWriter interface is handled through the System.IO namespace and allows us to interface to the files in the file system on a given machine. The Debug class interfaces with these output objects through listener objects. The job of any listener object is to collect, store up, and send the stored output to text files, logs, and the Output window. In our example, we will use the TextWriterTraceListener interface.

As we will see, the StreamWriter object opens an output path to a text file, and by binding the StreamWriter object to a listener object we can direct debug output to a text file.

Trace listeners are output targets and can be a TextWriter, an EventLog, or can send output to the default Output window (which is DefaultTraceListener). The TextWriterTraceListener accommodates the WriteLine method of a Debug interface by providing an output object that stores up information to be flushed to the output stream, which we setup by the StreamWriter interface.

The following table lists some of the commonly used methods from the `StreamWriter` object:

Method	Description
Close	Closes the `StreamWriter`.
Flush	Flushes all content of the `StreamWriter` to the output file designated upon creation of the `StreamWriter`.
Write	Writes byte output to the stream. Optional parameters allow designation of where in the stream (offset).
WriteLine	Writes characters followed by a line terminator to the current stream object.

The following table lists some of the methods associated with the `Debug` object, which provides the output mechanism for our text file example to follow:

Method	Description
Assert	Checks a condition and displays a message if `False`
Close	Executes a flush on the output buffer and closes all listeners
Fail	Emits an error message in the form of an Abort/Retry/Ignore message box
Flush	Flushes the output buffer and writes it to the listeners
Write	Writes bytes to the output buffer
WriteLine	Writes characters followed by a line terminator to the output buffer
WriteIf	Writes bytes to the output buffer given a specific condition is `True`
WriteLine IF	Writes characters followed by a line terminator to the output buffer if a specific condition is `True`

Below is an example of how we can open an existing file (called `mytext.txt`) for output and assign it to the `Listeners` object of the `Debug` object so it can catch our `Debug.WriteLine` statements:

```
Sub LoggingExample2()
  Dim objWriter As New _
      IO.StreamWriter(File.Open("c:\mytext.txt", FileMode.Open))
  Debug.Listeners.Add(New TextWriterTraceListener(objWriter))
  Try
    Throw (New EntryPointNotFoundException())
  Catch objA As System.EntryPointNotFoundException
    Debug.WriteLine(objA.Message)
    objWriter.Flush()
    objWriter.Close()
    objWriter = Nothing
  End Try
End Sub
```

Looking in detail at our code above, we first create a `StreamWriter` that is assigned to a file in our local file system:

```
Dim objWriter As New _
    IO.StreamWriter(File.Open("c:\mytext.txt",FileMode.Open))
```

We then assign our `StreamWriter` to a debug listener by using the `Add` method:

```
Debug.Listeners.Add(New TextWriterTraceListener (objWriter))
```

In our example above, we force an error condition and catch it, writing the `Message` property of the `Exception` object (which is `Entry point was not found.`) to the debug buffer through the `WriteLine` method:

```
Debug.WriteLine(objA.Message)
```

We finally flush the listener buffer to the output file and free our resources.

```
objWriter.Flush()
objWriter.Close()
objWriter = Nothing
```

Debugging and Measuring Performance

The .NET Framework has enhanced the capabilities we have to debug and measure the performance of our applications.

The debug capabilities have been expanded by not only the use of the `Debug` object as we illustrated earlier, but with some system events that we can generate. Debugging our application will always go beyond the development stage, as we can never anticipate everything that users will do with an application.

We discussed and illustrated in the previous logging and trace file examples how we can use the `Debug` statements in the VS.NET environment to develop output to event logs and files. In this section, we'll expand that capability by coupling it with the use of the `Trace` class. We can now trace the performance of our application via the use of this class. It is important that an application have the ability to have its performance measured so that we can make improvements as our application environment changes, as it always will over time.

The major difference between what we have seen with using our `Debug` statements and using tracing techniques is in their respective purpose. The `Debug` class is primarily used to write information to log files after an error has occurred or in order to be able to track information during program execution about variables. The use of the `Trace` class and tracing techniques described in this section allows us to see how well a piece of code or an entire application is performing. The two classes have many of the same properties and methods, and both even use listener objects to accomplish output. The biggest difference is that `Trace` class statements are compiled into release versions of code while `Debug` statements are not.

The topic of debugging and measuring performance brings up the subject of **instrumentation**. Instrumentation is a widely used term, which simply means that an application has a built-in ability to give the programmer feedback on what's going on within it as it runs. It is important to build these features into our programs, but at the same time, we must consider the overhead of doing the instrumentation constantly. This consideration brings up two points – first, that we must strategically place our instrumentation and second, that we should use conditional compilation statements and trace switches to trigger our instrumentation activity.

Conditional compilation statements have been around for quite a while, and come in quite handy when we want to run code only if certain conditions are met. Basically, a piece of code that is included in a conditional compilation section is surrounded by an #If ... #End If block. If the condition within the #If is met then the code is executed, otherwise it is skipped. There are two ways of setting up conditions to be tested in our #If statements: #Const directives and trace switches:

❑   A #Const directive is simply setting up a constant in the code with a #CONST statement. For instance, if we wanted to test for whether the version of code we had was the English version we would include a #Const EnglishVersion at the top of our code and then we could use an #If EnglishVersion within our code.

❑   Trace switches are objects we set up in our code that allow us to check a condition and generate our tracing output based on that condition. Our examples in this section will illustrate the use of trace switches and conditional compilation tests further.

Measuring Performance via the Trace Class

The trace tools in the .NET Framework evolve around the Trace class, which provides properties and methods that help us trace the execution of our code. By default, tracing is enabled in VB.NET, so not unlike our previous debug discussion, all we have to do is setup the output and utilize its capabilities.

We can specify the detail level we want to perform for our tracing output by configuring trace switches. Trace switches can be either BooleanSwitch or TraceSwitch. BooleanSwitch has a value of either 0 or 1, and is used to determine if tracing is off or on respectively; while TraceSwitch allows us to specify a level of tracing based on five enumerated values. We can manage a BooleanSwitch or TraceSwitch as an environment variable. Once a switch is established, we can create and initialize it in code and use it with either trace or debug.

A TraceSwitch can have five enumerated levels that can be read as 0-4 or checked with four properties provided in the switch class interface. The four properties return a Boolean value based on whether the switch is set to a certain level or higher. The five enumerated levels for TraceSwitch are:

Level	Description
0	None
1	Only error messages
2	Warning and error messages
3	Information, warning, and error messages
4	Verbose, information, warning, and error messages

The four properties are TraceError, TraceWarning, TraceInfo, and TraceVerbose. For example, if our switch was set at number 2 and we asked for the TraceError or TraceWarning properties they would return True, while the TraceInformation and TraceVerbose properties would return False.

An environment variable is either managed via the command line or under My computer | Properties | Advanced within the Environment Variables button.

Within the Environment Variables button, you add a new User variable, giving it the SwitchName and Value for that switch.

From the command line, type:

```
Set _Switch_MySwitch = 0
```

The value on the left of the equals is the name of the switch, and the value on the right of the equals is either 0 or 1 for a BooleanSwitch or 0-4 for a TraceSwitch. Note that there is a space between the word Set and the leading underscore of _Switch. Once you have typed the above line, if you follow that by the plain SET command at the command line it will show your new switch as an environment variable as shown in the following screen shot:

For the example that follows, we have the output directed to the default Output window:

```
Sub TraceExample1()
  Dim objTraceSwitch As TraceSwitch
  objTraceSwitch = New TraceSwitch("ExampleSwitch", "Test Trace Switch")
  objTraceSwitch.Level = TraceLevel.Error
  Try
    Throw (New EntryPointNotFoundException())
  Catch objA As System.EntryPointNotFoundException
    Trace.WriteLineIf(objTraceSwitch.TraceVerbose, _
        "First Trace " & objA.Source)
    Trace.WriteLineIf(objTraceSwitch.TraceError, _
        "Second Trace " & objA.Message)
  End Try
End Sub
```

We begin by assigning our switch to an existing registry entry and set its level:

```
objTraceSwitch = New TraceSwitch("ExampleSwitch", "Test Trace Switch")
objTraceSwitch.Level = TraceLevel.Error
```

After we throw our exception, we first cause our trace output listener to catch the Source property of our Exception object based on whether the value of our switch is TraceVerbose or better:

```
Trace.WriteLineIf(objTraceSwitch.TraceVerbose, _
    "First Trace " & objA.Source)
```

Since the tracing level is set to Error the above line is skipped and we continue by writing a trace to the Output window to include the message information if the level is set to Error:

```
Trace.WriteLineIf(objTraceSwitch.TraceError, _
    "Second Trace " & objA.Message)
```

As we can see in our Output window shown, we successfully wrote only the second trace line based on the level being Error on our trace switch:

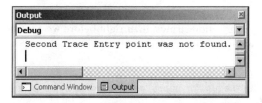

The other thing we want the ability to do is to determine the performance of our application. Overall, our application might appear to be working fine, but it is always a good thing to be able to measure the performance of our application so that environment changes or degradation over time can be counteracted. The basic concept here is to use conditional compilation so that we can turn on and off our performance-measuring code:

```
Sub TraceExample2()
  Dim connInfo As New Connection()
  Dim rstInfo As New Recordset()
  #Const bTrace = 1
  Dim objWriter As New _
    IO.StreamWriter(File.Open("c:\mytext.txt", FileMode.OpenOrCreate))
  connInfo.ConnectionString = "Provider = sqloledb.1" & _
    ";Persist Security Info = False;" & "Initial Catalog = Northwind;" & _
    "DataSource = LocalServer"
  connInfo.Open(connInfo.ConnectionString, "sa")
  Trace.Listeners.Add(New TextWriterTraceListener(objWriter))
  #If bTrace Then
    Trace.WriteLine("Begun db query at " & now())
  #End If
  rstInfo.Open("SELECT CompanyName, OrderID, " & _
    "OrderDate FROM Orders AS a LEFT JOIN Customers" & _
    " AS b ON a.CustomerID = b.CustomerID WHERE " & _
```

```
      "a.CustomerID = 'Chops'", connInfo, _
      CursorTypeEnum.adOpenForwardOnly, _
      LockTypeEnum.adLockBatchOptimistic)
    #If bTrace Then
      Trace.WriteLine("Ended db query at " & now())
    #End If
    Trace.Listeners.Clear()
    objWriter.Close()
    rstInfo.Close()
    connInfo.Close()
    rstInfo = Nothing
    connInfo = Nothing
End Sub
```

This subroutine uses ADO, so be sure to add a reference to an ADO library and an `Imports` `ADODB` *statement in the declarations section of the module.*

In this simple example we are trying to measure the performance of a database query using a conditional constant defined as bTrace by the following code:

```
#Const bTrace = 1
```

We establish our database connection strings, then right before we execute our query we write to a log file based on whether we are in tracing mode or not:

```
#If bTrace Then
  Trace.WriteLine("Begun db query at " & now())
#End If
```

Again, after our query returns we'll write to our log only if we are in tracing mode:

```
#If bTrace Then
  Trace.WriteLine("Ended db query at" & now())
#End If
```

It is always important to remember that tracing will potentially slow the application down, so we want to use this functionality only when troubleshooting and not let it run all the time.

Summary

In this chapter we reviewed the exception handler provided with the CLR and went over the methods it gives us to handle exceptions through the Try...Catch...Finally model. We discussed:

❑ Nested Try structures

❑ The Exit Try statement

❑ Properties and methods of the Exception object including: Message, StackTrace, Source, InnerException, HelpLink

- ❑ Handling `Exception` objects as returned from unmanaged code
- ❑ Error logging to event logs and trace files
- ❑ Instrumentation and measuring performance
- ❑ Tracing techniques

We used several examples in each section to illustrate the use of each method, property, and technique. It is most important to understand that error handling within VB.NET has been standardized and that the process has changed significantly from previously with VB6. As we work through these improvements, the sophistication and completeness provided by the CLR will increase the ability to lower overall critical messages that appear in applications.

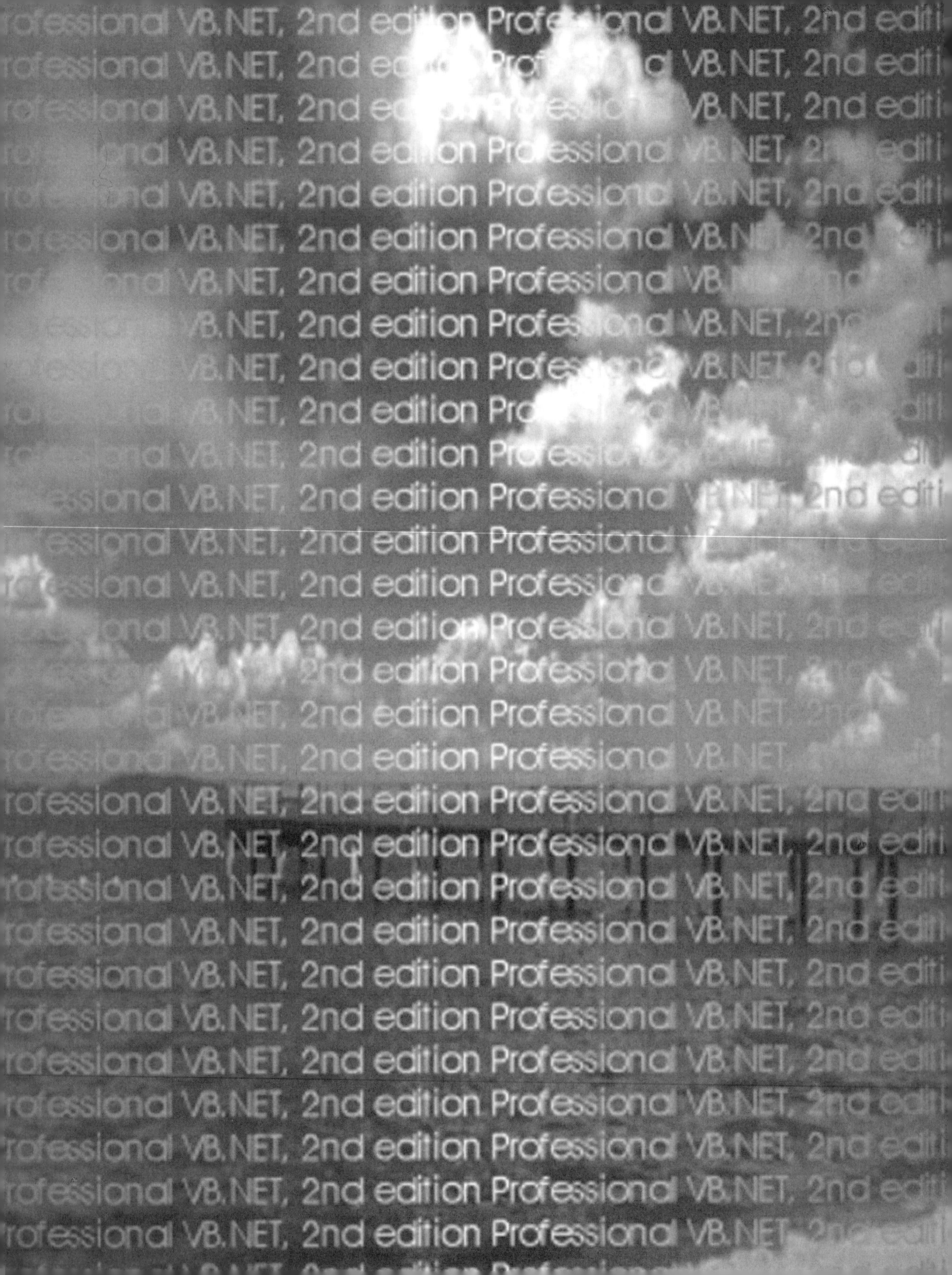
Professional VB.NET, 2nd edition

10

Using XML in VB.NET

In this chapter we'll look at how we can generate and manipulate **Extensible Markup Language (XML)** using VB.NET. However, using XML in VB.NET is a vast area to cover; the .NET Framework exposes five XML specific namespaces that contain over a hundred different classes. In addition, there are dozens of other classes that support and implement XML related technologies such as ADO.NET, SQL Server, and BizTalk. Consequently, we'll concentrate on the general concepts and the most important classes.

VB.NET relies on the classes exposed in the following XML-related namespaces in order to transform, manipulate, and stream XML documents:

- ❑ `System.Xml` – provides core support for a variety of XML standards (including DTD, namespace, DOM, XDR, XPath, XSLT, and SOAP).

- ❑ `System.Xml.Serialization` – provides the objects used to transform objects to and from XML documents or streams using serialization.

- ❑ `System.Xml.Serialization.Schema` – provides a set of objects that allow schemas to be loaded, created, and streamed. This support is achieved using a suite of objects that support the in-memory manipulation of the entities that compose an XML schema.

- ❑ `System.Xml.XPath` – provides a parser and evaluation engine for the **XML Path Language (XPath)**.

- ❑ `System.Xml.Xsl` – provides the objects necessary when working with, **Extensible Stylesheet Language (XSL)**, and **XSL Transformations (XSLT)**.

The XML-related technologies utilized by VB.NET include other technologies that generate XML documents and allow XML documents to be managed as a data source:

❑ **ADO** – the legacy COM objects provided by ADO have the ability to generate XML documents in stream or file form. ADO can also retrieve a previously persisted XML document and manipulate it. (Although ADO will not be used in this chapter, ADO and other legacy COM APIs can be accessed seamlessly from VB.NET.)

❑ **ADO.NET** – this uses XML as its underlying data representation: the in-memory data representation of the ADO.NET `DataSet` object is XML; the results of data queries are represented as XML documents; XML can be imported into a `DataSet` and exported from a `DataSet`. (ADO.NET will be covered in Chapter 11.)

❑ **SQL Server 2000** – XML specific features were added to SQL Server 2000 (`FOR XML` queries to retrieve XML documents and `OPENXML` in order to represent an XML document as a rowset). VB.NET can use ADO.NET in order to access SQL Server's XML-specific features (the documents generated and consumed by SQL Server can then be manipulated programmatically).

In this chapter we'll make sense of this range of technologies by introducing some basic XML concepts and demonstrating how VB.NET, in conjunction with the .NET Framework, can make use of XML. Specifically, we will:

❑ Understand the rationale behind XML

❑ Look at the namespaces within the .NET Framework class library that deal with XML and XML-related technologies

❑ Take a closer look at some of the classes contained within these namespaces

❑ Gain an overview of some of the other Microsoft technologies that utilize XML, particularly SQL Server and ADO.NET

At the end of this chapter, you will be able to generate, manipulate, and transform XML using VB.NET.

> *If you want to learn more about XML in general, an excellent starting point is* Professional XML, Second Edition *(Wrox Press, ISBN 1861005059). You can learn more about how XML is used in* Professional XML for .NET Developers *(Wrox Press, ISBN 1861005318).*

An Introduction to XML

XML is a tagged markup language similar to HTML. This means that XML leverages one of the most useful features of HTML – readability. However, XML differs from HTML in that XML *represents* data while HTML is a mechanism for *displaying* data. The tags in XML *describe* the data, for example:

```xml
<?xml version="1.0" encoding="utf-8"?>
<presciptions>
    <WXClientPrescription dentistName="Dr. Jam" medicationID="1"
                          quantity="21">
    </WXClientPrescription>
    <WXClientPrescription dentistName="Dr. Jam" medicationID="2"
                          quantity="22">
    </WXClientPrescription>
</presciptions>
```

This XML document is used to represent a set of medical prescriptions written by a dentist. The standard used to represent a prescription would be useful to dentists, doctors, insurance companies, government run medical systems, and pharmacies. This information can be shared using XML because:

❑   The data tags in XML are self describing

❑   XML is an open standard

XML supports the parsing of data by applications not familiar with the contents of the XML document. XML documents can also be associated with a description (a **schema**) that informs an application as to the structure of the data within the XML document.

At this stage, XML looks simple – it's just a human readable way to exchange data in a universally accepted way. The essential points that you should understand about XML are:

❑   XML data can be stored in a plain text file.

❑   A document is said to be **well formed** if it adheres to the XML standard.

❑   Tags are used to specify the contents of a document – for example,
    `<WXClientPrescription>`.

❑   XML **elements** (also called **nodes**) can be thought of as the objects within a document.

❑   Elements are the basic building blocks of the document. Each element contains a start tag and
    end tag. A tag can be both a start and an end tag such as – for example,
    `<WXClientPrescription/>`. Such a tag is said to be **empty**.

❑   Data can be contained in the element (the element content) or within **attributes** contained in
    the element.

❑   XML is hierarchical. One document can contain multiple elements, which can themselves contain
    child elements, and so on. However an XML document can only have one **root element**.

This last point means that the XML document hierarchy can be thought of as a tree containing nodes:

❑   Our example document has a root node, `<presciptions>`

❑   The branches of the root node are elements of type `<WXClientPrescription>`

❑   The leaves of the XML element, `<WXClientPrescription>`, are its attributes:
    `dentistName`, `quantity`, and `medicationID`

Of course, we're interested in the practical use of XML by VB.NET. A practical manipulation of our example XML would be to display for the staff of the dental clinic a particular prescription in some application – so that a pharmacy could fill the prescription, and then save the information to a database. In this chapter, we'll look at how we can perform such tasks using the functionality provided by the .NET Framework class library.

XML Serialization

The simplest way to demonstrate VB.NET's support for XML is not with a complicated technology such as SQL Server or ADO.NET. Instead, we will demonstrate a practical use of XML by serializing a class.

The **serialization** of an object means that it is written out to a stream, such as a file or a socket (this is also known as **dehydrating** an object). The reverse process can also be performed: an object can be de-serialized (or re-hydrated) by reading it from a stream.

> The type of serialization we are discussing in this chapter is XML serialization, where XML is used to represent a class in serialized form.

In order to understand XML serialization, let's examine a class named `WXClientPrescription` (which can be found in the code download from http://www.wrox.com). This class is implemented in VB.NET and is used by a dentist in order to write a prescription for medication. This class could be instantiated on a dentist's PDA, laptop, or even mobile phone (so long as the .NET Framework was installed).

An instance of `WXClientPrescription` corresponding to each prescription could be serialized to XML and sent over a socket using the PDA's cellular modem. (If the dentist's PDA did not have a cellular modem, the instance of `WXClientPrescription` could be serialized to a file.) The prescription could then be processed when the PDA was dropped into a docking cradle and synced. What we are talking about here is data in a propriety form – an instance of `WXClientPrescription` – being converted into a generic form – XML – that can be universally understood.

The `System.Xml.Serialization` namespace contains classes and interfaces that support the serialization of objects to XML and the deserialization of objects from XML. Objects are serialized to documents or streams using the `XmlSerializer` class. Let's look at how we can use `XmlSerializer`. First, we need to define an object that implements a default constructor, such as `WXClientPrescription`:

```
Public Class WXClientPrescription

    ' These are Public because we have yet to implement
    ' properties to provide program access

    Public dentistName As String
    Public medicationID As Integer
    Public quantity As Integer


    Public Sub New()
    End Sub

    Public Sub New(ByVal dentistName As String, _
                ByVal medicationID As Integer, _
                ByVal quantity As Integer)
      Me.dentistName = dentistName
      Me.medicationID = medicationID
      Me.quantity = quantity
    End Sub
```

```
End Class
```

Then create an instance of XmlSerializer, specifying the object to serialize and its type in the constructor:

```
Dim serialize As XmlSerializer = _
  New XmlSerializer(GetType(WXClientPrescription))
```

Create an instance of the same type as was passed as parameter to the constructor of XmlSerializer:

```
Dim prescription As WXClientPrescription = _
  New WXClientPrescription("Dr. Jam", 101, 10)
```

Call the Serialize method of the XmlSerializer instance and specify the stream to which the serialized object is written (parameter one, Console.Out) and the object to be serialized (parameter two, prescription):

```
serialize.Serialize(Console.Out, prescription)
Console.Out.WriteLine()
```

The output generated by this code is:

```
<?xml version="1.0" encoding="IBM437"?>
<WXClientPrescription xmlns:xsd="http://www.w3.org/2001/XMLSchema"
                      xmlns:xsi="http://www.w3.org/2001/XMLSchema-instance">
  <dentistName>Dr. Jam</dentistName>
  <medicationID>101</medicationID>
  <quantity>10</quantity>
</WXClientPrescription>
```

This output demonstrates the default way that the Serialize method serializes an object:

❑ Each object serialized is represented as an element with the same name as the class – in this case WXClientPrescription

❑ The individual data members of the class serialized are contained in elements named for each data member – in this case dentistName, medicationID, and quantity

Also generated is:

❑ The specific version of XML generated – in this case 1.0

❑ The encoding used – in this case IBM437

❑ The schemas used to describe our serialized object – in this case http://www.w3.org/2001/XMLSchema-instance and http://www.w3.org/2001/XMLSchema

A schema can be associated with an XML document and describes the data it contains (name, type, scale, precision, length, and so on). Either the actual schema or a reference to where the schema resides can be contained in the XML document. In either case, an XML schema is a standard representation that can be used by all applications that consume XML. This means that applications can use the supplied schema to validate the contents of an XML document generated by the Serialize method of XmlSerializer.

Our code snippet that demonstrated the Serialize method of XmlSerializer displayed the XML generated to Console.Out. Clearly, we do not expect an application to use Console.Out when it would like to access a WXClientPrescription object in XML form. The basic idea shown was how serialization can be performed in just two lines of code (one call to a constructor and one call to method). The entire section of code responsible for serializing the instance of WXClientPrescription is:

```vb
Try
    Dim serialize As XmlSerializer = _
                New XmlSerializer(GetType(WXClientPrescription))
    Dim prescription As WXClientPrescription = _
            New WXClientPrescription("Dr. Jam", 101, 10)

    serialize.Serialize(Console.Out, prescription)
    Console.Out.WriteLine()
Catch ex As Exception
    Console.Error.WriteLine(ex.ToString())
End Try
```

The Serialize method's first parameter is overridden so that it can serialize XML to a file (the filename is given as type String), a Stream, a TextWriter, or an XmlWriter. When serializing to Stream, TextWriter, or XmlWriter a third parameter to the Serialize method is permissible. This third parameter is of type XmlSerializerNamespaces and is used to specify a list of namespaces that qualify the names in the XML generated document. The permissible overrides of the Serialize method are:

```vb
Public Sub Serialize(Stream, Object)
Public Sub Serialize(TextWriter, Object)
Public Sub Serialize(XmlWriter, Object)
Public Sub Serialize(Stream, Object, XmlSerializerNamespaces)
Public Sub Serialize(TextWriter, Object, XmlSerializerNamespaces)
Public Sub Serialize(XmlWriter, Object, XmlSerializerNamespaces)
```

An object is reconstituted using the Deserialize method of XmlSerializer. This method is overridden and can de-serialize XML presented as a Stream, a TextReader, or an XmlReader. The overloads for Deserialize are:

```vb
Public Function Deserialize(Stream) As Object
Public Function Deserialize(TextReader) As Object
Public Function Deserialize(XmlReader) As Object
```

Before demonstrating the Deserialize method, we will introduce a new class, WXClientMultiPrescription. This class contains an array of prescriptions (an array of WXClientPrescription objects). WXClientMultiPrescription, is defined as follows:

```
Public Class WXClientMultiPrescription

    Public presciptions() As WXClientPrescription

    Public Sub New()
    End Sub

    Public Sub New(ByVal presciptions() As WXClientPrescription)
        Me.presciptions = presciptions
    End Sub
End Class
```

The `WXClientMultiPrescription` class contains a fairly complicated object: an array of `WXClientPrescription` objects. The underlying serialization and de-serialization of this class is more complicated than that of a single instance of a class that contains several simple types. However, the programming effort involved on our part is just as simple as before.

The following code demonstrates an object of type `WXClientMultiPrescription` being de-serialized (or re-hydrated) from a file, `justaddwater.xml`. This object is de-serialized using this file in conjunction with the `Deserialize` method of `XmlSerializer`:

```
' Open file, ..\justaddwater.xml
Dim dehydrated As FileStream = _
    New FileStream("..\justaddwater.xml", FileMode.Open)

' Create an XmlSerializer instance to handle deserializing,
' WXClientMultiPrescription
Dim serialize As XmlSerializer = _
            New XmlSerializer(GetType(WXClientMultiPrescription))

' Create an object to contain the deserialized instance of the object
Dim prescriptions As WXClientMultiPrescription = _
        New WXClientMultiPrescription()

' Deserialize object
prescriptions = serialize.Deserialize(dehydrated)
```

Once de-serialized, the array of prescriptions can be displayed:

```
Dim prescription As WXClientPrescription

For Each prescription In prescriptions.presciptions
    Console.Out.WriteLine("{0}, {1}, {2}", _
                        prescription.dentistName, _
                        prescription.medicationID, _
                        prescription.quantity)
Next
```

The file, `justaddwater.xml`, was created using code found in VBNetXML03, which is available in the code download. It is just code that serializes an instance of type, `WXClientMultiPrescription`. The output generated by displaying our de-serialized object containing an array of prescriptions is as follows:

```
Dr. Jam, 1, 11
Dr. Jam, 2, 12
Dr. Jam, 3, 13
Dr. Jam, 4, 14
```

XmlSerializer also implements a CanDeserialize method. The prototype for this method is:

```
Overridable Public Function CanDeserialize(ByVal xmlReader As XmlReader) _
    As Boolean
```

If CanDeserialize returns True, then the XML document specified by the xmlReader parameter can be de-serialized. If the return value of this method is False, then the specified XML document cannot be de-serialized.

The FromTypes method of XmlSerializer facilitates the creation of arrays that contain XmlSerializer objects. This array of XmlSerializer objects can be used in turn to process arrays of the type to be serialized. The prototype for FromTypes is:

```
Public Shared Function FromTypes(ByVal types() As Type) As XmlSerializer()
```

Before we further explore the System.Xml.Serialization namespace we need to take a moment to consider the various uses of the term, attribute.

Source Code Style Attributes

Thus far we have seen attribute applied to a specific portion of an XML document. Visual Basic has its own flavor of attribute, as does C# and each of the other .NET languages. These attributes refer to annotations to the source code that specify information that can be used by other applications accessing the original code. We will call such attributes **Source Code Style** attributes.

In the context of the System.Xml.Serialization namespace Source Code Style attributes can be used to change the names of the elements generated for the data members of a class or to generate XML attributes instead of XML elements for the data members of a class. In order to demonstrate this we will use a class called WXLaClientLaPrescription, which contains data members named dentistName, medicationID, and quantity. It just so happens that the default XML generated when serializing this class is not in a form that can be readily consumed by our external application – a French development team has written this external application and hence the XML element and attribute names are in French rather than in English.

In order to rename the XML generated for data member, dentistName, a Source Code Style attribute will be used. This Source Code Style attribute would specify that when WXLaClientLaPrescription is serialized the dentistName data member would be represented as an XML element, <LaDentistLaName>. The actual Source Code Style attribute that specifies this is:

```
<XmlElementAttribute("LaDentistLaName")> Public dentistName As String
```

WXLaClientLaPrescription also contains other Source Code Style attributes:

❑ `<XmlAttributeAttribute("LaMedicationLaID")>` – specifies that `medicationID` is to be serialized as an XML attribute named `LaMedicationLaID`.

❑ `<XmlAttributeAttribute("LaHowLaMuch")>` – specifies that `quantity` is to be serialized as an XML attribute named `LaHowLaMuch`.

The author of this chapter is American and takes full responsibility for the accuracy of the French translation.

`WXLaClientLaPrescription`, is defined as follows:

```
Public Class WXLaClientLaPrescription

    ' These are Public because we have yet to implement
    ' properties to provide program access
    <XmlElementAttribute("LaDentistLaName")> Public dentistName As String
    <XmlAttributeAttribute("LaMedicationLaID")> _
        Public medicationID As Integer
    <XmlAttributeAttribute("LaHowLaMuch")> Public quantity As Integer

    Public Sub New()
    End Sub

    Public Sub New(ByVal dentistName As String, _
                   ByVal medicationID As Integer, _
                   ByVal quantity As Integer)
        Me.dentistName = dentistName
        Me.medicationID = medicationID
        Me.quantity = quantity
    End Sub
End Class
```

`WXLaClientLaPrescription` can be serialized as follows:

```
Dim serialize As XmlSerializer = _
    New XmlSerializer(GetType(WXLaClientLaPrescription))
Dim prescription As WXLaClientLaPrescription = _
    New WXLaClientLaPrescription("Dr. Jam", 101, 10)

serialize.Serialize(Console.Out, prescription)
```

The output generated by this code reflects the Source Code Style attributes associated with class, `WXLaClientLaPrescription`:

```
<?xml version="1.0" encoding="IBM437"?>
<WXLaClientLaPrescription xmlns:xsd="http://www.w3.org/2001/XMLSchema"
                xmlns:xsi="http://www.w3.org/2001/XMLSchema-instance"
                LaMedicationLaID="101" LaHowLaMuch="10">
  <LaDentistLaName>Dr. Jam</LaDentistLaName>
</WXLaClientLaPrescription>
```

The value of medicationID is contained in an XML attribute, LaMedicationLaID, and the value of quantity is contained in an XML attribute, LaHowLaMuch. The value of dentistName is contained in an XML element, LaDentistLaName.

Our example has only demonstrated the Source Code Style attributes exposed by the XmlAttributeAttribute and XmlElementAttribute classes in the System.Xml.Serialization namespace. A variety of other Source Code Style attributes exist in this namespace that also control the form of XML generated by serialization. The classes associated with such Source Code Style attributes include: XmlTypeAttribute, XmlTextAttribute, XmlRootAttribute, XmlIncludeAttribute, XmlIgnoreAttribute, and XmlEnumAttribute.

System.Xml Document Support

The System.Xml namespace implements a variety of objects that support standards-based XML processing. The XML-specific standards facilitated by this namespace include: XML 1.0, Document Type Definition (DTD) Support, XML Namespaces, XML schemas, XPath, XSL/T, DOM Level 2 (Core implementation) and SOAP 1.1, SOAP Contract Language, and SOAP Discovery. The System.Xml namespace exposes over thirty separate classes in order to facilitate this level of XML standard's compliance.

With respect to generating and navigating XML documents, there are two styles of access:

❑   Stream-based – System.Xml exposes a variety of classes that read XML from and write XML to a stream. This approach tends to be a fast way to consume or generate an XML document because it represents a set of serial reads or writes. The limitation of this approach is that it does not view the XML data as a document composed of tangible entities such as nodes, elements, and attributes. An example of where a stream could be used would be when receiving XML documents from a socket or a file.

❑   **Document Object Model (DOM)**-based – System.Xml exposes a set of objects that access XML documents as data. The data is accessed using entities from the XML document tree (nodes, elements, and attributes). This style of XML generation and navigation is flexible but may not yield the same performance as stream-based XML generation and navigation. DOM is excellent technology for editing and manipulating documents. For example, the functionality exposed by DOM might make merging your checking, savings, and brokerage accounts simpler.

XML Stream-Style Parsers

When demonstrating XML serialization we alluded to XML stream-style parsers. After all, when an instance of an object was serialized to XML it had to be written to a stream, and when de-serialized it was read from a stream. When an XML document is parsed using a stream parser, the parser always points to the current node in the document. The basic architecture of stream parsers is as follows:

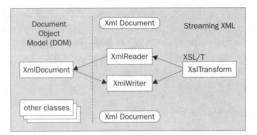

The classes that access a stream of XML (read XML) and generate a stream of XML (write XML) are contained in the `System.Xml` namespace and are as follows:

❑ `XmlWriter` – this abstract class specifies a non-cached, forward-only stream that writes an XML document (data and schema).

❑ `XmlReader` – this abstract class specifies a non-cached, forward-only stream that reads an XML document (data and schema).

Our diagram of the classes associated with the XML stream-style parser referred to one other class, `XslTransform`. This class is found in the `System.Xml.Xsl` namespace and is not an XML stream-style parser. Rather, it is used in conjunction with `XmlWriter` and `XmlReader`. This class will be reviewed in detail later.

The `System.Xml` namespace exposes a plethora of additional XML manipulation classes in addition to those shown in the architecture diagram. The classes shown in the diagram include:

❑ `XmlResolver` – this abstract class resolves an external XML resource using a URI. `XmlUrlResolver` is an implementation of an `XmlResolver`.

❑ `XmlNameTable` – the abstract class provides a fast means by which an XML parser can access element or attribute names.

Writing an XML Stream

An XML document can be created programmatically. One way to perform this task is by writing the individual components of an XML document (schema, attributes, elements, and so on) to an XML stream. Using a unidirectional write-stream means that each element and its attributes must be written in order – the idea is that data is always written at the head of the stream. In order to accomplish this we would use a writable XML stream class (a class derived from `XmlWriter`). Such a class ensures that the XML document we generate correctly implements the W3C *Extensible Markup Language (XML) 1.0* specification and the *Namespaces in XML* specification.

But why would this be necessary since we have XML serialization? We need to be very careful here to separate interface from implementation. XML serialization worked for a specific class, `WXLaClientLaPrescription`. The class is a proprietary implementation and not the format in which data is exchanged. For this one specific case the XML document generated when `WXLaClientLaPrescription` is serialized just so happens to be the XML format used when generating a prescription. `WXLaClientLaPrescription` was given a little help from Source Code Style attributes in order to conform to a standard XML representation of a prescription.

In a different application, if the software used to manage the entire dental practice wants to generate prescriptions, it will have to generate a document of the appropriate form. Our dental practice management software will achieve this by using an XML stream writer, XmlTextWriter. This class is derived from our XML stream writing class, XmlWriter, as follows:

```
Object
    XmlWriter
        XmlTextWriter
```

Before reviewing the subtleties of XmlTextWriter it is important to note that this class exposes over 40 methods and properties. The example presented in this section will provide an overview that touches on a subset of these methods and properties. This subset will allow an XML document that corresponds to a medical prescription to be generated.

The code that generates an XML document corresponding to a medical prescription is found in application VBNetXML02, which is included in the code download. Ultimately our instance of XmlTextWriter, prescriptionTextWriter, is a file on a disk. This means that the XML document generated is streamed to this file. Since the prescriptionTextWriter variable represents a file it must be:

❑   Created – the instance of XmlTextWriter prescriptionTextWriter, is created using New

❑   Opened – the file the XML is streamed to, PrescriptionsProgrammatic.xml, is opened by passing the filename to the constructor associated with XmlTextWriter

❑   Generated – the process of generating the XML document is described in detail at the end of this section

❑   Closed – the file (the XML stream) is closed using the Close method of XmlTextWriter

The basic infrastructure for managing the file (the XML text stream) is as follows:

```
Dim xmlTextWriter As XmlTextWriter = Nothing

prescriptionTextWriter = _
    New XmlTextWriter("..\PrescriptionsProgrammatic.XML", Nothing)

prescriptionTextWriter.Close()
```

Before writing the actual elements and attributes of our XML document certain properties of XmlTextWriter will be specified in order to make our document esthetically pleasing. Specifically, we will set the Formatting property to Formatting.Indent. This setting allows child elements of the XML document to be indented. We will also set IndentChar to the space character and the value of property Indentation to 4. These settings mean that the character used in child element indentation is the space character and the number of spaces indented is four. The code responsible for configuring our XML text stream in this manner is as follows:

```
prescriptionTextWriter.Formatting = Formatting.Indented
prescriptionTextWriter.Indentation = 4
prescriptionTextWriter.IndentChar = " "
```

With the preliminaries completed (file created and formatting configured), the process of writing the actual attributes and elements of our XML document can begin. The sequences of steps used to generate our XML document is as follows:

- ❑ Call the `WriteStartDocument` method in order to write the XML declaration and specify version 1.0. The XML generated by this method is:

```
<?xml version="1.0" standalone="no"?>
```

- ❑ Write an XML comment using the `WriteComment` method. This comment describes from whence the concept for this XML document originated and generates the following:

```
<!--Same as generated by serializing, WXClientPrescription -->
```

- ❑ Begin writing the XML element, `<WXLaClientLaPrescription>`, by calling the `WriteStartElement` method. We can only begin writing this element because its attributes and child elements must be written before the element can be ended with a corresponding, `</WXLaClientLaPrescription>`. The XML generated by the `WriteStartElement` method is:

```
<WXLaClientLaPrescription
```

- ❑ Write the attributes associated with `<WXLaClientLaPrescription>`, by calling the `WriteAttributeString` method twice. The XML generated by calling the `WriteAttributeString` method twice adds to our `WXLaClientLaPrescription` XML element that is currently being written to:

```
<WXLaClientLaPrescription LaMedicationLaID="101" LaHowLaMuch="10"
```

- ❑ Using the `WriteElementString` method, write the child XML element `<LaDentistLaName>` contained in the XML element, `<WXLaClientLaPrescription>`. The XML generated by calling this method is:

```
<LaDentistLaName>Dr. Jam</LaDentistLaName>
```

- ❑ Complete writing the `<WXLaClientLaPrescription>` parent XML element by calling the `WriteEndElement` method. The XML generated by calling this method is:

```
</WXLaClientLaPrescription>
```

Let's put all this together:

```
Dim prescriptionTextWriter As XmlTextWriter = Nothing

prescriptionTextWriter = _
    New XmlTextWriter("..\PrescriptionsProgrammatic.XML", Nothing)

With prescriptionTextWriter
  .Formatting = Formatting.Indented
  .Indentation = 4
  .IndentChar = " "
```

```
   .WriteStartDocument(False)
   .WriteComment( _
     "Same as generated by serializing, WXLaClientLaPrescription")
   .WriteStartElement("WXLaClientLaPrescription")
   .WriteAttributeString("LaMedicationLaID", "101")
   .WriteAttributeString("LaHowLaMuch", "10")
   .WriteElementString("LaDentistLaName", "Dr. Jam")
   .WriteEndElement() ' End WXLaClientLaPrescription

   .Close()
 End With
```

The XML document generated is persisted to a file name `PrescriptionsProgrammatic.XML`. The content of this file is:

```
<?xml version="1.0" standalone="no"?>
<!--Same as generated by serializing, WXLaClientLaPrescription-->
<WXLaClientLaPrescription LaMedicationLaID="101" LaHowLaMuch="10">
    <LaDentistLaName>Dr. Jam</LaDentistLaName>
</WXLaClientLaPrescription>
```

The previous XML document is the same in form as the XML document generated by serializing the `WXLaClientLaPrescription` class. Notice how in the previous XML document the `<LaDentistLaName>` element is indented four characters. This was achieved using the `Formatting`, `Indentation` and `IndentChar` properties of the `XmlTextWriter` class.

Our sample application, VBNetXML02, covered only a quarter of the methods and properties exposed by the XML stream writing class, `XmlTextWriter`. Other methods implemented by this class include methods that manipulate the underlying file – such as the `Flush` method – and methods that allow XML text to be written directly to the stream – such as the `WriteRaw` method.

The `XmlTextWriter` class also exposes a variety of methods that write a specific type of XML data to the stream. These methods include `WriteBinHex`, `WriteCData`, `WriteString`, and `WriteWhiteSpace`.

We can now generate the same XML document two different ways. We have used two different applications that took two different approaches to generating a document that represents a standardized medical prescription. However, there are even more ways to generated XML depending on circumstance. For example, we could receive a prescription from a patient's doctor and this prescription would have to be transformed from the XML format used by the doctor's office to our own prescription format.

Reading an XML Stream

XML documents can be read from a stream. The way a readable stream works is that data is traversed in the stream in order (first XML element, second XML element, and so on). This traversal is very quick because the data is processed in one direction and features such as write and move backwards in the traversal are not supported. At any given instance, only data at the current position in the stream can be accessed.

Before exploring how an XML stream can be read we understand why it should be read. To answer this question let's return to our dental office. Imagine that the application that manages the dental practice can generate a variety of XML documents corresponding to prescriptions, appointments, and laboratory work such as the making of crowns and dentures. All the documents (prescription, appointment, and laboratory work) can be extracted in stream form and processed by a report-generating application. This application prints up the schedule of appointments for a given day, the prescriptions that are outstanding for the scheduled patients, and the laboratory work required to treat the patients scheduled. The report generating application processes the data by reading in and parsing a stream of XML.

One class that can be used to read and parse such an XML stream is XmlTextReader. This class is derived from XmlReader. An XmlTextReader can read XML from a file (specified by a string corresponding to the file's name), a Stream, or an XmlReader. For demonstration purposes, we will use an XmlTextReader to read an XML document contained in a file. The application that will demonstrate this is VBNetXML01 (again, contained in the code download). Reading XML from a file and writing it to a file is not the norm when it comes to XML processing but a file is the simplest way to access XML data. This simplified access allows us to focus more on XML-specific issues.

The first step in accessing a stream of XML data is to create an instance of the object that will open the stream (the readOfficeInfo variable of type XmlTextReader) and to open the stream itself. Our application performs this as follows (where DentalManage.xml is the name of the file containing the XML document):

```
Dim readOfficeInfo As XmlTextReader

readOfficeInfo = New XmlTextReader("..\DentalManage.xml")
```

The basic mechanism for traversing each stream is to traverse from node-to-node using the Read method. Node types in XML include *element* and *whitespace.* Numerous other node types are defined but for the sake of our example we will focus on traversing XML elements and the white space that is used to make the elements more readable (carriage returns, linefeeds and indentation spaces). Once the stream is positioned at a node, the MoveToNextAttribute method can be called to read each attribute contained in an element. The MoveToNextAttribute method will only traverse attributes for nodes that contain attributes (nodes of type element). An example of an XmlTextReader traversing each node and then traversing the attributes of each node is as follows:

```
While readOfficeInfo.Read()
  ' Process node here
  While readOfficeInfo.MoveToNextAttribute()
  ' Process attribute here
  End While
End While
```

This code, which reads the contents of the XML stream, does not utilize any knowledge of the stream's contents. However, a great many applications know exactly what the stream they are going to traverse looks like. Such applications can use XmlReadText in a more deliberate manner and not simply traverse the stream without foreknowledge.

Once our example stream has been read, it can be closed using the Close method:

```
readOfficeInfo.Close()
```

The code that traverses an XML document is found in a subroutine named `WXReadXML`. This subroutine takes the filename containing the XML to read as a parameter. The code for subroutine is as follows and is basically the code we just outlined:

```
Private Sub WXReadXML(ByVal fileName As String)
   Dim readOfficeInfo As XmlTextReader

   readOfficeInfo = New XmlTextReader(fileName)
   While readOfficeInfo.Read()
     WXShowXMLNode(readOfficeInfo)
     While readOfficeInfo.MoveToNextAttribute()
       WXShowXMLNode(readOfficeInfo)
     End While
   End While
   readOfficeInfo.Close()
End Sub
```

For each node encountered after a call to the `Read` method, `WXReadXML`, calls the `WXShowXMLNode` subroutine. Similarly for each attribute traversed, the `WXShowXMLNode` subroutine is called. This subroutine breakdown each node into its sub-entities:

❑   Depth – the `Depth` property of `XmlTextReader` determines the level at which a node resides in the XML document tree. To understand depth, consider the following XML document composed solely of elements: `<A><B></B><C><D></D></C></A>`. Element `<A>` is the root element and when parsed would return a `Depth` of 0. Elements `<B>` and `<C>` are contained in `<A>` and are hence a `Depth` value of 1. Element `<D>` is contained in `<C>`. The `Depth` property value associated with `<D>` (depth of 2) should therefore be one more than the `Depth` property associated with `<C>` (depth of 1).

❑   Type – the type of each node is determined using the `NodeType` property of `XmlTextReader`. The node returned is of enumeration type, `XmlNodeType`. Permissible node types include: `Attribute`, `Element`, and `Whitespace`. (Numerous other node types can also be returned including: `CDATA`, `Comment`, `Document`, `Entity`, and `DocumentType`.)

❑   Name – the type of each node is retrieved using the `Name` property of `XmlTextReader`. The name of the node could be an element name such as `<WXLaClientLaPrescription>` or an attribute name such as `LaMedicationLaID`.

❑   Attribute Count – the number of attributes associated with a node is retrieved using the `AttributeCount` property of `XmlTextReader`'s `NodeType`.

❑   Value – the value of a node is retrieved using the `Value` property of `XmlTextReader`. For example the element node `<LaDentistLaName>` contains a value of, `Dr. Jam`.

Subroutine `WXShowXMLNode` is implemented as follows:

```
Private Sub WXShowXMLNode(ByVal reader As XmlReader)
   Dim depthCount As Integer

   If reader.Depth > 0 Then
     For depthCount = 1 To reader.Depth
       Console.Write("  ")
```

```
      Next
   End If

   If reader.NodeType = XmlNodeType.Whitespace Then
      Console.Out.WriteLine("Type: {0} ", reader.NodeType)
   ElseIf reader.NodeType = XmlNodeType.Text Then
      Console.Out.WriteLine("Type: {0}, Value: {1} ", _
                          reader.NodeType, _
                          reader.Value)
   Else
      Console.Out.WriteLine("Name: {0}, Type: {1}, " & _
                          "AttributeCount: {2}, Value: {3} ", _
                          reader.Name, _
                          reader.NodeType, _
                          reader.AttributeCount, _
                          reader.Value)
   End If
End Sub
```

Within the WXShowXMLNode subroutine, each level of node depth adds two spaces to the output generated:

```
If reader.Depth > 0 Then
   For depthCount = 1 To reader.Depth
      Console.Write("  ")
   Next
End If
```

We add these spaces in order to make the output generated human-readable (so we can easily determine the depth of each node displayed). For each type of node WXShowXMLNode displays the value of the NodeType property. The WXShowXMLNode subroutine makes a distinction between nodes of type Whitespace and other types of nodes. The reason for this is simple: a node of type Whitespace does not contain a name or attribute count. The value of such a node is any combination of white space characters (space, tab, carriage return, and so on). Therefore, it does not make sense to display the properties if the NodeType is XmlNodeType.WhiteSpace. Nodes of type Text have no name associated with them so for this type subroutine WXShowXMLNode only displays the properties, NodeType and Value. For all other node types, the Name, AttributeCount, Value, and NodeType properties are displayed.

A portion of the output generated is:

```
Name: DentalManageDump, Type: Element, AttributeCount: 0, Value:
  Type: Whitespace
  Name: WXClientMultiPrescription, Type: Element, AttributeCount: 0, Value:
    Type: Whitespace
    Name: presciptions, Type: Element, AttributeCount: 0, Value:
      Type: Whitespace
```

This example managed to use three methods and five properties of XmlTextReader. The output generated was informative but far from practical. XmlTextReader exposes over 50 methods and properties, which means that we have only scratched the surface of this highly versatile class. The remainder of this section will introduce a more realistic use of XmlTextReader and demonstrate how the classes of System.Xml handle errors.

Traversing XML Using XmlTextReader

An application can easily use XmlTextReader in order to traverse a document that is received in a known format. The document could thus be traversed in a deliberate manner. Recall we implemented a class that serialized arrays of prescriptions. Our next example will take an XML document containing multiple XML documents of that type and traverse them. Each prescription will be forwarded to the pharmacy by sending a fax. The document will be traversed as follows:

```
Read root element:  <DentalManageDump>
    Process each <WXClientMultiPrescription> element
        Read <presciptions> element
            Process each <WXClientPrescription>
                Send fax for each prescription here
```

The basic outline for our program's implementation is to open a file containing the XML document to parse and to traverse from element-to-element within this document:

```
Dim readOfficeInfo As XmlTextReader
Dim drName, medication, quantity As String

readOfficeInfo = New XmlTextReader(fileName)
readOfficeInfo.Read()
readOfficeInfo.ReadStartElement("DentalManageDump")
Do While (True)
    '*******************************************************
    ' * Process WXClientMultiPrescription elements here *
    '*******************************************************
Loop
readOfficeInfo.ReadEndElement() ' </DentalManageDump>
readOfficeInfo.Close()
```

The previous code opened the file using the constructor of XmlTextReader and closed the file using the Close method of this class. The previous code also introduced two methods of the XmlTextReaderClass:

- ❑ ReadStartElement(String) – verifies that the current in the stream is an element and that the element's name matches the string passed to method, ReadStartElement. If the verification is successful, the stream is advanced to the next element.

- ❑ ReadEndElement() – verifies that the current element is an end tab and if the verification is successful the stream is advanced to the next element.

The application knows that an element, <DentalManageDump>, will be found at a specific point in the document. The ReadStartElement method verifies this foreknowledge of the document format. Once all the elements contained in element <DentalManageDump> have been traversed the stream should point to the end tag </DentalManageDump>. The ReadEndElement method verifies this.

The code that traverses each element of type <WXClientMultiPrescription> similarly uses the ReadStartElement and ReadEndElement methods to indicate the start and end of the <WXClientMultiPrescription> and <presciptions> elements. The code that ultimately parses the list of prescription and faxes the pharmacy (using the WXFranticallyFaxThePharmacy subroutine) is as follows:

```
Dim readOfficeInfo As XmlTextReader
Dim drName, medication, quantity As String

readOfficeInfo = New XmlTextReader(fileName)
readOfficeInfo.Read()
readOfficeInfo.ReadStartElement("DentalManageDump")
Do While (True)
    readOfficeInfo.ReadStartElement("WXClientMultiPrescription")
    readOfficeInfo.ReadStartElement("presciptions")
    Do While (True)
        readOfficeInfo.ReadStartElement("WXClientPrescription")
        drName = readOfficeInfo.ReadElementString()
        medication = readOfficeInfo.ReadElementString()
        quantity = readOfficeInfo.ReadElementString()
        readOfficeInfo.ReadEndElement() ' clear </WXClientPrescription>
        WXFranticallyFaxThePharmacy(drName, medication, quantity)
        ' Should read next WXClientPrescription node
        ' else we quit
        readOfficeInfo.Read()
        If ("WXClientPrescription" <> readOfficeInfo.Name) Then
            Exit Do
        End If
    Loop

    readOfficeInfo.ReadEndElement() ' clear </presciptions>
    readOfficeInfo.ReadEndElement() ' clear </WXClientMultiPrescription>
    ' Should read next WXClientMultiPrescription node
    ' else we quit
    readOfficeInfo.Read() ' clear </DentalManageDump>
    If ("WXClientMultiPrescription" <> readOfficeInfo.Name) Then
        Exit Do
    End If
End If
Loop
readOfficeInfo.ReadEndElement() ' </DentalManageDump>
readOfficeInfo.Close()
```

Three lines within the previous code contain a call to the ReadElementString method:

```
drName = readOfficeInfo.ReadElementString()
medication = readOfficeInfo.ReadElementString()
quantity = readOfficeInfo.ReadElementString()
```

While parsing the stream, it was known that an element existed named <dentistName> and that this element contained the name of the dentist. Rather than parsing the start tag, getting the value, and parsing the end tag, it was easier just to get the data using the ReadElementString method. This method retrieves the data string associated with an element and advances the stream to the next element. The ReadElementString method was also used to retrieve the data associated with the XML elements <medicationID> and <quantity>.

The output of this example was a fax, which we won't show as the emphasis of this example was to show that it is simpler to traverse a document when its form is known. The format of the document is still verified by XmlTextReader as it is parsed.

The `XmlTextReader` class also exposes properties that give more insight into the data contained in the XML document and the state of parsing: `IsEmptyElement`, `EOF`, and `IsStartElement`. This class also allows data in a variety of forms to be retrieved using methods such as `ReadBase64`, `ReadHex`, and `ReadChars`. The raw XML associated with the document can also be retrieved using `ReadInnerXml` and `ReadOuterXml`. Once again, we have only scratched the surface of a class – `XmlTextReader` – that is rich in functionality.

Handling Exceptions

XML is text and could easily be read using mundane methods such as `Read` and `ReadLine`. A key feature of each class that reads and traverses XML is inherent support for error detection and handling. To demonstrate this, consider the following malformed XML document found in the file named `malformed.XML`:

```
<?xml version="1.0" encoding="IBM437"?>
<WXLaClientLaPrescription LaMedicationLaID="101", LaHowLaMuch="10">
  <LaDentistLaName>Dr. Jam</LaDentistLaName>
<WXLaClientLaPrescription>
```

This document may not immediately appear to be malformed. By wrapping a call to the method we developed (`WXReadXML`) we can see what type of exception is raised when `XmlTextReader` detects the malformed XML within this document:

```
Try
    WXReadXML("..\Malformed.xml")
Catch xmlEx As XmlException
    Console.Error.WriteLine("XML Error: " + xmlEx.ToString())
Catch ex As Exception
    Console.Error.WriteLine("Some other error: " + ex.ToString())
End Try
```

The methods and properties exposed by the `XmlTextReader` class raise exceptions of type `System.Xml.XmlException`. In fact, every class in the `System.Xml` namespace raises exceptions of type `XmlException`. Although this discussion of errors using an instance of type `XmlTextReader`, the concepts reviewed apply to all errors generated by classes found in the `System.Xml` namespace.

The properties exposed by `XmlException` include:

❑ `LineNumber` – the line within an XML document where the error occurred.

❑ `LinePosition` – the position within the line specified by `LineNumber` where the error occurred.

❑ `Message` – the error message that corresponds to the error that occurred. This error took place at the line in the XML document specified by `LineNumber` and within the line at the position specified by `LinePostion`.

The error displayed when subroutine `WXReadXML` processes `malformed.xml` is as follows:

```
XML Error: System.Xml.XmlException: The ',' character, hexadecimal value 0x2C,
cannot begin a name. Line 2, position 49.
```

Looking closely at our document there is a comma separating the attributes in element, `<WXLaClientLaPrescription>` (`LaMedicationLaID="101"`, `LaHowLaMuch="10"`). This comma is invalid. Removing the comma and running the code again gives the following output:

```
XML Error: System.Xml.XmlException: This is an unexpected token. Expected
'EndElement'. Line 5, position 27.
```

Once again, we recognize the precise error. We do not have an end element, `</WXLaClientLaPrescription>`, but have a opening element, `<WXLaClientLaPrescription>`.

The properties provided by the `XmlException` class (`LineNumer`, `LinePosition`, and `Message`) provide a useful level of precision when tracking down errors. The `XmlTextReader` class also exposes a level of precision with respect to the parsing of the XML document. This precision is exposed by the `XmlTextReader` through properties such as `LineNumber` and `LinePosition`.

Using the MemoryStream Object

A very useful class that can greatly help us when working with XML is `System.IO.MemoryStream`. Rather than needing a network or disk resource backing the stream (as in `System.Net.Sockets.NetworkStream` and `System.IO.FileStream`), `MemoryStream` backs onto a block of memory. Imagine we want to generate an XML document and e-mail it. The built-in classes for sending e-mail rely on having a `System.String` containing a block of text for the message body. But, if we want to generate an XML document, we need a stream.

If the document is reasonably sized, we should write the document directly to memory and copy that block of memory to e-mail. This is good from a performance and reliability perspective because we don't have to open a file, write it, rewind it, and read the data back in again. However, you must consider scalability in this situation because if the file is very large, or you have a great number of smaller files, you could run out of memory (in which case you'll have to go the "file" route).

In this section, we'll demonstrate how to generate an XML document to a `MemoryStream`. We'll read the document back out again as a `System.String` value and e-mail it. What we'll do is create a new class called `EmailStream` that extends `MemoryStream`. This new class will contain an extra method called `CloseAndSend` that, as its name implies, will close the stream and send the e-mail message.

First off, we'll create a new Console Application project called `EmailStream`. The first job is to create a basic `Customer` object that contains a few basic members and that can be automatically serialized by .NET through use of the `SerializableAttribute` attribute:

```vb
<Serializable()> Public Class Customer

    ' members...
    Public Id As Integer
    Public FirstName As String
    Public LastName As String
    Public Email As String

End Class
```

The fun part now is the `EmailStream` class itself. This needs access to the `System.Web.Mail` namespace, so you'll need to add a reference to the `System.Web` assembly. The new class should also extend `System.IO.MemoryStream`, as shown here:

317

```
Imports System.IO
Imports System.Web.Mail

Public Class EmailStream
    Inherits MemoryStream
```

The first job of `CloseAndSend` is to start putting together the mail message. This is done by creating a new `System.Web.Mail.MailMessage` object and configuring the sender, recipient, and the subject:

```
' CloseAndSend - close the stream and send the e-mail...
Public Sub CloseAndSend(ByVal fromAddress As String, _
                        ByVal toAddress As String, _
                        ByVal subject As String)

    ' create the new message...
    Dim message As New MailMessage()
    message.From = fromAddress
    message.To = toAddress
    message.Subject = subject
```

This method will be called once the XML document has been written to the stream, so we can assume at this point that the stream contains a block of data. To read the data back out again, we have to rewind the stream and use a `System.IO.StreamReader`. Before we do this, the first thing we should do is call `Flush`. Traditionally, streams have always been buffered – that is, the data is not sent to the final destination (the memory block in this case, but a file in the case of a `FileStream` and so on) each and every time the stream is written. Instead, the data is written in (pretty much) a non-deterministic way. Because we need all the data to be written, we call `Flush` to ensure that all the data has been sent to the destination and that the buffer is empty.

In a way, `EmailStream` is a great example of buffering. All of the data is held in a memory "buffer" until we finally send the data on to its destination in a response to an explicit call to this method:

```
' flush and rewind the stream...
Flush()
Seek(0, SeekOrigin.Begin)
```

Once we've flushed and rewound the stream, we can create a `StreamReader` and dredge all the data out into the `Body` property of the `MailMessage` object:

```
' read out the data...
Dim reader As New StreamReader(Me)
message.Body = reader.ReadToEnd()
```

After we've done that, we close the stream by calling the base class method:

```
' close the stream...
Close()
```

Finally, we send the message:

```
    ' send the message...
    SmtpMail.Send(message)

End Sub
```

To call this method, we need to add some code to the Main method. First, we create a new Customer object and populate it with some test data:

```
Imports System.Xml.Serialization

Module Module1

    Sub Main()

        ' create a new customer...
        Dim customer As New Customer()
        customer.Id = 27
        customer.FirstName = "Darren"
        customer.LastName = "Clarke"
        customer.Email = "darren@pretendcompany.com"
```

After we've done that, we can create a new EmailStream object. We then use XmlSerializer to write an XML document representing the newly created Customer instance to the block of memory that EmailStream is backing to:

```
        ' create a new e-mail stream...
        Dim stream As New EmailStream()

        ' serialize...
        Dim serializer As New XmlSerializer(customer.GetType())
        serializer.Serialize(stream, customer)
```

At this point, the stream will be filled with data, and after all the data has been flushed the block of memory that EmailStream backs on to will contain the complete document. Now we can call CloseAndSend to e-mail the document.

```
        ' send the e-mail...
        stream.CloseAndSend("matthew@dotnet247.com", _
            "matthew@dotnet247.com", "XML Customer Document")

    End Sub

End Module
```

You will probably already have Microsoft SMTP Service properly configured – this service is necessary to send e-mail. You also need to make sure that the e-mail addresses used in your code goes to your e-mail address! Run the project, check your e-mail, and you should see something like this:

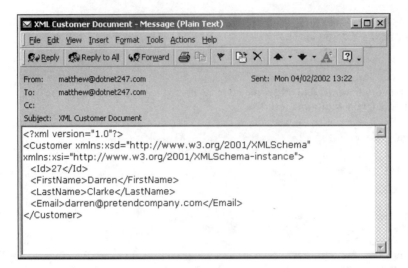

Document Object Model (DOM)

The classes of the System.Xml namespace that support the Document Object Model (DOM) interact as follows:

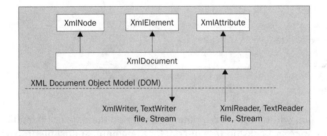

Within the previous diagram, an XML document is contained in a class named, XmlDocument. Each node within this document is accessible and managed using XmlNode. Nodes can also be accessed and managed using a class specifically designed to process a specific node's type (XmlElement, XmlAttribute, and so on). XML documents are extracted from XmlDocument using a variety of mechanisms exposed through such classes as XmlWriter, TextWriter, Stream, and a file (specified by filename of type String). XML documents are consumed by an XmlDocument using a variety of load mechanisms exposed through the same classes.

Where a DOM-style parser differs from a stream-style parser is with respect to movement. Using DOM, the nodes can be traversed forwards and backwards. Nodes can be added to the document, removed from the document, and updated. However, this flexibility comes at a performance cost. It is faster to read or write XML using a stream-style parser.

The DOM-specific classes exposed by System.Xml include:

- ❑ XmlDocument –corresponds to an entire XML document. A document is loaded using the Load method. XML documents are loaded from a file (the filename specified as type String), TextReader or XmlReader. A document can be loaded using LoadXml in conjunction with a string containing the XML document. The Save method is used in order to save XML documents. The methods exposed by XmlDocument reflect the intricate manipulation of an XML document. For example, the following self-documenting creation methods are implemented by this class: CreateAttribute, CreateCDataSection, CreateComment, CreateDocumentFragment, CreateDocumentType, CreateElement, CreateEntityReference, CreateNode, CreateProcessingInstruction, CreateSignificantWhitespace, CreateTextNode, CreateWhitespace, and CreateXmlDeclaration. The elements contained in the document can be retrieved. Other methods support the retrieving, importing, cloning, loading, and writing of nodes.

- ❑ XmlNode – corresponds to a node within the DOM tree. This class supports data types, namespaces, and DTDs. A robust set of methods and properties are provided to create, delete, and replace nodes: AppendChild, CloneNode, InsertAfter, InsertBefore, PrependChild, RemoveAll, RemoveChild, and ReplaceChild. The contents of a node can similarly be traversed in a variety of ways: FirstChild, LastChild, NextSibling, ParentNode, and PreviousSibling.

- ❑ XmlElement – corresponds to an element within the DOM tree. The functionality exposed by this class contains a variety of methods used to manipulate an element's attributes: GetAttribute, GetAttributeNode, RemoveAllAttributes, RemoveAttributeAt, RemoveAttributeNode, SetAttribute, and SetAttributeNode.

- ❑ XmlAttribute – corresponds to an attribute of an element (XmlElement) within the DOM tree. An attribute contains data and lists of subordinate data. For this reason it is a less complicated object than an XmlNode or an XmlElement. An XmlAttribute can retrieve its owner document (property, OwnerDocument), retrieve its owner element (property, OwnerElement), retrieve its parent node (property, ParentNode), and retrieve its name (property, Name). The value of an XmlAttribute is available via a read/write property named Value.

Given the diverse number of methods and properties (and there are many more than those listed here) exposed by XmlDocument, XmlNode, XmlElement, and XmlAttribute it should be clear that any XML 1.0 compliant document can be generated and manipulated using these classes. In comparison to their XML-stream counterparts, these classes afford more flexible movement within, and editing of XML documents.

A similar comparison could be made between DOM and data serialized and de-serialized using XML. Using serialization, the type of node (for example, attribute, or element) and the node name are specified at compile time. There is no on-the-fly modification of the XML generated by the serialization process.

Other technologies that generate and consume XML are not as flexible as DOM. This includes ADO.NET and ADO, which generate XML of a particular form. SQL Server does expose a certain amount of flexibility when it comes to the generation (FOR XML queries) and consumption of XML (OPENXML). The choice between using classes within DOM and using SQL Server is a choice between using a language such as VB.NET to manipulate objects or requiring SQL Server be installed and perform most XML manipulation in SQL.

DOM Traversing Raw XML Elements

Our first DOM example will load an XML document into an `XmlDocument` object using a string that contains the actual XML document. This scenario is typical of an application that uses ADO.NET to generate XML but then uses the objects of DOM to traverse and manipulate this XML. ADO.NET's `DataSet` object contains the results of ADO.NET data access operations. The `DataSet` class exposes a `GetXml` method. This method retrieves the underlying XML associated with the `DataSet`. The following code demonstrates how the contents of the `DataSet` are loaded into the `XmlDocument`:

```
Dim xmlDoc As New XmlDocument()
Dim ds As New DataSet()

' set up ADO.NET DataSet() here
xmlDoc.LoadXml(ds.GetXml())
```

This example will simply traverse each XML element (`XmlNode`) in the document (`XmlDocument`) and display the data accordingly. The data associated with this example will not be retrieved from a `DataSet` but will instead be contained in a string, `rawData`. This string is initialized as follows:

```
Dim rawData As String = _
    "<presciptions>" & _
    "  <WXClientPrescription>" & _
    "    <dentistName>Dr. Jam</dentistName>" & _
    "    <medicationID>1</medicationID>" & _
    "    <quantity>11</quantity>" & _
    "  </WXClientPrescription>" & _
    "  <WXClientPrescription>" & _
    "    <dentistName>Dr. Jam</dentistName>" & _
    "    <medicationID>2</medicationID>" & _
    "    <quantity>22</quantity>" & _
    "  </WXClientPrescription>" & _
    "</presciptions>"
```

The XML document in `rawData` is a portion of the XML hierarchy associated with a prescription written at our dental office. The basic idea in processing this data is to traverse each `<WXClientPrescription>` element in order to display the data it contains. Each node corresponding to a `<WXClientPrescription>` element can be retrieved from our `XmlDocument` using the `GetElementsByTagName` method (specifying a tag name of `WXClientPrescription`). The `GetElementsByTagName` method returns a list of `XmlNode` objects in the form of a collection of type `XmlNodeList`. Using the `For Each` statement to construct this list the `XmlNodeList` (`clientPrescriptionNodes`), can be traversed as individual `XmlNode` elements (`clientPrescriptionNode`). The code for handling this is as follows:

```
Dim xmlDoc As New XmlDocument()
Dim clientPrescriptionNodes As XmlNodeList
Dim clientPrescriptionNode As XmlNode

xmlDoc.LoadXml(rawData)
' Traverse each <WXClientPrescription>
clientPrescriptionNodes = _
    xmlDoc.GetElementsByTagName("WXClientPrescription")
```

```
For Each clientPrescriptionNode In clientPrescriptionNodes
    '*********************************************************
    ' Process <dentistName>, <medicationID> and <quantity> here
    '*********************************************************
Next
```

Each XmlNode can then have its contents displayed by traversing the children of this node using the ChildNodes method. This method returns an XmlNodeList (baseDataNodes) that can be traversed one XmlNode list element at a time:

```
Dim baseDataNodes As XmlNodeList
Dim baseDataNode As XmlNode
Dim bFirstInRow As Boolean

baseDataNodes = clientPrescriptionNode.ChildNodes
bFirstInRow = True
For Each baseDataNode In baseDataNodes
  If (bFirstInRow) Then
    bFirstInRow = False
  Else
    Console.Out.Write(", ")
  End If
  Console.Out.Write(baseDataNode.Name & ": " & baseDataNode.InnerText)
Next
Console.Out.WriteLine()
```

The bulk of the previous code retrieves the name of the node using the Name property and the InnerText property of the node. The InnerText property of each XmlNode retrieved contains the data associated with the XML elements (nodes) <dentistName>, <medicationID> and <quantity>. Our example displays the contents of the XML elements using Console.Out. Our XML document is displayed as follows:

```
dentistName: Dr. Jam, medicationID: 1, quantity: 11
dentistName: Dr. Jam, medicationID: 2, quantity: 22
```

Other, more practical, methods for using this data could have been implemented, including:

❏ The contents could have been directed to an ASP.NET Response object. The data retrieved could have been used to create an HTML table (<table> table, <tr> row and <td> data) that would be written to the Response object.

❏ The data traversed could have been directed to a ListBox or ComboBox Windows Forms control. This would allow the data returned to be selected as part of a GUI application.

❏ The data could have been edited as part of our application's business rules. For example, we could have used the traversal to verify that the <medicationID> matched the <quantity>. For example, if a medication must be taken three times a day then the quantity prescribed must be a multiple of three.

Our example in its entirety follows:

```
Dim rawData As String = _
  ' XML data not shown for reason of brevity
Dim xmlDoc As New XmlDocument()
Dim clientPrescriptionNodes As XmlNodeList
Dim clientPrescriptionNode As XmlNode
Dim baseDataNodes As XmlNodeList
Dim baseDataNode As XmlNode
Dim bFirstInRow As Boolean

xmlDoc.LoadXml(rawData)
' Traverse each <WXClientPrescription>
clientPrescriptionNodes = xmlDoc.GetElementsByTagName("WXClientPrescription")
For Each clientPrescriptionNode In clientPrescriptionNodes
  baseDataNodes = clientPrescriptionNode.ChildNodes
  bFirstInRow = True
  For Each baseDataNode In baseDataNodes
    If (bFirstInRow) Then
      bFirstInRow = False
    Else
      Console.Out.Write(", ")
    End If
    Console.Out.Write(baseDataNode.Name & ": " & baseDataNode.InnerText)
  Next
  Console.Out.WriteLine()
Next
```

DOM Traversing XML Attributes

This next example will demonstrate how to traverse data contained in attributes and how to update the attributes based on a set of business rules. In this example the XmlDocument object is populated by retrieving an XML document from a file. After the business rules edit the object, the data will be persisted back to the file:

```
Dim xmlDoc As New XmlDocument()

xmlDoc.Load("..\DentalOfficeReadyPrescriptionsV2.xml")
'*********************************************
' Busienss rules process document here
'*********************************************
xmlDoc.Save("..\DentalOfficeReadyPrescriptionsV2.xml")
```

The data contained in the file, DentalOfficeReadyPrescriptionsV2.xml, is a variation of the dental prescription. We have altered our rigid standard (for the sake of example) so that the data associated with individual prescriptions is contained in XML attributes instead of XML elements. An example this prescription data is as follows:

```
<WXClientPrescription dentistName="Dr. Jam" medicationID="1" quantity="11">
```

We have already demonstrated how to traverse the XML elements associated with a document so let's assume that we have successfully retrieved the XmlNode associated with the
<WXClientPrescription> element:

```
Dim attributes As XmlAttributeCollection
Dim attribute As XmlAttribute
Dim medicationID As Integer
Dim quantity As Integer

attributes = node.Attributes()
For Each attribute In attributes
  If 0 = String.Compare(attribute.Name, "medicationID") Then
    medicationID = attribute.InnerXml
  ElseIf 0 = String.Compare(attribute.Name, "quantity") Then
    quantity = attribute.InnerXml
  End If
Next
```

The previous code traverses the attributes of an XmlNode by retrieving a list of attributes using the Attributes method. The value of this method is used to set the attributes object (data type, XmlAttributeCollection). The individual XmlAttribute objects (variable, attribute) contained in attributes are traversed using a For Each loop. Within the loop the contents of the medicationID and the quantity attribute are saved for processing by our business rules.

Our business rules execute an algorithm that ensures that the medication in the prescription is provided in the correct quantity. This rule is that the medication associated with MedicationID=1 must be dispensed 21 tablets at a time. In the event of an invalid quantity, the code for enforcing this business rule uses the ItemOf property to look up the XmlAttribute object associated with the quantity attribute. The Value property of the XmlAttribute object is used to set the correct value of the medication's quantity. The code performing this business rule is as follows:

```
If medicationID = 1 Then
  ' medication must be taken 3 times a day for a week (21 times)
  If quantity <> 21 Then
    attributes.ItemOf("quantity").Value = "21"
  End If
End If
```

What is elegant about this example is that the list of attributes was traversed using For Each. Then, ItemOf was used to look up a specific attribute that had already been traversed. This would not have been possible if reading an XML stream with an object derived from the XML stream reader class, XmlReader.

We can use this code as follows:

```
Sub WXTraverseAttributes(ByRef node As XmlNode)
    Dim attributes As XmlAttributeCollection
    Dim attribute As XmlAttribute
    Dim medicationID As Integer
    Dim quantity As Integer

    attributes = node.Attributes()
    For Each attribute In attributes
        If 0 = String.Compare(attribute.Name, "medicationID") Then
            medicationID = attribute.InnerXml
```

```
            ElseIf 0 = String.Compare(attribute.Name, "quantity") Then
                quantity = attribute.InnerXml
            End If
        Next

        If medicationID = 1 Then
            ' medication must be taken 3 times a day for a week (21 times)
            If quantity <> 21 Then
                attributes.ItemOf("quantity").Value = "21"
            End If
        End If
    End Sub

    Sub WXReadDentalDOM()
        Dim xmlDoc As New XmlDocument()
        Dim clientPrescriptionNodes As XmlNodeList
        Dim clientPrescriptionNode As XmlNode
        xmlDoc.Load("..\DentalOfficeReadyPrescriptionsV2.xml")
        ' Traverse each <WXClientPrescription>
        clientPrescriptionNodes = _
            xmlDoc.GetElementsByTagName("WXClientPrescription")
        For Each clientPrescriptionNode In clientPrescriptionNodes
            WXTraverseAttributes(clientPrescriptionNode)
        Next
        xmlDoc.Save("..\DentalOfficeReadyPrescriptionsV2.xml")
    End Sub
```

XSLT Transforms

XSLT is a language that is used to transform XML documents. We have performed a similar task before. When working with XML serialization we rewrote the WXClientPrescription class. This class was used to serialize a prescription object to XML using nodes that contained English-language names. The rewritten version of this class, WXLaClientLaPrescription, serialized XML nodes containing French names. Source Code Style attributes were used in conjunction with the XmlSerializer class in order to accomplish this transformation. Two words in this paragraph send chills down the spine of any experienced developer: *rewrote* and *rewritten*. The point of an XSL Transform is to use an alternate language (XSLT) to transform the XML rather than rewriting the source code, SQL commands, or some other mechanism used to generate XML.

Conceptually XSLT is straightforward. A file with an .xslt extension describes the changes (transformations) that will be applied to a particular XML file. Once this is completed an XSLT processor is provided with the source XML file and the XSLT file and performs the transformation. The System.Xml.Xsl.XslTransform class is such an XSLT processor.

The XSLT file is itself an XML document, although certain elements within this document are XSLT specific commands. There are dozens of XSLT commands that can be used in writing an XSLT file. In our first example, we will explore the following XSLT elements (commands):

❑   stylesheet – indicates the start of the stylesheet (XSL) in the XSLT file.

- ❏ `template` – this element denotes a reusable template for producing specific output. This output is generated using a specific node type within the source document under a specific context. For example the text, `<xsl:template match="/">`, selects all root notes ("/") for the specific transform template.

- ❏ `for-each` – this element applies the same template to each node in the specified set. Recall that we demonstrated a class (`WXClientMultiPrescription`) that could be serialized. This class contained an array of prescriptions. Given the XML document generated when a `WXClientMultiPrescription` is serialized, each prescription serialized could be processed using, `<xsl:for-each select = "WXClientMultiPrescription/presciptions/WXClientPrescription">`.

- ❏ `value-of` – retrieves the value of the specified node and inserts it into the document in text form. For example the following, `<xsl:value-of select="dentistName" />`, would take the value of XML element, `<dentistName>`, and insert it into the transformed document.

The `WXClientMultiPrescription` class when serialized generates XML such as the following (where . . . indicates where additional `<WXClientPrescription>` elements may reside):

```xml
<?xml version="1.0" encoding="us-ascii" ?>
<WXClientMultiPrescription>
    <presciptions>
        <WXClientPrescription>
            <dentistName>Dr. Jam</dentistName>
            <medicationID>1</medicationID>
            <quantity>11</quantity>
        </WXClientPrescription>
        ...
    </presciptions>
</WXClientMultiPrescription>
```

The previous XML document is used to generate a report that is viewed by the dental practice's managing doctor. This report is in HTML form so it can be viewed via the Web. The XSLT elements we previously reviewed (`stylesheet`, `template`, and `for-each`) are all the XSLT elements required to transform our XML document (in which data is stored) into an HTML file (show that the data can be displayed). An XSLT file, `WXDisplayThatPuppy.xslt`, contains the following text that is used to transform a serialized version `WXClientMultiPrescription`:

```xml
<?xml version="1.0" encoding="UTF-8" ?>
<xsl:stylesheet xmlns:xsl="http://www.w3.org/1999/XSL/Transform"
    version="1.0">
  <xsl:template match="/">
    <HTML>
      <TITLE>Who's prescribing what</TITLE>
      <BODY>
        <TABLE BORDER="1">
          <TR>
            <TD><B>Dentist</B></TD>
            <TD><B>Medication ID</B></TD>
            <TD><B>Quantity</B></TD>
          </TR>
          <xsl:for-each select=
```

```
                "WXClientMultiPrescription/presciptions/WXClientPrescription">
                <TR>
                    <TD><xsl:value-of select="dentistName" /></TD>
                    <TD><xsl:value-of select="quantity" /></TD>
                    <TD><xsl:value-of select="medicationID" /></TD>
                </TR>
                </xsl:for-each>
            </TABLE>
        </BODY>
    </HTML>
  </xsl:template>
</xsl:stylesheet>
```

In the previous XSLT file, the XSLT elements are marked in boldface. These elements perform operations on the source XML file containing a serialized `WXClientMultiPrescription` object and generate the appropriate HTML file. Our file contains a table (marked by the table tag, `<TABLE>`) that contains a set of rows (each row marked by a table row tag, `<TR>`). The columns of the table are contained in table data tags, `<TD>`. The previous XSLT file contains the header row for the table:

```
<TR>
    <TD><B>Dentist</B></TD>
    <TD><B>Medication ID</B></TD>
    <TD><B>Quantity</B></TD>
</TR>
```

Each row containing data (an individual prescription from the serialized object, `WXClientMultiPrescription`) is generated using the XSLT element, `for-each`, to traverse each `<WXClientPrescription>` element within the source XML document:

```
<xsl:for-each select=
    "WXClientMultiPrescription/presciptions/WXClientPrescription">
```

The individual columns of data are generated using the `value-of` XSLT element, in order to query the elements contained within each `<WXClientPrescription>` element (`<dentistName>`, `<quantity>`, and `<medicationID>`):

```
<TR>
    <TD><xsl:value-of select="dentistName" /></TD>
    <TD><xsl:value-of select="quantity" /></TD>
    <TD><xsl:value-of select="medicationID" /></TD>
</TR>
```

The code to create a displayable XML file using the `System.Xml.Xsl` namespace is as follows:

```
Dim myXslTransform As XslTransform = New XslTransform()
Dim destFileName As String = "..\ShowIt.html"

myXslTransform.Load("..\WXDisplayThatPuppy.xslt")
myXslTransform.Transform("..\OneWXClientMultiPrescriptions.xml", _
                    destFileName)
System.Diagnostics.Process.Start(destFileName)
```

328

This consists of only five lines of code with the bulk of the coding taking place in the XSLT file. Our previous code snippet created an instance of an `System.Xml.Xsl.XslTransform` object named `myXslTransform.`. The `Load` method of this class is used to load the XSLT file we previously reviewed, `WXDisplayThatPuppy.xslt`. The `Transform` method takes a source XML file as the first parameter which in our case was a file containing a serialized `WXClientMultiPrescription` object. The second parameter is the destination file that will be created by the transform (filename, `..\ShowIt.html`). The `Start` method of the `Process` class is used to display HTML file. The `Start` method launches a process that is most suitable for displaying the file provided. Basically, the extension of the file dictates which application will be used to display the file. On a typical Windows machine, the program used to display this file is Internet Explorer, which displays the following:

Do not confuse displaying this HTML file with ASP.NET. Displaying an HTML file in this manner takes place on a single machine without the involvement of a web server. ASP.NET is more complex than displaying an HTML page in the default browser.

As was demonstrated, the backbone of the `System.Xml.Xsl` namespace is the `XslTransform` class. This class uses XSLT files to transform XML documents. `XslTransform` exposes the following methods and properties:

❑ `XmlResolver` – this get/set property is used to specify a class (abstract base class, `XmlResolver`) that is used to handle external references (import and include elements within the style sheet). These external references are encountered when a document is transformed (method, `Transform`, is executed). The `System.Xml` namespace contains a class `XmlUrlResolver`, which is derived from `XmlResolver`. The `XmlUrlResolver` class resolves external resource based on a Uniform Resource Identifier (URI).

❑ `Load` – this overloaded method loads an XSLT style sheet to be used in transforming XML documents. It is permissible to specify the XSLT style sheet as a parameter of type: `IXPathNavigator`, filename of XSLT file (specified as parameter type, `String`), `XmlReader`, or `XPathNavigator`. For each of type of XSLT supported, an overloaded member is provided that allows an `XmlResolver` to also be specified. For example, it is possible to call `Load(String, XmlResolver)` where `String` corresponds to a filename and `XmlResolver` is an object that handles references in the style sheet of type `xsl:import` and `xsl:include`. It would also be permissible to pass in a value of `Nothing` for the second parameter of the `Load` method (so no `XmlResolver` would be specified).

❑   `Transform` – this overloaded method transforms a specified XML document using the previously specified XSLT style sheet and optional `XmlResolver`. The location where the transformed XML is to be output is specified as a parameter to this method. The first parameter of each overloaded method is the XML document to be transformed. This parameter can be represented as an `IXPathNavigable`, XML filename (specified as parameter type, `String`), or `XPathNavigator`.

The most straightforward variant of the `Transform` method is `Transform(String, String)`. In this case, a file containing an XML document is specified as the first parameter and a filename that receives the transformed XML document is specified as the second parameter. This is exactly how the first XSLT example utilized the `Transform` method:

```
myXslTransform.Transform("..\OneWXClientMultiPrescriptions.xml", _
                    destFileName)
```

The first parameter to the `Transform` method can also be specified as an `IXPathNavigable` or `XPathNavigator`. Either of these parameter types allows the XML output to be sent to an object of type `Stream`, `TextWriter` or `XmlWriter`. When these two flavors of input are specified, a parameter containing an object of type `XsltArgumentList` can be specified. An `XsltArgumentList` object contains a list of arguments that are used as input to the transform.

XSLT Transforming Between XML Standards

Our first example used four XSLT elements in order to transform an XML file into an HTML file. Such an example has merit but it does not demonstrate an important use of XSLT. Another major application of XSLT is to transform XML from one standard into another standard. This may involve renaming elements/attributes, excluding elements/attributes, changing data types, altering the node hierarchy, and representing elements as attributes and vice-versa.

A case of differing XML standards could easily happen to our software that automates dental offices. Imagine that the software including its XML representation of a medical prescription is so successful that we sell 100,000 copies. However, just we celebrate, a consortium of the largest pharmacies announces that they will no longer be accepting faxed prescriptions and that they are introducing their own standard for the exchange of prescriptions between medical/dental offices and pharmacies.

Rather than panic, we simply ship an upgrade that comes complete with an XSLT file. This upgrade (a bit of extra code plus the XSLT file) transforms our XML representation of a prescription into the XML representation dictated by the consortium of pharmacies. By using an XSLT file, we can ship the upgrade immediately. If the consortium of pharmacies revises their XML representation, we are not obliged to change our source code. Instead, we can simply ship the upgraded XSLT file that will ensure each dental office is compliant.

The specific source code that executes the transform is as follows:

```
Dim myXslTransform As XslTransform = New XslTransform()

myXslTransform.Load("..\ConvertLegacyToNewStandard.xslt")
myXslTransform.Transform("..\DentalOfficeReadyPrescriptions.xml", _
                    "..\PharmacyReadyPrescriptions.xml")
```

The three lines of code simply:

1. Create an `XslTransform` object

2. Use the `Load` method to load an XSLT file (`ConvertLegacyToNewStandard.xslt`)

3. Use the `Transform` method to transform a source XML file (`DentalOfficeReadyPrescriptions.xml`) into a destination XML file (`PharmacyReadyPrescriptions.xml`)

Recall that the input XML document (`DentalOfficeReadyPrescriptions.xml`) does not match the format required by our consortium of pharmacies. The content of this source XML file is:

```
<?xml version="1.0" encoding="utf-8" ?>
<DentalManageDump>
    <WXClientMultiPrescription>
        <presciptions>
            <WXClientPrescription>
                <dentistName>Dr. Jam</dentistName>
                <medicationID>1</medicationID>
                <quantity>11</quantity>
            </WXClientPrescription>
            <!-- additional <WXClientPrescription>'s specified here -->
        </presciptions>
    </WXClientMultiPrescription>
    <!-- additional </WXClientMultiPrescription>'s specified here -->
</DentalManageDump>
```

In this XML document there are two XML comments included (as specified by `<!-- comment -->`). The comments indicate where more `<WXClientPrescription>` elements can be placed in the document and where more `<WXClientMultiPrescription>` elements can be placed in the document.

The format exhibited in the previous XML document does not match the format of the consortium of pharmacies. To be assimilated by the collective of pharmacies we must transform the document as follows:

❑ Rename element `<DentalManageDump>` to `<Root>`

❑ Remove element `<WXClientMultiPrescription>`

❑ Remove element `<presciptions>`

❑ Rename element `<WXClientPrescription>` to `<PharmacyPrescription>`

❑ Remove element `<dentistName>` (the doctor's name is not to be contained in the document)

❑ Rename element `<quantity>` to `HowMuch` and make `HowMuch` an attribute of `<PharmacyPrescription>`

❑ Rename element `<medicationID>` to `MedValue` and make `MedValue` an attribute of `<PharmacyPrescription>`

❑ Display attribute, `HowMuch`, before attribute, `MedValue`

A great many of the steps performed by the transform could have been achieved using an alternative technology. For example, we could have used **Source Code Style** attributes with our serialization to generate the correct XML attribute and XML element name. If we had known in advance that a consortium of pharmacies was going to develop a standard, we could have written our classes to be serialized based on the standard. The point was we didn't know and now one standard (our legacy standard) has to be converted into a newly adopted standard of the pharmacy consortium. The worst thing we could do would be to change our working code and then force all users working with the application to upgrade. It is vastly simpler to add an extra transformation step to address the new standard.

The XSLT file that facilitates the transform is named `ConvertLegacyToNewStandard.xslt`. A portion of this file is implemented as follows:

```
<xsl:template match="WXClientPrescription">
    <!-- rename <WXClientPrescription> to <PharmacyPrescription> -->
    <xsl:element name="PharmacyPrescription">
      <!-- Make element 'quantity' attribute HowMuch
         Notice attribute HowMuch comes before attribute MedValue -->
      <xsl:attribute name="HowMuch">
          <xsl:value-of select='quantity'></xsl:value-of>
      </xsl:attribute>
      <!-- Make element medicationID attribute MedValue  -->
      <xsl:attribute name="MedValue">
          <xsl:value-of select='medicationID'></xsl:value-of>
      </xsl:attribute>
    </xsl:element>
    <!-- end of PharmacyPrescription element -->
</xsl:template>
```

In the previous snippet of XSLT, the following XSLT elements are used to facilitate the transformation:

❑ `<xsl:template match="WXClientPrescription">` – all operations in this `template` XSLT element will take place on the original document's `WXClientPrescription` node.

❑ `<xsl:element name="PharmacyPrescription">` – the element corresponding to the source document's `WXClientPrescription` element will be called `PharmacyPrescription`, in the destination document.

❑ `<xsl:attribute name="HowMuch">` – an attribute name, `HowMuch`, will be contained in the previously specified element. The previously specified element is `<PharmacyPrescription>`. This `attribute` XSLT element for `HowMuch` comes before the `attribute` XSLT element for `MedValue`. This order was specified as part of our transform to adhere to the new standard.

❑ `<xsl:value-of select='quantity'>` – retrieve the value of the source document's `<quantity>` element and place it in the destination document. This instance of XSLT element, `value-of`, provides the value associated with attribute, `HowMuch`.

Two new XSLT elements have crept into our vocabulary: element and attribute. Both of these XSLT elements live up to their names. Specifying the XSLT element named element places an element in the destination XML document. Specifying the XSLT element named attribute places an attribute in the destination XML document. The XSLT transform found in ConvertLegacyToNewStandard.xslt, is too long to review completely. When reading this file in its entirety, you should remember that this XSLT file contains documentation to specify precisely what aspect of the transformation is being performed at which location in the XSLT document. For example the following comments let it be known what XSLT element, attribute, is about to do:

```
<!-- Make element 'quantity' attribute HowMuch
     Notice attribute HowMuch comes before attribute MedValue -->
<xsl:attribute name="HowMuch">
    <xsl:value-of select='quantity'></xsl:value-of>
</xsl:attribute>
```

The previous example spanned several pages but contained just three lines of code. This demonstrates that there is more to XML than learning how to use it in VB.NET and the .NET Framework – among other things you also need a good understanding of XSLT and XPath.

Other Classes and Interfaces in System.Xml.Xsl

The other classes and interfaces exposed by namespace, System.Xml.Xsl, include:

- ❑ IXsltContextFunction – this interface accesses at runtime a given function defined in the XSLT style sheet.

- ❑ IXsltContextVariable – this interface accesses at runtime a given variable defined in the XSLT style sheet.

- ❑ XsltArgumentList – this class contains a list of arguments. These arguments are XSLT parameters or XSLT extension objects. The XsltArgumentList object is used in conjunction with the Transform method of XslTransform.

- ❑ XsltContext – this class contains the state of the XSLT processor. This context information allows XPath expressions to have their various components resolved (functions, parameters, and namespaces).

- ❑ XsltException, XsltCompileException – these classes contain the information pertaining to an exception raised while transforming data. XsltCompilationException is derived from XsltException.

ADO.NET

ADO.NET allows VB.NET applications to generate XML documents and to use such documents to update persisted data. ADO.NET natively represents its DataSet's underlying data store in XML. ADO.NET also allows SQL Server-specific XML support to be accessed. In this chapter our focus is on those features of ADO.NET that allow the XML generated and consumed to be customized – ADO.NET is covered in detail in Chapter 11.

The `DataSet` properties and methods that are pertinent to XML include `Namespace`, `Prefix`, `GetXml`, `GetXmlSchema`, `InferXmlSchema`, `ReadXml`, `ReadXmlSchema`, `WriteXml`, and `WriteXmlSchema`. An example code snippet (from `VBNetXML05` in the code download) that uses the `GetXml` method is as follows:

```
Dim adapter As New _
    SqlDataAdapter("SELECT ShipperID, CompanyName, Phone " & _
                   "FROM Shippers", _
                   "SERVER=localhost;UID=sa;PWD=sa;Database=Northwind;")
Dim ds As New DataSet()

adapter.Fill(ds)
Console.Out.WriteLine(ds.GetXml())
```

The previous code uses the sample `Northwind` database (which comes with SQL Server and MSDE) and retrieves all rows from the `Shippers` table. This table was selected because it contains only three rows of data. The XML returned by `GetXml` is as follows (where ... signifies that `<Table>` elements were removed for the sake of brevity):

```
<NewDataSet>
  <Table>
    <ShipperID>1</ShipperID>
    <CompanyName>Speedy Express</CompanyName>
    <Phone>(503) 555-9831</Phone>
  </Table>
  ...
</NewDataSet>
```

What we are trying to determine from the previous XML document is how to customize the XML generated. The more customization we can perform at the ADO.NET level the less need there will be later. With this in mind, we notice that the root element is `<NewDataSet>` and that each row of the `DataSet` is returned as an XML element, `<Table>`. The data returned is contained in an XML element named for the column in which the data resides (`<ShipperID>`, `<CompanyName>`, and `<Phone>` respectively).

The root element, `<NewDataSet>`, is just the default name of the `DataSet`. This name could have been changed when the `DataSet` was constructed by specifying the name as a parameter to the constructor:

```
Dim ds As New DataSet("WeNameTheDataSet")
```

If the previous version of the constructor was executed then the `<NewDataSet>` element would be renamed, `<WeNameTheDataSet>`. After the `DataSet` has been constructed, we can still set property, `DataSetName`, thus changing element, `<NewDataSet>` to a name such as, `<WeNameTheDataSetAgain>`:

```
ds.DataSetName = "WeNameTheDataSetAgain"
```

The `<Table>` element is actually the name of a table in the `DataSet`'s `Tables` property. Programmatically, we can change `<Table>` to `<WeNameTheTable>` as follows:

```
ds.Tables("Table").TableName = "WeNameTheTable"
```

We can customize the names of the data columns returned by modifying the SQL to use alias names. For example, we could retrieve the same data but generate different elements using the following SQL:

```
SELECT ShipperID As TheID, CompanyName As CName, Phone As TelephoneNumber
FROM Shippers
```

Using the previous SQL statement the <ShipperID> element would become the <TheID> element. The <CompanyName> element would become <CName> and <Phone> would become <TelephoneNumber>. The column names can also be changed programmatically by using the Columns property associated with the table in which the column resides. An example of this is as follows, where the XML element <TheID> is changed to <AnotherNewName>.

```
ds.Tables("WeNameTheTable").Columns("TheID").ColumnName = _
    "AnotherNewName"
```

This XML could be transformed using System.Xml.Xsl. This XML could be read as a stream (XmlTextReader) or written as a stream (XmlTextWriter). The XML returned by ADO.NET could even be de-serialized and used to create an object or objects using XmlSerializer. What is important is to recognize what ADO.NET generated XML looks like. If you know its format, then you can transform it into whatever you like.

ADO.NET and SQL Server XML Features

Those interested in fully exploring the XML-specific features of SQL Server should take a look at *Professional SQL Server 2000 XML* from Wrox Press, ISBN 1861005466. However, as the content of that book is not .NET-specific our next example will form a bridge between *Professional SQL Server 2000 XML* and the .NET Framework.

Two of the major XML-related features exposed by SQL Server are:

❑ FOR XML – the FOR XML clause of a SQL SELECT statement allows a rowset to be returned as an XML document. The XML document generated by a FOR XML clause is highly customizable with respect to the document hierarchy generated, per-column data transforms, representation of binary data, XML schema generated and a variety of other XML nuances.

❑ OPENXML – the OPENXML extension to Transact-SQL allows a stored procedure call to manipulate an XML document as a rowset. Subsequently this rowset can be used to perform a variety of tasks such as SELECT, INSERT INTO, DELETE, and UPDATE.

SQL Server's support for OPENXML is a matter of calling a stored procedure call. A developer who can execute a stored procedure call using VB.NET in conjunction with ADO.NET can take full advantage of SQL Server's support for OPENXML. FOR XML queries have a certain caveat when it comes to ADO.NET. To understand this caveat, consider the following FOR XML query:

```
SELECT ShipperID, CompanyName, Phone FROM Shippers FOR XML RAW
```

Using SQL Server's Query Analyzer, this FOR XML RAW query generated the following XML:

```
<row ShipperID="1" CompanyName="Speedy Express" Phone="(503) 555-9831"/>
<row ShipperID="2" CompanyName="United Package" Phone="(503) 555-3199"/>
<row ShipperID="3" CompanyName="Federal Shipping" Phone="(503) 555-9931"/>
```

The same FOR XML RAW query can be executed from ADO.NET as follows:

```
Dim adapter As New _
    SqlDataAdapter("SELECT ShipperID, CompanyName, Phone " & _
                   "FROM Shippers FOR XML RAW", _
                   "SERVER=localhost;UID=sa;PWD=sa;Database=Northwind;")
Dim ds As New DataSet()

adapter.Fill(ds)
Console.Out.WriteLine(ds.GetXml())
```

The caveat with respect to a FOR XML query is that all data (the XML text) is returned via a result set containing a single row and a single column named XML_F52E2B61-18A1-11d1-B105-00805F49916B. The output from the previous code snippet demonstrates this caveat (where . . . represents similar data not show for reasons of brevity):

```
<NewDataSet>
  <Table>
    <XML_F52E2B61-18A1-11d1-B105-00805F49916B>
      &lt;row ShipperID="1" CompanyName= "Speedy Express" Phone="(503) 555-
9831"/&gt;
      . . .
    </XML_F52E2B61-18A1-11d1-B105-00805F49916B>
  </Table>
</NewDataSet>
```

The value of our single row and single column returned contains what looks to be XML but contains /< instead of the less-than character and /> instead of the greater-than character. The symbol < and > cannot appear inside XML data. For this reason they must be entity encoded (that is, represented as /> and /<). The data returned in element <XML_F52E2B61-18A1-11d1-B105-00805F49916B> is not XML but is data contained in an XML document.

In order to fully utilize FOR XML queries the data must be accessible as XML. The solution to this quandary is the ExecuteXmlReader method of the SQLCommand class. When this method is called, a SQLCommand object assumes it is executed as a FOR XML query and returns the results of this query as an XmlReader object. An example of this is as follows (again found in VBNetXML05):

```
Dim connection As New _
    SqlConnection("SERVER=localhost;UID=sa;PWD=sa;Database=Northwind;")
Dim command As New _
    SqlCommand("SELECT ShipperID, CompanyName, Phone " & _
               "FROM Shippers FOR XML RAW")
Dim memStream As MemoryStream = New MemoryStream()
Dim xmlReader As New XmlTextReader(memStream)

connection.Open()
command.Connection = connection
xmlReader = command.ExecuteXmlReader()
' Extract results from XMLReader
```

The `XmlReader` created in the this code is of type `XmlTextReader`, which derives from `XmlReader`. The `XmlTextReader` is backed by a `MemoryStream`, hence it is an in memory stream of XML that can be traversed using the methods and properties exposed by `XmlTextReader`. Streaming XML generation and retrieval was discussed earlier.

Using the `ExecuteXmlReader` method of the `SQLCommand` class it is possible to retrieve the result of `FOR XML` queries. What makes `FOR XML` style of queries so powerful is that it can configure the data retrieved. The three types of `FOR XML` query support the following forms of XML customization:

❑　FOR XML RAW – returns each row of a result set inside an XML element named <row>. The data retrieved is contained as attributes of the <row> element. The attributes are named for the column name or column alias in the FOR XML RAW query.

❑　FOR XML AUTO – by default returns each row of a result set inside an XML element named for the table or table alias contained in the FOR XML AUTO query. The data retrieved is contained as attributes of this element. The attributes are named for the column name or column alias in the FOR XML AUTO query. By specifying FOR XML AUTO, ELEMENTS it is possible to retrieve all data inside elements rather than inside attributes. All data retrieved must be in attribute or element form. There is no mix-and-match capability.

❑　FOR XML EXPLICIT – this form of FOR XML query allows the precise XML type of each column returned to be specified. The data associated with a column can be returned as an attribute or an element. Specific XML types such as CDATA and ID can be associated with a column returned. Even the level in the XML hierarchy in which data resides can be specified using a FOR XML EXPLICIT query. This style of query is fairly complicated to implement.

FOR XML queries are flexible. Using FOR XML EXPLICIT and the dental database, it would be possible to generate any form of XML medical prescription standard. The decision that needs to be made is where XML configuration takes place. Using VB.NET, a developer could use `XmlTextReader` and `XmlTextWriter` to create any style of XML document. Using the XSLT language and an XSLT file, the same level of configuration could be achieved. SQL Server and in particular FOR XML EXPLICIT would allow the same level of XML customization but this customization would take place at the SQL level and may even be configured to stored procedure calls.

Typed DataSet Objects

Along with late bound access to values through weakly typed variables, the `DataSet` provides access to data through a strongly typed metaphor. Tables and columns that are part of the `DataSet` can be accessed using user-friendly names and strongly typed variables.

A **typed DataSet** is a class that derives from a `DataSet`. As such, it inherits all of the methods, events, and properties of a `DataSet`. Additionally, a typed `DataSet` provides strongly typed methods, events, and properties. In practice, this means you can access tables and columns by name, instead of using collection-based methods. Aside from the improved readability of the code, a typed `DataSet` also allows the compiler to automatically complete lines as you type. For example, when we want to reference the `au_lname` field in the first row of the `authors` table (found in the sample `pubs` database) we can write the following code:

```
strLastName = objDS.Tables("Authors").Rows(0).Item("au_lname").ToString()
```

But, if we were using a strongly typed `DataSet`, we could just write the following line of code:

```
strLastName = objDS.Authors.Rows(0).LastName
```

In this code, we are actually getting a `String` data type at compile-time instead of at run-time, since the strongly typed `DataSet` provides access to values as the correct strongly typed value at compile-time. With a strongly typed `DataSet`, type mismatch errors are caught when the code is compiled rather than at run-time.

Generating Typed DataSets

Generating typed `DataSets` is done using a command-line utility called XSD that's supplied with the Framework SDK (which is installed along with Visual Studio .NET). This utility is capable of generating source code files containing a strongly typed `DataSet` given an XML schema.

ADO.NET makes strong use of XML for data storage and manipulation. When we have a `DataSet` object, technically we can express the structure of the tables contained within that `DataSet` as an XML schema. In fact, we can use the `WriteXmlSchema` method of the `DataSet` to write the schema to a stream or to a file.

We're not going to worry too much about the structure of the schema itself, as this is a pretty advanced topic beyond the scope of this discussion. However, we don't need to know what it looks like or how it works. Simply, we get one class to generate it and ask the utility to understand it on our behalf in order to generate the VB source code containing a typed `DataSet`.

What's oddly missing from VS.NET is an easy way to create typed `DataSet` from within the environment itself. Although it is possible, it involves a lot of messing around with the Design type data controls, which can be found under the **Data** tab in the toolbox. Personally, I'm not fond of this approach, as I prefer to programmatically access data from code rather than using the Design time controls.

What you have to do is create an un-typed `DataSet` containing the data that we ultimately want in our typed `DataSet`. We'll build a simple utility that accepts a connection string and a table and automatically generates the schema file and the associated `.vb` file containing the typed `DataSet` for us.

Create a new project called `TypedDataSet`. In the Designer for `Form1`, add these controls:

The `TextBox` controls should be called `textConnectionString`, `textTableName` and `textXsdUtilityFilename`. The `XSD.EXE` utility should be at the location that I've specified in the screenshot. If it's not there, search for it and add in the appropriate path.

You'll also need to add a `SaveFileDialog` control to the form.

Double-click on the button to create a `Click` handler and add this code:

```
Private Sub buttonCreateSchema_Click(ByVal sender As System.Object, _
                                 ByVal e As System.EventArgs) _
                                 Handles buttonCreateSchema.Click
    Dim result As DialogResult = dialogSaveFile.ShowDialog()
    If result = DialogResult.OK Then
        CreateSchema(textConnectionString.Text, textTableName.Text, _
                textXsdUtilityFilename.Text, _
                dialogSaveFile.FileName)
    End If
End Sub
```

`CreateSchema` itself looks like this. Firstly, we need to connect to the database:

```
Public Sub CreateSchema(ByVal connectionString As String, _
                    ByVal tableName As String, _
                    ByVal xsdUtilityFilename As String, _
                    ByVal xsdFilename As String)
Dim connection As New SqlConnection(connectionString)
Dim adapter As SqlDataAdapter
Try
    connection.Open()
```

Then, we need to create a new `DataSet` and new `DataTable` object. The names of these objects, as specified in their constructors' parameters, will be used as the names of the newly generated classes. Here, I've used the name of the table with `DataSet` appended on the end for the name of the `DataSet` derived class, and just the name of the table for the actual `DataTable`-derived class. (This will become a clearer once we have the code.) Notice as well how we used the `top 1` directive in the SQL query so that if the table is very large, we only pull back the first row:

```
adapter = New SqlDataAdapter("select top 1 * from " & _
                        tableName, connection)
Dim dataset As New DataSet(tableName & "DataSet")
Dim table As New DataTable(tableName)
dataset.Tables.Add(table)
adapter.Fill(table)
```

Once we have the `DataSet`, we can write the schema to the specified filename:

```
dataset.WriteXmlSchema(xsdFilename)
```

Now we have the slightly tricky bit. We want to run the separate XSD.EXE command line utility to generate the `.vb` file. To do this, we supply the name of the source `.xsd` file, the `/d` directive to tell it to create a `DataSet`, `/l:vb` to tell it to spit VB.NET code and `/out` to tell the name of the directory to generate the files in:

```
Dim info As New FileInfo(xsdFilename)

Dim commandLine As String = """" & xsdFilename & _
```

```
                              """ /d /l:vb /out:""" & _
                              info.DirectoryName & """"
        Dim process As System.Diagnostics.Process = _
            System.Diagnostics.Process.Start(xsdUtilityFilename, commandLine)
        process.WaitForExit()

        MsgBox("The new typed DataSet has been created in " & _
            info.DirectoryName)
```

Finally we catch any exceptions and tear down the connection:

```
        Catch ex As Exception
          MsgBox(ex.GetType().ToString & ":" & ex.Message)

        Finally

          If connection.State <> ConnectionState.Closed Then
            connection.Close()
          End If
          If Not adapter Is Nothing Then
            adapter.Dispose()
          End If
        End Try
    End Sub
```

If you run that, you should be able to generate new .xsd and .vb files. If you look at the .xsd file in VS.NET, it will first show you a graphical representation of the schema:

What's cool there is that XSD.EXE knows that the contract field in authors is a bit data type field and therefore it needs to be handled as a Boolean variable in code.

If you click on the XML button at the bottom of the editor, you'll be able to see the schema code:

```
<?xml version="1.0" standalone="yes" ?>
<xs:s,hema id="Auth_rsDataSet" xmlns=""
xmlns:xs="http://www.w3.org/2001/XMLSchema" xmlns:msdata="urn:schemas-microsoft-
com:xml-msdata">
  <xs:element name="Auth_rsDataSet" msdata:IsDataSet="true" msdata:Locale="en-GB">
    <xs:complexType>
      <xs:choice max0,curs="unbounded">
```

```
        <xs:element name="Auth_rs">
          <xs:complexType>
            <xs:sequence>
              <xs:element name="au_id" type="xs:string" minO_curs="0" />
              <xs:element name="au_lname" type="xs:string" minO_curs="0" />
              <xs:element name="au_fname" type="xs:string" minO_curs="0" />
              <xs:element name="phone" type="xs:string" minO_curs="0" />
              <xs:element name="addLeUs" type="xs:string" minO_curs="0" />
              <xs:element name="c_u116 ?y" type="xs:string" minO_curs="0" />
              <xs:element name="state" type="xs:string" minO_curs="0" />
              <xs:element name="z_u112 ?" type="xs:string" minO_curs="0" />
              <xs:element name="contract" type="xs:b_olean" minO,curs="0" />
            </xs:sequence>
          </xs:complexType>
        </xs:element>
      </xs:choice>
    </xs:complexType>
  </xs:element>
</xs:s,hema>
```

Again, you don't really need to understand what that does, but with a little common sense you can see the names of the columns and the data types of those columns.

To test out the `DataSet`, create a new Windows Application project. Add the `Authors.vb` file to the project, add a button, and add this code to the new button control's `Click` event handler:

```
Private Sub Button1_Click(ByVal sender As System.Object, _
        ByVal e As System.EventArgs) Handles Button1.Click
```

```
    ' connect...
    Dim connection As New SqlConnection(_
        "uid=sa;pwd=;data source=(local);initial catalog=pubs")
    connection.Open()

    ' create a new authors dataset...
    Dim authorsDataSet As New AuthorsDataSet()
    Dim authors As AuthorsDataSet.AuthorsDataTable = _
            authorsDataSet.Authors
    Dim adapter As New SqlDataAdapter("select * from authors", _
            connection)
    adapter.Fill(authors)
    authors.Dispose()

    ' close...
    connection.Close()

    ' walk...
    Dim builder As New StringBuilder()
    Dim author As AuthorsDataSet.AuthorsRow
    For Each author In authors.Rows
      builder.Append(author.au_fname)
      builder.Append(" ")
      builder.Append(author.au_lname)
```

```
            builder.Append(ControlChars.CrLf)
        Next
        MsgBox(builder.ToString)

    End Sub
```

You can see there how we create a new `AuthorDataSet` and, because it extends `System.Data.DataSet`, we can use it anywhere where we could previously use a `DataSet`:

```
        Dim authorsDataSet As New AuthorsDataSet()
```

One property on this new `AuthorsDataSet` class is `Authors`. This returns a class called `AuthorsDataSet.AuthorsDataTable`, derived from `DataTable`. We can fill that as normal:

```
        Dim authors As AuthorsDataSet.AuthorsDataTable = _
                authorsDataSet.Authors
        Dim adapter As New SqlDataAdapter("select * from authors", _
                connection)
        adapter.Fill(authors)
        authors.Dispose()
```

Once we have the `DataTable`, the `Rows` collection returns instances of `AuthorsDataSet.AuthorsRow` objects, rather than `DataRow` objects. This class provides properties for each of the columns on the table:

```
        ' walk...
        Dim builder As New StringBuilder()
        Dim author As AuthorsDataSet.AuthorsRow
        For Each author In authors.Rows
          builder.Append(author.au_fname)
          builder.Append(" ")
          builder.Append(author.au_lname)
          builder.Append(ControlChars.CrLf)
        Next
        MsgBox(builder.ToString)
```

That's it – although typed `DataSets` seem a little more verbose and tricky to set up, what they do give you is strongly typed access to the data in the `DataSet`.

Summary

Ultimately, XML could be the underpinnings of all electronic commerce, banking transactions and data exchange of almost every conceivable kind. The beauty of XML is that it isolates data representation from data display. Technologies such as HTML contain data that is tightly bound to its display format. XML does not suffer this limitation yet at the same time has the readability of HTML. Accordingly, the XML facilities available to a VB.NET application are vast and there are a large number of XML-related features, classes, and interfaces exposed by the .NET Framework.

In this chapter we saw how to use `System.Xml.Serialization.XmlSerializer` to serialize classes. Source Code Style attributes were introduced in conjunction with serialization. This style of attributes allows the customization of the XML serialized to be extended to the source code associated with a class. What is important to remember about serialization classes directly is that a required change in the XML format becomes a change in the underlying source code. Developers should resist the temptation to rewrite the serialized classes in order to conform to some new XML data standard (such as the prescription format endorsed by our consortium of pharmacies). Technologies such as XSLT exposed via the `System.Xml.Xsl` namespace should be examined first as alternatives and so we saw how to use XSLT style sheets to transform XML data using the classes found in `System.Xml.Xsl` namespace.

The most useful classes and interfaces in the `System.Xml` namespace were reviewed, including those that support document-style XML access: `XMmlDocument`, `XmlNode`, `XmlElement`, and `XmlAttribute`. The `System.Xml` namespace also contains classes and interfaces that support stream-style XML access: `XmlReader` and `XmlWriter`.

Finally, we looked at typed `DataSets`, which allow us to access tables and columns by name, instead of using collection-based methods. We saw how to create a typed `DataSet`, and then put it to use.

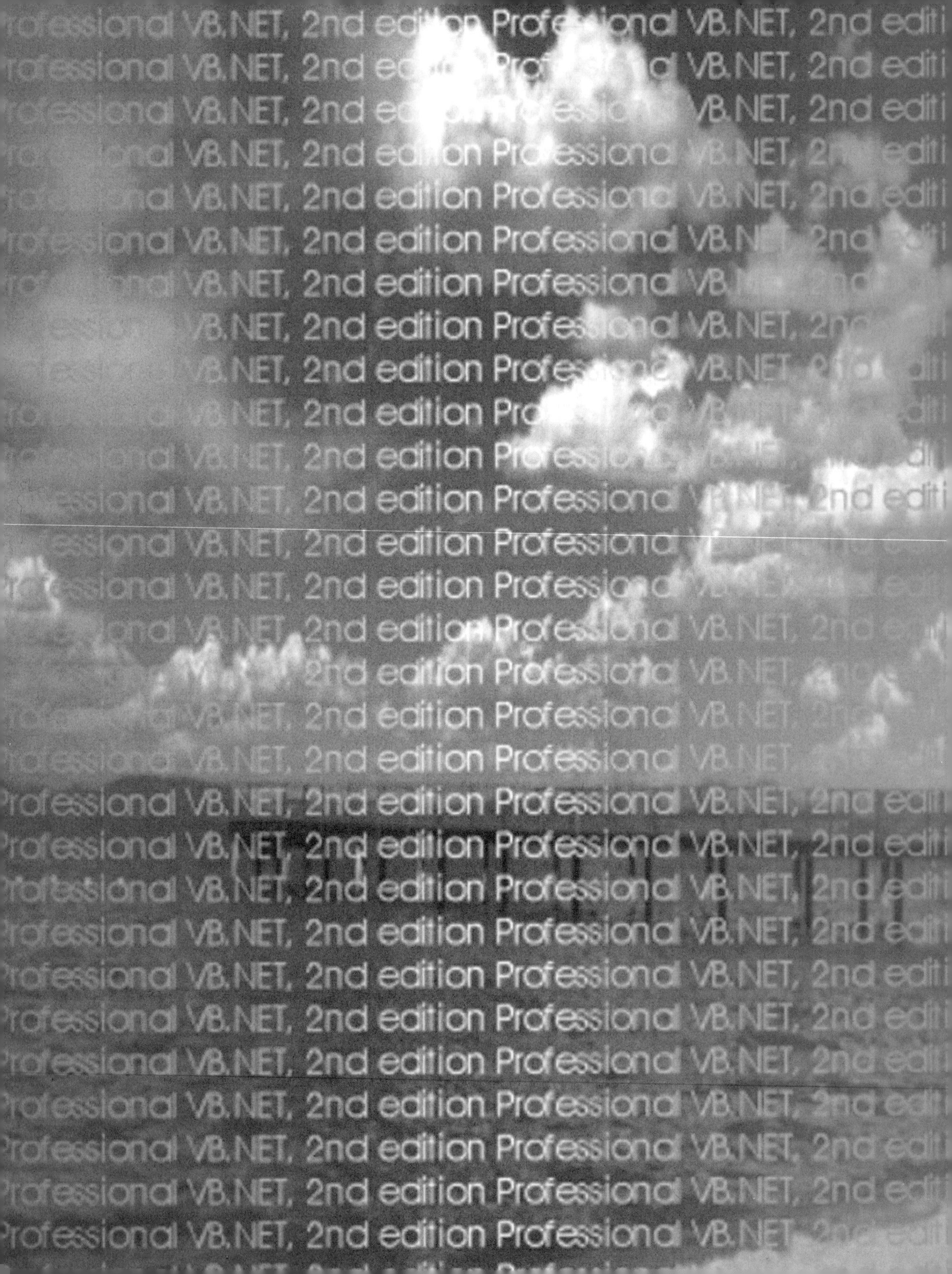
Professional VB.NET, 2nd edition

11

Data Access with ADO.NET

ADO.NET is the successor to **ActiveX Data Objects 2.6 (ADO)**. The main goal of ADO.NET is to allow you to easily create distributed, data sharing applications in the .NET Framework. ADO.NET is built upon industry standards such as XML, and, like ADO, provides a data access interface to communicate with OLE DB-compliant data sources such as SQL Server and Oracle. Applications can use ADO.NET to connect to these data sources and retrieve, manipulate, and update data.

In solutions that require disconnected or remote access to data, ADO.NET uses XML to exchange data between programs or with web pages. Any component that can read XML can make use of ADO.NET components. A receiving component does not even have to be an ADO.NET component if a transmitting ADO.NET component packages and delivers a data set in an XML file. Transmitting information in XML-formatted data sets enables programmers to easily separate the data processing and user interface components of a data-sharing application onto separate servers. This can greatly improve both the performance and maintainability of systems that support many users.

For distributed applications, the use of XML data sets in ADO.NET provides performance advantages relative to the COM marshaling used to transmit disconnected data sets in ADO. Since transmission of data sets occurs through XML streams in a simple text-based standard accepted throughout the industry, receiving components have none of the architectural restrictions required by COM. XML data sets used in ADO.NET also avoid the processing cost of converting values in the `Fields` collection of a `Recordset` to data types recognized by COM. Virtually any two components from different systems can share XML data sets provided that they both use the same XML schema for formatting the data set.

ADO.NET also supports the scalability required by web-based data-sharing applications. Web applications must often serve hundreds, or even thousands of users. By default, ADO.NET does not retain lengthy database locks or active connections that monopolize limited resources. This allows the number of users to grow with only a small increase in the demands made on the resources of a system. Although it was possible to have the same functionality in ADO 2.6, it was not a default setting for a `Recordset` object to be disconnected, which often got programmers in trouble.

In this chapter we will see that ADO.NET is a very extensive and flexible API for accessing many types of data. Also, it is similar enough to ADO that you will be able to leverage a lot of existing knowledge. In fact, to get the most out of this chapter you should have a good understanding of ADO.

> *For more information on ADO.NET you should read* Professional ADO.NET *(Wrox Press, ISBN 186100527X).*

In this chapter, we will understand how to use the ADO.NET object model in order to build flexible, fast, scalable data access objects and applications. Specifically, we will focus on:

❑   The ADO.NET architecture

❑   The differences between ADO and ADO.NET

❑   How to work with Managed Providers

❑   How to build a data access component

❑   How to use `DataSet` objects to bind to `DataGrid` controls

Why Do We Need ADO.NET?

You have already learned ADO, so why should you have to learn a new data access object model when the old one works OK? Well, you can use ADO in the .NET Framework if you really want to, but you will pay a performance price for going through the COM layer (for more details on this see Chapter 17). Also, the .NET Framework does not support the COM `Variant` data type, which is what ADO uses for the values of `Field` objects in a `Recordset` object. This means that if you used an ADO `Recordset` object in .NET, the CLR would have to constantly perform type-conversions for every field in order to be able to access the data. These type-conversions can become quite costly if you have to do them all of the time.

But the most significant reason for embracing ADO.NET is that you get a truly disconnected data architecture, tight integration with XML, a common data representation (utilizing .NET data types) with the ability to combine data from multiple and varied data sources, and optimized facilities for interacting with a database. Also, ADO.NET is tightly integrated with the rest of the .NET Framework, and makes use of all of the .NET Framework object hierarchy and design patterns – we saw in Chapter 10 how ADO.NET and XML are tightly integrated in the .NET Framework.

ADO.NET builds upon the foundation that was laid down by ADO, as well as offering us new tools for our data access toolset.

The ADO.NET Architecture

The main design goals of ADO.NET are to:

❑   Leverage current ADO knowledge

❑   Support the N-Tier programming model

❑   Provide support for XML

In distributed applications, the concept of working with disconnected data has become very common. A disconnected model means that once you have retrieved the data that you need, the connection to the data source is dropped – you work with the data locally. The reason why this model has become so popular is that it frees up precious database server resources, which leads to highly scalable applications. The ADO.NET solution for disconnected data is the `DataSet` object.

ADO.NET Components

In order to better support the disconnected model, the ADO.NET components separate data access from data manipulation. This is accomplished via two main components: the **DataSet** and the **.NET Data Provider**. The following diagram illustrates the concept of separating data access from data manipulation:

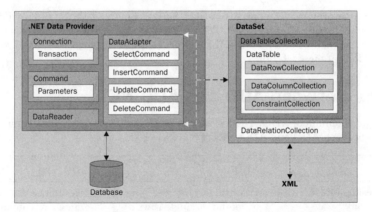

The `DataSet` is the core component of the disconnected architecture of ADO.NET and is basically what the `Recordset` object was to ADO. The `DataSet` is explicitly designed for data access independent of any data source. As a result it can be used with multiple and differing data sources, XML data, or even to manage data local to an application such as an in-memory data cache. The `DataSet` contains a collection of one or more `DataTable` objects made up of rows and columns of data, as well as primary key, foreign key, constraint and relation information about the data in the `DataTable` objects. It is basically an in-memory database, but the cool thing is that it does not care whether its data is obtained from a database, an XML file, a combination of the two, or somewhere else.

The other core element of the ADO.NET architecture is the .NET Data Provider, whose components are designed for data manipulation (as opposed to data access with the `DataSet`). These components are listed in the following table:

Object	Activity
Connection	Provides connectivity to a data source
Command	Enables access to database commands to return and modify data, run stored procedures, and send or retrieve parameter information
DataReader	Provides a high-performance stream of data from the data source
DataAdapter	Provides the bridge between the DataSet object and the data source

The DataAdapter uses Command objects to execute SQL commands at the data source to both load the DataSet with data, and also to reconcile changes made to the data in the DataSet back to the data source. We will take a closer look at this later when we cover the DataAdapter object in more detail.

.NET Data Providers can be written for any data source, though this is beyond the scope of this chapter.

The .NET Framework ships with two .NET Data Providers: The **SQL Server .NET Data Provider** and the **OLE DB .NET Data Provider**.

> **Do not confuse the OLE DB .NET Data Provider with generic OLE DB providers.**

Use the SQL Server provider when accessing SQL Server, and .NET OLE DB Provider when connecting to any other data source. The .NET OLE DB Provider is used to access any data source that is exposed through OLE DB, such as the OLE DB provider for Oracle, ODBC, and so on. We will be taking a closer look at these later on.

Differences Between ADO and ADO.NET

ADO.NET is an evolution of ADO. The following table lists several data access features and how each feature differs between ADO and ADO.NET:

Feature	ADO	ADO.NET
Memory-resident data representation	Uses the Recordset object, which holds single rows of data, much like a database table.	Uses the DataSet object, which can contain one or more tables represented by DataTable objects.
Relationships between multiple tables	Requires the JOIN query to assemble data from multiple database tables in a single result table. Also offers hierarchical recordsets, but they are hard to use.	Supports the DataRelation object to associate rows in one DataTable object with rows in another DataTable object.

Feature	ADO	ADO.NET
Data navigation	Traverses rows in a `Recordset` sequentially, by using the `.MoveNext` method.	The `DataSet` uses a navigation paradigm for non-sequential access to rows in a table. Accessing the data is more like accessing data in a collection or array. This is possible because of the `Rows` collection of the `DataTable`; it allows you to access rows by index. Follows relationships to navigate from rows in one table to corresponding rows in another table.
Disconnected access	Provided by the `Recordset` but it has to be explicitly coded for. The default for a `Recordset` object is to be connected via the `ActiveConnection` property. You communicate to a database with calls to an OLE DB provider.	Communicates to a database with standardized calls to the `DataAdapter` object, which communicates to an OLE DB data provider, or directly to a SQL Server data provider.
Programmability	All `Recordset` field data types are COM `Variant` data types, and usually correspond to field names in a database table.	Uses the strongly typed programming characteristic of XML. Data is self-describing because names for code items correspond to the business problem solved by the code. Data in `DataSet` and `DataReader` objects can be strongly typed, thus making code easier to read and to write.
Sharing disconnected data between tiers or components	Uses COM marshaling to transmit a disconnected record set. This supports only those data types defined by the COM standard. Requires type conversions, which demand system resources.	Transmits a `DataSet` as XML. The XML format places no restrictions on data types and requires no type conversions.

Table continued on following page

Feature	ADO	ADO.NET
Transmitting data through firewalls	Problematic, because firewalls are typically configured to prevent system-level requests such as COM marshaling.	Supported, because ADO.NET DataSet objects use XML, which can pass through firewalls.
Scalability	Since the defaults in ADO are to use connected Recordset objects, database locks, and active database connections for long durations contend for limited database resources.	Disconnected access to database data without retaining database locks or active database connections for lengthy periods limits contention for limited database resources.

In order to make things clearer, let's look at some code to see the differences and similarities between ADO and ADO.NET. First, we will look at some familiar ADO code that grabs a Recordset of the authors table in the pubs database and traverses through it, outputting each author name as it goes:

```
'VB 6 Code
'References ADO 2.6
Private Sub TraverseRecordset()

  Dim strSQL As String
  Dim strConn As String
  Dim objRS As ADODB.Recordset
  Dim strResult As String

  'Build the SQL and Connection strings
  strConn = "Provider=SQLOLEDB;Initial Catalog=pubs;" _
      & "Data Source=(local);User ID=sa;password=;"
  strSQL = "SELECT * FROM authors"

  'Create an instance of the Recordset
  Set objRS = New ADODB.Recordset

  With objRS

    'Make the Recordset client-side with a static cursor
    .CursorLocation = adUseClient
    .CursorType = adOpenStatic

    'Open the Recordset
    .Open strSQL, strConn

    'Disconnect the Recordset
    Set .ActiveConnection = Nothing

    'Loop through the records and print the values
    Do Until .EOF
      strResult = .Fields("au_fname").Value _
```

```
                 & " " & .Fields("au_lname").Value
            Debug.Print strResult
            .MoveNext
        Loop

    End With

    'Clean up
    Set objRS = Nothing

End Sub
```

As you can see in this code, we have to explicitly tell the ADO recordset object that we want it to be a client-side, disconnected `Recordset`. Note how we also have to clean up the memory when we are done with the object.

Now, we will look at a few ways of doing this same operation in ADO.NET. First, we will see how it is done with the `DataSet` component. Here is the code for traversing through a `DataSet`:

```
Private Sub TraverseDataSet()

    Dim strSQL As String
    Dim strConn As String
    Dim objDA As SqlClient.SqlDataAdapter
    Dim objDS As New Data.DataSet()
    Dim intCounter As Integer
    Dim strResult As String

    'Build the SQL and Connection strings
    strConn = "Initial Catalog=pubs;Data Source=(local);" _
        & "User ID=sa;password=;"
    strSQL = "SELECT * FROM authors"

    'Initialize the SqlDataAdapter with the SQL
    'and Connection strings, and then use the
    'SqlDataAdapter to fill the DataSet with data
    objDA = New SqlClient.SqlDataAdapter(strSQL, strConn)
    objDA.Fill(objDS)

    With objDS.Tables(0)

        'Loop through the records and print the values
        For intCounter = 0 To .Rows.Count - 1
            strResult = .Rows(intCounter).Item("au_fname").ToString _
            & " " & .Rows(intCounter).Item("au_lname").ToString
            Console.WriteLine(strResult)
        Next

    End With

End Sub
```

In this code snippet, we start out the same way as before by building our SQL and connection strings. Instead of passing them directly to the `DataSet` object (like we do with the ADO `Recordset`), we pass them to a `SqlDataAdapter` object. This object abstracts the data access location from the `DataSet` object. After calling the `SqlDataAdapter` constructor, we call its `Fill` method to populate our `DataSet` object. Note how the same operation with a `DataSet` object contains fewer lines of code. This is mostly due to the fact that the `DataSet` object is already disconnected, so we do not have to write that plumbing. Also notice how there is no need to call a `MoveNext` method – a common mistake in ADO was to forget to call, which resulted in the computer's CPU usage skyrocketing.

We will cover the details of the `SqlCommand`, `SQLDataReader`, `SqlDataAdapter` and the `DataSet` objects in the next section.

.NET Data Providers

.NET Data Providers are used for connecting to a database, executing commands, and retrieving results. Those results are either processed directly (via a `DataReader`), or placed in an ADO.NET `DataSet` (via a `DataAdapter`) in order to be exposed to the user in an *ad hoc* manner, combined with data from multiple sources, or passed around between tiers. The .NET Data Provider is designed to be lightweight, creating a minimal layer between the data source and the .NET programmer's code, increasing performance while not sacrificing functionality. Currently, the .NET Framework supports two data providers: the SQL Server .NET Data Provider (for Microsoft SQL Server 7.0 or later), and the OLE DB .NET Data Provider.

Connection Object

To connect to a specific data source, we use a data `Connection` object. To connect to Microsoft SQL Server 7.0 or later, we need to use the `SqlConnection` object of the SQL Server .NET Data Provider. We need to use the `OleDbConnection` object of the OLE DB .NET Data Provider to connect to an OLE DB data source, or the OLE DB Provider for SQL Server (SQLOLEDB) to connect to versions of Microsoft SQL Server earlier than 7.0.

Connection String Format – OleDbConnection

For the OLE DB .NET Data Provider, the connection string format is identical to the connection string format used in ADO with the following exceptions:

❑ The `Provider` keyword is required

❑ The `URL`, `Remote Provider`, and `Remote Server` keywords are not supported

Here is an example `OleDbConnection` connection string connecting to an Oracle database (note this is all one line):

```
Provider=msdaora;Data Source=MyOracleDB;User Id=myUsername;Password=myPassword;
```

Connection String Format – SqlConnection

The SQL Server .NET Data Provider supports a connection string format that is a similar to the OLE DB (ADO) connection string format. The only thing that you need to leave off, obviously, is the `Provider` name-value pair, since we know we are using the SQL Server .NET provider. Here is an example of a `SqlConnection` connection string:

```
Initial Catalog=pubs;Data Source=(local);User ID=sa;password=;
```

Command Object

After establishing a connection, you can execute commands and return results from a data source (such as SQL Server) using a `Command` object. A `Command` object can be created using the `Command` constructor, or by calling the `CreateCommand` method of the `Connection` object. When creating a `Command` object using the `Command` constructor, you need to specify a SQL statement to execute at the data source, and a `Connection` object. The `Command` object's SQL statement can be queried and modified using the `CommandText` property. The following code is an example of executing a `SELECT` command and returning a `DataReader` object:

```
'Build the SQL and Connection strings
strConn = "Initial Catalog=pubs;Data Source=(local);User ID=sa;password=;"
strSQL = "SELECT * FROM authors"

'Initialize the SqlDataReader with the SQL
'and Connection strings, and then use the
'SqlDataAdapter to fill the DataSet with data
objCommand = New SqlClient.SqlCommand(strSQL, New
SqlClient.SqlConnection(strConn))

'Open the connection
objCommand.Connection.Open()

'Execute the query, return a SQLDataReader object.
'CommandBehavior.CloseConnection flags the
'DataReader to automatically close the db connection
'when it is closed.
objDR = objCommand.ExecuteReader(CommandBehavior.CloseConnection)
```

Like the `Command` object in ADO, the `CommandText` property of the `Command` object will execute all SQL statements in addition to the standard `SELECT`, `UPDATE`, `INSERT` and `DELETE` statements. For example, you could create tables, foreign keys, primary keys, and so on by executing the applicable SQL from the `Command` object.

The `Command` object exposes several `Execute` methods to perform the intended action. When returning results as a stream of data, `ExecuteReader` is used to return a `DataReader` object. `ExecuteScalar` is used to return a singleton value. `ExecuteNonQuery` is used to execute commands that do not return rows, which usually includes stored procedures that have output parameters and/or return values. (We'll talk about stored procedures in a later section.)

When using a `DataAdapter` with a `DataSet`, `Command` objects are used to return and modify data at the data source through the `DataAdapter` object's `SelectCommand`, `InsertCommand`, `UpdateCommand` and `DeleteCommand` properties.

> Note that the `DataAdapter` object's `SelectCommand` **property must be set before the** `Fill` **method is called.**

The `InsertCommand`, `UpdateCommand` and `DeleteCommand` properties must be set before the `Update` method is called. We will take a closer look at this when we look at the `DataAdapter` object.

DataReader Object

You can use the `DataReader` to retrieve a read-only, forward-only stream of data from the database. Using the `DataReader` can increase application performance and reduce system overhead because only one buffered row at a time is ever in memory. With the `DataReader` object, you are getting as close to the raw data as possible in ADO.NET; you do not have to go through the overhead of populating a `DataSet` object, which sometimes may be expensive if the `DataSet` contains a lot of data. The disadvantage of using a `DataReader` object is that it requires an open database connection and increases network activity.

After creating an instance of the `Command` object, a `DataReader` is created by calling `Command.ExecuteReader` to retrieve rows from a data source. Here is an example of creating a `DataReader` and iterating through it:

```
Private Sub TraverseDataReader()

    Dim strSQL As String
    Dim strConn As String
    Dim objCommand As SqlClient.SqlCommand
    Dim objDR As SqlClient.SqlDataReader
    Dim strResult As String

    'Build the SQL and Connection strings
    strConn = "Initial Catalog=pubs;Data Source=(local);User ID=sa;password=;"
    strSQL = "SELECT * FROM authors"

    'Initialize the SqlDataReader with the SQL
    'and Connection strings, and then use the
    'SqlDataAdapter to fill the DataSet with data
    objCommand = New SqlClient.SqlCommand(strSQL, _
            New SqlClient.SqlConnection(strConn))

    'Open the connection
    objCommand.Connection.Open()

    'Execute the query, return a SqlDataReader object.
    'CommandBehavior.CloseConnection flags the
    'DataReader to automatically close the db connection
    'when it is closed.
    objDR = objCommand.ExecuteReader(CommandBehavior.CloseConnection)
```

354

```
    With objDR

        'Loop through the records and print the values
        Do While .Read = True
            strResult = .GetString(1) & " " & .GetString(2)
            Console.WriteLine(strResult)
        Loop

        'Close the DataReader (and its db connection)
        .Close()

    End With

End Sub
```

In this code snippet, we use the `SqlCommand` object to execute our query via the `ExecuteReader` method. This method returns a populated `SqlDataReader` object to us, and then we loop through it and print out the author names. The main difference with this code compared to the previous `TraverseDataSet()` example is that we have to stay connected while we loop through the data in the `DataReader` object; this is due to the fact that `DataReader` reads in only a small stream of data at a time in order to conserve memory space.

> **At this point an obvious design question is whether to use the `DataReader` or the `DataSet`. The answer to this question really depends upon performance. If you want high-performance, and you are only going to access the data that you are retrieving once, then the `DataReader` is the way to go. If you need access to the same data multiple times, or if you need to model a complex relationship in memory, then the `DataSet` is the way to go. As always, you will need to test each option out thoroughly before deciding which is best.**

The `Read` method of the `DataReader` object is used to obtain a row from the results of the query. Each column of the returned row may be accessed by passing the name or ordinal reference of the column to the `DataReader`, or, for best performance, the `DataReader` provides a series of methods that allow you to access column values in their native data types (`GetDateTime`, `GetDouble`, `GetGuid`, `GetInt32`, and so on). Using the typed accessor methods when the underlying data type is known will reduce the amount of type conversion required (converting from type `Object`) when retrieving the column value.

The `DataReader` provides a non-buffered stream of data that allows procedural logic to efficiently process results from a data source sequentially. The `DataReader` is a good choice when retrieving large amounts of data; only one row of data will be cached in memory at a time. You should always call the `Close` method when you are through using the `DataReader` object, as well as closing the `DataReader` object's database connection, because otherwise the connection won't be closed until the Garbage Collector gets around to collecting the object. Note how we used the `CommandBehavior.CloseConnection` enumeration value on the `SqlDataReader.ExecuteReader` method. This tells the `SqlCommand` object to automatically close the database connection when the `SqlDataReader.Close` method is called.

> **If your Command contains output parameters or return values, they will not be available until the** `DataReader` **is closed.**

DataAdapter Objects

Each .NET Data Provider included with the .NET Framework has a `DataAdapter` object: the OLE DB .NET Data Provider includes an `OleDbDataAdapter` object, and the SQL Server .NET Data Provider includes a `SqlDataAdapter` object. A `DataAdapter` is used to retrieve data from a data source and populate `DataTables` and constraints within a `DataSet`. The `DataAdapter` also resolves changes made to the `DataSet` back to the data source. The `DataAdapter` uses the `Connection` object of the .NET Data Provider to connect to a data source, and `Command` objects to retrieve data from, and resolve changes to, the data source from a `DataSet` object. This differs from the `DataReader`, in that the `DataReader` uses the `Connection` to access the data directly, without having to use a `DataAdapter`. The `DataAdapter` essentially decouples the `DataSet` object from the actual source of the data, whereas the `DataReader` is tightly bound to the data in a read-only fashion.

The `SelectCommand` property of the `DataAdapter` is a `Command` object that retrieves data from the data source. The `InsertCommand`, `UpdateCommand`, and `DeleteCommand` properties of the `DataAdapter` are `Command` objects that manage updates to the data in the data source according to modifications made to the data in the `DataSet`. The `Fill` method of the `DataAdapter` is used to populate a `DataSet` with the results of the `SelectCommand` of the `DataAdapter`. It also adds or refreshes rows in the `DataSet` to match those in the data source. Below we look again at our example from the `TraverseDataSet()` method used previously that shows how to fill a `DataSet` object with information from the `authors` table in the `pubs` database:

```vb
Dim strSQL As String
Dim strConn As String
Dim objDA As SqlClient.SqlDataAdapter
Dim objDS As New Data.DataSet()

'Build the SQL and Connection strings
strConn = "Initial Catalog=pubs;Data Source=(local);User ID=sa;password=;"
strSQL = "SELECT * FROM authors"

'Initialize the SqlDataAdapter with the SQL
'and Connection strings, and then use the
'SqlDataAdapter to fill the DataSet with data
objDA = New SqlClient.SqlDataAdapter(strSQL, strConn)

objDA.Fill(objDS)

With objDS.Tables(0)

   'Loop through the records and print the values
   For intCounter = 0 To .Rows.Count - 1
     strResult = .Rows(intCounter).Item("au_fname").ToString & _
               " " & .Rows(intCounter).Item("au_lname").ToString
     Console.WriteLine(strResult)
   Next

End With
```

Note how we use the `SqlDataAdapter`'s constructor to pass in and set the `SelectCommand`, as well as passing in the connection string in lieu of a `SqlCommand` object that already has an initialized `Connection` property. We then just call the `SqlDataAdapter` object's `Fill` method and pass in an initialized `DataSet` object. If the `DataSet` object is not initialized, the `Fill` method will raise an exception (`System.ArgumentNullException`). Now, let's take a look at some code in which we use a `DataSet` to insert data from the `DataSet` data to the pubs database:

```
Private Sub UpdateDataSet()

  Dim strSQL As String
  Dim strConn As String
  Dim objDA As SqlClient.SqlDataAdapter
  Dim objDS As New Data.DataSet()
  Dim objCB As SqlClient.SqlCommandBuilder
  Dim objRow As Data.DataRow
  Dim intCounter As Integer
  Dim strResult As String

  'Build the SQL and Connection strings
  strConn = "Initial Catalog=pubs;Data Source=(local);" & _
            "User ID=sa;password=;"
  strSQL = "SELECT * FROM authors"

  'Initialize the SqlDataAdapter with the SQL
  'and Connection strings
  objDA = New SqlClient.SqlDataAdapter(strSQL, strConn)

  'Initialize the SQLCommandBuilder by passing in
  'our DataAdapter. This will build the INSERT, UPDATE,
  'and DELETE commands for the DataAdapter object.
  objCB = New SqlClient.SqlCommandBuilder(objDA)

  'Use the SqlDataAdapter to fill the DataSet with
  'the authors table
  objDA.Fill(objDS, "Authors")

  'Add a new author to the local table in memory
  objRow = objDS.Tables("Authors").NewRow
  objRow("au_id") = "335-22-0707"
  objRow("au_fname") = "Tim"
  objRow("au_lname") = "McCarthy"
  objRow("phone") = "760-930-0075"
  objRow("contract") = 0
  objDS.Tables("Authors").Rows.Add(objRow)

  'Write the update back to the server
  objDA.Update(objDS, "Authors")

  'Indicate success
  Console.WriteLine("New author added!")
  Console.ReadLine()

  With objDS.Tables(0)
    'Loop through the records and print the values
```

```
      For intCounter = 0 To .Rows.Count - 1
        strResult = .Rows(intCounter).Item("au_fname").ToString & _
                    " " & .Rows(intCounter).Item("au_lname").ToString
        Console.WriteLine(strResult)
      Next
      Console.ReadLine()
    End With
  End Sub
```

This code starts out exactly the same as the `TraverseDataSet` method did. It starts to differ when we use a `CommandBuilder` object. This is a helper object which will internally build the `INSERT`, `UPDATE`, and `DELETE` commands for our `DataAdapter` object for us. The only caveat is that we have to make sure that our `SELECT` command has the primary key of the table that we are working on, in this case the au_id field. To use the `CommandBuilder` object, simply pass in the initialized `DataAdapter` object to the `CommandBuilder`'s constructor. We then call the `Fill` method of the `DataAdapter`, and specify that we are filling the Authors `DataTable` (we will cover this in more detail later).

Now comes the interesting part. In order to add the new row to the Authors table, we use the `DataTable`'s `NewRow` method to return an initialized `DataRow` object. We then reference the fields in the `DataRow` object by the column name, and set their respective values. Once we have finished setting the fields, we then have to add the new `DataRow` to the Authors `DataTable`. This is done by calling the `Add` method of the `DataTable`'s `Rows` property. So far everything we have done in this update has been offline; nothing has been written to the database. In order to write the changes to the database, we simply call the `Update` method of our `DataAdapter` object, and pass in the `DataSet` and the name of the `DataTable` (Authors) to update. By doing this, the `DataAdapter` will implicitly invoke the `INSERT` command that was built for us by the `CommandBuilder` object. The next part of the code is the same as the `TraverseDataSet` method; it simply writes out the names of the authors to the screen.

SQL Server .NET Data Provider

The SQL Server .NET Data Provider uses **Tabular Data Stream (TDS)**, to communicate with SQL Server. This offers a great performance increase, since TDS is SQL Server's native communication protocol. As an example of how much of an increase you can expect, when I ran some simple tests accessing the authors table of the pubs database we saw the SQL Server .NET Data Provider perform about 70% faster than the OLE DB .NET Data Provider.

The SQL Server .NET Data Provider is lightweight and it performs very well, mainly thanks to not having to go through the OLE DB or ODBC layer. What it actually does is establishes a networking connection (usually sockets based, see Chapter 23 for more information) and drags data from this directly into managed code – and vice versa.

> **This is very important, since going through the OLE DB or ODBC layers means that the CLR has to marshal (convert) all of the COM data types to .NET CLR data types each time data is accessed from a data source. By using the SQL Server .NET Data Provider, everything runs within the .NET CLR, and the TDS protocol is faster than the other network protocols previously used for SQL Server.**

To use this provider, you need to include the `System.Data.SqlClient` namespace in your application. Also, it will only work for SQL Server 7.0 and above. I highly recommend using SQL Server .NET Data Provider any time you are connecting to a SQL Server 7.0 and above database server. The SQL Server .NET Data Provider requires the installation of MDAC 2.6 or later.

OLE DB .NET Data Provider

The OLE DB .NET Data Provider uses native OLE DB through COM Interop (see Chapter 17 for more details) to enable data access. The OLE DB .NET Data Provider supports both manual and automatic transactions. For automatic transactions, the OLE DB .NET Data Provider automatically enlists in a transaction and obtains transaction details from Windows 2000 Component Services. The OLE DB .NET Data Provider does not support OLE DB 2.5 interfaces. OLE DB Providers that require support for OLE DB 2.5 interfaces will not function properly with the OLE DB .NET Data Provider. This includes the Microsoft OLE DB Provider for Exchange and the Microsoft OLE DB Provider for Internet Publishing. The OLE DB .NET Data Provider requires the installation of MDAC 2.6 or later. To use this provider, you need to include the `System.Data.OleDb` namespace in your application.

The DataSet Component

The `DataSet` object is central to supporting disconnected, distributed data scenarios with ADO.NET. The `DataSet` is a memory-resident representation of data that provides a consistent relational programming model regardless of the data source. The `DataSet` represents a complete set of data including related tables, constraints, and relationships among the tables – basically like having a small relational database residing in memory.

> Since the `DataSet` contains a lot of metadata in it, you need to be careful about how much data you try to stuff into it, since it will be consuming memory.

The methods and objects in a `DataSet` are consistent with those in the relational database model. The `DataSet` can also persist and reload its contents as XML and its schema as XSD. It is completely disconnected from any database connections; therefore, it is totally up to you to fill it with whatever data you need in memory.

DataTableCollection

An ADO.NET `DataSet` contains a collection of zero or more tables represented by `DataTable` objects. The `DataTableCollection` contains all of the `DataTable` objects in a `DataSet`.

A `DataTable` is defined in the `System.Data` namespace and represents a single table of memory-resident data. It contains a collection of columns represented by the `DataColumnCollection`, which defines the schema and rows of the table. It also contains a collection of rows represented by the `DataRowCollection`, which contains the data in the table. Along with the current state, a `DataRow` retains its original state and tracks changes that occur to the data.

DataRelationCollection

A `DataSet` contains relationships in its `DataRelationCollection` object. A relationship (represented by the `DataRelation` object) associates rows in one `DataTable` with rows in another `DataTable`. The relationships in the `DataSet` can have constraints, which are represented by `UniqueConstraint` and `ForeignKeyConstraint` objects. It is analogous to a `JOIN` path that might exist between primary and foreign-key columns in a relational database. A `DataRelation` identifies matching columns in two tables of a `DataSet`.

Relationships enable you to see what links information within one table to another. The essential elements of a `DataRelation` are the name of the relationship, the two tables being related, and the related columns in each table. Relationships can be built with more than one column per table, with an array of `DataColumn` objects for the key columns. When a relationship is added to the `DataRelationCollection`, it may optionally add `ForeignKeyConstraints` that disallow any changes that would invalidate the relationship.

ExtendedProperties

`DataSet` (as well as `DataTable` and `DataColumn`) has an `ExtendedProperties` property. `ExtendedProperties` is a `PropertyCollection` where a user can place customized information, such as the `SELECT` statement that was used to generate the resultset, or a date/time stamp of when the data was generated. Since the `ExtendedProperties` contains customized information, this is a good place to store extra, user-defined data about the `DataSet` (or `DataTable` or `DataColumn`), such as a time when the data should be refreshed. The `ExtendedProperties` collection is persisted with the schema information for the `DataSet` (as well as `DataTable` and `DataColumn`). The following code is an example of adding an expiration property to a `DataSet`:

```
Private Sub DataSetExtended()

    Dim strSQL As String
    Dim strConn As String
    Dim objDA As SqlClient.SqlDataAdapter
    Dim objDS As New Data.DataSet()


    'Build the SQL and Connection strings
    strConn = "Initial Catalog=pubs;Data Source=(local);" & _
            "User ID=sa;password=;"
    strSQL = "SELECT * FROM authors"

    'Initialize the SqlDataAdapter with the SQL
    'and Connection strings, and then use the
    'SqlDataAdapter to fill the DataSet with data
    objDA = New SqlClient.SqlDataAdapter(strSQL, strConn)
    objDA.Fill(objDS)

    'Add an extended property called "expiration"
    'Set its value to the current date/time + 1 hour
    objDS.ExtendedProperties.Add("expiration", DateAdd(DateInterval.Hour, _
                1, Now))
    Console.Write(objDS.ExtendedProperties("expiration").ToString)
```

```
    Console.ReadLine()

  End Sub
```

This code starts out by filling a `DataSet` with the `authors` table from the `pubs` database. We then add a new extended property, called `expiration`, and set its value to the current date and time plus one hour. We then simply read it back. As you can see, it is very easy to add extended properties to `DataSet` objects. The same pattern also applies to `DataTable` and `DataColumn` objects.

Creating and Using DataSet Objects

The ADO.NET `DataSet` is a memory-resident representation of data that provides a consistent relational programming model regardless of the source of the data it contains. A `DataSet` represents a complete set of data including the tables that contain, order, and constrain the data, as well as the relationships between the tables. The advantage to using a `DataSet` over using an ADO 2.6 `Recordset` object is that the data in a `DataSet` can come from multiple sources, and it is fairly easy to get the data from multiple sources into the data set. Also, you can define your own constraints between the data tables in a `DataSet`. With ADO `Recordset` objects, it was possible to have data from multiple sources, but it did require a lot more work. Also, constraints were not supported in ADO `Recordset` objects, which made it harder to model data from a database when you were disconnected from the data source.

There are several methods of working with a `DataSet`, which can be applied independently or in combination. You can:

❏ Programmatically create `DataTables`, `DataRelations` and `Constraints` within the `DataSet` and populate them with data

❏ Populate the `DataSet` from an existing relational database management system using a `DataAdapter`

❏ Load and persist the `DataSet` using XML

Here is a typical usage scenario for a `DataSet` object:

1. A client makes a request to a Web Service

2. Based on this request, the Web Service populates a `DataSet` from a database using a `DataAdapter` and returns the `DataSet` to the client

3. The client can then view the data and make modifications

4. When finished viewing and modifying the data, the client passes the modified `DataSet` back to the Web Service, which again uses a `DataAdapter` to reconcile the changes in the returned `DataSet` with the original data in the database

5. The Web Service may then return a `DataSet` that reflects the current values in the database

6. (Optional) The client can then use the `DataSet` class's `Merge` method to merge the returned `DataSet` with the client's existing copy of the `DataSet`; the `Merge` method will accept successful changes and mark with an error any changes that failed

The design of the ADO.NET `DataSet` makes this scenario fairly easy to implement. Since the `DataSet` is stateless, it can be safely passed between the server and the client without tying up server resources such as database connections. Although the `DataSet` is transmitted as XML, Web Services and ADO.NET automatically transform the XML representation of the data to and from a `DataSet`, creating a rich, yet simplified, programming model. In addition, because the `DataSet` is transmitted as an XML stream, non-ADO.NET clients can consume the same Web Service as that consumed by ADO.NET clients. Similarly, ADO.NET clients can interact easily with non-ADO.NET Web Services by sending any client `DataSet` to a Web Service as XML and by consuming any XML returned as a `DataSet` from the Web Service. One thing to be careful of is the size of the data; if there are a large number of rows in the tables of your `DataSet`, then it will eat up a lot of bandwidth.

Programmatically Creating DataSet Objects

Just like with the ADO `Recordset` object, you can programmatically create a `DataSet` object to use as a data structure in your programs. This could be quite useful if you have complex data that needs to be passed around to another object's method. For example, when creating a new customer, instead of passing twenty arguments about the new customer to a method, you could just pass the programmatically created `DataSet` object with all of the customer information to the object's method.

In ADO, you could programmatically create hierarchically `Recordset` objects using the `Shape` syntax, but most people did not like dealing with the complexity of this syntax. The `DataSet` object offers a much richer, and easier to use model for building complex data representations. Let's take a look at some sample code to programmatically build a shaped `Recordset` in ADO, and then we will contrast the code with how we build the same type in ADO.NET.

Here is some (VB6) ADO code to programmatically build a shaped `Recordset` of data containing customer order information. This sample will build a `DataSet` containing customer order information for one customer and one order, and it will output the data to the screen as XML:

```
Sub ADOShapeSyntax()

    Dim cnShape As ADODB.Connection
    Dim rstCustomers As ADODB.Recordset
    Dim rstCustomerOrders As ADODB.Recordset
    Dim stmXML As ADODB.Stream
    Dim strRSShape As String
    Dim strXML As String

    'Initialize ADO objects
    Set cnShape = New ADODB.Connection
    Set rstCustomers = New ADODB.Recordset
    Set stmXML = New ADODB.Stream

    strRSShape = "SHAPE APPEND NEW adInteger AS CustomerID," & _
                 " NEW adVarChar(100) AS FirstName," & _
                 " NEW adVarChar(100) AS LastName," & _
                 " NEW adVarChar(100) AS Phone," & _
                 " NEW adVarChar(255) AS Email," & _
                 " ((SHAPE APPEND NEW adInteger AS CustomerID," & _
                 " NEW adInteger AS OrderID," & _
                 " NEW adCurrency AS OrderAmount, " & _
                 " NEW adDate AS OrderDate)" & _
```

```
              " AS rstCustomerOrders RELATE CustomerID TO CustomerID) "

    cnShape.Open "Provider=MSDataShape;Data Provider=NONE;"
    rstCustomers.Open strRSShape, cnShape, adOpenStatic, adLockOptimistic

    With rstCustomers
      .AddNew
      .Fields("CustomerID").Value = 1
      .Fields("FirstName").Value = "Miriam"
      .Fields("LastName").Value = "McCarthy"
      .Fields("Phone").Value = "555-1212"
      .Fields("Email").Value = "tweety@hotmail.com"
      Set rstCustomerOrders = .Fields("rstCustomerOrders").Value
      rstCustomerOrders.AddNew
      rstCustomerOrders.Fields("CustomerID").Value = 1
      rstCustomerOrders.Fields("OrderID").Value = "12345"
      rstCustomerOrders.Fields("OrderAmount").Value = 22.22
      rstCustomerOrders.Fields("OrderDate").Value = #11/10/2001#
      rstCustomerOrders.Update
      .Save stmXML, adPersistXML
    End With

    'Get the XML string
    With stmXML
      .Type = adTypeText
      .Charset = "ascii"
      strXML = .ReadText
      Debug.Print strXML
    End With

    'Clean up
    Set cnShape = Nothing
    Set rstCustomers = Nothing
    Set rstCustomerOrders = Nothing
    Set stmXML = Nothing

End Sub
```

Notice how relatively complex the shaped provider syntax code is. Here is the code for accomplishing the exact same thing using an ADO.NET DataSet object:

```
Private Sub BuildDataSet()

    Dim objDS As New Data.DataSet("CustomerOrders")
    Dim dtCustomers As Data.DataTable = objDS.Tables.Add("Customers")
    Dim dtOrders As Data.DataTable = objDS.Tables.Add("Orders")
    Dim objDR As Data.DataRow

    With dtCustomers
      .Columns.Add("CustomerID", Type.GetType("System.Int32"))
      .Columns.Add("FirstName", Type.GetType("System.String"))
      .Columns.Add("LastName", Type.GetType("System.String"))
      .Columns.Add("Phone", Type.GetType("System.String"))
```

```
        .Columns.Add("Email", Type.GetType("System.String"))
    End With

    With dtOrders
        .Columns.Add("CustomerID", Type.GetType("System.Int32"))
        .Columns.Add("OrderID", Type.GetType("System.Int32"))
        .Columns.Add("OrderAmount", Type.GetType("System.Double"))
        .Columns.Add("OrderDate", Type.GetType("System.DateTime"))
    End With

    objDS.Relations.Add("r_Customers_Orders", _
                        objDS.Tables("Customers").Columns("CustomerID"), _
                        objDS.Tables("Orders").Columns("CustomerID"))

    objDR = dtCustomers.NewRow()
    objDR("CustomerID") = 1
    objDR("FirstName") = "Miriam"
    objDR("LastName") = "McCarthy"
    objDR("Phone") = "555-1212"
    objDR("Email") = "tweety@hotmail.com"
    dtCustomers.Rows.Add(objDR)

    objDR = dtOrders.NewRow()
    objDR("CustomerID") = 1
    objDR("OrderID") = 22
    objDR("OrderAmount") = 0
    objDR("OrderDate") = #11/10/1997#
    dtOrders.Rows.Add(objDR)

    Console.WriteLine(objDS.GetXml())
End Sub
```

Here is what the resulting XML of the `DataSet` looks like:

```
<CustomerOrders>
  <Customers>
    <CustomerID>1</CustomerID>
    <FirstName>Miriam</FirstName>
    <LastName>McCarthy</LastName>
    <Phone>555-1212</Phone>
    <Email>tweety@hotmail.com</Email>
  </Customers>
  <Orders>
    <CustomerID>1</CustomerID>
    <OrderID>22</OrderID>
    <OrderAmount>0</OrderAmount>
    <OrderDate>1997-11-10T00:00:00.0000</OrderDate>
  </Orders>
</CustomerOrders>
```

Notice how the ADO.NET code is much easier to read and more logical. We start out by first defining a `DataSet` object (`objDS`) named `CustomerOrders`. We then create two tables, one for Customers (`dtCustomers`), and one for Orders (`dtOrders`), and we then define the columns of the tables. Notice how we call the `Add` method of the `DataSet`'s Tables collection. We then define the columns of each of the tables, and create a relation in the `DataSet` between the `Customers` table and the `Orders` table on the `CustomerID` column. Finally, we create instances of `Rows` for the tables, add the data, and then append the `Rows` to the `Rows` collection of the `DataTable` objects. This operation contained fewer lines of code than the ADO example, was much more object-oriented, and as a result, is much easier to follow. This will usually result in code that is faster to write, easier to read, and less bug-prone.

> **If you create a** `DataSet` **object with no name, it will be given the default name of** `NewDataSet`.

ADO.NET DataTable Objects

A `DataSet` is made up of a collection of tables, relationships, and constraints. In ADO.NET, `DataTable` objects are used to represent the tables in a `DataSet`. A `DataTable` represents one table of in-memory relational data. The data is local to the .NET application in which it resides, but can be populated from a data source such as SQL Server using a `DataAdapter`.

The `DataTable` class is a member of the `System.Data` namespace within the .NET Framework class library. You can create and use a `DataTable` independently or as a member of a `DataSet`, and `DataTable`, objects can also be used by other .NET Framework objects including the `DataView`. You access the collection of tables in a `DataSet` through the `DataSet` object's `Tables` property.

The schema, or structure, of a table is represented by columns and constraints. You define the schema of a `DataTable` using `DataColumn` objects as well as `ForeignKeyConstraint` and `UniqueConstraint` objects. The columns in a table can map to columns in a data source, contain calculated values from expressions, automatically increment their values, or contain primary key values.

If you populate a `DataTable` from a database, it will inherit the constraints from the database so you do not have to do all of that work manually. A `DataTable` must also have rows in which to contain and order the data. The `DataRow` class represents the actual data contained in the table. You use the `DataRow` and its properties and methods to retrieve, evaluate and manipulate the data in a table. As you access and change the data within a row, the `DataRow` object maintains both its current and original state.

You can create parent/child relationships between tables within a database, like SQL Server, using one or more related columns in the tables. You create a relationship between `DataTable` objects using a `DataRelation`, which can then be used to return a row's related child or parent rows.

Connection Pooling in ADO.NET

Pooling connections can significantly enhance the performance and scalability of your application. Connection pooling is a great story in ADO.NET – it comes for free! Both the SQL Client .NET Data Provider and the OLE DB .NET Data Provider automatically pool connections using Windows 2000 Component Services and OLE DB Session Pooling, respectively. The only requirement is that you must use the exact same connection string each time if you want to get a pooled connection.

Universal Data Link (UDL) files can be used to supply OLE DB connection information to the OLE DB Provider.

> **UDL files are analogous to DSN files for ODBC connections.**

However, since UDL files can be modified externally to any ADO.NET client program, connections that use UDL files are not pooled. This is because the connection information can change without the ADO.NET client being aware of the change. As a result, for connection strings that contain UDL files, ADO.NET will parse the connection information found in a UDL file every time a connection is opened. Therefore, it is strongly suggested that you use a static connection string instead of a UDL file when using the OLE DB .NET Data Provider.

The SQL Client .NET Data Provider relies on Windows 2000 Component Services to provide connection pooling using an implicit pooling model by default.

Using Stored Procedures with ADO.NET

In this section, we'll take a quick look at how to use stored procedures, before delving into a more complex illustration of how we can build a reusable data access component that also uses stored procedures.

The motivation for using stored procedures is simple. Imagine you have this code:

```
select au_lname from authors where au_id='172-32-1176'
```

If you pass that to SQL Server using `ExecuteReader` on `SqlCommand` (or any execute method, for that matter), what happens is that SQL Server has to compile the code before it can run it, in much the same way that VB6 or VB .NET applications have to be compiled before they can be executed. This compilation takes SQL Server time, so it's a pretty obvious leap to deduce that if you can reduce the amount of compilation that SQL Server has to do, database performance should be increased. (Compare the speed of execution of a compiled application against interpreted code.)

That's what stored procedures are all about: we create a procedure, store it in the database and because the procedure is known of and understood ahead of time, it can be compiled ahead of time ready for use in our application.

Stored procedures are very easy to use, but the code to access them is (in my opinion) horribly verbose. In the next section we'll see some code that can make accessing stored procedures a little more straightforward, but to make things a little clearer we'll start by building a simple application that demonstrates how to create and call a stored procedure.

Creating a Stored Procedure

To create a stored procedure, you can either use the tools in Visual Studio .NET, or you can use the tools in SQL Server's Enterprise Manager. (Although technically you can use a third party tool or do it programmatically as well.)

For our example, we'll build a stored procedure that returns all of the columns for a given author ID. The SQL to do this will look like this:

```
select au_id, au_lname, au_fname, phone, address, city, state, zip, contract
  from authors where au_id=whatever author ID we want
```

The *whatever author ID we want* part is important. When using stored procedures, we typically have to be able to provide parameters into the stored procedure and use them from within code. This isn't a book about SQL Server, so I'm only going to show you in principle how to do this. There are many resources on the Web about building stored procedures (they've been around a very long time, and they're most definitely not a .NET-specific feature).

Variables in SQL Server are prefixed by the @ symbol. So, if we have a variable called `authorId`, our SQL will look like this:

```
select au_id, au_lname, au_fname, phone, address, city, state, zip, contract
  from authors where au_id=@authorId
```

My personal preference is to use camel casing for variable names in stored procedures, although feel free to choose your own convention.

In SQL Server, stored procedures can be accessed using the **Stored Procedures** object in the management tree. In this screenshot, you'll see a number of stored procedures already loaded. Those prefixed with `dt_` are the built-in SQL stored procedures. `byroyalty` is a stored procedure provided by the `pubs` database developers.

To create a new stored procedure, right-click on the **Stored Procedures** object and select **New Stored Procedure**. This will display the editor window.

A stored procedure can be either a single SQL statement, or a complex set of statements. T-SQL supports branches, loops and other variable declarations, which can make for some pretty complex stored procedure code. However, our stored procedure is just a single line of SQL. We need to declare the parameter that we want to pass in (`@authorId`), and the name of the procedure: `GetAuthorById`. (I prefer to use Pascal casing for stored procedure names, but again this is up to you.)

If the screenshot isn't clear, here's the complete code:

```
CREATE PROCEDURE GetAuthorById
(
   @authorId varchar(11)
)
AS
select au_id, au_lname, au_fname, phone, address, city, state, zip, contract
   from authors where au_id=@authorId
```

Click **OK** to save the stored procedure in the database. We're now able to access this stored procedure from code.

Calling the Stored Procedure

Calling the stored procedure is just an issue of creating a `SqlConnection` object to connect to the database and a `SqlCommand` object to run the stored procedure.

My preferred pattern for doing this is to create a separate class in the project called something like `Sprocs` and to add shared methods to this class to access each stored procedure. This gives me maximum potential for reuse. In addition to this, I like to create two versions of each method: one that takes a connection string and creates its own `SqlConnection` object, and one that takes a specific `SqlConnection` object.

If I'm running a complex piece of code that needs a `SqlConnection` object consistently (such as a batch reporting procedure), I'll establish a `SqlConnection` at the top of the routine and dispose of it at the end. This saves me from having to continually reopen the connection as I work through the code. However, if I'm running some code that doesn't need a `SqlConnection` object to be open all of the time, I want to create `SqlConnection` objects as I need them. The two versions of the stored procedure access method in `Sprocs` give me this flexibility.

Create a new project now called `LookupAuthor`. To this new project, add a new class called `Sprocs`.

Now we have to decide what we want to return out of the method. As when we supply an ID we're only ever going to get zero or one `DataRow` objects back, it makes sense to return either the `DataRow` that we found, or `Nothing` out of the method, which is what we'll do. However, as `SqlDataAdapter` will expect to fill a table, we'll create another helper method in `Sprocs` that strips out the first row and returns that or `Nothing`.

Here's the first version of the `GetAuthorById` method. The wrinkle here is that we have to tear down the connection should an exception be thrown from the other version of the method that runs the stored procedure. Notice how we don't want to handle the exception, which is why there's no `Catch` clause, but we do need a `Finally` clause to tear down the connection. Also, notice how that in addition to the connections string parameter, this method takes the same parameters as the stored procedure itself.

```
Public Shared Function GetAuthorById(ByVal connectionString As String, _
                                     ByVal authorId As String) As DataRow

    Dim connection As SqlConnection
    Dim result As DataRow
    Try
       connection = New SqlConnection(connectionString)
       connection.Open()
       result = GetAuthorById(connection, authorId)
    Finally
       If connection.State <> ConnectionState.Closed Then
         connection.Close()
       End If
    End Try

    Return result
End Function
```

Accessing the stored procedure is more verbose (but not more difficult) than accessing a normal SQL statement through the methods we've discussed thus far. The approach is:

❑   Create a `SqlCommand` object

❑   Configure it to access a stored procedure by setting the `CommandType` property

❑   Add parameters that exactly match those in the stored procedure itself

❑   Create a `SqlDataAdapter` and fill a results object of some kind (a `DataTable` in our case)

```
Public Shared Function GetAuthorById(ByVal connection As SqlConnection, _
                                     ByVal authorId As String) As DataRow
```

```
      Dim command As SqlCommand
      Dim adapter As SqlDataAdapter
      Dim result As DataRow
      Try
        command = New SqlCommand("GetAuthorById", connection)
        command.CommandType = CommandType.StoredProcedure

        Dim authorIdParam As SqlParameter = _
            command.Parameters.Add("@authorId", SqlDbType.VarChar)
        authorIdParam.Direction = ParameterDirection.Input
        authorIdParam.Value = authorId

        Dim datatable As New DataTable()
        adapter = New SqlDataAdapter(command)
          adapter.Fill(datatable)
          result = GetRowFromTable(datatable)

      Finally
        If Not adapter Is Nothing Then
          adapter.Dispose()
        End If
        If Not command Is Nothing Then
          command.Dispose()
        End If
      End Try

      Return result
    End Function
```

Here's the method to return the top row in a table:

```
    Protected Shared Function GetRowFromTable(ByVal table As DataTable) _
        As DataRow
      If table Is Nothing OrElse table.Rows.Count = 0 Then
        Return Nothing
      Else
        Return table.Rows(0)
      End If
    End Function
```

There's no real need to build an impressive UI for this application, as we're about to move on to a far more interesting discussion. To Form1, add a button and add this code to its Click handler:

```
      Private Sub Button1_Click(ByVal sender As System.Object, _
                                ByVal e As System.EventArgs) _
                                Handles Button1.Click

        Try
          Dim author As DataRow = Sprocs.GetAuthorById(ConnectionString, _
                                                "409-56-7008")
          MsgBox(author("au_fname") & " " & author("au_lname"))
```

```
        Catch ex As Exception
          MsgBox(ex.GetType().ToString() & ":" & ex.Message)
        End Try

    End Sub
```

Here I've hard-coded an author ID of 409-56-7008. Run the code now and you should see this:

Now that you understand how to create and use stored procedures, let's build something really cool.

Building a Data Access Component

In order to better demonstrate what we have learned so far about ADO.NET, we are going to build a data access component. This component is designed to abstract the processing of stored procedures. The component we are building will be targeted at SQL Server, and it is assumed that all data access to the database will be through stored procedures. The idea of only using stored procedures to access data in a database has a number of advantages, such as scalability, performance, flexibility, security, etc. The only disadvantage is that you have to use stored procedures, and not SQL strings. Through the process of building this component we will see how stored procedures are implemented in ADO.NET. We will also be building on the knowledge that we have gained from the previous chapters.

This component's main job is to abstract stored procedure calls to SQL Server, and one of the ways we do this is by passing in all of our stored procedure parameter metadata as XML. We will look at this XML later in this section. The other job of the component is to demonstrate the use of some of the new objects in ADO.NET.

> The code for this project is quite extensive and we will only examine the key parts of it in this chapter. The full source is available in the code download.

Let's start with the beginning of the component. The first thing we do is declare our namespace, our class, and the private members of the class:

```
Option Explicit On
Option Strict On

Imports System.Data.SqlClient
Imports System.Xml

Namespace IK.Data

  Public NotInheritable Class SQLServer
```

```
Inherits System.ComponentModel.Component

'Private members
Private mobjConnection As SqlConnection
Private mstrSPConfigXML As String
Private mstrSPConfigXMLFile As String
Private mstrModuleName As String
Private mblnDisposed As Boolean = False

Private Const EXCEPTION_MSG As String = "There was an error in " _
& "the method. Please see the Application Log for details."
```

We start out with our `Option` statements. Note that we are using the `Option Strict` statement. This helps prevent logic errors and data loss that can occur when you work between variables of different types. Next, we import the namespaces that we need for our component. In this case, most of our dependencies are on `System.Data.SqlClient`. We declare a namespace here, `IK.Data`, but you can use any unique namespace that you wish. We then proceed to declare our class and derive it from `System.ComponentModel.Container`, and it is this inheritance that makes our class a component. We will call our class `SQLServer`, to indicate that it wraps data access calls to SQL Server. Next, we declare our private data members. We use the `EXCEPTION_MSG` constant to indicate a generic error message for any exceptions that we throw.

Constructors

Now we get to declare our constructors for the `SQLServer` class. This is where we can really take advantage of function overloading, and it gives us a way to pass data to our class upon instantiation. First, we declare a default constructor:

```
Public Sub New()

    MyBase.New()

    'Initialize private members
    mstrSPConfigXML = ""
    mstrSPConfigXMLFile = ""
    mstrModuleName = Me.GetType.ToString

End Sub
```

In this constructor, as well as all constructors in VB, we call `MyBase.New()`, the default constructor of our base class. Next, we initialize our private members' data. Notice how we use the `GetType()` method of `Object` so we know at run-time what the name of our class is.

The next constructor we create allows for a database connection string to be passed in. By abstracting the database connection string out of this component, we give users of our component more flexibility in how they decide to store and retrieve their database connection strings. Here is the code for the constructor:

```
    Public Sub New(ByVal ConnectionString As String)

            'Call the base class constructor
            MyBase.New()

            'Initialize private members
            mobjConnection = New SqlConnection(ConnectionString)
            mstrSPConfigXML = ""
            mstrSPConfigXMLFile = ""
            mstrModuleName = Me.GetType.ToString

    End Sub
```

The only difference between this constructor and the default constructor is that we are passing in a database connection string and assigning it to the constructor of our mobjConnection (SqlConnection) object.

In the last constructor, we pass in both a database connection string and a string of XML representing the stored procedure parameters for the stored procedure we want to call. Here is the code for the constructor:

```
    Public Sub New(ByVal ConnectionString As String, ByVal SPConfigXML As String)

            'Call the base class constructor
            MyBase.New()

            'Initialize private members
            mobjConnection = New SqlConnection(ConnectionString)
            mstrSPConfigXML = SPConfigXML
            mstrSPConfigXMLFile = ""
            mstrModuleName = Me.GetType.ToString

    End Sub
```

This constructor simply sets the database connection and stored procedure parameter configuration for private members.

Properties

Now, let's look at the properties of our object. Our object contains the following properties: DBConnection, SPConfigXML, and SPConfigXMLFile. The DBConnection and SPConfigXML properties are added in case the user of our object did not want to supply them via a constructor call. The DBConnection property creates a new SqlConnection instance and returns the underlying connection string of the SqlConnection object (mobjConnection). The SPConfigXMLFile property allows the user of the object to pass in a valid file name containing the XML representing the stored procedure parameter metadata. All of the properties are read-write.

Here is the code for the DBConnection property:

```
    Public Property DBConnection() As String

            Set(ByVal Value As String)
```

373

```
            mobjConnection = New SqlConnection(Value)
        End Set
        Get
            Try
                Return mobjConnection.ConnectionString
            Catch
                Return ""
            End Try
        End Get

    End Property
```

Stored Procedure XML Structure

Rather than having the user of our object be responsible for populating the `Parameters` collection of a `Command` object, in this case we will abstract it out into an XML structure. The structure is very simple; it basically allows you to store the metadata for one or more stored procedures at a time. This has a huge advantage in the fact that you can change all of the parameters on a stored procedure without having to recompile this object. Below is what the XML structure for the metadata looks like:

```xml
<StoredProcedures>
  <StoredProcedure name>
   <Parameters>
    <Parameter name size datatype direction isNullable value />
   </Parameters>
  </StoredProcedure>
</StoredProcedures>
```

Here is what some sample data for the XML structure looks like:

```xml
<?xml version="1.0"?>
<StoredProcedures>
  <StoredProcedure name="usp_Get_Authors_By_States">
   <Parameters>
    <Parameter name="@states" size="100" datatype="VarChar"
     direction="spParamInput" isNullable="True" />
    <Parameter name="@state_delimiter" size="1" datatype="Char"
     direction="spParamInput" isNullable="True" />
   </Parameters>
  </StoredProcedure>
</StoredProcedures>
```

The valid values for the `direction` attribute are: `spParamInput`, `spParamOutput`, `spParamReturnValue`, and `spParamInputOutput`. The valid values for the `datatype` attribute are: `BigInt`, `Binary`, `Bit`, `Char`, `DateTime`, `Decimal`, `Float`, `Image`, `Int`, `Money`, `NChar`, `NText`, `NVarChar`, `Real`, `SmallDateTime`, `SmallInt`, `SmallMoney`, `Text`, `Timestamp`, `TinyInt`, `UniqueIdentifier`, `VarBinary`, `VarChar`, and `Variant`. These values map directly to the SQL data types in SQL Server 2000. We will call this file `PubsStoredProcedures.xsd` and save it in the root directory of our project.

Methods

Now, let's turn our attention to the methods of our object.

ExecSPReturnDS

This public function executes a stored procedure and returns a `DataSet` object. It takes a stored procedure name (`String`) and an optional list of parameter values (`ArrayList`). Here is the code for `ExecSPReturnDS`:

```
Public Function ExecSPReturnDS(ByVal SPName As String, Optional ByVal _
                   ParamValues As ArrayList = Nothing) As DataSet

        Dim objCommand As SqlCommand
        Dim objDA As SqlDataAdapter
        Dim objDS As New DataSet()

        Try

            'Make sure that the object has not been disposed yet
            If mblnDisposed = True Then
                Throw New ObjectDisposedException(mstrModuleName, _
                "This object has already been disposed.")
            End If

            'Make sure we are getting a valid stored procedure name.
            ValidateSPName(SPName)

            'Initialize the SQLCommand object
            objCommand = New SqlCommand(SPName, mobjConnection)
            objCommand.CommandType = CommandType.StoredProcedure

            'Build the parameters, if any
            BuildParameters(objCommand, ParamValues)

            'Initialize the SQLDataAdapter with the
            'SQLCommand object
            objDA = New SqlDataAdapter(objCommand)

            'Fill the DataSet
            objDA.Fill(objDS)

            'Return the value
            Return objDS

        Catch objException As Exception

            LogError(objException)
            Throw New Exception(EXCEPTION_MSG, objException)

        Finally

            'Close the connection and return the value
```

```
                    objCommand.Connection.Close()

        End Try

    End Function
```

This function uses three objects to accomplish its mission: the SqlCommand, SqlDataAdapter, and the DataSet objects. We first wrap everything in a Try-Catch-Finally block to make sure that we trap any exceptions that are thrown. The first thing we do is to make sure our object did not have its Dispose method called on it yet. Here is the code for the Dispose method:

```
    Public Overloads Sub Dispose()

        If mblnDisposed = False Then

            Try

                'Free up the database connection resource by
                'calling its Dispose method
                mobjConnection.Dispose()

            Finally

                'Call the base type's Dispose() method.
                MyBase.Dispose()

                'Because this Dispose method has done the necessary
                'cleanup, prevent the Finalize method from being called.
                GC.SuppressFinalize(Me)

                'Let our class know that Dispose() has been called
                mblnDisposed = True

            End Try

        End If

    End Sub
```

We do this by checking the mblnDisposed private variable. If it is True, then we throw an exception. The Dispose method closes the current connection (mobjConnection) if it is open by calling the base type's Dispose method, and then prevents the Finalize method from being called. Finally, we set the mblnDisposed private member to the value of True.

The next thing we do in ExecSPReturnDS is to make sure that the stored procedure name that we receive is a valid stored procedure name. We do this by calling the ValidateSPName private method. Here is the code for ValidateSPName:

```
    Private Sub ValidateSPName(ByRef SPName As String)

        'The name must be between 1 and 128 characters long.
```

```
      If Len(SPName) < 1 Or Len(SPName) > 128 Then
        Throw New Exception("A valid stored procedure name must " _
                & "be provided.")
      End If

   End Sub
```

This method just performs a check to make sure that the stored procedure name is between 1 and 128 characters long, in accordance with the SQL Server object naming conventions. If it is not, then we throw an exception. Looking back at the code for ExecSPReturnDS, we then call the SqlCommand object's constructor and pass in the stored procedure name, and then set its Connection and CommandType properties.

```
'Initialize the SQLCommand object
        objCommand = New SqlCommand(SPName, mobjConnection)
        objCommand.CommandType = CommandType.StoredProcedure
```

We make sure that we pass in the CommandType.StoredProcedure enumeration value, since we are executing a stored procedure. Once the SqlCommand object is properly initialized, we pass it by reference to the BuildParameters method. We will take a look at this method in more detail later.

```
'Build the parameters, if any
      BuildParameters(objCommand, ParamValues)
```

After the parameters have been added to the SqlCommand object, the next step is to pass the SqlCommand object to the SqlDataAdapter's constructor:

```
'Initialize the SQLDataAdapter with the
      'SQLCommand object
      objDA = New SqlDataAdapter(objCommand)
```

After doing this, we then call the Fill method of the SqlDataAdapter to fill our DataSet object:

```
'Fill the DataSet
      objDA.Fill(objDS)
```

We then return the DataSet object back to the caller:

```
'Return the value
      Return objDS
```

If there was an exception caught, then we log the exception data to the Application Log via the LogError private method, and then throw a new exception with our generic exception message. We nest the original exception inside of the new exception via the innerException constructor parameter:

```
Catch objException As Exception

      LogError(objException)
      Throw New Exception(EXCEPTION_MSG, objException)
```

377

In the `Finally` block, we close the `SqlCommand` object's `connection` property.

```
Finally

    'Close the connection and return the value
    objCommand.Connection.Close()
```

BuildParameters

This private method is the heart of this object, and does the most work. It is responsible for parsing the stored procedure parameter XML and mapping all of the parameter properties into the `Parameters` property of the `SqlCommand` object. Here is the signature of the method:

```
Private Sub BuildParameters(ByRef Command As SqlCommand, _
          ByRef ParamValues As ArrayList)
```

You will notice that both of its arguments, `SqlCommand` and `ArrayList`, are passed in by reference. Since it is a private method, there is no need to copy the state of these objects, so we just pass them `ByRef`. The `ParamValues` argument is an `ArrayList` of the values for each of the parameters, and these values must be in the same order as their corresponding parameters in the XML. The first thing we do in this method is to see if in fact there is any XML being passed in or not. Here is the code that checks for the XML:

```
'See if there is an XML string or XML file of
'parameters() for the stored procedure
If Len(mstrSPConfigXML) = 0 And Len(mstrSPConfigXMLFile) = 0 Then

    'No parameters to add, so exit
    Exit Sub

End If
```

The code above simply checks if there is an XML string or an XML file name in the object's private variables. If it cannot find either one, then we exit the method. It is entirely possible that users of this object may have stored procedures with no parameters at all.

After we pass this test, we then try to load whatever XML we have into an `XmlDocument` object. We have chosen an `XmlDocument` object (`objDOM`) to parse the XML as loading all of the stored procedure XML into memory will not hurt performance; it is a small amount of data. As an alternative, we could have used an `XmlReader` object to load in only what we needed into memory at runtime. Here is the code to load the XML:

```
'See if there is an XML string of parameters
'for the stored procedure
If Len(mstrSPConfigXML) > 0 Then

    'Try to load the XML into a DOM
    Try
        objDOM.LoadXml(mstrSPConfigXML)

    Catch objXMLException As XmlException
```

```
            'Throw an exception if the load failed
            Throw objXMLException

        End Try

    End If

    'See if there is an XML file of parameters
    'for the stored procedure
    If Len(mstrSPConfigXML) = 0 And Len(mstrSPConfigXMLFile) > 0 Then

        'Try to load the XML into a DOM
        Try
            objDOM.Load(mstrSPConfigXMLFile)

        Catch objXMLException As XmlException

            'Throw an exception if the load failed
            Throw objXMLException

        End Try

    End If
```

First we try to load the XML string, and then we try to load the XML file. If any of these operations fail, we throw an `XmlException` object.

The next step is to get the name of the stored procedure and clear the `SqlCommand` object's `Parameters` collection:

```
    'Now we have a DOM Document in memory

    'Get the name of the stored procedure
    strSPName = Command.CommandText

    'Clear the parameters collection for the SQLCommand
    Command.Parameters.Clear()
```

We then use the name of the stored procedure as the key in our XPath query of the XML, and then execute the XPath query:

```
    'Get the node list of <Parameter>'s for the stored procedure
    strXPathQuery = "/StoredProcedures/StoredProcedure[@name='" _
        & strSPName & "']/Parameters/Parameter"
    objParameterNodes = objDOM.SelectNodes(strXPathQuery)
```

This query is executed off the `XmlDocument` object and returns an `XmlNodeList` object. We then start the loop through the `Parameter` elements in the XML and retrieve all of the mandatory `Parameter` attributes:

```
    'Loop through the stored procedure <Parameter> elements
    For Each objNode In objParameterNodes
```

379

```
'Get the attribute values for the <Parameter> element.

'name
Try
  strParameterName = objNode.Attributes.GetNamedItem("name").Value
Catch
  Throw New Exception("Error getting the 'name' attribute " _
          & "for the <Parameter> element.")
End Try

'size
Try
  intParameterSize = CInt(objNode.Attributes.GetNamedItem("size").Value)
Catch
  Throw New Exception("Error getting the 'size' attribute " _
          & "for the <Parameter> element.")
End Try

'datatype
Try
  intSQLDataType = GetSQLDataType _
          & (objNode.Attributes.GetNamedItem("datatype").Value)
Catch
  Throw New Exception("Error getting the 'datatype' attribute " _
          & "for the <Parameter> element.")
End Try

'direction
Try
  intParameterDirection = GetParamDirection _
          & (objNode.Attributes.GetNamedItem("direction").Value)
Catch
  Throw New Exception("Error getting the 'direction' attribute " _
          & "for the <Parameter> element.")
End Try
```

Since these attributes are mandatory, if any of them are missing, we throw an exception. Notice the two helper functions being called, `GetSQLDataType` and `GetParamDirection`. These functions simply convert the string value from the XML into the proper enumeration value.

Next, we get the optional attributes:

```
'Get the optional attribute values for the <Parameter> element

'isNullable
Try
  blnIsNullable = _
    CBool(objNode.Attributes.GetNamedItem("isNullable").Value)
Catch
  blnIsNullable = False
End Try

'precision
```

```
Try
    bytPrecision = CByte(objNode.Attributes.GetNamedItem("precision").Value)
Catch
    bytPrecision = 0
End Try

'scale
Try
    bytScale = CByte(objNode.Attributes.GetNamedItem("scale").Value)
Catch
    bytScale = 0
End Try
```

These attributes are optional mainly because of their data types. Since they are Boolean and Byte data types, we just go ahead and convert them to `False` and `0` if they are missing.

Now that we have the `Parameter` attributes, the next step is to get the corresponding value for the `Parameter`:

```
'Get the value of the parameter. This could be passed in from
'one of the public methods, or it could be an attribute value
'in the XML <Parameter> element.
Try
    'Check the XML first
    objParameterValue = objNode.Attributes.GetNamedItem("value").Value
Catch
    'Now check the ParamValues ArrayList
    Try
        objParameterValue = ParamValues.Item(intParamCounter)
    Catch
        Throw New Exception("Error getting the corresponding value for " _
                & "the '" & strParameterName _
                & "' <Parameter> element.")
    End Try
End Try
```

We first check to see if the value was passed in along with the XML via the value attribute. If it was not, then we check to see if there is a corresponding value in the `ArrayList` of values. If we still do not get a `Parameter` value, then we throw an exception.

Now we are ready to create the `SqlParameter` object and set its `Direction` property. We do so with the following code:

```
'Create the parameter object. Pass in the name, datatype,
'and size to the constructor.
objParameter = New SqlParameter(strParameterName, intSQLDataType, _
                intParameterSize)

'Set the direction of the parameter.
objParameter.Direction = intParameterDirection
```

We then set the optional property values of the `SqlParameter` object:

```
'If the optional attributes have values, then set them.
If bytPrecision > 0 Then
  objParameter.Precision = bytPrecision
End If
If bytScale > 0 Then
  objParameter.Scale = bytScale
End If
```

Finally, we set the `Value` property of the `SqlParameter` object, add the `SqlParameter` object to the `SqlCommand` object's `Parameters` collection, increment our counter, complete our loop, and finish the method:

```
'Set the value of the parameter
objParameter.Value = objParameterValue

'Add the parameter to the SqlCommand's parameter collection
Command.Parameters.Add(objParameter)

'Increment the counter
intParamCounter = intParamCounter + 1

Next 'Each objNode In objParameterNodes

End Sub
```

Next we are going to look at `ExecSPReturnDR`. This function is almost identical to `ExecSPReturnDS`, except that it returns a `SqlDataReader` object instead of a `DataSet` object.

ExecSPReturnDR

As in the previous function, this public function executes a stored procedure and returns a `SqlDataReader` object. Also, it takes a stored procedure name (`String`) and an optional list of parameter values (`ArrayList`). Here are the code snippets for `ExecSPReturnDR` which differ from `ExecSPReturnDS`:

```
Public Function ExecSPReturnDR(ByVal SPName As String, _
Optional ByVal ParamValues As ArrayList = Nothing) As SqlDataReader

  Dim objCommand As SqlCommand
  Dim objReader As SqlDataReader

  Try

...

    'Build the parameters, if any
    BuildParameters(objCommand, ParamValues)

    'Open the connection (required for the ExecuteReader method).
    mobjConnection.Open()

    'Execute the sp and get the SqlDataReader.
```

```
        objReader = objCommand.ExecuteReader

        'Return the value
        Return objReader

    Catch objException As Exception

 ...

    End Function
```

This function uses two objects to accomplish its mission: the `SqlCommand` and `SqlDataReader` objects. The only part where this function differs from `ExecSPReturnDS` is right after we call the `BuildParameters` private method. In this case, we have to make sure that the `SqlCommand` object's `SqlConnection` is opened. This is because the `SqlDataReader` requires an open connection. We then call the `ExecuteReader` method of the `SqlCommand` object to get our `SqlDataReader` object. Since this method returns a `SqlDataReader` object, which requires an open database connection, we do not close the connection in this method. It is up to the caller to close the `SqlDataReader` and the connection when finished. This can be accomplished via the `Dispose` method on our object. Otherwise, the connection will be closed when the last reference to `SqlConnection` falls out of scope and is collected by the Garbage Collector.

The next function we are going to look at, `ExecSPReturnXML`, is almost identical to the last two functions, except that it returns a string of XML instead of a `DataSet` or a `DataReader`.

ExecSPReturnXML

This public function executes a stored procedure and returns a string of XML. This function requires that the stored procedure contains a `FOR XML` clause in its SQL statement. Once again, it takes a stored procedure name (`String`) and an optional list of parameter values (`ArrayList`). The code that differs from the previous examples is:

```
Public Function ExecSPReturnXML(ByVal SPName As String, _
        Optional ByVal ParamValues As ArrayList = Nothing) As String

    Dim objCommand As SqlCommand = Nothing
    Dim objXMLReader As XmlReader = Nothing
    Dim strXML As String

    Try

      ...

      'Build the parameters for the SqlCommand object.
      BuildParameters(objCommand, ParamValues)

  'Open the connection (required for the ExecuteXmlReader method).
            mobjConnection.Open()

            'Execute the sp and get the XmlReader.
            objXMLReader = objCommand.ExecuteXmlReader()
```

```
            'Build the string of XML.
            Do Until objXMLReader.Read = False
                strXML += objXMLReader.ReadOuterXml
            Loop

            'Return the XML.
            Return strXML

    Catch objException As Exception

    ...

    End Function
```

This time the two objects used to accomplish this function are the `SqlCommand` and `XmlReader` objects. In this case, the only part where this function differs is right after we call the `BuildParameters` private method. In this case, we have to make sure that the `SqlCommand` object's `SqlConnection` is opened, as the `XmlReader` requires an open connection. We then call the `ExecuteXmlReader` method of the `SqlCommand` object to get our `XmlReader`. Next, we loop through the `XmlReader`'s data to build a string of XML that we return. Finally, we close the `XmlReader` and the `SqlConnection` objects.

Next we turn to `ExecSP` which only needs the `SqlCommand` object to get its work done, to execute stored procedures that do not return result sets.

ExecSP

This public method executes a stored procedure and does not return a value. It takes a stored procedure name (`String`) and an optional list of parameter values (`ArrayList`) for its arguments. Here is the code for `ExecSP`:

```
Public Sub ExecSP(ByVal SPName As String, _
          Optional ByVal ParamValues As ArrayList = Nothing)

    Dim objCommand As SqlCommand = Nothing

    Try

    ...

        'Build the parameters for the SqlCommand object.
        BuildParameters(objCommand, ParamValues)

        'Open the connection (required for the ExecSP method).
        mobjConnection.Open()


        'Execute the stored procedure, and do not return any rows
        objCommand.ExecuteNonQuery()

    Catch objException As Exception
```

```
    . . .

End Sub
```

It is almost identical to the other `Exec*` functions, except for when it executes the stored procedure. It uses the `SqlCommand` object's `ExecuteNonQuery` method. This ensures that the `SqlCommand` does not return any type of `DataReader` object to read the results. This method will be mostly used to execute `INSERT`, `UPDATE`, and `DELETE` queries that do not return any results.

Finally, the last public function we are going to create is `ExecSPOutputValues`.

ExecSPOutputValues

This last public function in our component executes a stored procedure and returns an `ArrayList` object that contains output parameter values. It is not meant for stored procedures that return result sets. As with the previous examples, this function takes a stored procedure name (`String`) and an optional list of parameter values (`ArrayList`) for its arguments. Here is the code for `ExecSPOutputValues`:

```
Public Function ExecSPOutputValues(ByVal SPName As String, _
        Optional ByVal ParamValues As ArrayList = Nothing) As ArrayList

    Dim objCommand As SqlCommand = Nothing
    Dim arlParameters As New ArrayList()
    Dim objParameter As SqlParameter = Nothing

    Try

        . . .

        'Open the connection (required for the ExecOutputValues method).
        mobjConnection.Open()


        'Execute the stored procedure, and do not return any rows
        objCommand.ExecuteNonQuery()

        'Build the ArrayList of output values
        For Each objParameter In objCommand.Parameters
          If objParameter.Direction = ParameterDirection.Output Then
            arlParameters.Add(objParameter.Value)
          End If
        Next

        'Return the output values
        Return arlParameters

    Catch objException As Exception

    . . .

    End Function
```

This function is almost identical to ExecSP, except after SqlCommand.ExecuteNonQuery is called. Then, we iterate through the SqlCommand object's Parameters collection and look for all of the parameters that are output parameters. Next, we take the values of the output parameters and add them to the ArrayList object that we return.

Using DataSet Objects to Bind to DataGrids

Now that we have built our data access component, it is time to test it.

> Be sure to run the **UDF.sql** file – available with the code download – in your SQL Server's Query Analyzer before testing the data access component. This will create the necessary stored procedure and function in the **pubs** database.

A nice way to test it is to call the ExecSPReturnDS function, take the DataSet object that was created, and then bind the DataSet to a DataGrid. (You can find more about data binding in Chapter 16.) We also get to see how easily the DataSet object and the DataGrid control integrate together. To do this, create a new Windows Application solution, and add references to IK.Data, System, System.Data, System.Drawing, System.EnterpiseServices, System.Windows.Forms, and System.XML. Now import IK.Data, add a Button (named btnTest) and a DataGrid (named DgdAuthors) to your form, and bind the DataGrid to the DataSet object. Here is what your form should look like:

Here is what your references should look like:

Lastly, here is the code for the test application:

```vb
Imports IK.Data

Public Class frmTest
    Inherits System.Windows.Forms.Form

    ' Windows Form Designer generated code

    Private Sub btnTest_Click(ByVal sender As System.Object, _
                       ByVal e As System.EventArgs) _
                       Handles btnTest.Click

        Dim strConn As String
        Dim objDS As DataSet
        Dim objSQL As SQLServer
        Dim objArrayList As New ArrayList()
        Dim strError As String

        Try

            'Set the SQL Managed Provider connection string
            strConn = "Initial Catalog=pubs;Data Source=VICKB1;" & _
                    "User ID=sa;password=sa;"

            'Call the SQLServer component constructor and
            'pass the db connection string
            objSQL = New SQLServer()
            objSQL.DBConnection = strConn

            'Set the XML file property
            objSQL.SPConfigXMLFile = Application.StartupPath & _
                                "\PubsStoredProcedures.xml"

            'Add the two parameter values
            objArrayList.Add("CA")
            objArrayList.Add("^")
```

```
                'Execute the sp, and get the DataSet object back
                objDS = objSQL.ExecSPReturnDS("usp_Get_Authors_By_States", _
                                              objArrayList)

                'Bind the DataGrid to the DataSet object
                dgdAuthors.SetDataBinding(objDS.Tables(0), Nothing)

                'Call dispose to free db connection (just in case)
                'objSQL.Dispose()

            Catch objException As Exception

                'Display the exception message
                strError = objException.Message
                If Not IsNothing(objException.InnerException) Then
                    strError += objException.InnerException.Message
                End If
                MsgBox(strError)

            End Try

        End Sub
    End Class
```

We start out the code by supplying a database connection string to the SQLServer object constructor. We then set the XML file property of the SQLServer object by placing our XML file (PubsStoredProcedures.xml) in the path of the assembly. After that, we add two parameter values to the ArrayList object; these values are in the same order that the parameters are in the XML file. Next, the ExecSPReturnDS method of the SQLServer object is called so that a populated DataSet object is returned based upon a stored procedure that returns rows. Once we have the DataSet object, we simply call the SetDataBinding method of our DataGrid object. The SetDataBinding method takes two arguments, a data source (Object), and a data member (String). In this case, we do not have a data member, so we pass in Nothing. If you try to pass in an empty string, an exception will be thrown.

Finally, the results should look like:

au_id	au_lname	au_fname	phone	address	city
172-32-1176	White	Johnson	408 496-7223	10932 Bigge	Menl
213-46-8915	Green	Marjorie	415 986-7020	309 63rd St.	Oakl
238-95-7766	Carson	Cheryl	415 548-7723	589 Darwin L	Temp
267-41-2394	O'Leary	Michael	408 286-2428	22 Cleveland	San
274-80-9391	Straight	Dean	415 834-2919	5420 College	Oakl
341-22-1782	Smith	Meander	913 843-0462	10 Mississipp	Lawr
409-56-7008	Bennis	Abraham	415 658-9932	6223 Batema	Berk
427-17-2319	Dull	Ann	415 836-7128	3410 Blonde	Palo
472-27-2349	Gringlesby	Burt	707 938-6445	PO Box 792	Cove
486-29-1786	Locksley	Charlene	415 585-4620	18 Broadway	San
527-72-3246	Greene	Morningstar	615 297-2723	23 Graybar H	Nash
648-92-1872	Blotchet-Halls	Reginald	503 745-6402	55 Hillsdale B	Corv
672-71-3249	Yokomoto	Akiko	415 935-4228	3 Silver Ct	Walc

Test

Summary

In this chapter, we have taken a look at how ADO has evolved into ADO.NET. We have seen and used the main objects in ADO.NET that you need to quickly get up and running in order to build data access into your .NET applications. We took a fairly in-depth look at the `DataSet` object, since this is the core object of ADO.NET, and we also compared and contrasted ADO and ADO.NET so you could actually see the easier programming model.

We looked at stored procedures: how to create them in SQL Server and how to access them from our code. Finally, we built our own custom data access component, which made it easy to separate data access code from the rest of business logic code in a .NET application.

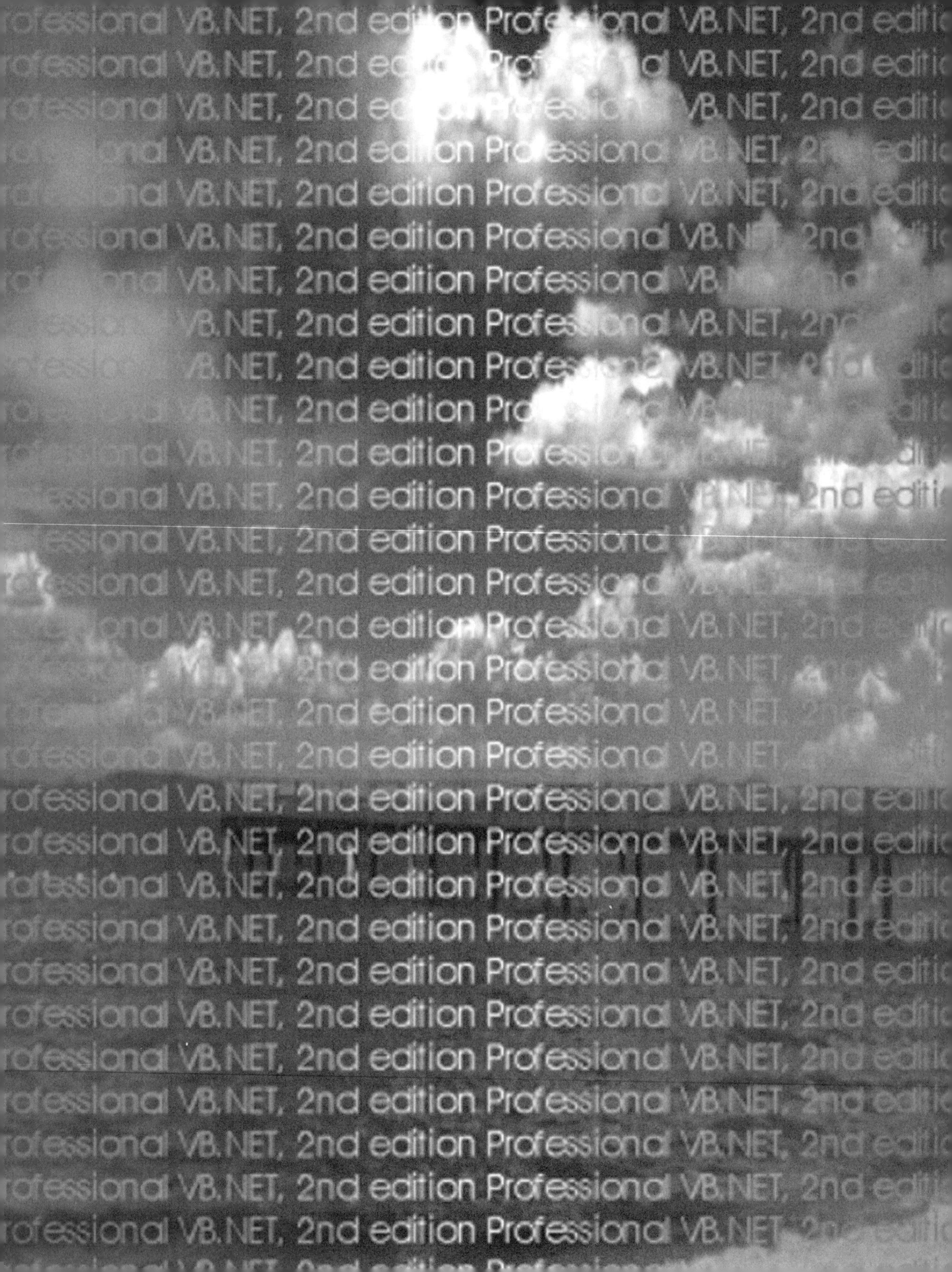
Professional VB.NET, 2nd edition

12

Windows Forms

Windows Forms (often abbreviated to **WinForms**) is the segment of the .NET framework used to create applications for the Win32 client. It is quickly obvious when you start developing a Windows application that the Microsoft development team made some fabulous improvements over the Visual Basic of old. Yes, some of your familiar controls have been retired, but no functionality has been lost. Believe me – you'll love the new world!

This chapter will concentrate primarily on forms and built-in controls. We'll discuss what is new and what has been changed from previous versions of Visual Basic. We'll start by talking a bit about the `System.Windows.Forms` namespace.

> While this chapter assumes you'll be writing a Windows application using Visual Studio .NET, it is possible to write a .NET windows application using nothing more than a text editor, and still take full advantage of everything Windows Forms have to offer.

The System.Windows.Forms Namespace

Before we immediately discuss a VB.Net windows application, let's first review a couple of points about a VB6 application to serve as a comparison. A VB6 standard EXE application begins with the immediate ability to create forms and controls built in from the start. Every VB6 application comes complete with all the user interface capability even if it's never used. For instance, even though you develop a VB6 application with no user interface whatsoever, VB6 still compiles in the entire VB6 runtime which includes all the code for the UI. This forces you to distribute an unnecessarily large application.

VB.NET, however, allows you to precisely select the assemblies you need, thus minimizing the unnecessary bulk of your finished application. It's possible, therefore, to create a VB application not only with no user interface, but also no user interface *code* compiled into the application. If you've flipped to this chapter, however, you're obviously not interested in an application without a user interface, so we'd better introduce the pieces you'll need in order to add forms and controls to your program.

In order to create an application that has a user interface, you need to reference the `System.Windows.Forms.dll` assembly, thus gaining access to the `System.Windows.Forms` namespace. This namespace is the source for all the rich capability you need for a windows application, from menus to message boxes.

> **When you create a new VB.NET application, you are presented with a list of possible application types. Your choice in this menu determines what assemblies will be pre-selected for you. Selecting the Windows Application type, for example, automatically gives you a reference to the** `System.Windows.Forms.dll` **namespace.**

For a quick browse of what's in the `System.Windows.Forms` namespace, create a new windows application, and then use the **Object Browser**. Expand the **System.Windows.Forms/System.Windows.Forms** tree and you'll see all the types defined within. The following figure shows the **Object Browser** expanded to the **Form** type:

If you scroll through the namespace, you'll notice all sorts of familiar controls such as **CheckBox** and **Button**.

The `System.Windows.Forms` *namespace makes frequent use of another namespace,* `System.Drawing`*. The* `System.Drawing` *namespace contains all the information about fonts, colors, pens, printing, and so on, and is a useful namespace if you want to start drawing your own controls. We'll cover this in Chapter 13.*

Forms as Classes

Before we explore forms in VB.NET, let's step back to VB6 for a moment. If you pay close attention to forms in VB6, you will probably notice that a form and a class are essentially the same thing, with forms having the added feature of a user interface. Visual Basic has always done a tremendous job of hiding the complexities of setting a form up for you. When people make the realization that a form is really just a class, they start to wonder where and how Visual Basic defines and instantiates the form variable. They start questioning how it became possible to simply start using the variable `Form1` in code, without ever actually declaring it anywhere in their code. Why didn't you ever have to write the following line anywhere?

```
Public WithEvents Form1 As New Form1
```

For example, if you want to use a class called `Class1`, you must first declare a variable, and then instantiate the object as follows:

```
Dim objMyClass As Class1
Set objMyClass = New Class1
```

When you start using a form, however, you magically get a variable already defined and instantiated for you. Visual Basic has always hidden the line `Public WithEvents Form1 As New Form1` from you. (VB experts aware of this hidden assignment often choose not to use it in order to more precisely control the lifetime of their forms.)

In VB.NET, all forms are now true classes, and it's abundantly obvious. There are no more secrets going on behind the scenes. All the properties are defined directly in code, instead of via a special series of settings in the `.frm file`. When you make a change to your form using the design window, you will see it appear in the code itself.

Pay very special attention to the fact that you no longer get a 'free of charge' variable set up for you. A form called `Form1` is now a class name, *and only a class name*. If you want to use it throughout your application, you'll need to set up your own object variable to reference it.

What is a Form in .NET?

Now that VB supports inheritance, forms take part in an inheritance structure that provides all the functionality you expect. You can also see where all that ability comes from. Forms in .NET are classes in the truest sense of the word.

In VB6, forms were saved as .frm files (forms were clearly objects that could be created and destroyed, but you never really saw their code as such). By contrast, forms in VB.NET are saved in .vb files just like any other class. It's the functionality they inherit that makes a class a *form*, as opposed to just any class. In essence, calling something a "form" is just a simple way of saying a "class that has the ability to display a rich user interface".

If you view the object hierarchy of a form, you can see that it's really a subclass seven levels removed from the Object class. The following tree shows the superclasses of the Form class with a brief description of what the Form class inherits from each.

Class Hierarchy	Description
Object	The highest superclass from which all .NET objects inherit.
MarshalByRefObject	Used by applications that support remote access. This class provides access to objects across application boundaries.
Component	Provides the base implementation of the IComponent interface, and allows for object sharing between applications.
Control	The base class for all components with a visual interface.
ScrollableControl	Provides auto-scrolling ability.
ContainerControl	Allows a component to contain other controls.
Form	The main window for an application.

Forms at Design Time

A very nice change to VB.NET is the design time placement of controls that have no immediate user interface. The Timer control in VB6, for instance, would be sited directly on your form as a small icon. In VB.NET, these controls are placed in their own special 'tray' beneath the form in the design window. A simple form with a Timer control appears as follows:

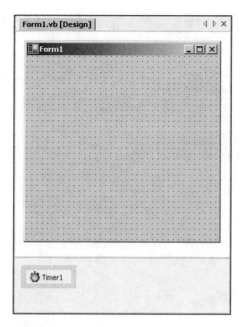

The Design Time Grid

The design time grid is the series of small dots that appear on a form in the designer. In VB6 this grid was set globally. In VB.NET, each form can uniquely manage how the grid affects its controls using the following properties of a form:

- ❑ ShowGrid: Toggles the display of the grid

- ❑ SnapToGrid: Determines if child controls will automatically align and size to the nearest grid point when they are moved and resized at design time

- ❑ GridSize: Sets the distance, in pixels, between the dots of the grid

To change the default values of these setting, open the Tools | Options screen and select the Windows Forms Designer section.

Setting the Startup Form

To define which form will be loaded first when your application runs, you need to open the Properties window for the project and set the Startup object setting. Do this using the Project | Properties menu. You can also invoke the window by right-clicking the project name in the Solution Explorer, and selecting Properties from the context menu.

If the Properties menu item doesn't appear under your Project menu, open the Solution Explorer (Ctrl-Alt-L), highlight the project name (it will be in bold font), then try again.

Form Borders

Changing the `FormBorderStyle` property of a form affects the way it can be manipulated by the user. The following table outlines the differences between the different `FormBorderStyle` settings, and the effect these settings have on other properties of the form:

FormBorderStyle Setting	Appearance	Effect on Other Form Properties
None	No border User cannot resize form	HelpButton: none MaximizeBox: none MinimizeBox: none SizeGripStyle: none
FixedSingle	Single 3D border User cannot resize form	HelpButton: toggles help button in toolbar (only if maximize and minimize buttons are disabled)
		MaximizeBox: enables/disables
		MinimizeBox: enables/disables
		SizeGripStyle: no effect

FormBorderStyle Setting	Appearance	**Effect on Other Form Properties**
Fixed3D	3D border User cannot resize form 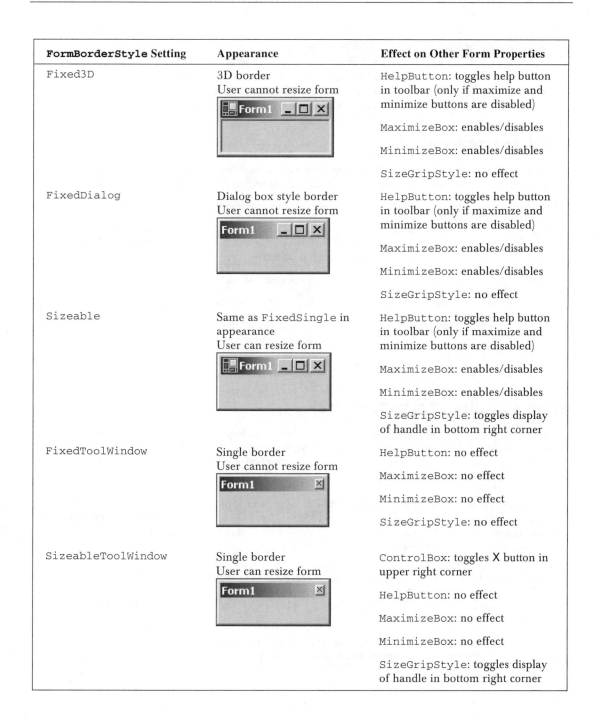	HelpButton: toggles help button in toolbar (only if maximize and minimize buttons are disabled) MaximizeBox: enables/disables MinimizeBox: enables/disables SizeGripStyle: no effect
FixedDialog	Dialog box style border User cannot resize form	HelpButton: toggles help button in toolbar (only if maximize and minimize buttons are disabled) MaximizeBox: enables/disables MinimizeBox: enables/disables SizeGripStyle: no effect
Sizeable	Same as FixedSingle in appearance User can resize form	HelpButton: toggles help button in toolbar (only if maximize and minimize buttons are disabled) MaximizeBox: enables/disables MinimizeBox: enables/disables SizeGripStyle: toggles display of handle in bottom right corner
FixedToolWindow	Single border User cannot resize form	HelpButton: no effect MaximizeBox: no effect MinimizeBox: no effect SizeGripStyle: no effect
SizeableToolWindow	Single border User can resize form	ControlBox: toggles X button in upper right corner HelpButton: no effect MaximizeBox: no effect MinimizeBox: no effect SizeGripStyle: toggles display of handle in bottom right corner

Always on Top

Some applications have the ability to remain visible at all times, even when they do not have the focus. To accomplish this effect in VB6, you needed an API call. In VB.NET, forms have been given a new property called TopMost. Set it to True to have a form overlay others even when it is inactive.

Startup Location

Often you'll want a form to be centered on the screen when it first appears. VB.NET does this automatically for you when you set the StartPosition property. Here are the settings and their meanings:

StartPosition Value	Effect
Manual	Show the form positioned at the values defined by the form's Location property
CenterScreen	Show the form centered on the screen
WindowsDefaultLocation	Show the form at the windows default location
WindowsDefaultBounds	Show the form at the windows default location, with the windows default bounding size
CenterParent	Show the form centered in its owner

Form Opacity (Transparency)

A fun new property to Windows Forms is the Opacity property of any rich control such as a form. The opacity measures how opaque or transparent a form is. A value of 0% makes the form fully transparent. A value of 100% makes the form fully visible. Any value between 0 and 100 makes the form partially visible as if it was a ghost.

I'm not sure how practical this property will be in a business application, but it makes for some nice UI glitz. The following block of code shows how to fade a form out and back in when the user clicks a button named Button1. You may have to adjust the Step value of the array depending on the performance of your computer:

```
Private Sub Button1_Click(ByVal sender As System.Object, _
                          ByVal e As System.EventArgs) _
                          Handles Button1.Click
    Dim i As Double
    For i = -1 To 1 Step 0.005
        ' Note - opacity is a value from 0.0 to 1.0 in code
        Me.Opacity = System.Math.Abs(i)
    Next i
End Sub
```

Visual Inheritance

By inheriting from `System.Windows.Forms.Form`, any class automatically gets all the properties, methods, and events that a form based on Windows Forms is supposed to have. However, a class does not have to inherit directly from the `System.Windows.Forms.Form` class in order to become a Windows Form. It can become a form by inheriting from another form, which itself inherits from `System.Windows.Forms.Form`. In this way controls originally placed on one form can be directly inherited by a second form. Not only is the design of the original form inherited, but also any code associated with these controls (the processing logic behind an **Add New** button, for example). This means that it is possible to create a base form with processing logic required in a number of forms, and then create other forms which inherit the base controls and functionality.

VB.NET provides an Inheritance Picker tool to aid in this process. It should be noted at this point, however, that a form must be compiled into either an `.EXE` or `.DLL` file before it can be used by the Inheritance Picker. Once that is done, the addition of a form that inherits from another form in the project can be performed via the **Project | Add Inherited Form**.

MDI Forms

Multiple Document Interface (MDI) forms are able to contain other forms. An MDI application consists of a parent MDI form and multiple children MDI forms. The child forms are kept contained within the parent and move when the parent moves.

To set up an MDI application you need a form that will act as the MDI parent. First, create a new windows application, set the `IsMdiContainer` property of the form to `True`. Next, add a new form to your project, and name it `ChildForm`.

To open a form as a child within your parent, you need to set its `MDIParent` property to the parent form. Use the following code in `Form1` to display the child form within it:

```
Public Class Form1
    Inherits System.Windows.Forms.Form

' Windows Form Designer generated code
    Private WithEvents ChildForm1 As ChildForm
    Private WithEvents ChildForm2 As ChildForm
    Private Sub ParentForm_Load(ByVal sender As System.Object, _
                                ByVal e As System.EventArgs) _
                                Handles MyBase.Load
        ChildForm1 = New ChildForm()
        ChildForm1.MdiParent = Me
        ChildForm1.Show()
        ChildForm2 = New ChildForm()
        ChildForm2.MdiParent = Me
        ChildForm2.Show()
    End Sub
End Class
```

Windows Menu

To provide a menu item that will list the available child windows that are owned by the parent, add a new `MainMenu` control to `Form1`. (See the section on *Menus* for further details on this.) Create a menu item (usually called **Windows**) and set its `MdiList` property to `True`. This property will cause the list of child windows to automatically appear as menu items beneath the **Windows** menu, automatically switch between child windows when the user selects an item, and automatically update itself when child windows are added and removed from the parent.

Arranging Child Windows

MDI parent forms have a method called `LayoutMDI` that will automatically arrange child forms in the familiar cascade or tile layout. Add a menu item to your Windows menu called **Tile Vertical** and insert the following code into your form to handle it:

```
Me.LayoutMdi(System.Windows.Forms.MDILayout.TileVertical)
```

When you're done, your application will look like the image on the left. Selecting **Tile Vertical** from the menu will yield the result on the right:

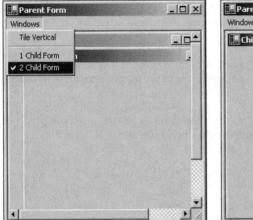

Your code should look something like this:

```
Public Class Form1
    Inherits System.Windows.Forms.Form
' Windows Form Designer generated code
    Private WithEvents ChildForm1 As ChildForm
    Private WithEvents ChildForm2 As ChildForm
    Private Sub Form1_Load(ByVal sender As System.Object, _
                ByVal e As System.EventArgs) _
                Handles MyBase.Load
        ChildForm1 = New ChildForm()
        ChildForm1.MdiParent = Me
        ChildForm1.Show()
        ChildForm2 = New ChildForm()
```

```
        ChildForm2.MdiParent = Me
        ChildForm2.Show()
    End Sub
    Private Sub MenuItem2_Click(ByVal sender As System.Object, _
                      ByVal e As System.EventArgs) _
                      Handles MenuItem2.Click
        Me.LayoutMdi(System.Windows.Forms.MdiLayout.TileVertical)
    End Sub
End Class
```

Setting Limits on the Form Size

In previous versions of Visual Basic, preventing a user from shrinking or expanding a form beyond a certain limit required you to check the size of the form in the `Resize` event, and essentially reset the height and width of the form only after it had exceeded the limits. This resulted in a terrible flickering effect. VB.NET now has `MaximumSize` and `MinimumSize` properties on the form to handle this for you. Simply set them to the sizes you desire. Use `0,0` for no limit.

Scrollable Forms

When designing forms, many users will ask to have countless (or so it seems) fields on a single screen. Try as you may, no amount of reorganizing and reducing spaces between the fields helps the situation. While you could split the data entry into multiple screens, it is often done with regret. (Imagine what the web surfing would be like if scrolling a web page was impossible.)

Forms in VB.NET are based on a class called `ScrollableControl`. This base class will give you, free of charge, scroll bars to pull controls into view that are off the edge of your forms.

The scrollable control class on which a form is based automatically gives a form scrollbars when it is sized smaller than the child controls sited on it. To enable this feature, set the `AutoScroll` property of your form to `True`. When you run your program, resize the form to make it smaller than the controls require and presto – instant scrolling.

> You cannot have both **Autoscroll** and **IsMdiContainer** both set to **True** at the same time.

Forms at Runtime

The lifecycle of a form is like that of all objects. It is created, and later destroyed. Forms have a visual component, so they use system resources, such as handles. These are created and destroyed at interim stages within the lifetime of the form. Forms can be created and will hold state as a class, but will not appear until they are activated. Likewise, closing a form doesn't destroy its state.

The following table summarizes the states of a form's existence, how you get the form to that state, the events that occur when the form enters a state, and a brief description of each:

Code	Events Fired	Description
MyForm = New Form1	None	The form's New() method will get called (as will InitializeComponent)
MyForm.Show() or MyForm.ShowDialog()	HandleCreated	Use Show() for modeless display
		Use ShowDialog() for modal display
	Load	
	VisibleChanged	The HandleCreated event only fires the first time the form is shown, or after it has previously been closed
	Activated	
MyForm.Activate()	Activated	A form can be activated when it is visible but does not have the focus
MyForm.Hide()	Deactivate	Hides the form (sets the Visible property to False)
	VisibleChanged	
MyForm.Close()	Deactivate	Closes the form and calls Dispose to releases the windows resources
	Closing	
	Closed	During the Closing event, you can set the CancelEventArgs.Cancel property to True to abort the close
	VisibleChanged	
	HandleDestroyed	
	Disposed	Also called when the user closes the form using the control box or X button
		The Deactivate event will only fire if the form is currently active
		Note: There is no longer an Unload event. Use the Closing or Closed event instead
MyForm.Dispose()	None	Use the Close() method to finish using your form
MyForm = Nothing	None	Releasing the reference to the form flags it for garbage collection. The garbage collector will call the form's Finalize() method

Controls

As expected, VB.NET introduces controls and features to make meeting your deliverables and requirements easier. Some controls have been renamed, others have been replaced, but nothing has been lost. This section will cover the features that all controls use (such as docking), and then address each of the standard controls available to you, as well as the important changes from previous versions of VB of which to be aware.

Control Tab Order

A wonderful new feature of the design environment is a tool that allows you to set the tab order of the controls on a form simply by clicking on them in sequence. To activate the feature, open a form in the designer, and select the View | Tab Order menu item. This will show a small number in the upper left corner of each control on your form representing the tab index of that control.

To set the values simply click on each control in the sequence you want the tab flow to operate. The following screenshot shows a simple form with the tab order feature enabled:

> In VB.NET it is possible to have two or more controls with the same tab index value. At run time, VB will break the tie by using the z-order of the controls. The control that is highest in the z-order will receive the focus first. The z-order can be changed by right-clicking the control and selecting **Bring to Front**.

Control Arrays

Control arrays, as you understood them in previous versions of VB, are gone in VB.NET. However, you now have a better way to do it. There were two good reasons why you wanted to use them:

❑ To have a single method handle the events of multiple controls

❑ To dynamically add new controls to your form at runtime

In order to make all this work, VB.NET now allows you to totally customize, *at runtime*, the methods that handle the events of your controls.

The first thing to notice is that you can no longer assign the same name to multiple controls on your form. Furthermore, the Index property is gone from the standard set of control properties.

To get the control array effect, you need to connect a single method to multiple control events. Then, since you are without the Index property, your handler will need a way to determine what control fired the event. To do this, simply use the Sender parameter.

A simple example is helpful to see how to set this up. First, create a new windows application, and add two buttons to the form as follows:

Double click Button1, to switch over to the code that handles the Button1.Click event. In order to make this method respond to the Button2.Click event as well, simply add the Button2.Click event handler to the end of the Handles list, and then add some simple code to display a message box indicating what button triggered the event:

```
' Note the change in the method name from Button1_Click. Since
' two objects are hooked up, it's a good idea to avoid having the
' method specifically named to a single object.
Private Sub Button_Click(ByVal sender As System.Object, _
            ByVal e As System.EventArgs) _
        Handles Button1.Click, Button2.Click
    Dim buttonClicked As Button
    buttonClicked = CType(sender, Button)
    ' Tell the world what button was clicked
    MessageBox.Show("You clicked """ & buttonClicked.Text & """")
End Sub
```

Run the program and click on the two buttons. Each one will trigger the event and display a message box.

Next, we'll enhance the program to add a third button dynamically at run time. First, add another button to your form that will trigger the addition of Button3 as follows:

Call your new button `addNewButton` and add the following code to handle its `Click` event:

```
Private Sub addNewButton_Click(ByVal sender As System.Object, _
                ByVal e As System.EventArgs) _
                Handles addNewButton.Click

    Dim newButton As Button

    ' Create the new control
    newButton = New Button()

    ' Set it up on the form
    newButton.Location = New System.Drawing.Point(184, 16)
    newButton.Size = New System.Drawing.Size(75, 23)
    newButton.Text = "Button3"

    ' Add it to the form's controls collection
    Me.Controls.Add(newButton)

    ' Hook up the event handler
    AddHandler newButton.Click, AddressOf Me.Button_Click
End Sub
```

When the `addNewButton` button is clicked, the code creates a new button, sets its size and position, and then does two essential things. Firstly, it adds it to the form's controls collection, and secondly it connects the `click` event to the method that will handle it.

With this done, run the program and click the `addNewButton` button. **Button3** will appear. Then, simply click **Button3** to prove that the click event is being handled. You should get the following result:

Automatic Resizing and Positioning Controls

In VB6 there were some third party controls that can be used to automatically resize controls when the form is resized – and some do a pretty good job of it actually (some not so good). VB.NET offers this feature built in, and is probably the first feature that makes people say "Oh wow, finally!" when they start playing around with the form designer.

If you've tried resizing and moving controls at runtime, you'll quickly come to realize that it's not as simple as it seems. Some controls need to move, some need to stretch, some need to do both. VB.NET covers these needs by way of docking, and anchoring.

Docking

Docking refers to gluing a control to the edge of a parent control. If the parent control moves or is stretched, the docked control will do the same. A perfect example of a docked control is a menu bar or a status bar, docked top and bottom of a form respectively. Docking is similar to the `Align` property of controls such as the VB6 status bar.

To work through an example, create a new windows application, and place a label on a form. We've set the background color to white, placed a solid border around, and set its `TextAlign` to `MiddleCenter` in order to have something that looks like this:

It would be great to glue this label to the top of the form. To do this, view the `Dock` property of the label. If you pull it down you'll see a small graphic like this:

Simply click the top section of the graphic to tell the label to stick to the top of the form. The other sections give you other effects. (A status bar would use the bottom section, for example.) The label control will immediately 'stick' to the top of your form. When you run your program, and stretch the window sideways, you'll get the following effect:

> If you attempt to dock multiple controls to the same edge, VB.NET must decide how to break the tie. Precedence is given to controls in reverse z-order. In other words, the control that is furthest back in the z-order will be the first control that is next to the edge. If you dock two controls to the same edge and want to switch them, right-click the control you want docked *first* and select **Send To Back**.

If you want a gap between the edge of your form and the docked controls, set the DockPadding property of the parent control. You can set a different value for each of the four directions (Left, Right, Top, Bottom). You can also set all four properties to the same value using the All setting.

Anchoring

Anchoring is similar to docking, except you can specifically define the distance each edge of your control will maintain from the edges of a parent.

To get the effect, add a button to the program started above as follows:

AutoResize Demo
Automatic Resizing Rocks!

Button1

Dropping down the Anchor property of the button gives you this graphic:

The four rectangles surrounding the center box allow you to toggle the anchor settings of the control. The above graphic shows the default anchor setting of TopLeft for all controls.

When the setting is on (dark gray), the edge of your control will maintain its starting distance from the edge of the parent as the parent is resized. If you set the anchor to two opposing edges (such as the left and right edges) the control will stretch to accommodate this:

AutoResize Demo
Automatic Resizing Rocks!

Button1

> Note that you should set the `Anchor` properties of your controls *after* you have designed the entire form since the anchoring effect occurs at design time as well. It can be very frustrating at design time when you need to adjust the size of your form but don't want the controls to move around.

The Splitter Control

The splitter control is a great new tool that helps with resizing as well. A splitter lets a user decide the width (or height) of sections that make up a form. Windows Explorer uses a splitter to divide the folder tree view and folder content windows.

Placing a splitter on your form at design time is a bit tricky if you're new to the feature. To save yourself some frustration, follow this basic sequence of steps:

❏ Place one panel on the form that will act as the left half of the form, and set its `Dock` property to `Left`

❏ Place the splitter control on the form – it will automatically dock. Be sure the splitter is sited on the form itself, and not within the panel. Place a button in the panel, and set the button's `Anchor` property to `Top, Left, Right`

❏ Your form should now look something like this (we've made the splitter extra fat and turned on their borders so you can see them):

❏ Next, add another panel that will act as the right panel, and set its dock property to `Fill`. This tells it to take up the remaining space on the form

❏ Add a button to the right panel, and as with the first, set its `Anchor` property to `Top, Left, Right`

When you run the form, the splitter will automatically operate and adjust sizes of the two panels, and in turn, the size of the two buttons.

> It's a good idea to change the back color of the splitter to a bright color like red at design time. This will make it easier to see and select. At run time, change the color to something less vibrant.

Validating Data Entry and the Error Provider

Most controls that you place on a form require that their content be validated in some way. A text box might require a numeric value only, or simply require that the user provide any value and not leave it blank.

VB.NET gives you some new features that make this task significantly easier than it was in previous versions. Most especially is the addition of the `ErrorProvider` control.

To illustrate the use of this control, create a new Windows application project and place on it two text boxes that will hold a user name and password as follows:

In the next few pages, we'll add code that will simply verify that the user has filled in both text boxes before proceeding.

The Validating Event

The `Validating` event fires when your control begins its validation. It is here that you need to place your code that will validate your control. Insert the following code to see this in action:

```
Private Sub UserNameTextBox_Validating(ByVal sender As Object, _
                        ByVal e As System.ComponentModel.CancelEventArgs) _
                        Handles userNameTextbox.Validating
    If userNameTextbox.Text = "" Then
      MessageBox.Show("User name cannot be blank")
    End If
End Sub
Private Sub PasswordTextBox_Validating(ByVal sender As Object, _
                        ByVal e As System.ComponentModel.CancelEventArgs) _
                        Handles passwordTextbox.Validating
    If userNameTextbox.Text = "" Then
      MessageBox.Show("Password cannot be blank")
    End If
End Sub
```

Run the program and tab between the controls without entering any text to get the error message. It is simple, and perhaps too effective. Imagine the effect on a large form with dozens of text boxes that is designed to handle high-speed data entry. The users will probably hate this design if they're interrupted with a message box on every mistake. This is addressed in the next few sections.

409

The Validated Event

The Validated event is fired once the validation of your control has finished running the validating events.

The CausesValidation Property

The CausesValidation property determines if the control will participate in the validation strategy on the form. In effect, a control with a CausesValidation setting of True (it is True by default) will have two effects:

- ❑ The control will have its Validating/Validated events fired when appropriate
- ❑ The control will trigger the Validating/Validated events for other controls

It is important to understand that the validation events fire for a control, *not when the focus is lost*, but when the focus shifts to a control that has a CausesValidation value of True.

To see this effect, set the CausesValidation property of the password text box in your application to False (be sure to leave it True for the username and OK button). When you run the program, tab off the username text box and again to the OK button. Notice that it isn't until the focus reaches the OK button that the validating event of the username text box fires. Also, notice that the validating event of the password field *never* fires.

Ultimately, if you determine that the control is not valid, you need to decide how to act. The simplest solution is to set the focus to the control and display an error message indicating what is wrong, but users often hate this interruption, especially if they're entering a screen full of data. The solution to this dilemma is the ErrorProvider control, which we'll add to our application next.

The Error Provider

How many times has a user approached you with the following requirement: show me graphically all the fields that are wrong and what is wrong with them, but don't interrupt the data entry process until I reach the end of the form and try to press the OK button.

While this desired behavior is definitely a valid request, it often leads to some rather interesting challenges. For instance, what if half the fields are wrong? How do you display a single message box for a dozen errors? Nobody will read a single gigantic message listing all the errors. You can try displaying only the first error, but then the user will fix it, only to get another one.

You then might attempt to highlight the invalid fields. Text boxes are easy – just set the background color to red perhaps. But what about list boxes? Setting the background color on such a large control would look horrible. And what about controls that have no background color? How do you indicate an error for those?

VB.NET addresses this problem with the ErrorProvider control. Adding this control to a form allows you to set an error message for each control on your form that can be shown in a tooltip when the field is not valid. To indicate which fields are invalid, the ErrorProvider control will automatically display a small icon next to each control. Placing the mouse over this icon will invoke the tooltip.

Back in the application we've started, set the CausesValidation property back to True for the password field, and then add an ErrorProvider control to your form. (The error provider control has no specific user interface, so it will be added to the section beneath your form.)

To hook it up to your fields, use the `SetError` method. Change the code in the `Validating` events of the two text boxes as follows:

```
    Private Sub UserNameTextBox_Validating(ByVal sender As Object, _
                        ByVal e As System.ComponentModel.CancelEventArgs) _
                        Handles UserNameTextBox.Validating
    If userNameTextbox.Text = "" Then
        ErrorProvider1.SetError(UserNameTextBox, "User Name cannot be blank")
    Else
        ErrorProvider1.SetError(UserNameTextBox, "")
    End If
End Sub
Private Sub PasswordTextBox_Validating(ByVal sender As Object, _
                        ByVal e As System.ComponentModel.CancelEventArgs) _
                        Handles PasswordTextBox.Validating
    If passwordTextbox.Text = "" Then
        ErrorProvider1.SetError(PasswordTextBox, "Password cannot be blank")
    Else
        ErrorProvider1.SetError(PasswordTextBox, "")
    End If
End Sub
```

Run the application and tab through the fields. Position the mouse over the error icon of the password field and you should see the following result:

The properties of the error provider allow you to change things such as the icon used, and where the icon will appear in relation to the field that has the error. For instance, you might want the icon to show up beneath a field instead. You can also have multiple error providers on your form. Often you may only want to warn a user that something doesn't look quite right. A second error provider with a yellow icon could be used to provide this feature.

Menus

Designing menus in VB.NET is yet another area that has been completely redesigned. A menu is now a control that you add to your form like any other control.

The menu designer is extremely intuitive – the menu appears on your form just as it would at run time, and you simply fill in the menu items you need.

Main Menus

Main menus are the standard menus you see that remain docked at the top of a form. Create a new Windows application and add a text box to your form. Set its `Multiline` property to `True` and stretch it out. This example will create a trivial text editor to demonstrate the use of menus.

Next, add a `MainMenu` control to your form. The menu designer will activate and you simply type your menu items and use the properties window to set the parameters.

Create the following **File** and **Edit** menu items. To set the properties of the individual menu items, simply click to select them and the properties window will show you the specific properties for that item:

*To create the separator in the **Edit** menu, enter a hyphen as the text of a menu item.*

The following code runs the menus of our sample app so far:

```
Private Sub copyMenuItem_Click(ByVal sender As System.Object, _
                               ByVal e As System.EventArgs) _
                               Handles copyMenuItem.Click

    TextBox1.Copy()
End Sub

Private Sub pasteMenuItem_Click(ByVal sender As System.Object, _
                                ByVal e As System.EventArgs) _
                                Handles pasteMenuItem.Click

    TextBox1.Paste()
End Sub

Private Sub closeMenuItem_Click(ByVal sender As System.Object, _
                                ByVal e As System.EventArgs) _
                                Handles closeMenuItem.Click

    Me.Close()
```

```
    End Sub

    Private Sub clearAllMenuItem_Click(ByVal sender As System.Object, _
                            ByVal e As System.EventArgs) _
                            Handles clearAllMenuItem.Click

        TextBox1.Text = ""
    End Sub
```

Context Menus

Next, we'll add a simple context menu that will allow the user to change the color of the text box. Context menus appear as small popup menus when the user right-clicks on a form or control.

When you add a context menu to the form, it is edited in the same way a main menu is – at the top of the form. At design time, this positioning is only done to give you a place to edit the menu. At run time, the context menu will appear in a specific location on the form, which we'll see in the code example that follows.

Double-click the ContextMenu control in the toolbox to add a new context menu to the form. Set up the context menu as follows:

To create the radio button indicators beside a menu item requires two properties to be set. The Checked property tells VB that the menu item will display a checkmark, while the RadioCheck property will tell VB that the checkmark should be displayed as a dot.

It is a standard to use radio checks when the selections are mutually exclusive, and checkmarks when more than one item can be chosen at the same time. However, VB.NET will not prevent you from having two menu items with a radio check next to them at the same time. It is up to you to manage this in code.

To hook up the context menu to appear when the user right-clicks the text box, simply set the ContextMenu property of the text box to the context menu you added to the form – that's all there is to it.

When you run the application and right-click on the text box, you will have the following result:

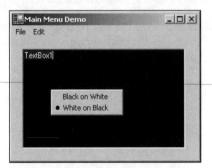

The following code can be used when you select the items in the context menu. Note the change of the `Checked` property. VB will not do this for you even though it is a very common standard that radio buttons are mutually exclusive:

```
Private Sub blackOnWhiteMenuItem_Click(ByVal sender As System.Object, _
                                       ByVal e As System.EventArgs) _
                                       Handles blackOnWhiteMenuItem.Click
    TextBox1.ForeColor = System.Drawing.Color.Black
    TextBox1.BackColor = System.Drawing.Color.White

    ' toggle the radio check
    blackOnWhiteMenuItem.Checked = True
    whiteOnBlackMenuItem.Checked = False
End Sub

Private Sub whiteOnBlackMenuItem_Click(ByVal sender As System.Object, _
                                       ByVal e As System.EventArgs) _
                                       Handles whiteOnBlackMenuItem.Click
    TextBox1.ForeColor = System.Drawing.Color.White
    TextBox1.BackColor = System.Drawing.Color.Black

    ' toggle the radio check
    blackOnWhiteMenuItem.Checked = False
    whiteOnBlackMenuItem.Checked = True
End Sub
```

Run the application, right-click the text box and select the **White on Black** option. If you open the context menu again, you'll see that the radio check has been changed:

Dynamically Manipulating Menus at Runtime

Menus can be adjusted at runtime using code. Context menus, for instance, may need to change depending on the state of your form.

The following code shows how to add a new menu item to the context menu, and also how to clear the menu items. Although simple, it can be expanded for more advanced uses. For instance, you may want to store a list of recently accessed files in the registry. When your application loads, you could read this list back, and insert a menu item into the file menu for each item, and use the same event handler for each:

```
' Add a new menu item at the top of ContextMenu1
Private Sub AddMenuItemExample()
    Dim newMenuItem As MenuItem

    ' Create the new menu item
    newMenuItem = New MenuItem("New Menu Item!")

    ' Set up the event that will handle it's click event
    AddHandler newMenuItem.Click, AddressOf Me.NewMenuItem_Click

    ' Add it to the menu
    ContextMenu1.MenuItems.Add(0, newMenuItem)
End Sub

' This method is here to handle the click event of a new menu item that
' is added dynamically at runtime
Private Sub NewMenuItem_Click(ByVal sender As System.Object, _
                            ByVal e As System.EventArgs)
    MessageBox.Show("New menu item clicked!")
End Sub

' Remove all the menu items from ContextMenu1
Private Sub ClearMenuExample()
    ContextMenu1.MenuItems.Clear()
End Sub
```

Duplicating Menus

Another task that you can perform with menus at runtime is cloning. You may, for instance, want to have a context menu duplicate the functionality of the Edit menu in a MainMenu control. To accomplish this, use the CloneMenu() method. The following example will replace the context menu of the text box in the application above with the same edit menu from MainMenu1:

```
Private Sub CloneMenuExample()
    Dim newContextMenu As ContextMenu

    newContextMenu = New ContextMenu()
    newContextMenu.MenuItems.Add(editMenuItem.CloneMenu())

    TextBox1.ContextMenu = newContextMenu
End Sub
```

> Since `CloneMenu()` clones the object in its entirety, all the event handlers will be cloned as well. You don't need to copy the event handler connections for all the menu items in the cloned menu.

To switch back, simply reassign `ContextMenu1` to the `ContextMenu` property of the text box as follows:

```
TextBox1.ContextMenu = ContextMenu1
```

Toolbars

The `Toolbar` control has definitely undergone some big improvements. It now hosts a collection of `ToolBarButton` objects, each with its own set of properties and behaviors. In VB6, you could try using a `ToolBar` control for limited functionality, or perhaps the `CoolBar` control, but neither were really as clean as the new version in VB.NET.

As with previous examples so far, create a new windows application to begin a simple demonstration on how to use the `ToolBar` control. Add a `ToolBar` control to your form and then expand the `Buttons` property to invoke the collection designer. `ToolBar`, as you might expect, hosts a collection of `ToolBarButton` objects. For now, simply add three buttons to your toolbar, and give each the names seen in the screenshot below. You'll have the following result:

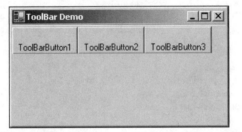

Next, we'll make the first button simply close the application, the second will act as a separator, and the third will be a dropdown that will invoke a context menu control. To do this reopen the `Toolbar` Button collection designer and make the following changes:

❑   Change the `Text` property of the first button to `Close`

❑   Change the `Style` property of the second button to `Separator`

❑   Change the `Text` property of the third button to `Background Color`, and the `Style` property to `DropDownButton`

When you're done, your form will appear as follows:

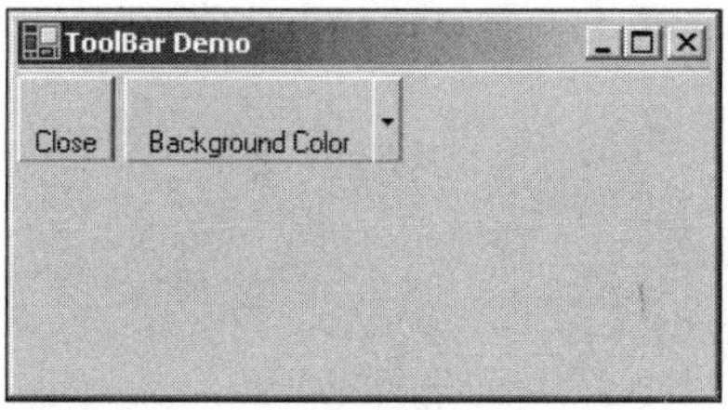

To capture the `Click` event of the `Close` button, add the following code to your form. Note the approach used to identify which button was clicked:

```
Private Sub ToolBar1_ButtonClick(ByVal sender As System.Object, _
            ByVal e As System.Windows.Forms.ToolBarButtonClickEventArgs) _
            Handles ToolBar1.ButtonClick
    Select Case ToolBar1.Buttons.IndexOf(e.Button)
        Case 0 ' Close button
            Me.Close()
    End Select
End Sub
```

When you run your application and click the `Close` button, your application will exit.

Next, we'll set up the dropdown button. Add a context menu to the form (see above section) and design it to contain two items – gray and white. If you like, assign radio checks to each as was done in the context menu sample above. In the form's `Load` event, add the following code:

```
Private Sub Form1_Load(ByVal sender As System.Object, _
                    ByVal e As System.EventArgs) Handles MyBase.Load
    ToolBarButton3.DropDownMenu = ContextMenu1
End Sub
```

That's all there is to it. You can, of course, add code similar to that shown above to handle the events of the context menu. Run the application and click the dropdown toolbar button:

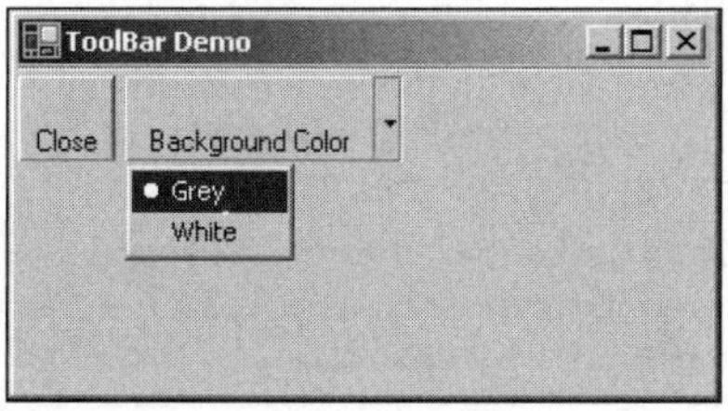

The toolbar buttons provide many other useful features to make them much nicer than the simple example shown above – images can be assigned to the buttons, the text can be aligned to the right instead of below, and the buttons themselves can appear flat if you prefer.

417

While the new toolbar is certainly a big improvement over the old version, there are still a few features that it lacks. One in particular is a combo box. A workaround you can try would involve placing a combo box on a panel, and docking the panel to the top of the form.

Common Dialogs

VB.NET provides you with seven common dialog controls. Each is a control that will open a predefined form that is identical to the one used by the operating system. The sections below outline the use and basic properties of each control that customize their use.

OpenFileDialog and SaveFileDialog

These two controls will open the standard dialog control that allows a user to select files on the system. They are virtually identical except for the buttons and labels that appear on the actual dialog box when it is shown to the user. Each prompts the user for a file on the system, by allowing the user to browse the files and folders available.

Use the following properties to set up the dialogs:

Property	Comments
InitialDirectory	Defines the initial location that will be displayed when the dialog box opens. For example: `OpenFileDialog1.InitalDirectory = "C:\Program Files"`
Filter	String that defines the 'Files of type' list. Separate items using the pipe character. Items are entered in pairs with the first of each pair being the description of the file type, and the second half as the file wildcard. For example: `OpenFileDialog1.Filter = "All Files|*.*|Text Files|*.txt|Rich Text Files|*.rtf"`
FilterIndex	Integer that specifies the default filter item to use when the dialog box opens. For example, with the above filter used, default to text files as follows: `OpenFileDialog1.FilterIndex = 2`
RestoreDirectory	Boolean value that, if `True`, will force the system's default directory to be restored to its location as it was when the dialog box was first opened. This is `False` by default.
Filename	Holds the full name of the file that the user selected, including the path.
ShowDialog()	Displays the dialog.

The following code will open the standard dialog box asking the user to select a file that currently exists on the system, and simply displays the choice in a message box upon return:

```
OpenFileDialog1.InitialDirectory = "C:\"
OpenFileDialog1.Filter = "Text files|*.txt|All files|*.*"
OpenFileDialog1.FilterIndex = 1
OpenFileDialog1.RestoreDirectory = True
OpenFileDialog1.ShowDialog()
MessageBox.Show("You selected """ & OpenFileDialog1.FileName & """")
```

ColorDialog Control

As the name obviously implies, this control gives the user a dialog box from which they can select a color. Use the following properties to set up the dialogs:

Property	Comments
Color	The System.Drawing.Color that the user selected. You can also use this to set the initial color selected when the user opens the dialog.
AllowFullOpen	Boolean value that, if True, will allow the user to select any color. If False, the user is restricted to the set of default colors.
ShowDialog()	Displays the dialog.

Using this property looks something like this:

```
ColorDialog1.Color = TextBox1.BackColor
ColorDialog1.AllowFullOpen = True
ColorDialog1.ShowDialog()
TextBox1.BackColor = ColorDialog1.Color
```

FontDialog Control

This control will display the standard dialog box allowing a user to select a font. Use the following properties to set up the dialogs:

Property	Comments
Font	The System.Drawing.Font that the user selected. Also used to set the initial font.
ShowEffects	Boolean value that, if True, will make the dialog box display the text effects options of underline and strikeout.
ShowColor	Boolean value that, if True, will make the dialog box display the combo box of the font colors. The ShowEffects property must be True for this to have an effect.
FixedPitchOnly	Boolean value that, if True, will limit the list of font choices to only those that have a fixed pitch (such as courier, or lucida console).
ShowDialog()	Displays the dialog.

Using these properties looks like this:

```
FontDialog1.Font = TextBox1.Font
FontDialog1.ShowColor = True
FontDialog1.ShowEffects = True
FontDialog1.FixedPitchOnly = False
FontDialog1.ShowDialog()
TextBox1.Font = FontDialog1.Font
```

Printer Dialog Controls

There are three more common dialog controls: `PrintDialog`, `PrintPreviewDialog`, and `PageSetupDialog`. They can all be used to control the output of a file to the printer. You can use these in conjunction with the `PrintDocument` component to run and control print jobs.

Drag and Drop

Implementing a drag and drop operation in .NET is accomplished using a short sequence of events. Typically it begins in a `MouseDown` event of one control, and always ends with the `DragDrop` event of another.

To demonstrate the process, we'll begin with a new windows application. Add two list boxes to your form and add three items to the first using the `Items` property designer. This application will allow you to drag the items from one list box into the other.

The first step in making drag and drop work is specifying whether or not a control will accept a drop. By default, all controls will reject such an act and not respond to any attempt by the user to drop something onto them. In our case, set the `AllowDrop` property of the second list box (the one without the items added) to `True`.

The next item of business is to invoke the drag and drop operation. This is typically (although you're not restricted to it) done in the `MouseDown` event of the control containing the data you want to drag. This is done using the `DoDragDrop` method. The `DoDragDrop` method defines the data that will be dragged, and the type of dragging that will be allowed. In our situation, we'll drag the text of the selected list box item, and we'll permit both a move and a copy of the data to occur.

Switch over to the code window of your form and add the following code to the `MouseDown` event of `ListBox1`:

```
Private Sub ListBox1_MouseDown(ByVal sender As Object, _
                        ByVal e As System.Windows.Forms.MouseEventArgs) _
                        Handles ListBox1.MouseDown
    Dim DragDropResult As DragDropEffects
    If e.Button = MouseButtons.Left Then
        DragDropResult = ListBox1.DoDragDrop( _
                    ListBox1.Items(ListBox1.SelectedIndex), _
                    DragDropEffects.Move Or DragDropEffects.Copy)
        ' Leave some room here to check the result of the operation
        ' (We'll fill it in next)
    End If
End Sub
```

You'll notice the comment above about leaving room to check the result of the operation. We'll fill that in shortly. For now, calling the DoDragDrop method has got us started.

The next step involves the recipient of the data – in our case, ListBox2. There are two events here that will be important to monitor – the DragEnter and DragDrop event.

As can be predicted by the name, the DragEnter event will occur when the user first moves over the recipient control. The DragEnter event has a parameter of type DragEventArgs that contains an Effect property and a KeyState property.

The Effect property allows you to set the display of the drop icon for the user to indicate if a move or a copy will occur when the mouse button is released. The KeyState property allows you to determine the state of the *Ctrl*, *Alt*, and *Shift* keys. It is a Windows standard that when both a move or a copy can occur, a user is to indicate the copy action by holding down the *Ctrl* key. Therefore, in this event we will check the KeyState property and use it to determine how to set the Effect property.

Add the following code to the DragEnter event of ListBox2:

```
Private Sub ListBox2_DragEnter(ByVal sender As Object, _
                                ByVal e As DragEventArgs) _
                                Handles ListBox2.DragOver
    If e.KeyState = 9 Then ' Control key
        e.Effect = DragDropEffects.Copy
    Else
        e.Effect = DragDropEffects.Move
    End If
End Sub
```

Note that you can also use the DragOver event if you want, but it will fire continuously as the mouse moves over the target control. In this situation, you only need to trap the initial entry of the mouse into the control.

The final step in the operation occurs when the user lets go of the mouse button to drop the data in its destination. This is captured by the DragDrop event. The parameter contains a property holding the data that is being dragged. It's now a simple process of placing it into the recipient control as follows:

```
Private Sub ListBox2_DragDrop(ByVal sender As Object, _
                                ByVal e As System.Windows.Forms.DragEventArgs) _
                                Handles ListBox2.DragDrop
    ListBox2.Items.Add(e.Data.GetData(DataFormats.Text))
End Sub
```

One last step – we can't forget to manipulate ListBox1 if the drag and drop was a move. Here's where we'll fill in the hole we left in the MouseDown event of ListBox1. Once the DragDrop has occurred, the initial call that invoked the procedure will return a result indicating what ultimately happened. Go back to the ListBox1_MouseDown event and enhance it to remove the item from the listbox if it was moved (and not simply copied):

```
Private Sub ListBox1_MouseDown(ByVal sender As Object, _
            ByVal e As System.Windows.Forms.MouseEventArgs) _
```

```
            Handles ListBox1.MouseDown
    Dim DragDropResult As DragDropEffects

    If e.Button = MouseButtons.Left Then
        DragDropResult = ListBox1.DoDragDrop( _
                    ListBox1.Items(ListBox1.SelectedIndex), _
                    DragDropEffects.Move Or DragDropEffects.Copy)
          ' If operation is a move (and not a copy) then remove then
          ' remove the item from the first list box
          If DragDropResult = DragDropEffects.Move Then
            ListBox1.Items.RemoveAt(ListBox1.SelectedIndex)
          End If
        End If
    End If
End Sub
```

When you're done, run your application and drag the items from Listbox1 into Listbox2. Try a copy by holding down the control key when you do it. The following screenshot shows the result after Item1 has been moved, and Item3 has been copied a few times:

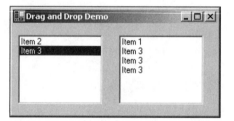

Summary of Standard Windows.Forms Controls

VB.NET of course contains most of the controls which you are accustomed to using in previous versions. The following few pages list out the basic controls that are generally quite intuitive and didn't warrant a full example to explain. Where appropriate, the important differences from previous versions of VB are stated.

Button

❑   Formerly known as CommandButton.

❑   Now uses the Text property instead of Caption.

❑   Can now display both an icon and text simultaneously. The image is set using the Image property (instead of Picture). The image position can be set using the ImageAlign property (left, right, center, and so on).

❑   Text on the button can be aligned using the TextAlign property.

❑   Can now have different appearances using the FlatStyle property.

❑   No longer has the Default and Cancel properties. These are now managed by the form itself using the AcceptButton and CancelButton properties.

CheckBox

- ❑ Now uses the `Text` property instead of `Caption`

- ❑ Can now appear as a toggle button using the `Appearance` property

- ❑ Checkbox and text can now be positioned within the defined area using the `CheckAlign` and `TextAlign` properties

- ❑ Uses the `CheckState` property instead of `Value`

- ❑ Has a `FlatStyle` property controlling the appearance of the checkbox

CheckedListBox

- ❑ A list box that has checkboxes beside each item (see `Listbox`)

ComboBox

- ❑ As with the new `ListBox` control, can now hold a collection of objects instead of an array of strings, (see `ListBox`)

- ❑ Now has a `MaxDropDownItems` property that specifies how many items to display when the list opens

DataGrid

- ❑ This has been significantly upgraded from its predecessor in VB6. In essence, the DataGrid is a front-end user interface to the data objects in .NET.

- ❑ You can find more information on this control in Chapter 16.

DateTimePicker

- ❑ Formerly known as a `DTPicker`

DomainUpDown - New!

- ❑ A simple one line version of a list box

- ❑ Can hold a collection of objects, and will display the `ToString()` result of an item in the collection

- ❑ Can wrap around the list to give a continuous scrolling effect using the `Wrap` property

GroupBox

- ❑ Formerly known as a Frame

HelpProvider – New!

- ❑ Allows quick and easy help configuration. Adding a `HelpProvider` control to your form puts extra properties in your other controls where you can set various help properties of the controls such as help text that will appear when the user presses *F1*, and links into compiled (`.chm`) help files or HTML help files.

HScrollBar

❑   Unchanged

ImageList

❑   Same as previous versions, but with an improved window for managing the images within the list. The `MaskColor` property is now `TransparentColor`.

Label

❑   Essentially the same as previous versions.

❑   `Caption` is now `Text`.

❑   Can now display an image and text.

❑   The `TextAlign` property is especially useful. The text of a label beside a text box in VB6 would always be a few pixels higher than the text in the text box. Now by setting the label's `TextAlign` property so that the vertical alignment is `Middle`, this problem is solved.

❑   Can now specify if a mnemonic should be interpreted (if `UseMnemonic` is `True`, the first ampersand (`&`) in the `Text` property will indicate to underline the following character and have it react to the *Alt* key shortcut, placing the focus on the next control in the tab order that can hold focus such as a text box).

LinkLabel – New!

❑   Identical to a label, but behaves like a hyperlink with extra properties such as `LinkBehavior` (for example, `HoverUnderline`), `LinkColor`, and `ActiveLinkColor`

ListBox

❑   A list box can now hold a collection of objects instead of an array of strings. Use the `DisplayMember` property to specify what property of the objects to display in the list, and the `ValueMember` property to specify what property of the objects to use as the values of the list items. (This is similar to the `ItemData` array from previous versions) For example, the combo box can store a collection of, say employee objects, and display to the user the `Name` property of each, as well as retrieve the `EmployeeId` as the value of the item currently selected.

❑   Can no longer be set to display checkboxes using a `Style` property. Use the `CheckedListBox` control instead.

ListView

❑   Same functionality as the VB6 version but with an improved property editor that allows you to define the list view item collection *and* its sub-items at design time

❑   Sub-items can have their own font display properties

❑   New `HeaderStyle` property instead of `HideColumnHeaders`

MainMenu

❑   See the *Menus* section

MonthCalendar

❑ Formerly known as `MonthView`

NotifyIcon – New!

❑ Great new control that gives you an icon in the system tray

❑ Tooltip of the icon is set by the `Text` property of the control

❑ Popup menus are set using a `ContextMenu` control (see section on *Menus* earlier in chapter)

NumericUpDown – New!

❑ A single line text box that displays a number and up/down buttons that increment/decrement the number when clicked

Panel – New!

❑ The panel control is essentially nothing more than a container for other controls. You can use it to group controls together for resizing needs (see the section on the *Splitter Control*), or simply to easily make visible, or invisible many controls at once simply by showing or hiding the panel on which they are all sited.

PictureBox

❑ `Image` property defines the graphic to display instead of `Picture`

❑ Use the `SizeMode` property to auto stretch, or center the picture

ProgressBar

❑ Now has a `Step()` method that automatically increments the value of the progress bar by the amount defined in the `Step` property

RadioButton

❑ Formerly known as `OptionButton`

❑ Use `Checked` property to specify value (formerly `Value`)

❑ Use `CheckAlign` and `TextAlign` to specify where the radio button and text appears in relation to the area of the control

RichTextBox

❑ Essentially the same control as before with a few new properties such as `ZoomFactor`, `WordWrap`, `DetectURLs` and `AutoWordSelection`

❑ Use the `Lines()` array to get or set specific individual lines of text of the control

Splitter

❑ See previous section

StatusBar

❑ Has a Panels collection and a ShowPanels property. If False, the status bar will display only the Text property. This would be equivalent to setting the VB6 status bar control Style property to sbrSimple.

❑ The StatusBar control docks to the bottom of the parent control by default. (See section on *Docking*.) You could change this if you want (although we're not sure how intuitive a floating status bar would be).

TabControl

❑ Formerly known as the TabStrip control.

❑ Now has a TabPages collection of TabPage objects. A TabPage object is a subclass of the Panel control specialized for use in the TabControl.

❑ Uses the Appearance property to display the tabs as buttons if desired (formerly the Style property of the TabStrip control).

TextBox

❑ Now has a CharacterCasing property that can automatically adjust the text entered into upper or lower case.

❑ ReadOnly property now used to prevent the text from being edited. This used to be theLocked property.
Note: The Locked property now determines if the control can be moved or resized.

❑ Now has Cut, Copy, Paste, Undo, and ClearUndo methods.

Timer

❑ Essentially unchanged from previous versions

❑ The timer is now *dis*abled by default

❑ You cannot set the interval to zero to disable it

ToolBar

❑ See previous section

ToolTip – New!

❑ Adding a tooltip control creates a new property for the various controls on your form. For instance, if your tooltip control is called ToolTip1, and you have a text box on your form, the text box will have a new property called Tooltip on Tooltip1. If you assign some text to this property, the text box will automatically display it as its tooltip. You can have multiple tooltip controls on your form if you wish, but assigning text to both of them for the same control will give you two overlapping tooltips on the screen – something to obviously avoid.

TrackBar

❑ Formerly known as the Slider control, essentially unchanged

TreeView

❑ Same functionality as in VB6 but with a new **Node Tree Editor** that allows you to visually design the tree

VScrollBar

❑ Unchanged

Retired Controls

Some controls have also been 'retired'. The following list outlines the controls from VB6 that you won't find in VB.Net, and how to reproduce their functionality:

Spinner

❑ Use the `DomainUpDown` or `NumericUpDown` control

Line and Shape

❑ VB.NET has no line or shape control, nor any immediate equivalent. A 'cheap' way of reproducing a horizontal or vertical line is to use a label control. Set its background color to that of the line you want, and then either the `Size.Height` or `Size.Width` value to 1.

❑ Diagonal lines and shapes must be drawn using GDI+ graphics methods.

DirListBox, FileListBox, DriveListBox

❑ You would typically use these controls to create a file system browser similar to windows explorer. VB.NET has no equivalent controls. You can use the `OpenFileDialog` and `SaveFileDialog` (see previous section) to accomplish your needs in most circumstances.

Image

❑ Use the `PictureBox` control

Using ActiveX Controls

While VB.NET is optimized to use Windows Forms controls, you can certainly place an ActiveX control on your form and use it as well. You'll see how to do this in Chapter 17.

Other Handy Programming Tips

Here are some other handy programming tips for using Windows Forms:

❑ **Switch the Focus to a Control** – Use the `.Focus()` method. To set the focus to `TextBox1`, for example, use the following code:
```
TextBox1.Focus()
```

❑ **Change the Cursor** – To switch the cursor to an hourglass, for example, use the `Cursor` object as follows:
```
Cursor.Current = Cursors.WaitCursor ' hourglass
Cursor.Current = Cursors.Default ' pointer
```

427

- ❑ **Quickly Determine the Container Control or Parent Form** – With the use of group boxes and panels, controls are often contained many times removed from the ultimate form. You can now use the `FindForm` method to immediately get a reference to the form. Use the `GetContainerControl` method to access the immediate parent of a control.

- ❑ **Traversing the Tab Order** – Use the `GetNextControl` method of any control to get a reference to the next control on the form in the tab order.

- ❑ **Convert Client Coordinates to Screen Coordinates (and back)** – Want to know where a control is in screen coordinates? Use the `PointToScreen` method. Convert back using the `PointToClient` method.

- ❑ **Change the Z-Order of Controls at Runtime** – Controls now have both `BringToFront` and `SendToBack` methods.

- ❑ **Where is the Mouse Pointer?** – The control class now exposes a `MousePosition` property that returns the location of the mouse in screen coordinates.

- ❑ **Managing Child Controls** – Container controls such as a group box or panel can use the `HasChildren` property and `Controls` property to determine the existence of, and direct references to, child controls respectively.

- ❑ **Maximize, Minimize, Restore a Form** – Use the form's `WindowState` property.

Summary

The new features and improvements to Windows Forms in VS.NET mean that countless tasks required by virtually every application that used to be awkward are now simple and elegant. It would seem that the Windows Forms team at Microsoft just never let up when it comes to improving the tools.

This chapter has run through all of the significant enhancements to Windows Forms which are now available in VB.NET, and how developers can take advantage of these when either updating existing applications or indeed writing new ones – using these tools should prove both enjoyable and productive.

13

Creating Windows Controls

The new options for deployment of form-based interfaces in the .NET Framework mean that user interfaces created with Windows Forms are less costly to install and support compared to VB6. Windows Forms also possess greatly enhanced functionality compared to that available in VB6, which enables us to design better interfaces that improve the user's experience.

Windows Forms interfaces are based on using **controls**. A control is simply a special type of .NET class (just as forms are). A control inherits (either directly or indirectly) from a base class called `System.Window.Forms.Control` that ensures that certain functionality will be available to all controls.

In this chapter we will look at the nature of Windows Forms user interfaces, and the three main techniques available to developers in creating user interfaces, namely:

- ❏ Inheriting from another control
- ❏ Building a composite control
- ❏ Writing a control based on the `Control` class

Then we'll go on to look in more detail at the base `Control` and `UserControl` classes, and consider a number of examples in order to illustrate how these can be used in developing custom Windows Forms controls.

Sources of Controls

There are four primary sources of controls for use on Windows Forms interfaces:

❑ Controls packaged with the .NET Framework (which we'll call **built-in controls**)

❑ Existing ActiveX controls that are imported into Windows Forms (like we saw in Chapter 12)

❑ Third-party .NET-based controls from a software vendor

❑ Custom controls that we create for a specific purpose

Built-In Controls

The set of built-in controls that comes with the .NET Framework is comparable to the set offered with previous versions of Visual Basic (although with some changes and additions). Chapter 12, on Windows Forms, covered the basics of using these controls.

Many Windows Forms interfaces can be built completely with built-in controls. The stability and fast implementation of the built-in controls make them attractive for a wide variety of purposes.

Existing ActiveX Controls

It is relatively straightforward to use existing ActiveX controls in Windows Forms. They can be referenced in the same way as .NET controls, and a wrapper for them will be automatically created.

However, performance considerations suggest that ActiveX controls should only be used when it is impractical to find or create an appropriate .NET control.

We'll see how to use an existing ActiveX control in Chapter 17, when we look at working with classic COM.

Third-Party Controls

If the set of built-in controls proves insufficient for the needs of a particular application, another option is to acquire more visual controls from a commercial software vendor. Such third-party controls have been available in previous versions of Visual Basic for many years, and continue to be an option for VB.NET.

A wide variety of controls from reputable vendors are available; they are often richer in functionality than the built-in controls, but just as robust.

Custom Controls

When neither built-in controls nor third-party controls are sufficient to meet our needs, the next option is to create custom controls.

This option was also possible in previous versions of Visual Basic by developing ActiveX controls (UserControls). However, custom controls in VB.NET have two main advantages over VB6 UserControls: simpler development and greater flexibility.

Developing Custom Controls in .NET

There are three basic techniques for creation of custom Windows Forms controls in .NET, corresponding to three different starting points. This range of options gives us the flexibility to choose a technique that allows an appropriate balance between simplicity and flexibility. We can:

- ❏ Inherit from another control
- ❏ Build a composite control
- ❏ Write a control from scratch

Inherit From Another Control

The simplest technique starts with a complete Windows Forms control that is already developed. A new class is created that inherits the existing control. (See Chapter 6 for a complete discussion of inheritance in .NET.) This new class has all the functionality of the base class from which it inherits and new logic can be added to create additional functionality in this new class or, indeed, to override functionality from the parent (when permitted).

Most of the built-in Windows Forms controls can be used as the base class for such an inherited control (there are a few that cannot be inherited from, such as the `NotifyIcon` control, and the `ProgressBar`). Third-party controls may also be candidates for extension into new custom controls through inheritance.

Here are some examples where it might make sense to extend an existing Windows Forms control:

- ❏ A text box with built-in validation for specific types of information
- ❏ A self-loading list box, combo box, or data grid
- ❏ A picture control that chooses a new image at random from a directory each time it appears on a form
- ❏ A menu control that varies its options based on the current user
- ❏ A `NumericUpDown` control that generates a special event when it reaches 80% of its maximum allowed value

The more times such functionality is needed, the more sense it makes to package it in a custom control. If a text box that needs special validation or editing will only be used in one place, it probably doesn't make sense to create an inherited control. In that case, simply adding some logic in the form where the control is used to handle the control's events and manipulating the control's properties and methods is probably sufficient. But where such functionality is needed in many locations in an application, packaging the functionality in an inherited control can centralize the logic and facilitate reuse, thereby removing maintenance headaches.

Build a Composite Control

In some cases, a single existing control does not furnish the needed functionality, but a combination of two or more existing controls does. Here are some typical examples:

❑   A set of text boxes to hold a name, address, and phone number, with the combined information formatted in a particular way

❑   A set of buttons with related logic that are always used together

❑   A set of option buttons with a single property exposed as the chosen option

❑   A data grid together with buttons that alter its appearance or behavior in specific ways

As with inherited controls, composite controls are only appropriate for situations that require the same functionality in multiple places. If the functionality is only needed once, then simply placing the relevant controls on the form and including appropriate logic in the form itself is usually better.

Composite controls are the closest relative to VB6 UserControls and, because of that, they are sometimes referred to as UserControls. In fact, the base class used to create composite controls is the UserControl class in .NET.

Write a Control From Scratch

If a control needs to have special functionality not related to any existing control, then it can be written from scratch to draw its own interface and implement its own logic. This option requires more work, but allows us to do just about anything that is possible in form design within .NET.

To write a control from scratch it is necessary to inherit from the Control class, which gives basic functionality such as properties for colors and size. With this basic functionality already built in, the main tasks to be performed to get a custom control working are to add on any specific properties and methods needed for this control, to write the rendering logic that will paint the control to the screen, and to handle mouse and keyboard input to the control.

The Base Classes for Control Creation

There are two classes that are used in different circumstances as a starting point to create a control. It is helpful to understand something about the structure of these classes to see when use of each is appropriate.

> The classes discussed in this chapter are all in the **System.Windows.Forms** namespace. There are similarly named classes for some of these in the **System.Web.UI** namespace (which is used for Web Forms), but these classes should not be confused with anything discussed in this chapter. We will cover the creation of Web controls in Chapter 15.

The Control Class

The `Control` class is contained within the `System.Windows.Forms` namespace and contains base functionality to define a rectangle on the screen, provide a handle for it, and process routine operating system messages. This gives the class the ability to perform such functions as handling user input through the keyboard and mouse. The `Control` class serves as the base class for any component that needs a visual representation on a Win32-type graphical interface. Besides custom controls that are inherited from the `Control` class, the `Form` class also ultimately derives from the `Control` class.

In addition to these low-level capabilities, the `Control` class also includes such visually related properties as `Font`, `ForeColor`, `BackColor`, and `BackGroundImage`. Many of these are familiar to Visual Basic developers because these are also members of the standard VB6 form. The `Control` class has additional properties that are used to manage layout of the control, such as docking and anchoring.

> **The `Control` class does not contain any logic to paint to the screen and, while it does offer access to the keyboard and mouse, it does not contain any actual input processing logic. The developer of a custom control based on the `Control` class must provide all of these capabilities.**

Here are some of the most important members of the `Control` class (from the perspective of a VB developer):

Property	Description
`AllowDrop`	If set to `True` then this control will allow drag and drop operations and events to be used
`Anchor`	Determines which edges of the control are anchored to the container's edges
`BackColor` `Font` `ForeColor`	Visual properties which are the same as corresponding properties in Visual Basic 6 and earlier
`CanFocus`	A read-only property that indicates whether the control can receive focus
`Causes Validation`	A new property of forms and controls that indicates whether entering the control causes validation on the control itself or on controls contained by this control that require validation
`Controls`	A collection of child controls which this control contains
`Dock`	Controls to which edge of the container this control is docked to
`Enabled`	Property indicating whether the control is currently enabled
`Handle`	The `HWND` handle that this control is bound to
`Location` `Size`	Properties that relate to the size and position of the control
`Visible`	Property that indicates whether the control is currently visible on the screen

Table continued on following page

Method	Description
BringToFront	Brings this control to the front of the z-order
DoDragDrop	Begins a drag and drop operation
Focus	Attempts to set focus to this control
Hide	Hides the control by setting the visible property to False
Refresh	Forces the control to repaint itself, and to force a repaint on any of its child controls
Show	Makes the control display by setting the visible property to True
Update	Forces the control to paint any currently invalid areas
WndProc	A very important method that allows access to Windows messages; since this is implemented in the Control class, all Windows Forms classes can have easy access to Windows messages

Event	Description
Click DoubleClick GotFocus KeyDown KeyPress KeyUp MouseDown MouseEnter MouseMove MouseUp Resize	Same as corresponding events in Visual Basic 6 and earlier
DragDrop DragEnter DragLeave DragOver	Events relating to drag and drop operations
Leave	Occurs when the control is left (focus is lost)
MouseHover	New mouse event to determine when the mouse cursor has hovered over the control
Paint	Occurs when the control is forced to repaint itself to the screen
PropertyChanged	Occurs when a property of the control has changed

The UserControl Class

The built-in functionality of the Control class is a great starting point for controls that will be built from scratch, with their own display and keyboard handling logic. However, there is no capability in the Control class to make it into a container. A custom control derived from the Control class cannot contain multiple controls – it can only manage a rectangular window that represents a single control.

That means that composite controls cannot use the `Control` class as a starting point. Composite controls combine two or more existing controls, so the starting point must be a container. The class that meets this requirement is the `UserControl` class. Since it ultimately derives from the `Control` class, it has all of the properties and methods we listed.

However, the `UserControl` class does not derive directly from the `Control` class. It derives from the `ContainerControl` class, which, in turn, derives from the `ScrollableControl` class. The class hierarchy looks like this:

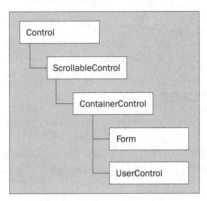

As the name suggests, the `ScrollableControl` class adds support for scrolling the client area of the control's window. Almost all the members implemented by this class relate to scrolling. They include `AutoScroll`, which turns scrolling on or off, and controlling properties such as `AutoScrollPosition`, which gets or sets the position within the scrollable area.

The `ContainerControl` class derives from `ScrollableControl` and adds the ability to support and manage child controls. It manages the focus and the ability to tab from control to control. It includes properties such as `ActiveControl` to point to the control with the focus, and `Validate`, which validates the most recently changed control that has not had its validation event fired.

Neither `ScrollableControl` nor `ContainerControl` are usually inherited from directly; they add functionality that is needed by their more commonly used child classes: `Form` and `UserControl`.

The `UserControl` class can contain other child controls, but the interface of `UserControl` does not automatically expose these child controls in any way. Instead, the interface of `UserControl` is designed to present a single, unified interface to outside clients such as forms or container controls. Any object interface that is needed to access the child controls must be specifically implemented in your custom control – the following example demonstrates this.

The external interface of the `UserControl` class consists exclusively of members inherited from other classes, though it does overload many of these members to gain functionality suitable for its role as a base class for composite controls.

Inheriting From Another Control

Now that we have some background on the options for creating custom controls, we are ready to look in depth at the procedures used for their development. First, we will look at creating a custom control by inheriting from an existing control and extending it with new functionality.

We will start by describing the general steps needed to create a custom control via inheritance, and then illustrate this with two examples. It is important to understand that many of the techniques described for working with a control created through inheritance also apply to the other ways that a control can be created. Whether inheriting from the Control class, the UserControl class, or from an existing control, a control is a .NET class. Creating properties, methods, and events, and coordinating these members with the VS.NET designers, is done in a similar fashion regardless of the starting point.

Overview of the Process

Here are the general steps involved in the creation of a custom control via inheritance:

1. In a new Windows Control Library project, the class that is created will inherit from the System.Windows.Forms.UserControl namespace. The line that specifies the inherited class must be changed to inherit from the control that is being used as the starting point.

2. The class file then gets new logic added as necessary to add new functionality, before the project is compiled with a Build operation in order to create a DLL containing the new control's code.

3. The control is now ready to be used. It can be placed in the Windows Forms toolbox with the Customize Toolbox option in Visual Studio. From that point forward, it can be dragged onto forms like any other control.

Creating a Numeric-Only Text box

As our first example, we will create a text box that only allows the user to put in a numeric entry. The starting point will be a normal Windows Forms text box that allows entry of any character. The new, inherited control will have additional logic to restrict input to those characters appropriate for numeric entry.

The basic requirements for the control are to:

❑ Allow digits

❑ Allow entry of one decimal point only

❑ Allow a minus sign, but only at the first position in the text box

❑ Throw away (or ignore) all other characters entered by the user

Step-By-Step Process to Create the Control

1. Start a new Windows Control Library project in VS.NET. Give it the name NumericTextBox, rename the resulting project module NumericTextBox.vb (by default it will be named UserControl1.vb), and bring up the code window for this class.

2. The first two lines of the class will look like this:

```
Public Class UserControl1
    Inherits System.Windows.Forms.UserControl
```

As we need to inherit from a text box, these lines should be changed to:

```
Public Class NumericTextBox
    Inherits System.Windows.Forms.TextBox
```

3. Next, we need to add the code for our new functionality. In our case, this is just one extra event routine which excludes the keys that we don't want to handle. To do that, place an event routine for the KeyPress event in the code. This is accomplished by opening the left-hand dropdown box in the code window and selecting the option **Base Class Events**, before selecting the **KeyPress** event in the right-hand dropdown box of the code window. Here is a sample screen showing the KeyPress event about to be selected:

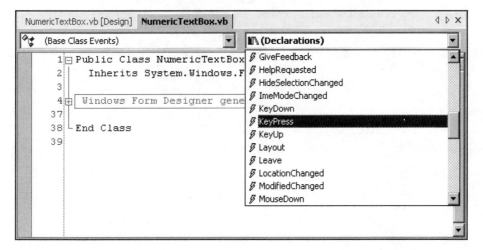

This action will cause the following code for an empty KeyPress event to be generated (the code below has line continuation characters added to facilitate readability):

```
Private Sub NumericTextBox_KeyPress(ByVal sender As Object, _
    ByVal e As System.Windows.Forms.KeyPressEventArgs) Handles _
    MyBase.KeyPress

End Sub
```

4. The following code should be added to the `KeyPress` event to monitor keystrokes from the user:

```
Private Sub NumericTextBox_KeyPress(ByVal sender As Object, _
  ByVal e As System.Windows.Forms.KeyPressEventArgs) _
  Handles MyBase.KeyPress
```

```
  Dim KeyAscii As Integer
  KeyAscii = Asc(e.KeyChar)

  Select Case KeyAscii

    Case 48 To 57, 8, 13        ' these are the digits 0-9, backspace,
      ' and carriage return
      ' we're OK on these, don't do anything

    Case 45                     ' minus sign

      ' The number can only have one minus sign, so
      ' if we already have one, throw this one away
      If InStr(Me.Text, "-") <> 0 Then
        KeyAscii = 0
      End If

      ' if the insertion point is not sitting at zero
      ' (which is the beginning of the field), throw away the minus
      ' sign (because it's not valid except in first position)
      If Me.SelectionStart <> 0 Then
        KeyAscii = 0
      End If

    Case 46                     ' this is a period (decimal point)

      ' if we already have a period, throw it away
      If InStr(Me.Text, ".") <> 0 Then
        KeyAscii = 0
      End If

    Case Else
      ' provide no handling for the other keys
      KeyAscii = 0

  End Select

  ' If we want to throw the keystroke away, then set the event
  ' as already handled. Otherwise, let the keystroke be handled normally.
  If KeyAscii = 0 Then
    e.Handled = True
  Else
    e.Handled = False
  End If

End Sub
```

5. Build the project to create a DLL containing the `NumericTextBox` control.

6. Create a new Windows Application project to test the control. Name the new project anything you like. Now right-click on the **Windows Forms** tab in the **Toolbox**, and select **Customize Toolbox...**, and then click the tab for **.NET Framework Components**. Hit the **Browse** button and navigate to the directory containing your `NumericTextBox` project, in order to select the `NumericTextBox.dll` file (found in the `/bin` subdirectory). Return to the **Customize Toolbox** dialog, check the box, and click the **OK** button.

7. Scroll to the bottom of the controls on the Windows Forms tab. The `NumericTextBox` control should be there.

8. Drag a `NumericTextBox` control onto the form as you would a normal `TextBox`. Start the project. Test the `NumericTextBox` to check that it only accepts numeric input.

Changing the Logic in a Custom Control

Since you created a new Windows Application project to test the `NumericTextBox`, you should be aware that, when you accessed `NumericTextBox.dll`, the new project made a copy of it in its own directory. This is necessary to run the application (see Chapter 25 to understand why this is the case).

> If you change the logic in the `NumericTextBox` control and then build a new version of it, that new version will not be automatically supplied to the Windows Application project used to test the control. It will be necessary to remove the control from the toolbox (via **Customize Toolbox**) and then refer to the changed version of the control.

Debugging a Custom Control

Since the process described in the previous section is tedious and prone to error, it is easier to test new controls by adding a new Windows Application to the same project that is being used to create the control. Then, when new versions of the control are built, the Windows Application in the project automatically uses the new version. This is the recommended technique to use during development of any type of custom control, and we will use it for the remaining examples in the chapter.

There is one additional step needed if a new Windows Application is added to a solution to test a custom control. The Windows Application project must be set as the startup project in the solution properties (this can be done by right-clicking on the project name in the **Solution Explorer** window and selecting **Set as Startup Project**). Otherwise, the default startup is the control project, and you will receive an error message if you try to execute the solution with the control still designated as the startup project.

Adding Additional Logic to a Custom Control

While the first example above is completely functional and can be useful, most custom controls are not so simple. Typically, a custom control has more complex logic to add capability to the base control.

Besides handling base class events, as in the first example above, custom controls can have new logic added via any of the following:

❑ Overriding properties and methods in the base class

❑ Creating new properties and methods in the child control class

❑ Defining new events that the child control class will generate for handling in a Windows Form that contains the control

Overriding a property or method in the base class is used when the functionality in that property or method is not sufficient for the new class. In the overriding logic, it is often necessary to call the original property or method in the base class using the MyBase keyword (further details on the MyBase keyword can be found in Chapter 5).

More commonly, however, a custom control needs to have properties, methods, and events that the base control does not possess. The following section discusses defining custom properties and methods for an inherited control and, after the next example, the process for defining a custom event is covered.

Creating a Property for a Custom Control

Creating a property for a custom control is just like creating a property for any other class.

Once a property is created for a control, it automatically shows up in the Properties window for the control. However, there are some additional capabilities that you can use to make the property work better with the designers and windows in VS.NET.

Setting Default Values and Creating Attributes for a Property

Properties typically need a **default value**, that is, a value the property will take on automatically when a control is instantiated. As you might expect, you can use your own internal logic in a control to set a default value for a property. Typically this means creating a module-level variable or constant initialized to the default value. Alternatively, you can initialize the default value in the constructor for the control. These techniques work fine, and are especially useful if the default value is different for different instantiations of the control, as in the case where the default Text property for a button is the name of the button.

If all instantiations of your control will have the same default value for a particular property, there is another technique for creating the default value that is often preferable. This involves using an attribute. There are various attributes that can be assigned in metadata to classes, properties, and methods. The one for creating a default value is called, appropriately enough, DefaultValue. It will be used in the next example to assign a default value to a property. The following code shows a DefaultValue attribute being set:

```
<DefaultValue(100)> Public Property MyProperty() As Integer
   Get
      Return mnMyProperty
   End Get
   Set(ByVal Value As Integer)
      mnMyProperty = Value
   End Set
End Property
```

In this case, the default value for `MyProperty` is set to 100. Including this line will cause the value of 100 to show up in the Properties window for a control as soon as it is dragged onto a form.

`DefaultValue` is not the only attribute that is useful for properties. The `Description` attribute is also one that should be used with most properties. It contains a text description of the property that shows up in the Properties windows when a property is selected. To include a `Description` attribute, the declaration of the property above would look like this:

```
<DefaultValue(100), _
Description("This is a description for my property")> _
Public Property MyProperty() As Integer
```

Attributes reside in namespaces, just as components do. To use one, it is necessary to refer to the appropriate namespace. The attributes above are available by referring to the `System.ComponentModel` namespace with the following line at the top of the class' code:

```
Imports System.ComponentModel
```

If you start to use an attribute and get a build error, the most likely reason (assuming that your syntax for the attribute is correct) is that the namespace for the attribute is not yet referred to in your project.(To add a new namespace to a project, simply click on the **References | Add Reference** menu in the **Solution Explorer** window.)

Once a property has an attribute, the attribute can be fetched in code. First, you need a reference to the attributes collection for the property, and then you can get to the individual attribute. The following code demonstrates how to fetch the `DefaultValue` attribute property for `MyProperty`:

```
Dim attributes As AttributeCollection = _
    TypeDescriptor.GetProperties(Me)("MyProperty").Attributes

' Now need a reference to the DefaultValue attribute, which is
' in the collection we just referenced above.
Dim myAttribute As DefaultValueAttribute = _
    CType(attributes(GetType(DefaultValueAttribute)), DefaultValueAttribute)
```

Making Properties Work Well with the Designer

There are two main ways that properties of classes interact with the Visual Studio environment. Firstly, properties are displayed in the Properties window, and they can be edited there. Secondly, the visual designers in VS.NET create code in form modules to set the properties of the controls contained on the form. (You can see this code when you expand the section of a form's code labeled `Windows Forms Designer generated code`.)

Serializing a Property in Code

However, the visual designers do not insert code to set all the properties of every control. Some controls have dozens of properties, and setting them all would require many lines of code. So the designers only generate code to set those properties that need a value other than their default value. That is, if you edit a property in the Properties window, and you set it to a value other than the default, the designer will generate code for that property. If the property is left with its default value, the designer will not generate code for it.

Generating code to set a property is called **serializing** the property. Designers check to see if a property needs to be serialized by using a method on the control containing the property. The method returns a Boolean value that indicates whether a property needs to be serialized (True if it does, False if it does not).

If a property is named MyProperty, then the method to check serialization is called ShouldSerializeMyProperty. It would typically look something like this:

```
Public Function ShouldSerializeMyProperty() As Boolean
  If mnMyProperty = mnMyPropertysDefaultValue Then
    Return False
  Else
    Return True
  End If
End Function
```

If a property in a custom control does not have a related ShouldSerializeXXX method, then the property is always serialized. Code for setting the property's value will always be included by the designer in the generated code for a form. For that reason, it's a good idea to always include such a method for every new property created for a control.

Note that the above code example shows the default value of the property being held in a module level variable. The default value can also be held in and called from a DefaultValue attribute.

Providing a Reset Method for a Control Property

It is also possible to relate a method to reset the property's value to the default to a property in a control. As an example of this, in the case of a property named MyProperty, the reset method is named ResetMyProperty. It typically looks something like this:

```
Public Sub ResetMyProperty()
  mnMyProperty = mnMyPropertysDefaultValue
End Sub
```

As with the ShouldSerializXXX method, the default property value can be called from an attribute if one has been included with the property declaration.

Defining a Custom Event for the Inherited Control

Adding events to classes was covered in Chapter 5. In summary, the process was is as follows:

❑ Declare the event in the control. The event can have any arguments that are appropriate, but they cannot have named arguments, optional arguments, or arguments that are ParamArrays. Here is code for declaring a generic event:

```
Public Event MyEvent(ByVal MyFirstArgument As Integer, _
                     ByVal MySecondArgument As String)
```

❑ Elsewhere in the control's code, implement code to raise the event. The location and circumstances of this code vary depending on the nature of the event, but a typical line that raises the event above looks like this:

```
RaiseEvent MyEvent(nValueForMyFirstArgument, sValueForMySecondArgument)
```

Often this code will be in a method that raises the event. This allows the raising of the event to be done in a uniform fashion. If the event will be raised from several places in your control, doing it with a method is preferred. If the event will only be raised in one place, the code to do it can just be placed in that location.

❑ The form that contains the control can now handle the event. The process for doing that is the same as handling an event for a built-in control.

The following example creates a custom property and a custom event in a control.

Creating a Checked ListBox that Limits the Number of Selected Items

Our next example inherits the built-in CheckedListBox control, and extends its functionality. If you are not familiar with this control, it works just like a normal ListBox control, except that selected items are indicated with a check in a checkbox at the front of the item rather than highlighting the item.

To extend the functionality of this control, we will create a property called MaxItemsSelected. This property will hold a maximum value for the number of items that a user can select. The event that fires when a user checks on an item is then monitored to see if the maximum has already been reached.

If selection of another item would exceed the maximum number, the selection is prevented, and an event is fired to let the consumer form know that the user has tried to exceed the maximum limit. The code that handles the event in the form can then do whatever is appropriate. In our case, we are just putting up a message box to tell the user that no more items can be selected.

We will place DefaultValue and Description attributes on our MaxItemsSelected property to assist in the designer. We will also implement methods for ShouldSerializeMaxItemsSelected and ResetMaxItemsSelected.

Here is the step-by-step construction of our example:

1. Start a new Windows Control Library project in VS.NET. Give it the name LimitedCheckedListBox and name the resulting project module LimitedCheckedListBox.vb, before bringing up the code window for this class.

2. Ensure that the following line is in the declarations at the top of the class (before the line declaring the class):

```
Imports System.ComponentModel
```

This allows us to utilize the attributes that we require from the System.ComponentModel namespace. The class declaration needs to be altered so that it reads as follows:

```
Public Class LimitedCheckedListBox
    Inherits System.Windows.Forms.CheckedListBox
```

3. We are ready to begin adding our own code. First, we need to implement the `MaxSelectedItems` property. We need a module level variable to hold the property's value, so insert this line just under the two lines in step 2:

```
Private  mnMaxSelectedItems As Integer = 4
```

4. Now create the code for the property itself. Insert the following code into the class just above the line that says `End Class`:

```
<DefaultValue(4), _
Description("The maximum number of items allowed to be checked")> _
Public Property MaxSelectedItems() As Integer
  Get
     Return mnMaxSelectedItems
  End Get
  Set(ByVal Value As Integer)
    mnMaxSelectedItems = Value
  End Set
End Property
```

This code sets the default value of the `MaxSelectedItems` property to 4, and sets a description for the property to be shown in the **Properties** window when the property is selected there.

5. Now we need to declare the event that will be fired when a user selects too many items. The event will be named `MaxItemsExceeded`. We will include arguments in our event to indicate the maximum that was exceeded (this is just for illustration – that number could be fetched from the control's properties). Just under the code for step 3, insert the following line:

```
Public Event MaxItemsExceeded(ByVal MaxAllowed As Integer)
```

6. Next, we need to insert code into the event routine that fires when the user clicks on an item. For the `CheckedListBox` base class, this is called the `ItemCheck` property. Open the left-hand dropdown in the code window and select the option **Base Class Events**. Then select the **ItemCheck** event in the right-hand dropdown of the code window. The following code will be inserted to handle the `ItemCheck` event:

```
Private Sub LimitedCheckedListBox_ItemCheck(ByVal sender As Object, _
        ByVal e As System.Windows.Forms.ItemCheckEventArgs) _
        Handles MyBase.ItemCheck

End Sub
```

7. The following code should be added to the `ItemCheck` event to monitor it for too many items:

```
Private Sub LimitedCheckedListBox_ItemCheck(ByVal sender As Object, _
        ByVal e As System.Windows.Forms.ItemCheckEventArgs) _
        Handles MyBase.ItemCheck
```

```
      If (Me.CheckedItems.Count >= mnMaxSelectedItems) _
         And (e.NewValue = CheckState.Checked) Then
         RaiseEvent MaxItemsExceeded(mnMaxSelectedItems)
         e.NewValue = CheckState.Unchecked
      End If
   End Sub
```

8. Now create code to deal with serialization and resetting of the `MaxSelectedItems` property. Insert this code just above the `End Class` line:

```
Public Function ShouldSerializeMaxSelectedItems() As Boolean
   If mnMaxSelectedItems = DefaultMaxSelectedItems() Then
       Return False
   Else
       Return True
   End If
End Function

Public Sub ResetMaxSelectedItems()
   mnMaxSelectedItems = DefaultMaxSelectedItems()
End Sub

Private Function DefaultMaxSelectedItems() As Integer
   ' Get default for MaxSelectedItems.
   ' First need a reference to the attributes collection
   ' for the property.
   Dim attributes As AttributeCollection = _
      TypeDescriptor.GetProperties(Me)("MaxItemsSelected").Attributes

   ' Now need a reference to the DefaultValue attribute, which is
   ' in the collection we just referenced above.
   Dim myAttribute As DefaultValueAttribute = _
       CType(attributes(GetType(DefaultValueAttribute)),
             DefaultValueAttribute)

   ' Finally, return the default value
   Return CInt(myAttribute.Value)
End Function
```

Notice that we are getting the default value for the property from the attributes collection. We have constructed a function to hold the logic that does that. If you expect this function to be called a lot, you might want to use a static variable in the function so that the process of getting the default from the attributes collection is only done once. In that case, the function would look like this:

```
Private Function DefaultMaxSelectedItems() As Integer
   Static nHoldDefault As Integer
   If nHoldDefault <> 0 Then
       Return nHoldDefault
   End If

   ' Get default for MaxSelectedItems.
   ' First need a reference to the attributes collection
   ' for the property.
```

```
    Dim attributes As AttributeCollection = _
        TypeDescriptor.GetProperties(Me)("MaxItemsSelected").Attributes

    ' Now need a reference to the DefaultValue attribute, which is
    ' in the collection we just referenced above.
    Dim myAttribute As DefaultValueAttribute = _
        CType(attributes(GetType(DefaultValueAttribute)),
            DefaultValueAttribute)

    ' Finally, set the default value to a variable to use
    nHoldDefault = myAttribute.Value
    Return CInt(nHoldDefault)
End Function
```

9. Build the project to create a DLL containing the `LimitedCheckedListBox` control.

10. Add a new Windows Application project to the solution (using the **File | Add Project | New Project...** menu) to test the control. Name the new project anything you like. Right-click on the solution (not the project) in the **Solution Explorer**, and select **Properties**. In the dialog box that comes up, change the dropdown under **Single Startup Project** to select your new Windows Application project.

11. In the new Windows Forms project, right-click on the **Windows Forms** tab in the **Toolbox**, and select **Customize Toolbox**. In the dialog box that appears, click the tab for **.NET Framework Components**, and browse to select the `LimitedCheckedListBox.dll` file. Return to the **Customize Toolbox** dialog, check the box and click the **OK** button.

12. Scroll to the bottom of the controls on the **Windows Forms** tab. The `LimitedCheckedListBox` control should be there.

13. The Windows Application will have a `Form1` that was created automatically. Drag a `LimitedCheckedListBox` control onto `Form1`, just as you would a normal list box. Change the `CheckOnClick` event for the `LimitedCheckedListBox` to True (to make testing easier). This property was inherited from the base `CheckedListBox` control.

14. In the **Items** property of the `LimitedCheckedListBox`, click the button to add some items. Insert the following list of colors: Red, Yellow, Green, Brown, Blue, Pink, and Black. At this point, your Windows Application Project should have a `Form1` that looks something like this:

15. Bring up the code window for `Form1`. In the left-hand dropdown above the code window, select **CheckedListBox1** to get to its events. Then, in the right-hand dropdown, select the **MaxItemsExceeded** event. The empty event will look like this:

```
Private Sub LimitedCheckedListBox1_MaxItemsExceeded(
    ByVal MaxAllowed As Integer) _
    Handles LimitedCheckedListBox1.MaxItemsExceeded

End Sub
```

16. Now insert the following code to handle the event:

```
MsgBox("You are attempting to select more than " & _
       CStr(MaxAllowed) & _
       " items. You must uncheck some other item " & _
       " before checking this one.")
```

17. Now start the Windows Application project. Check and uncheck various items in the list box to see that the control works as it is supposed to. You should get a message box whenever you attempt to check more than four items. (Four items is the default maximum, and we have not changed it.) If you uncheck some items, then you can check items again until the maximum is once again exceeded. When finished, close the form to stop execution.

18. Look at the code in the `Window Form Designer` generated code region and examine the properties for `LimitedCheckedListBox1`. Note how there is no line of code that sets `MaxSelectedItems`.

19. Go back to the design mode for `Form1` and select `LimitedCheckedListBox1`. In the **Properties** window, change the `MaxSelectedItems` property to 3.

20. Now, return to the code window and look again at the code that declares the properties for `LimitedCheckedListBox1`. Note that there is now a line of code that sets `MaxSelectedItems` to the value of 3.

21. Go back to the design mode for **Form1** and select **LimitedCheckedListBox1**. In the **Properties** window, right-click the **MaxSelectedItems** property. In the popup menu, select **Reset**. The property will change back to a value of 4, and the line of code that sets the property that you looked at in the step just above will be gone.

These last few steps showed that the `ShouldSerializeMaxSelectedItems` and the `ResetMaxSelectedItems` methods are working as they should.

A Composite UserControl

Sometimes inheriting an existing control is not sufficient to get the functionality you need. The next step up in complexity and flexibility is to combine more than one existing control to become a new control. This is similar to the process of creating a UserControl in VB6, but it is easier to do in VB.NET.

The main steps in the process of creating a UserControl are:

❑ Start a new Windows Control Library project, and assign names to the project and the class representing the control.

❑ The project will contain a design surface that looks a lot like a form. You can drag controls onto this surface just as you would a form. Write logic loading and manipulating the controls as necessary, very much like you would with a form. It is usually particularly important to create resize logic that will reposition and resize the controls on your UserControl when it is resized on the form containing it.

❑ Create properties of the UserControl to expose functionality to a form that will use it. This typically means creating a property to load information into and get information out of the control. Sometimes properties to handle cosmetic elements are also necessary.

❑ Build the control and refer to it in a Windows Application exactly as we did for the inherited controls discussed earlier.

> There is a key difference between this type of development and inheriting a control as we did in the examples above. A **UserControl** will not by default expose the properties of the controls it contains. It will expose the properties of the **UserControl** class plus any custom properties that we give it. If we want properties for contained controls to be exposed, we must explicitly create logic to expose them.

Creating a Composite UserControl

To demonstrate the process of creating a composite UserControl, we will build one that looks like this:

This type of layout is common on wizards and in other user interfaces that require selection from a long list of items. The control has one list box holding a list of items that can be chosen (on the left), and another list box containing the items chosen so far (on the right). Buttons allow items to be moved back and forth.

Loading this control means loading items into the left list box, which we call `lstSource` and refer to as the source list box. Getting selected items back out will involve exposing the items that are selected in the right list box, named `lstTarget` and referred to in our discussion as the target list box.

The buttons in the middle that transfer elements back and forth will be called `btnAdd`, `btnAddAll`, `btnRemove`, and `btnClear`, from top to bottom respectively.

There are lots of ways to handle this kind of interface element in detail. A production-level version would have the following characteristics:

- ❑ Buttons would gray out (disable) when they are not appropriate. For example, `btnAdd` would not be enabled unless an item is selected in `lstSource`.

- ❑ Items that have been transferred from `lstSource` to `lstTarget` would not be shown in `lstSource`. If they are removed from `lstTarget`, they should show in `lstSource` again.

- ❑ Items could be dragged and dropped between the two list boxes.

- ❑ Items could be selected and moved with a single double-click.

Such a production-type version contains too much code to discuss in this chapter. For our example, we are making the following allowances:

- ❑ Buttons do not gray out when they should be unavailable.

- ❑ Items transferred from `lstSource` will not disappear from the list. This means that it will be possible to add duplicate items to `lstTarget`.

- ❑ Drag-and-drop is not supported.

- ❑ No double-clicking is supported.

This leaves us with the following general tasks to make the control work:

- ❑ Create a `UserControl` project.

- ❑ Add the list boxes and buttons to the `UserControl` design surface.

- ❑ Add logic to resize the controls when the `UserControl` changes size.

- ❑ Add logic to transfer elements back and forth between the list boxes when buttons are pressed. (More than one item may be selected for an operation so several items may need to be transferred when a button is pressed.)

- ❑ Expose properties to allow the control to be loaded and selected items to be fetched by the form that contains the control.

How Does Resize Work?

The steps we just outlined are fairly straightforward. Even the resize logic is made easy by using the built-in capabilities of Windows Forms controls. The list boxes can be docked to the sides to help manage their resizing; then only their width needs to be managed. The buttons need to have an area set aside for them and then to be properly positioned within the area, but the sum total of this logic is far less than would be required with a similar control in VB6 (I know – I wrote one just like this in VB6 and getting the resize logic right was one of the more tedious aspects).

Setting a Minimum Size for Controls

Since we need the buttons to always be visible our UserControl needs to have a minimum size. To take care of that, we will add logic in our Resize event to prevent the width and height of the control from dropping below certain minimums.

Exposing Properties of Sub-Controls

Most of our controls contained in our composite control do not need to expose their interfaces to the form that will be using the composite control. The buttons, for example, are completely private to the UserControl – none of their properties or methods need to be exposed.

The easiest way to load up the control is to expose the appropriate properties of the source list box. Similarly, the easiest way to allow access to the selected items is to expose the appropriate properties of the target list box. In this way the UserControl will expose a limited number of their properties.

As an example, we have also implemented a Clear method that clears both list boxes simultaneously. This allows the control to be flushed and reused by a form that consumes it.

Stepping Through the Example

Here is the step-by-step procedure to build our composite UserControl:

1. Start a new Windows Control Library project. Name it **SelectComboControl**.

2. In the class file that is generated, change the name of the class to **SelectCombo**, and change the name of the associated VB module to SelectCombo.vb.

3. Go to the design surface for the control. Drag two list boxes and four buttons onto the control and arrange them so that they look something like this:

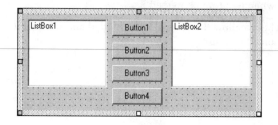

4. Change the names and properties of these controls as follows:

Original Name	New Name	Properties to set for control
Listbox1	lstSource	Dock = Left
Listbox2	lstTarget	Dock = Right
Button1	btnAdd	Text = "Add >"
		Size = 80,24 (80 twips wide by 24 twips high)
Button2	btnAddAll	Text = "Add All >>"
		Size = 80,24 (80 twips wide by 24 twips high)
Button3	btnRemove	Text = "< Remove"
		Size = 80,24 (80 twips wide by 24 twips high)
Button4	btnClear	Text = "<< Clear"
		Size = 80,24 (80 twips wide by 24 twips high)

5. Set up variables to hold the minimum size for the control and the size of the area for the buttons. That code should go just under the class declaration lines, and should look like this:

```
' Make the width of the area for the buttons 100 twips
Dim mnButtonAreaWidth As Integer = 100


' Set minimum height and width for the control
Dim mnMinControlWidth As Integer = 200
Dim mnMinControlHeight As Integer = 200
```

6. Set up resize logic to arrange these controls when the composite control is resized. Go to the code window for the class. Get an empty Resize event by selecting **Base Class Events** in the left-hand dropdown, and then **Resize** in the right-hand box. Place this code in the Resize event:

```
Private Sub SelectCombo_Resize(ByVal sender As Object, _
                              ByVal e As System.EventArgs) _
                              Handles MyBase.Resize
    ' Check for minimum width and height.
    ' Throw exception if new width or height too small
    Dim sError As String
    SError = "Attempted to make SelectCombo user control too small."

    If MyBase.Size.Width < mnMinControlWidth Then
       Dim eComboException As New ApplicationException(sError)
       eComboException.Source = Me.ToString
    End If
    If MyBase.Size.Height < mnMinControlHeight Then
```

```
        Dim eComboException As New ApplicationException(sError)
        eComboException.Source = Me.ToString
    End If

    'Set source and target list boxes to appropriate width. Note that
    'docking the list boxes makes their height the right size automatically.
    Dim nListboxWidth As Integer
    nListboxWidth = CInt(0.5 * (Me.Size.Width - mnButtonAreaWidth))
    lstSource.Size = New Size(nListboxWidth, lstSource.Size.Height)
    lstTarget.Size = New Size(nListboxWidth, lstSource.Size.Height)

    'Now position the buttons between the list boxes.
    Dim nLeftButtonPosition As Integer
    nLeftButtonPosition = nListboxWidth + _
        ((mnButtonAreaWidth - btnAdd.Size.Width) \ 2)
    btnAdd.Location = New Point(nLeftButtonPosition, btnAdd.Location.Y)
    btnAddAll.Location = New Point(nLeftButtonPosition, _
                                  btnAddAll.Location.Y)
    btnRemove.Location = New Point(nLeftButtonPosition, _
                                  btnRemove.Location.Y)
    btnClear.Location = New Point(nLeftButtonPosition, btnClear.Location.Y)
End Sub
```

7. Put logic in the class to transfer items back and forth between the list boxes and clear the target list box when `btnClear` is pressed. This logic is surprisingly short because it involves manipulating the collections of items in the list boxes. Here are the click events for each of the buttons:

```
Private Sub btnAdd_Click(ByVal sender As Object, _
                         ByVal e As System.EventArgs) _
                         Handles btnAdd.Click
    Dim objItem As Object
    For Each objItem In lstSource.SelectedItems
        lstTarget.Items.Add(objItem)
    Next objItem
End Sub

Private Sub btnAddAll_Click(ByVal sender As Object, _
                            ByVal e As System.EventArgs) _
                            Handles btnAddAll.Click
    Dim objItem As Object
    For Each objItem In lstSource.Items
        lstTarget.Items.Add(objItem)
    Next objItem
End Sub

Private Sub btnClear_Click(ByVal sender As Object, _
                           ByVal e As System.EventArgs) _
                           Handles btnClear.Click
    lstTarget.Items.Clear()
End Sub

Private Sub btnRemove_Click(ByVal sender As Object, _
```

```
                              ByVal e As System.EventArgs) _
                              Handles btnRemove.Click
      ' Have to go through the collection in reverse
      ' because we are removing items.
   Dim nIndex As Integer
   For nIndex = lstTarget.SelectedItems.Count - 1 To 0 Step -1
      lstTarget.Items.Remove(lstTarget.SelectedItems(nIndex))
   Next nIndex
End Sub
```

The logic in the `Click` event for `btnRemove` has one oddity to take into account the fact that items are being removed from the collection. We must go through the collection in reverse because if we remove items, the looping enumeration is then messed up and a runtime error will be generated.

8. Create the public properties and methods of the composite control. In our case, we need the following members:

Member	Purpose
`Clear` method	Clears both list boxes of their items
`Add` method	Adds an item to the source list box
`AvailableItem` property	An indexed property to read the items in the source list box
`AvailableCount` property	Exposes the number of items in the source list box
`SelectedItem` property	An indexed property to read the items in the target list box
`SelectedCount` property	Exposes the number of items available in the target list box

The code for these properties and methods is as follows:

```
Public ReadOnly Property SelectedItem(ByVal iIndex As Integer) As Object
   Get
      Return lstTarget.Items(iIndex)
   End Get
End Property

Public ReadOnly Property SelectedCount() As Integer
   Get
      Return lstTarget.Items.Count
   End Get
End Property

Public ReadOnly Property AvailableCount() As Integer
   Get
      Return lstSource.Items.Count
   End Get
```

```
    End Property

    Public Sub Add(ByVal objItem As Object)
      lstSource.Items.Add(objItem)
    End Sub

    Public ReadOnly Property AvailableItem(ByVal iIndex As Integer) As Object
      Get
        Return lstSource.Items(iIndex)
      End Get
    End Property

    Public Sub Clear()
      lstSource.Items.Clear()
      lstTarget.Items.Clear()
    End Sub
```

9. Build the control. Then create a Windows Application project to test it in. As in previous examples, it will be necessary to refer to the control using **Customize Toolbox**. Then it can be dragged from the toolbox, have items added, be resized, and so on. When the project is run, the buttons can be used to transfer items back and forth between the list boxes, and the items in the target list box can be read with the `SelectedItem` property.

Keep in mind that you can also use the techniques for inherited controls in composite controls too. You can create custom events, apply attributes to properties, and create `ShouldSerialize` and `Reset` methods to make properties work better with the designer. (That wasn't necessary here because most of our properties were `ReadOnly`.)

Building a Control From Scratch

The last technique to discuss is to derive a control from the `Control` class. Such a control gets a fair amount of base functionality from the `Control` class. We saw a partial list of properties and methods of the `Control` class earlier in the chapter. These properties arrange for the control to automatically have visual elements such as background and foreground colors, fonts, window size, and so on.

However, such a control does not automatically use any of that information to actually display anything. A control derived from the `Control` class must implement its own logic for painting the control's visual representation. In all but the most trivial examples, such a control also needs to implement its own properties and methods to gain the functionality it needs.

The techniques we used in the earlier example for default values and the `ShouldSerialize` and `Reset` methods all work fine with controls created from the `Control` class, so we will not go over that capability again. Instead, we will concentrate on the capability that is very different in the `Control` class – the logic to paint the control to the screen.

Painting a Custom Control with GDI+

The base functionality used to paint visual elements for a custom control is in the part of .NET called GDI+. A complete explanation of GDI+ is too complex for this chapter, but here is an overview of some of the main concepts needed.

GDI+

GDI+ is an updated version of the old GDI (Graphics Device Interface) functions provided by the Windows API. GDI+ provides a new API for graphics functions, which then takes advantage of the Windows graphics library.

The GDI+ functions can be found in the `System.Drawing` namespace. Some of the classes and members in this namespace will look familiar if you have used the Win32 GDI functions. Classes are available for such items as pens, brushes, and rectangles. Naturally, the `System.Drawing` namespace makes these capabilities much easier to use than the equivalent API functions.

The `System.Drawing` namespace enables you to manipulate bitmaps and indeed utilize various structures for dealing with graphics such as `Point`, `Size`, `Color`, and `Rectangle`. In addition to this there are a number of classes available to developers, including:

- ❑ `Cursors` – contains the various cursors that you would need to set in your application, such as an hourglass or an insertion `I-beam` cursor

- ❑ `Font` – includes capabilities like font rotation

- ❑ `Graphics` – contains methods to perform routine drawing constructs, including lines, curves, ellipses, and so on.

- ❑ `Icon`, `Pen`, and `Brush`

- ❑ The `Pen` and `Brush` classes

The System.Drawing Namespace

The `System.Drawing` namespace includes many classes and it also includes some subsidiary namespaces. We will be using one of those in our example: `System.Drawing.Text`. First, let's look at important classes in `System.Drawing`.

The System.Drawing.Graphics Class

Many of the important drawing functions are members of the `System.Drawing.Graphics` class. Methods like `DrawArc`, `DrawEllipse`, and `DrawIcon` have self-evident actions. There are over forty methods that provide drawing related functions in the class.

Many drawing members require one or more points as arguments. A point is a structure in the `System.Drawing` namespace. It has X and Y values for horizontal and vertical positions, respectively. When a variable number of points are needed, an array of points may be used as an argument. The next example below uses points.

The `System.Drawing.Graphics` class cannot be directly instantiated. That is, you can't just enter code like this to get an instance of the `Graphics` class:

```
Dim grfGraphics As New System.Drawing.Graphics()
```

That's because the constructor for the class is private. It is only supposed to be manipulated by objects that can set the Graphics class up for themselves. There are several ways to instantiate a Graphics class, but the one most commonly used in the creation of Windows controls is to get a reference to a graphics object for a window out of the arguments in a Paint event. That technique is used in our example further down. For now, to understand the capabilities of GDI+ a little better, let's do a quick example on a standard Windows Form.

Using GDI+ Capabilities in a Windows Form

Here is an example of a form that uses the System.Drawing.Graphics class to draw some graphic elements on the form surface. The example code runs in the Paint event for the form, and draws an ellipse, an icon (which it gets from the form itself), and two triangles, one in outline and one filled.

Start a Windows Application project in VB.NET. On the Form1 that is automatically created for the project, place the following code in the Paint event for the form:

```
Dim grfGraphics As System.Drawing.Graphics
grfGraphics = e.Graphics

' Need a pen for the drawing. We'll make it violet.
Dim penDrawingPen As New _
    System.Drawing.Pen(System.Drawing.Color.BlueViolet)

' Draw an ellipse and an icon on the form
grfGraphics.DrawEllipse(penDrawingPen, 30, 150, 30, 60)
grfGraphics.DrawIcon(Me.Icon, 90, 20)

' Draw a triangle on the form.
' First have to define an array of points.
Dim pntPoint(3) As System.Drawing.Point

pntPoint(0).X = 150
pntPoint(0).Y = 150

pntPoint(1).X = 150
pntPoint(1).Y = 200

pntPoint(2).X = 50
pntPoint(2).Y = 120

grfGraphics.DrawPolygon(penDrawingPen, pntPoint)

' Do a filled triangle.
' First need a brush to specify how it is filled.
Dim bshBrush As System.Drawing.Brush
bshBrush = New SolidBrush(Color.Blue)

' Now relocate the points for the triangle.
' We'll just move it 100 twips to the right.
pntPoint(0).X += 100
pntPoint(1).X += 100
pntPoint(2).X += 100
```

```
    grfGraphics.FillPolygon(bshBrush, pntPoint)
```

Then start the program and, when it comes up, the form will look something like this:

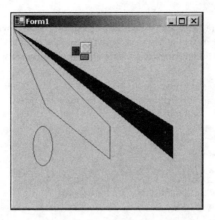

As you can see, the graphics functions are not difficult to use. The hardest part is figuring out how to initialize the objects needed, such as the graphics object itself, and the necessary brushes and pens.

As an example, we will create a custom control that functions as a label, but allows the text to be rendered at any angle.

First, create a new Windows Control Library. The created module will have a class in it named UserControl1. Rename the default class to TextRotator and change the Inherits statement like so:

```
Public Class TextRotator
    Inherits System.Windows.Forms.Control
```

Our TextRotator control needs to know the angle to rotate the text. So we need a module-level variable and a property procedure to support a RotationAngle property. First of all, place a declaration right under the line that causes the class to inherit the System. Windows.Forms.Control class.

```
Private msngRotationAngle As Single = 0
```

Then insert the following property procedure in the class to create the RotationAngle property:

```
Public Property RotationAngle() As Single
  Get
    Return msngRotationAngle
  End Get
  Set(ByVal Value As Single)
    If (msngRotationAngle >= -180) And (msngRotationAngle <= 180) Then
      msngRotationAngle = Value
      Me.Invalidate() ' Forces a repaint of the window
      ' This is a method of the Control class
    Else
```

```
            ' Should raise an error here
        End If
    End Set
End Property
```

Now, place code to handle the `Paint` event, that is, to draw the text when the control repaints. We will use some code similar to that in the section on drawing with the GDI+ (above). To provide a place for this code, we override the `OnPaint` method of the `Control` base class:

```
Protected Overrides Sub OnPaint(_
    ByVal e As System.Windows.Forms.PaintEventArgs)
    ' Declare a brush, a font, and a graphics
    ' object to use.
    Dim bshBrush As Brush
    Dim fntFont As Font

    ' We can get the graphic object directly from
    ' the PaintEventArgs parameter of the event.
    Dim grfGraphics As Graphics = e.Graphics

    ' Fix up the brush and the font.
    bshBrush = New SolidBrush(Me.ForeColor)
    fntFont = Me.Font

    ' Need to see how far to shift the drawing of the text
    ' so that it becomes visible. This calculation can be very
    ' complex, but we will simplify it for the example by making
    ' the starting point the center of the window for the control.
    ' (Code below assumes Option Strict is Off).
    Dim ShiftHorizontal As Single
    Dim ShiftVertical As Single
    ShiftHorizontal = Me.Size.Width * 0.5
    ShiftVertical = Me.Size.Height * 0.5

    ' Now draw some rotated text.
    grfGraphics.RotateTransform(RotationAngle)
    grfGraphics.DrawString(Me.Text, fntFont, bshBrush, _
                        ShiftHorizontal, ShiftVertical)
    grfGraphics.ResetTransform()
End Sub
```

We also need to repaint the control when the text is changed in it, so we need to place code in the `OnTextChanged` event of the base class. Get an empty `OnTextChanged` event and place the following code in it:

```
Private Sub TextRotator_TextChanged(ByVal sender As Object, _
                        ByVal e As System.EventArgs) _
                        Handles MyBase.TextChanged
    Me.Invalidate()
End Sub
```

The `Invalidate` method of the control forces a complete redraw of the control. As we discuss shortly, this type of logic should, ideally, be placed in all of the events that affect the rendering of the control, such as a font change event.

Build the control library. Then, start a new Windows Application project and right-click on the Windows Forms tab in the Toolbox. In the Customize Toolbox dialog, first make sure that the .NET Components tab is selected, and then use the Browse button to point to the deployed DLL for the control library. The Toolbox should now contain the `TextRotator` control.

Drag the `TextRotator` control onto the form in the Windows Application project. Notice that its property window includes a `RotationAngle` property. Set that to 20, for 20 degrees. Set the Text property to anything you like. When you run the project, the `TextRotator` control will display the string in its `Text` property at a 20 degree angle. Here's a sample screen:

This control can now be manipulated in code just like any other control.

A Full Implementation of this Control

For simplicity, we have left off many things that should be done for a production level control. You'll note that the `RotationAngle` property notes a place to declare an error if the rotation angle is out of bounds. Also, there are many events that should force a repaint of the control. We included one of those above (the `TextChanged` event), but there are a number of others, such as the `FontChanged` event.

The painting logic needs additional refinement also. Getting all the GDI+ positioning and painting logic correct is very fussy programming.

This need to take care of details means that doing a control this way takes more work than the earlier techniques. On a more positive note, however, this technique offers the ultimate in flexibility, and is sometimes required to get the functionality that a custom control needs.

Extending the TreeView Control

In this last section, we'll take a quick look at how we can develop our own user control that extends the `TreeView` control. This new control, called `FileTreeView`, will display a list of the folders and files contained within a given drive or directory. This will not only demonstrate how to extend one of the more complex controls supplied with the .NET Framework, but will also show us how to navigate the file system.

Create a new Windows Control Library project called `FileTreeView`. This project will contain all of the classes needed to support the new `TreeView`. Create a new User Control named `FileTreeView` and change the `Inherits` directive so that the new control extends `System.Windows.Forms.TreeView`, rather than `UserControl`:

```
Public Class FileTreeView
    Inherits System.Windows.Forms.TreeView
```

To the existing solution, create a new Windows Application project called `FileTreeHost`. To the new `Form1`, add a `FileTreeView` control:

You'll notice that the control looks identical to a normal `TreeView` – that's exactly what we want. Now we can turn our attention to adding our new functionality to the control.

Scanning Files and Directories

The file system can be manipulated using classes in the `System.IO` namespace. Specifically, we can use `System.IO.FileInfo` to manipulate files and `System.IO.DirectoryInfo` to manipulate folders.

To work with a folder we need to create an instance of `DirectoryInfo`, passing in the complete path of the folder. We can retrieve the name using the `Name` property, the full name of the folder (that is, the path to the folder, including the names of the parent folders) with the `FullName` property and – importantly for our example – we can retrieve a list of subdirectories using the `GetDirectories` method, and a list of files using the `GetFiles` method.

The first thing we need is a way of telling the control what folder we want to load as the root folder of the control. We'll do this by adding a property called `RootFolderName`. This property will be a simple string property, and we'll make it available for editing in the Properties window by using the `Browsable`, `Category` and `DesignerSerializationVisibility` attributes (for which you'll need to import `System.ComponentModel`):

First off, add this code:

```
Imports System.ComponentModel
Imports System.IO


Public Class FileTreeView
    Inherits System.Windows.Forms.TreeView


    Private _rootFoldername As String
```

When we're in design mode, we do not want to scan the folders. Scanning the folders will take time and as we can't actually manipulate the tree from the Designer there's no point in loading it. We'll use the protected DesignMode property of the control to detect if the control is running inside the Designer or inside the target application. If it's in the Designer, we'll add a node that contains simple text:

```
<Browsable(True), _
DesignerSerializationVisibility(DesignerSerializationVisibility.Visible), _
Category("Behavior")> _
Property RootFolderName() As String
  Get
    Return _rootFoldername
  End Get
  Set(ByVal Value As String)
    ' clear the nodes...
    Nodes.Clear()
    _rootFoldername = Value
    ' are we design mode?
    If Me.DesignMode = True Then
      Nodes.Add(Value)
    Else
      ' anything?
      If Value <> "" Then
          ' More to come here shortly
      End If
    End If
  End Set
End Property
```

If you build the project now, you'll be able to set the root folder. (When testing, select a folder that doesn't contain a vast number of files. I'm going to use C:\Program Files\Microsoft Office.)

You'll be able to see the root node in the tree:

A good design pattern to use with the `TreeView` control is to create a new node class that extends `System.Windows.Forms.TreeNode` for every type of node that the tree should display. In our case we need to: `FolderTreeNode` and `FileTreeNode`.

Create a new class called `FolderTreeNode`. Make it extend `TreeNode`, add a namespace import reference to `System.IO` and also add a private field to hold a `DirectoryInfo` instance.

```
Imports System.IO

Public Class FolderTreeNode
  Inherits TreeNode

    Private _folder As DirectoryInfo
```

We'll also need a read-only property to return the folder:

```
    Public ReadOnly Property Folder() As DirectoryInfo
      Get
        Return _folder
      End Get
    End Property
```

In the constructor for the class we'll scan all of the subfolders of the folder and create new `FolderTreeNode` objects for each subfolder. This will set up a recursion. Each time we create a new `FolderTreeNode`, that new instance will be able to find all of the subfolders and create further new instances of `FolderTreeNode` objects. The result is that by creating the top-level item, we'll automatically get all of the child, sub-children, sub-sub-children, and so on folders:

```
Public Sub New(ByVal folder As DirectoryInfo)

    ' set the name...
    _folder = folder
    Text = _folder.Name

    ' scan the subfolders...
    Dim subFolder As DirectoryInfo
    For Each subFolder In folder.GetDirectories()
      Nodes.Add(New FolderTreeNode(subFolder))
    Next
```

As well as adding all of the folders, we also need to add the files. For each file contained within the folder we'll create new `FileTreeNode` objects and add them to the current node.

```
    ' scan the files...
    Dim file As FileInfo
    For Each file In folder.GetFiles()
      Nodes.Add(New FileTreeNode(file))
    Next

End Sub
```

`FileTreeNode` is just as simple as `FolderTreeNode`:

```
Imports System.IO

Public Class FileTreeNode
  Inherits TreeNode

  ' members...
  Private _file As FileInfo

  Public Sub New(ByVal file As FileInfo)
    _file = file
    Text = file.Name
  End Sub

End Class
```

Add the following code to `FileTreeView` to link everything up:

```
        If Value <> "" Then
          ' create the new root node...
          Dim rootNode As New FolderTreeNode(New DirectoryInfo(Value))
```

```
        rootNode.Text = rootNode.Folder.FullName
        Nodes.Add(rootNode)
    End If
```

Now if you run the project you'll see all of the subfolders and files contained within the folder you initially specified.

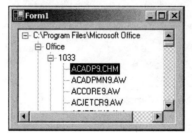

Running Programs

As the last part of this control demonstration, I'll quickly show you how to open any of the files by double-clicking on a `FileTreeNode`.

When you double-click on the control, `TreeView` will fire its `DoubleClick` event. We can intercept this by overriding the `OnDoubleClick` method. If this happens, we want to look what node was selected and, if it's a `FileTreeNode`, we call the `Open` method. (We'll build `Open` in a moment.)

```
    Protected Overrides Sub OnDoubleClick(ByVal e As System.EventArgs)
        ' what kind of node do we have?
        If SelectedNode.GetType() Is GetType(FileTreeNode) Then
            CType(SelectedNode, FileTreeNode).Open()
        End If
    End Sub
```

To open a document in .NET, we can use the `Start` method on `System.Diagnostics.Process`. This method will look up the associated application and automatically start it. For example, if we open a `.doc` file, Microsoft Word will be started. If we open a `.html` file, Internet Explorer will be opened, and so on.

Add this method to `FileTreeNode`:

```
    Public Sub Open()
        System.Diagnostics.Process.Start(_file.FullName)
    End Sub
```

Now if you run the application you'll be able to open files displayed on the tree with a double-click.

Summary

In this chapter we discussed the creation of custom controls in VB.NET, and illustrated how much easier it is to do this in comparison with previous versions of Visual Basic – the advent of full inheritance capabilities in VB.NET means that it is a lot easier for developers to utilize functionality simply by inheriting from the namespaces built into the .NET Framework. It is probably best to start by overriding these existing controls in order to learn the basics of creating properties and coordinating them with the designer, building controls and testing them, and so on. These techniques can then be extended by the creation of composite controls, as we have illustrated with worked examples within this chapter.

We saw how to create controls by:

❑ Inheriting from another control

❑ Building a composite control

❑ Writing a control from scratch, based on the `Control` class, although this took more work than the other two methods

We rounded off the chapter by looking at the type of practical use custom controls can be put to – we create a custom version of a `TreeView` control, and reused much of the functionality provided by the original control.

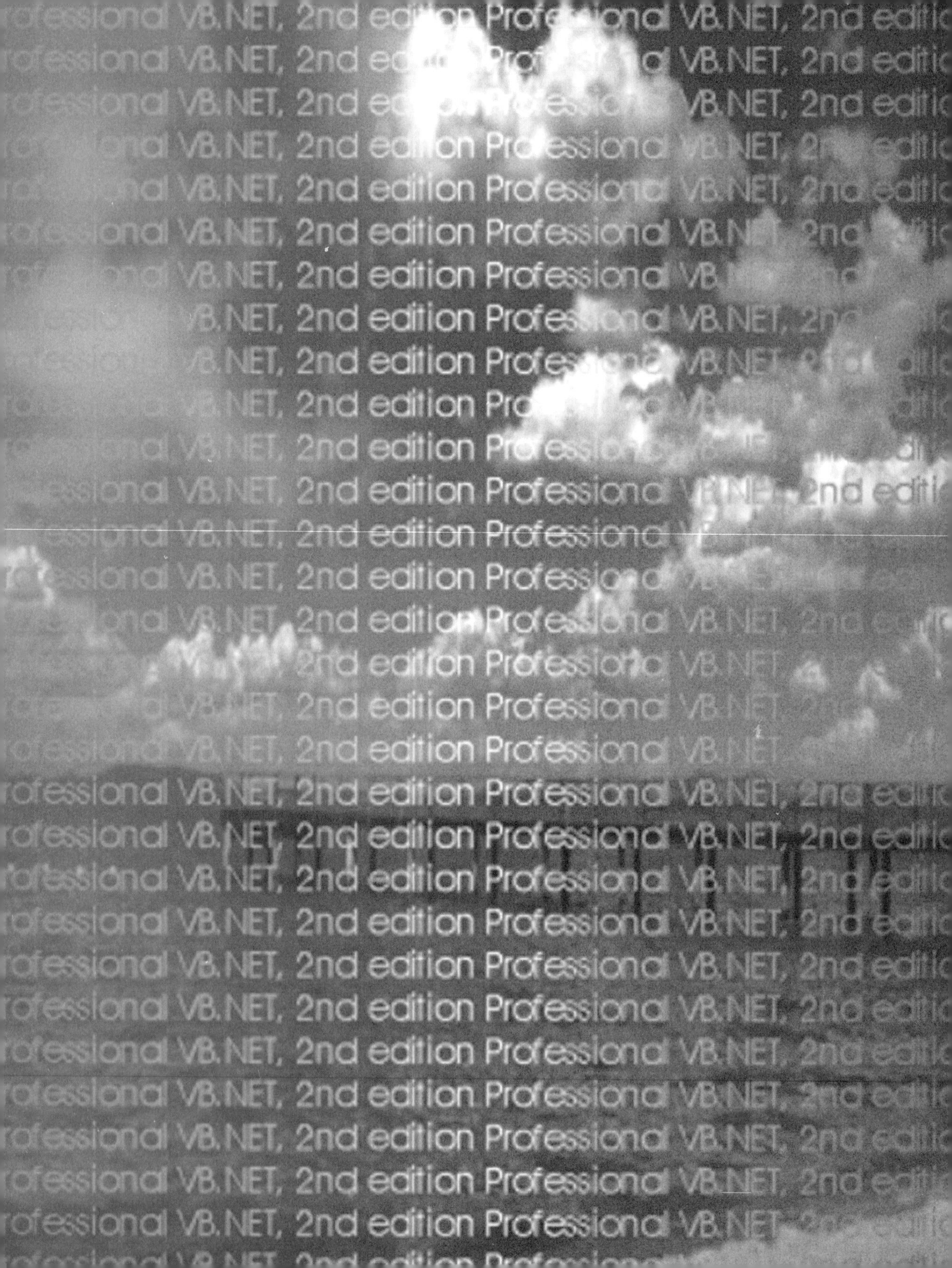
Professional VB.NET, 2nd edition

14

Web Forms

As a Visual Basic developer, the chances are that you are developing more and more applications that deal with the World Wide Web. Visual Basic programmers gravitated naturally to Microsoft's Active Server Pages (ASP) technology as a means to develop web applications. This is because of the similarity between programming VB and VBScript.

Unfortunately, ASP did not have a visual metaphor for creating web interfaces like the VB form (Visual InterDev was, at best, a poor first attempt by Microsoft). With .NET, Microsoft has bridged that gap by merging Visual InterDev within Visual Basic and has provided VB programmers with a visual ability for generating web interfaces, using **Web Forms**.

> **This chapter explores Web Forms and how you can benefit from their use but it is only meant to whet your appetite. If you want to learn more, you should read** *Professional ASP.NET 1.0 Special Edition* **(Wrox Press, ISBN 1861007035).**

Web Forms are part of the new **ASP.NET** technology. They allow us to use one of several different languages to quickly create web pages that combine visual HTML forms with server-side code. In a manner very similar to a VB Windows Form – which has a visual element (the form and its controls) and the code behind it – a Web Form also has an HTML form, that is visible within a browser, as well as server-side code encapsulated within a code class file.

A Web Form in Action

The easiest way to learn about Web Forms is to see them in action, and then take them apart to see how they are constructed. Let's look at a very simple Web Form – the quintessential Hello World example.

Setting Up the Environment

To be able to create ASP.NET applications and Web Forms you will need to be running **Internet Information Services (IIS)**. In addition, Microsoft strongly recommends that the server computer be formatted with NTFS (NT File System) rather than FAT (File Allocation Table). This results in better performance and substantially greater security, as well as offering additional options for source code control.

The HelloWorld Web Form

Create a new ASP.NET Web Application project in VS.NET. Name the project HelloWorld and make sure that you select the default http://localhost/ as your location for the project:

Click **OK** and you will be presented with a new solution. By default, VS.NET has created a new Web Form for you, called WebForm1.aspx (.aspx is the new extension for ASP.NET files).

When you clicked **OK**, a few things happened. Apart from creating a new folder in your Visual Studio Projects directory, VS.NET also established a web application on the target web server (in this case, the local web server, localhost). On the web server, VS.NET:

❑   Creates a duplicate physical folder under the \inetpub\wwwroot directory, named after your project

❑   Marks the folder as an IIS application, allowing script to be executed

❑ Creates a FrontPage Web if you have FrontPage Server Extensions installed – allowing you to author the web via FrontPage

You can treat the Web Form in front of you as a normal VB form, dropping controls on to it by dragging them from the toolbox. For now, drag a `Label` control from the toolbox and drop it onto the top left of the form. Use the **Properties** windows to set its caption (its `Text` property) to "Hello World". Your screen will look like this:

For this example, that's all we need to do. We can now execute our application. Normally, VS.NET executes applications in a special debug mode that allows you to monitor the progress of your application. For now, we simply want to execute our application in release mode, or production mode so change the **Solution Configurations** dropdown menu on your toolbar from **Debug** to **Release**. Click on the **Start** icon on the toolbar, or select **Debug | Start** from the menu. If all goes well, your browser will open the `WebForm1.aspx` file and you will see the following:

Right-click on the browser and select **View Source** to see what the output produced by our solution looks like. You will see that it is pure HTML, generated at run time by our `aspx` file (tidied up a bit here):

```
<!DOCTYPE HTML PUBLIC "-//W3C//DTD HTML 4.0 Transitional//EN">
<html>
  <head>
    <title>WebForm1</title>
    <meta name="GENERATOR" content="Microsoft Visual Studio.NET 7.0">
    <meta name="CODE_LANGUAGE" content="Visual Basic 7.0">
    <meta name="vs_defaultClientScript" content="JavaScript">
    <meta name="vs_targetSchema"
          content="http://schemas.microsoft.com/intellisense/ie5">
  </head>
  <body ms_positioning="GridLayout">
    <form name="Form1" method="post" action="WebForm1.aspx" id="Form1">
     <input type="hidden" name="__VIEWSTATE"
            value="dDwtMTU3ODAzNTQ4MDs7PnAT1yEqaPCDokleAQXc9nDhpJ7t" />
      <span id="Label1" style="width:91px;Z-INDEX: 101; LEFT: 18px;
                               POSITION: absolute; TOP: 22px">
        Hello World
      </span>
    </form>
  </body>
</html>
```

Notice that there is an HTML form within our page, even though we did not ask for one. We'll look at this more closely later on in this chapter. Our label is included within the span tag:

```
<span id="Label1" style="width:91px;Z-INDEX: 101; LEFT: 18px;
                         POSITION: absolute; TOP: 22px">
  Hello World
</span>
```

The span tag acts as a container to hold our label and its style attribute defines its location and size. Let's return to our VS.NET solution to see what makes this Web Form tick. Web Forms are very similar to Windows Forms, and we'll see how much alike they are with this next example.

Within our application, we have a single Web Form, WebForm1.aspx. Let's create a new one with a little more to it.

From the menu, select Project | Add Web Form. In the Add New Item dialog box that pops up, make sure you have selected Web Form and that its name is WebForm2.aspx. Click Open and you will have a new Web Form in your solution. Add a Label to this new form and also add a Button control to the form underneath the Label. Widen the width of the label by clicking on it and dragging its resizing handles.

From the Properties window, set the ID property of the Label (which defines its name) to be lblText. Leave its Text property as Label. Then click on the Button and set its ID property to btnSubmit. Click once on the button and press the *Enter* key, or right-click on the button and select View Code. You will be taken to the code behind the form. Wait a minute, though. This isn't a Windows Form, so how can buttons have code behind them?

In ASP.NET, controls *do* have code behind them. As you can see, we have a subroutine called btnSubmit_Click that will be executed when the button is clicked. This code is executed – on the server, not the client browser – whenever the form is submitted to the server. We'll see more details later on. For now, enter the following as the code for the click event:

```
Private Sub btnSubmit_Click(ByVal sender As System.Object, _
                          ByVal e As System.EventArgs) _
                          Handles btnSubmit.Click
    lblText.Text = "Hello World"
End Sub
```

Notice how IntelliSense works when you type in this line. Although ASP programmers had this functionality with InterDev, VS.NET's IntelliSense provides more HTML elements for use in your code.

Close the code window and return back to the design mode for the form. Change the Text property of the button to Submit and we are ready to view this form in action.

If you try to use the **Start** button to run the project, it will open up WebForm1.aspx since that is the starting form for the project. In order to view the second Web Form, set it to be the starting form by right-clicking on its name in the Solution Explorer and selecting **Set As Start Page** from the popup menu. Then press the **Start** button.

The new Web Form – WebForm2.aspx – opens up in the browser, displaying a label and a button. The label has the default caption of **Label**. Click on the **Submit** button and the text **Hello World** will appear within the label:

When you clicked on the submit button, the code behind the button was executed – just like a Windows Form.

The Anatomy of a Web Form

Web Forms bridge the gap between VB programming and traditional ASP programming. By offering a visual technique to drag and drop controls onto a page, and code for events behind the controls, Web Forms bring a very familiar metaphor to web development.

A Web Form is made up of two components: the visual elements that you can see in the design view and the code behind the controls and the page. The visual elements form the template for the presentation of the web page in the end user's browser. The code is executed on the server when the page loads and in response to other events that you have coded for.

If you try to create a Web Form by hand, using a text editor, you will probably end up creating both these components within the same physical file (this is fine as long as it has an .aspx extension). With VS.NET, however, the visual elements are defined in the .aspx file, while the code elements are defined in the .vb file that accompanies the Web Form.

The following figure shows the two components that make up our WebForm2.aspx Web Form within our example Web Application:

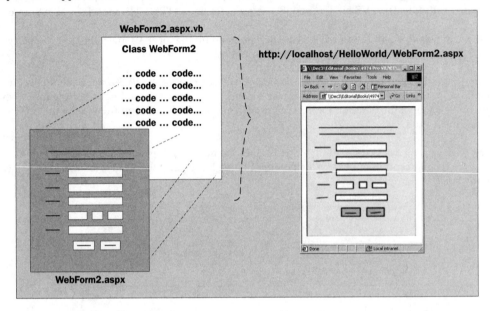

By dividing the components into separate files and, therefore, within the VS.NET environment, into separate views, Web Forms provide a very familiar environment for the VB programmer. With traditional VB, you first paint the form by dragging and dropping controls, and then write code for the events that the controls expose. When developing Web Forms, you first create the look of your web page by dragging and dropping controls onto the page, and then you write code for the events exposed by the controls.

The Template for Presentation

The .aspx file forms the User Interface component of the Web Form and serves as a template for its presentation in the browser. This .aspx file is the **Page** and it contains HTML markup and Web Forms specific elements. You can drag and drop several types of controls onto a Web Form, including:

- ❑ HTML controls
- ❑ Web Form controls
- ❑ Validation controls
- ❑ Data related controls
- ❑ COM and .NET components registered on your machine
- ❑ Items from your clipboard

We'll look at these different kinds of controls later on in this chapter.

The Code Component

If you code with VS.NET, the `.vb` file that accompanies the `.aspx` file forms the code component of your Web Form. To view this file, click on the **Show All Files** icon in the toolbar along the top of the **Solution Explorer**. Then expand the **WebForm2.aspx** node, to reveal **WebForm2.aspx.vb**. This `.vb` file contains a single `Public Class` named after your Web Form. In the `WebForm2.aspx` example, the `WebForm2.aspx.vb` code component has the following initial structure:

```
Public Class WebForm2
    Inherits System.Web.UI.Page
    Protected WithEvents lblText As System.Web.UI.WebControls.Label
    Protected WithEvents btnSubmit As System.Web.UI.WebControls.Button
```

Our `WebForm2` class inherits from the `System.Web.UI.Page` class. This allows the code within our Web Form to access the built-in `Request`, `Response`, `Session`, `Application`, and `Server` objects.

Every control that you place on the form and, consequently, in the `.aspx` file, is represented within the `.vb` file as an event code if it exposes an event that can be handled via server-side code. This is very much reminiscent of the way that VB code-behind forms work.

In our case, we have the `Click` event of our `btnSubmit` button represented by this fragment of code:

```
Private Sub btnSubmit_Click(ByVal sender As System.Object, _
                    ByVal e As System.EventArgs) _
                    Handles btnSubmit.Click
    lblText.Text = "Hello World"
End Sub
```

Before going on to look at the processing flow of ASP.NET pages, let's take a look at another example that will drive home the point that Web Forms make web development uncannily like VB development.

A More Complex Example

Suppose that we wish to display a calendar for the current month in a web page. Generating a dynamic calendar for a traditional ASP page involves writing at least 50 to 100 lines of code. You have to create a table to host the calendar, figure out the month and the year, and output the days of the week header. Then you need to figure out what day the current month begins with and how many days there are in the month. Finally, you can output the days of the month starting with 1 and going on till the end of the month. When you output the days, you need to make sure that you are placing each week horizontally in one row (a `<TR>` tag) of a table. When you reach the end of one week, you need to close the row (a `</TR>` tag) and begin a new one. Finally, when you are done with the days of the month, you probably need to output a few blank days to make the table appear even and look good on the screen. All this takes up a lot of ASP code, especially if you want the calendar to be generated dynamically.

There was an alternative before Web Forms. You could simply use a client-side ActiveX control – a Calendar control in your web page. However, this had its own problems.

ActiveX controls are not supported by all browsers – in fact, only IE on Windows really supports them. The Calendar control may not exist on your user's computer, so you have to worry about distributing it. Also, an ActiveX control will only work on the Windows platform, so your web site users on Macs, for example, will not be able to view the page properly.

> **Web Forms bring the ease of development with an ActiveX control to the world of ASP and web development but they output standard HTML on demand.**

In our HelloWorld project, add a new Web Form. By default, this form will be called `WebForm3.aspx`; accept the default name. Then, open up the Web Form in design view. From your toolbox, look for the `Calendar` control under the **Web Forms** group. Double-click or drag it onto the form. That's it, you now have a fully functional calendar in your web page – albeit a very plain looking one:

Before we run this Web Form, let's make it look a little better. Using the **Properties** window, set the following properties like so:

Property	Setting
ID	myCal
BackColor	A light yellow (#FFFFC0)
BorderColor	Black
BorderStyle	Solid
BorderWidth	1px
DayHeaderStyle, BackColor	Light orange (#FFC080)
DayHeaderStyle, BorderColor	Dark red (#C00000)
DayHeaderStyle, BorderStyle	Inset

Property	Setting
DayHeaderStyle, BorderWidth	1px
DayHeaderStyle, Font, Bold	True
DayNameFormat	Short
Font, Name	Verdana
Font, Size	X-Small
NextPrevFormat	ShortMonth
OtherMonthDayStyle, ForeColor	Silver
SelectedDayStyle, BackColor	Dark blue (#0000C0)
SelectedDayStyle, ForeColor	White

Alternatively, you can select one of the predetermined formats available for the calendar. Click on the Calendar control and, under the Properties window, click on the link marked AutoFormat. Select an option from the AutoFormat window to inherit the same look for your Calendar control.

When you are done, repeat the process we did earlier – set this page to be the start up page and then run the project.

All you did was drag and drop a calendar control onto a web page in your design environment and set a few properties to make it look different. In your browser, you should have a web page that looks like this:

This is not a static calendar painted on the browser. It is fully interactive. Click on any day and it becomes highlighted in blue. Click on another day and the selection changes. Click on the other months listed at the top of the calendar and the month view automatically changes.

Our Web Form contains the Calendar control that is being executed at run time.

The `Calendar` control is a Web Form server control that is outputting plain HTML to be viewed in the browser (IE and Netscape version 4.0 or above). And we developed it using VB.NET, just like developing and deploying a VB.NET Windows Form.

The Processing Flow of ASP.NET Web Forms

Traditional web development, especially ASP development, has always involved generating an HTML page and adding script code to it. An ASP page in traditional ASP (ASP versions prior to ASP.NET) was therefore a plain text file separated into blocks of ASP code and HTML code. When a browser requested an ASP page from the web server, the ASP engine kicked in and parsed the page, before its output was sent back to the browser. At run time, the ASP engine would interpret the ASP code one line at a time. It would execute each line that contained ASP script code, and would output unchanged every line that contained plain HTML text. The traditional ASP web development model was therefore one of HTML pages with code added to them.

The diagram below shows a simplistic view of how the processing flow takes place in traditional ASP:

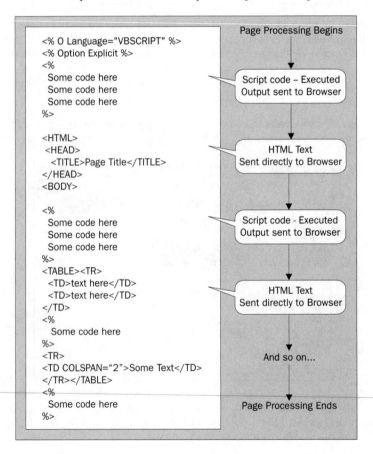

Web Forms turn this paradigm of web development upside down. With Web Forms, every page is actually an executable program. The page's execution results in HTML text being outputted. We can therefore focus on developing with controls and code elements that output HTML, instead of worrying about interspersing code around HTML text.

So, what exactly is a Web Form? Well, a VB.NET Web Form *is* an ASP.NET page. As we've already seen, Web Forms (or ASP.NET pages) are text files with an `.aspx` extension. On a .NET server (or indeed any IIS server where the .NET Framework has been installed), when a browser requests an `.aspx` file, the ASP.NET runtime parses and compiles the page. This process is similar to the way that the ASP engine in ASP 3.0 and below parsed the page. The main difference is that the ASP.NET runtime compiles the page into a .NET class file. The code is compiled and not interpreted line by line each time the page is executed using a script engine. This results in improved runtime performance since the web page code is compiled and stored in cache for reuse.

A typical Web Application project (that is, a project that contains Web Forms) developed in VB.NET will have at least one `.aspx` file. If you incorporate controls and code on the form, the code itself is placed in the `.vb` file. That is, if your Web Form is called `WebForm1`, you will end up with `WebForm1.aspx` and `WebForm1.aspx.vb`. The `.aspx` file corresponds to the traditional ASP `.asp` file and contains primarily HTML code that defines your web page. The `.aspx.vb` file contains the code-behind-the-web page VB code.

In addition, a Web Application project usually has a `Global.asax` and a `Web.config` file. The `Global.asax` file is the .NET counterpart of the `Global.asa` file used in ASP web applications. It contains code for event handlers that fire when the Application and the Session begin and end. A complete description of this file and its uses is available in *Professional ASP.NET 1.0 Special Edition* (Wrox Press, ISBN 1861007035).

The `Web.config` file is new to .NET. It is an XML formatted file that stores the configuration settings for your web application. This includes features such as debug mode and compiling options.

These files are actually located in two separate places. The files need to be executed on the web server and, therefore, their primary location is the web server. However, VS.NET also keeps a copy in its local cache. VS.NET synchronizes the files between its local cache and the server. When you work with a file in VS.NET and then save it, VS.NET automatically updates both the local cache as well as the file on the web server. Some local cache files serve a temporary purpose (they may be intermediary files, for example), and these are not written to the server.

When you use VS.NET to deploy your Web Application, it uses the standard model for VB applications – your project is compiled and the resulting files are deployed. In the case of a Web Application, all of the code files (but not the `.aspx` files) for each Web Form are compiled into a DLL along with all other executable files in your project. The DLL is then deployed to the web server as a single unit, without the source code. When the browser requests the `.aspx` file, the DLL file and the `.aspx` file are compiled into a new class and then run.

Let's take our HelloWorld example at the point at which we added the second Web Form to our application and ran it. We had the following files in our project:

- ❑ `WebForm2.aspx`
- ❑ `WebForm2.aspx.vb`
- ❑ `Global.asax`

- ❑   `Global.asax.vb`
- ❑   `Web.config`

Remember, we did not write any code for the `Global.asax` file and its code file `Global.asax.vb`. VS.NET automatically creates them for us with placeholders for code.

When we deploy this project, by pressing the **Start** button, the following files are copied to the Web Server with no change or compilation:

- ❑   `WebForm2.aspx`
- ❑   `Global.asax`

When we deploy this project, the following files are compiled into a single DLL called `HelloWorld.dll`:

- ❑   `WebForm2.asax.vb`
- ❑   `Global.asax.vb`

At this time, our web server contains the following three files for this Web Application:

- ❑   `WebForm2.aspx`
- ❑   `Global.asax`
- ❑   `HelloWorld.dll`

When we request the `.aspx` file in our browser, ASP.NET dynamically generates a temporary `.cls` class file out of the contents of the `.aspx` file. This temporary `.cls` file is then compiled into a temporary `.dll` file. This temporary `.dll` file inherits from the `HelloWorld.dll` file and, therefore, has access to all of the code within `HelloWorld.dll`. The temporary `.dll` file finally invokes the `HelloWorld.dll` file that contains the compiled code from the `WebForm2.vb` file. This results in the HTML that is rendered by the browser.

Remember, the .NET Framework exposes a number of classes from which .NET applications derive functionality and definitions. The root class includes the `System` class that provides system level functionality. Web Forms derive their look-and-feel functionality, or UI elements, from the `System.Web.UI` class. Each `.aspx` file represents one web page in a Web Application. When a browser requests an `.aspx` file for the very first time, ASP.NET generates the temporary `.cls` class file dynamically for the page by inheriting from the `System.Web.UI.Page` namespace. This class exposes the `Request`, `Response`, `Server`, `Application`, and `Session` objects, properties, and methods that classic ASP programmers are familiar with.

The above steps may seem like a lot of work. However, these steps are performed only once for each page. When the class is dynamically generated, it is also cached in a special directory so that subsequent requests for the same page are executed much faster. Once a page has been compiled into a class, it is cached until the next time that you make a change to the page. Therefore, as long as a page's code does not change, the page executes using the class file.

The following diagram shows how the processing flow takes place in ASP.NET for a Web Form:

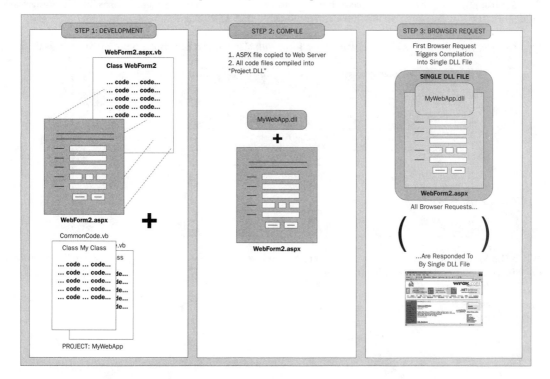

The Controls Available in Web Forms

Web Form controls are different to controls used in VB.NET Windows Forms. This is because Web Form controls operate within the ASP.NET page framework. There are four kinds of controls for use in Web Forms:

- ❏ HTML Server Controls
- ❏ ASP.NET Server Controls
- ❏ Validation Controls
- ❏ User Controls

Before we take a look at these types, let's examine the idea behind server-side controls.

The Concept of Server-Side Controls

Like in traditional ASP, you can use the <% and the %> tags to separate ASP code from plain HTML code. However, if you rely on these tags to delimit ASP code, you will be responsible for maintaining state when the page is submitted back to the server.

This means that, if you want to create an interactive web application, you will be responsible for obtaining the data from the Request object, passing it back to the browser when the page returns, and keeping track of it. This task – maintaining state – has been a big worry for ASP programmers up till now.

For example, consider the case where you have a form with a single text box and a button that submits the form:

When the form is submitted, assume that it returns back with the value of the text box intact. To be able to do this, you will need to code a form in this manner:

```
<html>
<head>
   <title>A Form</title>
</head>

<body>
  <form action="testForm.asp">
    What is your name?
    <input type="text" name="nm" value="<%= Request("nm") %>" size="40"
           maxlength="40"><br>
    <input type="submit" name="cmd" value=" Submit ">
  </form>
</body>
</html>
```

The programmer is responsible for maintaining the value of the text entered in the text box and returning it back to the browser:

```
value="<%= Request("nm") %>"
```

We do this by obtaining the value of the text box (named "nm") from the Request object, and using that value as the value attribute of the text box. The first time around, since the Request object does not have a value named nm, it will be blank and so the user will see a blank text box. When the user enters a value and presses the submit button, the same form is returned back but, this time, with the value of the text box filled in.

With Web Forms, Microsoft has introduced a new concept that takes care of managing state automatically without having to write any incremental code. Web Forms allow you to indicate that a particular form control needs to automatically maintain state when submitted by the user.

You do this by using the `runat="server"` attribute for the form controls as well as the form.

This one line change makes your form controls behave like **server-side controls** rather than just client-side controls. To take our example from above, we can change the code to the following:

```
<html>
<head>
  <title>A Form</title>
</head>

<body>
  <form action="testForm.aspx" runat="server">
    What is your name?
    <asp:textbox runat="server" name="nm"
                 size="40" maxlength="40" /><br>
    <input type="submit" name="cmd" value=" Submit ">
  </form>
</body>
</html>
```

Save the file with an `.aspx` extension (to make sure that the ASP.NET runtime handles its processing correctly) and we will get automatic state maintenance without writing any further code. Notice the differences. First, it is an `.aspx` file. Second, the FORM tag itself has an indication `runat="server"`:

```
<form action="testForm.aspx" runat="server">
```

This causes the ASP.NET runtime to create additional code to handle the state. This is done via a hidden form field that is appended to your form. If you chose to view the source of your file in the browser, this is what you would see in place of the form tag code:

```
<form name="_ctl0" method="post" action="testForm.aspx" id="_ctl0">
<input type="hidden" name="__VIEWSTATE"
       value="dDwyMTA1NTI4MTE3Ozs+6qY4WCGFNZ2KiocirrqUZX1z7Lo=" />
```

The ASP.NET runtime has added additional code, including a form NAME and an ID, as well as a hidden field called __VIEWSTATE. ASP.NET uses this hidden field to transfer state information between the browser and the web server. It compresses the information needed into a cryptic field value. All controls on the web page that need their state information maintained are automatically tagged within this single hidden field value.

Notice too that, instead of using a simple INPUT tag for our text box, we used the special `asp:textbox` tag. This is required to make sure that the text box behaves like a server-side control.

HTML Server Controls

HTML Server Controls are HTML elements exposed to the server by using the `runat="server"` attribute. In VS.NET, HTML Server Controls are included within the **Web Forms** group of the **Toolbox**. The regular HTML Form Controls (TextBox, CheckBox, Listbox, and so on) are available within the HTML group.

HTML Server Controls are identical to regular HTML Form controls in look, feel, and behavior, except that the presence of the `runat="server"` enables you to program them within the Web Forms page framework.

HTML Server Controls are available for the HTML elements most commonly used on a web page to make it interactive – such as the `FORM` tag, the HTML `<input>` elements (`TextBox`, `CheckBox`, `Submit` button), `ListBox` (`select`), `Table`, and `Image`. These pre-defined HTML Server Controls share the basic properties of the generic controls and, in addition, each control typically provides its own set of properties and its own event.

In the VS.NET environment, you can create a regular HTML control by clicking on the **HTML** group within your toolbox and then dragging a **Text Field** control on to the Web Form. Then give it the name `txtFirst_Name` by changing its `ID` property. This will result in a regular HTML control with something like the following code:

```
<input style="Z-INDEX: 102; LEFT: 221px; POSITION: absolute; TOP: 249px"
       type="text">
```

To convert a regular HTML control to an HTML Server Control (and vice versa), simply right-click on the control in the design mode and select (or uncheck) the menu option **Run As Server Control**. If you select it, you will see the following:

```
<input style="Z-INDEX: 102; LEFT: 221px; POSITION: absolute; TOP: 249px"
       type="text"
       id="Text1" name="Text1" runat="server">
```

Notice the difference – the final attribute that denotes that this is a server control.

HTML controls are created from classes in the .NET Framework class library's `System.Web.UI.HtmlControls` namespace. Regular HTML controls are parsed and rendered simply as HTML elements. For example, a regular `Text Field` HTML control will be parsed and rendered as an HTML text box.

By converting HTML controls to HTML Server Controls, you gain the ability to:

❑ Write code for events generated on the control that are executed on the server-side, rather than on the client-side. For example, you can respond with server-side code to the `Click` event of a `Button`.

❑ Write code for events in client script. Since they are displayed as standard HTML form controls, they retain the ability to handle client-side script as always.

❑ Automatically maintain the values of the control on a round-trip when the browser submits the page to the server.

❑ Bind the value of the control to a field, property, method, or expression in your server-side code.

HTML Server Controls are included for backward compatibility with existing ASP applications. They make it easier to convert traditional ASP applications to ASP.NET (Web Forms) applications.

However, everything that can be done with HTML Server Controls can be done – with more programmatic control – by using the new ASP.NET Server Controls.

ASP.NET Server Controls

HTML controls are just wrappers around regular HTML tags and do not offer any programmatic advantage in terms of controlling their look and feel. ASP.NET Server Controls, on the other hand, do not necessarily map to a single HTML element and provide a much richer UI output. We have already seen this with our Calendar ASP.NET Server Control.

VB.NET ships with over twenty ASP.NET Server Controls, ranging from simple controls like TextBox, Button, and Label, to more complex Server Controls such as the AdRotator, Calendar, and DataGrid. These controls can all be found in the System.Web.UI.WebControls namespace.

When you drag and drop each of these controls onto your Web Form, they display their own distinctive UI. For example, a TextBox may simply be visible as a text box, but the Calendar control or the DataGrid control will appear as a tabular construct.

Behind the scenes, these controls are prefixed with the asp: tag. For example, in WebForm1.aspx, when we placed a Label on the page and set its **Text** property to **Hello World**, our Label uses the following code to define it:

```
<asp:label id="Label1"
           style="Z-INDEX: 101; LEFT: 18px; POSITION: absolute; TOP: 22px"
           runat="server" width="91px">
   Hello World
</asp:label>
```

You can view the HTML source of any control by right-clicking anywhere on the page and selecting **View HTML Source** from the context menu. Similarly, when we dragged a Button onto the form, instead of obtaining the normal HTML INPUT TYPE="SUBMIT" text, we get the following:

```
<asp:Button id=cmdSubmit runat="server" Text="Button"></asp:Button>
```

Notice that the code does not represent a regular HTML control, but rather, an ASP.NET control. The attributes refer to the ASP.NET control's properties. At run time, the ASP.NET control is rendered on the web page by using plain HTML, which depends on the browser type as well as the settings on the control. For example, the button above may be rendered on the target browser either as an INPUT TYPE="SUBMIT" HTML element, or as a <BUTTON> tag, depending on the browser type.

The following ASP Server Controls ship with VB.NET and are available for use in a Web Form, and are found in the **Web Forms** section of the **Toolbox**:

Control	Purpose
Label	Displays non-editable text
TextBox	Displays editable text in a box

Table continued on following page

Control	Purpose
Button	Displays a button, usually used to carry out an action
LinkButton	Behaves like a button, but appears like a hyperlink
ImageButton	Displays a button with an image rather than with text
HyperLink	Creates a hyperlink for navigation
DropDownList	Presents a list in a dropdown combo box
ListBox	Presents a list of items in a scrollable box
DataGrid	Displays information (usually from a database) in a tabular format with rows and columns
DataList	Displays information from a database, very similar to the Repeater control
Repeater	Displays information from a database using HTML elements that you specify, repeating the display once for each record
CheckBox	Displays a single checkbox allowing users to check on or off
CheckBoxList	Displays a set of checkboxes as a group; useful when you want to bind it to data from a database
RadioButton	Displays a single radio button
RadioButtonList	Displays a group of radio buttons where only one radio button from the group can be selected
Image	Displays an image
Panel	Creates a bounding box on the Web Form that acts as a container for other controls
Calendar	Displays an interactive calendar
AdRotator	Displays a sequence of images, either in pre-determined or random order
Table	Creates a table

Validation Controls

Validation Controls are different from HTML or ASP.NET Server Controls in that they do not posses a visual identity. Their purpose is to provide easy client-side or server-side validation for other controls. For example, you may have a text box that you need the user to fill in, and you may need to only accept certain entries. For example, it could be a text box that requires a date in a certain format, like DD/MM/YY. Validation Controls allow you to generate validation scripts (client- or server-side) with a few clicks.

To use Validation Controls, you first attach the Validation Control to an input control and then set its parameters, so as to test for things like:

- ❑ Data entry in a required field
- ❑ Specific values or patterns of characters
- ❑ Entries between ranges

VB.NET ships with the following Validation Controls, also in the Web Forms section of the Toolbox:

Control	Purpose
RequiredFieldValidator	Ensures that the user does not leave a field blank
CompareValidator	Compares the user's entry against another value – a constant, the property of another control, or even a database value
RangeValidator	Makes sure that the user's entry is between the lower and upper boundary values specified
RegularExpressionValidator	Checks to make sure that the entry matches a pattern defined by the developer
CustomValidator	Checks the user's entry against validation logic that you code

The easiest way to understand the power and capability of Validation Controls is to see them in action.

Add a new Web Form to your HelloWorld solution (by default, it will be called WebForm4.aspx. Drag a TextBox control on to the Web Form and change its ID property to txtName. Then drag a RequiredFieldValidator control from your toolbox onto the Web Form, right next to the TextBox. Then, add a Button control onto the form, below the TextBox, and set its Text property to Submit.

Now, let's set the properties for the Validation Control. Change its ID to rfvTxtName, to signify to ourselves that it is going to be bound to the TextBox we just created. Then click on the ControlToValidate property and select the txtName TextBox from the dropdown list that appears. By doing so, we have bound the Validation Control to the txtName TextBox ASP.NET Server Control. Finally, change the ErrorMessage property to the text that we want to display if the user is in error: "Required Field. Please enter your name."

When you are done, your screen should look like:

Set the `WebForm4.aspx` as the start up page and run the project. You should see the page in the browser with just a textbox and a button visible. Do not type anything into the text box and just click the button to simulate a user submitting the form without entering a required field: our form submission is not accepted and we get a red error message reminding us that the field is required:

If you check the code behind this page, you will find that the Validation Controls write a lot of client-side JavaScript code to handle the data validation. However, we did not have to worry about it – we just dragged and dropped the Validation Control. The other Validation Controls also work in the same way: drop a Validation Control, attach it to a Server Control, and set the validation parameters.

User Controls

The final set of controls available is the User Controls. Similar to traditional VB User Controls, these are Web Forms that you create and then use within other Web Forms. This allows you to build visual components for your Web Forms – useful when creating toolbars, template UI elements, and so on.

User controls are covered in Chapter 15.

Events in Web Forms

Events in the world of Windows Forms are triggered by one of three different circumstances. An event can occur when the user makes an action: moves the mouse, uses the keyboard, and so on. An event can occur when the system makes an action: loads a page, reacts to another process or application, and so on. Finally, an event can occur without the engagement of either users or system, simply being caused by the passage of time.

In the world of the Web, however, the very stateless nature of the HTTP protocol forces web pages to have different event handling strategies. Consider the following:

❑ A browser requests a web page

❑ The web server serves the page by processing its code in a linear fashion

❑ The output of the server processing is sent back to the browser as HTML

❑ The browser renders the page on the screen based on the HTML output

❑ At this point, the page no longer exists on the server

❑ The user takes some action on the web page

❑ If the server has to react to this action, the page has to be posted back to the web server before the web server can react to the action

❑ This process continues over and over...

Web Forms expose events to the web developer, allowing you to write code for the events. This code is different from client-side script. The code for the event is evaluated and executed on the server.

If a Web Form can trigger an event for the mouse activity on a button, for instance, in such a way that the server can take action on the event, then the form will need to be posted every time the user moves the mouse. This is not practical and because of this, Web Forms expose very limited events for different controls (usually only the Click event).

The Web Form's Lifecycle

VB developers trying to create Web Forms face a few shocks, the first of which is the concept of a Web Form's lifecycle. Imagine developing a traditional VB form that goes through the following event code each time you display it on screen:

1. Form_Initialize: No problem.

2. Form_Load: No problem.

3. Form_QueryUnload: Huh?

4. Form_Unload: What?

5. Form_Terminate: No kidding?

This is the VB6 form's equivalent of the ASP.NET Web Form's cycle. This would be nonsensical for a VB6 form because it would load itself and then unload immediately afterwards.

In the case of Web Forms, when a browser requests a page, the Web Form is first loaded, then its events are handled, and finally it is discarded or unloaded from memory before the HTML output is sent to the browser. So, a Web Form goes through the cycle of load and unload each time that a browser makes a request for it.

Let's take a look at the stages in the life of a Web Form on the web server before its output is sent to the browser:

❑ **Configuration** – This is very similar to the Form_Initalize and the Form_Load stages of a VB6 form. This is the first stage of a Web Form's lifecycle on the web server. During this stage, the page and control state is restored and then the page's Page_Load event is raised.

The Page_Load event is built into every page. Since it occurs in the first stage of a Web Form's processing, this event is a useful tool for the web developer. The Page_Load event can be used to modify control properties, set up data binding or database access, and restore information from previously saved values before the page is visible on the browser.

❑ **Event handling** – If this is the first time that the browser has requested the page, no further events need to be handled. However, if this page is called in response to a form event, then the corresponding event handler in the page is called during this stage. Code within the event handler is then executed.

❑ **Cleanup** – This is the final stage in the page's lifecycle. It is the equivalent of the `Form_Unload` and `Form_Terminate` events of traditional VB. Remember, in the case of a Web Form, at the end of its processing, the page is discarded. The cleanup stage handles the destruction by closing files, database connections, by invoking the `Page_Unload` event. Like the `Page_Load` event, the `Page_Unload` event is built into every page. It can be used to clean up – delete variables and arrays from memory, remove objects from memory, close database connections, and so on.

Event Categories

Events in Web Forms can be classified into different categories:

❑ Intrinsic events

❑ Client-side events versus server-side events

❑ Postback versus non-postback events

❑ Bubbled events

❑ Application and session events

Intrinsic Events

Most Web Form controls support a click-type event. This is necessitated by the fact that, in order for an event to be processed, the Web Form needs to be posted back to the server. Some Web Form controls also support an `OnChange` event that is raised when the control's value changes.

Client-Side Versus Server-Side Events

ASP.NET Server Controls only support server-side events. However, the HTML elements that are outputted by these Server Controls support client-side events themselves. For example, the `MouseOver` event is used to change the source of an `Image` control and display a different image when the user rolls the mouse over the control. If you decide to use the ASP.NET `ImageButton` Server Control, you will be able to write code for the `ImageButton`'s `Click` event, which will be processed on the server. However, you can also write client-side code for the `MouseOver` event of the `ImageButton` to handle the rollover. If you write code for both the client- and server-side event, only the server-side event will be processed.

Postback Versus Non-Postback Events

Server-side event processing happens when the form is posted back to the server. By default, these click-type events are postback events. The `OnChange` event is raised when a control's value changes. For example, if you write code for the `OnChange` event of a `TextBox`, when the user changes its value, the event is not fired immediately. Instead, these changes are cached by the control until the next time that a post occurs. When the Web Form is posted back to the server, all the pending events are raised and processed. On the server-side, all of the `OnChange` events – that were cached and raised *before* the `Click` event that posted the form – are processed before the posting `Click` event.

Client-side events are automatically processed in the client browser without making a round trip to the browser. So, for example, validation client-side scripts do not need a postback to the server.

Bubbled Events

ASP.NET server controls such as the `Repeater`, `DataList`, and `DataGrid` controls can contain child controls that themselves raise events. For example, each row in a `DataGrid` control can contain one or more buttons. Events from the nested controls are **bubbled**, that is, they're sent to the container. The container in turn raises a generic event called `ItemCommand` with parameters that allow you to discover which individual control raised the original event. By responding to this single event, you can avoid having to write individual event handlers for child controls.

Application and Session Events

Continuing the tradition of ASP application and session events, VB.NET Web Forms support the same high-level events. These events are not specific to a single page but, rather, work at the user and/or web application level. These events include the `ApplicationStart` and `ApplicationEnd` events for the application level scope, and the `SessionStart` and `SessionEnd` events for the session (individual user) level scope. You can write code for these special events within the `Global.asax` file.

Web Forms Versus ASP

It is very easy to think of Web Forms (ASP.NET) as the next version of ASP – that Microsoft has released a new version of ASP and is just calling it ASP.NET to equate it to the other .NET initiatives. ASP 3.0, for instance, was basically the previous version (ASP 2.0) but with new functionality, performance improvements, and one new object. This is most definitely not the case with ASP.NET and ASP 3.0.

While Web Forms *are* the next version of ASP (ASP ceases to exist as a separate offering from Microsoft with the introduction of ASP.NET, though it will continue to be supported), it is not just an update. It is vastly different.

Let's consider the differences between ASP.NET and ASP 3.0:

❑ ASP was an interpreted application. This leads to poor performance, as compared to executable Windows desktop applications.

Web Forms are compiled into class `.dll` files and are invoked as 'applications' on the web server. This leads to vastly improved performance. The performance drop you see when you test your application for the very first time is, in fact, indicative of this change. ASP.NET checks to see if the source code for the page has changed in any way. If it has (like in your testing mode), it recompiles the page and saves the compiled output for all subsequent requests.

❑ In ASP, you are entirely responsible for managing view state and control state via code. If you want a form control to display the value entered by the user before the form is posted, you have to obtain the value from the `Request` object and use it as part of the `VALUE` attribute of the control. The onus is entirely on the web developer.

Web Forms provide automatic maintenance of view state and control state. By simply using server-side controls, you automatically obtain the ability to retain state for the control during server round trips.

❑ With ASP, you can only write code with scripting languages such as VBScript and JScript. These languages do not support typed variables or early binding on objects.

Web Forms support VB.NET code as well as C# code. You can use a coding language that supports typed variables (Dim x As Integer) as well as early binding on objects (Dim objRS As ADODB.Recordset). This results in additional benefits, like IntelliSense making it easier to assign property values and invoke methods on objects.

❑ With ASP, you are responsible for generating client-side validation code. When you have forms with large numbers of controls that need validation, this can be a cumbersome task – even if you have created custom routines that can simply be copy-and-pasted. You still need to write the code yourself to invoke these routines.

Web Forms provide a very robust, drag and drop, validation control feature. Not only can you drag and drop your way to setting up validation parameters – required fields, types of accepted input, range of accepted input, and so on – Web Forms also write the client-side validation routines for you. If you have used COM components with ASP applications, you know that, every time you need to change and update the COM component on the web server, you need to release the component from the web server (or COM+) before you can overwrite it with the new component. ASP programmers are used to bringing down the web server or stopping and starting the COM+ services to allow such changes.

With Web Forms, because of just-in-time compiling to native code, components can be updated without having to stop and start the web services.

❑ ASP configuration settings are stored in the metabase (meta information database) of the IIS web server. This makes it difficult to port the ASP application from one server to another. The metabase configuration settings have to be set up individually on the new web server each time you move the ASP application.

With Web Forms, all configuration settings are stored in an XML-formatted text file that can be easily moved from one web application directory to another. The XML-formatted Config.web file allows you to create portable configuration settings.

❑ Debugging of ASP applications has always been a daunting task. The only surefire way to debug ASP applications running on a web server is to pepper the ASP page with response.write statements, to output the values of variables in your code. This is similar to peppering a VB form with Debug.Print statements.

Web Forms provide an automatic tracing capability. When you set the Trace and the TraceMode properties of a Web Form, ASP.NET automatically maintains a log of actions performed, and their timestamp. When the page is rendered on the browser, ASP.NET automatically appends an HTML table listing all of the trace activity. You can also write your own tracing code to be appended to this log.

Transferring Control Among Web Forms

Earlier in this chapter, we mentioned that VB developers would get a shock when they try to create Web Forms because the familiar metaphor of VB development is turned upside down in the world of Web Form development. Well, get ready for shock number two!

In a traditional VB application, suppose you have two forms, Form1 and Form2. If you want the application to transfer control from Form1 (which is currently open on the screen) to Form2, all it takes is this code:

```
Load Form2
Form2.show
```

Of the two lines above, the first line is optional. You can use the first line if you plan to set some properties for Form2's controls, or invoke a subroutine within Form2 before showing it.

How do you do the same with a Web Form? Can you 'show' WebForm2 from WebForm1? The answer will surprise you. No, you can't. Not in the way that you can with traditional VB.

There are two ways to transfer control from one Web Form to another:

❑ **Hyperlink** – In WebForm1, you can create a hyperlink to allow the user to navigate to WebForm2 by using a Hyperlink HTML tag (<A>). If you wish, you can pass additional arguments to the second form when navigating to it, by using the Query String (the portion of the URL that appears after the question mark in a browser's address bar). This technique of transferring control is very fast, since it transfers control to the second page directly without having to post the first page and process its events/contents.

❑ **Redirecting** – The second technique is to use the server-side Response.Redirect method to transfer control to a second page. The Response.Redirect issues an Object Moved command to the browser, forcing the browser to request the second page via a client-side request. Another similar technique is to use the Server.Transfer method to transfer control to a second page. The Server.Transfer method directly transfers control and session state to the second page without making a client round trip.

A Final Example

We'll wrap up this chapter by building a small Web Forms application. Our application is a *Loan Slicer* application. Consider the scenario – you have a current home mortgage loan and you pay a certain sum of money as your monthly payment towards the loan. However, by simply making one additional payment per year towards the principal repayment, you can drastically reduce the life of the loan and pay it off faster. This is loan slicing. We want to build a Web Form application that will allow an end user to figure out not only what the monthly payment for a mortgage loan will be (that would be a wimpy little application), but also to see how the loan gets sliced off if the user wishes to pay an additional sum each month towards the principal.

We begin by asking the user to enter the principal loan amount, the interest rate per annum, and the number of years for which the loan will be taken.

We then calculate the monthly payment due for the loan, and display a table of how the payments slowly eat their way through the loan till the loan is fully paid off. If the user wishes to view the 'loan slicing' effect, he can specify a new monthly payment value higher than the original amount, and see how quickly the loan gets paid off.

We'll build this loan slicer using the US mortgage loan formula.

So, let's begin. Start VS.NET and select **New Project**. Select the project type to be ASP.NET Web Application and give it the name **LoanSlicer**. Ensure that the target server is localhost (your own computer).

VS.NET creates a default Web Form, `WebForm1.aspx`. Before we start adding controls to the form, right-click on the Web Form and select **Properties** to view the **DOCUMENT Property Pages** window. Then change the **Page Layout** to **FlowLayout**:

Now click **OK**. FlowLayout enables you to treat the Web Form as if it were a word processing document. You can insert text and paragraph marks, and the result is translated into HTML. Controls are placed where the cursor currently is in the text.

Drag a `Label` control onto this form and position it at the top left (you can move it around by inserting or deleting paragraph marks, just as you would move an inserted object in a Microsoft Word file). Set its:

❑   `ID` property to be `lblTitle`

❑   `Text` property to be `"Acme Loan Slicer"`

❑   `Font, Size` property to `Large`

❑   `Font, Bold` property to `True`

❑   `Font, Name` property to `Verdana`

Press *Enter* to the right of the `Label` to create a new paragraph. Then – in sequence – insert a `Label` control, a `TextBox` control, and a `RequiredFieldValidator` control. Your Web Form should look like this:

Set the properties for these controls as follows:

Control	Property	Value
Label	ID	Leave this unchanged.
	Text	Principal Amount ($):
	Font, Bold	True
	Font, Name	Verdana
TextBox	ID	txtPrincipal
RequiredFieldValidator	ID	rfvPrincipal
	ControlToValidate	txtPrincipal
	ErrorMessage	(Required. Please try again.)

Insert two more rows of Label and TextBox and RequiredFieldValidator controls, placing each set underneath the one above. To move to the next line without creating a new paragraph, use *Shift+Enter* to create a soft return (
 tag).

Set the properties for the second row of controls as follows:

Control	Property	Value
Label	ID	Leave this unchanged.
	Text	Interest Rate (%):
	Font, Bold	True
	Font, Name	Verdana
TextBox	ID	txtInterest
RequiredFieldValidator	ID	rfvInterest
	ControlToValidate	txtInterest
	ErrorMessage	(Required. Please try again.)

Set the properties for the third row of controls like so:

Control	Property	Value
Label	ID	Leave this unchanged.
	Text	Period (Years):
	Font, Bold	True
	Font, Name	Verdana
TextBox	ID	txtYears
RequiredFieldValidator	ID	rfvYears
	ControlToValidate	txtYears
	ErrorMessage	(Required. Please try again.)

Underneath these three sets of controls, place another row with a **Label** and a **TextBox** control, with these properties:

Control	Property	Value
Label	ID	Leave this unchanged.
	Text	Loan Slicer Monthly Amount ($):
	Font, Bold	True
	Font, Name	Verdana
TextBox	ID	txtSlicerAmount

Underneath these four rows of controls, place a `Button` with these properties:

Control	Property	Value
Button	ID	btnCalculate
	Text	Calculate

Next, place a `Label` control beneath the `Button` and set its properties:

Control	Property	Value
Label	ID	lblMonthlyPayment
	Text	Monthly Payment:
	Font, Bold	True

Control	Property	Value
	Font, Name	Verdana
	BackColor	Light blue (#C0FFFF)

And, finally, underneath the label, place a `DataGrid` control. For the `DataGrid` control, first set the following minimal but very important properties:

Control	Property	Value
DataGrid	ID	dgValues
	Visible	False

To set the appearance of the `DataGrid` control, instead of setting individual properties, click the **AutoFormat** link at the bottom of the **Properties** window. From the list, experiment with the look you want. The screenshot below shows **Professional 1**:

Before we go any further, let's test out this Web Form. We have not placed any code in it and so it shouldn't do much, but at least we can make sure that it looks fine. Before you proceed, make sure that you select **Release** from the **Solution Configurations** dropdown box on your toolbar. This will ensure that you run in final release mode, rather than in **Debug** mode.

Click the **Start** button to run the project. You should get the Web Form displayed in a browser. The `DataGrid` and the `RequiredFieldValidator` controls should be invisible. Go ahead and click on the `Calculate` button without entering any values in any of the text boxes. You should get the red error messages next to each text box, as shown here:

497

We are all set. Now let's proceed to write code for the form.

Calculating the monthly payment for a mortgage loan is a little convoluted to explain, but very simple to code. Here is the formula:

$$MP = P * (MI / 1 - (1 + MI)^{(-N)})$$

Assuming the following (where * is multiply, / is divide, and ^ is 'raise to the power of'):

Variable Name	Represents
MP	Monthly payment
P	Principal loan amount (the amount borrowed)
MI	Monthly interest rate in decimals (that is, the annual interest rate divided by 1200)
N	Number of months in the loan

This is the formula that we will be using for calculating our monthly payment. Once we calculate the monthly payment, it is simple to construct a grid containing the following information:

A	B	C	D	E	F	G	H	I
Month / Year	Loan Amount	Original Payment	Interest Paid	Principal Paid	Balance Loan	New Payment	New Principal Paid	New Balance Loan

Let's begin by adding code to our Calculate button. Double-click on the button to add a call to a subroutine we will be building as part of the next step:

```
Private Sub btnCalculate_Click(ByVal sender As System.Object, _
                               ByVal e As System.EventArgs) _
                               Handles btnCalculate.Click
    CalculateValues()
End Sub
```

At the bottom of the WebForm1 class, before the End Class statement, add this CalculateValues subroutine:

```
Private Sub CalculateValues()
  Dim dblPrincipal As Double
  Dim dblInterest As Double
  Dim lngYears As Long
  Dim dblMonthlyPayment As Double
  Dim dblMonthlyInterest As Double
  Dim lngN As Long

  ' -- Get our values from the text boxes
  dblPrincipal = Me.txtPrincipal.Text
  dblInterest = Me.txtInterest.Text
  lngyears = Me.txtYears.Text
  ' -- Calculated intermediary values
  dblMonthlyInterest = (dblInterest / (12 * 100))
  lngN = lngYears * 12
  ' -- Monthly Payment calculation:
  dblMonthlyPayment = (dblPrincipal * (dblMonthlyInterest / (1 - (1 + _
      dblMonthlyInterest) ^ (-lngN))))

  ' -- Assign the value to the Blue label
  Me.lblMonthlyPayment.Text = "Monthly Payment: " & _
      format(dblMonthlyPayment, "$#,##0.00")

End Sub
```

After declaring all the variables we will be using, we first obtain our values from the text boxes on the form:

```
dblPrincipal = Me.txtPrincipal.Text
dblInterest = Me.txtInterest.Text
lngyears = Me.txtYears.Text
```

We then calculate the intermediary variable values:

```
dblMonthlyInterest = (dblInterest / (12 * 100))
lngN = lngYears * 12
```

Finally, we are ready to calculate the monthly payment:

```
dblMonthlyPayment = (dblPrincipal * (dblMonthlyInterest / (1 - (1 + _
    dblMonthlyInterest) ^ (-lngN))))
```

We store this in the variable `dblMonthlyPayment`. We output this value as the `Text` property of the blue label on the screen, performing some formatting so that it is presented as a dollar amount:

```
Me.lblMonthlyPayment.Text = "Monthly Payment: " & _
    format(dblMonthlyPayment, "$#,##0.00")
```

That was the easy part. Let's test it again by running our application. Enter the following values: **Principal =** **100000**, **Interest Rate = 6.75**, **Years = 10**. You should get the output shown in the following figure:

Now comes the more difficult part – populating the `DataGrid` with our values.

Before we look at the code, let's understand what we are trying to do. We need to display a `DataGrid` full of rows and columns that represent our loan payouts. We want to display the current loan amount, the monthly payment, the interest paid, the principal paid, and the balance loan amount for every month of every year in the loan period.

In addition, if the user has entered a **Loan Slicer Monthly Amount** – an amount that he/she is willing to pay that is larger than the monthly payment due – we need to also figure out how the new monthly payment will pay off the loan faster – and therefore 'slice' it.

Normally, a `DataGrid` is bound to a database. We don't have a database in this scenario. We could dump the values into a database and have the `DataGrid` then read the database. But that would be very inefficient. A better way would be to create our own 'database' on the fly. We can do that by creating a `DataTable` object and populating it with values. Our `DataGrid` can be bound to a `DataView` object at run time. To do so, we need to write code as follows:

```
OurDataGridObject.DataSource = OurDataViewObject
```

A `DataView` object can be created and initialized by an existing `DataTable` object. Therefore, we can create a `DataView` object by using a `DataTable` object, as follows:

```
OurDataViewObject = New DataView(OurDataTableObject)
```

A `DataTable` object in turn consists of rows and columns, or rather `DataRow` objects and `DataColumn` objects. To create a row for a table, we use a `DataRow` object as follows:

```
OurDataTable.Rows.Add OurDataRow
```

The `DataColumn` objects can also be created at runtime by using the following code:

```
OurDataTable.Columns.Add OurDataColumn
```

And finally, we can create a `DataColumn` object by passing the `Column` definition as follows:

```
OurDataColumn = New DataColumn(strColumnName, ColumnDataType)
```

We can put all of this code together in the following `BuildPayoutGrid` subroutine. Add the following code to the bottom of the `CalculateValues` subroutine, immediately before the `End Sub`:

```
BuildPayoutGrid(dblPrincipal, dblMonthlyInterest, dblMonthlyPayment)
```

Then add the code for the `BuildPayOutGrid` subroutine itself:

```
Private Sub BuildPayoutGrid(ByVal dblP As Double, ByVal dblMI As Double, _
                            ByVal dblM As Double)
    ' -- Variables to hold our output data
    Dim dtPayout As DataTable
    Dim drPayout As DataRow
    Dim datMonthYear As Date
    Dim dblSlicerAmount As Double
    Dim dblNewBalance As Double
    Dim dblMonthlyInterestPaid As Double

    ' -- Make sure we have the new "Loan Slicer" monthly amount
    dblSlicerAmount = Me.txtSlicerAmount.Text
    ' -- if the user has not entered one, add one additional payment
    ' -- per year as the new slicer amount
    If dblSlicerAmount = 0 Then
      dblSlicerAmount = dblM + (dblM / 12)
    End If
    Me.txtSlicerAmount.Text = dblSlicerAmount
    ' -- Create a new DataTable
    dtPayout = New DataTable()
    ' -- Create nine string columns
    dtPayout.Columns.Add(New DataColumn("Month/Year", GetType(String)))
    dtPayout.Columns.Add(New DataColumn("Loan Amount", GetType(String)))
    dtPayout.Columns.Add(New DataColumn("Original Payment", _
        GetType(String)))
    dtPayout.Columns.Add(New DataColumn("Interest Paid", GetType(String)))
    dtPayout.Columns.Add(New DataColumn("Principal Paid", GetType(String)))
    dtPayout.Columns.Add(New DataColumn("Balance Amount", GetType(String)))
```

```
        dtPayout.Columns.Add(New DataColumn("New Payment", GetType(String)))
        dtPayout.Columns.Add(New DataColumn("New Principal Paid", _
            GetType(String)))
        dtPayout.Columns.Add(New DataColumn("New Balance Amount", _
            GetType(String)))

        dblNewBalance = dblP
        ' -- Populate it with values
        ' -- Start with current Month/Year
        datMonthYear = Now()
        Do While dblP > 0
          ' -- Create a new row for our table
          drPayout = dtPayout.NewRow()

          drPayout(0) = MonthName(Month(datMonthYear)) & ", " & _
              Year(datMonthYear)
          drPayout(1) = Format(dblP, "$#,##0.00")
          drPayout(2) = Format(dblM, "$#,##0.00")

          dblMonthlyInterestPaid = (dblP * dblMI)

          drPayout(3) = Format(dblMonthlyInterestPaid, "$#,##0.00")
          drPayout(4) = Format(dblM - dblMonthlyInterestPaid, "$#,##0.00")
          drPayout(5) = Format(dblP - (dblM - dblMonthlyInterestPaid), _
              "$#,##0.00")
          ' -- new values
          If dblNewBalance >= 0 Then
            drPayout(6) = Format(dblSlicerAmount, "$#,##0.00")
            drPayout(7) = Format(dblSlicerAmount - dblMonthlyInterestPaid, _
                "$#,##0.00")
            drPayout(8) = Format(dblNewBalance - (dblSlicerAmount - _
                dblMonthlyInterestPaid), "$#,##0.00")
          Else
            drPayout(6) = "PAID"
            drPayout(7) = "IN"
            drPayout(8) = "FULL"
          End If
          ' -- Add the row to the table
          dtPayout.Rows.Add(drPayout)
          ' -- Next month
          datMonthYear = DateAdd(DateInterval.Month, 1, datMonthYear)
          ' -- Starting Loan Amount is previous month's Ending balance
          dblP = (dblP - (dblM - dblMonthlyInterestPaid))
          dblNewBalance = (dblNewBalance - (dblSlicerAmount - _
              dblMonthlyInterestPaid))

        Loop
        ' -- Create a new DataView and bind it to the DataGrid
        With dgValues
          .Visible = True
          .DataSource = New DataView(dtPayout)
          .DataBind()
        End With
    End Sub
```

Let's examine this code piece by piece.

We begin by declaring the variables we will need:

```
Dim dtPayout As DataTable
Dim drPayout As DataRow
Dim datMonthYear As Date
Dim dblSlicerAmount As Double
Dim dblNewBalance As Double
Dim dblMonthlyInterestPaid As Double
```

We first make sure that we have a 'Loan Slicer' amount in the text box on the screen. If not, we simply add one additional monthly payment per year to calculate a new, larger monthly payment. We then update the textbox with the new 'slicer' amount:

```
dblSlicerAmount = Me.txtSlicerAmount.Text
' -- if the user has not entered one, add one additional payment
' -- per year as the new slicer amount
If dblSlicerAmount = 0 Then
    dblSlicerAmount = dblM + (dblM / 12)
End If
Me.txtSlicerAmount.Text = dblSlicerAmount
```

We then create a blank `DataTable`:

```
dtPayout = New DataTable()
```

We make sure that our `DataTable` has the columns we need. We add `DataColumns` to the `DataTable`. These `DataColumns` are created on the fly by passing column definition arguments to the `DataColumn` that we create:

```
dtPayout.Columns.Add(New DataColumn("Month/Year", GetType(String)))
dtPayout.Columns.Add(New DataColumn("Loan Amount", GetType(String)))
dtPayout.Columns.Add(New DataColumn("Original Payment", _
    GetType(String)))
dtPayout.Columns.Add(New DataColumn("Interest Paid", GetType(String)))
dtPayout.Columns.Add(New DataColumn("Principal Paid", GetType(String)))
dtPayout.Columns.Add(New DataColumn("Balance Amount", GetType(String)))

dtPayout.Columns.Add(New DataColumn("New Payment", GetType(String)))
dtPayout.Columns.Add(New DataColumn("New Principal Paid", _
    GetType(String)))
dtPayout.Columns.Add(New DataColumn("New Balance Amount", _
    GetType(String)))
```

We store the loan amount in a new variable to calculate the effect of the new 'slicer' amount also:

```
dblNewBalance = dblP
```

We are now ready to populate the `DataTable` columns with values, and the `DataTable` with rows. To do so, we begin with the current month:

```
datMonthYear = Now()
```

We need to dump the output as long as there is an outstanding balance on the loan. Therefore, we use a `Do...While...Loop` till our loan amount reduces to zero:

```
Do While dblP > 0
```

We begin the process of creating our 'database on the fly' by creating a new row for our `DataTable`. This new row will automatically have nine columns addressed by the column numbers 0 to 8:

```
drPayout = dtPayout.NewRow()
```

We set the values for each column in the current row. This is relatively simple. We know the initial loan amount and the monthly payment. We calculate the monthly interest on the outstanding loan amount and, from that, we can figure out how much of our monthly payment is interest and how much is the payoff of the principal itself. The balance is the amount of the loan left:

```
drPayout(0) = MonthName(Month(datMonthYear)) & ", " & _
    Year(datMonthYear)
drPayout(1) = Format(dblP, "$#,##0.00")
drPayout(2) = Format(dblM, "$#,##0.00")

dblMonthlyInterestPaid = (dblP * dblMI)

drPayout(3) = Format(dblMonthlyInterestPaid, "$#,##0.00")
drPayout(4) = Format(dblM - dblMonthlyInterestPaid, "$#,##0.00")
drPayout(5) = Format(dblP - (dblM - dblMonthlyInterestPaid), _
    "$#,##0.00")
```

We calculate the last three columns of figures based on our new 'slicer' amount using the same logic as the original amount. What this means is that the first six columns will show the loan being paid out month after month, based on the bank's monthly payment figure, while the last three columns will show the loan getting sliced and paid off much faster because of the larger monthly payment. Since we know that the loan will get sliced, we also add logic to display a text "PAID IN FULL", instead of negative numbers when the loan balance reaches zero.

```
If dblNewBalance >= 0 Then
    drPayout(6) = Format(dblSlicerAmount, "$#,##0.00")
    drPayout(7) = Format(dblSlicerAmount - dblMonthlyInterestPaid, _
        "$#,##0.00")
    drPayout(8) = Format(dblNewBalance - (dblSlicerAmount - _
        dblMonthlyInterestPaid), "$#,##0.00")
Else
    drPayout(6) = "PAID"
    drPayout(7) = "IN"
    drPayout(8) = "FULL"
End If
```

Once we have filled nine columns with figures, we are ready to add the row to the `DataTable`:

```
dtPayout.Rows.Add(drPayout)
```

Since we are in a loop, we need to get our data ready for the next pass. We increment the date by one month and update the value of our loan amount to the balance amount remaining. We do the same for the new sliced loan balance. We then complete the loop:

```
datMonthYear = DateAdd(DateInterval.Month, 1, datMonthYear)
' -- Starting Loan Amount is previous month's Ending balance
dblP = (dblP - (dblM - dblMonthlyInterestPaid))
dblNewBalance = (dblNewBalance - (dblSlicerAmount - _
    dblMonthlyInterestPaid))

Loop
```

When we finish processing the loop, we have a `DataTable` filled with values. We create a `DataView` based on the `DataTable` and assign it to the `DataSource` property of the `DataGrid`, all in one swoop. We also make sure that the `DataGrid` is visible (remember, in design mode, we had set it to be invisible). Finally, we invoke the `Bind` method to actually bind the `DataGrid` to the `DataView` created on the fly:

```
With dgValues
    .Visible = True
    .DataSource = New DataView(dtPayout)
    .DataBind()
End With
```

That's it, we get a neat HTML table filled with rows and columns of output from our `DataGrid`. Run the application and enter a **Principal Amount** of 100000, an **Interest Rate** of 6.75, a **Period** value of 10 and a **Loan Slicer Amount** value of 1500. You should see:

If we scroll down the page, we can see that our calculations are on the mark. At the end of 10 years, we have completely paid off our loan amount. However, because of our Loan Slicing feature, we see that, by simply paying (about) an additional $350 per month, we can cut down our loan from 10 years to around 7.5 years. Our `DataGrid` ends when the principal loan amount reduces to zero. Long before that, our Loan Slicer indicates that we have **PAID IN FULL** our loan:

WebForm1 - Microsoft Internet Explorer							
April, 2009	$35,443.64	$1,148.24	$199.37	$948.87	$34,494.77	$1,500.00	$1,300.63	$3,891.75
May, 2009	$34,494.77	$1,148.24	$194.03	$954.21	$33,540.56	$1,500.00	$1,305.97	$2,585.78
June, 2009	$33,540.56	$1,148.24	$188.67	$959.58	$32,580.99	$1,500.00	$1,311.33	$1,274.45
July, 2009	$32,580.99	$1,148.24	$183.27	$964.97	$31,616.02	$1,500.00	$1,316.73	-$42.28
August, 2009	$31,616.02	$1,148.24	$177.84	$970.40	$30,645.61	PAID	IN	FULL
September, 2009	$30,645.61	$1,148.24	$172.38	$975.86	$29,669.75	PAID	IN	FULL
October, 2009	$29,669.75	$1,148.24	$166.89	$981.35	$28,688.41	PAID	IN	FULL

And there you have it. A simple Web Forms application with a slight twist. You also saw how to bind a `DataGrid` to a non-database source that you are calculating on the fly.

Summary

Web Forms are the future for web development in the Microsoft .NET Framework and this chapter gave you an overview of what you can accomplish with them in VB.NET. Web Forms provide you with the power of Rapid Application Development for developing web applications. They are to web applications what Visual Basic was to windows applications when it was first released.

Web Forms are built on the Common Language Runtime and provide all the benefits of those technologies, including a managed execution environment, type safety, inheritance, and dynamic compilation for improved performance. Web Forms provide a familiar 'code behind forms' design metaphor for Visual Basic programmers. They automatically manage state and values for controls when a web page is posted back to the server. Additionally, Web Forms can generate an enormous amount of HTML code and client-side JavaScript code for data validation with a few clicks of your mouse.

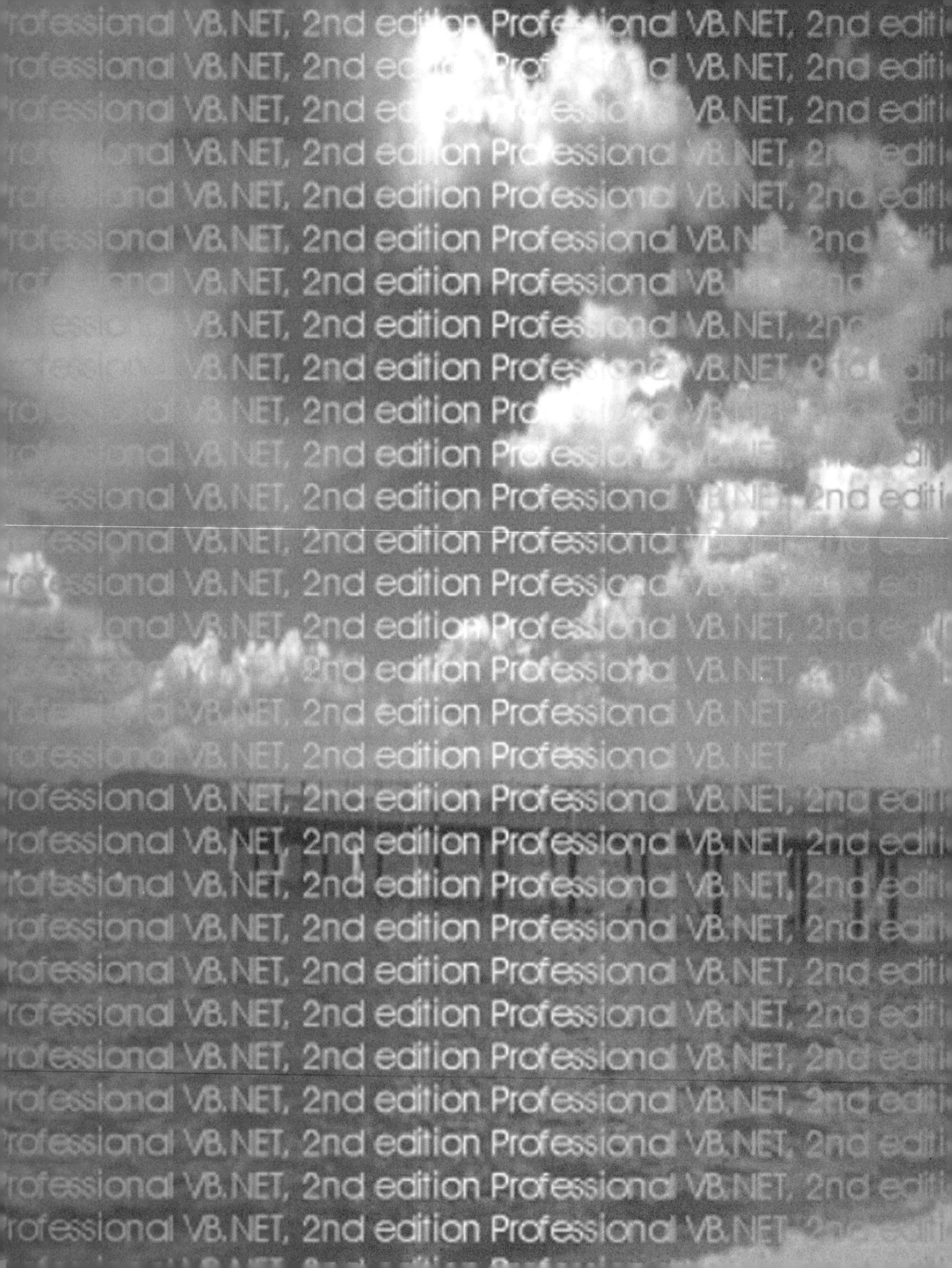
Professional VB.NET, 2nd edition

15

Creating Web Controls

It's probably only fair to warn you that creating **web controls** could easily be the subject of its own book, as it encompasses an entirely new form of Visual Basic control development. Custom web controls are likely to become one of the biggest arenas for third-party control development, as various vendors vie to fill the large gap in functionality left by the controls in the basic HTML specifications. This isn't meant as a slight to the controls that Microsoft has provided, by the way, but rather to point out the contrast between the rich functionality available in the Win32 controls and the basic functionality supported by the W3C's native HTML controls.

Microsoft has actually done an excellent job of wrapping up the basic functionality of the standard HTML controls and extending the most practical into server controls for .NET. They've also added some impressive new controls (such as the web calendar control) that take ASP web development into areas of functionality and sophistication typically reserved for desktop applications.

However, there are times when we will want to go beyond what the W3C and Microsoft have provided for us. In this chapter we'll look at:

- ❑   When we should create our own controls
- ❑   The different types of controls that we can create
- ❑   How to create and use a custom control
- ❑   How to reuse existing code in a custom control
- ❑   How to expose properties and methods of a control
- ❑   How to create and handle events of a control

❏   How to add a custom control to the Visual Studio .NET Toolbox

We'll begin by looking at why we would need to create our own controls.

Why Create Your Own Controls?

In each new web project, we come across problems that require novel solutions – problems that range from maintaining state in an essentially stateless environment to rolling out a consistent, robust site in a short space of time. As we saw in the previous chapter, .NET has responded to the first problem by providing us with state mechanisms that are built right into the platform. .NET has responded to the second problem by providing us with an extensible set of classes to help us build reusable web controls and components for our web sites.

Imagine a day when web site developers can stop worrying about which browser the client is using and which OS that browser is running on. A day, for instance, when a web site developer can drag a menu control onto a web form and let the control determine whether the client's browser is capable of rendering a DHTML menu or whether the menu should be output as a list of text-based hyperlinks. That's the philosophy of custom web controls in .NET. Smart controls that abstract the vagaries of HTML (or WML and so on) and allow web developers to focus on providing the best possible user experience, benefiting both the developer and the end user.

There are other benefits to creating custom web controls as well. We can create controls that meet our requirements, encapsulate our code, and re-use it. For instance, you may have developed a login form at one time or another; you might have also experienced the hassle of having to redevelop that login form for successive web sites. With .NET, we are now able to turn the login form into a class and take advantage of all of the benefits of object-oriented design, including inheritance and encapsulation.

So the benefits of creating custom web controls are fairly obvious in that they are centered around three of the four tenets of object-oriented design: abstraction, encapsulation, and inheritance.

> *Custom web controls also take advantage of polymorphism, especially when participating in ASP page control management.*

When to Create Your Own Controls

According to Microsoft, there are four basic scenarios where we might want to create our own custom web control:

❏   We have an ASP.NET page (or a portion of one) that provides a user interface (UI) or some functionality that we would like to reuse.

❏   We have an existing Web Forms control that meets most of our requirements. We want to customize it by adding, altering, or removing functionality until it meets all of our requirements.

❏   We need a control that combines the functionality of two or more existing Web Forms controls.

❑　　We need a web control with functionality that can't be found in an existing Web Form control or even in a combination of existing Web Form controls.

We should also add a fifth scenario to Microsoft's list – one that is likely to come into play in larger team development environments:

❑　　We want to use the functionality of a control written in one language on an ASP.NET page that uses a different language.

Types of Custom Web Controls

.NET offers us four different types of custom web controls that we can use to address these scenarios:

❑　　Web User Controls

❑　　Sub-classed controls

❑　　Composite controls

❑　　Templated controls

Let's take a look at each type in turn and discuss where they might fit into the development scenarios.

Web User Controls

Web User Controls (WUCs) in the web environment are different from Windows Forms User Controls. WUCs are portions of a web page that typically combine HTML and server-side script. They have almost all of the characteristics of the ASPX page class in that they support design time HTML, Codebehind, and dynamic compilation. (In fact, they are so close to ASPX pages that Microsoft originally called them **Pagelets**.) In contrast, Windows Forms User Controls are strictly class-based and, while they make use of the Windows Forms Designer, they do not allow for separation of code and content like WUCs do.

WUCs are extremely easy to create. You can build one from scratch by adding a Web User Control item to a web project and working with it exactly the same way as you would an ASPX page. More frequently, though, you'll take a portion of UI and/or functionality from one of your existing ASP.NET pages, place it into a separate file with an .ascx extension. That's it, you've created a WUC. It really is that simple to create an abstracted, encapsulated, and reusable component!

A WUC may require some tweaking if you've copied certain directives (any of the @ Page directives or the @ OutputCache directive) or if you've included <HTML> or <BODY> tags – we'll discuss the necessary modifications later on.

Of course, like most things we've seen in .NET, the ease with which we can create a WUC doesn't take away from the power and flexibility that they can offer. It's just that WUCs have been designed from the ground up to be simple yet extensible!

In previous versions of ASP, you might have used a Server-Side Include (SSI) to achieve the same effect as a WUC. In fact, in ASP.NET you could still use an SSI to encapsulate common functionality or UI elements, but WUCs provide much greater flexibility and extensibility. They offer several advantages over SSIs:

❑ WUCs provide their own namespace behind the scenes. This means that variables, methods, events, and constituent controls in the WUC will not conflict with identically named counterparts on the hosting page or within other instances of the same WUC.

❑ WUCs can be parameterized, which means that other developers can set properties for the control by specifying attributes in the element that inserts the WUC on the hosting page.

❑ WUCs can be written in any .NET compliant programming language, even if it's not the same server-side language used by the page that hosts it.

Once we've created our WUC, we can then choose to create or expose properties, methods, and events to the page that hosts the control – or not! A WUC can be a black box that reveals nothing of its inner workings or it can fully expose its contents. The choice is up to us.

Sub-Classed Controls

Sub-classed controls represent the most basic form of custom web control development. They are created as classes and create their HTML output directly through methods of the `HtmlTextWriter` class, a utility class provided by the hosting page for writing to the HTML response stream. A fairly typical example of a sub-classed control would be the `ImageButton` control, which inherits most of its functionality from the `Image` control and then adds support for a click event and a command event with associated command properties.

Don't let the phrase 'the most basic form of custom web control development' mislead you, though. Controls of this type can be very complex and detailed. 'Basic' merely refers to the fact that sub-classed controls do not use complex techniques like **class composition** or **templating** in rendering themselves. We'll discuss class composition and templating in the next two sections.

Typically, sub-classed controls are created by inheriting from one of the following base classes in the `System.Web.UI` namespace, or from one of their derivatives:

❑ `System.Web.UI.WebControls.WebControl` – for controls with a UI

❑ `System.Web.UI.Control` – for controls without a UI

We might also choose to inherit from the `System.Web.UI.HTMLControls.HTMLControl` class to create a server control for an HTML tag that Microsoft didn't include in the `HtmlControls` namespace, but there is not much point in doing this. .NET has the `HTMLGenericControl` class if we want to create a server control for an HTML tag that isn't already represented in the `System.Web.UI.HTMLControls` namespace. The `HTMLGenericControl` class has a `TagName` property to determine which tag it renders, which gives us the ability to create a server control for any HTML tag that we'd like.

By inheriting from these classes, sub-classed controls get all of the plumbing necessary to interact with the `Page` class, as well as the abilities to maintain state, to data bind, and to participate in server-side events.

Composite Controls

A composite control is a **container control** for other controls created by **class composition**. Class composition means that a composite control creates its child controls programmatically as classes, rather than as nested HTML or XML (the way that WUCs do) or as parameters within its element tag (the way that templated controls do). Composite controls are more or less equivalent to WUCs with the exception that they are compiled solely from a class file and persisted as part of an assembly, whereas WUCs are compiled on demand from an ASCX file (and, optionally, a Codebehind class file) and are not persisted in an assembly. Being a container control means that composite controls act as a host control for other controls. A typical example of a container class would be a `Panel` web control.

Composite controls are created through the standard class mechanisms in .NET. They can be created either by inheriting from the controls in the `System.Web.UI` namespace or by implementing one or more of the interfaces in the `System.Web.UI` namespace.

> *While implementing interfaces is an option for creating custom web controls, it is far too complex a subject to deal with here.*

Composite controls typically start by inheriting from the `System.Web.UI.Control` class (although you could certainly use one of its derivatives). The `Control` class provides the `Controls` collection to store child controls in and it also provides methods for rendering the child controls. All that is required of us when we develop a composite control is that we override the base class' `CreateChildControls` method to create instances of the child control classes and add them to the `Controls` collection. Once the child controls have been added to the `Controls` collection, the built-in functionality of the `Control` class will handle rendering them for us.

> *For more information on composite controls, see* Professional ASP.NET 1.0 Special Edition *(Wrox Press, ISBN 1861007035).*

Templated Controls

The last of the four types, templated controls, are types of container controls also referred to in the Microsoft documentation as **lookless controls**. These are controls that separate their UI from their behavior, allowing the page author to customize the appearance of their constituent controls without the use of code. Some examples of templated controls in the `System.Web.UI.WebControls` namespace are the `Repeater` and `Datalist` classes.

The requirements for a templated control are that it implements the `INamingContainer` interface and that it exposes one or more properties of type `System.Web.UI.ITemplate`. The name of each of these **template properties** can then be mapped to the tag name of a **template element** nested inside the templated control. Then, within the template element, the page author can specify whatever they would like for the appearance of that portion of the templated control, from literal text right on up to complex combinations of nested elements.

It might seem like the first sentence of the previous paragraph is a mistake. A property whose type is an interface? What's going on here? Let's take a look at the listing for a page with a `Repeater` control on it, and the output that it produces, and see if we can't make a little more sense of this:

```
<%@ Page Language="vb" %>
<html>
  <head>
    <script runat="server">
      Private Sub Page_Load(ByVal sender As System.Object, _
          ByVal e As System.EventArgs) Handles MyBase.Load
        Dim strCastArray() As String = {"Dorothy", _
                                        "The Wizard", _
                                        "Toto", _
                                        "etc."}
        Repeater1.DataSource = strCastArray
        Repeater1.DataBind()
      End Sub
    </script>
  </head>
  <body>
    <asp:repeater id="Repeater1" runat="server">
      <headertemplate>
        <h3>The Cast</h3>
      </headertemplate>
      <itemtemplate>
        <div><%# Container.DataItem %></div>
      </itemtemplate>
      <alternatingitemtemplate>
        <div style="background-color: silver">
          <%# Container.DataItem %>
        </div>
      </alternatingitemtemplate>
    </asp:repeater>
  </body>
</html>
```

This generates the following HTML source code (formatted here for clarity):

```
<html>
  <head></head>
  <body>
    <h3>The Cast</h3>
    <div>Dorothy</div>
    <div style="background-color: silver">The Wizard</div>
    <div>Toto</div>
    <div style="background-color: silver">etc.</div>
  </body>
</html>
```

which looks like this in Internet Explorer 6:

Notice that the `Repeater` control has `HeaderTemplate`, `ItemTemplate`, and `AlternatingItemTemplate` elements, none of which actually exist as either server objects or client elements. The reason for this is that, when the control parser for the page comes across unknown elements nested within a control that implements the `INamingContainer` interface, it checks the container control for a property with the same tag name as the unknown element. If the parser finds a matching property name, it then makes use of reflection (a technique for inspecting the structure of an object) to determine whether the property is of type `ITemplate`.

The parser then creates the unknown element as a special template builder control, either of type `CompiledTemplateBuilder` or `TemplateBuilder`, both of which implement `ITemplate`. It associates the nested content with the template builder control and passes the template builder control into the templated control as the value for the template property.

So what's happening here is that we have a specialized control that implements the interface being created behind the scenes, and then gets passed into our templated control. This is how we come to have properties of an interface type. It is a bit of an odd concept to wrap one's head around, but essentially this is what allows us to map specific data elements of our templated control to elements or element attributes provided by the user of our control.

> *For thorough coverage of templated controls, see* Professional ASP.NET 1.0 Special Edition *(Wrox Press, ISBN 1861007035).*

Now that we've covered the basic types of custom web controls, let's discuss where each type might fit in the development cycle.

When To Use Custom Web Controls

The easiest path to follow when creating custom web controls is to develop standard ASP.NET pages and, when we determine that we have something that can be re-used, separate it off into a WUC.

515

You could stop at this point, already having taken advantage of the abstraction and encapsulation provided by the WUC control. But if we want to use our control in multiple sites and still have a single set of source code for our control, we'll want to look at re-writing the control as one of the class-based custom web control types. This is because we can deploy the compiled code for a class-based control to multiple sites or to the Global Assembly Cache (GAC) for a given web server. If we change the source code, it is a simple thing to manage versions and to re-deploy the updated assembly. WUCs, on the other hand, require that their ASCX files exist locally within each web application that uses them. This means that we would need to copy any changes to the ASCX file manually to each web site that uses the control and, hopefully, not accidentally overwrite any other changed versions.

> **The best part of this is that the same code that you write for your ASP.NET page or your WUC will still work with minor modifications when you port it over to a sub-classed, composite, or templated control.**

Aside from migrating a WUC, we could also look at developing a class-based control when we want greater control over the HTML elements that comprise a control and the behavior of those elements (as well as the behavior of the control as a whole). Sub-classed controls make sense when we are building single element output, enhancing the functionality of an existing control, or generating unstructured or loosely structured output. Composite controls are excellent when we want to combine multiple controls or when we are looking at building complex or repeated combinations of other controls. Templated controls offer us a way of giving the consumer of our control a structured method for altering its appearance. Remember too that class-based custom web controls also take advantage of much of the same framework used to create custom Windows Forms controls, so you can leverage the skills that you gain in both areas. In fact, it is one of Microsoft's stated design goals to make web control development accessible even to developers who do not have a great deal of familiarity with HTML.

We will concentrate on web user controls and sub-classed controls for the rest of this chapter.

Creating a Web User Control

If you take a look around the web for any length of time you'll come across a whole host of standard UI functionality that would make for great custom web controls. Some examples would be:

- ❑ Login forms
- ❑ Menus
- ❑ Search widgets
- ❑ Headers, footers, and copyright notices
- ❑ Tables of contents
- ❑ Site navigation elements

Let's take an example from the Wrox web site and see if we can wrap it up into a WUC. If you navigate to http://www.wrox.com, you'll see a vertical navigation bar something like this:

What we have here is a vertical list of hyperlinks nested in a table with a red background. If you happen to be on a page that matches one of the hyperlink addresses from the list, then the corresponding element becomes rendered with white text with no text decoration (that is no underline).

For the purposes of our example, we're going to alter the Wrox navigation bar's functionality a bit. We'll make our example into a navigation bar that lists the rest of the examples that we're going to build in this chapter. We'll reduce the number of entries in the bar and we'll take advantage of some of the ASP.NET Hyperlink server control's behaviors to simplify our implementation.

> *For convenience sake, from this point forward in this chapter, you can assume that, unless specifically stated otherwise, any reference to a server control is a reference to an ASP.NET server control.*

When we're finished, we'll have a page that looks like this:

We'll need a web application to work from, so open up Visual Studio and create a new Web Application project called WebControls. Let's start with an existing web page and work our way through creating a WUC from it.

Download the code samples from http://www.wrox.com. Then add the file named
OriginalPage.aspx, which you'll find in the directory for this chapter, as an existing item to the
WebControls project (via the Project | Add Existing Item menu).

Visual Studio will inform you that the class file for this web form isn't in the project and will offer to
create one for you:

You can decline the offer, as this particular page doesn't actually use a Codebehind page. This probably
won't be typical of the pages you write in ASP.NET, but we're going to work without Codebehind for
this section.

Rename the file from OriginalPage.aspx to Default.aspx in order for the code to work properly,
and then double-click on Default.aspx to open it up in the Design View. Select View | HTML Source
so that we can look at the code listing:

```
<%@ Page Language="vb" AutoEventWireup="true" %>
<%@ Import Namespace="System.Drawing" %>
<html>
  <head>
    <title>User Control Example</title>
    <script runat="server" id="Script1">

    Sub Page_Load(Source As Object, E As EventArgs)
      Dim strPath As String = Request.Path.ToLower
      SetCurrentLink(strPath, hypHome)
      SetCurrentLink(strPath, hypExample1)
      SetCurrentLink(strPath, hypExample2)
      SetCurrentLink(strPath, hypExample3)
      SetCurrentLink(strPath, hypExample4)
      SetCurrentLink(strPath, hypExample5)
    End Sub

    Private Sub SetCurrentLink(ByVal strPath As String, _
                 ByRef hypToTest As HyperLink)
      With hypToTest
      If .NavigateUrl.ToLower().IndexOf(strPath) > -1 Then
        .NavigateUrl = String.Empty
        .ForeColor = Color.Yellow
      End If
      End With
    End Sub

    </script>
  </head>
<body style="font-family:verdana;font-size:10pt">
```

```
<form id="Form1" method="post" runat="server">
  <table cellspacing="10" width="99%" border="0" height="100%"
         style="font-family:verdana;font-size:10pt">
    <tr>
      <td width="200" valign="top">
        <table id="tblNavBar" bgcolor="#cc0033" width="100%"
               height="100%" style="font-family:verdana;font-size:10pt">
          <tr>
            <td colspan="2">
              <asp:hyperlink runat="server" id="hypHome"
                             navigateurl="/WebControls/Default.aspx"
                             font-bold="True" forecolor="white">
              Creating Web Controls
              </asp:hyperlink>
            </td>
          </tr>
          <tr>
            <td width="5px">
               
            </td>
            <td>
              <asp:hyperlink runat="server" id="hypExample1"
                     navigateurl="/WebControls/SubClassingAControl.aspx"
                     forecolor="white">
              Sub-classing a Control
              </asp:hyperlink>
            </td>
          </tr>
          <tr>
            <td>
               
            </td>
            <td>
              <asp:hyperlink runat="server" id="hypExample2"
                     navigateurl="/WebControls/ExtendingAControl.aspx"
                     forecolor="white">
              Extending an Existing Control
              </asp:hyperlink>
            </td>
          </tr>
          <tr>
            <td>
               
            </td>
            <td>
              <asp:hyperlink runat="server" id="hypExample3"
                             navigateurl="/WebControls/Clock.aspx"
                             forecolor="white">
              Creating a UI-less Control
              </asp:hyperlink>
            </td>
          </tr>
          <tr>
            <td>
```

```
                       
                    </td>
                    <td>
                      <asp:hyperlink runat="server" id="hypExample4"
                              navigateurl="/WebControls/CompositeControl.aspx"
                              forecolor="white">
                      Creating a Composite Control
                      </asp:hyperlink>
                    </td>
                  </tr>
                  <tr>
                    <td>
                       
                    </td>
                    <td>
                      <asp:hyperlink runat="server" id="hypExample5"
                              navigateurl="/WebControls/TemplatedControl.aspx"
                              forecolor="white">
                      Templated Control Sample
                      </asp:hyperlink>
                    </td>
                  </tr>
                  <tr>
                    <td colspan="2" height="100%">
                      <!-- This row takes up any slack space at the
                          end of this table -->
                       
                    </td>
                  </tr>
                </table>
              </td>
              <td valign="top">
                <h3>
                  Creating Custom Web Controls
                </h3>
                <p>
                  The navigation bar on the left of the page is (or will be) an
                  example of a User Control...
                </p>
              </td>
            </tr>
          </table>
        </form>
      </body>
    </html>
```

The code in this example is intentionally simplified so that we can concentrate on the specifics of creating a WUC. All the same, let's take a quick tour of the highlights.

Since we are not using a Codebehind window, we need to set the AutoEventWireup attribute of the @ Page directive to True to tell ASP.NET to use the Page_Load method to handle the firing of the Page_Load event.

You can also manually add the `Handles MyBase.EventName` *statement after each event that you want to wire up, but setting the* `AutoEventWireup` *attribute of the* `@ Page` *directive to* `True` *instructs the page to do this for you behind the scenes for any procedures named in the* `Object_EventName` *style.*

If you intend to use the `Handles` *statement you must specifically set the* `AutoEventWireup` *attribute to* `False`. *If you set it to* `True` *or omit it, your* `Object_EventName` *event handler will be called twice.*

For readability and troubleshooting purposes, you should probably choose one technique or the other and stick with it. Bear in mind that, if you foresee moving event handling procedures out of an ASPX page and into a Codebehind page, you should probably use the `Handles` *statement. That way your procedures will not require editing in order to be wired up in the Codebehind class.*

We also set the default language for the page, and import the `System.Drawing` namespace so that we don't have to fully qualify references to its members in our code:

```
<%@ Page Language="vb" AutoEventWireup="true" %>
<%@ Import Namespace="System.Drawing" %>
```

The code works by comparing the path of the currently displayed page to the URLs specified for the `Hyperlink` server controls in our navigation bar. It does this during the `Page_Load` event by calling a helper procedure named `SetCurrentLink` and passing it the path of the currently requested page along with a reference to the hyperlink object that we want to check it against:

```
Sub Page_Load(Source As Object, E As EventArgs)
   Dim strPath As String = Request.Path.ToLower
   SetCurrentLink(strPath, hypHome)
   SetCurrentLink(strPath, hypExample1)
   SetCurrentLink(strPath, hypExample2)
   SetCurrentLink(strPath, hypExample3)
   SetCurrentLink(strPath, hypExample4)
   SetCurrentLink(strPath, hypExample5)
End Sub
```

`SetCurrentLink` does its comparison by using the `String` object's built-in `IndexOf` method. We can write it this way because the `NavigateUrl` property is of type `String` and therefore naturally has all of the methods and properties of any other string object:

```
Private Sub SetCurrentLink(ByVal strPath As String, _
            ByRef hypToTest As HyperLink)
   With hypToTest
     If .NavigateUrl.ToLower().IndexOf(strPath) > -1
       .NavigateUrl = String.Empty
       .ForeColor = Color.Yellow
     End If
   End With
End Sub
```

We could have used the `InStr()` function to do the same thing but this is more in keeping with VB.NET's stronger focus on object-oriented programming. We had to use the `ToLower` method because the `IndexOf` method does not have an overloaded version that supports case-insensitive comparisons. We also used `ToLower` when we assigned the request path to `strUrl` so that we would be comparing one lowercase string with another lowercase string.

If the code finds a `Hyperlink` control with a matching path, it causes the control to be rendered as an anchor instead of as a hyperlink. It does this by resetting the `Hyperlink` control's `NavigateUrl` property to an empty string.

This can be a little confusing if you aren't familiar with the history of HTML. In SGML, the precursor to HTML, the "A" in an `<A>` tag stood for Anchor and the tag was used as a placeholder in a document (like a bookmark in Microsoft Word). When the tag was defined in HTML, it was assigned two duties: you could assign an anchor tag a name and use that name to refer to a given spot in a document (called an anchor), or you could specify a hyperlink reference for the tag and then click on the tag to navigate to another page (in which case it's called a hyperlink). In order to differentiate between the two tasks that the `<A>` tag can perform, browsers typically underline hyperlinks and they leave an anchor tag's formatting alone.

This is a prime example of how server controls can simplify web page development.

When the `Hyperlink` server control goes to render itself it takes into account that, if its `NavigateUrl` property is an empty string, then it shouldn't add the `href` attribute to the `<A>` tag. This causes the client's browser to render the tag as an anchor instead of as a hyperlink.

If we tried to do the same thing with basic HTML, we'd have to insert an inline conditional clause in the middle of our HTML to determine whether or not to include the `href` attribute, for example:

```
<% If Len(thisUrl) = 0 Then %>
<a id="hypHome">Chapter 15</a>
<% Else %>
<a id="hypHome" href="/WebControls/Default.aspx">Chapter 15</a>
<% End If %>
```

This also means that we don't need to specifically turn off the text decoration for the anchor tag, as the browser will automatically turn off the underline for us.

We also want to give another visual signal that this link represents our current location in the hierarchy by setting its `ForeColor` to the `System.Drawing.Color` collection constant `Yellow`:

```
.NavigateUrl = String.Empty
.ForeColor = Color.Yellow
```

Note that we didn't have to fully qualify the reference to the `Color` collection, thanks to the `@ Import` directive that we put at the top of the page.

That's pretty much it. It's a simple example but it gives us plenty of room for enhancements later on as we look deeper into the features available in WUCs.

Now it's probably a good idea to make sure that our page works before we go through with converting it to a WUC. We could just open a browser and navigate to http://localhost/WebControls/default.aspx, but let's get our project set up for debugging first. Right-click on `Default.aspx` in the Solutions Explorer window and select the **Set As Start Page** option. Now, when we click the **Start** button, Visual Studio will compile the web project, launch a browser window, start our web application, and display `Default.aspx`.

Adding a Web User Control Item to the Project

Hopefully, everything has worked up to now so we can go ahead and create our WUC. The first step is to add a file for the WUC to the project. Right-click on the **WebControls** project in the **Solution Explorer** and choose **Add | Add New Item…** from the context menu. Create a new **Web User Control** named `NavBar.ascx`. The WUC file should now be open in the **Design View**. Switch to the **HTML View**.

Next we'll want to cut the HTML and code from `Default.aspx` that makes our WUC tick and paste it into our newly created `ascx` file. Delete the existing text in `NavBar.ascx` and move the following sections over from `Default.aspx`:

```
<%@ Page Language="vb" AutoEventWireup="true" %>
<%@ Import Namespace="System.Drawing" %>
```

We're taking the above section because we still want to set the default language for our control, we still want to have ASP.NET associate our event code with the events that it is supposed to handle, and because we still want to get easy access to the `Color` collection in the `System.Drawing` namespace.

We'll also need the script block that does all of the setup work:

```
<script runat="server" ID="Script1">

  Sub Page_Load(Source As Object, E As EventArgs)
    Dim strPath As String = Request.Path.ToLower
    SetCurrentLink(strPath, hypHome)
    SetCurrentLink(strPath, hypExample1)
    SetCurrentLink(strPath, hypExample2)
    SetCurrentLink(strPath, hypExample3)
    SetCurrentLink(strPath, hypExample4)
    SetCurrentLink(strPath, hypExample5)
  End Sub

  Private Sub SetCurrentLink(ByVal strPath As String, _
            ByRef hypToTest As HyperLink)
    With hypToTest
    If .NavigateUrl.ToLower().IndexOf(strPath) > -1 Then
      .NavigateUrl = String.Empty
      .ForeColor = Color.Yellow
    End If
    End With
  End Sub

</script>
```

And the inner table that holds our navigation elements:

```
<table id="tblNavBar" bgcolor="#cc0033" width="100%"
       height="100%" style="font-family:verdana;font-size:10pt">
  <tr>
    <td colspan="2">
      <asp:hyperlink runat="server" id="hypHome"
                     navigateurl="/WebControls/Default.aspx"
                     font-bold="True" forecolor="white">
      Creating Web Controls
    </asp:hyperlink>
    </td>
  </tr>
  <tr>
    <td width="5px">
       
    </td>
    <td>
      <asp:hyperlink runat="server" id="hypExample1"
             navigateurl="/WebControls/SubClassingAControl.aspx"
             forecolor="white">
      Sub-classing a Control
    </asp:hyperlink>
    </td>
  </tr>
  <tr>
    <td>
       
    </td>
    <td>
      <asp:hyperlink runat="server" id="hypExample2"
                 navigateurl="/WebControls/ExtendingAControl.aspx"
                 forecolor="white">
      Extending an Existing Control
    </asp:hyperlink>
    </td>
  </tr>
  <tr>
    <td>
       
    </td>
    <td>
      <asp:hyperlink runat="server" id="hypExample3"
                     navigateurl="/WebControls/Clock.aspx"
                     forecolor="white">
      Creating a UI-less Control
    </asp:hyperlink>
    </td>
  </tr>
  <tr>
    <td>
       
    </td>
    <td>
```

```
            <asp:hyperlink runat="server" id="hypExample4"
                    navigateurl="/WebControls/CompositeControl.aspx"
                    forecolor="white">
          Creating a Composite Control
        </asp:hyperlink>
      </td>
    </tr>
    <tr>
      <td>
         
      </td>
      <td>
        <asp:hyperlink runat="server" id="hypExample5"
                    navigateurl="/WebControls/TemplatedControl.aspx"
                    forecolor="white">
        Templated Control Sample
      </asp:hyperlink>
      </td>
    </tr>
    <tr>
      <td colspan="2" height="100%">
        <!-- This row takes up any slack space at the
            end of this table -->
         
      </td>
    </tr>
  </table>
```

All that should be left in the `Default.aspx` page are the `html`, `head`, and `body` tags, and the outer table.

Reusing Code in a Web User Control

We only need to make a few modifications to get code from an ASP.NET web form to work in a WUC. The differences between the two are:

- ❑ WUCs don't allow a couple of directives aimed specifically at pages. The directives that are not allowed are @ Page and @ OutputCache.

- ❑ It isn't recommended to include `<html>`, `<head>`, or `<body>` elements in a WUC. It isn't forbidden, but it will make your WUC unfriendly to any page that already contains these elements.

- ❑ It is also recommended not to put `<form>` tags in a WUC. The reason for this is that your WUC could not then be placed inside a form on the hosting page (ASP.NET doesn't allow for nested server forms).

- ❑ You may optionally change any page event handlers from `Page_EventName` to `Control_EventName`. The WUC will still work whether you change this or not though.

You may wish to ignore the third recommendation if you are creating a login form or a self-contained search form, you know that you won't be nesting the control in another form, and you want the action and other attributes of the form to remain consistent throughout every instance of the control. Since we didn't include any of the `<html>`, `<head>`, `<body>` or `<form>` elements, the only change we need to make in `NavBar.ascx` is to change the @ Page directive to an @ Control directive:

```
<%@ Control Language="vb" AutoEventWireup="true" %>
```

For consistency, though, we'll change the `Page_Load` procedure name to `Control_Load`:

```
Sub Control_Load(Source As Object, E As EventArgs)
```

The @ Control Directive

The @ `Control` directive supports all of the same attributes that the @ `Page` directive does, with the exception of the `AspCompat` attribute and the tracing attributes (`trace` and `traceMode`). ASP compatibility and tracing can only be set at the page or web site level. We haven't included either of these attributes in our navigation bar example so we don't need to make any other modifications to the @ `Control` directive.

As a point of interest, ASP.NET will actually interpret any `<%@ %>` directive that does not specify the directive name as an @ `Page` or an @ `Control`, based on whether it is in an ASPX or an ASCX file, respectively. So, the following statement would work in both file types without modification:

```
<%@ Language="vb" AutoEventWireup="true" %>
```

The question, of course, is whether this will continue to be supported in future versions of ASP.NET!

That's it. You've created your first WUC and, yes, they can really be that easy. Let's head back to the `Default.aspx` page and add our new WUC to it.

Web User Controls and the @ Register Directive

We'll need to register our new control with the page before we'll be able to add it to the page. Place the following line at the top of `Default.aspx`:

```
<%@ Register TagPrefix="WebControlsuc" TagName="NavBar" src="NavBar.ascx"%>
```

The @ `Register` directive tells the compiler how to identify the element tags for our custom controls and where to locate their code. The `TagPrefix` and `TagName` attributes tell the compiler the syntax we'll use when we create elements for our WUC. The `src` attribute identifies the file that contains the code for the WUC and can be either a relative or absolute reference. So the page now knows that it should create any tag of the form `<tagprefix:tagname runat="server">` as an instance of the WUC found at the location specified in `src`.

In the left cell of the two cell table that we used to contain our original navigation bar elements, type in the following XML-style element declaration:

```
<body>
  <form id="Form1" method="post" runat="server">
    <table cellspacing="10" width="99%" border="0" height="100%">
      <tr>
        <td width="200" valign="top">
          <WebControlsuc:navbar id="MyNavBar" runat="server" />
```

```
        </td>
        <td valign="top">
          <h3>
            Welcome to the home page for the chapter
            on creating custom web controls!
          </h3>
          <p>
            The navigation bar on the left of the page
            is (or will be) an example of a User Control...
          </p>
        </td>
      </tr>
    </table>
  </form>
```

You could alternatively write the highlighted line as:

```
<WebControlsuc:navbar id="MyNavBar" runat="server">
</WebControlsuc:navbar>
```

The page will accept either empty tags or tag pairs but, since the control that we've created isn't meant to contain nested text or HTML elements, the former is more appropriate. It's a strong indicator to anyone else who looks at our page that they aren't expected to include any additional content within our element.

As we've seen above, WUCs are very simple to create. Creating one doesn't even require writing any additional code. They don't have to remain simple, though. In the following sections, we'll take a look at some of the more advanced techniques that we can use when creating WUCs.

Reaching Into a Web User Control

The way our WUC stands now, it is pretty much a black box as far as our page is concerned. Well, that's not entirely true. By virtue of being a WUC, it inherits the standard methods, properties, and events of the `System.Web.UI.UserControl` class, but there is no direct way to access the controls or the code it contains. It could contain nothing but the literal text "Hello World!" or it could contain a highly complex collection of elements and script but, without exposing any custom properties, methods, or events, the hosting page would never know.

So how do we expose custom properties, methods, and events? Pretty much the same way as we would for any other class. Any members of a WUC marked as `Public` will be available to the hosting page. That means that we can expose any variables, property statements, functions, procedures, and events we choose in a manner consistent with the rest of the VB.NET architecture.

Exposing Custom Properties

As an example, let's expose a custom property on our WUC that sets the background color of our navigation bar's table. We'll call it `BackColor` to keep it consistent with the rest of the ASP.NET server controls:

```
Protected _BackColor As Color = ColorTranslator.FromHtml("#cc0033")

Public Property BackColor As String
```

```
    Get
       Return ColorTranslator.ToHtml(_BackColor)
    End Get
    Set
       _BackColor = ColorTranslator.FromHtml(value)
    End Set
 End Property
```

What we've done is to create a protected variable of type `System.Drawing.Color` and initialize it with the Wrox Press red background color. Why not just create a variable of type string, though? By using the `Color` type, we're allowing our user to specify any of the named colors known to .NET, an RGB (Red-Green-Blue) value, a hex value, or an ARGB (Alpha-RGB) value. The `Color` class will also ensure that only valid named colors and color values can be assigned to our property. For instance, trying to assign either `PurpleHaze` or `#gg0000` to `BackColor` will generate run-time exceptions because they don't represent valid colors.

When we go to initialize the `BackColor` property, or to make use of it in an HTML tag, we run into a bit of a wrinkle, though. The `Color` class is based on 32-bit ARGB values while HTML uses 24-bit RGB or named colors. Now, if we were using `BackColor` to set the color on an ASP.NET server control, this wouldn't be a problem at all! The server controls automatically render any property that uses the `Color` type in an HTML friendly fashion, as either a hex value or a known color name. The HTML controls are another matter though – in order to have them render correctly, we need to convert from the ARGB values of the `Color` class to HTML friendly values manually.

To do this we can use the `System.Drawing.ColorTranslator` class like so:

```
    Return ColorTranslator.ToHtml(_BackColor)
```

To set the `BackColor` property in our hosting page, we specify it as an attribute in the element for the control:

```
    <WebControlsuc:navbar id="MyNavBar" runat="server"
                          backcolor="purple" />
```

Go ahead and add this `backcolor` attribute to the `MyNavBar` element and check it out in your browser. (Maybe we'll stick to red after all.)

Next, let's set up a property that will allow the consumer of our control to specify the current link directly. We'll add a little spice to the example by exposing the property complete with an enumeration of the available controls. Then we'll finish it up by modifying our existing code to make use of the new property. We'll start by putting in a couple of private, module-level variables to help us maintain and control the use of the new property:

```
    Private mblnLinksHaveBeenChecked As Boolean
    Private mlclCurrentLink As LinkControlList = LinkControlList.Default
```

We've declared `mlclCurrentLink` as a variable of type `LinkControlList` and initialized it to one of `LinkControlList`'s members. `LinkControlList` is the enumeration type representing the `Hyperlink` controls in the WUC that we're going to create next:

```
Public Enum LinkControlList
    [Default] = -1
    Home
    Example1
    Example2
    Example3
    Example4
    Example5
End Enum
```

If you aren't familiar with it already then the code for the enumeration type will probably seem pretty strange. The square brackets around the name of the first member of the enumeration (Default) allow us to take advantage of VB.NET's ability to allow us to use keywords and reserved words for the names of properties, procedures, and variables. That's probably not the most bizarre looking portion of the enumeration though.

The only member that we've specifically assigned a value to is Default. That's because any enumeration member that is not specifically set *automatically* takes on a value of one plus the previous member's value. So Home is one plus the value of Default, Example1 is one plus the value of Home, and so on. This behavior comes in extremely handy when we go to add a new member to the list, as we don't have to waste time manually renumbering the members that come afterwards.

> **If we were willing to start the enumeration list at zero, we wouldn't even have to assign a value to the first member.**

Now on to the property definition:

```
Public Property CurrentLink() As LinkControlList
    Get
        Return mlclCurrentLink
    End Get
    Set(ByVal Value As LinkControlList)
        If mblnLinksHaveBeenChecked Then
            Throw New Exception("The current link has already been rendered.")
        ElseIf Not System.Enum.IsDefined(mlclCurrentLink.GetType(), Value) Then
            Throw New ArgumentOutOfRangeException("CurrentLink", _
                Value, "Not a valid CurrentLink value! " & _
                "Please select a member from the LinkControlIndex enumeration.")
        Else
            mlclCurrentLink = Value
        End If
    End Set
End Property
```

In the Set portion of the property declaration, we do a little exception checking before setting the internal variable to the new property value:

```
If mblnLinksHaveBeenChecked Then
    Throw New Exception("The current link has already been rendered.")
```

529

The first section of the `If` statement checks to see if our control has already called the `SetCurrentLink` method or not. If it has, then we throw an exception to alert the consumer of our control that it is too late in the control's lifecycle to set the current link.

In the next section, the `ElseIf` statement checks to make sure that the value that has been passed in to us is actually a member of the `LinkControlIndex` enumeration:

```
ElseIf Not System.Enum.IsDefined(mlclCurrentLink.GetType(), Value) Then
    Throw New ArgumentOutOfRangeException("CurrentLink", _
        Value, "Not a valid CurrentLink value! " & _
        "Please select a member from the LinkControlIndex enumeration.")
```

> **Even though the System namespace has been imported by default, we still have to qualify the reference to the System.Enum class to distinguish it from the Enum keyword.**

If the hosting page has tried to set the index to an unacceptable value, for example 5, then this will cause our property to throw one of the standard system exception types. We use one of the constructor methods of the `ArgumentOutOfRangeException` class to expose as much information about the exception as possible.

This constructor takes three arguments. The first is the name of the argument that caused the exception, which we'll use to pass back the name of the property. The second passes in a reference to the invalid argument itself and exposes it through the `ActualValue` property of the exception. The third argument is a custom message that we'll use to give back an exception message that's slightly more informative than the default one.

If the new value makes it past our validation code, we set our internal variable equal to it:

```
Else
    mlclCurrentLink = Value
End If
```

At this point, the property is available to the hosting page but it doesn't do much yet. We'll need to make some changes to the rest of the code to implement it and, while we're at it, we might as well make a few optimizations. We can start by switching from using the `Load` event to making use of the `PreRender` event instead. Just like with an ASPX `Page` object, the `PreRender` event happens well after the `Load` event and just before the controls on the WUC are actually written to the HTML output stream. `PreRender` and `Load` have the same event signature so all we have to do is change the procedure name:

```
Sub Control_PreRender(ByVal sender As Object, ByVal e As System.EventArgs)
    Dim strPath As String
```

By doing this, we delay the calls to `SetCurrentLink` until as late as possible, giving script in the host container as much opportunity as possible to set the `CurrentLink` property.

It's time to implement the functionality behind the property. We're going to be replacing most of the existing code in the PreRender event procedure:

```
Sub Control_PreRender(ByVal sender As Object, ByVal e As System.EventArgs)
    Dim strPath As String
    Dim i As Integer
    Dim mLinkControls() As HyperLink = {hypHome, _
                                        hypExample1, _
                                        hypExample2, _
                                        hypExample3, _
                                        hypExample4, _
                                        hypExample5}

    If mlclCurrentLink = LinkControlList.Default Then
        strPath = Request.Path.ToLower
        For i = 0 To mLinkControls.GetUpperBound(0)
            If SetCurrentLink(strPath, mLinkControls(i)) Then
                mlclCurrentLink = CType(i, LinkControlList)
                Exit For
            End If
        Next
    Else
        strPath = mLinkControls(mlclCurrentLink).NavigateUrl.ToLower
        SetCurrentLink(strPath, mLinkControls(mlclCurrentLink))
    End If
    mblnLinksHaveBeenChecked = True
End Sub
```

The If *statement expects a return value from the* SetCurrentLink *procedure. We'll be converting* SetCurrentLink *to a function shortly.*

The first major change is that we need to be able to access our Hyperlink controls via the indices created in the LinkControlList enumeration. To do that we create the mLinkControls() array of type Hyperlink and initialize it with references to our Hyperlink server controls:

```
    Dim mLinkControls() As HyperLink = {hypHome, _
                                        hypExample1, _
                                        hypExample2, _
                                        hypExample3, _
                                        hypExample4, _
                                        hypExample5}
```

The next step is to check and see if the CurrentLink property has been set, by comparing it to the LinkControlList.Default member. If it hasn't been set, then we loop through the array calling SetCurrentLink for each of the hyperlink objects, until we find one whose NavigateURL property matches the request path:

```
    If mlclCurrentLink = LinkControlList.Default Then
        strPath = Request.Path.ToLower
        For i = 0 To mLinkControls.GetUpperBound(0)
            If SetCurrentLink(strPath, mLinkControls(i)) Then
```

```
        mlclCurrentLink = CType(i, LinkControlList)
        Exit For
     End If
  Next
```

This differs from the original code that we had because we are now using a For loop to walk an array of controls, where previously we had hard coded the calls for each control. This is obviously more flexible than the previous technique as all we need to do to add a new control to the list is to add it to the array and add a corresponding entry in the LinkControlList enumeration. This automatically includes the new control in the For loop. It also allows us to make an easy optimization by giving us a simple way to stop checking the rest of the hyperlink objects once a matching path has been found.

We'll do one more thing once we've found the current link and that is to set the internal variable for the CurrentLink property. Now if code in the container cares to inquire as to which link was actually set, it will be able to get the value back out.

If it turns out that the CurrentLink property has been set, we'll skip looping through the controls and call SetCurrentLink directly for the indicated control:

```
  Else
     strPath = mLinkControls(mlclCurrentLink).NavigateUrl.ToLower
     SetCurrentLink(strPath, mLinkControls(mlclCurrentLink))
  End If
```

We needed to force the path comparison to be equal in SetCurrentLink, so we set the strPath variable equal to the path of the control that we are passing in. It's a bit of a hack, but it keeps the example simple.

Finally, we have to set the mblnLinksHaveBeenChecked flag so that we can prevent any attempts to set the current link after this code has finished:

```
  mblnLinksHaveBeenChecked = True
```

We do need to go back and change one more thing before we can test our new code. We've added an If statement up above that looks for a return value from SetCurrentLink to determine whether the item being tested is actually the current link. Since SetCurrentLink is defined as a sub procedure and not a function, we need to change its declaration and modify it so that it returns a value of True when it finds the current link:

```
  Private Function SetCurrentLink(ByVal strPath As String, _
                        ByRef hypToTest As HyperLink) As Boolean
     With hypToTest
        If .NavigateUrl.ToLower().IndexOf(strPath) > -1 Then
           .NavigateUrl = String.Empty
           .ForeColor = Color.Yellow
           Return True
        End If
     End With
  End Function
```

To test our changes, add the following server-side script block to the Default.aspx page:

```
<head>
  <script runat=server language="vb">
    Sub Page_Load(ByVal Sender As System.Object, _
                  ByVal e As System.EventArgs)
      MyNavBar.CurrentLink = MyNavBar.LinkControlList.Example3
    End Sub
  </script>
  <title>User Control Example</title>
</head>
```

When you run the project, the current link will be set to Example3 and you'll get a page that looks like this:

Exposing a Custom Method

Exposing a custom method is again a matter of taking a private sub or function and marking it as available to other objects outside of the current class. Let's try it out by creating a sub-procedure that sets the style of all of the Hyperlink controls in our WUC. Here is the code for the procedure:

```
Public Sub SetLinkStyle(ByRef MasterStyle As Style, _
                        Optional ByVal Merge As Boolean = True)
  Dim objControl As Control
  For Each objControl In Me.Controls
    If TypeOf objControl Is HyperLink Then
      If Merge Then
        CType(objControl, Hyperlink).MergeStyle(MasterStyle)
      Else
        CType(objControl, Hyperlink).ApplyStyle(MasterStyle)
      End If
    End If
  Next
End Sub
```

> The goal of an example is to illustrate the topic at hand clearly, and not necessarily to write examples that are fully optimized for performance. Considering how important efficient code is to web application scalability, though, I would like to point out that, while having the **If** statement in the **For** loop is easier to read, it is not very efficient. In production grade code, this should be written with a top level **If** statement that determines whether to branch off and run a loop that merges the style or to run a loop that applies the style.

The important part for us right now is declaring the sub-procedure as `Public`. After that, we've exposed the method and the rest is just implementation details.

The way that the procedure works is by taking in two parameters. The first is a `System.Web.UI.WebControls.Style` object that has been set up with all of the attributes that we want to apply. The second parameter is used to indicate how to combine the attributes of the `Style` object that has been passed in with the `Style` object of each of our `Hyperlink` controls. If we want to keep all of the non-blank style attributes of each `Hyperlink` control and only add attributes from the passed in `Style` object, we'll set the `Merge` parameter to `True`. If, instead, we want to copy all of the non-blank attributes of the `NewStyle` object over to each `Hyperlink`, overwriting any matching attributes, then we'll want to set the `Merge` parameter to `False`.

The procedure itself cycles through all of the server controls in our WUC looking for ones of the `Hyperlink` type. When it finds one, it casts the generic `Control` type to the `Hyperlink` type so that it can get access to the appropriate `MergeStyle` or `ApplyStyle` method. Test our new method by adding this to the script block in Default.aspx:

```
Sub Page_PreRender(ByVal sender As Object, ByVal e As System.EventArgs)
    MyNavBar.CurrentLink = MyNavBar.LinkControlList.Example3

    Dim objStyle As New Style()
    objStyle.Font.Italic = True
    MyNavBar.SetLinkStyle(objStyle, False)
End Sub
```

The resulting form should look like this:

Creating an Event

At its most basic, creating a new event in a WUC is a fairly simple task. All it takes is a declaration of the event and then you raise the event from somewhere in the code.

> Although not strictly a requirement for creating an event, it is a strongly encouraged convention to provide a protected overridable **OnEventName** method that is called internally to raise the event rather than raising it directly. This convention makes our control easier to work with when it is inherited from, by allowing other developers to modify the event raising logic (that is, adding their own code or events that run before, after, or instead of our event).

Add the following in the declarations section of NavBar.ascx:

```
Public Event CurrentLinkProcessed(ByVal Sender As System.Object, _
                                  ByVal e As System.EventArgs)
```

This declares a new event called CurrentLinkProcessed, which we'll raise at the end of the Control_PreRender code. It's a good idea to keep the event signature (the parameter declarations) consistent with the ASP.NET standard for web control events. That standard is to pass the object that triggered the event and an instance of a class that gives information about the event itself to the event handler. Typically, that class is the EventArgs class or a class that derives from it. You may use any class you like, but it really is the best practice to at least inherit from the EventArgs class.

Now let's add the event raising method mentioned above:

```
Protected Overridable Sub OnCurrentLinkProcessed( _
                       ByVal e As System.EventArgs)
  RaiseEvent CurrentLinkProcessed(Me, e)
End Sub
```

Remember that, by marking the method as Protected, *we are making this method available only to code within our class and to classes that inherit from it. By marking it as* Overridable, *we are allowing any classes that derive from this to sink, modify, or replace the event.*

We use the RaiseEvent syntax to differentiate this from a call to an ordinary procedure. Having declared the event, we still need to call our event raising method from somewhere in our code. Add this line at the end of the Control_PreRender event:

```
  mblnLinksHaveBeenChecked = True
  OnCurrentLinkProcessed(EventArgs.Empty)
End Sub
```

Here we pass in an EventArgs object and we let the OnCurrentLinkProcessed method pass along the reference to the current instance of our WUC. Since we don't have any additional information about the event that we want to include, we use the shared Empty field (a public variable) of the EventArgs object to return an EventArgs object with its ExtendedInfo property set to Nothing.

So now that we've created the CurrentLinkProcessed event, let's see what it takes for the hosting container to respond to it.

Handling Web User Controls' Events

When we work with controls that have been created via tags in an ASPX page, creating event handlers is an exceptionally simple process. If we create a control programmatically, the process is a bit more involved but still reasonably simple. The good news with custom web controls and WUCs is that nothing is different with event handling. We can use the exact same techniques.

So, for our example, we only need to write the procedure that we want to use to respond to the event:

```
Public Sub MyNavBar_CurrentLinkProcessed(ByVal Sender As System.Object, _
                                ByVal e As System.EventArgs)
  Dim strMessage as String = "CurrentLink is: " & _
                        CStr(Sender.CurrentLink)& "<BR>"
  Response.Write(strMessage)
End Sub
```

Then wire it up by specifying it in an OnEventName attribute of the given element:

```
<WebControlsuc:navbar id="MyNavBar" runat="server"
  onCurrentLinkProcessed="MyNavBar_CurrentLinkProcessed" />
```

The UserControl class that our control is inherited from takes care of delegating the event handler for us and all we need to do is sit back and watch.

> If you are used to the way that Internet Explorer wires up client-side events for us, it might surprise you to discover that you can't just create a procedure for a server event called **MyNavBar_OnCurrentLinkProcessed** and have it wired up automatically.
>
> While you can call the procedure whatever you want, if you're *not* using Codebehind, you will always need to specify the name of the handling function in the **OnEventName** attribute of the element tag. If you *are* using a Codebehind class, then you can keep with the .NET standard and use the **Handles** statement.

We've essentially finished our WUC demo now and all that remains is to test it out. View the Default.aspx page in your browser and you should get results like the following:

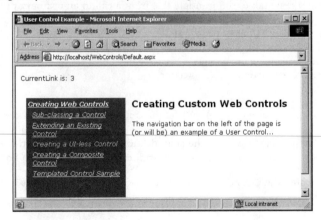

If you look at the top of the page, you'll see the `Response.Write` output indicating that the `CurrentLinkProcessed` event has fired. Since we've specifically set the current link to `Example3`, the index value for the `CurrentLink` property is 3, of course.

Comment out the line in the `Control_PreRender` event that sets the current link, so that the `NavBar` control will go back to determining the link based on the current location:

```
'MyNavBar.CurrentLink = MyNavBar.LinkControlList.Example3
```

Now view the page and you should get this output instead:

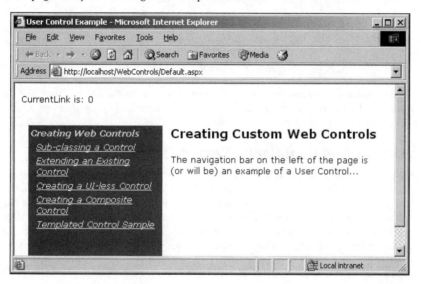

As expected, the `CurrentLinkProcessed` event fires whether we manually set the current link or not. Here we get the index value 0 indicating that `hypHome` is the current link.

> If you've used previous versions of ASP, you may be wondering why the `Response.Write` output is at the top of the page. This happens because the `CurrentLinkProcessed` event is firing before any HTML has actually been written to the output stream.

ASP.NET provides the `PlaceHolder` control for positioning dynamically added controls. The `PlaceHolder` control has no UI of its own but serves only as a light-weight container control for other server controls.

To use a `PlaceHolder` control, add the control from the Toolbox to the **Design View** of an ASPX page. Position the control where you want your dynamically added controls to go. Then, in code, call the `Add` or `AddAt` methods of the `PlaceHolder.Controls` collection.

The next couple of sections cover some additional topics that should be of interest to you as you continue to work with WUCs, before we move on to discuss sub-classed custom web controls.

Reaching out of a Web User Control

Reaching out of a WUC can be a fairly simple process if all you are looking for is the standard members of the hosting page or parent control (if our custom control is nested inside of other server controls). The UserControl class that our control inherits from exposes a Page field and a Parent field, respectively, for accessing the container hierarchy above us. So, if you want to know what the value of the hosting page's IsValid property is, refer to it with the following syntax:

```
If Me.Page.IsValid Then
    'Code to use if the host page passed validation
    ...
Else
    'Code to use if the host page did not pass validation
    ...
End If
```

Similarly, if you want access to one or more of the controls on a host container (maybe you're looking for other instances of your WUC), remember that you have access to the container's FindControl method and the Controls collection.

Casting to the Hosting Container's Type at Runtime

Be forewarned that, if you want to access a variable, property, or method that you've added to a page or a hosting container, you'll need to cast the object returned by the Page or Parent fields to the appropriate type first. In other words, the Page and Parent fields return objects of the base class Page and Control types. Any custom members of the specific instance of the page or control in question are not directly available through these objects. If you want to get access to, say, a public variable on the hosting page called strTestVar, you can't just use the following:

```
Response.Write(Me.Page.strTestVar)
```

If you do, you'll get a compiler error telling you that, "**The name 'strTestVar' is not a member of 'System.Web.UI.Page'.**" So, in order to get to strTestVar, we need to get a reference to the class of the ASP.NET page itself instead of the reference to its base class, System.Web.UI.Page. We can't use the CType function to convert between the two because we would need the type name from the current ASP page. Since that type name changes whenever our control is hosted by another page, we need a method to convert one object to another type – one that works even if we don't know the type until runtime. The shared method ChangeType(), from the System.Convert class, can do this for us:

```
Dim objPageInstance as Object = System.Convert.ChangeType(Me.Page, _
                                            Me.Page.GetType)
```

ChangeType takes two arguments – the object you want to convert and the type that you want to convert it to. In this case we get the object from Me.Page and we use the same object's GetType method to get at the type that the object was originally instanced from. Now we have access to *all* of the public members of the hosting page. We can rewrite our Response.Write statement as:

```
Response.Write(objPageInstance.strTestVar)
```

As long as the hosting page actually has an strTestVar string field or property, we'll get the value back instead of an error.

Other Web User Control Features

WUCs offer a wealth of features and functionality; more, really, than we could expect to cover even in an entire chapter dedicated solely to their use and development. So, to give the other control types their fair share of discussion we'll close off this section with a brief overview of some of the more salient topics.

Web User Control Namespaces

In the section that introduced WUCs, it was mentioned that they provide their own namespace. This means that we'll never have a naming conflict with any of the child controls created in a WUC. If you take a look at the source code from the example we've been working with, you'll find that each named element from our custom control has been given a new ID, one that is unique throughout the hosting page. This is accomplished by concatenating the unique ID of our WUC with the ID of the constituent element, creating a new unique ID!

To illustrate this, take a look at this portion of the source code that our WUC sample generates:

```
<a id="MyNavBar_hypHome"
   style="color:Yellow;font-weight:bold;font-style:italic;">
  Creating Web Controls
</a>
```

Notice that the client side ID generated for this element is the ID of the WUC, an underscore, and the ID of the hyperlink server control from within the WUC. This combination should guarantee us a unique ID on the client side for each of the server controls in the WUC, no matter how many instances of the WUC are added to the page.

This happens because the base `UserControl` class implements the `INamingContainer` interface, a tagging interface that instructs the hosting container to create a separate naming scope for each instance of a WUC. This interface will also come in handy later as we develop other types of container controls, since its use is not limited to WUCs.

Adding Web User Controls Programmatically

WUCs can also be added programmatically. Because they don't reside in class files there is a special method used to load them, though. The method is called `LoadControl` and it is available in every page and container control. The `LoadControl` syntax is:

```
HostingContainer.LoadControl("SomePath/MyUserControl.ascx")
```

Where `HostingContainer` is the page or other container object that we want to add the WUC to, and where `SomePath/MyUserControl.ascx` is the virtual path to the file where the WUC is saved.

The important thing to keep in mind as you read the remainder of the chapter is that WUCs share almost all of the features and functionality of the class-based forms of custom web control development. So, if you see something cool in the remaining portion of this chapter, chances are it applies to WUCs as well.

Creating a Sub-Classed Control

There are actually a couple of variations on basic sub-classed controls that we can create. We can roll our own by inheriting from the `System.Web.UI.WebControl` class (custom web controls), we can inherit from one of the controls in the `System.Web.UI.Webcontrols` or `System.Web.UI.HTMLcontrols` (extending an existing control), or we can inherit from the `System.Web.UI.Control` class (creating a control without a UI). We'll discuss them all, but let's cover a little bit of setup first.

Setting up a Test Bed Project

Let's start off our class-based examples by setting up our web control library and adding a test bed project to it. Create a new **Web Control Library** named `SubClassedControls`.

We're going to use the default namespace (which is the same as the project name) so we don't need to change any of the project settings. If you wanted to change the namespace though, you could right-click on the project in the **Solution Explorer** and select **Properties**. In the **General** properties section of the **SubClassedControls Property Pages** dialog box is the text box for the **Root Namespace** of the project.

Select **File | Add Project | Existing Project From Web...** from the menu bar. Enter the URL of the server that is currently hosting the `WebControls` web application (although the dialog box only says to enter the URL of the server, you can type in the full address of the application if you prefer):

Open the `WebControls.vbproj` file when the **Add Existing Project** dialog box displays. Once the web application project has loaded, right-click on the **WebControls** project in the **Solution Explorer** window and select **Set as Startup Project**. We need to do this so that we'll have an executable project when we click the **Start** button.

Right-click on the **WebControls** project again, this time selecting the **Add Reference** menu option. In the **Add Reference** dialog box, go to the **Projects** tab. **SubClassedControls** should already be displayed in the list box:

Double-click on the SubClassedControls project to add it to the Selected Components list box and then click OK. We've now made it so that the two projects will be built together when the project is run and that the SubClassedControls.dll will be copied to the WebControls web application's Bin folder.

Now that we've set up our test bed project let's move into the next section and start authoring our first sub-classed control.

Sub-Classed Controls and the Web Custom Control Template

To become familiar with the basics of class-based custom web control development in VB.NET, let's start off by examining the custom web control template provided with .NET.

First, change the name of the class file that was created for us to SubClassedControl.vb. If the file isn't open already, double-click on it to open it up in the code editor window. Now do a search for WebCustomControl1 and replace each occurrence with SubClassedControl.

Now let's take a look at the code that has been created for us. Believe it or not, this is all the code we need to build a custom web control. We could compile this code right now and it would work just fine. It might be a bit boring, but it would work.

These first two lines import some namespaces that will be of value to us as we develop our custom web control:

❑ System.ComponentModel – contains classes for implementing and licensing components, including the MemberAttribute class that allows us to describe properties of our class like the default property and how our class should appear in the design environment. While it is possible to write a custom web control that doesn't draw on this namespace, it would seriously hamper its use in development environments like Visual Studio.

❑ System.Web.UI – contains the ASP.NET classes, including the state management classes, enumerations for attributes, styles, tags, output caching, and persistence, and the text writer classes that we'll be using to write our control's output to the response stream.

```
Imports System.ComponentModel
Imports System.Web.UI
```

The next line declares our class and defines some attributes that tell the design environment how to represent our control:

```
<DefaultProperty("Text"), ToolboxData("<{0}:WebCustomControl1
runat=server></{0}:WebCustomControl1>")> Public Class WebCustomControl1
```

Let's review these attributes:

❑ `DefaultProperty` – tells the design environment which property to highlight in the property window when a control based on our class is selected.

❑ `ToolboxData` – this attribute gives the design environment a template for inserting the element tags of our control when it is added to an ASP.NET page from the toolbox. If we are writing a control that is intended as an empty tag – like the <br> or <img> tags – then we would change this attribute to something like `ToolboxData("<{0}:SubClassedControl runat=server/>")>`.

Changing the `ToolboxData` attribute to insert a self-closing tag does not change the output that is rendered for the client. If you need to override your control's closing tag characteristics, you should create a new control builder class for your control. For more information see *Professional ASP.NET 1.0 Special Edition* (Wrox Press, ISBN 1861007035).

Following our class declaration is the instruction to inherit from the base class `WebControl`. This one line gives us access to all of the properties, methods, and events that will facilitate the creation of the UI for our control, and it provides all of the plumbing necessary for the control to be hosted by an ASP.NET page:

```
Inherits System.Web.UI.WebControls.WebControl
```

> **Next comes a block of code to define a custom property for our control, its attributes, and the internal variable to store the property value in. It could just as easily have been called the Message property, but Text is more consistent with the naming conventions for control properties.**

```
Dim _text As String
```

The first portions of the property declaration are again attributes (or metadata) to help with the proper use of our control:

❑ `Bindable` – is used by the compiler to determine whether or not this property can participate in data binding.

❑ `Category` – is intended for the design environment and tells it how to group the property in the **Properties** window.

❑   DefaultValue – is metadata that identifies what the default value of the property is supposed to be. It is typically used by the design environment to identify when the value of the property has been changed.

> **DefaultValue** does *not* set the value of the property! It only describes what that value should be.

```
    <Bindable(True), Category("Appearance"), DefaultValue("")> _
    Property [Text]() As String
      Get
        Return _text
      End Get

      Set(ByVal Value As String)
        _text = Value
      End Set
    End Property

    Protected Overrides Sub Render(_
        ByVal output As System.Web.UI.HtmlTextWriter)
      output.Write([Text])
    End Sub
End Class
```

The Render Method

The interesting part is what happens when we override the Render method. The hosting container calls the Render method of our control when it is ready to insert our control into the **output stream**. The output stream is a buffer for holding the characters that will form our HTML response to the client browser. The page passes the Render method an HtmlTextWriter object in its output argument, which we use as the mechanism for writing to the output buffer (we'll come back to the HtmlTextWriter class in a moment).

Generally, you'll end up overriding one or more of the rendering methods of the base class (Render, RenderBeginTag, RenderContents, RenderChildren, or RenderEndTag) in most of the subclassed controls that you create. Overriding the control's rendering methods gives us the opportunity to create our own custom content; otherwise we'd end up with the base control's rendering of the control. In the template, the version of the Render method supplied overrides the base Render method to write literal text output. By doing so it prevents the WebControl from rendering the tags that it normally produces, and prevents any of the attributes that would normally be added to that tag from being rendered as well:

```
    Protected Overrides Sub Render( _
        ByVal output As System.Web.UI.HtmlTextWriter)
      output.Write([Text])
    End Sub
```

So now we have a control that writes its Text property directly to the output stream without adornment or modification.

> This is not a recommended practice! Although you'll frequently see examples and demos that write directly to the output stream like this, it is a gross simplification. In real-world code development, you should only use this technique for outputting literal text. For any other output, especially outputting beginning and ending tags, use the specialized writing and rendering methods of the **HtmlTextWriter** class.

Writing a control where all of the output is done through the HtmlTextWriter.Write() method will either prevent or seriously hamper your control from enjoying the benefits of the ASP.NET framework. Specifically, this approach would mean that:

❑ The control would require its own attribute writing and style handling logic

❑ It would require its own client-side naming and namespace handling conventions

❑ It could introduce non-standard behavior when working with other controls or ASP.NET pages

❑ It could even prevent the control from being properly rendered in browsers that support upcoming versions of the HTML standard

The temptation always exists to resort to using HtmlTextWriter.Write when outputting a simple set of tags or text. After all, if all you want to do is write a simple <br> or <hr> tag, it's easier to type in:

```
output.Write("<br>")
```

than it is to type in:

```
output.RenderBeginTag(HtmlTextWriterTag.Hr)
output.RenderEndTag()
```

It's a false economy, though. Aside from the fact that the utility methods of HtmlTextWriter can take care of so much of the coding, if you use them, you can count on having controls that will render correctly in browsers that are compliant with new HTML standards.

ASP.NET Delivers Different Code for Different Standards

We've already seen in the previous chapter that ASP.NET server controls change how they are rendered based on the version of HTML supported by the client's browser. The Page class manages this automatic process with assistance from classes that derive from HtmlTextWriter. When a request comes in from a client, the ASP.NET page determines the type of browser that the client has and uses that to decide which type of HtmlTextWriter object to create. Currently, if the client is considered to be **downlevel**, then the page creates an Html32TextWriter object to render HTML 3.2 compliant mark up. Otherwise, it creates an HtmlTextWriter object that will render HTML 4.01 compliant output.

So, as browsers come out with support for new standards, Microsoft (or third-party vendors) will supply new HTML text writers that override the utility methods and shared constants of the HtmlTextWriter base class to comply with those standards. Once the Page class has been updated to be aware of new sub-classes of HtmlTextWriter, a control created with the utility methods will, in most cases, automatically render output that is compliant with the new standard.

The Rendering Methods Subset

When we look at examples illustrating custom web control development, frequently the only output method of a control that gets customized is the Render method. While this technique works for keeping demonstrations simple, it can leave something to be desired when we want to start developing professional quality controls. To create a sub-classed control that takes better advantage of the controls in the WebControls namespace, we need to examine the subset of rendering methods that the base class provides.

The web control architecture is designed to allow fine-grained control of how we want to inherit rendering behavior. It's designed so that we can choose exactly the parts of the rendering process that we want to customize. The way that the web control architecture works is that the base WebControl class (and all of the controls derived from it) provides five separate methods that correspond to the various stages of control rendering. In order of execution they are:

- ❑ RenderBeginTag – responsible for outputting the opening character of the tag and the tag name, this method also calls AddAttributesToRender. It uses the read-only TagName property of the control to determine which tag to output and uses it in a call to the HtmlTextWriter's RenderBeginTag method.

- ❑ AddAttributesToRender – this method adds the identification, style, and standard tag attributes to the HtmlTextWriter's internal attribute collections by repeatedly calling the HtmlTextWriter's AddAttribute and AddStyleAttribute methods. Note that none of the AddAttributesToRender, AddAttribute, or AddStyleAttribute methods actually produce output; instead they prepare the attributes for later rendering, by the HtmlTextWriter.RenderBeginTag method, by adding items to the HtmlTextWriter's internal collections.

- ❑ RenderContents – produces the content after the beginning tag and before the ending tag. If the tag contains nested server controls then this method will instead call the RenderChildren method and let it handle creating the inner content. It will not call RenderChildren if the tag does not support nested controls (for example, controls like the Image control).

- ❑ RenderChildren – handles creating the child control content, by cycling through this control's Controls collection and calling each Render method of each child control in the collection.

- ❑ RenderEndTag – outputs the closing tag if necessary through a call to the HtmlTextWriter.RenderEndTag method. Typically, whether the control requires a closing tag or not is determined by the HtmlTextWriter and the control builder class associated with the control. Whether your control requires a closing tag or not, it should either implement the RenderEndTag behavior or inherit it from its base class.

> **The control's rendering methods are only responsible for invoking the associated methods of the HtmlTextWriter object. In all of the control's rendering methods, it is only the HtmlTextWriter object that actually adds to the output stream.**

All of the methods in the rendering subset take the HtmlTextWriter instance for the control as their only argument. With the exception of RenderChildren, they each make use of public constants from the HtmlTextWriter class to determine how their tag is written (that is, HtmlTextWriter.TagLeftChar for the opening chevron of the opening and closing tags, HtmlTextWriter.SelfClosingTagEnd for the forward slash and closing chevron of a self-closing element, etc.).

As for the Render method itself, it acts as a wrapper for the other five methods. Its main purpose is typically not to produce the control's output but, instead, to invoke the RenderBeginTag, RenderContents, and RenderEndTag methods (with RenderBeginTag and RenderContents calling AddAttributesToRender and RenderChildren in turn).

Developing Sub-Classed Controls

We've been working with the Web Custom Control template so far but, now that we've examined the rendering methods in greater detail, why don't we redevelop the template to take advantage of them?

By overriding the Render method directly and not invoking the rest of the web control rendering method subset members, or calling the HtmlTextWriter's rendering methods directly, the template creates a literal text control (for example, the Text property without any surrounding tags). If we want to create a label control, we need to modify the template's code to have it create tags and attributes, as well as output the contents of the Text property. The best way to do this is to override the RenderContents method and move the output write statement there. So remove the Render method override from the SubClassedControl class and replace it with the following:

```
Protected Overrides Sub RenderContents( _
      ByVal writer As System.Web.UI.HtmlTextWriter)
   writer.Write([Text])
End Sub
```

With this one change, we go from a literal text control to a control that outputs a complete tag – including support for the full set of tag and style attributes. To see which tag we get from the default WebControl implementation, let's add a host page to out project and check out the results.

Creating a Hosting Page

Right-click on the WebControls project and select Add | Add Web Form from the context menu. Call the new web form SubClassingAControl.aspx. Then right-click on SubClassingAControl.aspx in the Solution Explorer and select Set As Start Page.

To keep from adding a whole bunch of positioning attributes to our control when we add it to the design surface, right-click on the design surface and select Properties. Now change the page layout property to FlowLayout.

Now we're ready to add our control.

Adding a Custom Web Control to the Toolbox

Our control's class declaration includes metadata that tells the Toolbox how to write the control's element tags to the page. It would be nice to see that in action so let's add our control to the Toolbox.

We can only add compiled components to the Toolbox, so we need to build SubClassedControls into a DLL before we can add the SubClassedControl. Right-click on the SubClassedControls project and select Build.

In the Toolbox, select the tab that you want to display the control on. Since it should still be relatively uncluttered, let's choose the General tab. Right-click anywhere on the General tab's surface and pick Customize Toolbox... from the context menu.

In the Customize Toolbox dialog box, select the .NET Framework Components tab. Click on the Browse button and locate `SubClassedControls.dll` in the `SubClassedControls\Bin` folder. Check its box, then press OK:

The `SubClassedControl` should now be displayed in the Toolbox. Drag it onto the `SubClassingAControl.aspx` page. The control should now appear on the page, looking as though we have added an empty literal text server control:

It is useful to keep the Show details for non-visible elements setting turned on so that you can be sure that your server controls are within the form tags. If you want to turn this setting on or off in your copy of Visual Studio, you can find it under the Display settings in the HTML Designer folder, reached via Tools | Options.

Let's switch to the HTML view mode and we'll take a look at the code that the Toolbox has added for us. You should find a set of element tags like the following in the body of the page:

```
<form id="Form1" method="post" runat="server">
  <cc1:subclassedcontrol id="SubClassedControl1" runat="server">
  </cc1:subclassedcontrol>
</form>
```

The element tag is based on the template provided in the `ToolboxData` attribute for the class. It looks essentially the same as the template except that Visual Studio has substituted a tag prefix for the `{0}` placeholder and has assigned a unique ID to the element.

Of course, if you dragged the control onto the page and the page is set up for grid layout, you'll also have a bunch of positioning attributes.

> The **Toolbox** does not get updated with the latest value of your control's `ToolboxData` attribute when you rebuild your solution. If you change the `ToolboxData` attribute between builds, you'll need to remove the control from the **Toolbox** and then re-add it before you'll see your changes.

Custom Controls and the @ Register Directive

Just below the @ `Page` directive at the top of the file, you'll also find an @ `Register` directive like the following:

```
<%@ Register TagPrefix="cc1" Namespace="SubClassedControls"
             Assembly="SubClassedControls" %>
```

This version of the @ `Register` directive is a little different from the one that we saw in the WUCs section. For one thing, it doesn't have an `src` attribute – it has an `Assembly` attribute instead. The `src` and `Assembly` attributes serve the same purpose, though, and that is to identify the location of the controls in the namespace to the compiler and to the design environment. In the case of a WUC, that location was a file but, in the case of our sub-classed control, the location is an assembly containing the compiled code for our control.

Earlier, we discussed why the compiler needs to know the location of our control, but why does the design environment need to know it? When we first open the page, Visual Studio puts us into a graphical design mode. Now, when we add a custom control to the page, Visual Studio wants to be able to provide a graphical representation of our control in the **Design** view. So, when we first enter **Design** view, Visual Studio actually instantiates our control and asks it to render itself – which is why the design environment also needs to know where to find our control.

The second reason that we need the @ `Register` directive is to define a tag prefix so that we can uniquely identify the controls that belong to any given namespace in an assembly. Visual Studio has picked a tag prefix for us, although it's not very informative. Let's use the tag prefix `WebControlscwc` (which stands for Custom Web Controls) instead:

We'll need to change it in two places. First, in the @ `Register` directive:

```
<%@ Register TagPrefix="WebControlscwc" Namespace="SubClassedControls"
             Assembly="SubClassedControls" %>
```

And also in the element tags:

```
<WebControlscwc:subclassedcontrol id=SubClassedControl1 runat="server">
</WebControlscwc:subclassedcontrol>
```

Don't forget to make the tag prefix change in both the opening and closing tags.

Specifying a Default TagPrefix for the Assembly

If you don't like the default tag prefix that the design environment provides, we can instruct it to use a default `TagPrefix` value. We can assign a default tag prefix for each namespace in our assembly through the use of the `TagPrefix` attribute. The `TagPrefix` attribute can be added to the `AssemblyInfo.vb` file and it uses the following syntax:

```
<Assembly: System.Web.UI.TagPrefix("NamespaceName", "TagPrefix")>
```

So, in our case, we would add the following to the `AssemblyInfo.vb` file for the `SubClassedControls` project:

```
<Assembly: System.Web.UI.TagPrefix("SubClassedControls", "WebControlscwc")>
```

If you don't want to have to fully qualify `TagPrefix`, you can add a statement to import `System.Web.UI` at the top of the `AssemblyInfo.vb` file.

Save the file, close it, and compile the project. The next time that a control from `SubClassedControls` is added to a new page from the **Toolbox**, it will also add an @ `Register` directive with its `TagPrefix` attribute set to `WebControlscwc`.

Using the Control

All right, so we've written our control and we've put it on a hosting page. All that is left to do is to give it some text to display. In the opening tag of our control, add some content in the `Text` attribute (feel free to type in "Hello world" if you're a traditionalist):

```
<WebControlscwc:subclassedcontrol id=SubClassedControl1 runat="server"
  text="Sub-classed control with attribute text!">
</WebControlscwc:subclassedcontrol>
```

Now start the application and see what we get in the browser. Your page should look very similar to this:

Now let's see what kind of tag the `WebControl` base class created for us. Right-click on the page and select **View Source**. You shouldn't need to look too far to find our control's output. When you do, it should look something like this:

```
<span id="SubClassedControl1">Sub-classed control with attribute text!</span>
```

So `<span>` is the default tag name for the `WebControl` class, but what if we had wanted our control to use a `<div>` or an `<h1>` tag instead? If we were sub-classing from any other control, we would want to override the `RenderBeginTag` method and call the `HtmlTextWriter`'s `RenderBeginTag` method with the appropriate tag name. Since we are inheriting directly from the `WebControl` class, we can take advantage of the extra constructors that `WebControl` has to offer.

The WebControl Constructors

`WebControl` offers two additional constructors over and above the basic constructor. They are:

❑   `New(ByVal tag As HtmlTextWriterTag)` – this constructor takes a member from the `HtmlTextWriterTag` enumeration and uses that value to initialize the read-only `TagKey` and `TagName` properties

❑   `New(ByVal tag As String)` – this constructor takes in the tag name as a string and uses that value to initialize the read-only `TagKey` and `TagName` properties

So, if we want to render a control that inherits directly from `WebControl` as any tag other than a `<span>`, we should override the default class constructor and supply the appropriate tag to the constructor of our base class. To have our control rendered as a `<div>`, we'll supply the following constructor:

```
Public Sub New()
   MyBase.New(HtmlTextWriterTag.Div)
End Sub
```

We call the base class' tag key constructor instead of its tag name constructor because using a tag key offers the greatest extensibility. Should our control be hosted in any other form of output stream, we can supply it with a customized `HtmlTextWriter` class that maps any unsupported tag keys to an equivalent tag name. With a tag name, what we supply is always what we'll get!

Start the application again and let's see if we get the results that we want. The screen output should look pretty much the same but, when we view the source, we should see that the control has now been output as a `<div>` element:

```
<div id="SubClassedControl1">
  Sub-classed control with attribute text!
</div>
```

So far, so good. Earlier, when we set the display text for our new control, we used the `text` attribute to pass in the value to our control. Take a moment and change the control tags so that the text is now nested between them instead:

```
<WebControlscwc:subclassedcontrol id=SubClassedControl1 runat="server">
  Sub-classed control with nested text!
</WebControlscwc:subclassedcontrol>
```

Now try running the application. You should get a parser error:

This is because Microsoft has disallowed nesting in the base WebControl class by default. It seems to be a bit of an odd choice, considering that most people who are familiar with HTML will expect to be able to nest content within our tags, rather than specifying content through attributes. Since we'd probably like to give them the choice to use either technique, let's see how we can change the default behavior of our control in this regard.

Allowing/Disallowing Nested Controls

If we want to allow controls or literal text to be nested within our control, there is an attribute that can be added to the class declaration. The attribute that we want is the ParseChildren attribute. If we add it to the class declaration like so:

```
<DefaultProperty("Text"), ToolboxData( _
        "<{0}:SubClassedControl runat=server></{0}:SubClassedControl>"), _
        ParseChildren(False)> _
Public Class SubClassedControl
```

We are telling the compiler to add the attribute to the metadata for the class so that the page parser can determine at runtime whether the control is allowed to have nested (child) controls or not. Now, by default the WebControl class has its ParseChildren attribute set to True, which means it does not allow nested elements unless they correspond to properties of the control (typically this setting would be used in a data bound control like the Repeater control).

By setting it to False in our class, we are instructing the parser to convert any nested text into LiteralText controls, to instantiate any nested server controls, and to add everything to a collection of child controls for our control. After that, it is up to us as control developers to determine whether to render some, none, or all of the child controls in the collection.

> Any nested tags that are not marked with the **runat="server"** attribute will be treated as literal text and will not be instantiated as HTML server controls. In other words, the elements will still be output on the client-side, but we won't have access to them in server-side script.

Special Cases in Rendering Content

So now, by adding the ParseChildren(False) attribute to our class definition, nested content will no longer cause a parser error. Since we've overridden the method in the base control that would call the RenderChildren method, we still need to add code to our method to actually render that content. We need to go back to the RenderContents method and make use of some of the collections and state properties that we have inherited from the System.Web.UI.Control class.

The Control class, which WebControl inherits from, includes a collection to contain child controls, as well as two properties that indicate special states for that collection. The collection is (not surprisingly) called Controls and the two properties are HasControls and IsLiteralContent. The purpose of the Controls collection has already been discussed above, so we'll just take a look at the two properties here. HasControls and IsLiteralContent are essentially shortcuts that avoid the overhead associated with having to call upon the Controls collection directly. HasControls indicates whether we have any nested controls and it is equivalent to:

```
Controls.Count > 0
```

IsLiteralContent checks for the special case where we have nested content, but where none of that content defines server controls. In other words, we have either plain text or client-side HTML (which server-side code treats as though it were literal text) between the beginning and ending tags of our control. To give us access to the content on the server-side, ASP.NET stores it all in a single LiteralControl and adds that control to our Controls collection. So IsLiteralControl is shorthand for:

```
Controls.Count = 1 And TypeOf Controls(0) Is LiteralControl
```

> *It's more efficient to call HasControls and IsLiteralContent because they have already been evaluated during the parsing stage.*

So, to decide what to do with nested elements in our control, we'll add the following to our overridden RenderContents method:

```
Protected Overrides Sub RenderContents( _
        ByVal writer As System.Web.UI.HtmlTextWriter)
    If Not HasControls Then
      writer.Write([Text])
    ElseIf IsLiteralContent Then
```

```
      writer.Write(CType(Controls(0), LiteralControl).Text)
    Else
      MyBase.RenderChildren(writer)
    End If
  End Sub
```

The conditional statements above first check to see if we have any nested content. If we don't then, as before, we output the value of the Text property. If we *do* have nested content, then we check for the special case where the content doesn't have any nested server controls and output the Text property of the LiteralText control directly. Finally, if we have more than one control in the collection or we have one control but it isn't a LiteralText control, then we call on the RenderChildren method of our base control to walk through our Controls collection and render each child control in turn.

> *We haven't chosen to output the Text attribute when we have nested content because that is the way that the .NET server controls with a Text property generally behave.*

When the only nested content that we have is literal text or client-side HTML, it's good practice to expose that content on the server-side by setting the Text property equal to the nested content. So we'll go back to the Text property procedures and modify them to make them aware of the IsLiteralText special case:

```
<Bindable(True), Category("Appearance"), DefaultValue("")> _
Property [Text]() As String
  Get
    If IsLiteralContent Then
      Return CType(Controls(0), LiteralControl).Text
    Else
      Return _text
    End If
  End Get

  Set(ByVal Value As String)
    If IsLiteralContent Then
      CType(Controls(0), LiteralControl).Text() = Value
    Else
      _text = Value
    End If
  End Set
End Property
```

This way, if code in the hosting container retrieves or changes the Text property it will get access to the text that will actually be displayed on the page.

Summary

In this chapter, we've taken a long look at the various forms of custom web control development that are available in the .NET Framework. We've seen how the web development process has been designed, from the ground up, to leverage existing skill sets and to take full advantage of the powerful new object-oriented features in VB.NET.

We've examined the basic structure of web user and sub-classed controls, and covered some best practices for control design. We also took a brief look at composite and templated controls.

This chapter should act as a good starting point for your exploration of the wealth of web control development options that .NET has to offer.

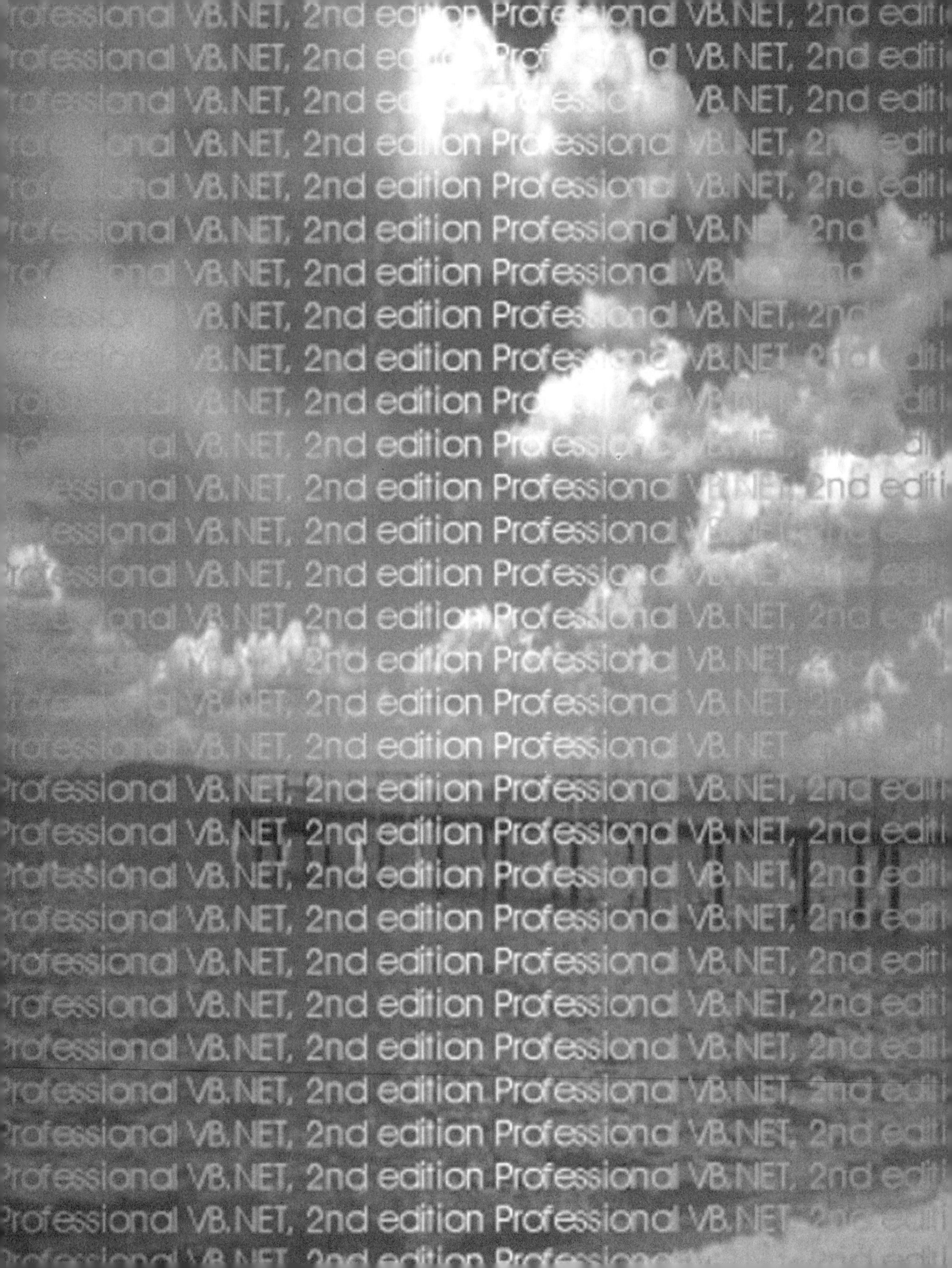
Professional VB.NET, 2nd edition

16

Data Binding

One extremely common requirement of applications is the ability to extract data from a data source (a database, Web service, XML file, or whatever) and display it on the screen. Once there, the user expects to be able to use user interface controls to manipulate and change the data, potentially to save any changes back to a data source.

.NET provides 'data binding' to make this process a little easier. It allows the automatic population of controls with data from an underlying data source and also provides a mechanism for updating the underlying data source in response to any changes the user may make. In this chapter, we're going to take a look at Windows Forms data binding.

Presenting Data

One basic way of presenting database data is in a tabular format. You've probably already seen tools such as SQL Server Enterprise Manager display information in this way, for example:

We can replicate that view more or less instantly by using the DataGrid Windows Forms control.

To start, we'll need a new Windows Application project. Call it DataGridDemo. To the default Form1 form, add a DataGrid control from the toolbox. Set its name property to datagridAuthors and its Dock property to Fill.

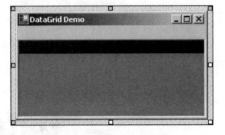

Add a MainMenu control to the form. Set its Name property to menuMain. Add a single top-level menu item to this menu. Set its Name property to menuRefresh and set its Text property to &Refresh:

Double-click on the new menu item to create a new event handler. Add this code:

```
Private Sub menuRefresh_Click(ByVal sender As System.Object, _
        ByVal e As System.EventArgs) Handles menuRefresh.Click
    RefreshData()
End Sub
```

Now, add a new Load event handler for the form itself and add this code:

```
Private Sub Form1_Load(ByVal sender As System.Object, _
        ByVal e As System.EventArgs) Handles MyBase.Load
    RefreshData()
End Sub
```

The RefreshData method itself simply connects to the database and populates a DataSet. Before that, we need to add some constants to Form1. The first defines the SQL Server connection string and you'll need to modify this to suit your own needs. The second defines the SQL string that will be used to return all of the authors back from the database.

```
Imports System.Data.SqlClient

Public Class Form1
    Inherits System.Windows.Forms.Form
```

```
Public Const ConnectionString As String = _
    "integrated security=sspi;initial catalog=pubs;data source=corrado"
    Protected Const GetAllAuthorsSqlString As String = "select au_id, au_lname,
au_fname, phone, address, city, state, zip, contract from authors order by
au_lname, au_fname"
```

Once `RefreshData` has established a connection to the database and populated the `DataSet`, we give the entire `DataTable` to the `DataGrid` control by setting the `DataGrid` control's `DataSource` property. This results in the data in the table being added to the `DataGrid` so that the user can see the data:

```
Public Sub RefreshData()
    Dim connection As New SqlConnection(ConnectionString)
    connection.Open()
    Dim adapter As New SqlDataAdapter(GetAllAuthorsSqlString, _
                        connection)
    Dim dataset As New DataSet()
    adapter.Fill(dataset)
    adapter.Dispose()
    connection.Close()
    Dim table As DataTable = dataset.Tables(0)
    datagridAuthors.DataSource = table
End Sub
```

Run the project now and the `DataGrid` will duly display the data:

	au_id	au_lname	au_fname	phone	address	city	state	zip	contract	
▶	409-56-7008	Bennet	Abraham	415 658-9932	6223 Batema	Berkeley	CA	94705	☑	
	648-92-1872	Blotchet-Halls	Reginald	503 745-6402	55 Hillsdale B	Corvallis	OR	97330	☑	
	238-95-7766	Carson	Cheryl	415 548-7723	589 Darwin L	Berkeley	CA	94705	☑	
	722-51-5454	DeFrance	Michel	219 547-9982	3 Balding Pl.	Gary	IN	46403	☑	
	712-45-1867	del Castillo	Innes	615 996-8275	2286 Cram Pl	Ann Arbor	MI	48105	☑	
	427-17-2319	Dull	Ann	415 836-7128	3410 Blonde	Palo Alto	CA	94301	☑	

As you can see, using data binding to display a table of information in a Windows Form application is very simple indeed.

The `DataGrid` has functionality built in that enables it to understand the `DataTable`. Although we can bind all sorts of data (which is a topic we'll look at later in this chapter), what it's really doing here is getting a `DataTable` and saying, "OK, I know what to do with that. I know that I can get a list of columns from the `Columns` collection in the `DataTable`, and I also know how to iterate through the rows and display them."

However, what we can't do there is change the data. Or rather, we can, but we cannot marshal the changes back into the database. What happens is if you change the data on this view, the column in the underlying `DataRow` does indeed get changed, because the `DataGrid` knows that when changes are made to the UI, those changes need to be passed back to the underlying, in-memory store of the data. What we need to do is copy the changes out of the in-memory store and back into SQL Server.

559

Saving Changes

When we load the data inside `RefreshData`, we disconnect the database connection after the read:

```
Public Sub RefreshData()
    Dim connection As New SqlConnection(ConnectionString)
    connection.Open()
        '...
    connection.Close()
        '...
End Sub
```

This is great from a scalability perspective, but presents a slight problem when we want to save the data back. When we need to save, we establish a connection to the database again and give a new `SqlDataAdapter` the rows that have changed (we'll see how to tell which rows have changed in a moment).

Before we do this, though, we need a way of telling the application that the data does need to be saved. We'll do this by adding a menu item. What would be cool though is if we only enabled this menu item when the data had actually changed. First off though, we need the menu item, so add a new menu item to `menuMain`. Set its `Name` property to `menuSaveChanges`, its `Text` property to `&Save Changes` and its `Enabled` property to `False`:

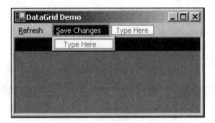

We can detect when the user changes the data by listening for an event on the `DataTable` object itself! `DataTable` raises these events: `ColumnChanged`,`ColumnChanging`, `RowChanged`, `RowChanging`, `RowDeleted`, and `RowDeleting`.

We'll hook into the `ColumnChanged` event, which will be sent when the user changes a value in any column. Add this code to `RefreshData`:

```
Public Sub RefreshData()
    '...
    connection.Close()
    Dim table As DataTable = dataset.Tables(0)
    AddHandler table.ColumnChanged, _
            New DataColumnChangeEventHandler(AddressOf ColumnChanged)
    datagridAuthors.DataSource = table
End Sub
```

Now, add the `ColumnChanged` method:

```
Protected Sub ColumnChanged(ByVal sender As Object, _
                    ByVal e As DataColumnChangeEventArgs)
    menuSaveChanges.Enabled = True
End Sub
```

Add this handler to `menuSaveChanges`:

```
Private Sub menuSaveChanges_Click(ByVal sender As System.Object, _
                    ByVal e As System.EventArgs)
    SaveChanges()
End Sub
```

The job of `SaveChanges` is to look through every `DataRow` on the bound `DataTable` examining the `State` property. If this is not `DataRowState.Unchanged`, then we need to ask a new `SqlDataAdapter` to marshal the changes back into the database. First off, when we start walking the collection we add any changed rows that we find to an `ArrayList`. If at the end of walking the collection we find that there are no changed rows, we return:

```
Public Sub SaveChanges()
    Dim table As DataTable = CType(datagridAuthors.DataSource, _
                DataTable)
    Dim changedRows As New ArrayList()
    Dim row As DataRow
    For Each row In table.Rows
        If row.RowState <> DataRowState.Unchanged Then
            changedRows.Add(row)
        End If
    Next
    If changedRows.Count = 0 Then
        Return
    End If
```

Once we have the list, we connect to the database:

```
Dim connection As New SqlConnection(ConnectionString)
connection.Open()
```

We used a `SqlDataAdapter` to get the data out of the database and into a `DataSet`, and so now we're going to do the reverse – that is, we're going to use a `SqlDataAdapter` to put data back into the database. To do this, we only need the original SELECT SQL statement that we used to retrieve the data (this technique only works if we select a single table at a time). We can use a `System.Data.SqlClient.SqlCommandBuilder` object to examine that SELECT SQL statement and build us a new UPDATE SQL statement (which, if you ask me, is pretty smart!). The object will also build us new INSERT and DELETE statements too. To do this, we just create a new `SqlCommandBuilder` and pass the `SqlDataAdapter` into the constructor:

```
Dim adapter As New SqlDataAdapter(GetAllAuthorsSqlString, _
                connection)
Dim builder As New SqlCommandBuilder(adapter)
```

We use the `Update` method on `SqlDataAdapter` to provide the data that should be updated (somewhat confusingly, this 'Update' method will also 'Insert' and 'Delete' rows as appropriate). If we give it an entire `DataSet`, what the adapter actually does is look through all the rows on all the tables in much the same way as we've done in the first part of this method. Instead, we'll use the alternative version of this method that takes an array of `DataRow` objects:

```
        Dim rows() As DataRow = _
                    CType(changedRows.ToArray(GetType(DataRow)),DataRow())
        adapter.Update(rows)
```

Finally, we close the connection and disable the menu item:

```
        ' close...
        adapter.Dispose()
        connection.Close()

        ' flag...
        menuSaveChanges.Enabled = False
    End Sub
```

Now try running the project again. In this screen shot, I've changed Cheryl Carson's city from Berkeley, CA to Tempe, AZ:

If you click the **Save Changes** button, the data will be saved back into the database. You need to select another row in the `DataGrid` in order for the changes to be made to the `DataSet`, so if you don't do this **Save Changes** will have no effect. If you click **Refresh**, this will prove that the data has indeed been changed – but the skeptical amongst you may wish to look in the database itself:

Profiling the Update Statement

I personally get a little concerned when I ask .NET to do something for me and I have no idea what it's doing behind the scenes. This is particularly important with thinking about database access. For example, when I ask `SqlDataAdapter` to fill a `DataSet` for me, I give it the SQL statement to use or (better yet) I give it a stored procedure to use. However, when I ask `SqlDataAdapter` to persist the changes back into the database, I'm using `SqlCommandBuilder` and, frankly, the fact that I don't know what that's doing concerns me.

Database access is one of those things in commercial software development that's both absolutely necessary, but can cause a tremendous amount of problems. A badly formed SQL query has the potential to kill the performance of an otherwise well-written application, and it's for this reason that we spend so much time carefully thinking about what queries to run and when to run them. It's also why we spend so much time with stored procedures. I personally don't enjoy having to mess around with complex blocks of code responsible for providing parameters to and executing stored procedures, but they are a necessary evil because they run so quickly and efficiently.

`SqlCommandBuilder` is a tricky one to call. In about five seconds, I can use one in my code, but what is it actually doing?

You can discover the query that it's built by messing around with the debugger, but an easier way is to use SQL Server's Profiler tool. This tool enables you to see what the queries being executed against a particular server are. By attaching Profiler to our server and saving the changes back into the database, we can see exactly what is happening.

You can find the Profiler from the Start menu: Start – Programs – Microsoft SQL Server – Profiler. When it starts, select File – New – Trace and connect it to the database server:

Profiler is actually a far more powerful tool than we're going to give it credit for here. If you'd like to learn more about how it works you should read Professional SQL Server 2000.

When you connect, you'll be asked to create a **trace**. Profiler will save events into this trace for later use – although in our case we're just going to watch the events unfold on the display as we run our application.

Click Run. A ton of stuff will display on the screen, which we can ignore. Select Edit – Clear Trace Window.

Run the `DataGrid` application. At this point, the application will connect to the database and query for the authors. If you look at the Profiler, you'll find some trace events. The ones coming from SQLAgent – Alert Engine you can ignore. But, the ones coming from .Net SqlClient Data Provider are important. These are the ones from our application:

EventClass	TextData	ApplicationName
RPC:Completed	exec sp_reset_connection	.Net SqlClient Data Provider
RPC:Completed	exec sp_executesql N'select au_id, ...	.Net SqlClient Data Provider
RPC:Completed	exec sp_reset_connection	.Net SqlClient Data Provider
RPC:Completed	exec sp_executesql N' SET FMTONLY O...	.Net SqlClient Data Provider
RPC:Completed	exec sp_executesql N'UPDATE authors...	.Net SqlClient Data Provider

Look at the second .NET event. It'll look like this:

```
exec sp_executesql N'select au_id, au_lname, au_fname, phone, address, city,
state, zip, contract from authors order by au_lname, au_fname'
```

That's exactly the statement that we supplied, with the curious exception that SQL Server appears to be running a built-in stored procedure called sp_executesql and passing in our SQL statement as a parameter. This is 'one of those things' and nothing to worry about.

Change some data in the DataGrid application and select **Save Changes**. You'll find an UPDATE statement that looks like this:

```
exec sp_executesql N'UPDATE authors SET city = @p1 , state = @p2 WHERE ( (au_id =
@p3) AND ((au_lname IS NULL AND @p4 IS NULL) OR (au_lname = @p5)) AND ((au_fname
IS NULL AND @p6 IS NULL) OR (au_fname = @p7)) AND ((phone IS NULL AND @p8 IS NULL)
OR (phone = @p9)) AND ((address IS NULL AND @p10 IS NULL) OR (address = @p11)) AND
((city IS NULL AND @p12 IS NULL) OR (city = @p13)) AND ((state IS NULL AND @p14 IS
NULL) OR (state = @p15)) AND ((zip IS NULL AND @p16 IS NULL) OR (zip = @p17)) AND
((contract IS NULL AND @p18 IS NULL) OR (contract = @p19)) )', N'@p1
varchar(5),@p2 char(2),@p3 varchar(11),@p4 varchar(6),@p5 varchar(6),@p6
varchar(6),@p7 varchar(6),@p8 char(12),@p9 char(12),@p10 varchar(14),@p11
varchar(14),@p12 varchar(7),@p13 varchar(7),@p14 char(2),@p15 char(2),@p16
char(5),@p17 char(5),@p18 bit,@p19 bit', @p1 = 'Tempe', @p2 = 'AZ', @p3 = '238-95-
7766', @p4 = 'Carson', @p5 = 'Carson', @p6 = 'Cheryl', @p7 = 'Cheryl', @p8 = '415
548-7723', @p9 = '415 548-7723', @p10 = '589 Darwin Ln.', @p11 = '589 Darwin Ln.',
@p12 = 'Berkley', @p13 = 'Berkley', @p14 = 'CA', @p15 = 'CA', @p16 = '94705', @p17
= '94705', @p18 = 1, @p19 = 1
```

That's a long SQL statement! The first line is telling us that SqlCommandBuilder is only changing the values for city and state, which is right because when I ran this statement I changed city from Berkeley to Scottsdale and state from CA to AZ. However, the rest of the statement is a bit of mishmash. It appears that SqlCommandBuilder couldn't work out what the primary key on the table was, because the statement should look like this:

```
exec sp_executsql N'UPDATE authors SET city=@p1, state=@p2 WHERE au_id=@p3',
    N'@p1 varchar(10), @p2 char(2)',
    @p1 = 'Scottsdale', @p2 = 'AZ', @p3 = '238-95-7766'
```

Better yet, we should have a custom stored procedure that just knows to update the city and state for a given author, if this is going to be a common activity that's worth optimizing.

This rather illustrates my point. Without actually spending the time to write the code that has an understanding that the au_id column is the primary key, SqlCommandBuilder is going to flounder around trying to find a close approximation.

Use `SqlCommandBuilder` with care and caution, and optimize the way your application uses the database to precisely fit your needs!

Master/Details Data Binding

A very common design pattern in data-centric applications is the 'master/details' view. In this kind of view, the 'top-level' data is shown in one UI element (for example, a list of books published). When this UI element is manipulated, another element or set of elements showing the detail is updated to display the detail 'within' the top-level data (for example, the sales for the selected book).

There are two ways of doing this – one relatively ugly and quite difficult to use from the user's perspective (although very easy to code), the other being a slightly more elegant solution (but slightly more difficult to code).

Multiple, Related Tables in a Single DataGrid

The first solution we'll look at (although ugly) shows some functionality of the `DataGrid` related to the fact that a `DataSet` can in fact contain multiple tables of data. For example, if we wanted we could create a single `DataSet` that loads data from a collection of different databases, and loads data from XML files, and even holds data created programmatically:

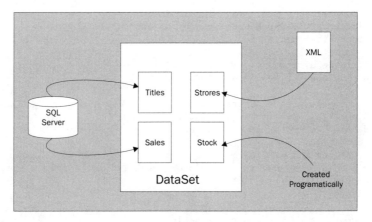

In the above example, we gave the `DataGrid` control just the table that we had bound to through the `DataSource` member. We could have given it the entire `DataSet`, in which case the control would have provided a list of tables for us to choose from. As there was only one table in the list, the list would have contained just one item.

In this next section, we'll take a look at using the `titles` table to retrieve a list of books that the publisher has published and we'll combine this with the `sales` table so that for a given book we can see what sales have been made.

We can use the same VS .NET project, as the code to drive this example will be similar to the previous one. First off, we need SQL statements to load all of the data from the `titles` table and from the `sales` table:

```
Public Class Form1
    Inherits System.Windows.Forms.Form
    ' const...
    Public Const ConnectionString As String = "integrated security=sspi;initial
catalog=pubs;data source=corrado"
    Protected Const GetAllAuthorsSqlString = "select au_id, au_lname, au_fname,
phone, address, city, state, zip, contract from authors order by au_lname,
au_fname"
    Protected Const GetAllTitlesSqlString As String = "select title_id, title,
type, pub_id, price, advance, royalty, ytd_sales, notes, pubdate from titles"
    Protected Const GetAllSalesSqlString As String = "select stor_id, ord_num,
ord_date, qty, payterms, title_id from sales"
```

To load the data this time round, we want to explicitly create the DataTable objects and use the
SqlDataAdapter to fill the table. Previously, we didn't create the tables and told the
SqlDataAdapter to fill the DataSet. All that happened here was that SqlDataAdapter discovered
no tables in the DataSet and created a new one for its purposes. Notice as well how we specifically
give the DataSet a name of Book Sales and how we do the same with the two tables. Finally, notice
how we bind datagridTitles (I've changed the name from datagridAuthors) to the DataSet, not
to an individual table:

```
Public Sub RefreshData()

    ' connect...
    Dim connection As New SqlConnection(ConnectionString)
    connection.Open()

    ' create a dataset...
    Dim dataset As New DataSet("Book Sales")

    ' manually create a titles table...
    Dim titlesTable As New DataTable("Titles")
    dataset.Tables.Add(titlesTable)

    ' get the titles back...
    Dim adapter As New SqlDataAdapter(GetAllTitlesSqlString, connection)
    adapter.Fill(titlesTable)
    adapter.Dispose()

    ' do the same for the sales table...
    Dim salesTable As New DataTable("Sales")
    dataset.Tables.Add(salesTable)

    ' get the sales back...
    adapter = New SqlDataAdapter(GetAllSalesSqlString, connection)
    adapter.Fill(salesTable)
    adapter.Dispose()

    ' close...
    connection.Close()

    ' bind...
```

```
            datagridTitles.DataSource = dataset
    End Sub
```

Run the project and you'll see a view with a plus button. Click this plus button and you'll see a list of tables:

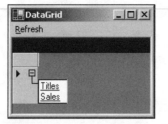

If you click in the Titles table, you'll see all of the titles:

title_id	title	type	pub_id	price	advance	royalty	ytd_sales	notes	pubdate
BU1032	The Busy Exe	business	1389	19.99	5000	10	4095	An overview	12/06/1991
BU1111	Cooking with	business	1389	11.95	5000	10	3876	Helpful hints	09/06/1991
BU2075	You Can Co	business	0736	2.99	10125	24	18722	The latest me	30/06/1991
BU7832	Straight Talk	business	1389	19.99	5000	10	4095	Annotated an	22/06/1991
MC2222	Silicon Valley	mod_cook	0877	19.99	0	12	2032	Favorite recip	09/06/1991

Book Sales:

The small left arrow button on the DataGrid control's toolbar acts as a back button, so you can use this to go back and see the Sales table.

That's pretty cute, but it doesn't really solve our problem, as we can't see which sales *specifically relate* to titles in the database. To solve this, we have to add a relation to the DataSet that defines how titles and sales are related. We do this by creating a new System.Data.DataRelation instance and adding it to the Relations collection of the DataSet. All we need to know is the name of the column from the master table and the name of the matching column in the details table. Here's the code:

```
    ' close...
    connection.Close()

    ' relate the tables...
    Dim relation As New DataRelation("TitleSales", _
        titlesTable.Columns("title_id"), salesTable.Columns("title_id"))
    dataset.Relations.Add(relation)

    ' bind...
    datagridTitles.DataSource = dataset
    End Sub
```

Now if you look at the titles table you'll find that small plus buttons appear next to each of the rows. Expanding one of these buttons gives you the option to view the sales:

Clicking on the link displays the related data:

Personally, I feel that this view in day-to-day use is pretty useless. The display of the master data displayed in the headers is squashed as best, unreadable at worst. Plus, you have to keep using the back button to go back to the master rows if you want to see sales for another book. Here's a better solution.

A More Usable Solution

A better solution is to have two `DataGrid` controls. The master list is always visible and changing the selection on this row leads to the selection being changes on the details list.

To do this, delete the `DataGrid` from `Form1` and add a new `Panel` control. Set the `Panel` control's `Dock` property to `Top`. Then, add a `Splitter` control, setting its `Dock` property to `Top` as well. Finally, add a new `Panel` control to the blank region at the bottom of the form and set its `Dock` property to `Fill`:

Then, add two new `DataGrid` controls to each of the two panels. Call the top one `datagridTitles` and the bottom one `datagridSales`. Set the `Dock` property of each to `Fill`:

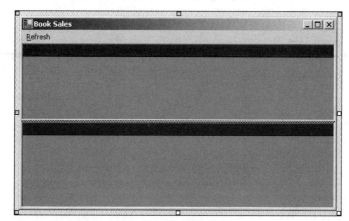

One of the issues with using the first ('ugly') approach was that not only did we have to load the entire `titles` table into memory, but we also had to load the entire `sales` table. This isn't particularly elegant if you consider that not only might this `sales` table be very large, but also that we don't need all of the data in that table to be loaded. It would be better to use an on-demand approach where the relevant sales data is loaded only when a title is selected.

However, our first job is to load the titles (these are the 'master' records). To do this, remove the lines of code from `RefreshData` that query data from `sales` and change the binding statement so that `datagridTitles` is bound to `tableTitles`. You'll also need to remove the line that creates the `DataRelation`:

```
Public Sub RefreshData()

    ' connect...
    Dim connection As New SqlConnection(ConnectionString)
    connection.Open()

    ' create a dataset...
    Dim dataset As New DataSet("Book Sales")

    ' manually create a titles table...
    Dim titlesTable As New DataTable("Titles")
    dataset.Tables.Add(titlesTable)

    ' get the titles back...
    Dim adapter As New SqlDataAdapter(GetAllTitlesSqlString, connection)
    adapter.Fill(titlesTable)
    adapter.Dispose()

    ' close...
    connection.Close()

    ' bind...
```

```
            datagridTitles.DataSource = titlesTable

    End Sub
```

Run the project and you'll see the titles. However, you can't see the sales data. The first thing we need to do to remedy that is to listen for CurrentCellChanged events being sent by the datagridTitles control. When we receive those messages, we can load the data and update the datagridSales control.

Finding out what title is selected in the datagridTitles control is actually quite difficult. You would think that the DataGrid control would expose a CurrentRow property that returned the current DataRow. In fact, it doesn't do this, mainly because the DataGrid control is not specifically tied to displaying data from a DataTable, and of course, a CurrentRow property only makes sense if you do have a list containing DataRow objects.

What we have to do instead is find out what title is selected by actually examining the row information loaded into the control. We are told when the selection changes what row number we're looking at. However, this does not map to a row number in the underlying DataTable as the user may have used the header of the DataGrid to resort the data by the columns (in which case the data won't marry up – originally row 16 in the DataTable would have matched row 16 in the DataGrid, but after the sort this may not be true). If we have the row number, we can look for the cell at column 0 at that row number, which will contain the title ID providing the user hasn't changed its value (you can set the DataGrid to be read-only by using the ReadOnly property):

```
    Private Sub datagridTitles_CurrentCellChanged(ByVal sender As Object, _
        ByVal e As System.EventArgs) Handles _
        datagridTitles.CurrentCellChanged

        ' what row?
        Dim titleId As String = _
        datagridTitles.Item(datagridTitles.CurrentCell.RowNumber, 0)

        ' form the sql...
        Dim sql As String = "select stor_id, ord_num, ord_date, qty, payterms,
        title_id from sales where title_id='" & titleId & "'"

        ' connect...
        Dim connection As New SqlConnection(ConnectionString)
        connection.Open()

        ' fill...
        Dim adapter As New SqlDataAdapter(sql, connection)
        Dim dataset As New DataSet()
        adapter.Fill(dataset)
        adapter.Dispose()

        ' close...
        connection.Close()

        ' show...
        datagridSales.DataSource = dataset.Tables(0)

    End Sub
```

With that code in place, run the application. You'll find that when you select titles from the master list, the matching sales information is displayed in the details list:

Forms

We've seen how data can be bound and displayed as tables. We've also seen how we can save the data back into the database once the user has changed it. What we haven't seen is how we can work with data that's displayed using a form.

Using forms in this way is a very common design pattern, and also gives rise to expectations in the user as to how the form should work. Typically, such forms use VCR (or in this day and age, DVD) buttons to allow the user to move through the records. Typically we have 'first', 'previous', 'next' and 'last' buttons. The user also expects to be told when data has been changed, and have the opportunity to save or to discard the data when they change the selection.

To keep track of things, we need to hold a `DataTable` containing the authors, and the index of the record that they are currently looking at. We also need to know whether they have changed the data in the underlying `DataTable` by changing the text in the form's `TextBox` controls so that we can prompt the user to save or discard the changes.

For this, you can either create a new project or use the existing one. Either way, you'll need to create a new form and add a number of `TextBox`, `Label` and `Button` controls. Also, if you are using a new project add a **Refresh** menu item again as before, otherwise keep the existing item:

Name the TextBox controls like this: textAuthorId, textLastName, textFirstName, textPhone, textAddress, textCity, textState and textZip. I've made the textAuthorId control read-only as it's unlikely the user will want to change this – or rather the user may potentially 'break' the data if she does change this.

Name the Button controls like this: buttonFirst, buttonPrevious, buttonNext, buttonLast and buttonSave. buttonSave should have its Enabled property set to False. Finally, set the Name property of the Label control in the bottom-right to labelPosition:

As a private field of Form1, create _authors:

```
Imports System.Data.SqlClient
Public Class Form1
    Inherits System.Windows.Forms.Form


    Private _authors As DataTable
```

When the form loads, call RefreshData. This method loads the entire authors table into a new DataTable and sets the Authors property (we'll build this property in a moment):

```
    Private Sub Form1_Load(ByVal sender As System.Object, _
                  ByVal e As System.EventArgs) Handles MyBase.Load
        RefreshData()
    End Sub
    Public Sub RefreshData()

        ' connect...
        Dim connection As New SqlConnection(ConnectionString)
        connection.Open()

        ' create and fill...
        Dim table As New DataTable()
        Dim adapter As New SqlDataAdapter(GetAllAuthorsSqlString, _
                      connection)
        adapter.Fill(table)
```

```
            adapter.Dispose()

            ' close...
            connection.Close()

            ' bind...
            Authors = table
    End Sub
```

The `Authors` property is responsible for setting the _authors field, but is also responsible for establishing the data binding. Add this code:

```
    Public Property Authors() As DataTable
        Get
            Return _authors
        End Get
        Set(ByVal Value As DataTable)

            ' set it...
            _authors = Value

            ' update the bindings...
            UpdateBindings()
        End Set
    End Property
```

The Windows Forms data binding is very flexible, but I find it a little hard to get my head around, so try and fully understand the next few points before moving on. The idea is that if you have a control, you can use data binding to 'tie' a property on that control together with an 'item' in the underlying data source. In our case, the 'item' we want to tie into is a specific column on the current row of the underlying `DataTable`. Without getting too far ahead of myself, there is a mechanism for discovering and changing the current row, which is how we'll move through the records, but we're going to do that in the next section.

You can nominate pretty much any property on a control to data bind to, providing that that property can accept the data type you're trying to use. (For example, you can't put a `varchar` field into a Boolean property.) In our case, we're going to use the `Text` property. So, when we start data binding we're going set the `Text` property to the associated value – the result of which is the value that will appear on the screen. When the user changes this value, the `Text` property will be read and the underlying `DataRow` will have the relevant column changed. Likewise, as we move through the rows in the table, the properties will be automatically updated.

The `DataBindings` property is defined on the `System.Windows.Forms.Control` class. All of the Framework controls (including `Form`) extend this class, so `DataBindings` is pretty much universally available on all controls. It's by manipulating this property that we can control the data binding. The first step is to remove any existing data bindings, and then add new data bindings that associated the `Text` property of each control with the relevant column from the _authors DataTable.

```
    Protected Sub UpdateBindings()

        ' remove the bindings...
```

```
        textAuthorId.DataBindings.Clear()
        textLastName.DataBindings.Clear()
        textFirstName.DataBindings.Clear()
        textPhone.DataBindings.Clear()
        textAddress.DataBindings.Clear()
        textCity.DataBindings.Clear()
        textState.DataBindings.Clear()
        textZip.DataBindings.Clear()

        ' do we have an author?
        If Not _authors Is Nothing Then

            ' bind the data to the text boxes...
            textAuthorId.DataBindings.Add("Text", _authors, "au_id")
            textLastName.DataBindings.Add("Text", _authors, "au_lname")
            textFirstName.DataBindings.Add("Text", _authors, "au_fname")
            textPhone.DataBindings.Add("Text", _authors, "phone")
            textAddress.DataBindings.Add("Text", _authors, "address")
            textCity.DataBindings.Add("Text", _authors, "city")
            textState.DataBindings.Add("Text", _authors, "state")
            textZip.DataBindings.Add("Text", _authors, "zip")
        End If
    End Sub
```

Run the project now and you'll find the first record displayed in the form:

What's happening here is that after we've loaded the data in, when we establish the data bindings the `TextBox` control is dredging the data from the underlying `DataTable` and using it to set the `Text` properties against each control.

Moving Through the Records

Now that we can display a record, we need to configure our form so that the user can move through the records. Although getting it to do this is remarkably easy, actually understanding what's happening behind the scenes is a little strange.

When working with data binding in this way, we're in a situation where the eight TextBox controls all have to be synchronized to the same data source. In our case, we've bound the Text properties of each to different 'items' (in our specific case, 'columns') on the same underlying data source (in our specific case again, a 'DataTable'). However, a table has two dimensions, which means that something has to keep track of which row is actually selected. That same 'something' also has to be manipulate-able from code so that we can change the row when the user clicks the VCR buttons.

The form maintains a collection of **binding managers**, which keep the various bindings synchronized. The base class is System.Windows.Forms.BindingManagerBase and there are two default derivations from this defined in the Framework: CurrencyManager and PropertyManager. CurrencyManager is a slightly odd name, because it refers to 'that which is current', not the way I always think of it as 'money'!

> For the time being, you can ignore **PropertyManager**. We'll cover this later.

The form itself is asked by the control for a binding manager through the BindingContext property. This property is implemented on System.Windows.Forms.Control and returns a BindingContext object. This object in turn supports an Item property, and if we give this property the data source that we want to bind to, it will either return a new binding manager or give us one that's already in use. So, in our case, when we bind textAuthorId for the first time, the collection is empty so a new CurrencyManager is created, configured to work with the authors DataTable and is added to the collection. When we bind to textLastName, because the same underlying data source is used, that *same* CurrencyManager is used, and so therefore *both controls are bound to the same binding manager*.

To see this in action, we need to wire up the buttons. These buttons will be responsible for changing the value of the AuthorIndex property, which will in turn be responsible for manipulating the data bindings such that a different record is displayed. Add new handlers for the four navigation buttons:

```
Private Sub buttonFirst_Click(ByVal sender As System.Object, _
        ByVal e As System.EventArgs) Handles buttonFirst.Click
    If CheckSave() = True Then
        AuthorIndex = 0
    End If
End Sub
Private Sub buttonPrevious_Click(ByVal sender As System.Object, _
        ByVal e As System.EventArgs) Handles buttonPrevious.Click
    If AuthorIndex <> 0 Then
        If CheckSave() = True Then
            AuthorIndex -= 1
        End If
    End If
End Sub
Private Sub buttonNext_Click(ByVal sender As System.Object, _
        ByVal e As System.EventArgs) Handles buttonNext.Click
    If AuthorIndex < AuthorCount - 1 Then
        If CheckSave() = True Then
            AuthorIndex += 1
        End If
    End If
End Sub
```

```
      Private Sub buttonLast_Click(ByVal sender As System.Object, _
            ByVal e As System.EventArgs) Handles buttonLast.Click
        If CheckSave() = True Then
            AuthorIndex = AuthorCount - 1
        End If
    End Sub
```

The `CheckSave` method will eventually check to see if the user wants to save any changes, but for now add this stub implementation:

```
    Protected Function CheckSave() As Boolean
        Return True
    End Function
```

`AuthorCount` will return the number of `DataRow` objects in the `DataTable`. If we don't have a `DataTable` available, we return zero:

```
    Public ReadOnly Property AuthorCount() As Integer
        Get
            If Not _authors Is Nothing Then
                Return _authors.Rows.Count
            End If
            Return 0
        End Get
    End Property
```

When we set the `Authors` table, we want to show the first record, which we will do by setting the to-be-built `AuthorIndex` to 0:

```
    Public Property Authors() As DataTable
        Get
            Return _authors
        End Get
        Set(ByVal Value As DataTable)

            ' set it...
            _authors = Value

            ' update the bindings...
            UpdateBindings()

            ' position at zero...
            AuthorIndex = 0
        End Set
    End Property
```

`AuthorIndex` is responsible for enabling and disabling the navigation buttons (we don't want to display the 'previous' button if we're at the first record in the table, for example) and also for setting the `Position` property of the `CurrencyManager` that's associated with the `DataTable`. When we change this value, the values in the `TextBox` controls will magically update. In effect, they detect when the position has changed, and rebind themselves to the new values.

576

To access the binding manager, we'll add a new property called `AuthorBindingContext`. This will cast the return value to a `CurrencyManager` and also check to make sure that we do have a `DataTable` of authors loaded:

```
Protected ReadOnly Property AuthorBindingContext() As CurrencyManager
    Get
        If Not _authors Is Nothing Then
    Return CType(BindingContext(_authors), CurrencyManager)
        Else
            Return Nothing
        End If
    End Get
End Property
```

Now the `AuthorIndex` code. This is mostly UI stuff, but take note of the point at which we set the `Position` property of the binding manager, because this is the point at which the actual record is changed. If the index is the first record (0), we disable the buttons that allow the user to move back. If the index is the last record (`AuthorCount - 1`) we disable the buttons that allow the user to move forward:

```
Public Property AuthorIndex() As Integer
    Get
        If Not AuthorBindingContext Is Nothing Then
            Return AuthorBindingContext.Position
        End If
    End Get
    Set(ByVal Value As Integer)

        ' do we have anything loaded?
        If _authors Is Nothing Then
            buttonFirst.Enabled = False
            buttonPrevious.Enabled = False
            buttonNext.Enabled = False
            buttonLast.Enabled = False
            labelPosition.Text = ""
            Return
        End If

        ' do the buttons...
        Dim enableBack As Boolean = False
        If Value > 0 Then
            enableBack = True
        End If
        Dim enableForward As Boolean = False
        If Value < AuthorCount - 1 Then
            enableForward = True
        End If
        buttonFirst.Enabled = enableBack
        buttonPrevious.Enabled = enableBack
        buttonNext.Enabled = enableForward
        buttonLast.Enabled = enableForward

        ' get the binding manager...
        Dim manager As CurrencyManager = AuthorBindingContext
```

```
          If Not manager Is Nothing Then

               ' have we actually changed?
               If manager.Position <> Value Then
                   manager.Position = Value
               End If
          End If

          ' position...
          labelPosition.Text = _
                 String.Format("{0} of {1}", Value + 1, AuthorCount)
     End Set
End Property
```

Run the project now and you'll be able to page through the records.

Saving Changes

To save the changes back into the database, we have to do virtually what we did before. When the user changes information in the form, we need to listen for ColumnChanged events coming off of the DataTable and at some point prompt them to save the data. This prompt will either be overt – that is, when they try to move off of a modified record, we'll pop up a message box asking if they want to save the changes – or we'll give them the opportunity to click the Save button to explicitly save the changes.

When the record needs to be saved, we'll keep a flag on the form itself that records that the record is 'dirty'. We'll simply use the Enabled state of buttonSave to do this. When the button is enabled, the form is dirty. When disabled, it is not. Here's the property:

```
     Public Property IsDirty() As Boolean
          Get
               Return buttonSave.Enabled
          End Get
          Set(ByVal Value As Boolean)
               buttonSave.Enabled = Value
          End Set
     End Property
```

When the authors are first loaded by setting the Authors property, we need to signal that the record is 'clean' by setting IsDirty to False (which will also disable the Save button):

```
     Public Property Authors() As DataTable
          Get
               Return _authors
          End Get
          Set(ByVal Value As DataTable)

               ' set it...
               _authors = Value

               ' update the bindings...
```

```
                UpdateBindings()

                ' position at zero...
                AuthorIndex = 0

                ' reset "isdirty"...
                IsDirty = False
            End Set
        End Property
```

We've already said that when the data is changed we'll get a ColumnChanged event fired. This would seem like a good point to set IsDirty to True. However, there's a strange wrinkle in the Framework that we have to consider.

We mentioned before that each row has a RowState property that returns an enumeration value indicating if the row is unchanged (DataRowState.Unchanged), or if the row is new (DataRowState.Added), deleted (DataRowState.Deleted), modified (DataRowState.Modified) or 'detached' (DataRowState.Detached) (This last one means that the row is not associated with a collection, typically a state indicating that it has just been created.)

SqlDataAdapter will ignore any row with a state of Unchanged (as you would expect). However, when ColumnChanged is fired RowState remains Unchanged even though data has been changed. RowState is a read-only property, so you can't just say "Your state is now *whatever*". Instead, we have to call EndEdit on the row to make the change permanent in memory and change the RowState value to Modified:

```
        Protected Sub ColumnChanged(ByVal sender As Object, _
                        ByVal e As DataColumnChangeEventArgs)

            ' accept the change...
            e.Row.AcceptChanges()
            IsDirty = True
        End Sub
```

> We didn't have to worry about this problem before, because the **DataGrid** already has the proper behavior built in. In this example, we start from scratch, so we have to replicate the behavior for our own purposes.

Of course, we have to actually add the handlers for this event. This should also be done in the Authors property:

```
        Public Property Authors() As DataTable
            Get
                Return _authors
            End Get
            Set(ByVal Value As DataTable)

                ' set it...
                _authors = Value
```

```
                    ' update the bindings...
                    UpdateBindings()

                    ' position at zero...
                    AuthorIndex = 0

                    ' listen for data changes...
                    AddHandler _authors.ColumnChanged, _
                        New DataColumnChangeEventHandler(AddressOf ColumnChanged)

                    ' reset "isdirty"...
                    IsDirty = False
                End Set
            End Property
```

If you run the project now, you'll find that if you change the value of a field the button will change. The events are only fired when the keyboard focus moves off of the TextBox control that you are editing. For example, change a value, press *Tab* and the **Save** button will become enabled as the IsDirty property is set to True:

To save the changes, we need to wire up the buttonSave control and also implement a proper version of CheckSave. Here's the Click event handler for buttonSave:

```
    Private Sub buttonSave_Click(ByVal sender As System.Object, _
            ByVal e As System.EventArgs) Handles buttonSave.Click
        SaveChanges()
    End Sub
```

CheckSave will return False if the user wants to cancel the navigation. For example, if the user changes a record, clicks buttonNext and when prompted, "Do you want to save changes?" presses **Cancel**, then the navigation needs to be stopped:

```
    Protected Function CheckSave() As Boolean         ' do we need to save?
        If IsDirty = False Then
            Return True
        End If
```

```
        ' ask the user?
        Dim result As DialogResult = _
            MsgBox("Do you want to save changes to this record?", _
            MsgBoxStyle.YesNoCancel Or MsgBoxStyle.Question)
        If result = DialogResult.Cancel Then
            Return False
        End If

        ' do we want to save?
        If result = DialogResult.Yes Then
            SaveChanges()
        Else
            IsDirty = False
        End If

    ' return...
    Return True

End Function
```

SaveChanges is very similar to the last SaveChanges method we built. However, this time rather than breaking out the rows that need to be saved, we pass the entire DataTable object over to the new SqlDataAdapter and ask it to work out what rows actually need to be saved.

```
    Public Sub SaveChanges()

        ' do we have authors?
        If _authors Is Nothing Then
            Return
        End If

        ' connect...
        Dim connection As New SqlConnection(ConnectionString)
        connection.Open()

        ' create an adapter...
        Dim adapter As New SqlDataAdapter(GetAllAuthorsSqlString, _
                        connection)
        Dim builder As New SqlCommandBuilder(adapter)
        adapter.Update(_authors)
        adapter.Dispose()

        ' close...
        connection.Close()

        ' flag...
        IsDirty = False
    End Sub
```

And that's it!

What Data Can Be Data Bound?

To round of this chapter, I'm going to talk about what kinds of data can be data bound. We've dealt exclusively with binding to `DataSet`, `DataTable` and `DataRow` objects. In fact, data binding can be done with pretty much any form of data.

Lists of Items

First off, we'll think about lists of objects. Although `DataTable` contains a list of `DataRow` objects, we can actually bind to any form of list, providing that they give us the correct interfaces.

With .NET, the two most common way to represent lists of objects is the 'array' or the 'collection'. An array is always derived from `System.Array`, whereas we have a bit more flexibility when it comes to the collection. `System.Array` supports these interfaces:

❑ `System.ICloneable` – provides a mechanism for copying the array

❑ `System.Collections.IEnumerable` – provides a mechanism for walking all of the objects contained within the array in turn, typically with a `For Each` loop

❑ `System.Collections.ICollection` – derived from `IEnumerable`, provides a mechanism for returning the number of objects contained within the array and also some other functionality for synchronizing the array for use in multiple threads

❑ `System.Collections.IList` – derived from `ICollection`, `IList` provides mechanisms for adding and removing items from the array

By and large, with the built-in controls, if the object supports `IEnumerable` you can data bind to it. Although I won't go through this in much detail, if we add a `ListBox` control to a form, we can bind an array of string objects to it like this:

```
Private Sub Form1_Load(ByVal sender As System.Object, _
                ByVal e As System.EventArgs) Handles MyBase.Load

    ' create an array of names...
    Dim names() As String = _
            {"Matthew", "Len", "Darren", "Edward", "Disraeli"}

    ' bind the list to the array...
    listNames.DataSource = names
End Sub
```

If we run the project, we see this:

That happens because the array supports one of the interfaces needed by the control. In this case, IEnumerable is used to walk each of the objects in turn. ToString is called on each one to get a string representation and the string value is added to the Items collection of the control itself.

In this case, the DataSource property is inherited from System.Windows.Forms.ListControl, the base class of both ListBox and ComboBox. This tells us that both of these controls will bind to a list of data in the same way.

Properties of Objects

We mentioned way back that DataBindings is implemented on System.Windows.Forms.Control, and as most of the Windows Forms controls are derived from this, it makes sense that most of the Windows Forms controls support data binding. However, this is not the form of data binding that we've just seen where a list is automatically iterated and presented. It's the kind of data binding where a property on the control is bound to a value on some other object.

Before, we saw how this kind of data binding could be used to bind a TextBox control's Text property to a column in a row of a DataTable. The other object doesn't have to be a DataRow – it can be anything that exposes a property.

Imagine we have this class:

```
Public Class Customer

    ' members...
    Private _id As Integer
    Private _firstName As String
    Private _lastName As String
    Public Property Id() As Integer
        Get
            Return _id
        End Get
        Set(ByVal Value As Integer)
            _id = Value
        End Set
    End Property
    Public Property FirstName() As String
        Get
            Return _firstName
        End Get
        Set(ByVal Value As String)
            _firstName = Value
        End Set
    End Property
    Public Property LastName() As String
        Get
            Return _lastName
        End Get
        Set(ByVal Value As String)
            _lastName = Value
        End Set
    End Property
End Class
```

We can bind any *property* (it must be a property, not just a public member) of that class to another property on a control, providing that the data types are compatible. For example:

```
Public Sub UpdateBindings()

    ' create the customer object...
    Dim customer As New Customer()
    customer.Id = 27
    customer.FirstName = "Eric"
    customer.LastName = "Ewing"

    ' bind it...
    buttonBind.DataBindings.Add("Text", customer, "FirstName")
End Sub
```

If we call UpdateBindings, what happens is that the text of the button will display the value stored in FirstName of the bound object.

Summary

In this chapter we took a look at how to use data binding in our Windows Forms application and saw some important design patterns that are common when building data-centric applications.

We started by examining the DataGrid control. This is a sophisticated control for presenting tables of data in applications. We found that binding a DataTable to this control was very easy, resulting in the table being displayed to the user. We then saw how we could save changes made back to the database.

We then saw two ways to build the classic master/detail view, at first using a single DataGrid control bound to a DataSet containing two related tables, and then using two separate DataGrid controls. We also saw how we could discover what SQL statements were actually being executed against the database by our application.

Finally, we looked at how to present data to the user in a form, offering them the classic VCR navigation buttons so common to form-entry applications. Finally we looked at the various list interfaces supported by the Framework and saw how we were not limited to just working with DataSet objects and its associates when data binding.

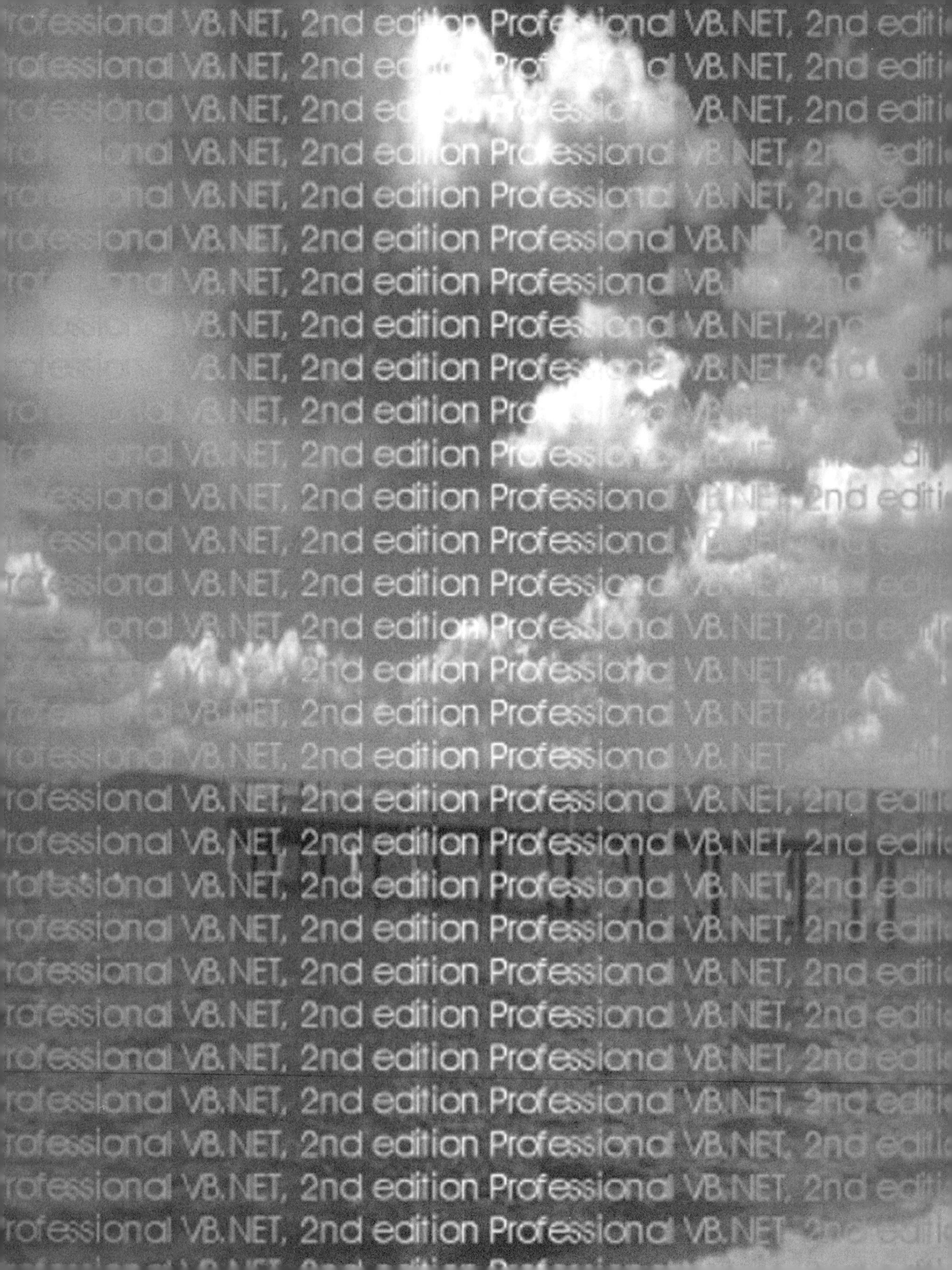
Professional VB.NET, 2nd edition

17

Working with Classic COM and Interfaces

However much as we try, we just can't ignore the vast body of technology surrounding Microsoft's **Component Object Model**, or **COM**. This model has been the cornerstone of so much Microsoft-related development over many years that we have to take a long, hard look at how we are going to integrate all that stuff into the new world of .NET.

In this chapter, then, we're going to start by taking a brief backward glance at COM. We're then going to compare it with how components interact in .NET, and see what tools Microsoft have provided us with to help link the two together. Having looked at the theory, we'll then try it out by building a few example applications. Firstly, we'll take a legacy basic COM object and run it from a VB.NET program. Then we'll repeat the trick with a full-blown ActiveX control. Finally, we'll turn things around and try running some VB.NET code in the guise of a COM object.

> **More information on how to make COM and VB6 code interoperate with the .NET platform can be found in** *Professional Visual Basic Interoperability: COM and VB6 to .NET* **(Wrox Press, ISBN 1861005652).**

As we do all this, try to remember one thing: COM is, to a large extent, where .NET came from. In evolutionary terms, COM's kind of like Lucy, the *Australopithecus* from ancient Ethiopia. So, if it seems a little clunky at times, let's not to be too hard on it. In fact, let's not refer to it as "Nasty, tired, clunky old COM" at all. Let's simply call it "Classic COM".

Classic COM

Before we look into COM-.NET interoperability, we should make sure that we are aware of the main points about COM itself. We won't attempt to do anything more than skim the surface here, however. Whilst the basic concepts are fundamentally simple, the underlying technology is anything but. Some of the most impenetrable books on software that have ever been written have COM as their subject, and I have no wish to add to these.

COM was pretty well Microsoft's first attempt at creating a language-independent standard for programming. The idea was that interfaces between components would be defined according to a binary standard. This would mean that you could, for the first time, invoke a VB component from a VC++ application, and vice versa. It would also be possible to invoke a component in another process or even on another machine, via Distributed COM (DCOM). We won't be looking at out-of-process servers here, however, as the vast majority of components developed to date are in-process. To a large extent, DCOM was fatally compromised by bandwidth, deployment, and firewall problems and never achieved a high level of acceptance.

A COM component implements one or more **interfaces**, some of which are standard ones provided by the system and some of which are custom interfaces defined by the component developer. An interface defines the various methods that an application may invoke. Once specified, an interface definition is supposed to be inviolate so that, even if the underlying code changes, applications that use the interface don't need to be rebuilt. If the component developers find that they have left something out, they should define a new interface containing the extra functionality in addition to that in the original interface. This has in fact happened with a number of standard Microsoft interfaces. For example, the IClassFactory2 interface extends the IClassFactory interface by adding features for managing the creation of licensed objects.

The key to getting applications and components to work together is **binding**. COM offers two forms of binding: early and late:

❑ In **early-binding**, the application uses a **type library** at compile time to work out how to link in to the methods in the component's interfaces. A type library can either come as a separate file, with extension .tlb, or as part of the DLL containing the component code.

❑ In **late-binding**, no connection is made between the application and its components at compile time. Instead, the COM runtime searches through the component for the location of the required method when the application is actually run. This has two main disadvantages: it's slower and it's unreliable. If a programming error is made (for example, the wrong method is called, or the right method with the wrong number of arguments), it doesn't get caught at compile time.

If a type library is not explicitly referred to, there are two ways in which to identify a COM component: by **class ID**, which is a GUID, and by **ProgID**, which is a string and looks like "MyProject.MyComponent". These are all cross-referenced in the registry. In fact, COM makes extensive use of the registry to maintain links between applications, their components, and their interfaces. (All experienced COM programmers know their way around the registry blindfold.)

VB6 has a lot of COM features embedded into it, to the extent that many VB6 programmers aren't even aware that they are developing COM components; for instance, if you create a DLL containing an instance of a VB6 class, you will in fact have created a COM object without even asking for one. We'll see how easy this is during the course of this chapter.

There are clearly similarities between COM and .NET. So, all we've got to do (pretty much) to make them work together is put a wrapper around a COM object to make it into an assembly, and vice versa.

COM and .NET in Practice

It's time to get serious and see if all this seamless integration really works. In order to do this, we're going to have to simulate a legacy situation. Let's imagine that our enterprise depends on a particular COM object that was written for us a long time ago by a wayward genius (who subsequently abandoned software development and has gone to live in a monastery in Tibet). Anyway, all we know is that the code works perfectly and we need it for our .NET application.

We have one, or possibly two, options here. If we have the source (which is not necessarily the case) and we have sufficient time (or, to put it another way, money), we can upgrade the object to .NET and continue to maintain it under VS.NET. For the purist, this is the ideal solution for going forward. However, maintaining the source as it is under VS.NET isn't really a viable option; VS.NET does offer an upgrade path, but it doesn't cope well with COM objects using interfaces specified as abstract classes.

If upgrading to .NET isn't an option, all we can do is simply take the DLL for our COM object, register it on our .NET machine, and use the .NET interoperability tools. This is the path that we're going to take.

So what we need is a genuine legacy COM object, and what we're going to have to use is genuine legacy VB6. For the next section, then, we're going to be using VB6. If you've already disposed of VB6, or never had it in the first place, feel free to skip this section. The DLL is available as part of the code download, in any case.

A Legacy Component

For our legacy component, we're going to imagine that we have some kind of analytics engine that requires a number of calculations. Because of the highly complex nature of these calculations, their development has been given to specialists, while the user interface for the application has been given to UI specialists. A COM interface has been specified that all calculations must confirm to. This interface has the name IMegaCalc and has the following methods:

Method	Description
Sub AddInput (InputValue as Double)	Add input value to calculation
Sub DoCalculation ()	Do calculation
Function GetOutput () as Double	Get output from calculation
Sub Reset ()	Reset calculation for next time

Step 1: Defining the Interface

The first thing we have to do is define our interface. In VB6, the way to do this is to create an abstract class, that is, one without any implementation. So, let's create an ActiveX DLL project called MegaCalculator. Within this, we'll create a class called IMegaCalc. This is what the code looks like:

```
Option Explicit

Public Sub AddInput(InputValue As Double)
End Sub

Public Sub DoCalculation()
End Sub

Public Function GetOutput() As Double
End Function

Public Sub Reset()
End Sub
```

From the main menu, select File | Make MegaCalculator.dll to define and register the interface.

Step 2: *Implementing Our Component*

For the purposes of this demonstration, the actual calculation that we're going to perform is going to be fairly mundane: in fact, we're going to calculate the mean of a series of numbers. So let's create another ActiveX DLL project, called MeanCalculator this time. We need to add a reference to the type library for the interface that we're going to implement, so select the **MegaCalculator** DLL via the References dialog that appears when you select **Project | References**.

Having done that, we can go ahead and write the code for the mean calculation. We do this in a class called MeanCalc:

```
Option Explicit

Implements IMegaCalc

Dim mintValue As Integer
Dim mdblValues() As Double
Dim mdblMean As Double

Private Sub Class_Initialize()
  IMegaCalc_Reset
End Sub

Private Sub IMegaCalc_AddInput(InputValue As Double)
  mintValue = mintValue + 1
  ReDim Preserve mdblValues(mintValue)
  mdblValues(mintValue) = InputValue
End Sub

Private Sub IMegaCalc_DoCalculation()
  Dim iValue As Integer
  mdblMean = 0#

  If (mintValue = 0) Then Exit Sub

  For iValue = 1 To mintValue
```

```
    mdblMean = mdblMean + mdblValues(iValue)
  Next iValue

  mdblMean = mdblMean / mintValue

End Sub

Private Function IMegaCalc_GetOutput() As Double
  IMegaCalc_GetOutput = mdblMean
End Function

Private Sub IMegaCalc_Reset()
  mintValue = 0
End Sub
```

As before, we select File | Make MeanCalculator.dll to build and register the component. It has a default interface called MeanCalc (which contains no methods, and is thus invisible to the naked eye), plus an implementation of IMegaCalc.

Step 3: Registering Our Legacy Component

We now have our legacy component. If we're developing our new .NET application on the same machine, we don't need to do anything more, because our component will already have been registered by the build process. However, if we're working on an entirely new machine, we'll need to register it there. The easiest way to do this is to open up a command box, and register it with the following command:

```
regsvr32 MeanCalculator.dll
```

And we should see this result:

Because MeanCalculator implements an interface from MegaCalculator, we'll also have to repeat the trick with that DLL:

```
regsvr32 MegaCalculator.dll
```

We're now ready to use our component from a .NET application.

The .NET Application

For our .NET application, all we're going to do is instantiate a MeanCalc object, and get it to work out a mean for us. So let's create a Windows Application project in VB.NET called CalcApp. This is what the form looks like:

The two text boxes are called `txtInput` and `txtOutput` respectively; the second one is not enabled for user input. The three command buttons are `btnAdd`, `btnCalculate`, and `btnReset` respectively.

Referencing the Legacy Component

Before we dive into writing the code behind those buttons, we need to make our new application aware of the `MeanCalculator` component. So we have to add a reference to it, via the Project | Add Reference menu item. This brings up a dialog with three tabs: .NET, COM, and Projects. Select MeanCalculator and MegaCalculator from the COM tab:

Now hit the OK button. Notice that, in the list of references in the Solution Explorer, we can now see both MeanCalculator and MegaCalculator:

Inside the .NET Application

Now that we've successfully got our component referenced, we can go ahead and finish coding up our application. First of all, we add a global variable (mobjMean) to hold a reference to an instance of the mean calculation component:

```
Public Class Form1
    Inherits System.Windows.Forms.Form

    Dim mobjMean As MeanCalculator.MeanCalc
```

Next, we need to open up the section labeled Windows Form Designer generated code, and add the following instruction to New:

```
Public Sub New()
  MyBase.New()

  'This call is required by the Windows Form Designer.
  InitializeComponent()

  'Add any initialization after the InitializeComponent() call

  mobjMean = New MeanCalculator.MeanCalc()

End Sub
```

This is where we actually create the component that we're going to use.

Finally, we need to add the code behind the buttons. First of all, the Add button:

```
Private Sub btnAdd_Click(ByVal sender As Object, _
                         ByVal e As System.EventArgs) _
                         Handles btnAdd.Click
  mobjMean.AddInput(CDbl(txtInput.Text))
End Sub
```

All we're doing here is adding whatever's in the input text box into the list of numbers for the calculation. Next, here's the code behind the Calculate button:

```
Private Sub btnCalculate_Click(ByVal sender As Object, _
                                 ByVal e As System.EventArgs) _
                                 Handles btnCalculate.Click
    mobjMean.DoCalculation()
    txtOutput.Text = mobjMean.GetOutput()
End Sub
```

This performs the calculation, retrieves the answer, and puts it into the output text box. Finally, the code behind the Reset button simply resets the calculation:

```
Private Sub btnReset_Click(ByVal sender As Object, _
            ByVal e As System.EventArgs) Handles btnReset.Click
    mobjMean.Reset()
End Sub
```

Trying It All Out

Of course, the proof of the pudding is in the eating, so let's see what happens when we run our application. First of all, let's put one value in, say 2, and click on Add. Now enter another value, say 3, and click on Add once more. When you click on Calculate, you'll get the mean of the two values (2.5 in this case):

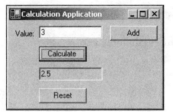

Using TlbImp Directly

In the preceding example, there's actually quite a lot going on under the covers. Every time that we import a COM DLL into VS.NET, it's creating a **default interop assembly**, which is basically a .NET assembly that acts as a wrapper for the COM object. If we're doing this a lot, it might be better to do the wrapping once and for all, and then let our application developers import the resulting .NET assembly instead. Let's see how we might do that.

The process that creates the default interop assembly on behalf of VS.NET is called TlbImp.exe. The name stands for **Type Library Import**, and that's pretty much what it does. It comes as part of the .NET Framework SDK, and you might find it convenient to extend the PATH environment variable to include the \bin directory of the .NET Framework SDK.

TlbImp takes a COM DLL as its input and generates a .NET assembly DLL as its output. By default, the .NET assembly has the same name as the type library, which will – in the case of VB6 components – always be the same as the COM DLL. This means that we'll have to explicitly specify a different output file. We do this by using the /out: switch. So that we can see what's going on at each step in the process, we'll also specify /verbose:

```
tlbimp MeanCalculator.dll /out:MeanCalculatorNet.dll /verbose
```

Let's see what happens:

Notice that `TlbImp` has encountered a reference to another COM type library, `MegaCalculator`, and it has very kindly imported that one as well. Note that the imported DLL retains the name `MegaCalculator.dll`. This means that if you happen to be storing both DLLs in the same place, `TlbImp` is going to find itself attempting to overwrite the COM version of `MegaCalculator.dll` with the .NET one (it won't actually do this, by the way, and the import will fail). The way around this is to explicitly run `TlbImp` on `MegaCalculator` first, specifying `MegaCalculatorNet.dll` as your output.

Having converted our COM DLLs into .NET assemblies, we can reference them in an application as we would any other .NET DLL.

Late-Binding

We've seen that we can successfully do early-binding on COM components within a .NET application. But what if we want to do late-binding? What if we don't have access to a type library at application development time? Can we still make use of the COM components? Does the .NET equivalent of late-binding even exist?

The answer is that, yes, it does, but, no, it's nothing like as transparent as with VB6. Let's take a look at what we used to do in VB6. If we wanted to do early-binding, what we would do is this:

```
Dim myObj As MyObj
Set myObj = New MyObj ' or Set myObj = CreateObject (•MyLibrary.MyObject•)

MyObj.MyMethod (...)
```

For late-binding, it would look like this instead:

```
Dim myObj As Object
Set myObj = new MyObj ' or Set myObj = CreateObject (•MyLibrary.MyObject•)

MyObj.MyMethod (...)
```

There's actually an enormous amount of stuff going on under the covers here; if you're interested in looking into this further, try *VB COM: Visual Basic 6 Programmer's Introduction to COM* (Wrox Press, ISBN 1861002130).

An Example for Late-Binding

For our sample, let's extend the calculator to a more generic framework that can feed inputs into a number of different calculation modules rather than just the fixed one. We'll keep a table in memory of calculation ProgIDs and present the user with a combo box to select the right one.

The Sample COM Object

The first problem we encounter with late-binding is that you can only late-bind to the default interface, which in our case is MeanCalculator.MeanCalc, not MeanCalculator.IMegaCalc. So we're going to have to re-develop our COM object as a stand-alone library, with no references to other interfaces.

As before, we'll build a DLL under VB6, copy it over to our .NET environment and re-register it there. We'll call this VB6 DLL MeanCalculator2.dll, and the code in the class (called MeanCalc) should look like this:

```
Option Explicit

Dim mintValue As Integer
Dim mdblValues() As Double
Dim mdblMean As Double

Private Sub Class_Initialize()
  Reset
End Sub

Public Sub AddInput(InputValue As Double)
  mintValue = mintValue + 1
  ReDim Preserve mdblValues(mintValue)
  mdblValues(mintValue) = InputValue
End Sub

Public Sub DoCalculation()
  Dim iValue As Integer
  mdblMean = 0#

  If (mintValue = 0) Then Exit Sub

  For iValue = 1 To mintValue
    mdblMean = mdblMean + mdblValues(iValue)
  Next iValue

  mdblMean = mdblMean / mintValue

End Sub

Public Function GetOutput() As Double
  GetOutput = mdblMean
End Function

Public Sub Reset()
  mintValue = 0
End Sub
```

As before, we'll need to move this across to our .NET machine and register it using `RegSvr32`.

The Calculation Framework

For our generic calculation framework, we'll create a new application in VB.NET called `CalcFrame`. We'll basically use the same dialog as last time, but with an extra combo box at the top:

The new combo box is called `cmbCalculation`. We've also disabled the controls `txtInput`, `btnAdd`, `btnCalculate`, and `btnReset`, until we know if the selected calculation is valid.

We'll start off by importing the `Reflection` namespace; we'll need this for handing all the late-binding:

```
Imports System.Reflection
```

Then we add a few member variables:

```
Public Class Form1
    Inherits System.Windows.Forms.Form

    Private mstrObjects() As String
    Private mnObject As Integer
    Private mtypCalc As Type
    Private mobjCalc As Object
```

Next, we need to add a few lines to `New`:

```
Public Sub New()
  MyBase.New()

  'This call is required by the Windows Form Designer.
  InitializeComponent()

  'Add any initialization after the InitializeComponent() call

  mnObject = 0
  AddObject("Mean", "MeanCalculator2.MeanCalc")
  AddObject("StdDev", "StddevCalculator.StddevCalc")

  If (mnObject > 0) Then
    cmbCalculation.SelectedIndex = 0
  End If

End Sub
```

What we're doing here is building up a list of calculations. Once we've finished, we select the first one in the list. Let's just take a look at that subroutine `AddObject`:

```
Private Sub AddObject(ByVal strName As String, ByVal strObject As String)
   cmbCalculation.Items.Add(strName)
   mnObject = mnObject + 1
   ReDim Preserve mstrObjects(mnObject)
   mstrObjects(mnObject - 1) = strObject
End Sub
```

Here, we're adding the calculation name to the combo box and its ProgID to an array of strings. Neither of these is sorted, so we get a one-to-one mapping between them.

Let's see what happens when we select a calculation via the combo box:

```
Private Sub cmbCalculation_SelectedIndexChanged(ByVal sender As Object, _
                                    ByVal e As System.EventArgs) _
                     Handles cmbCalculation.SelectedIndexChanged
   Dim intIndex As Integer
   Dim bEnabled As Boolean

   intIndex = cmbCalculation.SelectedIndex
   mtypCalc = Type.GetTypeFromProgID(mstrObjects(intIndex))

   If (mtypCalc Is Nothing) Then
      mobjCalc = Nothing
      bEnabled = False
   Else
      mobjCalc = Activator.CreateInstance(mtypCalc)
      bEnabled = True
   End If

   txtInput.Enabled = bEnabled
   btnAdd.Enabled = bEnabled
   btnCalculate.Enabled = bEnabled
   btnReset.Enabled = bEnabled

End Sub
```

There are two key calls here. The first is to `Type.GetTypeFromProgID`. This takes the incoming ProgID string and converts it to a `Type` object. This may either succeed or fail; if it fails, we disable all controls and let the user try again. If it succeeds, however, we go on to create an instance of the object described by the type. We do this in the call to the static method `Activator.CreateInstance`.

So let's assume that our user has selected a calculation that we can successfully instantiate. What next? The next thing is that the user enters a number and clicks on the **Add** button:

```
Private Sub btnAdd_Click(ByVal sender As Object, _
                   ByVal e As System.EventArgs) _
                   Handles btnAdd.Click
   Dim objArgs() As Object
```

```
    objArgs = New Object(0) {CDbl(txtInput.Text)}
    mtypCalc.InvokeMember("AddInput", BindingFlags.InvokeMethod, _
                        Nothing, mobjCalc, objArgs)
End Sub
```

The important call here is to `InvokeMember`. Let's take a closer look. There are five parameters here:

❑ The first parameter is the name of the method that we want to call: `AddInput` in this case. So instead of going directly to the location of the routine in memory, we ask the .NET run-time to find it for us.

❑ The value from the `BindingFlags` enumeration tells it that we want it to invoke a method for us.

❑ The next parameter is to provide language-specific binding information, which isn't needed in this case.

❑ The fourth parameter is a reference to the COM object itself (the one that we instantiated using `Activator.CreateInstance` above).

❑ Finally, the fifth parameter is an array of objects representing the arguments for the method. In this case, there's only one argument: the input value.

Something very similar to this is going on underneath VB6 late-binding, except that here it's exposed to us in all its horror. In some ways, that's no bad thing, because it should bring it home to you that late-binding is something to avoid if at all possible. Anyway, let's carry on and complete the program. Here are the remaining event handlers:

```
Private Sub btnCalculate_Click(ByVal sender As Object, _
        ByVal e As System.EventArgs) Handles btnCalculate.Click
    Dim objResult As Object
    mtypCalc.InvokeMember("DoCalculation", BindingFlags.InvokeMethod, _
                        Nothing, mobjCalc, Nothing)
    objResult = mtypCalc.InvokeMember("GetOutput", _
            BindingFlags.InvokeMethod, Nothing, mobjCalc, Nothing)
    txtOutput.Text = objResult
End Sub
```

```
Private Sub btnReset_Click(ByVal sender As Object, _
        ByVal e As System.EventArgs) Handles btnReset.Click
    mtypCalc.InvokeMember("Reset", BindingFlags.InvokeMethod, _
                        Nothing, mobjCalc, Nothing)
End Sub
```

Running the Calculation Framework

OK, let's quickly complete the job by running the application. Here's what happens when we select the non-existent calculation StdDev:

And here's what happens when we repeat our earlier calculation using Mean:

One final word about late-binding. We took care to ensure that we checked to see that the object was successfully instantiated. In a real-life application, we would also need to take care that the method invocations were successful, ensuring that all exceptions were caught – we don't have the luxury of having the compiler find our bugs for us.

ActiveX Controls

Let's move on from basic COM objects to ActiveX controls. These are still COM objects, with the crucial extension that they have to implement a whole further set of interfaces relating to user interface characteristics. We're going to do pretty much the same as we did with the basic COM component (apart from late-binding, which has no relevance to ActiveX controls) – build a legacy control using VB6 and then import it into a VB.NET project.

A Legacy ActiveX Control

For our legacy control, we're going to build a simple button-like object that is capable of interpreting a mouse click and can be one of two colors according to its state. We do this by taking a second foray into VB6; once again, if you don't have VB6 handy, feel free to skip the next section, download the OCX file, and pick it up when we start developing our .NET application.

Step 1: Create the Control

This time, we need to create an ActiveX Control project. We'll call the project Magic, and the control class MagicButton, so as to give a proper impression of its remarkable powers. From the toolbox, we select a Shape control and place it on the UserControl form that VB6 provides us with. Rename the shape to shpButton, and change its properties as follows:

Property	Value
FillStyle	0 – Solid
Shape	4 – Rounded Rectangle
FillColor	Gray (&H008F8F8F&)

Add a label on top of the shape control and rename this to lblText. Change its properties as follows:

Property	Value
BackStyle	0 – Transparent
Alignment	2 – Center

Switch to the code view of MagicButton.

Now we need to add two properties called Caption and State, and an event called Click, as well as code to handle the initialization of the properties and persisting them, to ensure that the shape resizes correctly and that the label is centered. We also need to handle mouse clicks. The code in MagicButton should look like this:

```
Option Explicit

Public Event Click()

Dim mintState As Integer

Public Property Get Caption() As String
  Caption = lblText.Caption
End Property

Public Property Let Caption(ByVal vNewValue As String)
  lblText.Caption = vNewValue
  PropertyChanged ("Caption")
End Property

Public Property Get State() As Integer
  State = mintState
End Property

Public Property Let State(ByVal vNewValue As Integer)
  mintState = vNewValue
  PropertyChanged ("State")
```

601

```
   If (State = 0) Then
     shpButton.FillColor = &HFFFFFF&
   Else
     shpButton.FillColor = &H8F8F8F&
   End If
End Property

Private Sub UserControl_InitProperties()
  Caption = Extender.Name
  State = 1
End Sub

Private Sub UserControl_ReadProperties(PropBag As PropertyBag)
  Caption = PropBag.ReadProperty("Caption", Extender.Name)
  State = PropBag.ReadProperty("State", 1)
End Sub

Private Sub UserControl_WriteProperties(PropBag As PropertyBag)
  PropBag.WriteProperty "Caption", lblText.Caption
  PropBag.WriteProperty "State", mintState
End Sub

Private Sub UserControl_Resize()
   shpButton.Move 0, 0, ScaleWidth, ScaleHeight
   lblText.Move 0, (ScaleHeight - lblText.Height) / 2, ScaleWidth
End Sub

Private Sub lblText_Click()
   RaiseEvent Click
End Sub

Private Sub UserControl_MouseUp(Button As Integer, Shift As Integer, _
                                X As Single, Y As Single)
   RaiseEvent Click
End Sub
```

If we build this, we'll get an ActiveX control called `Magic.ocx`.

Step 2: Registering Our Legacy Control

We now have our legacy control. As before, if we're developing our new .NET application on the same machine, we don't need to do anything more, because our control will already have been registered by the build process. However, if we're working on an entirely new machine, we'll need to register it there. As before, we need to open up a command box and register it with this command:

```
regsvr32 Magic.ocx
```

Having done that, we're ready to build our .NET application.

A .NET Application, Again

This .NET application is going to be even more straightforward than the last one. All we're going to do this time is show a button that will change color whenever the user clicks on it. Let's create a Windows Application project in VB.NET called `ButtonApp`. Before we start to develop it, however, we need to extend the toolbox to incorporate our new control. We do this via the Tools I Customize Toolbox menu item:

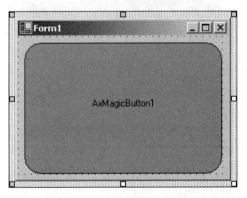

When we click on the OK button, we can see that our magic button class is now available to us in the toolbox. Let's add one to our form:

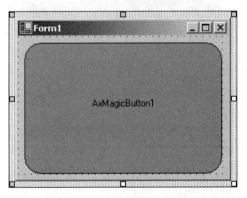

Notice that references to `AxMagic` and `Magic` have just been added to the project, in the Solution Explorer window. All we need to do now is initialize the `Caption` property to `ON`, change the `Text` of the form to `Button Application`, and code up a handler for the mouse click event:

```
Private Sub AxMagicButton1_Click(ByVal sender As System.Object, _
          ByVal e As System.EventArgs) Handles AxMagicButton1.ClickEvent
   AxMagicButton1.CtlState = CType(1 - AxMagicButton1.CtlState, Short)
   If (AxMagicButton1.CtlState = 0) Then
      AxMagicButton1.Caption = "OFF"
   Else
      AxMagicButton1.Caption = "ON"
   End If
End Sub
```

Something slightly peculiar happened here. In the course of importing our control into .NET, the variable State mutated into CtlState. This happened because there is already a class in the AxHost namespace called State, which is used to encapsulated the persisted state of an ActiveX control. (So maybe we should have called it something else.)

Trying It All Out, Again

So what happens when we run this one? First of all we see this:

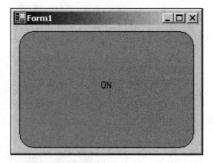

And if we click on the control, it changes to this:

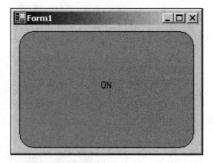

Using .NET Components in the COM World

So, we've established beyond all doubt that we can use our COM legacy components in the brave new .NET world. We don't have to throw everything out *quite* yet. It's now time to consider the opposite question: can we run .NET components in the COM world?

Actually, the question we should first be asking is probably this one: why on earth should we want to run .NET components in the COM world? It's not immediately obvious, in fact, because migration to .NET would almost certainly be application-led in most cases, rather than component-led. However, it's possible (just) to imagine a situation where a particularly large application remains non-.NET while component development moves over to .NET. Well, let's pretend that that's the case for the next section. The technology's quite cool, anyway.

A .NET Component

Let's take a look at our definitely non-legacy component. We'll implement an exact copy of the functionality that we did earlier with `MegaCalculator` and `MeanCalculator`, except using VB.NET rather than VB6.

Start off by creating a Class Library project called `MegaCalculator2`. This is the entire code of the class library:

```
Public Interface IMegaCalc

    Sub AddInput(ByVal InputValue As Double)
    Sub DoCalculation()
    Function GetResult() As Double
    Sub Reset()

End Interface
```

Next, we create another Class Library project, called `MeanCalculator3`. This will contain a class called `MeanCalc` that is going to implement the `IMegaCalc` interface, in a precise analogue of the `MeanCalc` in our original VB6 `MeanCalculator` project. As before, we'll need to add a reference to `MegaCalculator2` first. This is what the code looks like:

```
Public Class MeanCalc
  Implements MegaCalculator2.IMegaCalc

  Dim mintValue As Integer
  Dim mdblValues() As Double
  Dim mdblMean As Double

  Public Sub AddInput(ByVal InputValue As Double) _
      Implements MegaCalculator2.IMegaCalc.AddInput
    mintValue = mintValue + 1
    ReDim Preserve mdblValues(mintValue)
    mdblValues(mintValue - 1) = InputValue
  End Sub
```

605

```
   Public Sub DoCalculation() _
       Implements MegaCalculator2.IMegaCalc.DoCalculation
     Dim iValue As Integer

     mdblMean = 0

     If (mintValue = 0) Then Exit Sub

     For iValue = 0 To mintValue - 1 Step 1
       mdblMean = mdblMean + mdblValues(iValue)
     Next iValue

     mdblMean = mdblMean / iValue

   End Sub

   Public Function GetResult() As Double Implements _
                   MegaCalculator2.IMegaCalc.GetResult
     GetResult = mdblMean
   End Function

   Public Sub Reset() Implements MegaCalculator2.IMegaCalc.Reset
     mintValue = 0
   End Sub

   Public Sub New()
     Reset()
   End Sub

 End Class
```

This is all quite similar to the VB6 version, apart from the way in which `Implements` is used. Let's build the assembly.

Now we come to the interesting part: how do we register the resulting assembly so that a COM-enabled application can make use of it?

RegAsm

The tool provided with the .NET Framework SDK to register assemblies for use by COM is called `RegAsm`. RegAsm is very simple to use. If all you're interested in is late-binding, then you simply run it like this:

```
Visual Studio .NET Command Prompt                              _ □ ×
C:\>regasm MeanCalculator3.dll
Microsoft (R) .NET Framework Assembly Registration Utility 1.0.3705.0
Copyright (C) Microsoft Corporation 1998-2001.  All rights reserved.

Types registered successfully
C:\>
```

However, there's probably even less reason for late-binding to an exported .NET component than there is for early-binding, so we'll move on to look at early-binding. For this, we need a type library, so we need to add another parameter, /tlb:

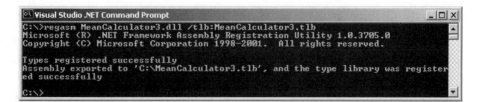

If we now take a look in our target directory, we see that not only do we have the original `MeanCalculator3.dll`, but we've also acquired a copy of the `MegaCalculator2.dll` and two type libraries: `MeanCalculator3.tlb` and `MegaCalculator2.tlb`. We'll need both of these, so it was good of `RegAsm` to provide them for us. We need the `MegaCalculator2` type library for the same reason as .NET needed the `MegaCalculator` assembly because it contains the definition of the `IMegaCalc` interface that `MeanCalculator` is using.

Testing with a VB6 Application

Turning the tables again, we need to build a VB6 application to see if this is really going to work. Let's copy the type libraries over to our pre-.NET machine (if that's where VB6 is running) and create a Standard EXE project in VB6. We'll call this `CalcApp2`. We'll need to create references to our two new type libraries, so we go to the References dialog and select them:

Now we've got all we need to create our application. Let's create the same as we did for the VB.NET `CalcApp`:

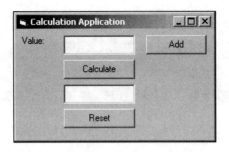

As before, the text boxes are `txtInput` and `txtOutput`, respectively, and the command buttons are `btnAdd`, `btnCalculate`, and `btnReset`.

And here's the code behind it:

```
Option Explicit

Dim mobjCalc As MeanCalculator3.MeanCalc
Dim mobjMega As MegaCalculator2.IMegaCalc

Private Sub btnAdd_Click()
  mobjMega.AddInput (txtInput.Text)
End Sub

Private Sub btnCalculate_Click()
  mobjMega.DoCalculation
  txtOutput.Text = mobjMega.GetResult
End Sub

Private Sub btnReset_Click()
  mobjMega.Reset
End Sub

Private Sub Form_Load()
  Set mobjCalc = New MeanCalculator3.MeanCalc
  Set mobjMega = mobjCalc
End Sub
```

Notice that, this time, we have to explicitly get hold of a reference to the interface `IMegaCalc`. The default interface of the component, `MeanCalc`, is entirely empty.

We make the executable via the File | Make CalcApp2.exe menu item, and then we can move it back to our .NET machine (unless, of course, we're already there). Let's run it up and see what happens:

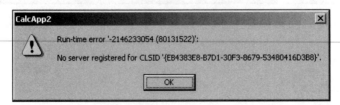

Well, that's not *quite* what we expected. What's happened here?

In COM, the location of the DLL containing the component is available via the registry. In .NET, the assembly always has to be either in the current directory or the global assembly. All the registry is doing for us here is converting a COM reference to a .NET one; it's not finding the .NET one for us.

But it's easy to sort out. All we have to do to resolve matters is move the two assemblies, for `MegaCalculator3` and `MeanCalculator2`, to our current directory, and try again:

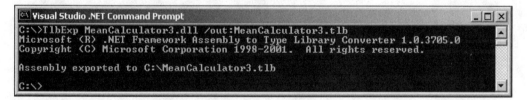

That's better. So we've established that in the unlikely event of having to run .NET from a COM-oriented application, Microsoft have provided us with the tools.

TlbExp

In fact, Microsoft have provided us with not one, but *two* alternative tools. The other one is `TlbExp`, which – as its name suggests – is the counterpart of `TlbImp`. This is how we can use `TlbExp` to achieve the same result as `RegAsm` in the previous section:

```
C:\>TlbExp MeanCalculator3.dll /out:MeanCalculator3.tlb
Microsoft (R) .NET Framework Assembly to Type Library Converter 1.0.3705.0
Copyright (C) Microsoft Corporation 1998-2001.  All rights reserved.

Assembly exported to C:\MeanCalculator3.tlb

C:\>
```

Summary

COM isn't going to go away for quite some time yet, so .NET applications have to interoperate with COM, and they have to do it well. In this chapter, we have looked at how all this works in practice.

- ❏ We managed to make a .NET application early-bind to a COM component, using the import features available in VB.NET
- ❏ We looked at the underlying tool, `Tlbimp`
- ❏ We managed to make it late-bind as well, although it wasn't a pleasant experience
- ❏ We incorporated an ActiveX control into a .NET user interface, again using the features of VB.NET
- ❏ We looked at using `Regasm` and `TlbExp` to export type libraries from .NET assemblies, so as to enable VB6 applications to use .NET assemblies as if they were COM components

609

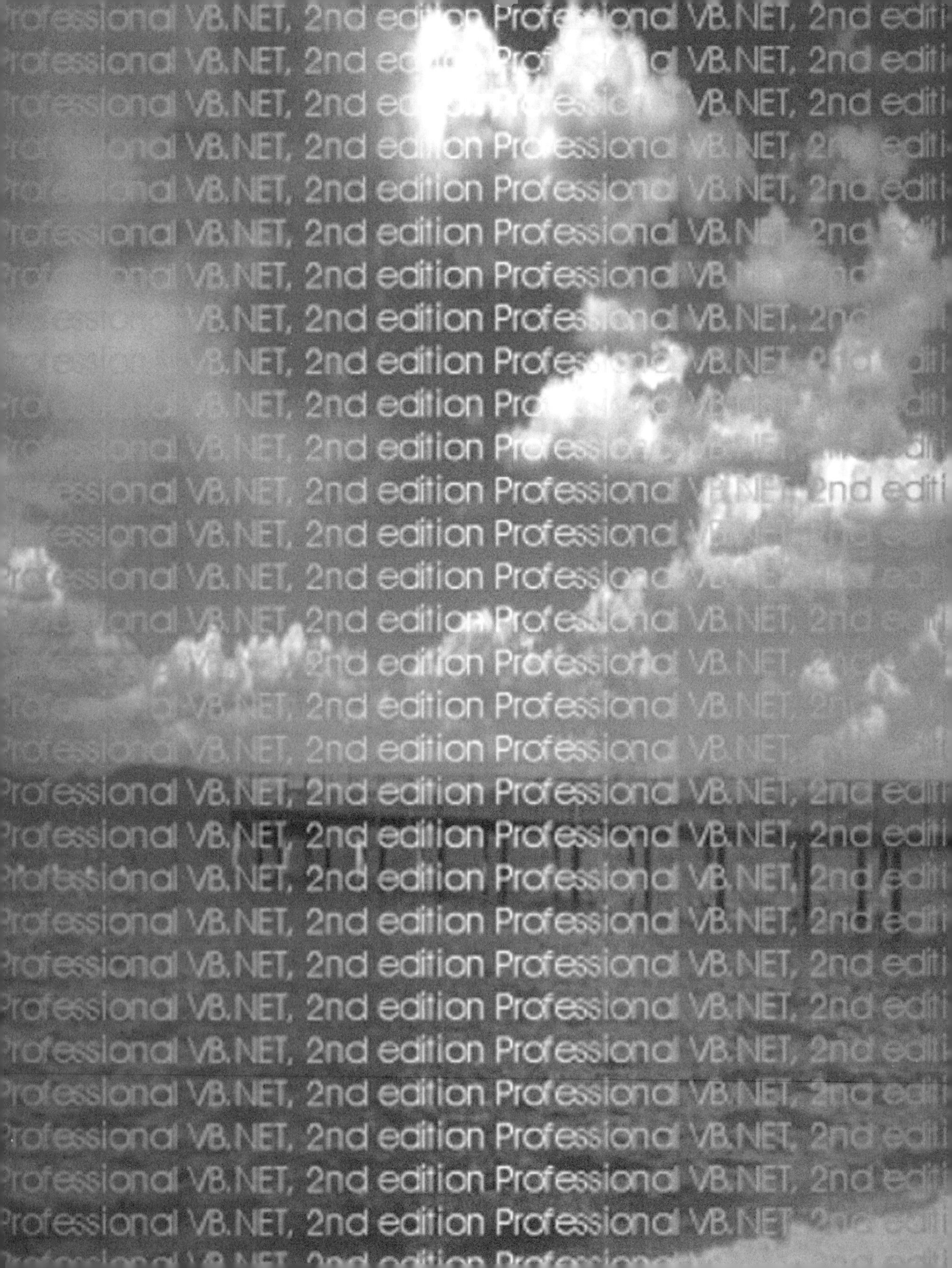
Professional VB.NET, 2nd edition

18

Component Services

In the previous chapter, we explored the vast hinterland of legacy software known as COM. We're now going to look at "what COM did next" and how it fits into the world of .NET, in the shape of **.NET Component Services**. You would be forgiven for thinking that Component Services is yet another version of legacy software, except that much of it hasn't been around for long enough to be considered as legacy. However, there is more to it than that. The end result is something of a compromise between the old COM world and .NET.

To understand Component Services, we need to go back in time to around 1997. Microsoft had, by this time, become by far the dominant supplier to the PC market, and was looking for something else to do. The obvious thing was to move into the enterprise server market, and a number of initiatives began to emerge from Microsoft. Amongst these, in no particular order, were **Microsoft Transaction Server (MTS)**, **Microsoft Message Queuing (MSMQ)**, and **Microsoft Clustering Services**. The aim of these developments was to bring something that had previously been esoteric, specialized, and generally mainframe-based within the scope of standard PC technology.

Handling transactions involved a considerable extension to the NT/COM runtime. It also involved the introduction of several new standard COM interfaces: some to be used or implemented by transactional components, and some to be used or implemented by the underlying resource managers, such as SQL Server. These additions, along with some other innovations relating to areas like asynchronous COM, came to be known as **COM+**.

There must have been considerable debate as to whether this vast infrastructure should be completely re-implemented within .NET or whether it should be tacked onto the side. In the event, pragmatism seems to have won the day because, under .NET, the **Component Services** (as they have been renamed) sit slightly uneasily between pure .NET and the kind of legacy COM stuff that we saw in the previous chapter. The end result is perfectly acceptable from an operational point of view (although it's debatable as to how elegant it is).

In this chapter we're going to explore the .NET Component Services. In particular, we're going to look at transaction processing and queued components. This is an enormous subject that could easily fill a whole book by itself. In this chapter, we will only be able to scratch the surface of it. However, by the end of the chapter, you will understand how all the various pieces fit together.

Let's start by looking at what transactions are, and how they fit into VB.NET.

> **You can find more information about transactions in .NET in *Professional VB.NET Transactions* (Wrox Press, 1861005954).**

Transactions

A **transaction** is one or more linked units of processing placed together as a single unit of work, which either succeeds or fails. If the unit of work succeeds, the work is then committed. If the unit fails, then every item of processing is rolled back and the process is placed back to its original state.

The standard transaction example involves transferring money from account A to account B. The money must either end up in account B (and nowhere else), or – if something goes wrong – stay in account A (and go nowhere else). We don't want the case in which we have taken money from account A but haven't put it in account B.

The ACID Test

Transaction theory starts with **ACID**. According to the ACID theory, all transactions should have the following properties:

❑ **Atomicity** – A transaction is **atomic** (that is, everything is treated as one unit). However many different components the transaction involves, and however many different method calls on those components there are, the system treats it as a single operation that either entirely succeeds or entirely fails. If it fails, the system is left in a state as if the transaction had never happened.

❑ **Consistency** – All changes are done in a consistent manner. The system goes from one valid state to another.

❑ **Isolation** – Transactions that are going on at the same time are isolated from each other. If transaction A changes the system from state 1 to state 2, transaction B will see the system in either state 1 or 2, but not some half-baked state in between the two.

❑ **Durability** – If a transaction has been committed, the effect will be permanent, even if the system fails.

Let's illustrate this with a concrete example. Imagine that, having spent a happy afternoon browsing in your favorite bookstore, you decide to shell out some of your hard-earned dollars for a copy of – yes – *Professional VB.NET 2ⁿᵈ Edition* (wise choice). You take the copy to the checkout, and you ask if they happen to have a less dog-eared one. A transaction is going on here: you pay money, and the store provides you with a book.

There are only two reasonable outcomes: either you get the book and the store gets their money, or you don't get the book and the store doesn't get their money. If, for example, there is insufficient credit on your card, you'll walk out of the shop without the book. If, on the other hand, there are no more copies of the book in the stockroom, you don't hand over your card at all. In either case, the transaction doesn't happen. The only way for the transaction to complete is for you to get the book and the store to get their money. This is the principle of atomicity.

If, on the other hand, the store decides to provide you with a copy of, say, Neal Stephenson's *Cryptonomicon* instead, you might reasonably feel that you have ended up with an outcome that wasn't originally on the agenda. This would be a violation of the principle of consistency.

Let's now imagine that there is one copy of the book in the storeroom. However, another potential buyer has gone up to the till next to you. As far as the person at the next till is concerned, your respective transactions are isolated from each other (even though you are competing for the same resource). Either your transaction succeeds or the other person's does. What very definitely *doesn't* happen is that the bookstore decides to exert the wisdom of Solomon and give you half each.

Once you have taken the book home, let's imagine that the bookstore calls you up and asks you if they could have the book back. Apparently, some important customer (well, far more important than you, anyway) needs a copy. You would feel that this was a tad unreasonable, and a violation of the principle of durability.

At this point, it's worth considering what implications all this is likely to have on the underlying components. How can you ensure that all of the changes in the system can be unwound if the transaction is aborted at some point? Perhaps you're in the middle of updating dozens of database files, and something goes wrong.

There are three aspects to rescuing this situation with transactions. First of all, we have to know that something has gone wrong. Secondly, we need to know how to perform the recovery. Thirdly, we need to co-ordinate the process of recovery. The middle part of the process is handled by the resource managers themselves – the likes of SQL Server and Oracle are fully equipped to deal with two-phase commit and rollback (even if the resource manager in question is re-started part-way through a transaction), and we don't need to worry about any of that. The last part of the process, co-ordination, is handled by the .NET runtime (or at least the Component Services part of it). The first part, knowing that something is wrong, is shared between the components themselves and the .NET runtime. This isn't at all unusual: sometimes a component can detect that something has gone wrong itself and signal that recovery is necessary whilst, on other occasions, it may not be able to do so, because it has crashed.

We'll see how all this works as we build our first transactional application. However, before we do that, we need to look at how transactions are implemented within .NET component services.

Transactional Components

But what actually are the components that are managed by Component Services? What purpose do they serve? To answer that, we need to consider what a typical real-world *n*-tier application looks like. The bottom tier is the persistent data store – typically an industry-standard database such as SQL Server or Oracle. The software here is concerned with maintaining the integrity of the application's data and providing rapid and efficient access to it. The top tier is the user interface. This is a completely different specialization, and the software here is concerned with presenting a smooth, easy to follow front-end to the end-user. This layer shouldn't actually do any data manipulation at all, apart from whatever formatting is necessary to meet each user's presentational needs. The interesting stuff is in the tiers in between – in particular, the business logic. In the .NET/COM+ transactional model, the software elements that implement this are components running under the control of the Component Services runtime.

Typically, these components are called into being to perform some sort of transaction and then – to all intents and purposes – disappear again. For example, a component might be called into play to transfer information from one database to another in such a way that the information was either in one database or the other, but not both. This component might have a number of different methods, each of which did a different kind of transfer. However, each method call would carry out a complete transfer:

```
Public Sub TransferSomething()
   TakeSomethingFromA
   AddSomethingToB
End Sub
```

Crucially, this means that most transaction components have no concept of **state**: there are no properties that hold values between method calls. Persistence is left to the outside tiers in this model. This takes a little bit of getting used to at first, because it runs counter to everything that we learnt in first grade object-orientation classes, so let's take a minute or two to consider what we're actually gaining from this. The business logic is the area of the system that requires all the transactional management. Anything that happens here needs to be monitored and controlled to ensure that all the ACID requirements are met. The neatest way to do this in a component-oriented framework is to develop the business logic as components that are required to implement a standard interface. The transaction management framework can then use this interface to monitor and control how the logic is implemented from a transactional point of view. The transaction interface is a means for the business logic elements to talk to the transaction framework and for the transaction framework to talk back to the logic elements.

So what's all this about not having state? Well, if we maintain state inside our components, then we've immediately got ourselves a scaling problem. The middle tiers of our application are now seriously resource-hungry. If you want an analogy from another area of software, consider why the Internet scales so well. The reason that it does is because HTTP is a stateless protocol. Every HTTP request stands in isolation, so no resources are tied up in maintaining any form of session. It's the same with transactional components.

This is not to say that you can't ever maintain state inside your transactional components. You can. However, it's not recommended, and we certainly won't be doing it in the examples in this chapter.

Before we move on into some practical examples, there's one other thing we need to talk about. We said earlier that transactional components are called into being, do their thing, and then disappear. This isn't the most efficient way of doing things, as instantiating a component takes a fair amount of effort. It would be better if we had a whole pool of components sitting there waiting to be used. In fact, it turns out that we can do just this. We'll see how it works in practice later.

An Example of Transactions

For our transaction example, we're going to build a simple business logic component that transfers data from one bank account (Wrox's in fact) to another one (mine, of course). Wrox's bank account will be represented by a row in one database (BankOfWrox), whilst mine will be represented by a row in another one (BankOfJon – it's kind of a sideline).

There's one important point that we should make right from the start. You can't have transactions without any resource managers. It's very tempting to think that you can experiment with transactional component services without actually involving, say, a database, because (as we shall see) none of the methods in the transactional classes makes any explicit references to one. However, if you do try to do this, you will find that your transactions don't actually trouble the system's statistics. Fortunately, you don't need to go out and lay out your hard-earned cash for a copy of SQL Server (nice though that is), because Visual Studio .NET comes with a stripped-down (but fully functional) copy of SQL Server, which goes under the name of **Microsoft Database Engine**, or **MSDE**.

Creating Our Databases

The first thing we have to do, then, is set up our databases. Move your cursor over the Server Explorer window, and you'll see the start of a tree of servers. Your computer should be in there; open up this node, and you should see **SQL Servers**. Open this up, and you should see something like MYCOMPUTER\NETSDK. OK, you've found your SQL Server:

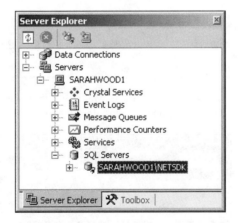

The next thing to do is right-click on this, and select New Database from the menu. You should see a dialog box like this appear:

We enter our database name (BankOfWrox), and elect to use SQL Server Authentication (the login name provided with MSDE is sa, with no password).

You should now see BankOfWrox in the tree below MYCOMPUTER\NETSDK. The next thing to do is set up the database. If you open up the new node, you should see a number of other nodes, including Tables. Right-click on this, and select New Table from the menu. You should now see a dialog something like this:

Create two columns, Name and Amount, as shown. Make sure that Name is set up to be the primary key. When you click on the close box, you'll see a dialog like this:

As suggested, use the name Accounts for the table. You should now see a child node called Accounts below Tables in the tree.

OK, that's BankOfWrox created. Repeat the whole process for BankOfJon. The structure is exactly the same (although it doesn't need to be for the purposes of this example).

Populating Our Databases

The next thing we need to do is populate our databases. If we right-click over Accounts, and select Retrieve Data from Table from the menu, we will see a grid which will enable us to add rows and initialize the values of their columns:

dbo.Accounts ...DK.BankOfWrox)	
Name	Amount
▶ Pro VB.NET	5000
Pro XML 2e	5000
✳	

Entered two accounts in BankOfWrox, Pro VB.NET and Pro XML 2e, and allocate $5000 to each. We repeat the process for BankOfJon, setting up one account, Jon, with $0 in it. (So Jon is either (a) broke or (b) wise enough not to leave any cash lying around in this sort of account. Go figure.)

The Business Logic

The next step is to create our transactional component to support our business logic. Create a new Class Library project called TransSample. Then add a reference to System.EnterpriseServices.

We're going to need this reference because, in order to come under the control of the Component Services runtime, our component needs to inherit from the System.EnterpriseServices.ServicedComponent class:

```
Imports System.EnterpriseServices

Public Class TransSample
  Inherits ServicedComponent
```

Here's the main function in our component, TransferMoney:

```
    Public Function TransferMoney(ByVal intDollars As Integer) As Boolean
      If TakeFromWrox(intDollars) = True Then
        If AddToJon(intDollars) = True Then
          ContextUtil.SetComplete()
          TransferMoney = True
        Else
          ContextUtil.SetAbort()
          TransferMoney = False
        End If
      Else
        ContextUtil.SetAbort()
        TransferMoney = False
      End If
    End Function
  End Class
```

Ignoring, for the moment, the references to ContextUtil, we can see that we have effectively divided up the logic into two halves: the half that takes money from the Wrox account (represented by the private function TakeFromWrox), and the half that adds it to Jon's account (represented by the private function AddToJon). For the function to complete successfully, each of the two halves must complete successfully.

617

So what does `ContextUtil` do? The `ContextUtil` class represents the context of the transaction. Within that context, there are basically two bits that control the behavior of the transaction from the point of view of each participant: the **consistent** bit and the **done** bit. The done bit determines whether or not the transaction is finished, so that resources can be re-used (we'll have more to say on this later, when we talk about Just-In-Time Activation and Object Pooling). The consistent bit determines whether or not the transaction was successful from the point of view of the participant. This is established during the first phase of the two-phase commit process. In complex distributed transactions involving more than one participant, the overall consistency and doneness are voted on, so that a transaction is only consistent or done when everyone agrees that it is. If a transaction completes in an inconsistent state, it is not allowed to proceed to the second phase of the commit.

In this case, we only have a single participant, but the principal remains the same: we can determine the overall outcome by setting these two bits, and we do this via `SetComplete` and `SetAbort`, which are static methods in the `ContextUtil` class. Both of these set the done bit to `True`. `SetComplete` also sets the consistent bit to `True`, whereas `SetAbort` sets the consistent bit to `False`. In our example, `SetComplete` is only set if both halves of the transaction are successful.

The First Half of the Transaction

Now let's see what's going on in the two halves of the transaction itself. First of all, here's the function that takes the money out of the Wrox account:

```
Private Function TakeFromWrox(ByVal intDollars As Integer) As Boolean
    Dim strConn As String
    Dim strCmd As String

    Dim objConn As SqlClient.SqlConnection
    Dim objAdapter As SqlClient.SqlDataAdapter
    Dim objBuilder As SqlClient.SqlCommandBuilder

    Dim objDataset As DataSet
    Dim objTable As DataTable
    Dim objRow As DataRow

    Dim intBalance As Integer
```

We start off by establishing a connection to our database, and extracting the entire table from it:

```
    strConn = "DATABASE=BankOfWrox;SERVER=(local)\NETSDK;UID=sa;PWD=;"
    strCmd = "Select * From Accounts"

    objConn = New SqlClient.SqlConnection(strConn)
    objAdapter = New SqlClient.SqlDataAdapter(strCmd, objConn)
    objBuilder = New SqlClient.SqlCommandBuilder(objAdapter)
```

The call to `SqlCommandBuilder` sets up the default SQL commands that will be used when we update the database. Next, we extract the first row (which should be Pro VB.NET) into a `DataRow` object:

```
    objDataset = New DataSet()
    objAdapter.Fill(objDataset)
```

```
objTable = objDataset.Tables(0)
objRow = objTable.Rows(0)
```

We get the current balance, and see if we can afford to transfer the amount that we've asked for. If not, we set the result of the function to `False`:

```
intBalance = CInt(objRow("Amount"))

If intDollars > intBalance Then
  TakeFromWrox = False
```

Otherwise, we subtract the amount, and update the table accordingly, setting the result to `True`:

```
Else
  intBalance = intBalance - intDollars

  objRow("Amount") = intBalance
  objAdapter.Update(objTable)

  TakeFromWrox = True
End If
```

Finally, we close the database:

```
objConn.Close()
End Function
```

The Second Half of the Transaction

The second half of the transaction is similar, except that the failure conditions are slightly different. First of all, Jon has stipulated that he doesn't want fiddly bits of loose change from Wrox, and so won't accept any transfer of less than $500. Secondly, we've inserted a bug such that an attempt to transfer a negative amount will cause a divide by zero. We'll see why we did this rather bizarre act of sabotage in a little while.

Here's the code:

```
Private Function AddToJon(ByVal intDollars As Integer) As Boolean
    Dim strConn As String
    Dim strCmd As String

    Dim objConn As SqlClient.SqlConnection
    Dim objAdapter As SqlClient.SqlDataAdapter
    Dim objBuilder As SqlClient.SqlCommandBuilder

    Dim objDataset As DataSet
    Dim objTable As DataTable
    Dim objRow As DataRow

    Dim intBalance As Integer

    If intDollars < 0 Then
```

```
      intDollars = intDollars / 0
   ElseIf intDollars < 500 Then
      AddToJon = False
   Else
      strConn = "DATABASE=BankOfJon;SERVER=(local)\NETSDK;UID=sa;PWD=;"
      strCmd = "Select * From Accounts"
      objConn = New SqlClient.SqlConnection(strConn)
      objAdapter = New SqlClient.SqlDataAdapter(strCmd, objConn)
      objBuilder = New SqlClient.SqlCommandBuilder(objAdapter)

      objDataset = New DataSet()
      objAdapter.Fill(objDataset)

      objTable = objDataset.Tables(0)
      objRow = objTable.Rows(0)

      intBalance = CInt(objRow("Amount"))

      intBalance = intBalance + intDollars

      objRow("Amount") = intBalance
      objAdapter.Update(objTable)

      objConn.Close()

      AddToJon = True
   End If
End Function
```

Our business logic component is complete. Let's see how we bring it under the control of Component Services. First of all, of course, we need to build our DLL in VS.NET.

The RegSvcs Tool

Because the Component Services infrastructure is COM-oriented, we need to use a tool that does two things: it needs to expose the .NET component as a COM component, and it then needs to register that COM component with Component Services. Component Services handles all transaction coordination. In other words, you only have to declare your required scripts and components, and then Component Services tracks any changes and restores data should the transaction fail. The tool to do this is called RegSvcs. It's part of the .NET Framework, like the other tools (such as RegAsm) that we encountered in the previous chapter. There are a number of different options associated with the RegSvcs tool and they are outlined in the following table:

Option	Description
/appname:(name)	Specifies the name of the COM+ 1.0 for the target application
/c	Creates the target application or gives an error message if it already exists
/componly	Configures components only, without methods or interfaces
/exapp	Expects an existing application

620

Option	Description
/extlb	Uses an existing type library
/fc	Finds or creates the target application (default)
/help or /?	Displays a usage message containing tool options and command syntax
/nologo	Suppresses the Microsoft logo output
/noreconfig	Doesn't reconfigure the existing target application
/parname:(name)	Specifies the name or ID of the target partition
/quiet	Specifies quiet mode; suppresses the logo and success output
/reconfig	Reconfigures an existing target application (default)
/tlb:(typelibrary file)	Specifies the filename for the type library to install
/u	Uninstalls the target application

This is what happens when we run with the following command (you'll have to change this depending on the location of TransSample.dll):

```
regsvcs C:\7167\TransSample\TransSample.dll
```

Actually, that wasn't really what we wanted to see. RegSvcs is telling us that our DLL doesn't have a strong name.

You can find more information about strong names and assemblies in general in Chapter 25.

The problem that we are facing is that the assembly that we've just created is a private assembly. In order to make it available to the transaction framework, we need to turn it into a shared assembly. To do this, we need to give the assembly a **cryptographically strong name**, generally referred to as its **shared name**.

Cryptographically strong means that the name has been signed with the private key of a dual key pair. This isn't the place to go into a long discussion on dual key cryptography, but the essence of this is as follows:

❑ A pair of keys are generated, one public and one private. If something is encrypted using the private key, it can only be decrypted using the public key from that pair

This means that it is an excellent tool for preventing tampering with information. If, for example, the name of an assembly were to be encrypted using the private key of a pair, then the recipient of a new version of that assembly could verify the origin of that new version, and be confident that it was not a rogue version from some other source. This is because only the original creator of the assembly retains access to its private key.

This is slightly scary stuff, because we don't usually expect to get involved in cryptography unless we're either (a) paranoid or (b) routinely working in the field of security. However, it's not a big deal in .NET, because Microsoft has helpfully provided us with a tool to generate key pairs. The tool is called sn, which stands for strong name.

The sn Tool

sn is another of those command line tools that come as part of the .NET package. This one is located in the \bin subdirectory from the .NET Framework SDK path. It's a very simple tool to use if all we want to do is generate a key pair. We use the -k command line option, plus the name of the key file that we want to create. For example:

```
sn -k C:\7167\TransSample\sgKey.snk
```

Let's run it and see what happens:

Giving the Assembly a Strong Name

We now have to make sure that our assembly uses the strong name. Add the following to Assemply.vb:

```
<Assembly: AssemblyKeyFile("C:\7167\TransSample\sgKey.snk")>
```

This new line tells .NET where to find the file containing the strong name that the assembly should be signed with.

Registering with Component Services

Once we've built the DLL again, we can run RegSvcs once more. This is what we see this time:

This is better. We could have given it a different application name by passing it into the command line:

```
regsvcs C:\7167\TransSample\TransSample.dll TransSampleApp
```

We could also have changed the name of the type library that it generated as well by passing this as the third parameter. The type library, of course, is only there because Component Services talks COM, and not native .NET.

The Component Services Console

The **Component Services Console** is the control interface for Component Services. This is an MMC snap-in, which you can find (on Windows 2000) by selecting Control Panel | Administrative Tools | Component Services. If you open it up, you'll see something like this:

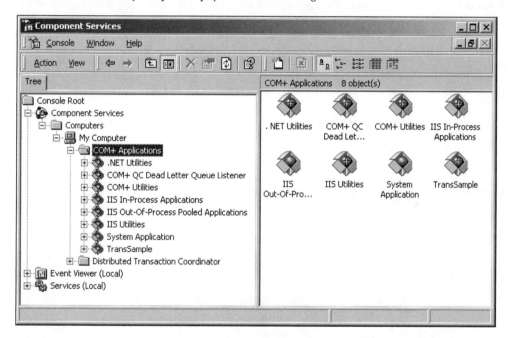

Hey! That's the name of our sample, under COM+ Applications. A COM+ application is a set of related COM+ components that have been packaged together. RegSvcs creates a new application for every component that it registers. If you want to bundle together a series of components from separate DLLs, you can do this, but you can only do it by creating a new application via the Component Services Console (try right-clicking on COM+ Applications and then selecting New). We'll explore the console a little more as we go on.

That's all very nice, but we're missing a couple of things. First of all, we need a test application. Secondly, and more importantly, we need to tell Component Services that we're interested in transactions.

A Test Application

Let's deal with the first problem straight away. We'll create a Windows Application project called TransApp and make a very simple form, like so:

The text field is called txtDollars and the command button is called btnConfirm.

In order to access our transactional component, we need to add references to a couple of DLLs. First of all, we need to add a reference to the transactional component DLL itself. We'll need to browse for this, as it isn't currently in the global assembly cache.

Secondly, in order to access the objects in this DLL, we'll also need to make our application aware of the System.EnterpriseServices assembly, so we'll need to add a reference to that as well.

Having done that, we need to import TransSample into our application:

```
Imports TransSample.TransSample

Public Class Form1
    Inherits System.Windows.Forms.Form
```

Here's the code behind our Confirm button:

```
Private Sub btnConfirm_Click(ByVal sender As System.Object, _
                        ByVal e As System.EventArgs) _
                        Handles btnConfirm.Click
    Dim objTrans As TransSample.TransSample
    objTrans = New TransSample.TransSample()

    If objTrans.TransferMoney(CInt(txtDollars.Text)) = True Then
      MsgBox("Transfer complete")
    Else
      MsgBox("Transfer failed")
    End If

    objTrans = Nothing
End Sub
```

The Transaction Attribute

We now need to tell Component Services how we wish our component to enter a transaction. There are two ways of doing this. Firstly, we can do it via the Component Services Console. First of all, we need to open up the explorer tree to locate the TransSample component, thus:

Next, we right click over this, and select **Properties** from the menu, then the **Transactions** tab:

We can then select one of the available options; we'll discuss what these all mean in a moment.

However, it's a little tiresome to require our system manager to do this every time, especially if we already know that our component is always going to have the same transaction characteristics. So there's an alternative mechanism available to us: we can explicitly set up an attribute in the code for our component.

Attributes are items of declarative information that can be attached to elements of code, such as classes, methods, data members, and properties. Anything that uses these can query their values at runtime. One such attribute is called `TransactionAttribute`, and – unsurprisingly – this is used for specifying the transaction characteristics of a component class. The value of this attribute is taken from an enumeration called `TransactionOption`. Both `TransactionAttribute` and `TransactionOption` are found within the `System.EnterpriseServices` namespace. That enumeration can take the following values:

Value	Description
Disabled	Ignore any transaction in the current context; this is the default.
NotSupported	Create the component in a context with no governing transaction.
Required	Share a transaction if one exists; create a new transaction if necessary.
RequiresNew	Create the component with a new transaction, regardless of the state of the current context.
Supported	Share a transaction if one exists. If it doesn't, create the component in a transaction-free context.

The available values are exactly the same as the ones shown in the Transaction tab. In our case, we've got a stand-alone transaction, so either `RequiresNew` or `Required` is equally valid.

Let's go back to our `TransSample` project, make the change, rebuild, de-register and then re-register the component:

```
<Transaction(TransactionOption.RequiresNew)> _
Public Class TransSample
    Inherits ServicedComponent
```

Before we start running our application, open up the section of the explorer tree in the Component Services Console labeled Distributed Transaction Coordinator, and select Transaction Statistics. You should see something like this:

Now run the application.

Enter 1000 and hit the Confirm button. You should see the number of current active transactions briefly go from none to one, followed by the number of committed transactions and the total both going up by one. Great, we've implemented our first transaction. And if we check the two databases, we can see that the amount in BankOfWrox's Pro VB.NET account has been reduced to $4000, whereas Jon's account in BankOfJon has been increased by $1000. ("Because I'm worth it", says Jon.)

Invalid Data

So what happens if we enter a value that we know to be invalid? There are two options here: either we try to transfer more money than there is in the Pro VB.NET account, or we try to transfer less than Jon will accept. Let's run the application again and try to transfer $100. As expected, the transaction will fail, and no changes will be made to the accounts. Pro VB.NET still has $4000, and Jon still has $1000. This isn't too much of a big deal, because the invalid condition is spotted before any database manipulation is carried out. If we look at the transaction statistics, we can see that the number of *aborted* transactions has been incremented this time.

However, let's try to transfer $10000. This time around, the first part of the transaction is successful, but the *second* part fails. Again, the number of aborted transactions is incremented. But what's happened to the database? Well, fortunately for everyone concerned, we see that there is still $4000 in the Pro VB.NET account, and still $1000 in Jon's. The *entire* transaction has failed.

Something Goes Wrong

Remember that bit of mindless vandalism that we did to the `AddToJon` function, so that it would divide by zero if we entered a negative value? Here's where we get to try it out.

Run the application again, and try to transfer $-1. This time we get a rather unpleasant response:

```
Microsoft Development Environment

⚠  An unhandled exception of type 'System.OverflowException' occurred in
   mscorlib.dll

   Additional information: Arithmetic operation resulted in an overflow.

        Break          Continue        Ignore          Help
```

But we were halfway through a transaction! Never mind, because if we look at the transaction statistics, we see that the aborted count has gone up by one. More importantly, if we check the databases, we see that Pro VB.NET *still* has $4000, and Jon still has $1000. So we're protected against software failures as well.

Other Aspects of Transactions

There are a number of other things that we can do with transactions that we should briefly cover here. We will first of all discuss how manual transactions differ from automatic ones, and then look at Just In Time activation and Object Pooling.

Manual Transactions

So far in this chapter, we have in fact been talking about **automatic transactions**. That is, transactions where Component Services determines when a transaction is about to start, according to the transaction attributes of the components taking part. In most cases, this is the sort of transaction that we'd be using by choice. However, there are also **manual transactions**, which are transactions that are started whenever we want them to. For example, within ADO.NET, you can use the `BeginTransaction` method on the `Connection` object to start a manual transaction. This returns a reference to a `Transaction` object, and you can use the `Commit` or `Rollback` methods on this to determine its outcome.

Just In Time

Creating and deleting components takes time. So, instead of discarding the component when we've finished with it, why not keep it around in case another instance is required? The mechanism by which we do this is called **Just In Time (JIT) activation**, and it's set by default for all automatic transactional components (it's unset by default for all other COM+ components, however).

We know by now that all good transactional components are entirely stateless. However, real life dictates differently, because – for example – we might want to maintain a link to our database, one that would be expensive to set up every time. The JIT mechanism provides us with a couple of methods that we can override in the `ServicedComponent` class in this case.

The method that gets invoked when a JIT component gets activated is called `Activate`, and the component that gets invoked when it is deactivated is called – unsurprisingly – `Deactivate`. In `Activate` and `Deactivate` you should put the things that you would normally put in your constructor and deconstructor. In addition, JIT can be activated by adding the `JustInTimeActivation` attribute to any class within `ServicedComponent`.

Object Pooling

We can, if we want, take this a stage further and maintain a pool of objects already constructed and prepared to be activated whenever required. When the object is no longer required or deactivated, it is returned to the pool until the next time it is required. By retaining objects, we do not have to continually create them from new, which in turns reduces the performance costs of our application. We can use the `ObjectPoolingAttribute` attribute within our class to determine how the pool is to operate:

```
<TransactionAttribute(TransactionOption.RequiresNew), _
ObjectPoolingAttribute (MinPoolSize=5, MaxPoolSize=20, _
                 CreationTimeOut=30)> Public Class TransSample
```

Holding Things Up

A JIT-activated component will be deactivated whenever the current method call returns, unless we tell it otherwise. The way that we control this is by means of methods in the `ContextUtil` class. The `ContextUtil` is the favored method to obtain information about the context of the COM+ 1.0 object.

If we invoke `ContextUtil.DisableCommit`, we are effectively telling Component Services that we are not finished yet; in other words, we're setting the consistency and done bits of the transaction to `False`. The transaction is in an indeterminate state for the time being. Once we are happy that everything is complete, we can call `ContextUtil.EnableCommit`, setting the consistency to `True` and the done bit to `False`. This says that we are happy for the component to be deactivated at the end of the current method call. However, it doesn't say whether or not the transaction is complete or not. It's up to us to invoke either `SetComplete`, setting both the consistency and done parts to true, or `SetAbort`, which sets the consistency to false and done to true – in other words, aborting the call.

As has been shown, `ContextUtil` allows us to control the activity of the object and retrieve any information about its context.

Queued Components

The traditional component programming model is very much a **synchronous** one. Put simply, you invoke a method and you get a result. However, a little thought reveals the unfortunate fact that an awful lot of real-world problems are inherently **asynchronous**. You can't always wait for a response to your request before moving on to the next task. So if we are to be able to tackle everything that the real world throws at us, we need to introduce an asynchronous component model.

Actually, it's a little more complicated than that. The synchronous model is quite simple to manage, because the three possible outcomes of a request are quite straightforward to handle. First of all, the request can be successful. Secondly, the software can crash. Finally, the software can simply not respond at all; in which case, we will have to time it out. However, if we are dealing with asynchronous requests, we have to handle all manner of unusual conditions. For example, the target system may not currently be operational, so we will have to take a decision on how long to wait before it comes back up again. Each outstanding request will take up system resources, so we will have to manage these resources carefully. We need to be able to know when the response comes back. And so on.

We are in fact dealing with a whole new infrastructure here, an infrastructure to handle reliable messaging. Microsoft's product to tackle this type of problem is MSMQ, or Microsoft Message Queue.

The idea behind reliable messaging is that once you have sent a message to a given target, you can effectively forget about it. The system will handle storing and forwarding of messages to their target, and will handle retries and timeouts for you, eventually giving up and returning messages to your dead letter queue if all else fails. MSMQ is in fact a whole technology in itself, but we're not going to cover it in any great detail here. However, we are going to look at where it impinges on .NET Component Services – welcome to **queued components**.

The principle behind queued components is quite simple. With standard component technology, every method call is entirely synchronous. You invoke the method and you wait for the response. If something fails along the way, you may have to wait a long time, but the system will eventually time you out. This is – generally speaking – all well and good if we are dealing with a single, self-contained system. However, once we get out into the distributed computing world, things get a little messier. We have to consider the possibility that it isn't sensible to wait for a response before moving on to the next task. This is where queued components come in. The idea is that you just invoke the method and then continue processing.

Naturally, this places some restrictions on the kind of component that we can use for this kind of thing. For example, we can't have any output arguments, and we can't have any return value. However, there are some cool things that we can do, and we're going to explore them in the next section.

> In order to run the Queued Components examples, MSMQ is needed, which comes with Windows 2000 and XP.

An Example of Queued Components

We're going to write a very simple logging component that takes a string as its input, and writes it out to a sequential file, as well as outputting it in a message box. For the purposes of a simple example, the client and the server will be on the same machine; however, in a production scenario they would be separate. So let's create a Class Library project called `Reporter`. As usual with component services, we need to add a reference to the `System.EnterpriseServices` namespace. The first thing we do is define an interface:

```
Imports System.IO
Imports System.EnterpriseServices


Public Interface IQReporter
```

```
      Sub Log(ByVal strText As String)
  End Interface
```

We need to separate out the interface from the implementation because the implementation, residing on the server, is going to be sitting on another machine somewhere. The client isn't the slightest bit interested in the details of this; all it needs to know is how to interface to it.

Let's take a look at the actual implementation. As with our transactional component, we inherit from `ServicedComponent`, and we also implement the interface that we have just defined. However, notice the `<InterfaceQueuing()>` attribute that indicates to the component services runtime that the interface can be queued (we did the same for the interface):

```
  <InterfaceQueuing(Interface:="IQReporter")> Public Class ImplReporter
    Inherits ServicedComponent
    Implements IQReporter
```

In the logging method, all we do is output a message box, open up a `StreamWriter` component to append to our log file, and then close it again.

```
      Sub Log(ByVal strText As String) Implements IQReporter.Log

        MsgBox(strText)

        Dim objStream As StreamWriter
        objStream = New StreamWriter("C:\account.log", True)

        objStream.WriteLine(strText)
        objStream.Close()

      End Sub

  End Class
```

And that's it for the code for the component. Let's take a look at what we have to do to the assembly definition:

```
  Imports System.Reflection
  Imports System.Runtime.InteropServices
  Imports System.EnterpriseServices

  ' General Information about an assembly is controlled through the following

  ...

  <Assembly: AssemblyTitle("")>
  <Assembly: AssemblyDescription("")>
  <Assembly: AssemblyCompany("")>
  <Assembly: AssemblyProduct("")>
  <Assembly: AssemblyCopyright("")>
  <Assembly: AssemblyTrademark("")>
  <Assembly: AssemblyKeyFile("C:\7167\Reporter\sgKey.snk")>
  <Assembly: ApplicationQueuing(Enabled:=True, QueueListenerEnabled:=True)>
```

```
<Assembly: ApplicationAccessControl(Value:=False, _
              Authentication:=AuthenticationOption.None)>
<Assembly: ApplicationActivation(ActivationOption.Server)>
<Assembly: ApplicationName("Reporter")>
<Assembly: CLSCompliant(True)>
```

The first addition is a reference to the `EnterpriseServices` namespace. In the actual assembly code, the first reference we need to make is to our old friend, the strong name key file. Next, we ensure that queuing is correctly enabled for this component. The next line is a special line to enable message queuing to work correctly in a workgroup environment, by switching off authentication. If we didn't do this, we would need to set up an entire domain structure. (In a production scenario, that's exactly what we would use, so you would need to remove this line.) Finally, we ensure that the component runs as a server, rather than as a library. This was optional in the case of transactional components, but it's mandatory for queued components. We'll see why soon.

Consoles Again

We're ready to build our component. As before, we register it using `RegSvcs`. Let's take a look at the Component Services Console to see how we're doing:

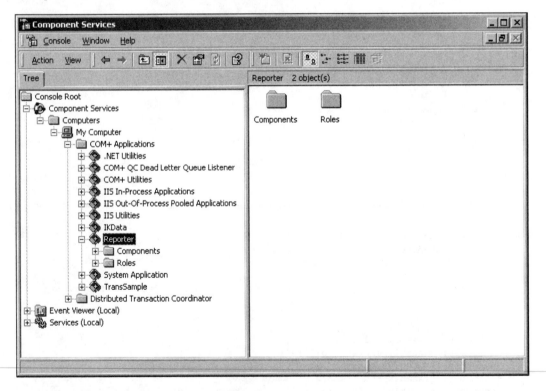

That looks fine, but there's one other console that we should be looking at right now. This is the **Computer Management Console**. You can get to this either from the system console, or by right-clicking on the My Computer icon, and selecting Manage from the menu. This is what it looks like:

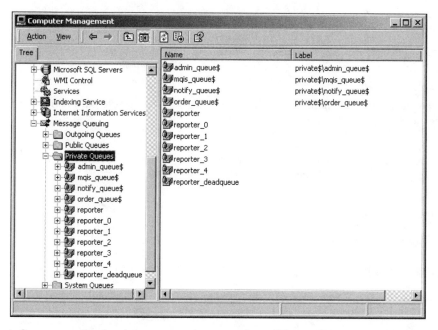

Tucked away, right at the bottom, is the part we're interested in. You'll need to open up **Services and Applications** to find it. Let's take a closer look:

Excellent, Component Services has set up some queues for us. There are five queues feeding into the main one, so we've got our infrastructure ready. Remember, by the way, that all this would be running on the server machine in a production scenario, not the client.

The Client

Let's build our client now. This is where it gets unexpectedly messy, so hang on to your hats. The problem is that all of this is built on top of the MSMQ infrastructure, which is – inevitably – a COM infrastructure. Worse, the kind of things that we are going to do involve **marshaling** COM objects into a stream suitable for inserting into a queued message. For the purposes of this discussion, we can think of marshaling as basically intelligently serializing the contents of a method invocation on an interface. We do this in such a way that they can then be deserialized at the other end and turned into a successful invocation of the same method in a remote implementation of the interface. We get COM to do this for us by constructing a **moniker**, which is basically an intelligent name.

We'll start by creating a Windows application project called `QueuedApp`. We need to add a reference to our `Reporter` component, in the usual manner. Here's the form:

The text box is called `txtMessage`, and the button is called `btnSend`.

Here's the code:

```
Imports System.Runtime.InteropServices
Imports Reporter

Public Class Form1
  Inherits System.Windows.Forms.Form

  Private Sub btnSend_Click(ByVal sender As System.Object, _
                        ByVal e As System.EventArgs) _
                        Handles btnSend.Click
```

Here's the crucial line. The important things to note are the references to our interface and its implementation. Everything else remains the same:

```
Dim iQReporter As Reporter.Reporter.IQReporter
iQReporter = CType(Marshal.BindToMoniker(_
                "queue:/new:Reporter.ImplReporter"), _
                Reporter.IQReporter)
```

Here's the queued call:

```
iQReporter.Log(txtmessage.text)
```

Finally, we have to release the reference to the underlying COM object:

```
Marshal.ReleaseComobject(iQReporter)
End Sub

'...
End Class
```

Like I said, it's not pretty, but you only have to do it once to be able to do it many times over.

Queuing Invocations

Let's try running it, shall we, and enter a suitable message:

We click on the Send button and ... nothing happens. Let's take a look at our message queue:

We've definitely created a message. So that represents our invocation. If we were to be able to read it, we would see "Hello everyone" embedded somewhere in it. (Unfortunately, the console only allows us to inspect the start of the message, but if we do so, we can see the name of our component in there.)

But why hasn't it been actioned? The answer is that we haven't actually started our server. Remember that we said that our component had to run as a server? This is why. The server has to sit there all the time, serving the incoming queue. So let's go to the Component Services Console, right-click on Reporter, select Start from the menu, and we're off. Lo and behold, there's our message box:

And if we look in C:\account.log we can see that it has been updated as well. Now, if we run our application, we'll see the message boxes popping up straight away.

Transactions with Queued Components

Now why did we call that file account.log? The thing is that MSMQ is, like SQL Server, a resource manager, and it can take part in transactions. At first, this is a little counter-intuitive, because how on earth can anything so asynchronous as MSMQ have anything to do with transactions? The point is that it is *reliable*. If we take the transaction to go up to the point at which a message is securely in the queue, we have definitely got something that can participate. What happens at the other end of the queue is an entirely separate transaction. Of course, if something goes wrong there, we may need to look at setting up a compensating transaction coming back the other way to trigger some kind of rollback.

For our final example, then, we're going to take our original transactional component, and add in a queued element, so that not only does the transfer of money take place, but the fact also gets logged to a remote file. We'll use exactly the same queued component as last time. And that's why we called the file account.log.

We start off by making a clone of TransSample, called TransSample2. We need to add a reference to Reporter and a couple more imports:

```
Imports System.EnterpriseServices
Imports System.Runtime.InteropServices
Imports Reporter
```

We also need a new private subroutine:

```
Private Sub ReportTransfer(ByVal intDollars As Integer)
  Dim iQReporter As Reporter.IQReporter
  iQReporter = _
    CType(Marshal.BindToMoniker("queue:/new:Reporter.ImplReporter"), _
    Reporter.IQReporter)

  iQReporter.Log("Transferring $" + CStr(intDollars))

  Marshal.ReleaseComobject(iQReporter)
End Sub
```

This may look kind of familiar to the previous queued component example application. Finally, we add a call to this:

```
Public Function TransferMoney(ByVal intDollars As Integer) As Boolean
    ReportTransfer(intDollars)

    If TakeFromWrox(intDollars) = True Then
        If AddToJon(intDollars) = True Then
```

So we're including a queued component into our transaction. It's been deliberately placed at the start to see if it genuinely takes part in the two-phase committal. If the transaction fails, we shouldn't see any messages come through. So that the queued component takes part in the transaction it must be marked with the Transaction attribute:

```
<InterfaceQueuing(Interface:="Reporter.IQReporter"), _
Transaction(TransactionOption.Required)> _
Public Class ImplReporter
```

If we transfer $1000, we eventually see the message box from our queued component:

So we know it's OK for valid transfers. What happens if we try to transfer $100? As we know from the earlier example, this will fail.

Summary

In this chapter, we have looked at the .NET Component Services, those parts of .NET that address issues required for serious enterprise computing. To begin with, we looked at transactions, what they are and the ACID (Atomicity, Consistency, Isolation, Durability) theory that describes the properties of transactions. This was followed by an example showing how transactions are controlled and monitored via the Component Services Console. Included here, we introduced and described the RegSvcs tool used to register components with Component Services.

After we had finished our transactional components example, we then went on to look at some of the other activities that could be carried out with transactions including manual transactions, just in time attributes, object pooling, and the ContextUtil class.

We also looked at how the two-phase commit is organized so that the failure of a single participant in the transaction causes the entire transaction to be abandoned. Then we looked at queued components, and how these can be used for asynchronous method invocations. Finally, we looked at how these could be combined with transactions.

Professional VB.NET, 2nd edition Professional VB.NET, 2nd editi

19

Threading

One of the things that the move from 16-bit to 32-bit computing gave us was the ability to write code that made use of threads, but although Visual C++ developers have been able to use threads for some time, Visual Basic developers haven't had a really reliable way to do so, until now. Previous techniques involved accessing the threading functionality available to Visual C++ developers. Although this worked, without adequate debugger support in the Visual Basic environment actually developing multithreaded code was nothing short of a nightmare.

This chapter will introduce you to the various objects in the .NET Framework that enable any .NET language to be used to develop multithreaded applications.

What is a Thread?

The principle of a thread is that it allows parts of your program to run independently of other parts. As you probably know, in Windows (NT, 2000, or XP) your program runs in a separate **process**. This is an artificial division that gives your program isolation from other programs so that no problem can indirectly affect each other's operation. (We talk about this more later.) A thread is in effect an execution pointer, which allows Windows to keep track of which line of your program is running at any one time. This pointer starts at the top of the program and moves through each line, branching and looping when it comes across decisions and loops and, at a time when the program is no longer needed, the pointer steps outside of the program code and the program is effectively stopped.

In threading, you have multiple execution pointers. This means that two or more parts of your code can run *simultaneously*. The classic example of **multithreaded** functionality is Microsoft Word's spell checker. When the program starts, the execution pointer starts at the top of the program and eventually gets itself into a position where you're able to start writing code.

However, at some point Word will start another thread and create another execution pointer. As you type, this new thread examines the text and flags any spelling errors as you go, underlining them with a red wavy line:

The principle of a thread is that it allows parts of your program to run independently of other parts. As you probably know, in Windows (NT, 2000, or XP) your program runs in a separate prooooocess.

Every application has one primary thread. This thread serves as the main process thread through the application. Imagine you have an application that starts up, loads a file from disk, performs some processing on the data in the file, writes a new file and then quits. Functionally, it might look like this:

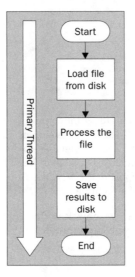

In this simple application, we only need to use a single thread. When the program is told to run, Windows creates a new process and also creates the **primary thread**. To understand more about exactly what it is a thread does, we need to understand a little more about how Windows and the computer's processor deal with different processes.

Processes versus Threads

Windows is capable of keeping many programs in memory at once and allowing the user to switch between them. These programs manifest themselves as applications and services. The difference between applications and services is the user interface – services don't usually have a user interface that allows the user to interact with them, whereas applications do. (In this way Microsoft Word is an example of an application, whereas Internet Information Server is an example of a service.) The ability to run many programs at once is called **multitasking**.

Each of these programs that your computer keeps in memory runs in a single process. The process is started when the program starts and exists for as long as the program is running. As Windows is an operating system that supports **multithreading**, a program is able to create separate threads within its own process. However, multitasking and multithreading are not necessarily the same thing.

Multitasking means that the operating system can keep multiple programs in memory at once and give each of them an opportunity to run (more on this later), but multithreading specifically means this ability to create more than one thread inside a process.

To support a multitasking environment, both the operating system and the processor have to work together to divide up the available computing power between all of the executing processes. We're going to over simplify our description of how Windows divides up its processing time as the finer minutiae of this topic is beyond the scope of this discussion. However, let's take a broad look at how time-slicing works.

Imagine we have two processes running on Windows. In a given time period, Windows will give 50% of the processing power to the primary thread on the first process, and the remaining 50% to the primary thread on the second process.

This division of processing power leads on to the concept of **process priority**. Setting priority on a process tells Windows to bias time-sharing towards a process of higher priority. This is useful in situations where you have a process that requires a lot of processor muscle, but it doesn't matter how long the process takes to do its work. An example of this is the Intel/United Devices Cancer Research Project. This project is based on having thousands of computers around the world running an algorithm that tries to match drug molecules with target proteins associated with the spread of cancer. This program runs continuously, but the actual calculations involve a great deal of math that tends to use a lot of processor power. However, this process runs at a very low priority, so if we need to use Word or Outlook or another application, Windows gives more processor time to these applications and less time to the research application. This means the computer can work smoothly when the user needs it to, letting the research application take up the slack.

> *You can learn more about the Intel/United Devices Cancer Research Project at* http://www.ud.com/.

Let's say we have **granularity** on our time slice of three seconds, in other words that, in a given time-slice divided between two processes, Process A is run for a second-and-a-half then Process B gets to run for a second-and-a-half. At the end of the period, Process A gets another chance to run for another second-and-a-half, then Process B gets to run. If another process is started, Processes A, B and C all get the opportunity to run for a single second. If Process B and Process C end, Process A gets all of the processor to itself, until another process is started.

What's critical to understand about time slicing is that the processes don't have to actively participate in this process. If we have three processes running and a granularity of three seconds, at the end of the first section, Process A doesn't have to say to Windows "OK, my time is up, I'll wait". Instead, Windows just stops allocating time to the process and, effectively, it stops until it gets another opportunity to run. This is known as **preemptive multitasking**.

Time slicing applies to threads as well. As you know, when a process is started it is given a primary thread. As a thread runs, it has the opportunity to **spin up** other threads to do work. Imagine now that Process A and Process B both have a single thread, but the primary thread of Process C has started another thread and has a total of two threads:

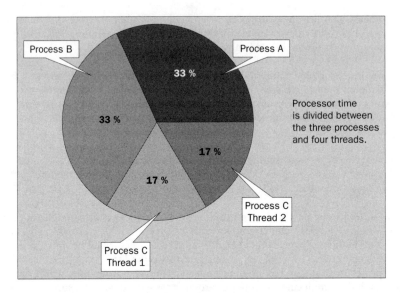

In this example, Process C is still getting one-third of the processing power per time slice. However, because Process C comprises two threads, the first thread is getting the first half of the one-third (17%) and the second thread is getting the second half of the one-third (again, 17%). So, at time "2 seconds", Windows stops executing Process B and starts executing the first thread of Process C. At time "2.5 seconds", Windows suspends the first thread of process C and moves onto the second thread. At time "3 seconds", the second thread of Process C is suspended and Process A is resumed. (Again, this is an oversimplification.) This is illustrated in the following figure:

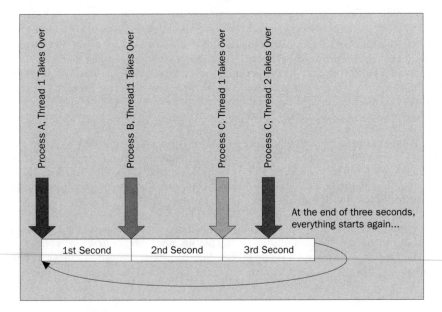

So why is all this important? Well, time slicing gets you to a point where all the processing power is shared equally. Without time slicing you can easily end up in a situation where you're at the mercy of badly behaving processes. If Windows wasn't capable of saying "OK, time to suspend this process and resume this different process" then it would have to say "I'll wait until you appear to be idle as being idle implies you've finished this bit of work, then I'll move on and start running this other process". If Windows relies on processes being well behaved, it's easy for a process to 'hijack' the system and give an unfair priority to its own process. This can have a catastrophic effect if the process has gone into an endless loop, like this:

```
n = 2
Do While n = 2
Loop
```

If the operating system were waiting for this process to be idle before starting another process, no other running process would ever get a chance to finish. This would hang the entire machine. This scenario is described by **cooperative multitasking**. This was the multitasking paradigm used by 16-bit versions of Windows, such as Windows 3.1. It relied on the program giving the operating system the opportunity to run another program.

The other side to this is that the operating system runs more 'smoothly'. Since Windows is taking an active interest in how processes run, no process gets an unfair distribution of the processing power. Although this seems like a pretty nebulous concept, achieving this 'smoothness' is one of the reasons for using threads.

When to Use Threads

If we regard computer programs as being either application software or service software, we find there are different motivators for each one.

Application software uses threads primarily to deliver a better user experience. Common examples are:

- ❑   Microsoft Word – background spell checker
- ❑   Microsoft Word – background printing
- ❑   Microsoft Outlook – background sending and receiving of e-mail
- ❑   Microsoft Excel – background recalculation

You can see that in all of these cases, threads are used to do 'something in the background'. This provides a better user experience. For example, I can still edit a Word document while Word is spooling another to the printer. Or, I can still read e-mails while Outlook is sending my new e-mail. As an application developer, you should use threads to enhance the user experience. Below is a diagram showing the threads involved when the Word spell checker is utilized:

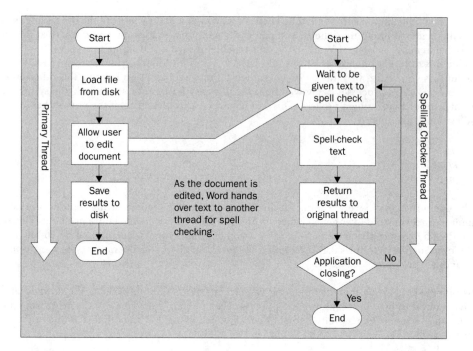

At some point during the application startup, code running in the primary thread would have spun up this other thread to be used for spell checking. As part of the 'allow user to edit the document' process, we give the spell checker thread some words to check. This thread separation means that the user can continue to type, even though spell checking is still taking place.

Service software uses threads to deliver scalability and improve the service offered. For example, imagine I had a Web server that receives six incoming connections simultaneously. That server needs to service each of the requests in parallel, otherwise the sixth thread would have to wait for me to finish threads one through five before it even got a look in. Here's how IIS might handle incoming requests:

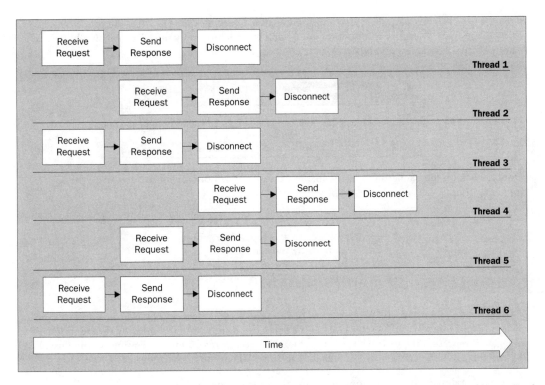

In this diagram, we've got six worker threads that exist only to help service requests from clients. Each request is handled by exactly one thread. This diagram doesn't show the other application threads that handle managing these threads. For example, the primary application thread will wait around for Windows to signal that the service needs to be stopped for various reasons. Another thread will listen to the incoming connection, and will either create a new thread, or find an existing thread that can service the requests. (Most server software uses thread pooling, a topic we discuss at the end of this chapter.)

ASP and ASP.NET development is a classic example of a situation where you don't care about threading, even though you're running in a multithreaded environment. Whenever your .asp or .aspx page is called you're only running in a pretty isolated fashion – you don't care what any of the other threads are doing. Even with ASP.NET, you're going to run in a very procedural way – in other words, from the start of the page to the bottom of the page.

A Threading Example

Creating a thread in .NET is extremely easy. All we have to do is create an instance of a System.Threading.Thread object and call the Start method. However, to do this we need a demonstration application. What we're going to do is build a simple application with a button and a text box. We'll start the thread when the button is clicked and from within the button, we'll set the text on the text box.

Create a new Windows Application project and call it ThreadExample. After the project has been created, the Form Designer will open to the default Form1 form. Lay out Form1 with a button called btnStartThread and a text box called txtResult:

Double-click on the background of the form to create a new Load event handler. Add the following code:

```
Private Sub Form1_Load(ByVal sender As System.Object, _
                       ByVal e As System.EventArgs) _
                       Handles MyBase.Load
    Me.Text &= " - Thread #" & _
        System.Threading.Thread.CurrentThread.GetHashCode
End Sub
```

The shared CurrentThread property can be used to access a Thread object that represents the currently executing thread. As this code will be running from within the primary thread, this Thread object will represent the primary thread. GetHashCode returns a unique identifier of the thread. When we run the code, the caption will, in effect, display the ID of the primary thread.

Once you've done that, we can look at getting the thread running.

Creating ThreadWorker

My preferred method for handling threads is to create a separate class for managing the starting and stopping of a thread. This class contains a private member called _thread that holds an instance of a System.Threading.Thread object. Instances of this worker class can then be instantiated by the main application and controlled exclusively through its methods. This encapsulates the threading functionality, meaning that the caller doesn't really have to worry about controlling the thread's lifetime.

Create a new class called ThreadWorker and add this code:

```
Imports System.Threading

Public Class ThreadWorker

    Public TextBox As TextBox
    Private _thread As Thread

End Class
```

ThreadWorker will have a public method called SpinUp that will go ahead and start the thread. But, in order for a thread to start you need to provide an entry point by means of a **delegate** that references a method on our ThreadWorker class.

 The thread will call this delegate as soon as it's ready to start work. This is conceptually similar to the startup method that VB6 projects had. In fact, the startup method is the entry point for the primary thread. As it's unlikely that any other threads will want to use the same entry point, we have to create a new one; hence our work here. Our delegate will be called Start (you are free to choose any name you like, I just like Start) and will be defined like this:

```
Private Sub Start()
  TextBox.Text = "Hello, world from thread #" & _
          Thread.CurrentThread.GetHashCode() & "!"
End Sub
```

Again, here we're using CurrentThread to get a Thread object that executes the currently executing thread. As this code should be running from within the new thread, the IDs should not match.

You can see that we don't have to do anything special from within Start to support the thread. Remember, you've already been writing code that runs in a thread – it's just that up until now you've only ever had a single thread.

Here's the code for the SpinUp method inside ThreadWorker that will start the thread:

```
Public Sub SpinUp()

  ' create a thread start object that refers to our worker...
  Dim threadStart As ThreadStart
  threadStart = New ThreadStart(AddressOf Me.Start)

  ' now, create the thread object and start it...
  _thread = New Thread(threadStart)
  _thread.Start()

End Sub
```

That's it. To start the thread all we have to do is create a System.Threading.ThreadStart object, give it a delegate that references our entry point, and pass it to a new System.Threading.Thread object. When we call Thread.Start the new thread will be created and our ThreadWorker.Start delegated method will be called as the entry point.

Calling SpinUp

To call SpinUp we need to wire in some code behind the button. Add this code:

```
Private Sub btnStartThread_Click(ByVal sender As Object, _
                      ByVal e As System.EventArgs) _
                      Handles btnStartThread.Click
    ' create a new worker...
    Dim worker As New ThreadWorker()
    worker.TextBox = txtResult()

    ' spin up the thread...
    worker.SpinUp()
End Sub
```

Since `txtResult` is a private member, we can't access it directly from the `ThreadWorker`. Instead, we use the `TextBox` property to pass a text box control to our instance of `ThreadWorker`. Code running inside of the thread can then set the `Text` property of this control to update the display.

To test the solution, run the project and click the **Start Thread** button. You should see something like this:

You can see that the IDs shown in the caption and in the text box are different. This proves that the code to set the caption and the code to set the text in the text box are indeed running on different threads.

Now we can look at why developing multithreaded applications requires more than a casual approach.

Synchronization

Windows provides isolation between different processes. What this means is that a process cannot directly affect another process, or rather, a process can only be affected in a controlled and well-understood manner.

For example, if I run up a process that crashes, in theory all the other processes should continue running. If I run up a process that tries to hog all of the processor for itself, other processes will continue running.

> *Again, a caveat: the way that Windows divides time is in reality more complex than the way that we've illustrated it here. Windows will in fact attempt to divide time based on the perceived need of the process. This means that if a process seems to need a lot of the processor and it's running at the same priority as other processes, Windows may not give processor share to the other applications. This leads to the apparent effect that no other processes can run.*

The most important aspect of process isolation, in relation to this discussion, is that of memory isolation. As a process, I am given my own block of memory. I cannot simply call into another process's allocated memory, either to read the memory or change it. This is great from both security and stability standpoints. Imagine an application that a user keys credit card numbers into. As a malicious programmer, I could theoretically start a process that continuously monitored the memory of the credit card application process. If I can watch the memory, I could extract the credit card information. Alternatively, my application might have a bug that inadvertently changes the memory of another process causing it to crash. Process isolation stops this from happening.

Changing memory in an uncontrolled manner can lead to catastrophic results. Most software is written with forward knowledge of how its memory should look, for example "I expect to see an object that provides a database connection at this address in memory".

If I was another process and I was able to affect another process's memory, I could move or change that other process's memory causing it to crash.

When we're writing multithreaded code, the hardest issue is that of managing access to the memory allocated to the process. You don't, for example, want two threads writing to the same piece of memory at the same time. Equally, you don't want a group of threads reading memory that another thread is in the process of changing. This management of memory access is called **synchronization**. It's properly managing synchronization that makes writing multithreaded code difficult.

Blocking, Wait States, and Signaling

Think back to our discussion about time slicing. Remember how we said that Windows automatically suspends and resumes our threads depending on its perceived processing needs, the various priority settings, and so on. Say we're running one process containing two threads. If we can somehow mark the second thread as **dormant** (in other words, tell Windows that it has nothing to do), there's no need for Windows to allocate time to it. Effectively, the first thread will receive 100% of the processor horsepower available to that process. When a thread is marked as dormant we say it's in a **wait state**.

Windows is particularly good at managing processes and threads. It's a core part of Windows' functionality and so its developers have spent a lot of time making sure that it's super-efficient and as bug free as software can be. This means that creating and spinning up threads is very easy to do and happens very quickly. Threads also only take up a small amount of system resources. However, there is a caveat you should be aware of.

The activity of stopping one thread and starting another is called **context switching**. This switching happens relatively quickly, but only if you're relatively careful with the number of threads you create. If you spin up too many threads, the process will spend all of its time switching between different threads, perhaps even getting to a point where the code in the thread doesn't get a chance to run because as soon as you've started the thread it's time for it to stop again.

Creating thousands of threads is not the right solution. What you need to do is find a balance between the amount of threads that your application needs and the amount of threads that Windows can handle. There's no magic number or right answer to the question of "How many threads should I create?" You just need to be aware of context switching and experiment a little.

Take the Microsoft Word spell check example. The thread that performs the spell check is around all the time. Imagine you have a blank document containing no text. At this point, the spell check thread is in a wait state. Imagine you type a single word into the document and then pause. At this point, Word will pass the word over to the thread and signal it to start working. The thread will use its own slice of the processor power to examine the word. If it finds something wrong with the word, it will tell the primary thread that a spelling problem was found and that the user needs to be alerted. At this point, the spell check thread drops back into a wait state until more text is entered into the document. Word doesn't spin up the thread whenever it needs to perform a check – rather the thread runs all the time but, if it has nothing to do, it drops into this efficient wait state. (We'll talk about how the thread starts again later.)

Again, we've oversimplified this. Word will 'wake up' the thread at various times. However, the principle is sound – the thread is given work to do, it reports the results and then it starts waiting for the next chunk of work to do.

Principles of Blocking

When a thread is in a wait state, a blocking operation of some sort has usually put it there. Some system event will usually release the block, causing the thread to come out of the wait state and start doing something. When we say 'event' we are *not* talking about a VB.NET event. Although the naming convention is unfortunate, the principle is the same – something happens and we react to it.

Although blocking can be used to control the execution of threads, it's primarily used to control access to resources, including memory. This is the basic idea behind synchronization – if we need something, we block until we can access it

To understand how threads share memory, imagine we have this code:

```
Public Class Adder

    Private Shared _value As Integer = 1

    Public Sub Increment()
      Dim n As Integer = _value
      n += 1
      _value = n
    End Sub

End Class
```

We have a shared member called _value there, which means that all instances of Adder will use the same instance of _value. Therefore, if we have two instances of the class, the first of which changes _value to 27, all other instances of the class will also see _value as 27.

Now look at the Increment method. There's nothing complicated about this at all – we get the value from _value, store it locally in n, add one to it and then set _value to n.

But, with our multithreaded hat on, we can see that there's a problem with this. Imagine we have two instances of the class, each instance created in a separate thread. If we call Increment on both objects *simultaneously*, we won't get the results we want.

What we want to happen is that each time Increment is called we want 1 to be added to the shared _value. If we call the code like this:

```
Dim adder As New Adder
adder.Increment()
adder.Increment()
```

then we can guarantee that at the end, _value will be 3 (provided _value was initialized to a value of 1). However, if we have two threads acting on _value simultaneously, we can't guarantee this. If the calls are perfectly simultaneous, both threads will get 1 from _value when Increment is called. Both threads will add 1 to this value and both threads will set _value to 2. Even though we've called the method twice, we only feel the effect of having called it once.

In fact, the problem is much worse than this. We can't guarantee that calls are not made simultaneously across threads. We also can't guarantee that threads run at the same speed. Basically, unless we have absolute control over the synchronization, weird problems are going to occur.

650

Critical Sections

To get around this problem, we want to mark a block of code as accessible to only one thread at a time. This guarantees that each time we call `Increment`, the entire operation occurs. This way, we guarantee that each call to `Increment` will properly affect _value and, therefore, all the weird problems should go away.

This kind of block is called a **critical section**. To use it, a thread tries to enter the critical section. If no other thread is inside the critical section, the thread can go straight on and do its work. If another thread tries to get into the block while the first thread is inside it, that second thread will be blocked until the first thread leaves the critical section, as shown in the following diagram:

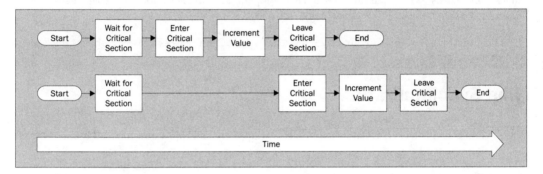

One problem with critical sections is that they create bottlenecks. Imagine we had 16 threads all trying to call `Increment`. Effectively, because only one thread can enter the critical section at a time, we have single-threaded code, and so get no advantage of multithreading. In fact, this thread will run slower than single-threaded code as we have the overhead of dealing with the extra threads and all of the context switching. What we need is a thread that understands more about what we want to do, something we'll look at now.

Reader/Writer Locks

If we were trying to access a file from a disk, we'd usually give Windows an indication of what we wanted to do with the file. This **mode** gives us certain permissions, but also enables sharing. For example, if we open a file for reading, there's no reason why another thread wanting to open the same file for reading cannot do so. In fact, ignoring operating system limitations, there's no limit to the number of times the file can be opened.

Compare this to writing the file. Only one thread should ever be able to write to the file, and this is on the proviso that no other thread is reading or writing to the file. If we're writing, we want exclusive access to the file. Although we've been talking about files, the same applies to memory:

❑ There's no limit to the number of threads that can read from _value at any given moment

❑ Only one thread at a given moment can write to _value, providing that no other thread is reading from it or writing to it

The .NET Framework provides a reader/writer lock that achieves this in the guise of an object called `System.Threading.ReaderWriterLock`. We'll see this in action in a moment.

Interestingly, a reader/writer lock won't actually help us reduce the bottleneck in the example we've seen so far. In all cases, this thread needs to write to _value, so we'll always need an exclusive lock that behaves in the same way as a critical section. However, in the majority of cases, using reader/writer locks is the most appropriate synchronization method and we'll look shortly at an example.

On-Demand Blocking

We've examined the concept of blocking from the perspective of writing code that automatically blocks when attempting to access a lock of some kind, either a critical section lock or a reader/writer lock. Blocking is also used in an on-demand basis to pause and resume threads. Coming back to our Word spell checker example, we spin up the thread when the application starts then block until we need to check some words. We wait until we're signaled and, at that point, start doing the spell check. When we've finished, we block until we're signaled again, and so on.

This kind of block is achieved with a System.Threading.ManualResetEvent object. We'll see this in a moment, too.

Trying Synchronization

To illustrate what we've talked about so far, we're going to build a new Windows Application and build a very simple spell checker. Create a new Windows Application project now and call it SpellChecker.

We're going to use the default Form1 form to build our application. Add controls, as listed below, to the form until you get something that looks like this:

Here are the names of the controls that need to have their names changed:

- ❑ `txtText` – the text box that contains the text that should be spell checked; set the `MultiLine` property of this control to `True`

- ❑ `txtThreadStatus` – a read-only text box that the thread will use to report back the time a spell check was performed

- ❑ `txtInvalidWords` – a text box that displays the invalid words that were found by the spell checker

- ❑ `tmrTextChanged` – a timer that will be enabled whenever the text in `txtText` changes

- ❑ `tmrUpdateInvalidWords` – a timer that will be used to update the invalid word list

> **You need to add the timers from the Components tab of the Toolbox, not the Windows Forms tab.**

Whenever Word finds a word that it thinks is spelled incorrectly, it underlines it with a red wavy line. To do this, Word has to have control over the various UI objects that actually render the page onto the screen. In our example, we don't have this fine level of control – we're using the standard `System.Windows.Forms.TextBox` control object, and without going through a considerable number of hoops, it's not easy for us to duplicate the wavy-line functionality.

What Word does is maintain a list of the words that it thinks are invalid. (If the word is valid, Word doesn't care about it. It only needs to keep track of one list, and as the invalid word list is likely to be shorter, this is the one that it uses.) As text is typed into the document, Word adds the newly typed words into a queue that the spell checker thread periodically examines. The results of the spell check are then passed back to the main application thread as a list of invalid words. As Word renders each word, it checks to see if the word it's rendering appears in its invalid word list. If it does, it draws a red wavy line under the text.

To get a similar effect, we're going to use another text box on our form to tell the user which words typed into the main edit area are invalid. As the text in `txtText` changes, we'll pass the whole lot over to a separate thread that will scan the words and create a list of invalid words. This list will then be passed back to `Form1` through a delegate, whereupon a constantly running timer will take the list and add the contents to `txtInvalidWords`.

Creating WordList

The first object we're going to build is an object that contains a list of words. We're not going to call this `Dictionary`, as veteran ASP developers will already be familiar with another object called `Dictionary`, and new .NET developers will want to avoid name clashes.

`WordList` is simply going to hold a list of words in a `System.Collections.ArrayList` object. This object provides a very fast search facility called a binary search, so we should be OK if we end up working with a very large dictionary. The caveat with using binary searches is that the list must be sorted alphabetically before we can search.

To populate `WordList`, we're going to read a file from disk. This file should contain a single word on each line, like this:

```
this
is
a
list
of
words
that
we
will
use
in
the
spell
checker
```

Create a list of words yourself, and save the file with the name `wordlist.txt` in the same build folder as your project. Note that this will be a list of valid words, so any word that the user types that is not in this list will be returned by the spellchecker as invalid. You can find a more meaningful list of words at http://www.insidemedicine.com/words.html.

Next, create a new class called `WordList` and add this code:

```
Imports System.IO

Public Class WordList
End Class
```

We'll be using the `System.IO` namespace to load the list of words into the word array. Now, add this code to define a new private member that will contain the collection, another to flag whether or not the list has been sorted and a method that can be used to add words to the collection:

```
Public Class WordList

    Private _wordList As New ArrayList()
    Private _isSorted As Boolean

    Public Sub Add(ByVal word As String)

      word = word.ToLower
      If Not _wordList.Contains(word) Then
        _wordList.Add(word.ToLower)
      End If
      _isSorted = False

    End Sub

End Class
```

To keep this example simple, we're going to ignore the problem of dealing with capitalization, by assuming that anything we ever work with will be lowercase. This is why we're using `ToLower` to convert the word to lowercase text, before adding it to the list. We also check to make sure that the word isn't already in the list when we add it.

Next we need to create the method to load the word list from disk. This method should be added to the `WordList` class. We'll start this with a `Try...Catch` block that will detect any problems with opening the file:

```
Public Sub Load(ByVal filename As String)

   Try

      Dim stream As New FileStream(filename, FileMode.Open)
      Dim reader As New StreamReader(stream)
```

The `System.IO.StreamReader` class contains a `ReadLine` method that will come in quite handy when we're loading up the file. Once we have the file, we can proceed to read in each word and add it to the list:

```
      _wordList.Clear()

      Do While True

         Dim buf As String = reader.ReadLine
         If buf = "" Then Exit Do

         _wordList.Add(buf)

      Loop
```

To make this code a little more efficient, we're not going to use the `Add` method we built earlier to add words to the list. If you recall, `Add` will transform the string into lowercase and scan the collection to make sure a word isn't already contained within it. What we want to do here is quickly populate the array. We'll assume that the words contained in `wordlist.txt` have already been qualified, and will always appear in lowercase with no words repeated.

Once we've worked through the file, we should close the reader and the stream. We'll also mark the list as not sorted:

```
      reader.Close()
      stream.Close()

      _isSorted = False
```

Marking the list as unsorted wouldn't be 100% appropriate in a production system. Just as we're assuming that the list is properly qualified insofar as it contains all lowercase, non-repeated words, we should also assume that it's sorted. However, for this example it will be easier on you to assume the list is not sorted. That way, as you're experimenting with the data, you won't have to worry about inserting new values into the correct place in `wordlist.txt`.

Finally, we can close off the method:

```
   Catch

      MsgBox("The file '" & filename & _
```

```
                "' could not be loaded. (" & _
            Err().GetException.Message & ")")

    End Try

End Sub
```

The last method we need on `WordList` is one that checks to see if a word is valid or not. We'll use the super-fast `BinarySearch` method on `ArrayList` to achieve this. What we'll do before we look for the word is sort the list if it's marked as unsorted:

```
' Contains - is the word in the word list?
Public Function Contains(ByVal word As String) As Boolean

  ' do we need to sort the list?
  If _isSorted = False Then
    _wordList.Sort()
    _isSorted = True
  End If

  ' do the search...
  Dim result As Integer = _wordList.BinarySearch(word)
  If result >= 0 Then
    Return True
  Else
    Return False
  End If

End Function
```

Effectively, checking to see if the list is sorted at this point means that the first time `Contains` is called, the list will be sorted and `BinarySearch` will work in an optimal fashion. (`BinarySearch` will return the index of the item in the list, or zero if the item is not in the list.) As it's unlikely that the list will be modified using `Add` before subsequent calls to `Contains`, the sort will only ever happen once.

Creating Checker

We're going to create our own self-contained class for handling the spell check process. `Checker` will also manage its own threading, meaning that aside from synchronization issues, we can pretty much rely on `Checker` properly starting and stopping its own thread.

Create a new class called `Checker` and add this code:

```
Imports System.Text
Imports System.Threading
Imports System.Collections.Specialized

Public Class Checker
End Class
```

To handle lists of words, we're going to be using a
`System.Collections.Specialized.StringCollection` object. This object makes it very easy to
work with lists of strings. Of course, we could use an `ArrayList` object as we did before, but our
primary motivation for using that was to obtain the binary search functionality.

Our object is going to need quite a number of members. First off, three members that will help us
handle the thread:

```
Public Class Checker
```

```
    Private _thread As Thread
    Private _isCancelled As Boolean
    Private _paused As New ManualResetEvent(False)
```

`Thread` (or `System.Threading.Thread`) you've already met, but you won't have met
`System.Threading.ManualResetEvent`. This object will provide a way for the application to tell
the thread to start spell checking. We'll see this in action later.

To do its work, we're going to give `Checker` a list of words to check. In this example, we're going to
always pass it the complete contents of `txtText.Text`, namely the entire document. In contrast, Word
will only pass new and changed words, not the entire document. We'll hold this list using these members:

```
    Private _checkList As New StringCollection()
    Private _checkListLock As New ReaderWriterLock()
```

The `System.Threading.ReaderWriterLock` object provides the synchronization access that we've
been talking about. We'll use this to synchronize access to `_checkList` as we add words to it from the
main application thread and as we check words in it from the thread itself. There is no natural
relationship between these two objects. Rather, the code that we write will cause these two objects to
work together to get the synchronization effect that we want.

Finally, we'll need a set of member fields that will help us communicate with `Form1`:

```
    Public WordList As New WordList()
    Public OwnerForm As Form1
    Public OnCheckComplete As CheckComplete
```

Delegates

Delegates can be used to create a free-form entry point into some piece of code in your application. In
this instance, we're going to use a delegate to tell `Form1` that the thread has finished checking through
the words, and also use it to pass through a `StringCollection` containing a list of invalid words. To
do this, we need to define the delegate. Add this code to `Checker`:

```
    Public Delegate Sub CheckComplete( _
        ByVal newInvalidWords As StringCollection)
```

Starting the Thread

The first method we need to add is `SpinUp`. This will tell the thread to start. In a short while, we're
going to define the `Start` method, but for now just add this code to `Checker`:

```
Public Sub SpinUp()

   Dim start As New ThreadStart(AddressOf Me.Start)

   _thread = New Thread(start)
   _thread.Name = "Spell checker"
   _thread.Start()

End Sub
```

This is very similar to the example we saw earlier in the chapter.

One thing we need this thread to do is report back to us to tell us when it's running, and when it has run. This is quite important in helping us understand what's happening behind the scenes. Add this write-only property:

```
Public WriteOnly Property ThreadStatus() As String
   Set(ByVal Value As String)
      OwnerForm.ThreadStatus = Now().ToString & ": " & Value
   End Set
End Property
```

We haven't built Form1.ThreadStatus yet, but when we do, it will simply change the Text property on txtThreadStatus to reflect whatever the thread wants to say.

Notice that we're ignoring synchronization problems with ThreadStatus, even though there is an argument that says we need to synchronize this block of code because the Text property can be accessed by more than one thread. For simplicity, we're going to ignore it and concentrate instead on resolving synchronization problems for the spell checking logic.

Add this code to kick off the Checker.Start method. Remember, this method will be called as the entry point for our new thread:

```
Private Sub Start()

   ThreadStatus() = "Thread started"

   Do While True

      ThreadStatus() = "Waiting..."

      _paused.WaitOne()
```

As soon as we hit WaitOne, we'll drop into a super-efficient wait state again. When this happens, Windows will stop allocating time to the thread, effectively freeing up processing power for other threads in the process. _paused is a System.Threading.ManualResetEvent object, which means its purpose in life is to provide a way for threads to be dropped in and out of wait states by a process called **signaling**. When the object is **non-signaled**, we'll block. When the object is **signaled**, the thread will start running again by moving the execution pointer down to the next line. We'll see this in action in a moment.

When we signal _paused, we start running again by virtue of the fact that Windows starts allocating us time slices again. The first thing we do is see if we're cancelled and, if we are, we drop out of the loop:

```
If _isCancelled = True Then Exit Do
```

If we're not cancelled, we have to check the words. To do this, we have to assume that the person who resumed us has used methods on the object that we haven't built yet to create a list of words to check in the _checkList string collection. We need to iterate through this collection, checking to see if any of the words are in our WordList object. If we find a word that's invalid, we'll add it to a collection called invalidWords:

```
Dim invalidWords As New StringCollection()
```

However, before we can look at _checkList, we have to synchronize access to it and try to acquire a reader lock. This will mean that other threads can read the list, but no other threads can write it (in this instance, we're not going to have other threads reading the list at the same time, but we could well have something trying to write to it):

```
_checkListLock.AcquireReaderLock(-1)
```

That's all we have to do to acquire a lock on _checkListLock. The integer parameter that AcquireReaderLock takes is a timeout. Here, we've specified –1, which means that we want to wait for an infinite amount of time for the lock to become available. If we specified 1000, we'd wait for one second (1000 milliseconds) for the lock to become available. We might under other circumstances want to wait only, say 30 seconds for the lock to become available. This brings up an important issue called **deadlocking** that we talk about at the end of this exercise.

Walking through the list of words is very easy:

```
Dim word As String
For Each word In _checkList
    If Not WordList.Contains(word) Then invalidWords.Add(word)
Next
```

Once we've done that, we need to release the reader lock.

> **It is critically important that you release any lock that you acquire.**

If we, for example, didn't unlock the reader at the end of this process, no one would ever be able to acquire a writer lock:

```
_checkListLock.ReleaseReaderLock()
```

You are probably using exception handling in your applications. We've omitted it to keep things easier, but you must pay attention to the way you release your locks. Make sure that you release your locks in a Finally clause. As Finally is called irrespective of whether an exception was thrown or not, it's guaranteed to get called.

Once we've unlocked the list and done our work, we can pass the list of invalid words back to the primary application thread through the delegate we were given when we were configured:

```
OnCheckComplete.Invoke(invalidWords)
```

At the end of this process, we can loop back to the beginning of the thread handler code and wait for a new request to do some work. Before we do this, we need to reset the _paused ManualResetEvent object and put it back into a non-signaled state (we'll talk about this in a moment):

```
_paused.Reset()
```

Finally, we can finish the Start method:

```
    Loop

    ThreadStatus() = "Thread stopped"

End Sub
```

Resuming the Thread

When the thread first starts, we call _paused.WaitOne and the result of this is that the thread drops into a wait state. _paused represents an instance of a ManualResetEvent object. This kind of object can either be signaled or non-signaled. When we created it, we created it with this line:

```
Private _paused As New ManualResetEvent(False)
```

The Boolean parameter on the constructor indicates the initial state of the object, and in this case we've said "Signaled = False".

Now that we've completed Start, we need to look at the method that instructs the thread to start checking the _checkList collection. Add this method to Checker:

```
Public Sub StartChecking()
    _paused.Set()
End Sub
```

By calling Set, as we are doing from StartChecking, we're signaling the object. By calling Reset, as we are doing from the end of the main thread loop implemented in Start, we're putting the object back into a non-signaled state. Set method always puts the object in a signaled state and Reset always puts it in a non-signaled state irrespective of the current state of the object.

If we call WaitOne on a non-signaled object, the thread will drop into a wait state until the thread is signaled again. As we create _paused in a non-signaled state, as soon as the thread starts, WaitOne will be called and the thread will drop into a wait state. When we call StartChecking from the primary application thread, _paused will be signaled, WaitOne will then return and the processing will start. After the processing is complete, we reset _paused, the loop jumps back up to the top and WaitOne is called again.

Together, this arrangement gives us a fine level of control over the execution of the thread.

Cancelling and Stopping the Thread

When the application closes, we want to gracefully exit the thread. To do this, we need to get the infinite loop implemented in Start to drop out. If you recall, Start is actually called by the thread manager. As soon as Start returns, the thread is said to be dormant and is ready to be cleaned up.

Here's the code to cancel the thread. Add this method to Checker:

```
Public Sub Cancel()
  _isCancelled = True
  StartChecking()
End Sub
```

As soon as we call this method, it will return, irrespective of whether the thread has actually managed to quit the loop, and get to the end of the Start method. Ideally, we want to make sure that the thread has shut down properly. To do this, we need another method:

```
Public Sub SpinDown()

  Cancel()

  _thread.Join()
  _thread = Nothing

End Sub
```

The Join method on _thread is a blocking call that drops the system into a wait state until the thread has finished executing and has got to a point where Windows has deleted it from its own internal threads subsystem. For this reason, SpinDown should not be called from the thread itself, but must be called from the primary application thread. As this call blocks, we're guaranteed that, by the time it returns, the thread has properly reached the end of Start and has finished its work.

Populating _checkList

All that remains now is to create some methods that update _checkList. These methods are pretty straightforward. First, let's look at the one that resets the list:

```
Public Sub ClearCheckList()

  _checkListLock.AcquireWriterLock(-1)
  _checkList.Clear()
  _checkListLock.ReleaseWriterLock()

End Sub
```

Notice how we're asking _checkListLock for a writer lock this time round. Also notice that we have to release the lock in the same way as we did for a reader lock.

Second, let's look at a method that adds a single word to the list. In this example, we're changing the word into all lowercase characters:

```
Public Sub AddWordToCheckList(ByVal word As String)

  word = word.ToLower

  _checkListLock.AcquireWriterLock(-1)
  If Not _checkList.Contains(word) Then
    _checkList.Add(word)
  End If
  _checkListLock.ReleaseWriterLock()

End Sub
```

Lastly, we need a method that can take an entire block of text and strip out everything that's not an alphanumeric character. As this method comes across a word, the word will be added to the list through AddWordToCheckList. To use the spell checker, the primary thread will make life easy for itself and give us a block of text. We'll be expected to transform it into a list of words that the spell check algorithm can work through:

```
Public Sub AddToCheckList(ByVal buf As String)

  Dim safeBuf As New StringBuilder()
  Dim n As Integer

  For n = 0 To buf.Length - 1

    If Char.IsLetterOrDigit(buf, n) Then
      safeBuf.Append(buf, n, 1)
    Else
      safeBuf.Append(" ")
    End If

  Next

  ' split up the words...
  Dim words() As String = safeBuf.ToString.Split(" ".ToCharArray)

  ' go through each word and add it...
  Dim word As String

  For Each word In words

    ' trim the word and only add it if it's not blank...
    word = word.Trim
    If word <> "" Then
      AddWordToCheckList(word)
    End If

  Next

End Sub
```

That brings us to the end of the Checker object. Now we just need to wire it into the main application.

Using Checker

To use the `Checker` object, we need to hold an instance of it in the form, and we also need to have somewhere to store our list of invalid words. Remember, the way we're going to work this is handing over a list of words for `Checker` to take a look at, and when it's finished, we'll be passed a list of invalid words. Before we do that, we need to add some namespaces:

```
Imports System.IO
Imports System.Text
Imports System.Threading
Imports System.Collections.Specialized

Public Class Form1
   Inherits System.Windows.Forms.Form
```

Now, add these members to `Form1`:

```
Public Class Form1
   Inherits System.Windows.Forms.Form

   Private _checker As New Checker()
   Private _invalidWords As New StringCollection()
   Private _invalidWordsLock As New ReaderWriterLock()
```

`Checker` will use a delegate to call back into the primary thread (the thread that's running the form). We need to define a method on `Form1` that has the same signature as this delegate, like this:

```
Public Sub OnCheckComplete(ByVal newInvalidWords As StringCollection)

   _invalidWordsLock.AcquireWriterLock(-1)
   _invalidWords = newInvalidWords
   _invalidWordsLock.ReleaseLock()

End Sub
```

When `OnCheckComplete` is called, it will be called from the spell checking thread, not the primary application thread. As we're now accessing the same data from different threads, we need to use the synchronization techniques we've already outlined to make sure everything stays in working order. Here, we're acquiring a writer lock, and keeping a reference to the string collection that the thread creates.

We now need to change the constructor of `Form1` to wire in the `Checker` object. You'll find the constructor hidden within the `Windows Form Designer generated code` region, so you may have to expand this out to find it. After the constructor has called `InitializeComponent`, we need to tell the `Checker` object who it belongs to:

```
Public Sub New()
   MyBase.New()

   'This call is required by the Windows Form Designer.
   InitializeComponent()
```

```
        _checker.OwnerForm = Me
```

Then, we need to pass a reference to `OnCheckComplete` so that the delegate can be called:

```
        _checker.OnCheckComplete = AddressOf Me.OnCheckComplete
```

Next, we need to load the word list. We're going to do this by using the
`Application.ExecutablePath` property. We'll also use a `System.IO.FileInfo` object to help us
extract the folder name from this path. You'll need to make sure that your `wordlist.txt` is stored in
the same folder that the executable will be compiled into by VS.NET. (By default, this will be the `bin`
folder within the folder containing your project files.)

```
        Dim filename As String
        Dim fileInfo As New FileInfo(Application.ExecutablePath)
        filename = fileInfo.DirectoryName & "\wordlist.txt"
```

After we have the filename, we can tell `WordList` to load it:

```
        _checker.WordList.Load(filename)
```

Finally, we can start the thread:

```
        _checker.SpinUp()

    End Sub
```

At this point, the thread will be running, but we have no way of telling it to check for words. For
completeness, we also need to be able to stop the thread when the application window is closed. To do
this we need to add the following code to `Form1`:

```
    Protected Overrides Sub OnClosing( _
        ByVal e As System.ComponentModel.CancelEventArgs)

      _checker.SpinDown()

    End Sub
```

Reporting Status

We created a property called `ThreadStatus` on the `Checker` object? We need to create this property
on `Form1` that supports `Checker`'s property:

```
    Public Property ThreadStatus() As String
      Get
        Return txtThreadStatus().Text
      End Get
      Set(ByVal Value As String)
        txtThreadStatus().Text = Value
      End Set
    End Property
```

Running the Spell Checker

To tell the spell checker to run, we need to use a combination of the `txtText.TextChanged` event, and the `tmrTextChanged` timer. When you create this timer, its `Enabled` property should be **False**, and its interval should be **500**.

When the text changes, we want to start the timer:

```
    Private Sub txtText_TextChanged(ByVal sender As System.Object, _
                                    ByVal e As System.EventArgs) _
                                    Handles txtText.TextChanged
        tmrTextChanged().Enabled() = True
    End Sub
```

This means that whenever we start typing text, half a second after that the timer will fire. When the timer fires, we need to stop the timer, populate the check list on `Checker` and then tell the thread to start running:

```
    Private Sub tmrTextChanged_Tick(ByVal sender As System.Object, _
        ByVal e As System.Timers.ElapsedEventArgs) _
        Handles tmrTextChanged.Elapsed

        tmrTextChanged().Enabled = False

        _checker.ClearCheckList()
        _checker.AddToCheckList(txtText().Text)

        _checker.StartChecking()

    End Sub
```

Viewing the Results

We're not going to build a custom view of the text that's underlined with a red wavy line. Instead, we're going to set up another timer that constantly examines the `_invalidWords` collection and adds the contents to the `txtInvalidWords` text box control.

> The **tmrUpdateInvalidWords** timer control should be enabled, and have an interval of **100**.

Add the following code to set up this timer:

```
    Private Sub tmrUpdateInvalidWords_Tick(ByVal sender As System.Object, _
        ByVal e As System.Timers.ElapsedEventArgs) _
        Handles tmrUpdateInvalidWords.Elapsed

        _invalidWordsLock.AcquireReaderLock(-1)

        Dim builder As New StringBuilder(Now().ToString)
```

```
builder.Append(" [")
builder.Append(Environment.TickCount.ToString)
builder.Append("]: ")

Dim word As String, isFirst As Boolean = True
For Each word In _invalidWords
  If isFirst = True Then
    isFirst = False
  Else
    builder.Append(", ")
  End If
  builder.Append(word)
Next

txtInvalidWords().Text = builder.ToString

_invalidWordsLock.ReleaseReaderLock()

End Sub
```

The code is careful to put a reader lock around any access to _invalidWords. Checker will periodically update this value by calling OnCheckComplete, so we have to make sure that access is synchronized. Once we have confirmed that we can access it, we loop through it and update the display, effectively showing the user a list of invalid words.

Now that we've done that, we can try running the application. Here's what you'll see:

Thread status effectively shows the time that the thread last checked, and you can see that, by the way we have it set up, it runs as soon as the application starts because _paused is initially set as being signaled. Invalid words displays a list of the invalid words, so any word displayed here will *not* be in the CheckWords file. You'll also notice that this value is being constantly updated. The large integer value comes from the Environment.TickCount property, which gives the number of milliseconds that the computer has been running.

That brings us to the end of our simple spell check application. Remember to add words to wordlist.txt to vary the results.

Deadlocking

As a multithreaded developer, you should have considerable respect for two things: synchronization and deadlocking. I hope I've illustrated how synchronization can bite you, but let's look at deadlocking.

Both synchronization and deadlocking have the same effect on your development efforts – each can create bizarre bugs that are incredibly hard to track down. By getting synchronization wrong, you can get your program 'out of step' and end up breaking or crashing the code several steps away from where you actually caused the problem. Deadlocking can result in your entire program freezing, again several steps away from where you caused the problem.

Deadlocking occurs when, for some reason, locks are not released. If you lock a reader/writer lock for writing and another thread wants to do the same, the second thread will stop executing until you release it. However, what happens if the second thread never gets access to the lock because the first lock never releases it? Either the second thread will wait for an infinite amount of time for the lock to become available, or it will timeout. Either way, the second thread won't get access to the resource it needs to do its work, so something won't work properly. The other, more insidious deadlocking problem is where the first thread is waiting for a lock that the second thread has, but the second thread won't release that lock until it can obtain the lock on an object that the first thread has. In this case, neither thread can find a resolution to the problem and both threads stop completely.

> **Make sure that you unlock your locks when you're finished!**

Thread Pooling

We've seen how to create threads, and how to properly synchronize data access between threads. We've also seen a fairly complete implementation on using threads within a typical desktop application. What we haven't seen is how to use threads in a service.

Most service applications work by providing a thread that sits around waiting for an incoming connection of some kind. Once a connection is received, a new thread is created and that new thread is asked to service the new connection, as shown below:

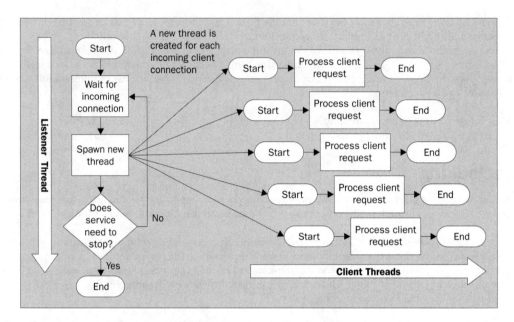

One way to streamline this process is to remove the overhead of creating a new thread each time a connection is created. This is done using a **thread pool** – a set of threads that sit around in memory waiting to be given some work, as illustrated in the following figure:

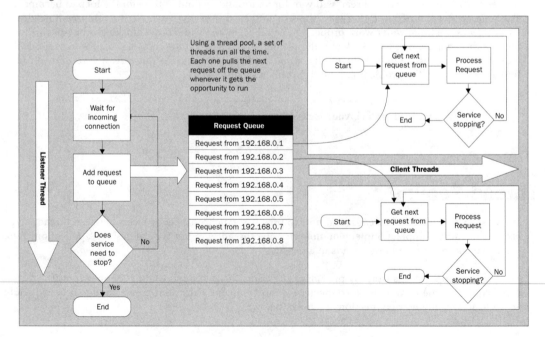

Under Windows and the .NET Framework, each process is automatically given a thread pool through the `System.Threading.ThreadPool` class. Each process can only have up to one thread pool, which can be shared between many different activities. In the classic service scenario that we're looking at, the thread pool may well be exclusively used to service incoming connections. However, the thread pool could also be used to run periodic activities, for example, examine the disk space on the server to make sure that it is not running low, check e-mail, and so on, as well as servicing client connections.

Interestingly, thread pools make threading even easier than we've already seen. Obviously, we still need to deal with synchronization, but we don't need to actually create threads – .NET does all that for us.

Next, we're going to create a new application that simulates the work of a server.

The Worker Object

Create a new Visual Basic Windows Application project called `Pooling` and then create a new class called `Worker`.

The `Worker` object is our conceptual object that is given some activity to do. In fact, we're not going to ask the object to do anything at all – rather we're going to ask it to sleep for a given period of time. In a server application, these objects would be created in response to an incoming connection, such as for a Web server, but we'll create a new `Worker` object and give it a socket that it can use to pass data between itself and the client.

First of all, let's give the namespaces to the object, and also create some members:

```
Imports System.Threading

Public Class Worker

    Public Id As Integer
    Public SleepPeriod As Integer
    Public Owner As Form1
    Public OnWorkerStart As WorkerStart
    Public OnWorkerEnd As WorkerEnd
    Private _isCancelled As Boolean
```

Here's a break down of the members:

- ❑ `Id` – used to store a system unique ID for the worker, we'll use this when debugging to keep track of what's happening

- ❑ `SleepPeriod` – the period of time that the worker should 'pretend' to work for

- ❑ `Owner` – the main application

- ❑ `OnWorkerStart` – a delegate provided by the owner that `Worker` will use to signal the start of work

- ❑ `OnWorkerEnd` – a delegate provided by the owner that `Worker` will use to signal the end of work

- ❑ `_isCancelled` – a Boolean that indicates whether the `Worker` has been cancelled

Next, let's define the delegates that the owner will use to communicate with the worker:

```
Public Delegate Sub WorkerStart(ByVal workerObject As Worker, _
                                ByVal workerThread As Thread)
Public Delegate Sub WorkerEnd(ByVal workerObject As Worker, _
                              ByVal workerThread As Thread)
```

To add an item to the thread pool, all we have to do is provide a delegated method that matches the signature of System.Threading.WaitCallback. This is a delegate definition contained in the .NET Framework class library that we need to use in order to work with the pool. We pass this method to the ThreadPool using a shared method, like this:

```
Public Sub Go()
   ThreadPool.QueueUserWorkItem(AddressOf Me.Start)
End Sub
```

When we're using the ThreadPool, we don't have to manage the lifetime of the thread. We only need to provide an entry point and the .NET Framework itself does everything else for us.

After we've called Go and subsequently called QueueUserWorkItem, the thread pool manager will wait for an opportunity for us to start running. If the thread pool is empty, or the pool determines that another thread will be created, a new thread will be spun up. Alternatively, if a thread is in the pool but isn't working through a work item, this existing thread will be used. It's this use of existing threads that makes using the thread pool efficient as we don't have the overhead of creating threads *every* time. When this happens, our delegate will be called. We can't actually control when this will happen – all we know is that it will happen at some point in the future.

We now need to implement Start. All this method needs to do is call an AddToLog function that we'll build in a moment, and call the delegates. We also pretend to do work by using the Thread.Sleep method:

```
Public Sub Start(ByVal state As Object)

   AddToLog("Started")
   If Not OnWorkerStart Is Nothing Then
     OnWorkerStart.Invoke(Me, Thread.CurrentThread)
   End If

   If _isCancelled = False Then
     thread.Sleep(SleepPeriod)
   End If

   If Not OnWorkerEnd Is Nothing Then
     OnWorkerEnd.Invoke(Me, Thread.CurrentThread)
   End If
   AddToLog("Stop")

End Sub
```

This method will only be called when a thread becomes available in the pool. That's why we have to use Thread.CurrentThread to get hold a thread object – it's the only way we can determine which thread we're running in.

Notice how we're using If statements to see if a delegate has been provided. This means that the developer doesn't have to provide delegates if she doesn't want to; for example, the developer might not need to know when a worker has started. This is quite a neat technique to use that may well help developers down the line use the object more easily.

We're going to use the txtStatus control on the application's form to let the worker provide status information to the user. Add this method:

```
Public Sub AddToLog(ByVal buf As String)
   Owner.AddToLog("[id:" & Id.ToString & ", thread:" & _
                  Thread.CurrentThread.GetHashCode.ToString & "] " & buf)
End Sub
```

Thread.GetHashCode is a useful method that will give you a unique identifier for the thread. This will let us keep track of how many threads are running during debugging, but in practical day-to-day running it is typically of little use. We'll see this working when we run the application.

Finally, we need to create a method that can cancel the worker:

```
Public Sub Cancel()
   _isCancelled = True
End Sub
```

The reason why we need this ability to cancel the worker is because if the application closes before the worker has started running, we need to be able to 'short circuit' the code that actually does the activity that by virtue of the fact the application is not running, no longer needs to be performed.

Creating Worker Objects

I've made this part of the exercise a little more complicated than it should be, simply to make it easier to understand what's happening inside the pool.

First of all, this is the layout of the form:

Here are the controls:

- ❑ txtStatus – a text box control that the workers use to report their progress.

- ❑ trkNumWorkers – a TrackBar control that varies the number of workers. Set Minimum to 1, Maximum to 256, Value to 16, and TickFrequency to 10.

- ❑ lblNumWorkers – a label that reports the number of workers selected on the TrackBar control.

- ❑ trkSleepPeriod – a TrackBar control that varies the number of milliseconds passed to Thread.Sleep by the worker. Set the Minimum to 0 and the Maximum to 2500, the Value to 250, and the TickFrequency to 100.

- ❑ lblSleepPeriod – a label that reports the number of milliseconds selected on the TrackBar control.

- ❑ lblNumActive – a label control used to report the number of active threads and the number of pending workers.

- ❑ lstThreads – a list box control used to report the number of running threads.

- ❑ btnClear – a button control used to clear txtStatus.

- ❑ btnGo – a button control used to create Worker objects.

- ❑ btnStop – a button control used to cancel all of the pending workers.

Now that the form has been designed, we can go ahead and define a few members. You also need to include the namespace import directive in the top of the code listing:

```
Imports System.Threading

Public Class Form1
    Inherits System.Windows.Forms.Form

    Private _workerId As Integer
    Private _statusLock As New ReaderWriterLock()
    Private _threadList As New Hashtable()
    Private _completeWorkerList As New ArrayList()
    Private _activeWorkerList As New ArrayList()
    Private _threadListLock As New ReaderWriterLock()
```

Here's what they will do:

- ❑ _workerId – provides an area to store the system unique worker ID

- ❑ _statusLock – used to synchronize access to txtStatus.Text

- ❑ _threadList – used to store a list of the threads that are being used and have ever been used

- ❑ _completeWorkerList – used to store a list of the workers that are being processed or that need to be processed

- ❑ _activeWorkerList – used to store a list of the workers that are currently being processed

- ❑ _threadListLock – used to synchronize access to _threadList, _completeWorkerList and _activeWorkerList

We need a few methods that provide simple UI updates. Add these methods and event handlers to your code:

```
Public Sub AddToLog(ByVal buf As String)
    _statusLock.AcquireWriterLock(-1)
    txtStatus().Text &= Now().ToString & ": " & buf & Chr(13) & Chr(10)
    _statusLock.ReleaseWriterLock()
End Sub


Private Sub trkNumWorkers_Scroll(ByVal sender As System.Object, _
                                 ByVal e As System.EventArgs) _
                                 Handles trkNumWorkers.Scroll
    lblNumWorkers().Text = trkNumWorkers().Value.ToString
End Sub


Private Sub trkSleepPeriod_Scroll(ByVal sender As System.Object, _
                                  ByVal e As System.EventArgs) _
                                  Handles trkSleepPeriod.Scroll
    lblSleepPeriod().Text = trkSleepPeriod().Value.ToString
End Sub


Private Sub btnClear_Click(ByVal sender As System.Object, _
                           ByVal e As System.EventArgs) _
                           Handles btnClear.Click
    txtStatus().Text = ""
    lstThreads.Items.Clear()
End Sub
```

Creating the Workers

One thing that it's important to understand is that we're not creating threads when we use the thread pool. We're creating workers by creating instances of objects from the `Worker` class, and we're then asking those objects to ask the thread pool to allocate time in the pool for us some time in the future. This is an important distinction – in everything we've done so far we've had a fine degree of control over when the thread will actually be created, (in other words we've created a new `Thread` object and called `Start`). When using a thread pool we're saying "run me when you can", and when we get executed will depend on server load. We also don't have control over how big the pool gets, so we might queue 10,000 worker objects, but the pool may only create four threads.

Here's the start of the handle for `btnGo` that will go on to create the workers:

```
Private Sub btnGo_Click(ByVal sender As System.Object, _
            ByVal e As System.EventArgs) Handles btnGo.Click

    Dim numWorkers As Integer = trkNumWorkers().Value
    Dim sleepPeriod As Integer = trkSleepPeriod().Value
```

To create the workers, we just have to use a simple loop. We provide an ID, the period of time each worker should sleep for when it's running and references to our delegated methods:

```
        Dim n As Integer
        For n = 1 To numWorkers

          Dim worker As New Worker()
          worker.Id = _workerId
          _workerId += 1
          worker.SleepPeriod = sleepPeriod
          worker.Owner = Me
          worker.OnWorkerStart = AddressOf Me.WorkerStart
          worker.OnWorkerEnd = AddressOf Me.WorkerEnd
```

We want to keep a list of workers that have been created and are either running, or are waiting to start:

```
          _threadListLock.AcquireWriterLock(-1)
          _completeWorkerList.Add(worker)
          _threadListLock.ReleaseWriterLock()
```

Finally, we can tell the worker to start working and close off the event handler:

```
          worker.Go()
        Next

    End Sub
```

Now we've done that, we can create the delegates that manage the list of working threads.

Creating the Delegates

As a user of a thread pool, you might not actually care what threads are running or what workers are currently being processed. However, for this example we want to try and illustrate what's going on behind the scenes so we're going to use our WorkerStart and WorkerEnd delegates to provide notification of what's happening in the threads so we can report back to the user.

We're going to maintain a list of the threads in _threadList (we're going to hold on to the integer ID of the thread, not a Thread object as you might expect). We're going to use this list to keep track of all the threads that we've ever seen. We can't tell when Windows has removed a thread from its own internal threading subsystem, so threads that actually no longer exist may well appear as idle. Don't forget, this exercise has been designed to show you how the thread pool works – some of the functionality we include in this application will rarely be used in the real world. This will give us an idea of how big the thread pool is growing in response to our usage. We also keep a list of the workers that are being processed in _activeWorkerList. Here's the code for WorkerStart:

```
      Public Sub WorkerStart(ByVal workerObject As Worker, _
                             ByVal workerThread As Thread)

        _threadListLock.AcquireWriterLock(-1)
        Try
          _threadList.Add(workerThread.GetHashCode, workerObject.Id)
        Catch
          _threadList.Item(workerThread.GetHashCode) = workerObject.Id
        End Try
```

```
        _activeWorkerList.Add(workerObject)

        UpdateThreadView()

        _threadListLock.ReleaseWriterLock()

    End Sub
```

We use a `Try...Catch` block to make it easier to update the list. If we try and add an item to the list and that item is already in there, an exception will be thrown in which case we can perform an update. We haven't seen `UpdateThreadView` yet, but we'll build it in a moment.

You can see that we're using a `Hashtable` object to keep track of the threads. We index this table against the thread object itself, and against each thread we store the ID of the thread that we're working with. Notice that we're careful to maintain locking against these lists so that everything is properly synchronized.

Here's the code for `WorkerEnd`:

```
    Public Sub WorkerEnd(ByVal workerObject As Worker, _
                        ByVal workerThread As Thread)

        _threadListLock.AcquireWriterLock(-1)
        _threadList(workerThread.GetHashCode) = 0

        _completeWorkerList.Remove(workerObject)
        _activeWorkerList.Remove(workerObject)

        UpdateThreadView()

        _threadListLock.ReleaseWriterLock()

    End Sub
```

You can see that this method removes the worker from both the complete and active list. Notice as well how rather than removing the thread from _threadList we set the ID of its worker to zero. This allows us to keep track of the threads that aren't actually doing anything at a given moment in time, but as we said we actually can't determine whether or not a thread still exists.

To report back on the status of the threads, we need to add this method:

```
    Public Sub UpdateThreadView()

        ' lock the list for reading...
        _threadListLock.AcquireReaderLock(-1)

        ' change the list...
        lstThreads().Items.Clear()

        ' go through the items...
        Dim item As Object
```

```
For Each item In _threadList.Keys

    ' create the string...
    Dim buf As String = "Thread " & item.ToString
    If CType(_threadList(item), Integer) <> 0 Then
        buf &= " working with Worker " & _threadList(item).ToString
    Else
        buf &= " is idle"
    End If

    ' add that...
    lstThreads().Items.Add(buf)

Next

' tell it how many are active...
lblNumActive().Text() = "Active: " & _
                        _activeWorkerList.Count.ToString & _
                        ", Pending: " & _
                        _completeWorkerList.Count.ToString

' release the lock...
_threadListLock.ReleaseReaderLock()

End Sub
```

With all that in place, we can test it.

Testing the Solution

To try it the first time, keep the number of threads set to 16 and keep the sleep period at 250 milliseconds. Click Go. This will create sixteen Worker objects and each worker object will pause for quarter-of-a-second when it runs.

You'll see that the thread pool runs all of the workers in a single thread, up until the last few workers are executed. Windows uses a heuristic routine to determine how many threads should be in the pool, and how many threads should be running concurrently. In this example, it will create the second thread when demand for the first thread reaches a certain point.

> **Due to the various factors that affect the thread pool, you may find it tricky to exactly duplicate the results as seen here. Play with the sliders until you see the effect you want. If you're running a highly specified multiprocessor machine, you may not get the same effect that you can see here. Windows may well decide it can afford to kick off more threads initially because you have more than one process and no amount of fiddling with the sliders will get this effect.**

What's really important to understand when talking about the thread pool is that although we're only running at most two workers at a time, all sixteen are queued almost immediately and that the first thread starts sometime after our loop has finished.

(This is because our loop is very quick to run. If our loop took longer to execute, or we were waiting for inbound connections, we may well find that the first thread starts before the last worker is queued.) In effect, the sixteenth worker has to wait quite a long time to get a chance to execute.

Now, without quitting, change the number of workers to 32 and set the sleep period to 1000 and try again. You'll see that immediately we start using two threads. That's because the second time round we already have two threads in the pool ready to go. Since we've told each thread to take a longer period of time to do the processing, there's more demand on the pool so we end up with more threads. You'll see this effect if you click Go for a third time. This time, however, all five threads allocated to the pool will start working.

Now that you've seen how to use the thread pool to make handling multiple asynchronous operations easier to handle, lets look at how the thread pool can improve on our spell checker example.

Cancelling Pending Workers

One of the issues with the thread pool is that once a work item has been queued, it cannot be un-queued. If you decide at some point that you don't want your work item to be processed, you need to flag it as cancelled. This is likely to happen if you decide to close down your application or the work that the worker was asked to do is no longer required or relevant.

We maintain a list of pending and active workers in _completeWorkerList for just this reason. Should we need to cancel all or some of the workers, we can iterate through this list and call Cancel for each one. Here's the code for the btnStop.Click handler:

```
Private Sub btnStop_Click(ByVal sender As System.Object, _
                          ByVal e As System.EventArgs) _
                          Handles btnStop.Click

    ' go through our worker list and tell every worker object to cancel...
    _threadListLock.AcquireReaderLock(-1)
    Dim worker As Worker
    For Each worker In _completeWorkerList
        worker.Cancel()
    Next

    ' release the lock...
    _threadListLock.ReleaseReaderLock()

End Sub
```

As each work item is asked to work, we already check to see if _isCancelled is set to True, (in other words that at some point someone has called Cancel). If this has happened, we drop out of the end of the work item. Notice how we still continue to call OnWorkerStart and OnWorkerEnd. This lets our caller keep track of the list of workers and threads in the normal manner.

Using the Thread Pool to Improve on the ManualResetEvent.WaitOne Scenario

You'll recall that with our spell checker we created a separate thread that sat around waiting for a `ManualResetEvent` object to be signaled. In reality, that thread didn't actually spend much of its lifetime working and so was in a wait state for the majority of its life.

Although there's no serious problem with this approach, it's not as efficient as it might be. Rather, we could use the thread pool to allocate a thread to us whenever we needed to go away and run a spell checker. This would mean that we were, effectively, creating a thread on demand.

But there's a wrinkle here – although the thread pool object is around all the time by virtue of a shared function, the thread pool contains no threads until the first work item is queued at which time a thread is created and calls into a delegate to start the work. That gives us no advantage over our previous approach, save for the fact that the thread pool will close down threads that have been idle for a period of time, restarting them should they be needed later on.

If you have a number of threads that behave in the same way as the spell checker thread, you may well find it advantageous to use the thread pool. Again, there are no hard and fast rules about how many threads you need to get the advantage – experimentation is key.

Another Demonstration

As we're nearing the end of the discussion, we're going to look at a fairly simple example of how to use the thread pool to handle a scenario where we have 64 workers that periodically need to run in a thread. Create a new Windows Application project and call it `RegisterExample`.

We're going to create another class called `RegisterWorker` to handle our work objects. This will be fairly similar to the one we just worked with. Create the new class now and add this code:

```
Imports System.Threading

Public Class RegisterWorker

   Public Id As Integer
   Private _event As New ManualResetEvent(False)
   Public OnWorkerStart As WorkerStart
   Public OnWorkerEnd As WorkerEnd

   Public Delegate Sub WorkerStart(ByVal workerObject As RegisterWorker, _
                     ByVal workerThread As Thread)
   Public Delegate Sub WorkerEnd(ByVal workerObject As RegisterWorker, _
                     ByVal workerThread As Thread)

End Class
```

To register the worker, we have to use the `ThreadPool.RegisterWaitForSingleObject` method. This method can be configured to fire whenever an object is signaled, or when a given period of time elapses. This timeout feature is particularly useful.

Imagine you have a thread that needs to check for e-mail every five minutes, but you also might want to tell the thread to check for e-mail on demand. This technique is perfect for this – create a new `ManualResetEvent` object, register it with the thread pool, but give it a timeout of five minutes. (This timeout period is the time between you registering the object with the thread pool and it being automatically started.) You can then either signal the `ManualResetEvent` object by using its `Set` method, or you can wait for it to timeout and start running.

Just like we've seen throughout these examples, we need to register a delegate that will be used to kick off the work. Add this code to `RegisterWorker`:

```
Public Sub Register()

  ' make sure that we're reset...
  _event.Reset()

  ' register the object with the thread pool...
  Dim callback As WaitOrTimerCallback = AddressOf Me.Start
  threadpool.RegisterWaitForSingleObject(_event, callback, _
                                          Nothing, -1, True)

End Sub
```

We take the parameters in order for `RegisterWaitForSingleObject`: firstly, we need to give it the `ManualResetEvent` object. This object must be non-signaled for this to work, so we call `Reset` to make sure that it is. Otherwise, the worker would be registered with the pool immediately. Secondly, we give it the delegate we want to call into. Thirdly, we give it a state object. We don't need to use this, so we'll use `Nothing`. Next, we supply a timeout value of −1, meaning that we want to wait forever. Finally we indicate if we want to receive only one notification during the lifetime of the object. We've set this to `True`, meaning that when we signal the event our delegate will only ever be called once. If we don't do this, our delegate will get called constantly, which is not what we want. What we have to do is tell it to call us once and then re-register the event after we've done our work. The 'timeout' is a once only occurrence, so as soon as it's fired once, it will never be fired again. That's why we have to register it again. We'll see this in a moment.

Next, we need a method that will kick off the worker. When we added _event to the thread pool, it was non-signaled. This signals the object, so the thread pool will recognize it, find a thread to run it, and use the `Start` method as the entry point.

```
Public Sub Go()
  _event.Set()
End Sub
```

Finally, we need to do some work. This is pretty similar to the way we did it before:

```
Private Sub Start(ByVal state As Object, ByVal wasSignalled As Boolean)

  ' tell the caller we've started...
  If Not OnWorkerStart Is Nothing Then _
            OnWorkerStart.Invoke(Me, thread.CurrentThread)

  ' here's where we'd do some work!
  Thread.Sleep(1000)
```

```
    ' tell the caller we've finished...
    If Not OnWorkerEnd Is Nothing Then _
                OnWorkerEnd.Invoke(Me, thread.CurrentThread)

    ' tell the worker to start waiting again...
    Register()

End Sub
```

Notice how we're calling `Register` again at the end of the method. This will allow us to re-signal the worker at a later time if we need it to do something else. Notice how we reset _event at the beginning of `Register`. This keeps everything in order for the next time we want to run.

Creating the UI

For this example, we're going to create 64 workers. To simulate these workers being started, we're going to create 64 buttons on a form. Since VB.NET no longer supports control arrays, the best way to create our 64 buttons is to do it programmatically from within the form's constructor. Before we build the button, we need to add a text box called `txtStatus` to the form:

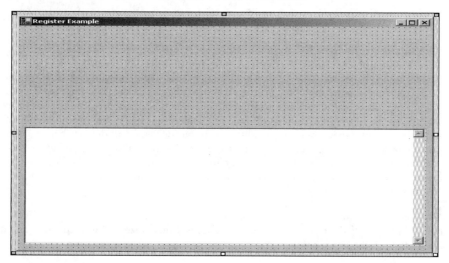

We also need to create a new version of the button control that is tied into a specific worker and can automatically call `Worker.Go` whenever the button is pressed. Create a new class called `WorkerButton` and add this code:

```
Imports System.Windows.Forms

Public Class WorkerButton
    Inherits Button

    Private _worker As RegisterWorker

    ' Constructor...
    Public Sub New(ByVal worker As RegisterWorker)
```

```
_worker = worker
    Text() = _worker.Id.ToString
End Sub

' OnClick - called when the button is clicked...
Protected Overrides Sub OnClick(ByVal e As EventArgs)

    ' tell the worker to do something...
    _worker.Go()

End Sub

End Class
```

Add these members to Form1, along with the following namespace declaration at the top of the code listing:

```
Imports System.Threading

Public Class Form1
    Inherits System.Windows.Forms.Form

    Const NumWorkers As Integer = 64
    Private _workers(NumWorkers) As RegisterWorker
    Private _workerButtons(NumWorkers) As Button
    Private _statusLock As New ReaderWriterLock()
```

To use this button, we need to modify the form's constructor. Find the **New** method and add this code:

```
Public Sub New()
    MyBase.New()

    'This call is required by the Windows Form Designer.
    InitializeComponent()

    ' set our caption so we know what thread we are...
    Me.Text &= " - Main Application Thread: " & _
            thread.CurrentThread.GetHashCode
```

The first thing we've done is to modify the form's caption to report the ID of the current thread. As New is called from the primary thread in the process, the caption will always display the ID of the primary thread. This will assure us that the workers are indeed running in their own threads.

Next, we need to define some metrics about how we'll be laying out the controls:

```
Dim spacing As Integer = 10
Dim x As Integer = spacing
Dim y As Integer = spacing
Dim width As Integer = 30
Dim height As Integer = 20
```

Now we can start creating the workers:

```
Dim n As Integer
For n = 0 To NumWorkers - 1

    ' create a worker object...
    _workers(n) = New RegisterWorker()
    _workers(n).OnWorkerStart = AddressOf Me.WorkerStart
    _workers(n).OnWorkerEnd = AddressOf Me.WorkerEnd
    _workers(n).Id = n
```

After we've created the worker, we can register it:

```
    _workers(n).Register()
```

Now we can create a new instance of our button control, position it on the form and add it to the form's control array:

```
    _workerButtons(n) = New WorkerButton(_workers(n))
    _workerButtons(n).Left = x
    _workerButtons(n).Top = y
    _workerButtons(n).Width = width
    _workerButtons(n).Height = height

    Controls().Add(_workerButtons(n))
```

After positioning the control, we can move to the next position and repeat the loop. At the end of each line, we move down to the left-most position of the next line:

```
    x += (width + spacing)
    If x > Me.Width - (width + spacing) Then
        x = spacing
        y += (height + spacing)
    End If
Next
```

Finally, we need to adjust the position of txtStatus so that it occupies the remaining space on the screen:

```
    txtStatus().Top = y + (height + spacing)
    txtStatus().Height = Me.Height - txtStatus().Top - (3 * spacing)

End Sub
```

We need to provide code for the delegated methods, and also build a helper to add log messages to txtStatus:

```
Public Sub WorkerStart(ByVal workerObject As RegisterWorker, _
                       ByVal workerThread As Thread)
    AddToLog("Worker " & workerObject.Id.ToString & _
             " started in thread " & workerThread.GetHashCode)
End Sub
```

```
Public Sub WorkerEnd(ByVal workerObject As RegisterWorker, _
                     ByVal workerThread As Thread)
  AddToLog("Worker " & workerObject.Id.ToString & " finished")
End Sub

Public Sub AddToLog(ByVal buf As String)
  _statusLock.AcquireWriterLock(-1)
  txtStatus().Text &= Now().ToString & ": " & buf & Chr(13) & Chr(10)
  _statusLock.ReleaseWriterLock()
End Sub
```

Testing the Solution

That's all we need to do to get this solution started. Run it up, click on one or two of the buttons and you'll see something like this:

You'll see that because we signaled the two objects consecutively we ended up with the same thread being reused. If you try clicking lots of different buttons quickly, you'll see that at some point another thread or two will be added to the pool to service the requests.

Summary

In this chapter, we took a fairly involved look at the subject of threading in .NET and how VB.NET developers now have access to a rich set of threading functionality. We started off by looking at how threads can be created, how they relate to processes and then briefly touched on the differences between multitasking and multithreading. We then worked through a sample application to illustrate threading in operation.

Our focus then moved on to the rather tricky subject of thread synchronization, in order to manage multithreaded code effectively, with details regarding the associated topics of blocking, wait state and signaling. To illustrate these principles we then developed a Spell Checker sample application.

In the final part of the chapter we looked at the nature of thread pools in relation to service applications, considering both how thread pools can be used to make the job of managing multiple asynchronous threads easier, and how the same pool can be used to look after multiple blocking event objects.

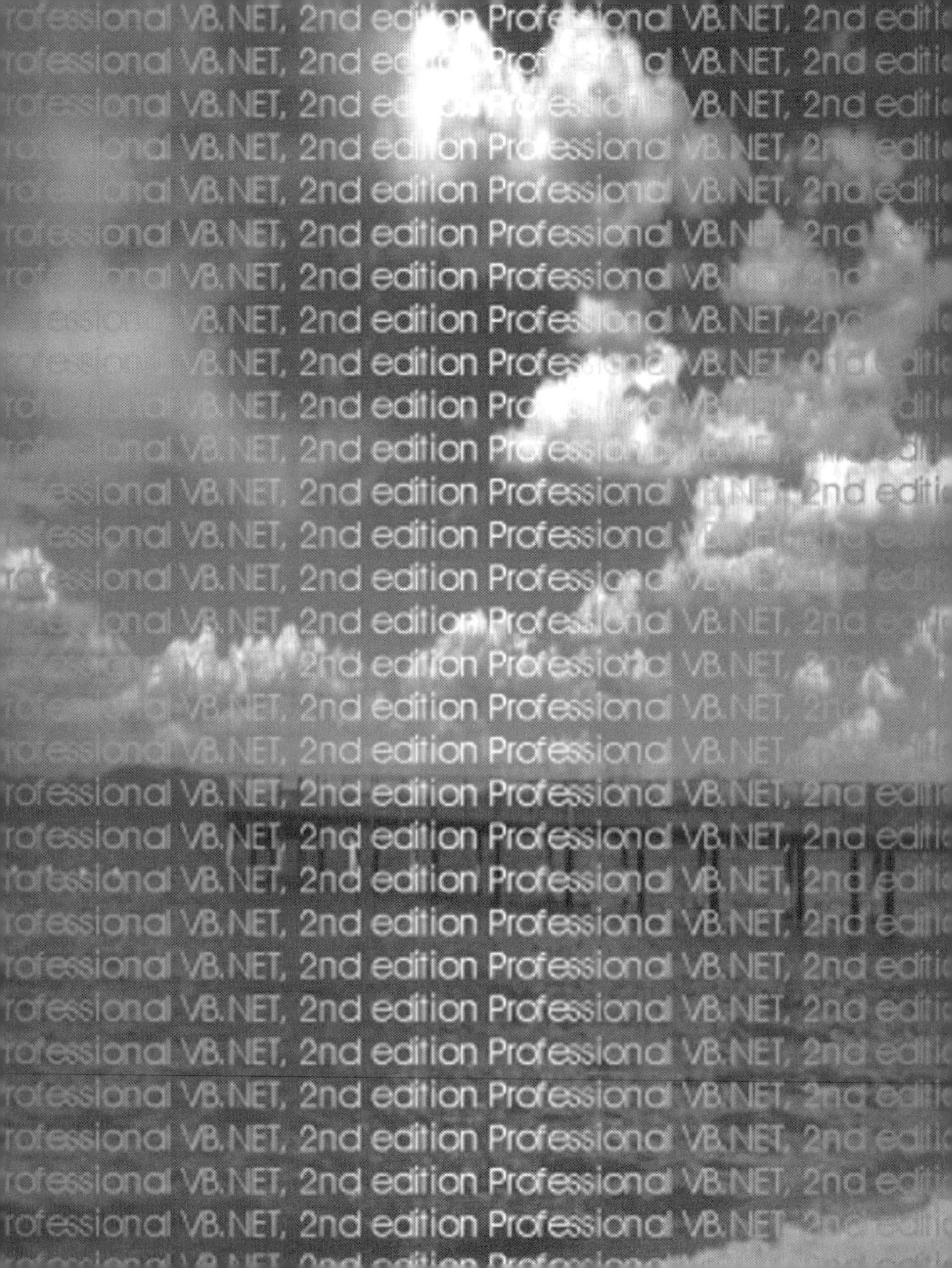
Professional VB.NET, 2nd edition

20

Remoting

Remoting is the .NET technology that allows code in one application domain to call into the methods and properties of objects running in another application domain. A major use of remoting is in the classic 3-tier desktop approach where presentation code on the desktop needs to access objects running on a server somewhere on the network. In terms of code, remoting is related to Web Services. However, although these two technologies share a lot of the same classes and principals, Remoting is designed to be an extensible technology that's not bound by the limitations of the SOAP/HTTP approach.

SOAP's biggest problem is that it is not lightweight. It's designed with maximum platform interoperability in mind, and this puts certain limits on how data can be transferred. For example, imagine that Platform A stores integer variables as a four-byte block of memory, with the lowest-value byte appearing first. Now imagine that Platform B also uses a four-byte block of memory, but this time the highest-value byte appears first. Without some form of conversion, if we copy that block of bytes from Platform A to Platform B, because the encoding of the value is different, the platforms won't be able to agree on what the number actually is. In this scenario, one platform will think it's got the number 4, whereas the other thinks that the number is actually 536870912.

SOAP gets around this problem by representing numbers (and everything else) as strings of ASCII characters – as ASCII is a text-encoding standard that most platforms can understand. However, this means that the native binary representations of the numbers have to be converted to text each time the SOAP document has to be constructed. In addition, the values themselves have to be packaged in something that we can read (with a little bit of effort). This leads to two problems: massive bloat (a four byte value starts taking hundreds of bytes to store) and wasted CPU cycles in converting from native encoding to text encoding and back again.

We can live with all these problems if we only want to run our Web Service on, say, Windows 2000, and have it accessed through a client running on a cell phone. SOAP is designed to do this kind of thing.

However, if we have a Windows XP desktop application that wants to use objects hosted on a Windows 2000 server (using the same platform), the bloated network traffic and wastage in terms of conversion is sub-optimal at best, and ridiculous at worst.

Remoting lets us enjoy the same power of Web services but without the downside. If we want, we can connect directly to the server over TCP and send binary data without having to do any conversions. If one Windows computer has a four-byte block of memory holding a 32-bit integer value, we can safely copy the bit pattern to another Windows computer and both will agree on what number is. In effect, network traffic sanity is restored and we're not wasting processor time doing conversions.

Now that you know what Remoting is, we're ready to understand its architecture.

Remoting Overview

Before we go on, we need to understand what we mean by certain terms. A **remote object** is an object that's been made available over Remoting. These objects are exactly the same kinds of objects that you build normally. All that we need to do to use them with Remoting is register them with the Remoting subsystem.

A **channel** is a way of communicating between two machines. Out-of-the-box, .NET comes with two channels: TCP and HTTP. The TCP channel is a lightweight channel designed for transporting binary data between two computers. (You need to think of the 'TCP channel' as being different to the TCP protocol that HTTP also uses.) It works using sockets, something we talk about in much more detail in Chapter 23. HTTP is, as you already know, the protocol that web servers use. In typical use, you'd expect to see clients connecting to remote objects over TCP when they are behind the firewall of a private network. It's likely you'd use HTTP when the client is outside of the network and on the public Internet, perhaps using a VPN connection into the private network, or just using an open port on your firewall. You can build your own networks to suit your own needs.

A **formatter** is how an object is 'crunched' into a format so that it can be squirted down the channel. This is serialization and de-serialization, which we'll talk more about later. Out-of-the-box, we have two formatters: Binary and SOAP. Binary is typically used in combination with the TCP channel, whereas SOAP is typically used in combination with the HTTP channel. You can also build your own formatters for your own needs. In fact, you can mix and match channels, so if you want to use the SOAP formatter with the binary channel you can, and so on. However, the HTTP/SOAP and TCP/Binary combinations are recommended by Microsoft.

A **message** is a communication between client and server. It holds the information about the remote object and the method or property that's being invoked as well as any parameters.

A **proxy** is used on the client-side to call into the remote object. To use Remoting, you don't typically have to worry about creating the proxy – .NET does it all for you. However, there's a slightly confusing split between something called a **transparent proxy** and a **real proxy**. A transparent proxy is so called because 'you can't see it'. When you request a remote object, a transparent proxy is what you get. It looks like the remote object (that is, it has the same properties and methods as the original), which means that your client code can use the remote object or a local copy of the would-be-remote object without you having to make any changes, and without you knowing that there is any difference. The transparent proxy defers the calls to the real proxy. The real proxy is what actually constructs the message, sends it to the server, and waits for the response. You can think of the transparent proxy as a 'fake' object that contains the same methods and properties that the real object contains.

The real proxy is effectively a set of helper functions that manage the communications. You don't use the real proxy directly – instead the transparent proxy calls into the real proxy on your behalf.

A **message sink** (and personally I find this a confusing name) is an 'interceptor object'. Before messages go into the channel, these are used to do some further processing on them, perhaps to attach more data, reformat data before it is sent, route debugging information or perform security checking. On the client-side, we have an 'envoy sink'. On the server-side, we have a 'server context sink' and an 'object context sink'. In typical use, you can ignore these.

Message sinks are a pretty advanced topic that allow for some powerful extensions to the Remoting model. Unfortunately, they're out of the scope of this book.

The following figures show how these concepts fit together:

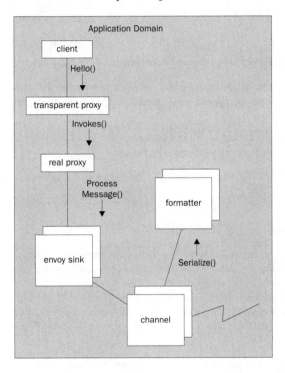

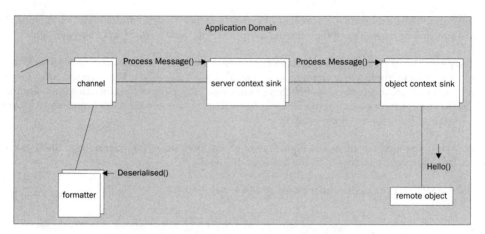

The next step is to look at the way that Remoting treats objects. In Remoting, objects are roughly divided into two camps: **service** objects and **client-activated** objects:

❑ Service objects run on the server and perform a service for the remote application, such as *give me a list of all the customers* or *create and invoice*. They have to be explicitly connected to.

❑ Client-activated objects are objects that just happen to run on a remote server. Rather then being explicitly connected to, all creation requests for classes that are registered as client-activated are automatically passed to the server.

Service objects are further divided into two types: **singleton** and **single** call. We'll discuss the difference between them next.

Singleton versus Single Call

Singleton objects are by far the most useful for the business-tier in the classic 3-tier design. The most accepted design pattern for this tier – in order to achieve maximum scalability – is to treat every method on the object like a self-contained method that has no state. In effect, business-tier objects should be designed in a rather non-OO manner – the object simply groups the methods together – rather than providing a way of changing the state of the object (as is typified by the way objects are used on the desktop). As an example, consider what a call to StartCar might do to an internal field in class Car called engineRunning.

With singleton objects, even if you have 10,000 clients requesting the object, only *one* instance is ever created. This is perfect from a scalability perspective. You can double the number of clients and no more memory is used to hold the objects. (This is actually a little simplistic – you can still run into problems if resources that the object uses, such as database connections, cannot handle the required number of clients.) Compare this to a scenario where each client requires their own instance of the object – that's a huge scalability problem. In addition, the object is completely free-threaded. There may be any number of threads running through a given method simultaneously. This means that you have to be very careful with thread synchronization should you choose to maintain state inside the object.

This is an important point. If you do choose to hold state, then the way that you handle the synchronization is important.

If you have a method that creates an exclusive write lock as the first statement and releases it at the last statement, you're effectively only going to allow one thread (that is, one client) to call that method at any one time. This can cause scalability problems, as the more clients you add, the more contention there is to this one method. In addition, if you establish a lock and then experience an exception that prevents you from unlocking, potentially none of the clients will ever be able to enter the lock, bringing down the entire application.

> **With singleton objects: on the first request, a single instance is created that exists throughout the life of the host process and is shared across all clients.**

Single-call objects are slightly different. They exist for a single call. When the call is received, an object is created, the method executed and at some point the garbage collector will clean up the object. It's not as good as singleton objects on the scalability front, because you can have more than one object required in memory at any one time.

> **We're going to be chiefly concerned with using singleton objects in the business-tier of a classic 3-tier design. You'll find that this is the most useful object in this scenario.**

Client-Activated Objects

Client-activated objects are, as their name implies, activated by the client. They are released from memory a while after the proxy has been garbage collected on the client side. We won't be looking at these in much detail in this chapter as their use is very specific and not massively useful from a classic 3-tier perspective.

Basically with client-activated objects, what you can do is say, *create any object of this given type on the server, instead of creating it locally in this application domain.* Whenever the application attempts to instantiate an object of a type that is registered as located locally, the object is actually instantiated remotely and you are given a proxy through which you can make calls to the remote object.

A Simple Client/Server Example

An excellent use of Remoting is hosting the business tier objects in a classic 3-tier design. In this example, we'll look at how we can build a stateless, singleton business object in the business tier and have that object called from a client. We'll make the object available over both the TCP and HTTP built-in channels.

The object we build, `Customers`, will contain a single method called `CreateCustomer`. This method will simply return a random integer number that represents the ID of the customer – that way we can keep the focus of the example on remoting.

Building the Server

First off, create a new Console Application project called `MyServer`.

With 3-tier, the presentation and the data portions of the application are separated. A good way to implement a Remoting solution is to further split the business tier into "host" and "object" sections. This is usually a good plan because, when we're debugging, we like the business objects themselves to be hosted in an environment where they can be easily debugged, but when the application goes into production we like those same objects to be hosted in an environment where they are more managed:

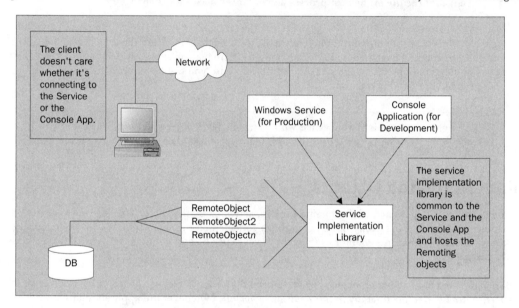

Console applications, for example, are great for debugging. They start quickly, you can set breakpoints in them right away, and their process can be killed if something goes wrong. On the other hand, Windows Service applications are very hard to debug.

A good way to split the application is to put the business objects in a separate class library project. Then we can create a Console Application host for debugging and create a Windows Service application for production. In both the debugging and the production cases, we can use the same object library.

So, add a Class Library project called `MyObjects` to the same solution as the `MyServer` project. Delete the default `Class1` class, because we won't need this.

To use Remoting in the server application, we need to import an assembly containing the various classes, and also add a number of namespace import declarations:

Your solution will now look like this:

Create a new class in the MyObjects project. Call it Customers. This will be the object that we make available over Remoting. In order for the object to be accessible as either a single-call or singleton object, it has to extend System.MarshalByRefObject. This tells .NET that the class should never move out of its application domain – and in this case you can take it to mean that if it's created on the server in response to a request from the client, the object does not move over the wire to the client – it stays where it is. For debugging, we'll add code to the constructor and finalizer so that we can see what's happening with the lifetime of the object:

```
Public Class Customers
    Inherits MarshalByRefObject
    Public Sub New()
        Debug("Created")
    End Sub
    Protected Overrides Sub Finalize()
```

```
        Debug("Finalized")
        MyBase.Finalize()
    End Sub
    Protected Sub Debug(ByVal buf As String)
        Console.WriteLine("[" & Me.GetHashCode() & "] " & buf)
    End Sub
End Class
```

Finally, we'll add the `CreateCustomer()` method itself. This simply returns an integer that represents the ID of the new customer:

```
    Public Function CreateCustomer() As Integer
        ' choose an ID...
        Dim random As New Random()
        Dim customerId As Integer = random.Next(1000)
        ' debug...
        Debug("Created customer #" & customerId)
        ' create and return...
        Return customerId
    End Function
```

Registering the Object with Remoting

Although that's all we have to do to make the object available over Remoting, we still have to register that object with the Remoting subsystem so that remote clients can connect to it.

There are two main ways that we can register objects with Remoting. We can either provide a separate configuration file that contains the registration details, or we can do it programmatically using various methods on various objects in the `System.Runtime.Remoting` and child namespaces.

My preferred pattern is to do this programmatically, as I prefer to have a single file containing the code and configuration data, rather than having an architecture where there are several files that have to be absolutely correct to get the application running. (In fact, where there is dynamic data that needs to be configured centrally, such as a database connection string or the ports used in a Remoting architecture such as this, I prefer to have a central Web Service available that the clients can pull the dynamic configuration data from.)

When we want to register classes for Remoting programmatically, we have to make repeated calls into a shared method called `RegisterWellKnownServiceType` on `System.Runtime.Remoting.RemotingConfiguration`. I personally feel this is too much work, so the pattern I'm going to demonstrate here uses Reflection to walk through all the types in a set of given assemblies looking for those marked with a certain attribute. When this attribute is found, the type is registered with Remoting using the `RegisterWellKnownServiceType`.

First off, we'll build our attribute, which we'll call `RemotingServiceAttribute`. This attribute can only be assigned to classes and takes a single parameter indicating whether or not the class should be registered as a singleton or single call service. Add this class to your `MyObjects` project:

```
    Imports System.Runtime.Remoting

    <AttributeUsage(AttributeTargets.Class)> _
```

```
Public Class RemotingServiceAttribute
  Inherits Attribute
  ' members...
  Public ObjectMode As WellKnownObjectMode
  ' Constructor...
  Public Sub New(ByVal objectMode As WellKnownObjectMode)
    Me.ObjectMode = objectMode
  End Sub
End Class
```

Now, add the attribute to the Customers class:

```
<RemotingService(System.Runtime.Remoting.WellKnownObjectMode.Singleton)> _
Public Class Customers
```

The RemotingBootstrapper object is responsible for walking a list of assemblies, scanning the types for the RemotingServiceAttribute attribute, and registering the objects when they are found. (Reflection was covered in Chapters 3 and 5.) As standard the .NET Framework doesn't support a collection of System.Reflection.Assembly objects, so we'll extend System.Collections.CollectionBase and add our own implementation to the MyObjects project:

```
Imports System.Reflection

Public Class AssemblyCollection
  Inherits CollectionBase
  Public Sub Add(ByVal newAssembly As [Assembly])
    list.Add(newAssembly)
  End Sub
  Public Sub Remove(ByVal oldAssembly As [Assembly])
    list.Remove(oldAssembly)
  End Sub
  Default Public Property Item(ByVal index As Integer) As [Assembly]
    Get
      Return CType(list.Item(index), [Assembly])
    End Get
    Set(ByVal Value As [Assembly])
      list.Item(index) = Value
    End Set
  End Property
End Class
```

Configuring an application to use Remoting involves a number of namespaces. These namespaces, together with System.Reflection, should be imported into the new RemotingBootstrapper class:

```
Imports System.Reflection
Imports System.Runtime.Remoting
Imports System.Runtime.Remoting.Channels
Imports System.Runtime.Remoting.Channels.Http
Imports System.Runtime.Remoting.Channels.Tcp
```

The class also needs to hold an instance of an AssemblyCollection object, and needs to provide a read-only property to access this collection:

```
Public Class RemotingBootstrapper

    ' members...
    Private _includeAssemblies As New AssemblyCollection()

    ' IncludeAssemblies property...
    Public ReadOnly Property IncludeAssemblies() As AssemblyCollection
      Get
        Return _includeAssemblies
      End Get
    End Property
```

As you would expect, the TCP channel and HTTP channels each have to be on their own, unique port. I'm going to use 8081 and 8082 here respectively. However, when you run the code, if you get an exception when creating or registering the channels, these ports may also be being used by another service on the computer. In a production application, you would need to perform some exception checking here to detect this problem. Alternatively, before registering the channel you can try and create a socket using the port that you wish to use. Chapter 23 shows you how to create sockets to listen for inbound connections, although it doesn't specifically talk about this scenario. Creating the channels is simply a matter of creating them, supplying the port as a parameter to the constructor, and calling System.Runtime.Remoting.ChannelServices.RegisterChannel:

```
Public Sub Start()

    ' create the channels...
    Dim channel As IChannel = New TcpChannel(8081)
    ChannelServices.RegisterChannel(channel)
    channel = New HttpChannel(8082)
    ChannelServices.RegisterChannel(channel)
```

Next, we loop through each of the assemblies in the IncludeAssemblies collection:

```
    ' go through the assemblies in the list...
    Dim scanAssembly As [Assembly]
    For Each scanAssembly In IncludeAssemblies
```

Then we loop through each type:

```
        ' go through each type...
        Dim scanType As Type
        For Each scanType In scanAssembly.GetTypes()
```

Then we look through each attribute. If we find an instance of a RemotingServiceAttribute is available on the type, we know that this type needs to be registered with Remoting:

```
        Dim scanAttribute As Object
        For Each scanAttribute In _
                    scanType.GetCustomAttributes(False)
            ' match?
            If scanAttribute.GetType() Is _
                    GetType(RemotingServiceAttribute) Then
```

If this happens, we need to do three things. We need to get hold of the attribute itself so we can find out if the object should be singleton or single call. Then we need to create a URI that we can use to access the object (and here I'm going to use the full name of the type with .rem tacked onto the end). Finally, we register the object through a call to RegisterWellKnownServiceType on System.Runtime.Remoting.RemotingConfiguration:

```
            Console.WriteLine("Registering: " & _
              scanType.ToString())
            ' get the attribute...
            Dim serviceAttribute As RemotingServiceAttribute = _
                CType(scanAttribute, RemotingServiceAttribute)
            ' register this object with remoting...
            Dim uri As String = scanType.ToString & ".rem"
            Console.WriteLine("    " & uri)
            RemotingConfiguration.RegisterWellKnownServiceType( _
                    scanType, uri, serviceAttribute.ObjectMode)
        End If
```

Finally we close off the loop and close the sub:

```
            Next
          Next
        Next
      End Sub
  End Class
```

Our motivation for including RemotingBootstrapper in the MyObjects library was so that we can easily use it from either the production or the debugging host. To do this, first off we need to add a reference to the MyObjects project from the MyServer project, so that we can access the RemotingBootstrapper class:

Now add this code inside Module1 of MyServer. Notice how we add the main MyObjects assembly to the IncludeAssemblies collection before calling Start.

(This approach relies on the remote objects being hosted in the same project as the bootstrapper objects themselves. If your remote objects are in a different project, you'll need to add a reference to the assembly containing the remote objects.)

```
Imports MyObjects

Module Module1
    Sub Main()
        ' create the bootstrapper...
        Dim boot As New RemotingBootstrapper()
        boot.IncludeAssemblies.Add(boot.GetType().Assembly)
        boot.Start()

        ' wait...
        Console.ReadLine()
    End Sub
End Module
```

Now run the project, and you should see this:

What this is telling us is that the `MyObjects.Customers` class is now accessible over Remoting. The URI displayed in the debugging text tells us how we can access the object. If we know what ports are being used (and we do: TCP is running on port 8081 and HTTP is on port 8082), and we know the hostname of the computer hosting the objects (`localhost`), we can access the object through tcp://localhost:8081/MyObjects.Customers.rem and http://localhost:8082/MyObjects.Customers.rem.

To test this out, take the HTTP URL and add ?WDSL on to the end. Web services and Remoting share a lot of code in .NET, so if we do this what we'll actually get back is the WSDL document of the remote object. This isn't particularly useful from an implementation perspective, but it does prove that the object is available. If you dig through the WSDL document, you'll find the method that we exposed:

![Internet Explorer window showing http://localhost:8082/MyObjects.Customers.rem?wsdl](image)

```xml
<?xml version="1.0" encoding="UTF-8" ?>
- <definitions name="Customers"
    targetNamespace="http://schemas.microsoft.com/clr/nsassem/MyObjects/MyObjects%
    2C%20Version%3D1.0.769.26087%2C%20Culture%3Dneutral%2C%
    20PublicKeyToken%3Dnull" xmlns="http://schemas.xmlsoap.org/wsdl/"
    xmlns:tns="http://schemas.xmlsoap.org/wsdl/"
```

Building the Client

So we have the object running in its own host console application, and we know that we can access this object through Internet Explorer. Now it's time to create a client application that can access this remote object.

Open a new instance of Visual Studio .NET and create a new Console Application project called `MyClient`. This client will, simply, create an instance of the remote object and display the return value from a call to `CreateCustomer`.

The curious issue with Remoting is that, at least in the pattern we're following here, the actual business tier object implementations that run on the server have to also be installed on the client, even though the client-side objects won't ever be used in the traditional sense. What Remoting needs is the 'metadata' for the class that describes the methods and properties. The methods and properties themselves will never be called directly; instead all calls will be deferred to the server for processing. We'll talk a little bit more about this topic later but for now, add a reference to the `MyObjects` assembly to `MyClient`. Remember, don't add a reference to the project – add a reference to the actual assembly. (Although you can technically add a reference to the project, you'll find that if you have two copies of Visual Studio .NET open with the same project loaded into each of the two solutions, you can run into issues where VS.NET will detect changes in one and keep asking you to reload the project in the other, and so on. It's easier just to add a reference to the assembly itself.)

To access the remote object, you need to have the URL. The Remoting subsystem will determine what channel should be used from the protocol in the URL (in our case, either `tcp:` or `http:`). Again, here I've hard-coded the URL into the project, which isn't great practice. A better plan would be to have the hostname and port numbers in the application configuration file or, as I mentioned before, use a Web Service to dynamically provide the URLs down to the client when they start up.

Once you have the URL, use `System.Activator.GetObject` to request a connection to the server-side object. You'll be passed back a transparent proxy that automatically marshals the call to the server and marshals the response back into your code. The elegant part of this technique is that whether you're using the proxy or the real object, the client side code doesn't change apart from the instantiation method. (You could implement a factory pattern here, where you could switch Remoting on or off, using the `GetObject` or `CreateInstance` method depending on whether you wanted to use Remoting or not.)

Here's all of the client-side code:

```
Imports MyObjects

Module Module1
  Sub Main()

    ' form the url...
    Dim url As String = "http://localhost:8082/MyObjects.Customers.rem"

    ' connect to the object...
    Dim customers As Customers = _
        CType(Activator.GetObject(GetType(Customers), url), Customers)

    ' call the method...
    Dim customerId As Integer = customers.CreateCustomer()
    Console.WriteLine("The customer ID is: " & customerId)
```

```
' wait...
   Console.ReadLine()
  End Sub
End Module
```

Run the server again, and then start up the project. You'll see something like this on the client:

You'll see this on the server:

The fact that we see debugging information in the server console application proves that the object is being accessed and is running remotely. Notice as well how the object is automatically created on the server in response to the call. The debugging information shows the hash code of this object in brackets ([74] in my case). If you close the client and run it again, you'll see that the same object is reused for the new client:

One object instance is shared between all clients, and we've proven this by creating a separate client and connecting to the same object. To run this example as using SingleCall objects instead, we need only make one change to our code in the Customers class:

```
<RemotingService(System.Runtime.Remoting.WellKnownObjectMode.SingleCall)> _
Public Class Customers
```

Now, if we run the example again, we can see that we create a new object each time (in this case, [47] and [58] are the hash codes for the objects that are created):

You'll notice that in either case the first connection takes a short while to execute. This is the point at which .NET sets up the client-side proxy and does other configuration activities, so there is a slight delay. You'll find that on subsequent calls the call is made much faster. You can demonstrate this by adding a loop to the client that calls `CreateCustomer` a number of times.

Passing By Reference and By Value

When an object extends `MarshalByRefObject`, what we're actually telling .NET is that we don't ever want that object to move outside of the Application domain in which it's created. If we want to use that object outside of the Application domain in which it was created (and in our case, our server process and our client process each contain exactly one Application domain), we have to pass a 'reference' to that object and consume it from a proxy. Our `Customer` object extends `MarshalByRefObject`; this is how we tell Remoting that the object should be created on the server (or rather, inside the Application domain in the server-side process that established the Remoting channel), and that the object should always stay inside this application domain – that is, it should remain remote and should never become 'local' to the client.

In some cases, we might actually want the object to 'move' from one Application domain to another. In this case, what we want to do is pass the object by 'value'. In this section, we'll take a look at how we can return an object by value from server-side code and use that object in client-side code.

When using Remoting, we need to pass the request through a stream and we also receive the response through a stream. Thanks to the way the proxies work, we don't usually worry about these streams – they're created for us as a response to the calls that we make.

However, although we can ignore streams when working with Remoting, we can't ignore serialization. This is the process in which an object is prepared for transmission using a stream. Basically, it converts an object to a string of bytes that can either be sent using a network stream to a server (and back again), or written to a file stream for de-serialization later, and so on.

If we want to transfer complex objects between Remoting client and server, we have to deal with serialization. We talked about serialization in the context of the `System.Xml.Serialization.XmlSerializer` class back in Chapter 10, but when we're dealing with serialization in terms of Remoting, we have to get a bit more complex.

We saw in Chapter 10 how adding the `Serializable` attribute to the class was a requirement before `XmlSerializer` could work with it. That's just half the problem when working with complex serialization, but it's a good place to start.

The Serializable Attribute

The concept behind the `Serializable` attribute is that you're telling .NET that this object should be serializable and de-serializable. What it actually means is that you don't need to do anything special to get the object serialized or de-serialized. Not all objects can be serialized and de-serialized in this way, and we talk more about that in the next section. For now, however, I want to demonstrate how to move a complex object from server to client and then use that same object in client-side code.

First off, we're going to create a class called `Order` that represents an order, and add it to the `MyObjects` project.

This `Order` class will have properties such as `OrderId`, `CreatedDate`, `TaxRate`, and so on. The `Order` class will also contain a collection of `OrderLine` objects. Each `OrderLine` expresses details like `ProductId`, `UnitPrice`, and so on.

First, add this class to the `MyObjects` project:

```
Public Class Order

    ' members...
    Public OrderId As Integer
    Public CreatedDate As DateTime
    Public PaidDate As DateTime
    Public Lines As New OrderLineCollection()
    Public TaxRate As Double
    Public Shipping As Double

    ' Tax...
    Public ReadOnly Property Tax() As Double
      Get
          Return LineTotal * TaxRate
      End Get
    End Property

    ' LineTotal...
    Public ReadOnly Property LineTotal() As Double
      Get
          Dim line As OrderLine
          Dim total As Double
          For Each line In Lines
            total += line.LineTotal
          Next
          Return total
      End Get
    End Property

    Public ReadOnly Property Total() As Double
      Get
          Return LineTotal + Tax + Shipping
      End Get
    End Property

End Class
```

Then, add the `OrderLine` class:

```
Public Class OrderLine

    ' members...
    Public ProductId As Integer
    Public Description As String
    Public Quantity As Integer
    Public UnitPrice As Double

    Public ReadOnly Property LineTotal() As Double
```

```
Get
        Return Quantity * UnitPrice
    End Get
  End Property

End Class
```

Finally, we need the `OrderLineCollection` class. This class will hold a strongly typed collection of `OrderLine` objects and will extend `System.Collections.CollectionBase`:

```
Public Class OrderLineCollection
  Inherits CollectionBase
  Public Sub Add(ByVal line As OrderLine)
    list.Add(line)
  End Sub
  Public Sub Remove(ByVal line As OrderLine)
    list.Remove(line)
  End Sub
  Default Public Property Item(ByVal index As Integer) As OrderLine
    Get
        Return CType(list.Item(index), OrderLine)
    End Get
    Set(ByVal Value As OrderLine)
      list.Item(index) = Value
    End Set
  End Property
End Class
```

As before, we're not worried about building a database for this example that we can use as our source of data. Instead, we'll build a new class called `Orders` that contains a method called `GetOrder`. This `GetOrder` method will return a new `Order` object populated with dummy data. As we need this object accessible over Remoting, we need to extend `MarshalByRefObject` and also apply the `RemotingServiceAttribute` attribute:

```
<RemotingService(Runtime.Remoting.WellKnownObjectMode.Singleton)> _
Public Class Orders
  Inherits MarshalByRefObject
  Public Function GetOrder(ByVal orderId As Integer) As Order

    ' create a new dummy order...
    Dim order As New Order()
    order.OrderId = orderId
    order.PaidDate = Date.Now.AddDays(-1)
    order.CreatedDate = order.PaidDate.AddMonths(-1)
    order.TaxRate = 0.085
    order.Shipping = 25

    ' add a line...
    Dim orderLine As New OrderLine()
    orderLine.ProductId = 27
    orderLine.Description = "Widget"
    orderLine.Quantity = 10
    orderLine.UnitPrice = 20
```

```
        order.Lines.Add(orderLine)

        ' add another line...
        orderLine = New OrderLine()
        orderLine.ProductId = 28
        orderLine.Description = "Widget"
        orderLine.Quantity = 5
        orderLine.UnitPrice = 95
        order.Lines.Add(orderLine)

        ' return it...
        Return order
    End Function
End Class
```

If you run the `MyServer` host at this point, you'll notice that both objects have been made available over Remoting:

At this point, you can either build a new client-side Console Application, or delete the sample code from the existing application that calls `CreateCustomer` and replace it with the code below. In our code download, we've created a new Console Application called `MyClient2`. This new code asks for an Order object to be returned from the server (the `GetOrder` call) and contains debugging code to display the details of the order to the user:

```
Imports MyObjects

Module Module1
    Sub Main()

        ' form the url...
        Dim url As String = "http://localhost:8082/MyObjects.Orders.rem"

        ' connect to the object...
        Dim orders As Orders = CType(Activator.GetObject(GetType(Orders), url), _
Orders)

        ' call the method...
        Dim order As Order = orders.GetOrder(1004)

        ' write the header...
        Console.WriteLine(String.Format("Order ID: {0}", order.OrderId))
        Console.WriteLine(String.Format("Created: {0}", order.CreatedDate))
        Console.WriteLine(String.Format("Paid: {0}", order.PaidDate))
        Console.WriteLine(String.Format("Line total: {0}", order.LineTotal))
        Console.WriteLine(String.Format("Tax: {0} ({1}%)", order.Tax, _
            (order.TaxRate * 100)))
```

```
    Console.WriteLine(String.Format("Shipping: {0}", order.Shipping))
    Console.WriteLine(String.Format("Total: {0}", order.Total))
    Console.WriteLine()

    ' details...
    Dim line As OrderLine
    For Each line In order.Lines
        Console.WriteLine(String.Format("{0} of {1} [{2}] @ {3} = {4}", _
                line.Quantity, line.Description, line.ProductId, _
                line.UnitPrice, line.LineTotal))
    Next

    ' wait...
    Console.ReadLine()
  End Sub
End Module
```

Start up the client application now and – disaster – you'll see this exception:

Notice particularly how the exception has been thrown on the *client-side*.

Microsoft has done a superb job here with handling exceptions that happen in remote, server-side code. This SerializationException exception is actually thrown on the server. However, notice that the server application is still running and you can prove that it's still running by viewing the WSDL document using the trick I demonstrated before. Although this is a problem with the server-side code, it is being felt on the client. Most importantly of all, the server-side process is still running and clients can still use the remote objects as normal!

The reason why we're seeing this exception is because we haven't marked the Order object as serializable. (You can see this in the actual message sent with the exception.) Let's do this now.

Adding the 'Serializable' Attribute

Stop both the client-side and server-side projects and add the Serializable attribute to Order, OrderLine and OrderLineCollection:

```
<Serializable()> Public Class Order
<Serializable()> Public Class OrderLine

<Serializable()> Public Class OrderLineCollection
```

Now run the server again, and try to connect to it with the client. This time, the objects will be serialized properly and you'll see the response on the client:

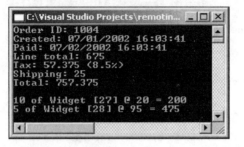

Complex Serialization

What's happening in the previous example is that .NET is able to serialize the object to the network stream and de-serialize it back into an object again at the client-side so that it can be used. In some cases, the object may not be serializable (for reasons we're about to explore), or you may want to impose a level of control over the serialization process. In both cases, it's down to you to write some custom code to manage the serialization.

XmlSerializer works on the concept of calling each of the public properties on an object in turn, forming an XML document that can be sent down a stream. You can use various attributes attached to the property definitions to control this. Serialization is sometimes known as deep serialization because rather than iterating and calling each property using Reflection, deep serialization peeks into the object and grabs the state of *every* field, adding it to the document. (It's not technically a document, but it's a sound metaphor so I'll stick with it.) This *includes* private and protected members, which is a very important point to appreciate.

At the other end (de-serialization), a new instance of the object is created, and the values against each member stored in the document are assigned to their relevant fields.

Where serialization gets tricky is when you're dealing with types that cannot be serialized. For example, System.IO.FileStream cannot be serialized. If you pass an object from one computer to another, the file handle on the original computer won't make sense on the new computer. What this means is that if you have a type like this:

```
<Serializable()> Public Class MyObject
   Private _stream As FileStream
End Class
```

FileStream cannot be serialized; even through the Serialization subsystem can access _stream despite it being private. In order to serialize and de-serialize MyObject, we actually have to take responsibility for the serialization process away from .NET and do it ourselves. As a rule, if your object has a member that cannot be serialized, you must take responsibility for the serialization process, roll up your sleeves, and write some code.

You won't find MSDN documentation that tells you which classes can and cannot be de-serialized – it's a case of trial and error.

Let's take a look at how to manage our own serialization/de-serialization process.

Controlling Serialization

To signal that we want to control serialization of the objects, not only do we need to mark the object with the Serializable attribute, we also have to implement the `System.Runtime.Serialization.ISerializable` interface. This interface contains a single method, `GetObjectData` and when this method is called it's up to you to tell .NET what information should be included in the document for transmission.

Our `Order`, `OrderLine` and `OrderLineCollection` objects each support serialization without us having to write custom code. Although it's a fairly artificial example, I'll demonstrate how we can add custom serialization to `OrderLineCollection`.

In the `MyObjects` project, add this namespace reference and tell the object that it should implement `ISerializable`:

```
Imports System.Runtime.Serialization

<Serializable()> Public Class OrderLineCollection
   Inherits CollectionBase
   Implements ISerializable

   Public Sub Add(ByVal line As OrderLine)
      list.Add(line)
   End Sub
```

Use the dropdown lists at the top of the code editor to add a stub method to implement `GetObjectData`.. (Select **ISerializable** from the left-hand list and **GetObjectData** from the right-hand list.) What we want to do is build an array of `OrderLine` objects and tell .NET to serialize the array. One of the two parameters to `GetObjectData` is called `info` and is a `SerializationInfo` instance. You can think of this as a 'bag' into which you can drop the data to be serialized. You'll be given this bag back again on de-serialization. In our case, we build the array and then add the entire array to the bag. For Remoting serialization, you can usually ignore the context parameter:

```
Public Sub GetObjectData(ByVal info As _
      System.Runtime.Serialization.SerializationInfo, _
      ByVal context As System.Runtime.Serialization.StreamingContext) _
      Implements System.Runtime.Serialization.ISerializable.GetObjectData

   ' create an array of orderline objects, and serialize that...
   Dim orderLines(Count - 1) As OrderLine
   Dim n As Integer
   For n = 0 To Count - 1
      orderLines(n) = Item(n)
   Next

   ' add this array...
   info.AddValue("OrderLines", orderLines)
End Sub
```

When I was first looking into custom serialization, I was baffled as to how you do de-serialization – there's no `SetObjectData` on `ISerializable`. What you have to do is implement a new constructor for the object that is called when the object needs to be de-serialized. This constructor gives you the 'bag' back again. The reason it is done this way is that if you didn't have a special custom constructor for serialization, the object would have to be instantiated *before* de-serialization. This approach gives you maximum flexibility – specifically, you don't *have* to have a parameter-less, public constructor available. But in Remoting, as well as the de-serialization constructor, we actually do need a parameter-less public constructor as otherwise we won't be able to create instances of the object on the server side. To clarify, if you think of serialization as being a technology that you can use when you're not using Remoting (to save application user documents, for example), you don't have to have a parameter-less public constructor as you'll always be controlling the lifetime of the object. However, with Remoting we need a parameter-less public constructor as we don't control the object's lifetime.

In the constructor, we get the array back and then repeatedly call `Add()` to fill the collection back up again:

```
' Normal constructor...
Public Sub New()
End Sub

' Deserialization constructor...
Protected Sub New(ByVal _
        info As System.Runtime.Serialization.SerializationInfo, _
        ByVal context As System.Runtime.Serialization.StreamingContext)

  ' get the data back...
  Dim orderLines() As OrderLine = _
    CType(info.GetValue("OrderLines", GetType(OrderLine())), OrderLine())

  ' add each item...
  Dim n As Integer
  For n = 0 To orderLines.Length - 1
    Add(orderLines(n))
  Next
End Sub
```

If you run the project, this will work as normal. However, if you want to debug the client-side code to see what's happening with the de-serialization process, you'll need to remove the reference to the `MyObjects` assembly and add the `MyObjects` project to the solution so that you can set breakpoints.

Using CallContext

On occasion, you may want to pass information across the Remoting boundary (or the Application domain boundary) with each and every call, but you may not want to muddy your object design by requiring extra parameters on each call. For example, imagine we implement a pattern whereby we create a security token, expressed as a `System.String`, which identifies the client. On the server-side, we may need that token available inside of the method in order to verify the client's security privileges.

If we go with the extra parameters technique, we'll end up with methods that look like this:

```
Public Function CreateCustomer(ByVal securityToken As String) As Integer
```

Or even:

```
Public Function CreateCustomer( _
    ByVal securitySettings As MySecuritySettings) As Integer
```

If requiring a clean object model that isn't peppered with these kinds of parameters seems a little purist, remember that the calling code also gets more complex. Each time a method is called, the security settings have to be retrieved and sent to the client, which will make your client-side code harder to read. A better approach is to add security information to the context of the client-side thread that is automatically made available on the server-side. We can do this by using the System.Runtime.Remoting.Messaging.CallContext object.

We can put anything we like into the call context, providing that it can be serialized. Of course, the lower the payload the less network traffic there is. Security tokens tend to be good for this kind of thing. You can ask the server to authenticate the user, store security settings in the database, and return a security token to access those settings back to the user. When the server-side code receives the token from the client, it can look up the information from the database and determine the security privileges.

In this next example, we're going to create a new client application that simulates six clients connecting to the server. Rather than being called from different processes, each client call will be executed in a separate thread in the same process. Each client will be given a name, and that name will be the security token. At the start of the thread we'll set that token into the call context of the thread and call a method called PingSecurityToken. On the server-side, we'll retrieve the token from the call context and return it back to the client. If everything's working properly, we'll have a single instance of Customers on the server processing requests from each of the six clients and the token that the client sends should be returned from PingSecurityToken.

Creating SecurityToken

In MyObjects, we need a new class called SecurityToken. In order for a class to work with the call context, that class has to be configured such that it can be transferred over the wire (that is, it has to be serializable), and the class also has to implement System.Runtime.Remoting.Messaging.ILogicalThreadAffinative. This interface is curious in that it doesn't have any members – simply marking the class as supporting this interface is enough.

The SecurityToken class will support a single member field called _token, accessed through a read-only property called Token. Here's the class that should be added to MyObjects:

```
Imports System.Runtime.Remoting.Messaging

<Serializable()> Public Class SecurityToken
    Implements ILogicalThreadAffinative

    ' members...
    Private _token As String
    Public Sub New(ByVal token As String)
        _token = token
    End Sub
```

```
Public ReadOnly Property Token() As String
   Get
      Return _token
   End Get
 End Property
 Public Overrides Function ToString() As String
    Return Token
 End Function
End Class
```

It would be great if we could just add a string to the call context, but because System.String doesn't implement ILogicalThreadAffinative, the string would not get passed from the client to the server. This interface tells Remoting that the object should be made available in the context of the remote call, and without this the object will be added to the local call context but it will not be available in the remote call context. However, this approach is a little more extensible as we can just add new properties to SecurityToken should we develop the need to flow more information over to the server.

Creating the Client

We need a new client application to do this, because up until this point our client application only makes a single request and disconnects. We need our new client to spin up a number of threads, each of which needs to make a call to the server. Create a new Console Application project and call it MyThreadedClient. This new application needs a reference to the MyObjects assembly, as before.

In this new application, we'll add a class that acts as a self-contained client. It will create a thread for itself, call the remote method, and display the results. We'll need to import these namespaces:

```
Imports System.Text
Imports System.Threading
Imports System.Runtime.Remoting.Messaging
Imports MyObjects
```

As member variables, the class needs to hold a reference to the System.Threading.Thread object that's running the client call, and also needs a MyObjects.SecurityToken object. We also need the URL pointing to the remote object, and a constructor that creates the SecurityToken object:

```
Public Class Client
  ' members...
  Private _thread As Thread
  Private _securityToken As SecurityToken

  ' const...
  Public Const Url As String = _
      "http://localhost:8082/MyObjects.Customers.rem"

  ' Constructor...
  Public Sub New(ByVal securityToken As String)
    _securityToken = New SecurityToken(securityToken)
  End Sub
```

The SpinUp method will create the new thread:

```
' SpinUp method...
Public Sub SpinUp()

    ' create and spin up a thread...
    _thread = New Thread(AddressOf ThreadEntryPoint)
    _thread.Start()
End Sub
```

Now we get to the interesting part. When we get inside ThreadEntryPoint, the first thing we do is add the SecurityToken object held in _securityToken to the call context. We do this through a call to the shared SetData method of System.Runtime.Remoting.Messaging.CallContext. In traditional Microsoft style, this is the class name/value paradigm – in other words, we retrieve the object at the other end by calling GetData, passing in the same name that acts as a key against the value:

```
' ThreadEntryPoint...
Private Sub ThreadEntryPoint()

    ' configure the call context...
    CallContext.SetData("SecurityToken", _securityToken)
```

Once we do that, we make the call and write the results to the console:

```
' get the object and make the call...
Dim customers As Customers = _
    CType(Activator.GetObject(GetType(Customers), Url), Customers)
Dim pingedToken As String = customers.PingSecurityToken()

' debug...
Dim builder As New StringBuilder()
builder.Append("[")
builder.Append(GetHashCode())
builder.Append("] [")
builder.Append(Thread.CurrentThread.GetHashCode())
builder.Append("] Ping: [")
builder.Append(_securityToken)
builder.Append("] Pong: [")
builder.Append(pingedToken)
builder.Append("]")
Console.WriteLine(builder.ToString())
End Sub
```

So, all we're doing there is making a call to PingSecurityToken. Remoting will automatically flow the SecurityToken instance across the Remoting boundary to the server, and our server-side code will explicitly return this value back as the return value from PingSecurityToken. This somewhat artificial application is all about proving that we can flow the security token to the server and read that token in server-side code.

Before we write PingSecurityToken, we need to actually create and spin up the clients. Add this code to Module1 of MyThreadedClient:

```
Sub Main()

    ' names of people...
    Dim names() As String = {"Darren", "Edward", "Steph", "Zoe", _
                             "Charlotte", "Tim"}

    ' go through each name and create a client...
    Dim name As String
    For Each name In names

        ' create a client...
        Dim client As New Client(name)

        ' run it...
        client.SpinUp()
    Next

    ' wait...
    Console.ReadLine()
End Sub
```

Adding PingSecurityToken to the Server

There are two things that we want to do on the server:

❑   We want to edit Debug such that the ID of the thread that is processing the server-side call is displayed – this will give us a greater insight as to what happens in a singleton object when the call context is used

❑   We need to actually write PingSecurityToken

First off, we import the necessary namespaces:

```
Imports System.Threading
Imports System.Runtime.Remoting.Messaging

<RemotingService(System.Runtime.Remoting.WellKnownObjectMode.Singleton)> _
Public Class Customers
    Inherits MarshalByRefObject
```

Secondly, we tweak Customers.Debug such that the thread ID is written to the console:

```
Protected Sub Debug(ByVal buf As String)
    Console.WriteLine("[" & Me.GetHashCode() & "] [" & _
                  Thread.CurrentThread.GetHashCode() & "] " & buf)
End Sub
```

PingSecurityToken is pretty basic. We use CallContext.GetData to get the data back, write it to the debugger, and return the token back as a System.String to the caller.

```
Public Function PingSecurityToken() As String
```

```
' get the token...
  Dim securityToken As SecurityToken = _
    CType(CallContext.GetData("SecurityToken"), SecurityToken)
  Debug("Called PingSecurityToken [" & securityToken.Token & "]")
  Return securityToken.Token
End Function
```

Run up both client and server, and you'll see six calls come through on the server. Against each call, you'll see the security token that was retrieved:

In our debugging information, the first number is the hash code of the singleton object used on the server. Notice how this is the same for every call. Second is the thread ID. Notice here how, in my case, thread #49 has been used three times. Even though the same thread has been used three times against the same object, the security token is different each time. Remoting properly manages the call context so that you're guaranteed that the values you have in the call context on the server-side are the same as those added in the affinitive call context on the client-side.

If the client-side code works, the token sent to the server should be the same as the return value from PingSecurityToken – in other words, the name written after Ping should match the name written after Pong:

There we have it: conclusive proof that the client-side call context is flowed automatically across the Remoting boundary and made available on the server-side.

Where Should We Put Metadata?

One major issue with Remoting is where to put the metadata. Throughout this chapter, we've built objects and run them on the server. We've used those same assemblies on the client. That's because we need the metadata on the client so that we can call the server code.

Metadata contains a 'map' of the types supported in an assembly, and all of the members of those types. We can use Reflection to walk through this metadata, but Remoting needs it in order to build the proxy. You can find more information on metadata in Chapter 3.

That might strike you as bad practice – why should we have multiple copies of business-tier code being copied around all the desktops in the enterprise? Why should our business partners using our apps have access to the business-tier assemblies (especially with MSIL being so readily readable with a quick de-compile).

In some cases, keeping the desktops clear of these technically server-side assemblies may be a little purist. In a closed setting (such as those in which only trusted computers have the code on them) it might not actually be a problem at all. You might even trust your business partners sufficiently not to worry about this issue.

However, because it can be a problem, I'll present a solution. The pattern we need to implement is to put together a separate set of interfaces for each of the business-tier classes and build two libraries – one designed for the server-side and the other designed for the client-side.

Rather than confuse the code we've already seen, I'll build a new business-tier class called `Catalog`. This class will contain a single method called `CreateProduct`. In addition, we need a new project in the `MyServer` solution called `MyMetadata` that contains a single interface called `ICatalog`.

`MyMetadata.ICatalog` is pretty basic:

```
Public Interface ICatalog
    Function CreateProduct(ByVal productName As String) As Integer
End Interface
```

`MyObjects.Catalog` implements this interface, and is also configured for Remoting:

```
<RemotingService(Runtime.Remoting.WellKnownObjectMode.Singleton)> _
Public Class Catalog
  Inherits MarshalByRefObject
  Implements MyMetaData.ICatalog
  Public Function CreateProduct(ByVal productName As String) As Integer _
                     Implements MyMetaData.ICatalog.CreateProduct

    ' debug...
    Console.WriteLine("CreateProduct called")

    ' create the product here...

    ' return the id...
    Return 27
  End Function
End Class
```

If you run the server now, you'll notice the object gets registered with Remoting – all's well and good.

The problem now is that if we add a reference to the `MyObjects` assembly, so that we can call `CreateProduct`, .NET will require a copy of the `MyObjects` assembly to be copied to the folder containing the client-side `MyClient.exe` assembly. This is *not* what we want. Instead, we add a reference to the `MyMetadata` assembly, as we did earlier; this assembly is copied over locally to the client-side code.

Now that we've done this, if we only ever refer to the interfaces in the client-side code, we'll never need the server-side code available locally. We just need the metadata in order to build the proxies and the interfaces themselves describe everything we need to know.

Create a new **Console Application**, and place the following code into the `Module1.vb` file:

```
Imports MyMetadata

Module Module1
    Sub Main()
    ' form the url...
    Dim url As String = "http://localhost:8082/MyObjects.Catalog.rem"

    ' get the product...
    Dim catalog As ICatalog = _
        Activator.GetObject(GetType(ICatalog), url)
    Dim productId As Integer = catalog.CreateProduct("Grommet")

    ' create the product...
    Console.WriteLine("The new product id is: " & productId)

    ' wait...
    Console.ReadLine()
End Module
```

If you now run both client and server, you'll notice everything works as normal. However, a quick glance in the `bin` folder for the project will prove that the server-side assemblies are not needed in order to run the application.

The caveat here is that in some cases we need more than just the metadata available on the client. If we're actually passing objects back from server to client (as we did before with `Order`), we do physically need the implementations on the client. If you still want to keep as much code as possible on the server-side, you'll need to further split the business tier into *client OK* and *client not OK* objects.

Summary

In this chapter, we took a pretty detailed look at how to use Remoting in classic 3-tier application design. We started by looking at the basic architecture of Remoting and launched pretty quickly into building a basic server and client that used a singleton object for answering client requests into the business tier.

We then looked at how to use serialization to return more complex objects from the server to the client. We looked at how to get .NET to do the serialization for us, and how we could control it ourselves by implementing `ISerializable`. We then saw how to use the call context for passing extra data from client to server along with each call without having to change the object model and finally looked at how to build a solution for separating the metadata and logic used in remote objects.

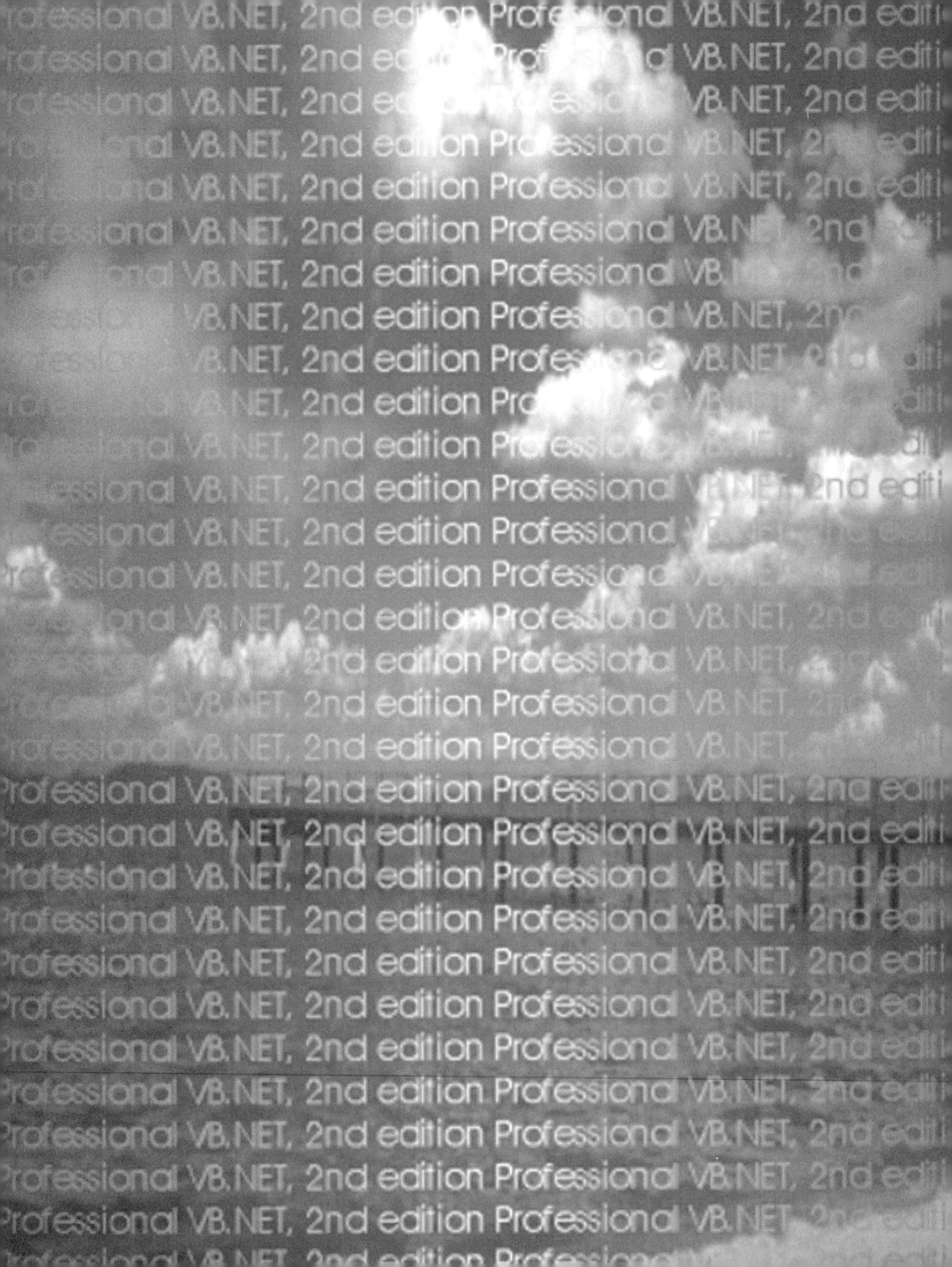
Professional VB.NET, 2nd edition

21

Windows Services

Modern, multi-tasking operating systems often need to run applications that operate in the background and which are independent of the user who is logged in. In Windows NT, Windows 2000, and Windows XP, such applications are called **Windows Services** (formerly known as NT Services). The tasks carried out by Windows Services are typically long running and have little or no direct interaction with a user (so they don't usually have user interfaces). Such applications may be started when the computer is booted, and often continue to run until the computer is shut down.

In this chapter we're going to look at:

❑   The characteristics of a Windows Service

❑   How we can interact with a Windows Service using VS.NET and the management applets in the Windows Control Panel

❑   How we can create, install, and communicate with a Windows Service using VB.NET

❑   How we can debug a Windows Service from within VS.NET

As VB6 did not offer direct support for the creation of Windows Services, you may be unfamiliar with such applications. So, to help understand the variety of such applications, we'll examine some scenarios in which a Windows Service application is a good solution.

Example Windows Services

SQL Server, Exchange Server, Internet Information Server (IIS), and anti-virus software all use Windows Services to perform tasks in response to events on the system. Only a background service, which runs no matter which user is logged in, could perform such operations.

Consider these Windows Services:

❑ **A File Watcher** – Suppose we are running an FTP server that places files it receives in a particular directory. We could use a Windows Service to monitor and process files within that directory. The service would run in the background and detect when files are changed within the directory, and then extract information from these files in order to process orders, or update address and billing information. We'll see an example of such a Windows Service later in this chapter.

❑ **An Automated Stock Price Reporter** – We could build a system that extracts stock prices from a web site and then e-mails the information to users. We could set thresholds so that an e-mail is only sent out if the stock price reaches a certain price. Our Windows Service could be automated to extract the information every ten minutes, or every ten seconds, and so on. Because a Windows Service can contain any logic that does not require a user interface, we have a lot of flexibility in constructing such applications.

❑ **Microsoft Transaction Server (MTS)** – MTS (part of COM+ Services in Windows 2000 and later) is an object broker that manages instances of components and is used regularly by professional developers. This service runs constantly in the background and manages components as soon as the computer is booted, just like IIS or Exchange Server.

Characteristics of a Windows Service

To properly design and develop a Windows Service, it's important to understand how a Windows Service differs from a typical Windows program. Here are the most important characteristics of a Windows Service:

❑ A Windows Service can start before a user logs on. The system maintains a list of Windows Services, and services can be set to start at boot time. Services can also be installed so that they require a manual startup and will not start at boot.

❑ A Windows Service can run under a different account from that of the current user. Most Windows Services provide functionality that needs to be running all the time and some load before a user logs on, so they cannot depend on a user being logged on to run.

❑ A Windows Service has its own process. It does not run in the process of a program communicating with it (Chapter 20 has more information on processes).

❑ A Windows Service typically has no user interface. This is because the service may be running under a different account from that of the current user, or the service may start at boot time, which would mean that the calls to put up a user interface might fail because they are out of context (it is possible to create a Windows Service with a user interface, but Visual Basic .NET cannot be used to do it; we'll discuss why later on).

❑ A Windows Service requires a special installation procedure; just clicking on a compiled EXE won't run it. The program must run in a special context in the operating system, and a specific installation process is required to do the configuration necessary for a Windows Service to be run in this special context.

❑ A Windows Service works with a **Service Control Manager** (which we'll discuss shortly). The Service Control Manager is required to provide an interface to the Windows Service. External programs that want to communicate with a Windows Service (for example, to start or stop the service) must go through the Service Control Manager. The Service Control Manager is an operating-system-level program, but it has a user interface that can be used to start and stop services, and this interface can be accessed through the Computer Management section of the Control Panel.

Interacting with Windows Services

You can view the services that are used on your computer by opening the Services Control Manager user interface. This can be done in Windows 2000 via Administrative Tools | Services in the Control Panel, and in Windows XP via Programs | Administrative Tools | Services from the Start button. Using the Services Control Manager, a service can be set to automatically start up when the system is booted, or a service can be started manually. Services can also be stopped or paused. The list of services contained in the Services Control Manager includes the current state for each service. The following screenshot show the Services Control Manager in Windows 2000:

The Status column indicates the current state of the service. If this column is blank, the service has not been started since the last time the computer was booted. Other possible values for Status are Started, Stopped, and Paused. You can get access to additional settings and details concerning a service by double-clicking on it.

When a service is started, it can automatically log into the system using either a user or system account:

❑ The user account is a regular NT account that allows the program to interact with the system – in essence, the service will impersonate a user

❑ The system account is not associated with a particular user

The Services Control Manager seen in the previous figure is part of the operating system (which is what supports Windows Services); it is not a part of .NET. Any service run by the operating system is exposed through the Services Control Manager, no matter how the service was created or installed. We can also interact with Windows Services via the Server Explorer in Visual Studio .NET. We'll cover this technique later on.

Creating a Windows Service

Prior to .NET, most Windows Services were created with C++. Third party toolkits were available to allow Windows Services to be created in VB6 and earlier, but deployment problems and threading issues meant that few developers went down this route.

In .NET the functionality needed to interface to the operating system is wrapped up in .NET Framework classes, so any .NET language can be used to create a Windows Service.

The .NET Framework Classes for Windows Services

There are several base classes that are needed to create a Windows Service:

❑ System.ServiceProcess.ServiceBase – Provides the base class for the Windows Service. The class that contains the logic that will run in the service inherits from ServiceBase. A single executable can contain more than one service, but each service in the executable will be a separate class that inherits from ServiceBase.

❑ System.Configuration.Install.Installer – This is a generic class that performs the installation chores for a variety of components. One class in a Windows Service process must inherit and extend Installer in order to provide the interface necessary to install the service under Windows XP, 2000, and NT.

Each class that inherits from Installer will need to contain an instance of each of these classes:

❑ System.ServiceProcess.ServiceProcessInstaller – This class contains the information needed to install a .NET executable that contains Windows Services (that is, an executable that contains classes that inherit from ServiceBase). The .NET installation utility for Windows Services (InstallUtil.exe, which we will discuss later) calls this class to get the information it needs to perform the installation.

❑   System.ServiceProcess.ServiceInstaller – This class also interacts with the
    InstallUtil.exe installation program. Whereas ServiceProcessInstaller contains
    information needed to install the executable as a whole, ServiceInstaller contains
    information on a specific service in the executable. If an executable contains more than one
    service, an instance of ServiceInstaller is needed for each one.

For many Windows Services we can leave VS.NET to take care of Installer,
ServiceProcessInstaller, and ServiceInstaller. We'll just need to set a few properties. The
class we need to thoroughly understand is ServiceBase as the class that contains the functionality of a
Windows Service must inherit from it.

The ServiceBase Class

ServiceBase contains several useful properties and methods, but initially it's more important to
understand the events of ServiceBase. Most of these events are fired by the Service Control Manager
when the state of the service is changed. The most important events are:

Event	How and when the event is used
OnStart	Occurs when the service is started. This is where the initialization logic for a service is usually placed.
OnStop	Occurs when the service is stopped. Cleanup and shutdown logic is generally placed here.
OnPause	Occurs when the service is paused. Any logic required to suspend operations during a pause goes here.
OnContinue	Occurs when a service continues after being paused.
OnShutdown	Occurs when the operating system is being shut down.
OnPowerEvent	Occurs when the system's power management software causes a change in the power status of the system. Usually used to change the behavior of a service when a system is going in or out of a 'suspended' power mode.
OnCustomCommand	Occurs when an external program has told the Service Control Manager that it wishes to send a command to the service. The operation of this event is covered in *Communicating with the Service*.

The events used most frequently are OnStart, OnStop, and OnCustomCommand. The OnStart and
OnStop events are used in almost every Windows Service written in VB.NET, and the OnCustomCommand
is used if any special configuration of the service needs to be done while the service is running.

All of these are Protected events, so they are only available to classes that inherit from
ServiceBase. Because of the restricted context in which it runs, a Windows Service component that
inherits from ServiceBase often lacks a public interface. While we can add public properties and
methods to such a component, they are of limited use because outside programs cannot obtain an object
reference to running Windows Service component.

To be active as a Windows Service, an instance of `ServiceBase` must be started via the shared `Run` method of the `ServiceBase` class. However, normally we don't have to write code to do this because the template code generated by VS.NET places the correct code in the `Main` subroutine of the project.

The most commonly used property of `ServiceBase` is the `AutoLog` property. This `Boolean` property is set to `True` by default. If `True`, then the Windows Service automatically logs the `Start`, `Stop`, `Pause`, and `Continue` events to an event log. The event log used is the Application Event Log and the Source in the log entries is taken from the name of Windows Service. This automatic event logging is stopped by setting `AutoLog` to `False`.

The File Watcher example that follows goes into more detail about the automatic logging in a Windows Service, and about event logs in general.

Installation-Oriented classes

The `Installer`, `ServiceProcessInstaller`, and `ServiceInstaller` classes are quite simple to use. A menu option (**Add Installer**, accessed by right-clicking on the design surface for the `ServiceBase` class for the project) creates all the code necessary to use them.

The `Installer` class (named `ProjectInstaller` by default in a Windows Service project) generally needs no interaction at all – it is ready to use when created by VS.NET. However it may be appropriate to change some properties of the `ServiceProcessInstaller` and `ServiceInstaller` classes. The properties that are typically modified for `ServiceProcessInstaller` include:

❑ `Account` – specifies the type of account under which the entire service application will run. Different settings give the services in the application different levels of privilege on the local system. We'll use the highest level of privilege, `LocalSystem`, for most of our examples to keep them simple. If this property is set to `User` (which is the default), then we must supply a username and password, and that user's account is used to determine privileges for the service. If there is any possibility that a service could access system resources that should be 'out-of-bounds', then using the `User` setting to restrict privileges is a good idea.

❑ `Username` – If Account is set to `User`, then this property determines the user account to use in determining the privileges the system will have and how it interacts with other computers on the network. If this property is left blank it will be requested when the service is installed.

❑ `Password` – This property determines the password to access the user account specified in the `Username` property. If the password is left blank it will be requested when the service is installed.

❑ `HelpText` – The information about the service that will be displayed in certain installation options.

If the `Account` property is set to `User` it is good practice to set up a special user account for the service, rather than relying on some existing account that is intended for a live user. The special account can be set up with exactly the appropriate privileges for the service. It also is not as vulnerable to having its password or its privileges inadvertently changed in a way that would cause problems in running the service.

For the `ServiceInstaller` class, the properties we might change include:

❑ `DisplayName` – The name of the service as displayed in the **Service Manager** or the **Server Explorer**. Can be different from the class name and the executable name if desired, though it's a good convention to make this name the same as the class name for the service.

❏   StartType – Specifies how the service is started. The default is Manual, which means we must start the service manually. If we want the service to always be started when the system starts, we can change this property to Automatic. The **Service Manager** can be used to override the StartType setting.

❏   ServiceName – The name of the service that this ServiceInstaller handles during installation. If we changed the class name of the service after using the **Add Installer** option, we would need to change this property to correspond to the new name for the service.

We don't normally need to understand or manipulate the methods of either ServiceProcessInstaller or ServiceInstaller. They are used as necessary during the installation process.

Multiple Services In One Executable

It is possible to place more than one class that inherits from ServiceBase in a single Windows Service executable. Each such class then allows for a separate service than can be started, stopped, and so on independently of the other services in the executable.

If a Windows Service executable contains more than one service, it needs to contain one ServiceInstaller for each service. Each ServiceInstaller is configured with the information used for its associated service, such as the displayed name and the start type (automatic or manual). However, the executable still only needs one ServiceProcessInstaller, which works for all the services in the executable. It is configured with the account information that will be used for all the services in the executable.

The ServiceController Class

Another important Framework class for working with Windows Services is the System.ServiceProcess.ServiceController class. This class is not used when constructing a service. It is used by external applications to communicate with a running service, allowing operations such as starting and stopping the service. The ServiceController class is described in detail in *Communicating with the Service*.

Other Types of Windows Service

The ServiceBase and ServiceController classes can be used to create typical Windows Services that work with high-level system resources such as the file system or performance counters. However, some Windows Services need to interact at a deeper level. For example, a service may work at the kernel level, fulfilling functions such as that of a device driver.

This version of the .NET classes for Windows Services cannot be used to create such services, which rules out both VB and C# as tools to create them. C++ is typically the tool of choice for these types of services. If the .NET version of C++ is used, the code for such services would typically run in unmanaged mode.

Another type of service that cannot be created with the Framework classes is one that interacts with the Windows Desktop. Again, C++ is the preferred tool for such services.

We'll look at the types of services that *are* possible again when we cover the ServiceType property of the ServiceController class, in *Communicating with the Service*.

Creating a Windows Service with VB.NET

Let's create and use a Windows Service with VB.NET, using the Framework classes we discussed. We will demonstrate these tasks later in a detailed example. Here is a high-level description of the necessary tasks:

1. Create a new project of the type **Windows Service**. The service will be in a module named `Service1.vb` by default. The service can be renamed as with any other .NET module. (The class that is automatically placed in `Service1.vb` will be named `Service1` by default, and it will inherit from `ServiceBase`.)

2. Place any logic needed to run when the service is started in the `OnStart` event of the service class.

3. Add any additional logic that the service needs to carry out its operation. Logic can be placed in the class for the service, or in any other class module in the project. Such logic is typically called via some event that is generated by the operating system and passed to the service, such as a file changing in a directory, or a timer tick.

4. Add an installer to the project. This module provides the interface to Windows 2000, Windows XP, or Windows NT to install the module as a Windows Service. The installer will be a class that inherits from `System.Configuration.Install.Installer`, and it will contain instances of the `ServiceProcessInstaller` and `ServiceInstaller` classes.

5. Set properties of the installer modules as necessary. The most common settings needed are the account under which the service will run and the name the service will display in the Service Control Manager.

6. Build the project. This will result in an EXE file. If the service were named `WindowsService1`, then the executable file would be named `WindowsService1.exe`.

7. Install the Windows Service with a command line utility named `InstallUtil.exe`. (As previously mentioned, a service cannot be started by just running the EXE file.)

8. Start the Windows Service with the **Service Control Manager** (available in the **Control Panel | Administrative Tools** folder in Windows 2000, or the **Start | All Programs | Administrative Tools** folder in Windows XP) or with **Server Explorer** in Visual Studio .NET.

You can also start a service from the command console if the proper paths to .NET are set. The command is "`NET START <servicename>`". Note that the `<servicename>` used in this command is the name of the service, not the name of the executable in which the service resides.

Depending on the configuration of your system, a service being started with any of the methods above will sometimes fail with an error message that says the service did not start in a timely fashion. This may be because the .NET libraries and other initialization tasks did not finish fast enough to suit the **Service Control Manager**. If this happens, attempt the start the service again, and it will usually succeed the second time.

Note that steps 2 thru 5 can be done in a different order. It doesn't matter if the installer is added and configured before or after the logic that does the processing for the service is added.

At this point, a service is installed and running. The **Service Manager** or the **Server Explorer** can stop the service, or it will be automatically stopped when the system is shut down. The command to stop the service in a command console is "NET STOP <servicename>".

The service will not automatically start up the next time the system is booted unless the service is set for that. This can be done by setting the StartType property for the service to "Automatic" when developing the service or it can be done in the **Service Manager**. Right-clicking on the service in the **Service Manager** gives access to this capability.

This process outlined above is superficially similar to doing most other VB.NET projects. There are a few important differences, however:

❑ We cannot debug the project in the environment as you normally would a VB.NET program. The service must be installed and started before it can be debugged. It is also necessary to attach to the process for the service to do debugging. Details are included in *Debugging the Service*.

❑ Even though the end result of the development is an EXE, we should not include any message boxes or other visual elements in the code. The Windows Service executable is more like a component library in that sense, and should not have a visual interface. If you include visual elements such as message boxes, the results can vary. In some cases, the UI code will have no effect. In others cases, the service may hang when attempting to write to the user interface.

❑ Finally, we should be especially careful to handle all errors within the program. Since the program is not running in a user context, a runtime error has no place to report itself visually. We should handle all errors with structured exception handling, and use an event log or other offline means to record and communicate run-time errors.

Creating a Counter Monitor Service

To illustrate the steps we outlined, we'll create a simple service. The service will check the value of a performance counter, and when the value of the counter exceeds a certain value, the service will beep every three seconds. This is a good example for stepping through the process of creating, installing, and starting a Windows Service. It contains very little logic, and we can easily tell when it is working.

In the first phase of the example, we'll create a service that always beeps. Then in the second phase, we'll add logic to monitor the performance counter and only beep when the counter exceeds a value of 5:

1. Start a new VB project in Visual Studio of type **Windows Service**. Name the project CounterMonitor.

2. In the **Solution Explorer**, rename Service1.vb to CounterMonitor.vb.

3. Click on the design surface for CounterMonitor.vb. In the **Properties** window, change the (Name) property to CounterMonitor, and change the ServiceName property from Service1 to CounterMonitor (the (Name) property changes the name of the class on which the service is based, while the ServiceName property changes the name of the service as known to the **Service Control Manager**).

4. Right-click on the project for the service (not the solution, but the project), and select **Properties**. Under **Startup Object**, select `CounterMonitor`.

5. The **Designer** fails to change one reference to the old `Service1`. This is intentional. The `Sub Main` for the project can start multiple services, so the **Designer** cannot be sure when to change the name of the service or services being started. Consequently, you will need to change your service name manually in one line. Go into the code generated by the **Designer**, and look for this line:

```
ServicesToRun = New System.ServiceProcess.ServiceBase() {New Service1()}
```

Change the name "`Service1`" at the end of the line to "`CounterMonitor`". The line will then look like this:

```
ServicesToRun = New System.ServiceProcess.ServiceBase() _
                                        {New CounterMonitor()}
```

6. Open the **Toolbox**, and click on the **Components** (not the **Windows Forms**) tab. Drag a `Timer` control from the **Toolbox** onto the `CounterMonitor` component. It will appear on the design surface with the name `Timer1`.

7. In the **Properties** window for `Timer1`, change the `Interval` property to a value of 3000 (that's 3000 milliseconds, which will cause the timer to fire every 3 seconds).

8. Go to the code for `CounterMonitor.vb`. Inside the `OnStart` event handler (which is already created for you in the code), enter the following code:

```
Timer1.Enabled = True
```

9. In the `OnStop` event for the class, enter the following code:

```
Timer1.Enabled = False
```

10. Create an `Elapsed` event for timer by highlighting `Timer1` in the left-hand dropdown box at the top of the code editor window, and then selecting the `Elapsed` event in the right-hand dropdown.

11. In the `Elapsed` event, place the following line of code:

```
Beep()
```

12. Now add an installer to the project. Go back to the design surface for `CounterMonitor` and right-click on it. Select **Add Installer**. A new component called `ProjectInstaller1` is created and added to the project. It will have two additional components added to its design surface, named `ServiceProcessInstaller1` and `ServiceInstaller1`:

13. On the `ProjectInstaller1` design surface, highlight the `ServiceProcessInstaller1` control. In its **Properties** window, change the `Account` property to `LocalSystem`.

14. Highlight the `ServiceInstaller1` control. In its Properties window, change the `DisplayName` property to `CounterMonitor`.

15. Now build the project. An EXE for the service will be created named `CounterMonitor.exe`.

Installing the Service

Now we are ready to install the service. The utility for doing this must be run from a command line. The utility is called `InstallUtil.exe`, and it is located in the .NET utilities directory, which will typically be named `C:\WINNT\Microsoft.NET\Framework\v1.0.3705` on Windows 2000 and NT systems, or `C:\Windows\Microsoft.NET\Framework\v1.0.3705` on Windows XP.

You can easily access this utility (and all the other .NET utilities in that directory) using an option off of the Programs Menu that is installed with VS.NET. Choose **Microsoft Visual Studio.NET | Visual Studio .NET Tools | Visual Studio .NET Command Prompt**. This will result in display of a command window. Change to the directory that contains `CounterMonitor.exe` and run the following command:

```
InstallUtil CounterMonitor.exe
```

You should look at the messages generated by `InstallUtil.exe` to make sure that the installation of the service was successful. The utility will generate several lines of information, and if it is successful, the last two lines will be:

```
The Commit phase completed successfully.

The transacted install has completed.
```

If these two lines do not appear, you will need to read all the information generated by the utility to find out why the install did not work. Reasons might include a bad path name for the executable, or trying to install the service again when it is already installed (it must be uninstalled before it can be reinstalled – see below).

Starting the Service

Later in this chapter, we will create our own 'control panel' screen to start and stop the service. But to test it, we will use the **Server Explorer** in Visual Studio .NET. Open the Server Explorer in Visual Studio .NET and expand the Service node. The resulting screen will look something like this:

727

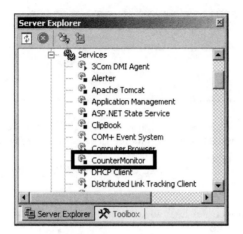

If the CounterMonitor service does not appear in the list, the installation was unsuccessful. Try the installation again and check the error messages.

Right-click on the CounterMonitor service. Select the **Start** menu option. You will hear the service begin beeping every three seconds. You can stop the service by right-clicking on it again, and selecting the **Stop** menu option.

You can also use the **Service Control Manager** built-in to Windows to start the CounterMonitor service:

Start CounterMonitor by right-clicking on it and selecting **Start**. As before, you will hear your computer begin to beep every three seconds. You can stop the service by right-clicking on CounterMonitor and selecting **Stop**. Note that if you already started the service via the Server Explorer (as discussed above), then it will be in a **Started** state when you go into the **Service Control Manager** program.

Uninstalling the Service

Uninstalling the service is very similar to installing it. The service must be in a stopped state before it can be uninstalled, but the uninstall operation will attempt to stop the service if it is running. The uninstall operation is done in the same command window as the install operation, and the command used is the same as the one for installation, except that the option /u is included just before the path for the service:

```
InstallUtil.exe /u C:\MyServices\CounterMonitor.exe
```

You can tell that the uninstall was successful if the information displayed by the utility contains the line:

```
Service CounterMonitor was successfully removed from the system.
```

If the uninstall is unsuccessful, you should read the rest of the information to find out why. Besides typing in the wrong path name, another common reason for failure is trying to uninstall a service that is in a running state and could not be stopped in a timely fashion.

Once you have uninstalled CounterMonitor, it will no longer show up in the list of available services to start and stop (at least after a refresh it won't).

> **A Windows Service must be uninstalled and reinstalled every time you make changes to it. You should uninstall CounterMonitor now because we're about to add new capabilities to it.**

Monitoring a Performance Counter

Performance counters are a system-level function of Windows 2000, XP, and NT. They are used to track usage of system resources. Performance counters can be expressed as counts (number of times a web page was hit), or percentages (how much disk space is left), or other types of information. Many counters are automatically maintained by the operating system, but applications can create and manage their own performance counters.

To demonstrate how services can interact with system-level functionality, we will add the capability to our CounterMonitor to monitor a particular performance counter, and only beep when the performance counter exceeds a certain value.

Performance counters can be monitored by a user with the Performance Monitor. There are a variety of performance counters built-in to the operating system, providing access to information such as the number of threads currently active on the system, or the number of documents in a print queue. Any of these, and any custom performance counters, can be graphed in the Performance Monitor.

Creating a Performance Counter

We will create a performance counter named `ServiceCounter`. Then we will change `CounterMonitor` to check that counter and only beep when its value is over 5. To test it, we will create a small Windows Forms application that increments and decrements the counter.

Performance counters are typically accessed in Visual Studio.NET through the **Server Explorer** tab. To see the available performance counters, open the **Server Explorer**, which will look much like the following screen:

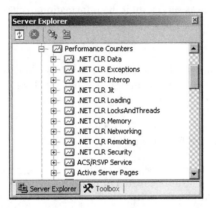

To see the categories of performance counters, click the plus sign next to the **Performance Counters** option in the **Server Explorer**. Several dozen categories will be shown. You can look at the counters in any particular category by clicking on the plus sign next to the category.

You can also create new categories and new counters. For this example, you need to create a new category for our counter called `Service Counters`. To do that, right-click on the **Performance Counters** option in the **Server Explorer** and select the **Create New Category** ... option. In the resulting dialog, enter the name of the category as `Service Counters`, and create a new counter by clicking the **New** button and entering `TestCounter` for the name.

Integrating the Counter into the Service

Using a performance counter in the `CounterMonitor` service is straightforward. Open the `CounterMonitor` project, and go to the design surface for `CounterMonitor`. Then open the **Server Explorer** so that it shows the `TestCounter` that we created. Click on `TestCounter` and drag it onto the `CounterMonitor` design surface.

A new control named `PerformanceCounter1` will be shown. The performance counter is now ready to use. Change the logic in the `Elapsed` event for `Timer1` to look like this:

```
If PerformanceCounter1.RawValue > mnMaxValue Then
    Beep()
End If
```

The `RawValue` property being used in this code fetches the unformatted value of the counter. For counters that track whole numbers (such as the number of times a web page is hit), the `RawValue` property is normally used to get the value of the counter for testing or display. Some other types of counters use a `NextValue` method to get a formatted value. See the `CounterType` property of the `PerformanceCounter` class for more on the types of performance counters available.

Next, put this statement in the code module just under the line that begins with `Inherits`:

```
Dim mnMaxValue As Integer = 5
```

Now build the service again, and install it as we did before. Start the service. It should not beep at this point, because the value in the performance counter is zero. You can leave the counter running at this point, because we will now create a program to change the value in the performance counter, and thus make the service begin beeping.

Changing the Value in the Performance Counter

To manipulate the performance counter, we will build a small forms-based application. Close the `CounterMonitor` solution in Visual Studio, and start a new **Windows Application** Project named `CounterTest`. Place two buttons on `Form1` and change their properties as follows:

Name	Text
btnIncrement	Increment Counter
btnDecrement	Decrement Counter

Then open the **Server Explorer** and drag the `TestCounter` onto the form, just as you did with the `CounterMonitor` project. As with all non-visible components from the toolbox, the counter will appear in the component tray (just under the form) rather than on the form design surface.

The `PerformanceCounter1` control for `CounterTest` needs one property change. The `ReadOnly` property of the control needs to be set to `False`. This will allow the application to manipulate the counter. (This change was unnecessary for the `CounterMonitor` Windows Service project, because that project only reads the value of the performance counter and does not change it.)

Now double-click `btnIncrement` to get to its click event. Place the following code in the event:

```
PerformanceCounter1.Increment()
```

Double-click the `btnDecrement` to get to its click event. Place the following code in the event:

```
PerformanceCounter1.Decrement()
```

Run the program and click the increment button six times. If the `CounterMonitor` service is running, on the sixth click it will begin beeping because the value in the counter has exceeded five. Then click the decrement button a couple of times, and the beeping will stop.

If you want to monitor the current value of the counter, select Control Panel I Administrative Tools I Performance. This program, the Performance Monitor, allows the value of counters to be graphed. You add a counter for display by right-clicking on the right-hand portion of the Performance Monitor, and adding a counter in the dialog that pops up. You can use the help for this program for more details on displaying counters in the Performance Monitor.

Communicating with the Service

Up to this point, we've seen how to:

❑ Create a service with Visual Basic .NET

❑ Start and stop a service with the Server Explorer in Visual Studio .NET or the Service Control Manager in the control panel

❑ Make a service work with a system level function such as a performance counter

If it is sufficient to start, stop, and check on the service through the Server Explorer or Service Control Manager, and there is no need to do any other communication with the service, then the above procedures are all you need. But it is often helpful to create a specialized application to manipulate your service. This application will typically be able to start and stop a service, and to check on its status. It may also need to communicate with the service to change its configuration. Such an application is often referred to as a **control panel** for the service, even though it does not necessarily reside in the operating system's Control Panel. A commonly-used example of such an application is the SQL Server Service Manager, whose icon appears in the tray on the Taskbar (normally in the lower right section of the screen) if you have SQL Server 2000 installed.

Such an application needs a way to communicate with the service. The .NET Framework base class that is used for such communication is the ServiceController class. It is in the System.ServiceProcess namespace. You need to add a reference to System.ServiceProcess.dll (which contains this namespace) before a project can use the ServiceController class.

The ServiceController class provides an interface to the Service Control Manager, which coordinates all communication with Windows Services. However, we don't have to know anything about the Service Control Manager to use the ServiceController class. We just manipulate the properties and methods of the ServiceController class, and any necessary communication with the Service Control Manager is accomplished on our behalf behind the scenes.

It's a good idea to use exactly *one* instance of the ServiceController class for each service you are controlling. Multiple instances of ServiceController that are communicating with the same service can have timing conflicts. Typically, that means using a module-level object variable to hold the reference to the active ServiceController, and instantiating the ServiceController during the initialization logic for the application. The following example uses this technique.

The ServiceController Class

The constructor for the ServiceController requires the name of the Windows Service with which it will be communicating. This is the same as the name that was placed in the ServiceName property of the class that defined the service. We'll see how to instantiate the ServiceController class shortly.

The ServiceController class has several members that are useful in manipulating services. Here are the most important methods:

Method	Purpose
Start	A method to start up the service.
Stop	A method to stop the service.
Refresh	A method to make sure the ServiceController object contains the latest state of the service (needed because the service might be manipulated from another program).
ExecuteCommand	A method used to send a custom command to the service. We will cover this method in the section on *Custom Commands* below.

Here are the most important properties:

Property	Purpose
CanStop	A property indicating whether the service can be stopped.
ServiceName	A property containing the name of the associated service.
Status	An enumerated property that indicates whether a service is stopped, started, in process of being started, and so on. The ToString method on this property is useful for getting the status in a string form for text messages. The possible values of the enumeration are: ContinuePending – The service is attempting to continue Paused – The service is paused PausePending – The service is attempting to go into a paused state Running – The service is running StartPending – The service is starting Stopped – The service is not running StopPending – The service is stopping

Table continued on following page

Property	Purpose
ServiceType	A property that indicates the type of service. The result is an enumerated value. The enumerations are: Win32OwnProcess – The service uses its own process (this is the default for a service created in .NET). Win32ShareProcess – The service shares a process with another service (this advanced capability is not covered here). Adapter, FileSystemDriver, InteractiveProcess, KernelDriver, RecognizerDriver – These are low-level service types that cannot be created with Visual Basic .NET because the ServiceBase class does not support the types. However, the value of the ServiceType property may still have these values for services created with other tools.

Integrating a ServiceController into the Example

To manipulate the service, we'll enhance the CounterTest program we created earlier. Here are step-by-step instructions to do that:

1. Add three new buttons to the CounterTest form, with the following names and text labels:

Name	Text
btnCheckStatus	"Check Status"
btnStartService	"Start Service"
btnStopService	"Stop Service"

2. Add a reference to the DLL that contains the ServiceController class. To do this, select **Project | Add Reference**. On the .NET tab, highlight the **System.ServiceProcess.dll** option, and press the **Select** button. Then press the **OK** button.

3. Add this line at the top of the code for Form1:

```
Imports System.ServiceProcess
```

4. As we discussed, the project needs to use only one instance of the ServiceController class. Create a module-level object reference to a ServiceController class by adding the following line of code:

```
Dim myController As ServiceController
```

5. Create a `Form Load` event in `Form1`, and place the following line of code in it to instantiate the `ServiceController` class:

```
myController = New ServiceController("CounterMonitor")
```

We now have a `ServiceController` class named `myController` that we can use to manipulate the `CounterMonitor`. In the click event for `btnCheckStatus`, place the following code:

```
Dim sStatus As String
myController.Refresh()
sStatus = myController.Status.ToString

MsgBox(myController.ServiceName & " is in state:" & sStatus)
```

In the click event for `btnStartService`, place the following code:

```
Try
    myController.Start()
Catch exp As Exception
    MsgBox("Could not start service")
End Try
```

In the click event for `btnStopService`, place the following code:

```
If myController.CanStop Then
    myController.Stop()
Else
    MsgBox("Service cannot be stopped")
End If
```

Run and test the program. The service may already be running because of one of your previous tests. Make sure the performance counter is high enough to make the service beep, and then test starting and stopping the service.

More About ServiceController

`ServiceController` classes can be created for any Windows Service, not just those created in .NET. For example, you could instantiate a `ServiceController` class that was associated with the Windows Service for Internet Information Server (IIS), and use it to start, pause, and stop IIS. The code would look just like the code used above for the application that controlled the `CounterMonitor` service. The only difference is that the name of the service would need to be changed in the line that instantiates the `ServiceController` (step 5 above).

It's also useful to emphasize that the `ServiceController` is not communicating directly with the service. It must go through the **Services Control Manager**. That means the requests from the Service Controller to start, stop, or pause a service do not behave synchronously. As soon as the `ServiceController` has passed the request to the `ServicesControlManager`, it continues to execute its own code without waiting for the **Service Control Manager** to pass on the request, or for the service to act on the request.

Custom Commands

Some services need additional operations besides starting and stopping. For example, for our CounterMonitor, we might want to set the threshold value of the performance counter that causes the service to begin beeping, or we might want to change the interval between beeps.

With most components, we would implement such functionality through a public interface. That is, we would put public properties and methods on the component. However, we cannot do this with a Windows Service, because it has no public interface that we can get to from outside the service.

To deal with this need, the interface for a Windows Service contains a special event called OnCustomCommand. The event arguments include a numeric code that can service as a command sent to the Windows Service. The code can be any number in the range 128 to 255. (Those numbers under 128 are reserved for use by the operating system.)

To fire the event and send a custom command to a service, the ExecuteCommand method of the ServiceController is used. The ExecuteCommand method takes the numeric code that needs to be sent to the service as a parameter. When this method is accessed, the ServiceController class tells the **Service Control Manager** to fire the OnCustomCommand event in the service, and to pass it the numeric code.

To see this process in action, let's go through an example. Suppose we want to be able to change the interval between beeps for our CounterMonitor service. We cannot directly send the beep interval that we want, but we can pick various values of the interval, and associate a custom command numeric code with each.

Suppose we want to be able to set intervals of one second, three seconds (the default), or ten seconds. We could set up the following correspondence:

Custom command numeric code	Beep interval
201	One second (1000 milliseconds)
203	Three seconds (3000 milliseconds)
210	Ten seconds (10000 milliseconds)

The correspondence between code and times we have chosen is completely arbitrary. We could use any codes between 128 and 255 to associate with our beep intervals. The ones above were chosen because they are easy to remember.

First, we need to change the CounterMonitor service so that it is able to accept the custom commands for the beep interval. To do that, first make sure the CounterMonitor service is uninstalled from any previous installs. Then open the Visual Studio .NET project for the CounterMonitor service.

Create an OnCustomCommand event in the service. To do this, first open the code window for CounterMonitor.vb. Then select **(Overrides)** in the left dropdown above the code window, and select **OnCustomCommand** in the right dropdown. This will generate the shell event. In the OnCustomCommand event, place the following code:

```
        Timer1.Enabled = False
        Select Case command
            Case 201
                Timer1.Interval = 1000
            Case 203
                Timer1.Interval = 3000
            Case 210
                Timer1.Interval = 10000
        End Select
        Timer1.Enabled = True
```

Now build the CounterMonitor service, re-install it, and start it.

Now we can enhance our CounterTest application that we created earlier to set the interval. To allow the user to pick the interval, we will use radio buttons. On the CounterTest program Form1 (which currently contains five buttons), place three radio buttons. Set their text labels as follows:

```
RadioButton1.Text   "One second"
RadioButton2.Text   "Three seconds"
RadioButton3.Text   "Ten seconds"
```

Then place a button directly under the option buttons. Name it btnSetInterval, and set its text to Set Interval. In the click event for this button, place the following code:

```
        Dim nIntervalCommand As Integer = 203
        If RadioButton1.Checked Then
            nIntervalCommand = 201
        End If
        If RadioButton2.Checked Then
            nIntervalCommand = 203
        End If
        If RadioButton3.Checked Then
            nIntervalCommand = 210
        End If
        myController.ExecuteCommand(nIntervalCommand)
```

At this point, Form1 should look something like the sample screen below:

Start the `MonitorTest` control program, and test the ability to change the beep interval. Remember to make sure the performance counter is high enough so that the `CounterMonitor` service beeps. Also remember that every time you stop and restart the service, it will reset the beep interval to three seconds.

Passing Strings to a Service

Since the `OnCustomCommand` event only takes numeric codes, we cannot directly pass strings to the service. For example, if we wanted to reconfigure a directory name for a service, we could not just send the directory name over.

Instead it would be necessary to place the information to be passed to the service in a file in some known location on disk. Then a custom command for the service could instruct it to look at the standard file location, and read the information in the file. What the service did with the contents of the file would, of course, be customized for the service.

Creating a File Watcher

Now let's step through another example to illustrate what a Windows Service can do and how to construct one. We will build a service that monitors a particular directory, and reacts when a new or changed file is placed in the directory. The example Windows Service application waits for those files, extracts information from them, and then logs an event to a system log to record the file change.

As before, we create a Windows Service from the built-in template named **Windows Service** in the **New Project** screen. Start by creating a new project and selecting the **Windows Service** template. Name this project **FileWatcherService** and click on **OK**. This will create a new service class called `Service1.vb`. Rename this to `FileWatcherService.vb`. Then right-click on the design surface, select **Properties**, and set the `ServiceName` property to `FileWatcherService`.

As in the first example, you will need to reset the project's start object to `FileWatcherService`, and to change the name `Service1` to `FileWatcherService` in the designer code that starts the service.

Writing Events Using an Eventlog

We will make sure the service is doing its job by having it write events to a system event log. Event logs are available under Windows NT, Windows 2000, and Windows XP. As with many other system-level features, the use of event logs is simplified in .NET because a .NET Framework base class does most of the work.

There are three event logs on the system: `Application`, `Security`, and `System`. Normally, your applications should only write to the `Application` log. A property of a log entry called `Source` identifies the application writing the message. This property does not have to be the same as the executable name of the application, but is often given that name to make it easy to identify the source of the message.

You can look at the events in the event log by using the Event Viewer. It is in Control Panel | Administrative Tools | Event Viewer on Windows 2000, and Start | All Programs | Administrative Tools | Event Viewer on Windows XP. We will use the event viewer in our example below to make sure our service is generating events.

The AutoLog Property

Early in the chapter, we briefly mentioned that the `AutoLog` property of the `ServiceBase` class determines whether the service automatically writes events to the Application log. The `AutoLog` property instructs the service to use the application event log to report command failures, as well as information for `OnStart`, `OnStop`, `OnPause`, and `OnContinue` events on the service. What is actually logged to the event log is an entry saying Service started successfully and Service stopped successfully, and any errors that might have occurred.

We can turn off the event log reporting by setting the `AutoLog` property to `False` in the Properties window for the service. However, we will leave it set to `True` for our example. That means some events will be logged automatically (without us including any code for them). Then we will add some code to our service to log other events not covered by the `AutoLog` property.

First, though, we need to implement a file monitoring control into our project.

Creating a FileSystemWatcher

For performance reasons, we should do all of our work on a separate thread to our main application thread. We want to leave our main application free to accept any requests from the user or operating system. We can do this by using some of the different components that create their own threads when they are launched. The `Timer` component and the `FileSystemWatcher` component are two examples. When the `Timer` component fires its `Elapsed` event, a thread is spawned and any code placed within that event will work on that newly created thread. The same thing happens when the events for the `FileSystemWatcher` component fire.

You can learn more about threading .NET in Chapter 19.

The FileSystemWatcher Component

The `FileSystemWatcher` component is used to monitor a particular directory. The component implements `Created`, `Changed`, `Deleted`, and `Renamed` events, which are fired when files are placed in the directory, changed, deleted or renamed, respectively.

The operation that takes place when one of these events is fired is up to the application developer. Most often, logic is included to read and process the new or changed files. However, we are just going to write a message to a log file.

To implement the component in the project, drag-and-drop a `FileSystemWatcher` control from the Components tab of the Toolbox onto the designer surface of `FileWatcherService.vb`. This control will automatically be called `FileSystemWatcher1`.

The EnableRaisingEvents Property

The `FileSystemWatcher` control should not generate any events until the service is initialized and ready to handle them. To prevent this, set the `EnableRaisingEvents` property to `False`. This will prevent the control from firing any events. We will enable it during the `OnStart` event in the service.

These events fired by the `FileSystemWatcher` are controlled using the `NotifyFilter` property, discussed below.

The Path Property

Next, the path that we want to monitor is the TEMP directory on the C: drive, so set the Path property to C:\TEMP (be sure to check that there is a TEMP directory on your C: drive). Of course, this path can be changed to monitor any directory depending on your system, including network or removable drives.

The NotifyFilter Property

We only want to watch for when a file is freshly created, or the last modified value of a file has changed. To do this we set the NotifyFilter property to **FileName, LastWrite**. We could also watch for other changes such as attributes, security, size, and directory name changes as well, just by changing the NotifyFilter property. Note that we specify multiple changes to watch for by including a list of changes separated by commas.

The Filter Property

The types of files that we will look for are text files. This is done by setting the Filter property to *.txt.

The IncludeSubdirectories Property

If we wanted to watch subdirectories, we would set the IncludeSubdirectories property to True. In this sample, we're leaving it as False, which is the default value.

You should have the following properties set:

Adding FileSystemWatcher Code to OnStart and OnStop

Now that we have some properties set, let's add some code to the OnStart event. We need to start the FileSystemWatcher1 component so it will start triggering events when files are created or copied into the directory we're monitoring, so we set the EnableRaisingEvents property to True:

```
Protected Overrides Sub OnStart(ByVal args() As String)

    ' Start monitoring for files
    FileSystemWatcher1.EnableRaisingEvents = True
End Sub
```

Once our file monitoring properties are initialized, we are ready to start the monitoring.

When the service stops we need to stop the file monitoring process. Add this code to your OnStop event:

```
Protected Overrides Sub OnStop()
    ' Stop monitoring for files
    FileSystemWatcher1.EnableRaisingEvents = False

End Sub
```

The EventLog component

Now we are ready to place an EventLog component in the service to facilitate logging of events. Drag and drop an EventLog control from the **Components** tab of the **Toolbox** onto the designer surface of FileWatcherService.vb. This control will automatically be called EventLog1.

Set the Log property for Eventlog1 to Application, and set the Source property to FileWatcherService.

The Created Event

Next, we will place some logic in the Created event of our FileSystemWatcher component to log when a file has been created. This event will fire when a file has been placed or created in the directory that we are monitoring. This event fires because the last modified information on the file has changed.

Select **FileSystemWatcher1** from the **Class Name** drop down and select **Created** from the **Method Name** drop down, and the Created event will be added to your code. Add code to the Created event as follows:

```
Public Sub FileSystemWatcher1_Created(ByVal sender As Object, _
        ByVal e As System.IO.FileSystemEventArgs) _
        Handles FileSystemWatcher1.Created
    Dim sMessage As String
    sMessage = "File created in directory - file name is " + e.Name
    EventLog1.WriteEntry(sMessage)
End Sub
```

Notice that the event arguments object (the object named "e" in the event parameters) includes a property called Name. This property holds the name of the file that generated the event.

At this point, we could add the other events for FileSystemWatcher (Changed, Deleted, Renamed) in a similar way and create corresponding log messages for those events. To keep the example simple, we'll just do the Created event in this service.

We need to add an Installer class to this project to install the application. This is done as it was in the earlier CounterMonitor example, by right-clicking on the design surface for the service and selecting **Add Installer**. Don't forget to change the Account property to LocalSystem, or set it to User and fill in the Username and Password properties.

As before, you must install the service using InstallUtil.exe. Then you can start it with the **Server Explorer** or the **Service Manager**.

Upon successful compilation of these steps, we will get a message logged for any file with a `.txt` extension that we copy or create in the monitored directory. So, after dropping some sample text files into our monitored directory, we can use the **Event Viewer** to check and make sure the events are present.

Here is an example screen showing the **Event Viewer** with several example messages created by our service:

If you right-click on one of the events for `FileWatcherService`, you'll see a detail screen. Notice that the message corresponds to the event log message we constructed in the `Created` event of the `FileSystemWatcher` control in the service:

Debugging the Service

Because a service must be run from within the context of the Services Control Manager rather than from within VS.NET, debugging a service is not as straightforward as debugging other Visual Studio .NET application types. To debug a service, we must start the service and then attach a debugger to the process in which it is running. We can then debug your application using all of the standard debugging functionality of VS.NET.

> You should not attach to a process unless you know what the process is and understand the consequences of attaching to and possibly killing that process.

To avoid going through this extra effort, you may want to test out most of the code in your service in a standard Windows Forms application. This test-bed application can have the same components (FileSystemWatchers, EventLogs, Timers, and so on) as the Windows Service, and thus will be able to run the same logic in events. Once you have checked out the logic in this context, you can just copy and paste it into a Windows Service application.

However, there will be some occasions for which the service itself needs to be debugged directly. So it's important to understand how to attach to the service's process and do direct debugging. The rest of this section explains how to do that.

The only time you can debug a service is when it's running. When you attach the debugger to the service, you are interrupting the service. The service is suspended for a short period while you attach to it. The service will also be interrupted when you place breakpoints and step through you code.

Attaching to the service's process allows you to debug most, but not all, of the service's code. For instance, because the service has already been started, you cannot debug the code in the service's OnStart method this way, or the code in the Main method that is used to load the service. To debug the OnStart event or any code under the Component Designer generated code region, you have to add a dummy service and start that service first. In the dummy service, you would create an instance of the service that you want to debug. You can place some code in a Timer object and create the new instance of the object that you want to debug after thirty seconds or so. You want to allow yourself enough time to attach to the debugger before the new instance is created. Meanwhile, you can place breakpoints in your startup code to debug those events.

To Debug a Service

Follow these steps to debug a service:

1. Install your service.

2. Start your service, either from the Services Control Manager, Server Explorer, or from code.

3. In VS.NET, load the solution for the service. Then select Processes from the Debug menu. The Processes dialog box appears:

4. For a Windows Service, the process you want to attach to is not a foreground process, so you must check the checkbox next to the Show system processes option.

5. In the Available Processes section, click on the process indicated by the executable name for your service, and then the Attach button. The Attach to Process dialog box appears:

6. Make sure that just the **Common Language Runtime** option is selected and then click **OK**. You will return to the **Processes** dialog. Before you close the **Processes** dialog, you have the option to select either **Detach from this process** or **Terminate this process**, once debugging is finished. If you select the first option, your service will still run once you stop debugging. In this case, select **Terminate this process** and select **Close**. You can now debug your process.

7. Place a break point in the code for the service at the place you want to debug. Cause the code in the service to execute (by placing a file in a monitored directory, for example).

8. When finished, select **Stop Debugging** from the **Debug** menu. You can also select **Processes** from the **Debug** menu, click on your debugged process, and then click **Detach** or **Terminate**.

Let's go through an actual scenario, using our earlier `CounterMonitor` example. Bring up both the `CounterMonitor` project and the `CounterTest` project in separate instances of the VS.NET IDE. Then make sure that the `CounterMonitor` service has been started. It is best if you hear it beeping – that way you know it is working. If necessary, remember to increment the performance counter to make it beep.

In the `CounterMonitor` project, go to the **Debug** menu and select **Processes...**; you'll get a dialog that shows a list of the foreground processes on the system. Check the checkbox next to "Show system processes".

Once you do this, the list of processes will expand, and one of the processes in the list will be `CounterMonitor.exe`. That's the process you want. Highlight it and press the **Attach** button.

You'll then get a dialog asking you what program types you are interested in debugging. Since we are working solely within .NET, check the box next to **Common Language Runtime** and leave the rest unchecked. Then press the **OK** button on this dialog, and press the **Close** button on the **Processes** dialog. You are now attached to the process running `CounterMonitor` in the background.

Place a breakpoint on the first line of the `OnCustomCommand` event:

```
Timer1.Enabled = False
```

Now we are ready to check debugging. Bring up the `CounterTest` program, and start it. Press one of the radio buttons to change the beep interval. You will hear the beeping stop, because `CounterMonitor.exe` has entered debugging mode. Switch back to the `CounterMonitor` project, and the cursor will be on the breakpoint line in `OnCustomCommand`. You can use the normal commands at this point to step through the code.

Summary

In this chapter, we have seen a general overview of what a Windows Service is and how to create one with Visual Basic .NET. The techniques in this chapter can be used for many different types of background service. A few examples are:

❑ Automatically moving statistical files from a database server to a web server

❑ Pushing general files across computers and platforms

❑   A watchdog timer to ensure that a connection is always available

❑   An application to move and process FTP files, or indeed files received from any source

While Visual Basic .NET cannot be used to create every type of Windows Service, it is effective at creating many of the most useful ones. The .NET Framework classes for Windows Services make this creation relatively straightforward. The designers generate much of the routine code needed, and you as a developer can concentrate on the code that is specific to your particular Windows Service.

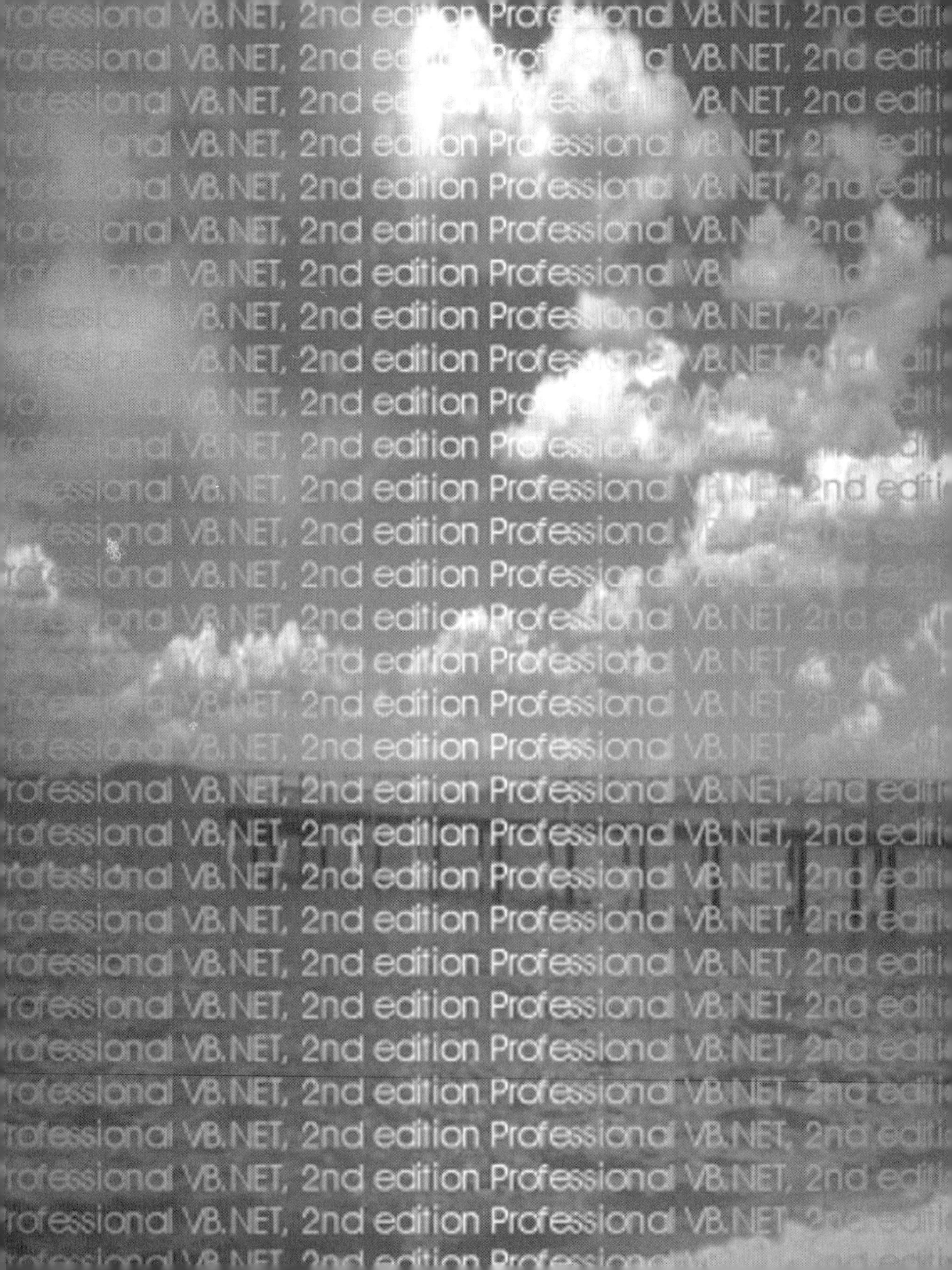
Professional VB.NET, 2nd edition

Web Services

To start this chapter, we're going to dive into short a history of multi-tier architecture and network operating systems. We'll discuss the early days of the network-as-the-computer, and some of the future. The reason for this diversion is so that we can understand the rationale behind **Web Services**.

We'll go on to look at a sample Web Service, make it accessible to the Internet, and access it from a client application – both with the VS .NET IDE and using command line tools. From there we'll move on to a key feature of Web Services – the **Service Repository**, **discovery**, and **UDDI** (**Universal Description, Discovery, and Integration**) – features which allow remote programmers to correctly access Web Services.

We'll get into more in-depth topics when we discuss the four namespaces found in the .NET Framework class library (`System.Web.Services`, `System.Web.Description`, `System.Web.Services.Discovery`, and `System.Web.Services.Protocols`) that deal with Web Services, and how to access them with Visual Basic .NET. Then we will move to a discussion of the serious topics, such as security, transactions, and the downsides of any distributed architecture (including Web Services). Finally, we'll wrap up with a short discussion of where we go from here, and how we get there.

Introduction to Web Services

A Web Service is a group of functions, packaged together for use in a common framework throughout a network. This is shown in the following diagram, where Web Services provide access to information through standard Internet Protocols via a **WSDL (Web Services Description Language)** contract – that is, an XML description of the service.

This simple concept provides for a very wide variety of potential uses by developers of Internet and enterprise applications alike:

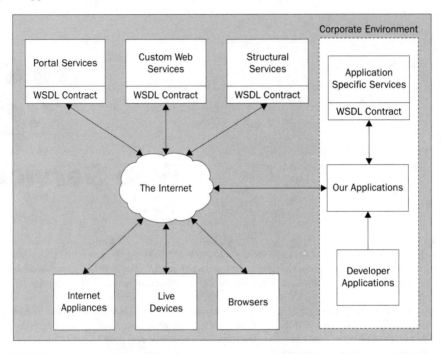

Web Services are going to be the heart of the next generation of systems architecture because they are:

❑   Architecture neutral – Web Services don't depend on a proprietary wire format, schema description, or discovery standard.

❑   Ubiquitous – Any service that supports the standards can support the service.

❑   Simple – Creating Web Services is easy, quick and can be free. The data schema is human readable. Any language can participate.

❑   Interoperable – Since the Web Services all speak the same standards, they can all speak to one another.

In basic terms, a Web Service is an object with an XML document describing all of the methods, properties, and events sitting between the code and the caller. Any body of code written in just about any language can be described with this XML document, and then any application that understands **SOAP (Simple Object Access Protocol)** can access the object. That's because the parameters you'd type after the function name are passed via XML to the Web Service and because SOAP is an open standard.

Microsoft has put a wrapper around all of the XML schemas that support Web Services (including SOAP and WSDL) so that they look like .NET or COM objects. We'll talk about how the world views a Web Service, then how Microsoft views Web Services.

Early Architectural Designs

An understanding of the history of the search for a decent **remote method invocation (RMI)** protocol is imperative to our understanding of why Web Services are so important. Each of the RMI systems created before Web Services solved a particular set of problems, and we will see how Web Services crosses platform boundaries to solve them all.

The Network Angle

Throughout the history of computing, the networking operations were largely handled by the operating system. UNIX, the networking host of early computing, featured a body of shell operations that gave remarkable user control over the operations of the network. Personal computing was slower to catch up: Microsoft and Apple software didn't inherently support networking protocols until the mid 1990s. Third party add-ons by Novell and Banyan were available earlier, but they were only adjunct to the operating system. The concept of the network being the computer didn't fully infiltrate the development community until the expansion of the World Wide Web.

Application Development

Let's break from networking for a minute and look at how application development progressed through this time. Early Time Sharing Operation systems allowed several people to use the same application with its built-in data. These single tier systems didn't allow for growth in the system size, and data redundancy became the standard, with nightly batch jobs synchronizing the data becoming commonplace through the 70s and early 80s.

Eventually, the opportunity presented by networks became the overriding factor in systems development, and enterprise network developers began offering the loosely termed **Object Request Brokers (ORBs)** on their systems: Microsoft's MTS, **CORBA (Common Object Request Broker Architecture)**, and the like. These ORBs allowed for the separation of the user interface from the business logic using tightly coupled method pooling. This three-tier architecture brings us to the present in development terms, so let's step back for a second and let networking catch up.

Merging the Two with the Web

The HTTP protocol was born in 1990. There had been several other information delivery protocols before, like Gopher, but what made HTTP different were the extensibility of the related language, HTML, and the flexibility of the transport layer, TCP/IP. Suddenly movement of many formats of data was possible in a stateless, distributed way. Software-as-a-service was on its way.

Over the next decade, low-level protocols supported by network systems and the Internet became a staple in applications, with SMTP and FTP providing file and information transfer among distributed servers. **Remote procedure calls (RPC)** took things to the next level, but were platform specific, with UNIX implementations in CORBA and Microsoft's **Distributed COM (DCOM)** leading the pack.

Enterprise development took a clue from the emerging technologies in WAN networking and personal computing, and development for these large-scale business systems began to mature. As usage of networks grew, developers began to solve problems of scalability, reliability, and adaptability, with the traditional flat-format programming model. Multi-tier development began to spread the data, processing, and user interface of applications over several machines connected by local area networks.

This made applications more scalable and reliable by allowing for growth and providing redundancy. Gradually, vendor compliance and the Java programming language provided adaptability, allowing the applications to run in a variety of circumstances on a variety of platforms.

However, there was a dichotomy between the capabilities of the network and the features of the programming environment. Specifically, after the introduction of XML there still existed no 'killer app' using its power. XML is a subset of Standard Generalized Markup Language (SGML), an international standard that describes the relationship between a document's content and its structure. It allows developers to create their own tags for hierarchical data transport in an HTML-like format. With HTTP as a transport and SOAP as a protocol, there still needed to be an interoperable, ubiquitous, simple, broadly supported system for the execution of business logic throughout the world of Internet Application development.

The Foundations of Web Services

The hunt began with a look at existing protocols. As has been the case for years, the Microsoft versus Sun Alliance debate was heating up among RPC programmers. CORBA versus DCOM was, and continues to be, a source of continuing argument for developers using those platforms for distributed object development. After Sun added Remote Method Invocation to Java with Java-RMI, we had three distributed object protocols that fit none of the requirements we set out.

First, let's focus on DCOM and RMI, because they are manufacturer-specific. CORBA is centrally managed by the Object Management Group, so it is a special case and should be considered separately.

RMI and DCOM provide distributed object invocation for their respective platforms – extremely important in this era of distributed networks. Both allow for the enterprise-wide reuse of existing functionality, which dramatically reduces cost and time-to-market. Both provide encapsulated object methodology, preventing changes to one set of business logic from affecting another. Finally, similar to ORB-managed objects, maintenance and client weight are reduced by the simple fact that applications using distributed objects are by nature multi-tier.

DCOM

DCOM's best feature is the fact that it is based on COM – surely the most prevalent desktop object model in use today. COM components are shielded from one another, and calls between them are so well-defined by the OS specific languages that there is practically no overhead to the methods. Each COM object is instantiated in its own space, with the necessary security and protocol providers. If an object in one process needs to call an object in another process, COM handles the exchange by intercepting the call and forwarding it though one of the network protocols.

When you use DCOM, all you are doing is making the wire a bit longer. In NT4 Microsoft added the TCP/IP protocol to the COM network architecture and essentially made DCOM Internet-savvy. Aside from the setup on the client and server, the inter-object calls are transparent to the client, and even to the programmer.

Any Microsoft programmer can tell you, though, that DCOM has its problems. First, there is a customer wire transport function, so most firewalls will not allow DCOM calls to get through – even though they are by nature quite benign. There is no way to query DCOM about the methods and properties available unless you have the opportunity to get the source code or request the remote component locally. In addition, there is no standard data transfer protocol (though that is less of a problem since DCOM is mostly for Microsoft networks).

Remote Method Invocation in Java

RMI is Sun's answer to DCOM. Java relies on a really neat, but very proprietary, protocol called Java Object Serialization, which protects objects marshaled as a stream. The client and server both need to be constructed in Java for this to work, but it simplifies remote method invocation even more, as Java doesn't care if the serialization takes place on one machine or across a continent. Similar to DCOM, RMI allows the object developer to define an interface for remote access to certain methods.

CORBA

CORBA uses Internet Inter-ORB Protocol to provide remote method invocation. It is remarkably similar to Java Object Serialization in this regard. Since it is only a specification, though, it is supported by a number of languages on diverse operating systems. With CORBA, the ORB does all the work, such as finding the pointer to the parent, instantiating it so that it can receive remote requests, carrying messages back and forth, and dispute arbitration and trash collection. The CORBA objects use specially designed sub-ORB objects balled Basic or Portable Object Adapters to communication with remote ORBs, allowing developers more leeway in code reuse.

At first sight, it seems CORBA is our ace-in-the-hole. Only one problem – it doesn't really work that way. CORBA suffers from the same thing the web browsers do – poor implementations of the standards, causing lack of interoperability between Object Request Brokers. With IE and Netscape, a little differential in the way the pages display is written off as cosmetic. If there is a problem with the CORBA standard though, it is a *real* problem. Not just looks are affected, but network interactions too, as if there were 15 different implementations of HTTP.

The Problems

The principal problem of the DCOM/CORBA/RMI methods is the complexity of the implementation. The transfer protocol of each of these is based on manufacturer standards, generally preventing interoperability. In essence, the left hand has to know what the right hand is doing. This prevents a company using DCOM from communicating with a company using CORBA, emphasizing platform as a reason for doing business with one another.

First, we have the problem of wire format. Each of these three methods uses an OS-specific wire format that encompasses information only supplied by the operating system in question. The problem with this is that two diverse machines cannot usually share information. The benefit is security; since the client and server can make assumptions about the availability of functionality, data security can be managed with API calls to the operating system.

The second problem is the number of issues associated with describing the format of the protocol. Aside from the actual transport layer, we have to have a schema or layout for the data that moves back and forth. Each of the three contemporary protocols makes great assumptions between the client and server. DCOM, for instance, provides ADO/RDS for data transport, whereas RMI has JDBC. While we can endlessly argue the benefits of one over the other, we'll agree on the fact that they don't play well together.

The third problem is how to know where to find broadly available services, even within your own network. We've all faced the problem of having to call up the COM+ MMC panel so we could remember how to spell this component or that method. When the method is resident on a server ten buildings over and we don't have access to the MMC console, the next step is digging through the text documentation – if there is any.

753

The Other Players

On a path to providing these services we stumble across a few other technologies. While **Java Applets** and Microsoft's **client-side ActiveX** aren't technically distributed object invocation, they do provide distributed computing and provide important lessons. Fortunately, we can describe both in the same section since they are largely the same, with different operating systems as their backbone.

Applets and client-side ActiveX are both attempts to use the HTTP protocol to send thick clients to the end user. In a circumstance where a user can provide a platform previously prepared to maintain a thicker-than-HTML client base to a precompiled binary, the ActiveX and Applet protocols pass small applications to the end user, usually running a web browser. These applications are still managed by their servers, at least loosely, and usually provide custom data transmission, utilizing the power of the client to manage the information distributed, as well as display it.

This concept was taken to the extreme with **Distributed Applet-based Massively Parallel Processing**, a strategy that used the power of the Internet to complete processor-intense tasks like 3D rendering or massive economic models with a small application installed on the user's computer. If you view the Internet as a massive collection of parallel processors – sitting mostly unused – you have the right idea. An example of this type of processing is provided by United Devices (http://www.ud.com).

What we learned here is that HTTP can provide distributed computing. The problem we discovered is that the tightly coupled connection between the client and server had to go, given the nature of today's large enterprises. The HTTP angle did show developers that using an industry recognized transport method did solve problem number one – wire format. Using HTTP meant that no matter what the network, the object could communicate. The client still had to know a lot about the service being sent, but the network didn't.

The goal is *Distributed Object Invocation Meets the World Wide Web.* The problems that face us are wire format, protocol, and discovery. The solution is a standards-based, loosely-coupled method invocation protocol with a huge catalog. Microsoft, IBM, and Ariba set out in 1999 to create just that, and generated the RFC for Web Services.

What All the Foundations Missed

You may notice that in reviewing the majority of the above services we have not mentioned much about language. This is because it was a problem that was overlooked by the foundations. Even RMI didn't see reality that you can't make everyone use the same language, even if it is a great language.

HTTP – A Language Independent Protocol

What we really need is a language independent protocol that allows for a standard wire transfer, protocol language, and catalog service. Java and Remote Scripting and ActiveX taught us that HTTP is the wire transfer of choice.

Why is this? What does HTTP do that is so great? First, it is simple. The header added to a communication by HTTP is straightforward enough that a power user could type it at a command prompt if he had to. Second, it doesn't require a special data protocol – it just uses ASCII text. Finally, it is extensible. Additional headers can be added to the HTTP header for application specific needs, and intermediary software just ignores it.

XML – Cross-Language Data Markup

Now that we have the standard wire transfer protocol that we know works, we need a language and a transport mechanism. Existing languages don't really have data description functions, aside from the data management object models like ADO. XML fits the bill because it is self-describing. There's no need for the left hand to know what the right hand is doing. An XML file transported over HTTP doesn't need to know the answering system's network protocol or its data description language. The concepts behind XML are so light and open; everyone can agree to support them. In fact, almost everyone has. XML has become the ASCII of the Web.

XML is important to Web Services because it provides a universal format for information to be passed from system to system. We knew that, but Web Services actually uses XML as the object invocation layer, changing the input and output to tightly formatted XML so to be platform and language independent.

SOAP – The Transfer We Need

Enter Simple Object Access Protocol (SOAP), which uses HTTP to package essentially one-way messages from service to service in such a way that business logic can interpolate a request/response pair. In order for your web page to get the above listing, for instance, a SOAP request would look something like this:

```
POST /Directory HTTP/1.1
Host: Ldap.companyname.com
Content-Type: text/xml;
charset="utf-8"
Content-Length: 33
SOAPAction: "Some-URI"

<SOAP-ENV:Envelope
 xmlns:SOAP-ENV="http://schemas.xmlsoap.org/soap/envelope/"
 SOAP-ENV:encodingStyle="http://schemas.xmlsoap.org/soap/encoding/">
  <SOAP-ENV:Body>
    <m:FindPerson xmlns:m="Some-URI">
      <NAME>sempf</NAME>
    </m: FindPerson>
  </SOAP-ENV:Body>
</SOAP-ENV:Envelope>
```

This is an HTTP page request, just like you'd see for an HTML page except the `Content-Type` specifies XML and there is the addition of the `SOAPAction` header. SOAP has made use of the two most powerful parts of HTTP – content neutrality and extensibility. Here is the response statement from the server:

```
HTTP/1.1 200 OK
Content-Type: text/xml;
charset="utf-8"
Content-Length: 66

<SOAP-ENV:Envelope
 xmlns:SOAP-ENV="http://schemas.xmlsoap.org/soap/envelope/"
 SOAP-ENV:encodingStyle="http://schemas.xmlsoap.org/soap/encoding/"/>
  <SOAP-ENV:Body>
    <m:FindPersonResponse xmlns:m="Some-URI">
```

```
        <DIRECTORY>Employees
        <PERSON>
           <NAME>Bill Sempf</NAME>
           <FUNCTION>Architect
              <TYPE>Web Services</TYPE>
           </FUNCTION>
           <CONTACT>
              <PHONE TYPE=CELL>123-456-7890</PHONE>
              <PHONE TYPE=HOME>555-111-2222</PHONE>
           </CONTACT>
        </PERSON>
        </DIRECTORY>
        </m: FindPersonResponse >
     </SOAP-ENV:Body>
  </SOAP-ENV:Envelope>
```

SOAP allows us to send the XML files back and forth among remote methods. It is tightly similar to XML-RPC, a protocol developed by Dave Winer in parallel with the SOAP protocol. Both protocols provide similar structures, but it is the official SOAP protocol that is used by VB.NET.

SOAP isn't specific to .NET, either. The SOAP Toolkit is a set of tools that Microsoft's Web Services Team provides free of charge. It contains a wonderful WSDL editor, retrofit objects for Windows 2000 and NT4 boxes, and more. You can find it at http://msdn.microsoft.com/webservices.

Web Services Description Language

A Web Services Description Language (WSDL) document is a set of definitions. Six elements are defined and used by the SOAP protocol: `types`, `message`, `portType`, `binding`, `port`, and `service`. Essentially adding another layer of abstraction, the purpose of WSDL is to isolate remote method invocations from their wire transport and data definition language. Once again, it is a specification, not a language, so it is much easier to get companies to agree to its use.

As WSDL is just a set of descriptions in XML; it has not so much a protocol as a grammar. Below you'll find the sample service contract for the `UpdateRemote` Web Service we'll be building later in the chapter. You will be able to see this file by surfing to http://localhost/WebService1/Service1.asmx?WSDL after you install the samples:

```
<?xml version="1.0" encoding="utf-8" ?>
<definitions xmlns:s="http://www.w3.org/2001/XMLSchema"
  xmlns:http="http://schemas.xmlsoap.org/wsdl/http/"
  xmlns:mime="http://schemas.xmlsoap.org/wsdl/mime/"
  xmlns:tm="http://microsoft.com/wsdl/mime/textMatching/"
  xmlns:soap="http://schemas.xmlsoap.org/wsdl/soap/"
  xmlns:soapenc="http://schemas.xmlsoap.org/soap/encoding/"
  xmlns:s0="http://Localhost/WebService1"
  targetNamespace="http://Localhost/WebService1"
  xmlns="http://schemas.xmlsoap.org/wsdl/">
<types>
 <s:schema attributeFormDefault="qualified" elementFormDefault="qualified"
    targetNamespace="http://Localhost/WebService1">
  <s:import namespace="http://www.w3.org/2001/XMLSchema" />
  <s:element name="AcceptUpdate">
   <s:complexType>
```

```
    <s:sequence>
     <s:element minOccurs="1" maxOccurs="1" name="dsDataSet"
                nillable="true">
       <s:complexType>
        <s:sequence>
        <s:element ref="s:schema" />
        <s:any />
       </s:sequence>
      </s:complexType>
     </s:element>
    </s:sequence>
   </s:complexType>
  </s:element>
  <s:element name="AcceptUpdateResponse">
   <s:complexType>
    <s:sequence>
     <s:element minOccurs="1" maxOccurs="1" name="AcceptUpdateResult"
       type="s:boolean" />
    </s:sequence>
   </s:complexType>
  </s:element>
</s:schema>
  </types>
<message name="AcceptUpdateSoapIn">
 <part name="parameters" element="s0:AcceptUpdate" />
</message>
<message name="AcceptUpdateSoapOut">
 <part name="parameters" element="s0:AcceptUpdateResponse" />
</message>
<portType name="Service1Soap">
 <operation name="AcceptUpdate">
  <input message="s0:AcceptUpdateSoapIn" />
  <output message="s0:AcceptUpdateSoapOut" />
 </operation>
</portType>
<portType name="Service1HttpGet" />
 <portType name="Service1HttpPost" />
  <binding name="Service1Soap" type="s0:Service1Soap">
   <soap:binding transport="http://schemas.xmlsoap.org/soap/http"
     style="document" />
   <operation name="AcceptUpdate">
   <soap:operation soapAction="http://Localhost/WebService1/AcceptUpdate"
     style="document" />
  <input>
   <soap:body use="literal" />
  </input>
  <output>
   <soap:body use="literal" />
  </output>
 </operation>
</binding>
<binding name="Service1HttpGet" type="s0:Service1HttpGet">
 <http:binding verb="GET" />
  </binding>
```

757

```
<binding name="Service1HttpPost" type="s0:Service1HttpPost">
 <http:binding verb="POST" />
</binding>
<service name="Service1">
 <port name="Service1Soap" binding="s0:Service1Soap">
  <soap:address location="http://localhost/WebService1/Service1.asmx" />
 </port>
 <port name="Service1HttpGet" binding="s0:Service1HttpGet">
  <http:address location="http://localhost/WebService1/Service1.asmx" />
 </port>
 <port name="Service1HttpPost" binding="s0:Service1HttpPost">
  <http:address location="http://localhost/WebService1/Service1.asmx" />
 </port>
</service>
</definitions>
```

This is what makes it all work. You'll notice that each of the inputs and outputs of the
`AcceptUpdateResponse` function are defined as elements in the schema. .NET uses this to build
library files that understand how best to format the outgoing requests – so no matter what operating
system develops the WSDL, as long as it is well formed, a Windows application can consume it with
SOAP and .NET.

In fact, IIS with the .NET Framework is set up to use the WSDL to provide a great user interface for
developers and consumers to check out and test Web Services. If you remove the ?wsdl from the above
URL you'll see a very nicely formatted documentation screen for the service. Click on the function
name and you'll get the screen shown below. This is all dynamically generated from the WSDL
document, which is dynamically generated from ASP.NET code. Abstraction makes it all work:

The benefit to knowing how WSDL works is being able to define your own descriptions. More documentation would be available on the listing of functions screen before this one, had we added it to the WSDL. Also, we could manually define HTTP POST and GET schemas – though it wouldn't do much good since the sole function of this particular service is to pass a Microsoft-specific DataSet.

Building a Web Service

Building Web Services with VS .NET is *incredibly* easy. Microsoft has made it a cakewalk to put together a new Web Service application and expose methods off of that Web Service.

To get started, all you need is an ASP.NET Web Service application. Visual Studio will ask you for the location of the web server. Enter this as http://localhost/MyWebService.

Unlike an ASP.NET Web Application project, Visual Studio will create an .asmx file rather than an .aspx file. .asmx is short for Active Server Methods, and its name comes from the fact that what we're going to do is add methods that will be exposed through the Web Service.

By default, the Designer for the new **Service1.asmx** file will appear. Right-click on the Designer and select **View Code**; you'll notice a commented out HelloWorld method. You'll also notice that this method is decorated with <WebMethod()>. This attribute (System.Web.Services.WebMethodAttribute) is what we use to tell ASP.NET that we want to expose this method over the Web Service.

Un-comment the HelloWorld method, leaving the WebMethod attribute in place.

```
<WebMethod()> Public Function HelloWorld() As String
   HelloWorld = "Hello World"
End Function
```

Next, add a new method called GoodbyeWorld, without a WebMethod attribute:

```
Public Function GoodbyeWorld() As String
   GoodbyeWorld = "Goodbye World"
End Function
```

Run the project and VS .NET will open the **Service1.asmx** file. By default, Web Services display a test interface that lets you see which methods are available, and also lets you execute the methods:

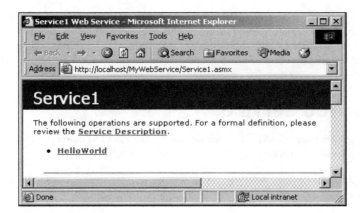

Notice how we can only see the `HelloWorld` method. This is the only method decorated with the `WebMethod` attribute, hence the reason why `GoodbyeWorld` and all of the inherited methods on the `Service1` class were not displayed.

If you click on the link, you'll be given the option to invoke the method:

If you do this, the URL http://localhost/MyWebService/Service1.asmx/HelloWorld? will be requested, which happens to be the URL for this specific method. You'll then see a SOAP document containing the results of the call:

```
<?xml version="1.0" encoding="utf-8" ?>
<string xmlns="http://tempuri.org/">Hello World</string>
```

That's pretty much all there is to Web Services from an implementation perspective in .NET. .NET deals with all of the plumbing that we discussed in the first part of this chapter (SOAP, WSDL, and so on), which means that all we have to do is add properly decorated methods to the service.

In the next section, we'll take a look at doing something a little more useful with Web Services.

A More Realistic Example

Although the example we saw before was very easy to implement, it doesn't demonstrate a real world application of Web Services. Let's look at a more realistic example by building a Web Service that updates a web site from the data in an intranet. For the sake of example, we'll imagine that a third party provider hosts the site. Our SQL Server and the hosting company's SQL Server are behind firewalls, and the Internet Information Server is in a De-Militarized Zone – a safe, though exposed, network position.

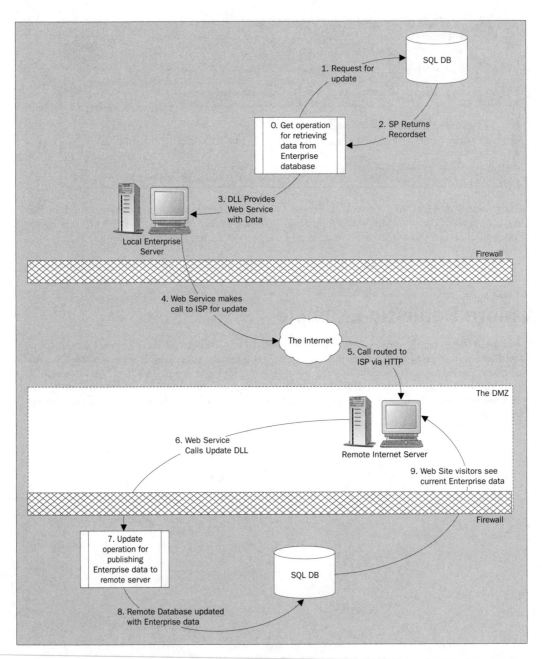

In order to get the data from our site to the remote site, we'll call a Web Service on the remote web server from our intranet. Since the SOAP envelope is sent via HTTP, our firewall will allow it through, and ADO.NET on the IIS box will handle the actual database manipulation. The remote firewall will allow database calls only from the IIS box, and our data will be updated safely through the security.

In real life, the class file `UpdateRemote` would be local to our intranet server, and the database file would be a SQL Server on a second PC. Across the Internet, as shown in the diagram, the Web Service would be on an IIS box sitting outside the network firewall. The DLL that actually provides the data functions would be on an application server inside the firewall and the database would again be on a separate machine.

For our application, though, we'll have two SQL Server databases (called `ItemsLocal` and `ItemsRemote`) on the same server. Both databases will have a single table, `Items`. This will have fields called `ItemId`, `Description`, and `Quantity`. Open the `ItemsLocal` file and add a few sample items.

Using Visual Studio .NET to Build Web Services

The VS .NET IDE shows a marked improvement from the add-ins provided for Visual Studio 6 in the SOAP Toolkit. For instance, Web Services are shown as references on a project, rather than in a separate dialog. The discovery process, discussed later, is used to its fullest, providing much more information to the developer. In short, it is nearly as easy to consume a Web Service with VB.NET as it is to use DLLs.

After providing a URL, VB.NET creates five new files, including a blank `.asmx` file called `Service1.asmx`, a `Global.asax` file, a `Web.config` file, and a discovery file called `WebService1.vsdisco`. Quite a bit of the code you need has been pre-entered for you. For instance, the `.disco` file will be preset for dynamic discovery based on the known protected directories of your server:

```
<?xml version="1.0" encoding="utf-8" ?>
<dynamicDiscovery xmlns="urn:schemas-dynamicdiscovery:disco.2000-03-17">
<exclude path="_vti_cnf" />
<exclude path="_vti_pvt" />
<exclude path="_vti_log" />
<exclude path="_vti_script" />
<exclude path="_vti_txt" />
<exclude path="Web References" />
</dynamicDiscovery>
```

Make a DataSet

For simplicity we'll use the DataSet Designer feature of VS.NET. The DataSet Designer will allow us to quickly and easily create the data access we need, without having to dig through lots of ADO.NET code.

Right-click on the **WebService1** project in the Solution Explorer and select **Add | Add New Item**. One of the options is a new DataSet – accept the default name of `Dataset1.xsd`. This creates a new DataSet schema on the fly, and it's already strongly typed for us.

In the Server Explorer window, right-click on **Data Connections** and select **Add Connection**. Make sure you select the **Microsoft OLE DB Provider for SQL Server** from the first tab, and your server's name and login information in the **Connection** tab. Select **ItemsRemote** as the database to which we want to connect and click on **OK**.

If it's not already open; double-click on the **Dataset1.xsd** file in the Solution Explorer. Then, go back to the Server Explorer, expand the data connection we just made and drag the `Items` table on to the designer surface of `Dataset1.xsd`.

The layout of our table appears in the schema file, and we have access to the data we need. This database should be empty of data, since we didn't put anything in it, but we'll change that when we consume the service.

Build the Service

Click on the **View Code** button in the Solution Explorer to view the ASP.NET code behind `Service1.asmx`. Rename the `HelloWorld` function to `AcceptUpdate` and have it take a `DataSet` as a parameter. Add a namespace parameter so that our function can be distinguished from other services on the web. Then we simply add code to merge the DataSet in the class file, which we just added, to the DataSet passed to the method. The block of IDE code in the `#Region` segment remains unchanged:

```
<WebService(Namespace:="http://localhost/WebService1")> _
Public Class Service1
  Inherits System.Web.Services.WebService


  '...


  <WebMethod()> _
  Public Function AcceptUpdate(ByVal dsDataSet As DataSet) As Boolean

    Dim dsRemoteDataset As New Dataset1()
    dsRemoteDataset.Merge(dsDataSet)
    dsRemoteDataset.AcceptChanges()
    dsRemoteDataset = Nothing

  End Function

End Class
```

Right-click on the **Service1.asmx** file in the Solution Explorer and select **Build and Browse**. If there are no errors, you'll see a simple screen listing `AcceptUpdate` as the sole method of the service. Click on **AcceptUpdate** and you'll get a screen like that earlier shown in the *Web Services Description Language* section. No HTTP form is provided because our service doesn't support HTTP POST or GET. Complex objects are only served by SOAP.

Consuming the Service

For our consuming application, we will provide a class file called `UpdateRemote` – so create a new Class Library project and the class within it both with that name. For now, we'll have a single function called `sendData`. This time we'll code the DataSet by hand, since we need to use the `DataAdapter` to fill it with data from the local database.

Add a Web Reference

The only bit of magic here is the adding of a web reference with the VS.NET IDE. As we'll see below, we are really creating a proxy DLL with the WSDL file of the service and referencing it in the project, but the IDE makes it very easy.

Right-click on the **UpdateRemote** project in the Solution Explorer and select **Add Web Reference**. You'll see a simple form that advertises Microsoft UDDI services. Enter the URL of our service in the **Address** bar – this would be at the ISP in our real life scenario, but if you've been following along it'll be http://localhost/webservice1/service1.asmx:

The service description page we've just seen when we built our service appears in the left pane, with .NET specific information in the right. Click on the **Add Reference** button at the bottom of the window to add this to the project. The service appears in a new folder in the Solution Explorer, **Web References**:

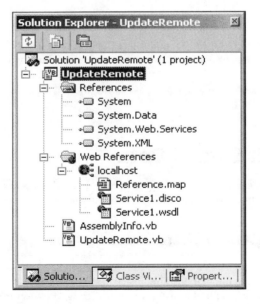

One Line of Code

The COM architecture continually promised 'one line of code' to generate great results. Web Services live up to the promise, minus the declarations.

We now need only call the referenced Web Service and pass the generated DataSet, and we are done. Compared to the scores of lines of XML we would have to write to pass the DataSet in the existing Microsoft technologies, this is a breeze.

Add the `sendData` function to the `UpdateRemote` class:

```
Public Class UpdateRemote

  Function sendData() As Boolean
    Dim wsRemoteUpdate As New localhost.Service1()
    Dim dsLocalData As DataSet = New DataSet()

    Dim strSQL As String
    Dim strConn As String
    Dim objDA As SqlClient.SqlDataAdapter

    strConn = "Data Source=(local);User ID=sa;password=;" & _
              "Initial Catalog=ItemsLocal"
    strSQL = "SELECT * FROM Items"

    objDA = New SqlClient.SqlDataAdapter(strSQL, strConn)
    objDA.Fill(dsLocalData, "Items")

    'Call the Web Service, passing the DataSet
    wsRemoteUpdate.AcceptUpdate(dsLocalData)
  End Function

End Class
```

Right-click on the **UpdateRemote** project and select **Build**. If there are no errors, generate a test container and the `UpdateRemote.dll`. You'll need to use the following lines of code:

```
Dim objRemote As New UpdateRemote.UpdateRemote()
objRemote.sendData()
```

Returning Rich Sets of Data

So far we've seen that we can return something as simple as a string (as in our first example) and that we can also return and pass more complicated objects around, like a DataSet.

> **Web services can handle any type of data that can be serialized.**

In Chapter 21 we spent some time talking about serialization. Specifically, we were talking about how the process can take a rich object and transform it into a string of bytes for transmission down a wire. We also spoke about the HTTP/SOAP and TCP/Binary channel/formatter combinations.

Remoting and Web Services share a common code base (in fact, Remoting is like an extensible, semi-proprietary Web Services implementation).

What actually happens when we prepare a string or a DataSet to be sent from client to server or from server to client is that we're using the same SOAP formatter used with Remoting. Therefore, any object that can be serialized can be sent back as a return value from a Web Service.

To the MyWebService solution, add the MyObjects project that we used in the *Remoting* chapter. If you recall, this project contains an Order object that describes an order, and that this Order object contains a number of fields and a collection of OrderLine objects. As well as adding the project itself, add a reference to the MyObjects project from the MyWebService project. You'll also need to add the MyMetaData project to the solution as well as a reference to MyMetaData.dll (from Chapter 20) in the MyObjects project.

To Service1, add a reference to the MyObjects namespace:

```
Imports System.Web.Services
Imports MyObjects

<WebService(Namespace := "http://tempuri.org/")> _
Public Class Service1
    Inherits System.Web.Services.WebService
```

Then, add this method:

```
<WebMethod()> Public Function GetOrder(ByVal orderId As Integer) _
            As Order

    ' create it...
    Dim orders As New Orders()
    Return orders.GetOrder(orderId)

End Function
```

What we're seeing here is not only a demonstration of how easy it is to return rich sets of data through Web Services, but also a classic example of code reuse. We've already spent some time building the Orders business object, and here we are consuming that object from another application. In fact, although we're loading this object locally, we could, if we wanted, consume the object through Remoting, as we discussed in Chapter 20.

Run the project and click on the GetOrder method link. Enter an ID into the invoke form and click Invoke:

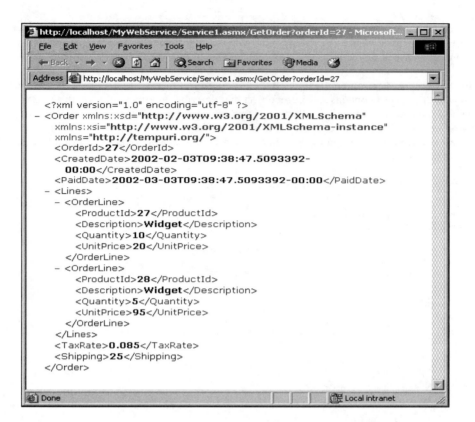

Because `Order` is decorated with the `Serializable` attribute, the SOAP formatter
(`System.Runtime.Remoting.Formatters.Soap.SoapFormatter`) is able to create a SOAP
document describing the order. This is returned as a SOAP document back to the caller for consumption.

If you go back and look at the WSDL document for the service you'll find these elements:

```
<s:complexType name="Order">
 <s:sequence>
  <s:element minOccurs="1" maxOccurs="1" name="OrderId" type="s:int" />
  <s:element minOccurs="1" maxOccurs="1" name="CreatedDate"
            type="s:dateTime" />
  <s:element minOccurs="1" maxOccurs="1" name="PaidDate" type="s:dateTime" />
  <s:element minOccurs="0" maxOccurs="1" name="Lines"
            type="s0:ArrayOfOrderLine" />
  <s:element minOccurs="1" maxOccurs="1" name="TaxRate" type="s:double" />
  <s:element minOccurs="1" maxOccurs="1" name="Shipping" type="s:double" />
 </s:sequence>
</s:complexType>
<s:complexType name="ArrayOfOrderLine">
 <s:sequence>
  <s:element minOccurs="0" maxOccurs="unbounded" name="OrderLine"
            nillable="true" type="s0:OrderLine" />
 </s:sequence>
</s:complexType>
```

```
<s:complexType name="OrderLine">
 <s:sequence>
  <s:element minOccurs="1" maxOccurs="1" name="ProductId" type="s:int" />
  <s:element minOccurs="0" maxOccurs="1" name="Description"
            type="s:string" />
  <s:element minOccurs="1" maxOccurs="1" name="Quantity" type="s:int" />
  <s:element minOccurs="1" maxOccurs="1" name="UnitPrice" type="s:double" />
 </s:sequence>
</s:complexType>
```

These are schema elements that describe the format of the response. Notice how they match the fields used in serialization of the document.

VB .NET and System.Web.Services

The SOAP toolkit provided a number of wizards to accomplish most of the obstacle course required to set up a Web Service, but the .NET Framework class library provides the abstract classes. The System.Web.Services namespace provides four classes and three other namespaces that allow programmatic exposure of methods to the web.

System.Web.Services Namespace

The System.Web.Services namespace includes these component classes:

❑   WebService

❑   WebMethodAttribute

❑   WebServiceAttribute

❑   WebServicesBindingAttribute

The WebService class is the base class from which all the ASP.NET services are derived, and includes access to the public properties for Application, Context, Server, Session, Site, and User. ASP programmers will recognize these objects from the ASP namespace. Web Services can access the IIS object model from the WebService class, such as application-level variables:

```
<%@ WebService Language="VB" Class="Util"%>
    Imports System.Web.Services

Public Class Util
    Inherits WebService

<WebMethod(Description = "Application Hit Counter", _
        EnableSession = "False")> _
Public Function HitCounter() As String

    If (Application("HitCounter") = null) Then
      Application("HitCounter") = 1
    Else
      Application("HitCounter") = Application("HitCounter") + 1
    End If
```

```
        HitCounter = Application("HitCounter")

    End Function

    End Class
```

`WebService` is an optional base class. If you don't need access to ASP.NET objects, you don't have to use it. The `WebMethodAttribute` class, however, is a necessity if you want your class to be available over the Web.

The `WebServiceAttribute` class is similar to the `WebMethodAttribute` class in that it allows you to add the description string to an entire class, rather than method by method. We'd add it before the class declaration above:

```
<WebService(Description="Common Server Variables")> _
Public Class ServerVariables
    Inherits WebService
```

Instead of using WSDL in the contract to describe these services, the `System.Web.Services` namespace provides programmatic access to these properties. IIS Service Discovery will use these descriptions when queried. This way we have removed the necessity to struggle with the myriad of protocols surrounding Service Contract Language and SOAP.

System.Web.Services.Description Namespace

The `System.Web.Services.Description` namespace provides a host of classes that provide total management of the WSDL Descriptions for your Web Service. This object manages every element in the WSDL schema as a class property.

Let's look at an example. In our discussion above on the benefits of WSDL description, we mentioned the benefits of being able to query a Web Service about its methods and parameters. The `System.Web.Services.Description` namespace provides methods for the discovery of methods and parameters, gathering the information from the service contract and providing it to the object model in our VB.NET code.

If we are working on the HTTP-GET protocol (as opposed to SOAP, for instance), the `HttpGetRequestResponseInfo` class provides access to the information we can find in the contract in the `<requestResponse>` element. In the `serviceDescription` element, we find all parameter info for all three protocols, including HTTP GET.

```
    <httpget xmlns="urn:schemas-xmlsoap-org:get-sdl-2000-01-25">
     <service>
      <requestResponse name="IsValidEmail"
         href="http://aspx.securedomains.com/sempf/validate.asmx/IsValidEmail">
        <request>
         <param name="sEmail"/>
        </request>
        <response>
         <mimeXml ref="s0:boolean"/>
        </response>
```

```
        </requestResponse>
      </service>
    </httpget>
```

The parameter, sEmail, is shown in the schema as a request element. This is available to us in our VB.NET code through the Request property of the HttpGetRequestResponseInfo object:

```
Imports System.Web.Services.Description

ReadOnly Property ExpectedParameters() As String
  Get
    ExpectedParameters = HttpGetRequestResponseInfo.Request
  End Get
End Property
```

System.Web.Services.Discovery Namespace

The System.Web.Services.Discovery namespace provides access to all of the wonderful features of the .disco files on a dynamic basis. Since Microsoft is currently trying to integrate Web Services as a remoting protocol and not pushing the public service side as much, we don't see the use of .disco files as often in the Microsoft side of things. Your business partner might be using them, though, so this namespace proves useful. For instance, you can access the DiscoveryDocument using the Discovery class:

```
Imports System.Web.Services.Discovery

ReadOnly Property DiscoveryDocument(strURL As String) As DiscoveryDocument
  Get
    DiscoveryDocument = DiscoveryClientProtocol.Discover(strURL)
  End Get
End Property
```

Like the System.Web.Services.Description namespace, the System.Web.Services.Discovery namespace provides many tools to build a .disco document on the fly.

System.Web.Services.Protocols Namespace

All of the wire service problems we solved above with HTTP and SOAP are handled here in the System.Web.Services.Protocols namespace. Handling references to classes also referenced in other Web Services namespaces, the System.Web.Services.Protocols namespace will prove to be a handy tool. The objects referenced by the System.Web.Services.Protocols namespace include (among others):

❑ Cookies per RFC 2019

❑ HTML forms

❑ HTTP request and response

❑ MIME

❑ Server

❑ SOAP, including SOAPException, our only error handling mechanism

❑ URI and URLs

❑ XML

The `System.Web.Services.Protocols` namespace is particularly handy for managing the connection type by a client. A consumer of a Web Service can use HTTP GET or HTTP POST to call a service, as well as HTTP SOAP. Microsoft's .NET initiative focuses on SOAP. The `System.Web.Services.Protocols.SoapDocumentMethodAttribute` class allows the developer to set special attributes of a public method for when a client calls it using SOAP:

```
<%@ WebService Language="VB" class="MyUser" %>

Imports System;
Imports System.Web.Services;
Imports System.Web.Services.Protocols;

Public Class MyUser
    Inherits WebService

  <SoapDocumentMethod(Action="http://MySoapmethod.org/Sample", _
   RequestNamespace="http://MyNameSpace.org/Request", _
   RequestElementName="GetUserNameRequest", _
   ResponseNamespace="http://MyNameSpace.org/Response", _
   ResponseElementName="GetUserNameResponse") _
   WebMethod(Description="Obtains the User Name")> _
  Public Function GetUserName()
    '...
  End Function
End Class
```

Architecting with Web Services

Web Services impart two remarkable benefits to users – one more obvious, another less so. First, they will replace common binary RPC formats, such as DCOM, CORBA, and RMI. Since these use a proprietary communication protocol, they are significantly less architecturally flexible than Web Services. With appliances utilizing more and more of the Internet, platform neutrality will be a great advantage.

Less obvious but more importantly, Web Services will be used to transfer structured business communication in a secure manner – potentially ending the hold Sterling has had on the EDI market. HTTPS with 128 bit SSL can provide the security necessary for intra-company information transfer.

Why Web Services?

So why Web Services? First, they are remarkably easy to deploy with VB.NET. The key to remoting with Web Services is the SDL contract – written in the dense WSDL protocol we looked at earlier.

IIS 5.0 does that for you in conjunction with the .NET Framework, analyzing your VB code, and dynamically generating the WSDL code for the contract.

Also, they are inherently cross-platform, even if created with Microsoft products. Yes, we've heard this before, but so far this seems to be true. Since the standard XML schemas are centrally managed, and IBM mostly built the WSDL specification, Microsoft seems to have toed the line on this one.

Finally, they best represent where the Internet is going – toward an architecturally neutral collection of appliances, rather than millions of PCs surfing the World Wide Web. Encapsulating code so that you can simply and easily allow cell phones to use your logic is a major boon to developers – even if they don't know it yet.

How This All Fits Together

It is important to note that Web Services are not a feature of the .NET Framework per se. In fact, Web Services run fine on Windows NT4 SP6, with SOAP Toolkit installed. You can do most anything we are doing here with VB6 and IIS 4.0.

However, the .NET Framework encapsulates the Web Services protocol into objects. It is now an integrated part of the strategy, rather than an add-on. If you are currently working in a VB6 environment, take a look at the SOAP toolkit, and understand that the services you build are available not only to different flavors of Windows, but to IBM and Sun platforms as well.

The goal of Web Services is to provide a loosely coupled, ubiquitous, universal information exchange format. Toward that end, SOAP is not the only mechanism for communicating with Web Services – HTTP GET and HTTP POST are also supported by .NET. Response is via HTTP, just like normal RPCs with SOAP. This allows legacy web applications to make use of Web Services without the benefit of the .NET Framework.

Web Service Proxies

Visual Studio .NET generates proxies invisibly, just like the creation of DLL files for normal COM+ projects. In fact, the Web Proxies *are* DLL files, because you are generating a library for use by the application. However, since .NET no longer requires the registration of DLL files we can toss them around like popcorn.

Enemies of the State

State refers to the status of any object at a given time. Stateful applications persist the existence of their objects so as to provide access to properties or to watch for events. While methods can use state, they don't need to. A good example is a connection to a database, which can be maintained in situ to reduce the overhead of opening and closing. If you maintain the database connection, you don't need to re-lookup the cursors each and every time the user accesses data – because they start where they left off.

Maintaining state makes it easier on the programmer but *much* harder on the operating system. Each persisted object package takes up a thread, which has its own overhead.

If you suddenly go from 100 users to 1000 users with a stateful system, you may need to significantly increase RAM, because each user maintains a lock on a portion of memory.

Stateless objects are more difficult to design, but they provide one of the four key needs of today's applications – scalability. With our above example, the growth from 100 to 1000 users will increase the strain on the system, but since each object is closed moments after the application is done with it there is little expansion of memory use. Object pooling takes things to the next step, providing an artful 'waiting period' for objects to be reused in before being closed.

Now – step from the world of Visual Basic to the world of the Web. It's bad enough for a corporate intranet to have persisted objects hanging around tying up memory and network resources, but if Web Services use state, then we'll have persisted objects tying up Internet resources. Stateful objects send messages between the client and server to maintain their store of information – be it on the same machine, over the LAN, or over the Internet. In short – methods only for Web Services, please.

Using DNS as a Model

How does any computer know where to find a web page? Every machine doesn't know every location of every page. Rather, there is a big catalog called **DNS** that is replicated by most Internet Service Providers, which translates domain names (like yahoo.com) into IP numbers (like 204.71.200.74).

The benefit of the DNS system is that is offers a further level of abstraction between the marketing and the wires. It's a lot easier to remember yahoo.com than 204.71.200.74. With Web Services, it becomes even more important, as there is not only a function name, but also the parameters that we must remember.

Three things make up the **Web Service Repository**: a standard format, a language, and a database. We have already discovered the language, WSDL. This can be used to layout the discovery information we need to publicize our Web Services. The format of choice is called **DISCO** (short for DISCOvery of all things). Finally, and most exciting, is the Web Services answer to DNS – **UDDI** (**Universal Description, Discovery, and Integration**). Let's talk about DISCO first.

DISCO

One way to enable a repository is to have applications that look for services. In order to implement this, we drop a DISCO document into the Web Service directory – a file that an application can look for that enables the discovery of the Web Services present in that directory, or on that machine. Alternatively, we can mark each particular service we would like to enable.

Web Service discovery is the process of locating and interrogating Web Service descriptions, which is a preliminary step for accessing a Web Service. It is through the discovery process that Web Service clients learn that a Web Service exists, what its capabilities are, and how to properly interact with it.

Dynamic Discovery with IIS

Admittedly not as fun as it sounds, **dynamic discovery** is Web Services' answer to the robots.txt file. Dynamic discovery automatically exposes Web Services beneath a given URL on a web site. By placing this document at the root of your service's directories you give a prospective consumer the opportunity to obtain information about all services contained in that directory or subdirectories.

To enable dynamic discovery for your Web Services, you'll create a <filename>.disco document at the root of your Web Services directory.

This XML file contains the *excluded* directories within the hierarchy, so that the dynamic discovery process knows where not to go to gather information about Web Services:

```xml
<?xml version="1.0" ?>
<dynamicDiscovery xmlns="urn:schemas-dynamicdiscovery:disco.2000-03-17">
<exclude path="_vti_cnf"/>
<exclude path="_vti_pvt"/>
<exclude path="_vti_log"/>
<exclude path="_vti_script"/>
<exclude path="_vti_txt"/>
</dynamicDiscovery>
```

In order for the dynamic discovery to be noticed by visiting consumers, you should refer to it in the <head> of your default HTML or ASP document:

```html
<head>
  <link type='text/xml' rel='alternate' href='Default.disco'/>
  <title></title>
</head>
```

Or, if you have an XML page as your default:

```xml
<?xml-stylesheet type="text/xml" alternate="yes" href="default.disco" ?>
```

Dynamic discovery is the way to go with IIS; the discovery process is very well tuned. If you work with another web server, though, or are a hands-on sort, you can roll-your-own discovery documents for each Web Service.

A **discovery document** is just an XML file with references listed in the discovery hierarchy. Within the hierarchy, you can add as many service contracts as you have services, and references to other DISCO documents throughout the server:

```xml
<?xml version="1.0" ?>
<disco:discovery xmlns:disco="http://schemas.xmlsoap.org/disco"
                 xmlns:scl="http://schemas.xmlsoap.org/disco/scl">
  <scl:contractRef ref="http://ServerName/ServiceName.asmx?SDL"/>
  <scl:contractRef ref="http://ServerName/AnotherName.asmx?SDL"/>
  <scl:contractRef ref="http://ServerName/ThirdName.asmx?SDL"/>
  <disco:discoveryRef ref="Folder1/default.disco"/>
  <disco:discoveryRef ref="Folder2/default.disco"/>
  <disco:discoveryRef ref="Folder3/default.disco"/>
</disco:discovery>
```

This is essentially what IIS will do for you using Dynamic Discovery.

The DISCO concept depends on the client knowing where to start. If you don't know that a business offers a particular Web Service, you won't know where to look for a DISCO document. UDDI is all about changing that.

The UDDI Project

The DISCO format allows crawlers to index Web Services just as they index web sites. The `robots.txt` approach, however, is dependent on the ability of a crawler to locate each web site and the location of the service description file on that web site. The current system relies upon the interlocking nature of web sites to crawl from site to site – there is no such visible connection between Web Services. This leaves the programmer having to know where to begin looking for a Web Service before he starts.

UDDI takes an approach that relies upon a distributed registry of businesses and their service descriptions implemented in a common XML format. You can learn all about UDDI at http://www.uddi.org, but we'll give you an intro to it here and talk about how it relates to Microsoft in general and VB.NET in particular.

UDDI is basically a group of web-based registries similar to DNS servers, where businesses provide descriptions of their Web Services in terms of an XML file with white, yellow, and green pages:

❑ The **white pages** include how and where to find the service

❑ The **yellow pages** include ontological classifications and binding information

❑ The **green pages** include the technical specification of the service

In the XML schema for UDDI, this breaks into four elements: `businessEntity`, `businessService`, `bindingElements` and metadata, or `tModels`. The `tModels` provide additional important technical information that falls outside the `bindingElements` element, but that is necessary for the consumption of the service once bound.

You can find the XML schema for this at http://www.uddi.org/schema/uddi_1.xsd but you don't have to understand it because UDDI provided an API that is built into the .NET Framework, as we'll see in the next section. Generally, though, each API function represents a publicly accessible SOAP message used to get or place information about a registry entry. For instance, the `findService` SOAP message lists available services based on the conditions specified in the arguments:

```
<find_service businessKey="uuid_key" generic="1.0" [ maxRows="nn" ]
              xmlns="urn:uddi-org:api" >
  [<findQualifiers/>]
  <name/> | <categoryBag/> | <tModelBag/>
</find_service>
```

The parameters it accepts include `maxRows`, `businessKey`, `findQualifiers`, `name`, `categoryBag`, and `tModelBag`. On success, it returns a `serviceList` as a SOAP response object. On the whole, it's not that much different from what we are used to in the COM world, except it is entirely an open standard.

Using UDDI

The best thing about UDDI is how easy it is to use. Many of us who started early in the Internet field remember filling out the InterNIC's domain add/change forms, and having our own representative at the 'NIC to help us when we were stuck. Now, though, the Web handles registration of services – you only need to really have a grasp of the discovery schema if you are going to build a registration site.

In fact, Microsoft has a UDDI mirror if its own at http://uddi.microsoft.com/ where you can register your Web Services, just like adding them to DNS or a search engine. Of course, you'll have to have a Microsoft Passport (another UDDI registered Web Service) to do it, but it is rather a simple task. After registering against your Passport, you enter business and contact information that is stored in your UDDI registry. Then you can add your Web Services.

Where UDDI is Headed

UDDI is the invisible fourth layer in the stack of protocols that represent Web Services. Like DNS and HTTP, UDDI provides a needed interface between the SOAP messaging and the ubiquity of the service that is so important, but difficult to achieve.

Going forward, UDDI as an organization sees itself being a global provider of discovery services for the business-to-business Web Services market, hosted throughout the world. For instance, software companies can build applications that customize themselves based on services information in the UDDI registry on installation. Online marketplaces can back their market sites with UDDI technology; to better serve the growing needs of B2B value-added services.

Future services planned by UDDI include extension of the technology far beyond the specifications in the Open Draft. Eventually, regional and hierarchical searches will be accomplished through simple, effective conventions. Their goal is much farther reaching than InterNIC's was at the beginning – truly using the lessons learned in the past to shape the future.

Security in Web Services

When you open up a procedure call to remoting, you have the potential to fall prey to accidents, poor end-user implementation, and crackers. Any application design needs to include some level of security. Web Services demand inclusion of security.

Security problems with Web Services fall into two categories – that of interception, and that of unauthorized use. SOAP messages intercepted by crackers potentially expose private information like account numbers and passwords to the public. Unauthorized use at best costs money and at worst wreaks havoc within a system.

Very few of the concepts we are discussing here are things we would like to see in the hands of those wearing the black hats. Even the simple validation service handles e-mail addresses – a valuable commodity in this world of 'opt in' spamming. If you add Social Security or account numbers to the service, is becomes even more of a concern. Fortunately, the wire transport of choice – HTTPS – provides a 128-bit solution to our problems.

The Secure Sockets Layer

The Secure Sockets Layer, or SSL, is a protocol consumed by HTTP in the transfer of Internet data from web server to browser. On the Web, the process works like this:

1. The user calls a secure web document, and a unique public key is generated for the client browser, using the server's root certificate

2. A message, encrypted with the server's public key, is sent from the browser

3. The server can decrypt the message using its private key

The protocol in the URI represents HTTP; if it were changed to HTTPS:

```
<address uri="https://aspx.securedomains.com/sempf/Validate.asmx" />
```

Then the service would make an SSL call to the server. Remember that SSL is significantly slower than HTTP, so you will suffer a performance hit. Given the sensitivity of much of the information passing over Web Services, it is probably worth the slowdown.

Directory Level Security

We also have the option to code security into our applications. This solves different problems from SSL, and in fact you may wish to combine the two services for a complete security solution.

Unauthorized access is a potential problem for any remote system, but for Web Services even more so. The open architecture of the system provides crackers with all the information they need to plan an attack. Fortunately, simplicity is often the best defense. Use of the NT security options already on your server is your best bet to defend against unauthorized users.

You can use NTFS permissions for individual directories within an application, and require users to provide a valid username and password combination if they wish to access the service.

> *Web Service security is a large area to cover. For more information you should refer to the documentation included with the .NET Framework SDK and* Professional ASP.NET Web Services *(Wrox Press, ISBN 1861005458).*

The best approach to security is to use SSL and directory level security together. Though slow and at times inconvenient, it is a small price to pay for the heightened level of security. Though this is different from the traditional role-based COM+ security, it is still very effective for running information across the wire.

Other Types of Security

The Windows platform also provides for other forms of security. For instance, the Windows CryptoAPI supplies access to most of the commonly used encryption algorithms – outside from the protocols used in Secure Sockets Layer. Digital Certificates (sort of a personal form of SSL ServerCertificates) is now rapidly becoming a powerful force in security.

The Down Side

There is a down side to any distributed architecture. We've covered most of them in this chapter thus far and suggested workarounds – security, state, speed, and connectivity. Let's go over them once more to help make sure that Web Services are the way to go.

Security

The issue and solution of security problems is the management of client expectations. If Web Services are built securely to begin with, there will be no instances to draw concern or scrutiny. Consider the security of everything you write. It's fairly easy, and the payoff is great.

State

State is less of a problem because in Windows DNA, Microsoft has been saying for years that n-tier statefulness has to go. Most developers are used to the idea and if you aren't then you need to get on the boat with the rest of us. Don't use properties. Don't watch for events. Architect your solutions to be loosely coupled. That's what Web Services are made to do. You can do other things with Web Services, but you shouldn't.

Transactions

Web Services are not made for transactional systems. If our Web server at MyCompany.com were to access a database at UPS for example, and the connection dropped in the middle, the lock on the database would remain without giving the network system at UPS a chance to solve the problem. Web Services are by nature loosely coupled. They are not designed for tight transactional integration.

A common use of Web Services, communication between differing systems, prompted a number of technology architects to design a number of XML transaction protocols like 2PC. These packages provide for a code of understanding between two systems that can assume that the network link will remain stable.

Speed and Connectivity

Speed and connectivity is going to be a continuing problem until we have the ubiquitous bandwidth George Gilder talks about in Telecosm. Right now, the majority of internet devices that could really benefit from Web Services – cell phones, PDAs – are stuck at the paltry 14,000 bits per second currently supported by most wireless providers.

For application development, this is a concern because when the router goes down, the application goes down. Right now, our intranets continue to function when our ISP drops the ISDN. With Web Services running the links to our customers and suppliers, that ISDN line becomes the company lifeline. Redundancy of connections and a firm partnership with your service provider are the only solution.

Where We Go From Here

The cell phone is a listening device. It listens for a call to its network address from the cell network. When it receives one, it follows some logic to handle the call. Sound familiar? This works just like the RPC architecture, and will be the format for a new host of devices that listen for our Web Services calls over the G3 wireless network.

The first lines of the W3C XML group's charter says:

> **"Today, the principal use of the World Wide Web is for interactive access to documents and applications. In almost all cases, such access is by human users, typically working through web browsers, audio players, or other interactive front-end systems. The Web can grow significantly in power and scope if it is extended to support communication between applications, from one program to another."**

New business communication will be via XML and Web Services, rather than EDI and VANs. Micropayment may actually become a reality. There are scores of promises that the Internet made since its inception that can be fulfilled with Web Services and XML. It won't stop there though. The power of listening devices will bring Web Services development into user-to-user markets from business-to-business.

It sounds far-fetched, I know, but I hope you can see how the power of Web Services on .NET could make it possible. SOAP isn't just about replacing the RPC architecture already out there. It is a fundamentally different way to think about the network as the platform.

Summary

In this chapter, we've looked at the need for an architecturally neutral, ubiquitous, easy-to-use, and interoperable system to replace DCOM, RMI, and CORBA. We've discussed how Web Services fill the gaps successfully because HTTP is used as the language independent protocol, XML is its language (in WSDL) and transport mechanism, and SOAP allows us to package up messages for sending over HTTP.

Then we moved on to look at how to create and consume our Web Services programmatically using VB.NET. We discussed the abstract classes provided by the .NET Framework class library to set up and work with Web Services. In particular, we looked at the `WebService`, `WebServiceAttribute`, `WebMethodAttribute`, and `WebServiceBindingAttribute` component classes of the `System.Web.Services` namespace, in addition to the `System.Web.Services.Description`, `System.Web.Services.Discovery`, and `System.Web.Services.Protocols` namespaces.

Next, we took a high-level look at some of the technologies supporting Web Services – namely DISCO and UDDI – before briefly covering security in Web Services.

Finally, we talked about some of the downsides to using any distributed architecture (Web Services included) but we finished with an optimistic note on where Web Services might take us in the future.

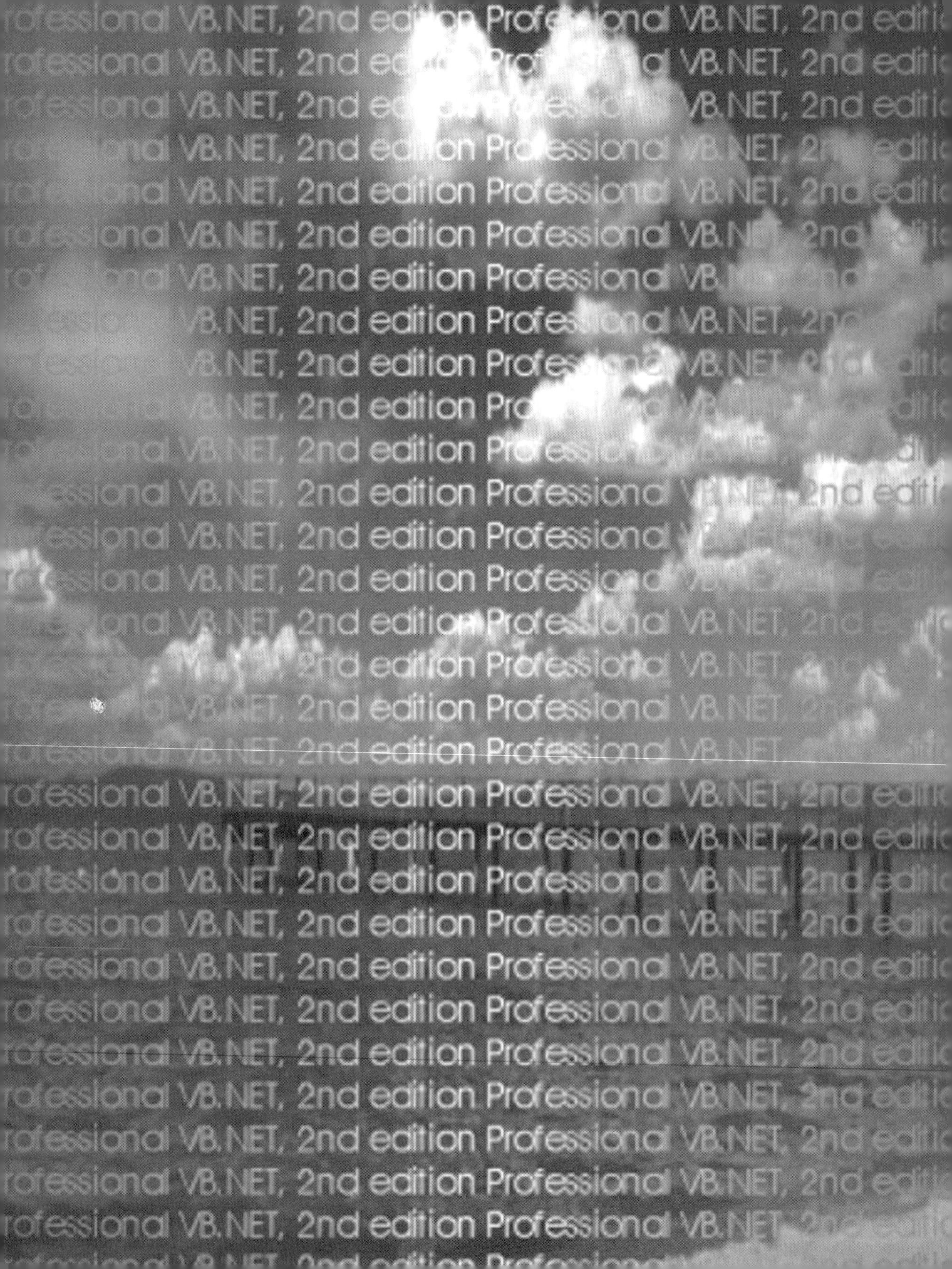
Professional VB.NET, 2nd edition

VB.NET and the Internet

In today's network-centric world, it's very likely that our applications will need to work with other computers over a private network, the public Internet, or both.

In this chapter, we'll be looking at how we can:

❑ Download resources from the Web

❑ Design our own communication protocols

❑ Reuse Internet Explorer in our applications

A good place to start working with network resources is to look at how we can download content from the Web.

Downloading Internet Resources

Downloading content from the web is very easy, so we'll throw together a basic application before getting onto some more meaty topics. Our application will download the HTML from a web page and display it in a text box. Later on we'll look at how we can display HTML properly by hosting Internet Explorer (IE) in our Windows Forms applications, but for now we'll just use plain text.

In order to download a web page, we need to be able to identity the remote page that we wish to download, make a request of the Web server that can provide that page, listen for the response, and download the data for the resource.

The classes we're interested here are `System.Uri`, `System.Net.WebRequest`, `System.Net.HttpWebRequest` and `System.Net.HttpWebResponse`:

❑ `System.Uri` is a useful general-purpose class for expressing a **Uniform Resource Identifier (URI)**. A **URL (Uniform Resource Locator)** is a type of URI (although in reality the terms are so confused that they are often used interchangeably). A URI, however is 'more than' a URL, which is why the .NET class is `Uri` not `Url`. `System.Uri` has many properties for decoding a URI. For example, if we had a string like http://www.pretendcompany.com:8080/myservices/myservice.asmx?WSDL, we could use the `Port` property to extract the port number, the `Query` property to extract the query string, and so on.

❑ A `WebRequest` expresses some kind of Internet resource (so in my opinion a better name for this class would be `InternetRequest`, as the classes aren't specifically related to the web protocol).

❑ Protocol-specific descendants of `WebRequest` carry out the actual request: `HttpWebRequest` expresses an HTTP download and `FileWebRequest` expresses a file download, for example `file:c:\MyFile.txt`.

❑ An `HttpWebResponse` is returned once a connection to the web server has been made and the resource is available to download.

There are another two major classes related to working with the Internet in the Framework. One is `System.Net.WebClient` and the other is `System.Net.WebProxy`. `WebClient` is basically a helper class that wraps the request and response classes I've just mentioned. As this is a Professional level book, I'm going to show you what to do behind the scenes – in effect, re-engineer what `WebClient` can do. I'll talk about `WebProxy` later, which allows us to explicitly define a proxy server to use for Internet communications.

Let's use these classes to build an application. Create a new Windows Application, create a new form, and add controls to it like this:

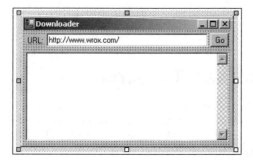

The control names are: `textUrl`, `buttonGo` and `textData`. The `Anchor` properties of the controls are set so that the form resizes properly. `textUrl` should be set to `Top`, `Left`, `Right`, `buttonGo` to `Top`, `Right`, and `textData` to `Top`, `Left`, `Bottom`, `Right`.

Add these namespace import declarations to the form's code:

```
Imports System.IO
Imports System.Net
Imports System.Text
```

To keep our code simple we'll include all the functionality into the `Click` handler of `buttonGo`. In an ideal world you want to break the code in the handler out to a separate method. This enriches the interface of the object and promotes good reuse:

The first thing we do here is create a new `System.Uri` based on the URL the user enters into the text box:

```
Private Sub buttonGo_Click(ByVal sender As System.Object, _
    ByVal e As System.EventArgs) Handles buttonGo.Click
Dim uri As New Uri(textUrl.Text)
```

Then we'll illustrate some of the useful properties of `System.Uri`:

```
Dim builder As New StringBuilder()
builder.Append("AbsolutePath: " & uri.AbsolutePath & ControlChars.CrLf)
builder.Append("AbsoluteUri: " & uri.AbsoluteUri & ControlChars.CrLf)
builder.Append("Host: " & uri.Host & ControlChars.CrLf)
builder.Append("HostNameType: " & uri.HostNameType.ToString() & _
            ControlChars.CrLf)
builder.Append("LocalPath: " & uri.LocalPath & ControlChars.CrLf)
builder.Append("PathAndQuery: " & uri.PathAndQuery & ControlChars.CrLf)
builder.Append("Port: " & uri.Port & ControlChars.CrLf)
builder.Append("Query: " & uri.Query & ControlChars.CrLf)
builder.Append("Scheme: " & uri.Scheme)
MsgBox(builder.ToString())
```

The shared `Create` method of `System.Net.WebRequest` is used to create the actual object that we can use to download the web resource. Notice how we don't create an instance of `HttpWebRequest`; we're working with a return object of type `WebRequest`. However, we'll actually be given `HttpWebRequest` object – `WebRequest` chooses the most appropriate class to return based on the URI. This allows us to build our own handlers for different network resources that can be used by consumers who simply supply an appropriate URL.

To make the request and get the response back from the server (so ultimately we can access the data), we call the `GetResponse` method of `WebRequest`. In our case, we'll get an `HttpWebResponse` object – once more it's up to the implementation of the `WebRequest`-derived object – in this case `HttpWebRequest` – to return an object of the most suitable type.

If the request is not OK, we'll get an exception (which for the sake of simplicity we won't bother processing). If the request is OK, we can get the length and the type of the response using properties of the `WebResponse` object:

```
Dim request As WebRequest = WebRequest.Create(uri)
Dim response As WebResponse = request.GetResponse()
builder = New StringBuilder()
builder.Append("Request type: " & request.GetType().ToString() & _
            ControlChars.CrLf)
builder.Append("Response type: " & response.GetType().ToString() & _
            ControlChars.CrLf)
builder.Append("Content length: " & response.ContentLength & _
            " bytes" & ControlChars.CrLf)
builder.Append("Content type: " & response.ContentType & _
            ControlChars.CrLf)
MsgBox(builder.ToString())
```

It just remains for us to download the information. We can do this through a stream (WebResponse
objects return a stream by overriding GetResponseStream), and what's more, we can use a
System.IO.StreamReader to download the whole lot in a single call by calling the ReadToEnd
method. This method will only download text, so if you want to download binary data you'll have to use
the methods on the Stream object directly, or use a System.IO.BinaryReader.

```
        Dim stream As Stream = response.GetResponseStream()
        Dim reader As New StreamReader(stream)
        Dim data As String = reader.ReadToEnd()
        reader.Close()
        stream.Close()
        textData.Text = data
    End Sub
```

If you run the application, enter a URL of http://www.wrox.com, and click the Go button, you'll see
debugging information about the URL:

This is a simple URL. Our application tells us that the scheme is http, and the host name type is Dns. If, for
example, we enter an IP into the URL to be requested rather than a host name, this type will come back as
IPv4. This tells us where the host name came from – in this case, it's a general Internet hostname.

Next, our application provides information about the response:

Finally, we get to see the data itself:

This application has shown how easy it is to download data from a web server. However, we've skipped a lot of the exception handling and threading issues related to downloading network resources in a reliable manner.

Perhaps the most important exception to be aware of when using these classes is the `System.Net.WebException` exception. If anything goes wrong on the `WebRequest.GetResponse` call, this exception will be thrown. Among other things, this exception provides access to the `WebResponse` object through the `Response` property. The `StatusCode` property of `WebResponse` tells you what actually happened through the `HttpStatusCode` enumeration. For example, `HttpStatusCode.NotFound` is the equivalent of the HTTP 404 status code.

Sockets

There may be times when you need to transfer data across a network (either a private network or the Internet) when the existing techniques and protocols don't exactly suit your needs. For example, you wouldn't be able to download resources using the techniques discussed at the start of this chapter; and you can't use Web Services (as described in Chapter 22) or Remoting (as described in Chapter 20). When this happens, the best course of action is to roll your own protocol using **sockets**.

TCP/IP, and therefore the Internet, is based on sockets. The principle is simple – establish a port at one end and allow clients to 'plug in' to that port from the other end. Once the connection is made, applications can send and receive data through a stream. For example, HTTP nearly always operates on port 80. So, a web server opens a socket on port 80 and waits for incoming connections (web browsers – unless told otherwise – attempt to connect to port 80 in order to make a request of that web server).

In .NET, sockets are implemented in the `System.Net.Sockets` namespace, and use classes from `System.Net` and `System.IO` to get the stream classes. Although working with sockets can be a little tricky outside of .NET, the Framework includes some superb classes that enable you to open a socket for inbound connections (`System.Net.TcpListener`) and for communication between two open sockets (`System.Net.TcpClient`). These two classes, in combination with some threading shenanigans, allow us build our own protocol, through which we can send any data we like. With our own protocol, we have ultimate control over the communication.

To demonstrate these techniques we're going to build Wrox Messenger, a very basic instant messenger application similar to .NET Messenger.

Building the Application

We'll wrap all the functionality of our application into a single Windows Application. This application will act as both a server that waits for inbound connections and as a client that established outbound connections.

Create a new project called **WroxMessenger**. Change the title of `Form1` to `Wrox Messenger` and add a `TextBox` control called `textConnectTo` and a `Button` control called `buttonConnect`:

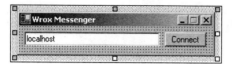

We'll talk about this in more detail in a little while, but for now you need to know that it's very important that all of our UI code runs in the same thread, and that the thread is actually the main application that creates and runs Form1.

To keep track of what's happening, we'll add a field to Form1 that allows us to store the ID of the startup thread, and also report that ID on the caption. This will help our understanding of the thread/UI issues that we discuss later. We'll also need some namespace imports and a constant specifying the ID of the default port. Add this code to Form1:

```
Imports System.Net
Imports System.Net.Sockets
Imports System.Threading

Public Class Form1
  Inherits System.Windows.Forms.Form

  Private Shared _mainThreadId As Integer

  Public Const ServicePort As Integer = 10101
```

Next, open the **Windows Form Designer** generated code region and add this code to the constructor that populates the field and changes the caption:

```
Public Sub New()
  MyBase.New()

  'This call is required by the Windows Form Designer.
  InitializeComponent()

  'Add any initialization after the InitializeComponent() call
  _mainThreadId = Thread.CurrentThread.GetHashCode()
  Text &= " - " & _mainThreadId.ToString()

End Sub
```

To listen for incoming connections, we'll create a separate class called Listener. This class will use an instance of System.Net.Sockets.TcpListener to wait for incoming connections. Specifically, this will open a TCP port that *any* client can connect to – sockets are absolutely not platform specific. Although connections are always made on a specific, known port, the actual communication takes place on a port of the TCP/IP subsystems choosing, which means you can support many inbound connections at once, despite the fact that each of them connects to the same port. Sockets are an open standard available on pretty much any platform you care to mention. For example, if we publish the specification for our protocol, developers working on Linux would be able to connect to our Wrox Messenger service.

When we detect an inbound connection, we'll be given a System.Net.Sockets.TcpClient object. This is our gateway to the remote client. To send and receive data, we need to get hold of a System.Net.NetworkStream object (returned through a call to GetStream on TcpClient), which returns us a stream that we can use.

Create a new class called Listener. This thread needs members to hold an instance of a System.Threading.Thread object, and also a reference back to the Form1 class that is the main form in the application. We won't go into a discussion of how to spin up and spin down threads, nor are we going to talk about synchronization – you should refer back to Chapter 19 if you need information.

Here's the basic code for our Listener class:

```
Imports System.Net.Sockets
Imports System.Threading

Public Class Listener

   Private _main As Form1
   Private _listener As TcpListener
   Private _thread As Thread

   Public Sub New(ByVal main As Form1)
      _main = main
   End Sub

   Public Sub SpinUp()

      ' create and start the new thread...
      _thread = New Thread(AddressOf ThreadEntryPoint)
      _thread.Start()
   End Sub
End Class
```

The obvious missing method here is ThreadEntryPoint. This is where we need to create the socket and wait for inbound connections. When we get them, we'll be given a TcpClient object, which we need to pass back to Form1 where the conversation window can be created.

To create the socket, we create an instance of TcpListener and give it a port. In our application, the port we're going to use is 10101. This port should be free on your computer, but if your debugger breaks on an exception when you instantiate TcpListener or call Start, try another port. Once we've done that and called Start to configure the object to listen for connections, we drop into an infinite loop and call AcceptTcpClient. This method will block until the socket is closed, or a connection becomes available. If we get Nothing back, either the socket is closed or there's a problem, so we drop out of the thread. If we get something back, then we pass the TcpClient over to Form1 through a call to (not yet built) ReceiveInboundConnection method:

```
   ' ThreadEntryPoint...
   Protected Sub ThreadEntryPoint()

      ' create a socket...
      _listener = New TcpListener(Form1.ServicePort)
```

```
        _listener.Start()

        ' loop infinitely, waiting for connections...
        Do While True

            ' get a connection...
            Dim client As TcpClient = _listener.AcceptTcpClient()
            If client Is Nothing Then
                Exit Do
            End If

            ' process it...
            _main.ReceiveInboundConnection(client)
        Loop
    End Sub
```

It's in the `ReceiveInboundConnection` method that we'll create the **Conversation** form that the user can use to send messages.

Creating Conversation Windows

When we build Windows Forms applications that support threading we can run into a problem with the Windows messaging subsystem. This is a very old part of Windows (the idea has been around since version 1.0 of the platform, although the implementation on modern Windows versions is far removed from the original) that powers the Windows user interface.

Even if you're not familiar with old school Windows programming, such as MFC, Win32 or even Win16 development, you should be familiar with events. When we move a mouse over a form, we get `MouseMove` events. When we close a form, we get a `Closed` event. There's a mapping between these events and the messages that Windows passes around to support the actual display of the windows. For example, whenever we receive a `MouseMove` event, a message called `WM_MOUSEMOVE` is sent to the window, by Windows, in response to the mouse driver. In .NET, and in other RAD development environments like VB and Delphi, this message is converted into an event that we can write code against.

Although this is getting way off topic – we know how to build Windows Forms applications by now and don't need to get into the details of messages like `WM_NCHITTEST` or `WM_PAINT` – it has an important implication. In effect, Windows creates a message queue for each thread into which it posts the messages that the thread's windows have to work with. This queue is looped on a virtually constant basis, and the messages are distributed to the appropriate window (remember, small controls like buttons and text boxes are also windows). In .NET, these messages are turned into events, but unless the message queue still gets looped the messages don't get through.

Imagine that Windows needs to paint a window. It will post a `WM_PAINT` message to the queue. A message loop implemented on the main thread of the process containing the window detects the message and dispatches it on to the appropriate window where it is processed. Now imagine that the queue isn't looped. The message never gets picked up, and the window will never get painted.

In a Windows application, a single thread is usually responsible for message dispatch. This thread is usually (although it doesn't have to be) the main application thread – the one that's created when the process is first created. If we create windows in a different thread then that new thread has to support the message dispatch loop so that messages destined for the windows get through. However, with `Listener`, we have no code for processing the message loop and there's little point in writing any because the next time we call `AcceptTcpClient` we're going to block and everything will stop working.

The trick then is to create the windows only in the main application thread, which is the thread that created `Form1` and that is processing the messages for all the windows created in this thread. We can pass calls from one thread to the other by calling the `Invoke` method of `Form1`.

This is where things start to get complicated. We have to write an awful lot of code to get to a point where we can see that the socket connection has been established and get conversation windows to appear. Here's what we need to do:

- ❏ Create a new **Conversation** form. This form will need controls for displaying the total content of the conversation, plus a `TextBox` control for adding new messages.

- ❏ The **Conversation** window will need to be able to send and receive messages through its own thread.

- ❏ `Form1` needs to be able to initiate new connections. This will be done in a separate thread that is managed by the thread pool. When the connection has been established, a new **Conversation** window needs to be created and configured.

- ❏ `Form1` also needs to receive inbound connections. When it gets one of these, a new **Conversation** needs to be created and configured.

Let's look at these problems one at a time.

Creating the Conversation Form

The simplest place to start is to build the new **Conversation** form. This needs three `TextBox` controls (`textUsername`, `textMessages` and `textMessage`) and a `Button` control (`buttonSend`). Here's the form:

This class requires a number of fields and an enumeration. It needs fields to hold the username of the user (which we'll default to `Darren`), the underlying `TcpClient`, the `NetworkStream` returned by that client. The enumeration indicates the direction of the connection (which will help us when debugging):

```
Imports System.Net
Imports System.Net.Sockets
Imports System.Text
Imports System.Threading
Imports System.Runtime.Serialization.Formatters.Binary

Public Class Conversation
  Inherits System.Windows.Forms.Form

  Private _username As String = "Darren"
  Private _client As TcpClient
  Private _stream As NetworkStream
  Private _direction As ConversationDirection

  Public Enum ConversationDirection As Integer
    Inbound = 0
    Outbound = 1
  End Enum
```

We won't look into the issues of establishing a thread for exchanging messages at this stage, but we will look at implementing the ConfigureClient method. This method will eventually do more work than this, but for now it sets a couple of fields and calls UpdateCaption:

```
Public Sub ConfigureClient(ByVal client As TcpClient, _
                           ByVal direction As ConversationDirection)

  ' set it up...
  _client = client
  _direction = direction

  ' update the window...
  UpdateCaption()
End Sub

Protected Sub UpdateCaption()

  ' set the text...
  Dim builder As New StringBuilder(_username)
  builder.Append(" - ")
  builder.Append(_direction.ToString())
  builder.Append(" - ")
  builder.Append(Thread.CurrentThread.GetHashCode())
  builder.Append(" - ")
  If Not _client Is Nothing Then
    builder.Append("Connected")
  Else
    builder.Append("Not connected")
  End If
  Text = builder.ToString()
End Sub
```

One debugging issue that we have is that if we're connecting to a conversation on the same machine, we need a way of changing the name of the user sending each message, otherwise things will get confusing. That's what the top-most TextBox control is for. In the constructor, set the text for the textUsername.Text property:

```
Public Sub New()
  MyBase.New()

  'This call is required by the Windows Form Designer.
  InitializeComponent()

  'Add any initialization after the InitializeComponent() call
  textUsername.Text = _username
End Sub
```

On the TextChanged event for this control, update the caption and the internal _username field:

```
Private Sub textUsername_TextChanged(ByVal sender As System.Object, _
                                     ByVal e As System.EventArgs) _
                                     Handles textUsername.TextChanged
  _username = textUsername.Text
  UpdateCaption()
End Sub
```

Initiating Connections

Form1 needs to be able to both initiate connections and receive inbound connections – the application is both a client and a server. We've already created some of the server portion by creating Listener and now we'll look at the client side.

The general rule when working with sockets is that any time we send anything over the wire, we must perform the actual communication in a separate thread. Virtually all calls to send and receive do so in a blocking manner – that is, they block until data is received, block until all data is sent and so on.

If threads are used well, the UI will keep running as normal, irrespective of the problems that may occur during transmit and receive. This is why in the InitiateConnection method on Form1 we defer processing to another method called InitiateConnectionThreadEntryPoint that is called from a new thread:

```
Public Sub InitiateConnection()
  InitiateConnection(textConnectTo.Text)
End Sub

Public Sub InitiateConnection(ByVal hostName As String)

  ' give it to the threadpool to do...
  ThreadPool.QueueUserWorkItem(AddressOf _
  Me.InitiateConnectionThreadEntryPoint, hostName)
End Sub

Private Sub buttonConnect_Click(ByVal sender As System.Object, _
```

793

```
                                          ByVal e As System.EventArgs) _
                                          Handles buttonConnect.Click
        InitiateConnection()
    End Sub
```

Inside the thread, we try to convert the host name that we're given into an IP address (`localhost` is used as the host name in the demonstration, but it could be the name of a machine on the local network or a hostname on the Internet). This is done through the shared `Resolve` method on `System.Net.Dns` and returns a `System.Net.IPHostEntry` object. As a hostname can point to multiple IP addresses, we'll just use the first one that we're given. We take this address expressed as an IP (for example, `192.168.0.4`) and combine it with the port number to get a new `System.Net.IPEndPoint`. We create a new `TcpClient` from this `IPEndPoint` and try to connect.

If at any time an exception is thrown (which can happen because the name couldn't be resolved, or the connection could not be established), we'll pass the exception over to `HandleInitiateConnectionException`. If it succeeds, we'll pass it to `ProcessOutboundConnection`. Both of these methods will be implemented shortly:

```
    Private Sub InitiateConnectionThreadEntryPoint(ByVal state As Object)

        Try

            ' get the host name...
            Dim hostName As String = CStr(state)

            ' resolve...
            Dim hostEntry As IPHostEntry = Dns.Resolve(hostName)
            If Not hostEntry Is Nothing Then

                ' create an end-point for the first address...
                Dim endPoint As New IPEndPoint(hostEntry.AddressList(0), _
                    ServicePort)

                ' create a tcp client...
                Dim client As New TcpClient()
                client.Connect(endPoint)

                ' create the connection window...
                ProcessOutboundConnection(client)
            Else
                Throw New ApplicationException("Host '" & hostName & _
                  "' could not be resolved.")
            End If
        Catch ex As Exception
            HandleInitiateConnectionException(ex)
        End Try
    End Sub
```

When it comes to `HandleInitiateConnectionException` we start to see the inter-thread UI problems that were mentioned earlier. When there is a problem with the exception, we need to tell the user, which means that we need to move the exception from the thread pool managed thread into the main application thread. The principle for this is the same – we need to create a delegate and call that delegate through the `Invoke` method of the form. This method does all the hard work in marshaling the call across to the other thread.

Here's what the delegates look like. They have the same parameters of the calls themselves. As a naming convention I tend to use the same name as the method and tack the word Delegate on the end:

```
Public Class Form1
    Inherits System.Windows.Forms.Form

    Private Shared _mainThreadId As Integer

    ' delegates...
    Protected Delegate Sub HandleInitiateConnectionExceptionDelegate( _
                                          ByVal ex As Exception)
```

In the constructor for Form1, we capture the thread callers thread ID and store it in _mainThreadId. Here's a method that compares the captured ID with the ID of the current thread:

```
Public Shared Function IsMainThread() As Boolean
    If Thread.CurrentThread.GetHashCode() = _mainThreadId Then
        Return True
    Else
        Return False
    End If
End Function
```

The first thing we do at the top of HandleInitiateConnectionException is to check the thread ID. If it doesn't match, we create the delegate and call it. Notice how we set the delegate to call back into the same method, as the second time it's called we would have moved to the main thread, therefore IsMainThread will return True and we can process the exception properly:

```
Protected Sub HandleInitiateConnectionException(ByVal ex As Exception)

    ' main thread?
    If IsMainThread() = False Then

        ' create and call...
        Dim args(0) As Object
        args(0) = ex
        Invoke(New HandleInitiateConnectionExceptionDelegate(AddressOf _
            HandleInitiateConnectionException), args)

        ' return...
        Return
    End If

    ' show it...
    MsgBox(ex.GetType().ToString() & ":" & ex.Message)
End Sub
```

The result is that when the call comes in from the thread pool managed thread, IsMainThread returns False, and the delegate is created and called. When the method is entered again as a result of the delegate call, IsMainThread returns True and we see the message box.

When it comes to `ProcessOutboundConnection`, we have to again jump into the main UI thread. However, the magic behind this method is implemented in a separate method called `ProcessConnection`, which can handle either inbound or outbound connections. Here's the delegate:

```
Public Class Form1
    Inherits System.Windows.Forms.Form

    Private Shared _mainThreadId As Integer
    Private _listener As Listener

    Protected Delegate Sub ProcessConnectionDelegate(ByVal client As _
            TcpClient, ByVal direction As Conversation.ConversationDirection)
    Protected Delegate Sub HandleInitiateConnectionExceptionDelegate(ByVal _
            ex As Exception)
```

Here's the method itself, which creates the new Conversation form and calls the `ConfigureClient` method:

```
    Protected Sub ProcessConnection(ByVal client As TcpClient, _
        ByVal direction As Conversation.ConversationDirection)

        ' do we have to move to another thread?
        If IsMainThread() = False Then

            ' create and call...
            Dim args(1) As Object
            args(0) = client
            args(1) = direction
            Invoke(New ProcessConnectionDelegate(AddressOf ProcessConnection), _
                    args)

            Return
        End If

        ' create the conversation window...
        Dim conversation As New Conversation()
        conversation.Show()
        conversation.ConfigureClient(client, direction)
    End Sub
```

Of course, `ProcessOutboundConnection` needs to defer to `ProcessConnection`:

```
    Public Sub ProcessOutboundConnection(ByVal client As TcpClient)
        ProcessConnection(client, Conversation.ConversationDirection.Outbound)
    End Sub
```

Now that we can connect to something on the client-side, let's look at how to receive connections (on the server-side).

Receiving Inbound Connections

We've already built `Listener`, but we haven't created an instance of it, nor have we spun up its thread to wait for incoming connections. To do this, we need a field in `Form1` to hold an instance of the object, and we also need to tweak the constructor. Here's the field:

```
Public Class Form1
    Inherits System.Windows.Forms.Form

    Private _mainThreadId As Integer
    Private _listener As Listener
```

Here is the new code that needs to be added to the constructor:

```
Public Sub New()
    MyBase.New()

    'This call is required by the Windows Form Designer.
    InitializeComponent()

    'Add any initialization after the InitializeComponent() call
    _mainThreadId = Thread.CurrentThread.GetHashCode()
    Text &= " - " & _mainThreadId.ToString()

    ' listener...
    _listener = New Listener(Me)
    _listener.SpinUp()
End Sub
```

When inbound connections are received, we'll get a new `TcpClient` object. This is passed back to `Form1` through the `ReceiveInboundConnection` method. This method, like `ProcessOutboundConnection`, defers to `ProcessConnection`. As `ProcessConnection` already handles the issue of moving the call to the main application thread, `ReceiveInboundConnection` looks like this:

```
Public Sub ReceiveInboundConnection(ByVal client As TcpClient)
    ProcessConnection(client, Conversation.ConversationDirection.Inbound)
End Sub
```

If you run the project now, you should be able to click on the **Connect** button and see two windows – one inbound and one outbound:

If you close all three windows, the application will keep running because we haven't written code to close down the listener thread, and having an open thread like this will keep the application open. Use the **Debug | Stop Debugging** menu option in VS.NET to close the application down by killing all running threads.

By clicking the **Connect** button, we're calling `InitiateConnection`. This spins up a new thread in the pool that resolves the given host name (`localhost`) into an IP address. This IP address, in combination with a port number, is then used in the creation of a `TcpClient` object. If the connection can be made, `ProcessOutboundConnection` is called, which results in the first of the conversation windows being created and marked as 'outbound'.

Our example is somewhat artificial, as the two instances of Wrox Messenger should be running on separate computers. On the remote computer (if we're connecting to `localhost` this will be the same computer) a connection is received through the `AcceptTcpClient` method of `TcpListener`. This results in a call to `ReceiveInboundConnection`, which in turn results in the creation of the second conversation window, this time marked as 'inbound'.

Sending Messages

Next we have to work out how to exchange messages between the two Conversation windows. We already have a `TcpClient` in each case so all we have to do is squirt binary data down the wire on one side and pick it up at the other end. As both Conversation windows act as both client and server, both need to be able to send and receive.

We have three problems to solve:

- ❑ We need to establish one thread to send and another thread to receive data
- ❑ Data sent and received needs to be reported back to the user so that they can follow the conversation
- ❑ The data that we want to send has to be converted into a wire-ready format, which in .NET terms usually means serialization

The power of sockets means that we can define whatever protocol we like for data transmission. If we wanted to build our own SMTP server we could implement the (publicly available) specifications, set up a listener to wait for connections on port 25 (the standard port for SMTP), wait for data to come in, process it, and return responses as appropriate.

If you are building your own server protocols, it's best to work in this way. Unless you have very strong reasons for not doing so, you want to make your server as open as possible, meaning that it's not tied to a specific platform. This is the way that things are done on the Internet. To an extent, things like Web Services should negate the need to build our own protocols; as we go forward, we will rely instead on the 'remote object available to local client' paradigm.

You may be thinking ahead to the idea of using the serialization features of .NET to transmit data across the network. After all, we've already seen this in action in Web Services and Remoting. We can take an object in .NET, use serialization to convert it to a string of bytes and squirt that string down to a Web Service consumer, or Remoting client, or even to a file.

In Chapter 20, we learned about `BinaryFormatter` and `SoapFormatter`. We could use either of those classes, or create our own custom formatter, to convert data for transmission and reception. In this case, we're going to create a new class called `Message` and use `BinaryFormatter` to crunch it down into a wire-ready format and convert it back again for processing.

This approach isn't ideal from the perspective of interoperability, as the actual protocol used is lost in the implementation of the .NET Framework, rather than being under our absolute control.

If we want to build an open protocol, this is *not* the best way to do it. Unfortunately the best way to do it is out of the scope of this book but a good place to start is to look at existing protocols and standards and model any protocol on their approach. `BinaryFormatter` is quick and dirty, which is why we're going to use it.

The Message Class

The `Message` class contains two fields, _username and _message, which form the entirety of the data that we want to transmit. The code for this class follows; notice how the `Serializable` attribute is applied to it so that `BinaryFormatter` can change it into a wire-ready form, and how we've provided a new implementation of `ToString`:

```
Imports System.Text
<Serializable()> Public Class Message

  Private _name As String
  Private _message As String

  Public Sub New(ByVal name As String)
    _name = name
  End Sub

  Public Sub New(ByVal name As String, ByVal message As String)
    _name = name
    _message = message
  End Sub

  Public Overrides Function ToString() As String
    Dim builder As New StringBuilder(_name)
    builder.Append(" says:")
    builder.Append(ControlChars.CrLf)
    builder.Append(_message)
    builder.Append(ControlChars.CrLf)
    Return builder.ToString()
  End Function
End Class
```

Now all we have to do is spin up two threads – one for transmission and one for reception–updating the display. We need two threads per *conversation*, so if we have ten conversations open, we'll need twenty threads plus the main UI thread, plus the thread running `TcpListener`.

Receiving messages is pretty easy. When we call `Deserialize` on `BinaryFormatter`, we give it the stream returned to us from `TcpClient`. If there's no data, this blocks. If there is data, it's decoded into a `Message` object that we can display. If we have multiple messages coming down the pipe, `BinaryFormatter` will keep processing them out until the pipe is empty. Here's the method for doing this, and this should be added to `Conversation`. Remember, we haven't implemented `ShowMessage` yet:

```
    Protected Sub ReceiveThreadEntryPoint()

      ' create a formatter...
      Dim formatter As New BinaryFormatter()
```

```
         ' loop...
      Do While True

         ' receive...
         Dim message As Message = formatter.Deserialize(_stream)
         If message Is Nothing Then
           Exit Do
         End If

         ' show it...
         ShowMessage(message)
      Loop
   End Sub
```

Transmitting messages is a touch more complex. What we want is a queue (managed by a `System.Collections.Queue`) of outgoing messages. Every second, we'll examine the state of the queue and if we find any messages, we'll use `BinaryFormatter` to transmit them. As we'll be accessing this queue from multiple threads, we'll use a `System.Threading.ReaderWriterLock` to control access. To minimize the amount of time we spend inside locked code, we'll quickly transfer the contents of the shared queue into a private queue that we can process at our leisure. This allows the client to continue to add messages to the queue through the UI even though existing messages are being sent by the transmit thread.

First, add these members to `Conversation`:

```
Public Class Conversation
    Inherits System.Windows.Forms.Form

   Private _username As String = "Darren"
   Private _client As TcpClient
   Private _stream As NetworkStream
   Private _direction As ConversationDirection
   Private _receiveThread As Thread
   Private _transmitThread As Thread
   Private _transmitQueue As New Queue()
   Private _transmitLock As New ReaderWriterLock()
```

Now add this method, again to `Conversation`:

```
   Protected Sub TransmitThreadEntryPoint()

      ' create a formatter...
      Dim formatter As New BinaryFormatter()
      Dim workQueue As New Queue()

      ' loop...
      Do While True

         ' wait for the signal...
         Thread.Sleep(1000)

         ' go through the queue...
```

```
         _transmitLock.AcquireWriterLock(-1)
         Dim message As Message
         workQueue.Clear()
         For Each message In _transmitQueue
           workQueue.Enqueue(message)
         Next
         _transmitQueue.Clear()
         _transmitLock.ReleaseWriterLock()

         ' loop the outbound messages...
         For Each message In workQueue

           ' send it...
           formatter.Serialize(_stream, message)

         Next

       Loop

     End Sub
```

When we want to send a message, we call one version of the SendMessage method. Here are all of the implementations, and the Click handler for buttonSend:

```
     Private Sub buttonSend_Click(ByVal sender As System.Object, _
       ByVal e As System.EventArgs) Handles buttonSend.Click
       SendMessage(textMessage.Text)
     End Sub

     Public Sub SendMessage(ByVal message As String)
       SendMessage(_username, message)
     End Sub

     Public Sub SendMessage(ByVal username As String, ByVal message As String)
       SendMessage(New Message(username, message))
     End Sub

     Public Sub SendMessage(ByVal message As Message)

       ' queue it...
       _transmitLock.AcquireWriterLock(-1)
       _transmitQueue.Enqueue(message)
       _transmitLock.ReleaseWriterLock()

       ' show it...
       ShowMessage(message)
     End Sub
```

ShowMessage is responsible for updating textMessages so that the conversation remains up to date (notice how we add the message both when we send it and when we receive it so that both parties have an up-to-date thread). This is a UI feature, so it is good practice to pass it over to the main application thread for processing. Although the call in response to the button click comes off of the main application thread, the one from inside ReceiveThreadEntryPoint does not. Here's what the delegate looks like:

```
Public Class Conversation
  Inherits System.Windows.Forms.Form

  ' members...
  Private _username As String = "Darren"
  Private _client As TcpClient
  Private _stream As NetworkStream
  Private _direction As ConversationDirection
  Private _receiveThread As Thread
  Private _transmitThread As Thread
  Private _transmitQueue As New Queue()
  Private _transmitLock As New ReaderWriterLock()

    Public Delegate Sub ShowMessageDelegate(ByVal message As Message)
```

Here's the method implementation:

```
    Public Sub ShowMessage(ByVal message As Message)

      ' thread?
      If Form1.IsMainThread() = False Then

        ' run...
        Dim args(0) As Object
        args(0) = message
        Invoke(New ShowMessageDelegate(AddressOf ShowMessage), args)

        ' return...
        Return
      End If

      ' show it...
      textMessages.Text &= message.ToString()
    End Sub
```

All that remains now is to spin up the threads. This should be done from within `ConfigureClient`. Before the threads are spun up, we need to get hold of the stream and store it in the private `_stream` field. After that, we create new `Thread` objects as normal:

```
    Public Sub ConfigureClient(ByVal client As TcpClient, _
        ByVal direction As ConversationDirection)

      ' set it up...
      _client = client
      _direction = direction

      ' update the window...
      UpdateCaption()

      ' get the stream...
      _stream = _client.GetStream()
```

```
        ' spin up the threads...
        _transmitThread = New Thread(AddressOf TransmitThreadEntryPoint)
        _transmitThread.Start()
        _receiveThread = New Thread(AddressOf ReceiveThreadEntryPoint)
        _receiveThread.Start()
    End Sub
```

At this point if you run the application you should be able to connect and exchange messages:

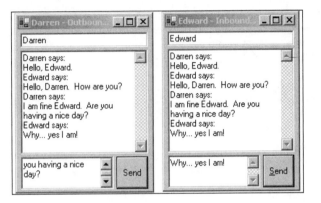

Notice how in these screenshots I've changed the username of the inbound connection to Edward using the textUsername text box so that I can follow which half of the conversation comes from where.

Shutting Down the Application

We've yet to solve the problem of neatly closing the application, or in fact dealing with one person in the conversation closing down their window indicating that they wish to end the conversation. When the process ends (whether 'neatly' or forcefully), Windows automatically mops up any open connections and frees up the port for other processes.

If we close our window (imagine, if you will, that we have two computers, one window per computer as we would in a production environment), we're indicating that we want to end the conversation. We need to close the socket and spin down the transmission and reception threads. At the other end, we should be able to detect that the socket has been closed, spin down the threads and tell the user that the other user has terminated the conversation.

This all hinges on being able to detect when the socket has been closed. For some reason, Microsoft has actually made this very hard thanks to the design of the TcpClient class. TcpClient effectively encapsulates a System.Net.Sockets.Socket class, providing methods for helping to manage the connection lifetime and communication streams. However, TcpClient does not have a method or property that answers the question, "Am I still connected?" What we need to do is get hold of the Socket object that TcpClient is wrapping and then we can use its Connected property to find out if the connection has been closed.

TcpClient does support a property called Client that returns a Socket. However, this property is protected, meaning that we can only access it by inheriting a new class from TcpClient. But, there is another way – we could use Reflection to get at the property and call it without having to inherit a new class.

803

Microsoft claims that this is a legitimate technique, even though it appears to violate every rule in the book about encapsulation. Reflection is designed not only for finding out which types are available, and learning which methods and properties each type supports, but also for invoking those methods and properties whether they're protected or public.

So, in `Conversation` we need to store the socket:

```
Public Class Conversation
    Inherits System.Windows.Forms.Form

    Private _username As String = "Darren"
    Private _client As TcpClient
    Private _socket As Socket
```

In `ConfigureClient`, we need to use `Reflection` to peek in to the `Type` object for `TcpClient` and dig out the `Client` property. Once we have a `System.Reflection.PropertyInfo` for this property, we can retrieve its value by using the `GetValue` method. Here's the code. You'll also need to include the `System.Reflection` namespace:

```
Public Sub ConfigureClient(ByVal client As TcpClient, _
                            ByVal direction As ConversationDirection)

    ' set it up...
    _client = client
    _direction = direction

    ' update the window...
    UpdateCaption()

    ' get the stream...
    _stream = _client.GetStream()

    ' get the socket through reflection...
    Dim propertyInfo As PropertyInfo = _
        _client.GetType().GetProperty("Client", _
        BindingFlags.Instance Or BindingFlags.NonPublic)
    If Not propertyInfo Is Nothing Then
        _socket = propertyInfo.GetValue(_client, Nothing)
    Else
        Throw New Exception("Couldn't retrieve Client property from _
                        TcpClient")
    End If

    ' spin up the threads...
    _transmitThread = New Thread(AddressOf TransmitThreadEntryPoint)
    _transmitThread.Start()
    _receiveThread = New Thread(AddressOf ReceiveThreadEntryPoint)
    _receiveThread.Start()
End Sub
```

Applications are able to check the state of the socket either by detecting when an error occurs because we've tried to send data over a closed socket, or by actually asking if the socket is connected. If we either don't have a Socket available in _socket (that is, it is Nothing), or if we have one and it tells us we're disconnected, we give the user some feedback and exit the loop. By exiting the loop, we effectively exit the thread, which is a neat way of quitting the thread. Notice as well that we might not have a window at this point (we might be the one that closed the conversation by closing the window), so we wrap the UI call in a Try...Catch (the other side will see a <disconnect> message):

```
Protected Sub TransmitThreadEntryPoint()

    ' create a formatter...
    Dim formatter As New BinaryFormatter()
    Dim workQueue As New Queue()

    ' name...
    Thread.CurrentThread.Name = "Tx-" & _direction.ToString()

    ' loop...
    Do While True

        ' wait for the signal...
        Thread.Sleep(1000)

        ' disconnected?
        If _socket Is Nothing OrElse _socket.Connected = False Then
            Try
                ShowMessage(New Message("Debug", "<disconnect>"))
            Catch
            End Try
            Exit Do
        End If

        ' go through the queue...
```

ReceiveThreadEntryPoint also needs some massaging. When the socket is closed, the stream will no longer be valid and so BinaryFormatter.Deserialize will throw an exception. Likewise, we quit the loop and therefore neatly quit the thread:

```
Protected Sub ReceiveThreadEntryPoint()

    ' create a formatter...
    Dim formatter As New BinaryFormatter()

    ' loop...
    Do While True

        ' receive...
        Dim message As Message = Nothing
        Try
            message = formatter.Deserialize(_stream)
        Catch
        End Try
```

```
        If message Is Nothing Then
          Exit Do
        End If

        ' show it...
        ShowMessage(message)
     Loop
   End Sub
```

So how do we deal with actually closing the socket? Well, we tweak the `Dispose` method of the form itself and if we have a _socket object we close it:

```
    Protected Overloads Overrides Sub Dispose(ByVal disposing As Boolean)
      If disposing Then
        If Not (components Is Nothing) Then
          components.Dispose()
        End If
      End If

      ' close the socket...
      If Not _socket Is Nothing Then
        _socket.Close()
        _socket = Nothing
      End If

      MyBase.Dispose(disposing)
    End Sub
```

Now you'll be able to start a conversation and if you close one of the windows, <disconnect> will appear in the other. In the background, the four threads (one transmit, one receive per window) will spin down properly:

However, the application itself will still not close properly, even if you close all the windows. That's because we need to stop the `Listener` when `Form1` closes. To do this, we'll make `Listener` implement `IDisposable`. First of all:

```
    Public Class Listener
        Implements IDisposable
```

Then we add the following:

```
Public Sub Dispose() Implements System.IDisposable.Dispose

  ' stop it...
  Finalize()
  GC.SuppressFinalize(Me)

End Sub

Protected Overrides Sub Finalize()

  ' stop the listener...
  If Not _listener Is Nothing Then
    _listener.Stop()
    _listener = Nothing
  End If

  ' stop the thread...
  If Not _thread Is Nothing Then
    _thread.Join()
    _thread = Nothing
  End If

  ' call up...
  MyBase.Finalize()

End Sub
```

Now all that remains is to call `Dispose` from within `Form1`. A good place to do this is in the `Closed` event handler:

```
Protected Overrides Sub OnClosed(ByVal e As System.EventArgs)
  If Not _listener Is Nothing Then
    _listener.Dispose()
    _listener = Nothing
  End If
End Sub
```

After you compile again, you'll find that you'll now be able to properly close down the application.

Using Internet Explorer in your Applications

A common requirement of modern applications is to display HTML files and other files commonly used with Internet applications. Although the Framework has considerable support for common image formats (such as GIF, JPEG and PNG), working with HTML is a touch trickier.

We don't want to have to write our own HTML parser so using an existing component to display HTML pages is in most cases your only option. Internet Explorer was implemented as a standalone component comprised of a parser and a renderer all packaged up in a neat COM object. The Internet Explorer application that we all use 'simply' hosts this COM object. There's nothing to stop us using this COM object in our own applications, and in this section that's exactly what we're going to do.

Yes, I said COM object. There is no managed version of Internet Explorer for use with .NET. If you consider the issue that writing an HTML parser is extremely hard, and writing a renderer is extremely hard you'll come to the conclusion that I did that I'd rather use interop to get to Internet Explorer in my .NET applications than have Microsoft try and rewrite a managed version of it just for .NET. I'm confident that we will see 'Internet Explorer .NET' within the next year or two, but for now we do have to use Interop.

Internet Explorer Interop Design Pattern

My preferred design pattern for using IE in Windows Forms applications is to create a separate library containing a 'mini-browser'. This is a separate control that contains the Internet Explorer COM control, a toolbar and a status bar in one. I can just drop this into my applications as and when I need it. I'll demonstrate how to build this mini-browser control in the following sections. In some cases, you might want to display HTML pages without giving the user the UI widgets like toolbar or the ability to enter their own URLs. An extension to this pattern (which we're not going to see here), would include properties to turn off the toolbar and status bar and route status bar text change messages through to a control of your choosing.

Creating the Project

Create a new **Windows Control Library**. In the library, we need a new `MiniBrowser` control class. Delete the default `UserControl1` and create a new user control called `MiniBrowser`.

To gain access to the IE COM object, we need to create a COM wrapper for the object. Visual Studio can do this for us, which makes our lives a bit easier. With the **Designer** open, right-click on the **Toolbox** and select **Customize Toolbox**; then with the COM Components tab selected, scroll down until you find **Microsoft Web Browser** and check it on.

You may be prompted to create a new interop wrapper for the control, in which case indicate that you do. This will result in the control being added to the **Toolbox**:

Open the **Designer** for `MiniBrowser`. Draw a new **Explorer** control onto it. As well as the new control appearing on the surface of the Designer, new assemblies will be added to the list of references for the project. These references point to assemblies that VS.NET has created to host the control. In fact, `AxSHDocVw` (implemented in the new `AxInterop.ShDocVw.dll` assembly, which you can find in the project's bin folder) contains a class called `WebBrowser`. This class is inherited from `System.Windows.Forms.AxHost`, a class that understands how to host ActiveX, or rather 'COM' components. (Again, this is a curious .NET nomenclature issue. ActiveX is actually a deprecated name – the proper name is now COM. More properly, this class should be called `ComControlHost`.) This class contains the same methods and properties that the contained COM component implements, and the class itself maps the calls into the managed methods and properties and into the unmanaged COM object:

To the **Designer**, add a `StatusBar` control. This will automatically dock at the bottom of the control and you should ensure that the bar does not obscure the `WebBrowser` control. The `StatusBar` usually looks better if we use the panels, so set the `ShowPanels` property to `True`. Using the `Panels` property, add a new **Panel**. Set the `Text` property of the **Panel** to `Ready`, the `Name` property to `panelStatus` and `AutoSize` to `Spring`:

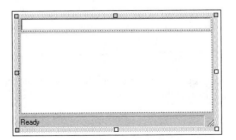

We'll build the toolbar buttons a bit later, but for now we need an address bar. To the top of the control, add a **TextBox** control. Clear its `Text` property, set its `Name` property to `textUrl` and set its `Anchor` property to `Top, Left, Right`.

Finally, to implement the resizing set the Anchor property of the `WebBrowser` control to `Left, Right, Top, Bottom`. In addition, set its `Name` property to `Ie`:

To test the control we need to get it to load a page. We'll add a `HomeUrl` property and make it navigate to that location when the control is loaded. Add these members to `MiniBrowser`:

```
Public Class MiniBrowser
    Inherits System.Windows.Forms.UserControl

    Private _url As String
    Private _homeUrl As String = "http://www.wrox.com/"
```

When the `HomeUrl` property is set, we'll just update the `_homeUrl` field. However, when the `Url` is set we'll take the opportunity to ask the `WebBrowser` control to navigate to the URL:

```
    Public Property HomeUrl() As String
      Get
        Return _homeUrl
      End Get
      Set(ByVal Value As String)
        _homeUrl = Value
      End Set
    End Property

    Public Property Url() As String
      Get
        Return _url
      End Get
      Set(ByVal Value As String)
        Ie.Navigate(Value)
      End Set
    End Property
```

Notice how we can just call the `Navigate` method on `WebBrowser`. This will call straight through to the matching `Navigate` method on the underlying COM control. Also, notice how we don't update the `_url` field whenever we set the `Url` property. We'll do this later, once IE tells us that navigation is complete.

So that we can navigate to the URL of our choice, we need to tweak the `textUrl` control. Set the `AcceptsReturn` property of this control to `True`. Add a handler for the `KeyPress` event of `textUrl` and add this code to check whether the user has hit the return key whilst editing the text in the control:

```
    Private Sub textUrl_KeyPress(ByVal sender As Object, _
      ByVal e As System.Windows.Forms.KeyPressEventArgs) _
      Handles textUrl.KeyPress
      If e.KeyChar = Chr(13) Then
        Url = textUrl.Text
      End If
    End Sub
```

To test the control we need a host application. Create a Windows Application project in the same solution and, to the newly created `Form1` form, add a `MiniBrowser` control. Set its `Dock` property to `Fill`.

Run the project and enter a URL into the text box. Press the return key and IE will navigate to the URL that you supplied:

Updating the Text Property of textURL

You'll notice that when you click around the links, the text in textUrl is not updated and also the status bar doesn't update itself. We can fix this by listening for events coming off of the IE control and adding handlers to the control.

Updating the status bar text is easy. We just have to listen for the StatusTextChange event and update the Text property on panelStatus:

```
Private Sub Ie_StatusTextChange(ByVal sender As Object, _
   ByVal e As AxSHDocVw.DWebBrowserEvents2_StatusTextChangeEvent) _
   Handles Ie.StatusTextChange
   panelStatus.Text = e.text
End Sub
```

When IE has finished opening a resource, the DownloadComplete event will be fired. We can listen for this and update the _url field and the text on textUrl. That way when the user clicks through the links, her position on the site will be properly updated. However, this event doesn't return the URL through as a parameter. We have to use the LocataionURL property of WebBrowser to return this information:

```
Private Sub Ie_DownloadComplete(ByVal sender As Object, _
                                ByVal e As System.EventArgs) _
                                Handles Ie.DownloadComplete
   _url = Ie.LocationURL
   textUrl.Text = Url
End Sub
```

Now if you run the application you'll find that the status bar and address bar work as they do in IE:

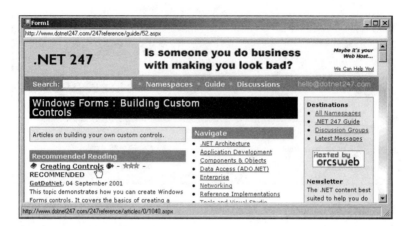

The Toolbar

To round off our discussion on building the mini-browser, we'll add a simple toolbar to the top of the control that gives us the usual features we'd expect from a web browser – that is, back, forward, stop, refresh and home.

Rather than using the `ToolBar` control, we'll add a set of button controls at the top of the control where we've currently got the address bar. Add five buttons to the top of the control, like this:

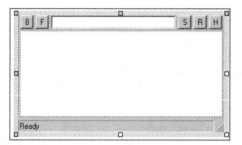

I've just changed the text on the button to indicate their function. Of course, you can use a screen capture utility to 'borrow' button images from IE and use those. The buttons should be named `buttonBack`, `buttonForward`, `buttonStop`, `buttonRefresh` and `buttonHome`. To get the resizing to work properly, make sure you set the `Anchor` property of the three buttons on the right to `Top`, `Right`.

On startup, `buttonBack`, `buttonForward` and `buttonStop` should be disabled. The IE COM control will tell us explicitly when to enable and disable the Back and Forward buttons, depending on where the user is in the page stack. We'll enable the Stop button whenever the download starts, and disable again when it stops. Curiously, the Refresh button has to be enabled when the Stop button is disabled and vice versa.

First off though, we'll add the functionality behind the buttons. It's good practice to have separate methods for each of the handlers rather than coding directly into the event handlers. The `WebBrowser` class itself implements the methods that we need, so this is all very straightforward:

```
    Private Sub buttonBack_Click(ByVal sender As System.Object, _
      ByVal e As System.EventArgs) Handles buttonBack.Click
      GoBack()
    End Sub

    Public Sub GoBack()
      Ie.GoBack()
    End Sub

    Private Sub buttonForward_Click(ByVal sender As System.Object, _
      ByVal e As System.EventArgs) Handles buttonForward.Click
      GoForward()
    End Sub

    Public Sub GoForward()
      Ie.GoForward()
    End Sub

    Private Sub buttonStop_Click(ByVal sender As System.Object, _
      ByVal e As System.EventArgs) Handles buttonStop.Click
      StopDownload()
    End Sub

    Public Sub StopDownload()
      Ie.Stop()
    End Sub

    Private Sub buttonRefresh_Click(ByVal sender As System.Object, _
      ByVal e As System.EventArgs) Handles buttonRefresh.Click
      RefreshBrowser()
    End Sub

    Public Sub RefreshBrowser()
      Ie.Refresh2()
    End Sub

    Private Sub buttonHome_Click(ByVal sender As System.Object, _
      ByVal e As System.EventArgs) Handles buttonHome.Click
      Ie.GoHome()
    End Sub
```

To manage the enable and disabling of the buttons, we have to key into a couple of events. As we mentioned before, whenever downloading begins, we need to enable Stop and disable Refresh. Add an event handler for the DownloadBegin event of Ie that contains code to enable and disable the buttons:

```
    Private Sub Ie_DownloadBegin(ByVal sender As Object, _
                                 ByVal e As System.EventArgs) _
                                 Handles Ie.DownloadBegin
      buttonStop.Enabled = True
      buttonRefresh.Enabled = False
    End Sub
```

We already have a handler for DownloadComplete, but we need to add a call to switch the buttons around when this is received:

```
Private Sub Ie_DownloadComplete(ByVal sender As Object, _
   ByVal e As System.EventArgs) Handles Ie.DownloadComplete
   _url = Ie.LocationURL
   textUrl.Text = Url
   buttonStop.Enabled = False
   buttonRefresh.Enabled = True
End Sub
```

The CommandStateChange event lets IE tell us when we should update the enabled or disabled states of our buttons. This event provides an ID so we know which button and a Boolean flag indicating whether or not we should enable it or disable it. Here's the code:

```
Private Sub Ie_CommandStateChange(ByVal sender As Object, _
    ByVal e As AxSHDocVw.DWebBrowserEvents2_CommandStateChangeEvent) _
    Handles Ie.CommandStateChange

   ' do what?
   Dim control As Control = Nothing
   Select Case e.command
     Case 1
       control = buttonForward
     Case 2
       control = buttonBack
   End Select

   ' set it...
   If Not control Is Nothing Then
     control.Enabled = e.enable
   End If
End Sub
```

Run the project now and visit a web page and click through a few links. You should be able to use the toolbar to enhance your browsing experience.

Summary

In this chapter we kicked off by looking at just how easy it is to download resources from a web server using classes built into the Framework. System.Uri lets us express a URI, and System.Net.WebRequest, in combination with System.Net.HttpWebRequest and System.Net.HttpWebResponse, lets us physically get hold of the data.

In the second section we took a look at how we could build our own network protocol by using sockets, implemented in the System.Net.Sockets namespace. We looked at how TcpListener and TcpClient make it relatively easy to work with sockets. We also spent a lot of time working with threads and the various UI issues that that kind of work throws up in order to make the application as usable as possible.

Finally we looked at how we could reuse the COM-based Internet Explorer control in our own application through .NET's interop layer.

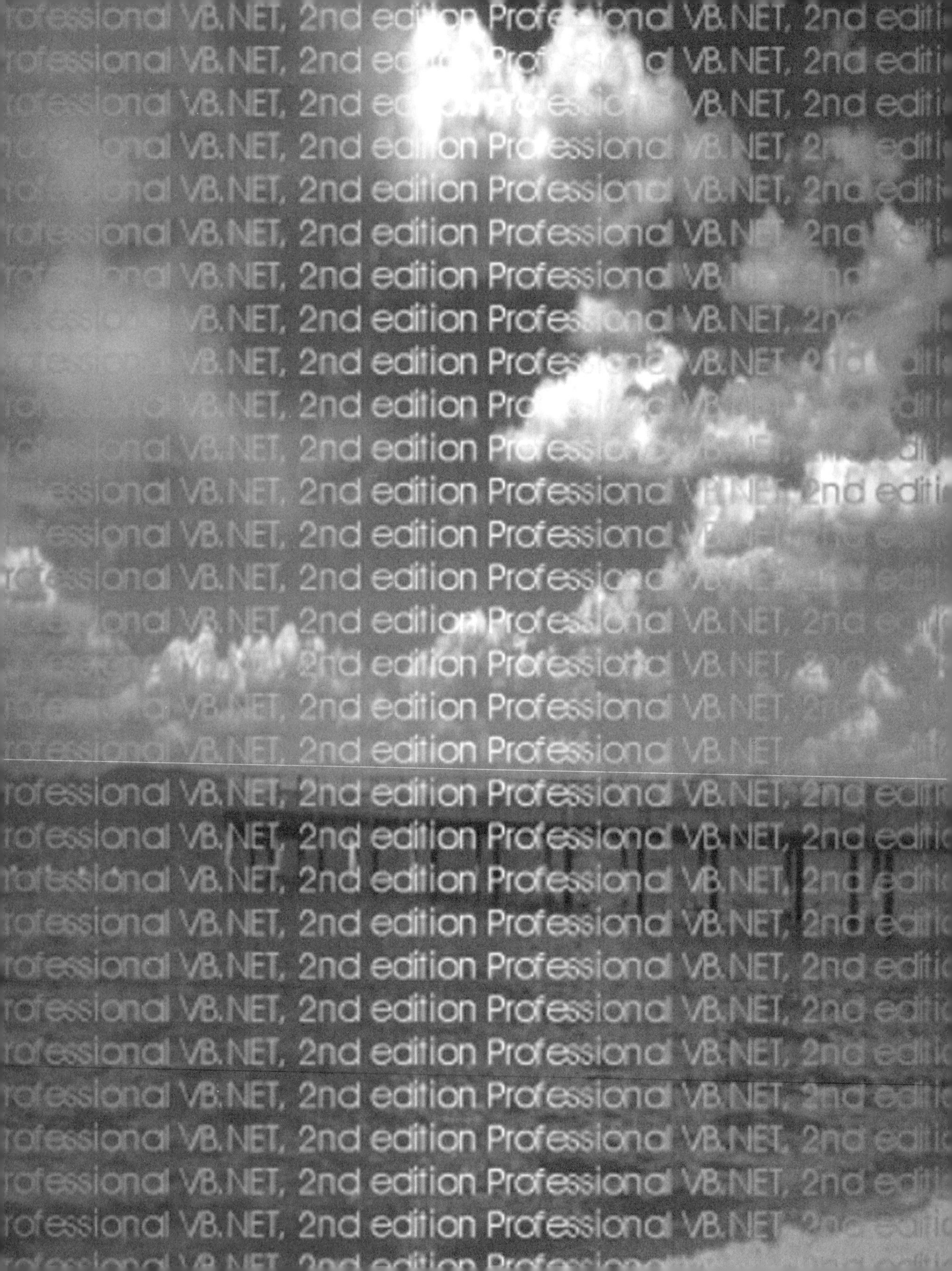
Professional VB.NET, 2nd edition

24

Security in the .NET Framework

This chapter will cover the basics of security and cryptography. We'll begin with a brief discussion of the .NET Framework's security architecture, because this will have an impact on the solutions that we may choose to implement.

The .NET Framework provides us with additional tools and functionality with regard to security. We now have the `System.Security.Permissions` namespace, which allows us to control code access permissions along with role based and identity permissions. Through our code, we can control access to objects programmatically, as well as receive information on the current permissions of objects. This security framework will assist us in finding out if we have permissions to run our code, instead of getting half way through execution and having to deal with permission based exceptions. In this chapter we will cover:

- ❏ Concepts and definitions
- ❏ Permissions
- ❏ Roles
- ❏ Principals
- ❏ Code Access Permissions
- ❏ Role Based Permissions
- ❏ Identity Permissions
- ❏ Managing Permissions
- ❏ Managing Policies
- ❏ Cryptography

Cryptography is the cornerstone of .NET Web Services security model, so in the second half of this chapter we discuss the basis of cryptography, and how to implement it. Specifically, we will cover:

❑ Hash algorithms

❑ SHA

❑ MD5

❑ Secret key encryption

❑ Public key cryptography standard

❑ Digital signatures

❑ Certification

❑ Secure Sockets Layer communications

Let's begin the chapter by taking a look at some security concepts and definitions.

> **As always, the code for this chapter is available for download from http://www.wrox.com, which you'll need in order to follow along.**

Security Concepts and Definitions

Before going on, let's detail the different types of security that we will be illustrating in this chapter and how they can relate to real scenarios:

Security Type	Related concept in `Security.Permissions` namespace or utility	Purpose
NTFS	None	Lock down specific files on any given machine.
Security Policies	`Caspol` utility, `PermView` utility	Set up overall security policy for a machine or user from an operating system level.
Cryptographic	Strong name and assembly, generation, `SignCode` utility	Use of Public-Key infrastructure and Certificates.

Security Type	Related concept in `Security.Permissions` namespace or utility	Purpose
Programmatic	Groups and Permission Sets	For use in pieces of code that are being called into. Provides extra security to prevent users of calling code from violating security measures implemented by the program that are not provided for on a machine level.

There are many approaches to providing security on our machines where our shared code is hosted. If multiple shared code applications are on one machine, each piece of shared code can get called from many front-end applications. Each piece of shared code will have its own security requirements for accessing environment variables – such as the registry, the file system, and other items – on the machine that it is running on. From an NTFS perspective, the administrator of our server can only lock down those items on the machine that are not required to be accessed from *any* piece of shared code running on it. Therefore, some applications will want to have additional security built in to prevent any calling code from doing things it is not supposed to do. The machine administrator can further assist the programmers by using the utilities provided with .NET to establish additional machine and/or user policies that programs can implement. As a further step along this line, the .NET environment has given us programmatic security through **Code Access** security, **Role Based** security, and **Identity** security. As a final security measure, we can use the cryptographic methods provided to require the use of certificates in order to execute our code.

Security in the .NET infrastructure has some basic concepts that we will discuss here. Code security is managed and accessed in the .NET environment through the use of security policies. Security policies have a relationship that is fundamentally tied to either the machine that code is running on, or to particular users under whose context the code is running. To this end, any modifications to the policy are done either at the machine or user level.

We establish the security policy on a given set of code by associating it with an entity called a **group**. A group is created and managed within each of the machine and user based policies. These group classifications are set up so that we can place code into categories. We would want to establish new code groups when we are ready to categorize the pieces of code that would run on a machine, and assign the permissions that users will have to access the code. For instance, if we wanted to group all Internet applications and then group all non-Internet applications together, we would establish two groups and associate each of our applications with its respective group. Now that we've got the code separated into groups we can define different permission sets for each group. If we wanted to limit our Internet applications' access to the local file system, we could create a permission set that limits that access and associates the Internet application group with the new permission set. By default, the .NET environment gives us one code group named `All Code` that is associated with the `FullTrust` permission set.

Permission sets are unique combinations of security configurations that determine what each user with access to a machine can do on that machine. Each set determines what a user has access to – for instance, whether they can read environment variables, the file system, or execute other portions of code. Permission sets are maintained at the machine and user levels through the utility `Caspol.exe`. Through this utility, we can create our own permission sets, though there are seven permission sets that ship with the .NET infrastructure that are also useful, as shown in the following table:

Permission Set	Explanation
FullTrust	Allows full access to all resources – adds assembly to a special list that has FullTrust access
Everything	Allows full access to everything covered by default named permission sets, only differs from FullTrust in that the group does not get added to the FullTrust Assembly List
Nothing	Denies all access including Execution
Execution	Allows execution only access
SkipVerification	Allows object to bypass all security verification
Internet	Grants default rights that are normal for Internet applications
LocalInternet	Grants rights that are not as restricted as Internet, but not full trust

Security that is used within the programming environment also makes use of permission sets. Through code, we can control access to files in a file system, environment variables, file dialogs, isolated storage, reflections, registry, sockets, and UI. Isolated storage and virtual file systems are new operating system level storage locations that can be used by programs and are governed by the machine security policies. These file systems keep a machine safe from file system intrusion by designating a regulated area for file storage. The main access to these items is controlled through Code Access Permissions.

Although many methods that we use in VB.NET give an identifiable return value, the only return value that we will get from security methods is if the method fails. If a security method succeeds, it will not give a return value. If it fails, it will return an exception object reflecting the specific error that occurred.

Permissions in the System.Security.Permissions Namespace

The System.Security.Permissions namespace is the namespace that we will use in our code to establish and use permissions to access many things such as the file system, environment variables and the registry within our programs. The namespace controls access to both operating system level objects as well as code objects. In order to use the namespace in our project we need to include the Imports System.Security.Permissions line with any of our other Imports statements in our project. Using this namespace gives us access to using the CodeAccessPermissions, and PrincipalPermissions classes for using Role Based permissions and also utilizing information supplied by Identity permissions. CodeAccessPermission is the main class that we will use as it controls access to the operating system level objects our code needs in order to function. Role Based permissions and Identity permissions grant access to objects based on the identity that the user of the program that is running carries with them.

In the following table, those classes that end with Attribute, such as EnvironmentPermissionAttribute, are the classes that allow us to modify the security level at which our code is allowed to interact with each respective object. The attributes that we can specify reflect either Assert, Deny, or PermitOnly permissions.

If permissions are asserted we have full access to the object, while if we have specified `Deny` permissions we are not allowed to access the object through our code. If we have `PermitOnly` access, only objects within our program's already determined scope can be accessed, and we cannot add any more resources beyond that scope. In our table we also deal with security in regard to **Software Publishers**. A Software Publisher is a specific entity that is using a digital signature to identify itself in a web-based application. The following is a table of the namespace members that apply to Windows Forms programming with an explanation of each:

Class	Description
CodeAccessSecurityAttribute	Specifies security access to objects such as the registry and file system
EnvironmentPermission	Controls ability to see and modify system and user environment variables
EnvironmentPermissionAttribute	Allows security actions for environment variables to be added via code
FileDialogPermission	Controls ability to open files via a file dialog
FileDialogPermissionAttribute	Allows security actions to be added for File Dialogs via code
FileIOPermission	Controls ability to read and write files in the file system
FileIOPermissionAttribute	Allows security actions to be added for file access attempts via code
IsolatedStorageFilePermission	Controls ability to access a virtual file system within the isolated storage area of an application
IsolatedStorageFilePermissionAttribute	Allows security actions to be added for virtual file systems via code
IsolatedStoragePermission	Controls ability to access the isolated storage area of an application
IsolatedStoragePermissionAttribute	Allows security actions to be added for the isolated storage area of an application
PermissionSetAttribute	Allows security actions to be added for a permission set
PrincipalPermissionAttribute	Allows for checking against a specific user. Security principals are a user and role combination used to establish security identity
PublisherIdentityPermission	Allows for ability to access based on the identity of a software publisher

Table continued on following page

Class	Description
PublisherIdentityPermissionAttribute	Allows security actions to be added for a software publisher
ReflectionPermission	This controls the ability to access non-public members of a given type
ReflectionPermissionAttribute	Allows for security actions to be added for public and non-public members of a given type
RegistryPermission	Controls the ability to access registry keys and values
RegistryPermissionAttribute	Allows security actions to be added for registry keys and values
SecurityAttribute	Controls which security attributes are representing code, used to control the security when creating an assembly
SecurityPermission	The set of security permission flags for use by .NET; this collection is used when we want to specify a permission flag in our code
SecurityPermissionAttribute	Allows security actions for the security permission flags
UIPermission	Controls ability to access user interfaces and use the windows clipboard
UIPermissionAttribute	Allows security actions to be added for UI Interfaces and the use of the clipboard

Code Access Permissions

Code access permissions are controlled through the CodeAccessPermissions class within the System.Security namespace, and its members make up the majority of the permissions we'll use in our attempt to secure our code and operating environment. The following is a table of the class methods and an explanation of their use:

Method	Description
RevertAll	Reverses all previous assert, deny or permit only methods
RevertAssert	Reverses all previous assert methods
RevertDeny	Reverses all previous deny methods

Method	Description
RevertPermitOnly	Reverses all previous permit only methods
Assert	Sets the permission to full access so that the specific resource can be accessed even if the caller hasn't been granted permission to access the resource
CheckDemand	Checks the current permissions to determine if the resource can be accessed in a specific manner
Copy	Copies a permission object
Demand	Returns whether or not all callers in the call chain have been granted the permission to access the resource in a given manner
DemandImmediate	Returns whether the immediate caller has been granted the permission to access the resource in a given manner
Deny	Denies all callers access to the resource
Equals	Determines if a given object is the same instance of the current object
FromXML	Establishes a permission set given a specific XML encoding. This parameter is an XML encoding
GetHashCode	Returns a hash code associated with a given object
GetType	Returns the type of a given object
Intersect	Returns the permissions two permission objects have in common
IsSubsetOf	Returns result of whether the current permission object is a subset of a specified permission
PermitOnly	Determines that only those resources within this permission object can be accessed even if code has been granted permission to other objects
ToString	Returns a string representation of the current permission object
ToXML	Creates an XML representation of the current permission object
Union	Creates a permission that is the union of two permission objects

Role-Based Permissions

Role-based permissions are permissions granted based on the user and role that code is being called with. Users are generally authenticated within the operating system platform and hold a **Security Identifier (SID)** that is associated within a security context. The SID can further be associated with a role, or a group membership that is established within a security context. The .NET role functionality supports those users and roles associated within a security context and also have support for generic and custom users and roles through the concept of principals. A principal is an object that holds the current caller credentials, which is termed the identity of the user. Principals come in two types – **Windows** principals and **non-Windows** principals. Windows based Principal objects are objects that store the Windows SID information regarding the current user context associated with the code that is calling into the module where we are using Role-Based permissions. Non-Windows Principals are principal objects that are created programmatically via a custom login methodology which are made available to the current thread.

Role based permissions are not set against objects within our environment like code access permissions. They are instead a permission that is checked within the context of the current user and role that a user is part of. Within the System.Security.Permissions namespace, the concept of the principals and the PrincipalPermission class of objects are used to establish and check permissions. If a programmer passes the user and role information during a call as captured from a custom login, the PrincipalPermission class can be used to verify this information as well. During the verification, if the user and role information is Null then permission is granted regardless of user and role. The PrincipalPermission class does not grant access to objects, but has methods that determine if a caller has been given permissions according to the current permission object through the Demand method. If a security exception is generated then the user does not have sufficient permission.

The following is the table of the methods in the PrincipalPermission class and a description of each:

Method	Description
Copy	Copies a permission object
Demand	Returns whether or not all callers in the call chain have been granted the permission to access the resource in a given manner
DemandImmediate	Returns whether the immediate caller has been granted the permission to access the resource in a given manner
Deny	Denies all callers access to the resource
Equals	Determines if a given object is the same instance of the current object
FromXML	Establishes a permission set given a specific XML encoding
GetHashCode	Returns a hash code associated with a given object
GetType	Returns the type of a given object

Method	Description
Intersect	Returns the permissions two permission objects have in common specified in parameter
IsSubsetOf	Returns result of whether the current permission object is a subset of a specified permission
IsUnrestricted	Returns result of whether the current permission object is unrestricted
ToString	Returns a string representation of the current permission object
ToXML	Creates an XML representation of the current permission object
Union	Creates a permission that is the union of two permission objects

As an example of how we might use these, here is a code snippet which captures the current Windows principal information and displays it to the screen in the form of a message box output. Each element of the principal information could be used in a program to validate against, and thus restrict code execution based on the values in the principal information. In our example we have inserted an `Imports System.Security.Principal` line at the top of our module so we could use the identity and principal objects:

```
Imports System.Security.Principal
Imports System.Security.Permissions

...

Private Sub btnRoleBasedPermissions_Click _
     (ByVal sender As System.Object, ByVal e As System.EventArgs)
   Dim objIdentity As WindowsIdentity = WindowsIdentity.GetCurrent
   Dim objPrincipal As New WindowsPrincipal(objIdentity)
   MessageBox.Show(Str(objPrincipal.Identity.IsAuthenticated))
   MessageBox.Show(Str(objIdentity.IsGuest))
   MessageBox.Show(objIdentity.ToString)
   objIdentity = Nothing
   objPrincipal = Nothing
End Sub
```

In this code we have illustrated a few of the properties that could be used to validate against when a caller wants to run our code. Sometimes we want to make sure that the caller is an authenticated user, and not someone who bypassed the security of our machine with custom login information. This is achieved through the following line of code:

```
MessageBox.Show(Str(objPrincipal.Identity.IsAuthenticated))
```

and will output in the `MessageBox` as either **True** or **False**.

Another piece of information to ensure that our caller is not bypassing system security would be to check and see if the account is operating as a guest. We do this by this line of code:

```
MessageBox.Show(Str(objIdentity.IsGuest))
```

Once again, the `IsGuest` returns either `True` or `False`, based on whether the caller is authenticated as a guest.

Our final `MessageBox` in our example displays the `ToString` value for the identity object. This is a value that tells us what type of identity it is, either a Windows Identity or non-Windows Identity. The line of code that executes is:

```
MessageBox.Show(objIdentity.ToString)
```

The output from the `IsString` method is shown in the following screenshot:

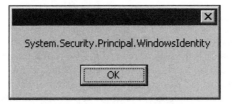

Again, the principal and identity objects are used in verifying the identity or aspects of the identity of the caller that is attempting to execute our code. Based on this information we can lock down or release certain system resources. We will show how to lock down and release system resources through our code access permissions examples coming up.

Identity Permissions

Identity permissions are pieces of information, also called **evidence**, by which a piece of code can be identified. Examples of the evidence would be the strong name of the assembly or the digital signature associated with the assembly.

> *A strong name is a combination of the name of a program, its version number, and its associated cryptographic key and digital signature files.*

Identity permissions are granted by the runtime based on information received from the trusted host, or someone who has permission to provide the information. Therefore, they are permissions that we don't specifically request. Identity permissions provide additional information to be used by the runtime when we configure items in the `Caspol` utility. The additional information that the trusted host can supply includes the digital signature, the application directory, or the strong name of the assembly.

Managing Code Access Permissions

In this section we'll be looking at the most common type of permissions – that of programmatic access – permissions, and how they are used. As our example we created a Windows Form and placed three buttons on it. This Windows Form will be used to illustrate the concept we previously mentioned, namely that, if a method fails, an exception object is generated which contains our feedback. Note at this point, that in the case of a real-world example we would be setting up permissions for a calling application. In many instances we don't want a calling application to be able to access the registry, or we want a calling application to be able to read memory variables, but not change them. However, in order to demonstrate the syntax of our commands, in our examples that follow we have placed the attempts against the objects we have secured in the same module. In our examples, we first set up the permission that we want and grant the code the appropriate access level we wish it to be able to utilize. Then we use code that accesses our security object to illustrate the effect our permissions have on the code that accesses the objects. We'll also be tying together many of the concepts discussed so far by way of these examples.

To begin with, let's look at an example of trying to access a file in the file system, which will illustrate the use of the `FileIOPermission` class in our `Permissions` namespace. In the first example, the file `C:\testsecurity\testing.txt` has been secured at the operating system level so that no one can access it. In order to do this, the system administrator would set the operating system security on the file to no access:

```
Imports System.Security.Principal
Imports System.Security.Permissions
Imports System.IO


...


Private Sub btnFileIO_Click(ByVal sender As System.Object, _
                            ByVal e As System.EventArgs)
Dim oFp As FileIOPermission = New _
   FileIOPermission(FileIOPermissionAccess.Write, "C:\testsecurity\testing.txt")


oFp.Assert()
Try
    Dim objWriter As New IO.StreamWriter _
        (File.Open("C:\testsecurity\testing.txt", IO.FileMode.Open))
    objWriter.WriteLine("HI There")
    objWriter.Flush()
    objWriter.Close()
    objWriter = Nothing
Catch objA As System.Exception
    MessageBox.Show(objA.Message)
End Try


End Sub
```

Let's walk through the code. In this example, we are going to attempt to open a file in the `C:\testsecurity` directory called `testing.txt`. We set the file access permissions within our code so that the method, irrespective of who called it, should be able to get to it with the following lines:

```
Dim oFp As FileIOPermission = New _
   FileIOPermission(FileIOPermissionAccess.Write, "C:\testsecurity\testing.txt")

oFp.Assert()
```

We used the `Assert` method, which declares that the resource should be accessible even if the caller has not been granted permission to access the resource. However, in this case, since the file is secured at the operating system level (by the system administrator), we get the following error that was caught in our exception handling:

Now, let's look at that example again with full operating system rights, but the code permissions set to `Deny`:

```
Protected Sub btnFileIO_Click(ByVal sender As
Object, ByVal e As System.EventArgs)

Dim oFp As FileIOPermission = New
FileIOPermission(FileIOPermissionAccess.Write,
"C:\testsecurity\testing.txt")
oFp.Deny()

Try

Dim objWriter As New IO.StreamWriter
(File.Open("C:\testsecurity\testing.txt",
IO.FileMode.Open))
      objwriter.WriteLine("HI There")
      objWriter.Flush()
      objWriter.Close()
      objWriter = Nothing

Catch objA As System.Exception
      messagebox.Show(objA.Message)

End Try
End Sub
```

The `Deny` method denies all callers access to the object regardless of whether the operating system granted them permission. With the `Deny` method, we catch the following error in our exception handler:

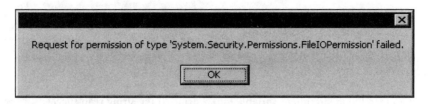

As you can see, this error differs from the first by reflecting a
`Security.Permissions.FileIOPermission` failure as opposed to an operating system
level exception.

Now let's look at an example of how we would use the `EnvironmentPermission` class of the
namespace to look at `EnvironmentVariables`.

```
Protected Sub btnTestEnvironmentPermissions_Click _
    (ByVal sender As Object, ByVal e As System.EventArgs)

    Dim oEp As EnvironmentPermission = New EnvironmentPermission _
        (environmentpermissionaccess.read, "Temp")

    Dim sEv As String
    oEp.assert()

    Try
        sEv = environment.GetEnvironmentVariable("Temp")
        Console.WriteLine("Assert was a success")

    Catch objA As System.Exception
        Console.WriteLine("Assert failed")

    End Try

    oep.revertassert()
    oep.Deny()

    Try
        sEv = environment.GetEnvironmentVariable("Temp")
        Console.WriteLine("Deny was a success")

    Catch objA As System.Exception
        Console.WriteLine("Deny failed")

    End Try

    Console.WriteLine(oep.ToString)

End Sub
```

There is a lot going on in this example, so let's look at it carefully. We first establish an environment
variable permission and use the `assert` method to ensure access to the code that follows:

```
Dim oEp As EnvironmentPermission = New EnvironmentPermission _
    (environmentpermissionaccess.read, "Temp")

Dim sEv As String
oEp.assert()
```

We then try to read the environment variable into a string. If the string read succeeds we write a line to the console to reflect the success. If the read fails we write a line to the console reflecting the failure:

```
Try
    sEv = environment.GetEnvironmentVariable("Temp")
    Console.WriteLine("Assert was a success")

Catch objA As System.Exception
    Console.WriteLine("Assert failed")

End Try
```

Next, we revoke the assert we previously issued by using the RevertAssert method and establish Deny permissions:

```
oep.RevertAssert()
oep.Deny()
```

We then try again to read the variable, and write the appropriate result to the console:

```
Try
    sEv = environment.GetEnvironmentVariable("Temp")
    Console.WriteLine("Deny failed")
Catch objA As System.Exception
    Console.WriteLine("Deny was a success")
End Try
```

We finally write the ToString of the method to the console. Below is the output on the console as a result of running our subroutine. The first two lines of our console output below give us the feedback from our Assert and Deny code, followed by the output of our ToString method:

```
Assert was a success
Deny failed
<Permission class="System.Security.Permissions.EnvironmentPermission, mscorlib,
Ver=1.0.2204.21, Loc=", SN=03689116d3a4ae33" version="1">
  <Read>Temp</Read>
</Permission>
```

As you can see, the ToString method is an XML representation of the permission object that is currently in effect. The first and second lines in the output are the system information of the version of the VB.NET security environment that was running at the time the button was clicked. The third line is the environment variable name surrounded by the Read tags, which was the permission in effect at the time the ToString method was executed.

Let's look at one more example of where the permissions would affect us in our program functionality, that of accessing the registry. We would generally access the registry on the computer that was the central server for a component in our Windows Forms application.

When we use the EventLog methods to create entries in the machine event logs we access the registry. To illustrate this concept, in the following code example we'll deny permissions to the registry and see the result:

```
Protected Sub btnTestRegistryPermissions_Click(ByVal sender As Object, _
                                    ByVal e As System.EventArgs)

Dim oRp As New _
    RegistryPermission(Security.Permissions.PermissionState.Unrestricted)
oRp.Deny()

Dim objLog As New EventLog()
Dim objLogEntryType As EventLogEntryType

Try
    Throw (New EntryPointNotFoundException())
    Catch objA As System.EntryPointNotFoundException
    Try
      If Not objLog.SourceExists("Example") Then
        objLog.CreateEventSource("Example", "System")
      End If
      objLog.Source = "Example"
      objLog.Log = "System"
      objLogEntryType = EventLogEntryType.Information
      objLog.WriteEntry("Error: " & objA.message, objLogEntryType)
    Catch objB As System.Exception
        MessageBox.Show(objB.Message)
    End Try
End Try

End Sub
```

As we walk through our code, we start with setting up registry permission and setting it to Deny access:

```
Dim oRp As New _
    RegistryPermission(Security.Permissions.PermissionState.Unrestricted)
oRp.Deny()
```

Next we set up to Throw an exception on purpose in order to set up writing to an event log:

```
Throw (New EntryPointNotFoundException())
```

When the exception is caught, it checks the registry to make sure a specific type of registry entry source is already in existence:

```
If Not objLog.SourceExists("Example") Then
  objLog.CreateEventSource("Example", "System")
End If
```

And at this point our code fails with the following error message:

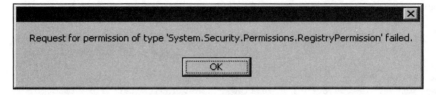

Request for permission of type 'System.Security.Permissions.RegistryPermission' failed.

These examples can serve as a good basis for use in developing classes that access the other objects within the scope of the Permissions namespace, such as reflections and UI permissions.

Managing Security Policy

As we stated in the introduction to the chapter, we have two new command line utilities (caspol.exe and permview.exe) that help us configure and view security policy at both machine and user levels. When we manage security policy at this level we are doing so as an administrator of machine or user policy for a machine that is hosting code that will be called from other front-end applications. Caspol.exe is a command line utility that has many options to give us ability to configure our security policies (Caspol stands for Code Access Security Policy). User and machine policy are associated with groups and permission sets. There is one group that is provided for us – the AllCode Group.

The Caspol utility has two categories of commands for us to review. The first category listed in the following table is the set of commands that give us feedback on what the current security policy is:

Command	Short Command	Parameters	Effect
-List	-l	None	This lists the combination of the following three options
-ListGroups	-lg	None	This will list only groups
-ListPset	-lp	None	This will list only permission sets
-ListFulltrust	-lf	None	This will list only assemblies which have full trust privileges

Command	Short Command	Parameters	Effect
-Reset	-rs	None	This will reset the machine and user policies to the default for .NET. This is handy if a policy creates a condition that is not recoverable. Use this command carefully as you will lose all changes made to the current policies
-ResolveGroup	-rsg	Assembly File	This will list what groups are associated with a given assembly file
-ResolvePerm	-rsp	Assembly File	This will list what permission sets are associated with a given assembly file

Let's look at some examples of output from our above listed commands.

If we wanted to list the groups active on our local machine at the DOS prompt we would type:

```
Caspol -Machine -ListGroups
```

The output will look similar to the following (though will differ slightly depending upon the machine you are working on):

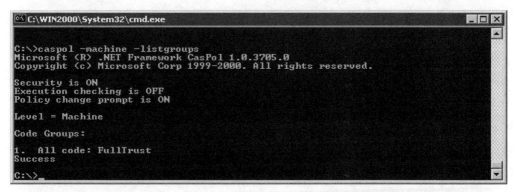

Let's talk about the above screen, so that we know some of the other things that are listed besides what we specifically requested. On the third line we see that code access security checking is on. On the following line we see that the machine is not checking for the user's right to execute the Caspol utility, since Execution checking is off. The Policy change prompt is on, so if the user executes a Caspol command that will change system policy there will be an "Are You Sure?" style prompt which appears to confirm that this is really intentional.

The level is also listed on our screen prior to our requested output, which is detailed at the bottom listing the groups present on the machine. There are two levels that the policies pertain to, those being the machine and the user. When changing policy, if the user is not an administrator, the user policy is affected unless the user specifically applies the policy to the machine through use of the -machine switch as illustrated in our screenshot. If the user is an administrator the machine policy is affected unless the user specifically applies the policy to the user level through the use of the -user switch.

Let's now look at another request result example. This time we will ask for a listing of all of the permission sets on our machine. At the command prompt we would type:

```
Caspol -machine -listpset
```

And we would see the output similar to the following screenshot. The output below has been shortened for space considerations, but the output would contain a listing of all of the code explicitly set to execute against the seven permission sets that we mentioned in our definitions section. Also note that the output is an XML representation of a permission object. The listing details the named permission sets and what each one has as active rights. For instance the first permission set is named LocalInternet, while the next lines detail the Permission class, being an environment permission with read access to the three environment variables – UserName, Temp and Tmp. The next class detail is regarding FileDialogpermissions, and it lists those as being unrestricted. The screenshot then goes on to detail the effective settings for IsolatedStorage and others:

Let's now look at the second category of commands that go with the `Caspol` utility as shown in the following table. These commands are those we will use to actually modify policy:

Command	Short Command	Parameters	Effect
-AddFullTrust	-af	Assembly File Name	Adds a given Assembly file to the full trust permission set.
-AddGroup	-ag	Parent Label, Membership, Permission Set Name	Adds a code group to the code group hierarchy.
-AddPSet	-ap	Permission Set Path, Permission Set Name	Adds a new named permission set to the policy; the permission set should be an XML file.
-ChgGroup	-cg	Membership, Permission Set Name	Changes a code group's information.
-ChgPset	-cp	File Name, Permission Set Name	Changes a named permission set's information.
-Force	-f		This option is not recommended. It forces `Caspol` to accept policy changes even if the change could cause `Caspol` itself not to be able to be executed.
-Recover	-r		Recovers policy information from a backup file that is controlled by the utility.
-RemFullTrust	-rf	Assembly File Name	Removes a given Assembly file from the full trust permission set.
-RemGroup	-rg	Label	Removes a code group.
-RemPSet	-rp	Permission Set Name	Removes a permission set. The seven default sets cannot be removed.

Let's begin our discussion of these commands with a few more definitions that will help us understand the parameters that go with our commands. An **assembly file** is created within VB.NET each time we do a build where our version is a release version. An assembly needs to have a strong name associated with it in order to be used in our permissions groupings. An assembly gets a strong name from being associated with a digital signature uniquely identifying the assembly. We carry out this association in addition to providing other pieces of evidence to be used with the strong name within the property pages of our application.

Open the SecurityApp application from the source code for this chapter. Below is the screenshot of the project's property page that pertains to building the assembly with a strong name:

The strong name configuration screen is where we associate our assembly with an existing originating key file in order for VS.NET to generate a strong name during the build process. During the build, VS.NET has generated the strong name, and then we can add our assembly to our security configuration. Place the executable, SecurityApp.exe, which was created from our build, into the C:\testsecurity directory on the local machine for use with our policy method illustrations.

If we wanted to add our assembly to the fulltrust permission set we would type:

```
Caspol -addfulltrust C:\testsecurity\SecurityApp.exe
```

The following is a screenshot of the outcome of our command:

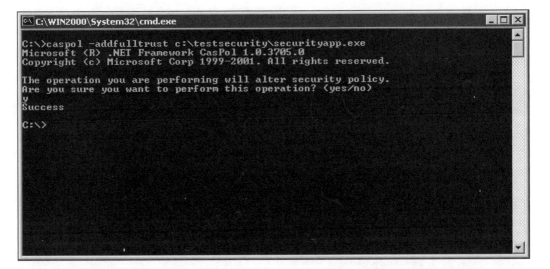

As we can see, we were prompted before our command altered our security policy, and then our new application was added to the `fulltrust` assembly list. We can confirm it was added by issuing the following command:

```
Caspol -listfulltrust
```

The excerpt of output from our command that includes our new assembly would look like:

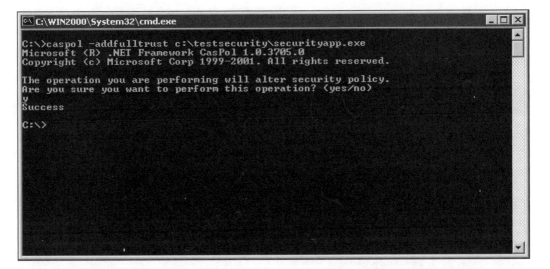

In the screenshot, we can see our application name, version, and key information that was associated with our `.exe` file when we did our build.

Now, let's look at the creation and addition of a permission set to our permission sets in our security policy. Permission sets can be created by hand, in any text editor, in an XML format and saved as an .xml file. Below is a listing from one such file that was created for this example:

```
<PermissionSet class="System.Security.NamedPermissionSet" version="1">
<Permission class="System.Security.Permissions.FileIOPermission, mscorlib, _
          SN=03689116d3a4ae33" version="1">
   <Read> C:\TestSecurity </Read>
</Permission>
<Permission class="System.Security.Permissions.EnvironmentPermission, _
          mscorlib, SN=03689116d3a4ae33" version="1">
   <Read> [TEMP] </Read>
</Permission>
   <Name>SecurityExample</Name>
   <Description>Gives Full File Access</Description>
</PermissionSet>
```

The listing has multiple permissions within the permission set. The listing sets up read file permissions within one set of tags as shown below:

```
<Permission class="System.Security.Permissions.FileIOPermission, mscorlib, _
          SN=03689116d3a4ae33" version="1">
   <Read> C:\TestSecurity </Read>
</Permission>
```

We then set up read access to our Temp environment variable in the second set of permission tags:

```
<Permission class="System.Security.Permissions.EnvironmentPermission, _
          mscorlib, SN=03689116d3a4ae33" version="1">
   <Read> [TEMP] </Read>
</Permission>
```

The listing also gives our custom permission set the name of SecurityExample with a description:

```
   <Name>SecurityExample</Name>
   <Description>Gives Full File Access</Description>
```

When we want to add our permission set to our policy, we would type:

```
Caspol -addpset C:\testsecurity\securityexample.xml securityexample
```

In the above command, we are issuing the -addpset flag to indicate that we want to add a permission set, followed by the XML file containing our permission set, followed finally by the name of our permission set. The outcome of our command looks like the following screenshot:

We can then list our security permission sets by typing `Caspol -listpset`. Here is the excerpt that shows our new security permission set:

As you can see, typing `Caspol -listpset` gives a listing of just the permission sets within our policy. Our named permission set `SecurityExample` shows up under the `Named Permission Sets` heading, and its description is listed just after its name.

Now that we have a permission set, we can add a group that our assembly object fits into and which enforces our new permission set. We add this group by using the `AddGroup` switch in `Caspol`. The `AddGroup` switch has a couple of parameters that need more explanation. The first parameter is `parent_label`. When we look at the group screenshot that follows, we can see our `All code` group has a `1.` before it. The labels within code groups have a hierarchy that gets established when we add groups, and so we need to specify what our parent label would be. In our case since the only one that exists is `1.`, that is what we'll be designating.

Since we designate 1, the new group will become a child of 1. The second parameter is `membership`. The `membership` parameter has a certain list of options that we can put in based on the table below. Each option designates a piece of information we are providing about the pieces of code that we will add to our group. For instance we would state that we will only be adding code that had a specific signature with the `-Pub` option, or add only code in a certain application directory with the `-AppDir` option:

Option	Description
-All	All Code
-Pub	Code that has a specific signature on a certificate file
-Strong	Code that has a specific strong name, as designated by a file name, code name, and version
-Zone	Code that fits into the following zones: MyComputer, Intranet, Trusted, Internet, or Untrusted
-Site	Originating on a web site
-Hash	Code that has a specific assembly hash
-AppDir	A specific application directory
-SkipVerif	Code that requests the `skipverification` permission
-URL	Originating at a specific URL

The third parameter to the `AddGroup` command is the permission set name that we want associated with our group. Our group that we will create will be under parent label 1, and we will designate the `-Zone` parameter as being `MyComputer` since our code lives on a local drive. We will also associate the new group with our `SecurityExample` permission set by typing the following command:

```
Caspol -addgroup 1. -Zone MyComputer SecurityExample
```

We can see that our output from the command was successful in the following screenshot:

In our screenshot that follows, we use the -listgroups command to list our new group:

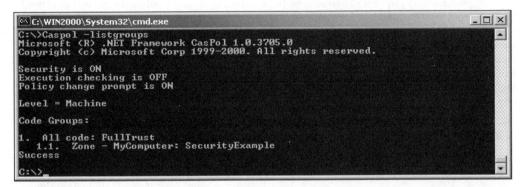

In the screenshot we can see that a 1.1 level was added with our SecurityExample permission set attached to all code that fits into the **MyComputer Zone**. Now let's verify that our assembly object fits into the **MyComputer Zone** by using our resolveperm command:

As we can see at the bottom of the screenshot it lists which **ZoneIdentityPermission** the assembly object has been associated with – **MyComputer**. In addition each assembly will get a URLIdentityPermission specifying the location of the executable.

Not only do we have the utility that helps us with managing security permission sets and groups, but we also have a utility that views the security information regarding an assembly called Permview.exe. (Permview stands for Permissions Viewer.)

Permview is not as complex as Caspol because its main purpose is to give a certain type of feedback regarding the security requests of assemblies. In fact, the Permview utility only has two switches, one for the output location, and one for declarative security to be included in the output. In order to specify an output location the switch is /Output and then a file path is appended to the command line after the switch. The Permview utility brings up another concept we have yet to cover – that of declarative security. Declarative security is displayed in the Permview utility with the /Decl switch, and is security that a piece of code requests at an assembly level. Since it is at the assembly level, the line which requests the security is at the top of the VB.NET module, even before our Imports statements. We can request one of three levels of security as shown in the following table:

Level	Description
RequestMinimum	Permissions the code must have in order to run
RequestOptional	Permissions that code may use, but could run without
RequestRefused	Permissions that you want to ensure are never granted to the code

Requesting permissions at the assembly level will help ensure that the code will be able to run, and not get permission based security exceptions. Since we have users calling our code, the declarative security ensures the callers have proper security to do all that our code requires, otherwise a security exception will be thrown. The following is an example of the syntax of how we would request minimum permissions, and the code would be placed at the top of our procedure. This example also illustrates syntax as described in the table at the beginning of our chapter regarding permissions in the Security.Permissions namespace. It also illustrates the use of a security constant, SecurityAction.RequestMinimum for the type of security we are requesting:

```
<Assembly: SecurityPermissionAttribute(SecurityAction.RequestMinimum)>
```

Once this line is added to our assembly, Permview will report on what the assembly requested by listing minimal, optional, and refused permission sets – including our security permission set under the minimal set listing.

Security Tools

Microsoft provides many security tools in its .NET SDK. Most of these tools are console based utility applications. These can be used to help implement the security processes outlined above. We won't be discussing the use of these tools in great detail.

There are two groups of tools provided with the SDK:

❑ Permissions and assembly management tools

❑ Certificate management tools

Permissions and Assembly Management Tools

Program Name	Function
Caspol.exe	Stands for Code Access Security Policy tool. Lets you view and modify security settings.
Signcode.exe	File signing tool; lets you digitally sign your executable files.
Storeadm.exe	Administration tool for isolated storage management. Restricts code access to filing system.
Permview.exe	Displays assembly's requested access permissions.
Peverify.exe	Checks if the executable file will pass the runtime test for type safe coding.
Secutil.exe	Extracts a public key from a certificate and puts it in a format that is usable in your source code.
Sn.exe	Creates assemblies with strong names; that is, digitally signed namespace and version info.

Certificate Management Tools

Program Name	Function
Makecert.exe	Creates a X.509 certificate for testing purposes.
Certmgr.exe	Assembles certificates into a CTL (Certificate Trust List). Can also be used for revoking.
Chktrust.exe	Validates a signed file containing data, its PKCS#7 hash and a X.509 certificate.
Cert2spc.exe	Creates an SPC (Software Publisher Certificate) from a X.509 certificate.

Now that we've covered the permissions side of .NET security, let's take a look at cryptography.

Cryptography Basics

Rather than being a general exposition of cryptography, this section is meant to familiarize you with basic techniques required to deal with .NET security and protecting your Web Services through encryption. The three building blocks we need are hashing algorithms, secret key encryption, and an understanding of the Public Key Cryptographic System (PKCS).

Hashing algorithms digest long sequences of data into short **footprints**, the most popular being 64 bit hash keys. The two most popular hashing algorithms are SHA (Secured Hash Algorithm) and MD5 (Message Digest version 5). These hash keys are used for signing digital documents – in other words, the hash is generated and encrypted using a **private key**.

Secret key encryption is commonly used to protect data through passwords and pass phrases (long phrases that would be difficult to guess). Secret key encryption is suitable for situations where the encrypted data needs to be accessed by the same person who protected it.

Public Key Cryptography is most widely used in protecting the data through encryption. It is also used for digital signatures. Public Key Cryptography is based on asymmetric keys. This means that you always have a pair of keys. One is known to all and is called the **public key**. The other key of the pair is kept secret and is known only to the owner. This is called the **private key**. If we use the public key to encrypt data, it can only be decrypted using the corresponding private key of the key pair, and vice versa.

The public key is known to all, so any one can decrypt the information. However, the private key is known only to the owner, so this process acts as a **digital signature**. In other words, if the public key decrypts the message, we know that the sender was the owner of the private key. As we hinted, rather than encrypting the whole document using the private key, a hash algorithm is used to digest the data into a compact form, and this is then encrypted using the private key. The result of this process is called the digital signature of the digital document.

If the data is encrypted using the public key, it can then only be decrypted by the corresponding private key, which means that only the owner of the private key will be able to read the unencrypted data. This can be used for encryption purposes.

The cryptographic namespace of .NET Framework is `System.Security.Cryptography`.

Hash Algorithms

Hash algorithms are also called **one–way functions**. This is because of their mathematical property of non-reversibility. The hash algorithms reduce large binary strings into a fixed length binary byte array. This fixed length binary array is used for computing digital signatures as explained above.

To verify a piece of information, the hash is recomputed and compared against a previously computed hash value. If both the values match, the data has not been altered. The cryptographic hashing algorithms map a large stream of binary data to a much shorter fixed length, so it is theoretically possible to have two different documents having the same hash key.

Although, in theory, it is possible that two documents may have the same MD5 hash key and a different check sum, it is computationally impossible to create a forged document having the same hash key as the original hash value. Take the case of a virus attack on an executable code. In the late 80's the state-of-art was to create a check sum or a CRC (Cyclic Redundancy Check) as a protection measure against accidental or malicious damage to the code integrity.

> *Virus makers drew cunning designs to create viruses that added padding code to the victim's files so that the check sum and CRC remained unchanged in spite of the infection. However, using MD5 hash values, this kind of stealth attack is rendered unfeasible.*

Windows Meta Files (WMF), still use check sums in the file header. For example, the .NET Framework class `System.Drawing.Imaging.WmfPlaceableFileHeader` has a read/write property of type `short` called `Checksum`. However, due to ease of computation, this check sum is used as a cheap mode of protection against accidental damage rather than against malicious attacks.

Here is a simple program to calculate a check sum:

```
' Cryptography/Checksum.vb

Imports System
Imports System.IO

Module Module1
```

This is the entry point for the program. Here, we check to see if we've received the correct argument from the command line to run the program, and stop the program if we haven't:

```
Public Sub Main(ByVal CmdArgs() As String)
    If (CmdArgs.Length <> 1) Then
        Console.WriteLine("usage: Checksum <filename>")
        End
    End If
```

First, we open the file for which the check sum is to be computed:

```
    Dim fs As FileStream = File.OpenRead(CmdArgs(0))
```

We then compute the check sum and close the file, and then output the result to the screen:

```
    Dim sum As Short = compute(fs)
    fs.Close()
    Console.WriteLine(sum)
End Sub
```

The method below computes the check sum:

```
Function compute(ByVal strm As Stream)
    Dim sum As Long = 0
    Dim by As Integer
    strm.Position = 0
    by = strm.ReadByte
    While (by <> -1)
        sum = (((by Mod &HFF) + sum) Mod &HFFFF)
        by = strm.ReadByte
    End While
    Return CType((sum Mod &HFFFF), Short)
End Function
End Module
```

Compile this program with:

```
vbc Checksum.vb
```

And run it with:

```
Checksum <filename>
```

Due to their unsafe nature, check sum and CRC are sometimes termed as poor cousins of cryptographic hash algorithms. We will now look into classes provided by .NET Framework to cater for cryptographic grade algorithms.

Cryptographic Hash Algorithms

The abstract class `System.Security.Cryptography.HashAlgorithm` represents the concept of cryptographic hash algorithms within the .NET Framework. The framework provides seven classes which extend the `HashAlgorithm` abstract class. These are:

- ❑ `MD5CryptoServiceProvider` (extends abstract class `MD5`)
- ❑ `SHA1CryptoServiceProvider` (extends abstract class `SHA1`)
- ❑ `SHA256Managed` (extends abstract class `SHA256`)
- ❑ `SHA384Managed` (extends abstract class `SHA384`)
- ❑ `SHA512Managed` (extends abstract class `SHA512`)
- ❑ `HMACSHA` (extends abstract class `KeyedHashAlgorithm`)
- ❑ `MACTripleDES` (extends abstract class `KeyedHashAlgorithm`)

The last two classes belong to a class of algorithm called **keyed hash algorithms**. The keyed hashes extend the concept of cryptographic hash with the use of a shared secret key. This is used for computing the hash of a data transported over an unsecured channel.

The following is an example of computing a hash value of a file:

```
' Cryptography/TestKeyHash.vb

Imports System
Imports System.IO
Imports System.Security.Cryptography
Imports System.Text
Imports System.Runtime.Serialization.Formatters

Module Module1
    Public Sub Main(ByVal CmdArgs() As String)
        If (CmdArgs.Length <> 1) Then
            Console.WriteLine("usage: TestKeyHash <filename>")
            End
        End If
```

Here, we create the object instance of the .NET SDK Framework class, with a salt (a random secret to confuse a potential snooper):

```
        Dim key() As Byte = Encoding.ASCII.GetBytes( _
                          "My Secret Key".ToCharArray())
        Dim hmac As HMACSHA1 = New HMACSHA1(key)
        Dim fs As FileStream = File.OpenRead(CmdArgs(0))
```

The next four lines compute the hash, convert the binary hash into a printable base 64 format, close the file, and then print the base 64 encoded string as the result of hashing to the screen:

```
        Dim hash() As Byte = hmac.ComputeHash(fs)
        Dim b64 As String = Convert.ToBase64String(hash)
        fs.Close()
        Console.WriteLine(b64)
    End Sub
End Module
```

The code can be compiled at the command line using the following:

```
vbc TestKeyHash.vb
```

To execute the code, give the following command at the console prompt:

```
TestKeyHash TestKeyHash.vb
```

This should produce the following output:

```
IOEj/D0rOxjEqCD8qHoYm+yWw6I=
```

The previous example uses an instance of the HMACSHA1 class. The output displayed is a Base64 encoding of the binary hash result value. Base64 encoding is widely used in MIME and XML file formats to represent binary data. To recover the binary data from a Base64 encoded string, we could use the following code fragment:

```
byte[] orig = Convert.FromBase64String(b64);
```

The XML parser, however, does this automatically. We will come across this in later examples.

SHA

SHA is a block cipher and operates on a block size of 64 bits. However, the subsequent enhancements of this algorithm have bigger key values, thus increasing the value range and therefore enhancing the cryptographic utility. We must note that the bigger the key value sizes, the longer it takes to compute the hash. Moreover, for relatively smaller data files, smaller hash values are more secure. To put it another way, the hash algorithm's block size should be less than or equal to the size of the data itself.

The hash size for the SHA1 algorithm is 160 bits. Here is how to use it, which is similar to the HMACSHA1 code discussed previously:

```
' Cryptography/TestSHA1.vb

Imports System
Imports System.IO
Imports System.Security.Cryptography
Imports System.Text
Imports System.Runtime.Serialization.Formatters

Module Module1
    Public Sub Main(ByVal CmdArgs() As String)
        If (CmdArgs.Length <> 1) Then
            Console.WriteLine("usage: TestSHA1 <filename>")
            End
        End If
        Dim fs As FileStream = File.OpenRead(CmdArgs(0))
        Dim sha As SHA1 = New SHA1CryptoServiceProvider()
        Dim hash() As Byte = sha.ComputeHash(fs)
        Dim b64 As String = Convert.ToBase64String(hash)
        fs.Close()
        Console.WriteLine(b64)
    End Sub
End Module
```

The .NET Framework provides bigger key size algorithms as well, namely SHA256, SHA384 and SHA512. The numbers at the end of the name indicate their block size.

The class `SHA256Managed` extends the abstract class `SHA256`, which in turn extends the abstract class `HashAlgorithm`. The Forms Authentication module of ASP.NET security (`System.Web.Security.FormsAuthenticationModule`) uses SHA1 as one of its valid formats to store and compare user passwords.

MD5

MD5 stands for Message Digest version 5. It is a cryptographic, one way hash algorithm. The MD5 algorithm competes well with SHA. MD5 is an improved version of MD4, devised by Ron Rivest of RSA fame. In fact, FIPS PUB 180-1 states that SHA-1 is based on similar principals to MD4. The salient features of this class of algorithms are:

❑   It is computationally unfeasible to forge an MD5 hash digest

❑   MD5 is not based on any mathematical assumption such as the difficulty of factoring large binary integers

❑   MD5 is computationally cheap, and therefore suitable for low latency requirements

❑   It is relatively simple to implement

The MD5 is the de facto standard for hash digest computation, due to the popularity of RSA.

The .NET Framework provides an implementation of this algorithm through the class `MD5CryptoServiceProvider` in the `System.Security.Cryptography` namespace. This class extends the `MD5` abstract class, which in turn extends the abstract class `HashAlgorithm`. This class shares a common base class with SHA1, so the examples previously discussed can be modified easily to accommodate this:

```
Dim fs As FileStream = File.OpenRead(CmdArgs(0))
    Dim md5 As MD5 = New MD5CryptoServiceProvider()
    Dim hash() As Byte = md5.ComputeHash(fs)
    Dim b64 As String = Convert.ToBase64String(hash)
    fs.Close()
    Console.WriteLine(b64)
```

Secret Key Encryption

Secret key encryption is widely used to encrypt data files using passwords. The simplest technique is to seed a random number using a password, and then encrypt the files with an XOR operation using this random number generator.

The .NET Framework represents the secret key by an abstract base class `SymmetricAlgorithm`. Four concrete implementations of different secret key algorithms are provided by default:

❑   `DESCryptoServiceProvider` (extends abstract class `DES`)

❑   `RC2CryptoServiceProvider` (extends abstract class `RC2`)

❑   `RijndaelManaged` (extends abstract class `Rijndael`)

❑   `TripleDESCryptoServiceProvider` (extends abstract class `TripleDES`)

Let's explore the `SymmetricAlgorithm` design. As will be clear from the following example code, two separate methods are provided to access encryption and decryption. Here is a console application program that encrypts and decrypts a file given a secret key:

```
' Cryptography/SymEnc.vb

Imports System.Security.Cryptography
Imports System.IO
Imports System.Text
Imports System
Module Module1
    Public Sub Main(ByVal CmdArgs() As String)
        If (CmdArgs.Length <> 4) Then
            UsageAndExit()
        End If
```

Here, we compute the index of the algorithm that we'll use:

```
        Dim algoIndex As Integer = CmdArgs(0)
        If (algoIndex < 0 Or algoIndex >= algo.Length) Then
            UsageAndExit()
        End If
```

We open the input and output files (the file name represented by `CmdArgs(3)` is the output file, and `CmdArgs(2)` is the input file):

```
        Dim fin As FileStream = File.OpenRead(CmdArgs(2))
        Dim fout As FileStream = File.OpenWrite(CmdArgs(3))
```

849

We create the symmetric algorithm instance using the .NET Framework class `SymmetricAlgorithm`. This will use the algorithm name indexed by the `CmdArgs(0)` parameter. After this, we'll set the key parameters, and display them on-screen for information:

```
Dim sa As SymmetricAlgorithm = _
    SymmetricAlgorithm.Create(algo(algoIndex))
sa.IV = Convert.FromBase64String(b64IVs(algoIndex))
sa.Key = Convert.FromBase64String(b64Keys(algoIndex))
Console.WriteLine("Key " + CType(sa.Key.Length, String))
Console.WriteLine("IV " + CType(sa.IV.Length, String))
Console.WriteLine("KeySize: " + CType(sa.KeySize, String))
Console.WriteLine("BlockSize: " + CType(sa.BlockSize, String))
Console.WriteLine("Padding: " + CType(sa.Padding, String))
```

At this point, we check to see which operation is required, and execute the appropriate static method:

```
    If (CmdArgs(1).ToUpper().StartsWith("E")) Then
        Encrypt(sa, fin, fout)
    Else
        Decrypt(sa, fin, fout)
    End If
End Sub
```

Here is where the encryption itself takes place:

```
    Public Sub Encrypt(ByVal sa As SymmetricAlgorithm, _
                    ByVal fin As Stream, _
                    ByVal fout As Stream)
    Dim trans As ICryptoTransform = sa.CreateEncryptor()
    Dim buf() As Byte = New Byte(2048) {}
    Dim cs As CryptoStream = _
        New CryptoStream(fout, trans, CryptoStreamMode.Write)
    Dim Len As Integer
    fin.Position = 0
    Len = fin.Read(buf, 0, buf.Length)
    While (Len > 0)
        cs.Write(buf, 0, Len)
        Len = fin.Read(buf, 0, buf.Length)
    End While
    cs.Close()
    fin.Close()
End Sub
```

Here's the decryption method:

```
    Public Sub Decrypt(ByVal sa As SymmetricAlgorithm, _
                    ByVal fin As Stream, _
                    ByVal fout As Stream)
    Dim trans As ICryptoTransform = sa.CreateDecryptor()
    Dim buf() As Byte = New Byte(2048) {}
    Dim cs As CryptoStream = _
        New CryptoStream(fin, trans, CryptoStreamMode.Read)
```

```
            Dim Len As Integer
            Len = cs.Read(buf, 0, buf.Length)
            While (Len > 0)
                fout.Write(buf, 0, Len)
                Len = cs.Read(buf, 0, buf.Length)
            End While
            fin.Close()
            fout.Close()
    End Sub
```

This next method prints usage information:

```
    Public Sub UsageAndExit()
        Console.Write("usage SymEnc <algo index> <D|E> <in> <out> ")
        Console.WriteLine("D =decrypt, E=Encrypt")
        Dim i As Integer
        For i = 0 To (algo.Length - 1)
            Console.WriteLine("Algo index: {0} {1}", i, algo(i))
        Next i
        End
    End Sub
```

The static parameters used for object creation are indexed by CmdArgs(0). How we arrive at these magic numbers will be discussed shortly:

```
    Dim algo() As String = {"DES", "RC2", "Rijndael", "TripleDES"}
    Dim b64Keys() As String = { _
        "YE32PGCJ/g0=", _
        "vct+rJ09WuUcR61yfxniTQ==", _
        "PHDPqfwE3z25f2UYjwwfwg4XSqxvl8WYmy+2h8t6AUg=", _
        "Q1/lWoraddTH3IXAQUJGDSYDQcYYuOpm"}
    Dim b64IVs() As String = { _
        "onQX8hdHeWQ=", _
        "jgetiyz+pIc=", _
        "pd5mgMMfDI2Gxm/SKl5I8A==", _
        "6jpFrUh8FF4="}
End Module
```

After compilation, this program can encrypt and decrypt using all four of the symmetric key implementations provided by the .NET Framework. The secret keys and their initialization vectors (IV) have been generated by a simple source code generator, which we will examine shortly.

The commands given below encrypt and decrypt files using the DES algorithm. With the first command, we take a text file, 1.txt, and use the DES algorithm to create an encrypted file called 2.bin. The next command decrypts this file back and stores it into 3.bin:

```
SymEnc 0 E 1.txt 2.bin
SymEnc 0 D 2.bin 3.bin
```

The first parameter of the SymEnc program is an index to the string array, which determines the algorithm to be used:

```
Dim algo() As String = {"DES", "RC2", "Rijndael", "TripleDES"}
```

The string defining the algorithm is passed as a parameter to the static `Create` method of the abstract class `SymmetricAlgorithm`. This class has an abstract factory design pattern:

```
Dim sa As SymmetricAlgorithm = _
    SymmetricAlgorithm.Create(algo(algoIndex))
```

To encrypt, we get an instance of the `ICryptoTransform` interface by calling the `CreateEncryptor` method of the `SymmetricAlgorithm` class extender:

```
Dim trans As ICryptoTransform = sa.CreateEncryptor()
```

Similarly, for decryption, we get an instance of the `ICryptoTransform` interface by calling the `CreateDecryptor` method of the `SymmetricAlgorithm` class instance:

```
Dim trans As ICryptoTransform = sa.CreateDecryptor()
```

We use the class `CryptoStream` for both encryption and decryption. However, the parameters to the constructor differ. For encryption we use:

```
Dim cs As CryptoStream = _
    New CryptoStream(fout, trans, CryptoStreamMode.Write)
```

Similarly, for decryption we use:

```
Dim cs As CryptoStream = _
    New CryptoStream(fin, trans, CryptoStreamMode.Read)
```

We call the `Read` and `Write` methods of the `CryptoStream` for decryption and encryption respectively. For generating the keys we use a simple code generator, listed below:

```vb
' Cryptography/SymKey.vb

Imports System.Security.Cryptography
Imports System.Text
Imports System.IO
Imports System
Imports Microsoft.VisualBasic.ControlChars

Module Module1
    Public Sub Main(ByVal CmdArgs() As String)
        Dim keyz As StringBuilder = New StringBuilder()
        Dim ivz As StringBuilder = New StringBuilder()
        keyz.Append("Dim b64Keys() As String = { _" + crlf)
        ivz.Append(crlf + "Dim b64IVs() As String = { _" + crlf )
```

The algorithm names for symmetric keys used by .NET SDK are given the correct index values here:

```
Dim algo() As String = {"DES", "RC2", "Rijndael", "TripleDES"}
```

For each of the algorithms, we generate the keys and IV:

```
Dim i As Integer
Dim comma As String = ", _" + crlf
For i = 0 To 3
    Dim sa As SymmetricAlgorithm = _
        SymmetricAlgorithm.Create(algo(i))
    sa.GenerateIV()
    sa.GenerateKey()
    Dim Key As String
    Dim IV As String
    Key = Convert.ToBase64String(sa.Key)
    IV = Convert.ToBase64String(sa.IV)
    keyz.AppendFormat(tab  + """" + Key + """" + comma)
    ivz.AppendFormat(tab  + """" + IV + """" + comma)
    If i = 2 Then comma = " "
Next i
```

Here, we print or emit the source code:

```
    keyz.Append("}")
    ivz.Append("}")
    Console.WriteLine(keyz.ToString())
    Console.WriteLine(ivz.ToString())
    End Sub
End Module
```

The above program creates a random key and an initializing vector for each algorithm. This output can be inserted directly into the SymEnc.vb program. The simplest way to do this is to type this:

```
SymKey > keys.txt
```

This will redirect the information into a file called keys.txt, which you can then use to cut and paste the values into your program. We use the StringBuilder class along with the control character crlf (carriage return and line feed) to format the text so that it can be inserted directly into your program. We then convert the binary data into Base64 encoding using the public instance method ToBase64String of the class Convert. Kerberos, the popular network authentication protocol supported by Windows 2000 and all of the UNIX flavors, uses secret key encryption for implementing security.

In this next section we will look into public key encryption.

PKCS

The Public Key Cryptographic System is a type of asymmetric key encryption. This system uses two keys, one private and other public. The public key is widely distributed whereas the private key is kept secret. One cannot derive or deduce the private key by knowing the public key, so the public key can be safely distributed.

The keys are different, yet complementary. That is, if you encrypt data using the public key, only the owner of the private key can decipher it, and vice versa. This forms the basis of PKCS encryption.

If the private key holder encrypts a piece of data using their private key, any person having access to the public key can decrypt it. The public key, as the name suggests, is available publicly. This property of the PKCS is exploited along with a hashing algorithm, such as SHA or MD5, to provide a verifiable digital signature process.

The abstract class `System.Security.Cryptography.AsymmetricAlgorithm` represents this concept in .NET Framework. Two concrete implementations of this class is provided by default, and they are:

❑ `DSACryptoServiceProvider` which extends the abstract class `DSA`.

❑ `RSACryptoServiceProvider` which extends the abstract class `RSA`.

DSA (Digital Signature Algorithm) was specified by NIST (National Institute of Standards and Technology) in January 2000. The original DSA standard was, however, issued by NIST, way back in August 1991. DSA cannot be used for encryption and is good for only digital signature. We will discuss digital signature in more detail in the next sub section.

RSA algorithms can also be used for encryption as well as digital signatures. RSA is the de facto standard and has much wider acceptance than DSA. RSA is a tiny bit faster than DSA as well.

RSA algorithm is named after its three inventors Rivest, Shamir and Adleman. It was patented in the USA, but the patent expired on 20th September. 2000. RSA can be used for both digital signature and data encryption. It is based on the assumption that large numbers are extremely difficult to factor. The use of RSA for digital signatures is approved within the FIPS PUB 186-2 and defined in the ANSI X9.31 standard document.

To gain some practical insights into RSA implementation of the .NET Framework, consider the following code:

```
' Cryptography/TestRSAKey.vb

Imports System.Security.Cryptography.Xml
Module Module1
    Sub Main()
        Dim RSA As RSAKeyValue = New RSAKeyValue()
        Dim str As String = RSA.Key.ToXmlString(True)
        System.Console.WriteLine(str)
    End Sub
End Module
```

This code creates a pair of private and public keys and prints it out at the command line in XML format. To compile the above code, simply open a console session, run `corvar.bat` (if necessary) to set the .NET SDK paths, and compile the program by typing the following command:

```
Vbc /r:System.Security.dll TestRSAKey.vb
```

This should produce a file called `TestRSAKey.exe`. Execute this program and redirect the output to a file such as `key.xml`:

```
TestRSAKey > key.xml
```

The file `key.xml` contains all the private and public members of the generated RSA key object. You can open this XML file in Internet Explorer 5.5 or above. If you do so, you will notice that the private member variables are also stored in this file. The binary data representing the large integers is encoded in `Base64` format.

The program listed above uses an `RSAKeyValue` instance to generate a new key pair. The class `RSAKeyValue` is contained in the `System.Security.Cryptography.Xml` namespace. This namespace can be thought of as the XML face of the .NET cryptographic framework. It contains a specialized, lightweight implementation of XML for the purpose of cryptography, and the model allows XML objects to be signed with a digital signature.

The `System.Security.Cryptography.Xml` namespace classes depend upon the classes contained in the `System.Security.Cryptography` namespace for the actual implementation of cryptographic algorithms.

The `key.xml` file, generated by redirecting the output of the VB.NET test program `TestRSAKey`, contains both private and public keys. However, we need to keep the private key secret while making the public key widely available. Therefore we need to separate out the public key from the key pair. Here is the program to do it:

```vb
' Cryptography/TestGetPubKey.vb

Imports System.Text
Imports System.Security.Cryptography
Imports System.IO
Imports System.Security.Cryptography.Xml
Imports System
Module Module1
    Public Sub Main(ByVal CmdArgs() As String)
        If (CmdArgs.Length <> 1) Then
            Console.WriteLine("usage: TestGetPubKey <key pair xml>")
            End
        End If
        Dim xstr As String = File2String(CmdArgs(0))
```

The following code creates an instance of the RSA implementation and re-initializes the internal variables through the XML formatted string:

```vb
        Dim rsa As RSACryptoServiceProvider = New RSACryptoServiceProvider()
        rsa.FromXmlString(xstr)
        Dim x As String = rsa.ToXmlString(False)
        Console.WriteLine(x)
    End Sub
    Public Function File2String(ByVal fname As String)
        Dim finfo As FileInfo = New FileInfo(fname)
        Dim buf() As Byte = New Byte(finfo.Length) {}
        Dim fs As FileStream = File.OpenRead(fname)
        fs.Read(buf, 0, buf.Length)
        Return (New ASCIIEncoding()).GetString(buf)
```

```
        End Function
    End Module
```

This program is logically similar to `TestRSAKey.vb`, except that it has to read the key file and pass a different parameter in the `ToXmlString` method.

The cryptography classes use a lightweight XML implementation, thus avoiding the elaborate ritual of parsing the fully-formed generic XML data containing serialized objects. This has another advantage of speed because it bypasses the DOM parsers.

To compile the previous code, type:

```
vbc /r:System.Security.dll TestGetPubKey.vb
```

This should produce the file `TestGetPubKey.exe`. Run this file, giving `key.xml` as the name of the input file, and redirect the program's output to `pub.xml`. This file will contain an XML formatted public key. The binary data, basically binary large integers, are `Base64` encoded. You may recall that `key.xml` contains both the public and private key pairs, and was generated by redirecting the output of `TestRSAKey.exe`. The following line will redirect `key.xml`'s public key to `pub.xml`:

```
TestGetPubKey key.xml > pub.xml
```

Now, let's write a program to test the encrypt and decrypt feature of the RSA algorithm:

```vb
' Cryptography/TestCrypt.vb

Imports System
Imports System.IO
Imports System.Security.Cryptography.Xml
Imports System.Security.Cryptography
Imports System.Text
Module Module1
    Public Sub Main(ByVal CmdArgs() As String)
        If (CmdArgs.Length <> 4) Then
            Console.WriteLine("usage: TestCrypt <key xml> <E|D> <in> <out>")
            Console.WriteLine(" E= Encrypt, D= Decrypt (needs private key)")
            End
        End If
```

Here, we read the public or private key into memory:

```vb
        Dim xstr As String = File2String(CmdArgs(0))
```

We create an instance of an RSA cryptography service provider and initialize the parameters based on the XML lightweight file name passed in `CmdArgs(0)`:

```vb
        Dim RSA As New RSACryptoServiceProvider()
        RSA.FromXmlString(xstr)
```

We display the key file name:

```
Console.WriteLine("Key File: "+args[0]);
string op = "Encrypted";
```

We read the input file and store it into a byte array:

```
Dim info As FileInfo = New FileInfo(CmdArgs(2))
Dim inbuflen As Integer = CType(info.Length, Integer)
Dim inbuf() As Byte = New Byte(inbuflen-1) {}
Dim outbuf() As Byte
Dim fs As FileStream = File.OpenRead(CmdArgs(2))
fs.Read(inbuf, 0, inbuf.Length)
fs.Close()
```

We either encrypt or decrypt depending on CmdArgs(1) option:

```
If (CmdArgs(1).ToUpper().StartsWith("D")) Then
    op = "Decrypted"
    outbuf = rsa.Decrypt(inbuf, False)
Else
    outbuf = rsa.Encrypt(inbuf, False)
End If
```

We'll write back the result in the output buffer into the file, and display the result:

```
fs = File.OpenWrite(CmdArgs(3))
fs.Write(outbuf, 0, outbuf.Length)
fs.Close()
Console.WriteLine(op + " input [" + CmdArgs(2) + "] to output [" _
                + CmdArgs(3) + "]")
End Sub
```

Here's a helper method to read the file name passed as an argument and convert the content to string:

```
Public Function File2String(ByVal fname As String)
    Dim finfo As FileInfo = New FileInfo(fname)
    Dim buf() As Byte = New Byte(finfo.Length) {}
    Dim fs As FileStream = File.OpenRead(fname)
    fs.Read(buf, 0, buf.Length)
    fs.Close()
    Return (New ASCIIEncoding()).GetString(buf)
End Function
End Module
```

This test program encrypts or decrypts a short file depending on the parameters supplied to it. It takes four parameters; the XML formatted private or public key file, option E or D standing for encrypt or decrypt options respectively and input and output file names.

This program can be compiled with the following command.

```
vbc /r:System.Security.dll TestCrypt.vb
```

The above command will produce a PE file `TestCrypt.exe`. To test the encrypt and decrypt functions, we'll create a small plain text file called `1.txt`. Recall that we had also created two other files `key.xml` and `pub.xml`. The file `key.xml` contains a key pair and `pub.xml` contains the public key extracted from the file `key.xml`.

Let's encrypt the plain text file `plain.txt`. To do so use the following command:

```
TestCrypt pub.xml E 1.txt rsa.bin
```

Note that we have used the public key file to encrypt it. You can type the output on the console, but this won't make any sense to us because it contains binary data. You could use a binary dump utility to dump out the file's content. If you do this, you will notice that the total number of bytes is 128 compared to the input of 13 bytes. This is because the RSA is a block cipher algorithm and the block size equals the key size, so the output will always be in multiples of the block size. You may wish to re-run the above examples with larger files to see the resulting encrypted file length.

Let us now decrypt the file to get back the original text. Use the following command to decrypt:

```
TestCrypt key.xml D rsa.bin decr.txt
```

Note that we used the `key.xml` file, which also contains the private key, to decrypt. That's because we use the public key to encrypt and private key to decrypt. In other words, anyone may send encrypted documents to you if they know your public key, but only you can decrypt the message. The reverse is true for digital signatures, which we will cover in the next section.

Digital Signature Basics

Digital signature is the encryption of a hash digest (for example MD5 or SHA-1) of data using a public key. The digital signature can be verified by decrypting the hash digest and comparing it against a hash digest computed from the data by the verifier.

As noted earlier, the private key is known only to the owner, so the owner can sign a digital document by encrypting the hash computed from the document. The public key is known to all, so anyone can verify the signature by recomputing the hash and comparing it against the decrypted value, using the public key of the signer.

The .NET Framework provides DSA and RSA digital signature implementations by default. We will consider only DSA, as RSA was covered in the previous section. Both of the implementations extend the same base class, so all programs for DSA discussed below will work for RSA as well:

We will go through the same motions of producing a key pair and a public key file and then sign and verify the signature:

```
' Cryptography/GenDSAKeys.vb

Imports System
Imports System.Security.Cryptography
Imports FileUtil
```

```
Module Module1
    Public Sub Main(ByVal CmdArgs() As String)
        Dim dsa As DSACryptoServiceProvider = New DSACryptoServiceProvider()
        Dim prv As String = dsa.ToXmlString(True)
        Dim pub As String = dsa.ToXmlString(False)
        Dim fileutil As FileUtil = New FileUtil()
        fileutil.SaveString("dsa-key.xml", prv)
        fileutil.SaveString("dsa-pub.xml", pub)
        Console.WriteLine("Created dsa-key.xml and dsa-pub.xml")
    End Sub
End Module
```

This code generates two XML formatted files dsa-key.xml and dsa-pub.xml, containing private and public keys respectively. Before we can run this, however, we need to create the FileUtil class used to output our two files:

```
' Cryptography/FileUtil.vb

Imports System.IO
Imports System.Text

Public Class FileUtil
    Public Sub SaveString(ByVal fname As String, ByVal data As String)
        SaveBytes(fname, (New ASCIIEncoding()).GetBytes(data))
    End Sub

    Public Function LoadString(ByVal fname As String)
        Dim buf() As Byte = LoadBytes(fname)
        Return (New ASCIIEncoding()).GetString(buf)
    End Function

    Public Function LoadBytes(ByVal fname As String)
        Dim finfo As FileInfo = New FileInfo(fname)
        Dim length As String = CType(finfo.Length, String)
        Dim buf() As Byte = New Byte(length) {}
        Dim fs As FileStream = File.OpenRead(fname)
        fs.Read(buf, 0, buf.Length)
        fs.Close()
        Return buf
    End Function

    Public Sub SaveBytes(ByVal fname As String, ByVal data() As Byte)
        Dim fs As FileStream = File.OpenWrite(fname)
        fs.SetLength(0)
        fs.Write(data, 0, data.Length)
        fs.Close()
    End Sub
End Class
```

The following code signs the data:

```
' Cryptography/DSASign.vb

Imports System
Imports System.IO
Imports System.Security.Cryptography
Imports System.Text
Imports FileUtil

Module Module1
    Public Sub Main(ByVal CmdArgs() As String)
        If CmdArgs.Length <> 3 Then
            Console.WriteLine("usage: DSASign <key xml> <data> <sign>")
            End
        End If
        Dim fileutil As FileUtil = New FileUtil()
        Dim xkey As String = fileutil.LoadString(CmdArgs(0))
        Dim fs As FileStream = File.OpenRead(CmdArgs(1))
```

The DSA provider instance is created and the private key is reconstructed from the XML format using the following two lines of code:

```
        Dim dsa As DSACryptoServiceProvider = New DSACryptoServiceProvider()
        dsa.FromXmlString(xkey)
```

The next line signs the file:

```
        Dim sig() As Byte = dsa.SignData(fs)
        fs.Close()
        fileutil.SaveString(CmdArgs(2), Convert.ToString(sig))
        Console.WriteLine("Signature in {0} file", CmdArgs(2))
    End Sub
End Module
```

To verify the signature, we'll use the following sample code:

```
' Cryptography/DSAVerify.vb

Imports System
Imports System.IO
Imports System.Security.Cryptography
Imports System.Text
Imports FileUtil

Module Module1
    Public Sub Main(ByVal CmdArgs() As String)
        If CmdArgs.Length <> 3 Then
            Console.WriteLine("usage: DSAVerify <key xml> <data> <sign>")
            End
        End If
        Dim fileutil As FileUtil = New FileUtil()
        Dim xkey As String = fileutil.LoadString(CmdArgs(0))
        Dim data() As Byte = fileutil.LoadBytes(CmdArgs(1))
```

```
        Dim xsig As String = fileutil.LoadString(CmdArgs(2))
        Dim dsa As DSACryptoServiceProvider = New DSACryptoServiceProvider()
        dsa.FromXmlString(xkey)
        Dim xsigAsByte() As Byte = New Byte(xsig) {}
        Dim verify As Boolean
        verify = dsa.VerifyData(data, xsigAsByte)
        Console.WriteLine("Signature Verification is {0}", verify)
    End Sub
End Module
```

The actual verification is done using the highlighted code fragment.

The next four commands listed below compile the source files:

```
vbc /target:library FileUtil.vb
vbc /r:FileUtil.dll GenDSAKeys.vb
vbc /r:FileUtil.dll DSASign.vb
vbc /r:FileUtil.dll DSAVerify.vb
```

There are many helper classes within the System.Security.Cryptography, and the System.Security.Cryptography.Xml namespaces, which provide many features to help deal with digital signatures and encryption and, at times, provide overlapping functionality. Therefore, there is more than one way of doing the same thing.

X509 Certificates

X509 is a public key certificate exchange framework. A public key certificate is a digitally signed statement by the owner of a private key, trusted by the verifier (usually a certifying authority) that certifies the validity of the public key of another entity. This creates a trust relationship between two unknown entities. This is an ISO standard specified by the document ISO/IEC 9594-8. X.509 certificates are also used in SSL (Secure Sockets Layer), which is covered in the next section.

There are many certifying authority services available over the Internet. VeriSign (http://www.verisign.com) is the most popular one. This company was also founded by the RSA trio themselves. You can also run your own Certificate Authority (CA) service over an Intranet using Microsoft Certificate Server.

The Microsoft .NET Framework SDK also provides tools for generating certificates for testing purposes.

```
makecert -n CN=Test test.cer
```

This command generates a test certificate. You can view it by clicking on the test.cer file from the Windows Explorer.

From the same screen, you could also install this certificate on your computer.

Three classes dealing with X509 certificates are provided in the .NET Framework in the namespace System.Security.Cryptography.X509Certificates. Here is a program that loads and manipulates the certificate created above:

```
' Cryptography/LoadCert.vb

Imports System
Imports System.Security.Cryptography.X509Certificates

Module Module1
    Public Sub Main(ByVal CmdArgs() As String)
        If CmdArgs.Length <> 1 Then
            Console.Write("usage loadCert <cert file> ")
            End
        End If
        Dim cert As X509Certificate = _
            X509Certificate.CreateFromCertFile(CmdArgs(0))
        Console.WriteLine("hash= {0}", cert.GetCertHashString())
        Console.WriteLine("effective Date= {0}", _
                        cert.GetEffectiveDateString())
        Console.WriteLine("expire Date= {0}", _
```

```
                          cert.GetExpirationDateString())
        Console.WriteLine("Isseued By= {0}", cert.GetIssuerName())
        Console.WriteLine("Issued To= {0}", cert.GetName())
        Console.WriteLine("algo= {0}", cert.GetKeyAlgorithm())
        Console.WriteLine("Pub Key= {0}", cert.GetPublicKeyString())
    End Sub
End Module
```

The static method loads `CreateFromCertFile` the certificate file and creates a new instance of the class `X509Certificate`.

The next section deals with SSL, which uses X509 certificates for establishing the trust relationship.

Secure Sockets Layer

SSL (Secure Sockets Layer) protocol provides privacy and reliability between two communicating applications over the Internet. SSL is built over the TCP layer. In January 1999, IETF (Internet Engineering Task Force) adopted an enhanced version of SSL 3.0 and called it TLS, which stands for Transport Layer Security. TLS is backwardly-compatible with SSL, and is defined in RFC 2246. However, the name SSL stayed due to wide acceptance of this Netscape protocol name.

SSL provides connection-oriented security and has the following four properties:

❑ Connection is private and encryption is valid for that session only.

❑ Symmetric key cryptography, like DES, is used for encryption. However, the session secret key is exchanged using public key encryption.

❑ Digital Certificates are used to verify the identities of the communicating entities.

❑ Secure hash functions, like SHA and MD5, are used for message authentication code (MAC).

The SSL protocol sets the following goals for itself:

❑ **Cryptographic security** – Uses symmetric key for session and public key for authentication

❑ **Interoperability** – Interpolates OS and programming languages

❑ **Extensibility** – Adds new protocols for encrypting data which are allowed within the SSL framework

❑ **Relative efficiency** – Reduces computation and network activity by using caching techniques

The following is a simplified discussion of the SSL algorithm sequence.

Two entities communicating using SSL protocols must have a public-private key pair, optionally with digital certificates validating their respective public keys.

At the beginning of a session, the client and server exchange information to authenticate each other. This ritual of authentication is called the **Handshake Protocol**. During this, a session ID, the compression method and the cipher suite to be used are negotiated. If the certificates exist, they are then exchanged. Although certificates are optional, either the client or the server may refuse to continue with the connection and end the session in the absence of a certificate.

After receiving each other's public keys, a set of secret keys based on a randomly generated number is exchanged by encrypting it with each other's public keys. After this, the application data exchange can commence. The application data will be encrypted using a secret key, and a signed hash of the data is sent to verify the data integrity.

Microsoft implements the SSL client in the .NET Framework classes. However, the server side SSL can be used by deploying your service through the IIS web server.

The following code fragment can be used to access SSL protected web servers from the .NET platform:

```
WebRequest req = WebRequest.Create("https://www.microsoft.com");
WebResponse result = req.GetResponse();
```

Note that the above URL starts with https, which signals the WebRequest class to use SSL protocol. Interestingly, the same code is useful for accessing unsecured URLs as well.

The following is a program for accessing a secured URL. It takes care of the minor details such as encoding for us:

```
' Cryptography/GetWeb.vb

Imports System
Imports System.IO
Imports System.Net
Imports System.Text

Module Module1
    Public Sub Main(ByVal CmdArgs() As String)
        If CmdArgs.Length <> 1 Then
            Console.WriteLine("usage: GetWeb url")
            Console.WriteLine("example: GetWeb https://www.microsoft.com")
            End
        End If
        Dim ms As String
```

We call the Create() method (which we'll see in a moment) with a URL and an encoding format:

```
        Try
            ms = Create(CmdArgs(0), "utf-8")
        Catch x As Exception
            Console.WriteLine(x.StackTrace)
            Console.WriteLine("Bad URL: {0}", CmdArgs(0))
        End Try
        Console.WriteLine(ms)
    End Sub
```

Now we come to the Create() method. Using the .NET SDK WebRequest object, we create an HTTP secured request object and get its response stream:

```
    Function Create(ByVal url As String, ByVal encod As String) As String
        Dim req As WebRequest = WebRequest.Create(url)
```

```
        Dim result As WebResponse = req.GetResponse()
        Dim ReceiveStream As Stream = result.GetResponseStream()
```

We create an encoding instance from the .NET Framework object, `Encoding`:

```
        Dim enc As Encoding = System.Text.Encoding.GetEncoding(encod)
```

Here, we'll create the stream reader:

```
        Dim sr As StreamReader = New StreamReader(ReceiveStream, enc)
```

We read the stream fully – the entire web page or serialized object is read into the `response` String:

```
        Dim response As String = sr.ReadToEnd()
        Return response
    End Function
    Dim MaxContentLength As Integer = 16384 ' 16k
End Module
```

The above console application gets a secured (SSL) protected URL and displays the content on the console. To compile the code, give the following command:

```
vbc /r:System.dll GetWeb.vb
```

Summary

In this chapter we covered the basics of security and cryptography. We started with an overview of the security architecture of the .NET Framework, and looked at four types of security: NTFS, security policies, cryptographic, and programmatic.

We went on to examine the security tools and functionality that the .NET Framework provides. We examined the `System.Security.Permissions` namespace, and learned how we can control code access permissions, role based permissions, and identity permissions. We looked at how we can manage code access permissions and manage security policies for our code. We used two tools – `Caspol` and `Permview` – that help us to configure and view security at both the machine and user levels.

In the second half of the chapter we turned our attention to cryptography – both the underlying theory and how it can be applied within our applications. We looked at the different types of cryptographic hash algorithms, including SHA, MD5, Secret Key Encryption, and PKCS. We also understood how we can use digital certificates (specifically, X509 certificates) and Secure Socket Layers.

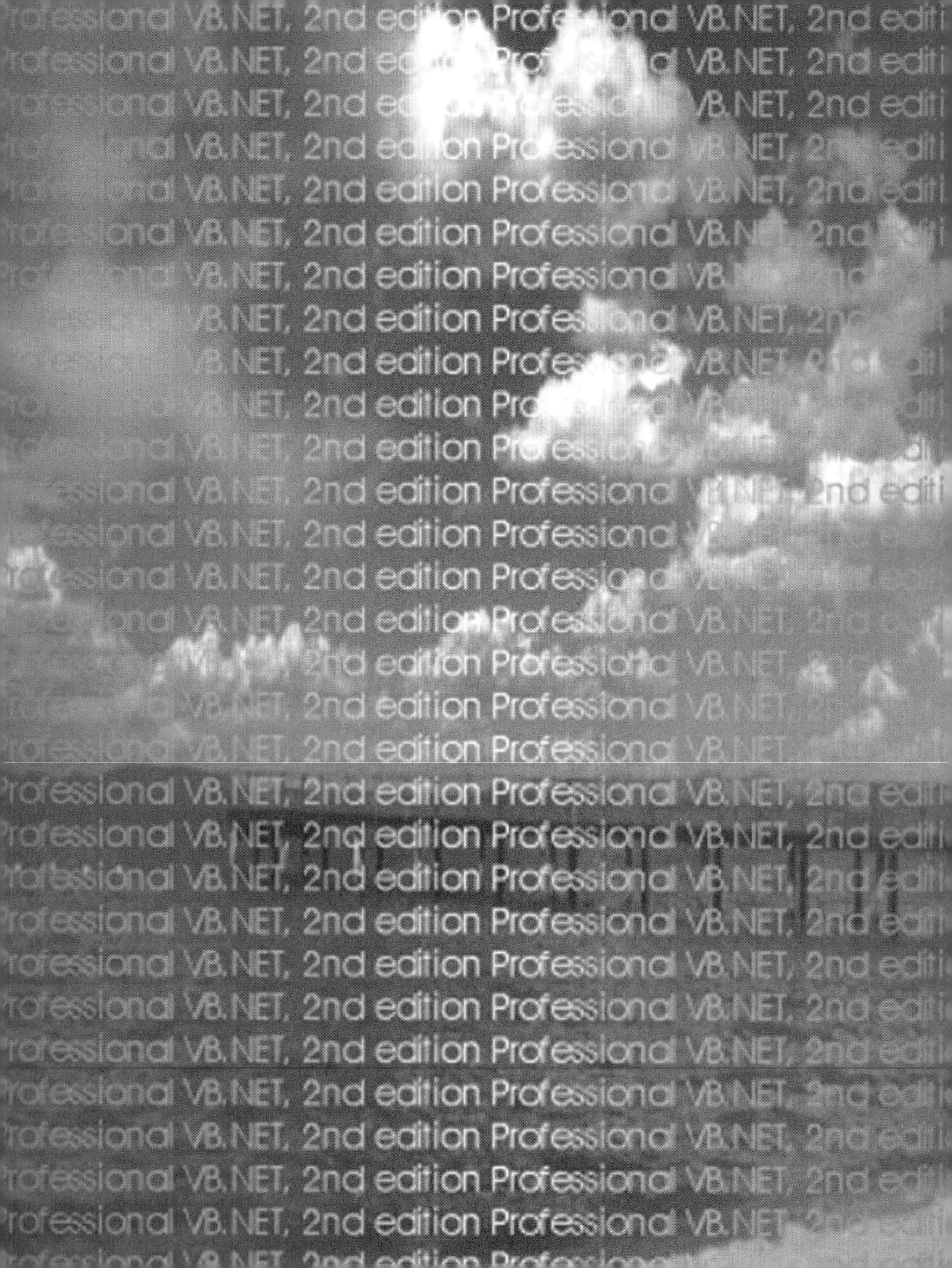
Professional VB.NET, 2nd edition

Assemblies and Deployment

When you create Windows applications other people will (hopefully) want to install and use them. However, all sorts of errors can occur when we try to run an application we've just created (and which worked perfectly on our machine) on another machine. Even more infuriating are problems that occur months later when a user has installed another piece of software that is totally unrelated to ours. You'll be pleased to hear that there are many new features in VS.NET and the CLR that make application deployment easier.

This chapter is going to look at what VS.NET and the CLR have to offer to help us. For many years application deployment wasn't treated as an integral part of the development lifecycle of an application. It was often treated as an after thought – not considered until the application had been finished. With the increasing componentization of products this lead to a number of problems for end users. This is not to say that it's the developer's fault that these problems occur. Often, they could be attributed to a form of growing pains as we moved towards a more component-based software architecture.

Specifically, we're going to look at:

- ❑ What assemblies are and how they are used
- ❑ How assemblies can be versioned
- ❑ The different ways that an application can be deployed
- ❑ How we can use VS.NET to create deployment projects for our applications

Assemblies

The assembly is used by the CLR as the smallest unit for:

❑ Deployment

❑ Version control

❑ Security

❑ Type grouping

❑ Code reuse

An assembly can be thought of as a logical DLL (assemblies can also be contained with an EXE file). It must contain a **manifest** (also referred to as the **assembly metadata**) and (optionally) any of the following three sections:

❑ Type metadata

❑ Microsoft Intermediate Language (MSIL) code

❑ Resources

An assembly can be just one file. The following figure details the contents of an assembly:

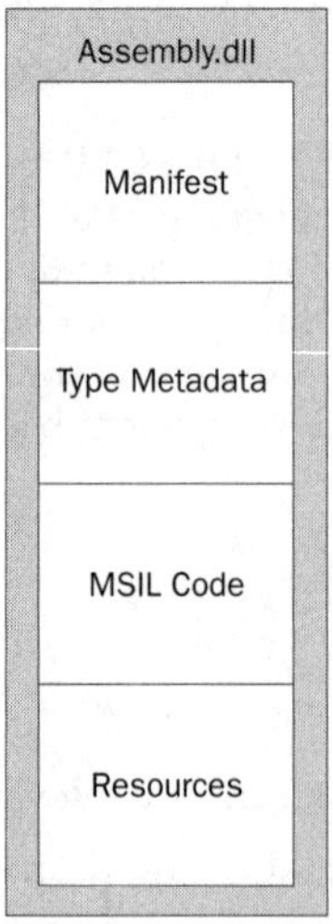

Alternatively, the structure can be split across multiple files as shown in the following figure (or any other combination that you would want):

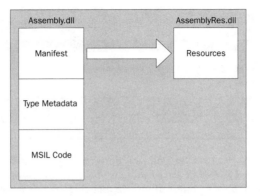

An assembly can only have one manifest section across all the files that make up the assembly. There is nothing stopping you, however, from having a resource section (or any of the other sections of Type Metadata, and MSIL Code) in each of the files that make up an assembly. The ability to split an assembly across multiple files can help with deployment and specifically on-demand downloading. The section of assemblies of most interest to us is the manifest.

The Manifest

The **manifest** is part of the mechanism by which an assembly is self-describing. The manifest includes the following sections (which will be covered later):

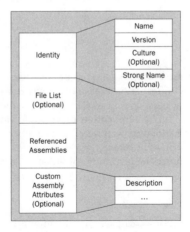

To look at what the manifest contains for a particular assembly we can use the **IL Disassembler** (Ildasm.exe) that is part of the .NET Framework SDK. When Ildasm.exe loads up, you can browse for an assembly to view by selecting Open from the File menu. Once an assembly has been loaded into Ildasm.exe it will disassemble the metadata contained within the assembly and present you with a treeview that you can use to navigate it:

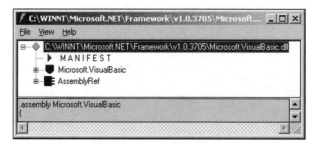

The full path of the assembly you are viewing will represent the root node. You will notice that the first node below the root is called M A N I F E S T and, as you probably have guessed, it contains all the information about the assembly's manifest. If you double-click on this node a new window will be displayed containing the information contained within the manifest:

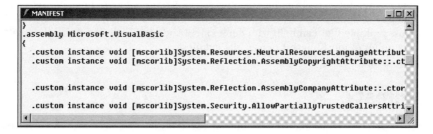

However, it's all very well knowing what sections are contained within the manifest and how to view them, but what are they used for?

The Identity Section

The **identity** section of the manifest is what is used to uniquely identify this particular assembly. The section can contain some optional information that may or may not be present. There are certain restrictions on the information that must appear in the identity section depending on the type of assembly. Assemblies come in two types: **application-private** and **shared**. (We will cover the differences between the two types shortly.) The identity section of an assembly can be found by looking for the .assembly (without a following extern) directive in the Manifest window of Ildasm.exe. In the above screenshot the line that denotes the beginning of the identity section is:

```
.assembly Microsoft.VisualBasic
```

From the earlier figure of the manifest we can see that the identity section can contain a number of subsections. Every assembly has a name that is declared as part of the .assembly directive; in the case of the above line, we can see the assembly is called Microsoft.VisualBasic. The name of the assembly is very important, as this is what the CLR uses to locate the actual file that contains the assembly. The extension .dll is appended to the assembly name to give the name of the file that contains the assembly manifest.

The Version Number

The identity section must also contain an entry that describes what version of the assembly it is. A version number for an assembly is presented by the `.ver` directive in `Ildasm.exe` and in the previous screenshot we can see that the `Microsoft.VisualBasic` assembly has a version number of 7:0:0:0 as indicated by the following entry in the `.assembly` section:

```
.ver 7:0:0:0
```

As you can see there are four parts to a version number:

```
Major : Minor : Build : Revision
```

Assemblies that have the same name but different version numbers are treated as completely different assemblies. If you have an assembly on your machine that has a version number of 1.5.2.3 and another version of the same assembly with a version number of 1.6.0.1 then the CLR will treat them as different assemblies. The version number of an assembly is part of what is used to define dependencies between assemblies.

Strong Names

The identity section can also contain an optional **strong name**. The strong name is not a name as such but is in fact a public key that has been generated by the author of the assembly in order to uniquely identify the assembly. A strong name is what is used to ensure that your assembly has a unique signature compared to other assemblies that may have the same name. Strong names were introduced to overcome the situation where you have created a component and another developer releases an assembly with exactly the same name that could be mistaken for being a new version of your component. Without strong names there is nothing you could do, the user would be unaware of this and blame you for any problems.

A strong name is based on public-private key encryption and creates a unique identity for your assembly. You can create a key pair that is used to create a strong name by using the **SN tool** included in the .NET Framework SDK (we saw how to do this in Chapter 17). The public key is stored in the identity section of the manifest. A signature of the file containing the assembly's manifest is created and stored in the resulting PE file. The .NET Framework uses these two signatures when resolving type references to ensure that the correct assembly is loaded at runtime. A strong name is indicated in the manifest by the `.publickey` directive in the `.assembly` section.

The Culture

The final part of an assembly's identity is its **culture,** which is optional. Cultures are used to define what country/language the assembly is targeted for.

The combination of name, strong name, version number, and culture is used by the CLR to enforce version dependencies. So, you could create one version of your assembly targeted at English users, another for German users, and so on.

Cultures can be general in the case of English or more specific in the case of US-English. Cultures are represented by a string that can have two parts to it: primary and secondary (optional). The culture for English is en and the culture for US-English is en-us.

If a culture is not indicated for an assembly, it is assumed that the assembly can be used for any culture. Such an assembly is said to be **culture-neutral**.

A culture can be assigned to an assembly by including the attribute `AssemblyCulture` from the `System.Reflection` namespace in your assembly's code (usually within the `AssemblyInfo.vb` file):

```
<Assembly: AssemblyCulture("en")>
```

The culture of an assembly is represented in the manifest by the `.locale` directive in the `.assembly` section:

```
.locale = (65 00 6E 00 00 00 )                          // e.n...
```

Referenced Assemblies

The next section of the manifest that we are going to look at is the **referenced assemblies** section. As the name suggests, this section is where information is recorded about all the assemblies that are referenced by ours. An assembly reference is indicated in the manifest by the use of the `.assembly extern` directive:

You can see from the above screenshot that various pieces of information are stored about an assembly when it is referenced. The first piece of information stored is the name of the assembly. This is included as part of the `.assembly extern` directive. The screenshot shows a reference to the `mscorlib` assembly. This name of the reference is used to determine the name of the file that contains the implementation of the assembly. The CLR takes the name of the assembly reference and appends `.dll`. So, in the example above, the CLR will look for a file called `mscorlib.dll` when it resolves the type references. The assembly `mscorlib` is a special assembly in .NET that contains all the definitions of the base types used in .NET and is referenced by all assemblies. We will talk about the process that the CLR goes through to resolve a type reference later on in this chapter.

The .publickeytoken Directive

If the assembly being referenced contains a strong name, then a **hash** of the public key of the referenced assembly is stored as part of the record to the external reference. This hash is stored in the manifest using the `.publickeytoken` directive as part of the `.assembly extern` section. The assembly reference shown in the figure above contains a hash of the strong name of the `mscorlib` assembly. The stored hash of the strong name is compared at runtime to a hash of the strong name (`.publickey`) contained within the referenced assembly to help ensure that the correct assembly is loaded. The value of the `.publickeytoken` is computed by taking the low 8 bytes of a hash (SHA1) of the strong name of the referenced assemblies.

The .Ver Directive

The version of the assembly being referenced is stored in the manifest. This version information is used with the rest of the information stored about a reference to ensure the correct assembly is loaded; this will be discussed later. If an application references version 1.1.0.0 of an assembly, it will not load version 2.1.0.0 of the assembly unless a version policy (discussed later) exists to say otherwise. The version of the referenced assembly is stored in the manifest using the `.ver` directive as part of a `.assembly extern` section.

The .Locale Directive

If an assembly that is being referenced has a culture then the culture information will also be stored in the external assembly reference section using the `.locale` directive. The combination of name, strong name (if it exists), version number, and culture that makes up a unique version of an assembly.

Assemblies and Deployment

So we've looked at the structure of assemblies, in particular we've looked at the contents of the assembly manifest and how this is used to help provide a mechanism of self-description for the assembly. But how does the concept of assemblies help with deployment and the issues of versioning and DLL Hell? This section answers this question.

Application-Private Assemblies

To start answering the above question we need to look at the two types of assemblies that can exist. The first is an **application-private assembly**. As the name implies this type of assembly is used by one application only and is not shared. This is the default style of assembly in .NET and is the main mechanism by which an application can be independent of changes to the system. The notion of private components was introduced with Microsoft Windows 2000 and the `.local` file. If a `.local` file is created in an application's directory and a component is requested from the application, the search for the component would be started in the application's directory first. If the component is found in the application's directory then it is used. If the component could not be found locally then it would be searched for in the `system` path.

Application-private assemblies are deployed into the application's own directory. As application-private assemblies are not shared they do not need a strong name. This means, at a minimum, they only need to have a name and version number in the identity section of the manifest. As the assemblies are private to the application, the application does not perform version checks on the assemblies, as the application developer has control over the assemblies that are deployed to the application directory. If strong names exist, however, the CLR will check that they match. If all the assemblies that an application uses are application-private and the CLR is already installed on the target machine, it is possible to simply copy the application's directory to the target machine, assuming there are no other dependencies that need to be created (such as databases, message queues, file associations, and shortcuts). This can be accomplished due to the fact that assemblies are self-describing and contain all the information that is needed to resolve references. There is no need to copy and then register any components. The self-describing aspect of assemblies removes the dependency on the Registry, which means that applications can be backed up and copied more easily. This is a form of XCOPY deployment and cannot be used if an application uses shared assemblies (which are described below) or requires any other dependencies that cannot be simply copied.

Shared Assemblies

The second type of assembly is the **shared assembly** and as the name suggests this type of assembly can be shared amongst several applications. This type of assembly can be used in situations where it is not necessary to install a version of an assembly for each application that uses it. For instance it is not necessary to install the `System.Windows.Forms.dll` assembly for each application that uses it – it is far better to install a shared version of the assembly.

There are certain requirements that are placed upon shared assemblies. The assembly needs to have a globally unique name, which is not a requirement of application-private assemblies. As mentioned earlier strong names are used to create a globally unique name for an assembly. As the assembly is shared, all references to the shared assembly are checked to ensure the correct version is being used by an application. Shared assemblies are stored in the **Global Assembly Cache (GAC)**, which is usually located in the `Assembly` folder in the `Windows` directory (for example, `C:\WINNT\Assembly`).

There need be no other changes to the code of the assembly to differentiate it from that of an application-private assembly. In fact, just because an assembly has a strong name does not mean it has to be deployed as a shared assembly; it could just as easily be deployed in the application directory as an application-private assembly.

You must have administrator rights to the machine you are installing a shared assembly on, which means that specific action must be taken ruling out the form of XCOPY deployment mentioned earlier.

The Global Assembly Cache (GAC)

Each computer that has the .NET runtime installed has a GAC. The strong name of an assembly is used when the shared assembly is placed into the GAC. A hash of the assembly is created using the public key stored as part of the metadata, which is then compared to the hash that was created when the component was compiled. If they differ, the component has been modified (since it was compiled) and it will not be installed.

> **An assembly must have a strong name to be placed in the GAC.**

The strong name is also used when an application resolves a reference to an external assembly. It checks that the public key stored in the assembly is equal to the hash of the public key stored as part of the reference in the application. If the two do not match then the application knows that the external assembly has not been created by the original author of the assembly.

You can view the assemblies that are contained within the GAC by navigating to the directory using the Windows Explorer:

The `gacutil.exe` utility that ships with .NET is used to add and remove assemblies from the GAC. To add an assembly into the GAC using the `gacutil.exe` tool, use the following command line:

```
gacutil.exe /i myassembly.dll
```

To remove an assembly, use the `/u` option like this:

```
gacutil.exe /u myassembly.dll
```

The `gacutil` utility offers much the same functionality as `shfusion.dll`, which provides the user interface you see when you navigate to the GAC via Windows Explorer. We can remove this DLL to reveal the real contents of the GAC.

Follow these steps to view the GAC as you see it in the following screenshot:

- ❑   Before you navigate to the GAC location, find `shfusion.dll` on your system and rename it

- ❑   If it returns an 'access denied', you will need to reboot and rename it as soon as it has rebooted

- ❑   Once renamed, point Windows Explorer to the GAC location

> **Do not tamper with any other files and directories located here as it may have undesirable results.**

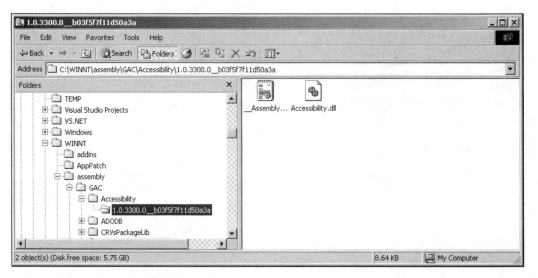

Now, you can see what is really behind the GAC. When you register an assembly into the GAC, a directory is made, the assembly copied into it, and a brief description is recorded into a GAC file. This helps the user interface for the GAC to show the nicely formatted view you can normally see. When trying to locate an assembly, the CLR probes the GAC and the files that it contains to check if the matching assembly is stored within it.

> Remember to rename **shfusion.dll** when you're finished.

Versioning Issues

Although COM was a landmark achievement in Windows programming history, it left much to be desired when it came to maintaining backward compatibility. COM used type libraries to describe its interfaces and each interface was represented by a GUID. Each interface ID was stored in the registry along with other related entries which made for a complex set of inter-related registry entries. The separation between the registry entries and the actual DLL on disk made it extremely easy for things to go wrong. A wrong registry entry or simply a mismatched GUID rendered the DLL useless. We were sometimes left with manual registry entry deletion or modification, which at its best was somewhat tedious.

The problem described here is that COM DLLs are not self-describing as they rely heavily on the registry having the correct entries. Another problem lies with the operating system not being able to best resolve differences between different DLL versions. Prior versions of Visual Basic rely on the `Server.coClass` and not the actual version of the DLL. Having the version information purely as information leaves nothing to decide what version differences there may be.

The frustrations caused by COM and its versioning policies have long plagued developers and administrators alike. In this section, we will attempt to give you some background into how the .NET Framework has attempted to resolve these issues and how we can utilize the methodology, tools, and policies that it provides.

Let's begin by looking at topics for a good solution to versioning issues of our .NET components:

❑   Application isolation

❑   Side-by-side execution

❑   Self-describing components

> **In .NET, a version policy can be thought of as a set of rules that the CLR enforces that enable it to find, load, and execute your component. The CLR policy sets out to find if you have the authority to load an assembly, to find the correct version, and more. The CLR does not enforce its versioning policies onto application-private assemblies but only on the shared assemblies.**

Application Isolation

In order for an application to be *isolated* it should be self-contained and independent. This means that the application should rely on its own dependencies for ActiveX controls, components, or files, and not have those files shared with other applications. The option of having **application isolation** is essential for a good solution to versioning problems.

If an application is isolated, components are owned, managed by, and used by the parent application alone. If a component is used by another application, even if it is the same version, it should have its very own copy. This ensures that each application can install and uninstall dependencies and not have it interfere with other applications.

> *Does this sound familiar? This is what most early Windows and DOS applications did until the emphasis was put into registering DLLs into the* system *directory. The wheel surely does turn! Also at that time, the registry started to replace our need for INI files, and now we will be moving back to the separate configuration file (which we will discuss later in this chapter) like the INI file, as it lends itself well to application isolation.*

The .NET Framework caters for application isolation by allowing us to create application-private assemblies that are for individual applications and are repeated physically on disk for each client. This means that each client is independent from the other. This non-sharing attitude works best for some scenarios.

Side-by-Side Execution

However, it is not always a good idea for an application to be completely isolated as sometimes code sharing is more beneficial and/or logical. If this is the case, the .NET Framework allows us to create and distribute shared assemblies. These assemblies must have versioning policies enforced as well as the ability to run side-by-side.

Side-by-side execution occurs when multiple versions of the same assembly can run at the same time. There are two side-by-side execution models. They are defined as being single machine execution in different processes and then more particularly within the same process.

The CLR is responsible for ensuring that assemblies are able to execute side-by-side. However side-by-side execution is not a CLR mechanism alone, as you can easily make unmanaged code execute side-by-side within the normal COM environment (known as **DLL/COM redirection**). Components that are to execute side-by-side must be installed within the application directory or a subdirectory of it. This ensures application isolation (as we discussed earlier).

Self-Describing

Many problems that we have had with COM components with regard to backward compatibility, resolving references, and versioning incompatibilities have largely been due to the way in which COM has traditionally stored information about the components it describes. Although the interfaces for a class are described together within a type library, the mechanism to find the owner of the class is left to registry entries. This means that the registry entries are often separate to the actual class and so become misaligned. Therefore one of the most important must haves for good versioning policies is that the component must describe itself completely. The assembly contains all the code (MSIL) and information the runtime requires to enforce a good versioning policy.

Version Policies

We discussed earlier that a version number is comprised of four parts: major, minor, build, and revision. The version number is used as part of the identity of the assembly. The combination of the major and minor parts of a version number indicates if a version is compatible with a previous version or not. When the version number of a component only changes by its build and revision parts, it is compatible. This is often referred to as **Quick Fix Engineering** (**QFE**).

When an application comes across a type that is implemented in an external reference, the CLR has to determine what version of the referenced assembly to load. What steps does the CLR go through to ensure the correct version of an assembly is loaded? To answer this question, we need to look at **version polices** and how they affect what version of an assembly is loaded.

The Default Versioning Policy

We will start by looking at the **default versioning policy**. This policy is what is followed in the absence of any configuration files on the machine that modify the versioning policy. The default behavior of the runtime is to consult the manifest for the name of the referenced assembly and the version of the assembly to use.

If the referenced assembly does not contain a strong name it is assumed that the referenced assembly is application-private and is located in the application directory. The CLR takes the name of the referenced assembly and appends .dll to create the filename that contains the referenced assembly's manifest. The CLR then searches in the application's directory for the filename and, if found, it will use the version that was found even if the version number is different from the one specified in the manifest. Therefore, the version numbers of application-private assemblies are not checked as the application developer, in theory, has control over which assemblies are deployed to the applications directory. If the file could not be found the CLR will raise a System.IO.FileNotFoundException.

Automatic Quick Fix Engineering Policy

If the referenced assembly contains a strong name, the process by which an assembly is loaded is different:

1. The three different types of assembly configuration files (discussed later) are consulted, if they exist, to see if they contain any settings that will modify which version of the assembly the CLR should load.

2. The CLR will then check to see if the assembly has been requested and loaded in a previous call. If it has, it will use the loaded assembly.

3. If the assembly is not already loaded the GAC is queried for a match and if found this will be used by the application.

4. If any of the configuration files contain a codebase (discussed later) entry for the assembly, the assembly is looked for in the location specified. If the assembly cannot be found in the location specified in the codebase, a TypeLoadException is raised to the application.

5. If there are no configuration files or there are no codebase entries for the assembly the CLR then moves on to probe for the assembly starting in the application's base directory.

6. If the assembly still hasn't been found, the CLR will ask the Windows Installer service if it has the assembly in question. If it does the assembly is installed and the application uses this newly installed assembly. This is a feature called **on-demand installation**.

If the assembly hasn't been found by the end of this process a TypeLoadException will be raised.

Although a referenced assembly contains a strong name this does not mean it has to be deployed to the GAC. This allows application developers to install a version with the application that is known to work. The GAC is consulted to see if it contains a version of an assembly with a higher *build.revision* number to enable administrators to deploy an updated assembly without having to re-install or rebuild the application. This is known as **Automatic Quick Fix Engineering Policy**.

Configuration Files

The default versioning policy described above may not be the most appropriate policy for our requirements. Fortunately, we can modify this policy with the use of XML configuration files to meet our specific needs. There are three types of configuration files that can be created:

❑ The first is an **application configuration file** and is created in the application directory. As the name implies, this configuration file applies to one application only. We create an application configuration file by creating a file in the application directory with the same name as the application filename and appending .config. For example, suppose we have an application called HelloWorld.exe installed in the C:\HelloWorld directory. The application configuration file would be: C:\HelloWorld\HelloWorld.exe.config.

❑ The second type of configuration file is called the **machine configuration file**. It is named machine.config and can be found in the <CLR INSTALL DIR>\Config directory. The machine.config file overrides any other configuration files on a machine and can be thought of as containing global settings.

❑ The third type of configuration file is the **security configuration file** and it contains information regarding the code access security system. The code access security system allows us to grant/deny access to resources by an assembly. This configuration file must be located within the Windows directory.

The main purpose of the configuration file is to provide binding-related information to the developer or administrator that wishes to override the default policy handling of the CLR.

Specifically, the configuration file, as it's written in XML, has a root node named <configuration> and must have the end node of </configuration> present in order to be syntactically correct.

The configuration file is divided into specific types of nodes that represent different areas of control. These areas are:

- ❑ Startup
- ❑ Runtime
- ❑ Remoting
- ❑ Crypto
- ❑ Class API
- ❑ Security

Although all of these areas are important, in this chapter we will look only at the first two.

The settings that we are going to discuss can be added to the application configuration file. Some of the settings (these will be pointed out) can also be added to the machine configuration file. If a setting in the application configuration file conflicts with that of one in the machine configuration file then the setting in the machine configuration is used. When we talk about assembly references in the following discussion of configuration settings, we are talking about shared assemblies (in other words, assemblies that have a strong name).

Startup Settings

The <startup> node of the application and machine configuration files has a <requiredRuntime> node that specifies the runtime version required by the application. This is because different versions of the CLR can run on a machine side-by-side. The example below shows how we would specify the version of the .NET runtime inside the configuration file:

```
<configuration>
  <startup>
    <requiredRuntime version="1.0.0.0" safeMode="true"/>
  </startup>
</configuration>
```

Runtime Settings

The runtime node, which is written as <runtime> (not to be confused with <requiredRuntime>), specifies the settings that manage how the CLR handles garbage collection and versions of assemblies. With these settings, we can specify which version of an assembly the application requires or redirect it to another version entirely.

Loading a Particular Version of an Assembly

The application and machine configuration files can be used to ensure that a particular version of an assembly is loaded. You can indicate whether this version should be loaded all the time or only to replace a specific version of the assembly. This functionality is supported through the use of the <assemblyIdentity> and <bindingRedirect> elements in the configuration file. For example:

```
<configuration>
  <runtime>
    <assemblyBinding xmlns="urn:schemas-microsoft-com:asm.v1">
      <dependentAssembly>
        <assemblyIdentity name="AssemblyName"
                          publickeytoken="b77a5c561934e089"
                          culture="en-us"/>
          <bindingRedirect oldVersion="*"
                           newVersion="2.0.50.0"/>
      </dependentAssembly>
    </assemblyBindings>
  </runtime>
</configuration>
```

The <assemblyBinding> node is used to declare settings for the locations of assemblies and redirections via the <dependentAssembly> node and also the <probing> node (which we will look at shortly).

In the example above, when the CLR resolves the reference to the assembly named AssemblyName it will load version 2.0.50.0 instead of the version that appears in the manifest. If you would like to only load version 2.0.50.0 of the assembly when a specific version is referenced then you can replace the value of the oldVersion attribute with the version number that you would like to replace (for example, 1.5.0.0). The publickeytoken attribute is used to store the hash of the strong name of the assembly to replace. This is used to ensure that the correct assembly is identified. The same is true of the culture attribute.

Defining the Location of an Assembly

The location of an assembly can also be defined in both the application and machine configuration files. We can use the <codeBase> element to inform the CLR of the location of an assembly. This enables us to distribute an application and have the externally referenced assemblies downloaded the first time they are used. This is called on-demand downloading. For example:

```
<configuration>
  <runtime>
    <assemblyBinding xmlns="urn:schemas-microsoft-com:asm.v1">
      <dependentAssembly>
        <assemblyIdentity name="AssemblyName"
                          publickeytoken="b77a5c561934e089"
                          culture="en-us"/>
          <codeBase version="2.0.50.0"
                    href="http://www.wrox.com/AssemblyName.dll/>
      </dependentAssembly>
    </assemblyBindings>
  </runtime>
</configuration>
```

From the example above we can see that whenever a reference to version 2.0.50.0 of the assembly AssemblyName is resolved (and the assembly isn't already on the users computer), the CLR will try to load the assembly from the location defined in the href attribute. The location defined in the href attribute is a standard URL and can be used to locate a file across the Internet or locally.

If the assembly cannot be found or the details in the manifest of the assembly defined in the href attribute do not match those defined in the configuration file, the loading of the assembly will fail and you will receive a TypeLoadException. If the version of the assembly in the above example is actually 2.0.60.0 then the assembly will load, as the version number is only different by build and revision number.

Providing the Search Path

The final use of configuration files that we will look at is that of providing the search path for use when locating assemblies in the application's directory. This setting only applies to the application configuration file. By default the CLR will only search for an assembly in the application's base directory, it will not look in any subdirectories. We can modify this behavior by using the <probing> element in an application configuration file. For example:

```
<configuration>
  <runtime>
    <assemblyBinding xmlns="urn:schemas-microsoft-com:asm.v1">
      <probing privatePath="regional"/>
    </assemblyBinding>
  </runtime>
</configuration>
```

The privatePath attribute can contain a list of directories relative to the application's directory (separated by a semi-colon) that you would like the CLR to search in when trying to locate an assembly. The privatePath attribute cannot contain an absolute pathname.

As part of an assembly reference being resolved, the CLR will check in the application's base directory for it. If it cannot find it, it will look through in order all subdirectories specified in the privatePath variable, as well as looking for a subdirectory with the same name as the assembly. If the assembly being resolved is called AssemblyName, the CLR will also check for the assembly in a subdirectory called AssemblyName, if it exists.

This isn't the end of the story though. If the referenced assembly being resolved contains a culture, the CLR will also check for culture specific subdirectories in each of the directories it searches in. For example, if the CLR is trying to resolve a reference to an assembly named AssemblyName with a culture of en, a privatePath equal to that in the above example, and the application being run has a home directory of C:\ExampleApp, the CLR will look in the following directories to find the assembly (in the order they are shown):

- ❑ C:\ExampleApp
- ❑ C:\ExampleApp\en
- ❑ C:\ExampleApp\en\AssemblyName
- ❑ C:\ExampleApp\regional\en
- ❑ C:\ExampleApp\regional\en\AssemblyName

As you can see, the CLR can probe quite a number of directories to locate an assembly.

When an external assembly is resolved by the CLR it consults the configuration files first to see if it needs to modify the process by which it resolves an assembly. As we discussed, the resolution process can be modified to suit your needs.

Now that we understand assemblies, we are going to start discussing the problems that occur when we deploy applications, along with a number of terms that are used when talking about application deployment. We will then move to look at what the CLR contains that helps us alleviate some of the deployment issues discussed previously. The remainder of the chapter will then focus on the practical aspects of creating deployment projects in VS.NET, which will include a number of walkthroughs.

Deployment in .NET is a huge topic and we couldn't hope to cover every aspect in the pages that we have for this chapter. What this chapter should give you is the understanding, basic knowledge, and the desire to learn more about the options available to you.

Application Deployment

We are going to start this section by discussing the main issues associated with application deployment and defining a few common terms that are used. We will then move on to discuss the deployment options available prior to .NET. Hopefully, this will give you an understanding of the issues to be overcome when considering deployment in .NET.

Firstly, though, what do we mean by the term 'application deployment'? In the context of this chapter, it means the process of taking an application, packaging it up, and installing it on another machine. This includes installing the application new, re-installing it or upgrading it. It applies to traditional Windows-based applications, Web-based applications that will need to be installed within the confines of another web server, and any of the other Visual Basic project templates.

DLL Hell

The two small words 'DLL' and 'Hell' describe what can be a very large problem for application developers. If you are aware of the problems that **DLL Hell** encompasses then please feel free to skip this section.

What does DLL Hell mean? The term is actually used to describe a number of problems that can arise when multiple applications share a common component. The common component is usually a .dll or a COM component. The problems usually arise for one of three reasons, which will be discussed below:

❑ The first common cause of DLL Hell is when you install a new application that overwrites a shared component with a version that is not compatible with the version that already resides on the computer. Any applications that relied on the previous version of the component could well be rendered unusable. This is often caused when you install an application that overwrites a system file (for example, MFC42.dll) with an older version. Any application that relied on the functionality of the newer version will stop working. When installing the application on the computer the installer should check that it is not overwriting a newer version of the component. However, not all installations do this check.

❑ The second cause occurs when a new version of a shared component is installed that is binary compatible (the public interface matches exactly) with the previous version, but in updating the functionality, a new bug has been introduced into the component which could cause any application that depends on the component to misbehave or stop working. This type of error can be very hard to diagnose.

❑ The third common cause occurs when an application uses a feature of a common component that is actually an undocumented and unexpected behavior of the component: a side effect. When this shared component is updated with a newer version the side effect may well have disappeared, breaking any applications that depended on it. There are many undocumented API calls available in DLLs; the problem is that, because they are undocumented, they may well disappear in a subsequent version without warning.

As the above discussion indicates, DLL Hell can be caused by a variety of reasons and the effects can be wide ranging. Applications may stop working but worse still, it could introduce subtle bugs that may lie undetected for some time. It may be some time before you realize an application has stopped working, which can make it significantly harder to detect the cause of the problem.

Microsoft has tried to address some of these issues with the latest versions of Windows by introducing Windows File Protection and Private DLLs:

❑ As the name suggests Windows File Protection is a mechanism by which the OS protects a list of system DLLs from being overwritten with a different version. Normally only service packs and other OS updates can update the DLLs that are protected, although this can be overridden by changing some registry keys. This should reduce some of the causes of DLL Hell that are caused by the overwriting of system DLLs.

❑ The second feature introduced is that of private DLLs. Private DLLs are used by one particular application only and are not shared amongst different applications. If an application relies on a specific version of a .dll or COM component then it can be installed in the application directory and a .local file created in the directory to inform that OS to look for private DLLs first and then move on to look for shared DLLs.

You will be pleased to hear that Microsoft has incorporated new features into the CLR and the .NET framework that will help to overcome DLL hell and make deployment easier. These new features will be discussed throughout the remainder of this chapter.

XCOPY Deployment

The term **XCOPY deployment** was coined to describe an ideal deployment scenario. Its name derives from the DOS xcopy command that is used to copy an entire directory structure from one location to another. XCOPY deployment relates to a scenario where all you have to do to deploy an application is to copy the directory (including all child directories) to the computer that you would like to run the program.

Why can't we use XCOPY deployment at present? The main reason is that the process of installing an application currently is a multi-step process. For example, any application that uses a COM component will require a number of steps to install it on another computer. First, the component needs to be copied to the machine, and then the component must be registered on the machine, creating a dependency between the component and the registry. The application requires the entry in the registry to activate the component. Because of this coupling between the component and the registry it is not possible to install the component by simply copying it from one machine to another.

All but the simplest of applications also require other dependencies (such as databases, message queues, document extensions) to be created on the new computer. The CLR tries to overcome the problem of the coupling between the registry and components but at present it cannot help with the dependencies that are required by more advanced applications. We are closer to XCOPY deployment with .NET and in some cases we may actually be able to achieve a form of it.

The issue of what runtime files need to be on a computer to run an application needs to be addressed. For a .NET application to run on a computer it needs to have the necessary core CLR files installed, as well as any files required by the application. Some people argue that if you need to install a runtime prior to installing an application then this can never be classed as true XCOPY deployment. To start with the CLR will be distributed as a downloadable installation routine (or distributed as part of an applications setup routine), but we can expect it to be included in future service packs and natively included as part of the operating system in future versions of Microsoft Windows. Once the CLR has been installed it will not need to be installed again, so perhaps we can define a requirement of an application to be that a particular version of the CLR is installed.

Deployment Options Prior to .NET

Prior to VS.NET there were a number of deployment options available to the developer, some supplied by Microsoft and others supplied by third party companies, each trying to ease the pain of deploying applications. In this section, we will take a brief look at some of these options.

Manual Installation

As the name suggests, the **manual installation** method involves copying all the files manually into the correct place and then completing any other steps that are required to complete the installation of the software, for example registering any COM components and adding any other registry entries. It could also mean setting up database connections, and so on. There is no automation in this deployment method and the steps have to be repeated on every computer that the application needs to be installed on. This installation method is time consuming and is not feasible for most applications, as it often requires advanced knowledge that perhaps the typical user of the application cannot be expected to have or learn. This is the installation method most commonly used when COM+ components are installed onto a server.

Custom Installer

The second deployment method we will look at is the use of a **custom installation program**. We can use the installation program to define the steps and actions that are required to install the application on a computer. The program then packages up all the required files including the instructions into an application the users can use to install the application on their machines.

The **Package and Deployment Wizard**, which was provided with VB6, is an example of such an application. You run the wizard, selecting the files that need to be copied and where they need to be copied to. The wizard then creates an installation that can be run on another computer.

Another variant often used to create an installation program is script based (for example, InstallShield). It packages up any files that need to be copied and allows us to write a script to define what needs to be done when the installer is run. The script-based approach is very flexible in that we can easily incorporate any additional processing that needs to be done when installing an application (for example, creating a new database).

There are many other variants on this theme of creating an installation program. As you can see there is no consistency between the installation programs; each program can offer different functionality (or lack of). Microsoft acknowledged this inconsistency and tried to come up with a solution, which we will discuss next.

Windows Installer

Microsoft introduced the **Windows Installer** service as part of Windows 2000 as the solution to the shortcomings of the existing installation programs. Although the Windows Installer service was released as part of Windows 2000, it can also be installed on previous version of Windows and is automatically installed with several Microsoft applications (such as Microsoft Office). The Windows Installer service is what Microsoft calls an **operating system component**. The service implements all the required rules that a setup needs (for instance: *do not overwrite a system file with an older version*).

Instead of creating an executable that contains all the rules to install the application, you create a file, called a **Windows Installer package file** (.msi), which describes what needs to be done to install your application. An application is described in the resulting Windows Installer package as being made up of three parts: components, features, and products. Each part is made up of any number of the previous parts. For example, a product is made up of several features, and a feature may contain one or more components. The component is the smallest part of the installation and contains a group of files and other resources that all need to be installed together. We will not be going into the underlying details of the Windows Installer architecture. If you are interested then you should take a look at the Windows Installer SDK documentation in MSDN.

The files that make up a product can be packaged externally in a number of cabinet files or the files can be packaged up into the resultant .msi file. As you will see later, there are a number of options within the deployment project templates that allow us to specify how the product's files are packaged. When the user requests that a particular application needs to be installed they can just double-click the .msi file (assuming the Windows Installer service is installed). If the Windows Installer service is not installed there is usually a Setup.exe file that will install the Windows Installer service first. The service will read the file and determine what needs to be done (such as which files need to be copied and where they need to be copied to) to install the application. All the installation rules are implemented centrally by the service and do not need to be distributed as part of a setup executable. The Windows Installer package file contains a list of actions (such as *copy file mfc40.dll to the windows system folder*) and what rules need to be applied to these actions. It does not contain the implementation of the rules.

The Windows Installer service also provides a rich API that developers can use to include features such as on-demand installing into their applications. One of the biggest complaints about previous installers is that if the installation fails, the user's computer is often left in an unstable state. The Windows Installer service overcomes this by providing a rollback method. If the installation fails for some reason, the Windows Installer service will rollback the computer to its original state – so we could say that the installation is transactional.

You can manually create a Windows Installer package file using the Windows Installer SDK tools. However, this is not very user-friendly, so Microsoft released the **Visual Studio Installer** (**VSI**) as an add-on for Visual Studio 6. The VSI integrated into the development environment and made the development of the Windows Installer package files easier. Three out of the four actual deployment/setup templates in VS.NET use Windows Installer technology. We will look at these in more detail later in the chapter.

Application Deployment in VS.NET

We've just looked at some background issues relating to application deployment and some of the deployment options that have been previously available to developers. We're now going to turn our attention to looking at how the CLR and the .NET Framework can help with deployment and resolve the issue of DLL Hell. Finally, we will take a look at the deployment project templates that are available within VS.NET.

VS.NET Deployment Projects

So you have decided that you need to package your application in some way so that it can be installed on other machines. The option of just zipping up the application directory is not satisfactory or not possible. What can you do? You will be pleased to hear that VS.NET provides a set of project templates that can be used to help package your application and deploy it. The remainder of this chapter will focus on these project templates. We will start by taking a look at the different templates and what they should be used for, after which we will take a practical look at their creation.

Project Templates

VS.NET includes five project templates that can be used for setup and deployment in .NET. Before we discuss the project templates we need to define the difference between setup and deployment. A **setup** is an application/process that you create that packages your application up and provides an easy mechanism by which it can be installed on another machine. **Deployment** is the process of taking an application and installing it on another machine, usually by the use of a setup application/process.

The five project templates available within VS.NET can be created by the same means as any other project in VS.NET, by using the New Project dialog box:

As you can see from the figure above you need to select the **Setup and Deployment Projects** node from the treeview of project types to the left of the dialog box. Out of the five available project templates there are four actual project templates:

- ❑ Cab Project
- ❑ Merge Module Project
- ❑ Setup Project
- ❑ Web Setup Project

and one wizard that can be used to help create one of the four project templates listed above:

- ❑ Setup Wizard

Let's now consider each of the project types in turn.

The Cab Project Template

As its name implies, the Cab Project template is used to create a **cabinet file**. A cabinet file (.cab) can contain any number of files. It is usually used to package components into a single file that can then be placed on a web server so that the cab file can be downloaded by a web browser.

Controls hosted within Internet Explorer are often packaged into a cabinet file and a reference added to the file in the web page that uses the control. When Internet Explorer encounters this reference it will check that the control isn't already installed on the user's computer, at which point it will download the cabinet file, extract the control, and install it to a protected part of the user's computer.

Cabinet files can be compressed to reduce their size and consequently the time it takes to download them.

The Merge Module Project Template

The Merge Module Project template is used to create a **merge module**, which is similar to a cabinet file in that it can be used to package a group of files. The difference is that a merge module file (.msm) cannot be used by itself to install the files that it contains. The merge module file created by this project template can be used within another setup project.

Merge modules were introduced as part of the Microsoft Windows Installer technology to enable a set of files to be packaged up into an easy to use file that could be re-used and shared between Windows Installer-based setup programs. The idea is to package up all the files and any other resources (for example, registry entries, bitmaps, and so on) that are dependent on each other into the merge module.

This type of project can be very useful for packaging a component and all its dependencies. The resulting merge file can then be used in the setup program of each application that uses the component.

Microsoft suggests that a merge module should not be modified once it has been distributed, which means a new one should be created. The notion of packaging everything up into a single re-distributable file can help alleviate the issues of DLL Hell as the package contains all dependencies.

The Setup Project Template

The Setup Project template is used to create a standard Windows Installer setup for an application. This type of project will probably be familiar to you if you have used the Visual Studio Installer add-on for Visual Studio 6. The Setup Project template can be used to create a setup package for a standard Windows application, which is normally installed in the `Program Files` directory of a user's computer.

The Web Setup Project Template

The Web Setup Project template is used to create a Windows Installer setup program that can be used to install a project into a virtual directory of a web server. It is intended to be used to create a setup program for a web application.

The Setup Wizard

The Setup Wizard can be used help guide you through the creation of one of the above four setup and deployment project templates. The steps that the wizard displays to you depend on whether the wizard was started to add a project to an existing solution or started to create a totally new project.

Creating a Deployment Project

A deployment project can be created in exactly the same way as any other project in VS.NET by using the New | Project option from the File menu or by using the New Project button on the VS.NET start page.

You can also add a deployment project to an existing solution by using the Add Project item from the File menu. You will then be presented with the Add New Project dialog box where you can select the deployment template of choice.

Walkthroughs

Now that we have looked at how we can create a deployment project, the next two sections are going to contain practical walkthroughs of the creation of two deployment projects. The two walkthroughs are going to cover:

❑ Desktop application

❑ Web application

Each these scenarios will detail a different deployment project template. They have been chosen as they are the most common deployment scenarios. You will be able to use the walkthroughs and apply or modify them to your own needs. We will not use the wizard to create the deployment projects in the walkthroughs. This decision has been taken so that you will be able to understand what is required to create a deployment project. The wizard can be used to help guide you through the creation of a deployment project and therefore hide from you some of the steps that we will be taking in the walkthroughs. However, the wizard can be very useful in providing the base for a deployment project.

Desktop Application

The first deployment scenario that we are going to look at is that of a desktop application where a user installs and runs an application on his machine. The application will be Windows-based and we will need to ensure that everything it needs is distributed with the application executable. This type of deployment scenario is one of the most typical that you will come across.

In this deployment scenario, the package needs to be created in such a way that it will guide the user through the process of installing the application on his or her machine. The best deployment template for this scenario is the **Setup Project** and this is what we will be using throughout this section.

Before we start getting into the specifics of this project type we need to create an application that will serve as our desktop application that we want to deploy. For this example we are going to use the Windows Application project type. Create a new project and choose **Windows Application** from the list of available Visual Basic project templates. We will not add any code to the project and will use it as the new project wizard created it. At the moment we have a solution with one project contained with in it.

Add a new project to the solution and choose **Setup Project** from the list of available **Setup and Deployment Project** templates. You will now have a solution containing two projects:

The deployment project does not contain any files at present, just a folder called **Detected Dependencies**, which we will discuss later. Notice also the buttons that appear along the top of the **Solution Explorer**. These are used to access the editors of this deployment project template and will be discussed later in this chapter.

Next, we need to add files to the setup project and in particular we need to look at how we can add the file created by the Windows application project. We can add files to the setup deployment project in two ways. The first is to make sure the setup project is the active project and then choose the **Add** item from the **Project** menu. The second method is to right-click the setup project file in the **Solution Explorer** and choose **Add** from the popup menu. Both these methods enable you to choose from one of four options:

❑ If you select **File** from the submenu, you will be presented with a dialog box that will allow you to browse for and select a particular file to add to the setup project. This method is sufficient if the file you are adding is not the output from another project within the solution. This option is very useful in web setup projects as it allows you include external business components (if they are used) and so on.

❑ The **Merge Module** option allows us to include a merge module in the deployment project. If you select this option, you will be presented with a dialog box that you can use to browse for and select a merge module to include in your project. Third-party vendors can supply merge modules or we can create our own with VS.NET.

❑ The **Assembly** option can be used to select a .NET component (assembly) to be included in the deployment project. If you select this option you will be presented with a window that you can use to select an assembly to include from those that are installed on your machine.

❑ If the deployment project is part of a solution (as in this walkthrough) you can use the **Project Output** submenu item. As the name implies, this allows you to add the output from any of the projects in the solution to the setup project.

We want to add the output of the windows application project to the setup project. So we need to select the **Project Output** menu item to bring up the dialog box that will enable us to accomplish this task:

The **Add Project Output Group** dialog box is split into several parts:

❑ The combo-box at the top contains a list of the names of all the non-deployment projects in the current solution. In our case there is only one project – **WindowsApplication**.

❑ Below the combo-box is a list box containing a list of all the possible outputs from the selected project. If you click on a possible output a description appears in the **Description** box at the bottom. The type of output we are interested in is the **Primary output** so make sure this is selected. The different types of output are summarized in the following table.

❑ Below the list of possible outputs is a combo-box that allows us to select the **Configuration** to use for the selected project. We will use the **(Active)** option as this will use whatever configuration is in effect when the project is built. The combo-box will also contain all the possible build configurations for the selected project.

Click **OK** to return to the solution.

Project Output	Description
Primary output	The primary output of a project is the resulting DLL or EXE that is produced by building the particular project.
Localized resources	The localized resource of a project is a DLL that contains only resources. The resources within the DLL are specific to a culture or locale. This is often called a satellite DLL.
Debug Symbols	When the particular project in question is compiled a special file is created that contains special debugging information about the project. These are called **debug symbols**. The debug symbols for a project have the same name as the primary output but with an extension of .pdb. The debug symbols provide information to a debugger when an application is being run through it.
Content Files	This project output is used only with ASP.NET Web Applications. The content files of a web application are the html, graphic files and so on that form the content of the web site.
Source Files	This will include all the source files for the selected project including the project file. The solution file is NOT included.

Now, not only has the output from the Windows application been added to the **Setup** project but the **Detected Dependencies** folder contains an entry.

Whenever you add a .NET component to this deployment project its dependencies are added to this folder. The dependencies of the dependencies will also be added and so on until all the required files have been added. This functionality has been included to help ensure that all the dependencies of an application are deployed along with the application. The files listed in the **Detected Dependencies** folder will be included in the resulting setup and, by default, will be installed into the application's directory as application-private assemblies. This default behavior helps to reduce the possible effects of DLL Hell by making the application use its own copies of dependent files:

If you do not want a particular dependency file to be included in the resulting setup you can exclude it by right-clicking on the particular entry under **Detected Dependencies** and selecting **Exclude** from the popup menu. The dependency will now have a little stop sign before its name to indicate that it has been excluded:

Dependencies can also be excluded by selecting the particular dependency and using the Properties *window to set the* Exclude *property to* True. *The listed dependencies will be refreshed whenever a .NET file is added to or removed from the setup project taking into account any files that have already been excluded.*

You may decide that you want to exclude a detected dependency from the setup of an application because you know that the dependency is already installed on the target computer. This is fine if you have tight control over what is installed on a user's machine. If you don't and you deploy the application with the missing dependency, your application could well be rendered unusable. In the previous screenshot you can see that there is one entry in the folder. The dotnetfxredist_x86_enu.msm file is a merge module dependency. As mentioned previously a merge module is used to package a group of files that are dependent on each other. This merge module contains a re-distributable version of the CLR and will be installed on the user's computer when the installation is run.

We can select an item in the setup project in the **Solution Explorer** and that particular item's properties will be displayed in the **Properties** window. For example, if we select the root node of the setup project (**Setup**), the **Properties** window will change to show us the details of the setup project:

Properties ⊓ ✕

Setup Deployment Project Properties ▾

⊟ Misc

AddRemoveProgr	(None)
Author	Wrox Press Ltd
Description	
DetectNewerInst	True
Keywords	
Localization	English (United States)
Manufacturer	Wrox Press Ltd

Misc

Properties ❷ Dynamic Help

> **As with any other project in VS.NET there are a set of project properties that can also be modified. The project properties are accessed by right-clicking the project file and choosing Properties from the popup menu. These properties will be covered later.**

We are not going to include a discussion of every single property of all the different project items as we could probably fill a whole book on the subject. Instead, we will take a look at the properties from the root setup node and each of the two different project items. We are going to start with the root setup node (**Setup**). Before we start our discussion, make sure that the node is selected and take some time to browse the list of available properties. The root setup node represents the resulting output from this deployment project type: Windows Installer package (`.msi`). Therefore, the Properties window contains properties that will affect the resulting `.msi` that is produced.

Properties of the Root Setup Node

The first property we are going to look at is `ProductName`. This property, as the name tells us, is used to set the textual name of the product that this Windows Installer package is installing. By default it is set to the name of the setup project (in our case `Setup`). The value of this property is used throughout the steps of the resulting setup. For instance, it is used for the text of the title bar when the resulting `.msi` file is run. The property is used along with the `Manufacturer` property to construct the default installation directory:

```
C:\Program Files\<Manufacturer>\<ProductName>
```

The `ProductName` property is also used by the Add/Remove Programs control panel applet, to show that the application is installed:

From this screenshot you can see there is a link that you can click on to get support information about the selected application:

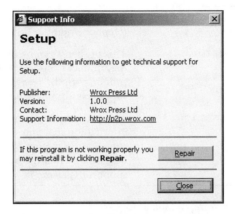

A number of the properties of the setup project can be used to customize the support information that is shown. The following table contains details of the how the properties relate to the support information that is shown:

Support Information	Related Properties	Description
Publisher	Manufacturer	The Manufacturer property is used to help create the default installation directory for the project and provide a textual display of the manufacturer of the application contained within the Windows Installer package.
	ManufacturerUrl	This property is used in conjunction with the Manufacturer property to make a hyperlink for the **Publisher** part of the support information. If a value is entered, the name of the **Publisher** will be underlined, which can then be clicked to allow you to visit the publisher's web site. If a value is not included the publisher's name does not act as a hyperlink.
Version	Version	This is the version number of the Windows Installer package. It can be changed to match the version number of the application that the package installs. But this has to be done manually.
Contact	Author	This property is used to hold the name of the company/person that created the Windows Installer package. By default this has the same value as the Manufacturer property.

Table continued on following page

Support Information	Related Properties	Description
Support Information	SupportPhone	This property can be used to provide a support telephone number for the application.
	SupportUrl	This property can be used to provide a URL for the product's support web site. The value of this property will be represented as a hyperlink in the support information window.
Comments	Description	This property can be used to include any information that you would like to appear in the support information window. For instance, it could be used to detail the opening hours of your support department.

The next property that we are going to look at for the root setup node is called `AddRemoveProgramsIcon`. As you can probably guess, this property allows us to set the icon that appears in the **Add/Remove Programs** control panel applet for the application contained within this Windows Installer package. We can select (None) from the dropdown list, which means that we do not want to change the icon and the default icon will be used. Alternatively, we have the option to (Browse...) for an icon, which brings up a window that allows us to find and select the particular icon we would like to use. We do not have to use a stand-alone icon file; we can use an icon from an executable or DLL that is contained within the project.

The remainder of the properties for the root setup node are summarized in the following table:

Property	Description
DetectNewerInstalledVersion	If this property is set to **True** and a newer version of the application is found on the machine then the installation will not continue. If the property is set to **False** then this check will not occur and the application will install even if there is a newer version on the computer already.
Keywords	This property enables you to set a number of keywords that can be used to locate this installer.
Localization	This property is used to set which locale this installer has been designed to run in. The values of this property will affect what string resources are used within the installation.
PackageCode	This property is a GUID that is used to uniquely identify this installer. This property is used to link the installer with a specific version of the application that it installs.
ProductCode	This property is a GUID that is used to uniquely identify the particular version of the application contained within it.

Property	Description
RemovePreviousVersion	If this property is set to True and an older version of the application is found on the machine then the installation will remove the old version and continue on with the installation. If the property is set to False then this check is not done.
SearchPath	This property is used to specify a search path that Visual Studio uses when it builds the setup project and needs to find the detected dependencies.
Subject	This property is used to provide an additional text string of what the installation is used for.
Title	This property is used to set the textual title of the application that is installed. By default this property will have the same name as the setup project.
Upgrade Code	This property is a GUID and is used to uniquely identify a product. This property should stay the same for all versions of the same application. The ProductCode and PackageCode properties change depending on the specific version of the product.

Properties of the Primary Output Project Item

We are now going to move on and take a quick look at the properties of the primary output project item in the following table:

Property	Description
Condition	This enables you to enter a condition that will be evaluated when the installation is run. If the condition evaluates to true then the file will be installed; likewise if the condition evaluates to false then the file won't be installed. If we only wanted a particular file to be installed if the installation was being run on Microsoft Windows 2000, we could enter the following for the condition: VersionNT >= 5.
Dependencies	Selecting this property will display a window that shows all the dependencies of the selected project output.
Exclude	You can use this property to indicate whether you want the project output to be excluded from the resulting Windows Installer package.
ExcludeFilter	This property enables you to exclude files from the project output using wildcards. For example, if you enter a wild card of *.txt, then all files that are part of the project output that have an extension of .txt will be excluded from the resulting Windows Installer package. Selecting this property will display a window that will allow you to enter any number of wildcards.
Folder	As mentioned previously this property allows you to select the target folder for the project outputs.

Table continued on following page

Property	Description
Hidden	This property allows you to install the files that make up the project output as hidden files. This property basically toggles on/off the hidden attribute of the files.
KeyOutput	This property expands to provide information about the main file that makes up the project output. In our case it will show information of the WindowsApplication.exe file.
Outputs	Selecting this property will display a window that lists all the files that are part of the project output and where these files are located on the development machine.
PackageAs	This property can be used to indicate whether the project output should be packaged according to what is defined in the project properties (vsdpaDefault) or externally (vsdpaLoose) to the resulting Windows Installer package. The default is to use the project properties setting.
Permanent	This property is used to indicate whether the files that make up the project output should be removed when the application is uninstalled (False) or left behind (True). It is advisable that all the files that are installed by an application be removed when the application is uninstalled. Therefore this property should be set to False, which it is by default.
ReadOnly	This property is used to set the read only file attribute of all the files that make up the project output. As the name suggests this makes the file read only on the target machine.
Register	This property allows you to instruct the Windows Installer to register the files contained within the project output as COM objects. This only really applies to projects (for example, Class Library project template) that have been compiled with the Register for COM Interop project property set.
SharedLegacy	This property indicates whether the files that make up the project output are to be reference counted once installed. This really only applies to files that are going to be shared across multiple applications. When the installation is removed the files will only be uninstalled if their reference count is equal to zero.
System	This property indicates that the files contained within the project output are to be treated as system files and protected by windows file protection.
Transitive	This property indicates whether the condition specified in the condition property is re-evaluated when the installation is re-run on the computer at a later date. If the value is true then the condition is checked on each additional run of the installation. A value of False will cause the condition only to be run the first time the installation is run on the computer. The default value is False.
Vital	This property is used to indicate that the files contained within the project output are vital to the installation – if the installation of these files fails then the installation as a whole should fail. The default value is True.

Properties of the Detected Dependency Items

We are now going to take a brief look at the properties of the `dotnetfxredist_x86_enu.msm` file in the **Detected Dependencies** folder. This file is a merge module dependency and the second is an assembly dependency. We will only cover the properties that are different to those of the project output item (discussed above). Most of the additional properties are read only and cannot be changed. They are used purely to provide information to the developer:

Property	Description
MergeModuleProperties	A merge module can contain a number of custom configurable properties. If the selected merge module contains any they will appear here. In the case of our example there are no custom properties.
Author	This property stores the name of the author of the merge module. Read only.
Description	This property is used to store a textual description of the merge module. Read only.
LanguageIds	This property is used to indicate what language the selected merge module is targeted at. Read only.
ModuleDependencies	Selecting this property will show a window that lists all the dependencies of the selected merge module. Read only.
ModuleSignature	This property will display the unique signature of the merge module. Read only.
Subject	This property is used to display additional information about the merge module. Read only.
Title	This property is used to simply state the title of the merge module. Read only.
Version	This property is used to store the version number of the selected merge module. The version number of the merge module usually changes as the version number of the files it contains changes. Read only.

Of course, some projects will also contain other `.dll` files in this folder. In this case, some of the additional properties that may be encountered for these files are as follows:

Property	Description
DisplayName	This contains the filename of the selected assembly. Read only.
Files	Selecting this property will display a window that will list all the files that make up the selected assembly. Read only.
HashAlgorithm	This property shows what hash algorithm was used by the manifest in hashing the files contents (to stop tampering). Read only.

Table continued on following page

Property	Description
Language	This property will show what language this assembly is targeted at. This property relates to the culture of an assembly. If the property is empty then the assembly is culture (language) independent. Read only.
PublicKey PublicKeyToken	These two properties are used to show information about the strong name of the selected assembly. If an assembly has a strong name then either of these two properties will contain a value (other than all 0s). One or the other of these properties are used and not normally both. Read only.
SourcePath	This property contains the location of where the selected assembly can be found on the development computer. Read only.
TargetName	This property contains the filename of the assembly, as it will appear on the target machine. Read only.
Version	This property shows you the version number of the selected assembly. Read only.

This has been a brief look at the **Setup Project** template. It uses all the project defaults and provides a standard set of steps to the user when they run the Windows Installer package. More often than not this simple approach of including a single application file and its dependencies is not good enough. Fortunately, the setup project can be customized extensively to meet our needs. We can create shortcuts, directories, registry entries and so on. These customizations and more can be accomplished using the set of built-in editors, which will be covered after the next walkthrough.

Web Application

The other deployment scenario we are going to look at is that of a web application that has been created using the Web Application project template. We are assuming that the web application is being developed on a development web server and that we will need to create a deployment project to transfer the finished application to the production web server. Although the previous deployment scenario is one of the most typical, this scenario has to come a very close second.

From the simple requirements defined above we can see that the best deployment template to use is the **Web Setup Project** template. There is one major difference between this template and the previous Setup Project template, in that the Web Setup Project will by default deploy the application to a virtual directory of the web server on which the setup is run, whereas a Setup Project will deploy the application to the `Program Files` folder on the target machine by default. There are obviously some properties that differ between the two project templates, but other than that they are pretty similar. They both produce a Windows Installer package and have the same set of project properties discussed later in the chapter.

As with the other walkthroughs, we need to create an application that we can use to deploy. Start a new project and make sure you select ASP.NET Web Application from the list of available project templates. We are not going to add any code to the project that we just created, as it is being used purely as a base for the deployment project. Now add a **Web Setup Project** template. Our solution contains two projects.

As with the previous walkthroughs the deployment project does not contain any files at present. There is also a folder called **Detected Dependencies** in the solution explorer that acts in exactly the same way as in the previous walkthrough:

The next step that we need to look at is adding the output of the web application to the deployment project. This is accomplished in pretty much the same way as the previous walkthrough. So to start with, add the **Primary output** from the web application to the deployment project using the method described in the previous walkthroughs.

If we built the solution now and tried to deploy the application onto the production web server it would not work. When adding the **Primary output** from a web application, only the compiled code of the web application including its detected dependencies are added to the deployment project. All the other files that make up a web application (HTML files, style sheets, and so on) are not included as part of the **Primary output** of the project.

To include these files in the deployment project we need to add another project output to the deployment project. This time we need to include the **Content Files** of the web application. The resulting project should look like this:

Now if we build the solution, the resulting Windows Installer package will include the compiled code of the web application along with its dependencies, as well as the other files that make up a web application, ASP.NET files, style sheets, and so on.

Most of the topics discussed in the last walkthrough apply to this walkthrough. As mentioned earlier the Setup Project and Web Setup projects are very similar and are only really different in where they install the application by default.

Modifying the Deployment Project

In the last two walkthroughs we created the default Windows Installer package for the particular project template. We didn't customize the steps or actions that were performed when the package was run. What if we had wanted to add a step into the installation process that displayed a ReadMe file to the user? Or what if we needed to create registry entries on the installation computer? The walkthroughs did not cover how to customize the installation to our needs, which is what this section is going to focus on. There are six editors that we can use to customize a Windows Installer-based deployment project:

- ❑ File System editor
- ❑ Registry editor
- ❑ File Types editor
- ❑ User Interface editor
- ❑ Custom Actions editor
- ❑ Launch Conditions editor

The editors are accessible through the View | Editor menu option or by using the corresponding buttons at the top of the Solution Explorer.

We can also modify the resulting Windows Installer package through the project properties window. In this section we are going to take a brief look at each of the six editors and the project properties, and how they can be used to modify the resulting Windows Installer package. We will only be able to cover the basics of each of the editors, enough to get you going. We will use the project created in the desktop application walkthrough in this section.

Project Properties

The first step we can take in customizing the Windows Installer package is to use the project properties. The project properties dialog box is accessed by right-clicking the root of the setup project and selecting Properties from the popup menu or by selecting the Properties item from the Project menu when the setup project is the active project. Both of these methods will bring up the project properties dialog box:

As you can see from the above screenshot there is only one page that we can use to set the properties of the project: Build.

The Build Page

We will now take a look at the Build page and how the options can be used to affect how the resulting Windows Installer package is built.

Build Configurations

The first thing to notice is that like most other projects in VS.NET we can create different build configurations. We can modify the properties of a project for the currently active build configuration or we can modify the properties for all the build configurations. We use the Configuration combo-box to change what build configuration we want to change the properties for. In the previous screenshot, notice that we are modifying the properties for the currently active build configuration: Debug. The button labeled Configuration Manager allows us to add, remove, and edit the build configurations for this project.

Moving on we can see an option called Output file name, which can be used to modify where the resulting Windows Installer package (.msi) file will be created. We can modify the filename and path directly or we can press the Browse button.

Package Files

By using the next setting, Package files, we can specify how the files that make up the installation are packaged up. The table below describes the possible settings:

Package:	Description
As loose uncompressed files	When we build the project, the files that are to be included as part of the installation are copied to the same directory as the resulting Windows Installer package (.msi) file. As mentioned above, this directory can be set using the Output file name setting.
In setup file	When the project is built, the files that are to be included as part of the installation are packaged up in the resulting Windows Installer package (.msi) file. By using this method we only have one file to distribute. This is the default setting.
In cabinet file(s)	With this option, when the project is built, the files that are to be included as part of the installation are packaged up into a number of cabinet files. The size of the resulting cabinet files can be restricted by the use of a number of options, which will be discussed later in this section. This option can be very useful if you want to distribute the installation program on a set of floppy disks.

What happens if we try to install the resulting Windows Installer package on a machine that does not have the Windows Installer services running on it? Not a great deal. Luckily, there is a project option that will help us overcome this problem: **Bootstrapper**. There are three options available from the combo-box:

❑   None

❑   Windows Installer Bootstrapper

❑   Web bootstrapper

If None is selected then only the Windows Installer package file will be produced when the setup project is built. If you select Windows Installer Bootstrapper then some additional files will be placed in the output directory when the setup project is built. These additional files will install the Windows Installer services on the machine that it is run on. With this option selected, four additional files will be added to the directory that contains the resulting Windows Installer package file. The table below details the additional files:

File	Description
Setup.exe	If a user does not have the Windows Installer service installed on his machine he can use this file to install the application. When running this file the Windows Installer services will be installed onto the machine (if it is not already installed) and then the .msi file will be run and the installation will continue as normal.
Setup.ini	This is a configuration file that is used by Setup.exe after it has installed the Windows Installer services (if needed) and contains one setting – the name of the .msi file to run.
InstMsiA.exe	This file is the installation for the Windows Installer services for a Windows 95 or 98 based machine.
InstMsiW.exe	This file is the installation for the Windows Installer services for a Windows NT, 2000, or XP based machine.

The final option is Web Bootstrapper. This option allows you produce a number of additional files that can be used to allow the application to be installed over the Internet. When you select this option a window will be presented to you:

This window is used to set two options of the web bootstrapper:

- The Setup folder URL setting is used to define the location of where the Windows Installer package file produced will be located when deployed. This setting needs to be the URL of a folder.

- The Windows Installer upgrade folder URL setting is where you can optionally set the location of where the two Windows Installer service installer files (InstMsiA.exe and InstMsiW.exe) are located. This setting (if used) needs to be the URL of a folder. If this setting is not used, it is assumed that the two files are located at the URL specified by the Setup folder URL setting.

When we build the setup project with this option, three additional files are created in the output directory: Setup.exe, InstMsiA.exe and InstMsiW.exe. The only file that has a different function from that discussed previously is the Setup.exe file, which we will discuss later in this section. The Windows Installer package (.msi) file that was created by the build needs to be copied to the web server so that it is available via the URL specified in the Setup folder URL setting. The InstMsiA.exe and InstMsiW.exe files need to be copied to the web server so they are accessible via the URL specified in the Windows Installer upgrade folder URL setting. If no value was specified for this property then they need to be copied to the same location as the Windows Installer package file. The Setup.exe file can then be distributed to anyone who wants to install your application.

When the user executes the Setup.exe file, it first checks that the correct version of the Windows Installer service is installed. If it is not, then the required setup (InstMsiA.exe or InstMsiW.exe) file is downloaded from the URL specified in the above settings and then installed. Once the correct version of the Windows Installer service is installed, the Setup.exe file then downloads the package file (.msi) from the location specified. Once the package has been downloaded, the installation continues as normal by executing this Windows Installer package. If the package file cannot be downloaded then you will receive an error informing you that it could not be downloaded. The installation will then end.

The advantage of using this technique is that you do not have to deploy the Windows Installer setup files to each of the clients; they are available centrally from one location over the Web. Several installers can share the same download location. The Windows Installer package file that contains your application is also not distributed to each client. They download it from a central location. This allows you to change the package and have the client pick up this change automatically when they install the application. The disadvantage to this approach is that anyone who installs your application will need to have an Internet connection and if the files are large, it could take a long time to download them.

Compression

We also have the option to modify the compression used when packaging up the files that are to be contained within the installation program. The three options (Optimized for speed, Optimized for size, and None) are pretty self-explanatory and will not be covered in this book. The default, however, is Optimized for speed.

Setting the Cabinet File Size

If we want to package the files in cabinet files then we have the option to specify the size of those resulting cabinet file(s):

❑   The first option we have is to let the resulting cabinet file be of an unlimited size. What this effectively means is that all the files will be packaged into one big cabinet file. The resulting size of the cabinet file will also be dependent on the compression method selected.

❑   If, however, creating one large cabinet file is not practical, especially if you want to distribute your application on floppy disks (1440Kb of space per floppy), you can use the second option to specify the maximum size of the resulting cabinet file(s). If you select this option you need to fill in the maximum size that a cabinet file can be (this figure is in Kb). If all the files that need to be contained within this installation exceed this size then multiple cabinet files will be created.

Using the Solution Signing Options

The final set of options are concerned with signing the resulting Windows Installer package using Authenticode. To enable Authenticode signing you must make sure the checkbox is checked. This will enable you to set the three settings that are required to sign the package file:

Setting	Description
Certificate file	This setting is used to define where the Authenticode certificate file can be found. This file is used to sign the package.
Private key file	This setting is used to define where the private key file is. This file contains what we call an encryption key that is used to sign the package.
Timestamp server URL	This setting allows you to optionally specify the URL of a timestamp server. The timestamp server will be used to get the time of when the package was signed.

We will not be covering Authenticode signing in this chapter. If you are interested in this option you should consult the MSDN documentation.

The File System Editor

Now that we have taken a look at the project properties we are going to move on to look at the editors that are available for us to use to customize the resulting Windows Installer package. You will need to make sure that the current active project is the setup project.

We are going to start by taking a look at the File System Editor, so start it via the View | Editor menu option. The File System Editor is used to manage all the file system aspects of the installation including:

- ❑ Creating folders on the user's machine

- ❑ Adding files to the folders defined

- ❑ Creating shortcuts

Basically, this is the editor we use to define what files need to be installed and where they are installed on the user's machine.

The File System Editor is split into two panes:

The left-hand pane shows a list of the folders that have been created automatically for the project (discussed earlier in the chapter). When you select a folder in the left pane, two things happen: firstly, the right-hand pane of the editor displays a list of the files that are to be installed into the selected folder, and secondly, the Properties windows will change to show you the properties of the currently selected folder.

Adding Items to a Folder

To add an item that needs to be installed to a folder, we can either right-click on the folder in the left-hand pane and choose Add from the popup menu, or we can select the required folder and right-click in the right-hand pane and again choose Add from the popup menu. You will be presented with four options, three of which have been discussed earlier in the walkthroughs:

- ❑ Project Output

- ❑ File

- ❑ Assembly

The fourth option (Folder) allows us to add a subfolder to the currently selected folder. This sub folder then becomes a standard folder that can be used to add files. If we add any .NET components or executables, the dependencies of these components will also be added to the installation automatically.

Adding Special Folders

When we create a new deployment project, a set of standard folders will be created for us (listed in the desktop application section). What if the folders created do not match our requirements? Well, we can also use the File System editor to add special folders. To add a special folder, right-click anywhere in the left-hand pane (other than on a folder) and you will be presented with a popup menu that has one item: Add Special Folder. Alternatively, it's also available through the Action | Add Special Folder menu option. This menu item expands to show you a list of folders that you can add to the installation (folders already added to the project will be grayed out):

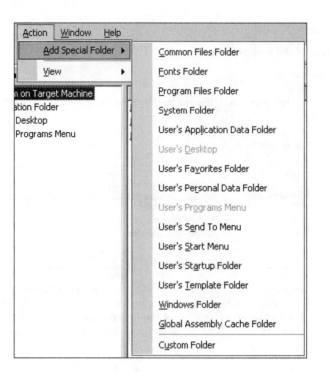

As you can see from the screenshot there are a number of system folders that we can choose from. They are summarized in the following table:

Name	Description	Windows Installer property
Common Files Folder	Files (non-system) that are shared by multiple applications are usually installed to this folder.	[CommonFilesFolder]
Fonts Folder	This folder is used to contain all the fonts that are installed on the computer. If your application used a specific font you want to install it into this folder.	[FontsFolder]
Program Files Folder	Most applications are installed in a directory below the program files folder. This acts as root directory for installed applications.	[ProgramFilesFolder]
System Folder	This folder is used to store shared system files. The folder typically holds files that are part of the OS.	[SystemFolder]
User's Application Data Folder	This folder is used to store data on a per-application basis that is specific to a user.	[CommonAppDataFolder]

Name	Description	Windows Installer property
User's Desktop	This folder represents the user desktop. This folder could be used to create and display a shortcut to your application that a user could use to start your application.	[DesktopFolder]
User's Favorite Folder	This folder is used as a central place to store links to the user's favorite web sites, documents, folders, etc.	[FavoritesFolder]
User's Personal Data Folder	This folder is where a user will store their important files. It is normally referred to as 'My Documents'.	[PersonalFolder]
User's Programs Menu	This folder is where shortcuts, etc. are created to applications that appear on the user's program menu. This would be an ideal place to create a shortcut to your application.	[ProgramMenuFolder]
User's Send To Menu	This folder stores all the user's send to shortcuts. A send to shortcut is displayed when you right-click a file in the Windows Explorer and choose Send To. The send to shortcut usually invokes an application passing in the pathname of the files it was invoked from.	[SendToFolder]
User's Start Menu	This folder can be used to add items to the user's start menu. This is not often used.	[StartMenuFolder]
User's Startup Folder	This folder is used to start applications whenever the user's logs into the computer. If you would like your application to start every time the user logs in, then you could add a shortcut to your application in this folder.	[StartupFolder]
User's Template Folder	This folder contains templates specific to the logged in user. Templates are usually used by applications like Microsoft Office 2000.	[TemplateFolder]
Windows Folder	This folder is the windows root folder. This is where the OS is installed.	[WindowsFolder]
Global Assembly Cache Folder	This folder is used to store all the shared assemblies on the user's computer.	

If none of the built-in folders match your requirements, you can even use the item at the bottom of the list to create your own custom folder. This is where the Windows Installer property column of the above table comes. Suppose we wanted to create a new directory in the user's favorites folder called **Wrox Press**. We could accomplish this by adding the correct special folder and then adding a subfolder to it. Another way to accomplish this is to create a custom folder, the process of which we will include below:

Right-click in the left-hand pane of the file editor and choose **Custom Folder** from the popup menu. The new folder will be created in the left-hand pane of the editor. The name of the folder will be edit mode, so enter the text **Wrox Press**. And press *Enter*.

The folder will now be selected and the **Properties** window will have changed to show the properties of the new folder. The properties of a folder are summarized in the table below:

Property	Description
(Name)	This is the name of the selected folder. The name property is used within the setup project as the means by which you select a folder.
AlwaysCreate	This property is used to indicate whether this folder should be created on installation even if it's empty (**True**). If the value is **False** and there are no files to be installed into the folder, then the folder will not be created. The default is **False**.
Condition	This enables you to enter a condition that will be evaluated when the installation is run. If the condition evaluates to true then the folder will be created, likewise if the condition evaluates to false then the folder won't be created.
DefaultLocation	This is where we define where the folder is going to be created on the target machine. We can enter a literal folder name (such as `C:\Temp`), or we can use a Windows Installer property, or a combination of the two. A Windows Installer property contains information that is filled in when the installer is run. In the above table of special folders there was a column called Windows Installer property. The property defined in this table would be filled in with the actual location of the special folder at runtime. Therefore, if we entered `[WindowsFolder]` as the text for this property, the folder created would represent the windows special folder.
Property	This property is used to define a Windows Installer property that can be used to override the `DefaultLocation` property of the folder when the installation is run.
Transitive	This property indicates whether the condition specified in the condition property is re-evaluated on subsequent (re-)installs. If the value is **True** then the condition is checked on each additional run of the installation. A value of **False** will cause the condition only to be run the first time the installation is run on the computer. The default value is **False**.

Set the `DefaultLocation` property to `[FavoritesFolder]\Wrox Press`.

We could now add some shortcuts to this folder using the technique described below. When the installation is run, a new folder will be added to the user's favorite folder called **Wrox Press**.

Creating Shortcuts

The final aspect of the File System Editor that we are going to look at is that of creating shortcuts. The first step in creating a shortcut is to locate the file that is to be the target of the shortcut. Select the target file and right-click on it. The popup menu that appears will include an option to create a shortcut to the selected file, which will be created in the same folder. Select this option.

To add the shortcut to the user's desktop we need to move this shortcut to the folder that represents the user's desktop. Likewise we could move this shortcut to the folder that represents the user's programs menu. Cut and paste the new shortcut to the User's Desktop folder in the left-hand pane of the editor. The shortcut will now be added to the user's desktop when the installation is run. You will probably want to rename the shortcut, which can be accomplished easily via the Rename option of the popup menu.

We have only taken a brief look at the File System Editor. I would encourage you to explore what can be accomplished by using the editor.

The Registry Editor

The next editor that we are going to look at is the Registry Editor, which is used to:

❑   Create registry keys

❑   Create values for registry keys

❑   Import a registry file

Like the File System Editor, the Registry Editor is split into two panes:

The left-hand pane of the editor represents the registry keys on the target computer. When you select a registry key, two things happen: the right-hand pane of the editor will be updated to show the values that are to be created under the selected registry key, and if the registry key selected is not a root key in the left-hand pane, the Properties window will be updated with a set of properties for this registry key.

When you create a new deployment project a set of registry keys will be created for you that correspond to the standard base registry keys of Windows. Notice in the screenshot that there is a key defined with a name of [Manufacturer]. When the installation is run, this will be replaced with the value of the Manufacturer property that we discussed earlier in the chapter. [Manufacturer] is a property of the installation and can be used elsewhere within the installation. There are a number of these properties defined that can be used in much the same way (you should consult the *Property Reference* topic in the MSDN documentation for a full list).

Adding a Value to a Registry Key

So what do we need to do to add a value to a registry key? We must first select the required registry key (or create it) that is going to hold the registry values and then there are a number of ways that we can add the registry value:

- ❏ We can right-click on the registry key and use the resulting popup menu
- ❏ We can right-click in the right-hand pane and use the resulting popup menu
- ❏ We can use the Action menu

The menu items contained within the Action menu will depend on where the current focus is. For illustrational purposes here, select one of the Software registry keys. The Action menu will contain one item, New, which contains a number of menu items:

- ❏ Key
- ❏ String Value
- ❏ Environment String Value
- ❏ Binary Value
- ❏ DWORD Value

Using this menu we can create a new registry key below the currently selected key (via Key), or we can create a value for the currently selected registry key using one of the four Value types: String, Environment String, Binary, and DWORD.

So let's take a look at how we can create a registry entry that informs the application whether or not to run in debug mode. The registry value must be applicable to a particular user, must be called Debug, and must contain the text True or False.

The first step that needs to be completed is to select the following registry key in the left-hand pane of the editor:

HKEY_CURRENT_USER\Software\[Manufacturer]

The registry key HKEY_CURRENT_USER is used to store registry settings that apply to the currently logged in user.

Now, we want to create a value so that it is applicable to only this application and not all applications created by us. What we need to do is create a new registry key below the HKEY_CURRENT_USER\Software\[Manufacturer] key that is specific to this product, so select the Action I New I Key menu item.

When the key is created, the key name will be editable, so give it a name of [ProductName] and press *Enter*. This will create a key that is given the name of the product contained within this Windows Installer package. The ProductName property of the setup was discussed earlier in this chapter.

Now that we have created the correct registry key, we need to create the actual registry value. Make sure that our new registry key is selected and choose String Value from the Action I New menu and give the new value a name of Debug.

Once the value has been created we can set a default value for it, in our case False. Make sure that the new value is selected, the Properties window will have changed to show you the details for this value. Notice that there is a property called Value, which we will use to set the initial value. Enter False as the value for the Value property and that's it:

When the Windows Installer package is run the Debug registry value will be created. As you can see manipulating the Windows Registry is straightforward.

We can move most keys and values in the Registry Editor around by using cut-and-paste or simply by dragging and dropping the required item.

> **If a value already exists in the registry, the Windows Installer package will overwrite the existing value with that defined in the Registry Editor.**

Importing Registry Files

If you already have a registry file that contains the registry settings that you would like to be created, you can import the file into the Registry Editor, which saves you having to manually enter the information. To import a registry file you need to make sure the root node (Registry on Target Machine) is selected in the left-hand pane of the editor. You can then use the Import item of the Action menu to select the registry file to import.

> **Registry manipulation should be used with extreme caution. Windows relies heavily on the registry and as a result of this you can cause yourself a great deal of problems if you delete/overwrite/change registry values and keys without knowing the full consequences of the action.**

If you want to create the registry entries that are required to create file associations you can use the editor covered next.

913

The File Types Editor

The File Types Editor can be used to create the required registry entries to establish a **file association** for the application being installed. A file association is simply a link between a particular file extension and a particular application. For example, the file extension .doc is normally associated with Microsoft WordPad or Microsoft Word.

When we create a file association, not only do we create a link between the file extension and the application, we also define a set of actions that can be performed from the context menu of the file with the associated extension. Looking at our Microsoft Word example, if we right-click on a document with an extension of .doc, we get a context menu that can contain any number of actions – for example, Open and Print. The action in bold (Open by default) is the default action to be called when we double-click on the file, so in our example double-clicking a Word document will start Microsoft Word and load the selected document.

Creating File Extensions

So how do we create a file extension using the editor? We will answer this question by walking through the creation of a file extension for our application. Let's say that our application uses a file extension of .set and that the file is to be opened in the application when we double-click on the file. To accomplish this we need to start the File Types editor, which unlike the last two editors, only has one pane to its interface:

To add a new file type we need to make sure the root element (File Types on Target Machine) is selected in the editor. We can then choose Add File Type from the Action menu. Give the new file type the name, Example File Type.

Before we continue we must set the extension and application that this file type uses. These are both accomplished using the Properties window:

Enter .set as the value for the Extensions property.

To associate an application with this file type we need to use the Command property. The ellipsis button for this property presents us with a dialog box where we can select an executable file contained within any of the folders defined in the File System Editor. In our case, we'll select the Primary Output from WindowsApplication (active) from the Application Folder as the value for Command.

When we created the new file type, a default action was added for us called &Open – select it. Now take a look at the Properties window again. Notice the Arguments property: we can use this to add command line arguments to the application defined in the last step. In the case of the default action that has been added for us, the arguments are "%1", where the value %1 will be replaced by the filename that invoked the action. We can add our own hard-coded arguments (such as /d). An action is set to be the default by right-clicking on it and selecting Set as Default from the popup menu.

The User Interface Editor

The User Interface Editor is used to manage the interface that the user uses to proceed through the installation of the application. The editor allows us to define the dialog boxes that are displayed to the user and in what order they are shown. The User Interface Editor looks like this:

The editor uses a treeview with two root nodes: Install and Admin. Below each of these nodes there are three nodes that represent the stages of installation: Start, Progress, and End. Each of the three stages can contain a number of dialog boxes that will be displayed to the user when the resulting Windows Installer package is run. A default set of dialog boxes is predefined when we create the deployment project. The default dialog boxes that are present depend on the type of deployment project: Setup Project or Web Setup Project. The above screenshot shows the dialog boxes that added by default to a Setup Project. If however you are creating a Web Setup Project the Installation Folder dialog will be replaced by an Installation Address dialog. Using the previous screenshot we will discuss the two modes that installer can be run in and what the three stages of the installation are.

Installation Modes

We'll start by taking a look at the two modes that the installation runs: Install and Admin. These basically distinguish between an end user installing the application and a system administrator performing a network setup.

> To use the **Admin mode** of the resulting Windows Installer package you can use **msiexec.exe** with the **/a** command line parameter:
>
> `msiexec.exe /a <PACKAGE>.msi`

The Install mode will be the one that is most used and is what we will use in this discussion. As mentioned earlier the steps the installation goes through can be split into three stages and are represented as sub nodes of the parent installation mode.

The Start Stage

The Start stage is the first stage of the installation and contains the dialog boxes that need to be displayed to the user before the actual installation of the files and so on begins. The Start stage should be used to gather any information from the user that may affect what is installed and where it is installed. This stage is commonly used to ask the user to select the base installation folder for the application and to ask the user what parts of the system he would like to install. Another very common task of this stage is to ask the user what their name is and what organization they work for. At the end of this stage the Windows Installer service will determine how much disk space is required on the target machine and check that this amount of space is available. If the space is not available, the user will receive an error and the installation will not continue.

The Progress Stage

The Progress stage is the second stage of the installer and is where the actual installation of the files occurs. There isn't usually any user interaction in this stage of installation. There is normally one dialog box that indicates the current progress of the installation. The current progress of the installation is calculated automatically.

The End Stage

Once the actual installation of the files and so on has finished the installer moves into the End stage. The most common use of this stage is to inform the user that the installation has completed successfully. It is often used to provide the option of running the application straight away or to view any release notes.

Customizing the Order of Dialog Boxes

The order in which the dialog boxes appear within the treeview determines the order in which they are presented to the user when the resulting Windows Installer package is run. Dialog boxes cannot be moved between the different stages.

The order of the dialog boxes can be changed by dragging the respective dialog boxes to the position in which we want them to appear. We can also move a particular dialog box up or down in the order in which it is shown by right-clicking on the dialog box and selecting either Move Up or Move Down.

Adding Dialog Boxes

A set of pre-defined dialog boxes have been added to the project for us, but what happens if these do not match our requirements? As well as being able to modify the order in which the dialog boxes appear, we can also add or remove dialog boxes from any of the stages.

When adding a dialog box we have the choice of using a built-in dialog box or importing one. To illustrate how to add a dialog box, we will look at an example of adding a dialog box to display a ReadMe file to the user of Windows Installer package. The ReadMe file will need to be displayed before the actual installation of the files and so on occurs.

The first step is to determine the mode in which the dialog box is to be shown: Install or Admin. In our case we are not interested in the Admin mode so we will use the Install mode. After this, we need to determine the stage at which the dialog box is to be shown. In our example, we want to display the ReadMe file to the user before the actual installation of the files occurs, which means we will have to show the ReadMe file in the Start stage. Make sure the Start node is selected below the Install parent node.

We are now ready to add the dialog box. Using the Action menu again, select the Add Dialog menu item, which will display a dialog box where you can choose from the built-in dialog boxes:

As you can see from the screenshot there are a number of built-in dialog boxes to choose from. Each dialog box has a short description that appears at the bottom of the window to inform you of its intended function. In the case of our example, we want to use the Read Me dialog box, so select it and click on OK.

New dialog boxes are always added as the last dialog box in the stage that they are added to, so now we need to move it into the correct position. In our case we want the Read Me dialog box to be shown immediately after the Welcome dialog box, so drag and drop it into position.

Properties of the Dialog Boxes

Like most other project items in VS.NET, dialog boxes have a set of properties that we can change to suit our needs using the Properties window. If you make sure a dialog box is selected, you will notice that the properties window changes to show the properties of the selected dialog box. The properties that appear depend on the dialog box selected. Details of all the properties of the built in dialog boxes can be found by looking at the *Properties of the User Interface Editor* topic in the MSDN documentation.

The Custom Actions Editor

The Custom Actions Editor is used for fairly advanced installations and allows us to define actions that are to be performed due to one of the following installation events: Install, Commit, Rollback, and Uninstall. For example, we can use this editor to define an action that creates a new database when the installation commits.

The custom actions that are added using this editor can be windows script-based or compiled executables or DLLs.

Before we continue with our discussion of this editor make sure that it is loaded. Once loaded you will notice that it uses a treeview to represent the information, much like the User Interface Editor. There are four nodes that represent each of the four installation events that you can add custom actions to:

As with the User Interface Editor, the order in which the actions appear determines the order in which they are run and this can be modified by simply dragging and dropping the actions, or by using the context menus of the actions to move them up or down.

Adding a Custom Action

To add a custom action we must select the node of the event into which we want to install the action. You can then use the Action menu to select the executable, DLL or script that implements the custom action. The four actions that are defined in the editor are defined in the following table:

Event	Description
Install	The actions defined for this event will be run when the installation of the files and so on has finished but before the installation has committed
Commit	The actions defined for this event will be run when the installation has been committed and has therefore been successful
Rollback	The actions defined for this event will be run when the installation fails and rolls back the machine to the same state as before the install was started
Uninstall	The actions defined for this event will be run when the application is being uninstalled from the machine

Suppose we wanted to start our application up as soon as the installation had been completed successfully. We could use the following process to accomplish this:

First we need to decide when the action must occur. Using the above table we can see that the Commit event will be run when the installation has been successful. Make sure this node is selected in the editor. We are now ready to add the actual action we would like to happen when the commit event is called. Using the Action menu again, select the Add Custom Action menu item, which will display a dialog box that we can use to navigate for and select a file (exe, .dll or windows script) from any that are included in the File System Editor. In the case of our example select Primary output from WindowsApplication (Active), which is contained within the Application Folder.

As with most items in the editors that we are discussing, the new custom action has a number of properties that we can use. These properties are summarized in the following table:

Property	Description
(Name)	This is the name given to the custom action selected.
Arguments	This property allows you to pass command line arguments into the executable that makes up the custom action. This only applies to custom actions that are implemented in executable files (.exe). By default the first argument passed in can be used to distinguish what event caused the action to run. The first argument can have the following values: /Install /Commit /Rollback /Uninstall
Condition	This enables you to enter a condition that will be evaluated before the custom action is run. If the condition evaluates to True then the custom action will run, likewise if the condition evaluates to False then the custom action will not run.
CustomActionData	This property allows you to pass additional information to the custom action.
EntryPoint	This property is used to define the entry point in the .dll that implements the custom action. This only applies to custom actions that are implemented in dynamic linked libraries (.dll). If no value is entered then the installer will look for an entry point in the selected DLL with the same name as the event that caused the action to run (Install, Commit, Rollback, Uninstall).
InstallerClass	If the custom action is implemented by an Installer class (consult the MSDN documentation for more information) in the selected component then this property must be set to True. If not it must be set to False.
SourcePath	This property will show the path to the actual file on the developer's machine that implements the custom action.

Set the InstallClass property to equal False as our application does not contain an installer class.

That's it. When we run the Windows Installer package and the installation is successful, our application will automatically start. The custom action that we implemented above is very simple, but custom actions can be used to accomplish any customized installation actions that you could want. I suggest that you take some time to play around with what can be accomplished using custom actions.

The Launch Conditions Editor

The Launch Conditions Editor can be used to define a number of conditions for the target machine that must be met before the installation will run. For example, if your application relies on the fact that the user must have Microsoft Word 2000 installed on their machine to run your application, you can define a launch condition that will check this.

You can define a number of searches that can be performed to help create launch conditions:

❑   File search

❑   Registry search

❑   Windows Installer search

As with the Custom Actions Editor, the Launch Conditions Editor uses a treeview to display the information contained within it:

There are two root nodes: the first (Search Target Machine) is used to display the searches that have been defined, the second (Launch Conditions) contains a list of the conditions that will be evaluated when the Windows Installer package is run on the target machine.

As with many of the other editors, the order in which the items appear below these two nodes determines the order in which the searches are run and the order in which the conditions are evaluated. If we wish, we can modify the order of the items in the same manner as previous editors.

> **The searches are run and then the conditions are evaluated as soon as the Windows Installer package is run, before any dialog boxes are shown to the user.**

We are now going to look at an example of adding a file search and launch condition to a setup project. For argument's sake, let's say that we want to make sure that our users have Microsoft Word 2000 installed on their machine before they are allowed to run the installation for our application.

Adding a File Search

We begin by searching for the Microsoft Word 2000 executable:

Making sure the **Search Target Machine** node is currently selected in the editor, add a new file search by selecting the **Add File Search** item from the **Action** menu. The new item will need to be given a meaningful name, so enter **Word2KSearch**:

Modifying the File Search Properties

Like most items contained within the editors mentioned in this chapter, the new file search item has a set of properties that we can modify using the Properties window. The properties of the file search item determine the criteria that will be used when searching for the file. Most of the properties are self-explanatory and have been covered in previous sections and will not be covered in this chapter.

In our example here, we need to search for the Microsoft Word 2000 executable, which means that a number of these properties will need to be modified to match our own search criteria.

The first property that we need to modify is `FileName`, which is used to define the name of the file that the search will look for. In our case we need to search for Microsoft Word 2000 executable, so enter `winword.exe` as the value for this property. Previous versions of Microsoft Word used the same filename.

There is no need for us to search for the file from the root of the hard drive. The `Folder` property can be used to define the starting folder for the search. By default, the value is `[SystemFolder]`, which indicates that the search will start from the Windows `system` folder. There are a number of these built-in values that we can use; if you are interested then you can look up what these folders correspond to in *Adding Special Folders* section.

In our example, we do not want to search the Windows `system` folder as Microsoft Word is usually installed in the `Program Files` folder, so set the value of the `Folder` property to `[ProgramFilesFolder]` to indicate that this should be our starting folder.

When the search starts it will only search the folder specified in the `Folder` property as indicated by the default value (0) of the `Depth` property. The `Depth` property is used to specify how many levels of subfolders the search will look in from the starting folder specified above for the file in question. There are performance issues relating to the `Depth` property. If a search is performed for a file that is very deep in the file system hierarchy, it can take a long time to find the file. Therefore it is advisable that wherever possible you should use a combination of the `Folder` and `Depth` properties to decrease the possible search range. The file that we are searching for in our example will probably be at a depth of greater than 1, so change the value to 3.

There may be different versions of the file that we are searching for on a user's machine. We can use the remaining properties to specify a set of requirements for the file that must be met for it to be found, for example, minimum version number, minimum file size.

We are searching for the existence of Microsoft Word 2000; this means that we will need to define the minimum version of the file that we want to find. To search for the correct version of `winword.exe` we need to enter `9.0.0.0` as the value for the `MinVersion` property. This will ensure that the user has Microsoft Word 2000 or later installed and not an earlier version.

921

The result of the file search will need to be assigned to a Windows Installer property so that we can use it to create a launch condition later. This is going to be a bit of a tongue-twister. We need to define the name of the Windows Installer property that is used to store the result of the file search using the Property property. Enter WORDEXISTS as the value for the Property property. If the file search is successful, the full path to the found file will be assigned to this Windows Installer property, otherwise it will be left blank.

Properties	⼚ ×
Word2kSearch Launch Condition Properties	▼

⊟ Misc	
(Name)	Word2kSearch
Depth	3
FileName	winword.exe
Folder	[ProgramFilesFolder]
MaxDate	
MaxSize	
MaxVersion	
MinDate	
MinSize	
MinVersion	9.0.0.0
Property	WORDEXISTS

Property
Specifies a named property that can be accessed at installation run time to modify the installation based on search results

Creating a Launch Condition

A file search alone is pretty useless. Which takes us on to the second step of the process of ensuring the user has Microsoft Word 2000 installed, creating a launch condition. We can use the results of the file search described above to create a launch condition.

Make sure the Launch Conditions node is selected in the editor and add a new launch condition to the project by selecting Add Launch Condition from the Action menu. We need to give this new item a meaningful name and in the case of our example we will give it a name of Word2KExists:

Launch Conditions (Setup)

This new item has a number of properties that we will need to modify. The first property we will change is called Message and is used to set the text of the message box that will appear if this condition is not met. Enter any meaningful description that describes why the installation cannot continue.

The next property that we will need to change is called `Condition` and is used to define a valid deployment condition that is to be evaluated when the installation runs. The deployment condition entered must evaluate to `True` or `False`. When the installer is run, the condition will be evaluated, if the result of the condition is `False` then the message defined will be displayed to the user and the installation will stop.

For our example, we need to enter a condition that takes into account if the `winword.exe` file was found. We can use the Windows Installer property defined above (`WORDEXISTS`) as part of the condition. As the property is empty if the file was not found and non-empty if the file was found, we can perform a simple test on whether the property is empty to create the condition. Enter `WORDEXISTS <> " "` as the value for the `Condition` property.

Hopefully, from the above discussion of this search you will be able to apply the knowledge gained, to understand how to use the other searches and create your own launch conditions.

We have now finished our brief discussion of the editors that we can use to modify the resulting Windows Installer package to our needs. We have only looked briefly at the functionality of the editors but they are extremely powerful so I advise you to spend some time playing around with them.

Building

The final step is concerned with how to build the deployment or setup project you have created. There is basically no difference between how you build a VB.NET application and deployment/setup project. If the project is the only project contained within the solution then you can just use the Build item from the Build menu, which will cause the project to be built. As with the other projects you will be informed of what is happening during the build through the Output window.

The deployment/setup project can also be built as part of a multi-project solution. If the Build Solution item is chosen from the Build menu, all the projects in the solution will be built. Any deployment or setup projects will be built last. This is to ensure that if they contain the output from another project in the solution that they pick up the latest build of that project.

As with most other project templates in VS.NET, you can set the current build configuration to be used when building the project. This will not be covered in this chapter as it has been covered previously in the book. As you can see building a setup/deployment project is basically the same as building any other project template.

Summary

We started by looking at the structure of an assembly and how it contains metadata that enables it to describe itself. This mechanism of self-description will help us when we come to deploy our applications by removing dependencies on the registry, unlike COM components. If a machine has the CLR installed on it, it is more feasible that an application can be deployed to a machine simply by copying the files (although this does not apply if the application must install shared assemblies).

We also looked at how the identity of an assembly is used to allow multiple versions of an assembly to be installed on a machine and how this aids the side-by-side use of assemblies. We covered how an assembly is versioned and the process by which the CLR resolves an external assembly reference and how we can modify this process through the use of configuration files.

We also looked at how an assembly stores information such as version number, strong name, and culture about any external assemblies that it references. We also looked at how this information is checked at runtime to ensure that the correct version of the assembly is referenced and how we can use versioning policies to override this in the case of a buggy assembly. The assembly is the single biggest aid in reducing the errors that can occur due to DLL Hell and in helping with deployment.

We also covered a number of topics relating to deployment and deployment issues, including:

❑ How assemblies are used as the foundations of deployment in .NET

❑ How assemblies are structured to help reduce the problems of deployment, known as DLL Hell

❑ How assemblies move us towards the goal of true XCOPY deployment

❑ VS.NET setup and deployment project types

❑ Setup/Deployment project editors

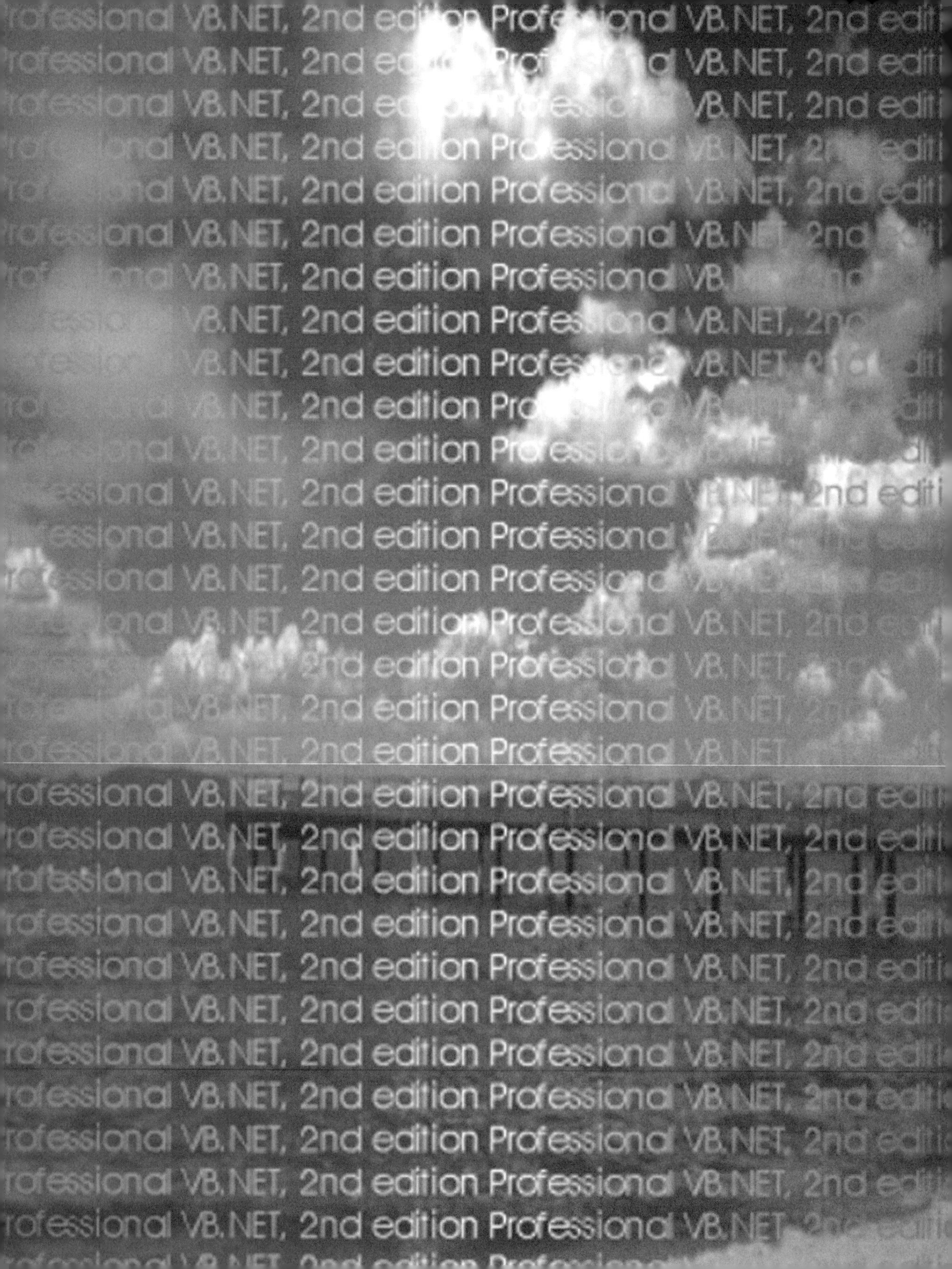
Professional VB.NET, 2nd edition

Using the Visual Basic Compatibility Library

The Visual Basic Compatibility Library is provided in the .NET environment in order to assist in the conversion of existing code, as well as providing backward compatibility and support for developers who are transitioning to the new version. There has been much said about the newest version of VB, and how we should handle our legacy code. Many are saying that anything new should be started in the latest version, and anything old should be rewritten from ground up instead of being run through a conversion. Regardless of which way we choose to handle our VB6 code, the compatibility library will come in handy along the way. While the compatibility library is a very nice tool, please keep in mind as we go through this chapter that our main goal should be to use it as a temporary solution to the learning curve presented by new software revisions. Please also keep in mind that the compatibility library is not all-inclusive and therefore may not assist in all instances when a programmer is undergoing the task of converting code to VB.NET.

What is the Compatibility Library?

The compatibility library is a library made up of the VB6 functions that have been replaced in VB.NET due to reorganization into different libraries, syntax changes or just that they weren't deemed necessary anymore. At the end of the chapter is a complete list, including information about what each function was replaced by. The library is used by the conversion tools and can also be used by adding a reference to it within a VB.NET project.

When the Library is Used by the Conversion Tools

The compatibility library is referenced automatically in any project that has run through the conversion tool. This occurs when you open an existing VB6 project in Visual Studio .NET, or can be accessed manually using the VBUpgrade.exe program included with the Visual Studio .NET installation. During the conversion, if a function is no longer supported, it has a note by it and the VB6 compatibility library equivalent is used. The notes that appear in the code are comments right by the line of code where the issue is. For instance, when the conversion tool was run on the VB6 version of the VBBank DLL the conversion tool placed the following note in the Account class module due to a change in support of the GetObjectContext.SetAbort statement:

'UPGRADE_ISSUE: COM expression not supported: Module methods of COM objects. Click for more: ms-help://MS.MSDNVS/vbcon/html/vbup1060.htm.

It is important to review code that is noted and replace it with the newer code syntax because the older code will not be as efficient.

A couple of examples of when the library has been used by the conversion tools follow. The examples are taken from running the VBBank sample (included in the Visual Studio .NET installation) through the conversion utility and comparing that to the new sample in the VB.NET samples library.

In the VB6 version of the VBBank there are a few things we can look at that have changed, encompassing the topics of default properties and object creation.

First of all, the default properties for fields in ADO recordsets have changed. In VB6 the code that was getting the Balance field from a recordset looked like:

```
lngBalance = adoRS.Fields("Balance").Value
```

When run through the conversion utility it changed to:

```
lngBalance = VB6.GetDefaultProperty & (adoRS.Fields("Balance").Value)
```

In the VB.NET version this same code is written as:

```
IntBalance = cint(adoRS.Fields("Balance").Value)
```

As you can see there are two important changes in the line of code written in VB.NET. Not only is there a change in where our default data type changes are reflected, but also the VB6.DefaultProperty does not need to be designated. The default property changes, as they relate to recordsets, are primarily for making code easy to read. For instance using the same VB.NET structure above, the default property is Item for the Fields object, so we didn't need to specify it as:

```
IntBalance = cint(adoRS.Fields.Item("Balance").Value)
```

(It should be noted, however that the Item designator would work.) In contrast, we can no longer take as many shortcuts as we used to. For instance below is an example that would not work, since, at the very least, the Fields collection must be designated now:

```
IntBalance = cint(adoRS("Balance").Value)
```

With respect to the changes in the way we create objects, the conversion utility incorporates the use of the compatibility library in the following way:

```
objCreateTable = VB6.CreateObject("VB6Bank.CreateTable")
```

The VB.NET code for this same type of instruction is as follows, illustrating the use of the new keyword in object creation:

```
Dim ct as New CreateTable
```

The main point to the object creation changes is to simplify the code used. As illustrated above, where we declared the object then set the variable equal to the created object, we now can use the New keyword in one line to accomplish the same task.

When to Use the Library in Projects

The compatibility library is primarily for transitioning to the new environment. As you will see outlined in the table at the end of the chapter, there are a *few* major changes to the language which drive *most* of the changes in syntax with regard to the functions. As mentioned before, the conversion tools automatically put the reference into a converted project, but we want to clean up our projects and remove the reference for stability and speed.

Referencing the Compatibility Library

The compatibility library can be added as a reference, and is located under the .NET Framework tab of the Add Reference dialog. It is listed as Microsoft.VisualBasic.Compatibility, as illustrated in the following screenshot:

Once the reference is added to the project you will need to add the following imports line to your code:

```
Imports Microsoft.VisualBasic.Compatibility
```

Compatibility Library Examples

Let's start with looking at FileIO operation changes, which make up a good deal of our compatibility library. We open, write to, read from, and close files differently now. We'll use a small sample executable project to illustrate how FileIO has changed. The code below our screenshot is taken from the Click event of the button:

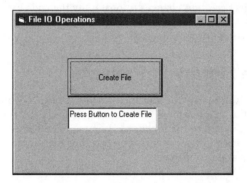

Our code simply opens a file, writes two lines to it and closes the file, populating a text box with status while working. Let's look at how the code was created in VB6:

```
'This is VB6 code
Private Sub cmdCreateFile_Click()
    Dim Handle As Integer
    Handle = FreeFile
Open "c:\Testing.txt" For Output As Handle
    txtCreate = "Writing File"
Write #Handle, "This is line 1"
Write #Handle, "This is line 2"
Close #Handle
    txtCreate = "File Written"
End Sub
```

Now, let's look at what the conversion tool did with our code:

```
Private Sub cmdCreateFile_Click(ByVal eventSender As System.Object, _
        ByVal eventArgs As System.EventArgs) Handles cmdCreateFile.Click
    Dim Handle As Short
    Handle = FreeFile()
    FileOpen(Handle, "c:\Testing.txt",OpenMode.Output)
    txtCreate.Text = "Writing File"
    WriteLine(Handle, "This is line 1")
    WriteLine(Handle, "This is line 2")
    FileClose(Handle)
```

```
        txtCreate.Text = "File Written"
    End Sub
```

There are a few alterations to our code that should interest us here. The conversion tool changed how our variable was dimensioned to Short instead of Integer due to the changes in data type definition.

In addition, we can see how our Open and Write functions have changed to FileOpen and WriteLine. In VB6 we opened a file with:

```
    Open "c:\Testing.txt" For Output As Handle
```

The conversion utility changed it to the syntax of the updated FileOpen function as:

```
    FileOpen(Handle, "c:\Testing.txt",OpenMode.Output)
```

As you can see, there is a syntactical difference between the two lines, changing to a function that has the OpenMode parameter within it. In addition, while in VB6 we write a line to the file using the following syntax:

```
    Write #Handle, "This is line 1"
```

In VB.NET the function now looks like:

```
    WriteLine(Handle, "This is line 1")
```

Along with those functions, the conversion tool has forced us to use property assignment with our text box because the default properties of Object are dealt with differently now, as illustrated by the following code:

```
    txtCreate.Text = "Writing File"
```

Now let's look at one approach we could use to do the same thing in VB.NET:

```
    Private Sub cmdCreateFile_Click(ByVal sender As System.Object, _
            ByVal e As System.EventArgs) Handles
    cmdCreateFile.Click
    Dim objWriter As New IO.StreamWriter(File.Open& _
        ("c:\Testing.txt",FileMode.OpenOrCreate))
    txtcreate.Text = "Writing File"
    objWriter.Write("This is Line 1")
    objwriter.Write("This is Line 2")
    objWriter.Flush()
    objWriter.Close()
    txtCreate.Text = "File Written"
    objWriter = Nothing
    End Sub
```

When working with the `StreamWriter` object and other associated file functions, we need to keep in mind that they have moved to the `System.IO` namespace. The major differences in how we do things include, using stream writers to create, read, and write files as well as having the open and close functions directly related to the stream writer interface instead of directly opening the file through a file handle.

The other major revision area that you will note from our reference table is the way we handle forms. Let's look specifically at how the constants and default properties have changed in comparison to VB6. The example shown below is the `Click` event of the button shown on the screenshot:

First, let's look at the code as it was in VB6. You will see we use VB constants which determine our message box style and the comparison in our `if` statement:

```
'This is VB6 code
   Private Sub cmdGoForIt_Click()
   Dim bRes As String
   bRes = MsgBox("Click OK for testing", vbOKCancel,& "Testing")
   If bRes = vbOK Then
       txtResult = bRes
   Else
       txtResult = "You should have hit OK"
   End If
   End Sub
```

Below is the code after running through the conversion utility. You will see that we have the `MsgBoxResult.OK` evaluation as well as the `MsgBoxStyle.OKCancel` method replacing `vbOKCancel`:

```
'Conversion tool code
Private Sub cmdGoForIt_Click (ByVal eventSender  & _
        As System.Object, ByVal eventArgs As System.EventArgs)
   Dim bRes As String
   bRes = CStr(MsgBox("Click OK for testing", MsgBoxStyle.OKCancel, "Testing"))
   If bRes = CStr(MsgBoxResult.OK) Then
       txtResult.Text = bRes
   Else
       txtResult.Text = "You should have hit OK"
   End If
End Sub
```

Now let's look at how we would do it in VB.NET:

```
'VB.NET code
Private Sub cmdGoForIt_Click(ByVal sender &_
        As Object, ByVal e As System.EventArgs)
   Dim bRes As Integer
   bres = (MessageBox.Show("Click OK for testing", & "Testing", _
           MessageBox.OKCancel))
   If bRes = DialogResult.OK Then
      txtResult.Text = str(bres)
   Else
      txtResult.Text = "You should have hit OK"
   End If
End Sub
```

When we look at our lines that evaluate the results of our message box, we can see how our code has been changed. The following VB6 code:

```
If bRes = vbOK Then
```

has been altered by the conversion utility so as to read:

```
If bRes = CStr(MsgBoxResult.OK) Then
```

It has also changed to be more specific to the functions that relate to the object the program is dealing with in VB.NET:

```
If bRes = DialogResult.OK Then
```

In summary, as you can see from the examples, the major areas which have changed have done so dramatically. As a result, it is important to choose wisely between code conversion and rewriting code completely, although the conversion utility can be nice to use as a source of information regarding what will need to be changed in our existing code. We have a nice tool in the compatibility library to help us through the change, but as always, learning the new coding styles will be the most efficient way to tackle projects in the future.

The following pages have a complete listing of the compatibility library and the reasons and replacements for the functions that are included.

Compatibility Library Reference Listing

This section provides a complete list of the compatibility functions and what they are replaced by in the .NET environment. As mentioned before, the .NET replacements fall into several categories. The categories we will reference here include declaration syntax changes, elements replaced by methods, data type change, Boolean operator changes, and class and interface changes.

Declaration Syntax Changes

Declaration syntax changes mainly encompass declaring multiple variables on one line. For instance, where in VB6 the following statement would evaluate to both variables being an integer:

```
Dim A as Integer, B as Integer
```

in VB.NET we can do the same thing without repeating the As Integer keywords:

```
Dim A, B as Integer
```

Elements Replaced by Methods

Method, Element	Changed Reason	New Method, Element, Namespace
CopyArray	Moved to Copy method of Array class	Copy method of Array class
FontChangeBold	Moved to Font class of System.Drawing namespace	Bold property of Font class relative to an object that the Font class is being applied to
FontChangeItalic	Moved to Font class of System.Drawing namespace	Italic property of Font class relative to an object that the Font class is being applied to
FontChangeName	Moved to Font class of System.Drawing namespace	Name property of Font class relative to an object that the Font class is being applied to
FontChangeSize	Moved to Font class of System.Drawing namespace	Size property of Font class relative to an object that the Font class is being applied to
FontChangeStrikeOut	Moved to Font class of System.Drawing namespace	StrikeOut property of Font class relative to an object that the Font class is being applied to
FontChangeUnderline	Moved to Font class of System.Drawing namespace	Underline property of Font class relative to an object that the Font class is being applied to
FontChangeWeight	Moved to Font class of System.Drawing namespace	Size property of Font class relative to an object that the Font class is being applied to
Math	Moved to Math class in System	
Oct	Moved to Math class	

Method, Element	Changed Reason	New Method, Element, Namespace
PixelstoTwipsX	Moved to System.Drawing namespace	See Point Converter class
PixelstoTwipsY	Moved to System.Drawing namespace	See Point Converter class

Data Type Changes

The data type changes that affect us most in the VB.NET environment surround the date and time functions, integer data type changes and the universal data type changes. The changes to date and time functionality are mainly data type changes to 8 byte formats. The Integer data types have been expanded and changed. What used to be an Integer in VB6 was a 16 bit size, and is now a 32 bit size. The 16 bit size has been changed to the Short data type. The previous Long data type was a 32 bit size, and is now a 64 bit size. Constant usage and support for the standard VB constants has changed as well. Constants from VB6, such as the familiar VBOK we used for messagebox feedback has changed to be supported within the objects they relate to. For instance, as we illustrated in our previous examples, what we used to see as a plain VBOK return from a message box is now declared as a DialogResult.OK.

Method, Element	Changed Reason	New Method, Element, Namespace
FixedLengthString	Data type change	Strings are no longer fixed length
ZorderConstants	Support changed for constants	

Boolean Operator Changes

In VB6 the And, Or, Not were used for Bitwise and Boolean operations. In the new version of VB they have added specific Bitwise operators so that our regular And, Or, Not and Xor are Boolean as contrasted with BitAnd, BitOr, BitNot, and BitXOr being Bitwise.

Method, Element	Changed Reason	New Method, Element, Namespace
And	Bitwise operation changes – expanded to have new Bitwise elements	And as well as BitAnd
Imp	Replaced by = operator	
EQV	Replaced by = operator	
Or	Bitwise operation changes – expanded to have new Bitwise elements	Or as well as BitOr

Method, Element	Changed Reason	New Method, Element, Namespace
Not	Bitwise operation changes – expanded to have new Bitwise elements	Not as well as BitNot
Xor	Bitwise operation changes – expanded to have new Bitwise elements	Xor as well as BitXOr

Class and Interface Changes

There are a couple of new classes which encompass the majority of our changes from generic VB6 functions to class-based functions in VB.NET. The System.Windows.Forms namespace holds all of the classes that make up the objects that we place on our forms and their properties. Also, the System.IO namespace has been added to encompass the file access functionality. The first table below relates to the System.Windows.Forms namespace, and the second table is an alphabetic listing of other namespaces that are affected:

Method, Element	Changed Reason	New Method, Element, Namespace
ButtonArray	Replaced by Button class in new System.Windows.Forms	
ComboBoxArray	Moved to CheckBox class in System.Windows.Forms	
CheckBoxArray	Moved to CheckBox class in System.Windows.Forms	
CheckedListBox Array	Moved to CheckBox class in System.Windows.Forms	
DirDrive	Moved to System.Windows.Forms	Use OpenFileDialog and SaveFileDialog methods
DirListBox	Moved to System.Windows.Forms	Use OpenFileDialog and SaveFileDialog methods
DirListBoxArray	Moved to System.Windows.Forms	Use OpenFileDialog and SaveFileDialog methods

Method, Element	Changed Reason	New Method, Element, Namespace
DriveListBox	Moved to System.Windows. Forms	Use OpenFileDialog and SaveFileDialog methods
DriveListBoxArray	Moved to System.Windows. Forms	Use OpenFileDialog and SaveFileDialog methods
FileListBox	Moved to System.Windows. Forms	Use OpenFileDialog and SaveFileDialog methods
FileListBoxArray	Moved to System.Windows. Forms	Use OpenFileDialog and SaveFileDialog methods
GetCancel	Moved to System.Windows. Forms	CancelButton property of Form
GetDefault	Moved to System.Windows. Forms	Default button has moved to be the Accept button property
GetFileDescription	Moved to System.Windows. Forms	FileVersionInfo.FileDescription property
GetItemData	Moved to System.Windows. Forms	Use ItemData property of object
GetItemString	Moved to System.Windows. Forms	Use GetItemText method
GroupBoxArray	Moved to System.Windows. Forms	Group Box Collection of GroupBox class
LabelArray	Moved to System.Windows. Forms	
ListBoxArray	Moved to System.Windows. Forms	
ListBoxItem	Moved to System.Windows. Forms	
MenuItemArray	Moved to System.Windows. Forms	

Table continued on following page

Method, Element	Changed Reason	New Method, Element, Namespace
PanelArray	Moved to System.Windows.Forms	
PictureBoxArray	Moved to System.Windows.Forms	
ShowForm	Moved to System.Windows.Forms	Changed to Form.Show
Support	Moved to System.Windows.Forms	
TabControlArray	Moved to System.Windows.Forms	
TabLayout	Moved to System.Windows.Forms	TabBase class
TextBoxArray	Moved to System.Windows.Forms	
TimerArray	Moved to System.Windows.Forms	
WhatsThisMode	Moved to System.Windows.Forms	
Zorder	Moved to System.Windows.Forms	

Method, Element	Changed Reason	New Method, Element, Namespace
BaseControlArray	Replaced by BaseControlBuilder Class	BaseControlBuilder with Array as type
BaseOCXArray	Replaced by BaseControlBuilder Class	BaseControlBuilder with OCX as type
BOF	Moved to File class in System.IO namespace	
Close	Replaced by System.IO namespace file operations	

Method, Element	Changed Reason	New Method, Element, Namespace
`Constants`	Collection of `Constants` is related to object relationships	
`CreateObject`	`New` keyword instantiates objects	Replace with usage of `New`
`EOF`	Moved to `File` class in `System.IO` namespace	
`FileAttr`	Moved to `File` class in `System.IO` namespace	`Attributes` property
`FileGet`	Moved to `File` class in `System.IO` namespace	
`FileGetObject`	Moved to `File` class in `System.IO` namespace	
`FilePut`	Moved to `File` class in `System.IO` namespace	
`FilePutObject`	Moved to `File` class in `System.IO` namespace	
`FileSystem`	Replaced by `System.IO` namespace functionality	Use overloaded `Open` methods
`Format`	Moved to `Format` method members of `System` namespace	Use individual methods of `System` namespace, such as `Decimal.format`
`GetActiveControl`	Moved into `ContainerControl` class	`ActiveControl` property
`GetEXEName`	Moved to `System.Reflection` namespace	Use `GetExecutingAssembly` method
`GetHInstance`	Moved to `System.Runtime.Interopservices` namespace	
`GetPath`	Moved to `System.IO` namespace	
`HscrollBarArray`	Replaced by `HscrollBar` class	
`LineInput`	Moved to `System.IO` namespace	
`Open`	Moved to `System.IO` namespace	
`OpenAccess`	Moved to `System.IO` namespace	
`OpenforAppend`	Moved to `System.IO` namespace	
`OpenforInput`	Moved to `System.IO` namespace	

Table continued on following page

Method, Element	Changed Reason	New Method, Element, Namespace
OpenforOutput	Moved to System.IO namespace	
OpenMode	Moved to System.IO namespace	
OpenShare	Moved to System.IO namespace	
SendKeys	Moved to System.IO namespace	SendKeys class
SetAppearance	Moved to System.IO namespace	Choose appropriate appearance property of object
SetBorderStyle	Moved to System.IO namespace	Use appropriate BorderStyle property for object
SetCancel	Moved to System.IO namespace	CancelButton property of Form
SetDefault	Moved to System.IO namespace	Default button has moved to be the Accept button property
SetDefault Property	Moved to System.IO namespace	DefaultPropertyattribute of field object
SetItemData	Moved to System.IO namespace	Use ItemDate property of object
SetItemString	Moved to System.IO namespace	Use SetItemText method
SetListBoxColumns	Moved to System.IO namespace	Columns property of listbox class
SetResourceBase Name	Moved to System.IO namespace	
Tag	Tag property of field no longer supported	
TwipsPerPixelX	Moved to System.Drawing namespace	See Point Converter class
TwipsPerPixelY	Moved to System.Drawing namespace	See Point Converter class
TwipsToPixelsX	Moved to System.Drawing namespace	See Point Converter class
TwipsToPixelsY	Moved to System.Drawing namespace	See Point Converter class
VScrollBarArray	Replaced by VscrollBar class	
Write	Moved to System.IO namespace	
WriteLine	Moved to System.IO namespace	

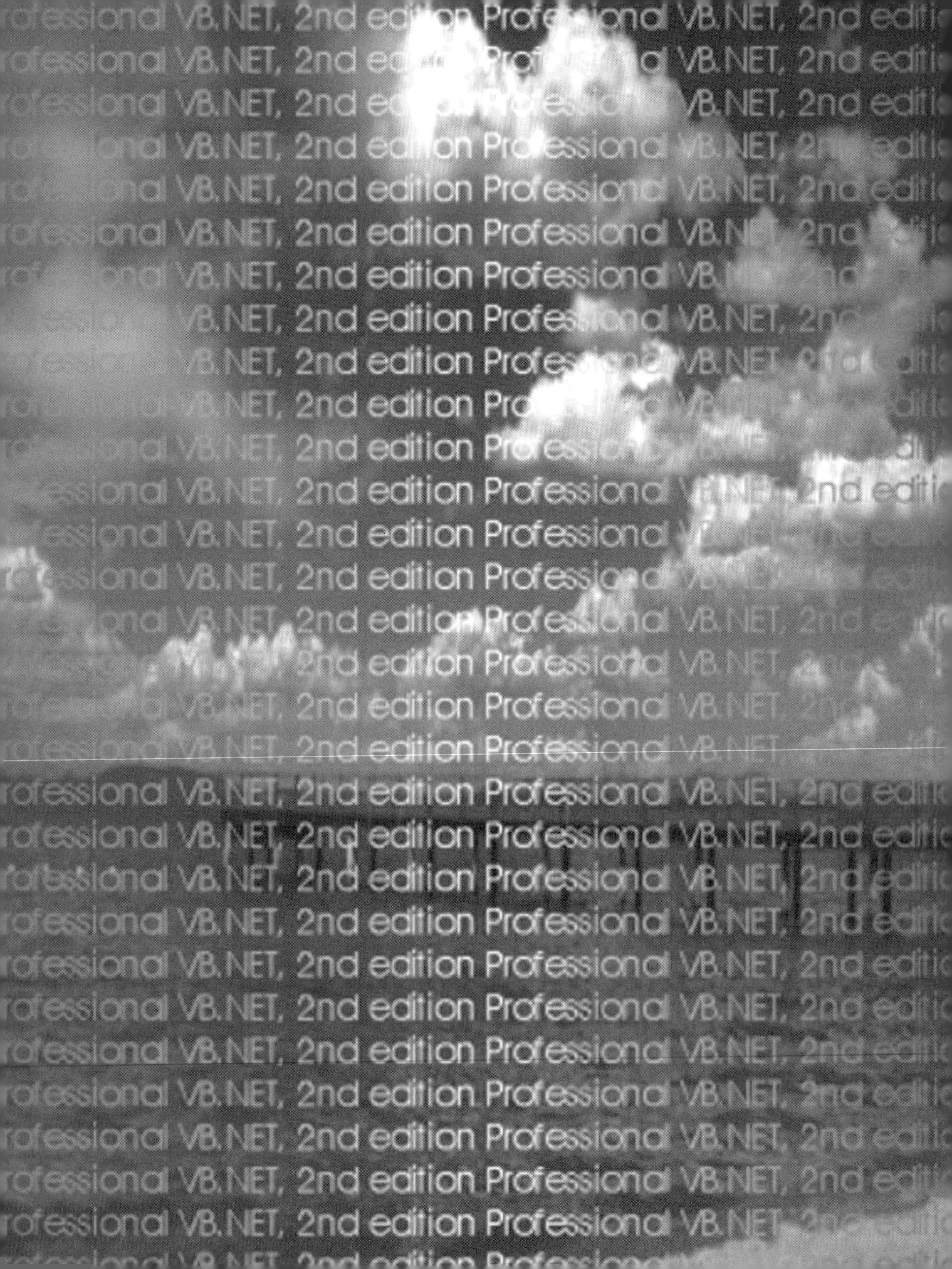
Professional VB.NET, 2nd edition

Index

A Guide to the Index

The index is arranged hierarchically, in alphabetical order, with symbols preceding the letter A. Most second-level entries and many third-level entries also occur as first-level entries. This is to ensure that users will find the information they require however they choose to search for it.

X

Notes

Notes

C# Today

The daily knowledge site for professional C# programmers

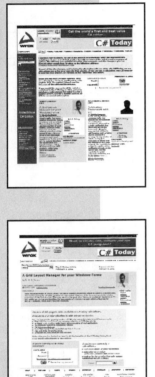

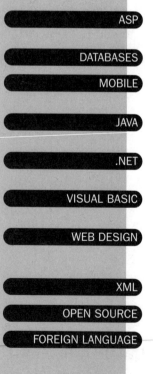

Got more Wrox books than you can carry around?

Wroxbase is the new online service from Wrox Press. Dedicated to providing online access to books published by Wrox Press, helping you and your team find solutions and guidance for all your programming needs.

The key features of this service will be:

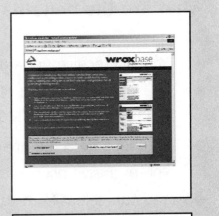

- Different libraries based on technologies that you use everyday (ASP 3.0, XML, SQL 2000, etc.). The initial set of libraries will be focused on Microsoft-related technologies.
- You can subscribe to as few or as many libraries as you require, and access all books within those libraries as and when you need to.
- You can add notes (either just for yourself or for anyone to view) and your own bookmarks that will all be stored within your account online, and so will be accessible from any computer.
- You can download the code of any book in your library directly from Wroxbase

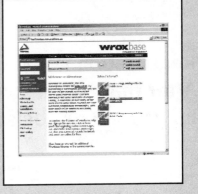

Visit the site at: www.wroxbase.com

wrox

Programmer to Programmer™

Registration Code: 7167KF7X264U8Q01

Wrox writes books for you. Any suggestions, or ideas about how you want information given in your ideal book will be studied by our team. Your comments are always valued at Wrox.

Free phone in USA 800-USE-WROX
Fax (312) 893 8001

UK Tel.: (0121) 687 4100   Fax: (0121) 687 4101

Pro VB .NET, 2nd edition – Registration Card

Name _____

Address _____

_____

_____

City _____ State/Region _____

Country _____ Postcode/Zip _____

E-Mail _____

Occupation _____

How did you hear about this book?

❏ Book review (name) _____

❏ Advertisement (name) _____

❏ Recommendation _____

❏ Catalog _____

❏ Other _____

Where did you buy this book?

❏ Bookstore (name) _____ City _____

❏ Computer store (name) _____

❏ Mail order _____

❏ Other _____

What influenced you in the purchase of this book?

❏ Cover Design ❏ Contents ❏ Other (please specify):

_____

How did you rate the overall content of this book?

❏ Excellent ❏ Good ❏ Average ❏ Poor

What did you find most useful about this book? _____

_____

_____

What did you find least useful about this book? _____

_____

Please add any additional comments. _____

_____

What other subjects will you buy a computer book on soon?

_____

What is the best computer book you have used this year?

_____

Note: This information will only be used to keep you updated about new Wrox Press titles and will not be used for any other purpose or passed to any other third party.

wrox

Programmer to Programmer™

Note: If you post the bounce back card below in the UK, please send it to:

Wrox Press Limited, Arden House, 1102 Warwick Road,
Acocks Green, Birmingham B27 6HB. UK.

Computer Book Publishers